THE Pictorial Field Book of the WAR OF 1812

THE PICTORIAL FIELD-BOOK

OF THE

WAR OF 1812;

OR,

ILLUSTRATIONS, BY PEN AND PENCIL, OF THE HISTORY, BIOGRAPHY, SCENERY, RELICS, AND TRADITIONS OF THE LAST WAR FOR AMERICAN INDEPENDENCE.

BY BENSON J. LOSSING.

VOLUME 1

WITH SEVERAL HUNDRED ENGRAVINGS ON WOOD, BY LOSSING AND BARRIT CHIEFLY FROM ORIGINAL SKETCHES BY THE AUTHOR.

A FIREBIRD PRESS BOOK

Gretna 2003

Firebird, Firebird Press, and 🐦 are imprints of Firebird Press, Inc.
a division of Pelican Publishing Company, Inc.

Manufactured in the United States of America
Published by Pelican Publishing Company, Inc.
1000 Burmaster Street, Gretna, Louisiana 70053

CHAPTER I.
EARLY DAYS OF THE REPUBLIC.

The Close of the Revolution; the States free, but not independent, 18; Why? Articles of Confederation, 19; the Public Debt, 20; Attitude of the States, 21; British Opinion concerning them, 22; Public Dangers, 23; Dissolution of the Republic threatened, 24; Washington's Forebodings; his Proposition for a Convention to reorganize Government, 25; Meeting of the Convention, 26; Proceedings of the Convention to form a National Constitution, 27-32; Ratification of the Constitution; its Opponents, 33; the Establishment of a Nation, 34.

CHAPTER II.
EVENTS IN THE NORTHWESTERN TERRITORY.

Foundations of Government in the Wilderness, 35; the Northwestern Territory; Settlements there, 36-37; the Indians and their British Allies, 38; Councils with the Indians, 39; British Intrigues and Indian Hostilities, 40; Expedition against the Indians in the Ohio Country, 41; Battle on the Maumee, 42; Visit to the Place of Conflict, 43-44; Expeditions of Scott and Wilkinson, 45; Forts built in the Wilderness, 46; St. Clair's Expedition, 47; his Battle with the Indians and Defeat, 48; how Washington received the News of St. Clair's Defeat, 49; his Justice and Generosity; Wayne's Expedition, 50; Interference of British Officials, 51; the British and Indians in armed Alliance, 52; Wayne's Expedition down the Maumee, 53, 54; Defeat of the Indians and treaty of Greenville, 55, 56.

CHAPTER III.
ESTABLISHMENT OF THE NATIONAL GOVERNMENT.

The national Policy and Power indicated, 58; Relations with France and England, 59; revolutionary Movements in France, 60, 61; diplomatic Intercourse with Great Britain and Spain, 62; Discourtesy of the British Government; mistaken Views concerning the American Government, 63; Acts in relation to the Public Debt, 64; Hamilton's financial Scheme; Currency, 65; Jefferson's Disappointment and Suspicions, 66; Progress of the French Revolution, 67; the political and religious Views of Jefferson and Adams, 68; Democracy in England, 69; Adams's Scheme of Government; Jefferson's Disgust and ungenerous Suspicions, 70; Paine's *Rights of Man;* a Newspaper War, 71; the *Federal* and *Republican* Parties formed, 72; Sympathy with the French Revolutionists, 73; Lafayette, 74; Monarchy in France overthrown, 75; the National Convention; Execution of the King, 76; Minister from the French Republic, 77; Washington's Proclamation of Neutrality, 78.

CHAPTER IV.
FOREIGN RELATIONS AND DOMESTIC POLITICS.

"Citizen Genet" and his Reception by his political Admirers, 79; his first Interview with Washington; Enthusiasm of the Republicans, 80; the American and the French Revolution compared, 81; Genet defies the American Government, 82; he is recalled; his Successor, 83; British "Rules" and "Orders in Council;" Armed Neutrality, 84; British Impressment of American Seamen, 85; Jay's Treaty with Great Britain, 86; Opposition to the Treaty, 87; the Whisky Insurrection; Democratic Societies, 88; Difficulties with Algiers, 89; an American Navy recommended, 90; Construction of a Navy; Unfriendliness of the French Directory, 91; Struggle between the Republicans and Federalists for political Power; Adams elected President, 92; open Rupture between France and the United States threatened, 93; Madness of Partisans, 94; Aggressions of the French Directory, 95; Preparations for War with France; Action in New York, 96; History of the Songs "Hail, Columbia!" and "Adams and Liberty," 97.

CHAPTER V.
WAR ON THE OCEAN.—POLITICAL STRUGGLES.

Washington appointed to the Command of the Army; Hamilton acting General-in-chief, 98; Envoys extraordinary sent to France, 99; Bonaparte in Power; American War-vessels afloat, 100; British Outrages; Obsequiousness of the American Government, 102; naval Engagements, 103; American Cruisers in the West Indies, 104; Truxtun's Victory; Honors to the Victor, 105; Peace; Divisions in the Federal Party, 106; Intrigues against Adams; Alien and Sedition Laws; Nullification Doctrines put forth, 107; State Supremacy asserted; Jefferson elected President, 108; Mortification of the Federalists; Death of Washington, 109; a public Funeral, 110; Washington's Person and Character, 111.

CONTENTS.

CHAPTER VI.
DIFFICULTIES WITH THE BARBARY POWERS.—ENGLAND AND FRANCE AT WAR.

Bonaparte's Career and Influence, 112; Obsequiousness of Englishmen, 113; Beginning of Jefferson's Administration; the National Capital, 114; Jefferson's Policy; political Proscription, 115; the Navy reduced, 116; Captain Bainbridge, the Dey of Algiers, and the Sultan, 117; Insolence and Exactions of the Barbary Rulers, 118; American Navy in the Mediterranean Sea and its Operations, 119–120; Bombardment of Tripoli, 121; Destruction of the *Philadelphia*, 122; Destruction of the *Intrepid*; Honors to Commodore Preble, 123; Commodore Barron's Squadron in the Mediterranean, 124; Eaton's Expedition in Northern Africa; Respect of the Barbary Powers for the American Flag, 125; Bonaparte and his Relations with England, 126; a French Invasion of England threatened, 127; a Struggle for political Supremacy; Bonaparte proclaimed Emperor, 128; Napoleon's Berlin Decree, 129.

CHAPTER VII.
EVENTS WEST OF THE ALLEGHANIES.—SEARCH AND IMPRESSMENT.

Organization of new States, 130; Americans disturbed by the Retrocession of Louisiana to France, 131; the secret Designs of the latter, 132; Jefferson's Letter and Bonaparte's Necessity; Purchase of Louisiana, 133; Events connected with the Purchase of Louisiana, 134; the Duel of Hamilton and Burr; the Acts of Burr's political Associates, 135; his ambitious Schemes; Blennerhassett and Wilkinson, 136; Burr's Operations, Trial for Treason, and Exile, 137; American commercial Thrift and British Jealousy, 138; British Perfidy defended by British Writers, 139; Unpleasant foreign Relations, 140; Memorial of Merchants concerning British Depredations, 141; Impressment of American Seamen and Right of Search, 142; diplomatic Correspondence on the Subject, 143; cruel Treatment of American Seamen, 144; farther diplomatic Action, 145, 146; national Independence and Honor in Peril, 147; Minister extraordinary sent to England, 148.

CHAPTER VIII.
SEARCH AND IMPRESSMENT.—EMBARGO.—PARTY SPIRIT.

Negotiations concerning the Impressment of American Seamen, 149; a Treaty agreed to, but not ratified; War on the Administration, 150, 151; The Continental System of Napoleon, 152; Aggressions on American Commerce and Neutrality by France and England, 153; Napoleon's Milan Decree and its Effects, 154; the Navy and the Gun-boat Policy, 155; British Cruisers in American Waters, 156; the Affair of the *Chesapeake*, 157; the Outrage resented, 158; Action of the American Government, 159; Action of the British Government, 160; fruitless Mission of a British Envoy, 161; political Complexion of the Tenth Congress; an Embargo established, 162; its Effects; Party Spirit violently aroused, 163; the Embargo vehemently denounced, 164; the British exact Tribute from neutral Nations, 165; Dangers of national Vanity, 166.

CHAPTER IX.
WAR BETWEEN THE UNITED STATES AND GREAT BRITAIN THREATENED.

Provisions for strengthening the American Navy, 167; Gun-boats; Opposition to a Navy, 168; British opposition to the Orders in Council, 169; Napoleon's Blow at American Commerce; Modification of the Orders in Council, 170; Actions concerning the Embargo, 171; Disunionists in New England, 172, 173; Embargo or War the proclaimed Alternative, 174; Cotton supposed to be the King of Commerce, 175; Just Arrangements for settling the Difficulties with Great Britain, 176; the British Government repudiates the Acts of its Agent, 177; an offensive British Minister sent to America, 278; the French Decrees and British Orders in Council, 179; England and France refuse to be just, 180; Outrage by a British Cruiser, 181; Method of signaling, 182, 183; Action between the *President* and *Little Belt*, 184; Testimony concerning the Affair, 185; Commodore Rodgers assailed and vindicated, 186.

CHAPTER X.
HOSTILITIES OF THE INDIANS IN THE NORTHWEST.

The Indiana Territory and Governor Harrison, 187; British Emissaries among the Indians, 188; Tecumtha and his Brother the Prophet, 189; Indian Confederation proposed; Harrison denounces the Prophet, 190; the Mission of Joseph Barron, 191; Tecumtha before Harrison at Vincennes, 192; roving Plunderers; Tecumtha alarmed, 193; Preparations for fighting the Indians, 194; Harrison marches up the Wabash with Troops; Deputation of friendly Indians, 195; Visit of the Author to the Region of threatened Hostilities, 196–200; Harrison approaches the Prophet's Town; the Indians alarmed, 201; Harrison's Encampment near the Tippecanoe, 202; the Prophet's Teaching, 203; Battle of Tippecanoe, 204, 205; The Prophet disgraced, 206; Actors in the Battle of Tippecanoe, 207; Author's Visit to the Battle-ground, 208, 209.

CHAPTER XI.
A WAR SPIRIT AROUSED.—DECLARATION OF WAR AGAINST GREAT BRITAIN.

The Twelfth Congress and its Composition, 210; the President's feeble War-trumpet, 211; Charges against Great Britain, 212; Action of the Committee on Foreign Relations, 213; Alarm on Account of the Slaves, 214; Randolph and Calhoun in Congress, 215; Policy of the Federalists, 216; Patriotism of some of their Leaders, 217; Debate concerning the Navy, 218; the President compelled to adopt War Measures, 219; a British Emissary in New England, 220; his Revelations and Rewards, 221; Action of the British Ministry on the Subject, 222; a new Embargo Act, 223; delusive Hopes of Justice, 224; a preliminary War Measure, 225; Report on the Causes of and Reasons for War, 226; Action of Congress on the Subject, 227; Declaration of War, 228; Protest of the Minority in Congress against the Measure, 229; Organization of a Peace Party, 230; Measures for carrying on the War, 231; public Acts in opposition to the War, 232.

CHAPTER XII.
BEGINNING OF THE WAR OF 1812.

The British Regency—Political Affairs in Europe, 233; the Troops and Fortifications on the Northern Frontier, 234; Sea-coast Defenses of the United States, 235-238; Fulton's Torpedoes and their Uses, 238-240; Fulton's Anticipations, 241; Effects of a Fear of Torpedoes, 242; the Action of State Governments concerning the War, 243; public Feeling in Canada, 244; Signs of Pacification, 245; conditional Revocation of the Orders in Council, 246; haughty Assumptions of the British Government on the Subject of Search and Imprisonment, 247; War inevitable and justifiable, 248; Choice of military Leaders, 249, 250.

CHAPTER XIII.
HULL'S CAMPAIGN AGAINST CANADA.

Canada to be invaded—Object of the Invasion, 251; Organization of an Army in Ohio—an active Frontiersman, 253; Author's Journey through Ohio, 254; General Hull takes Command of Ohio Volunteers, 255; regular and volunteer Troops in the Wilderness, 256; Hull's March to Detroit, 257; his Baggage and Papers captured, 258; how the British in Canada were informed of the Declaration of War, 259; Detroit in 1812, 260; Hull invades Canada, 261, 262; Reconnoissance toward Malden, 263; first Battle of the War, 264, 265; Distrust of General Hull, 266; first Blood shed in the War, 267; early Scenes at Mackinaw, 268, 269; Events at Mackinaw in 1812, 270; Employment of the Indians by the British, 271.

CHAPTER XIV.
CAMPAIGN ON THE DETROIT FRONTIER.

Alarming Facts and Rumors, 272; Preparations in Canada for resisting Invasion, 273; Alarm caused by the Invasion, 274; Symptoms of Disloyalty—General Brock's Influence, 275; Defeat of Americans under Van Horne at Brownstown, 276; mutinous Spirit evinced in Hull's Army, 277; Expedition to succor a Supply-train, 278; the March toward the River Raisin, 279; Battle of Maguaga, 280, 281; Disappointment and Disaffection of the American Troops, 282; Brock goes to Malden with Troops, 283; Preparations for attacking Detroit, 284; Hull deceived—an Effort to reach a Supply-train, 285; Hull summoned to surrender, and refuses, 286; the British proceed to attack Detroit, 287; Scenes within the Fort, 288; Hull surrenders the Fort, Garrison, and Territory, 289; Feeling of the Troops—Result of the Surrender, 290; Incidents of the Surrender, 291; British Occupation of Detroit and Michigan, 292; Account of the Surrender, and public Indignation, 293; Hull tried by a Court-martial, 294; a Consideration of Hull's public Character, 295; the Government more to blame than Hull, 296.

CHAPTER XV.
MILITARY EVENTS IN THE THEN FAR NORTHWEST.

The Author's Journey from Chicago to Detroit, 297; a Ride from Windsor to Amherstburg, 298; Historical Localities at Amherstburg or Malden, 299; Windsor and "Windsor Castle," 300; Pontiac's Siege of Detroit, 301; Chicago, its Name, Settlement, and Position, 302; Trading-house and Fort at Chicago, 303; an Indian Raid, 304; Troubles at Chicago, 305; Treachery of the Indians—a Warning, 306; Munitions of War and Liquor destroyed, 307; Massacre at Chicago, 308; Incident of the Conflict with the Savages—Bravery of Women, 309; Cruelties of the Indians—their British Allies, 310; Survivors of the Massacre, 311; Mrs. Kenzie and the Growth of Chicago, 312; Designs against Fort Wayne, 313; Attack on Fort Wayne, 314; Ravages of the Indians—Little Turtle, 315; Treachery of Indians at Fort Wayne, 316; Fort Harrison besieged, 317; brave Deeds at Fort Harrison, 318; Attack on Fort Madison, 319.

CHAPTER XVI.
WAR WITH THE BRITISH AND INDIANS IN THE NORTHWEST.

The Nation aroused—Enthusiasm of the People, 320; Harrison and the Kentuckians, 321; Harrison at the Head of Kentucky Volunteers, 322; Departure for the Wilderness, 323; Volunteers flock to Harrison's Standard, 324; Fort Wayne relieved—Destruction of Indian Villages, 325; Harrison's Popularity—he commands the Northwestern Army, 326; Winchester met by British and Indians in the Wilderness, 327; Re-enforcements gathering, 328; Harrison's proposed autumn Campaign, 329; reported Movement through the Wilderness, 330; Erection of Forts, 331; the Indians alarmed and humbled, 332; the Author's Visit to the Theatre of War, 333; Preparations for further Warfare, 334; Expedition against the Indians in the Illinois Country, 335; Expedition to the Wabash Region, 336; Sufferings of the Kentucky Soldiers, 337.

CHAPTER XVII.
WAR WITH THE BRITISH AND INDIANS IN THE NORTHWEST.

Harrison cheerfully meets Difficulties, 338; Difficulties of a winter Campaign, 339; Organization of the Army—the Western Reserve, 340; Preparations in Ohio against Invasion, 341; Energy and Patriotism of Colonel Wadsworth, 342; an Expedition to the Maumee, 343; stirring Events at the Maumee Rapids, 344; Services of friendly Indians, 345; Campbell's Expedition into the Wabash Region, 346; a Battle near the Mississiniwa, 347; Sufferings and Difficulties of Harrison's Army, 348, 349; Advance toward the Maumee Rapids, 350; Frenchtown on the Raisin River threatened, 351; Battle at Frenchtown, 352; Winchester arrives with Re-enforcements, 353; he disregards Warnings of Danger, 354; Massacre at Frenchtown, 355; Winchester compelled to surrender his Army, 356; Perfidy, Cowardice, and Inhumanity of the British Commander, 357; Massacre and Scalping allowed by him, 358; Incidents of the Massacre, 359; Author's Visit to Frenchtown, 360; historical Localities and Survivors of the War there, 361, 362; Harrison unjustly censured, 363; his Army at the Maumee Rapids, 364.

CHAPTER XVIII.
EVENTS ON THE NORTHERN AND NIAGARA FRONTIERS IN 1812.

First warlike Measures on the Northern Frontier, 365; the Militia of the State of New York, 366; Events on Lake Ontario and at Sackett's Harbor, 367; a hostile British Squadron off Sackett's Harbor, 368; a Skirmish and a Repulse of the British—Vessels of War on Lake Ontario, 369; Operations on the St. Lawrence Frontier, 370; hostile Squadrons on Lake Ontario, 370; Operations near Kingston—Commodore Chauncey, 372; General Brown sent to Ogdensburg, 373; the British attack Ogdensburg, 374; St. Regis, its capture by the Americans, 375; Honors to the Victors at Albany, 376; Eleazer Williams, or "The Lost Prince," 377; the Author's Visit to St. Regis, 378; Buffalo in 1812, 379; the Niagara Frontier, 380; American Troops on the Niagara Frontier, 381; an Armistice and its Effects, 383; Preparations for an Invasion of Canada, 384; Expeditions for capturing British Vessels, 385; Capture of the *Adams* and *Caledonia* near Fort Erie, 386; Incidents of the Exploit, 387; Feelings of the Americans and British, 388.

CHAPTER XIX.
EVENTS ON THE NIAGARA FRONTIER IN 1812.

Conduct of General Smyth, 389; Van Rensselaer prepares to attack Queenston, 390; British Force on the Niagara Frontier, 391; Expedition against Queenston delayed, 392; military Etiquette—Colonel Scott, 393; Passage of the Niagara River in the Dark, 394; Skirmish at Queenston Village, 395; Colonel Van Rensselaer wounded and Captain Wool in command, 396; the Americans scale Queenston Heights, 397; Battle on Queenston Heights and Death of General Brock, 398; Passage of the River by Re-enforcements, 399; Events on Queenston Heights, 400; another Battle—Wool wounded, 401; bad Conduct of the New York Militia, Colonel Scott in Command, 402; Heroes and Cowards made Prisoners of War, 403; Surrender of the American Army, 404; a triumphal and funeral Procession, 405; Honors to General Brock, 406; Colonel Solomon Van Rensselaer, 407; Events at the Mouth of the Niagara River, 408; Protection for American Prisoners of War, 409; General Smyth's injurious Pride and Folly, 410; his silly Proclamations ridiculed, 411.

CHAPTER XX.
EVENTS ON THE NIAGARA FRONTIER AND VICINITY IN 1812.

The Author's Visit to the Niagara Frontier, 412; Lewiston, Queenston, and Queenston Heights, 413; Brock's Monument, 414; an Evening on Queenston Heights, 415; Interview with the Chief of the Six Nations, 416; Journey from Queenston to Niagara, 417; Fort George and its Appurtenances, 418; Fort Mississaga—Return to Niagara Falls, 419; Journey from Niagara Falls to the Settlement of the Six Nations on the Grand River, 420; a Morning with the Chief of the Six Nations, 421; Indian Relics and Customs, 422; the Mohawk Church and Brant's Tomb, 423, 424; the Mohawk Institute—Communion-plate from Queen Anne, 425; British attack Black Rock, 426; Preparations for another Invasion of Canada, 427; the British forewarned—Passage of the Niagara River, 428; Incidents of the attempted Invasion, 429; Smyth's Incompetence and Folly, 430; the Invasion of Canada abandoned, 431; a Duel, and what came of it—exit Smyth, 432.

CHAPTER XXI.
NAVAL OPERATIONS IN 1812.

Acknowledged naval Superiority of Great Britain, 433; Character, Distribution, and Condition of the American War Marine, 434; Commodore Rodgers's Squadron—first Shot in the War, 435; Rodgers in European waters—British Squadron at Halifax, 436; Cruise of the *Constitution*, 437; how she eluded her Pursuers, 438; the *Essex* goes on a Cruise, 439; Cruise of the *Essex*, 440; how a Challenge was accepted by Commodore Porter, 441; the *Constitution* off the Eastern Coast, 442; Battle between the *Constitution* and *Guerriere*, 443, 444; Destruction of the *Guerriere*—Effects of the Victory, 445; Honors to Commodore Hull, 446; Effect of the Victory on the British Mind, 447; Hull's Generosity, 448; Cruise of the *Wasp*, 449; Fight between the *Wasp* and the *Frolic*, 450; both Vessels captured by the *Poictiers*, 451; Honors to Captain Jones, 452; Lieutenant Biddle honored and rewarded, 453.

CHAPTER XXII.
NAVAL OPERATIONS AND CIVIL AFFAIRS IN 1812.

Commodore Rodgers's second Cruise, 454; Battle between the *United States* and *Macedonian*, 455; Capture of the *Macedonian*—Decatur takes her to New York, 456; Honors to Decatur, 457; Bainbridge in Command of a Squadron, 458; his Cruise on the Coast of Brazil, 459; Battle between the *Constitution* and *Java*, 460; Loss of the *Java*—Incidents of the Battle, 461; Honors to Bainbridge, 462; Effects of the naval Battles in Great Britain, 463; meeting of the Twelfth Congress, 464; Madison re-elected—his Administration sustained, 465; Quincy's Denunciations and Clay's Response, 466; Measures for strengthening the Army and Navy, 467; Retaliation—Report of the Committee on Foreign Relations, 468; Manifesto of the Prince Regent and its Charges, 469; Mediation of the Emperor of Russia proposed, 470; Rejoicings over Napoleon's Misfortunes—Peace Commissioners, 471; Cabinet Changes, 472.

CHAPTER XXIII.
EVENTS ON THE MAUMEE RIVER.

Contemplated Expedition against Malden, 473; American Camp at the Maumee Rapids, 474; Interference of the Secretary of War with General Harrison, 475; General Clay's march to the Maumee, 476; Harrison assumes grave Responsibilities, 477; British and Indian Expedition against Fort Meigs, 478; the Mission of Captain Oliver, 479; Leslie Combs volunteers for perilous Duty, 480; Incidents of his Voyage down the Maumee, 481; Preparations for an Assault on Fort Meigs, 482; Attack on Fort Meigs, 483;

CONTENTS. vii

critical Situation of the Fort and Garrison, 484; Harrison's Plans against the Besiegers, 485; Dudley's Defeat and sad Results, 486; Arrival of Re-enforcements for Fort Meigs, 487; Effect of a Sortie from Fort Meigs, 488; the Author's Visit to the Maumee Valley, 490–493.

CHAPTER XXIV.
THE WAR IN NORTHERN OHIO—CONSTRUCTION OF PERRY'S FLEET.

Harrison's Provision for the Frontier Defenses, 494; Kentuckians under Colonel R. M. Johnson, 495; Tecumtha anxious for hostile Action, 496; Johnson's Troops at Fort Stephenson, 497; unsuccessful Attempt to capture Fort Meigs, 498; Fort Stephenson menaced, 499; Croghan determines to hold it, 500; it is summoned to surrender, 501; a Siege, 502; Fort Stephenson stormed, and the Assailants repulsed, 503; Incidents of the Night succeeding the Struggle—Honors to Croghan, 504; the Author's Visit to Sandusky, 505, 506; also to Fremont and Site of Fort Stephenson, 507; Journey to Toledo—Harrison's Character assailed and vindicated, 508; Captain Perry sent to Lake Erie, 509; Harbor of Erie or Presq' Isle, 510; Construction of a Lake Fleet begun there, 511; Perry's Services with Chauncey and in securing American Vessels, 512; Perry's earnest Call for Men, 513; Erie menaced, 514; first Cruise of Perry's Fleet, 515; Harrison visits Perry, 516; Perry's second Cruise, 517.

CHAPTER XXV.
THE BATTLE OF LAKE ERIE.

Perry prepares for Battle, 518; his final Instructions—British Squadron in sight, 519; Names and Character of the opposing Squadrons, 520; Change in the Order of Battle, 521; relative Position of the Squadrons—Opening of the Battle, 522; first Position of the Vessels in the Fight, 523; the Battle—Scenes on board the *Lawrence*, 524, 525; sad Condition of the *Lawrence*, 526; Perry goes from the *Lawrence* to the *Niagara*, 527; Perry breaks the British Line, 528; his Victory—British Ships vainly attempt to Escape, 529; Perry's famous Dispatch, 530; Surrender of the British Officers—Burial of the Dead, 531; sad Effects of the Battle, 532; Importance of Perry's Victory, 533; public Celebrations by the exultant Americans, 534; Honors to Elliott and his Subordinates, 535; a Plea for a British-Indian Alliance—Prediction by Washington Irving, 536; Author's Visit to Erie and Cleveland, 537; Preparations for unveiling a Statue of Perry at Cleveland, 538; surviving Soldiers of the War of 1812, 539; the Statue unveiled—a remarkable Dinner-party, 540; a sham naval Battle—early Residents of Cleveland, 541; Perry and his Captives, 542; Reception of Perry and Harrison at Erie, 543.

CHAPTER XXVI.
HARRISON'S INVASION OF CANADA—HIS HOME.

Arrangements for invading Canada, 544; Army of the Northwest in Motion, 545; it crosses Lake Erie, 546; Proctor, frightened, flees from Malden—Tecumtha's scornful Rebuke, 547; vigorous Pursuit of the British, 548; the Armies in the River Thames, 549; Destruction of Property, 550; the British and Indians make a Stand for Battle, 551; the Armies in battle Array, 552; Battle of the Thames, 553, 554; British defeated—Death of Tecumtha—who killed him, 555; Gallantry of Colonel Johnson, 556; Harrison and Proctor properly rewarded, 557, 558; Returns to Detroit—Effect of the Victory, 559; the Author's Visit to the Thames Battle-ground, 560, 561; Harrison on the Northern Frontier, 562; Harrison leaves the Army—Author's Journey in Ohio, 563; Antiquities at Newark, 564, 565; Columbus and the Scioto Valley, 566; Chillicothe and its Vicinity, 567, 568; Governor Worthington's Residence, 569; Visit to Batavia and North Bend, 570; North Bend and its early Associations, 571; Courtship and Marriage of Captain Harrison and Anna Symmes, 572; Harrison's Tomb and Dwelling, 573, 574.

CHAPTER XXVII.
EVENTS ON THE ST. LAWRENCE FRONTIER AND UPPER CANADA.

The Energies of Great Britain displayed, 575; Operations in the St. Lawrence Region, 576; Attack on Elizabethtown—Retaliation, 577; Attack on Ogdensburg, 578; Defense of the Town, 579; Ogdensburg captured, 580; the Village plundered and Citizens carried off, 581; Author's Visit to Ogdensburg and Prescott, 582; the Canadian Rebellion, 583; another Invasion of Canada contemplated, 584; Preparations for it, 585; Expedition against Little York, 586, 587; Americans land and drive the British to Little York, 588; Explosion of a Powder-magazine and Death of General Pike, 589; Capture of York and Escape of the British, 590; York abandoned—a Scalp as an Ornament, 591; the Author's Visit to Toronto, formerly Little York, 592; an Adventure among the Fortifications, 593; notable Men and Places at Toronto, 594; Passage across Lake Ontario—Journey to Niagara Falls, 595; Expedition against Fort George—the respective Forces, 596; Cannonade between Forts George and Niagara, 597; the American Squadron and the landing of Troops, 598; a severe Battle—Capture of Fort George, 599; the British retreat to the Beaver Dams and Burlington Heights, 600; British Property on the Niagara Frontier destroyed by themselves—Expedition toward Burlington Heights, 601; the Americans at Stony Creek, 602; Battle at Stony Creek, 603; Capture of Generals Chandler and Winder, 604; the Americans flee and are pursued, 605; Destruction of Property at Sodus—British Fleet off Oswego, 606.

CHAPTER XXVIII.
EVENTS AT SACKETT'S HARBOR AND ON THE NIAGARA FRONTIER IN 1813.

British Designs on Sackett's Harbor—its Defenses, 607; General Brown in Command at Sackett's Harbor, 608; Assembling of the Militia—Approach of the British, 609; Position of the Militia—a Panic and Flight, 610; a Conflict—Destruction of Public Stores, 611; the British retreat, 612; Sackett's Harbor and its Defenses, 614; the Author's Visit there—the Frigate *New Orleans*—a neglected Monument, 616; historical Localities around Sackett's Harbor—a Visit to Watertown and Brownsville, 617; the Story of Whittlesey and his Wife, 618; Movements on the Niagara Frontier, 619; Expedition against the British at the Beaver Dams, 620; Services of a patriotic Woman, 621; Defeat and Surrender of the Americans —Fort George invested, 622; the Author's Visit to the Beaver Dams Region, 623; a veteran Canadian

Soldier, 624; Visit to Stony Creek and Hamilton, 625; British and Indian Raids on the Niagara Frontier, 626; Battle at Black Rock, 627; Expedition to Burlington Heights and York, 628; Dearborn succeeded by Wilkinson, 629; Relations between Wilkinson, Armstrong, and Hampton, 630; Affairs on the Niagara Frontier, 631; Fort George menaced and Newark burnt, 632; just Indignation of the British—Retaliation proposed, 633; Fort Niagara captured—Desolation of that Frontier, 634; N. Y. Militia at Buffalo, 635; Battle near Black Rock and Destruction of Buffalo, 636; Horrors of retaliatory Warfare, 637.

CHAPTER XXIX.
EVENTS ON THE NORTHERN FRONTIER IN 1813.

Wilkinson concentrates his Forces, 638; General Dearborn moves into Canada, 639; Repulse of the British at La Colle—Colonel Carr, 640; Preparations for War on Lake Champlain, 641; Movements of Hampton in Northern New York, 642; Chauncey tries to engage Sir James Yeo on Lake Ontario, 643; a Battle at last, 644; Chauncey again searching for his Foe, 645; an Expedition for the St. Lawrence against Montreal—Disasters, 646; Hampton's Operations in the Chateaugay Region, 647; Wilkinson's Expedition on the St. Lawrence, 648; Battle off French Creek—the Expedition moves down the St. Lawrence, 649; the Flotilla passes Prescott, 650; General Brown invades Canada—Wilkinson in Peril, 651; Preparations for a Battle, 652; Battle of Chrysler's Field, 653; the Americans go down the St. Lawrence, 654; Character of some of the chief Leaders, 655; the Army in winter Quarters at French Mills, 656; its Sufferings there and Release, 657; Attempt to seduce American Soldiers from their Allegiance, 658; the Author's Visit to the St. Lawrence Region—Carleton Island, 659, 660; William Johnson of the Thousand Islands, 661; his Exploits, Arrest, and Imprisonment, 662; his Services in the War of 1812, 663; a Visit to French Mills and Vicinity, 664; Rouse's Point—La Colle, 665; a Visit to Chrysler's Farm, Prescott, and Ogdensburg, 666.

CHAPTER XXX.
PREDATORY WARFARE OF THE BRITISH ON THE COAST.

Blockade of the Chesapeake and Delaware Bays declared, 667; Operations of Blockaders in Chesapeake Bay, 668; Attack on Lewiston—Cockburn, the Marauder, 669; Capture of Frenchtown, 670; Attack on Havre de Grace, 671; the Town plundered and fired, 672; the Author's Visit to Havre de Grace—John O'Neill, 673; Cockburn plunders and destroys other Villages, 674; stirring Scenes in Hampton Roads, 675; a British Fleet enters the Roads, 676; Craney Island and its Defenders, 677; Preparations for Battle, 678; the British attack, are repulsed, and withdraw, 679; they turn upon Hampton, 680; they land and menace it, 681; a Struggle for the Possession of Hampton, 682; Americans driven out, and the Village given up to Rapine and Plunder, 683; the Author visits Craney Island and Norfolk, 684, 685; the Fortifications on Craney Island, 686; a Visit to Hampton, 687; a Daughter of Commodore Barron—a Veteran of 1812—Hampton destroyed by Virginia Rebels, 688; Cockburn in the Potomac and on the Coasts of the Carolinas and Georgia, 689; Secret Organizations among the Slaves, 690; Decatur runs the Blockade at New York, 691; blockading Squadron off New London, 692; Alarm produced by Torpedo Vessels, 693; the Coast of Connecticut blockaded—the local Militia, 694; Decatur in the Thames, 695; the Author's Visit to New London and its Vicinity, 696, 697.

CHAPTER XXXI.
WAR ON THE OCEAN IN 1813.

Battle between the *Hornet* and *Peacock*, 698; Victory of the *Hornet*—Prowess of the Americans respected, 699; Honors to Captain Lawrence and his Men, 700; Cruise of the *Chesapeake*—her Character, 701; Lawrence's last official Letter, 702; Broke's Challenge, 703; the *Chesapeake* and her Crew, 704; the *Chesapeake* goes out to fight, 705; Battle between the *Chesapeake* and *Shannon*—Death of Lawrence, 706; Treachery—Capture of the *Chesapeake*—she is taken to Halifax, 708; Exultation of the British, 709; Honors to Captain Broke, 710; Respect paid to the Remains of Lawrence and his Lieutenant, Ludlow, 711; funeral Ceremonies at Salem, 712; funeral Ceremonies at New York—Monuments, 713; stirring Scenes in Chesapeake Bay, 714; Cruise of the *Argus* in British Waters, 715; Battle between the *Argus* and *Pelican*, 716; Battle between the *Enterprise* and *Boxer*, 717; Funeral of the Commander of each at Portland, 718; Honors to Burrows and M'Call, 719; last Cruise of the *Enterprise*, 720.

CHAPTER XXXII.
CRUISE OF THE ESSEX.

Weakness of the American Navy, 721; the *Essex* starts on a long Cruise—a Search for Bainbridge, 722; she sails for the Pacific Ocean, 723; her Search for British whaling Vessels, 724; by capturing and arming British whaling Vessels, Porter creates a Squadron, 725; successful Cruise among the Gallapagos Islands, 726; Porter sails for the Marquesas Islands, 727; civil War in Nooaheevah, 728; Porter engages in the War, 729; the Women of Nooaheevah, 730; Incidents in the Harbor of Valparaiso, 731; Battle between the *Essex* and two British Ships, 732; the *Essex* captured—Porter returns Home, 733; Honors to Commodore Porter—his subsequent Career, 734; Rodgers's long Cruise in 1813—his Services to his Country, 735, 736; he makes another Cruise in the *President*—Honors to Rodgers, 737.

CHAPTER XXXIII.
WAR AGAINST THE CREEK INDIANS.

Insurrectionary Movements in Louisiana, 738; military Movements in West Florida, 739; Louisiana made a State—Insurrection in East Florida, 740; Action of United States Officials there—Expedition, 741; Surrender of Mobile to the Americans, 742; Tennessee Volunteers on the Mississippi, 743; they return to Nashville, 744; Tecumtha in the Creek Country—he exhorts the Creeks to make War on the White People, 746; the Creek Nation and their Position, 747; Civil War among the Creeks—White People in Peril, 748; the Militia in the Field—Battle of Burnt Corn Creek, 749; Preparations for Defense in Lower Alabama, 750; Fort Mims and its Occupants, 751; Rumors of impending Hostilities, 752; Fort Mims

CONTENTS.   ix

crowded with Refugees, 753; gathering of hostile Savages near, 754; furious Assault on Fort Mims, 755; Massacre at Fort Mims, 756; Horrors of the Massacre, 757; Response of the Tennesseeans to a Cry for Help, 758; General Andrew Jackson in the Field—Mobile threatened, but saved, 759.

CHAPTER XXXIV.
WAR AGAINST THE CREEK INDIANS.

Jackson heeds a Cry for Help from the Coosa, 760; the Army threatened with Famine—Affairs in the lower Creek Country, 761; Choctaw Allies—Expedition against Tallasehatche, 762; Battle of Tallasehatche, 763; Jackson hastens to the Relief of threatened Posts, 764; Battle at Talladega, 765; the dispirited Indians sue for Peace, 766; Destruction of the Hillabee Towns, 767; the Creek Country invaded from Georgia—Battle of Auttose, 768; Expedition under Captain Dale, 769; Dale's terrible Canoe Fight, 770; Fort Claiborne at Randon's Landing, 771; Battle of Econochaco, 772; Dissolution of the Armies in the Creek Country—new Volunteers, 773; Battle of Emucfau, 774; Battle on Enotochopco Creek, 775; Battle on the Calebee River, 776; East Tennesseeans and Choctaw Allies on the Way to the Creek Country, 777; Battle of the Horseshoe, 779; the Power of the Creek Nation broken there, 780; the subdued Indians sue for Peace—Weathersford in Jackson's Tent, 781; the Creek Nation ruined, 782.

CHAPTER XXXV.
CIVIL AFFAIRS IN 1813—EVENTS ON THE NORTHERN FRONTIER IN 1814.

Political Composition of Congress—Peace Commissioners, 783; illicit Traffic—Change in public Sentiment—Peace Party, 784; revolutionary Proposition—new Embargo Act, 785; Rumors of Peace—Embargo Act repealed, 786; Provisions for the increase of the Army, 787; Prisoners of War—retaliatory Measures proposed, 788; Campaign on the Northern Frontier and Lake Champlain, 789; Wilkinson marches on La Colle Mill, in Canada, 790; Battle of La Colle Mill, 791; end of Wilkinson's military Career, 792; Brown, moving toward the Niagara Frontier, perplexed by Orders from the War Department, 793; Naval Forces on Lake Ontario, 794; the British attack Oswego, 795; they capture Oswego, 796; Survivors of the War in Oswego, 797; Sackett's Harbor blockaded, 798; Woolsey at Big Sandy Creek with Stores for Sackett's Harbor, 799; Battle at Big Sandy Creek, 800; a great Cable carried to Sackett's Harbor—Author's Visit to Big Sandy Creek, 801; the Army on the Niagara Frontier—Red Jacket, 802; Fort Erie and the Invasion of Canada, 803; an Invasion of Canada from Black Rock, 804; Capture of Fort Erie, 805; Scott prepares for battle at Street's Creek, 806; preliminary Fighting, 807; Scott advances—the British Force, 808; the Battle of Chippewa, 809, 810; the British driven from Chippewa—Indians disheartened, 811; the Armies inspirited by the Victory, 812; Preparations to cross the Chippewa Creek, 813; the British retreat—Brown marches for Fort George, 814—he falls back to Chippewa, 815.

CHAPTER XXXVI.
WAR ON THE NIAGARA FRONTIER IN 1814.

The British, re-enforced, advance toward Chippewa, 816; Scott discovers them near Niagara Falls, 817; the British attack Scott, 818; Brown advances from Chippewa, 819; Colonel Miller captures a British Battery, 820; Appreciation of his Exploit, 821; desperate Struggle in the darkness—Victory for the Americans, 822; close of the Battle of Niagara Falls, 823; the Battle and the Victory considered, 824; Scott, wounded, proceeds to Washington, 825; Honors awarded him, 826; the Author's Visit to the Battle-grounds of Chippewa and Niagara Falls, 827, 828; the Army falls back and is ordered to Fort Erie, 829; the British again attack Black Rock, 830; Brown wounded—Gaines takes Command of the Army, 831; the American Troops at Fort Erie, 832; the British assail the Fort, 833; Battle of Fort Erie, 834, 835; Brown resumes Command, 836; a Sortie, 837; brilliant Success of General Porter, 838; Triumph of Miller and Upham, 839; the British abandon the Siege, 840; Honors awarded to General Brown, 841; Honors to Generals Porter and Ripley, 842; two remarkable Survivors of the Battle of Fort Erie, 843; General Izard sends Troops to the Niagara Frontier, 844; he takes Command there, 845; the American Troops withdraw from Canada, 846; the Author visits Fort Erie and its Vicinity, 847, 848; Holmes's Expedition into Canada—Battle of the Long Woods, 849; Expedition to the upper Lakes, 850; Operations in that Region, 851; M'Arthur's Raid in Canada, 852—his Bravery and Generosity, 853.

CHAPTER XXXVII.
EVENTS ON LAKE CHAMPLAIN IN 1814.

The Downfall of Napoleon, 854; English Troops released for Service in America, 855; Struggle for the Control of Lake Champlain, 856; Operations on the Canada Border, 857; alarming Order from the War Department, 858; Concentration of Troops at Plattsburg, 859; Position of American Works there, 860; the British advance on Plattsburg, 861; a Skirmish at Beekmantown, 862; another near Plattsburg, 863; the British checked at the Saranac Bridge, 864; British land—our naval Forces in motion, 865; Opening of naval Battle off Plattsburg, 866; Battle of Lake Champlain, 867–870; Victory for the Americans complete, 871; Casualties, 872; Movements of the land Troops—Battle of Plattsburg, 873; the British alarmed, 874; their hasty Flight into Canada, 875; Rejoicings because of Victory, 876; Honors to General Macomb, 877; Honors to Commodore Macdonough, 878; Effect of the Victory at Plattsburg, 879; the Author's Visit to the Scene of War on and near Lake Champlain, 880–884; Operations on Lake Ontario, 885; a heavy British Ship on the Lake, 886; close of Hostilities on the Northern Frontier, 887.

CHAPTER XXXVIII.
THE WAR ON THE NEW ENGLAND COAST IN 1814.

The Blockade of New London, 888; amphibious Warfare on the New England Coast, 889; New England sea-port Towns blockaded, 890; Portsmouth and Boston menaced, 891; Preparations for the Defense of Boston, 892; the British Squadron attacks Stonington, 893; Captain Holmes and his Gun, 894; a Deputation sent to the British Commander, 895; the British repulsed—impotency of the Attack, 896; a

CONTENTS.

British Force on the Coast of Maine, 897; Operations in Penobscot Bay and River, 898; Preparations at Hampden to oppose the British Invasion, 899; Panic and Flight of the Militia, 900; the British at Bangor, 901; Treatment of General Blake, 902; the British at Castine, 903; the Author's Visit to Places on the New England Coast—Observations at Boston, 904; at Salem and Marblehead, 905–907; Journey to the Penobscot, 908; Observations at Castine, 909; Voyage up the Penobscot, 910; Hampden, 911; Observations at Bangor, 912; Visit to New Bedford and Providence, 913; Stonington and Mystic, 914; Story of a faithful Daughter, 915.

CHAPTER XXXIX.
THE CAPTURE OF WASHINGTON CITY.

Apathy of the Government while the Capital was in peril, 916; feeble Preparations for its Defense, 917; General Winder in Command—a Call for Troops, 918; Tardiness of the Secretary of War—Apathy of the People, 919; Appearance of the British in Chesapeake Bay, 920; gathering of Troops—Destruction of Barney's Flotilla, 921; the Forces gathered for the Defense of Washington and Baltimore, 922; the British move on Washington from the Patuxent, 923; Battle Lines formed near Bladensburg, 924; Excitement in the national Capital, 925; the British advance on Bladensburg, 926; Arrangements to receive them, 926, 927; Dueling-ground near Bladensburg, 928; Battle of Bladensburg, 929, 930; Barney wounded and made Prisoner, 931; the victorious British march on Washington City, 932; Destruction of the public Buildings, 933; Destruction of the Navy Yard, 934; Flight of the President and his Cabinet—Patriotism of Mrs. Madison, 935; Object of the Invasion, 936; the British retreat from Washington, 937; Slavery the cause of the Disaster at Bladensburg, 938; a British Fleet passes up the Potomac, 939; Alexandria plundered—Torpedoes, 940; the British Squadron returns to Chesapeake Bay—Visit to the Battle-ground at Bladensburg, 941; Kalorama and Oak Hill Cemetery, 942; Congressional Burial-ground—Fort Washington, 943.

CHAPTER XL.
EVENTS AT BALTIMORE, PHILADELPHIA, AND NEW YORK IN 1814.

The British in Chesapeake Bay, 944; Exploits of Parker and Cockburn, 945; Operations of the British Fleet in Chesapeake Bay, 946; Baltimore threatened, 947; Preparations for the Defense of Baltimore, 948; Fortifications and Troops for its Defense, 949; the British land and advance on Baltimore, 950; Position of the contending Armies, 951; Battle of North Point—Death of the British Commander, 952, 953; the British Fleet moves up to attack Fort M'Henry, 954; Bombardment of the Fort, 955; the British Invaders driven off, 956; "The Star-spangled Banner," 957; the British land Troops march on Baltimore, 958; they retire to their Ships—the British Programme, 959; Honors to Colonel Armistead, 960; the Author's Visit to Baltimore and the historical Localities around it, 961–965; New York and Philadelphia relieved, 965; the Volunteer Companies of Philadelphia, 966; Organization of Troops and Establishment of Camps, 967; Patriotism of the Citizens of Philadelphia, 968; New York aroused—Committee of Defense, 969; the Citizens assist in casting up Fortifications—"The Patriotic Diggers," 970; the Fortifications around New York, 971–975; a floating Battery authorized by Congress, 976; the Steamship *Fulton the First*, 977.

CHAPTER XLI.
NAVAL WARFARE ON THE OCEAN IN 1814—AMERICAN PRIVATEERS.

New Vessels for the Navy—the *John Adams*, 978; Cruise of the *Wasp*—Capture of the *Reindeer*, 979; the *Wasp* and *Avon*—Loss of the *Wasp*, 980; Fight between the *Peacock* and *Epervier*, 981; Barney's Flotilla in Chesapeake Bay, 982; the *Constitution*, 983; Battle between the *Constitution*, *Cyane*, and *Levant*, 984; the *Constitution* and her Prizes—Honors to Commodore Stewart, 985; Stewart's Home in New Jersey, 986; Decatur's Squadron—he puts to Sea in the *President*, 987; Battle between the *President* and *Endymion*, 988; the rest of Decatur's Squadron puts to Sea, 989; Battle between the *Hornet* and *Penguin*, 990; Honors to Captain Biddle, 991; Cruise of the *Hornet* and *Peacock*—the Navy at the end of the War, 992; the first Privateers, 993; Cruise of the *Rossie*, 994; first Prize taken to Baltimore—the *Globe*, 995; Cruise of the *Highflyer*, *Yankee*, and *Shadow*, 996; Salem and Baltimore Privateers, 997; Privateering at the close of 1812, 998; remarkable Cruise of the *Comet*, 999; Cruise of the *Chasseur*, *Saratoga*, *Dolphin*, *Lottery*, and *Yankee*, 1000; Cruise of the *General Armstrong*, *Ned*, and *Scourge*, 1001; the *Teaser*—Capture of the *Eagle*—Cruise of the *Decatur*, 1002; Cruise of the *David Porter*, *Globe*, and *Harpy*, 1003; the Career of the *General Armstrong*, 1004; Honors to Captain Reid—Cruise of the *Prince de Neufchâtel*, 1005; Cruise of the *Saucy Jack* and *Kemp*, 1006; Cruise of the *Macdonough* and *Amelia*—the American Privateers and their Doings, 1007.

CHAPTER XLII.
CIVIL AFFAIRS IN 1814—OPERATIONS IN THE GULF REGION.

Boston the Centre of illicit Trade, 1008; the Peace Faction assails the Government and the Public Credit, 1009; Effects of the Conspiracy against the Public Credit, 1010; new financial Measures—Revival of the Public Credit, 1011; Measures for increasing the Army—Discontents in New England, 1012; the Hartford Convention, 1013–1015; the Members of the Hartford Convention, 1016; Jackson recalled to active Service in the Gulf Region, 1017; the Baratarians and their Leader, 1018; Jackson perceives Mischief at Pensacola, 1019; Fort Bowyer threatened by a British Squadron, 1020; the Fort attacked and the Assailants repulsed, 1021; the British at Pensacola—Jackson marches on that Post, 1022; Flight of the British and Indians, 1023; Jackson in New Orleans—Appearance of the British, 1024; Preparations to receive the Invaders, 1025; Capture of the American Flotilla on Lake Borgne, 1026; Jackson's Review of Troops in New Orleans and their Disposition, 1027; the British approach the Mississippi, 1028; they march on New Orleans—Response to Jackson's Call for Troops, 1029; Events below New Orleans, 1030; a night Battle, 1031; the British fall back, 1032; the Americans withdraw, 1034.

CONTENTS. xi

CHAPTER XLIII.
DEFENSE OF NEW ORLEANS—PEACE.

Jackson's Line of Defense, 1034 ; a gloomy Day for the Invaders—Arrival of General Pakenham, 1035 ; Seat of War in Louisiana and Florida, 1036 ; severe Battle on the 28th of December, 1037 ; the British vanquished—the American Lines of Defense, 1038 ; the British cast up Redoubts near the American Line, 1039 ; a heavy Battle, 1040 ; the British repulsed and then re-enforced, 1041 ; Jackson prepares to receive the increased British Forces, 1042 ; Character and Disposition of his own Forces—Position of his Army on the 7th of January, 1043 ; a British Detachment crosses the Mississippi, 1044 ; Battle of New Orleans, 1046–1049 ; Disposal of the Dead, 1050 ; Attack on Forts St. Philip and Bowyer—Jackson's Army in New Orleans, 1051 ; Honors accorded to Jackson and his Troops, 1052 ; Rumors of Peace and continuance of Martial Law, 1053 ; Incidents of Jackson's Trial for Contempt of Court, 1054 ; the Author's Journey to New Orleans—Lexington and "Ashland," 1055 ; Frankfort and its Cemetery, 1056 ; a Visit to Nashville and the "Hermitage," 1057 ; New Orleans and its historic Men and Places, 1058 ; Attack on Fort Sumter—Uprising of the People, 1059 ; Negotiations for Peace and the Commissioners, 1060 ; Ghent and the Sympathy of its Inhabitants with the Americans, 1061 ; the Treaty of Peace, 1062, 1063 ; Rejoicings of the American People, 1064 ; Commemorative Medals—its Ratification, 1065 ; Position of the Republic at the close of the War, 1067 ; Readjustment of National Affairs—Dartmoor Prisoners, 1068 ; Prosperity of the Republic and its Relations to other Nations, 1069 ; Text of the Treaty of Peace, 1071.

Illustrations

1. Illuminated Frontispiece.
2. Title-page.
3. Preface .... Page iii
4. Contents v
5. Illustrations xiii
6. Initial Letter 17
7. First Great Seal of the United States 20
8. War 22
9. Britannia aroused 22
10. Portrait of William Jackson 26
11. Jackson's Monument 27
12. Portrait and Signature of Gouverneur Morris 28
13. Signatures of the Members of the Constitutional Convention 30, 31, 32
14. Tail-piece 34
15. Initial Letter 35
16. Campus Martius 37
17. Portrait and Signature of Miss Heckewelder 37
18. Portrait and Signature of General St. Clair 38
19. Signature of Winthrop Sargent 38
20. Signature of Lord Dorchester 38
21. Fort Harmar 39
22. Fort Washington, on the Site of Cincinnati 41
23. Signature of Joseph Harmar 41
24. The Maumee Ford—Place of Harmar's Defeat 42
25. Map—Harmar's Defeat 43
26. Hall's Crossing-place 43
27. Apple-tree near Harmar's Ford 44
28. Map—Plan of St. Clair's Camp and Battle 47
29. Signature of Tobias Lear 49
30. Lowry's Monument 52
31. Map—Plan of Line of Wayne's March 54
32. Signature of A. M'Kee 54
33. Map—Battle of the Fallen Timbers 55
34. Turkey-foot Rock 55
35. Signature of Colonel Hamtramck 56
36. Colonel Hamtramck's Tomb 56
37. Tail-piece—Indian Implements 57
38. Initial Letter 58
39. Portrait and Signature of T. Pinckney 64
40. Liberty Cent 65
41. Portrait and Signature of General Hamilton 66
42. Portrait and Signature of Thomas Paine 69
43. A Bad Measure 69
44. An Assignat 74
45. Portrait of Louis XVI 76
46. Paine fitting Stays 76
47. Memorial Medal 76
48. Initial Letter 79
49. The Contrast 81
50. Portrait and Signature of Thomas Mifflin 82
51. Portrait and Signature of E. C. Genet 83
52. Portrait and Signature of John Jay 85
53. Signature of Alexander M'Kim 89
54. Seal of the Republican Society of Baltimore 89
55. Portrait and Signature of C. C. Pinckney 92
56. Portrait and Signature of John Adams 93
57. Portrait and Signature of Joel Barlow 94
58. Signature of Benjamin Stoddert .... Page 96
59. Initial Letter 98
60. John Bull taking a Lunch 99
61. Signature of Stephen Decatur 101
62. Portrait and Signature of John Barry 101
63. Commodore Barry's Monument 101
64. Naval Pitcher 104
65. Medal presented to Commodore Truxtun 105
66. Signature of Thomas Truxtun 105
67. Truxtun's Grave 105
68. The Lutheran Church in Philadelphia 110
69. Washington Medal 111
70. Tail-piece—M'Pherson Blue 111
71. Initial Letter 112
72. Portrait and Signature of Thomas Jefferson 114
73. Algiers in 1800 117
74. Portrait and Signature of Richard Dale 118
75. Dale's Monument 119
76. Portrait and Signature of Edward Preble 120
77. Tripolitan Weapon 121
78. Tripolitan Poniard 122
79. Medal given to Commodore Preble 123
80. Naval Monument 124
81. Signature of William Eaton 125
82. Initial Letter 130
83. Portrait and Signature of A. Burr 135
84. Signature of John Adair 136
85. Blennerhassett's Residence 136
86. Signature of Blennerhassett 136
87. Portrait and Signature of Rufus King 143
88. Portrait and Signature of William Pinkney 148
89. Initial Letter 149
90. Lynnhaven Bay 156
91. Portrait and Signature of Commodore Barron 159
92. Portrait and Signature of James Monroe 161
93. Initial Letter 167
94. Gun-boats 168
95. Portrait and Signature of Josiah Quincy 174
96. Portrait and Signature of James Madison 176
97. Fort or Battery Severn, at Annapolis 181
98. Commodore Rodgers's Residence 182
99. Signals, No. 1 182
100. Signal Book 182
101. Signals, No. 2 183
102. Signals, No. 3 183
103. Signals, No. 4 183
104. Signal Alphabet 183
105. Signal, No. 5 184
106. Portrait and Signature of Commodore Rodgers 185
107. Tail-piece—Gauntlet 186
108. Initial Letter 187
109. Birth-place of Tecumtha and his Brother 188
110. The Prophet 189
111. Joseph Barron 191
112. Indian Detecter 191
113. Portrait and Signature of General Boyd 194
114. Signature of Peter Funk 195
115. Fort Harrison 197
116. Signat're of Judge Naylor Page 198
117. Portrait and Signature of A. Whitlock 199
118. Portrait and Signature of William H. Harrison 200
119. View at Tippecanoe Battleground 202
120. Signature of J. Snelling 203
121. Map—Battle of Tippecanoe 205
122. Vignette to a Mournful Ballad 208
123. Tippecanoe Battle-ground 209
124. Tail-piece—Wigwam 209
125. Initial Letter 210
126. Portrait and Signature of H. Clay 211
127. The Gerrymander 211
128. Portrait and Signature of J. Randolph 215
129. Portrait and Signature of J. C. Calhoun 216
130. Signature of Josiah Quincy 217
131. Signature of James Emott 217
132. Signature of J. H. Craig 220
133. Fac-simile of a Newspaper Cut 224
134. Portrait and Signature of Governor Clinton 225
135. Governor Clinton's Tomb 226
136. Caricature—Josiah the First 228
137. Initial Letter 233
138. Portrait of George the Fourth 233
139. Signature of Jonathan Williams 235
140. Fort Independence 236
141. Castle Williams 237
142. Plan of Fort M'Henry 237
143. Torpedo, Plate 1 238
144. Torpedo, Plate 2 239
145. Torpedo, Plate 3 239
146. Torpedo, Plate 4 240
147. Destruction of the Dorothea 240
148. Portrait and Signature of Robert Fulton 242
149. Fulton's Birth-place 242
150. Signature of Edward Baynes 247
151. Portrait of Henry Dearborn 249
152. General Dearborn's Residence 250
153. The Parting Stone 250
154. Initial Letter 251
155. Portrait and Signature of William Hull 252
156. Portrait and Signature of John Johnston 253
157. Place of Hull's Rendezvous 254
158. Signature of Governor Meigs 255
159. View at Bloody Bridge 261
160. Colonel Babie's Residence 262
161. View at the Riviere aux Canards 264
162. Map—Detroit Frontier 266
163. Portrait and Signature of Duncan M'Arthur 267
164. Mackinack, from Round Island 267
165. Arch Rock, Mackinack 268
166. Fort Mackinack 269
167. Tail-piece—Canoe 271
168. Initial Letter 272
169. Fort Niagara, from Fort George 274
170. Portrait of Thomas B. Van Horne 275
171. Barracks at Sandwich 278
172. Maguaga Battle-ground 281
173. Tecumtha 282
174. Signature of J. B. Glegg 283
175. Portrait and Signature of D. Noon 292
176. Portrait and Signature of Lewis Cass 294
177. Tail-piece—Neglected Grave 296

ILLUSTRATIONS.

178. Initial Letter............Page 297
179. Signature of Jno. B. Laughton 298
180. View at Malden, Upper Canada...................................... 299
181. British Cannon at Detroit.... 300
182. Signature of Robt. Reynolds.. 300
183. Signature of C. Moran........ 302
184. Kinzie Mansion and Fort Dearborn......................... 303
185. The Black Partridge's Medal. 306
186. Map—Site of Chicago........ 308
187. Block-house at Chicago...... 312
188. Fort Wayne in 1812........... 315
189. The Little Turtle's Grave..... 315
190. Bridge at the Head of the Maumee.............................. 316
191. Portrait and Signature of Z. Taylor........................... 318
192. General Taylor's Residence... 319
193. Initial Letter................ 320
194. Fort Defiance................ 333
195. Site of Fort Defiance........ 333
196. Apple-tree at Defiance....... 334
197. Tail-piece — Indians at Ruins of a Village.................... 337
198. Initial Letter................ 338
199. Portrait and Signature of Simon Perkins..................... 340
200. Signature of Elijah Wadsworth......................... 340
201. Portrait and Signature of E. Whittlesey...................... 341
202. Signature of William Eustis.. 349
203. Winchester's Head-quarters.. 354
204. Map — Movements at Frenchtown............................. 358
205. Residence of La Salle........ 359
206. Monroe, from the Battleground.......................... 361
207. Signature of Laurent Durocher.............................. 362
208. Portrait and Signature of Jas. Knaggs........................... 363
209. Tail-piece — Tomahawk and Scalping-knife.................. 364
210. Initial Letter................ 365
211. Arsenal Building, Watertown 366
212. Signature of Colonel Benedict 367
213. Portrait of Captain William Vaughan......................... 368
214. Cipher Alphabet and Numerals............................... 370
215. Signature of Paul Hamilton.. 370
216. Signature of Richard Dodge.. 373
217. Appearance of Fort Presentation in 1812.................... 373
218. Design on Indian Pass....... 374
219. Signature of G. D. Young.... 376
220. Portrait and Signature of Eleazer Williams.................. 377
221. Old Church in St. Regis..... 378
222. Boundary Monument........ 379
223. The Port of Buffalo in 1813... 380
224. Remains at Fort Schlosser... 380
225. Signature of H. Dearborn... 381
226. Map of the Niagara Frontier. 382
227. Portrait and Signature of Stephen Van Rensselaer........ 384
228. Signature of William Howe Cuyler......................... 387
229. Portrait and Signature of Jesse D. Elliott................... 388
230. Tail-piece — Oar, Boardingpike, and Rope................ 388
231. Initial Letter................ 389
232. Signature of Alexander Smyth 389
233. Queenston in 1812............ 390
234. Signature of John R. Fenwick 391
235. View from the Site of Vrooman's Battery.................. 391
236. Signature of John Chrystie... 392
237. Signature of James Collier... 393
238. Landing-place of the Americans at Queenston............ 395
239. Russell's Law Office......... 396
240. Portrait and Signature of John E. Wool....................... 397
241. Signature of J. R. Mullany... 399
242. Portrait and Signature of John Brant........................... 401
243. Brant's Monument........... 401
244. Signature of Joseph G. Totten 403
245. Signature of J. Gibson....... 403
246. New Magazine at Fort George 405
247. Signature of R. H. Sheaffe... 405
248. Medal in Memory of General Brock........................... 406
249. Brock's Monument........... 406

250. Portrait and Signature of Solomon Van Rensselaer..Page 407
251. Signature of John Lovett..... 407
252. Tail-piece—Proclamation and Sword........................... 411
253. Initial Letter................ 412
254. Brock's Monument on Queenston Heights.................... 414
255. Monument where Brock fell.. 416
256. Signature of Solomon Vrooman.............................. 417
257. Present Outline of Fort George 418
258. French Magazine at Fort George........................... 418
259. Distant View of Fort Mississaga.............................. 419
260. Interior View—Fort Mississaga in 1860..................... 419
261. Mission-house on the Grand River........................... 421
262. Portrait and Signature of G. H. M. Johnson.................. 421
263. Ornamental Tomahawk...... 421
264. Deer-shank Weapon.......... 422
265. Silver Calumet............... 422
266. Ancient Scalping-knife...... 422
267. Mohawk Church, Grand River, C. W......................... 423
268. Interior of Mohawk Church.. 423
269. Communion Plate............ 425
270. General Porter's Residence, Black Rock.................... 426
271. Signature of George M'Feely. 426
272. Signature of Cecil Bisshopp.. 428
273. Signature of Samuel Angus... 428
274. Tail-piece — Snail on Mapleleaf.............................. 432
275. Initial Letter................ 433
276. Signature of R. Byron....... 436
277. The *Constitution* in 1860..... 436
278. Fac-simile of Commodore Porter's Writing................. 441
279. Portrait and Signature of Commodore Hull................ 442
280. Hull's Monument............ 442
281. Portrait of James Richard Dacres............................. 444
282. Hull's Medal................. 446
283. Portrait and Signature of Captain Jones..................... 449
284. Signature of Thos. Whitnyates 449
285. Signature of J. P. Beresford.. 451
286. A Wasp on a Frolic.......... 452
287. Medal awarded to Captain Jones........................... 452
288. The Biddle Urn.............. 453
289. Tail-piece—Eagle bearing off the Trident of Neptune..... 453
290. Initial Letter................ 454
291. Signature of John S. Carden. 456
292. Medal awarded to Decatur... 458
293. Portrait and Signature of Commodore Bainbridge...... 459
294. Bainbridge's Monument..... 459
295. Bainbridge's New York Gold Box............................. 462
296. Bainbridge's Albany Gold Box 462
297. Bainbridge's Medal.......... 463
298. Bainbridge's Urn............ 463
299. Tail-piece — Napoleon's Flag and Star descending....... 472
300. Initial Letter................ 473
301. Signature of C. Gratiot...... 474
302. Portrait and Signature of Green Clay.................... 476
303. View of Cincinnati from Newport in 1812.................. 476
304. Map—Fort Meigs and its Vicinity........................... 477
305. Fac-simile of Harrison's Letter.............................. 479
306. Portrait and Signature of Leslie Combs.................. 480
307. Up the Maumee Valley...... 481
308. Site of the British Batteries from Fort Meigs............. 482
309. Portrait and Signature of Wm. Christy.......................... 483
310. Plan of Fort Meigs........... 484
311. Signature of W. E. Boswell... 487
312. Map—Siege of Fort Meigs... 488
313. Remains of Walker's Monument............................. 489
314. Portrait of Peter Navarre.... 490
315. Ruins of Fort Miami......... 491
316. Up the Maumee from Maumee City............................ 492
317. Well at Fort Meigs........... 492

318. Tail-piece—A Scalp......Page 493
319. Initial Letter................ 494
320. Signature of R. M. Johnson.. 495
321. Johnson's Monument........ 496
322. Portrait and Signature of G. Croghan........................ 499
323. View at Fremont, or Lower Sandusky...................... 500
324. Plan of Fort Stephenson..... 503
325. Gold Medal awarded to General Croghan.................. 505
326. Lower Castalian Spring...... 506
327. Site of Fort Stephenson..... 507
328. Part of Short's Sword-scabbard............................. 507
329. Perry's Residence............ 509
330. Portrait and Signature of Daniel Dobbins.................. 509
331. Wayne's Block-house at Erie 510
332. Site of French Fort and Entrance to Erie Harbor........ 511
333. Mouth of Cascade Creek.... 511
334. Block-house................. 511
335. Map—Erie and Presq' Isle Bay 514
336. Portrait and Signature of Usher Parsons.................. 516
337. Put-in Bay.................. 517
338. Initial Letter................ 518
339. Perry's Look-out, Gibraltar Island......................... 518
340. Perry's Battle-flag........... 519
341. Portrait of O. H. Perry...... 521
342. View of Perry's Birth-place.. 521
343. Catafalco................... 521
344. Perry's Monument........... 521
345. The two Squadrons just before the Battle.................. 522
346. Portrait and Signature of S. Champlin....................... 523
347. First Position in the Action.. 523
348. Signature of J. J. Yarnall.... 524
349. Second Position in the Battle 526
350. Portrait and Signature of J. Chapman....................... 527
351. Signature of Thomas Holdup 528
352. Position of the Squadrons at the close of the Battle....... 529
353. Almy's Sword................ 529
354. Fac-simile of Perry's Dispatch 530
355. The Burial-place, Put-in Bay. 532
356. Queen Charlotte and Johnny Bull............................. 534
357. The Perry Medal............. 535
358. The Elliott Medal............ 535
359. Signature of Asel Wilkinson. 538
360. Portrait of Benjamin Fleming 538
361. Perry's Lantern.............. 539
362. Perry's Statue................ 540
363. Portrait and Signature of S. Sholes.......................... 541
364. Champlin's Chair............ 542
365. Perry's Quarters at Erie..... 543
366. Portrait of T. H. Stevens.... 543
367. Initial Letter................ 544
368. Portrait and Signature of C. S. Todd.......................... 548
369. Dolsen's.................... 549
370. View at the Mouth of M'Gregor's Creek.................... 550
371. M'Gregor's Mill.............. 550
372. Portrait of Oshawahnah..... 552
373. View on the Thames......... 553
374. Map—Battle of the Thames.. 554
375. Portrait and Signature of S. Theobald...................... 556
376. The Harrison Medal......... 558
377. The Shelby Medal........... 558
378. Tecumtha's Pistol........... 560
379. Thames Battle-ground....... 561
380. Remains of an ancient Coffin 564
381. The four Sides of the Holy Stone........................... 564
382. Stone Axes.................. 564
383. Sectional View of a Pyramid. 564
384. Great Earth-work near Newark............................. 565
385. The old State-house........ 567
386. General M'Arthur's Residence 568
387. Portrait and Signature of T. Worthington.................. 568
388. Adena, Governor Worthington's Residence............... 569
389. Portrait and Signature of Mrs. Harrison...................... 571
390. Pioneer House, North Bend.. 571
391. Block-house at North Bend.. 571
392. Harrison's Grave............. 573
393. Symmes's Monument........ 573

ILLUSTRATIONS. XV

394. Harrison's Residence at North Bend.................. Page 574
395. Initial Letter.................. 575
396. Block-house at Brockville.... 577
397. Parish's Store-house.......... 578
398. Portrait and Signature of D. W. Church................. 578
399. Site of Fort Presentation..... 579
400. Map—Operations at Ogdensburg................. 580
401. Portrait and Signature of J. York................. 580
402. Court-house, Ogdensburg.... 580
403. The battered Wind-mill...... 583
404. Wind-mill and Ruins near Prescott................. 584
405. Fort Wellington in 1860...... 584
406. Portrait and Signature of Z. Pike................. 586
407. Little York in 1813........... 587
408. Remains of the Western Battery................. 588
409. Powder-magazine at Toronto 589
410. Map—Attack on Little York.. 590
411. Signature of John Ross....... 592
412. Remains of old Fort Toronto. 593
413. Old Fort at Toronto in 1860... 593
414. View on the Niagara near Lewiston................. 595
415. Entrance to the Niagara River 597
416. Plan of Operations at the Mouth of the Niagara..... 599
417. A North River Steam-boat... 601
418. Portrait and Signature of W. H. Merritt................. 602
419. Battle-ground of Stony Creek 603
420. Tail-piece — Destruction of Store-houses................. 606
421. Initial Letter................. 607
422. Portrait and Signature of Jacob Brown................. 608
423. General Brown's Monument.. 608
424. Light-house at Horse Island.. 609
425. Signature of Capt. Mulcaster. 610
426. Map—Operations at Sackett's Harbor................. 612
427. Sackett's Harbor in 1814...... 613
428. Map—Sackett's Harbor and its Defenses................. 614
429. Signature of Henry Eckford.. 615
430. The *New Orleans*............. 616
431. Pike's Monument............. 616
432. Remains of Fort Pike......... 617
433. Block-house, Sackett's Harbor 617
434. Mansion of General Brown... 618
435. Whittlesey Rock, Watertown. 618
436. Signature of C. G. Bœrstler... 620
437. German Church............... 620
438. Portrait and Signature of Laura Secord................. 621
439. Beaver Dams Battle-ground and Surroundings......... 624
440. Signature of James Dittrick.. 624
441. Bisshopp's Monument........ 628
442. Interior of Fort Niagara..... 634
443. Signature of General A. Hall. 635
444. Tail-piece — Farm-house on fire................. 637
445. Initial Letter................. 637
446. Portrait and Signature of J. G. Swift................. 638
447. Signature of Joseph Bloomfield................. 639
448. Signature of A. De Salabery. 639
449. Portrait and Signature of Robert Carr................. 640
450. Portrait and Signature of Jas. Wilkinson................. 646
451. Signature of W. Hampton.... 648
452. Mouth of French Creek...... 649
453. Bald Island and Wilkinson's Flotilla................. 650
454. Chrysler's in 1855............. 652
455. Signature of Rob't Swartwout 652
456. Signature of J. A. Coles...... 653
457. Signature of J. Walbach...... 653
458. Map—Chrysler's Field....... 654
459. Signature of M. Myers....... 654
460. Place of Debarkation on the Salmon River................. 655
461. Lewis and Boyd's Head-quarters................. 656
462. Brown's Head-quarters...... 656
463. Fac-simile of written Placard 658
464. Remains of Fort Carleton.... 659
465. Indian Armlet................. 660
466. Light-house kept by Johnston 661
467. Peel Island................. 661
468. Portrait and Signature of W. Johnston................. Page 662
469. Johnston's Commission....... 663
470. French Mills in 1860.......... 664
471. Signature of James Campbell 665
472. The Block-house Well........ 665
473. Signature of Peter Brouse.... 666
474. Victoria Medal............... 666
475. Initial Letter................. 667
476. Interior of old Fort Norfolk.. 668
477. Signature of A. M'Lane...... 668
478. Signature of Admiral Cockburn................. 669
479. Landing-place of the British at Havre de Grace............. 671
480. The Pringle House........... 672
481. Episcopal Church............. 672
482. John O'Neil's Sword.......... 673
483. General View of Craney Island 675
484. Signature of Jos. Tarbell..... 675
485. Signature of J. Sanders...... 676
486. Portrait and Signature of W. B. Shubrick................. 676
487. Portrait and Signature of Robert Taylor................. 677
488. Signature of B. J. Neale...... 678
489. Portrait and Signature of Jas. Faulkner................. 678
490. Plan of Operations at Craney Island................. 679
491. Signature of Josiah Tattnall.. 680
492. The *Centipede*................. 680
493. View at Hampton Creek in 1853................. 681
494. Plan of Operations at Hampton................. 683
495. Head-quarters of Beckwith and Cockburn............. 683
496. British Consul's House....... 685
497. Oyster Fishing............... 685
498. Remains of Fortifications on Craney Island................. 686
499. Block-house on Craney Island 686
500. Magazine on Craney Island.. 686
501. Landing-place of the British at Murphy's................. 687
502. Kirby House................. 688
503. Soldiers' Monument at Point Pleasant................. 689
504. Osceola's Grave............... 690
505. Entrance to Bonaventure..... 691
506. Signature of T. M. Hardy.... 691
507. New London in 1813........... 692
508. Light-house at New London.. 694
509. Signature of H. Burbeck..... 694
510. Burbeck's Monument........ 694
511. Commodore Rodgers's Monument................. 696
512. Ancient Block-house at Fort Trumbull................. 697
513. New London Harbor from Fort Trumbull................. 697
514. The old Court-house.......... 697
515. Initial Letter................. 698
516. The Lawrence Medal......... 700
517. Hornet and Peacock.......... 700
518. Signature of Sam. Evans..... 701
519. Fac-simile of Lawrence's Letter................. 702
520. Fac-simile of Broke's Challenge................. 703
521. The *Chesapeake* disabled...... 706
522. Portrait of Captain Broke.... 707
523. *Shannon* and *Chesapeake* at Halifax................. 708
524. Portrait and Signature of Jas. Lawrence................. 709
525. Signature of Admiral Warren 709
526. Admiral Warren's Seal....... 709
527. Silver Plate presented to Captain Broke................. 710
528. Signature of George Budd.... 711
529. Coffins................. 712
530. Lawrence Memorial.......... 712
531. Monument of Lawrence and Ludlow................. 713
532. Lawrence's early Monument. 713
533. Portrait of W. H. Allen...... 715
534. Lieutenant Allen's Monument 716
535. Graves of Burrows, Blyth, and Waters................. 718
536. The Burrows Medal.......... 719
537. The M'Call Medal............. 720
538. Initial Letter................. 721
539. Portrait and Signature of D. Porter................. 721
540. The mighty Gattanewa....... 728
541. The *Essex* and her Prizes..... 729
542. Marquesas Drum............. Page 730
543. Battle of the *Essex*, *Phœbe*, and *Cherub*................. 733
544. David Porter's Monument.... 734
545. Initial Letter................. 738
546. Signature of Fulwar Skipwith 740
547. Signature of Hugh Campbell. 740
548. Portrait and Signature of General Robertson................. 747
549. Signature of Sam Dale....... 749
550. Map—Seat of War in Southern Alabama................. 751
551. Fort Mims................. 756
552. Portrait of John Coffee...... 759
553. Initial Letter................. 760
554. Map—Battle of Talladega.... 765
555. Claiborne Landing............. 770
556. Map—Seat of the Creek War in Upper Alabama......... 778
557. Map—Battle of the Horseshoe 780
558. Initial Letter................. 783
559. Signature of N. Macon....... 784
560. Embargo—a Caricature..... 785
561. Death of the Terrapin........ 787
562. Signature of J. Mason........ 788
563. Signature of C. Van De Venter 788
564. Signature of George Glasgow 788
565. Map—Affair at La Colle Mill. 790
566. La Colle Mill and Block-house 791
567. The dismantled *Superior*..... 794
568. Sir J. L. Yeo................. 795
569. Attack on Oswego........... 796
570. Signature of A. Bronson..... 796
571. Signature of H. Eagle........ 797
572. Signature of M. M'Nair...... 797
573. Fort at Oswego in 1855....... 798
574. Place of Battle at Sandy Creek 799
575. Otis's House, Sandy Creek... 800
576. Signature of Alfred Ely..... 800
577. Signature of Harmon Ehle... 801
578. Portrait of Jehaziel Howard.. 801
579. Red Jacket's Medal.......... 802
580. Portrait of Red Jacket....... 803
581. Profile and Signature of William M'Ree................. 803
582. Portrait and Signature of C. K. Gardner................. 805
583. Signature of General Riall... 805
584. Street's Creek Bridge....... 806
585. Remains of Tête-de-pont Battery................. 807
586. Signature of Joseph Treat.... 807
587. Street's Creek Bridge, looking North................. 808
588. General Towson's Grave..... 809
589. Map—Battle of Chippewa.... 810
590. Signature of Worth.......... 812
591. Worth's Monument.......... 812
592. Jones's Monument.......... 812
593. Mouth of Lyon's Creek...... 813
594. Initial Letter................. 816
595. View at Lundy's Lane....... 818
596. Portrait and Signature of J. Miller................. 820
597. Miller's Medal................. 821
598. Portrait of John M'Neil...... 821
599. Flag of the Twenty-fifth..... 822
600. Map—Battle of Niagara Falls 823
601. Scott's Medal................. 826
602. Signature of Winfield Scott.. 826
603. Signature of Jas. Cummings.. 827
604. Hospital near Lundy's Lane.. 828
605. Wooden Slab................. 828
606. Remains of Douglass's Battery and Fort Erie........ 830
607. Portrait and Signature of E. P. Gaines................. 831
608. Drummond's Secret Order... 832
609. Gaines's Medal................. 836
610. Portrait and Signature of P. B. Porter................. 838
611. Porter's Tomb................. 838
612. Map—Siege of Fort Erie..... 839
613. Wood's Monument............. 840
614. Brown's Medal................. 841
615. Brown's Gold Box............ 841
616. Signature of E. W. Ripley... 842
617. Porter's Medal................. 842
618. Seal of the City of New York. 842
619. Signature of De Witt Clinton 842
620. Ripley's Medal................. 843
621. Portrait of Robert White.... 844
622. Fac-simile of White's Writing 844
623. Portrait and Signature of G. Izard................. 845
624. Ruins of Fort Erie........... 846
625. Fort Erie Mills................. 847
626. Signature of James Sloan.... 847

ILLUSTRATIONS.

627. Soldiers' Monument.....Page 848
628. Riley's Monument............ 849
629. Signature of R. M'Douall..... 850
630. Map—M'Arthur's Raid....... 852
631. Portrait of General Scott..... 853
632. Initial Letter................ 854
633. Portrait and Signature of T. Macdonough................ 856
634. Judge Moore's House........ 857
635. Signature of D. Bissell....... 857
636. Signature of G. Prevost...... 858
637. Portrait and Sig. of B. Mooers 858
638. Portrait and Signature of A. Macomb.................... 859
639. Sampson's................... 859
640. Map—Fortifications at Plattsburg..................... 860
641. M. Smith's Monument....... 861
642. Howe's House................ 862
643. Platt's Residence............ 863
644. Old Stone Mill............... 864
645. The Saranac................. 865
646. Henley's Medal.............. 868
647. Cassin's Medal............... 868
648. Portrait and Signature of H. Paulding.................. 869
649. View from Cumberland Head 870
650. Map—Naval Action.......... 871
651. Macdonough's Dispatch...... 872
652. Portrait and Sig. of J. Smith. 872
653. Battle of Plattsburg.......... 873
654. The Saranac at Pike's Cantonment..................... 874
655. Ruins of Fort Brown......... 875
656. Artillery Quadrant........... 875
657. General Mooers's Grave...... 876
658. United States Hotel.......... 876
659. Macomb's Monument........ 877
660. Macomb's Medal............. 878
661. Macdonough's Medal......... 878
662. Macdonough's Farm-house... 879
663. Downie's Grave.............. 879
664. View in Beekmantown....... 880
665. Soldiers' Graves.............. 880
666. Map—Seat of War........... 881
667. Store-houses................. 882
668. Mooers's House.............. 882
669. Woolsey's House............. 883
670. Ball in Mooers's House...... 884
671. Portrait and Signature of F. Gregory................... 885
672. Portrait and Signature of M. Crane..................... 885
673. Crane's Monument........... 886
674. Portrait and Signature of I. Chauncey.................. 887
675. Chauncey's Monument....... 887
676. Initial Letter................ 888
677. Portrait and Signature of J. Montgomery............... 891
678. Fort Pickering............... 891
679. Carcass..................... 894
680. Stonington Flag.............. 894
681. The Cobb House.............. 896
682. Denison's Monument......... 896
683. Portrait and Signature of J. Sherbrooke................ 897
684. Fort Porter, Castine......... 897
685. Signature of R. Barrie........ 898
686. General Blake's House....... 898
687. Crosby's Wharf.............. 899
688. Portrait and Signature of C. Morris.................... 900
689. Morris's Monument.......... 901
690. Town-house, Hampden....... 902
691. Reed's Shop.................. 902
692. Remains of Fort George..... 903
693. Signature and Seal of G. Gosselin...................... 903
694. Yankee Doodle Upset......... 904
695. Billet-head of *Constitution*... 905
696. Fort Pickering, Salem........ 906
697. Remains of Fort Lee......... 906
698. Marblehead Harbor........... 907
699. Fort Sewall.................. 907
700. Portrait and Signature of Dr. Browne................... 908
701. Small Cannon................ 909
702. View from Fort George...... 909
703. Remains of Fort Castine..... 909
704. Remains at Fort Griffith..... 910
705. Fort Point................... 910
706. The Bacon Tree.............. 911
707. Mouth of the Kenduskeag.... 911
708. Portrait and Sig. of Van Meter 912
709. Remains of Fort Phœnix..... 913
710. Arsenal at Stonington........ 914
711. Portrait and Sig. of J. Holmes 914

712. Portrait and Signature of A. B. Holmes............Page 914
713. Denison's Grave............. 914
714. Tail-piece—Bomb-shell....... 915
715. Initial Letter................ 916
716. Signature of P. Stuart....... 916
717. Portrait and Signature of D. L. Clinch.................. 917
718. Portrait and Signature of W. H. Winder................. 918
719. Signature of H. Carbery..... 920
720. Signature of J. P. Van Ness.. 920
721. Signature of T. E. Stansbury. 921
722. Signature of J. Sterett....... 921
723. Signature of W. Smith....... 922
724. Signature of S. West......... 922
725. Signature of W. D. Beall..... 922
726. Signature of J. W. Scott..... 922
727. Signature of J. Tilghman.... 922
728. Old Mill, Bladensburg....... 924
729. Bridge at Bladensburg....... 927
730. Residence of J. C. Rives..... 927
731. Dueling-ground, Bladensburg 928
732. Signature of J. Davidson..... 928
733. Map—Battle of Bladensburg. 929
734. Portrait and Signature of J. Barney................... 930
735. Barney's Spring.............. 931
736. Bullet....................... 931
737. The Capitol in 1814.......... 932
738. Remains of the Capitol...... 933
739. Remains of the President's House..................... 934
740. Signature of T. Tingey....... 934
741. Portrait and Signature of D. Madison................... 935
742. Portrait and Signature of J. Barker................... 936
743. Portrait and Signature of G. R. Gleig................... 937
744. Signature of D. Wadsworth... 938
745. Fort Washington............. 939
746. Sketch of Torpedo........... 940
747. The Unknown................ 942
748. Barlow's Vault............... 942
749. Kalorama.................... 942
750. Cenotaph.................... 943
751. Gerry's Monument........... 943
752. Initial Letter................ 944
753. Portrait and Sig. of P. Parker. 946
754. Portrait and Sig. of S. Smith. 947
755. Montebello.................. 947
756. Rodgers's Bastion............ 949
757. Methodist Meeting-house.... 950
758. Portrait and Signature of J. Stricker................... 950
759. Portrait and Signature of D. M'Dougall................. 952
760. Battle of North Point........ 953
761. Battle-flag.................. 954
762. Signature of M. Bird......... 954
763. Fort M'Henry in 1861....... 954
764. Signature of J. H. Nicholson.. 955
765. Signature of S. Lane......... 955
766. Portrait and Signature of G. Armistead................. 955
767. Signature of F. S. Key....... 956
768. Star-spangled Banner........ 957
769. The Armistead Vase.......... 960
770. Armistead's Monument...... 960
771. Signature of W. K. Armistead 960
772. Battle Monument............ 961
773. The City Spring, Baltimore... 962
774. Portrait and Sig. of J. Lester. 963
775. North Point Battle-ground... 963
776. Monument where Ross fell... 964
777. Remains of Circular Battery.. 965
778. State Fencible............... 966
779. Signature of D. D. Tompkins. 970
780. Signature of Morgan Lewis... 970
781. Fort Stevens and Mill Rock.. 971
782. Tower at Hallett's Point..... 971
783. Fortifications around New York..................... 972
784. Mill Rock Fortifications..... 973
785. Fort Clinton................. 973
786. Fort Clinton and Harlem River 973
787. M'Gowan's Pass.............. 974
788. North Battery............... 974
789. View from Fort Fish......... 974
790. Courtenay's, and Tower...... 975
791. Remains of Block-house...... 975
792. M'Gowan's Pass in 1860...... 975
793. Signature of A. and N. Brown. 976
794. Iron-clad Vessel............. 976
795. Section of Floating Battery... 977
796. *Fulton the Second*............ 977
797. Initial Letter................ 978

798. Portrait and Signature of J. Blakeley................Page 979
799. Blakeley's Medal............ 980
800. Portrait and Signature of L. Warrington............... 981
801. Warrington's Medal......... 982
802. Billet-head of *Cyane*......... 985
803. Stewart's Medal............. 986
804. Stewart's Residence......... 986
805. Stewart's Sword............. 986
806. Portrait and Signature of C. Stewart................... 987
807. Portrait and Signature of S. Decatur................... 988
808. Decatur's Monument........ 989
809. Portrait and Sig. of J. Biddle 990
810. Biddle's Medal.............. 991
811. Privateer Schooner......... 993
812. Signature of Admiral Sawyer 994
813. Portrait and Signature of S. C. Reid................... 1004
814. Initial Letter............... 1008
815. Signature of A. J. Armstrong 1011
816. Portrait and Signature of A. J. Dallas................. 1011
817. Signature of T. Jesup....... 1013
818. Signatures of the Members of the Hartford Convention.. 1014
819. Caricature.................. 1015
820. The Hermitage.............. 1017
821. Portrait of W. C. C. Claiborne 1019
822. Portrait of A. Jackson...... 1020
823. Map—Attack on Fort Bowyer 1021
824. Jackson's City Head-quarters 1024
825. Portrait of Major Plauché... 1024
826. Patterson's Monument...... 1025
827. Map—Fight of Gun-boats and Barges................... 1026
828. Cathedral in New Orleans... 1027
829. Fort St. John................ 1028
830. Villeré's Mansion........... 1029
831. Portrait of De la Ronde..... 1030
832. Lacoste's Mansion.......... 1031
833. Map—Affair below N. Orleans 1032
834. Portrait of De Lacy Evans... 1032
835. A Tennessee Flag........... 1033
836. Initial Letter............... 1034
837. De la Ronde's Mansion...... 1034
838. Map—Seat of War in Louisiana...................... 1036
839. Jackson's Head-quarters..... 1037
840. Chalmette's Plantation...... 1039
841. Map—Battle of New Orleans 1040
842. Remains of a Canal......... 1042
843. Plauché's Tomb............. 1043
844. You's Tomb................. 1043
845. Map—Position of Troops.... 1044
846. Battle of New Orleans...... 1047
847. Monument.................. 1048
848. Pecan-trees................. 1050
849. Map—Fort St. Philip....... 1051
850. Jackson's Medal............. 1052
851. Jackson's Draft............. 1053
852. Signature of D. A. Hall..... 1054
853. The Old Court-house........ 1054
854. Ashland.................... 1055
855. Bodley's Grave.............. 1055
856. Jackson's Tomb............. 1055
857. Clay's Monument........... 1056
858. Grave of Daniel Boone...... 1056
859. Kentucky Soldiers' Monument..................... 1057
860. Portrait and Signature of F. Robertson................ 1058
861. Portrait of A. Henner....... 1058
862. Japan Plum................. 1059
863. Portrait of J. Q. Adams..... 1059
864. Portrait of J. A Bayard..... 1060
865. Adams's Homes............. 1060
866. View of Ghent.............. 1061
867. Cipher Writing............. 1061
868. Fac-simile of MS. of Treaty of Ghent................. 1062
869. Seal and Sig. of Gambier.... 1062
870. Seal and Sig. of Goulburn... 1062
871. Seal and Sig. of W. Adams.. 1062
872. Seal and Sig. of J. Q. Adams. 1062
873. Seal and Sig. of J. A. Bayard 1062
874. Seal and Sig. of H. Clay.... 1063
875. Seal and Sig. of J. Russell... 1063
876. Seal and Sig. of A. Gallatin.. 1063
877. Por't and Sig. of C. Hughes. 1063
878. Medal of Gratitude.......... 1065
879. Treaty of Peace Medal...... 1065
880. Allegorical Picture—Peace.. 1066
881. Dartmoor Prison............ 1068
882. Tail-piece — Civil and Military Power................ 1073

Preface

THE author of this volume said to the readers of his PICTORIAL FIELD-BOOK OF THE REVOLUTION, at the close of that work, "Should time deal gently with us, we may again go out with staff and scrip together upon the great highway of our country's progress, to note the march of events there." The implied promise has been fulfilled. The author has traveled more than ten thousand miles in this country and in the Canadas, with note-book and pencil in hand, visiting places of historic interest connected with the War of 1812, from the Great Lakes to the Gulf of Mexico, gathering up, recording, and delineating every thing of special value, not found in books, illustrative of the subject, and making himself familiar with the topography and incidents of the battle-fields of that war. Access to the archives of governments, state and national, and to private collections, was freely given him; and from the lips of actors in the events of that struggle he received the most interesting information concerning it, which might have perished with them.

The results of the author's researches and labors are given in this volume. The narrative of historic events is resumed where his work on the Revolution left it. An account is given of the perils of the country immediately succeeding the Revolution; the struggles of the new nation with the allied powers of British and Indians in the Northwest; the origin and growth of political parties in the United States, and their relations to the War of 1812; the influence of the French Revolution and French politics in giving complexion to parties in this country; the first war with the Barbary Powers; the effects of the wars of Napoleon on the public policy of the United States; the Embargo and kindred acts, and the kindling of the war in 1812.

The events of the war are given in greater detail than in any work hitherto published, and the narrative brings to view actors in the scenes whose deeds have been overlooked by the historian. The work is a continuation of the history of our country from the close of the Revolution in 1783 to the end of the Second War with Great Britain in 1815.

POUGHKEEPSIE, NEW YORK, JULY, 1868.

PICTORIAL FIELD-BOOK

OF

THE WAR OF 1812.

CHAPTER I.

"I see, I see,
Freedom's established reign; cities, and men,
Numerous as sands upon the ocean shore,
And empires rising where the sun descends!
The *Ohio* soon shall glide by many a town
Of note; and where the *Mississippi* stream,
By forests shaded, now runs sweeping on,
Nations shall grow, and states not less in fame
Than Greece and Rome of old. We, too, shall boast
Our Scipios, Solons, Catos, sages, chiefs,
That in the lap of Time yet dormant lie,
Waiting the joyous hour of life and light."

PHILIP FRENEAU, 1775.

UCH was the prophecy of an American poet when the war for his country's independence had just been kindled; and similar were the prescient visions of the statesmen and sages of that hour, who, in the majesty of conscious rectitude, decreed the dismemberment of a mighty empire and the establishment of a nation of freemen in the New World. Their rebellion instantly assumed the dignity of a revolution, and commanded the respect and sympathy of the civilized nations. Their faith was perfect, and under its inspiration they contended gallantly for freedom, and won. We, their children, have seen the minstrel's prophecy fulfilled, and all the bright visions of glory that gave gladness to our fathers paled by a splendor of reality that makes us proud of the title — AMERICAN CITIZEN.

When, on the 25th of November, 1783, John Van Arsdale, a sprightly sailor-boy of sixteen years, climbed the slushed flag-staff in Fort George, at the foot of Broadway, New York, pulled down the British ensign that for more than seven years had floated there, and unfurled in its place the banner of the United States,[1] the work of the Revolution was finished. As the white sails of the British squadron that bore away from our shores the last armed enemy to freedom in Amer-

---

[1] Before the British left Fort George they nailed their colors to the summit of the flag-staff, knocked off the cleets, and "slushed" the pole from top to bottom, to prevent its being climbed. Van Arsdale (who died in 1836) ascended by nailing on cleets, and applying sand to the greased flag-staff. In this way he reached the top, hauled down the British flag, and placed that of the United States in its position. It is believed by some that the nailing of the flag there by the British had a higher significance than was visible in the outward act, namely, a compliance with orders from the imperial government not to strike the flag, as in a formal surrender, but to leave it flying, in token of the claim of Great Britain to the absolute proprietorship of the country then abandoned. It was believed that the absence of British authority in the United States would be only temporary.

B

ica became mere specks upon the horizon in the evening sun to the straining eyes of eager thousands gazing seaward beyond the Narrows,[1] the idea of absolute independence took possession of the mind and heart of every true American. He saw the visible bonds of British thraldom fall at his feet, and his pulse beat high with the inspiration of conscious freedom, and the full assurance that the power and influence of British sovereignty had departed from his country forever.

Alas! those natural, and generous, and patriotic, and hopeful emotions were fallacious. They were born of a beautiful theory, but derived no real sustenance from sober facts. They were the poetry of that hour of triumph, entrancing the spirit and kindling the imagination. They gave unbounded pleasure to a disenthralled people. But there were wise and thoughtful men among them who had communed with the teachers of the Past, and sought knowledge in the vigorous school of the Present. They diligently studied the prose chapters of the great volume of current history spread out before them, and were not so jubilant. They reverently thanked God for what had been accomplished, adored him for the many interpositions of his providence in their behalf, and rejoiced because of the glorious results of the struggle thus far. But they clearly perceived that the peace established by the decrees of high contracting parties would prove to be only a lull in the great contest — a truce soon to be broken, not, perhaps, by the trumpet calling armed men to the field, but by the stern behests of the inexorable necessities of the new-born republic. The revolution was accomplished, and the political separation from Great Britain was complete, but absolute independence was not achieved.

The experience of two years wrought a wonderful change in the public mind. The wisdom of the few prophetic sages who warned the people of dangers became painfully apparent. The Americans were no longer the legal subjects of a monarch beyond the seas, yet the power and influence of Great Britain were felt like a chilling, overshadowing cloud. In the presence of her puissance in all that constitutes the material strength and vigor of a nation, they felt their weakness; and from many a patriot heart came a sigh to the lips, and found expression there in the bitter words of deep humiliation—We are *free*, but not *independent*.

Why not? Had not a solemn treaty and the word of an honest king acknowledged the states to be free and independent?

Yes. The Treaty of Peace had declared the confederated colonies "to be free, sovereign, and independent states;" and that the King of Great Britain would treat them as such, and relinquish "all claims to the government, propriety, and territorial rights of the same."[2] The king, in his speech from the throne,[a] had said, "I have sacrificed every consideration of my own to the wishes and opinion of my people. I make it my humble and earnest prayer to Almighty God that Great Britain may not feel the evils which might result from so great a dismemberment of the empire, and that America may be free from those calamities which have formerly proved, in the mother country, how essential monarchy is to the enjoyment of constitutional liberty. Religion, language, interest, affections may, and I hope will, yet prove a bond of permanent union between the two countries: to this end neither attention nor disposition shall be wanting on my part."[3]

[a] December 5, 1783.

---

[1] The passage from New York Harbor to the sea, between Long Island and Staten Island.

[2] See Article I. of the Treaty of Peace between the United States and Great Britain, signed at Paris on the 3d of September, 1783, by David Hartley in behalf of Great Britain, and Benjamin Franklin, John Adams, and John Jay for the United States.

[3] This acknowledgment was wrung from the king. He had long detested the very name of every thing American; and this feeling was strengthened by his intense personal hatred of Dr. Franklin, whose coolness and adroitness had given him the distinction of Arch-rebel. The king carried his prejudices so far that Sir John Pringle was driven to resign his place as President of the Royal Society in this wise: The king urgently requested the society to publish, with the authority of its name, a contradiction of a scientific opinion of the rebellious Franklin. Pringle replied that it was not in his power to reverse the order of nature, and resigned. The pliant Sir Joseph Banks, with the practice of a true courtier, advocated the opinion which was patronized by his majesty, and was appointed President of the Royal Society. See Wright's *England under the House of Hanover*, ii., 68.

Reception of John Adams in England.   Why the Americans were not independent.   Articles of Confederation.

This was all very kind, and yet the Americans were not independent.

Why not? Had not the representative of their independent sovereignty been appointed by the Congress to reside as the agent of the republic in the British capital, and been received with cordiality?

Yes. John Adams had been appointed[a] minister plenipotentiary to the Court of Great Britain, and had been ordered to leave sunny France for foggy England. The Duke of Dorset, the British embassador at Paris, had treated him most kindly at Auteuil, and had as kindly prescribed a gay court-dress to be worn by the embassador at his first presentation to the king on his majesty's birth-day. That plenipotentiary had been presented,[b] most graciously received, and affected almost to tears by these honest words of good King George: "I was the last man in the kingdom, sir, to consent to the independence of America; but, now it is granted, I shall be the last man in the world to sanction a violation of it."

[a] February 24, 1785.

[b] June 4, 1785.

This reception was significant, and this declaration of his majesty was explicit and sincere. Yet the Americans were not independent.

Why not? Because *they had not formed a nation, and thereby created a power to be respected;* because British statesmen were wise enough to perceive this weakness, and sagacious enough to take advantage of it. Without the honesty of the king, misled by the fatal counsels of the refugee loyalists who swarmed in the British metropolis, and governed wholly by the maxims and ethics of diplomacy, the ministry cast embarrassments in the way of the Confederation, neglected to comply with some of the most important stipulations of the Treaty of Peace, maintained a haughty reserve, and waited with complacency and perfect faith to see the whole fabric of government in the United States, cemented by the bonds of common interest and common danger while in a state of war, crumble into fragments, and the people return to their allegiance as colonists of Great Britain. Their trade and commerce, their manufactures and arts, their literature, science, religion, and laws were yet largely tributary to the parent country, without a well-grounded hope for a speedy deliverance. To this domination was added a traditional contempt of the English for their transatlantic brethren as an inferior people,[1] and the manifestation of an illiberal and unfriendly spirit, heightened by the consciousness that the Americans were without a government sufficiently powerful to command the fulfillment of treaty stipulations, or an untrammeled commerce sufficiently important to attract the cupidity and interested sympathies of other nations.

Such is a general statement of reasons why the United States were not independent of Great Britain after their total political separation from her. These gave to Dr. Franklin and others the consciousness of the incompleteness of the struggle commenced in 1775. When a compatriot remarked that the war for independence was successfully closed, Franklin wisely replied, "Say, rather, the war of the *Revolution.* The war for *independence* is yet to be fought."

I have remarked that our fathers had not formed a NATION on the return of peace, and in that fact was the inherent weakness of their government, and the spring of all the hopes of the royalists for their speedy return to colonial dependency. To illustrate this, let us take a rapid survey of events from the ratification of the Treaty of Peace in the autumn of 1784, to the formation of the National Constitution in the autumn of 1787.

The *Articles of Confederation,* suggested by Dr. Franklin in the summer of 1775, adopted by the Continental Congress in November, 1777, and finally settled by the ratification of all the states in the spring of 1781, became the organic law of the great American League of independent commonwealths, which, by the first article of that Constitution, was styled "The United States of America." In behalf of this Confeder-

---

[1] "Even the chimney-sweepers on the streets," said Pitt, in a speech in the House of Commons in 1763, "talk boastingly of their subjects in America."

acy, commissioners were appointed by the Continental Congress to negotiate for peace with Great Britain. That negotiation was successful, and, in September, 1783, a defin-
itive treaty was signed at Paris[a] by the respective commissioners[1] of the two governments. It was subsequently ratified by the Congress and the Crown. In the first article of the treaty all the states of the League were named, for the simple purpose of definitely declaring what provinces in the New World formed "The United States of America," as there were British, French, and Spanish provinces there not members of the League; and also because they were held to be, on the part of the English, independent republics, as they had been colonies independent of each other.[2]

[a] September 3, 1783.

The League now assumed a national attitude, and the powers of the Confederacy were speedily tested. The bright visions of material prosperity that gladdened the hearts of the Americans at the close of the war soon faded, and others more sombre appeared when the financial and commercial condition of the forming republic was contemplated with candor. A debt of seventy millions of dollars lay upon the shoulders of a wasted people. About forty-four millions of that amount was owing by the Federal government (almost ten millions of it in Europe), and the remainder by the individual states. These debts had been incurred in carrying on the war. Even while issuing their paper money in abundance, the Congress had commenced borrowing; and when, in 1780, their bills of credit became worthless, borrowing was the chief monetary resource of the government. This, of course, could not go on long without involving the republic in embarrassments and accomplishing its final ruin. The restoration of the public credit or the downfall of the infant republic was the alternative presented to the American people.

---

[1] See note 2, page 18.
[2] The advocates of the mischievous political doctrine known as supreme *state sovereignty*, whose fundamental dogma is that the states then forming the inchoate republic were absolutely *independent sovereignties*, have cited this naming of the several states in that treaty in support of their views. The states were independent *commonwealths*, but not *sovereignties*. That term implies no superior. The colonies and states had never been in that exalted position. They were dependencies of Great Britain until the Declaration of Independence was promulgated, when they immediately assumed the position of equals in a National League, acknowledging the general government which they thus established as the supreme controlling power, having a broad signet for the common use, bearing the words, "Seal of the United States,"

FIRST GREAT SEAL OF THE UNITED STATES.*

as its insignia of authority. When a treaty of peace was to be negotiated, the states did not each choose a commissioner for the purpose, but these agents were appointed by the General Congress, as representatives of the nationality of the Confederation, without reference to any particular states. And when, a few years later, the people ("We the PEOPLE" is the phrase) formed and ratified a *National Constitution*, they disowned all independent state *sovereignty*, and reserved to the states only municipal rights, the exercise of which should not be in contravention of the organic law of the land.

* For a history (with illustrations) of this first Great Seal of the United States, see a paper in *Harper's Magazine*, vol. xiii., p. 178, written by the author of this work.

With a determination to restore that public credit, the General Congress immediately put forth all its strength in efforts to produce such a result. A few weeks after the preliminary Treaty of Peace was signed, the Congress declared that "the establishment of permanent and adequate funds on taxes or duties, which shall operate generally, and, on the whole, in just proportion, throughout the United States, is indispensably necessary toward doing complete justice to the public creditors, for restoring public credit, and for providing for the future exigencies of the war."[1] Two months later[a] the Congress recommended to the several states, as "indispensably necessary to the restoration of public credit, and to the punctual discharge of the public debts," to vest the Congress with power to levy, for a period of twenty-five years, specified duties on certain imported articles, and an *ad valorem* duty on all others, the revenue therefrom to be applied solely to the payment of the interest and principal of the public debt. It was also proposed that the states should be required to establish for the same time, and for the same object, substantial revenues for supplying each its proportion of one million five hundred thousand dollars annually, exclusive of duties on imports, the proportion of each state to be fixed according to the eighth article of the organic law of the League.[2] This financial system was not to take effect until acceded to by every state.

[a] April 18, 1783.

This proposition was approved by the leading men of the country, but it was not adopted by the several states. They all took action upon it in the course of the succeeding three years, but that action was rather in the form of overtures—indications of what each state was willing to do—not of positive law. All the states except two were willing to grant the required amount, but they were not disposed to vest the Congress with the required power. "It is *money*, not *power*, that ought to be the object," they said. "The former will pay our *debts*, the latter may destroy our *liberties*."[3]

This first important effort of the Congress to assume the functions of sovereignty was a signal failure, and the beginning of a series of failures. It excited a jealousy between the state and general governments, and exposed the utter impotency of the latter, whose vitality depended upon the will of thirteen distinct legislative bodies, each tenacious of its own peculiar rights and interests, and miserly in its delegation of power. It was speedily made manifest that the public credit must be utterly destroyed by the inevitable repudiation of the public debt.

The League were equally unfortunate in their attempts to establish commercial relations with other governments, and especially with that of Great Britain. The Liberal ministry, under the Earl of Shelburne when the preliminary Treaty of Peace was signed, devised generous measures toward the Americans. Encouraged by a lively hope thereby engendered, American commerce began to revive. William Pitt, son of the eminent Earl of Chatham, then at the age of only twenty-four years, was Chancellor of the Exchequer. With a clear perception of the value to Great Britain of friendly relations between that government and the new republic, he introduced a bill into Parliament for the regulation of commerce between the two countries, by which trade with the British West India Islands and other colonial possessions of the crown was thrown open to the enterprise of the merchants of the United States.

In this proposed measure was involved a powerful element of solid peace and harmony between the two governments; but there seemed not to be wisdom enough among the statesmen of Great Britain for a practical perception of it. The shipping

---

[1] Journal of Congress, February 12, 1783. The last clause was necessary, because only *preliminary* articles of peace had been signed, and the war might continue.

[2] The following was the proposed apportionment: New Hampshire, $52,708; Massachusetts, $224,427; Rhode Island, $32,318; Connecticut, $132,091; New York, $128,243; New Jersey, $83,358; Pennsylvania, $205,189; Delaware, $22,443; Maryland, $141,517; Virginia, $256,487; North Carolina, $109,006; South Carolina, $96,183; Georgia, $16,030.

[3] The resolutions of Congress, and the proceedings of the several State Legislatures, with remarks thereon by "A Republican," were published in the *New York Gazetteer*, and afterward in pamphlet form, in the autumn of 1786, by *Carroll & Patterson*, 32 Maiden Lane, New York.

interest, then potential in Parliament, with strange blindness to its own welfare and that of the state, successfully opposed it; and the Liberal Shelburne ministry did not survive the proposition a month. It was dissolved, and, after a ministerial hiatus of several weeks, during which time faction threatened the peace if not the stability of the throne, a Cabinet was formed of materials the most discordant hitherto. North and Fox, Burke and Cavendish, Portland and Stormont, who had differed widely and debated bitterly on American affairs, coalesced, much to the astonishment of the simple, the scandal of political consistency, and the delight of satirists with pen and pencil.[1]

The new Cabinet listened to other counsels than those of the sagacious Pitt, and, instead of acting liberally toward the United States, as friends and political equals, they inaugurated a restrictive commercial policy, and assumed the offensive *hauteur* of lord and master in the presence of vassals or slaves. Echoing the opinions of the acrimonious Silas Deane, the specious Tory, Joseph Galloway, and Peter Oliver, the refugee Chief Justice of Massachusetts,[2] English writers and English statesmen made public observations which indicated that they regarded the American League as only alienated members of the British realm. Lord Sheffield, in a formidable pamphlet, gave expression to the views of the Loyalists and leading British statesmen, and declared his belief that ruin must soon overtake the League, because of the anarchy and confu-

---

WAR.

BRITANNIA AROUSED.

[1] The political satires and caricatures of the day indicate the temper of the people. Of these the war in America formed the staple subject at the time in question. The conduct of that war, its cessation or continuance, formed the topic of violent debates in Parliament, caused rancor among politicians, was the basis of new party organizations, and a source of great anxiety among the people. Among those who employed caricatures in the controversies Sayer and Gillray were the chief. The latter soon outstripped all competitors, and gave to the world more than twelve hundred caricatures, chiefly political. One of his earliest productions was issued at the period in question, in which the original positions of the different leaders of the coalition were exhibited in compartments. In one, entitled "War," Fox and Burke, in characteristic attitudes, are seen thundering against the massive Lord North. In another compartment, called "Neither Peace nor War," the three orators are, in the same attitudes, attacking the preliminary Treaty of Peace with the United States. Under them are the words "The Astonishing Coalition." Another caricature was called "The Loves of the Fox and the Badger; or, The Coalition Wedding." This popular caricature was a burlesque pictorial history of the sudden friendship between Fox and North. The latter was commonly known in political circles as "the badger." In another print Fox and North were represented under one coat, standing on a pedestal, and called "The State Idol." This the king (who detested the whole affair) was expected to worship. In another, the two are seen approaching Britannia (or the people) to claim her sanction. She rejects them, and their attention is directed to a gallows and block in the distance as their proper destination.

The coalition finally became unpopular, and Gillray, in a caricature entitled "Britannia Aroused; or, The Coalition Monsters Destroyed," represents her in a fury, grasping one of the leaders by the neck and the other by the leg, and hurling them from her as enemies to liberty. I have copied from Wright's *England under the House of Hanover* the most forcible portions of the two caricatures named.

[2] Silas Deane had been an active supporter of the American cause, and was sent to France, as an agent of the Continental Congress, early in 1776. In the autumn of that year he was associated with Dr. Franklin and Arthur Lee as commissioners to the French Court. Deane's unfitness for his station was soon made apparent, and he was recalled at the close of 1777. He went to England at the close of the war, and there vented his spleen against his countrymen.

Joseph Galloway was a Pennsylvanian, who espoused the republican cause, and was a member of the first Congress in 1774, but soon afterward abandoned his countrymen and went to England. He first joined the royal army in New York, and did not leave the country until 1778. He was a ready writer, and wrote much against the American cause in England, where he died in 1803.

Peter Oliver was past middle life when the Revolution broke out. He was appointed Chief Justice of Massachusetts in 1769, when his brother-in-law, Hutchinson, became governor of that province. He was impeached by the Massachusetts Assembly in 1774, and soon afterward went to England, where he died in 1791, aged 79 years.

sion in which they were involved in consequence of their independence. He assumed that the New England States in particular would speedily become penitent suppliants at the foot of the king for pardon and restoration as colonies. He saw the utter weakness and consequent inefficiency of the League as a form of government, and advised his countrymen to consider them of little account as a *nation*.[1] "If the American states choose to send consuls, receive them, and send a consul to each state. Each state will soon enter into all necessary regulations with the consul, and this is the whole that is necessary." In other words, the League has no dignity above that of a fifth-rate power, and the states are still, in fact, only dislocated members of the British Empire.[2]

In considering the more remote causes of the War of 1812, and the final independence of the United States achieved by that war, that pamphlet of Lord Sheffield, which gave direction to British legislation and bias to the English mind in reference to the American League, may be regarded as a most important one. It was followed by Orders in Council[3] by which American vessels were entirely excluded from the British West Indies; and some of the staple productions of the United States, such as fish, beef, pork, butter, lard, *et cetera*, were not permitted to be carried there except in British bottoms. These orders were continued by temporary acts until 1788, when the policy was permanently established as a commercial regulation by act of Parliament.

In view of this unfriendly conduct of Great Britain, the General Congress, in the spring of 1784, asked the several states to delegate powers to them for fifteen years, by which they might compel England to be more liberal by countervailing measures of prohibition.[4] Well would it have been for the people of the young republic had some restrictive measures been adopted, whereby British goods could have been kept from their ports, for in a very short time after the peace a most extravagant and ruinous trade with Great Britain was opened. Immense importations were made, and private indebtedness speedily added immensely to the evils which the war and an inadequate government had brought upon the people. But the appeal of the Congress was in vain. The states, growing more and more jealous of their individual dignity, would not invest the Congress with any such power; nor would they, even in the face of the danger of having their trade go into the hands of foreigners, make any permanent and uniform arrangements among themselves. Without public credit, with their commerce at the mercy of every adventurer, without respect at home or abroad, the League of States, free without independence, presented the sad spectacle of the elements of a great nation paralyzed in the formative process, and the coldness of political death chilling every developing function of its being.

Difficulties soon arose between the United States and Great Britain concerning the

---

[1] "It will not be an easy matter," he said (and he no doubt spoke the language of the English people in general), "to bring the American states to act as a nation; *they are not to be feared as such by us*. It will be a long time before they can engage or will concur in any material expenses. A stamp act, a tea act, or such act that can never again occur, would alone unite them. Their climate, their staples, their manners are different; their interests opposite; and that which is beneficial to one is destructive to the other. We might as reasonably dread the effects of combinations among the German as among the American states, and deprecate the resolves of the Diet as those of the Congress. In short, every circumstance proves that it will be extreme folly to enter into any engagements *by which we may not wish to be bound hereafter*. It is impossible to name any material advantage the American states will or can give us in return *more* than what we of course shall have. No treaty can be made with the American states that can be binding on the whole of them. The Act of Confederation does not enable Congress to form more than general treaties."—SHEFFIELD'S *Observations on the Commerce of the American States*, London, 1783.

[2] The estimation in which the League was held by the British government may be inferred by an inquiry of the Duke of Dorset, in reply to a letter from Messrs. Adams, Franklin, and Jefferson, on the subject of a commercial treaty, in March, 1785. His grace inquired "whether they were commissioned by Congress or their respective states, for it appeared to him that *each state was determined to manage its own matters in its own way*." It could not be expected that England would be in haste to form any important commercial relations with a government so uncertain in its character, for a league of independent governments was liable to dissolution at any moment.

[3] July, 1783. The British Privy Council consists of an indefinite number of gentlemen, chosen by the sovereign, and having no direct connection with the Cabinet ministers. The sovereign may, under the advice of this council, issue orders or proclamations, which, if not contrary to existing laws, are binding upon the subjects. These are for temporary purposes, and are called *Orders in Council*.

[4] See Journal of Congress, April 30, 1784.

inexecution of the Treaty of Peace, each charging the other with infractions of that treaty, or neglect to comply with its requirements.[1] An open rupture was threatened, and John Adams was sent to England,[a] clothed with the full powers of a plenipotentiary, to arrange all matters in dispute.

[a] February 24, 1785.

But Mr. Adams could accomplish little. Indeed his mission was almost fruitless. He found the temper of the British people, from the peasant up to the monarch, cold, if not positively hostile, toward the United States. He was never insulted, yet the chilliness of the social atmosphere, and the studied neglect of his official representations, often excited hot indignation in his bosom. But his government was so weak and powerless that he was compelled to bite his lips in silence. When he proposed to have the navigation and trade between all the dominions of the British crown and all the territories of the United States placed upon a basis of perfect and liberal reciprocity, the offer was not only rejected with scorn, but the minister was given to understand that no other would be entertained by the British government. When he recommended his own government to pass countervailing navigation laws for the benefit of American commerce, he was met with the fact that it possessed no power to do so. At length, believing his mission to be useless, and the British government steadily refusing to send a minister to the United States, he asked and received permission to return home.

Meanwhile matters were growing infinitely worse in the United States. The Congress had become absolutely powerless, and almost a by-word among the people. The states had assumed the attitude of sovereign, each for itself; and their interests were too diversified, and in some instances too antagonistic, to allow them to work in harmony for the general good. The League was on the point of dissolution, and the fair fabric for the dwelling of liberty, reared by Washington and his compatriots, was tottering to its fall. The idea of forming two or three distinct confederacies took possession of the public mind. Western North Carolina revolted, and the new State of Franklin,[2] formed by the insurgents, endured several months. A portion of Southwestern Virginia sympathized in the movement. Insurrection against the authorities of Pennsylvania appeared in the Wyoming Valley.[3] A Convention deliberated at Portland on the expediency of erecting the Territory of Maine into an independent state.[4] An armed mob surrounded the New Hampshire Legislature, demanding a remission of taxes;[5] and in Massachusetts, Daniel Shays, who had been a captain in the Continental army, placed himself at the head of a large body of armed insurgents, and defied the government of that state.[6] There was resistance to taxation every where, and disrespect for law became the rule and not the exception.

There was reason for this state of things. The exhaustion of the people was great on account of the war, and poverty was wide-spread. The farmer found no remunerative market for his produce, and domestic manufactures were depressed by foreign competition.[7] Debt weighed down all classes, and made them feel that the burden

---

[1] Against Great Britain it was charged that slaves had been carried away by her military and naval commanders subsequent to the signing of the treaty, and on their departure from the country.* It was also complained that the Western military posts had not been surrendered to the United States according to Article VII. of the treaty. Against the United States it was charged that legal impediments had been interposed to prevent the collection of debts due British merchants by Americans, and that the stipulations concerning the property of Loyalists, found in Articles V. and VI. of the treaty, had not been complied with. These criminations and recriminations were fair, for it has been justly remarked, "America could not, and Great Britain would not, because America did not, execute the treaty."—*Life and Works of John Adams*, i., 424.

[2] See Ramsey's *History of Tennessee;* Harper's *Magazine* for March, 1862.

[3] See Lossing's *Field-Book of the Revolution*.   [4] See Williamson's *History of Maine*.

[5] See Coolidge and Mansfield's *History of New Hampshire*.

[6] See Bradford's *History of Massachusetts;* Harper's *Magazine* for April, 1862.

[7] The idea was prevalent, at the close of the war, that the United States ought to be an exclusively agricultural nation, and that the old policy of purchasing all fabrics in Europe, to be paid for by the productions of the soil, would be the wiser one. Acting upon the belief that this would be the policy of the new government, the merchants imported largely, and, there being very little duty to be paid, domestic manufactures could not compete with those of Great Britain. The fallacy of the idea that exports would pay for the imports was soon made manifest, and almost universal bankruptcy

* See Article VII. of the treaty.

Washington's Views of Public Affairs. His Suggestions, and those of Alexander Hamilton. Propositions of the latter.

which the tax-gatherer would lay upon them would be the "feather" that would "break the camel's back." There was doubt, and confusion, and perplexity on every side; and the very air seemed thick with forebodings of evil. Society appeared to be about to dissolve into its original elements.

Patriots—men who had labored for the establishment of a wise government for a free people—were heart-sick. "Illiberality, jealousy, and local policy mix too much in all our public councils for the good government of the Union," wrote Washington. "The Confederation appears to me to be little better than a shadow without the substance, and Congress a nugatory body, their ordinances being little attended to. To me it is a solecism in politics; indeed, it is one of the most extraordinary things in nature, that we should confederate as a nation, and yet be afraid to give the rulers of that nation (who are the creatures of our own making, appointed for a limited and short duration, and who are amenable for every action, and may be recalled at any moment, and are subject to all the evils they may be instrumental in producing) sufficient powers to order and direct the affairs of the same. By such policy as this the wheels of government are clogged, and our brightest prospects, and that high expectation which was entertained of us by the wondering world, are turned into astonishment; and from the high ground on which we stood we are descending into the vale of confusion and darkness.

"That we have it in our power to become one of the most respectable nations upon earth, admits, in my humble opinion, of no doubt, if we would but pursue a wise, just, and liberal policy toward one another, and keep good faith with the rest of the world. That our resources are ample and increasing, none can deny; but while they are grudgingly applied, or not applied at all, we give a vital stab to public faith, and shall sink, in the eyes of Europe, into contempt."[1]

Other patriots uttered similar sentiments; and there was a feverish anxiety in the public mind concerning the future, destructive of all confidence, and ruinous to enterprises of every kind. Already grave discussions on the subject had occurred in the library at Mount Vernon, during which Washington had suggested the idea of a conjunction of the several states in arrangements of a commercial nature, over which the Congress, under the Articles of Confederation, had no control. The suggestion was luminous. It beamed out upon the surrounding darkness like a ray of morning light. It was the herald and harbinger of future important action—the key-note to a loud trumpet-call for the wise men of the nation to save the tottering republic. It was the electric fire that ran along the paralyzed nerves of the nation, and quickened into action a broader statesmanship, like that displayed by the youthful Hamilton, who, three or four years before, had induced the Legislature of New York to recommend the "assembling of a general Convention of the United States, specially authorized to revise and amend the Confederation, reserving the right to the respective Legislatures to ratify their determination."[2]

---

occurred among the importing merchants. The imports from Great Britain during the years 1784 and 1785 amounted in value to $30,000,000, while the exports thither did not exceed $9,000,000.

[1] Letter to James Warren, October 7, 1785.

[2] So early as 1780, Alexander Hamilton, then only twenty-three years of age, thoroughly analyzed the defects of the Articles of Confederation, in a long letter to James Duane, member of Congress from New York. It was dated, "Liberty Pole, September 3, 1780." He discussed the subject at great length, gave an outline sketch of a Federal Constitution, and suggested the calling of a Convention to frame such a system of government.* During the following year he published in the *New York Packet*, printed at Fishkill, Duchess County, a series of papers under the title of *The Constitutionalist*, which were devoted chiefly to the discussion of the defects in the Articles of Confederation. They excited great local interest; and Hamilton succeeded, in the summer of 1782, in having the subject brought before the Legislature of the State of New York while in session at Poughkeepsie. It was favorably received, and on Sunday, the 21st of July, that body passed a series of resolutions, in the last of which occurred the sentence above quoted.

On the 1st of April, 1783, Hamilton, in a debate in Congress, expressed an earnest desire for a general Convention, and the subject was much talked of among the members of Congress in 1784. In the same year Thomas Paine and Pelatiah Webster wrote on that subject. In the spring of 1784, Noah Webster, the lexicographer, in a pamphlet which he says he "took the pains to carry in person to General Washington," suggested a "new system of government, which

* See *The Works of Alexander Hamilton*, i., 150.

Convention of Representatives of the States at Annapolis and Philadelphia.

This recommendation had been seriously pondered by thoughtful men throughout the League, but the public authorities were not then ready to adopt it. Washington's proposition for a commercial Convention was favorably received, and in September, the following year,[a] five states were represented by delegates in such Convention, held at Annapolis, in Maryland.[1] Already a desire had been expressed in many parts of the country for a Convention having a broader field of consideration than *commerce*, only one of the elements of a nation's prosperity. So thought and felt members of the Convention at Annapolis—a Convention that proved a failure in a degree, inasmuch as only five of the thirteen states were represented. They adjourned after a brief session, first recommending the several states to call another Convention in May following; and performing the momentous service of preparing a letter to the General Congress, in which the defects of the Articles of Confederation were set forth.

[a] September 11, 1786.

In February following, the Congress took the proceedings of the Convention into consideration, and recommended a meeting of delegates from the several states, to be held at Philadelphia on the second Monday in the ensuing May; not, however, for the regulation of commerce, but really for the reconstruction of the national government.[2]

WILLIAM JACKSON.

On the 4th of July, 1776, a Congress of representatives of thirteen colonies met in the great room of the State House in Philadelphia, since known as Independence Hall, and declared those colonies free and independent states. On Monday, the 14th of May, 1787, a Congress of representatives of the same colonies, then become free and independent states, assembled in the same hall for the purpose of establishing the validity and power of that declaration, by dissolving the inefficient political League of the states, and constituting the inhabitants of all the states one great and indissoluble *nation*.

There were few delegates present on the appointed day of meeting; and it was not until the 25th that representatives from seven states (the prescribed quorum) appeared. Then Washington, a delegate from Virginia, was chosen president of the Convention, and William Jackson secretary.[3] On

---

should act, not *on the states, but directly on individuals*, and vest in Congress full power to carry its laws into effect." This pamphlet is entitled, "Sketches of American Policy." Thus thinking men all lamented the weakness of the general government, and foresaw the dangers of the doctrine of supreme state sovereignty, which has wrought so much mischief in our day.

[1] The following are the names of the representatives: *New York*—Alexander Hamilton, Egbert Benson; *New Jersey*—Abraham Clarke, William C. Houston; *Pennsylvania*—Tenche Coxe, James Schureman; *Delaware*—George Read, John Dickinson, Richard Bassett; *Virginia*—Edmund Randolph, James Madison, Jr., St. George Tucker.

[2] This action of the Congress took place on the 21st of February, 1787. The resolution (which was submitted by the delegates from Massachusetts) was as follows:

"*Resolved*, That in the opinion of Congress it is expedient that, on the second Monday in May next, a Convention of Delegates, who shall have been appointed by the several states, be held at Philadelphia, for the sole and express purpose of revising the Articles of Confederation, and reporting to Congress and the several Legislatures such alterations and provisions therein as shall, when agreed to in Congress and confirmed by the states, render the Federal Constitution adequate to the exigencies of government and the preservation of the Union."

[3] William Jackson was an eminent patriot, and one of Washington's most intimate personal friends. He entered the Continental army at the age of sixteen years, and served his country faithfully during the whole war for independence. He became an aid to the commander-in-chief, with the rank of major. In 1781 he accompanied his friend, Colonel John Laurens, on a diplomatic mission to France. At the close of the war he visited Europe, and on his return was appointed, on the nomination of Washington, secretary to the Convention that formed the National Consti-

the 28th, Edmund Randolph, of Virginia,[1] at the request of his colleagues, opened the business of the Convention in a carefully considered speech, in which he pointed out the serious defects in the *Articles of Confederation*, illustrated their utter inadequacy to secure the dignity, peace, and safety of the republic, and asserted the absolute necessity of a more energetic government. At the close of his speech he offered to the Convention fifteen resolutions, in which were embodied the leading principles whereon to form a new government according to his views.

I do not propose to consider in detail, nor even in a synoptical manner, the proceedings of that Convention, which occupied several hours each day for four months. I will merely direct attention to the really great men who composed it, and the measures that were adopted, and leave the reader to seek in other sources the interesting information concerning the events in the daily sessions of that remarkable congress of wise men, whose efforts bore noble fruit for the political sustenance of mankind.[2]

The venerable Dr. Franklin, then near the close of a long and useful life, was the most conspicuous member of that Convention next to Washington. Thirty-three years before he had elaborated a plan of union for the colonies, to which neither the crown nor the provinces would listen;[3] now he came to revive that plan, with full hope of success. Johnson, Rutledge, and Dickinson had been members of the Stamp-act Con-

JACKSON'S MONUMENT.

tution. His private record of the proceedings and debates is in the hands of his family. He became the private secretary of President Washington, and accompanied him on his tour through the Southern States in 1791. He held the office of surveyor of the port of Philadelphia and inspector of customs there until removed, for political causes, by Mr. Jefferson. He then started a daily newspaper, called "The Political and Commercial Register."

Major Jackson lived a life of unsullied honor, and at his death was buried in Christ Church yard, on Fifth Street, Philadelphia. A plain slab about three feet high marks the spot, and bears the following inscription: "Sacred to the memory of Major William Jackson: born March the 9th, 1759; departed this life December the 17th, 1828. Also to Elizabeth Willing, his relict: born March the 27th, 1768; departed this life August the 5th, 1858." Mrs. Jackson was ninety years of age at the time of her death.

I am indebted to Miss Ann Willing Jackson, daughter of Major Jackson, for the portrait given on the preceding page. It is copied from a miniature in her possession, painted by Trumbull. She also has a silhouette profile of her father, cut by Mrs. Mayo, of Richmond, Virginia, the mother of the late Mrs. General Winfield Scott.

The signature of Secretary Jackson is with those of the other signers of the Constitution, on page 32.

[1] Edmund Randolph was a son of an attorney general of Virginia before the Revolution. He was an eminent lawyer, and a warm patriot throughout the old war for independence. He was a member of the Continental Congress from 1779 until 1782. He was active in the Convention that formed the Constitution. He was elected Governor of Virginia in 1788, and Washington chose him for his first attorney general of the United States in 1789. He was secretary of state in 1794, but, in consequence of being engaged in an intrigue with the French minister, he retired from public life. He died in December, 1813.

[2] Rhode Island was not represented in the Convention. Ignorant and unprincipled men happened to control the Assembly of the state at that time, and they refused to elect delegates to the Convention. But some of the best and most influential men in Rhode Island joined in sending a letter to the Convention, in which they expressed their cordial sympathy with the objects of the movement, and promised their acquiescence in whatsoever measures the majority might adopt. The following were the names of the delegates from the several states:

New Hampshire.—John Langdon, John Pickering, Nicholas Gilman, and Benjamin West.
Massachusetts.—Francis Dana, Elbridge Gerry, Nathaniel Gorham, Rufus King, and Caleb Strong.
Connecticut.—William Samuel Johnson, Roger Sherman, and Oliver Ellsworth.
New York.—Robert Yates, John Lansing, Jr., and Alexander Hamilton.
New Jersey.—David Brearley, William Churchill Houston, William Paterson, John Neilson, William Livingston, Abraham Clark, and Jonathan Dayton.
Pennsylvania.—Thomas Mifflin, Robert Morris, George Clymer, Jared Ingersoll, Thomas Fitzsimmons, James Wilson, Gouverneur Morris, and Benjamin Franklin.
Delaware.—George Read, Gunning Bedford, Jr., John Dickinson, Richard Bassett, and Jacob Brown.
Maryland.—James M'Henry, Daniel of St. Thomas Jenifer, Daniel Carroll, John Francis Mercer, and Luther Martin.
Virginia.—George Washington, Patrick Henry, Edmund Randolph, John Blair, James Madison, Jr., George Mason, and George Wythe. Patrick Henry having declined his appointment, James M'Clure was nominated to supply his place.
North Carolina.—Richard Caswell, Alexander Martin, William Richardson Davie, Richard Dobbs Spaight, and Willie Jones. Richard Caswell having resigned, William Blount was appointed as deputy in his place. Willie Jones having also declined his appointment, his place was supplied by Hugh Williamson.
South Carolina.—John Rutledge, Charles Pinckney, Charles C. Pinckney, and Pierce Butler.
Georgia.—William Few, Abraham Baldwin, William Pierce, George Walton, William Houston, and Nathaniel Pendleton.

[3] "The Assemblies did not adopt it," said Franklin, "as they all thought there was too much *prerogative* in it; and in England it was judged to have too much of the *democratic.*"

gress in 1765, and the last two had been compatriots of Washington in the Congress of 1774. Livingston, Sherman, Read, and Wythe had shared the same honors. The last two, with Franklin, Sherman, Gerry, Clymer, Morris, and Wilson, had signed the Declaration of Independence. The Continental army was represented by Washington, Mifflin, Charles Cotesworth Pinckney, and Hamilton. The younger members, who had become conspicuous in public life after the Declaration of Independence, were Hamilton, Madison, and Edmund Randolph. The latter was then Governor of Virginia, having succeeded Patrick Henry, the "trumpet of sedition" when the states were British provinces.

The Convention was marked by long and warm debates, and with dignity suited to the occasion. The most prominent speakers were King, Gerry, and Gorham, of Massachusetts; Hamilton and Lansing, of New York; Ellsworth, Johnson, and Sherman, of Connecticut; Paterson, of New Jersey; Franklin, Wilson, and Morris, of Pennsylvania; Dickinson, of Delaware; Martin, of Maryland; Randolph, Mason, and Madison, of Virginia; Williamson, of North Carolina, and the Pinckneys, of South Carolina.

Such were the men, all conspicuous in the history of the republic, who assembled for the purpose of laying the broad foundations of a nation. They had scarcely a precedent in history for their guide. The great political maxim established by the Revolution was, that the original residence of all human sovereignty is in THE PEOPLE: it was for these founders of a great state to parcel out from the several commonwealths of which the new nation was composed, so much of their restricted power as the people of the several states should be willing to dismiss from their local political institutions, in making a strong and harmonious republic that should be at the same time harmless toward reserved state rights. This was the great problem to be solved. "At that time," says a recent writer, "the world had witnessed no such spectacle as that of the deputies of a nation, chosen by the free action of great communities, and assembled for the purpose of thoroughly reforming its Constitution, by the exercise and with the authority of the national will. All that had been done, both in ancient and in modern times, in forming, moulding, or modifying constitutions of government, bore little resemblance to the present undertaking of the states of America. Neither among the Greeks nor the Romans was there a precedent, and scarcely an analogy."[1]

Randolph suggested the chief business of the Convention in his proposition "that a NATIONAL government ought to be established, consisting of a supreme legislative, executive, and judiciary." Upon this broad proposition all future action was based; and they had not proceeded far before it was clearly perceived that the *Articles of Confederation* were too radically defective to be the basis of a stable government. Therefore, instead of trying to amend them, the Convention went diligently at work to form an entirely new Constitution. In this they made slow progress, opinions were so conflicting. Plans and amendments were offered, and freely discussed. Day after day, and week after week, the debates continued, sometimes with great courtesy, and sometimes with great acrimony, until the 10th of September, when all plans and amendments which had been adopted by the Convention were placed in the hands of a committee for revision and arrangement.[2] By

[1] Curtis's *History of the Origin, Formation, and Adoption of the Constitution of the United States.*
[2] This committee, appointed on the 8th, consisted of Messrs. Madison, Hamilton, King, Johnson, and Gouverneur Morris. They were directed to "revise the style of, and arrange, the articles agreed to by the House." They placed the matter in the hands of Gouverneur Morris for the purpose. In language and general arrangement, the National Constitution was the work of that eminent man.*

---

* Gouverneur Morris was born near the Westchester shore of the Harlem River, New York, at the close of January, 1752. He was educated at King's (now Columbia) College, in the city of New York, studied law under the eminent

Signing the Constitution.   Hesitation on the part of some.   Patriotic Course of Franklin, Hamilton, and others.

this committee a Constitution was reported to the Convention. It was taken up and considered clause by clause, discussed, slightly amended, and then engrossed. On the 15th it was agreed to by the delegates of all the states present. On the 17th a fair copy on parchment was brought in to receive the signatures of the members—an act far more important in all its bearings than the signing of the Declaration of Independence, eleven years before.[1]

In the performance of that act, as in the former, there was some hesitation on the part of a few. There had been serious differences of opinion during the whole session —so serious that at times there seemed a probability that the Convention would be an utter failure. There were still serious differences of opinion when the instrument was adopted, and delicate questions arose about signing it. A large majority of the members wished it to go forth to the people, not only as the act of the Convention collectively, but with the individual sanction and signature of each delegate. This was the desire of Dr. Franklin, and, with pleasant words, he endeavored to allay all irritation and bring about such a result. It was finally agreed, on the suggestion of Gouverneur Morris, that it might be signed, without implying personal sanction, in these closing words: "Done by consent of the states present. In testimony whereof, we have subscribed," etc.

Hamilton patriotically seconded the efforts of Franklin, notwithstanding the instrument did not have his approval, because it did not give power enough to the national government. "No man's ideas," he said, "are more remote from the plan than my own; but is it possible to deliberate between anarchy and confusion on one side, and the chance of good on the other?"

The appeals of Franklin and Hamilton, and the example of Madison and Pinckney, secured the signatures of several dissatisfied members; and all present, excepting Mason and Randolph, of Virginia,[2] and Gerry, of Massachusetts,[3] signed the Constitution.[4] While this important work was in progress, Franklin looked toward the chair occupied by Washington, at the back of which a sun was painted, and observed, "I have often and often, in the course of the session, and the vicissitudes of my hopes and fears as to its issue, looked at that sun behind the President without being able to tell whether it was rising or setting: at length I have the happiness to know that it is a rising sun."

The Convention, by a carefully worded resolution, recommended the Congress to lay the new Constitution before the *people* (not the *states*), and ask them, *the source of all*

William Smith, of that city, and was licensed to practice in 1771. He was an active patriot during the war, serving in the Continental Congress, on committees of safety, etc. He resided some time in Philadelphia. He was sent abroad on a diplomatic mission, and resided for a while in Paris. He afterward went to London on public business, and was finally appointed minister plenipotentiary at the French Court. He returned to America in 1798, was elected to the Senate of the United States, and was active in public and private life until his death in 1816.

[1] For a full account in detail of all the proceedings in relation to the Constitution, see the *History of the Origin, Formation, and Adoption of the Constitution of the United States, with Notices of its Principal Framers*, by George Ticknor Curtis, in two volumes: New York, Harper & Brothers.

[2] George Mason was Washington's neighbor and early personal friend. He was a statesman of the first order among those of his associates in Virginia, and a thorough republican. He was the framer of the Constitution of Virginia, and was active in the Convention that formed the National Constitution. He was so imbued with the state pride for which Virginians have always been noted, that he would not agree to that Constitution because it did not recognize individual state sovereignty—the very rock on which the new republic was then in danger of being wrecked. In conjunction with Patrick Henry, he opposed its adoption in the Virginia Convention, professing to believe that it would be the instrument for converting the government into a monarchy. He died at his seat on the Potomac (Gunston Hall) in the autumn of 1792, at the age of sixty-seven years.

[3] We shall have occasion to consider the public character of Mr. Gerry hereafter. He was Vice-President of the United States in 1812.

[4] The names of the delegates have been given in note 2, page 27. The names of those who signed the Constitution are given in our *fac-similes* of their signatures, which have been engraved from the original parchment in the State Department at Washington. It will be seen that Alexander Hamilton's name stands alone. His colleagues from New York (Yates and Lansing) had left the Convention in disgust on the 1st of July, and New York was considered not officially represented. But Hamilton, who had not swerved from duty, was there. The weight of his name was important, and in the place that should have been filled with the names of delegates from his state was recited, "Mr. Hamilton, of New York." It will be observed that the hand-writing of all seems defective, the lines appearing irregular. This is owing to the parchment on which their names are written, which did not receive the ink as freely as paper would have done. These irregularities have all been carefully copied, so as to give a perfect *fac-simile* of the originals.

Signatures to the National Constitution.

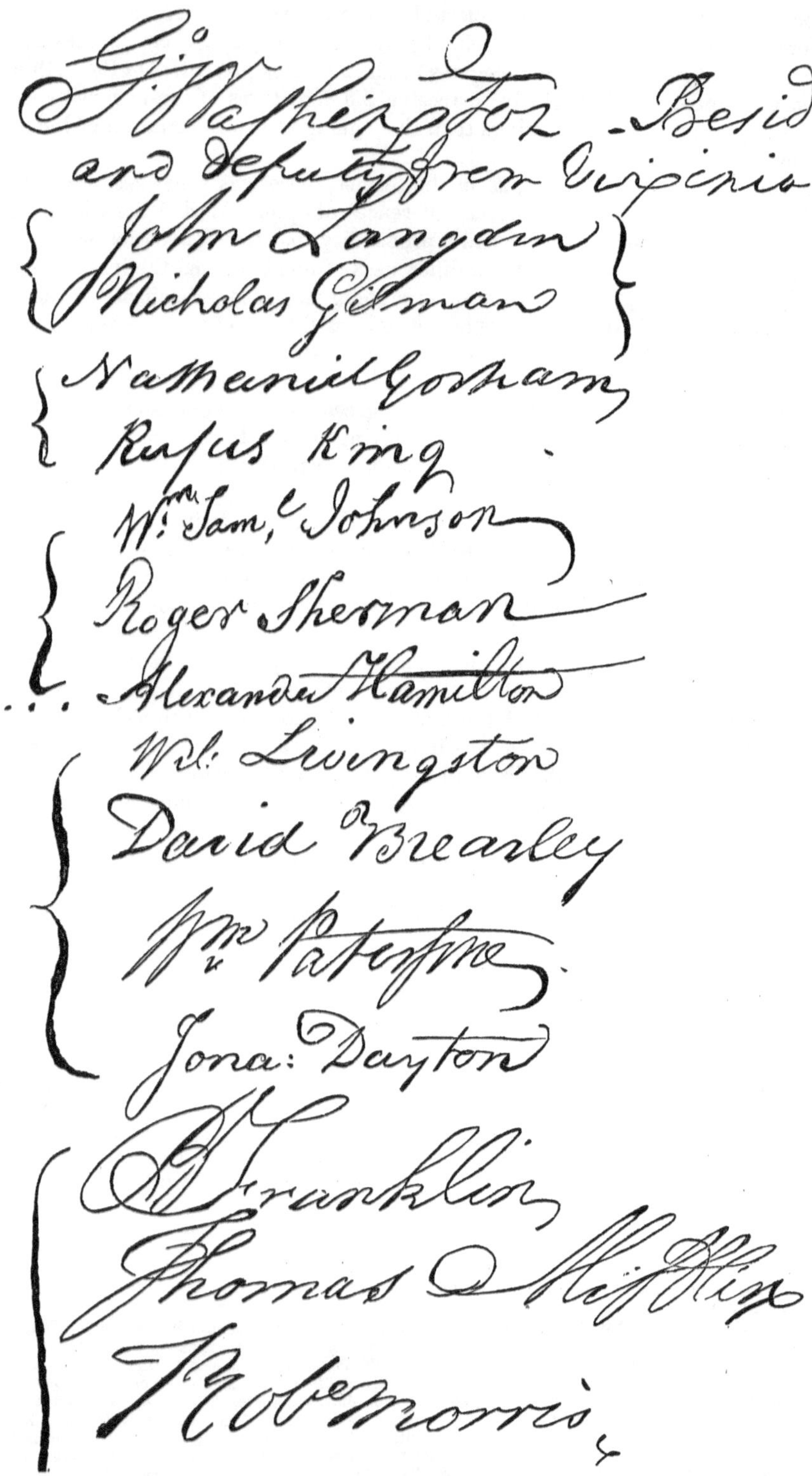

G. Washington—Presid'.
and deputy from Virginia

{ John Langdon
Nicholas Gilman }

{ Nathaniel Gorham
Rufus King }

{ W". Sam'. Johnson
Roger Sherman }

... Alexander Hamilton

{ Wil: Livingston
David Brearley
W". Paterson
Jona: Dayton }

{ B. Franklin
Thomas Mifflin
Rob'. Morris

OF THE WAR OF 1812.   31

Resolutions sent to the State Legislatures.   Signatures to the National Constitution.

sovereignty, to ratify or reject it.   The views of the great majority of the members of Congress were concurrent, and on the 28th of September that body

"*Resolved unanimously*, That the said report [of the Convention to the Congress], with the resolutions and letters accompanying the same, be transmitted to the several

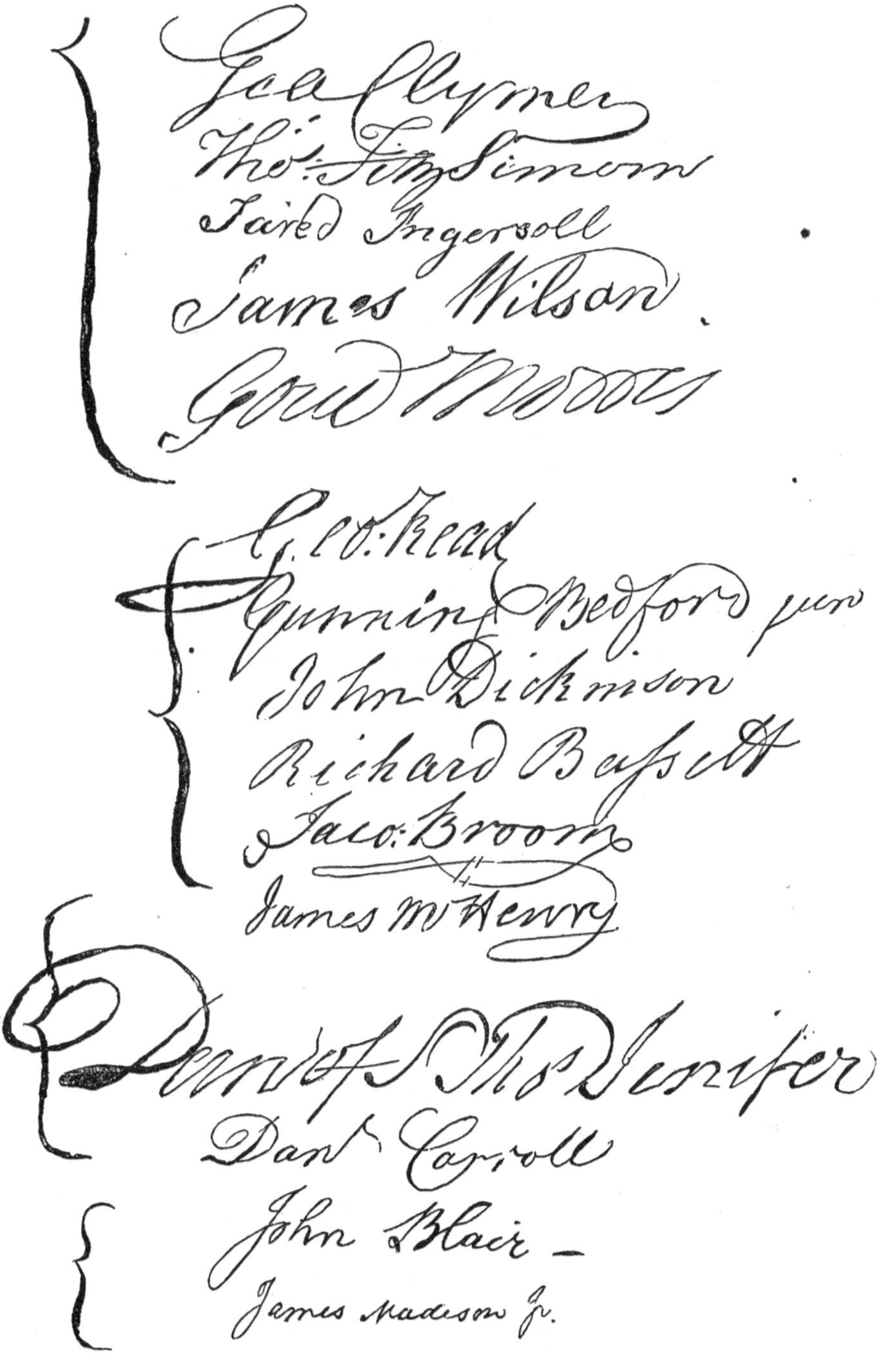

{ Geo Clymer
Thos FitzSimons
Jared Ingersoll
James Wilson
Gouv Morris

{ Geo: Read
Gunning Bedford jun
John Dickinson
Richard Bassett
Jaco: Broom
James McHenry

Danl of St Thos Jenifer
Danl Carroll

{ John Blair
James Madison Jr

Legislatures, in order *to be submitted to a Convention of Delegates chosen in each state by the people thereof,* in conformity to the resolves of the Convention made and provided in that case."

Conventions of the *people* were accordingly held in the several states to consider the Constitution. Long and stirring debates occurred in these Conventions, and at every public gathering and private hearth-stone in the land. Hamilton, Madison, Jay, and others fed the public understanding with able essays on government and in favor of the new Constitution.[1] That instrument was read and discussed every where. But it

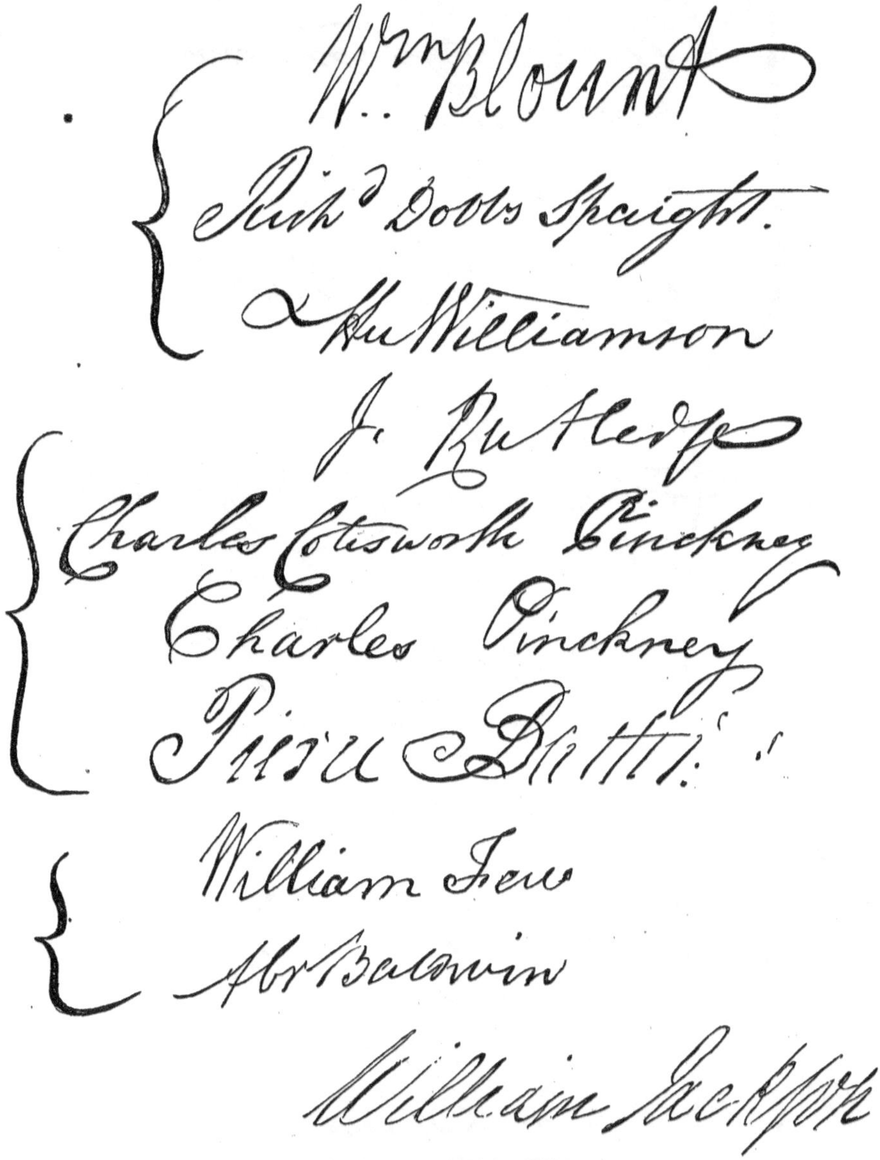

{ Wm Blount
Richd Dobbs Spaight.
Hu Williamson }

{ J. Rutledge
Charles Cotesworth Pinckney
Charles Pinckney
Pierce Butler }

{ William Few
Abr Baldwin }

William Jackson

SIGNATURES TO THE CONSTITUTION.

[1] The essays of Hamilton, Madison, and Jay were published under the general title of *The Federalist*. It was originally designed to comprise the series within twenty, or, at most, twenty-five numbers, but they extended to eighty-five. Of these Hamilton wrote sixty-five. The first number, written by Hamilton in the cabin of a Hudson River sloop, was

| Ratification of the Constitution. | Opposition to it. | The family and state Pride of the Virginians. |

was nine months after its adoption by the Convention, before the people of nine states ratified it—that number being necessary to make it the organic law of the land. That ninth state was New Hampshire, and the momentous act of the people occurred on the 21st of June, 1788. The General Congress was then in session, and, on the 2d of July, adopted measures "for putting the said Constitution into operation." They appointed the first Wednesday of the ensuing March as the day when the functions of the new government should commence their action. The people in the states that had ratified the Constitution chose their presidential electors in compliance with its provisions. These met on the first Wednesday in February, 1789, and elected George Washington chief magistrate of the new republic, and John Adams Vice-President. Washington was inaugurated on the 30th of April, and before the close of the year the inhabitants of all the states but one had ratified the National Constitution.[1]

After earnest deliberation—after the free discussion of every principle of government involving state rights and state sovereignty—after a careful comparison of the advantages and disadvantages of a consolidated nation and the confederacy they had fairly tried, it was solemnly declared that "WE, THE PEOPLE of the United States, in order to form a more perfect Union, establish Justice, insure domestic Tranquillity, provide for the common defense, promote the general Welfare, and secure the blessings of Liberty to ourselves and our Posterity, do ordain and establish this CONSTITUTION for the United States of America."[2]

---

published on the 27th of October, 1787, a little more than a month after the adjournment of the National Convention. They were published four times a week in a New York daily paper. Of these essays Washington wrote to Hamilton in August, 1788: "When the transient circumstances and fugitive performances which attend this crisis shall have disappeared, that work [*The Federalist*] will merit the notice of posterity, because in it are candidly and ably discussed the principles of freedom and the topics of government, which will be always interesting to mankind, so long as they shall be connected in civil society."

[1] That state was Rhode Island, which held out until the spring of 1790. The people in the several states ratified the Constitution in the following order: *Delaware*, December 7, 1787; Pennsylvania, December 12, 1787; New Jersey, December 18, 1787; Georgia, January 2, 1788; Connecticut, January 9, 1788; Massachusetts, February 6, 1788; Maryland, April 28, 1788; South Carolina, May 23, 1788; New Hampshire, June 21, 1788; Virginia, June 26, 1788; New York, July 26, 1788; North Carolina, November 21, 1788; Rhode Island, May 29, 1790. During the recess of Congress, in the autumn of 1789, President Washington visited the New England States. As Rhode Island yet remained a kind of foreign state, he avoided it.

[2] The Constitution was violently assailed by the "State Rights" or state sovereignty men—men who regarded allegiance to a state as paramount to that due to the national government. Their chief objection was that it destroyed (as it was intended to do) the alleged sovereignty of the several states, and constituted a consolidated nation. In Virginia, especially, such a result was looked upon by the proud aristocracy with great disfavor. Virginia was then the ruling state in the League, and her political power was swayed by a few families. These were exceedingly proud, and, down to the breaking out of the war for independence, they looked with disdain upon the people of the other colonies.* This feeling was somewhat modified by the operations of the war, and new men were found at the helm of the vessel of state. Yet much of the old pride remained, and the leading Virginians, with a few honorable exceptions, could not bear the thought of having the "Old Dominion," as they were proud to call the commonwealth, stripped of her independent sovereignty. The new leaders seized upon this dominant state pride and made it subservient to their wishes. Patrick Henry violently denounced the Constitution because of its destructive effects upon state sovereignty. He clearly understood its character when, with a loud voice, in the Virginia Convention, he demanded, "Who authorized the Convention to speak the language '*We, the people*,' instead of '*We, the states*?'" Even from that illustrious man who saved us by his valor, I would have a reason for his conduct." George Mason, in the same Convention, denounced the Constitution because, as he asserted, it "changed the confederation of states into a consolidation, and would annihilate the state governments."

The opposition in several other states was very powerful, for various reasons, and the Constitution and the friends of the Constitution were assailed with the most outrageous misrepresentations. Of the opponents in Virginia Washington wrote: "Their strength, as well as those of the same class in other states, seems to lie in misrepresentation, and a desire to inflame the passions and alarm the fears by noisy declamation, rather than to convince the understanding by sound arguments, or fair and impartial statements. Baffled in their attacks upon the Constitution, they have attempted to vilify and debase the characters who formed it, but I trust they will not succeed."

The papers, by Colonel Byrd (who was a member of the Colonial Council), above referred to, afford a glimpse of the sense of superiority to all the other colonists entertained by the leading families in Virginia, which was always the bane of progress and national feeling, and made large numbers of the politicians of that state disunionists from the beginning. In these papers the New Englanders were spoken of as "a puritanical sect, with pharisaical peculiarities in their worship and behavior." Trade was an unfit calling, and a trade eluding laws, though pronounced void, was justly regarded as demoralizing. Such, they charged, was much of the trade of the Eastern provinces. The dwellers of New York had no more favor. The Dutch were also traders—a "slippery people"—intruders on Virginia—encroachers and reformers. New Jersey, in a religious aspect, was not less obnoxious, peopled by "a swarm of Scots Quakers, who were not tolerated to exercise the gifts of the spirit in their own country;" by "Anabaptists," too, and some "Swedes." The merits of Penn were equivocal—he was not immaculate; but, though "Quakers had flocked to Pennsylvania in shoals," they had the virtues of "dilligence and frugality," and the "prudence" which became non-combatants. Mary-

* See Byrd's *Westover Papers*.

With the birth of the nation on the 4th of March, 1789, the Continental Congress, the representative of the League, expired. Its history is one of the most remarkable on record. It was first an almost spontaneous gathering of patriotic men, chosen by their fellow-citizens in a time of great perplexity, to consult upon the public good. They represented different provinces extending a thousand miles along the Atlantic coast, with interests as diversified as the climate and geography. With boldness unequaled and faith unexampled, they snatched the sceptre of rule over a vast dominion from imperial England, of whose monarch they were subjects, and assumed the functions of sovereignty by creating armies, issuing bills of credit, declaring the provinces free and independent states, negotiating treaties with foreign governments, and, finally, after eight long years of struggle, wringing from their former sovereign his acknowledgment of the independence of the states which they represented. The career of the Congress was meteor-like, and astonished the world with its brilliancy. It was also short. Like a half-developed giant exhausted by mighty efforts, it first exhibited lassitude, then decrepitude, and at last hopeless decay. Poor and weak, its services forgotten by those who should have been grateful for them, it lost the respect of all mankind, and died of political marasmus.

Out of its remains, phœnix-like, and in full vigor and grand proportions, arose a nation whose existence had been decreed by the will of true sovereignty—THE PEOPLE—and whose perpetuity depends upon that will. It immediately arrested the profound attention of the civilized world. It was seen that its commerce, diplomacy, and dignity were no longer exposed to neglect by thirteen distinct and clashing legislative bodies, but were guarded by a central power of wonderful energy. The prophecy of Bishop Berkeley was on the eve of fulfillment.[1] England, France, Spain, and Holland placed their representatives at the seat of the new government, and the world acknowledged that the new-born nation was a power—positive, tangible, indubitable.

---

land was a commodious retreat for Papists, for whom "England was too hot," and to whom, as a neighbor, Virginia was a little cold. The Carolinas, left "derelict by the French and Sapaniards," were the regions of pines and serpents —dismal in their swamps, and deadly in their malaria. "Thus, in the eyes of her favored few," says a late writer, "Virginia was the paradise of the New World." For a farther illustration of this subject, see *History of the Republic of the United States of America, as traced in the Writings of Alexander Hamilton and his Contemporaries,* by John C. Hamilton.

[1] When inspired with his transatlantic mission, Bishop Berkeley wrote his six "Verses on the Prospect of Planting Arts and Learning in America," in which he predicted the rising greatness of the New World, and employed the oft-quoted line,

"Westward the course of empire takes its way."

CHAPTER II.

> "Old burial-places, once sacred, are plundered,
> And thickly with bones is the fallow field strown;
> The bond of confederate tribes has been sundered—
> The long council hall of the brave overthrown.
> The Sac and Miami bowmen no longer
> Preserve at the door-posts unslumbering guard;
> We fought, but the pale-browed invaders were stronger;
> Our knife-blades too blunt, and their bosoms too hard."
>
> W. H. C. HOSMER.

E have seen the development of weak, isolated commonwealths into a powerful, consolidated nation, and are now to observe the growth of that nation in resources and strength until, by an exhibition of its powers in vindication of its rights before the world, it became absolutely independent, and was respected accordingly.

That assertion and vindication were made by the moral forces of legislation and the patriotism of the people, co-working with the material forces of army and navy. In this view is involved the whole drama of the contest known in history as the War of 1812, or the Second Struggle for Independence—a drama, many of whose characters and incidents appear upon the stage simultaneously with the persons and events exhibited in the preceding chapter. Looking back from the summer of 1812, when war against Great Britain was formally declared, the causes of the conflict appear both remote and near. The war actually began years before the President proclaimed the appeal to arms.

While statesmen and politicians were arranging the machinery of government, the people were laying broad and deep the visible foundations of the state, in the establishment of material interests and the shaping of institutions consonant with the new order of things, and essential to social and political prosperity. They had already begun to comprehend the hidden resources and immense value of the vast country within the treaty limits of the United States westward of the Alleghany Mountains. They had already obtained prophetic glimpses of a future civilization that should flourish in the fertile regions watered by the streams whose springs are in those lofty hills that stretch, parallel with the Atlantic, from the Lakes almost to the Gulf, across fourteen degrees of latitude. Pioneers had gone over the grand hills and sent up the smoke of their cabin fires from many a fertile valley irrigated by the tributaries of the Ohio and Mississippi. Already they had learned to regard the Father of Waters as a great aqueous highway for an immense inland commerce soon to be created, and had begun to urge the supreme authority of the land to treat with Spain for its free navigation. Already peace and friendship with the savage tribes on the remote frontiers of civilization had been promised by treaties made upon principles of justice and not fashioned by the ethics of the sword.[1]

---

[1] Necessity, if not conscience, recommended this policy, for at the close of the Revolution the "regular army" had been reduced to less than seven hundred men, and no officer was retained above the rank of captain. This force was soon still farther reduced to twenty-five men to guard the military stores at Pittsburg, and fifty-five to perform military duty at West Point and other magazines.

Peace was negotiated with most of the tribes which had taken part against the United States in the late war. A

Indian Treaties.　　　Anti-slavery Movements.　　　The Ordinance of 1787.　　　First Settlements in Ohio.

By treaty with the chief tribes between the Ohio River and the Great Lakes, and the cession by Virginia[1] to the United States of all claims to lands in that region, the general government became absolute possessor of a vast country, out of which several flourishing states have since been formed.[2]

While the National Convention was in session at Philadelphia in the summer of 1787, the Continental Congress, sitting at New York, feeble and dying, with only eight states represented, took up and disposed of in a satisfactory manner a subject second only in importance to that under discussion in the capital of Pennsylvania. They adopted,[a] by unanimous vote, "An Ordinance for the government of the Territory of the United States northwest of the Ohio."[3] In anticipation of this action, extensive surveys had been made in the new territory. Soon after the passage of the ordinance above mentioned, a sale of five millions of acres, extending along the Ohio from the Muskingum to the Sciota, were sold to the "Ohio Company," which was composed of citizens of New England, many of whom had been officers of the Continental army.[4] A similar sale was made to John Cleve Symmes, of New Jersey, for two millions of acres, in the rich and beautiful region between the Great and Little Miami Rivers, including the site of Cincinnati.

a July 13, 1787.

These were the first steps taken toward the settlement of the Northwestern Territory, in which occurred so many of the important events of the War of 1812. Hitherto New England emigration had been chiefly to Vermont, Northern New Hampshire, and the Territory of Maine. Now it poured, in a vast and continuous stream, into the Ohio country. General Rufus Putnam, at the head of a colony from Massachusetts, founded a settlement[5] (the first, of Europeans, in all Ohio, if we except the Moravian missionary stations[6]) at the mouth of the Muskingum River, and named it Marietta, in honor of

---

treaty was concluded at Fort Stanwix (now Rome, New York) in October, 1784, with the Six Nations. Another was concluded at Fort M'Intosh in January, 1785, with the Wyandots, Delawares, Chippewas, and Ottawas; and another with the Cherokees, at Hopewell, in November the same year. Dissatisfaction having arisen concerning remuneration for lands, two new treaties were made at Fort Harmar, on the Muskingum, Ohio, at the beginning of 1789, by which allowances were made for ceded lands. By treaty, the Indian titles to lands extending along the northern bank of the Ohio and a considerable distance inland, as far west as the Wabash River, were extinguished. This tract comprised about seventeen millions of acres.

1 The deed of cession, signed by Virginia commissioners, with Thomas Jefferson at their head, was executed on the first day of March, 1784. It stipulated that the territory ceded should be laid out and formed into states, not less than one hundred nor more than one hundred and fifty miles square; that the states so formed should be "distinct republican states," and admitted as members of the National Union, having the same rights of sovereignty, etc., as the older states.

After the cession was executed the Congress referred the matter to a committee, of which Mr. Jefferson was chairman. That committee reported an ordinance containing a plan for the government of the whole Western territory north and south of the Ohio, from the thirty-first degree of north latitude to the northern boundary of the United States, it being supposed that other states owning territory south of the Ohio would follow the example of Virginia. The plan proposed to divide the great Territory into seventeen states, and among the conditions was the remarkable one "that, after the year 1800, there shall be neither slavery nor involuntary servitude in any of the said states, other than in the punishment of crimes whereof the party shall have been duly convicted." This provision did not get the vote of nine states, the number necessary to adopt it. New York, New Jersey, and Pennsylvania, with the four New England States, voted for it; North Carolina was divided; Delaware and Georgia were unrepresented; Maryland, Virginia, and South Carolina voted against it. (See Journal of Congress, April 19, 1784.) After expunging this proviso the report was adopted, but the subject was not definitely acted upon.

2 Ohio, Michigan, Indiana, Illinois, and Wisconsin.

3 This ordinance was reported by a committee, of which Mr. Dane, of Massachusetts, was chairman. It contained Mr. Jefferson's anti-slavery proviso, with a clause relative to the rendition of fugitive slaves, similar in form to the one incorporated in the National Constitution a few weeks later.

4 This company was formed in Boston, and Rev. Manasseh Cutler, and Winthrop Sargent were the authorized agents of the association to make the contract with the United States Treasury Board. Among the associates were Generals Parsons and Rufus Putnam, of Connecticut; General Varnum and Commodore Whipple, of Rhode Island; General Tupper, of Massachusetts, and men of lesser note in public life.

5 Putnam and his party landed on the site of Marietta on the 7th of April, 1788. The governor of the territory had not yet arrived, so they established temporary laws for their own government. These were published by being written and nailed to a tree. Return J. Meigs, afterward governor of the state, was appointed to administer the laws. Such was the beginning of government in the State of Ohio.

6 These devoted missionaries were the first white inhabitants who took up their abode within the present limits of the State of Ohio. The Rev. John Frederick Post and Rev. John Heckewelder had penetrated the wilderness in this direction before the commencement of the Revolution. Their first visit was as early as 1761. Others followed, and they established three stations, or villages of Indian converts, on the Tuscarawas River, within the limits of the present county of that name. These were named Schoenbrun, Gnadenhutten, and Salem. The latter was near the present village of Port

Maria Antoinette, the queen of Louis the Sixteenth, of France. A stockade fort, called Campus Martius, was immediately commenced, as a protection against the hostile Indians.[1] In the autumn of the same year a party of settlers seated themselves upon Symmes's purchase, and founded Columbia, near the mouth of the Little Miami. Fort Washington was soon afterward built a short distance below, on the site of Cincinnati.

CAMPUS MARTIUS.

It has been estimated that within the years 1788 and 1789, full twenty thousand men, women, and children went down the Ohio in boats, to become settlers on its banks. Since then, how wonderful has been the growth of empire beyond the Alleghanies!

Soon after the organization of the Northwestern Territory, Major General Arthur St. Clair,[2] an officer in the old French War, and in the Continental army during the Revolution, was appointed its governor by the Congress, of which body he was then president. He accepted the position with reluctance. "The office of governor was in a great measure forced on me," he said, in a letter to a friend.[3] Yet, ever ready to go where duty to his country called him, he proceeded to the Territory in the summer of

Washington. There Heckewelder resided for some time, and there his daughter Johanna Maria was born, on the 6th of April, 1781. She was the first white child born in Ohio, and is yet living [1867] at Bethlehem, Pennsylvania, in full possession of her mental faculties. She has been deaf for a number of years, and uses a slate in conversation. Her hand is firm, and she writes with vigor, as her signature, carefully copied in the engraving, made at the close of 1859, attests. It was appended to an autograph note to the writer. The portrait was taken by the Daguerreian process at that time. In a diary kept by the younger pupils of the Bethlehem boarding-school, where Miss Heckewelder was educated, under date of December 23, 1788

(the year when Marietta was founded), occurs the following sentence: "Little Miss Polly Heckewelder's papa returned from Fort Pitt, which occasioned her and us great joy." See *Bethlehem Souvenir*, 1858, p. 67.

[1] This fort was a regular parallelogram, with an exterior line of seven hundred and twenty feet. There was a strong block-house at each corner, surmounted by a tower and sentry-box. Between them were dwelling-houses. At the outer corner of each block-house was a bastion, standing on four stout timbers. There were port-holes for musketry and artillery. These buildings were all made of sawed timbers. Twenty feet in advance of these was a row of very strong and large pickets,

Johanna Maria Heckewelder.

with gateways through them, and a few feet outside of these was placed a row of *abatis*.
[2] Arthur St. Clair was a native of Edinburg, in Scotland, where he was born in 1734. He came to America with Admiral Boscawen in 1759, and served under Wolfe as a lieutenant. After the peace in 1763 he was placed in command of Fort Ligonier, in Pennsylvania. When the Revolution broke out he espoused the patriot cause, and was appointed a colonel in the Continental army in January, 1776. He was active most of the time during that war, and after its close settled in Pennsylvania. He was President of the Continental Congress in 1787, and the following year was appointed governor of the newly-organized Northwestern Territory. His services in that region are recorded in the text. He survived his misfortunes there almost a quarter of a century, and then died, in poverty, at Laurel Hill, in Western Pennsylvania, in August, 1818, at the age of eighty-four years.
[3] William B. Giles, a member of Congress from Virginia.

SIGNATURE OF WINTHROP SARGENT.

1788, and took up his abode in Campus Martius,[a] with Winthrop Sargent as secretary or deputy, who acted as chief magistrate during the absence of the governor.

[a] July, 1788.

St. Clair at once instituted inquiries, in accordance with his instructions, concerning the temper of the Indians in the Territory. They were known to be exceedingly uneasy, and sometimes in frowning moods; and the tribes on the Wabash, numbering almost two thousand warriors, who had not been parties to any of the treaties, were decidedly hostile. They continued to make predatory incursions into the Kentucky settlements, notwithstanding chastisements received at the hands of General George Rogers Clarke, the "father of the Northwest," as he has been called; and they were in turn invaded and scourged by bands of retaliating Kentuckians. These expeditions deepened the hostile feeling, and gave strength and fierceness to both parties when, in after years, they met in battle.

It soon became evident that all the tribes in the Territory, numbering full twenty thousand souls, were tampered with by British emissaries, sent out from the frontier forts, which had not been given up to the United States in compliance with treaty stipulations. Sir John Johnson (son of Sir William, of the Mohawk Valley, and the implacable enemy of the United States[1]) was the Inspector General of Indian Affairs in America, and had great influence over the savages; and Lord Dorchester (formerly Sir Guy Carleton) was again governor general of those provinces,[2] and, by speeches at Quebec and Montreal, directly instigated the savages to war. These circumstances gave rise to the opinion that the British government, which yet refused to send a representative to the United States, and treated the new republic with ill-concealed contempt, was preparing the way for an effort to reduce the members of the League to colonial vassalage.

The Confederacy was but feebly prepared to meet hostilities on their northwestern frontier. The military force at the time the Territory was formed consisted of only about six hundred men, commanded by Brigadier General Harmar.[3] Of these there were two companies of artillery, formed of volunteers who enlisted to put down Shays's Rebellion in Massachusetts. The frontier military stations were Pittsburg, at the forks of the Ohio, Fort M'Intosh, on Beaver Creek, and Fort Franklin, on French Creek, near old Fort Venango, in Pennsylvania; Fort Harmar, at the mouth of the Mus-

---

[1] Sir John was the heir to the title and fortune of Sir William, and was at the head of the Loyalists in the Mohawk Valley at the beginning of the Revolution. He had lived some time in England, and returned to settle in Canada in 1785. He had suffered in person and estate at the hands of the republicans, having been expelled from his home, his property confiscated, and his family exiled. These circumstances made him a bitter and relentless foe, and ready to strike a blow of retaliation. His losses were made up by the British government by grants of land. He died at Montreal in 1830, at the age of eighty-eight years. For a detailed account of his career during the old war for independence, see Lossing's *Field-Book of the Revolution*, vol. i.

[2] Sir Guy Carleton was Governor of Canada when the old war for independence broke out, and continued there until its close. He was acquainted with all the affairs of the Indians, and had great influence over them.

[3] Appointed brigadier general on the 31st of July, 1787.

Council at Fort Harmar.   Little Turtle's Opposition.   Uneasiness of the Indians of the Gulf Region.

FORT HARMAR.

kingum River; Fort Steuben, on the Ohio River, now Jeffersonville, opposite Louisville; and Fort Vincennes, on the Wabash River.

Early in 1789[a] Governor St. Clair held a council at Fort Harmar[1] with chiefs and sachems of the Six Nations. He also held a council with the leading men of the Wyandots, Delawares, Ottawas, Chippewas, Pottawatomies, and Sacs. With all these representatives of thousands of Indians, scattered over the country from the Mohawk Valley to that of the Wabash, he made treaties, when old agreements were confirmed, and remunerations and boundaries were specified. The Six Nations (or, rather, five of the six nations, for the Mohawks, who were in Canada, were not represented) were faithful to the treaty; but the great body of the others, influenced by British emissaries and unscrupulous traders, refused to acknowledge the validity of the treaty made by their warriors and rulers.[2] Within a few weeks after the council at Fort Harmar, parties of them were out upon the war-path on the frontiers of Virginia and Kentucky.

[a] January 9.

Nearer the Gulf, the Creeks and Cherokees, brought into immediate contact with the wily Spaniards in Florida and at New Orleans, who were already preparing seductive temptations to the settlers in the trans-Alleghany valleys to leave the American League and join fortunes with the children of Old Spain, became first uneasy, and at the time in question were assuming a hostile attitude. The Creeks, led by the talented M'Gillivray, a half-breed, whose father was a Scotchman, had formed a close alliance with the Spaniards, and through them might receive arms and other military supplies. In view of all these circumstances, the portentous cloud of a threatened general Indian war was gathering in the western horizon at the close of 1789.

---

[1] This fort was commenced in the autumn of 1785, by a detachment of United States troops under the command of Major John Doughty. It was on the right bank of the Muskingum, at its junction with the Ohio, and was named in honor of Colonel Josiah Harmar, to whose regiment Major Doughty's corps was attached. It was the first military post of the kind erected within the limits of Ohio. The outlines formed a regular pentagon, embracing about three fourths of an acre. United States troops occupied it until 1790, when they left it to construct and occupy Fort Washington, on the site of Cincinnati. During the Indian wars that succeeded it was occupied by a few troops, and was finally abandoned after the treaty of Greenville in 1795.

[2] In the great council at Fort Greenville in 1795, Little Turtle, the most active of the chiefs in the Northwest, gave the following reason for their refusal to comply with the treaties: "You have told me," he said, "that the present treaty should be founded upon that of Muskingum. I beg leave to observe to you that that treaty was effected altogether by the Six Nations, who seduced some of our young men to attend it, together with a few of the Chippewas, Wyandots, Delawares, Ottawas, and Pottawatomies. I beg leave to tell you that I am entirely ignorant of what was done at that treaty."

Yet more threatening was the aspect of affairs on the Western frontier in the spring of 1790. Serious trouble was evidently brewing. Major Hamtramck, a small Canadian Frenchman, and a spirited officer in the United States army, was in command of the military post at Vincennes, an important point on the Wabash,[1] surrounded by French families, whose long residence made them influential among the Indians. Many of the latter spoke their language, and some had embraced the Roman Catholic religion. Taking advantage of this intimate relationship, Hamtramck sent out Antoine Gamelin, with speeches to the Wabash and Miami Indians from Governor St. Clair, offering them peace and friendship. In the course of his tour Gamelin obtained positive evidence of the influence of the British at Detroit over the savage mind in the West. He traversed the country from Post Vincennes along the Wabash, and eastward to the Miami village, where the conjunction of the St. Mary's and St. Joseph's Rivers forms the Maumee, or Miami of the Lakes, at the present city of Fort Wayne, Indiana. He made speeches himself, and offered them St. Clair's; but he was every where met with the reply that they could do nothing definitely until they could hear from Detroit. "You invite us to stop our young men," said the Kickapoos. "It is impossible to do it, being constantly encouraged by the British." "We are all sensible of your speech, and pleased with it," said Blue Jacket, chief warrior of the Shawnoese; "but we can not give you an answer without hearing from our father at Detroit." "We can not give a definite answer without consulting the commandant at Detroit," said Le Gris, the great chief of the Miamis. "The English commandant at Detroit is our father since he threw down our French father," said the Shawnoese.[2] And so, on all occasions, they were unwilling to accept proffers of peace with the United States without first consulting the commandant at Detroit, with whom Johnson and Carleton were in constant communication. Instigated by these men, these Western tribes insisted on the establishment of the Ohio River as the boundary between the Indians and the United States, and would listen to no other terms.[3]

Hamtramck was so well satisfied of these machinations of the British that he assured Governor St. Clair that a permanent peace with the savages was an impossibility. The governor, meanwhile, had received accounts of the depredations of the Indians along the Ohio from the Falls (Louisville) to Pittsburg. They infested the banks in such numbers, waylaying boats and plundering and wounding the voyaging emigrants, that an utter cessation of the navigation of the river seemed inevitable.

The principal rendezvous of the marauders was near the mouth of the Scioto, on the north bank of the Ohio, and to that point two hundred and thirty Kentucky volunteers and one hundred regular troops were sent, under General Harmar. They assembled at Fort Washington,[4] then not quite completed, and marched from thence to the Scioto.

---

[1] Vincennes was so named by the French traders, who established a trading-post there as early as 1730. The name is in honor of the Sieur de Vincennes, an officer sent to the Miamis as early as 1705, and who commanded the post on the Wabash, afterward called by his name. It was alternately in possession of the Americans and British during the Revolution, while the head-quarters of the latter were at Detroit. It is on the bank of the Wabash, one hundred miles from its mouth, and is the capital of Knox County, Indiana.

[2] Gamelin's Journal, cited by Dillon, in his *History of Indiana*, p. 226.

[3] This curtailment of the boundaries of the United States, so as to prevent their control of the upper lakes and the valuable fur trade of the country around them, was a favorite scheme of British statesmen. It was even proposed as a *sine qua non*, at one time, by the British commissioners who negotiated the Treaty of Peace in 1814, that the Indians inhabiting a portion of the United States within the limits established by the Treaty of 1783 should be included as the allies of Great Britain in the projected pacification; and that definite boundaries should be settled for the Indian territory, upon a basis which would have operated to surrender to a number of Indians, not probably exceeding a few thousands, the rights of sovereignty as well as of soil, over nearly one third of the territorial dominions of the United States, inhabited by more than one hundred thousand of its citizens.*

[4] Fort Washington was built on the site of a block-house erected by Ensign Luce within the limits of the present city of Cincinnati, which was first named Losantiville by a pedantic settler, from the words *le os anti ville*, which he interpreted as meaning "the village opposite the mouth"—mouth of Licking River. Luce was at North Bend with a detachment of troops, charged with selecting a site for a block-house. Judge Symmes wished it to be built there, but Luce, according to the judge, was led to Cincinnati, as Losantiville was then called, on account of his love for the beautiful wife of a settler, who went there to reside because of the attentions to her of the ensign at the Bend. Luce followed, and erected the

---

* See *American State Papers*, ix., 332 to 421, inclusive.

The Indians fled on their approach, and the expedition returned without accomplishing any thing.

A more formidable expedition, to penetrate the Miami country, was determined upon, and, at the close of September,[a] General Harmar left Fort Washington with over fourteen hundred troops,[1] and moved toward the heart of the hostile Indian country around the head waters of the Maumee. St. Clair, in obedience to instructions from President Washington, had previously sent a letter[b] to the British commandant at Detroit, courteously informing him that the expedition had no designs upon any possessions of the crown. He added that he had every reason to expect, after such a candid explanation, that the commandant would neither countenance nor assist the tribes in their hostilities. Of course this expectation was not realized.

[a] 1790.

FORT WASHINGTON, ON THE SITE OF CINCINNATI.

[b] September 19.

Harmar reached the Maumee at the middle of October. As he approached an Indian town the inhabitants fled, leaving it to be burned by the invaders. Colonel Hardin, with some Kentucky volunteers and thirty regulars, was sent in pursuit. He fell into an ambuscade of one hundred Indians, under *Mish-i-kin-a-kwa*, or Little Turtle (an eminent Miami chief), about eleven miles from the site of Fort Wayne, where the Goshen state road crosses the Eel River. The frightened militia fled without firing a gun, while the regulars stood firm until twenty-two of their number were slain. Captain Armstrong, who escaped, stood in mud and water up to his chin, and saw the savages dance in frantic joy because of their victory.

Harmar moved about two miles to Chillicothe[2] and destroyed it; then, after being

---

block-house there; and in 1790 Major Doughty built Fort Washington on the same spot. It was a rude but strong structure, and stood upon the eastern boundary of the town as originally laid out, between the present Third and Fourth Streets, east of Eastern Row, now Broadway, which was then a "two-pole alley." The celebrated English writer and traveler, Mrs. Trollope, resided in Cincinnati for a while, and had a noted bazar on the site of the fort. That work was composed of a number of strongly-built hewn-log cabins, a story and a half in height, arranged for soldiers' barracks. Some, better finished than the majority, were used by the officers. They formed a hollow square, inclosing about an acre of ground, with a strong block-house at each angle. One of these was Luce's. These were built of the timber from the ground on which the fort stood. In 1792 Congress reserved fifteen acres around it for the use of the garrison. In the autumn of 1790, Governor St. Clair arrived at Fort Washington, organized the County of Hamilton, and decreed that the little village of Cincinnati, commenced around the fort, should be the county seat. Thus commenced the Queen City of the West, as it has been called.

[1] These consisted of three battalions of Virginia militia, one battalion of Pennsylvania militia, one battalion of mounted light troops, and two battalions of regulars—in all, 1453. Of these, 320 were regulars.

[2] This has been mistaken for the present Chillicothe on the Scioto. Chillicothe was the name of one of the principal tribes of the Shawnoese, and was a favorite name for a village. There were several of that name in the country of the Shawnoese. There was Old Chillicothe, where Boone was a captive for some time. It was on the Little Miami, on the site of Xenia. There was another on the site of Westfall, in Pickaway County; and still another on the site of Frankfort, in Ross County. There was an Indian town of that name on the site of the present Chillicothe. All these were within the present limits of Ohio. It signified "the town," or principal one.

menaced by the Indians, he turned his face toward Fort Washington.[a] That night was a starry one, and Hardin, who was full of fight, proposed to Harmar a surprise of the Indians at the head of the Maumee, where they had a village on one side of the river and an encampment of warriors on the other side. Harmar reluctantly complied, and four hundred men were detached for the purpose.[1] Sixty of them were regulars, under Major Wyllys. They marched in three columns (the regulars in the centre), and pushed forward as rapidly as possible, hoping to fall upon the Indians before dawn. But it was after sunrise before they reached the bank of the Maumee. A plan of attack was soon arranged. Major Hall, with a detachment of militia, was to pass around the village at the bend of the Maumee, cross the St. Mary's and the St. Joseph's, gain the rear of the Indian encampment unobserved, and await an attack by the main body of the troops in front. These, consisting of Major M'Mullin's battalion, Major Fontaine's cavalry, and the regulars under Major Wyllys, were to cross the Maumee at and near the usual ford, and thus surround the savages. The game was spoiled by the imprudence of Major Hall, who fired prematurely upon a solitary Indian and alarmed the encampment. The startled Miamis were instantly seen flying in different directions. The militia under M'Mullin and the cavalry under Fontaine, who had crossed the river, started in pursuit, in disobedience of orders, leaving the regulars under Wyllys, who had also crossed the Maumee, unsupported. The latter were attacked by Little Turtle and the main body of the Indians, and driven back with great slaughter. Richardville, a half-blood and successor to Little Turtle, who was in the battle, and who died at Fort Wayne in 1840, often asserted that the bodies of the slain were so numerous in the river at the ford that he could have crossed over the stream upon them dryshod.[2]

[a] October 21, 1790.

THE MAUMEE FORD—PLACE OF HARMAR'S DEFEAT.

While this conflict was going on at the ford, M'Mullin and Fontaine, in connection with Hall, were skirmishing with parties of Indians a short distance up the St. Joseph's. Fontaine, with a number of his followers, fell at the head of his mounted militia, in making a charge. He was shot dead, and, falling from his horse, was immediately scalped. The remainder, with those under Hall and M'Mullin, fell back in confusion toward the ford of the Maumee, and followed the remnant of the regulars in their retreat. The Indians, having suffered severely, did not pursue.

General Harmar was informed of the disaster by a horseman who had outstripped the rest. A detachment of militia was immediately ordered to the assistance of the retreating parties; but such mortal fear had taken possession of these raw recruits that only thirty, willing to go, could be found among them. On his arrival at camp Hardin urged Harmar to proceed with his whole force to the Maumee. The latter, having lost all confidence in the militia, refused; and, as soon as preparations could be made, the whole army took up its march[b] for Fort Wash-

[b] October 23.

---

[1] Harmar's halting-place was on Nine-mile Creek, a tributary of the Maumee, nine miles south of Fort Wayne.
[2] Statement of John P. Hedges, of Fort Wayne, to the author.

ington, which they reached on the 4th of November.[1]

I visited the scene of the disaster at the Maumee Ford toward the close of September, 1860. I came up the Maumee Valley to Defiance on the night of the 24th, and, after visiting places of historic interest there the next morning (of which I shall hereafter write), I rode on to Fort Wayne upon the Toledo and Wabash Railway, a distance of forty-three miles. It was a delightful day, but the journey was very monotonous, because almost interminable forests covered the flat country over which we passed. I arrived

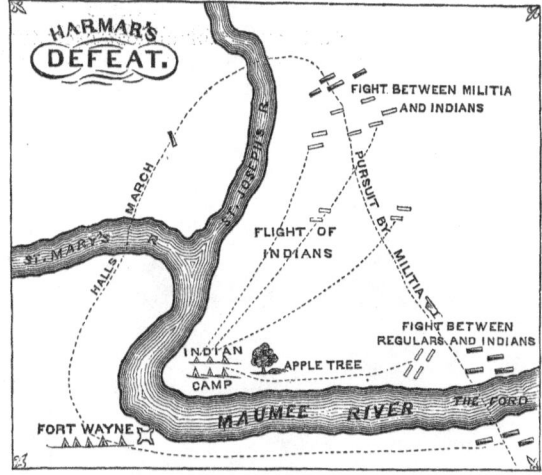

at the flourishing city of Fort Wayne, the shire town of Allen County, Indiana, late in the afternoon, and by twilight had visited the fords of the Maumee and St. Joseph's, made famous by the events of the 22d of October, 1790. I was accompanied by the Hon. F. P. Randall, the mayor of the city, who kindly offered his services as guide. We crossed the great bridge at the head of the Maumee, and rode first down that stream to the place yet known as "Harmar's Ford." It is about half a mile below the confluence of the St. Mary's and St. Joseph's at Fort Wayne. The river was not then fordable there, a dam having been built about half a mile below, making the water four feet deep at the old crossing-place. The road that led to and crossed the ford was along the margin of the Maumee, which was skirted by the same forest-trees in whose presence the battle was fought. They had grown to be grand and stately, and were made exceedingly picturesque by the trailing grape-vines.

HALL'S CROSSING-PLACE.

We returned to the bridge and rode up the St. Joseph's to the place where Major Hall and his detachment forded it. It is about half a mile above the bridge. There the St. Joseph's, with its banks fringed with a variety of graceful trees, swept in gentle curves, and presented to the eye pictures of great beauty. Near the spot here represented, on the east bank of the St. Joseph's, was once a stockade, built by the French, and occupied by the English in Pontiac's time.

The land of the point between the St. Joseph's and the Maumee, on which Little Turtle was encamped and the principal Miami village was situated, is a level bottom, and known as the Cole Farm. Much of it was covered with Indian corn of lux-

---

[1] Harmar lost, in this expedition, 183 killed and 31 wounded. Among the killed were Majors Wyllys and Fontaine. The loss of the Indians was supposed to be about equal to that of the white people. Criminations and recriminations grew out of this expedition. Harmar and Hardin were both tried by court-martial and both were acquitted. Harmar resigned his commission on the 1st of January, 1792. Hardin had been a lieutenant in Morgan's rifle corps in the Revolution, and was a brave soldier. He was a Virginian by birth, but settled in Kentucky after the war. He was killed by some Shawnoese while on a mission of peace to them in 1792, when he was in the thirty-ninth year of his age. A county in each of the states of Ohio and Kentucky bears his name, in his honor.

uriant growth; and I was told that there is evidence that a similar crop has been raised from it year after year for almost a century, and yet the soil was black, rich, and apparently inexhaustible. Here, it is said, was the place where the Miamis were accustomed to burn their prisoners.[1]

APPLE-TREE NEAR HARMAR'S FORD.

About three hundred yards westward from Harmar's Ford, on the site of the Indian camp, was a venerable apple-tree, full of fruit, its trunk measuring fifteen feet in circumference. Under this tree Chief Richardville, to whom allusion has been made, was born a little more than a hundred years ago.[2] It was a fruit-bearing tree then, and is supposed to have grown from a seed dropped by some French trader among these Twightwees, as the Miamis were called in early times.[3] In the sketch of the apple-tree the city of Fort Wayne is seen in the distance. The spires on the left are those of the Roman Catholic Cathedral.

We returned to Fort Wayne at twilight, and I spent the evening profitably with Mr. Hedges, one of the oldest and most intelligent of the inhabitants of that town.[4] He was there in the spring of 1812, while the old stockade was yet standing, and before a garrison of United States troops from Harrison's army arrived. He has seen the city bloom out into its present form and beauty from the folds of the dark forest, and its history and traditions are as familiar to him as those of his own biography. We chatted on the events of the past until a late hour, and parted with an agreement to visit the historic scenes together in the morning. The air toward midnight was as mild as early June, but a dappled sky prophesied a storm. At three o'clock in the morning I was aroused by heavy thunder-peals, and the dawning of the

---

[1] We have mentioned Mr. Gamelin's peace mission, on page 40. He was at this place, and only three days after he left (about the 1st of May, 1790), the savages, as if in derision of the United States authority, brought an American prisoner there and burned him.—See DILLON's *History of Indiana*.
About seventy years ago a white man was bound to the stake at this place. The mother of Chief Richardville, mentioned in the next note, and a woman of great influence, had made fruitless attempts to save him. The torch was applied. Richardville, then quite young, had been designated as their future chief. She appealed to him, and, placing a knife in his hand, bade him assert his chieftainship and cut the cords that bound the prisoner. He obeyed, and the prisoner was released. The kind-hearted Miami woman secreted the prisoner and sent him down the Maumee in a canoe, covered with furs and peltries, in charge of some friendly Indians. Many years afterward Richardville stopped at a town in Ohio. A man came to him and threw his arms affectionately around his neck. It was the rescued prisoner.—*Lecture before the Congregation of the First Presbyterian Church, Fort Wayne.*

[2] *Pis-he-wa* (Wildcat), or Jean Baptiste Richardville, was born in 1759. His father was Joseph Drouet de Richardville, a Frenchman, who traded at *Ke-ki-on-ga** (Fort Wayne) from 1750 to 1770. He was elected chief of the Miamis, on the death of Little Turtle, in 1811. He was a large, fine-looking man, of quite light complexion, and spoke English well. Richardville left a fortune at his death in 1840. I was told by an old resident of Fort Wayne, who knew him well, that he had received large sums of money and immense tracts of land, from time to time, in consideration of his signing treaties; and that, at his death, he had $200,000 buried where no one but his daughter could find it. He was a temperate man, with acquisitiveness largely developed. He was buried in Fort Wayne.

[3] The Twightwees once formed a powerful confederacy of tribes, and claimed to be the possessors of a vast territory. At the treaty with Wayne at Greenville, which we shall notice presently, Little Turtle thus defined the ancient boundary of the Twightwees or Miamis: "It is well known by all my brothers present that my forefather kindled the first fire at Detroit; from thence he extended his lines to the head waters of the Scioto; from thence to its mouth; from thence down the Ohio to the mouth of the Wabash; and from thence to Chicago, on Lake Michigan."—*American State Papers*, i., 570. This comprises about one half of Ohio, the whole of Indiana, and a part of Southern Michigan.

[4] John P. Hedges was employed in the commissary's department, under John H. Piatt, of Ohio, the contractor for the army of the Northwest, commanded by General Harrison. He was active in that department during the whole of the war, and became familiar with all the territory. He was with General M'Arthur in his campaign in Western Canada, and was with Harrison at the battle of the Thames. He was at the treaty with the Indians at Greenville in 1814, and distributed provisions to the savages on that occasion.

---

* *Ke-ki-on-ga* in the language of the Miamis, and *Kee-ki-ogue* in that of the Pottawatomies.

Indian Hostilities continued.   Expeditions of Generals Scott and Wilkinson.   Destruction of Villages and Crops.

28th was made dreary by a cold drizzle drifting upon a northeast wind. I went out alone, and made the sketches at the two fords and other drawings, and, after visiting the grave of Little Turtle, departed in the midday train for Indianapolis. Of Fort Wayne in 1812, and of Little Turtle and his grave, I shall hereafter write.

Although Harmar in his expedition had punished the Miamis and Shawnoese severely, and Hamtramck meanwhile had been up the Wabash to the mouth of the Vermilion River and destroyed some deserted villages, Indian hostilities in the Northwest were not even checked. The settlers along the Ohio were continually menaced and sometimes attacked by the savages, back of whom was distinctly heard the voice of the British commandant at Detroit. Western Virginia and Kentucky were threatened, and life and property on the frontiers were in jeopardy every hour. The Virginia Legislature adopted measures for the protection of the settlers, and the national government, awake to the importance of the subject, put forth all its available strength for the same purpose. General Knox, the Secretary of War, issued orders to proper authorities beyond the mountains "to impress the Indians with the power of the United States," and "to inflict that degree of punishment which justice may require."[1] Under these instructions, General Scott, of Kentucky, with eight hundred mounted men, crossed the Ohio,[a] and penetrated the Wabash country to the large village of Ouiatenon, situated about eight miles below the present village of Lafayette, Indiana, where several French families resided. There he found ample evidence of the Indians' connection with and dependence on the British at Detroit. Scott destroyed the town, and several villages in the neighborhood, and desolated the country. He killed thirty-two Indians, "chiefly warriors of size and figure," and took fifty-eight prisoners, without losing any of his own men.[2]

[a] May 23, 1791.

On the 1st of August Brigadier General James Wilkinson left Cincinnati (Fort Washington) with five hundred and twenty-five men, and penetrated the same region, by a different route, to the important Ouiatenon village of *Ke-na-pa-com-a-qua*, which the French called *L'Anguille* (The Eel), on the Eel River, about six miles from the present Logansport, Indiana.[3] He destroyed that village, desolated the country around as far as Tippecanoe, and then pushed forward to the great prairies that stretch away toward Lake Michigan. But deep morasses, into which he was sometimes plunged armpit deep, compelled him to return. He then destroyed another Kickapoo village of twenty houses, desolated all the crops, and, after a march of four hundred and fifty miles, reached the Falls of the Ohio (Louisville) on the 21st of August.[4]

The misfortune that befell the Indians under the lash of Scott and Wilkinson did not quiet them. The British emissaries stimulated their courage to a point of desperation by assuring them that the grand object of the United States was to exterminate the tribes and take possession of their lands.[5] Thus two most powerful incentives to war

---

[1] Instructions of the Secretary of War to Brigadier General Scott, of Kentucky, March 9, 1791.
[2] Scott's official report to the Secretary of War, June 28, 1791.
[3] Fort Ouiatenon, a stockade built by the French, was near the present city of Lafayette, Indiana.
[4] "I have destroyed," he said, "the chief town of the Ouiatenon nation, and made prisoners of the sons and sisters of the king. I have burned a respectable Kickapoo village, and cut down at least four hundred and thirty acres of corn, chiefly in the milk. The Ouiatenons, left without houses, home, or provisions, must cease to war, and will find active employ to subsist their squaws and children during the impending winter."—WILKINSON's *Official Report to Governor St. Clair*, August 24, 1791.
[5] The most active of these British emissaries were Simon Girty, Andrew M'Kee, and Mathew Elliott, three malignant Tories during the Revolution. The two latter were natives of Path Valley, Pennsylvania. Many a murder was justly charged to these men while the old war for independence was in progress. They carried on their depredations on the frontier with a high hand, and, for their faithfulness in inciting Indian hostilities during that war that led to frightful massacres, the British government rewarded them with official station. They married Indian women, and became thoroughly identified with the savages. At the time we are now considering Elliott and M'Kee were subordinate agents in the British Indian Department, and, with Girty, had homes near Malden, in Canada, on the Detroit River. We shall meet Elliott again. Girty was an unmitigated scoundrel. More brutal than the most savage Indian, he had not one redeeming quality. He was the offspring of crime. His father, an Irishman, was a sot; his mother was a bawd. He was nurtured among the warlike Senecas, and his innate cruelty had free scope for growth. With Elliott and M'Kee, who, with him, had been imprisoned at Pittsburg in 1778, he aroused the Indians in the Northwest with the same cry

were presented—self-preservation and patriotism. In defense of life and country they resolved to fight to the last. Little Turtle, of the Miamis, Blue Jacket, of the Shawnoese, and Buck-ong-a-helos, of the Delawares, put forth all their energies in the summer of 1791, as Pontiac had done thirty years before, to confederate all the Western tribes in an effort to drive every European from the soil north of the Ohio. The protestations of St. Clair that peace, friendship, and justice, not war, subjugation, and robbery, were the desire of the people and government of the United States, were of no avail; and he was compelled, for the sake of the national life on the frontier, to attempt to convince them, by the stern argument of arms, that they were governed by bad counselors at Detroit.

It was determined to establish a strong military post in the heart of the Miami country, on the site of the present city of Fort Wayne. Congress authorized the raising of sufficient troops for the purpose, and during the spring and summer of 1791, St. Clair was putting forth strong efforts in that direction, but with indifferent success. Enlistments were slow, and it was not until the beginning of September that he had collected a sufficient force to attempt the enterprise with an appearance of safety. These had been collected in the vicinity of Cincinnati, and placed under the immediate command, in camp, of Major Hamtramck, who was remarkable as a tactician and disciplinarian.[1] St. Clair took the field as commander-in-chief. Major General Richard Butler, of Pennsylvania, was his second in command, and Winthrop Sargent, Secretary of the Territory, was appointed adjutant general.

An army little more than two thousand strong, under the immediate command of General Butler, and accompanied by General St. Clair, moved forward on the 5th and 6th of September.[a] On the bank of the Great Miami, little more than twenty miles from Fort Washington, they halted and built Fort Hamilton, on the site of the present village of Hamilton. Forty-two miles farther on, at a point about six miles south of Greenville, in the present Darke County, Ohio, they built Fort Jefferson. When they moved from there, on the 24th of October, they began to encounter the subtle foe in small parties. It was evident that dusky scouts were hanging upon their flanks, and they became hourly more cautious and vigilant. The nights were frosty, but serene. The days were genial and brilliant. The summer warmth had been diffused over the whole of September; and now the forests were arrayed in all the gorgeous beauty of autumnal splendors peculiar to them.

[a] 1791.

At length, when dark clouds were overhead, and falling leaves were thick in their path, the invading army halted and encamped upon the borders of an unknown stream, which proved to be a chief tributary of the Upper Wabash. They were ninety-seven miles from Fort Washington, deep in the wilderness. A light fall of snow lay upon the ground—so light that it appeared like hoar-frost. Over a piece of rising ground, timbered with oak, ash, and hickory, the encampment was spread, with a fordable stream, forty feet in width, in front. The army lay in two lines, seventy yards apart, with four pieces of cannon in the centre of each. Across the stream, and beyond a rich bottom land three hundred yards in width, was an elevated plain, covered with an open forest of stately trees. There the militia—three hundred and fifty independent, half-insubordinate men, under Lieutenant Colonel Oldham, of Kentucky—were encamped.

Eight weary miles through the woods the soldiers had marched that day, and when the camp was arranged the sun was low in the cloudless sky of the west. The tired soldiers early sought repose, without suspicion of danger near. All around them

---

that now alarmed them: "The Americans want to take your lives and your lands." For more than twenty years the women and children of the Ohio country turned pale when his name was mentioned.

[1] Hamtramck was a poor rider. "He was crooked like a frog on horseback," said the venerable Major Whitlock, of Crawfordsville, to me, who knew him well, and had served under him. He had the faculty of inspiring the men with self-confidence, and, notwithstanding he was a most rigid disciplinarian, the troops all loved him, for he was kind-hearted, generous, and brave.

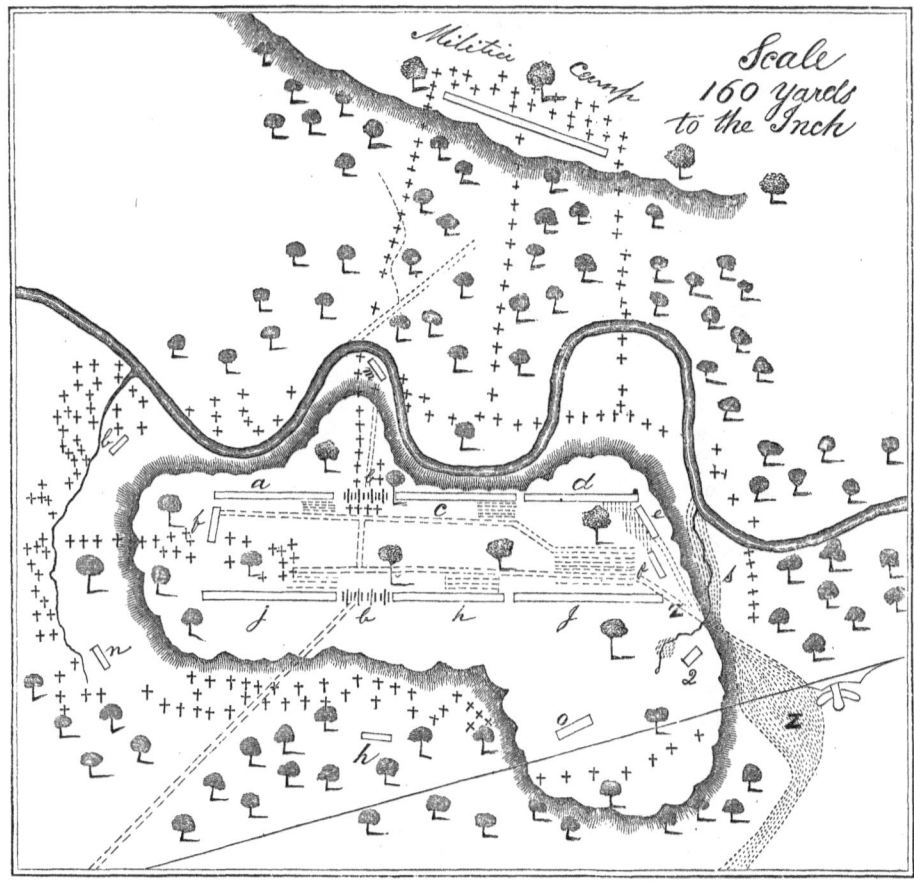

PLAN OF ST. CLAIR'S CAMP AND BATTLE.[1]

were evidences of old and recent Indian camps, and a few lurking savages had been seen by vigilant eyes; but no one knew whether Little Turtle and his confederates, with their followers, were near or far away.

They were near. Only a few miles distant the great Miami leader, Blue Jacket the Shawnoese chief, and Buck-ong-a-helos, the leader of the Delawares, with the cruel Girty and other white men in the British interest, were lying in wait, with two thousand fierce warriors at their beck.[2] These had been watching St. Clair's movements for several days, and were waiting for the proper moment to fall upon him like a bolt from the cloud.

The morning of the 4th dawned brilliantly. "Moderate northwest wind, serene atmosphere, and unclouded sky."[3] All night long the sentinels had been firing upon

---

[1] This sketch of St. Clair's encampment is from Winthrop Sargent's MS. Journal of the Campaign, kindly lent to me by his grandson, Winthrop Sargent, Esq., of Philadelphia. It is a *fac-simile* of Mr. Sargent's sketch.

EXPLANATION.—*a*, Butler's battalion; *b b*, artillery; *c*, Clarke's battalion; *d*, Patterson's battalion; *e*, Faulkner's rifle company; *f f*, cavalry; *g*, detachment of U. S. Second Regiment; *h*, Gaither's battalion; *j*, Beddinger's battalion; *b n p*, flank guards; *o* 2, pickets; *s*, swamp; *m*, camp guard. The numerous crosses represent the enemy; *z z*, troops retreating; the crooked stream, a tributary of the Wabash.

[2] The late Colonel John Johnson, of Dayton, mentioned hereafter, informed me that, from the best information he could obtain, the Indians numbered about two thousand. Some have estimated their number at one thousand, and others at three thousand. The principal tribes engaged in the battle were the Miamis, Delawares, Shawnoese, Wyandots, Ottawas, and a few Chippewas and Pottawatomies.

[3] Winthrop Sargent's MS. Journal, November 4, 1791.

prowling Indians, and the men, by order of the commanding general, had slept upon their arms.

The troops had been early mustered and dismissed from parade. They were preparing for breakfast, when, half an hour before sunrise, a body of Indians, with yells that wakened horrid echoes miles away through the forest, fell suddenly upon the militia. The assailed camp was immediately broken up, and the frightened soldiers, most of whom had never been in battle, rushed wildly across the bottom and the creek into the lines of the regulars, producing alarm and confusion there. The Indians closely followed, and fell upon the regulars. The savages were several times repulsed, but soon rallied, and directed their most effective shots upon the artillery in the centre. Every officer there was prostrated, and the cannon were silenced. The carnage among the Americans was terrible, yet they withstood the enemy with great gallantry for almost three hours. Finally, when full one half of the army had fallen, St. Clair ordered a retreat to an old Indian road or trail. This was accomplished after a furious charge as if to turn the enemy's flank.[1] The militia then led the van in the precipitate retreat, which soon became a flight.[2] The fugitive army was well covered by Major Clarke and his battalion; and the Indians, after following about four miles, turned back, wonderfully elated with their victory. Little Turtle was in chief command.

St. Clair behaved gallantly during the dreadful scene. He was so tortured with gout that he could not mount a horse without assistance. He was not in uniform. His chief covering was a coarse cappo coat, and a three-cocked hat from under which his white hair was seen streaming as he and Butler rode up and down the lines during the battle. He had three horses killed under him. Eight balls passed through his clothes. He finally mounted a pack-horse, and upon this animal, which could with difficulty be spurred into a trot, he followed in the retreat.

The fugitive army did not halt until safely within the palisades of Fort Jefferson. The panic was terrible, and the conduct of the army after quitting the ground was most disgraceful. Arms, ammunition, and accoutrements were almost all thrown away; and even officers, in some instances, threw away their arms, "thus setting an example for the most precipitate and ignominious flight."[3] They left the camp at nine o'clock in the morning, and at seven o'clock that evening they were in Fort Jefferson, twenty-nine miles distant. That evening Adjutant General Sargent wrote in his diary, "The troops have all been defeated; and though it is impossible, at this time, to ascertain our loss, yet there can be no manner of doubt that more than half the army are either killed or wounded."[4]

---

[1] There were quite a large number of the wounded so maimed that they could not walk or sit upon a horse, and their companions were compelled to leave them upon the field. "When they knew they must be left," says Sargent, "they charged their pieces with a deliberation and courage which reflects the highest honor upon them; and the firing of musketry in the camp after we had quitted it leaves little doubt that their latest efforts were professionally brave, and where they could pull a trigger they avenged themselves."—MS. Journal.
During the engagement, the Indians, as opportunity offered, plundered and scalped their victims. They also disfigured the bodies of the slain. Having been taught by the British emissaries that the Americans made war upon them for their lands, they crammed clay and sand into the eyes and down the throats of the dying and dead.—DILLON'S History of Indiana, p. 283. Among the slain was Major General Butler; and it has been authoritatively asserted that the miscreant, Simon Girty, instigated a savage warrior, while the general was yet alive on the field, to scalp him, and take out his heart for distribution among the tribes!

[2] The whole number of effective troops in the battle, according to Sargent's return, was 1748.

[3] Sargent's MS. Journal. There were almost two hundred female camp-followers, chiefly wives of the soldiers. Of these, fifty-six were killed; most of the remainder were in the flight. One of them, Mrs. Catharine Miller, who died in Cincinnati about the year 1838, was so fleet afoot that she ran ahead of the army. She had a great quantity of long red hair, that streamed behind her as she ran, and formed the *oriflamme* which the soldiers followed.—Statement of Major Whitlock, of Crawfordsville, Indiana.

[4] MS. Journal, Friday, November 4, 1791. Mr. Sargent was slightly wounded. According to his report, afterward made out carefully, thirty-six officers were killed and thirty wounded; and 593 privates were killed and missing, and 214 wounded. He did not think many Indians were lost—probably not more than one hundred and fifty killed and wounded. Several pieces of cannon, and all the baggage, ammunition, and provisions were left on the field, and became spoil for the savage victors. The value of public property lost, according to the report of the Secretary of War toward the close of 1792, was $32,810 75. The signature of the Adjutant General, of which a *fac-simile* is given on page 38, was cop-

At Fort Jefferson the flying troops found the First Regiment of the United States army, about three hundred strong. Leaving a well-provisioned garrison there, the remnant of St. Clair's force made their way to Fort Washington, where they arrived at noon on the 8th.[a]

[a] November, 1791.

Intelligence of St. Clair's defeat produced the greatest alarm among all the settlers in the West, even as far eastward as Pittsburg. It cast a gloom over society in all parts of the Union, and checked for a short time the tide of emigration in the direction of the Ohio.[1]

St. Clair was condemned in unmeasured terms by men of all classes and parties, and the indignation of President Washington was exceedingly hot. "Here," he said to Tobias Lear, his private secretary, "yes, HERE, on this very spot, I took leave of him. I wished him success and honor. You have your instructions, I said, from the Secretary of War. I had a strict eye to them, and will add but one word—*beware of a surprise!* I repeat it—BEWARE OF A SURPRISE! You know how the Indians fight us. He went off with that, as my last solemn warning, thrown into his ears.[2] And yet!! to suffer that army to be cut to pieces, hacked, butchered, tomahawked, by a surprise—the very thing I guarded him against!! O God, O God, he is worse than a murderer! How can he answer it to his country? The blood of the slain is upon him—the curse of widows and orphans—the curse of Heaven!"

The tone of Washington's voice was appalling as these vehement sentences escaped his lips. "It was awful!" said Mr. Lear. "More than once he threw his hands up as he hurled imprecations upon St. Clair." Mr. Lear remained speechless—awed into breathless silence.

"The roused chief," says the chronicler, "sat down on the sofa once more. He seemed conscious of his passion, and uncomfortable. He was silent; his wrath began to subside. He at length said, in an altered voice, 'This must not go beyond

---

ied from his report. In Howe's *Historical Collections of Ohio* may be found many particulars and anecdotes of this disastrous campaign.

Among the slain, as we have observed, was Major General Butler, a highly esteemed officer from Pennsylvania. He held the rank of colonel in the Continental army. In 1787 he was sent to the Ohio as agent for Indian affairs in that quarter. He was wounded early in the action, and before his wounds could be dressed, an Indian, who had penetrated the camp, ran up and tomahawked and scalped him. Butler was much beloved by the Indians who were friendly to the United States. Among those who loved him most was Big Tree, a Seneca chief in the Genesee Valley. He vowed to avenge the death of Butler by killing three of the hostile Indians. Because the treaty of peace at Greenville in 1795 thwarted his bloody purpose, Big Tree committed suicide.

[1] This event was the theme for oratory, the pulpit, poetry, art, and song. I have before me a dirge-like poem, printed on a broadside, and embellished with rude wood-cuts representing forty coffins at the head, a portrait of General Butler, a Miami village, an Indian with a bow, and the hideous skull and cross-bones. It is entitled "The Columbian Tragedy," and professes to give, in verse, "a particular and official account" of the affair. It was published "by the earnest request of the friends of the deceased worthies who died in defense of their country." According to this "official account," the battle was fought between two thousand United States troops "and near four thousand wild Indian savages, at Miami Village, near Fort Washington!" A pious tone runs through the mournful ballad, and the feelings of the writer may be imagined after the perusal of this single verse:

" My trembling hand can scarcely hold
My faint, devoted quill,
To write the actions of the Bold,
Their *Valor* and their *Skill*."

There was a famous song that was sung for many years afterward, entitled " Sinclair's Defeat," written, as the author thus informs us, by one of the soldiers:

" To mention our brave officers is what I write to do;
No sons of Mars e'er fought more brave, or with more courage true.
To Captain Bradford I belonged, in his Artillery;
He fell that day among the slain—a valiant man was he."

This song may be found in Howe's *Historical Collections of Ohio*, p. 136.

[2] This interview was on the 28th of March, 1791, the day when St. Clair left Philadelphia and proceeded to the frontier post of Pittsburg. Thence he went to Kentucky, and afterward to Fort Washington, every where endeavoring to enlist the sympathies and co-operation of the inhabitants for the campaign.

D

this room.' Another pause followed—a longer one—when he said, in a tone quite low, 'General St. Clair shall have justice. I looked hastily through the dispatches—saw the whole disaster, but not all the particulars. I will hear him without prejudice; he shall have full justice.'

"He was now," said Mr. Lear, "perfectly calm. Half an hour had gone by; the storm was over, and no sign of it was afterward seen in his conduct or heard in his conversation."[1]

Washington was both generous and just, and St. Clair found in him a most faithful friend. "The first interview of the President with the unfortunate general after the fatal 4th of November," says the late Mr. Custis, who was present, "was nobly impressive. St. Clair, worn down by age, disease, and the hardships of a frontier campaign, assailed by the press, and with the current of popular opinion setting hard against him, repaired to his chief as to a shelter from the fury of so many elements. Washington extended his hand to one who appeared in no new character, for, during the whole of a long life, misfortune seemed 'to have marked him for her own.' Poor old St. Clair hobbled up to his chief, seized the offered hand in both of his, and gave vent to his feelings in an audible manner."[2]

St. Clair's case was investigated by a committee of the House of Representatives, and he was honorably acquitted. But public sentiment had set against him in a current too strong to be successfully resisted, and he resigned his commission.[3] General Anthony Wayne, whose impetuosity exhibited during the old war for independence had gained him the title of "Mad Anthony," was appointed to fill his place. Wayne was then in the prime of manhood, and Congress and the people had confidence in his intelligence, courage, and energy. Congress authorized an increase of the regular army to a little over five thousand men, and a competent part of this force, to be called the Legion of the United States, was to be assigned to Wayne for an expedition against the Indians in the Northwest. He took post at Pittsburg early in the following June,[a] and appointed that place as the rendezvous of his invading army. It was soon perceived that it was easier to vote troops in the halls of Congress than to draw them out and muster them in the camp; and it was not until near the close of November that Wayne had collected a sufficient number to warrant his moving forward. He then went down the Ohio only about twenty miles, and there hutted his soldiers in a well-guarded camp, which he called Legionville. There he was joined by Lieutenant William Henry Harrison, afterward the distinguished general in the armies of the United States, and the ninth President of the republic. The

[a] 1792.

---

[1] *Washington in Domestic Life*, by Richard Rush, p. 67.
[2] *Recollections and Private Memoirs of Washington*, by his adopted son, G. W. P. Custis, p. 419.
[3] The late Hon. Elisha Whittlesey, of Ohio, First Auditor of the United States Treasury during a portion of the first term of Mr. Lincoln's administration, and a veteran soldier of 1812, furnished me with the following interesting account of his interview with St. Clair three years before his death:

"In May, 1815, four of us called upon him, on the top of Chestnut Ridge, eastwardly eight or ten miles from Greensburg, Westmoreland County, Pennsylvania. We were traveling on horseback to Connecticut, and being informed that General St. Clair kept tavern, we decided to call for entertainment during the night. We alighted at his residence late in the afternoon, and, on entering his log house, we saw an elderly, neat gentleman, dressed in black broadcloth, silk stockings, and small-clothes, shining shoes whose straps were secured by large silver buckles, his hair clubbed and powdered. On closing his book he rose, received us most kindly and gracefully, and pointing us to chairs, he asked us to be seated. On being asked for entertainment, he said, 'Gentlemen, I perceive you are traveling, and although I should be gratified by your custom, it is my duty to inform you I have no hay nor grain. I have good pasture, but if hay and grain are essential, I can not furnish them.'

"There stood before us a major general of the Revolution—the friend and confidant of Washington—late governor of the Territory northwest of the River Ohio—one of nature's noblemen, of high, dignified bearing, whom misfortune, nor the ingratitude of his country, nor poverty could break down nor deprive of self-respect—keeping a tavern in a log house, but could not furnish a bushel of oats nor a lock of hay. We were moved principally to call upon him to hear him converse about the men of the Revolution and of the Northwestern Territory, and our regret that he could not entertain us was greatly increased by hearing him converse about an hour. The large estate he sacrificed for the cause of the Revolution was within a short distance of the top of Chestnut Ridge, if not in sight. After he was governor he petitioned Congress for relief, but died before it was granted."*

* During the last two years of his life General St. Clair received a pension of sixty dollars a month from his government, and his latter days were made comfortable thereby. About 1856, Senator Brodhead, of Pennsylvania, procured from Congress an appropriation for the heirs of General St. Clair.

young Virginian soon exhibited qualities which caused Wayne to make him a member of his military family as his aid-de-camp.

Wayne remained at Legionville until the close of April, 1793, when his whole force proceeded to Cincinnati in boats, and took post near Fort Washington. There they remained all the summer and until the 7th of October, when Wayne moved forward and encamped[a] six miles in advance of Fort Jefferson, on the site of Greenville. His army then numbered three thousand six hundred and thirty men, exclusive of a small body of friendly Indians from the South, chiefly Choctaws, under the eminent warrior, Humming-bird.

[a] October 23.

While the army was making these tardy movements, the government was using its best endeavors to effect a pacification of the tribes, and to establish a solid peace without more bloodshed. These efforts promised success at times. With the aid of the pious Heckewelder, the Moravian, General Putnam made a treaty of peace and friendship with the Wabash and Illinois tribes, at Vincennes, on the 27th of September, 1792. At about the same time great numbers of the tribes on the Miami, the Maumee (or Miami of the Lakes), and Sandusky Rivers, assembled at the Maumee Rapids to hold a grand council, at which Red Jacket, Cornplanter, Big Tree, the aged Guasutha, and other representatives of the Six Nations appeared, at the request of the Secretary of War. Simon Girty was the only white man present. The savages, on consultation, determined, in conformity with the advice of the British, not to acknowledge any claim of the United States to lands northwest of the Ohio River.[1]

In the spring of 1793 a commission was sent by the President to treat with the hostile tribes.[2] Lieutenant Governor Simcoe, of Canada, professing to be friendly, and favorable to a pacification of the tribes, the commissioners went by the way of Niagara, a post yet held by the British. Simcoe received them courteously, and hospitably entertained them for five or six weeks, while the Indians were holding another grand council at the Rapids of the Maumee. While tarrying there, the commissioners were informed by a Mohawk Indian from the Grand River that Governor Simcoe had "advised the Indians to make peace, *but not to give up any of their lands.*"[3] The commissioners called Simcoe's attention to this. He did not deny the allegation, but replied, "It is of that nature that it can not be true," as the Indians had not "applied for his advice on the subject."[4] This subterfuge was well understood by the commissioners; and his admission that, "ever since the conquest of Canada," it had been "the principle of the British government to *unite the American Indians,*" was ominous of ulterior designs.

At Niagara, and at Captain Elliott's, near the mouth of the Detroit River, in Canada, the commissioners held councils with the Indians, but nothing satisfactory was accomplished. British influence was more powerful than ever, and the savages in council plainly told the commissioners that if they insisted upon the treaty at Fort Harmar, and claimed lands on the northern side of the Ohio, they might as well go home, as they would never agree to any other boundary than that river. So the commissioners, after several months of fruitless labor, turned homeward late in August. It was evident that the might of arms must make a final settlement of the matter, and to arms the United States resorted.

We left Wayne and his army near Fort Jefferson, eighty miles from Fort Washington, on the 23d of October. He was then embarrassed by a lack of sufficient convoys for his stores. Already a party detailed for this purpose had been attacked and se-

---

[1] The sentiments of the Indians, even the friendly ones, concerning the boundary, may be inferred from the following toast given by Cornplanter, at the table of General Wayne, at Legionville, in the spring of 1793: "My mind is upon that river," he said, pointing to the Ohio. "May that water ever continue to run, and remain the boundary of lasting peace between the Americans and Indians on the opposite shore."—HALL's *Memoir of W. H. Harrison*, p. 31.
[2] The commission consisted of Benjamin Lincoln, Beverly Randolph, and Timothy Pickering.
[3] Note of commissioners to Lieutenant Governor Simcoe, 7th June, 1793.
[4] Reply of Lieutenant Governor Simcoe to American commissioners, 7th June, 1793.

verely handled by a strong band of Indians under Little Turtle near Fort St. Clair. Lieutenant Lowry and fourteen of his companions were killed,[1] and all the horses attached to the wagons were carried off.

The season was now too far advanced to enter upon a campaign, so Wayne set his army to building a very strong fort on the spot where he was encamped. It was made impregnable against the Indians. There they went into winter-quarters.[2] Sufficient garrisons were placed in the forts at Vincennes, Cincinnati, and Marietta; and the return of spring was waited for with anxiety, for it was obvious that hostilities with the savages could not be long delayed.

A European war, to which we shall soon have occasion again to refer, was now having its effect upon the United States, complicating the difficulties which naturally attend the arrangement of a new system of government. Ill feeling between the United States and Great Britain was increasing, and evidences were not wanting that the latter was anxious for a pretense to declare hostilities against the former. Taking advantage of this state of things, Lord Dorchester (formerly Sir Guy Carleton), the Governor of Canada, encouraged the Indians in maintaining their hostile attitude. At a council of warriors from the West, held at Quebec early in 1794,[a] Dorchester, in a speech, said, "*Children*, since my return I find no appearance of a line remains; and from the manner in which the people of the states push on, and act, and talk on this side, and from what I learn of their conduct toward the sea, *I shall not be surprised if we are at war with them in the course of the present year; and if so, a line must then be drawn by the warriors*."

[a] February 10, 1794.

This was a suggestion for the savages to prepare for war. It was followed by an order from Dorchester to Lieutenant Governor Simcoe to establish a British military post at the rapids of the Maumee, fifty miles within the Indian country and the treaty limits of the United States. At the very time when this menacing attitude was assumed, the government of the new republic was exhibiting the most friendly feelings toward that of Great Britain by a position of strict neutrality.

Wayne was compelled to wait until late in the summer of 1794 before he felt strong enough to move forward. Meanwhile the Indians appeared in force. On the 30th of June, about a thousand of them, accompanied by a number of British soldiers and French Canadian volunteers,[3] made their appearance before Fort Recovery (mentioned in note 2 below), and during the day assailed the garrison several times. During these assaults the Americans lost fifty-seven men in killed, wounded, and missing, and two hundred and twenty-one horses. The Indians lost more, they said, than in their battle with St. Clair.

Less than a month after this engagement, Wayne was joined[b] by Major General Scott, with sixteen hundred mounted volunteers from Kentucky; and two days afterward[c] he moved forward with his whole force toward the

[b] July 26, 1794.
[c] July 28.

LOWRY'S MONUMENT.

[1] Fort St. Clair was at a point about a mile from the site of Eaton, in Preble County, Ohio. Between it and Eaton is a small cemetery, and therein, upon one of those ancient artificial mounds common in Ohio, a neat monument of Rutland marble, twelve feet in height, was erected by the citizens in commemoration of the slain at Fort Recovery. Lowry and his companions were buried in Fort St. Clair. His remains were removed to the little cemetery on the 4th of July, 1822, and there reinterred with the honors of war. They were afterward buried in the mound.

[2] This was called Fort Greenville, and covered a large part of the site of the present village of Greenville. The soldiers built several hundred log huts, in which they wintered comfortably. Each hut was occupied by six persons.

From Fort Greenville Wayne sent out eight companies, and a detachment of artillery to take possession of and fortify the place where St. Clair was defeated. They arrived on the ground on Christmas-day, and proceeded to build a strong stockade. They named it Fort Recovery, in commemoration of the fact that they had recovered the territory lost by St. Clair, as well as all but one of the cannon which he was compelled to leave behind. A company each of artillery and riflemen were left there as a garrison.

[3] Burnet, in his notes, asserts upon good authority that there were "a considerable number of British soldiers and Detroit militia with the Indians." Friendly Choctaws and Chickasaws with Wayne, who had been sent on a scout a few days before, saw a large body of Indians, among whom, they asserted, were many white men with their faces painted.

Wayne's Expedition down the Maumee.   His Offers of Peace rejected.   Conduct of Little Turtle.

Maumee. Admonished by the fate of St. Clair, he marched cautiously and slowly —so slowly and stealthily that the Indians called him The Blacksnake. Little Turtle was again upon the alert, with two thousand warriors of his own and neighboring tribes within call. The vigilant Wayne well knew this. He had faithful and competent scouts and guides, and by unfrequented ways and with perplexing feints, he moved steadily onward, leaving strength and security in his rear.

Twenty-five miles beyond Fort Recovery he built a stockade on the bank of the St. Mary's, and called it Fort Adams. From this point he moved forward on the 4th of August, and at the end of four days encamped on a beautiful plain at the confluence of the Au Glaize and Maumee Rivers, on the site of the present village of Defiance. There he found a deserted Indian town, with at least a thousand acres of corn growing around it.[1] There, as elsewhere on his march, the alarmed savages fled at his approach. He tarried there a week, and built a strong fortification, which he called Fort Defiance. Of this fort, and the appearance of its remains when I visited it in the autumn of 1860, I shall hereafter write.

Wayne was now at the most important and commanding point in the Indian country. "We have gained the grand emporium of the hostile Indians of the West without loss of blood," he wrote to the Secretary of War.[a] And there he gained full and positive information concerning the character, strength, and position of the British military post at the foot of the Maumee Rapids already alluded to.[2]   [a] August 14, 1794.

Once more peace and reconciliation were offered to the Indians. Notwithstanding he was in possession of full power to subjugate and destroy without fear of the British intruders below, Wayne, unwilling to shed blood unnecessarily, sent a message to the Indians down the Maumee with kind words. "Be no longer deceived or led astray," he said, "by the false promises and language of bad white men at the foot of the Rapids; they have neither the power nor the inclination to protect you." He offered them peace and tranquillity for themselves and their families, and invited them to send deputies to meet him in council without delay. His overtures were rejected, and by craftiness they endeavored to gain time. "Stay where you are," they said, "for ten days, and we will treat with you; but if you advance we will give you battle."

This defiance was contrary to the advice of the sagacious Little Turtle, who counseled peace.[3] For this he was taunted with accusations of cowardice. The false charge enraged him, and he was foremost in the conflict that immediately ensued. That conflict was unavoidable. The vigilant Wayne perceived that nothing but a severe blow would break the spirit of the tribes and end the war, and he resolved to inflict it mercilessly. For this purpose his legion moved forward on the 15th of August, and on the 18th took post at Roche de Bout, at the head of the Rapids, near the present town of Waterville, and there established a magazine of supplies and baggage, with protecting military works, which they called Fort Deposit. There, on the 19th, Wayne called a council of war, and adopted a plan of march and of battle submitted by his young aid-de-camp, Lieutenant Harrison, who, nineteen years afterward, as a general-in-chief, performed gallant exploits in that portion of the Maumee Valley.[4]

---

[1] "The very extensive and highly cultivated fields and gardens show the work of many hands. The margin of those beautiful rivers, the Miami of the Lakes [pronounced Maumee] and Au Glaize, appear like one continued village for a number of miles both above and below this place; nor have I ever before beheld such immense fields of corn in any part of America from Canada to Florida."—WAYNE's *Letter to the Secretary of War from Fort Defiance*, August 14, 1794.

[2] It was a strong work of earth and logs, mounting four 9-pounders, two large howitzers, six 6-pounders, and two swivels. The garrison, under Major Campbell, a testy Scotchman, consisted of 250 British regulars and 200 militia.

[3] "We have beaten the enemy twice, under separate commanders," said Little Turtle, in a speech. "We can not expect the same good fortune always to attend us. The Americans are now led by a chief who never sleeps. The night and the day are alike to him; and during all the time that he has been marching upon our villages, notwithstanding the watchfulness of our young men, we have never been able to surprise him. Think well of it. There is something whispers me it would be prudent to listen to the offers of peace."

[4] I am indebted to the Hon. John Francis Hamtramck Claiborne, of Mississippi, for the plan of the line of march and order of battle given in the text. In a letter to me, covering the drawings, dated "Bay St. Louis, Mississippi, August

Battle of the Fallen Timbers.   Devastations around Fort Miami.   The Punishment of M'Kee.

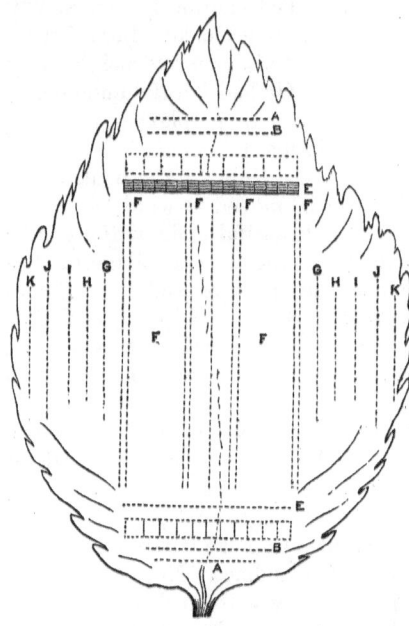

PLAN OF THE LINE OF MARCH.[1]

On the morning of the 20th, at eight o'clock, Wayne advanced with his whole army according to the adopted plan of march, having for his subordinate general officers Major General Scott, of the Kentucky volunteers, and Brigadier Generals Wilkinson, Todd, and Barber. They had proceeded about five miles when the advanced corps, under Major Price, were terribly smitten by heavy volleys from the concealed foe, and were compelled to fall back. The legion was immediately formed in two lines, principally in a dense wood on the borders of a wet prairie, where a tornado had prostrated a large number of trees, making the operations of cavalry very difficult. This fallen timber[2] afforded an admirable covert for the enemy, who, full two thousand strong, and composed of Indians and Canadian volunteers,[3] were posted in three lines, within supporting distance of each other. Wayne's troops fell upon the foe with fearful energy, and made them flee toward Fort Miami like a herd of frightened deer to a covert. In the course of an hour the victory was complete. The mongrel horde were driven more than two miles through the thick woods, and left forty of their number dead in the pathway of their flight. By the side of each body lay a musket and bayonet from British armories.[4]

Three days and three nights the victorious army remained below the Rapids, wielding the besom of destruction in defiance of the threats of the commandant of Fort Miami, within view of whose guns Wayne pitched his tents. On the site of the present Maumee City, near Fort Miami, Colonel M'Kee, the British agent already mentioned, and chief instigator of the war, had extensive store-houses and dwellings, for he was carrying on a most lucrative trade with the Indians. These, with their contents, were committed to the flames, while every product of the field and garden above and below the British fort was utterly destroyed.[5] Wayne's men sometimes ap-

---

20, 1860," Mr. Claiborne remarks: "This day, sixty-six years ago, was fought the great Battle of the Rapids. I send you the original 'Plan of the Line of March' and of the 'Order of Battle.' I found these diagrams among the papers of my father, the late General Claiborne, who was in the battle, a lieutenant and acting adjutant in the First Regiment United States Infantry, Colonel J. F. Hamtramck. I found them in a package of letters from Harrison to my father, the 'Plan of the Line of March' indorsed, in my father's handwriting, 'Lieutenant Harrison's Plan, adopted in council, August 19, '94.'

"Wayne, it appears, called a council of war on the 19th, and the plan, drawn up by Harrison, then a young man of twenty-one years, was adopted by the veteran officers the moment it was submitted—an homage to skill and talent rarely awarded to a subaltern."

[1] EXPLANATION OF THE PLAN.—A A, two squadrons of expert woodmen; B B, two squadrons of light dragoons; E E, two companies of infantry front and rear; G G, one troop of light dragoons on each flank; H H, one company of infantry on each flank; I I, one squadron of dragoons on each flank; J J, two companies of riflemen on each flank; K K, expert woodmen on the extreme of each flank. F F F F represent the main army in two columns, the legion of regular troops on the right, commanded by General Wilkinson, and the Kentucky volunteers, under Scott, on the left.

[2] This conflict is often called in history and tradition the Battle of the Fallen Timbers.

[3] There were about seventy white men, including a corps of volunteers from Detroit under Captain Caldwell.

[4] Among the officers mentioned by Wayne, in his dispatch to the Secretary of War, whose services demanded special mention, were Wilkinson and Hamtramck; his aids-de-camp De Butt, Lewis, and Harrison; Mills, Covington of the cavalry, Webb, Slough, Prior, Smith, Van Rensselaer, Rawlins, M'Kenney, Brook, and Duncan. His loss in killed and wounded was 133. Of these, 113 were regulars. The loss of the enemy was not ascertained. In their flight they left forty of their dead in the woods.

[5] Wayne's dispatch to the Secretary of War from Fort Defiance, August 28, 1794.

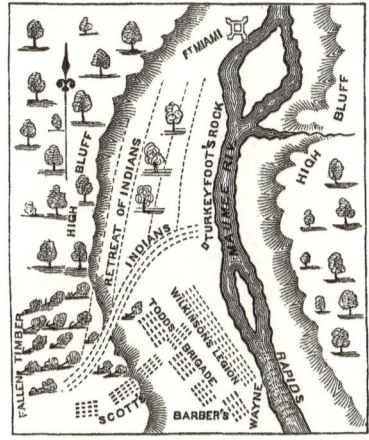

PLAN OF THE BATTLE OF THE FALLEN TIMBERS.

proached within pistol-shot of Fort Miami, but its guns prudently kept silence. Major Campbell, the commandant, contented himself with scolding and threatening, while Wayne coolly defied him and retorted with vigor. Their correspondence was very spicy, but harmless in its effects.

Among the brave warriors in the battle who was the last to flee before Wayne's legion, was Me-sa-sa, or Turkey-foot, an Ottawa chief, who lived on Blanchard's Fork of the Au Glaize River. He was greatly beloved by his people. His courage was conspicuous. When he found the line of the dusky warriors giving way at the foot of Presque Isle Hill, he leaped upon a small boulder, and by voice and gesture endeavored to make them stand firm. He almost immediately fell, pierced by a musket ball, and expired by the side of the rock. Long years afterward, when any of his tribe passed along the Maumee trail, they would stop at that rock, and linger a long time with manifestations of sorrow. Peter Navarre, a native of that region, and one of General Harrison's most trusted scouts during the War of 1812, who accompanied me to the spot in the autumn of 1860, told me that he had seen men, women, and children gather around that rock, place bits of dried beef, parched peas and corn, and sometimes some cheap trinket upon it, and, calling frequently upon the name of the beloved Ottawa, weep piteously. They carved many rude figures of a turkey's foot on the stone, as a memorial of the English name of the lamented Me-sa-sa. The stone is still there, by the side of the highway at the foot of Presque Isle Hill, within a few rods of the swift-flowing Maumee. Many of the carvings are still quite deep and distinct, while others have been obliterated by the abrasion of the elements.[1] Of this locality, so famous in the chronicles of the War of 1812, I shall have more to say hereafter.

TURKEY-FOOT'S ROCK.

---

[1] The above view of *Turkey-foot's Rock* is at the foot of the Maumee Rapids, looking up the stream. It is seen in the foreground, on the right, and over it the road passing over Presque Isle Hill. It was here, and farther to the right, that the Indians were posted among the fallen trees. On the left is seen the Maumee, which here sweeps in a graceful curve. The point across the Maumee at the bend is the river termination of a plain, on which General Hull's army was encamped while on its march toward Detroit in the summer of 1812. There the army crossed the Maumee.

Turkey-foot Rock is limestone, about five and a half feet in length and three feet in height. It is about three miles above Maumee City. In allusion to the event which the rock commemorates, Andrew Coffinberry, of Perrysburg, in a poem entitled "The Forest Ranger, a Poetic Tale of the Western Wilderness of 1794," thus wrote, after giving an account of Wayne's progress up to this time:

"Yet at the foot of red Presque Isle
Brave Me-sa-sa was warring still:

Having thoroughly accomplished his work, Wayne returned with his army to Fort Defiance,[a] while the Indians, utterly defeated and disheartened, retired to the borders of Maumee Bay, in the vicinity of Toledo, to brood over their misfortunes and ponder upon the future. At the middle of September the victors moved from Defiance to the head of the Maumee, and at the bend of that river, just below the confluence of the St. Mary's and St. Joseph's, which form it, they built a strong fortification, and named it Fort Wayne. It was completed on the 22d of October, and was immediately garrisoned with infantry and artillery, under Colonel Hamtramck.[1] This accomplished, the remainder of the troops left, some for Fort Washington, to be discharged from the service, and the others for Fort Greenville, where Wayne made his head-quarters for the winter. Thither deputations from the various tribes with whom he had been at war came to Wayne, and agreed upon preliminary terms of peace. They well remembered his assurance that the British had neither the power nor the inclination to help them—an assurance verified by the silence of Fort Miami's guns. They promised to meet him in council early in the ensuing summer, for the purpose of forming a definitive treaty of peace between the United States and the Indian tribes of the Northwest. Faithful to their promise, chiefs and sachems began to reach Fort Greenville early in June. A grand council was opened there on the 16th of that month, and was continued until the 10th

[a] August 27, 1794.

He stood upon a large rough stone,
Still dealing random blows alone;
But bleeding fast—glazed were his eyes,
And feeble grew his battle-cries;
Too frail his arm, too dim his sight,
To wield or aim his axe aright;
As still more frail and faint he grew,
His body on the rock he threw.
As coursed his blood along the ground,
In feeble, low, and hollow sound,
Mingled with frantic peals and strong,
The dying chief poured forth his song."

Here follows "The Death-song of the Sagamore."

[1] John Francis Hamtramck was a most faithful and useful officer. He was a resident of Northern New York when the Revolution broke out, and was a captain in the Continental army. He was appointed a major in the regular army of the United States in September, 1789, and was promoted to be lieutenant colonel commandant of the first sub-legion in February, 1793. He commanded the left wing under General Wayne in the battle of the Maumee, in August, 1794, and held the rank of lieutenant colonel in the First Infantry in 1796. He was retained as colonel on the reduction of the army in April, 1802, and on the 11th of April the following year he died and was buried at Detroit.

HAMTRAMCK'S TOMB.

While in Detroit, in the autumn of 1860, I visited the grave of Colonel Hamtramck, and made the accompanying sketch. It is in the grounds attached to St. Anne's Orphan Asylum, and between that institution and St. Anne's Church, both belonging to the Roman Catholics. The monument over his grave and the grounds around it were much neglected. The former was dilapidated, the latter covered with weeds and brambles. The monument is composed of a light freestone slab, grown dingy from the effects of the elements, lying upon a foundation of brick. It bears the following inscription:

"Sacred to the memory of JOHN FRANCIS HAMTRAMCK, Esq., Colonel of the First United States Regiment of Infantry, and Commandant of Detroit and its dependencies. He departed this life on the 11th of April, 1803, aged 45 years, 7 months, and 27 days. True patriotism, and zealous attachment to national liberty, joined to a laudable ambition, led him into military service at an early period of his life. He was a soldier even before he was a man. He was an active participator in all the dangers, difficulties, and honors of the Revolutionary War; and his heroism and uniform good conduct procured him the attention and personal thanks of the immortal Washington. The United States, in him, have lost a valuable officer and good citizen, and society a useful and pleasant member. To his family his loss is incalculable, and his friends will never forget the memory of Hamtramck. This humble monument is placed over his remains by the officers who had the honor to serve under his command: a small but grateful tribute to his merit and his worth."

of August. Almost eleven hundred Indians were present, representing twelve tribes.[1] A definitive and satisfactory treaty was signed by all parties on the 3d of August, and the pacification of the Indians of the Northwest was thereby made complete.[2] By the operations of a special treaty between the United States and Great Britain, the Western military posts were speedily evacuated by the British, and for fifteen years the most remote frontier settlements were safe from any annoyance by the Indians. This security gave an immense impetus to emigration to the Northwestern Territory, and the country was rapidly filled with a hardy population.

---

[1] Wyandots, Delawares, Shawnoese, Ottawas, Chippewas, Pottawatomies, Miamis, Weas, Kickapoos, Piankeshaws, Kaskaskias, and Eel River Indians.

[2] After the treaty had been twice read to the Indians, and every section explained by General Wayne, that officer said: "Brothers,—All you nations now present, listen! You now have had, a second time, the proposed articles of treaty read and explained to you. It is now time for the negotiation to draw to a conclusion. I shall, therefore, ask each nation individually if they approve of and are prepared to sign those articles in their present form, that they may be immediately engrossed for that purpose. I shall begin with the Chippewas, who, with the others who approbate the measure, will signify their assent. You, Chippewas, do you approve of these articles of treaty, and are you prepared to sign them? [A unanimous answer—yes.] You, Ottawas, do you agree? [A unanimous answer—yes.] You, Pottawatomies? [A unanimous answer—yes.] You, Wyandots, do you agree? [A unanimous answer—yes.] You, Delawares? [A unanimous answer—yes.] You, Shawnoese? [A unanimous answer—yes.] You, Miamis, do you agree? [A unanimous answer—yes.] You, Weas? [A unanimous answer—yes.] And you, Kickapoos, do you agree? [A unanimous answer—yes.] The treaty shall be engrossed; and, as it will require two or three days to do it properly on parchment, we will now part, to meet on the 2d of August. In the interim, we will eat, drink, and rejoice, and thank the Great Spirit for the happy stage this good work has arrived at."

After the treaty was signed, a copy of it on paper was given to the representative of each nation, and then a large quantity of goods and many small ornaments were distributed among the Indians present. On the 10th, at the close of the council, General Wayne said to them: "Brothers, I now fervently pray to the Great Spirit that the peace now established may be permanent, and that it may hold us together in the bonds of friendship until time shall be no more. I also pray that the Great Spirit above may enlighten your minds, and open your eyes to your true happiness, that your children may learn to cultivate the earth and enjoy the fruits of peace and industry. As it is probable, my children, that we shall not soon meet again in public council, I take this opportunity of bidding you all an affectionate farewell, and of wishing you a safe and happy return to your respective homes and families."

By this treaty the Indians ceded about twenty-five thousand square miles of territory to the United States, besides sixteen separate tracts, including lands and forts. In consideration of these cessions, the Indians received goods from the United States, of the value of $20,000, as presents, and were promised an annual allowance, valued at $9500, to be equitably distributed among all the tribes who were parties to the treaty.

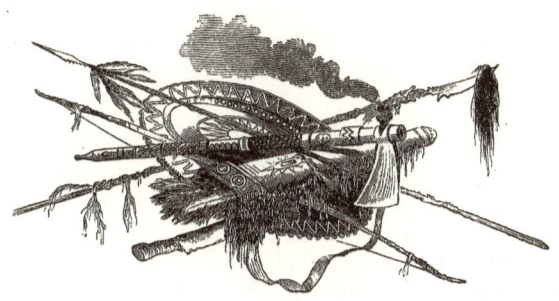

CHAPTER III.

"What constitutes a state?
. . . . . .
Men, who their duties know,
But know their rights, and, knowing, dare maintain;
Prevent the long-aimed blow,
And crush the tyrant while they rend the chain—
These constitute a *state*."
                                        Sir William Jones.

"There's a warfare where none but the morally brave
Stand nobly and firmly, their country to save.
'Tis the war of *opinion*, where few can be found,
On the mountain of principle, guarding the ground;
With vigilant eyes ever watching the foes
Who are prowling around them, and aiming their blows."
                                        Mrs. Dana.

HILE the arm of military power was removing the remains of a hoary barbarism from the beautiful region west of the Alleghanies, preparatory to the founding of great commonwealths there, the new national government was summoning its functions into energetic and beneficent action. Men were never called upon to perform duties of greater importance and momentous consequences. They were charged with the establishment of the foreign and domestic policy of a nation, "not for a day, but for all time." The President and the Legislature felt the responsibility, and in solemn earnestness they elaborated schemes for the future prosperity of the republic.

The earliest efforts of Congress, after its organization, were directed to the arrangement of a system of revenue, in order to adjust the wretched financial affairs of the country. Mr. Madison, the tacitly acknowledged leader in the House of Representatives, presented the plan of a temporary tariff upon foreign goods imported into the United States, with provisions favorable to American shipping; also a scheme of tonnage duties, in which great discriminations were made in favor of American vessels, as well as those of France, Holland, Sweden, and Prussia, the only nations having treaties of commerce with the United States. An efficient revenue system was speedily adopted and put in motion, for the consolidated government possessed inherent power to do so.

This first practical exhibition of sovereignty by the central government of the United States opened the eyes of British merchants and statesmen to the fact that the Americans had suddenly made a stride toward absolute independence—that their commerce was no longer subjected to the caprice of foreign powers, nor neglected because of the disagreements and jealousies of thirteen distinct Legislatures. They perceived that its interests were guarded and its strength nurtured by a central power of wonderful energy, and that the new republic had taken its place among the family of nations with just claims to the highest respect and consideration. Other nations yielded the same recognition, and its future career was contemplated with peculiar interest throughout the civilized world.

While the House of Representatives was engaged on the subject of revenue, the Senate was occupied in arranging a judiciary system. A bill for the purpose was offered in that body by Oliver Ellsworth, of Connecticut. After undergoing several amendments, it was concurred in by both houses of Congress, and a national judiciary

The Judiciary.   Amendments to the Constitution.   Cabinet Ministers.   Relations with France and England.

was established similar in all its essential features to that now in operation. It consisted of one chief justice and five associate justices, who were directed to hold two sessions annually at the seat of the national government. Circuit and district courts were also established, which had jurisdiction over certain specified cases. Each state was made a district, as were also the two Territories of Kentucky and Maine. The districts, excepting the two Territories, were grouped so as to form three circuits. A marshal and district attorney were appointed for each district by the President.[1]

The subjects of revenue and judiciary being well disposed of, Congress next turned its attention to the organization of executive departments. Only three—Treasury, War, and Foreign Relations—were established. The heads of these were styled Secretaries instead of Ministers, as in Europe. The President of the United States was clothed with power to appoint or dismiss them at his pleasure, with the concurrence of the Senate. They were designed to constitute a cabinet council, ever subject to the call of the President for consultation on public affairs, and bound to give him their opinions in writing when required.

The attention of Congress was next turned to the amendments of the Constitution proposed by the people of the several states, which amounted, in the aggregate, to one hundred and forty-seven, besides separate Bills of Rights proposed by Virginia and New York. Sixteen of the amendments were agreed to, and twelve of them were subsequently ratified by the people and became a part of the organic law of the nation. The profound wisdom of the framers of the Constitution and its own perfection are illustrated by the fact that, of these twelve amendments, not one of them, judged by subsequent experience, was of a vital character.

Before the adjournment of Congress on the 29th of September,[a] the President had appointed his Cabinet,[2] and the new government was fairly set in motion. Its foreign relations were, on the whole, satisfactory, and only in England were other than friendly feelings toward the United States manifested. These were met by corresponding ill feeling toward England on this side of the Atlantic. The resentments caused by the late long war were blunted, but by no means deprived of their strength; and, finally, the fact that the British government still held possession of Western military posts within the boundary of the United States, and that from these had gone out influences which had involved their country in a bloody and expensive war with the Indians, produced much irritation in the American mind. This was intensified by the wounds given to their national pride by the British government, in so long refusing to negotiate a commercial treaty with them, and declining to reciprocate the friendly advances of the United States by sending a minister to reside at the national capital.

[a] 1789.

With their old ally, France, the most perfect friendship still existed, but it was destined to a speedy interruption. Events in that country, and the position assumed by the President of the United States in relation to them, caused violent animosity to take the place of cordial good will, and were among the causes which gave birth to parties in America whose collisions, for several years, shook the republic to its centre, and at times threatened its existence. The animosities of these parties, and the collateral relations of national policy and events in France and England to them, will be found, as we proceed in our narrative, to have played an important part in the great drama we are considering, at the period immediately preceding and during the progress of the War of 1812.

---

[1] John Jay, of New York, was appointed Chief Justice of the United States; and John Rutledge, of South Carolina, James Wilson, of Pennsylvania, William Cushing, of Massachusetts, Robert H. Harrison, of Maryland, and John Blair, of Virginia, were appointed associate judges.

[2] Alexander Hamilton was appointed Secretary of the Treasury; Henry Knox, Secretary of War; and Thomas Jefferson, Secretary of Foreign Affairs, the duties of which were the same as now performed by the Secretary of State, or prime minister. The Navy Department was not created until 1798. Naval affairs were under the control of the Secretary of War. At that time the Attorney General and Postmaster General were heads of departments, but were not, as now, Cabinet officers. Edmund Randolph was appointed Attorney General, and Samuel Osgood Postmaster General.

At the very time when the fruits of the American Revolution were exhibiting their ripeness in the form of a free and vigorous nation full of promise, the Empire of France, made unsound to the core by social and political corruptions most foul, was shaken by a moral earthquake—a revolution severe at the beginning, and terrible in its subsequent course. The French monarch was weak, his advisers were wicked, and the dominant classes, through luxury and concomitant vices, were exceedingly corrupt. The good and the brave of the kingdom had long perceived the abyss of woe upon the brink of which their country was poised, and with a heroism which in the light of history appears almost divine, they resolved to sound the trumpet of political reform, and arouse king, nobles, and people to a sense of solemn duty as men and patriots.

At the head of these brave men was Lafayette, seconded chiefly by the Duke de Rochefoucauld and M. Condorcet. They wished to obtain for France a Constitution similar to that of England, which they regarded as the most perfect model of human government then known. They loved their king because of his many virtues, and would have advised him wisely had their voices been permitted audience in the Tuileries; but they loved France more than their king, and desired to see her crowned with true glory, based upon the welfare and prosperity of her people. To accomplish this, they placed their hopes on a virtuous constitutional monarchy.

For a long time Lafayette and his coadjutors had been elaborating their scheme. At length, in the Assembly of Notables, in April, 1789, that champion of rational liberty stood up in his place and boldly demanded a series of reforms in the name of the people, one of which was a representative National Assembly. "What!" exclaimed the Count D'Artois, one of the king's bad advisers, "do you make a motion for the States General?" "Yes, and even more than that," quickly responded Lafayette. That *more* was a charter from the king, by which the public and individual liberty should be acknowledged and guaranteed by the future States General. The proposition was received with unbounded enthusiasm. The measure was carried. Early in May a session of the States General was opened at Versailles, and they constituted themselves a National Assembly.

Now was the golden opportunity for King Louis. Slight concessions at that moment might have secured blessings for himself and his country. But he heeded the counsels of venal men more than the supplications of his real friends. He opposed the popular will, and took the road to ruin. He ordered the hall of the National Assembly to be closed, and placed a cordon of mercenary German troops around Paris to overawe the people. From that time until early in July the French capital was dreadfully agitated. Passion ruled the hour. The city was like a seething caldron. Every one felt that a terrible storm was about to burst.

The National Assembly was now sitting in Paris, and thoroughly sustained by the people. They called for the organization of forty-eight thousand armed militia. Within two days two hundred and seventy thousand citizens were enrolled. A state mayor was appointed by the town assembly, and the Marquis La Salle was named commander-in-chief.

Court dispatches were intercepted by the people by the arrest of royal couriers. Then they demanded arms. An immense assemblage went to the Hospital of the Invalids on the 10th of July, and demanded from the governor the instant delivery to them of all weapons there. He refused, and they seized thirty thousand muskets and twenty pieces of cannon. Then they visited the shops of the armorers and the depository of the *Garde-meuble*, and seized all the arms found there.

Higher and higher rose the tide of revolution. The girdle of soldiers around Paris was the chief cause for present irritation. The National Assembly sent a deputation to the king at Versailles to ask him to remove them. His good heart counseled compliance, but his weak head bowed to the demands of bad advisers. "I alone have

| Excitement in Paris. | Formation of a National Guard. | Treachery at the Bastile. | That Prison destroyed. |

the right to judge of the necessity, and in that respect I can make no change," was the haughty answer of the king borne back to the Assembly. This answer, and the dismissal of M. Necker, the controller of the treasury, and other patriotic ministers who favored reform, produced a crisis.

Paris was comparatively quiet on the night of the 13th of July. It was the ominous lull before the bursting of the tempest. The streets were barricaded. The people formed themselves into a National Guard, and chose Lafayette as their commander. Gun, sabre, scythe, and whatever weapon fell in their way was seized. Multitudes of men of the same opinion embraced each other in the streets as brothers, and, in an instant almost, a National Guard of one hundred thousand determined men was formed.

The morning of the 14th was serene. The sky was cloudless. But storms of passion were sweeping over Paris. The people were in motion at an early hour. Their steps were toward the Bastile, a hoary state prison, which was regarded as the stronghold of despotism. They stood before it in immense numbers. A parley ensued. The gates were opened, and forty leading citizens, as representatives of the populace, were allowed to enter. The bridges were then suddenly drawn, and volleys of musketry soon told a tale of treachery most foul. They were all murdered! That moment marks the opening of the terrible scenes of the French Revolution. With demoniac yells the exasperated populace dragged heavy cannon before the gates, and threatened the destruction of the Bastile. The terrified governor displayed a white flag, and invited a second deputation to enter the gates. These shared the fate of the former! The furious multitude would no longer listen to words of peace. They were treacherous all. A breach was soon made in the walls. The governor and other officers were dragged to execution, and their heads were paraded upon pikes through the streets. The great iron key of the Bastile was sent to the City Hall.[1] The National Assembly decreed the demolition of the hated prison, and very soon it was leveled to the ground.[2] Upon its site, now the *Place de Bastile*, stands the *Column of July*, erected by Louis Philippe to commemorate the Revolution in 1830, which placed him on the throne. Lafayette sent the key of the Bastile to Washington, who placed it in the broad passage at Mount Vernon, where it still hangs.

The National Assembly elected Lafayette commander-in-chief of the National Guard of all France, a corps of more than four millions of armed citizens. They voted him a salary of fifty thousand dollars a year, but, imitating Washington, he refused to accept any remuneration for his services. The humbled king approved his appointment, and the monarch, deserted by his evil counselors, threw himself upon the National Assembly. "He has been deceived hitherto," Lafayette proclaimed to the public, "but he now sees the merit and justice of the popular cause." The overjoyed people shouted "Long live the king!" and for a moment the Revolution seemed to be at an end and its purposes accomplished.

But Lafayette, who comprehended the labors and the dangers yet to be encountered, was filled with apprehension. The wily Duke of Orleans, who desired the destruction of the king for the base purpose of his own exaltation to the throne, was busied in sowing the seeds of distrust among the people.[3] The duke incited them to demand the monarch's presence at the Tuileries. Louis went voluntarily from Versailles to Paris, followed by sixty thousand citizens and a hundred deputies of the

---

[1] For a picture and description of this key, see Lossing's *Field-Book of the Revolution*, ii., 209.
[2] A picture of the Bastile may be found in Lossing's *Home of Washington and its Associations*, p. 221.
[3] "He does not, indeed, possess talent to carry into execution a great project," said Lafayette to John Trumbull, who was about to leave Paris, "but he possesses immense wealth, and France abounds in marketable talents. Every city and town has young men eminent for abilities, particularly in the law—ardent in character, eloquent, ambitious of distinction, but poor." Many of these were the men who composed the leaders in the Reign of Terror, and reddened the streets of Paris with human blood.

Assembly, and there formally accepted the Declaration of the Rights of Man, which was presented to him. The people were satisfied, and the duke was disappointed. Order reigned in Paris and throughout the kingdom. The bearing of these events upon our subject will be observed presently.

At this time a general European war seemed inevitable. A long-pending controversy between Great Britain and Spain remained unsettled. It was believed that France, with her traditional hatred of Great Britain, would side with Spain. This alliance would menace England with much danger. At the same time, Spain, a declining power, would necessarily be much embarrassed by war. Viewing this situation of affairs in Western Europe with the eye of a statesman, Washington concluded that it was a favorable time to urge upon Spain the claims of the United States to the free navigation of the Mississippi, concerning which negotiations had been for some time pending, and also to press upon Great Britain the necessity of complying with the yet unfulfilled articles of the Treaty of 1783. Mr. Carmichael, the American *Chargé des Affaires* at the Court of Madrid,[1] was instructed not only to press the point concerning the navigation of the Mississippi with earnestness, but to endeavor to secure to the United States, by cession, the island of New Orleans and the Floridas, offering as an equivalent the abiding friendship of the new republic, by which the territories of Spain west of the Mississippi might be secured to that government. At the same time, Gouverneur Morris, then in Paris, was directed by Washington to repair to London, and, with sincere professions of a desire on the part of the United States "to promote harmony and mutual satisfaction between the two countries," sound the British ministry on the subject of a full and immediate execution of the Treaty of 1783.[2]

Morris had a formal interview with the Duke of Leeds, the Secretary of Foreign Affairs, near the close of March, 1790. He was received with cordiality, and was assured of the earnest desire of Great Britain to cultivate friendly relations with the United States, and the determination of the king to send a minister to America. But when Morris attempted to hold explicit conversation on the subject of his semi-official mission he was met with evasion and reticence. It was immediately made evident to him that there was real reluctance on the part of Great Britain to fulfill the stipulations of the Treaty of 1783, or to make a fair commercial arrangement, and that there was a disposition to procrastinate while the difficulties between Great Britain and Spain remained unadjusted. He found great misapprehensions existing in England concerning the real character of the Americans and their government, even among the best informed. They overrated the importance to Americans of friendship with them. They believed that trade with Great Britain was of vital consequence to the Americans, and that the latter would make an international commercial treaty upon almost any terms to secure it. With this belief, a committee of Parliament, to whom had been referred the revenue acts of the United States, acting under the advice of the merchants of leading maritime towns of Great Britain, reported early in 1790, in favor of negotiating 'a commercial treaty with the Americans, but with the explicit declaration that the commissioners should not "submit to treat" for the admission of American vessels into any of the British islands or colonial ports. They actually believed that the necessities of the United States would make them acquiesce in an arrangement so ungenerous and partial.

While war with Spain seemed impending, the British ministers listened complacently to what Morris had to say about the frontier military posts, the impressment of American seamen into the British naval service under the plea that they were sub-

---

[1] William Carmichael went to Spain with Minister John Jay, as secretary of legation, in 1779, and when that functionary left, Mr. Carmichael remained as *Chargé des Affaires*. After the Treaty of Peace was signed in 1783, the Spanish government refused to acknowledge him as such, but finally, through the agency of Lafayette, they reluctantly consented to do so.

[2] Washington's letter to Gouverneur Morris, October 13, 1789.

jects of Great Britain, and the propriety of sending a full minister to the United States.[1] It was evident that the British were willing to allow their relations with the Americans to remain unchanged until they should have a definite perception of the course European affairs were likely to take. This evidence became more and more manifest in the autumn. The French government, embarrassed by its own troubled affairs, was disinclined to take part with Spain in its quarrel, and the latter, unable alone to cope with Great Britain, yielded every point in the controversy, and the dispute was settled. Relieved of this burden of perplexity, and regarding France as hopelessly crippled by her internal difficulties, Great Britain showed marked indifference concerning her relations with the United States. Nothing more was said about sending a minister to America, and Mr. Morris was treated with neglect, if not with positive discourtesy.

At the close of the year Mr. Morris left England. He had been there about nine months, endeavoring to obtain a positive answer to the simple questions, Will you execute the Treaty? will you make a treaty of commerce with the United States? At the end of that time the real views of the British government were as hidden as at the beginning. Ungenerous diplomacy had been employed all the time by the British ministry, while the American government was anxious to establish peaceful relations with Great Britain and all the world upon principles of exact justice. Its agents were unskilled in the low cunning of diplomatic art which at that time distinguished every court in Europe, and they lost the game. Both the government and people of the United States felt aggrieved and indignant at the course of Great Britain, and self-respect would not allow them to farther press the subject of diplomatic intercourse or treaty relations. They therefore resolved to pause in action until the republic should become strong enough to speak in decisive tones, and prepared to maintain its declarations by corresponding vigor of action.

Great changes are wrought by time. The march of stirring events in Europe now became majestic, for a new and important era was dawning; and the dignity and importance of the republic beyond the sea was too apparent to the world to allow the British government to maintain its indifference much longer without evil consequences to itself. Already France, Holland, and Spain, the real enemies of England, had placed representatives at the seat of our national government, and British pride was compelled to yield to expediency. In August, 1791, George Hammond arrived in Philadelphia, clothed with full ministerial powers as the representative of Great Britain, presented his credentials, and was formally received. In December following, diplomatic relations between the two governments were established by the

---

[1] Great Britain evidently apprehended an alliance of the United States with Spain, in the event of a war between the former and the latter power. Dorchester, the Governor of Canada, was employed to ascertain the disposition of the United States on that point. He accordingly asked permission to pass through New York on his way to England; and when it was readily granted, as he expected, he sent his aid-de-camp, Major Beckwith, to the seat of the United States government, under the pretext of making a formal acknowledgment, but really to seek information upon the subject in question. He first approached Mr. Hamilton, the Secretary of the Treasury. After expressing the thanks of Lord Dorchester, he, with apparent unconcern, remarked that his lordship had reason to fear that the delays which Mr. Morris experienced in England would be attributed to a lack of desire on the part of the British ministry to adjust every matter in dispute between the United States and Great Britain. In behalf of his lordship he was instructed to say, that there could be no doubt, not only of the friendly feeling of Great Britain, but of a desire on her part for an alliance with the United States. Major Beckwith then spoke of the rupture between Great Britain and Spain, and expressed his presumption that, in the event of war, the United States would find it to their interest to take part with Great Britain. He then, in the name of Dorchester, disclaimed any influence, under British authorities, over the Indian tribes in the West. The President laid the matter before his Cabinet, and it was agreed to draw out from the major as much information as possible by treating him and his communication very civilly. But he obtained no information of importance. The matter was so transparent that no one was deceived. "What they [the ministers] are saying to you," Jefferson wrote to Morris in August, "they are saying to us through Quebec; but so informally that they may disavow it when they please.... Through him [Major Beckwith] they talk of a minister, a treaty of commerce, and *alliance*. If the object of the latter be honorable, it is useless; if dishonorable, inadmissible. These tamperings prove that they view war as possible; and some symptoms indicate designs against the Spanish possessions adjoining us. The consequences of their acquiring all the country on our frontier from the St. Croix to the St. Mary's are too obvious to you to need development. You will readily see the dangers which would then environ us.... We wish to be neutral, and we will be so, *if they will execute the Treaty fairly* and *attempt no conquests adjoining us*."

appointment of Thomas Pinckney, of South Carolina, as American minister to the Court of St. James.[1]

At about this time two violently antagonistic parties had assumed definite shape and formidable proportions in the United States, the acknowledged heads of which were Alexander Hamilton and Thomas Jefferson, members of Washington's Cabinet. On the former, as Secretary of the Treasury, devolved the important duty to arrange a plan for

Thomas Pinckney

the establishment of the public credit.[2] Owing to long delay, and doubts and discouragements in the minds of the original holders of the evidences of the public debt, they had fallen into the hands of speculators at one sixth of their nominal value. It was therefore argued that, in the liquidation of these claims, there should be a scale of depreciation adopted, thereby making a saving to the public treasury. Hamilton would listen favorably to no suggestions of

that kind. With the sagacity of a statesman, the sincerity of an honest man, and the true heart of a patriot, he planted his foot firmly upon the ground of justice and honor, and declared that public credit could only be established by the faithful discharge of public obligations in strict conformity to the terms of the contract. These debts were originally due to officers and soldiers, farmers, mechanics, and patriotic capitalists, and were sacred in the estimation of honest men; and it was no just plea for their whole or partial repudiation that speculators would profit by the honesty of the government. It was not for the debtor to inquire into whose hands his written promises to pay were lodged, nor how they came there.[3] Upon this lofty foundation of principle Hamilton stood before hosts of his frowning countrymen, conscious of the importance of financial honor and integrity to the infant republic, and determined to secure for it the dignity which justice confers, at whatever cost of personal popularity.

[a] January 14, 1790.

He accordingly presented to Congress,[a] in an able report, a scheme "for the support of the public credit," whose principal feature was the funding of the public debt—a plan proposed by him to Robert Morris as early as 1782. He also proposed the assumption by the general government of the state debts incurred during the war, amounting, in principal and interest, to over twenty millions of dol-

---

[1] Thomas Pinckney was born in Charleston, South Carolina, 23d of October, 1750. He was educated in England. When the Revolution broke out he entered the military service, and was active until Gates's defeat near Camden, in August, 1780, when he was made a prisoner. He was Gates's aid. He was chosen Governor of South Carolina in 1787. In 1792 he went as minister to England. In 1794 he was sent in the same capacity to Spain, to treat concerning the navigation of the Mississippi. At the beginning of 1812 the President appointed him to the command of the Southern division of the army. After the war General Pinckney retired to private life. He died on the 2d of November, 1828, aged seventy-eight years.

[2] The impoverished condition of the country, and the wants of the public treasury at that time, may be comprehended by the fact that, at the close of 1789, the Attorney General and several members of Congress were indebted to the private credit of the Secretary of the Treasury to discharge their personal expenses. Even the President of the United States was obliged to pass his note to his private secretary, Mr. Lear, to meet his household expenses, which was discounted at the rate of two per cent. a month. Members of Congress were paid by due-bills, which the collectors were ordered to receive in payment of duties.—HAMILTON's *History of the Republic of the United States*, iv., 48.

[3] Hamilton argued that, besides motives of political expediency, there were reasons in favor of his view "which rest on the immutable principles of moral obligation; and, in proportion as the mind is disposed to contemplate, in the order of Providence, an ultimate connection between public virtue and public happiness, will be its repugnance to a violation of those principles. This reflection derives additional strength from the nature of the debt of the United States. IT WAS THE PRICE OF LIBERTY. The faith of America has been repeatedly pledged for it, and with solemnities that give peculiar force to the obligation."

Hamilton's Financial Scheme assailed.   Banking Capital in the United States.   A Decimal Currency adopted.

lars. His scheme included the establishment of a national bank,[1] a system of revenue from taxation, internal and external, and a sinking fund.

This scheme—just, patriotic, necessary, and beneficial—was assailed with the greatest vehemence, and the discussions which it elicited, especially upon the subject of the assumption of the state debts, in Congress, in the public press, and in private circles, fearfully agitated the nation, and created the first regular and systematic opposition to the principles on which the affairs of the republic were administered. Its propositions, especially the one relating to the assumption of state debts, were regarded with alarm by the late opponents of the Constitution and a consolidated government, because of their tendency to a centralization of power, as giving an undue influence to the general government by placing the purse as well as the sword in its hands, and as being also of doubtful constitutionality. Many believed that they saw in this scheme great political evils, because it secured the financial union of the states, and might lead to the establishment of a government as absolute as a constitutional monarchy. These suspicions were strengthened by the well-known fact that Hamilton regarded the British government as a model of excellence, and had advocated greater centralization of power, in the Convention of 1787. He was made the target for the shafts of personal and political malice, and his financial system was misrepresented and abused as a scheme for enriching a few at the expense of the many.[2] The war of opinion was fierce and uncompromising.

While Washington took no part in the discussion of Hamilton's scheme, it commanded his highest admiration, as the most perfect that human wisdom could devise for restoring the public credit and laying the foundation of national policy. He predicted great and lasting good from its adoption, and his prophecies were fulfilled. Confidence was revived, and that acted like magic upon industry; and then com-

---

[1] At that time the whole banking capital of the United States was only $2,000,000, invested in the *Bank of North America*, established in Philadelphia by Robert Morris, chiefly as a government fiscal agent; the *Bank of New York*, in New York City; and the *Bank of Massachusetts*, in Boston. In January, 1791, Congress chartered a national bank for the term of twenty years, with a capital of $10,000,000, to be located in the city of Philadelphia, and its management to be intrusted to twenty-five directors. It did not commence business operations in corporate form until in February, 1794.

The subject of currency had occupied the attention of the old Congress as early as 1782, when Gouverneur Morris presented an able report on the subject, written at the request of Robert Morris.* He proposed to harmonize the moneys of all the states. Starting with one ascertained fraction as a unit, for a divisor, he proposed the following table of money: Ten units to be equal to one penny; ten pence to one bill; ten bills, one dollar (about seventy-five cents of our present currency); and ten dollars, one crown. Mr. Jefferson, as chairman of a committee on the subject of coins, reported a table in 1784, in which he adopted Morris's decimal system, but entirely changed its details. He proposed to strike four coins, namely, a golden piece of the value of ten dollars, a dollar in silver, a tenth of a dollar in silver, and a hundredth of a dollar in copper. This report was adopted by Congress the following year, and this was the origin of our *cent*, *dime*, *dollar*, and *eagle*. The establishment of a mint for coinage was delayed, and no legislative action on the subject was taken until early in April, 1792, when laws were enacted for the preparation of one. For three years afterward the operations of the mint were chiefly experimental, while in Congress long debates were had concerning the devices for the new coins. The Senate proposed the head of the President of the United States who should occupy the chair of state at the time of the coinage. In the House, the head of Liberty was suggested, as being less aristocratic than the effigy of the President—less the stamp of royalty. The head of Liberty was finally adopted. During that interval of three years, several of the coins called "specimens," now so rare in cabinets, and so much sought after by connoisseurs, were struck. Of these the rarest is a small copper coin, known as the "Liberty-cap cent." The engraving is from one in my possession. The mint was first put into full operation, in Philadelphia, in 1795.

LIBERTY CENT.

[2] "The public paper suddenly rose, and was for a short time above par," says Marshall. "The immense wealth which individuals acquired by this unexpected appreciation could not be viewed with indifference."

---

* Robert Morris had considered the subject for more than a year. As early as July, 1781, he wrote to Benjamin Dudley, of Boston, an Englishman, requesting him to come to Philadelphia, that he might consult him about the coinage of money. In November Mr. Dudley was employed in assaying. Mr. Morris kept him engaged in experiments, and in the preparation of machinery for a mint. In these Mr. Dudley consulted Dr. Rittenhouse and Francis Hopkinson. A country blacksmith, named Wheeler, was employed to make the rollers for the mint, and it was July the following year before any machinery was perfected. Mr. Morris labored hard to get the mint in operation, but without success. Finally, on the 2d of April, 1783, Morris was enabled to write in his diary, "I sent for Mr. Dudley, who delivered me a piece of silver coin, being the first that has been struck as an American coin." Mr. Dudley was installed superintendent of the mint, having charge, also, of the preparation of the paper moulds, etc., in the manufacture of the currency printed by Hall & Sellers, the printers of the Continental money. Finally, in July, Mr. Morris gave up the idea of establishing a mint, and Mr. Dudley, after delivering up the dies to him, left his service.—ROBERT MORRIS'S *Diary*.

E

menced that wonderful development of material wealth which has gone on with few intermissions until the present time.

While these discussions were at their height, Jefferson arrived at the seat of government, to assume the duties of Secretary of State. He had but lately returned from France, where he had labored for several years in the diplomatic service of his country. He had

witnessed the uprising of the people there at the bidding of Lafayette and others a few months before. The example of his own country was the star of hope to the French revolutionists, and as the author of the *Declaration of Independence*, he was regarded as an oracle, and courted by the leaders of the constitutional party there. Fresh from the fields of political excitement in the French capital, and his inherent democratic principles and ideas intensified and enlarged by these experiences, he came home full of enthusiasm, expecting to find every body in his own country ready to speak a sympathizing word for, and to extend a helping hand to the *people* of France, the old ally of Americans in their efforts to establish for themselves a constitutional government.

But Mr. Jefferson was disappointed. When he arrived in New York, after a tedious journey of a fortnight on horseback, he was warmly welcomed by the leading families of the city, and became the recipient of almost daily invitations to social and dinner parties. The wealthier and more aristocratic classes in New York, who gave dinner parties at that time, were mostly Loyalists' families, who remembered the pleasant intercourse they had enjoyed with the British officers during the late war, and had always regarded the British form of government as the most perfect ever devised. Free from political restraint, their conversation was open and frank, and their sentiments were expressed without reserve. Mr. Jefferson was continually shocked by the utterance of opinions repugnant to his faith, and in contrast with his recent experience.[1]

Mr. Jefferson, who was sensitively and even painfully alive to the evils of despotism and the dangers of a government stronger than the people, took the alarm, and he became morbidly suspicious of all around him. The conservatism of Washington and his associates in the government, and their lack of enthusiasm on the subject of the French Revolution, which so filled his own heart, were construed by him as indifference to the diffusion of democratic ideas and the triumph of republican principles, for which the patriots in the war for independence had contended. He had scarcely taken his seat in the Cabinet before he declared that some of his colleagues held decidedly monarchical views, and it became a settled belief in his mind that there was a party in the United States constantly at work, secretly and sometimes openly, for the overthrow of republicanism. This idea became a sort of monomania, and haunted him until his death, more than thirty years afterward.

Events in France soon began to make vivid impressions upon the public mind in America. The fears of Lafayette were realized. The lull that succeeded the tempest of 1789, was only the precursor of a more terrible storm in 1791, that shook European society to its deepest foundations, and, like the great earthquake of 1755, was felt in almost every part of the globe.

---

[1] "I can not describe the wonder and mortification with which the table conversation filled me," Mr. Jefferson wrote. "Politics was the chief topic, and a preference for a kingly over republican government was evidently the favorite sentiment. An apostate I could not be, nor yet a hypocrite; and I found myself, for the most part, the only advocate on the republican side of the question, unless among the guests there chanced to be some member of that party from the legislative houses." This is the first mention that we any where find of a Republican Party in this country.

Formation of the Jacobin Club in Paris.   Demoralization of the National Guard.   A Constitution granted to the People.

Long before the meeting of the States-general at Versailles, forty intelligent men, whose feelings were intensely democratic, who avowed their hatred of kings and their attendant titles and privileges, and who ridiculed and contemned Christianity as an imposture, had met in the hall of the Jacobin monks in Paris, and from that circumstance were called the Jacobin Club. In the commotions that attended and followed the destruction of the Bastile, this club had gained immense popularity. They now published a newspaper, whose motto was LIBERTY AND EQUALITY, and whose design was to disseminate ultra democratic doctrines, irreligious ideas, and a spirit of revolt and disaffection to the king. They became potential—a power in the state. Their influence was every where seen in the laxity of public morals. The church was polluted with the contagion. A refractory spirit appeared among the National Guards, and the king and his family were insulted in public.

Disgusted with these evidences of demoralization, Lafayette resigned his command of the National Guard, but resumed it on the solicitation of sixty battalions. He was exceedingly popular, yet he could not wholly control the spirit of anarchy that was abroad. The king, alarmed, fled in disguise from Paris. Terror prevailed among all classes. The flight of the monarch was construed into a crime by his enemies, and he was arrested and brought back to Paris under an escort of thirty thousand National Guards. He excused his movement with the plea that he was exposed to too many insults in the capital, and only wished to live quietly, away from the scenes of strife.

The populace were not satisfied. Led by Robespierre, a sanguinary demagogue, and member of the Constituent Assembly, they met in the Elysian Fields, and petitioned for the dethronement of Louis. Four thousand of the National Guard fired upon them, and killed several hundred. The exasperation of the people was terrible, yet the popularity of Lafayette held the factious in check.[1]

The Constitution was completed in September. The trembling king accepted it, and solemnly swore to maintain it. Proclamation of the fact was made throughout the kingdom, and a grand fête, whereat one hundred thousand people sang and danced the Carmagnole in the Elysian Fields, was held at Paris, and salvos of cannon thundered along the banks of the Seine.[2]

There was wide-spread sympathy in the United States with these revolutionary movements in France. The spirit of faction, viewed at that great distance, appeared like patriotism. Half-formed and half-understood political maxims, floating upon the tide of social life in the new republic, began to crystallize into tenets, and assumed antagonistic party positions. The galvanic forces, so to speak, which produced these crystallizations, proceeded from the President's Cabinet, where Mr. Jefferson, the Secretary of State, and Mr. Hamilton, the Secretary of the Treasury, were at direct variance in their views of domestic public measures, and were making constant war upon each other. Jefferson, believing, with Thomas Paine (who now appeared in the field of political strife abroad), that a weak government and a strong people were the best guarantees of liberty to the citizen, contemplated all executive power with distrust, and desired to impair its vitality and restrain its operations. He thought he saw in the funding system arranged by Hamilton, and in the United States Bank and the excise law—creations of that statesman's brain—instruments for enslaving the people;

---

[1] "I am exposed to the envy and attacks of all parties," he wrote to Washington, "for this single reason, that whoever acts or means wrong finds me an insuperable obstacle. And there appears a kind of phenomenon in my situation—all parties against me, and a national popularity, which, in spite of every effort, has remained unchanged. . . . Given up to all the madness of license, faction, and popular rage, I stood alone in defense of the law, and turned the tide into the constitutional channel."

[2] Upon a tree planted on the site of the Bastile a placard was placed, in these words:

"Here is the epoch of Liberty;
We dance on the ruins of despotism;
The Constitution is finished—
Long live patriotism!"

and he affected to believe that the rights of the states and liberties of the citizens were in danger.

Hamilton, on the other hand, regarded the National Constitution as inadequate in strength to perform its required functions, and believed weakness to be its most radical defect; and it was his sincere desire and uniform practice so to construe its provisions as to give strength and efficiency to the Executive in the administration of public affairs.

Not content with an expression of his opinions, Jefferson charged his political opponents, and especially Hamilton, with corrupt and anti-republican designs, selfish motives, and treacherous intentions; and thus was inaugurated that system of personal abuse and vituperation which has ever been a disgrace to the press and political leaders of this country.

An unfortunate blunder made by John Adams, the Vice-President, at about this time, confirmed Jefferson in his opinions and fears. These men, compatriots in the events out of which the nation had been evolved, cherished dissimilar political ideas, and held widely differing religious sentiments. Mr. Jefferson was always a freethinker, and his latitudinarianism was greatly expanded by a long residence among the contemners of revealed religion in France. He admired Voltaire, Rousseau, and D'Alembert, whose graves were then green; and one of his most intimate companions was the Marquis of Condorcet, who "classed among fools those who had the misfortune to believe in a revealed religion."[1] He sympathized with the ultra Republicans of France, was their counselor in the early and later stages of the revolutionary movement of 1789, and opened his house to them for secret conclave. He was an enthusiastic admirer of a nation of enthusiasts.

Mr. Adams, on the contrary, was thoroughly imbued with the political and religious principles of New England Puritanism. He discovered spiritual life in every page of the Bible, and accepted the doctrines of revealed religion as an emanation from the fountain of Eternal Truth. His mind was cast in the mould of the English conservative writers, whom he admired. He detested the principles and practices of the French philosophers, whom Jefferson revered; and, from the outset, he detected in the revolutionary movements in France the elements of destructiveness which were so speedily developed. These views were indicated in a letter to the Rev. Dr. Price, of England, acknowledging the receipt of a printed copy of his famous discourse on the morning of the anniversary dinner of the English Revolution Society in 1789, in which the preacher, accepting the French Revolution as a glorious event in the history of mankind, said, "What an eventful period is this! I am thankful that I have lived to see it; and I could almost say, 'Lord, now lettest thou thy servant depart in peace, for mine eyes have seen thy salvation.' . . . I have lived to see thirty millions of people indignantly and resolutely spurning at slavery, and demanding liberty with an irresistible voice."

To this Adams replied, "I know that encyclopedists and economists—Diderot and D'Alembert, Voltaire and Rousseau—have contributed to this great event even more than Sidney, Locke, or Hoadley; perhaps more than the American Revolution: and I own to you I know not what to make of a republic of thirty millions of atheists. . . .

---

[1] Capefigue, ii., 82. Mr. Jefferson's religious views, at that time, may be inferred from the contents of a letter written at Paris on the 10th of August, 1787, to Peter Carr, a young relative of his in Virginia, wherein he lays down some maxims for his future guidance. He enjoins him to exalt reason above creeds. "Question with boldness," he says, "even the existence of a God; because, if there be one, he must more approve the homage of reason than of blindfold fear." He then advises him to read the Bible as he would Livy or Tacitus. "The facts which are within the ordinary course of nature you will believe on the authority of the writer, as you do those of the same kind in Livy or Tacitus." He then cautions him against a belief in statements in the Bible "which contradict the laws of nature." Concerning the New Testament, he said, "It is the history of a personage called Jesus. Keep in your eye the opposite pretensions, 1, of those who say he was begotten of God, born of a virgin, suspended and reversed the laws of nature at will, and ascended bodily into heaven; and, 2, of those who say he was a man of illegitimate birth, of a benevolent heart, enthusiastic mind, who set out with pretensions to divinity, ended in believing them, and was punished capitally for sedition by being gibbeted according to the Roman law."

An English Democrat's Discourse.   Burke's Reflections on the French Revolution.   Paine's "Rights of Man."

Too many Frenchmen, after the example of too many Americans, pant for equality of person and property. The impracticability of this, God Almighty has decreed, and the advocates for liberty who attempt it will surely suffer for it."[1]

---

[1] See Letter to Richard Price, April 19, 1790, in the *Life and Works of John Adams*, ix., 563.

Richard Price, D.D., LL.D., was an eminent English Dissenting minister, and at this time was preacher at the meeting-house in Old Jewry, London. He was then quite venerable in years, and with a mind as vigorous as when, in 1776, he wrote his famous "Observations on the War in America." He was an ultra democrat, and sympathized strongly with the French Revolution. He did not live to see that Revolution assume its huge proportions and hideous visage that so terrified Europe, for he died in the spring of 1791.

The discourse above alluded to was preached on the anniversary of the Revolution in 1688 (4th of November) which hurled James the Second from the throne. Dr. Price was an active member of the "Revolution Club," of which, at that time, the Earl of Stanhope was president. The discourse "On the Love of our Country" was preached before the members, and was subsequently printed. After alluding to the Revolution in France, he said, "I see the dominion of kings changed for the dominion of laws, and the dominion of priests giving way to the dominion of reason and conscience. Be encouraged, all ye friends of freedom and writers in its defense! The times are auspicious. Your labors have not been in vain. Behold kingdoms, admonished by you, starting from sleep, breaking their fetters, and claiming justice from their oppressors! Behold the light you have struck out, after setting America free, reflected to France, and there kindled into a blaze that lays despotism in ashes, and warms and illuminates Europe!"

The Society, at that meeting, on motion of Dr. Price, agreed, by acclamation, to send, in the shape of a formal address, "their congratulations to the National Assembly on the event of the late glorious Revolution in France." This action and the discourse of Dr. Price produced the greatest agitation throughout England. Auxiliary clubs were speedily formed in various parts of the kingdom, encouraged by men like Dr. Priestley, the eminent Unitarian minister at Birmingham. Monarchist and Churchman were greatly alarmed. The king was inclined to deny any more concessions to the Liberal party, making the Revolution in France a sufficient argument against reform in England, while the clergy of the hierarchy raised a cry that the Church was in danger from the revolutionizing and destructive machinations of the Dissenters. To the astonishment of all men, Edmund Burke raised his voice in the House of Commons in cadences never heard before from his lips. He had ever been the eloquent advocate of the rights of man. Now he declared that there was no such thing as natural rights of men, and he condemned the whole body of Dissenters in the strongest terms, as discontented people, whose principles tended to the subversion of good government. Nor did his denunciations rest there. He professed to regard Dr. Price's sermon with holy horror, and its author as a most dangerous agitator, and he brought to the task of disabusing the public mind of England concerning the real character of the revolt in Paris the whole powers of his mighty intellect. In an almost incredible short space of time he wrote his famous "Reflections on the French Revolution," the publication of which produced a most powerful effect. The king and ministry, and the Tory party, expressed unbounded admiration of this splendid defense of their policy, while all just men agreed that it was a monstrous exaggeration. It called forth many opposing writers—among them the powerful Priestley, the elegant Mackintosh, and the coarse but vigorous Paine. The war of words, and pen, and type was waged furiously for a long time, and satirical ballads and clever caricatures played a conspicuous part in the contest.

Thomas Paine, who had been in Paris some time, and participated in some of the revolutionary scenes there, had lately returned when Burke's "Reflections" appeared, and he lost no time in preparing an answer, which he entitled "The Rights of Man." The first part was published on the 1st of February, 1791, and produced great disturbance. It was sought after with the greatest avidity, and in proportion to its success was the alarm and indignation of the Tory party. There was ample food for the caricaturists, and Gillray's pencil was active. Fox and Sheridan, who were the leaders of the opposition in Parliament, were classed among the leaders of the Revolution Clubs, and appeared in pictures with Priestley and Paine. In May, 1791, Gillray burlesqued Paine in a caricature which he entitled "The Rights of Man; or, Tommy Paine, the American Tailor, taking the Measure of the Crown for a new pair of Revolution Breeches." Paine is seen with the conventional type of face given by the caricaturists to a French democrat. His tri-colored cockade bears the inscription, "*Vive la liberté!*" and from his mouth proceeds an incoherent soliloquy, as if from a man half drunk.* This was in allusion to his well-known intemperance. Paine was finally prosecuted by the government for libel on account of some remarks in his "Rights of Man," and was compelled to flee to France, where he was warmly received by the revolutionists. A Tory mob destroyed Dr. Priestley's church in Birmingham, and his dwelling and fine library a short distance in the country; also he and his family barely escaped with their lives.

A BAD MEASURE.

---

* The following is a copy of the soliloquy: "Fathom and a half! fathom and a half! Poor Tom! ah! mercy upon me! that's more by half than my poor measure will ever be able to reach! Lord! Lord! I wish I had a bit of the stay-tape [allusion to Paine's former business of staymaker] or buckram which I used to cabbage when I was a 'prentice, to lengthen it out. Well, well, who would ever have thought it, that I, who have served seven years as an apprentice, and afterward worked four years as a journeyman to a master tailor, then followed the business of an exciseman as much longer, should not be able to take the dimension of this bawble! for what is a crown but a bawble,

Mr. Adams had discerned with alarm the contagion of revolution which went out from Paris in the autumn of 1789. He saw it affecting England, and menacing the existence of its government; and he perceived its rapid diffusion in his own country with surprise and pain. It was so different in form and substance from that which had made his own people free, that he was deeply impressed with its dangers. With a patriotic spirit he sought to arrest the calamities it might bring upon his country, and with that view he wrote a series of articles for a newspaper, entitled "Discourses on Davila." These contained an analysis of Davila's *History of the Civil War in France*[1] in the sixteenth century. The aim of Mr. Adams was to point out to his countrymen the danger to be apprehended from factions in ill-balanced forms of government. In these essays he maintained that, as the great spring of human activity, especially as related to public life, was self-esteem, manifested in the love of superiority, and the desire of distinction, applause, and admiration, it was important in a popular government to provide for the moderate gratification of all of them. He therefore advocated a liberal use of titles and ceremonial honors for those in office, and an aristocratic Senate. To counteract any undue influence on the part of the Senate, he proposed a popular assembly on the broadest democratic basis; and, to keep in check encroachments of each upon the other, he recommended a powerful Executive. He thought liberty to all would thus be best secured.[2] From the premises which formed the basis of his reasoning, he argued that the French Constitution, which disavowed all distinctions of rank, which vested the legislative authority in a single Assembly, and which, though retaining the office of king, divested him of nearly all actual power, must, in the nature of things, prove a failure. The wisdom of this assumption has been vindicated by history.

The publication of these essays at that time was Mr. Adams's blunder.[3] His ideas were presented in a form so cloudy that his political system was misunderstood by the many and misinterpreted by the few. He was charged with advocating a monarchy and a hereditary Senate; and it was artfully insinuated that he had been seduced by Hamilton (whose jealous opponents delighted in pointing to him as the arch-enemy of republican government) from his loyalty to those noble principles which he had exhibited before he wrote his "Defense of the American Constitutions," published in London three years before.

Those essays filled Jefferson with disgust, and he cherished the idea that Hamilton, Adams, Jay, and others were at the head of a party engaged in a conspiracy to overthrow the republican institutions of the United States, and on their ruins to construct a mixed government like that of England, composed of a monarchy and aristocracy.[4]

---

[1] *Dell' Istoria delle Guerre Civili di Francia*, by Henrico Caterino Davila.

[2] This was only an amplification of the thought thus expressed in his *Defense of the American Constitutions:* "It is denied that the people are the best keepers, or any keepers at all, of their own liberties, when they hold collectively, or by representative, the executive and judicial power, or the whole uncontrolled legislature." He did not believe in the efficiency or safety of a government formed upon the simple plan of M. Thurgot and other clear-minded men of France, in which all power was concentrated in one body directly representing the nation. That was the doctrine and the practice of the French revolutionists, enforced by the logic of Condorcet and the eloquence of Mirabeau. Mr. Adams wished a system of checks and balances, which experience has proved to be the wisest.

[3] They were published in the *Gazette of the United States*, at Philadelphia, then the seat of the national government. Their more immediate object was a reply to Condorcet's pamphlet, entitled *Quatre Lettres d'un Bourgeois de New Haven, sur l'Unité de la Législation*. Mr. Adams soon perceived that his essays were furnishing the partisans of the day with too much capital for immediate use in the conflict of opinion then raging, and ceased writing before they were completed. Twenty years later, when a new edition was published, Mr. Adams wrote, "This dull, heavy volume still excites the wonder of its author—first, that he could find, amidst the constant scenes of business and dissipation in which he was enveloped, time to write it; secondly, that he had the courage to oppose and publish his own opinions to the universal opinion of America, and indeed of all mankind. Not one man in America then believed him. He knew not one, and has not heard of one since, who then believed him.—J. A., 1812."

[4] "The Tory paper, Fenno's," he wrote to Mr. Short, in Paris, "rarely admits any thing which defends the present form which we may see in the Tower for sixpence apiece? Well, although it may be too large for a tailor to take measure of, there's one comfort—he may make mouths at it, and call it as many names as he pleases! And yet, Lord! Lord! I should like to make it a Yankee-doodle night-cap and breeches, if it was not so d—d large, or I had stuff enough. Ah! if I could once do that, I would soon stitch up the mouth of that barnacled Edmund from making any more *Reflections* upon the Flints. And so, Flints and Liberty forever, and d—n the Dungs! Huzza!"

To thwart these fancied designs, and to inculcate the doctrines of the French Revolution which he so much admired, and on which he grounded his hopes of a stable government in his own country,[1] Jefferson hastened to have printed and circulated Thomas Paine's famous reply to Burke's "Reflections on the French Revolution," called "The Rights of Man," which had just been received from England. That essay, originally dedicated "To the President of the United States," was admired by Jefferson, and it was issued from the Philadelphia press, with a complimentary note from him.

This apparent indorsement of the essay by the government, in the persons of the President and Secretary of State, was very offensive to Great Britain, and produced a good deal of stir in the United States. Major Beckwith, the aid-de-camp of Lord Dorchester, already mentioned,[2] was in Philadelphia at that time, and expressed his surprise; but subsequent assurances that the President knew nothing of the dedication, and that Mr. Jefferson "neither desired nor expected" to have the note printed, soon smoothed the ripple of dissatisfaction so far as the British government was concerned.[3]

The political and personal feud between Jefferson and Hamilton became more intense every hour. Freneau's *United States Gazette*, believed to be under the control of the former, was filled with bitter denunciations of Hamilton and the leading measures of the administration; and Fenno's *National Gazette*, the supporter of the government policy, was made spicy by Hamilton's vigorous retorts.[4] The public mind was greatly excited thereby, and Washington was compelled to perceive (as he did with alarm and mortification) that there was a schism in his Cabinet, which threatened to be destructive of all harmony of action, and perilous to the public good. He anxiously sought to end the strife by assuming the holy office of peace-maker, but in

---

of government in opposition to his desire of subverting it, to make way for a king, Lords, and Commons. There are high names here in favor of this doctrine . . . Adams, Jay, Hamilton, Knox, and many of the Cincinnati. The second says nothing; the third is open. Both are dangerous. They pant after union with England, as the power which is to support their projects, and are most determined Anti-Gallicans. It is prognosticated that our republic is to end with the President's life; but I believe they will find themselves all head and no body."

[1] "You will have heard," Mr. Jefferson wrote to Edward Rutledge in August, 1791, "before this reaches you, of the peril into which the French Revolution is brought by the flight of their king. Such are the fruits of that form of government which heaps importance on idiots, and which the Tories of the present day are trying to preach into our favor. I still hope the French Revolution will issue happily. I feel that the permanence of our own leans in some degree on that, and that a failure there would be a powerful argument to prove that there must be a failure here."

[2] See note 1, page 63.

[3] The political sentiments of Paine's *Rights of Man* were in accordance with the feelings and opinions of the great body of the American people. The author sent fifty copies to Washington, who distributed them among his friends. His official position cautioned him to be prudently silent concerning the work. Richard Henry Lee, to whom Washington gave a copy, said, in his letter acknowledging the favor, "It is a performance of which any man might be proud; and I most sincerely regret that our country could not have offered sufficient inducements to have retained, as a permanent citizen, a man so thoroughly republican in sentiment and fearless in the expression of his opinions." See Lossing's *Home of Washington, or Mount Vernon and its Associations*, p. 262.

The note alluded to in the text was from Mr. Jefferson to a stranger to him (Jonathan Bayard Smith), to whom the owner of Paine's pamphlet, who lent it to the Secretary of State, desired him to send it. "To take off a little of the dryness of the note," Mr. Jefferson made some complimentary observations concerning the pamphlet, and expressed his satisfaction that something public would be said, by its publication, "against the political heresies which had lately sprung up." To the astonishment of Mr. Jefferson, this private note was printed with the pamphlet the next week. Mr. Jefferson acknowledged that his remarks in it were aimed at the author of the *Discourses on Davila*, and the affair produced a temporary estrangement between him and Mr. Adams.

Warm discussions arose, soon after the publication of Paine's pamphlet, on the doctrines which it promulgated. A series of articles in reply to the "Rights of Man" appeared in the Boston *Centinel*, over the signature of *Publicola*, which were attributed to John Adams, and were reprinted in London, in pamphlet form, with his name on the title-page. They were written by his son, the late John Quincy Adams. They were answered by several writers. "A host of champions," Jefferson wrote to Paine, "entered the arena immediately in your defense."

[4] Philip Freneau, a poet of some pretensions, and a warm Whig writer during the Revolution, was called from New York, where he was editing a newspaper, to fill the post of translating clerk in the State Department under Mr. Jefferson. A new paper, called *The National Gazette*, opposed to the leading measures of the administration, was started, and Freneau was made its editor. It was understood to be Mr. Jefferson's "organ," but it would be both ungenerous and unjust to believe that the bitter attacks made upon all the measures of the administration were approved by Mr. Jefferson; yet, when the Secretary well knew that the President, whom he professed to revere, was greatly hurt and annoyed by them, it was, as Mr. Irving justly remarks (*Life of Washington*, v., 164), "rather an ungracious determination to keep the barking cur in his employ." Fenno published the *United States Gazette*, the supporter of the measures of the administration.

vain.¹ The antagonisms of the Secretaries had become too violent to be easily reconciled. Their partisans were numerous and powerful, and had become arranged in tangible battle order, under the respective names of *Federalists* and *Republicans*—names which for many years were significant of opposing opinions: first, concerning the administration of the national government; secondly, on the question of a neutral policy toward the warring nations of Europe; and, thirdly, on the subject of the war with Great Britain declared in 1812.

The Federalists, called the "British party" by their opponents, were in favor of a strong central government, and were very conservative. They were in favor of maintaining a strict neutrality concerning the affairs of European nations during the exciting period of Washington's administration, and were opposed to the War of 1812. The Republicans, called the "French party," were favorable to a strong people and a weak government, sympathized warmly with the French revolutionists, and urged the government to do the same by public expressions and belligerent acts if necessary, and were favorable to the War of 1812 when it became an apparent national necessity. *Federal* and *Republican* were the distinctive names of the two great political parties in the United States during the first quarter of a century of the national existence, when they disappeared from the politician's vocabulary. New issues, growing out of radical changes in the condition of the country, produced coalitions and amalgamations by which the identity of the two old parties was speedily lost.

The zeal of the opposing parties was intensified by events in Europe during the summer and autumn of 1792; and at the opening of the last session of the second Congress, in November, the party divisions were perfectly distinct in that body.

All Europe was now effervescing with antagonistic ideas. The best and wisest men stood in wonder and awe in the midst of the upheaval of old social and political systems. Popular sentiment in the United States was mixed in character, and yet crude in form, and for a while it was difficult to discern precisely in what relation it stood to the disturbed nationalities of Europe. The blood of nearly all of them coursed in the veins of the Americans; and notwithstanding a broad ocean, and perhaps more than a generation of time, separated the most of them from the Old World, they experienced lingering memories or pleasant dreams of Fatherland.

France, the old ally and friend of the United States, was the centre of the volcanic force that was shaking the nations. The potentates of Europe, trembling for the stability of their thrones, instinctively arrayed themselves as the implacable enemies of the new power that held the sceptre of France, and disturbed the political and dynastic equilibrium. They called out their legions for self-defense and to utter a solemn protest. The *people* were overawed by demonstrations of power. The gleam of bayonets and the roll of the drum met the eye and ear every where, and in the autumn of 1792 nearly all Europe was rising in arms against France.

Revolution had done its work nobly, wisely, and successfully in the United States, and the experiment of self-government was working well. The memory of French arms, and men, and money that came to their aid in their struggle for liberty, filled the hearts of the Americans with gratitude, for they were not, as a people, aware of

---

ª August 23, 1792.

¹ Both ministers discharged their respective duties to the entire satisfaction of the President, and he felt greatly disturbed by their antagonisms, now become public. To Jefferson he wrote,ª after referring to the Indian hostilities, and the possible intrigues of foreigners to check the prosperity of the United States, "How unfortunate, and how much to be regretted is it, that while we are encompassed on all sides by armed enemies and insidious friends, internal dissensions should be harrowing and tearing our vitals. . . . My earnest wish and my fondest hope, therefore, is that, instead of wounding suspicions and irritating charges, there may be liberal allowances, mutual forbearances, and temporizing yieldings on all sides. Under the exercise of these, matters will go on smoothly, and, if possible, more prosperously. Without them, every thing must rub; the wheels of government will clog, our enemies will triumph, and, by throwing their weight into the disaffected scale, may accomplish the ruin of the goodly fabric we have been erecting."

Washington wrote to Hamilton in a similar strain, and from both he received patriotic replies. But the feud was too deep-seated to be healed. Jefferson would yield nothing. He harbored an implacable hatred of Hamilton, whom he had scourged into active retaliation, and whose lash he felt most keenly.

the utterly selfish motive of the Bourbon in giving that aid, and how little it had really contributed to their success in that struggle; and their own zeal for freedom, while enjoying the fruition of their efforts, awakened their warmest sympathies for those yet in the toils of slavery. Without inquiring, they cheered on the people of France, who were first led by the beloved Lafayette; and with corresponding detestation, heightened by the memory of old wrongs and the irritations of present unfriendliness, they saw Great Britain, so boastful of liberty, arrayed against the French people in their professed struggle for the establishment of a constitutional government like that of England.

But there were wise, and thoughtful, and prudent men in the United States and in Great Britain, who had made the science of government their study and human nature their daily reading, who clearly perceived the vast difference between the revolutions in America and France, and thought they observed in the latter no hope for the real benefit and prosperity of the people. These, in the United States, formed the leaders of the Federal or conservative party. Washington had hailed with great satisfaction the dawning of what he hoped to be the day of liberty in France, but, from the beginning, his own sagacity, and the gloomy forebodings manifested by Lafayette from time to time in his letters, made him doubtful of the success of the movement. He often expressed an earnest *wish* that republicanism might be established in France, but never breathed a *hope*, because he never felt it. And when, in the summer of 1792, he perceived the bloody and ferocious character of the French Revolution, and the departure of its course from the high and honorable path marked out for it by Lafayette and his compatriots, he and the conservative party, then fortunately holding the reins of executive and legislative power, resolved that the government of the United States should stand aloof from all entanglements with European politics.

Jefferson and his party, on the other hand, deeply sympathized with the French revolutionists, and bore intense enmity toward Great Britain. They were greater in numbers than the Federalists, and their warfare was relentless. They denounced every man and measure opposed to their own views with a fierceness and lack of generosity that appears almost incredible, and they shut their ears to the howling of that lawless violence that had commenced drenching the soil of France in blood. Even the dispatches of government agents abroad were sneered at as instruments of needless alarm, if not something worse.[1]

But "the inexorable logic of events" soon revealed to the people of the United States those terrible aspects of the French Revolution which made them for a moment recoil with horror. Anarchy had seized unhappy France, and the ferocious Jacobin Club reigned supreme in Paris. They were the enemies of the king and Constitution, and were determined to overthrow both. Incited by them, the populace of Paris, one hundred thousand in number, professedly incensed because the king had refused to sanction a decree of the National Assembly against the priesthood, and another for the establishment of a camp of twenty thousand men near Paris, marched to the Tuileries[a] with pikes, swords, muskets, and artillery, and demanded entrance. The gates were thrown open, and forty thousand armed men, many of them the vilest *sans-culottes* of the streets of Paris, went through the palace, and compelled the king, in the presence of his family, to put the *bonnet rouge*, or red cap of liberty, upon his head. [a] June 20, 1792.

Lafayette was then at the head of his army at Maubeuge, a fortified town in the Department of the North. He hastened to Paris, presented himself at the bar of the

---

[1] Gouverneur Morris, who had been appointed minister to France after Jefferson left, kept Washington continually informed of the scenes of anarchy and licentiousness in the French capital, and presented gloomy prognostications respecting the future of that country. Because of this faithfulness, and his testimony against the tendency of the French Revolution, Mr. Jefferson, in his blind devotion to that cause, and his ungenerous judgment concerning all who differed from him, spoke of Morris as "as a high-flying monarchy-man, shutting his eyes and his faith to every fact against his wishes, and believing every thing he desired to be true."

AN ASSIGNAT, OR PAPER-MONEY OF THE FRENCH REVOLUTIONISTS.

National Assembly, and in the name of the army demanded the punishment of those who had insulted the king and his family in the palace and violated the Constitution. But Lafayette was powerless. Paris was drunk with passion and unrestrained license.

| Monarchy in France overthrown. | Lafayette imprisoned. | The National Convention established. |

The doom of royalty was decreed. The populace and members of the Assembly demanded the deposition of Louis. The sittings of the Assembly were declared permanent until order should be restored. At midnight[a] the dreadful tocsin, or alarm-bell, was sounded, and the drums beat the *generale* in every direction. The streets were filled with the mad populace, and in the morning the Tuileries were attacked by them. The king, attended by the Swiss Guard, fled to the National Assembly for protection. Nearly every man of the guard was butchered. The monarch escaped unhurt, but the overawed Assembly decreed the suspension of the royal authority.[1] Monarchy in France was virtually overthrown, and with it fell Lafayette and the constitutional party. The Jacobins of the Assembly procured a decree for the arrest of the marquis. He and a few friends turned their faces toward Holland as a temporary refuge from the storm until they could escape to the United States. They were arrested on the way, and for three years Lafayette was entombed in an Austrian dungeon at Olmutz, while pretended republicans, with bloody hands, were holding the uncertain and slippery reins of anarchical power in his beloved France.

[a] August 9, 1792.

The Jacobins were not satisfied with the suspension of the king's authority. They felt unsafe while he lived. They conspired against his life and the lives of all who might sympathize with him. They filled the prisons with priests and nobles, and other suspected persons. These men were dangerous while their pulses beat healthily. Their prisons became human slaughter-houses. Thither the demoniac populace were sent on the evening of the 2d of September,[b] and before the dawn, at least eighteen hundred persons were slain!

[b] 1792.

The conspirators now took bolder steps. They abolished the Constituent Assembly, and constituted themselves a National Convention. The Hall of the Tuileries was their meeting-place, and there, in the palace of the kings, they assumed the executive powers of government. They decreed the abolition of royalty, and proclaimed France a republic.[c] With wonderful energy they devised and put in motion schemes of conquest and propagandism. They assumed to be the deliverers of the people of Europe from kingly rule. Frontier armies, with the aid of paper-money alone,[2] were speedily put in motion to execute the decree of Danton and his fellow-regicides that "there must be no more kings in Europe." They invaded Belgium and Savoy, and conquered Austrian Netherlands. At the sound of the Marseilles Hymn, sung by these knights-errant of the new chivalry, the people flocked to the standards of revolt.[3]

[c] September 23, 1792.

---

[1] The king wrote a touching letter to his brother, dated "August 12, 1792, seven o'clock in the morning." The following is a copy:

"My brother, I am no longer king; the public voice will make known to you the most cruel catastrophe. I am the most unfortunate of husbands and of fathers. I am the victim of my own goodness, of fear, of hope. It is an impenetrable mystery of iniquity. They have bereaved me of every thing. They have massacred my faithful subjects. I have been decoyed by stratagem far from my palace, and they now accuse me! I am a captive. They drag me to prison, and the queen, my children, and Madame Elizabeth [his sister] share my fate.

"I can no longer doubt that I am an object odious in the eyes of the French, led astray by prejudice. This is the stroke which is most insupportable. My brother, but a little while, and I shall exist no longer. Remember to avenge my memory by publishing how much I loved this ungrateful people. Recall one day to their remembrance the wrongs they have done me, and tell them I forgave. Adieu, my brother, for the last time."

This letter was sent in a bit of bread to a friend of the king. It was intercepted, and never reached his brother.—*Correspondence of Louis XVI.*, translated by HELEN MARIA WILLIAMS, iii., 45.

[2] This paper-money, a specimen of which is given on page 74, was called *Assignat*. It was first issued in 1789, and the basis for its credit was the property of the clergy and the emigrants, which the government had seized, and which was intended for sale. For three years it held a market value of over ninety per cent., but in 1792 it began to depreciate, and, like our own Continental money, soon became worthless. The first issue was to the amount of about $200,000,000. The amount that was finally put in circulation was about $1,750,000,000. This paper-money, which for a season played so important a part in the history of the world, was productive of the greatest evils. Specimens of it are now rarely to be found. The engraving represents one in the author's possession.

[3] In the National Convention, on the 28th of September, Danton declared, amid the loud applauses of the assembly, that "the principle of leaving conquered peoples and countries the right of choosing their own constitutions ought to be so far modified that we should expressly forbid them to give themselves kings. *There must be no more kings in Europe. One king would be sufficient to endanger general liberty;* and I request that a committee be established for the purpose of promoting *a general insurrection among all people against kings.*" They thus made a distinction between the monarchs and the people, and professed to be the deliverers of the latter. The Revolution Clubs of England affiliated with them in sentiment, and Dr. Priestley and Thomas Paine were elected members of the National Convention. Priestley de-

Egotism of the French Revolutionists.   Paine in France.   Execution of Louis XVI.

Success gave the revolutionists *prestige*, and, with egotism unparalleled, the National Convention, by acclamation, declared that, "in the name of the French nation, they would grant fraternity and assistance to all those peoples who wished to procure liberty;" and they charged the executive power "to send orders to the generals to give assistance to such people, and to defend citizens who had suffered, and were then suffering in the cause of liberty."

LOUIS XVI.

The revolutionists, flushed with victories, and emboldened by the obedience which their reign of terror inspired, soon executed a long-cherished plan of the Jacobins, and murdered their king in the presence of his subjects.[1] They declared war against England and Holland,[a] and soon afterward against Spain,[b] and with the battle-cry of "*Liberty and Equality*," they defied all Europe. For a

[a] Feb. 1, 1793.

[b] March 7.

moment England was alarmed, for she had numerous enemies in her own household, and the civilized world looked upon the sanguinary tragedy on the Gallic stage with dismay and horror.

The contagion of that bloody Revolution had so poisoned the circulation of the social and political system of the United States, that, strange as it may appear to us, when the proclamation of the French Republic, with all its attendant horrors of August and September, was made known here, followed speedily by intelligence of

---

clined, but Paine accepted, went over to France, and took his seat in that blood-thirsty assembly. This called forth squibs and caricatures in abundance. In one of the latter, entitled "Fashion for Ease; or, a Good Constitution sacrificed for a Fantastic Form," Paine is represented fitting Britannia with a new pair of stays, in allusion to the occupation of his early life. Over a cottage door on one side was a sign, "Thomas Paine, Stay-maker, from Thetford. Paris Modes by Express." Paine never ventured to return to England. His popularity in France was brief. In the National Convention he offended the ferocious Jacobins by advocating leniency toward the king. He incurred their hatred, and Robespierre and his associates cast him into prison, where he composed his "Age of Reason." He was saved from the guillotine by accident, escaped to the United States, and spent much of his time there, until his death, in coarse abuse of men and measures in that country and England.

[1] They went through the farce of a trial. The king was accused of treason to the people and the Constitution, and was found guilty, of course. Weak in intellect, and dissipated in habits as he was, Louis was innocent of the crimes alleged against him. He was beheaded by

PAINE FITTING STAYS.

the guillotine. When standing before the instrument of death, and looking upon the people with benignity, he said, "I forgive my enemies; may God forgive them, and not lay my innocent blood to the charge of the nation! God bless my people!" He was cut short by an order to beat the drums and sound the trumpets, when the brutal officer in charge called out to him, "*No speeches! come, no speeches!*"

The death of Louis was sincerely mourned. He was weak, but not wicked. He was an amiable man, and loved his country. His friends dared not make any public demonstrations of grief, or even of attachment. A small commemorative medal of brass was struck, and secretly circulated. These were cherished by the Loyalists for a generation with great affection. On one side is a head of Louis, with the usual inscription—LUD. XVI. REX GALL. DEI GRATIA. On the other side is a memorial urn, with "LOUIS XVI." upon it, and a fallen crown and sceptre at its base. Beneath is the date of his death, and over it the significant words, SOL REGNI ABIIT—"The sun of the kingdom has departed." The engraving is from a copy in the author's possession.*

MEMORIAL MEDAL.

* Louis was born on the 23d of March, 1754, and in 1770 married Maria Antoinette, of Austria. He ascended the throne of France, on the death of his grandfather, in 1774.

the conquest of Austrian Netherlands by a French army, there was an outburst of popular feeling in favor of the Gallic cause that seemed to be almost universal. They were blind to the total difference between their own Revolution and that in France. They were forgetful of the friendship of Holland during that struggle—a friendship far more sincere than that of the French; forgetful also of the spirit of true liberty which for centuries had prevailed in Holland, and made it an asylum for the persecuted for conscience' sake in all lands; and the people in several towns and cities celebrated these events with demonstrations of great joy.[1] With a similar spirit the death of the French king was hailed by the leaders of the Republican party in the United States; and the declaration of war against England and Holland by France awakened a most remarkable enthusiasm in favor of the old ally of the Americans, aroused old hatreds toward England, and called loudly for compliance with the letter and spirit of the treaty of 1778.[2]

These demonstrations were soon followed by the arrival of "Citizen Genet," as he was styled,[3] as minister of the French Republic to the United States. He came in a frigate, and landed at Charleston, South Carolina, early in April. His reception there was all that his ambition could have demanded; and his journey of three or four weeks by land from there to Philadelphia, the national capital, was a continued ovation. He was a man of culture and tact, spoke the English language fluently, and was frank, lively, and communicative. He was precisely the man for his peculiar mission. He mingled familiarly with the people, proclaimed wild and stirring doctrines, scorned all diplomatic art and reserve, and assured the citizens of the United States of the unbounded affection of his countrymen for the Americans. The Republican leaders hailed his advent with delight; and a large portion of the people were favorable to immediate and active participation by their government with France in its impending struggle against armed Europe. Many, in the wild enthusiasm of the moment, would not have hesitated an instant in precipitating their country into a war that might have proved its utter ruin.

It was fortunate for the country that a man like Washington, and his wise counselors, were at the helm and halliards of the vessel of state at that time, and endowed with courage sufficient to meet the dangerous popular gale. When intelligence of the declaration of war between France and other nations reached him, the President was at Mount Vernon. He had no confidence in the self-constituted rulers of France or their system of government. "They are ready to tear each other in pieces," he wrote to Governor Lee, of Virginia, "and will, more than probably, prove the worst foes the country has."

Perceiving the proclivity of the public mind in his own country, the President felt great anxiety, and he made immediate preparations to arrest, as far as possible, the terrible evils which a free course of the popular sympathy for the French might have.

---

[1] There was a grand fête held in Boston on the 24th of January, 1793. An ox was roasted whole. It was then decorated with ribbons, and placed upon a car drawn by sixteen horses. The flags of the United States and France were displayed from the horns of the ox. It was paraded through the streets, followed by carts bearing sixteen hundred loaves of bread and two hogsheads of punch. These were distributed among the people; and at the same time a party of three hundred, with Samuel Adams, then Lieutenant Governor of Massachusetts, at their head, assisted by the French consul, sat down to a dinner in Faneuil Hall. To the children of all the schools, who were paraded in the streets, cakes were presented, stamped with the words "*Liberty and Equality.*" By public subscription, the sums owed by prisoners in the jail for debt were paid, and the victims of that barbarous law were set free. In Philadelphia the anniversary of the French alliance, mentioned in the subjoined note, was commemorated by a public dinner. Governor (late General) Mifflin presided. At the head of the table a pike was fixed, bearing upon its point the *bonnet rouge*, with the French and American flags intertwined in festoons, and the whole surmounted by a dove and olive branch.

[2] A treaty of alliance, friendship, and commerce was entered into by the United States and France on the 6th of February, 1778, by which the former was bound to guarantee the French possessions in America; and by a treaty of commerce executed at the same time, French privateers and prizes were entitled to shelter in the American ports, while those of the enemies of France should be excluded.—See Article XVII. of the Treaty.

[3] The French Jacobins affected the simplicity of the republics of Greece and Rome. All titles were abolished, and the term *citizen* was universally applied to men. When the king was spoken of, his family name of Capet was used. He was called "Citizen Capet" or "Louis Capet." They affected to regard liberty as a divinity, and a courtesan, in the conventional costume of that divinity, was paraded in a car through the streets as the Goddess of Liberty.

[a] April 12, 1793. He sent[a] a most unwelcome letter to the Secretary of State. "War," he wrote, "having actually commenced between France and Great Britain, it behooves the government of this country to use every means in its power to prevent the citizens thereof from embroiling us with either of those powers, by endeavoring to maintain a strict neutrality." He required Mr. Jefferson to give the subject his careful thought, and lay his views before him on his arrival in Philadelphia. A similar letter was sent to the head of every other department.

Washington reached Philadelphia on the 17th of April, and on the 19th held a Cabinet council. It was agreed that the President should issue a proclamation of neutrality, warning citizens of the United States not to take part in the kindling war. At the same meeting it was agreed that the minister of the French Republic should be received.[1]

The President's proclamation of neutrality was issued on the 22d of April, and was assailed with the greatest vehemence by the "French party," as the Republicans were called. Reverence for the President's character and position was forgotten in the storm of passion that ensued. The proclamation was styled a "royal edict," a "daring and unwarrantable assumption of executive power," and was pointed at as an open manifestation by the President and his political friends of partiality for England, a bitter foe, and hostility to France, a warm friend and ancient ally. It is fair to infer, from the tone of his private letters at that time, that the Secretary of State (who voted very reluctantly in the Cabinet for the proclamation), governed by his almost fanatical hatred of Hamilton, and his sympathies with the French regicides, secretly promoted a public feeling hostile to the administration.[2]

---

[1] The following is a copy of the President's proclamation:

"Whereas it appears that a state of war exists between Austria, Prussia, Sardinia, Great Britain, and the United Netherlands on the one part, and France on the other, and the duty and interests of the United States require that they should, with sincerity and good faith, adopt and pursue a conduct friendly and impartial toward the belligerent powers:

"I have therefore thought fit, by these presents, to declare the disposition of the United States to observe the conduct aforesaid toward those powers respectively, and to exhort and to warn the citizens of the United States carefully to avoid all acts and proceedings whatsoever which may in any manner tend to contravene such disposition.

"And I do hereby make known, that whosoever of the citizens of the United States shall render himself liable to punishment or forfeiture under the law of nations, by committing, aiding, or abetting hostilities against any of the said powers, or by carrying to any of them those articles which are deemed contraband by the modern usage of nations, will not receive the protection of the United States against such punishment or forfeiture; and farther, that I have given instructions to those officers to whom it belongs to cause prosecutions to be instituted against all persons who shall, within the cognizance of the courts of the United States, violate the laws of nations with respect to the powers at war, or any one of them. In testimony whereof, etc., etc. Signed, GEORGE WASHINGTON."

[2] It is an unpleasant duty to arraign men whom the nation delights to honor as tried patriots, on a charge of complicity with those who at one time would have wrecked the government upon the rocks of anarchy, not designedly, perhaps, but nevertheless effectually. But historic truth sometimes demands it, as in the case before us. Mr. Jefferson was openly opposed to the policy of Washington's administration. This was manly. But it was not manly to be a covert enemy. He always denied any complicity with Freneau, his translating clerk, in his coarse abuse of Washington and his political friends, while Jefferson was Secretary of State; but the very minutes made by Mr. Jefferson himself, and printed in his *Anas*, sufficiently indicate his relative position to Freneau at that time. He says that at a Cabinet council Washington spoke harshly of Freneau, who impudently sent him three copies of his paper every day, filled with abuse of the administration. "He could see nothing in it," Jefferson recorded, "but an impudent design to insult him: he ended in a high tone." Again Jefferson says, "He [the President] adverted to a piece in Freneau's paper of yesterday. He said he despised all their attacks on him personally, but that there had never been an act of the government, not meaning in the executive line only, but in any line, which that paper had not abused. . . . He was evidently sore and warm, and I took his intention to be, that I should interpose in some way with Freneau, perhaps withdraw his appointment of translating clerk in my office. But I will not do it. His paper has saved our Constitution, which was galloping fast into monarchy, and has been checked by no one means so powerfully as by that paper. It is well and universally known that it has been that paper which has checked the career of the monocrats."—*Memoir and Correspondence of Jefferson*, London edition, iv., 497. But the evidence against Mr. Jefferson in this matter is not entirely circumstantial. The late Dr. John W. Francis, of New York, who was Freneau's physician in the latter years of his life, informed the author that it was one of the most poignant griefs of that journalist that he had seemed to be an enemy of Washington. He assured Dr. Francis that the *National Gazette* was entirely under the control of Mr. Jefferson, and that the Secretary *dictated or wrote the most violent attacks on Washington and his political friends.* The only excuse for the conduct of Mr. Jefferson at that time is political monomania.

CHAPTER IV.

"While France her huge limbs bathes recumbent in blood,
And society's base threats with wide desolation,
May Peace, like the dove who returned from the flood,
Find an ark of abode in our mild Constitution.
But though peace is our aim,
Yet the boon we disclaim
If bought by our Sovereignty, Justice, or Fame;
For ne'er shall the sons of Columbia be slaves
While the earth bears a plant, or the sea rolls its waves."
ROBERT TREAT PAINE.

HE wisdom and timeliness of Washington's proclamation of neutrality was soon made manifest. Genet came with blank commissions for naval and military service, and proceeded to fit out two privateers at Charleston. He was also empowered to give authority to every French consul in the United States to constitute himself a court of admiralty, to dispose of prizes captured by French cruisers and brought into American ports. In defiance of the proclamation, his privateers, manned principally by American citizens, sailed from Charleston, with the consent and good wishes of the governor and citizens, to depredate on British commerce.[1]

One of these privateers was *L'Embuscade*, the frigate that brought Genet to our shores. She went prowling up the coast, seizing several vessels, and at last captured a fine British merchantman, named *The Grange*, within the Capes of the Delaware, when she proceeded to Philadelphia in triumphant attitude.[a] Her arrival was greeted by a great assemblage of people on the brink of the river. "When the British colors were seen reversed," Jefferson wrote to Madison, "and the French flying above them, the people burst into peals of exultation." Upon her head, her foremast, and her stern, liberty-caps were conspicuous; and from her masts floated white burgees, with words that echoed the egotistic proclamation of the French National Convention.[2]

[a] May 2, 1793.

L'Embuscade was the precursor of the French minister, who arrived at Philadelphia fourteen days later.[b] According to preconcert, a number of citizens met him at the Schuylkill and escorted him to the city, in the midst of the roar of cannon and the ringing of bells. There he received addresses from societies and the citizens at large; and so anxious were his admirers to pay homage to their idol, that he was invited to a public dinner before he presented his credentials to the President of the United States!

[b] May 16.

At that presentation, which occurred on the 19th,[c] the minister's pride was touched, and his hopeful ardor was chilled. He found himself in an atmos-

[c] May.

---

[1] General William Moultrie, the heroic patriot of the Revolution, was then Governor of South Carolina. A wit of the day wrote:

"On that blest day when first we came to land,
Great Mr. Moultrie took us by the hand;
Surveyed the ships, admired the motley crew,
And o'er the envoy friendship's mantle threw;
Received the *sans-culotte* with soft embrace,
And bade him welcome with the kindliest grace."

[2] From her foremast were displayed the words, "Enemies of equality, reform or tremble;" from her mainmast, "Freemen, we are your friends and brethren;" from the mizzen-mast, "We are armed for the defense of the rights of man." *L'Embuscade* saluted the vast crowd with fifteen guns, and was responded to on shore by cheers, and gun for gun.

phere of the most profound dignity in the presence of Washington; and he was made to realize his own littleness while standing before that noble representative of the best men and the soundest principles of the American Republic. He withdrew from the audience abashed and subdued. He had heard sentiments of sincere regard for the French nation that touched the sensibilities of his heart, and he had felt, in the genuine courtesy and severe simplicity and frankness of the President's manner, wholly free from effervescent enthusiasm, a withering rebuke, not only of the adulators in public places, but also of his own pretentious aspirations and ungenerous duplicity.[1]

Genet affected to be shocked by the evidences of monarchical sympathies in the President's house.[2] He was supremely happy when he was permitted to escape from the frigidity of truth, virtue, and dignity into the fervid atmosphere of a banquet-hall filled with his "friends."[a] There his ears were greeted with the stirring Marseilles Hymn, an ode in French, composed for the occasion,[3] and toasts brimful of "Liberty and Equality." There his eyes were delighted with a "tree of liberty" upon the table, and the flags of the two nations in fraternal enfoldings. There his heart was made glad by having the red cap of liberty placed upon his own head first, and then upon the head of each guest, while the wearer, under the inspiration of its symbolism—

[a] May 23, 1793.

> "That sacred Cap, which fools in order sped
> In grand rotation, round from head to head"—

uttered some patriotic sentiment. There his hopes of success were made to bud anew as he saw the officers and sailors of the privateer receive a "fraternal embrace" from each guest, and bear away to the robber the flags of the two nations amid the cheers of the convivialists.

Genet's presence intensified the party spirit of the Republicans. "Democratic Societies," in imitation of the Jacobin Clubs of France, were formed, secret in their proceedings, and disloyal in the extreme in their practice at that time. In servile imitation of their prototypes, they adopted the peculiar phrases of the populace of Paris;[4] and a powerful faction was soon visible, more French than American in their habits of thought and political principles. By some strange infatuation, sensible and patriotic men were drawn into the toils of the charmer, and they sanctioned and participated in scenes which composed a most astounding and humiliating farce.[5]

---

[1] Genet's address to Washington was full of friendly professions. "It was impossible," Jefferson wrote to Madison, "for any thing to be more affectionate, more magnanimous than the purport of Genet's mission. . . . He offers every thing, and asks nothing." And yet, while making these professions, he had secret instructions in his pocket to foment discord between the United States and Great Britain, and to set the American government at defiance, if necessary, in the execution of his designs. He had already openly insulted that government by his acts at Charleston—a city which, on that occasion as on subsequent ones, earned the "bad eminence" of standing alone in the attitude of disloyalty to the national government.

[2] He was "astonished and indignant" at seeing a bust of Louis XVI. in the vestibule, and complained of it to his "friends" as an "insult to France." He was equally "astonished" by discovering in the President's parlor "certain medallions of Capet and his family;" and he was "shocked to learn" that the Marquis De Noailles (a relative of Madame Lafayette) and other emigrant Frenchmen had lately been admitted to the presence of Washington. Indeed he found most things disagreeable outside of the charmed circle of his "friends."

[3] This was written by "Citizen Duponceau," of Philadelphia, a worthy French gentleman, who came to America with the Baron De Steuben, and was for many years a distinguished citizen of Pennsylvania. The ode was translated into English at the table by Freneau, the translating clerk of the Secretary of State, and then sung again.

[4] "The title of *citizen*," says Griswold, "became as common in Philadelphia as in Paris, and in the newspapers it was the fashion to announce marriages as partnerships between Citizen Brown, Smith, or Jones and the *citess* who had been wooed to such an association."—*Republican Court*, p. 350.

[5] "At a dinner at which Governor Mifflin was present, a roasted pig received the name of the murdered French king, and the head, severed from the body, was carried round to each of the guests, who, after placing the liberty-cap on his own head, pronounced the word 'tyrant,' and proceeded to mangle with his knife that of the luckless creature doomed to be served for so unworthy a company. One of the Democratic taverns displayed as a sign a revolting picture of the mutilated and bloody corpse of Marie Antoinette."*—Republican Court*, p. 350. Strange as it may seem, Jefferson was so influenced by his prejudices at that time that he shut his eyes, apparently, to all passing events, and could write to Mad-

---

* Marie Antoinette, the unhappy queen of Louis XVI., became the victim of Jacobin malignity, and was beheaded on the 16th of October, 1793. She was a daughter of the Emperor of Austria, and is represented as a beautiful and accomplished woman. Her murderers accused and convicted her of crimes of which they knew she was innocent. She was taken to the scaffold on a cart. Her body was cast into the Magdalen church-yard, and immediately consumed with quick-lime! The fiends denied her a grave.

But the ludicrous picture of Genet's reception in Philadelphia was relieved by a dignified act. On the day of his arrival in that city, an address, signed by three hundred merchants and other substantial men of that city, in which was expressed the soundest loyalty to the letter and spirit of his proclamation of neutrality, was presented to President Washington.

Similar enthusiasm for the French cause was manifested in New York and a few other places, but the citizens were never obnoxious to the charge of overt disloyalty to the government. Although the *Carmagnole*[1] was sung hourly in the streets, and Democratic societies fanned the zeal for the Jacobin system of government into intemperate heat, the citizens, as such, remained loyal to the Constitution and the laws.[2]

The government, unawed by the storm of passion that beat upon it, went steadily forward in the path of right and duty. *The Grange* was restored to its British owners, and the privateers were ordered to leave the American waters. Orders were sent to the collectors of all the ports of the United States for the seizure of all vessels fitted out as privateers, and to prevent the sale of any prizes captured by such vessels. Americans from one of the privateers fitted out at Charleston were arrested and indicted for a violation of law; and Chief Justice Jay declared it to be the duty of grand juries to present all persons guilty of such violation of the laws of nations with respect to any of the belligerent powers.

These measures greatly irritated the French minister and his American partisans. He protested; and the Secretary of State, soon finding him to be a troublesome friend, reiterated the opinions of the President, and plainly told him that, by commissioning privateers, he had violated the sovereignty of the United States, and that it was expected that *The Genet* and *L'Embuscade* (the two privateers fitted out at Charleston) would leave the American waters forthwith.

ison, after expressing his opinion that Genet's magnanimous offers would not be received, "It is evident that one or two of the Cabinet [meaning Hamilton and Knox], at least, under pretense of avoiding war on the one side, have no great antipathy to run foul of it on the other, and to make a part in the confederacy of princes against human liberty."

[1] A dance, with singing, performed in the streets of Paris during the French Revolution. See page 60.
[2] These societies and the newspapers in their interest attempted to deceive the people by comparing the French Revolution to their own, as equally justified and holy. Many, totally ignorant of the facts, believed; but enlightenment and better counsels kept their passions in check. The informed and thoughtful saw no just comparison between the two Revolutions.

THE CONTRAST.

The aspect of dignity, decorum, gravity, order, and religious solemnity so conspicuous in the American Revolution was wholly wanting in that of the French. "When I find," Hamilton wrote to Washington, "the doctrines of atheism openly advanced in the Convention, and heard with loud applauses; when I see the sword of fanaticism extended to enforce a political creed upon citizens who were invited to submit to the arms of France as the harbingers of liberty; when I behold the hand of rapacity outstretched to prostrate and ravish the monuments of religious worship erected by those citizens and their ancestors; when I perceive passion, tumult, and violence usurping those seats where reason and cool deliberation ought to preside—I acknowledge that I am glad to believe there is no real resemblance between what was the cause of America and what is the cause of France." The difference between *American liberty* and *French liberty* was graphically illustrated by a print called *The Contrast*, of which our engraving is a reduced copy.

Genet, with offensive pertinacity, denounced this doctrine as contrary to right, justice, and the law of nations, and threatened "to appeal from the President to the people." The Republican papers sustained him in his course.[1] The Democratic societies became more bold and active; and Genet, mistaking the popular clamor in his favor for the deliberate voice of the nation, actually undertook to fit out as a privateer at Philadelphia, during the absence of the President at Mount Vernon, under the very eyes of the national government, a British vessel that had been captured and brought in there by *L'Embuscade*, and which he named in French *The Little Democrat*. Mifflin, the Democratic Governor of Pennsylvania, interfered, and threatened to seize the vessel if Genet persisted in his course. The minister refused to listen.

Jefferson begged him to desist until the return of the President. Genet spurned his kind words, and raved like a madman. He declared his determination to send *The Little Democrat* to sea, complained that he had been thwarted in all his undertakings by the government, denounced the President as unfaithful to the wishes of the people, and resolved to press him to call the Congress together to act upon the subjects in dispute.[2]

Genet's official and private conduct became equally offensive; and when, on Washington's return to the seat of government, it was recited to him, his indignation was aroused. "Is the minister of the French Republic to set the acts of the government at defiance *with impunity?*" he asked. His Cabinet answered No. Forbearance toward the insolent minister was no longer required by the most exacting courtesy, and it was agreed in Cabinet council that the French government should be requested to recall him because he was offensive to that of the United States. Jefferson had become disgusted with him, and the tone of popular sentiment soon became more sensible and patriotic. His reiterated threat of appealing from the President to the people—in other words, to excite an insurrection for the purpose of overthrowing the government—had shocked the national pride; and many considerate Republicans,

---

[1] A writer in Freneau's *Gazette* said, "I hope the minister of France will act with firmness and spirit. The *people* are his friends, or the friends of France, and he will have nothing to apprehend; for, *as yet*, the people are the sovereigns of the United States. Too much complacency is an injury done to his cause; for, as every advantage is already taken of France (not by the *people*), farther condescension may lead to farther abuse. If one of the leading features of our government is pusillanimity when the British lion shows his teeth, let France and her minister act as becomes the dignity of her cause, and the honor and faith of nations."

Freneau's paper, at that time, was assisted in its attacks upon the government by the *General Advertiser* (afterward known as the *Aurora*), edited by B. F. Bache, a grandson of Dr. Franklin, who had been educated in France. It was even more violent and abusive than its colleague, and even charged Washington with an intention of joining in the league of kings and priests against the French Republic!

[2] Genet was intrusted by his government with bolder schemes than the fitting out of privateers. He was to organize what are called in our day "filibustering expeditions," on an extensive scale, against the Spanish dominions, the object being no less than the seizure of Florida and New Orleans. An expedition against the former was to be organized in South Carolina, and against the latter in Kentucky. The one in the Mississippi Valley was to be led by General George Rogers Clarke, the conqueror of the Northwest, to whom was given the magniloquent title of "Major General in the Armies of France, and Commander-in-chief of the French Revolutionary Legions on the Mississippi." Funds for carrying on these expeditions were to be derived from the payment to the minister, by the United States, of a portion of the national debt due to France. French emissaries were employed in South Carolina and Kentucky, and in the latter district, the public mind, irritated by the Spanish obstructions to the navigation of the Mississippi, was very favorable to the movement. The failure of Genet's mission put an end to these schemes of conquest, not, however, until they had produced annoying effects upon the national government.

A Reaction.   *Genet recalled.*   *His Successor.*   *Biographical Sketch of Genet.*

who had been zealous in the cause of the Revolution in France, paused while listening to the audacious words of a foreigner who presumed to dictate the course of conduct to be pursued by the beloved Washington. The tide turned. Very soon there were demonstrations throughout the Union of agreement with the proclamation of neutrality, which the partisans of Genet never dreamed of, and a strong and irresistible reaction in favor of the national government speedily manifested itself on every hand.

Genet[1] was recalled, and M. Fouchet, a man equally indiscreet, was

appointed his successor. At the close of the year, Mr. Jefferson, whose views of French affairs had become much modified by the course of events at home and abroad, left the Cabinet and retired to private life, much to the regret of Washington, who found in him an able minister of state. Jefferson was a patriot, but, for several years, his jealousy and hatred of Hamilton and his friends made him a political monomaniac.

While the government of the United States, unswayed by the popular sentiment in favor of France, and national resentment against Great Britain, had hastened, on the breaking out of war between those two countries, to adopt a strictly neutral policy, thereby showing great magnanimity and a conciliatory spirit toward the late enemy in the field, that enemy, inimical still, was pursuing a selfish and ungenerous course, which the wisest and best men of England deplored. Regardless of the opinions of Europe expressed in the treaty for an armed neutrality in 1780,[2] she revived the rule of war laid down by herself alone in

---

[1] Mr. Genet never returned to France. At about the time of his recall, a change of faction had taken place in his country, and he thought it prudent not to return. He remained, married a daughter of George Clinton, Governor of the State of New York, and became an ornament to American society. It is only of his official conduct, while the minister of the French Jacobin government, that Americans have reason to complain of him. He was a man of eminent abilities. At the time of his arrival in the United States, he was a few months more than thirty years of age, having been born in January, 1763. He was a precocious boy, and from childhood was engaged in public employments. He was attached to the embassies at Berlin, Vienna, London, and St. Petersburg. Because of a spirited letter which he wrote to the Emperor of Russia, indignantly protesting against his expulsion from his dominions after the death of Louis XVI., he became a favorite of the French revolutionists. He was made adjutant general of the armies of France and minister to Holland, and was employed in revolutionizing Geneva and annexing it to France. He was finally sent to America as minister and consul general. He was twice married. His second wife was the daughter of Mr. Osgood, the first Postmaster General under the Constitution. He took great interest in agriculture, and his last illness was occasioned by his attendance at the meeting of an agricultural society of which he was president. He died at his seat on Prospect Hill, near Greenbush, opposite Albany, on the 14th of July, 1834.* One of his sisters was the celebrated Madame Campan, and another was Madame Anguie, mother-in-law of the distinguished Marshal Ney. Mr. Genet often spoke of the wisdom of Washington and his administration, the folly of his own countrymen at that time and of their admirers in America, and rejoiced that the proclamation of neutrality defeated his wild schemes.

[2] During the American Revolution the superior maritime power of Great Britain was able to damage the commerce

---

* Genet was buried in the grave-yard of the Reformed Dutch Church at Greenbush. Upon a plain marble tablet placed over his remains is the following inscription:

"Under this humble stone are interred the remains of EDMUND CHARLES GENET, late Adjutant General, Minister Plenipotentiary and Consul General from the French Republic to the United States of America. He was born at Versailles, parish of St. Louis, in France, January 8, 1763, and died at Prospect Hill, town of Greenbush, July 14, 1834.

"Driven by the storms of the Revolution to the shades of retirement, he devoted his talents to his adopted country, where he cherished the love of liberty and virtue. The pursuits of literature and science enlivened his peaceful solitude, and he devoted his time to usefulness and benevolence. His last moments were like his life, an example of fortitude and true Christian philosophy. His heart was love and friendship's sun, which has set on this transitory world, to rise with radiant splendor beyond the grave."

1756,[1] and first by a "provisional order in council," as it was called, issued in June, 1793,[2] and then by another order in council, issued in November following,[a] and secretly promulgated, she struck heavy blows at her antagonist, regardless of the fact that they fell almost as heavily upon those who favored her by neutrality. Citizens of the United States were then carrying on an extensive trade with the French West India Islands, whose ports had been opened to neutrals for the same reasons as in 1756, and felt no apprehension of interference from any source. But Great Britain had determined to again apply her starvation measures against her old enemy, and a secret order in council was issued, and silently circulated among the British cruisers, without the least notice or intimation to the American merchants, directing all vessels engaged in trading with any colony of France to be taken into British ports for adjudication in the courts of admiralty.[3]

[a] November 6, 1793.

This lawless invasion of neutral rights, conducted secretly and treacherously, prostrated at one blow a great portion of American commerce. The property of American merchants to the amount of many millions of dollars was swept from the seas into British ports and lost. This was regarded as little better than highway robbery, judged by the law of nations and common justice.

When intelligence of this high-handed measure reached the United States, it produced the hottest indignation throughout the land. Political strife instantly ceased, and both parties were equally zealous in denunciations of the treachery and aggressions of Great Britain, for which she offered no other excuse than expediency, growing out of her evident determination to maintain her boasted position of "mistress of the seas," regardless of the rights of all the rest of the world. Congress was then in session, and measures were proposed for retaliation, such as reprisals, embargoes, se-

---

of other European nations immensely. The British government revived the rule of 1756, below mentioned, and infringed largely upon neutral commerce. To resist these encroachments, and to protect neutral maritime rights, Russia, Sweden, Denmark, and Holland formed a treaty of alliance, which they denominated The Armed Neutrality, by which they pledged themselves to support, at the hazard of war, if necessary, the following principles: 1. That it should be lawful for any ships to sail freely from one port to another, or along the coast of the powers at war. 2. That all merchandise and effects belonging to the subjects of the belligerent powers, and shipped in neutral bottoms, should be entirely free; that is, free ships make free goods. 3. That no place should be considered blockaded except the besieging power had taken a station so as to expose to imminent danger any ship attempting to sail in or out of such ports. 4. That no neutral ships should be stopped without material and well-grounded cause; and, in such cases, justice should be done them without delay." The British navy triumphed over all opposition, the designs of the armed neutrality were defeated, and Holland was made a party to the war with the Americans and France. A similar attempt to restrict the maritime power of Great Britain was made in the year 1800, which resulted in the destruction of the Danish fleet before Copenhagen in April, 1801. Soon after this The Armed Neutrality was dissolved, and the dominion of the seas was accorded to England.

[1] When the war between Great Britain and France was formally declared in 1756, the former power announced, as a principle of national law, "that no other trade should be allowed to neutrals with the colonies of a belligerent in time of war than what is allowed by the parent state in time of peace." This was in direct opposition to the law of nations promulgated by Frederick the Great, of Prussia, namely, "the goods of an enemy can not be taken from on board the ships of a friend;" and also in direct violation of a treaty between England and Holland, in which it was stipulated expressly that "free ships make free goods"—that the neutral should enter safely and unmolested all the harbors of the belligerents, unless they were blockaded or besieged. England not only violated the treaty, but, having the might, exercised the right of invading the sovereignty of Holland, and capturing its vessels whose cargoes might be useful for her navy. This assumption—this dictation of law to the nations to suit her own selfish purposes—turned against England the denunciations of the civilized world, and which for more than a century she has never ceased to receive. At that time her "law" was aimed directly at France, then much the weaker naval power. Unable to maintain her accustomed trade with her West India Islands, she opened their ports to neutrals. It was to destroy the trade by neutrals, so lucrative to them and so beneficial to France, that Great Britain introduced that new principle of national law.

[2] This order, intended as a starvation measure against France, declared that all vessels laden wholly or in part with breadstuffs, bound to any port of France, or places occupied by French armies, should be carried into England, and their cargoes either disposed of there, or security given that they should be sold only in ports of a country in friendship with Great Britain. This order was issued on the 8th of June, 1793.

[3] The following is a copy of the order:

"George R.: Additional instructions to all ships of war, privateers, etc.:

"That they shall stop and detain all ships laden with goods the produce of any colony belonging to France, or conveying provisions or other supplies for the use of such colonies; and shall bring the same, with their cargoes, to legal adjudication in our courts of admiralty. By his majesty's command. Signed, DUNDAS.

"November 6, 1793."

So secretly was this order issued that the first account of its existence reached the London Exchange with the details of several captures which it authorized and occasioned. And Mr. Pinckney, the American minister, was unable to procure a copy of it until the 25th of December, more than six weeks after it was issued.—*Pinckney's letter to his government, December 26, 1793.*

questrations, and even war. The whole country was violently agitated; and the excitement was increased by events on the Indian frontier, already mentioned, showing the hand of British influence in the bloody battles in the Northwest.

Another and more serious element of discord between the two nations came up for consideration, and which, in after years, was one of the immediate causes of open hostilities between the two countries. This was the impressment of American seamen into the British service. In efforts to maintain her position of "mistress of the seas," Great Britain found herself under the necessity of announcing another "law of nations" to suit her particular case. High wages, humane treatment, and security from danger, to be found in the American merchant service, had attracted a great many British seamen to it. Their government, alarmed at the threatened weakening of its naval power by this drain, planted itself upon the theory that a subject can not expatriate himself—once an Englishman, always an Englishman; proclaimed the doctrine that in time of war the government had a right to the services of every subject; and that, at the command of their sovereign, every natural-born subject was bound to return and fight the battles of his country. In accordance with this doctrine a proclamation was issued, by which authority was given to the commanders of British ships of war to make up any deficiency in their crews by pressing into their service British-born seamen wherever found, not within the immediate jurisdiction of any foreign state. Under this authority many American merchant vessels were crippled, while in mid-ocean, by British seamen being taken from them. Nor were subjects of Great Britain alone taken. It was sometimes difficult to discover the nationality of English and American seamen; and as the British commanders were not very nice in their scrutiny, native-born Americans were frequently dragged on board British war vessels, and kept in servitude in the royal navy for years. This was a great and irritating grievance.

War with Great Britain now seemed inevitable. To avert it was Washington's most anxious desire. To do so, and maintain strict neutrality, was a difficult task. He resolved to try negotiation. He well knew that the temper of his countrymen would oppose it. With a moral heroism commensurate with the occasion, he nominated John Jay, the Chief Justice of the United States, as envoy extraordinary to the Court of Great Britain, to negotiate for a settlement of all matters in dispute between the two governments. The proposition was met with a storm of indignation. It was scouted as pusillanimous. The Democratic societies and Democratic newspapers were aroused into uncommon activity. The tri-colored cockade was seen on every side, and the partisans of the French regicides ruled the hour. Better counsels prevailed in the Senate, and on the 19th of April[a] that body confirmed the nomination by a vote of eighteen to eight. On the 12th of May following, Mr. Jay sailed from New York for London.

[a] 1794.

The French "Republic," meanwhile, had become offended with the United States because of the virtual dismissal of Genet, and demanded the recall of Mr. Morris.

| The Fall of the French Jacobins. | Minister Monroe in Paris. | Jay's Treaty with Great Britain. |

Washington prudently complied, and appointed James Monroe in his place. The latter arrived in France at an auspicious moment.[a] Intelligence of the new American mission to England had aroused the most bitter enmity toward the United States among the violent leaders of the National Convention. But their bloody rule was at an end. Robespierre and his fiendish associates had fallen. For some time they had been hated in the Convention. At length Billaud Varennes mounted the tribune, and, in a speech full of invective, denounced Robespierre as a tyrant.[b] The accused attempted to speak. "Down with the tyrant!" burst from many a lip, and he and his guilty colleagues were dragged to execution amid the shouts of the populace, who had huzzaed as loudly when the king was murdered. With their fall the dreadful Reign of Terror ended. The Jacobin society was suppressed. Reason and conscience were asserting their sway in the Convention. The nation breathed freer, and the curtain fell on one of the bloodiest tragedies in the history of the human race.

[a] August, 1794.
[b] July 26, 1794.

Monroe was received with great cordiality. He sent a judicious letter to the President of the Convention. Its sentiments were consonant with the feelings of the hour. When he afterward entered the hall of the Convention the president embraced him affectionately. It was decreed that the flags of the two nations should be entwined and hung up there, in token of international union and friendship; and Monroe, with reciprocal courtesy, presented the banner of his country to the Convention in the name of the American people. The Convention, in turn, resolved to present their national flag to the President of the United States.

Jay's mission to England was partially successful. He found many obstacles to contend with. He entered upon the business in June, with Lord Grenville, and on the 19th of November following, the contracting parties signed a treaty of amity, commerce, and navigation. Although Mr. Jay accomplished much less than his instructions directed him to ask for, the treaty was a long step in the direction of right, justice, and national prosperity, and led to the execution, to a great extent, of the Treaty of 1783. It also laid the solid foundation of the commercial policy of the United States.[1]

Jay's treaty was doomed to a severe trial, and, with it, the administration, the Constitution, and even the republic itself. The Democrats had resolved to oppose it, whatever might be its provisions, especially if it should remove all pretexts for a war

---

[1] The treaty provided for the establishment of commissions to determine the eastern boundary of the United States, then in dispute; the amount of losses incurred by British subjects by impediments being thrown in the way of collecting debts in the United States incurred before the Revolution; and to ascertain and estimate the losses of the Americans by irregular and illegal captures by British cruisers, such losses to be paid by the British government. It was provided that the Western military posts should be given up on the 1st of June, 1796, in consideration of the adjustment of the ante-Revolutionary debts. The Indian trade was left open to both nations, the British being allowed to enter all American harbors, with the right to ascend all rivers to the highest port of entry. This was not reciprocated in full. Americans were not allowed free navigation of the rivers in the Hudson's Bay Company's possessions, nor those of others of the British colonial possessions in America, except *above* the highest ports of entry. The citizens or subjects of each government holding lands in the dominions of the other government were to continue to hold them without alienage, nor were confiscations of the property of such persons to be allowed. In a word, the existing conditions of property should not be disturbed. Such are the substantial provisions in the first ten articles of the treaty, which were declared to be perpetual. The remaining eighteen, having special reference to commerce and navigation, were limited in their operations to two years after the termination of the war in which Great Britain was then engaged. American vessels were allowed to enter the British ports in Europe and the East Indies on equal terms with those of British vessels, while participation in the East India coasting-trade, and trade between European and British East Indian ports, was left to the contingency of British permission. The British were permitted to meet the discrimination in the American tonnage and import duties by countervailing measures. American vessels not exceeding seventy tons were allowed to trade to the British West Indies on condition that they should not, during the continuance of the treaty, transport from America to Europe any of the principal colonial products. British vessels were to be admitted into American ports on terms equal to the most favored nations. There were provisions made favorable to neutral property on the high seas, and that a vessel entering a blockaded port should not be liable to capture unless previously notified of the blockade. There were satisfactory arrangements made concerning enlistments; of courtesy between ships of war and privateers of the two countries; to prevent the arming of privateers of any nation at war with the two contracting parties, and the capture of goods in the bays and harbors of the parties. In the event of war between the two countries, the citizens or subjects of either should not be molested, if peaceable; and fugitives from justice, charged with high crimes, to be mutually given up.*

* The Treaty in full may be found in the *Statesman's Manual*, iv., 298.

Violent Opposition to the Treaty.   Its Friends assailed.   Secession proposed by Virginians.

with Great Britain. It reached the President early in March,[a] but the Senate were not convened to consider it until June.[b] Meanwhile an unfaithful Cabinet minister (Mr. Randolph, of Virginia) revealed enough of its character to warrant attacks upon it. The mad, seditious cry of faction was immediately raised in the Democratic societies and spread among the people.[1]

[a] March 5, 1795.
[b] June 8.

The Senate finally voted to ratify the treaty, and it was published to the world.[2] Then the opposition opened upon it their heaviest batteries of abuse. The chief targets for their shot were its provisions for the payment of honest debts contracted before the Revolution, and the omission to provide for the remuneration of slaveholders for their negroes carried away during that war. As the Constitution of the United States, and the public sentiment and judicial decisions of Great Britain did not recognize man as property,[3] the claim relating to slaves in the old treaty was passed over.

The author of the treaty, the approving senators, the administration, and the President personally, were violently assailed. The treaty was declared to be a token of national cowardice; an insult to the American people; a covert blow at France, their old ally. Bold attempts were made to intimidate the President and prevent his signing it. Public meetings were held all over the country, at which the most violent language and seditious suggestions and menaces were made. A mob in Philadelphia paraded in the streets with effigies of Jay and the ratifying senators.[4] A meeting in Boston denounced the treaty as containing not one article " honorable or beneficial to the United States." Hamilton and other speakers in favor of the treaty were stoned at a public meeting in New York, not only by a low mob, but by decent people.[5] South Carolinians called Jay a " traitor," longed for a guillotine, trailed the British flag in the dust of the streets of Charleston, and burned it at the door of the British consul; while Virginians, ever ready with the grand panacea of *disunion* for political evils, offered their prescription in emphatic if not elegant language.[6]

---

[1] The following is a specimen of those factious cries: "Americans, awake! Remember what you suffered through a seven years' war with the satellites of George the Third (and I hope the last). Recollect the services rendered by your allies, now contending for liberty. Blush to think that America should degrade herself so much as to enter into *any kind of treaty* with a power, now tottering on the brink of ruin, whose principles are directly contrary to the spirit of republicanism. The United States are a republic. Is it advantageous to a republic to have a connection with a monarch? Treaties lead to war, and war is the bane of a republican government.... France is our natural ally; she has a government congenial with our own.... The nation *on whom our political existence depends* we have treated with indifference bordering on contempt.... *Citizens,* your security depends on France.... Let us unite with France, and stand or fall together."

[2] The Senate, on voting to recommend the ratification of the treaty, removed the seal of secrecy, but forbade the publication of the treaty itself, for prudential reasons connected with measures for ascertaining the construction by the English of the order of the 8th of June, 1793 (see page 84), which, it was rumored, had just been renewed. Regardless alike of the rules of the Senate, of official decorum, and of personal honor, Senator Thomson Mason, of Virginia, sent a copy of it to the *Aurora* newspaper, the bitter enemy of the administration, and a full abstract of it was published therein on the 2d of July. A poet of the day thus ironically addressed Mr. Mason:

" Ah, Thomson Mason! long thy fame shall rise
With Democratic incense to the skies!
Long shall the world admire thy manly soul,
Which scorned the haughty Senate's base control;
Came boldly forward with thy weighty name,
And gave the treaty up for public game!"—*The Echo.*

[3] In 1697 an English court decided that "negroes being usually bought and sold among merchants as merchandise, and *also being infidels*, there might be a property in them sufficient to maintain trover." In 1702 Chief Justice Holt decided that "so soon as a negro lands in England he is free." To this Cowper alluded when he said, "Slaves can not breathe in England." Holt also decided that "there is no such thing as a slave by the law of England." Just before the kindling of the Revolution these decisions were reaffirmed by Chief Justice Lord Mansfield in the case of James Somerset, a native of Africa, who had been carried to Virginia, sold as a slave, and taken to England by his master, where he was induced to assert his freedom.

[4] That of Jay bore a pair of scales: one was labeled "*American liberty and independence*," and the other, which greatly preponderated, "*British gold.*" From the mouth of the figure proceeded the words, " *Come up to my price, and I will sell you my country.*"

[5] "These are hard arguments," said Hamilton, who was hit a glancing blow upon the forehead by one of the stones. "Edward Livingston," says the late Dr. Francis, in his *Old and New York* (" afterward so celebrated for his Louisiana Code"), was, I am informed, one of the violent young men by whom the stones were thrown."

[6] "Notice is hereby given," said a Richmond paper (July 31, 1795), "that in case the treaty entered into by that damned arch-traitor, John Jay, with the British tyrant should be ratified, a petition will be presented to the next General Assembly of Virginia at the next session, praying that the said state may recede from the Union, and be under the government of one hundred thousand free and independent Virginians.

"P.S. As it is the wish of the people of the said state to enter into a treaty of amity, commerce, and navigation with

None of these things moved Washington. He signed the treaty, and awaited calmly to see the storm pass by. It did so, and the foundations of the government were found to be stronger than ever. It was, says Lyman, "the first act of the government that proved the stability of the Federal Constitution. It was a severe trial, and the steadiness with which the shock was borne may be attributed, in some degree, to the personal character of the President."[1] In after years, when the republic was menaced by internal factions and external foes, the result of the conflict over "Jay's Treaty" was pointed to as a warrant for faith and hope.

While these unpleasant relations with Great Britain and France were exciting the people of the United States, the government was sorely perplexed by other events at home and abroad. At home there had been, for a long time, much discontent on account of excise laws which levied a duty on domestic distilled liquors. These discontents were fanned into a flame by the Democratic societies, and, in the summer of 1794, the inhabitants of some of the western counties of Pennsylvania arrayed themselves in armed opposition to the authority of the national government. A formidable insurrection prevailed. Buildings were burned, mails were robbed, and government officers were insulted and abused. At one time there were nearly seven thousand insurgents in arms, many of them being the militia of the country, who had assembled at the call of rebel leaders. The insurgent spirit also infected the border counties of Virginia.

The President perceived with alarm this imitation of the lawlessness of French politics, then so assiduously propagated, and took immediate steps to crush the growing monster. He first issued two warning proclamations.[a] They were unheeded. After exhausting all peaceable means for the restoration of order, he sent a large body of Pennsylvania, New Jersey, Virginia, and Maryland troops, under General Henry Lee (then Governor of Virginia), into the disaffected district. This argument was effectual; and very soon the outbreak, known in history as the "Whisky Insurrection," like that of Shays's in Massachusetts a few years earlier, was subdued and thoroughly allayed. This alarming insurrection was ended without the shedding of a drop of blood—a result chiefly due to the prompt energy and prudence of Washington. The government was amazingly strengthened by the event. Every good citizen expressed his reprobation of violent resistance to law, and the Democratic societies, the chief fomenters of the rebellion,[2] after that showed symptoms of a desire to become less conspicuous.[3]

[a] August 7 and September 25.

---

any other state or states of the present Union who are averse to returning again under the galling yoke of Great Britain, the printers of the (at present) United States are requested to publish the above notification."

[1] Lyman's *Diplomacy of the United States*, i., 208.

[2] "That the self-constituted societies," Washington wrote to John Jay, "which have spread themselves over this country, have been laboring incessantly to sow the seeds of distrust, jealousy, and of course discontent, thereby hoping to effect some revolution in the government, is not unknown to you.* That they have been the fomenters of the Western disturbances, admits of no doubt in the mind of any one who will examine their conduct."

"I consider this insurrection," he wrote to General Henry Lee on the 26th of August; "as the first formidable fruit of the Democratic societies, brought forth, I believe, too prematurely for their own views, which may contribute to the annihilation of them."

[3] I have before me the certificate of membership granted to Captain (afterward Commodore) Joshua Barney by the

* At that time there existed in the city of New York an association called the *Tammany Society, or Columbian Order*. It was formed by William Mooney, an upholsterer, residing in New York during the administration of Washington. Its first meeting was on the 13th of May, 1789. It took its name from the Indian chief Tammany, of whom it was said "he loved liberty more than life." Its officers were composed of a grand sachem and thirteen sachems, representing the President and the governors of the thirteen states. Besides these there was a grand council, of which the sachems were members. It was a very popular society, and its membership included most of the best men of New York. Its anniversary on the 12th of May came to be regarded as a holiday. No party politics were tolerated in its meetings. But when Washington denounced "self-constituted societies" for reasons above named, nearly all of the members left it, believing their society to be included in the just reproof. Mooney and others adhered to the organization, and from that time it became a political organization, and took part with Jefferson and the Democratic party. It is still in existence, and is known as a centre of Democratic organization, in the political sense of that name. Its head-quarters are Tammany Hall, fronting on the eastern side of the City Hall Park, at the junction of Nassau Street and Park Row. They met at first at Martling's Long Room, on the southeast corner of Nassau and Spruce Streets. In the year 1800 they determined to build a "wigwam." Tammany Hall was accordingly erected by them. The corner-stone was laid on the twenty-second anniversary of the society, in May, 1811, and was finished the following year. Of the original committee of thirteen appointed at the meeting in 1800 to carry out the design of erecting a building, only one now (1867) survives: that is the venerable Jacob Barker, of New Orleans.

Difficulty with Algiers.   British Interference.   Algerine Corsairs let loose upon American Commerce.

The new difficulty abroad was with Algiers, one of the Barbary Powers, on the southern coast of the Mediterranean Sea. The corsairs of those states, and especially of Algiers, had long depredated upon commerce in that region, and had grown bold by suffered impunity. When, at the close of the Revolution, American vessels began to find their way within the Pillars of Hercules, they frequently became the prey of these sea-robbers, who appropriated their cargoes and sold their crews into slavery, where they were held for ransom-money. President Washington called the attention of the national government to these piracies as early as 1790; and, in an able report, Secretary Jefferson laid before Congress important details touching the position of American interests in that part of the globe. Little, however, could be done, as the Americans had no navy; and the commerce of the United States in that quarter was for a long time dependent on the Portuguese fleet for protection.

Portugal was at war with Algiers for several years, and the fleet of the former confined the cruisers of the latter to the Mediterranean Sea. This barrier was broken in 1793, by British instrumentality acting secretly, for the avowed purpose of damaging France. Portugal was then seriously dependent on Great Britain, and had asked its aid in procuring a peace with Algiers. The British agent at the Court of the Dey was instructed to do so, and, without due authority being given him by Portugal to act in its behalf, he concluded a truce between the belligerents for one year. In that treaty was introduced the extraordinary stipulation that the Portuguese government *should not afford protection to any nation against Algerine cruisers!* This truce was immediate in its operations, and the robbers were released without notice being given to other powers.

The effect of this measure was disastrous to American commerce. Notwithstanding the British ministry disclaimed any intention to injure the United States, it was very evident that it was a part of a scheme to cripple the growing commerce of the Americans, or at least so to alarm it as to prevent its carrying supplies to France. And such was the result. The corsairs spread themselves over the Atlantic near the European coasts, and captured a large number of American vessels making their way to Portugal and other parts of the Continent, unsuspicious of any danger. The corsairs of Tunis joined those of Algiers, and thus a powerful fleet of pirate ships was formed.[1]

Democratic or Republican Society of Baltimore, with the seal of the society attached, by the side of which his name is written. The following is a copy of the certificate and seal:

"To all other Societies established on principles of LIBERTY and EQUALITY, UNION, PATRIOTIC VIRTUE, and PERSEVERANCE.

"We, the Members of the Republican Society of Baltimore, certify and declare to all Republican or Democratic Societies, and to all Republicans individually, that Citizen JOSHUA BARNEY hath been admitted and now is a member of our Society, and that, from his known zeal to promote Republican principles and the rights of humanity, we have granted him this our certificate (which he hath signed in the margin), and do recommend him to all Republicans, that they may receive him with fraternity, which we offer to all those who may come to us with similar credentials.

"In testimony whereof, etc.   Signed,   ALEXANDER M'KIM, *President.*
"GEORGE SEARS, *Secretary.*"

This certificate is dated the "twelfth day of August, and in the nineteenth year of the independence of the United States and the establishment of the American Republic," or 1795.

[1] The maritime force of Algiers at that time, according to O'Brien (see *American State Papers*, x., 328), consisted of four frigates, with an aggregate of 124 guns; one polacca (a vessel with three short masts, without tops, caps, or crosstrees to the upper yards), with 18 guns; one brig of 20; four xebecs (a small three-masted vessel used in the Mediter-

The Pride and Avarice of the Dey of Algiers.   An American Navy recommended.   First Steps toward its Creation.

The Americans felt justly indignant toward Great Britain because of the important part she had played in letting those robbers out of the Mediterranean. But the government was powerless to act. David Humphreys, who had been appointed commissioner for the United States to negotiate with the Dey of Algiers, had been treated with contempt by the haughty semi-barbarian, who was as avaricious as he was proud. "If I were to make peace with every body," he said, "what should I do with my corsairs? What should I do with my soldiers? They would take off my head for the want of other prizes, not being able to live on their miserable allowance!"

Such logic was unanswerable by words, and Humphreys wrote to his government at the close of 1793, at the suggestion of Captain Richard O'Brien,[1] "If we mean to have a commerce, we must have a navy to defend it." With the same recognition of the necessity for nautical power, Washington, in his message at the opening of Congress early in December,[a] said, when alluding to the war in Europe, and the delicate international questions arising out of the frontier relations of the republic, "There is a rank due to the United States among nations, which will be withheld, if not absolutely lost, by the reputation of weakness. If we desire to avoid insult, we must be able to repel it; if we desire to secure peace, one of the most powerful instruments of our prosperity, it must be known that we are at all times ready for war."

[a] 1793.

The President's wise counsels prevailed. In January,[b] 1794, a committee was appointed, with instructions to report the amount of force necessary to protect American commerce against the Algerine pirates, and the ways and means for its support.[2] This measure, and the general subject of British aggressions, elicited, as we have seen, long and warm debates, and party lines were very distinctly drawn. The feeling against Great Britain became intense, and in March[c] an embargo for a limited period was laid, chiefly for the purpose of obstructing the supply of provisions for the British fleet in the West Indies.[3] Then followed the appointment of Mr. Jay as minister extraordinary to Great Britain, already noticed.

[b] January 2.
[c] March 26, 1794.

There was a powerful and determined opposition to the creation of a navy. With strange ideas of national honor and national independence, some advocated the purchase of a peace with the Dey of Algiers, and the future security of his forbearance, by ransom and tribute money, rather than prepare for, and thus, as they believed, provoke a war. And these cowardly counsels had great influence; for when, finally, a bill was passed[d] providing for the construction of six frigates, it was encumbered with a clause commanding a suspension of labor upon them in the event of a peace with Algiers being secured. For the purchase of such peace a million of dollars were appropriated. An act was also passed for the fortification of the harbors of the republic.[4] These were the first steps toward the creation of the navy, army, and fortifications of the United States under the National Constitution.

[d] March 11, 1794.

---

ranean), with an aggregate of 168 guns; a brig on the stocks of 20 guns; three galliotas, with 4 guns each; and sixty gun-boats. The vessels were all manned at the rate of twelve men for each gun. Tunis had, at the same time, twenty-three corsairs, mounting from 4 to 24 guns each.

[1] Letter of O'Brien to Humphreys, dated "Algiers, November 12, 1793."—See *American State Papers*, Boston edition, 1817, x., 319.

[2] This was the first Committee of Ways and Means ever appointed by the Congress, questions of that sort having been hitherto referred to the Secretary of the Treasury. It was an opposition measure.

[3] First for thirty days, and afterward for sixty. At the end of that time the embargo expired by limitation, but a temporary act authorized the President to renew it at any time before the next session of Congress.

[4] The naval bill provided that four of the six frigates should carry 44 guns each, and the other two 36 guns each. About $700,000 were appropriated for the purpose. In the matter of harbor defenses, the President was authorized to commence fortifications at Portland, Portsmouth, Gloucester, Salem, Boston, Newport, New London, New York, Philadelphia, Baltimore, Annapolis, Alexandria, Norfolk, Ocracoke Inlet, Wilmington, Cape Fear River, Georgetown, S. C., Charleston, Savannah, and St. Mary's. But the whole amount of money appropriated for this purpose was the paltry sum of $136,000. True, this was only for the *commencement* of the fortifications. The President was authorized to purchase two hundred cannon, and artillery munitions for the forts, for which $96,000 were appropriated. For the establishment of arsenals and armories $81,000 were appropriated, and $340,000 were provided for the purchase of arms and

Building of Frigates.   Tribute to the Dey of Algiers.   Release of Captives.   The French Directory offended.

Perceiving an urgent necessity in the aspect of foreign affairs in relation to his own government, the President resolved to have the six frigates built immediately, and their keels were soon respectively laid in six different ports.[1] The work was going on briskly, when it was suspended, at the close of 1795, by the conclusion of a treaty of peace[a] with the African robber, which cost the government a million of dollars without ultimate advantage.[2] The work on the six frigates was suspended, and the mercantile marine of the United States lost all hope of protection in the event of a war with any foreign government.

[a] November 28, 1795.

At the beginning of 1796 the aspect of the foreign affairs of the republic was peaceful. The Indian war in the West had ceased; a better understanding with Great Britain prevailed than had been known since the close of the Revolution; and the French government, then in the hands of a Directory,[3] showed no special symptoms of enmity toward that of the United States. But clouds soon began to appear in that section of the political horizon. The ratification of Jay's treaty gave such offense to the Directory that they declared[b] the alliance between France and the United States at an end, and that Adet, the successor of Fouchet, should be recalled, to make room for a special minister. In July,[c] when intelligence was received that the Congress of the United States had made an appropriation for the due execution of Jay's treaty, the Directory issued a secret order authorizing French ships of war to treat neutral vessels in the same manner as they had suffered themselves to be treated by the English. Under this authorization, numerous American ships were seized in the West Indies by French cruisers. This was followed in

[b] February 15, 1796.

[c] July 2.

---

military stores. The importation of arms for two years was to be free, and no arms were allowed to be exported for a year.

[1] These were Portsmouth, N. H., Boston, New York, Philadelphia, Baltimore, and Norfolk. The President also proceeded to appoint the following officers, constructors, and navy agents:

Captains and Superintendents.	Naval Constructors.	Navy Agents.	For Ships to be built at
John Barry.	Joshua Humphreys.	Isaac Coxe.	Philadelphia.
Samuel Nicholson.	George Cleghorn.	Henry Jackson.	Boston.
Silas Talbot.	Forman Cheesman.	John Blagge.	New York.
Richard Dale.	John Morgan.	W. Pennock.	Norfolk.
Thomas Truxtun.	David Stodert.	Jeremiah Yillott.	Baltimore.
James Sever.	James Hackett.	Jacob Sheaffe.	Portsmouth.

[2] The relations of those African sea-robbers to the commerce of the world at that time was a disgrace to the civilized nations who suffered themselves to be made tributary to the piratical rulers of the semi-barbarian states on the southern shores of the Mediterranean Sea.

The first contact of those powers with the Americans was in 1785, when Algerine corsairs captured two vessels from the United States, and consigned their crews, twenty-one in number, to slavery. Measures were immediately taken by the diplomatic agents of the United States in Europe for their release. The rapacious Dey believed he had found a new mine of wealth, and he asked an enormous price for their ransom. The American government determined not to establish a precedent that would be followed by more exorbitant demands. In France was a religious order, called Mathurins, established in ancient times for the purpose of redeeming Christian captives in the hands of the infidels. On the solicitation of Mr. Jefferson, then minister of the United States at the French Court, the principal of this order undertook to procure a release of the American captives. He was unsuccessful. Others made similar attempts, with like results. The Dey refused to lower his demands, believing that the United States would pay any price rather than allow Americans to remain in bondage. Finally our government appropriated $40,000 for their ransom, and first John Paul Jones, and then Mr. Barclay, were appointed commissioners to negotiate for their release. Each died before he reached Algiers, and the business was placed in the hands of Colonel David Humphreys, American minister at Lisbon. This was at about the time when the truce between Portugal and Algiers, already mentioned, was concluded. The Algerine fleet was then upon the Atlantic and, within a month after the truce was agreed upon, ten American vessels were captured by them, and over one hundred American seamen consigned to slavery. Colonel Humphreys asked the Dey for a passport to Algiers. The elated ruler said that he would not make peace with the Americans on any terms, nor allow any American embassador to come to his capital. Humphreys hastened to the United States, when Congress appropriated about a million of dollars to be applied to the release of the captives. In the spring of 1795 Humphreys sailed for Europe, with Mr. Donaldson, consul for Tunis and Tripoli. While the former remained in France to obtain the aid of that government, Donaldson made a treaty with the Dey. The captives were finally released on the payment of a large sum of money, and an agreement on the part of the United States to pay to the Dey of Algiers an annual tribute. The amount to be paid down was $800,000, and, in addition, the United States agreed to present the Dey with a frigate worth one hundred thousand dollars. The amount of annual tribute-money was twenty-five thousand dollars. This treaty was humiliating to the United States, but it was in accordance with the usages of European nations, and could not then be avoided.

[3] The Directory was installed at the Luxembourg at Paris, under a new constitution of government, on the 1st of November, 1795, and was appointed to hold executive power for four years. It was composed of five members, and ruled in connection with the Chambers, namely, the Council of Ancients and the Council of Five Hundred.

America by Minister Adet's famous "cockade proclamation," calling upon all French residents in the United States, in the name of the Directory, to mount on their hats a tri-colored cockade. The call was loyally responded to, and many American Democrats, also, were seen with this token of their devotion to the French Republic.

Mr. Monroe, having failed to please either the French Directory or his own government, was superseded by Charles Cotesworth Pinckney, of South Carolina. That gentleman embarked as minister to France in September, bearing with him Monroe's letters of recall.

Washington's second administration was now drawing to a close, and he resolved to retire to private life. In September he issued his admirable Farewell Address to his countrymen—a political legacy of inestimable value. At the same time the first great struggle of the Federal and Democratic parties for power was going on, in the canvass for Washington's successor. The candidates were Adams and Jefferson; and every appeal which party spirit or party rancor could invent was made to the people all over the land. Adet, with unparalleled impudence, issued an inflammatory appeal to the people, containing a summary of alleged violations of friendship to France on the part of the United States government. It was chiefly intended to arouse the feelings of the Americans against Great Britain. Other partisans of Jefferson, in their zeal to injure the Federal party, made outrageous assaults upon Washington's character, charging him with using the public money for private use, and of being a traitor to his country.[1] The notorious Thomas Paine, lately released from a French prison, with his moral sensibilities all blunted by habitual dissipation, wrote a scurrilous letter to Washington, from under the roof of Monroe in Paris, in the summer of 1796. This was published in the United States for the purpose of promoting Jefferson's election. But Adams was successful. The attack on Washington strengthened the Federal party, and the last growl of the opposition toward him personally was given by a writer in the *Aurora* on the first President's retirement from office at the beginning of March, 1797, and on the eve of his departure for Mount Vernon.[2]

When Washington retired from public life the clouds of difficulty between the United States and France were thickening. French cruisers were inflicting great wrongs on American commerce, and near the close of the session of the Congress of 1796, '97, the Secretary of State laid before that body[a] a full

[a] February 27, 1797.

---

[1] "If ever a nation has been debauched by a man," said a writer in the *Aurora*, "the American nation has been debauched by Washington. If ever a nation was deceived by a man, the American nation has been deceived by Washington. Let his conduct, then, be an example to future ages. Let it serve to be a warning that no man may be an idol. Let the history of the Federal government instruct mankind that the mask of patriotism may be worn to conceal the foulest designs against the liberties of the people."

[2] "'Lord, now lettest thou thy servant depart in peace, for mine eyes have seen thy salvation,'" said this politician. "If ever there was a time that would license the reiteration of the exclamation of the pious Simeon," he said, "that time is now arrived; for the man who is the source of all the misfortunes of our country is this day reduced to a level with his fellow-citizens, and is no longer possessed of power to multiply evils upon the United States. . . . When a retrospect is taken of the Washingtonian administration for eight years, it is a subject of the greatest astonishment that a single individual should have cankered the principles of republicanism in an enlightened people just emerged from the gulf of despotism, and should have carried his designs against the public liberty so far as to have put in jeopardy its very existence. Such, however, are the facts, and, with them staring us in the face, this day ought to be a JUBILEE in the United States!"

exhibit of them. From that communication it appeared that not only were American vessels captured, but their crews were treated with great indignity, and even cruelty. Many bitter complaints were made against Commodore Joshua Barney, then in the French service, in command of two frigates in the West Indies, who was accused of treating his own captive countrymen with indifference and neglect. He was also charged with having insulted the American flag by hoisting it union down. And yet, when he arrived in Chesapeake Bay to learn and carry away to France the result of the Presidential election, though he boasted of having in his pocket the orders of the French Directory to capture American vessels, and declared that, if Jefferson were not elected, war would be proclaimed by France within three months, he was not the less on that account honored and feasted by infatuated politicians who read the *Aurora* and believed Washington to be a traitor![1]

Adams[2] came into office with a powerful party opposed to him—a party which lacked only two votes of giving the election to Mr. Jefferson, his rival, who became Vice-President. An open rupture with France was becoming more and more imminent. The accession of Spain to their alliance, and the victories of young Napoleon Bonaparte in Italy, gave the Directory strength, and their bearing toward other governments became more and more insolent. Their corsairs were depredating upon American commerce, and in their pride they declared that, until the United States had redressed certain alleged grievances of which they complained, no minister of the republic would be received by them. Pinckney, who had never been officially received as minister, was ordered to leave France. He retired to Holland, after sending a narrative of his bad treatment to his government, and there awaited farther orders.

The conduct of the French Directory soon wrought a great change in the public mind in the United States. Disappointed by the failure of Jefferson to be elected President, the Directory determined to punish the people who dared to thwart their plans. They issued a decree[a] which was almost tantamount to a declaration of war. It not only authorized the capture of American vessels under certain conditions, but declared that any American found on board of a hostile ship, though placed there without his consent by impressment, should be hanged as a pirate. American seamen, continually liable to impressment by the British, were to be subjected to a pirate's fate by the French! Strange to say, the eminent American,

[a] May 10, 1797.

---

[1] Hildreth's *History of the United States*, Second Series, i., 703.
[2] John Adams was born at Quincy, Massachusetts, October 13, 1735. He was educated at Harvard University, and at the age of twenty-two years commenced the practice of the law. He was brought prominently into public life by his defense of Captain Preston at Boston, who was engaged in the so-called "massacre," in the spring of 1770. He became a member of the Massachusetts Legislature, and in 1774 was elected to the Continental Congress. He was one of the most active men in that body until sent on diplomatic missions to Europe. He was the representative of the new republic abroad for many years, and was one of the negotiators for peace in 1783. In 1789 he was chosen Vice-President of the United States, and in 1797 was elevated to the seat of the President, as Washington's successor. He served one term, and retired to Quincy in 1801. He engaged but little in public life afterward. He and Jefferson died on the same day, July 4, 1826, just fifty years after they voted for the Declaration of Independence. Mr. Adams was then ninety-one years of age. The above portrait was painted by Stuart at about the time Adams was elected President.

Joel Barlow, at that time a resident in Paris, coolly wrote to a friend concerning this barbarous decree, "The government here is determined to fleece you to a sufficient degree to bring you to your feeling in the only nerve in which your sensibility lies, which is your pecuniary interest."[1]

President Adams had called an extraordinary session of Congress at the middle of May. The reaction every where had greatly strengthened the

administration party, and many Republicans talked with complacency of a war with France. But a majority of the Cabinet favored farther attempts at negotiation. John Marshall, a Federalist (afterward Chief Justice of the United States), and Elbridge Gerry, a Democrat (afterward Vice-President), were appointed envoys extraordinary to proceed to Europe, join Mr. Pinckney, and attempt to settle by diplomacy all matters in dispute between the United States and France. After a session of little more than six weeks, during which time provision was made for a small loan for calling out eighty thousand militia, and creating a small naval force, and acts against privateering were passed, Congress adjourned[a] in time to escape the yellow fever that ravaged Philadelphia that season.[2]

[a] July 10, 1797.

---

[1] Letter to his brother-in-law, Abraham Baldwin, of Georgia. Barlow, who went to France with a communication to the National Convention from a sympathizing society in England, was made a French citizen. By some commercial operations he accumulated a large fortune, lived in sumptuous style in Paris, and, being a thorough French Democrat, was the bitter enemy of the administrations of Washington and Adams. While at Hamburg, in 1793, he was invited to a Jacobin festival, and he furnished for the occasion a copy of the following song, written by Thelwall, a celebrated English Jacobin. It was sung on that occasion, and has been generally considered a composition by Mr. Barlow himself. It was entitled *God save the Guillotine*, and is a parody of the English national song* *God save the King*:

"God save the guillotine!
Till England's king and queen
Her power shall prove;
Till each anointed knob
Affords a clipping job,
Let no rude halter rob
The guillotine.

"France, let thy trumpet sound
Tell all the world around
How CAPET fell;
And when great GEORGE's poll

Shall in the basket roll,
Let mercy then control
The guillotine.

"When all the sceptred crew
Have paid their homage due
The guillotine,
Let Freedom's flag advance
Till all the world, like France,
O'er tyrants' graves shall dance,
And peace begin."

[2] At about this time a letter written by Jefferson to Philip Mazzei, an Italian republican, who had lived near him in Virginia for a while, was published in the Federal newspapers, and made a great stir. The letter was written a year before, and was translated and published by Mazzei in a Florentine journal. It contained a virtual indorsement of all the charges made against Washington and his political friends. Its publication brought to an end the friendship between Jefferson and the late President. Jefferson was placed in such an unpleasant dilemma by it that he prudently kept silence. It was used with great effect at the time, and was again brought up against him at the Presidential canvass in the year 1800. It was made the subject of a caricature called THE PROVIDENTIAL DETECTION. At a place for

---

* It may not be out of place here to remark that "God save the King," in words and air, did not originate with Handel in the time of George the First, as is generally supposed, but is a literal translation of a *cantique* which was always sung by the maidens of St. Cyr when Louis the Fourteenth entered the chapel of that establishment to hear the morning prayer. M. De Brinon was the author of the words, and the music was by the eminent Lulli, founder of the French opera. The following is a copy of the words:

"Grand Dieu sauve le Roi!
Grand Dieu venge le Roi!
Vive le Roi!
Que toujours glorieux,
Louis victorieux!
Voye ses ennemi
Toujours soumis!
Grand Dieu sauve le Roi!
Grand Dieu venge le Roi!
Vive le Roi!"

This air is still sung by the vine-dressers in the south of France.—See *Memoirs of Madame de Crequy*.

Pride of the French Directory. Attempt to extort Tribute from the Americans. Pinckney's Reply. A French Decree.

Darker and darker appeared the storm-clouds of European politics, and the muttering of their thunders shook the social fabric in America with some alarm. England, for a moment, seemed tottering to its fall. Its financial power was sorely smitten by the suspension of specie payments by the Bank of England, and its naval strength and supremacy seemed menaced by a great mutiny at the Nore. Bonaparte was making his splendid conquering marches in the direction of the Danube, and the Carpathian Mountains beyond, and Austria had already been compelled to make peace with his government. Success waited on French arms and French diplomacy every where; and when the three American envoys reached Paris in October,[a] and asked for an audience with the Directory, they met with a haughty refusal, unless they should first pay into the deficient French treasury a large sum as an equivalent for friendship. Overtures for this purpose were made by unofficial agents, and the sum demanded was two hundred and forty thousand dollars, besides an arrangement for purchasing from the French government a large amount of Dutch securities, which had been wrung from the Hollanders as the price of peace. Threats were made that, if these conditions were not complied with, the envoys might be ordered to leave France at any time with only twenty-four hours' notice, and that the coasts of the United States would be ravaged by French vessels from St. Domingo.

[a] October 4, 1797.

Delay followed delay. The envoys were firm; and the occasion was given for Pinckney to utter the noble sentiment, "Millions for defense, but not one cent for tribute!" At length the envoys, having presented a list of grievances of which their government complained, asked for their passports if they could not be recognized as ministers. These were finally granted[b] to the *Federal* envoys, but under circumstances of insult and indignity which amounted to virtual expulsion from the country. Gerry, the *Democrat*, who had held interviews with Talleyrand, the French premier, without the knowledge of his colleagues, and who doubtless encouraged him to believe that the "French party" in America were sufficiently numerous to avert a war with France, and insure a partial if not full compliance with her demands, was directed to remain in the character of an accepted minister.[1] He did so, and received the severest censures from his indignant countrymen. After being treated with mingled insolence and contempt by Talleyrand and his associates, Gerry also embarked for the United States.[c]

[b] March, 1798.

[c] July, 1798.

Meanwhile the French Directory had issued a decree[d] concerning neutrals on the ocean, more outrageous than any yet put forth, and calculated to effectually destroy American commerce in European waters.[2] This action, the indecent treatment of the envoys, and the continued depredations of the French cruisers, aroused a violent war spirit in the United States. It had been manifested, in a degree, at the opening of the Fifth Congress, and it increased with every fresh item of intelligence from France.

[d] January 18, 1798.

The President, in his first annual message,[e] had recommended preparations for war; and in Congress the administration grew stronger every hour. At length, at the middle of March, dispatches came from the envoys giving a history of the infamous proceedings of the French Directory.[3] A general outburst

[e] November 23, 1797.

---

burnt sacrifice called the "Altar of French Despotism," before which Jefferson is kneeling, a flame is seen, fed by papers marked *Age of Reason, Godwin, Aurora, Chronicle, J. J. Rousseau, Voltaire, Ruins of Volney, Helvetius,* etc. Around the altar lie sacks for consumption, marked AMERICAN *Spoliations, Dutch Restitution, Sardinia, Flanders, Venice, Spain, Plunder,* etc.

[1] Gerry was much petted while in France, while his colleagues were neglected. At a ball given by Talleyrand as early as January, 1798, at which General and Madame Bonaparte were present, Mr. Gerry appeared. His brother envoys not having been invited, he at first refused, but finally attended, he said, in compliance with the dictates of policy.

[2] It proclaimed that all vessels having merchandise on board, the production of England or her colonies, whoever the owner of the merchandise might be, were liable to seizure as good prizes; and any vessel which at any previous part of her voyage had touched at any English port or possession was forbidden to enter any French port. Just before the issuing of this decree an American at Nantes wrote to his friends at home that no less than sixty privateers were fitting out in that port alone to prey upon American commerce.

[3] The Directory at that time were Barras, Moulins, Siéyes, Gohier, and Roger Ducos. All but Barras were soon after-

of indignation followed. The people of the United States, as a nation, felt deeply insulted, and Pinckney's patriotic sentiment was repeated in every part of the republic. And yet there were those slavish enough to justify France and criminate their own government. In this cowardly course the *Aurora* took the lead. By some disloyal hand it was placed in possession of Talleyrand's rejoinder to the complaints of the envoys, and published it before it reached the government of the United States, for whom alone it was intended. It was argued that it would be better to comply with the demands of the Directory for money than to incur the risk of a war—better to purchase peace by humbly paying tribute, than to vindicate the claims of the nation to independence by asserting and maintaining its rights at all hazards!

Such logic did not suit the character nor temper of the American people at that time. The rampant war spirit, fed on every hand by fresh aggressions and patriotic appeals, was not to be appeased. The President issued a special message,[a] calling upon Congress to make provisions for hostilities. His appeal was responded to with alacrity. Means for administering chastisements for injuries received, and for repelling those which were threatened, were provided without hesitation. Provision was made for the organization of a regular provisional army, in magnitude sufficient for the exigencies of the case, and the employment of a volunteer force. Measures were also taken, on the recommendation of the Secretary of War, for strengthening the navy, and making it a power to be respected on the high seas.[1]

[a] March 19, 1798.

To a great extent party spirit disappeared in the National Legislature. Their proceedings were approved by the great majority of the people, and the President received addresses from all parts of the Union, warmly commending his course, and overflowing with the most fervid patriotism.[2] The young Federalists, with a spirit of defiant response to the Democrats, who still wore the badge of devotion to French politics ordered by Adet, mounted a black cockade, such as was worn by officers in the Revolution;[3] and between the wearers of these opposing decorations there was

---

ward driven from office; and when, in the autumn of 1799, Bonaparte usurped the government, he expelled from France the first two above named as utterly corrupt.

[1] After much manœuvring on the part of the opposition to prevent the adoption of these measures to meet any hostilities on the part of France, the men who in 1794—only four years before—were eager for war with England, and voted for preparations for it with alacrity, were now as vehement for peace—an inconsistency which many of their partisans throughout the country pointed at with scorn. Congress authorized a regular provisional army of about twenty thousand men, and gave the President authority to appoint officers for it; also to receive and organize volunteer corps, who should be exempted from ordinary militia duty. The sum of $800,000 was appropriated for the purchase of cannon, arms, and military stores. Provision was made for fortifying the harbors of the United States—a labor already commenced—and, for the farther security of ports, the purchase and equipment of ten galleys. The President was also authorized to cause twelve ships of not less than 32 guns each, twelve of not less than 20 nor exceeding 24 guns each, and six not exceeding 18 guns each, besides galleys and revenue cutters, to be built. A Navy Department, the duties of which the Secretary of War had hitherto performed, was created, and on the 30th of April, 1798, Benjamin Stoddert, of Georgetown, in the District of Columbia, was appointed the first Secretary of the Navy, and took his seat in the Cabinet.

Ben Stoddert

[2] The city of New York was greatly excited by the prospect of a war with France. Its commerce had suffered much by the depredations of French cruisers, and the mercantile classes were greatly exasperated. The Republicans or Democrats had a debating association, whose meetings were public, called "The Society of Free Debate." A meeting was called for the 27th of April, 1798, to discuss the question, "Would it be better policy, under existing circumstances, to lay an embargo [a scheme proposed by some as a less dangerous measure], than to arm in defense of our carrying-trade?" The Federalists went to the meeting in great numbers, and, by an overwhelming vote, elected Jacob Morton chairman. By ten to one they voted for arming. They expressed by resolutions full approbation of the conduct of the government, and their determination to support it. They appointed a committee, consisting of Colonel Jacob Morton, Colonel Ebenezer Stevens, Nicholas Evartson, John Cozine, and Josiah Ogden Hoffman, to draft an address to the President and Congress, expressive of their satisfaction with the course pursued toward France. After the adjournment a Quaker addressed the multitude.

On the 5th of May a meeting was held, and addressed by the late Chief Justice Samuel Jones. Nine hundred young men present pledged themselves to be in readiness, at a moment's warning, to offer their services to their country against the French.

On the 5th of June the New York Chamber of Commerce took action concerning the defenses of New York. They appointed a committee to confer with the military authorities and the Corporation. A conference was held the next day at the Tontine Coffee-house, and it was resolved to call a public meeting of citizens who might be ready to defend an "insulted country" and the "defenseless port." The call was made, and an invitation was given for such citizens to enroll themselves as an artillery corps, it having been ascertained that Colonel Stevens, an experienced artillerist of the Revolution, was willing to take the direction of them and to give them instructions.

[3] This gave them the name of "Black-cockade Federalists," which was a term of reproach until ten years after the War of 1812-'15.

intense hatred, which sometimes led to personal collisions. In the streets of cities opposing processions were seen; and all over the land the new songs of *Hail, Columbia!* and *Adams and Liberty*, were sung with unbounded applause.[1] The excitement against some of the opposition leaders in Congress soon became intense, and the most obnoxious of them, from Virginia, sought personal safety in flight, under the pretense of attention to their private affairs at home.

---

[1] The history of the origin and fate of these two songs is curious. The former, almost totally destitute of poetic merit, is still sung, and is regarded as a national song; the latter, full of genuine poetry, has been forgotten. *Hail, Columbia!* was written in the spring of 1798, when the war spirit of the nation was aroused by the irritating news from France. Mr. Fox, a young singer and actor in the Philadelphia Theatre, was to have a benefit. There was so little novelty at the play-house that he anticipated a failure. On the morning previous, he called upon Joseph Hopkinson, and said, "Not a single box has been taken, and I fear there will be a thin house. If you will write me some patriotic verses to the tune of the 'President's March,' I feel sure of a full house. Several people about the theatre have attempted it, but they have come to the conclusion that it can not be done. Yet I think you may succeed." Hopkinson retired to his study, wrote the first verse and chorus, and submitted them to Mrs. Hopkinson, who sang them with a harpsichord accompaniment. The time and words harmonized. The song was soon finished, and the young actor received it the same evening. The theatre placards the next morning announced that Mr. Fox would sing a new patriotic song. The house was crowded—the song was sung—the audience were wild with delight; for it touched the public heart with electrical effect at that moment, and eight times the singer was called out to repeat the song. When it was sung the ninth time the whole audience arose and joined in the chorus. On the following night (April 30, 1798) the President and his wife and some of the heads of departments were present, and the singer was called out time after time. It was repeated night after night in the theatres of Philadelphia and other places, and it became the universal song of the boys in the streets. On one occasion a crowd thronged the street in front of the author's residence, and suddenly "Hail, Columbia!" from five hundred voices broke the stillness of the midnight air.

In June following Robert Treat Paine was requested to write a song, to be sung at the anniversary of the "Massachusetts Charitable Fire Society." He wrote a political song adapted to the temper of the times, and called it "Adams and Liberty." At the house of Major Russell, editor of the *Boston Centinel*, the author showed it to that gentleman. "It is imperfect," said Russell, "without the name of Washington in it." Mr. Paine was about to take some wine, when Russell politely and good-naturedly interfered, saying, "You can have none of my wine, Mr. Paine, until you have written another stanza, with Washington's name in it." Paine walked back and forth a few moments, called for a pen, and wrote the finest verse in the whole poem—a verse which forms the epigraph of the chapter on the next page. This song, in nine stanzas, became immensely popular. It was sung all over the country, in theatres and public places, in workshops and drawing-rooms, and by the boys in the streets. The sale of it on "broadsides" yielded the author a profit of $750. The temper of the large majority of the American people at that time is expressed in the following verses of the ode:

> " While France her huge limbs bathes recumbent in blood,
>   And Society's base threats with wide dissolution;
> May Peace, like the dove, who returned from the flood,
>   Find an ark of abode in our mild Constitution.
>   But though Peace is our aim,
>   Yet the boon we disclaim,
> If bought by our Sov'reignty, Justice, or Fame.
>
> " 'Tis the fire of the flint, each American warms;
>   Let Rome's haughty victors beware of collision,
> Let them bring all the vassals of Europe in arms—
>   We're a world by ourselves, and disclaim a division.
>   While with patriot pride
>   To our laws we're allied,
> No foe can subdue us, no faction divide.
>
> " Our mountains are crowned with imperial oak,
>   Whose roots, like our liberties, ages have nourished;
> But long ere our nation submits to the yoke,
>   Not a tree shall be left on the field where it flourished.
>   Should invasion impend,
>   Every grove would descend
> From the hill-tops they shaded, our shores to defend.
>
> " Let our patriots destroy Anarch's pestilent worm,
>   Lest our Liberty's growth should be checked by corrosion;
> Then let clouds thicken round us, we heed not the storm,
>   Our realm fears no shock but the earth's own explosion.
>   Foes assail us in vain,
>   Though their fleets bridge the main,
> For our altars and laws with our lives we'll maintain.
> For ne'er shall the sons of Columbia be slaves
> While the earth bears a plant, or the sea rolls its waves."

Preparations for War.   Washington invited to command the Army.   He accepts.   Hamilton acting General-in-chief.

CHAPTER V.

"Should the tempest of war overshadow our land,
   Its bolts could ne'er rend Freedom's temple asunder;
For, unmoved, at its portal, would Washington stand,
   And repulse with his breast the assaults of the thunder!
        His sword from the sleep
        Of its scabbard would leap,
And conduct with its point ev'ry flash to the deep!
For ne'er shall the sons of Columbia be slaves
While the earth bears a plant, or the sea rolls its waves."
ROBERT TREAT PAINE.

AVING resolved on war, if necessary, for the dignity of the nation, the question arose spontaneously in the hearts of the American people, Who shall command our armies at this important crisis? All minds instinctively turned toward Washington as the only man who could command the respect of the *whole* nation and keep a dangerous faction in check.[1] "In such a state of public affairs," Hamilton wrote, "it is impossible not to look up to you. ... In the event of an open rupture with France, the public voice will again call you to command the armies of your country. ... All your past labor may demand, to give it efficacy, this farther, this great sacrifice."[2] "We must have your name, if you will in any case permit us to use it," President Adams wrote to him on the 22d of June. "There will be more efficiency in it than in many an army." And four days later, James M'Henry, the Secretary of War, wrote to him, "You see how the storm thickens, and that our vessel may soon require its ancient pilot. Will you—may we flatter ourselves that, in a crisis so awful and important, you will accept the command of all our armies? I hope you will, because you alone can unite all hearts and all hands, if it is possible that they can be united."

These intimations were followed by corresponding action. On the 7th of July President Adams, with the consent of the Senate, appointed Washington Lieutenant-general and commander-in-chief of all the armies raised and to be raised for the service of the United States. The venerated patriot, then sixty-five years of age, instantly obeyed the call of his country. "You may command me without reserve," he said to President Adams, qualifying the remark only by the expressed desire that he should not be called into active service until the public need should demand it. His friend, Mr. Hamilton, then forty-one years of age, was appointed first major general, and placed in active supreme command; and in November, Washington held a conference at Philadelphia with all the general officers, when arrangements were made for the complete organization of a provisional army on a war footing.

Washington all this while had looked upon the gathering tempest with perfect confidence that the clouds would pass by, and leave his country unscathed by the

---

[1] It was the settled conviction of many of the wisest men of that day that the leaders of the opposition wished to overthrow the Constitution. "It is more and more evident," Hamilton wrote to Washington late in May, 1798, "that the powerful faction which has for years opposed the government is determined to go all lengths with France. I am sincere in declaring my full conviction, as the result of a long course of observation, that they are ready to *new model* our Constitution under the *influence* or *coercion* of France, to form with her a perpetual alliance, *offensive* and *defensive*, and to give her a monopoly over trade by *peculiar* and *exclusive* privileges. This would be in substance, whatever it might be in name, to make this country a province of France. Neither do I doubt that her standard, displayed in this country, would be, directly or indirectly, seconded by them, in pursuance of the project I have mentioned."
[2] Hamilton to Washington, May 19, 1798.

lightning and the hail. Events soon justified his faith. The pride of the haughty Directory was speedily humbled, and the fears of England, toward whom many thoughtful men in America had looked as a possible friend and aid in the event of a war with France, were allayed. The victorious Bonaparte, who had threatened Great Britain with invasion, had gone off to Egypt on a romantic expedition, his avowed object being to march into Palestine, take possession of Jerusalem, rebuild the Temple, and restore the Jews to their beloved city and land. This he unsuccessfully attempted after the battle of the Nile, in which the proud Toulon fleet had been vanquished by Nelson.[a] A few weeks later Sir John Borlase Warren had scattered a French fleet[b] that hovered on the coast of Ireland to aid insurgents there; and many minor victories were accorded to English prowess.[1]

[a] August 1, 1798.
[b] October 12.

These successes of the English, intelligence of the war feeling in America, and the appointment of Washington as commander-in-chief of the armies of the United States, made the intoxicated Directory pause in their mad career. The wily Talleyrand began to think of conciliation. In letters to Pinchon,[c] French secretary of legation at the Hague, he intimated that any advances for negotiation that the government of the United States might make would be received by the Directory in a friendly spirit. These intimations, as intended, were communicated to William Vans Murray, the United States minister at the Hague, who transmitted them to his government.

[c] August 28 and September 28, 1798.

Without consulting his Cabinet, or taking counsel of national dignity, President Adams nominated Mr. Murray minister plenipotentiary to France. The country was astounded. It came upon the Cabinet, the Congress, and the people without premonition. The Cabinet opposed it, and the Senate resolved not to confirm it. No direct overtures had been made by the French government; and some of Mr. Adams's best friends, who regarded war as preferable to dishonor, deprecated a cowardly cringing to a half-relenting tyrant, and warmly remonstrated with him. He persisted, and they were estranged. He finally so far yielded to public opinion as to nominate three envoys extraordinary, Mr. Murray being one, to negotiate a settlement of all matters in dispute between the United States and France. These were confirmed by the Senate at near the close of the session, in February, 1799, not willingly, but from a conviction that a refusal to do so might endanger the existence of the Federal party, for Mr. Adams had many and powerful supporters. It was stipulated, however, that the two envoys yet at home (Chief Justice Oliver Ellsworth and Patrick Henry[2]) should

JOHN BULL TAKING A LUNCH.

[1] England had for some time trembled violently before the wonderful operations of Bonaparte on the Continent. For a while invasion of the island seemed imminent. But when the cloud disappeared in the autumn of 1798, and scarcely a day passed without bringing intelligence of some new success of the British navy, the feeling of exultation was intense. The pencil of Gillray, the great caricaturist, was exceedingly active, and in quick succession he brought out several prints illustrating John Bull as being surfeited with his immense captures. In one of these, entitled "John Bull taking a Luncheon; or, British Cooks cramming Old Grumble-gizzard with *Bonne Chère*," the representative of English nationality, a burly old fellow is seen sitting in a chair at a well-furnished table, while the naval cooks are zealous in their attentions. The hero of the Nile offers him a "fricassee à la Nelson," consisting of a large dish of battered French ships of the line. Another admiral offers him a "fricando à la Howe," "dessert à la Warren," "Dutch cheese a la Duncan," et cætera. John Bull is deliberately snapping up a frigate at a mouthful, and is evidently fattening on his diet. "What!" he exclaims, "more fricassees? Where do you think I shall find room to stow all you bring in?" By his side is an immense jug of brown stout to wash them down. Behind him is a picture of "Bonaparte in Egypt" suspended against the wall, nearly concealed by Nelson's hat, which is hung over it.*

[2] Mr. Henry declined the nomination because of his advanced age and increasing infirmities. Governor William R.

* The portion of this celebrated caricature here given, with the description, is copied from Wright's *England under the House of Hanover*, ii., 298.

not embark for Europe until authentic and satisfactory assurances should be given as to their reception. Such assurances were received by the government in October following, and in November Ellsworth and W. R. Davie (the latter having taken Mr. Henry's place) sailed for Europe. Fortunately for all parties, when the envoys reached France a change had taken place in the government of that country. The Directory was no more. Bonaparte had suddenly returned from the East, after great and brilliant movements with various results, and was hailed as the good genius of the Republic. He found, as he expected, his country rent by political dissensions, and the Directory in disrepute among the most powerful classes. With the assistance of a strong party, supported by bayonets, he dissolved the Assembly of Representatives and took the government into his own hands,[a] with the title of First Consul, which was at first conferred upon him for ten years, and afterward for life.

[a] November 8, 1799.

The audacity and energy of Bonaparte saved France from anarchy and ruin. To please the people he proclaimed a pacific policy, and opened correspondence with the powers then at war with the Republic with professions of peaceful desires. It was at this auspicious moment that the American envoys arrived[b] at Paris.

[b] March 2, 1800.

While these political movements were in progress, and preparations were making in the United States for a French invasion, war between the two nations actually commenced on the ocean, although hostilities had not been proclaimed by either. On the 7th of July, 1798, Congress declared the old treaties with France at an end, and two days afterward passed a law authorizing American vessels of war to capture French cruisers wherever they might be found. On the 11th, a new marine corps of nearly nine hundred men, rank and file, commanded by a major, was established by law, and a total of thirty active cruisers was provided for.

We have observed that some movements for strengthening the navy were begun early in 1797. The frigates *United States*, 44, *Constitution*, 44, and *Constellation*, 38,[1] were launched, and ordered to be put in commission that year. The *United States* first reached the water, and was the beginning of the American navy created after the adoption of the National Constitution. She was launched at Philadelphia on the 10th of July,[c] and was followed in September by the *Constellation* and *Constitution*. The former was set afloat on the 7th of that month, at Baltimore, and the latter on the 20th, at Boston;[2] yet none of these were ready for sea when, in the spring of 1798, war with France seemed inevitable.

[c] 1797.

An Indiaman, called the *Ganges*, was armed and equipped at Philadelphia as a 24-pounder, and placed in the command of Captain Richard Dale. She sailed on the 22d of May, to cruise along the coast from the east end of Long Island to the Capes of Virginia, to watch the approach of an enemy to the ports of New York, Philadelphia, and Baltimore. On the 12th of June Captain Dale received instructions off the Capes of Delaware to seize French cruisers and capture any of their prizes that might fall in his way.

The *Constellation*, 38, first went down the Patapsco on the morning of the 9th of April,[d] and early in June went to sea under the command of Captain Thomas Truxtun, in company with the *Delaware*, 20, Captain Decatur,[3] each having

[d] 1798.

Davie, of North Carolina, was appointed in Henry's place. The commission then stood: Murray, of Maryland; Ellsworth, of Connecticut; and Davie, of North Carolina. Mr. Murray, still at the Hague, was instructed to inform Talleyrand of the appointment.

[1] These numbers, 44, 38, etc., refer to the number of guns carried by each vessel, or, rather, the number they were rated at. The armament of vessels sometimes varies from the rate.

[2] The *Constellation* was constructed by David Stodert.

[3] Stephen Decatur was born at Newport, Rhode Island, in 1751. He commanded several privateers during the Revolution, and captured several English ships. He received a commission as captain in the United States navy in 1798, and served with distinction during the hostilities with the French cruisers. In 1800 he commanded a squadron of thirteen sail on the Guadaloupe station, his flag-ship being the *Philadelphia*, 38. He left the service in 1801, and engaged in

Capture of Le Croyable.   The *United States* and the *Constitution.*   Life and Services of Commodore Barry.

orders similar to Dale's. When only a few days out, Decatur fell in with the French corsair *Le Croyable*, 14, captured her, and sent her to Philadelphia as a prize. She was condemned by the prize court, added to the United States navy with the name of *Retaliation*, and placed under the command of Lieutenant William Bainbridge. She was the first vessel captured during the "French War of '98," so called, and was the first vessel taken by the present navy of the United States.

Early in July the *United States*, 44, Captain John Barry,[1] went to sea, and cruised eastward. She carried among her officers several young men who afterward became distinguished in the annals of naval warfare.[2] The government soon afterward determined to send a force to the West Indies, where American commerce was most exposed, and Captain Barry was ordered there with a small squadron, consisting of the *United States*, 44, *Delaware*, 20, and *Herald*, 18.

The *Constitution* (yet in the service) went to sea in July, in command of Captain Samuel Nicholson, and, in company with four revenue vessels, sailed in August to cruise off the coast southward of the Virginia Capes. One of these vessels was in command of Lieutenant (afterward Commodore) Preble.

In August the *Constitution*, Captain Trux-

---

commercial pursuits in Philadelphia, where he died in 1808. A plain slab, near the noble granite monument erected to the memory of his distinguished son in St. Peter's (Episcopal) Church burying-ground, marks the grave of the gallant captain and his wife, who died in 1812.

[1] John Barry was born in Ireland, County of Wexford, in 1745. He came to America in his youth, as a seaman. In 1775 he entered the naval service of Congress, and it is a disputed point whether he was the first of the commanders who got to sea at that period. He was in active service during the whole war. In the establishment of the new navy in 1794 he was named the senior officer, in which station, in command of the *United States*, he died on the 13th of September, 1803, in the city of Philadelphia. He died childless, at the age of fifty-eight years.

Commodore Barry's tomb is near the entrance to the cemetery of St. Mary's Roman Catholic Church, on Fourth Street, Philadelphia. The following is a copy of the inscription:

"Let the patriot, the soldier, and the Christian who visit these mansions of the dead, view this monument with respect. Beneath are deposited the remains of JOHN BARRY. He was born in the County of Wexford, in Ireland, but America was the object of his patriotism, and the theatre of his usefulness and honor. In the Revolutionary War, which established the independence of the United States, he bore the commission of a captain in their infant navy, and afterward became commander-in-chief. He fought often and once bled in the cause of freedom. But his habits of war

COMMODORE BARRY'S MONUMENT.

did not lessen in time the peaceful virtues which adorn private life. He was gentle, kind, just, and charitable; and not less beloved by family and friends than by his grateful country. In a full belief in the doctrines of the Gospel, he calmly resigned his soul into the arms of his Redeemer on the 13th of September, 1803, in the fifty-ninth year of his age. His affectionate widow hath caused this marble to be erected, to perpetuate his name after the hearts of his fellow-citizens have ceased to be the living record of his public and private virtues."

[2] Her first lieutenant was David Ross, who was last seen on the 30th of November, 1799; John Mullowny, who died in

tun, and the *Baltimore*, 20, Captain Phillips, performed signal service by safely convoying sixty American merchant vessels from Havana to the United States, in the face of several French cruisers lying in that port. Both the British and French authorities in the West Indies were surprised at the appearance of so many American cruisers in that region. At the close of the year 1798 the American navy consisted of twenty-three vessels, with an aggregate armament of four hundred and forty-six guns.

It was at this time that the first of the series of most flagrant outrages upon the American flag, which finally aroused the people of the United States to vindicate their honor and independence by an appeal to arms, was committed by a British commander. The American ship *Baltimore*, Captain Phillips, sailed out of Havana on the morning of the 16th of November, 1798, in charge of a convoy bound to Charleston, South Carolina, and in sight of Moro Castle met a British squadron. At that time the governments of the United States and Great Britain were on friendly terms, and Phillips bore up to the *Carnatick*, the flag-ship of his majesty's squadron, to speak to the commander. To his surprise, three of the convoy were cut off from the rest and captured by the British vessels. By invitation Phillips went on board the *Carnatick*, when he was informed that every man on board the *Baltimore* who had not a regular American protection should be transferred to the British flag-ship. Captain Phillips protested against the outrage, and declared that he would formally surrender his ship, and refer the matter to his government. His protest was of no avail. On returning to the *Baltimore*, he found a British officer mustering his men. He immediately ordered that gentleman and those who accompanied him to walk to the leeward, and then sent his men to their quarters. After consultation with a legal gentleman on board his ship, he determined to formally surrender her if his men were taken from him. Fifty-five of them were transferred to the *Carnatick*, and the colors of the *Baltimore* were lowered. Only five of her crew were retained by the British captain. These were pressed into the service of the king. The remainder were sent back, and the *Baltimore* was released. The British squadron then sailed away with the five captive seamen, and the three merchant vessels as prizes.

The *Baltimore* hastened to Philadelphia, and her case was laid before the government. At that time the trade between the United States and Great Britain was extremely profitable to American merchants; and the mercantile interest was such a power in the state that almost any indignity from the "mistress of the seas" would have been submitted to rather than provoke hostilities with that government.[1] The American Cabinet, in its obsequious deference to the British, had actually instructed the commanders of American cruisers on *no account*—not even to save a vessel of their own nation—to molest those of other nations, France excepted.[2] The government dismissed Captain Phillips from the navy without trial because he surrendered without a show of resistance; but the outrage of the British commander was passed by unnoticed!

At about the time of this occurrence near Havana, a small American squadron was

---

1801, was her second lieutenant; her third was James Barron, afterward commodore; and her fourth was Charles Stewart, the venerable commodore, yet (1862) living. Among the midshipmen were Decatur, Somers, and Caldwell, who distinguished themselves at Tripoli. Jacob Jones and William M. Crane joined her soon afterward, both of whom became commodores.

[1] The country had just entered upon a career of great commercial prosperity, notwithstanding many perils and hinderances beset that branch of national industry. American tunnage had doubled in ten years. American agricultural products found a ready market. The exports had increased from nineteen millions to almost ninety millions, and the imports in about the same proportion; and the amount of revenue from imports greatly exceeded the most sanguine anticipations.

[2] "The vessels of every other nation (France excepted"), ran the instructions of the Secretary of the Navy, "are on *no account* to be molested; and I wish particularly to impress on your mind that, should you ever see an American vessel captured by the armed ship of any nation at war with whom we are at peace, you can not lawfully interfere to prevent the capture, for it is to be taken for granted that such nation will compensate for such capture if it shall prove to have been illegally made."

cruising off Guadaloupe. One of the vessels was the captured *Le Croyable*, now the *Retaliation*, commanded by Lieutenant Bainbridge. They discovered some French cruisers, and mistook them for English vessels. The *Retaliation* reconnoitered them, and perceived her mistake too late to avoid trouble. She was attacked by two French frigates (the *Volontaire* and *Insurgente*), and was compelled to surrender. The *Insurgente*, to whom the *Retaliation* was a prize, was one of the swiftest vessels on the ocean. She immediately made chase after two of the American ships, who were pressing all sail in flight. Bainbridge was a prisoner on the *Volontaire*, and, with the officers of that vessel, witnessed the chase with great interest from the forecastle. The *Insurgente* continually gained upon the fugitives. "What are their armaments?" the commander of the *Volontaire* asked Bainbridge. "Twenty-eight twelves and twenty nines," he quickly responded. This false statement doubled their forces, and startled the commander. He was the senior of the captain of the *Insurgente*, and immediately signaled him to give up the chase. The order was reluctantly obeyed. The American vessels escaped, and Bainbridge's deceptive reply cost him only a few curses. In this affair the *Retaliation* gained the distinction of being the first cruiser taken by both parties during the war.

The strength of the navy was considerably increased during the year 1799. Many vessels were launched, and most of them were commissioned before the close of autumn. At the beginning of the year the active force in the West Indies was distributed into four squadrons. Commodore Barry, the senior officer in the service, was in command of ten vessels, with an aggregate of two hundred and thirty-two guns, whose general rendezvous was St. Rupert's Bay. Another squadron of five vessels, under Commodore Truxtun, in the *Constellation*, rendezvoused at St. Kitt's, and cruised to leeward as far as Porto Rico. Captain Tingey, with a smaller force, cruised between Cuba and St. Domingo; and Captain Decatur, with some revenue vessels, watched the interests of American commerce off Havana. These squadrons captured many French vessels during the year.

At meridian on the 9th of February,[a] while the *Constellation* was cruising off Nevis, a large vessel was discovered at the southward. Truxtun gave chase, and brought on an engagement at little past three in the afternoon. It lasted an hour and a quarter, when the antagonist of the *Constellation* struck her colors and surrendered. She was the famous French frigate *Insurgente*, Captain Barreault, just mentioned as the captor of the *Retaliation* a few weeks earlier. The gallant Frenchman did not yield until his fine ship was dreadfully shattered, and he had lost seventy men, killed and wounded. The *Constellation* had lost only three men wounded. The prize was put in charge of Lieutenant (afterward Commodore) Rodgers, and at the end of three days of tempest, danger, and suffering, she was taken into St. Kitt's[1] (St. Christopher), and received a salute from the fort.

[a] 1800.

This victory produced great exultation in the United States, and the navy was declared to be equal to any in the world. The *Insurgente* carried 40 guns and 409 men; the *Constellation* only 32 guns and 309 men. The battle was fought with great skill and bravery on both sides. The press was filled with eulogiums of Truxtun. He received congratulatory addresses from all quarters, and the merchants of Lloyd's Coffee-house, London, sent him a service of plate worth over three thousand dollars, on which a representation of the action was elegantly engraved.[2] The captives were loud in praises of Truxtun's courtesy and kindness;[3] and for a long time a

---

[1] Cooper's *Naval History of the United States*, i., 297; Truxtun's dispatch to the Secretary of the Navy.
[2] Wyatt's *Generals and Commodores of the American Army and Navy*, p. 197.
[3] "I am sorry," Captain Barreault wrote to Truxtun, "that our two nations are at war; but since I unfortunately have been vanquished, I felicitate myself and crew upon being prisoners to you. You have united all the qualities which characterize a man of honor, courage, and humanity. Receive from me the most sincere thanks, and be assured I shall make it a duty to publish to all my fellow-countrymen the generous conduct which you have observed toward us."

song, called "Truxtun's Victory," was sung every where, in private and at public gatherings.[1]

During the remainder of the year nothing of importance was performed by or befell our cruisers. In November Commodore Barry sailed from Newport[a] for France in the *United States*, having Messrs. Wolcott and Davie, the two envoys, on board. He met with no adventures, and performed his errand with satisfaction. Meanwhile our cruisers were busy in the West Indies, watching the interests of American commerce there, and making the French corsairs exceedingly cautious and circumspect. At length another victory gave lustre to the American navy, rendering it very popular, and causing many leading families of the country to place their sons in the service.[2]

[a] November 3, 1799.

The victory was again by Truxtun, in the *Constellation*. Early on the morning of the 1st of February, 1800, while off Guadaloupe seeking for the large French frigate *La Vengeance*, said to be in those waters, he discovered a sail to the south which he took to be an English merchantman. He ran up English colors, but receiving no response, he gave chase. The stranger pressed sail, and it was almost fifteen hours before the *Constellation* came within hailing distance of her. It was then discovered that she was a large French frigate. Truxtun, unabashed, prepared for action. It was opened by the Frenchman, at eight o'clock in the evening, by shots from the stern and quarter guns. A desperate engagement at pistol-shot distance ensued. It lasted until one in the morning, the combatants all the while running free, side by side, and pouring in broadsides. The French frigate suddenly ceased firing, and disappeared so completely in the gloom that Truxtun believed she had gone to the bottom of the sea. At that moment it was discovered that the *Constellation*'s shrouds had been nearly all cut away, and that the mainmast was ready to fall. A heavy squall came on, and the mast went by the board, carrying with it a midshipman and several topmen who were aloft. The stranger, dreadfully crippled, made her way to Curaçao, where she arrived on the 6th.[b] She was the sought-for frigate *La Vengeance*, carrying 54 guns and 400 men, including passengers. Captain Pitot, her commander, acknowledged that he had twice struck his flag during the engagement. She would have been a rich prize for the *Constellation*. It was lost only by the utterly helpless condition of that vessel's mainmast. Truxtun bore away for Jamaica, and it was some time before he knew the name and character of his antagonist, and the prize he had lost.[3]

[b] February, 1800.

---

[1] The song was not poetry, but touched a chord of popular sentiment which responded with great animation. The following is a single verse of the song, which contains eight:

"On board the *Constellation* from Baltimore we came;
We had a bold commander, and Truxtun was his name:
Our ship she mounted forty guns,
And on the main so swiftly runs,
To prove to France Columbia's sons
Are brave Yankee boys."

[2] "The Navy" became a favorite toast at public meetings, and pictures of naval battles and doggerel verses called "naval songs" were sold in the shops and streets. An enterprising crockery merchant had some pitchers of different sizes made in Liverpool, commemorative of the navy. One of them, before me, that belonged to the late W. J. Davis, Esq., of New York, is a white pitcher, about a foot in height. Under the spout, in a wreath, are the words, "SUCCESS TO THE INFANT NAVY," and below this the American eagle, in form like that on the great seal of the United States. On one side is a picture of a full-rigged vessel of war, and some naval emblems in the foreground. On the other side is a map of the United States, having on one side Washington and Liberty, in full-length figures, Fame, with trumpet and wreath, above it; and on the other side Franklin sitting making a record, and a helmeted female, representing America, near which stands Justice. This device was upon pitchers made at about the time of Washington's inauguration as the first President of the United States.

[3] *La Vengeance* had on board the Governor of Guadaloupe and his family, and two general officers, returning to France. She had also a full cargo of sugar and coffee, and a very large amount of specie. She lost, in killed and wounded, one hundred and sixty-two. The *Constellation* lost fourteen men killed and twenty-

NAVAL PITCHER.

OF THE WAR OF 1812.   105

Truxtun's Victory welcomed.   He is honored by Congress.   His public Services.

This second victory over a superior foe gave Truxtun great renown at home and abroad, and the Congress of the United States, by action approved on the 29th of March, 1800, authorized the President to present him a gold medal " emblematical of the late action," with the thanks of the nation.[1]

MEDAL PRESENTED TO COMMODORE TRUXTUN.

five wounded. Eleven of the latter died of their wounds. Among the lost was Midshipman Jarvis, of New York, who commanded the men in the top. He was warned by an old seaman that the mast would soon fall. He gallantly said, "Then we must go with it." They did so, and only one man was saved. Congress, by vote, recognized the bravery of young Jarvis, "who gloriously preferred certain death to an abandonment of his post."

[1] This medal is represented in the engraving, the exact size of the original. On one side is a profile bust of Truxtun in relief, with the legend, "PATRIÆ PATRES FILIO DIGNO THOMAS TRUXTUN." On the reverse are seen two ships of war (the French a two-decker), both shattered, and the rigging of both much cut up. Legend: "THE UNITED STATES FRIGATE CONSTELLATION, OF THIRTY-EIGHT GUNS, PURSUES, ATTACKS, AND VANQUISHES THE FRENCH SHIP LA VENGEANCE, OF FIFTY-FOUR GUNS, 1ST OF FEBRUARY, 1800."

Thomas Truxtun was born at Jamaica, Long Island, on the 17th of February, 1755. He went to sea at the age of twelve years. During his apprenticeship he was impressed into the British service, but was soon released. He commanded a vessel in 1775, and brought considerable powder to the colonies at that time. He was engaged in privateering from Philadelphia during the whole war. While carrying Mr. Barclay, consul general of the United States, to France, he had a successful engagement with a British man-of-war. In 1794 he was appointed by Washington one of the six naval commanders, and the *Constellation* was built under his superintendence at Baltimore. His exploits in her are related in the text. The cruise which resulted in the defeat of *La Vengeance* was his last. In 1802 he was ordered to the command of a squadron destined for the Mediterranean. Being denied a captain to command his flag-ship, he declined the service. His letter to this effect was construed by President Jefferson as a resignation, which was accepted, and the American navy was deprived of one of its brightest ornaments. He retired to a farm not far from Philadelphia, where he remained in quiet until 1816, when the citizens of Philadelphia elected him high sheriff. He held that office three years, and died on the 5th of May, 1822, in the sixty-seventh year of his age. He was buried in Christ Church-yard, Fifth Street, Philadelphia, where a plain upright slab of white marble marks his grave, on which is the following inscription: "Sacred to the memory of Commodore Thomas Truxtun, formerly of the United States Navy, who died May 5th, 1822, aged sixty-seven years." In considering the little sketch of Truxtun's grave, the spectator is supposed to be standing with his back to Fifth Street looking east.

TRUXTUN'S GRAVE.

Peace.　　Troubles among the Federalists.　　Character of President Adams.　　Opposition to Adams in his own Party.

Other victories of less magnitude were won by the American cruisers during the earlier months of the year 1800, and contributed to make the little navy of the United States a subject for praise and wonder in Europe. But its services were now less needed, and efforts to increase the navy were sensibly relaxed during the summer of that year. Active negotiations for peace and amity were in progress between the United States and the First Consul of France, which led to a settlement of difficulties. The American envoys were cordially received, and three plenipotentiaries, with Joseph Bonaparte at their head, were appointed to treat with them. Many difficulties arose, and sometimes an utter failure of the effort seemed inevitable. Finally a convention was concluded,[1] peace was established, the envoys returned home, and the provisional army of the United States was disbanded.

Allusion has been made to the divisions in the Federal party on account of President Adams's course in the appointment of diplomatic agents for negotiations with the French government before that government had officially signified its willingness to receive them. The instant dissatisfaction caused by that act only gave intensity to feelings already existing. Mr. Adams was an honest patriot, of much ability, but totally unfitted by temperament and disposition for the leadership of a great political party. He was excessively vain, and correspondingly sensitive and jealous. His vivid and sometimes eccentric imagination seldom yielded obedience to judgment. His prejudices were violent and inexorable, and his frankness made him indiscreet in his expressions of opinion concerning men and measures. He held resentment against Hamilton as relentless as did Jefferson, and he openly accused him of British proclivities, and hostility to the National Constitution. Because Wolcott, and Pickering, and Ames, and M'Henry, and other leading Federalists could not agree with him concerning public policy, the President regarded them as personal enemies, actuated by selfish objects, and desirous of defeating his most earnest wishes, namely, a re-election to the seat he then occupied. Cunning Democrats fanned the flame of discord; and they strengthened Adams's political aspirations by assuring him that he might unite the moderate and virtuous men of both parties, and thus crush the oligarchy of radical Federalists, to whom all national troubles should be attributed.[2]

It was not long before confidence among the members of the Federal party was almost destroyed. Such were their divisions in the House of Representatives that, notwithstanding they had a decided majority there, they were not able, as Jefferson exultingly wrote, to carry a single measure during the session of 1799–1800. The simple truth appears to be that Adams would not be controlled by the leaders who claimed to have elevated him and his party to power. He exercised his own judgment as President without regard to party. His most ardent political partisans, now become his opponents, reciprocated his own suspicions, and believed that his conduct was prompted by jealousy of Hamilton, and a disposition to secure his own re-election at whatever sacrifice of principle, or at whatever risk to the Federal party.[3]

These suspicions created zealous action. The most influential Federal leaders, two of whom (Timothy Pickering and James M'Henry) were in Adams's Cabinet, adopted a scheme for quietly preventing his re-election to the Presidency, which he ardently desired. The method of choosing the President and Vice-President, at that time, was

---

[1] This convention was signed at Paris on the 30th of September, 1800, by Oliver Ellsworth, William R. Davie, and William Vans Murray, on the part of the United States, and Joseph Bonaparte, Charles P. E. Fleurieu, and Pierre L. Rœderer, in behalf of France. It provided that the old treaties should remain inoperative until a new negotiation should decide concerning them as well as indemnities mutually claimed. It provided for the mutual restoration of captured public ships and property not already condemned; for the mutual payment of all debts due by the respective governments and individuals thereof; for reciprocal commercial relations to be equal to those of the most favored nations, and for security of American commerce against the vexatious pretensions of French cruisers. The convention also declared that *free ships should make free goods*, thus affirming the doctrine of Frederick the Great fifty years earlier, and denying that of England in her famous rule of 1756, revived in 1793.—See the convention in full in the *Statesman's Manual*, iv., 338.　　[2] Oliver Wolcott to Fisher Ames, Dec. 20, 1799.

[3] Hildreth's *History of the United States*, Second Series, ii., 355.

Plans of Federalists for defeating Adams.   Tactics of the Democrats.   The Alien and Sedition Laws.

for two persons to be voted for without distinction as to the office for which they were respectively intended; and the one receiving the highest number of votes was declared President, and the other Vice-President.[1] This plan gave facility to the scheme of Mr. Adams's opponents. A caucus of the Federal members of Congress resolved to place Mr. Adams and Charles Cotesworth Pinckney, of South Carolina, on the same ticket, with the understanding that both should receive the same number of votes, and thus cause the election to be carried to the House of Representatives, where Mr. Pinckney would have a considerable majority. Caution was necessary, for the foe was vigilant, and ever ready to take advantage of the weakness which dissensions would create in the Federal camp. Open opposition to Adams, whose high personal character was appreciated every where, and especially in New England, might have imperiled the success of the party. Mr. Adams, on the other hand, was aware of the intrigues against him, and that members of his Cabinet were leaders in the scheme; yet for once he was discreet enough not to denounce them openly, nor dismiss them from his council, for he was doubtful of his own strength in the powerful Middle States where they were popular, and where the Alien and Sedition Laws, which brought such odium upon his administration, were heartily detested. A Democratic caucus pursued a similar course, and selected Thomas Jefferson and Aaron Burr, but with the understanding that the former was the choice of the party for President.

The Alien and Sedition Laws just alluded to were used adroitly by the Democrats to excite the people against Adams's administration and the Federal party, and that use was made powerful in securing the election of Mr. Jefferson to the Presidency in the year 1800.[2]

---

[1] For the young reader, or a foreigner to whom the working of our political system in detail may not be familiar, an explanation here may be useful. The President of the United States is not voted for directly by the people. Persons in each state, in number equal to the respective senators and representatives in Congress, are elected by the people, and delegated with full powers to choose a President and Vice-President. These meet at a specified time, and form what is termed the Electoral College. Although the electors may vote for whom they please, the candidates named by the people are always voted for in the college, so that practically the people do vote directly for President and Vice-President. In the event of an equal number of votes being cast in the college for both candidates, the election is carried to the House of Representatives, in accordance with the provisions of the National Constitution, Article ii., section 1.

[2] The action of Virginia and Kentucky politicians in the matter were so powerful at the time, and remote, even to our day, in their influence upon public opinion in a portion of the republic concerning the theory of our government, as to warrant the introduction here of the following brief history of the affair:

In the year 1798, when war with France seemed to be unavoidable, Congress passed acts for the security of the government against internal foes. By the first act alien enemies could not become citizens at all. By the second, which was limited to two years, the President was authorized to order out of the country all aliens whom he might judge to be dangerous to the peace and safety of the United States. By a third act, in case of war declared against the United States, or an actual invasion, all resident aliens, natives or citizens of the hostile nation, might, upon a proclamation of the President issued according to his discretion, be apprehended, and secured or removed. These were known as *Alien Laws*. The President never had occasion to employ them, but several prominent Frenchmen, who felt that the laws were aimed at them, speedily left the country. Among them was the celebrated French writer, M. Volney, who, in the preface to his *View of the Soil and Climate of the United States of America*, complained bitterly of the "violent and public attacks made upon his character, with the connivance or instigation of a certain eminent personage," meaning President Adams.

In July, 1798, an act was passed for the punishment of sedition. It made it a high misdemeanor, punishable by a fine not to exceed $5000, imprisonment from six months to five years, and binding to good behavior at the discretion of the court, for any persons unlawfully to combine in opposing measures of the government properly directed by authority, or attempting to prevent government officers executing their trusts, or inciting to riot or insurrection. It also provided for the fining or imprisoning any person guilty of printing or publishing "any false, scandalous, and malicious writings against the government of the United States, or either House of Congress, or the President, with intent to defame them, or to bring them into contempt or disrepute." This was called the *Sedition Law*.

The laws brought out the heaviest batteries of denunciation from the opposition, and were deplored by many of the Federalists. The wise Hamilton perceived the dangers that might arise from the enactment of the Sedition Law, and immediately wrote a hurried note of warning to Wolcott on the 29th of June, saying, "LET US NOT ESTABLISH A TYRANNY. Energy is a very different thing from violence. If we take no false step, we shall be essentially united; but if we push things to the extreme, we shall then give to faction *body* and *solidity*." The fears of Hamilton were realized. Nothing contributed more powerfully to the speedy downfall of the Federal party than these extreme measures.

The Alien and Sedition Laws aroused individual resentments, and led to the public avowal of the doctrine of independent and supreme state sovereignty in its most dangerous form. The right of "nullification" was as distinctly proclaimed by Jefferson and others as it ever was by Calhoun or Hayne. In a series of resolutions drawn up under the seal of secrecy as to their authorship, Mr. Jefferson declared the National Constitution to be a mere compact made by sovereign states *as states*, each having the sole right of interpreting for itself the "compact," and bound by no interpretation but its own; that the general government has no final right, in any of its branches, to interpret the extent of its own powers, and that all its acts not considered constitutional by a state may be properly nullified by such state within

Most of the Presidential electors at that time were chosen by the respective State Legislatures, and not by the people, as now, and the contest was really commenced in the election of members to those bodies. New York was regarded as the custodian of the balance of political power, and the election of that state which occurred at the close of April, 1800, was looked to with great anxiety by both parties. A radical change had taken place. Burr, the most unscrupulous intriguer of the day, worked incessantly, and New York, which the year before gave the Federalists five hundred majority, now gave almost as great a majority for the Democrats. The latter were jubilant—the former were alarmed.

At this time the germ of a new party was distinctly visible in Virginia and the states south of it, which was born of slavery and the doctrine of independent state sovereignty. Virginia was its sponsor, and it allied itself to the Democratic party. And yet, strange as it may seem, Mr. Adams at this time looked to the Southern States for his forlorn hope in the coming election contest. Believing Pickering and M'Henry to be unpopular there, he abruptly called upon them to resign. M'Henry instantly complied, but Pickering refused. Adams dismissed him with little ceremony.[1] The event caused much excitement, and had considerable influence in reducing the Federal vote. Bitter animosities prevailed. Criminations and recriminations ensued.

The open war in the Federal party against Mr. Adams was waged by a few leaders, several of whom resided in Essex County, Massachusetts, the early home of Pickering, and on that account the irritated President called his assailants and opposers the "Essex Junto." He denounced them as slaves to British influence, some lured by monarchical proclivities, and others by English gold. Severe retorts followed; and a pamphlet from the pen of Hamilton, whom Adams had frequently assailed in conversation as a British sympathizer, and an enemy to the National Constitution, damaged the President's political prospects materially.

The result of the canvass was the triumph of the Democratic party. Jefferson was elected President of the United States, and Aaron Burr Vice-President,[2] to the great joy of their partisans, who chanted, in effect,

> "The *Federalists* are down at last!
> The *Monarchists* completely cast!
> The *Aristocrats* are stripped of power—
> Storms o'er the *British faction* lower.
> Soon *we Republicans* shall see
> Columbia's sons from bondage free.
> Lord! how the Federalists will stare
> At JEFFERSON in ADAMS' chair!"—*The Echo.*

---

its own boundaries. These resolutions were offered to the Kentucky Legislature; but the one avowing the absolute right of nullification was modified, or rather substituted by another, before the whole were put upon their passage. This action was in November, 1798. Within a month afterward John Taylor, of Caroline, an avowed secessionist, introduced into the Virginia Legislature a series of resolutions drawn by Mr. Madison, similar in spirit, but more cautious in expression. They were adopted, and, with a plea in their favor, were sent to the various State Legislatures. In some of them they were handled roughly, and all that responded condemned them as unwarrantable and mischievous, excepting already-committed Kentucky. These were the famous "Resolutions of '98," on which nullification in 1832 and secession in 1861 planted themselves and looked for justification. The whole movement was of a local and temporary nature. Jefferson and Madison were wielding dangerous weapons in their sturdy warfare for political power (for that was the animus of the whole matter); but they trusted the people, and believed, as Jefferson said in his inaugural, that great errors may be tolerated when reason is left free to combat them. That nullifiers and secessionists have no warrant for their doctrines in the action of the Virginia Legislature at that time Mr. Madison distinctly declared more than thirty years afterward. "The tenor of the debates," he said, "which were ably conducted, and are understood to have been revised for the press by most, if not all of the speakers, *discloses no reference whatever to a constitutional right in an individual state to arrest by force the operation of a law of the United States.*"—See letter to Edward Everett, August, 1830, in *Selections from the Private Correspondence of James Madison*, published by J. C. M'Guire, of Washington City, for private distribution.

[1] John Marshall, who was soon afterward appointed Chief Justice of the United States, took Pickering's place as Secretary of State, and Samuel Dexter was called to M'Henry's seat in the Cabinet as Secretary of War.

[2] The Electoral College met, and their vote stood as follows: Jefferson, 73; Burr, 73; Adams, 65; Pinckney, 64; John Jay, 1. The votes for Jefferson and Burr being equal, the election, as provided by the Constitution, was carried into the House of Representatives. The occasion presented exciting scenes. On the first ballot eight states voted for Jefferson, six for Burr, and two (Vermont and Maryland) were divided. Two or three members were so sick that they were brought to the House on beds. For seven days the members were occupied in balloting. The Federalists all voted for Burr, as the least offensive of the two candidates, but the friends of Jefferson were stronger than they.

Mortification of the Federalists.   Ins and Outs.   Announcement of the Death of Washington.   Its Effect.

The mortification of the defeated party was intense, and new elements of strife soon mingled with the old causes of contention between the two parties. At these John Quincy Adams hinted when he said, "The election of Mr. Jefferson to the Presidency was, upon sectional feelings, the triumph of the South over the North, of the slave representation over the free. On party grounds, it was the victory of professed Democracy over Federalism, of French over British influence. The party overthrown was the whole Federal party. The whole Federal party was mortified and humiliated at the triumph of Jefferson.[1]

After an existence of eight years as a distinct political organization, the original Federal party fell, never to rise again into power. Its noble monument is the machinery of the national government, which its wise men devised and set in motion, and which still performs its functions with admirable steadiness and increased power —machinery which the opposition declared to be weak and dangerous when they were in the minority, but which they adopted as sound and secure as soon as they came into power. The saying of English politicians, that a Tory in place becomes a Whig out of place, and a Whig when provided with a place becomes a Tory, was exemplified.[2]

While the nation was thus agitated by contending factions and menaced by the tempests of war, the great light of the republic, by whose steady planetary gleams the vessel of state had been long guided, and saved from the rocks and quicksands of faction and anarchy, suddenly went out. In the darkness that fell without twilight —without premonition—every discordant voice was for a moment hushed, for awe placed the finger of silence upon the lips of political partisans of every kind. The National Congress was then in session at Philadelphia. Early on the morning of the 18th of December[a]—a cold, crisp, winter morning—a courier with smoking steed dashed up to the Presidential mansion, and delivered a letter from the private secretary[3] of the great leader, who had already been called PATER PATRIÆ.[4] The President was at breakfast. The seal was black wax. It was broken hastily by Mr. Adams, who read, "It is with inexpressible grief that I have to announce to you the death of the great and good General WASHINGTON. He died last evening, between ten and eleven o'clock, after a short illness of about twenty-four hours."[5]

[a] 1799.

There was grief in the President's household. There was grief in Congress when John Marshall announced[b] "Our Washington is no more." There was grief in the streets of the national capital when the sad intelligence went from lip to ear all over the city within an hour after the arrival of the courier. There was grief throughout the nation when the knell of the funeral bells in cities and villages, with chilling monotone, fell upon the ears of the people. There was grief in Europe when, forty days afterward, it was known in England and on the Continent. Lord Bridport lowered to half mast the flags of his great English fleet

[b] December 19.

---

[1] See *Life of William Plummer*, p. 310.
[2] A London paper in 1813 contained the following poetic version of the maxim, under the head of *Definition of Parties:*

"WHIGS NEVER IN.
A *Whig* is never in! How strange the story!
Turn in a *Whig*—he turns in a *Tory!*

TORIES NEVER OUT.
A *Tory's* never out! Strange whirligig!
Turn out a *Tory*—he turns out a *Whig!*

INS AND OUTS.
Why then turn all our brains with senseless rout?
Tory and *Whig* are merely IN and OUT."

[3] Tobias Lear.
[4] The late G. W. P. Custis, the adopted son of Washington, in a letter to his foster-father written at Annapolis, where he was at school, on the 12th of July, 1798, after congratulating his guardian on his appointment to the command of the American army, said, "Let an admiring world again behold a Cincinnatus springing up from rural retirement to the conquest of nations; and the future historian, in recording so great a name, insert that of the 'Father of his Country.'"
[5] Dated "Mount Vernon, December 15, 1799."

of sixty vessels then lying in Torbay; and Bonaparte, just made First Consul of France, paid a beautiful tribute to the virtues of the beloved man in an order of the day to the French army, and in directing a funeral oration to be pronounced before him and the civil and military authorities.[1] The Congress of his own country, by joint resolutions, decreed[a] that a marble monument should be erected to his memory at the new Capitol on the Potomac; that there should be a funeral procession from Congress Hall to the German Lutheran Church, where an oration should be pronounced by one of the members of Congress; that the citizens of the United States should wear crape on their left arm as mourning for thirty days; and that the President should send a letter of condolence to Mrs. Washington, and request that her husband's remains might be interred at the Capitol of the nation.[2] They also recommended the people of the United States to assemble on the next anniversary of Washington's birthday,[b] " to testify their grief by suitable eulogies, orations, and discourses, or by public prayers."

[a] December 23, 1799.

[b] February 22, 1800.

THE LUTHERAN CHURCH IN PHILADELPHIA.

General Henry Lee, the personal friend of Washington, and son of that "Lowland Beauty" whom the great patriot loved in his early youth, was the chosen orator. With rare eloquence he charmed the vast audience that thronged the Lutheran Church, the largest in Philadelphia.[3] The *M'Pherson Blues*,[4] an elegant military corps of three hundred young men, were there as a guard of honor, and fired the accustomed military salute. On the ensuing 22d of February funeral orations were pronounced in many places throughout the country; and memorials of many kinds were speedily prepared, to perpetuate, by visible objects, the recollection of Washington's vir-

---

[1] This oration was delivered by Louis Fontaine in the Temple of Mars, at Paris, on the 8th of February, 1800. In allusion to the young general and chief ruler of France before him, the orator said, in his peroration, "Yes, thy counsels shall be heard, O Washington! O warrior! O legislator! O citizen without reproach! He who, *while yet young*, rivals thee in battles, shall, like thee, with his triumphant hands, heal the wounds of his country. Even now we have his disposition, his character for the pledge; and his warlike genius, unfortunately necessary, shall soon lead sweet peace into this temple of war. Then the sentiment of universal joy shall obliterate the remembrance of oppression and injustice. Already the oppressed forget their ills in looking to the future. The acclamations of every age will be offered to the hero who gives happiness to France, and seeks to restore it to a contending world."

[2] Mrs. Washington consented to the removal of her husband's remains to the National Capitol. But they have never been taken from his beloved Mount Vernon. They never should be. That home of the illustrious patriot is now the property of the patriotic women of America, and should ever be consecrated by the presence of his tomb. The HOME and TOMB of our beloved friend should be inseparable, and these words of Lunt should express the sentiments of every American:

"Ay, leave him alone to sleep forever,
Till the strong archangel calls for the dead,
By the verdant bank of that gushing river
Where first they pillowed his mighty head."

[3] That German Lutheran Church is yet standing on Fourth Street, Philadelphia, above Arch Street. Lee's oration was hastily prepared, but was an admirable production. In it he used those memorable words, "FIRST IN WAR, FIRST IN PEACE, FIRST IN THE HEARTS OF HIS COUNTRYMEN." This oration may be found in Custis's *Recollections of Washington*.

[4] This corps was composed of the elite of Philadelphia society. The costume is represented in an engraving in Lossing's *Home of Washington, or Mount Vernon and its Associations*. Six of those who were present on that occasion were yet living in January, 1862, and all were residents of Philadelphia, namely, Samuel Breck, aged ninety; S. Palmer, aged eighty-one; S. F. Smith, aged eighty-one; Charles N. Bancker, aged eighty-five; Quintan Campbell, aged eighty-five, and Robert Carr, aged eighty-four. John F. Watson, the annalist of Philadelphia and New York, and who died in De-

tues and illustrious deeds.[1] The faithful history of those deeds is his best eulogy.[2]

> "His glory fills the land—the plain,
>   The moor, the mountain, and the mart!
> More firm than column, urn, or fane,
>   His monument—the human heart.
> The Christian—patriot—hero—sage!
>   The chief from heaven in mercy sent;
> His deeds are written on the age—
>   His country is his monument."
>   GEORGE P. MORRIS.

cember, 1860, was a member. Colonel Carr, who was an officer in the War of 1812, informed me that he was one of the squad who fired the volleys on that occasion. The costume of the M'Pherson Blues is seen in the figure below.

[1] Among many other tokens of respect published at that time was a silver medal, a little larger and thicker than the Spanish quarter of a dollar. One of these is in the possession of the writer, and is represented in the engraving. On one side is a profile of Washington, inclosed in a wreath of laurel, and surrounded by the words, "HE IS IN GLORY, THE WORLD IN TEARS." On the reverse is a memorial urn, and

WASHINGTON MEDAL.

around it, forming two circles, are abbreviations, seen in the engraving, signifying "Born February 11, 1732; General of the American Army, 1775; resigned 1783; President of the United States of America, 1789; retired in 1796; General of the Armies of the United States, 1798; died December 14, 1799." This medal was designed by Dudley A. Tyng, the collector of customs at Newburyport at that time, and engraved and published, immediately after the death of Washington, by Jacob Perkins, the well-known ingenious mechanic and engraver. He cut dies for this design of two sizes.

[2] A contemporary wrote as follows concerning Washington's person and character:

"GENERAL WASHINGTON in his person was tall, upright, and well-made; in manner easy and unaffected. His eyes were of a bluish cast, not prominent, indicative of deep thoughtfulness, and, when in action on great occasions, remarkably lively. His features strong, manly, and commanding; his temper reserved and serious; his countenance grave, composed, and sensible. There was in his whole appearance an unusual dignity and gracefulness which at once secured for him profound respect and cordial esteem. He seemed born to command his fellow-men. In his official capacity he received applicants for favors, and answered their requests with so much ease, condescension, and kindness, as that each retired believing himself a favorite of his chief. He had an excellent and well-cultivated understanding; a correct, discerning, and comprehensive mind; a memory remarkably retentive; energetic passions under perfect control; a judgment sober, deliberate, and sound. He was a man of the strictest honor and honesty; fair and honorable in his dealings; punctual to his engagements. His disposition was mild, kind, and generous. Candor, sincerity, moderation, and simplicity were, in common, prominent features in his character; but, when an occasion called, he was capable of displaying the most determined bravery, firmness, and independence. He was an affectionate husband, a faithful friend, a humane master, and a father to the poor. He lived in the unvarying habits of regularity, temperance, and industry. He steadily rose at the dawn of day, and retired to rest usually at nine o'clock in the evening. The intermediate hours all had their proper business assigned them. In his allotments for the revolving hours religion was not forgotten. Feeling, what he so often publicly acknowledged, his entire dependence on God, he daily, at stated seasons, retired to his closet to worship at His footstool, and to ask His divine blessing. He was remarkable for his strict observation of the Sabbath, and exemplary in his attendance on public worship."

CHAPTER VI.

"The Dey of Algiers, not afraid of his ears,
   Sent to Jonathan once for some tribute:
'Ho! ho!' says the Dey, 'if the rascal don't pay,
   A caper or two I'll exhibit.
I'm the Dey of Algiers, with a beard a yard long;
I'm a Mussulman, too, and of course very strong:
For this is my maxim, dispute it who can,
That a man of stout muscle's a stout Mussulman.'"

EFFERSON'S administration commenced under favorable auspices.[a] There were omens of peace abroad, and these promised calmness and prosperity at home. The league of England and the Continental powers against Bonaparte had failed to impede his progress in the path toward universal dominion; on the contrary, he had brought nearly all Europe trembling at his feet. Within the short space of two years he made himself master of all Italy, and humbled proud Austria by a series of the most splendid victories on record. Within the circle of another two years he had returned from his Oriental campaigns to receive the homage of France, and accept its sceptre in republican form as First Consul. With the absolute power of an emperor, which title he speedily assumed, he prepared to bring to France still more wealth, territory, and glory, by extending her sway from Africa to the North Cape—from the Atlantic to the Ural Mountains. Old thrones shook; and when Bonaparte whispered peace all Europe listened eagerly, for they were words of hope for dynasties and nationalities.

[a] March 4, 1801.

The preliminary Treaty of Luneville,[1][b] affirming that of Campo-Formio,[2] made four years earlier,[c] rendered a reconstruction of the map of Europe necessary, for kings and princes had allowed the successful soldier to change the geographical lines of their dominions. Great Britain was left alone in armed opposition to the conquering Corsican. Even her late allies against him, always jealous of her maritime superiority, were now his foes. The league of Northern powers, known as the Armed Neutrality,[3] was re-established by treaty[d] at the instigation of the Emperor Paul, of Russia, and from their council went forth the spirit of Cato's words concerning the offending African city: *Delenda est Carthago*—"Carthage must be destroyed." They resolved to contradict by force her doctrine concerning the freedom of neutrals,[4] and naval armaments were put afloat. At the same time Bonaparte was threatening Great Britain with invasion, and her rich East India possessions with the tread of the conqueror.

[b] February 9, 1801.
[c] October 17, 1797.
[d] December 16, 1800.

Although burdened with taxation to a degree before unknown, and wearied with her long contest with France and the Irish rebellion under her own roof,[5] Britain

---

[1] The peace concluded at Luneville between the French Republic and the Emperor of Germany, after confirming the Treaty of Campo-Formio, stipulated that the Rhine to the Dutch Territories should form the boundaries of France, and recognizing the independence of the Bavarian, Helvetic, Ligurian, and Cisalpine Republics.

[2] In the Treaty of Campo-Formio, between France and Austria, the latter yielded the Low Countries and the Ionian Islands to the former, and Milan, Mantua, and Modena to the Cisalpine Republic which Bonaparte had established in Italy. By a secret article, the Emperor of Austria took possession of the Venitian dominions, in compensation for the Netherlands.   [3] See note 2, on page 83.   [4] See note 1, page 84.

[5] The Roman Catholics and the Protestant Dissenters in Ireland were subjected to cruel and insulting disabilities by the English in regard to both civil and religious privileges. In 1791 a society was formed, chiefly under the direction of Wolfe Tone, for the purpose of procuring Parliamentary reform in this matter. They were called "United Irishmen." They were also animated by republican sentiments, and a hatred of England as an oppressor. Inspired by events in

once more put forth her strength on the ocean. Parker and Nelson destroyed the Danish fleet at Copenhagen,[a] and brought that government to submission; the other powers of the league, alarmed, and deserted by Paul's successor, withdrew from the unequal contest, and left England still boasting, as in Waller's time, two hundred years ago, that her ships were

[a] April 2, 1801.

"Riding without a rival on the sea;"

or chanting, with the faith of Thomson, a hundred years later,

"When Britain first, at Heaven's command,
Arose from out the azure main,
This was the charter of the land,
And guardian angels sung the strain:
Rule Britannia; Britannia rules the waves!
Britons never shall be slaves."

England was willing to have peace, but not with the loss of an iota of her power. A peace ministry, with Mr. Addington at its head, assumed the reins of government in the spring of 1801. It looked with favor upon the dispersion of the war-clouds which had so long brooded over Europe. During that year one after another of the Continental powers wheeled into the line of amicable relations with Bonaparte,[1] and in March, 1802,[b] by treaty at Amiens,[2] he and George the Third became technical friends, much to the disgust of a powerful war party in England, who would not trust the word of the ambitious Corsican for an hour. They believed his object to be rest and gaining of time, while he should make preparations for more formidable blows for the subjugation of Europe. But they were compelled to yield to the greater faith, or the greater needs, of the government and the majority. There was sunlight abroad, and a bow of promise in the sky. It seemed as if universal peace was about to be established in Europe, and Bonaparte was hailed as a pacificator. England blazed with bonfires and illuminations; was resonant with speeches and sermons; feasted in public halls in testimony of her faith and joy, and enriched her literature with addresses and poems on the apparent dawning of a political millennium. Forgetful of the past deeds of Bonaparte, which they had denounced as *crimes*, Englishmen flocked to Paris to bow before the rising sun of power, and carried back with them French fashions in abundance, as tokens of their satisfaction. The sly Corsican, chuckling over their obsequiousness, and their blindness to his real designs, treated the most distinguished of his English admirers with marked respect, and received in turn such fulsome adulation that right-minded men in Great Britain blushed with shame.[3]

[b] March 25.

The machinery of government was all adjusted for the easy management of the

---

France, these "United Irishmen," whose society extended all over the kingdom, resolved to strike for liberty and establish a republican form of government for Ireland. In this they received the aid of France. They nominated an executive directory in 1797. Their plans, carried on with the utmost secrecy, were ripe for execution, when they were discovered and denounced by a government spy. Many of the leaders were arrested, but an open, armed rebellion was suddenly developed all over the kingdom in May, 1798. Great Britain put forth its military power, then strong at home, in anticipation of an invasion by the armies in France, and the insurrection was crushed in the course of a few months.

[1] France concluded a treaty of peace with Naples March 18, 1801; with Spain, March 21; with the Pope, July 15; with Bavaria, August 24; with Portugal, September 29; with Russia, October 4; with Turkey, October 9; and with Algiers, December 7.

[2] This was a treaty between Great Britain, Holland, France, and Spain. The preliminary treaty had been signed on the 1st of October, 1801. The definitive treaty was signed by Lord Cornwallis, for England; Joseph Bonaparte, for France; Azara, for Spain, and Schimmelpenninck, for Holland.

[3] Among those who went over at that time were Charles James Fox and his nephew, Lord Holland, Lords Erskine, Grey, and other leading men. These visits excited the ridicule of satirists. Gillray's pencil was active. Several caricatures from his brain were speedily published. He ridiculed the visit of Fox and his friends in a caricature entitled "*Introduction of Citizen Volprone and Suite at Paris*," in which Fox and his wife, Lord and Lady Holland, and Grey and Erskine, are seen stooping low before the new ruler of France. One of the most popular of his caricatures was entitled "*The first Kiss this ten years, or the meeting of Britannia and Citizen François*." Britannia, who has suddenly become corpulent, appears as a fine lady in full dress, her shield and spear leaning neglected against the wall. The citizen expresses his joy at the meeting in warm terms. "Madame," he says, "permittez me to pay my profound esteem to your engaging person, and to seal on your divine lips my everlasting attachment!!!" The lady, blushing deeply, replies, "Monsieur, you are a truly well-bred gentleman; and though you make me blush, yet you kiss so delicately I can not refuse you, though I was sure you would deceive me again!" On the wall just behind these two figures are portraits of King George and Bonaparte scowling at each other.—See Wright's *England under the House of Hanover*, ii., 391.

new President of the United States. The treasury had never been so full, nor the revenue so abundant as at that time, and he was enabled to signalize the commencement of his administration and to strengthen it by the repeal of the excise and other obnoxious acts, which were necessary at the beginning. Commerce, and all the industrial interests of the country, were flourishing, and the pathway of the new chief magistrate of the republic seemed plain, flowery, and luminous.

The seat of government had just been removed to the city of Washington, the new capital of the nation, and then an insignificant village on the bank of the Potomac, on the verge of a Maryland forest,[1] in the District of Columbia.[2] There, in one of the wings of the half-finished Capitol, the last session of Congress had been held; and there, on the 4th of March, 1801, Chief Justice Marshall administered to Mr. Jefferson the oath of office, and he became the third President of the United States.[3]

Although Jefferson was a radical Republican, he made no special changes in the inaugural ceremonies used by his predecessors. He abolished public levees at the Presidential mansion, and sent messages in writing to Congress, instead of

---

[1] "There is one good tavern about forty rods from the Capitol, and several other houses are built or erecting," Oliver Wolcott wrote to a friend in the autumn of 1800; "but I don't see how the members of Congress can possibly secure lodgings unless they will consent to live like scholars in a college or monks in a monastery, crowded ten or twenty in one house. The only resource for such as wish to live comfortably will be found in Georgetown, three miles distant, over as bad a road in winter as the clay grounds near Hartford. . . . There are, in fact, but few houses in any one place, and most of them small, miserable huts, which present an awful contrast to the public buildings. The people are poor, and, as far as I can judge, they live like fishes, by eating each other. . . . You may look in almost any direction, over an extent of ground nearly as large as the city of New York, without seeing a fence or any object except brick-kilns and temporary huts for laborers. . . . There is no industry, society, or business."

Mrs. Adams, wife of the President, wrote in November, 1800: "Woods are all you see from Baltimore until you reach the *city*, which is only so in name. Here and there is a small cot, without a glass window, interspersed among the forests, through which you travel miles without seeing a human being." Concerning the President's house, which she speaks of as "upon a grand and superb scale, requiring about thirty servants to attend and keep the apartments in proper order, and perform the ordinary business of the house and stables," she said, "If they will put me up some bells—there is not one hung through the whole house, and promises are all you can obtain—and let me have wood enough to keep fires, I design to be pleased. I could content myself almost any where for three months; but, surrounded with forests, can you believe that wood is not to be had, because people can not be found to cut and cart it! Briesler entered into a contract with a man to supply him with wood; a small part—a few cords only—has he been able to get. Most of that was expended to dry the walls of the house before we came in, and yesterday the man told him it was impossible to procure it to be cut and carted. He has had recourse to coals, but we can not get grates made and set. We have, indeed, come into a *new country*."

[2] The District of Columbia was a tract ten miles square, lying on each side of the Potomac, and ceded to the United States by the States of Maryland and Virginia, for the residence of the national government. The portion lying in Virginia was retroceded to that state a few years ago. The city of Washington was laid out in 1791, and the erection of the Capitol was commenced in 1793, when, on the 18th of April, President Washington laid the corner-stone, with masonic ceremonies. The two wings were completed in 1808. The government, which had resided ten years in Philadelphia, moved to Washington in the autumn of 1800.

[3] Thomas Jefferson was born at Shadwell, Albemarle County, Virginia, on the 13th of April, 1743. He was educated at William and Mary's College, studied law with the eminent George Wythe, and was admitted to the bar while yet a very young man. He was a member of the Virginia Assembly before the Revolution, and won fame as a vigorous thinker and writer. He was elected to the Continental Congress in 1775, and in 1776, at the request of a committee of which he was a member, he drew up the Declaration of Independence. He was offered an embassy to France, but declined it on account of feeble health. In 1779 he was elected Governor of Virginia, and in 1780 retired from public life, and devoted his time chiefly to literary and scientific pursuits. He was sent to France in 1783, to join Adams and Franklin, as representative of his country, and in 1785 succeeded Franklin as minister at the French Court. He remained there until 1789, when he returned, and entered Washington's Cabinet as Secretary of State. He remained in that position until 1793. He was elected Vice-President of the United States in 1796, and in 1801 was elected to the Presidency. He was

Mr. Jefferson foreshadows his Policy.   His Popularity.   A National Party desired.   Political Proscription begun.

delivering speeches in person, because he considered these customs too monarchical in form.[1]

A small military and civic escort conducted Mr. Jefferson to the Capitol, and there he read his inaugural address to a large crowd of delighted listeners. It had been looked for with anxiety, as it would foreshadow the policy of the new administration.[2] It was patriotic, conservative, and conciliatory, and allayed many apprehensions of his political opponents. "Every difference of opinion," he said, "is not a difference of principle. We have called by different names brethren of the same principle. We are all Federalists—we are all Republicans."[3]

In this spirit Mr. Jefferson commenced his administration. He set about the reform of public abuses, treated every body with kindness, and left most of the incumbents of public offices untouched for a while.[4] His political enemies were compelled to confess his forecast, wisdom, and faithfulness; and many Federalists, believing that he would not disturb their friends in office, joined the Republican party, and became the most vehement denunciators of their old partisans and their principles.[5]

Mr. Jefferson soon discovered that he was not wholly his own master. He had been elevated to power by a party whose leaders, like those of all parties, were lustful for office. He was compelled to listen to their clamors, and finally to yield acquiescence in their doctrine that "to the victor belongs the spoils."[6] He gradually filled many of the most important offices in his gift with his political friends, for whose accommodation faithful men, a large proportion of them appointed by Washington and retained by Adams, were removed. Thus was developed in alarming proportions that system of proscription commenced by the second President, which has worked mischievously in the administration of our general and state governments from that time until the present. It bore immediate fruit in the form of bitter partisanship. The Federalists, now become the opposition, and thereby having the advantage in controversy, began a relentless warfare upon the new administration as soon as its proscriptive policy was manifested. With that warfare, as a mere game of politics, we have nothing to do, except so far as it had a bearing upon

---

re-elected in 1805, and in 1809 retired to private life, from which he was never again drawn. He died at his residence at Monticello on the 4th of July, 1826, in the 84th year of his age. Like Adams, he departed on the fiftieth anniversary of the Declaration of Independence. The profile of Mr. Jefferson, given on page 114, is from an impression from a private plate made in aquatinta about the year 1804, and presented by the President to the Hon. D. C. Verplanck, who was a member of Congress from 1803 until 1809.

[1] The personal appearance of President Jefferson at this period may be imagined from the following description by William Plumer, United States senator from New Hampshire in 1802: "The next day after my arrival I visited the President, accompanied by some Democratic members. In a few moments after our arrival a tall, high-boned man came into the room. He was dressed, or rather undressed, in an old brown coat, red waistcoat, old corduroy smallclothes much soiled, woolen hose, and slippers without heels. I thought him a servant, when General Varnum surprised me by announcing that it was the President."—See *Life of William Plumer*, p. 242.

[2] In a letter to Nathaniel Macon, of North Carolina, on the 14th of May, Mr. Jefferson indicated his policy as follows: "1. Levees are done away with. 2. The first communication to the next Congress will be, like all subsequent ones, by message, to which no answer will be expected. 3. The diplomatic establishment in Europe will be reduced to three ministers. 4. The compensation of collectors depends on you [Congress], and not on me. 5. The army is undergoing a chaste reformation. 6. The navy will be reduced to the legal establishment by the last of this month. 7. Agencies in every department will be revised. 8. We shall push you to the uttermost in economizing. 9. A very early recommendation has been given to the Postmaster General to employ no printer, foreigner, or Revolutionary Tory in any of his offices."

[3] See the *Statesman's Manual*, i., 242, where the President's inaugural message is printed in full.

[4] Mr. Jefferson appointed James Madison Secretary of State, Henry Dearborn Secretary of War, and Levi Lincoln Attorney General. He retained Mr. Adams's Secretaries of the Treasury and Navy until the following autumn, when Albert Gallatin was appointed to the first, and Robert Smith to the second. These were both Republicans, and his Cabinet was now wholly so.

[5] Mr. Jefferson dreamed, patriotically, of a consolidated national party and a brilliant administration. In a letter to John Dickinson, two days after his inauguration, he wrote, "I hope to see shortly a perfect consolidation, to effect which, nothing shall be wanting on my part short of the abandonment of the principles of the Revolution. A just and solid republican government maintained here, will be a standing monument and example for the aim and imitation of the people of other countries." Yet he early resolved on rewards to friends. To Colonel Monroe he wrote on the 7th of March, "To give time for a perfect consolidation seems prudent. I have firmly refused to follow the counsels of those who have desired the giving of offices to some of the Federalist leaders in order to reconcile. I have given, and will give, only to Republicans, under existing circumstances."

[6] This doctrine was first announced in these words by the late William L. Marcy when he assumed the administration of the public affairs of the State of New York as governor in 1833.

public events during the few years immediately preceding the War of 1812, and held relationship thereto.

It seems proper at this point in our narrative to say, that the sketch of the rise and progress of the two great political parties which existed in the United States at the beginning of the present century, and whose animosities and aspirations had much to do in bringing about a war in 1812, has been given for the purpose, first, to afford our general subject that much-needed elucidation, and, secondly, to connect by dependent links of historic outlines the events of the FIRST with those of the SECOND WAR FOR INDEPENDENCE.

At the close of Mr. Adams's administration,[a] Congress passed a law[1] authorizing the President to place the navy on a rigid peace footing, by retaining only thirteen frigates,[2] and only six of these to be kept in active service. The act authorized him to dismantle and sell all others, and lay up seven of the thirteen in a way in which they might be carefully preserved. It also authorized him to reduce the complement of officers and men, by retaining in the service, in time of peace, only nine captains, thirty-six lieutenants, and one hundred and fifty midshipmen, including those employed on the six frigates kept in active service, and to discharge the remainder. Under this authority, and in accordance with his own judgment concerning rigid economy and the prospect of universal peace, Mr. Jefferson sold all but the thirteen frigates named, laid up seven of these, and discharged all the officers and men in excess after placing the service on a peace footing. And yet, in the matter of force, nearly four fifths was retained, for the vessels sold were mostly inferior, and only fourteen of them had been built expressly for the government service. The President also suspended work on six ships authorized by Congress in 1798. So little did the American people then seem to apprehend the value of a competent navy for the protection of their commerce every where, as well as the honor of the nation, that a majority of them applauded these measures, while many Federalists assailed them only for political effect. That strong arm of the government which had so protected commerce as to enable the Americans to sell to foreign countries, during the difficulties with France, surplus products to the amount of $200,000,000, and to import sufficient to yield the government a revenue exceeding $23,000,000, was thus paralyzed by an unwise economy in public expenditure.

[a] March, 1801.

The conduct of the Barbary Powers soon made the want of an efficient navy painfully apparent. The government of the United States had purchased, by the payment in full of a stipulated sum of money, the friendship, or rather the forbearance of the Bey of Tripoli, while to the Dey of Algiers and the Bey of Tunis tribute in money, military and maritime stores, and other presents was annually paid.[3] The submission of all the Christian nations of Europe to these exactions made those pirate-kings exceedingly insolent, and finally, in the spring of 1801, the President resolved to humble the pride and the power of those commercial marauders, release American commerce from their thrall in the Mediterranean, and assert the dignity of his country by ceasing to pay tribute to another. This resolution was strengthened by the

---

[1] Approved March 3, 1801.
[2] These were the *United States, Constitution, President, Chesapeake, Philadelphia, Constellation, Congress, New York, Boston, Essex, Adams, John Adams,* and *General Greene*. These had an aggregate armament of 364 guns. The vessels sold were the *George Washington, Ganges, Portsmouth, Merrimack, Connecticut*, of 24 guns each; the *Baltimore, Delaware,* and *Montezuma*, of 20 guns each; the *Maryland, Patapsco, Herald, Trumbull, Warren, Norfolk, Richmond,* and *Pinckney*, of 18 guns each; the *Eagle, Augusta,* and *Scammel*, 14 guns each; the *Experiment*, 9 guns, and nine galleys.—COOPER, i., 333–4.
[3] Colonel Ebenezer Stevens, an active and eminent merchant of New York, and who had been a meritorious artillery officer during the Revolution, was employed by the government as its factor in forwarding the stores to Tunis. In May, 1801, Secretary Madison wrote to Mr. Stevens on the subject, saying, "It is desirable that the remaining cargo of maritime and military stores due to the Regency of Tunis should be provided and shipped without loss of time. The powder will be given to you from the public magazines, and the Navy Department will give orders to its agent at New York or elsewhere, as may be most convenient, to supply the cannon and such other articles as you may want and can be spared."—*MS. letter*. How much *cheaper* and more *dignified* it would have been to have sent the materials in ships of war, fully prepared, as they might have been, to knock the capitals of those semi-barbaric rulers about their ears, and sink their corsairs in the deep waters of the Mediterranean!

insolent treatment of Commodore Bainbridge by the Dey of Algiers the previous year. In May, 1800, Bainbridge, in command of the *George Washington*, 24, went out with the usual tribute to the Algerine ruler. He arrived in the port of his capital in September, performed with courtesy the duties enjoined upon him, and was about to leave, when the Dey commanded him to carry an Algerine embassador to the Court of the Sultan at Constantinople. Bainbridge politely refused compliance, when the haughty and offended Dey said sternly, " You pay me tribute, by which you become my slaves, and therefore I have a right to order you as I think proper." The guns of the castle were looking out vigilantly upon Bainbridge's frigate, and without their permission he could not pass out of the harbor. He was compelled to yield to the force of circumstances, being assured by Mr. O'Brien, once a captive and then American consul there, that if he attempted to leave the harbor, the guns of the castle, heavy and well-manned, would open upon his vessel with destructive effect, his ship would be seized and used for the purpose, and war would ensue. To avoid these calamities Bainbridge bowed submissively to the humiliation; and he even complied

ALGIERS IN 1800.

with the haughty ruler's farther requisition, that he should carry the Algerine flag at the main, and that of the United States at the fore. He sailed out of the port of Algiers an obedient slave, and then, placing his own flag in the position of honor as a freeman, he bore the Algerine embassador to the Golden Horn. "I hope," he wrote to the Secretary of the Navy, "I shall never again be sent to Algiers with tribute, unless I am authorized to deliver it from the mouth of our cannon."

Under other circumstances this trip to the ancient city of Constantinople would have been a desirable one, for Bainbridge had the honor of displaying the stars and stripes for the first time before that famous seat of Ottoman empire. The Sultan and his great officers of state were astonished. They had never heard of the United States; but when, at length, they were made to comprehend that it was a country beyond the great sea, discovered by Columbus, of which they had heard vague and romantic rumors, Bainbridge was received with the greatest courtesy. He and the Turkish admiral became warm friends; and when Bainbridge was about to return to Algiers in January, the latter gave him a *firman* to protect him from farther insolence there. The Sultan, whose flag bore the crescent moon, drew a favorable omen from this visit of a banner bearing its neighbors, the stars of heaven. He believed the two nations must ever be friends, and so they have been.

On his return to Algiers[a] the Dey requested Bainbridge to go on another errand to Constantinople. Bainbridge peremptorily refused. The Dey flew into a rage, threatened war, and finally menaced the captain with personal violence. Bainbridge quietly produced his *firman*, when the fierce governor became lamb-like, and obsequiously offered to the man he had just looked upon as his slave,

[a] January 21, 1801.

The Dey of Algiers humbled.   Insolence of the Bey of Tunis.   Commodore Dale in the Mediterranean.

friendship and service. Taking advantage of this change, Bainbridge assumed the air of a dictator, and demanded the instant release of the French consul and fifty or sixty of his countrymen, who had lately been imprisoned by the Dey. When Bainbridge left he carried away with him all the French in Algiers. His compulsory visit to Constantinople resulted in great good to his fellow-men.

The Bey or Bashaw of Tripoli,[1] not content with the gross sum that had been paid him by the United States, when he learned that his neighbors had received larger bribes than he, demanded tribute in the autumn of 1800, and threatened war if his demand was not satisfied within six months. Accordingly, in May, 1801, he ordered the flag-staff of the American consulate to be cut down, and proclaimed war. In anticipation of these events, Commodore Dale had been sent with a small squadron, consisting of the *President*, 44, Captain James Barron; *Philadelphia*, 38, Captain Samuel Barron; *Essex*, 32, Captain Bainbridge, and *Enterprise*, 12, Lieutenant Commandant Sterrett. The *President* was Dale's flag-ship. The squadron sailed from Hampton Roads, and reached Gibraltar on the 1st of July. Dale soon proceeded eastward in company with the *Enterprise*, and appeared off Tripoli and Tunis, to the great astonishment of the rulers of those states. On the way the *Enterprise* fell in with, attacked, and captured a Tripolitan corsair called the *Tripoli*, reducing her, in the course of an engagement of three hours, almost to a wreck, and killing and wounding twenty of her men, without the loss of a single man on her side.[2] Meanwhile the *Philadelphia* was cruising in the Straits

of Gibraltar, to prevent two Tripolitan corsairs which were found there going out upon the Atlantic; and the *Essex* sailed along the northern shores of the Mediterranean, to convoy American merchant ships. Dale continued to cruise in the Mediterranean until autumn, and his presence exercised a most wholesome restraint over the corsairs.[3]

Another expedition was sent to the Mediterranean in 1802, under Commodore Richard V. Morris. It was a relief squadron, and consisted of the *Chesapeake*, 38, Lieutenant Chauncey, acting captain; *Constellation*, 38, Captain Murray; *New York*, 36, Captain James Barron; *John Adams*, 28, Captain Rodgers; *Adams*, 28, Captain Campbell, and *Enterprise*, 12, Lieutenant Commandant Sterrett. Morris hoisted his broad pennant on board the *Chesapeake*. The squadron did not go in a body, but proceeded one after another from February until September. Meanwhile the *Boston*,

---

[1] This was Jussuf Caramalli. He was a third son, and had obtained the seat of power by violence. He murdered his father and elder brother, and deposed his next brother, Hamet, the rightful heir, who at this time was an exile in Egypt, whither he fled to save his life, followed by quite a large number of adherents.

[2] The *rais* or commander of the *Tripoli* was Mahomet Sous. Three times during the engagement the *Tripoli* struck her colors, and as often treacherously renewed the combat, when Lieutenant Sterrett determined to sink her. She was too much of a wreck to be taken into port—indeed, according to instructions, she could not be made a prize—and she was dismantled under the direction of Lieutenant David Porter. When her commander reached Tripoli, wounded and heart-broken, he was subjected to great indignity. He was placed upon a jackass, paraded through the streets, and afterward received the bastinado.

[3] Richard Dale was born near Norfolk, Virginia, on the 6th of November, 1756. He went to sea at the age of twelve years, and continued in the merchant service until 1776, when he became lieutenant of a Virginia cruiser. He was an active officer during the whole war of the Revolution, and was with Paul Jones in his gallant action with the *Serapis* in September, 1779. He was then only about twenty-three years of age. He was a great favorite with Jones, and the latter presented to Dale the elegant gold-mounted sword which Jones received from the King of France. It is now in the possession of his grandson, Richard Dale, of Philadelphia, where I saw it in November, 1861. The handle, guard, and hilt,

commanded by the eccentric Captain M'Neill (son of Hector M'Neill, of the Revolutionary navy),[1] was cruising in the Mediterranean in an independent way, after conveying Robert R. Livingston, the United States minister, to France. The port of Tripoli was blockaded by her early in May, where she was joined by the *Constellation*. The latter vessel was soon left alone, as M'Neill avoided the company of others, and not long afterward she had a severe contest with a flotilla of seventeen Tripolitan gun-boats. She handled them severely, as well as some cavalry on the shore, with her great guns.

The *Chesapeake* reached Gibraltar on the 25th of May, and found the *Essex*, Captain Bainbridge, still blockading the two Tripolitan cruisers there. The arrival of the *Adams* late in July enabled the *Chesapeake*, in company with the *Enterprise*, to cruise along the north shore of the Mediterranean for the protection of American commerce. Finally orders were given for the different vessels of the squadron to rendezvous at Malta. They collected there in the course of the month of January, 1803, and during the spring appeared off the ports of the Barbary Powers, and effectually restraining their corsairs. Tripoli was blockaded by the *John Adams* in May. She had a severe engagement toward the close of the month with gun-boats and land batteries. These suffered severely, and the Americans lost twelve or fifteen in killed and wounded. An unsuccessful attempt to negotiate a peace was made the next day, and in June the movements of the Algerine and Tunisian corsairs induced the Americans to raise the blockade. But, before leaving, Commodore Rodgers, of the *John Adams* (then in chief command), with the *Enterprise*, attacked a large Tripolitan corsair lying in a sheltered bay, and drove her people to the shore. The corsair soon afterward blew up, with a large number of persons who had returned to her. The ships then all left the Barbary coast, and Commodore Morris returned home. He arrived toward the close of November, 1803. The conduct of affairs in the Mediterranean under his direction was not satisfactory. A court of inquiry decided that he had not " discovered due diligence and activity in annoying the enemy," and the President, with a precipitation difficult to be defended, dismissed him from the service without trial.[2]

The United States government had determined to act with more vigor against the Barbary Powers, and in May, 1803, Commodore Preble was appointed to the com-

DALE'S MONUMENT.

and the mountings of the scabbard are solid gold, with beautifully-wrought devices on them. Upon the blade is the following inscription: VINDICATI MARIS LUDIVICUS XVI. REMUNERATOR STRENUO VIRTUTI—"Louis XVI. rewarder of the valiant asserter of the freedom of the sea."

Dale left the service in 1780. In 1794 he was appointed one of the six naval captains by Washington. He was made commodore in 1801 by being placed in command of a squadron, and the following year he resigned. He retired with a competency, and spent the remainder of his days in Philadelphia, where he died in 1826, in the sixty-ninth year of his age.

The grave of Commodore Dale is in Christ Church-yard, on Fifth Street, Philadelphia. His monument is a marble slab, with the following inscription: "In memory of Commodore RICHARD DALE, born November 6, 1756, died February 24, 1826. An honest man, an incorruptible patriot, in all his relations conciliating universal love. A Christian without guile, he departed this life in the well-founded and triumphant hope of that blessedness which awaits all who, like him, die in the Lord." On the same slab is an inscription commemorative of the virtues of his wife, who died in September, 1832, at the age of sixty-five years. Very near this tomb is a handsome marble cross, erected to the memory of Montgomery, a son of Commodore Dale, also of the United States navy, who died in December, 1852, at the age of fifty-five years.

[1] See Lossing's *Field-Book of the Revolution*, ii., 640.

[2] Richard Valentine Morris was the youngest son of Lewis Morris, of Morrisania, New York, one of the signers of the Declaration of Independence. He entered the service in early life, and in June, 1798, he was commissioned a captain in the navy. He was retained as fifth in rank at the reduction of the navy in 1801. His dismissal from the service has ever been considered a high-handed political measure. He died while attending the Legislature at Albany in 1814.

mand of a squadron, consisting of the *Constitution*, 44, *Philadelphia*, 38, *Argus* and *Siren*, 16 each, and *Nautilus*, *Vixen*, and *Enterprise*, 12 each. Preble sailed in the *Constitution* at the middle of August, and the other vessels followed as fast as they were made ready. The *Philadelphia*, Captain Bainbridge, had sailed in July, and on the 26th of August captured the Moorish frigate *Meshboha*, found holding in possession an American merchant vessel which she had taken as a prize. It was discovered that her commander was acting under the orders of the Moorish Governor of Tangiers to cruise for American vessels. The *Philadelphia* returned to Gibraltar with her prize.

On the arrival of Preble he determined to sail for Tangiers and make inquiries respecting the hostile proceedings of the Moors. He was accompanied by Commodore Rodgers, and on the 6th of October the *Constitution*, *New York*, *John Adams*, and *Nautilus* entered the Bay of Tangiers. Preble had an interview with the Emperor of Morocco, who disavowed the act of the Governor of Tangiers, and expressed a desire to remain at peace with the United States.

The difficulty with Morocco being settled, Rodgers sailed for home, and Preble made energetic preparations to bring Tripoli to terms. A serious disaster soon occurred. On the morning of the 31st of October the *Philadelphia* chased a Tripolitan ship into the harbor of Tripoli. In endeavoring to beat off she struck on a rock not laid down in any of the charts. Every effort to get her off failed, and she was attacked and finally captured by the Tripolitans. Bainbridge and his officers and men were made prisoners, and two days afterward the ship was extricated and taken into the harbor. The officers were treated as prisoners of war, but the crew were made slaves.

Bainbridge found means to report his misfortune to Preble at Malta, and to suggest the destruction of the *Philadelphia*, which was being fitted for sea. Preble had recently appeared off Tripoli for the first time. On the 23d of December the *Enterprise*, Lieutenant Decatur, sailing in company with the flag-ship, captured a ketch called the *Mastico*, then belonging to the Tripolitans, and bound to Constantinople with a present of female slaves for the Sultan. Heavy storms arose, and Preble and Decatur sailed into Syracuse, where the ketch was appraised and taken into the service, with the name of the *Intrepid*.

Decatur had formed a plan for cutting out or destroying the *Philadelphia*. It was approved by Preble; and on the 3d of February, 1804, he left Syracuse with orders and preparations to destroy her. The *Intrepid* was chosen for the service, and seventy-four determined young men sailed in her for the port of Tripoli, accompanied by the brig *Siren*, Lieutenant Stewart. Heavy storms delayed their operations until the 16th, when, in the evening, the young moon shining brightly, the *Intrepid* sailed into the harbor, and was warped alongside the *Philadelphia* without exciting suspicion, she having assumed the character of a vessel in distress. Most of the officers and men were concealed until the ketch was placed alongside the *Philadelphia*. Then,

OF THE WAR OF 1812.   121

Destruction of the *Philadelphia*.   Tripoli bombarded.   A hand to hand Fight.   Gallantry of Decatur.

for the first, the Tripolitans suspected them. At the same moment Decatur and other officers sprang on board the frigate, followed by their men. In a few minutes the turbaned defenders of the vessel were all killed or driven into the sea. She was immediately set on fire, in the midst of the roar of cannon from the Tripolitan batteries and castle, and from two corsairs near. The scene was magnificent; and as the guns of the *Philadelphia* became heated they were discharged. The *Intrepid* was in imminent danger from the flames, but she escaped. Not one of the gallant Decatur's men was killed, and only four were wounded. In the light of the conflagration the *Intrepid*, by the aid of oars, swept out of the harbor, where the boats of the *Siren*, with their strong sweeps, were in readiness to aid in towing her off. Before a pleasant breeze both vessels sailed for Syracuse, where the American squadron and the people of the town welcomed them with strong demonstrations of joy. For this heroic act Decatur was promoted to captain, and several of the other officers who accompanied him were advanced.

This bold act greatly alarmed the Bey or Bashaw of Tripoli, and the ensuing blockade of his port by Commodore Preble made him exceedingly circumspect. Finally, at the close of July,[a] Preble entered the harbor of Tripoli with his squadron, and anchored the *Constitution* two and a half miles from the walled city, whose protection lay in heavy batteries mounting one hundred and fifteen cannon, nineteen gun-boats, a brig, two schooners, and some galleys, twenty-five thousand land-soldiers, and a sheltering reef of dangerous rocks and shoals. These did not dismay Preble. On the 3d of August, at three in the afternoon, he opened a heavy cannonade and bombardment from his gun-boats, which alone could get near enough for effective service. Conflict in closer range soon took place, and finally Lieutenant Decatur, commanding gun-boat *Number Four*, lay his vessel alongside one of the largest of those of the enemy, and boarded and captured her after a desperate struggle.[1] He immediately boarded another, when he had a most desperate personal encounter with the powerful Tripolitan captain. The struggle was brief but deadly. The captain was finally killed by Decatur at a moment of fearful peril, and the vessel was captured.[2] After a general conflict of two hours, during which time three of the enemy's gun-boats were sunk in the harbor, three of them captured, and a heavy loss of life had been suffered by the Tripolitans, the Americans thought it prudent to withdraw, but to renew the conflict four days afterward.

[a] 1804.

The second attack on Tripoli commenced at half past two o'clock in the afternoon of the 7th.[b] An hour afterward a hot shot from the town passed into the hull of gun-boat *Number Nine*, one of the prizes captured on the 3d, and fired her magazine. The vessel was destroyed, and with it her commander, Lieutenant Caldwell, of the *Siren*, Midshipman Dorsey, and eight of her crew. Six others were wounded. When the smoke cleared away her bow only was above water. On it were Midshipman Robert T. Spence and eleven men, busily engaged in loading the long 24-pounder with which she was armed. They gave three loud cheers, discharged the gun at the enemy, and a moment afterward were picked from the water by men in boats, for the wreck on which they stood, with its great gun, had gone to the bottom.

[b] August.

Again, after inflicting some damage upon the enemy, the Americans withdrew, but renewed the attack on the 24th of the same month. This was

TRIPOLITAN WEAPON.

---

[1] While Captain Decatur was thus gallantly assailing the enemy, his younger brother James, first lieutenant of the *Nautilus*, was as bravely emulating his example, in command of gun-boat *Number Two*. He had caused the surrender of one of the enemy's largest vessels, and was boarding her to take possession, when the captain of the surrendered vessel treacherously shot him and escaped. The miscreant's pistol was loaded with two balls connected by a wire. The wire struck Decatur on the forehead, and bending, the two balls entered his temples, one on each side, and killed him instantly. He was the only American officer killed in this engagement.

[2] Decatur attacked the Tripolitan captain with a pike. The assailed seized it and turned it upon his assailant. Deca-

brief, and without any important results. But on the 29th a fourth and more formidable attack was made by the American gun-boats, commencing at three o'clock in the morning. The conflict continued until daylight, with great fury on both sides, when the *Constitution* ran toward the harbor, under heavy fire from the Bashaw's castle and Fort English. She signaled the gun-boats to withdraw, correctly supposing their ammunition to be nearly exhausted. This was done under the fire of the *Constitution*, which, with grape and round shot, greatly damaged the gun-boats of the enemy and caused them to retreat. She then ran in, and opened a heavy fire upon the town, batteries, and castle. She soon silenced the guns of the castle and two batteries, sunk a Tunisian vessel, damaged a Spanish one, severely bruised the enemy's galleys and gun-boats, and then withdrew, without having a man hurt.

The American squadron lay at anchor off Tripoli until the 2d of September repairing damages. It then sailed for the harbor, where it arrived on the afternoon of the 3d. The enemy, profiting by experience, had adopted new tactics. The change compelled Preble to modify his own plan. At half past three in the afternoon the bomb-ketches opened the conflict by bombarding the town. The *Constitution* ran down to the rocky reef and opened a heavy fire, at grape-shot distance, upon the castle and the city. She poured in eleven effective broadsides, while the smaller vessels were carrying on the conflict at other points. The general engagement lasted an hour and a quarter, when, the wind rising freshly, the commander, in the exercise of prudence, gave a signal for the squadron to withdraw.

The ketch *Intrepid*, used in the destruction of the *Philadelphia*, had been converted into a floating mine, for the purpose of destroying the enemy's cruisers in the harbor of Tripoli. One hundred barrels of gunpowder were placed in a room below deck, and immediately above them a large quantity of shot, shell, and irregular pieces of iron were deposited. In other parts of the vessel combustibles were placed, and she was made in every way a most disagreeable neighbor. On the night succeeding the fifth bombardment of Tripoli she was sent into the harbor on her destructive mission, under the command of Captain Somers, who had behaved gallantly during the recent attacks on the town. He was assisted by Lieutenant Wadsworth, of the *Constitution*, and Mr. Israel, an ardent young officer, who got on board the ketch by stealth. These, with a few men to work the *Intrepid*, and the crews of two boats employed in towing her, composed the expedition.

At nine o'clock in the evening the *Intrepid* entered the harbor on her perilous mission. The night was very dark, and she soon disappeared in the gloom. Many eager eyes were turned in the direction where her shadowy form was last seen. All hearts in the squadron beat quickly with anxiety. Suddenly a fierce and lurid light streamed up from the dark bosom of the waters like volcanic fires, and illuminated with its horrid gleams the rocks, forts, flotilla, castle, town, and the broad expanse of the harbor, followed instantly by an explosion that made all surrounding objects tremble. Flaming masts and sails and fiery bombs rained upon the waters for a few moments,

tur drew his cutlass and attempted to cut off the head of the pike, when his weapon snapped at the hilt, and he was left apparently at the mercy of the Turk. He parried the thrust of the Tripolitan, and sprang upon and clutched him by the throat. A trial of strength ensued, and they both fell to the deck. The Tripolitan attempted, as they lay, to draw a small poniard from his sash. Decatur perceived the movement, grasped the hand that held the deadly steel, and drew from his own pocket a small pistol, which he passed round the body of his antagonist, pointed it inward, and shot him dead. During the affray, Reuben James, a quarter-gunner, performed a most self-sacrificing act. One of the Tripolitan crew, seeing the perilous condition of his commander, aimed a sabre-blow at Decatur's head. James, with both arms disabled from wounds and bleeding profusely, rushed between the Tripolitan and his commander, and received the sabre-stroke upon his own head. The blow was not fatal. Decatur took the dirk from his foe, and afterward presented it to Captain (now [1867] the venerable
TRIPOLITAN PONIARD.
Vice-Admiral) Charles Stewart—from which the annexed drawing was made. One of the weapons—a powerful though not large sort of a sword or long knife, in a shark-skin scabbard—which was taken from the enemy by Decatur at that time, is delineated in the engraving on page 121. It is in the possession of F. J. Dreer, Esq., of Philadelphia.—See Waldo's *Life of Decatur*, page 132.

when all was again silence and darkness three-fold greater than before. Anxious eyes and ears bent in the direction of the dreadful explosion. The boats were waited for until the dawn with almost insupportable impatience. They never came, and no man of that perilous expedition was heard of afterward. Whether the explosion was an accident or a sacrifice—whether a shot from the enemy, or a brand dropped from a patriotic hand to prevent the ketch and its freight of men and powder from falling into the hands of the Tripolitans—can never be known. For more than sixty years the matter has been shrouded in impenetrable mystery.[1]

Lack of powder and the approach of the stormy season of the year induced Commodore Preble to cease operations on the dangerous Barbary coast, other than the maintenance of the blockade of Tripoli. Not another shot was fired; and on the 10th of September[a] Preble was relieved by the arrival of Commodore Samuel Barron. He returned home late in February, 1805, bearing expressions of the highest regards from his officers, and received the homage of the nation's gratitude.[2] Congress voted thanks to the commodore, and all who had served under his orders. On Preble they bestowed a gold medal bearing appropriate devices and inscrip-

[a] 1804.

MEDAL GIVEN TO COMMODORE PREBLE.

[1] Waldo, in his *Life of Decatur*, page 146, says that an eye-witness informed him that the evening was unusually calm; that as the *Intrepid* moved silently into the inner harbor, two of the enemy's heaviest galleys, with more than a hundred men in each, captured the "infernal," wholly unconscious of her character. The impression was that Somers, knowing their fate to be miserable captivity if taken prisoners into the city, where Bainbridge and his men had then suffered for eleven months, considered death preferable, and with his own hand fired the magazine of the *Intrepid*. Under this impression a newspaper writer, after alluding to the capture, wrote with more feeling than poetry—

"In haste they board: see Somers stand,
Determined, cool, formed to command,
The match of death in his right hand,
Scorning a life of slavery.
And now behold! the match applied,
The mangled foe the welkin ride:
Whirling aloft, brave Somers cried,
'A glorious death or liberty!'"

[2] Edward Preble was born in Portland, Maine, on the 15th of August, 1761. He early evinced a passion for the sea, and engaged in the merchant service. He became a midshipman in the naval service in 1779 in the state ship *Protector*. He afterward became lieutenant of the sloop-of-war *Winthrop*, and remained in her during the remainder of the war for independence. He was the first lieutenant appointed in the new naval establishment in 1798, and soon afterward made two cruises in the brig *Pickering* as commander. In 1800 he was made captain and placed in command of the *Essex*, in which he sailed to the East Indies to convoy American vessels. On account of ill health he withdrew from active service until 1803, when he went to the Mediterranean Sea. After his successful operations there he again withdrew from the service. In 1806 he suffered severely from debility of the digestive organs, from which he never recovered. He died on the 25th of August, 1807, at the age of forty-six years. To his memory a friend wrote in 1807—

"Lamented chief! though death be calmly past,
Our navy trembled when he breathed his last!
Our navy mourns him, but it mourns in vain:
A Preble ne'er will live—ne'er die again!
Yet hope, desponding, at the thought revives—
A second PREBLE—a DECATUR lives!"

The likeness of Preble given on page 120 is from a portrait of him in Faneuil Hall, Boston.

tions.[1] Officers of the navy afterward caused a white marble monument to be erected at the government dock-yard near the National Capitol in memory of their brother officers who fell at Tripoli.[2]

Commodore Barron found himself in command of a much greater naval force than the Americans had ever put afloat in the Mediterranean Sea. It consisted of the *President*, 44, Captain Cox; *Constitution*, 44, Captain Decatur; *Congress*, 38, Captain Rodgers; *Constellation*, 38, Captain Campbell; *Essex*, 32, Captain J. Barron; *Siren*, 16, Captain Stewart; *Argus*, 16, Captain Hull; *Vixen*, 12, Captain Smith; *Enterprise*, 12, Lieutenant Commandant Robinson, and *Nautilus*, 12, Lieutenant Commandant Dent. The *John Adams*, 28, Captain Chauncey, and the *Hornet*, 12, Lieutenant Commandant Evans, with two bombs and twelve gun-boats, were expected to join the Mediterranean squadron. It will be perceived that in this squadron, in actual command, were many of those who attained to great distinction during the War of 1812.

---

[1] The engraving on the preceding page shows the exact size of the medal. On one side is a bust of the commodore, with the legend, "EDWARDO PREBLE, DUCI STRENUO COMITIA AMERICANA." On the reverse, the American fleet bombarding the town and forts of Tripoli; legend, "VINDICI COMMERCII AMERICANI." *Exergue*—ANTE TRIPOLI, 1804."

[2] The picture represents the monument as it appeared when first erected. It is of white marble, and with its present pedestal (not seen in the engraving) is about forty feet in height. It was mutilated when the navy yard at Washington was burned in 1814. It was afterward repaired, and removed to the west front of the Capitol in Washington, where it was placed upon a spacious brown-stone base in an oval reservoir of water. The monument, with this base, was removed to Annapolis, in Maryland, in 1860, and set up there in the grounds of the Naval Academy. In consequence of the Great Rebellion, in 1861, that academy was removed to Newport, Rhode Island. The monument was left. "It is situated," wrote Mr. William Yorke AtLee to the author in January, 1862, "on a hill in the northwestern portion of the naval school grounds. It is in a state of good preservation, and adds not a little to the beauty of the grounds."

The shaft is surmounted by the American eagle, bearing the shield. On its sides the representations of the bows of vessels are seen projecting, and by its pedestal is an allegorical figure of *Fame* in the attitude of alighting, with a coronal of leaves in one hand and a pen in the other. The form of the pedestal has been altered. On one side of the base, in relief, is a view of Tripoli and the American squadron; on the other the names of the heroes in whose memory the monument was erected. On three sides of the base are statues representing *Mercury* (Commerce), *History*, and *America*, the latter in the form of an Indian girl with a feather head-dress, half nude, and two children near. On the brown sandstone sub-base on which this monument now stands are the following inscriptions, upon three sides:

NAVAL MONUMENT.

1. "Erected to the memory of Captain Richard Somers, Lieutenants James Caldwell, James Decatur, Henry Wadsworth, Joseph Israel, and John Dorsey, who fell in the different attacks made on the city of Tripoli in the year of our Lord 1804, and in the twenty-eighth year of the independence of the United States."

2. "The love of country inspired them. *Fame* has crowned their deeds. *History* records the event. The *Children of Columbia* admire, and *Commerce* laments their fall."

3. "As a small tribute of respect to their memory, and admiration of their valor, so worthy of imitation, their brother officers have erected this monument."

Alliance with Hamet Caramalli. March across Northern Africa. Peace with Tripoli. The Barbary Powers humbled.

Barron's flag-ship was the *President.* Leaving some of his force to overawe the menacing Moors, he kept up the blockade of Tripoli during the autumn and winter of 1804–5. Meanwhile a land movement against Tripoli was conceived and executed under the management of Captain William Eaton, of the United States army, then consul at Tunis.

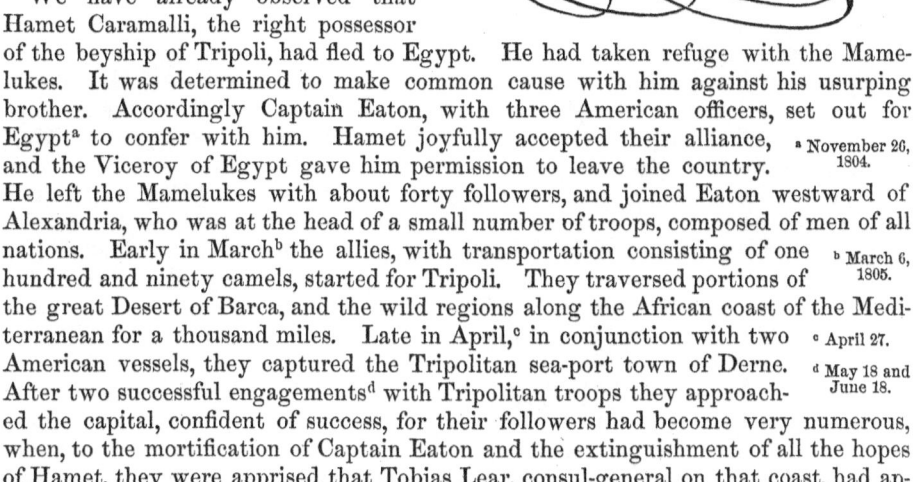

We have already observed that Hamet Caramalli, the right possessor of the beyship of Tripoli, had fled to Egypt. He had taken refuge with the Mamelukes. It was determined to make common cause with him against his usurping brother. Accordingly Captain Eaton, with three American officers, set out for Egypt[a] to confer with him. Hamet joyfully accepted their alliance, [a] November 26, 1804. and the Viceroy of Egypt gave him permission to leave the country. He left the Mamelukes with about forty followers, and joined Eaton westward of Alexandria, who was at the head of a small number of troops, composed of men of all nations. Early in March[b] the allies, with transportation consisting of one [b] March 6, 1805. hundred and ninety camels, started for Tripoli. They traversed portions of the great Desert of Barca, and the wild regions along the African coast of the Mediterranean for a thousand miles. Late in April,[c] in conjunction with two [c] April 27. American vessels, they captured the Tripolitan sea-port town of Derne. [d] May 18 and June 18. After two successful engagements[d] with Tripolitan troops they approached the capital, confident of success, for their followers had become very numerous, when, to the mortification of Captain Eaton and the extinguishment of all the hopes of Hamet, they were apprised that Tobias Lear, consul-general on that coast, had appeared before Tripoli in the *Essex,* and made a treaty[e] with the terrified [e] June 4. Bashaw.[1]

Thus ended the four years' war with Tripoli. The ruler of Tunis was yet insolent, and Commodore Rodgers, who had become commander of the squadron in consequence of the failing health of Barron, anchored thirteen vessels before his capital on the 1st of August. The haughty Bey was speedily humbled, and sent an embassador to the United States.

The power of the American government was now acknowledged and feared by all the barbarians of the northern shores of Africa, and the commerce of the Mediterranean Sea was relieved of great peril. Pope Pius the Seventh declared that the Americans had done more for Christendom against the North African pirates than all the powers of Europe united. The cruising and belligerent operations of the American navy in the Mediterranean had not only accomplished this great good for the world, but had been an admirable school for the military marine of the United States. The value of the lessons taught in that school was manifested a thousand times during the war with Great Britain that ensued a few years later.

While these events in the Mediterranean, connected in the practical service on the part of the Americans with the War of 1812, were transpiring, political changes had commenced in Europe which speedily aroused the United States to a sense of the necessity of strengthening the naval arm of the government.

We have observed that the beginning of 1802 saw a general pacification of Europe, and that England paid obsequious court to Bonaparte, whose fascinations allured thousands of Englishmen to France. This "*First* Kiss in Ten Years," celebrated by

---

[1] This treaty was not creditable. Although it was stipulated that the United States should pay no more tribute to Tripoli, it was agreed that $60,000 should be paid for captives then in possession of the Bashaw. Altogether better and less humiliating terms for the United States might have been obtained. All that Hamet gained was the release of his wife and children. He lost every thing else. He afterward came to the United States, and applied to Congress for remuneration for his services in favor of the Americans. His petition was denied, but $2400 were voted for his temporary relief.

the caricaturists, was the *last* for more than that space of time. First jealousy, then suspicion, and, finally, intense hatred of France and her ruler took possession of the English mind. These feelings were intensified by the act of the French Senate, who declared Bonaparte consul for life,[a] a declaration speedily sanctioned by the votes of three millions of Frenchmen. This was jealously regarded as a cautious step toward more absolute power, which England feared; and when, immediately afterward, first the Island of Elba,[b] then Piedmont,[c] then the Duchy of Parma,[d] were incorporated into the dominions of France, no one doubted that the First Consul would speedily set armies in motion for the greater aggrandizement of himself and the country of his adoption.

[a] August 3, 1802.
[b] August 15.
[c] September 11.
[d] October.

England professed to see in this accession of territory infringements of the Treaty of Amiens. Bonaparte retorted by accusing Great Britain of violating the spirit of treaties and endeavoring to disturb the peace of Europe, for which he was laboring, and assumed toward England a haughty and dictatorial tone that wounded her sensitive pride. He evinced a disposition to possess Malta; required England to drive royal French emigrants from her shores, where they had taken refuge; demanded a suppression of the liberties of the English press in its criticisms on French affairs, because it was regarded as his most dangerous enemy; and actually asked for a modification of the English Constitution.[1] He was charged with inciting another rebellion in Ireland, and distributing his secret emissaries, under the guise of consuls, all along the British coasts.[2]

The cup of Bonaparte's iniquity was finally made full to English comprehension when, at the beginning of March, 1803, he declared, in an official note to Lord Whitworth, the British embassador in Paris, that England, alone, can not now encounter France." That announcement, assuming the shape of a menace, raised a storm of patriotic indignation all over England, which found a loud echo in the House of Lords on the 9th of March. That indignation, not unmixed with alarm, became more intense when intelligence reached London that a *Senatus Consultum* on the 21st of March had placed one hundred and twenty thousand conscripts at the command of the French ruler. Still professing a desire for peace, the Addington ministry continued negotiations with Bonaparte. Finally, in May, the British minister at Paris, who had been personally insulted by the First Consul, and who had repeatedly warned his government that the negotiations on the part of the French ruler were deceptive, and contrived only to give time for hostile preparation, was ordered to leave the French capital. The British government immediately ordered the French minister to leave London, and on the 18th of May formally declared war against France, and put in immediate operation an embargo upon all French vessels in English ports. In retaliation, crowds of English visitors in the French dominion were seized and held as prisoners of war.[3] Immense bodies of troops were sent to the French coast, and menaced England with immediate invasion. Bonaparte superintended the preparations in person, established his head-quarters at Boulogne, on the roads to which finger-posts marked "*To London*" were erected, and every possible means were used to in-

---

[1] The English Constitution is not a permanent instrument embodying the foundations of all laws, like that of the United States, but comprehends the whole body of English laws enacted by Parliament, and by which the British people are governed. The Constitution of the United States is superior to the Congress or National Legislature; the Parliament or National Legislature of England is superior to the Constitution. What Parliament declares to be the Constitution of England is the Constitution of England: what the Parliament enacts the monarch must be governed by, and the courts can not adjudge to be unconstitutional and void. Sheridan comprehensively said, "The King of England is not seated on a solitary eminence of power; on the contrary, he sees his *equals* in the coexisting branches of the Legislature, and he recognizes his *superior* in the LAW."

[2] The latter charge was proven by the seizure of the papers of the French consul at Dublin, in whose secret instructions were the following passages: "You are required to furnish a plan of the ports of your district, with a specification of the soundings for mooring vessels. If no plan of the ports can be procured, you are to point out with what wind vessels can come in and go out, and what is the greatest draught of water with which vessels can enter the river deeply laden."

[3] About twelve thousand English subjects of all ages were committed to custody.

The English People excited against France.   Invasion of Great Britain by the French expected.   Witticisms.

flame the resentments of Frenchmen against their English neighbors across the Channel.

In England every art was also employed to excite the people against France and its ruler. Immense numbers of "loyal papers" and "loyal tracts" were scattered over the land, some being atrocious libels on Bonaparte and his family, fictitious accounts of his barbarities, and exaggerated pictures of his treatment of those countries which had bowed to his power; others were calm and dignified appeals to the patriotism and courage of the nation. It was evident to all that an invasion was probable, and yet wits, and satirists, and vulgar libelers hurled perpetual volleys of abuse and ridicule against Bonaparte and France, affecting, with ill-disguised trepidation, to look upon both with contempt.[1] This apparent gayety and unconcern was like the whistling of boys in the dark to keep their courage up. The government at the same moment was making immense preparations to repel the expected invasion, and the year 1803 was one of alarm and terror for all England.[2] She was the asylum of the Bourbon Royalists, who were the traditional enemies of all popular liberty and progress, the most implacable foes of the French ruler, and the sleepless and relentless conspirators against the lives of all who should stand in the way of their recovery of the throne from which the best of their lineage, Louis the Sixteenth, had been driven a few years before. These Royalists were petted by the English government and pit-

---

[1] Bonaparte was sometimes compared to a wild beast, at other times to a pigmy, and at all times as a blusterer to be laughed at. One morning London would be amused by a large placard announcing an exhibition thus: "Just arrived at Mr. Bull's Menagerie, in British Lane, the most renowned and sagacious *Man-tiger* or *Orang-outang*, called Napoleon Bonaparte. He has been exhibited in Holland, Switzerland, and Italy, and lately in Egypt," etc. Another morning chapmen would offer in the great thoroughfares songs with words like these:

"Come, I'll sing you a song, just for want of some other,
About a *small* thing that has made a *great* pother:
A mere *insect*—a *pigmy*. I'll tell you, my hearty,
'Tis the Corsican *hop-o'-my-thumb*, Buonaparté."

Or boastful ballads in words like these:

"Arm, neighbors, at length,
And put forth your strength
Perfidious, bold France to resist!
Ten Frenchmen will fly,
To shun a black eye,
If one Englishman doubles his fist!"

The theatres were resonant with patriotic songs. One of the most popular of those sung in the play-houses, called "The Island," began with this stanza:

"If the French have a notion
Of crossing the ocean,
  Their luck to be trying on land,
They may come if they like;
But we'll soon make 'em strike
  To the lads of the tight little Island!
Huzza for the boys of the Island!
The brave volunteers of the Island!
The fraternal embrace,
If foes want in this place,
We'll present all the *arms* in the Island!"

Gillray and other caricaturists were exceedingly active at this time in ridiculing all parties, but especially Bonaparte. Some of these caricatures, which were grossly personal, annoyed the Corsican exceedingly, for he was extremely sensitive to any thing like ridicule against himself and family. The one which gave him most offense was a broad parody on *Belshazzar's Feast*, by Gillray, which appeared in August, 1803, entitled "*The Handwriting on the Wall*." The First Consul and Josephine, his wife (the latter represented of enormous bulk), and other members of his family and court, are seated at table devouring the good things of England as a dessert. When Bonaparte first discovers the mysterious hand, his fork is stuck into St. James's, seen on his plate. Another is swallowing the Tower of London, while Josephine is drinking large bumpers of wine. On a plate bearing the inscription "Oh de roast beef of Old England!" is seen a head of King George. Above the feasters a hand holds the scales of Justice, in which the legitimate crown of France weighs down the red cap and its attendant chain—Despotism under the name of Liberty. Behind Josephine stand the three afterward princesses of the imperial family—Borghese, Louise, and Joseph Bonaparte. A copy of this caricature is given in full in Wright's *History of the House of Hanover, illustrated by Caricatures and Satires*. It is said to have greatly exasperated the First Consul and his friends.

[2] On the 23d of July the germ of another rebellion in Ireland appeared at Dublin. The chief leader was Robert Emmet, an eminent barrister, who was implicated, with his brother, in the rebellion there in 1798. His followers proved themselves so unworthy of himself and the cause (which was the independence of Ireland) that he fled in despair to the Wicklow Mountains. He might have evaded pursuit, but his love for his betrothed, the daughter of the famous Curran, caused him to linger. He was arrested, tried for and found guilty of treason, and hanged on the 20th of September following.

ied by the English people; and this offense, above all others, exasperated Bonaparte, for he regarded England as the accomplice of the conspirators against himself and human freedom.

The British declaration of war, said Meneval (who was always at the elbow of the First Consul), changed his whole nature.[1] He had been planning vast beneficent schemes for France under the serene skies of universal peace, when England, of all the nations loudest in her professions of concord and sentiments of Christian benevolence, was the first to disappoint him—the first to again disturb the peace of Europe by brandishing high in air the flaming sword of war, instead of the green olive-branch of amity and good will. Compelled to accept the challenge, he resolved to give her war to her heart's content.

Each party charged the other with acts of flagrant wrong against the peace and well-being of the world, and the record of impartial history implies that both spoke the truth. It is not our business to act as umpire on the question, or to delineate the events of the great war that ensued. We will simply consider the resulting effects of these international strifes on the peace and prosperity of the United States. The war was waged by both parties with an utter disregard of the rights of all other nations or the settled maxims of international comity. France and England entered the lists for the champion's belt—for the supremacy in the political affairs of the world—and they fought with the science, the desperation, and the brutality of accomplished pugilists.

On the 18th of May, 1804, Bonaparte was proclaimed Emperor of the French, in accordance with a decree of the Senate[a] and the votes of the people. To give more eminent sanction to the deed, the Pope was invited to perform the coronation ceremony. He consented, and on the 2d of December following Bonaparte was anointed by his holiness, at the great altar of Notre Dame, "The High and Mighty Napoleon the First." The republics which he had established by his sword were speedily changed into kingdoms, on the thrones of which members of his own family were placed. In May, the following year,[b] he was solemnly anointed King of Italy at Milan. Then he cast his eyes significantly over Europe, and contemplated a thorough reconstruction of its map. England, Russia, Austria, and Sweden, alarmed and provoked, coalesced against the "usurper," as Napoleon was called. Prussia was kept from the league only by a bribe, Napoleon having offered Hanover, which he had stolen from England, as the price of the king's friendship. Very soon a French army one hundred and eighty thousand strong was upon the Rhine. On the 2d of December the strength of the Corsican was tested. Against him, near Austerlitz, appeared two great armies, each led, like his own, by an emperor. They met in deadly conflict. Napoleon was the victor. The Continental Powers withdrew from the contest. Prussia received Hanover as her reward, and England was left to fight the Emperor of the French single-handed. Napoleon proceeded to distribute crowns and ducal coronets among his friends and favorite generals with a lavish hand, and induced no less than fourteen German princes, who ruled over sixteen millions of people, to form a league, under the supremacy of France, known as the Confederacy of the Rhine.

Early in 1806 the English government, under the premiership of Charles Fox, opened with Napoleon negotiations for peace, the restoration of Hanover being one of the proposed conditions. Napoleon considered it, and on that account the King of Prussia, alarmed and offended, joined the coalition of the Northern Powers against him. The exasperated emperor marched upon Prussia, and, after slaying more than twenty thousand of the king's subjects in arms, he entered Berlin,[c] his capital, in triumph. Meanwhile the Russians had been beaten back

a May 3.

b May 26, 1805.

c October 25, 1806.

---

[1] *History of the Second War between the United States of America and Great Britain,* by Charles J. Ingersoll. Second Series, i., 206.

through Poland, and he was in possession of Warsaw. Strong, bold, and defiant, and burning with a desire to humble "perfidious Albion," he issued from his camp at the Prussian capital[a] the famous manifesto known in history as the Berlin Decree,[1] which declared the ports of the whole of the British dominions in a state of blockade, while a French vessel of war scarcely dare appear on the ocean to enforce it. This brings us to the immediate consideration of events in the United States, and the effects of the strife abroad upon American affairs.

[a] November 21, 1806.

---

[1] The following is a copy of the decree:

"Imperial Camp, Berlin, November 21, 1806.
"Napoleon, Emperor of the French and King of Italy, considering:
"1. That England does not admit the right of nations as universally acknowledged by all civilized people;
"2. That she declares as an enemy every individual belonging to an enemy state, and, in consequence, makes prisoners of war not only of the crews of *armed* vessels, but those also of *merchant* vessels, and even the supercargoes of the same;
"3. That she extends or applies to merchant vessels, to articles of commerce, and to the property of individuals the right of conquest, which can only be applied or extended to what belongs to an enemy state;
"4. That she extends to ports not fortified, to harbors and mouths of rivers, the *right of blockade*, which, according to reason and the usages of civilized nations, is applicable only to strong or fortified ports;
"5. That she declares places blockaded before which she has not a single vessel of war, although a place ought not to be considered blockaded but when it is so invested that no approach to it can be made without imminent hazard; that she declares even places blockaded which her united forces would be incapable of doing, such as entire coasts and a whole empire.
"6. That this unequaled abuse of the right of blockade has no other object than to interrupt the communication of different nations, and to extend the commerce and industry of England upon the ruin of those of the Continent;
"7. That this being the evident design of England, whoever deals on the Continent in English merchandise favors that design, and becomes an accomplice;
"8. That this conduct in England (worthy only of the first stages of barbarism) has benefited her to the detriment of other nations;
"9. That it being right to oppose to an enemy the same arms she makes use of, to combat as she does when all ideas of justice and every liberal sentiment (the result of civilization among men) are disregarded,
"We have resolved to enforce against England the usages which she has consecrated in her maritime code.
"The present decree shall be considered as the fundamental law of the Empire until England shall acknowledge that the *rights of war* are the same on land as at sea; that they can not be extended to any private property whatever, nor to persons who are not military, and until the right of blockading be restrained to fortified places actually invested by competent forces.
"Art. 1. The British Islands are in a state of blockade.
"Art. 2. All commerce and correspondence with them is prohibited; consequently, all letters or packets written *in* England, or *to* an Englishman *written in the English language*, shall not be dispatched from the post-offices, and shall be seized.
"Art. 3. Every individual a subject of Great Britain, of whatever rank or condition, who is found in countries occupied by our troops or those of our allies, shall be made prisoner of war.
"Art. 4. Every warehouse, all merchandise or property whatever belonging to an Englishman, are declared good prize.
"Art. 5. One half of the proceeds of merchandise declared to be good prize and forfeited, as in the preceding articles, shall go to indemnify merchants who have suffered losses by the English cruisers.
"Art. 6. No vessel coming directly from England or her colonies, or having been there since the publication of this decree, shall be admitted into any port.
"Art. 7. Every vessel that by a false declaration contravenes the foregoing disposition shall be seized, and the ship and cargo confiscated as English property.
"Art. 8. [This article states that the Councils of Prizes at Paris and at Milan shall have recognizance of what may arise in the Empire and in Italy under the present decree.]
"Art. 9. Communications of this decree shall be made to the Kings of Spain, Naples, Holland, Etruria, and to our other allies, whose subjects as well as ours are victims of the injuries and barbarity of the English maritime code.
"Art. 10. Our ministers of foreign relations, etc., are charged with the execution of the present decree.
"NAPOLEON."
With a partiality toward the Americans that was practical friendship, the French cruisers did not, for a whole year, interfere with American vessels trading with Great Britain. On this point Alexander Baring, M.P., in his *Inquiry into the Causes and Consequences of the Orders in Council, and an Examination of the Conduct of Great Britain toward the Neutral Commerce of America*, said: "*No condemnation of an American vessel had ever taken place under it;* and so little did the French privateers interfere with the trade of America with this country, that the *insurance* on it was very little higher than in time of profound peace; while that of the American trade with the Continent of Europe has at the same time been doubled, and even trebled, by the conduct of our cruisers."

I

CHAPTER VII.

"Shall that arm which haughty Britain
　In its gristle found too strong—
That by which her foes were smitten—
　Shall that arm be palsied long?
See our sons of ocean kneeling
　To a tyrant's stripes and chains!
Partisan! hast thou no feeling
　When the hardy tar complains?
See the British press-gang seize him,
　Victim of relentless power!
Stout his heart is, but must fail him
　In this evil, trying hour."

　　　　　　　　　THE IMPRESSED SEAMAN'S APPEAL.

ENCOURAGED by promises of continued peace in Europe, and the relaxation of the "rule of 1756" by Great Britain,[1] the commerce and general business of the United States enjoyed a season of unexampled prosperity. The social and political power of the republic rapidly augmented. The Indians on the frontiers were peaceful; and the causes for irritation on the part of the inhabitants west of the mountains toward the Spaniards, who controlled the Lower Mississippi, were in a fair way of being speedily removed. The germs of new states were appearing in the late wilderness. That vast domain northwest of the Ohio, west of a line drawn from the mouth of the Kentucky River to Fort Recovery on St. Clair's battle-field, and thence due north to Canada, was erected into a Territory,[a] and named INDIANA. William Henry Harrison, Wayne's efficient aid in 1794 (who had been out of the army since 1798), was appointed governor of the germinal state, and established his capital at Vincennes, on the Lower Wabash.

[a] May 7, 1802.

At about the same time the Mississippi Territory, organized in 1798 by Winthrop Sargent, St. Clair's efficient secretary in the government of the Ohio country, was allowed a representative assembly,[b] and its political machinery was put in motion.

[b] May 10.

In the spring of 1802 the United States came into possession, by act of Georgia, of one hundred thousand square miles of territory, now constituting the State of Alabama. It was inhabited by the Creek and Cherokee Indians toward the east, and the Choctaw and Chickasaw tribes toward the west. With those philanthropic impulses which marked the character of Jefferson, he recommended measures for the well-being of those tribes, and for securing to them equal and exact justice.

Late in the same year the inhabitants within the present domain of Ohio, in representative convention held at Chilicothe, adopted a State Constitution,[c] and the Territory, called OHIO, became a peer among the states of the republic.

[c] November 29.

But these political organizations on soil within the domains of the United States, and over which a civilized population was rapidly spreading, were of small account when compared with the importance of a great acquisition of territory and political power which speedily followed. Louisiana, which once comprehended the vast and undefinable region of the Valley of the Mississippi and the domain watered by its

---

[1] See note 1, page 84.

Louisiana retroceded to France.   The Americans disturbed by the Act.   President Jefferson's View of the Subject.

tributaries, from the Gulf of Mexico to the forty-ninth parallel of latitude, and westward to the Pacific Ocean, or "South Sea," as it was then called, was a possession of France by right of discovery by secular and religious explorers, and was named in honor of the Gallic king Louis.

In 1763 France ceded to England the whole of that region east of the Mississippi except Florida, and to Spain all west of that river. By these cessions and the surrender of others, effected by compulsion at the end of a seven years' war, France abdicated territorial dominion in North America.

While the negotiations of the Treaty of Amiens were in progress, a rumor went abroad that Spain, by secret treaty, had retroceded, or would retrocede, to France all of Louisiana in her possession, and possibly the domain along the Gulf of Mexico known as East and West Florida, thus giving to that now rising, ambitious, and aggressive power the entire control of the navigation of the Mississippi, and a position to exercise an influence over the political affairs of the United States more potent and permanent than had ever been attempted. This gave the government and people much uneasiness, and the American ministers in London, Paris, and Madrid were immediately instructed to endeavor to defeat the measure. It was too late. The act of cession was accomplished, and the fact was made known to the President early in 1802.

President Jefferson, who loved his country and republican institutions intensely, and who desired its prosperity and grandeur with a patriot's warm devotion, wrote an earnest letter to Mr. Livingston,[a] the American embassador at Paris, on the subject. With wonderful sagacity he clearly comprehended the matter in all its bearings, immediate and prospective, and perceived the great evils to the republic which French occupation of the outlet of the Mississippi would inflict. "It would completely reverse," he said, "all the political relations of the United States, and would form a new epoch in our political career. Of all nations of any consideration, France is the one which hitherto has offered the fewest points on which we could have any conflict of right, and the most points of common interest. From these causes we have ever looked to her as our *natural friend*, as one with whom we never could have occasion of difference. Her growth, therefore, we viewed as our own, her misfortunes ours. There is on the globe one single spot the possessor of which is our natural and habitual enemy. It is New Orleans, through which the produce of three eighths of our territory must pass to market; and, from its fertility, it will ere long yield more than half of our whole produce, and contain more than half of our inhabitants. France, placing herself in that door, assumes to us the attitude of defiance. Spain might have retained it quietly for years. Her pacific dispositions, her feeble state would induce her to increase our facilities there, so that her possession of the place would be hardly felt by us, and it would not perhaps be very long before some circumstance might arise which might make the cession of it to us the price of something of more worth to her.

"Not so can it ever be in the hands of France; the impetuosity of her temper, the energy and restlessness of her character, placed in a point of eternal friction with us and our character, which, though quiet, and loving peace and the pursuit of wealth, is high-minded, despising wealth in competition with insult or injury. Enterprising and energetic as any nation on earth, these circumstances render it impossible that France and the United States can long continue friends when they meet in so irritable a position. . . . The day that France takes possession of New Orleans fixes the sentence which is to restrain her forever within her low-water mark. It seals the union of two nations who, in conjunction, can maintain exclusive possession of the ocean. From that moment we must marry ourselves to the British fleet and nation. We must turn all our attentions to a maritime force, for which our resources place us on very high ground; and, having formed and connected together a power which

[a] April 18, 1802.

Proposition for the Cession of Louisiana.   The secret Designs of France.   Talleyrand.   Atrocious Suggestions.

may render re-enforcement of her settlements here impossible to France, make the first cannon which shall be fired in Europe the signal for tearing up every settlement she may have made."¹

Mr. Jefferson suggested that if France considered the possession of Louisiana "indispensable for her views," she might be willing to cede to the United States, for a consideration, the Island of New Orleans, and the Floridas, and guarantee the free navigation of the Mississippi by both nations, thus removing, in a degree, "the causes of jarring and irritation" between the parties.²

Although the President's letter to Mr. Livingston was private, Mr. Jefferson chose to consider it as supplemental to the official instructions which were sent to the embassador, and he desired him to urge, on proper occasions, with the proper persons, and in a proper manner, the considerations and suggestions which the letter contained. As we have already observed, it was too late to prevent the cession. That act had been accomplished by secret treaty eighteen months before.³

Nothing now remained for the Americans to do to prevent the threatened evils of French occupation at the mouth of the Mississippi but to negotiate for the purchase of territory there. Such negotiations were speedily entered into. Mr. Livingston took important preliminary steps in that direction, and in January, 1803,ᵃ James Monroe was appointed to assist him in the negotiation. Their in-

ᵃ January 10.

---

¹ Letter to Robert R. Livingston, April 18, 1802.

² France had no really peaceful and friendly feelings toward the United States at that time. Among the dreams of glory which filled the mind of Bonaparte was the re-establishment of the ancient colonial Empire of France. His first essay was in St. Domingo; his next was to be in Louisiana. What would have been his instrumentalities there in extending his sway over the country west of the Alleghanies, may be inferred from the following extract of a memorial whose inspiration was supposed to be the First Consul, and Talleyrand the writer. This document was published in pamphlet form in Philadelphia in 1803, but was suppressed because of negotiations then pending for the purchase of Louisiana from France. It vindicates the wisdom and sagacity of Jefferson exhibited in the above letter to Mr. Livingston. On the forty-fifth page of the pamphlet it is observed:

"There is still another mean, however, by which the fury of THE STATES may be held at pleasure—by an enemy placed on their Western frontiers. The only aliens and enemies within their borders are not the *blacks*. They, indeed, are the most inveterate in their enmity; but the INDIANS are, in many respects, more dangerous inmates. *Their savage ignorance, their undisciplined passions, their restless and warlike habits*, their notions of ancient *rights, make them the fittest tools imaginable for disturbing* THE STATES. In the territory adjacent to the Ohio, Mississippi, and Missouri there are more than *thirty thousand men* whose trade is hunting, and whose delight is war. These men lie at the mercy of any civilized nation who live near them. Such a neighbor can gain their friendship or provoke their enmity with equal ease. He can make them inactive, or he can rouse them to fury; he can direct their movement in any way he pleases, and make it mischievous or harmless, *by supplying their fury with arms and with leaders*, or by withholding that supply.

"The pliant and addressful spirit of the French has always given them an absolute control over these savages. The office which the laziness or the insolence of the British found impracticable was easily performed by us, and will be still easier hereafter, since we shall enter on the scene with more advantages than formerly.

"We shall detach within, a sufficient force to maintain possession against all the efforts of THE STATES, should they, contrary to all their interests, proceed to war *with* or *without* provocation. We shall find in the Indian tribes an army permanently cantoned in the most convenient stations, *endowed with skill and temper best adapted to the nature and the scene of the war*, and armed and impelled with far less trouble and expense than an equal number of our own troops. *We shall find a terrible militia, infinitely more destructive while scattered through the hostile settlements than an equal force of our own*. We shall find in the bowels *of* THE STATES *a mischief that only wants the touch of a well-directed spark to involve in its explosion the utter ruin of half their nation*. Such will be the power we shall derive from a military station and a growing colony on the Mississippi. These will be certain and immediate effects, whatever distance and doubt there may be in the remoter benefits to France on which I have so warmly expatiated. As a curb on a nation whose future conduct in peace and war will be of great importance to us, this province will be cheaply purchased at ten times the cost to which it will subject us."

The writer made Bonaparte say: "My designs on the Mississippi will never be officially announced till they are executed. Meanwhile the world, if it pleases, may fear and suspect, but nobody will be wise enough to go to war to prevent them. I shall trust to the folly of England and America to let me go my way in my own time."

When the war between the United States and Great Britain broke out in 1812, British writers urged the government to employ the savages, with all their known blood-thirstiness and cruelty, as allies. One writer soundly berated the government for its apparent apathy toward their "Indian friends," and cited the above atrocious suggestions of the French minister as the true programme of action for the British to pursue in the war with the Americans!—See the *New Quarterly Review and British Colonial Register*, No. 4: J. M. Richardson, Cornhill, London.

³ There had been for some time indications of speedy hostilities between the United States and Spain, growing out of the territorial relations of the two countries on the Gulf of Mexico. By a treaty with Spain in 1795 that government had granted to the United States the right of deposit at New Orleans for three years, after which the privilege was either to be continued, or an equivalent place assigned on another part of the banks of the Mississippi. The Spaniards considered themselves masters of the province while it was unoccupied by the French, even after the cession was consummated. The privilege of deposit at New Orleans had been continued; but suddenly, in October, 1802, the Spanish intendant or governor declared by proclamation that the right of deposit at New Orleans no longer existed. This produced great excitement in the Western country, and the Americans, when certified of the treaty of cession, did not doubt that the Spanish intendant acted under orders from the French government.

structions only asked for the cession of New Orleans and the Floridas, and that the Mississippi should be divided by a line that should put the city of New Orleans within the territory of the United States, thus securing the free navigation of that river.

To the surprise of the American negotiators, M. Marbois, the representative of Bonaparte,[1] offered to treat for the sale of the *whole* of Louisiana. "Irresolution and deliberation," said the First Consul in his instructions to Marbois, "are no longer in season. I renounce Louisiana. It is not only New Orleans that I will cede, it is the whole colony, without any reservation. I know the price of what I abandon, and I have sufficiently proved the importance that I attach to this province, since my first diplomatic act with Spain had for its object the recovery of it. I renounce it with the greatest regret. To attempt to retain it would be folly. I direct you to negotiate this affair with the envoys of the United States."

The sagacious Bonaparte—the Man of Expediency—saw clearly which was the path of safety for him. Jefferson's covert menace of an American alliance with England against him, his ill success against St. Domingo,[2] and the storm-clouds of war that were again lowering darkly over Europe, caused the gorgeous dream of colonial dominion to fade from the mind of the First Consul. He needed troops at home, and he was more in want of money than far-off possessions held by doubtful tenure.[3]

Monroe arrived at Paris on the 12th of April, 1803. The negotiations immediately commenced. The intercourse between the three commissioners was very pleasant. Livingston and Marbois had known each other intimately more than twenty years before. Every thing went on smoothly; and in less than a fortnight a treaty was signed by which the United States came into the possession of a vast and, to some extent, undefined domain, containing a mixed free population of eighty-five thousand souls and forty thousand negro slaves, for the sum of $15,000,000. "We have lived long," said Mr. Livingston to Marbois, as he arose from his seat after signing the treaty, "but this is the noblest work of our whole lives. The treaty which we have just signed has not been obtained by art or force; equally advantageous to the two contracting parties, it will change vast solitudes into flourishing districts. From this day the United States take their place among the powers of the first rank; the English lose all exclusive influence in the affairs of America.".

Bonaparte, who had watched the progress of the negotiations with intense interest, held similar opinions. "It is true," he said to Marbois a few hours later, "the negotiation does not leave me any thing to desire; sixty millions [francs] for an occupation that will not perhaps last for a day! I would that France should enjoy this unexpected capital, that it may be employed in works beneficial to her marine.[4] This accession of territory," he continued exultingly, "strengthens forever the power of the United States; *and I have just given to England a maritime rival that will, sooner or later, humble her pride.*"

---

[1] Marbois was secretary to the French embassy to the United States during a portion of the American Revolution, and was now at the head of the French Treasury Department.

[2] Toussaint L'Ouverture, an able and courageous negro, seized the Spanish part of St. Domingo, and made it a colony of France, in January, 1801. He was declared President for life. This example was speedily followed by the black and colored population of Guadaloupe. They seized the governor sent out by Bonaparte, and established a provisional government in October, 1801. Meanwhile an insurrection had broken out in St. Domingo, and Bonaparte sent his brother-in-law, Le Clerc, to quell it. Toussaint regarded the army as an instrument for the enslavement of himself and his people. A new civil war ensued, while the French army was completely decimated by fever and sword. Twenty thousand soldiers perished, and sixty thousand white people of the island were massacred by the infuriated negroes. A momentary peace ensued. Toussaint, who deprecated these acts, was treacherously seized on the false charge of intention to excite another insurrection, taken to France, and died in prison there. By direct act of Bonaparte slavery was established in Guadaloupe (where his army was more successful), and the slave-trade was opened.

[3] "I require a great deal of money," the First Consul said to Marbois, "to carry on this war, and I would not like to commence with new contributions. If I should regulate my terms according to the value of those vast regions to the United States, the indemnity would have no limits. I will be moderate, in consideration of the necessity in which I am placed of making a sale. But keep this to yourself."

[4] The invasion of England and the prostration of her maritime superiority was then Bonaparte's favorite project.

Notwithstanding the acknowledged national advantages to be gained by the acquisition of Louisiana, the Federal politicians, especially those of New England, perceiving that it would strengthen the South, into whose hands the government had fallen, raised a loud outcry against it as the work of the Southern Democracy. They professed to regard the measure as inimical to the interests of the North and East; and having, while in power, become familiar with the prescription of disunion of the states, always put forth by the Southern political doctors as the great remedy for apparently incurable political evils, they resolved to try its efficiency in the case in question. All through the years 1803 and 1804 desires for and fears of a dissolution of the Union were freely expressed in what are now the free-labor states east of the Alleghanies;[1] and a select Convention of Federalists, to be held at Boston in the autumn of 1804, to consider the question of disunion, was contemplated early in that year. Alexander Hamilton was invited to attend it, but his emphatic condemnation of the whole plan, only a few months before his death, seems to have disconcerted the leaders and dissipated the scheme. "To his honor be it spoken," said Dewitt Clinton in the Senate of the State of New York in 1809, "it was rejected by him with abhorrence and disdain."

The acquisition of Louisiana by the United States was distasteful to the Spaniards. It brought the restless and enterprising Americans too near the Spanish provinces in Mexico to promise quietude to the latter. Yrugo, the Spanish minister at Washington, therefore entered a solemn protest against the entire treaty. Questions concerning the true boundary of Louisiana were speedily raised, and serious complications were threatened. The Spaniards were disposed to cling to all the territory east of the Mississippi included in West Florida, and thus hold possession of New Orleans. This disposition opened afresh the animosity of the inhabitants of the West against the occupants of the Lower Mississippi, and the United States contemplated the necessity of taking possession of New Orleans by the force of arms. Troops under General James Wilkinson, consisting of a few regulars, several companies of Mississippi volunteers, and a considerable number of Tennessee militia, marched from Nashville to Natchez.

But a peaceful transfer of the territory took place. Lausat, the commissioner of France to receive Louisiana from the Spaniards under the cession treaty, performed that duty, and a few days afterward he formally delivered the island and city of New Orleans to General Wilkinson and William C. C. Claiborne, the commissioners appointed for the purpose by the United States. The Spaniards were left in possession of the country along the Gulf of Mexico to the Atlantic Ocean, known as The Floridas, lying south of the thirty-first degree of north latitude, and east of a line nearly corresponding with the present boundary between Mississippi and Louisiana on the Pearl River.

Upon the soil thus acquired, and which was an important step in the direction of absolute independence of Great Britain on the part of the United States, some of the most stirring events of the War of 1812 occurred, and thereon was fought the last and most decisive battle of the Second War for Independence.

The acquisition of Louisiana created in the minds of adventurers visions of personal and national aggrandizement the influence of which it was difficult to resist. Among those who formed schemes of operation in that direction was Aaron Burr, the Vice-President of the United States, who in 1804, by the failure of his political aspirations, the general distrust of his political and personal integrity, the exposure of his immoral character, his hopeless financial embarrassments, and, above all, his cruel murder of

---

[1] Jefferson, who was a strict constructionist of the Constitution, was a little embarrassed by this treaty. The acquisition of territory he thought unconstitutional, and he proposed an amendment of that instrument so as to sanction this important act. But nothing of the kind was done. All parties coincided in the measure, and on the 20th of October, 1803, the Senate ratified the treaty by a vote of twenty-four to seven. The purchase of Louisiana became a precedent, and its accession was one of the glories of Mr. Jefferson's administration.

Aaron Burr. His Murder of Hamilton. Virginians honor him for it. Specially honored by Jefferson and his Friends.

the great and honored Hamilton in a duel, had become a desperate man, and a fugitive from society and from justice, moral and legal. When the correspondence between Burr and Hamilton immediately preceding the duel was published, it was evident that the former had committed a murder by forcing the combat upon his victim.[1] The public indignation was intense—so intense that Burr fled before its fury to Georgia by sea, "merely," as he wrote to his daughter Theodosia, a planter's wife in South Carolina, " to give a little time for passion to subside, not from any apprehensions of the final effects of proceedings in courts of law."

Burr found himself in a congenial atmosphere in the South. He was fêted and caressed; and when, finally, he made his way toward Washington City, to take his seat as President of the Senate by virtue of his office, he was treated to ovations. A public dinner was given him at Petersburg, in Virginia, to honor him as "the destroyer of the arch-foe of democracy."[2] Attended by a retinue of Democrats he visited the theatre in the evening, where the audience rose and received him with cheers.[3] At Washington City he was received with great deference. The "President (Jefferson) seems to have been *more* complaisant than usual;"[4] and at Burr's request General Wilkinson was appointed Governor of Louisiana, and Dr. Brown secretary. These were the Vice-President's warm friends.

At the close of his official career in the spring of 1805, Burr was a ruined man, socially, politically, and pecuniari-

---

[1] The political intrigues and social immoralities of Burr had become so generally known in 1804 that his future success in any political schemes was extremely doubtful. He offered himself as an independent candidate for Governor of the State of New York in the spring of 1804, and was defeated, as he believed, through the powerful influence of Alexander Hamilton, who was convinced that he was unfit for any important place of honor or profit. That failure imbittered him. This feeling was intensified by the consciousness that he was suspected and distrusted every where. Hamilton, whom he regarded as his arch-enemy, was at the same time honored and trusted. His integrity was not doubted by his most uncompromising political enemies. This contrast was like glowing embers upon the head of Burr, and he was resolved to destroy his antagonist. A pretext for action to that end was not long wanting. A zealous partisan of Burr's competitor in the late election, in his zeal during the canvass, declared in print that Hamilton had said that the Vice-President was a "dangerous man, who ought not to be trusted with the reins of government." Again he wrote, "I could detail you a more despicable opinion which General Hamilton has expressed of Burr."

These alleged expressions were made the basis of a challenge, on the part of Burr, to mortal combat. Hamilton perceived at the beginning that Burr was determined to force him to fight, against his own convictions of the wrongfulness of dueling and the necessities of the case. He took honorable means to avoid a meeting. His malignant enemy could not be appeased. At length, compelled by the wretched custom of society then prevailing, called "the code of honor," he accepted the challenge, met Burr on the western shore of the Hudson near Weehawken early on the morning of the 11th of July, 1804, and received a mortal wound. He declared his intention not to fire at Burr, and adhered to his resolution, while the murderer took deliberate aim, and accomplished his errand to the field of blood. Hamilton was conveyed across the river to the house of a friend, where he died after suffering for twenty-four hours. The coroner returned a verdict of willful murder. A bill of indictment for that crime was found against him in New Jersey, within the jurisdiction of which the duel was fought, and the Grand Jury of New York found bills against him and his seconds for being concerned in a duel, the punishment for which, by a recent act of that state, was disfranchisement and incapacity to hold office for twenty years. Burr fled to Philadelphia, and from thence to Georgia.

[2] Parton's *Life of Aaron Burr*, page 372.   [3] The same.

[4] The same, page 373. Senator Plumer wrote in November, 1804, "Mr. Jefferson has shown him more attention, and invited him oftener to his house within the last three months, than he ever did for the same time before. Mr. Gallatin [Secretary of the Treasury] has waited upon him oftener at his lodgings, and one day was closeted with him more than two hours. Mr. Madison, formerly the intimate friend of Hamilton, has taken his murderer into his carriage, and accompanied him on a visit to the French minister.... The Democrats of both houses are remarkably attentive to Burr. What office they can give him is uncertain. Mr. Wright, of Maryland, said in debate, 'The first duel I ever read of was that of David killing Goliath. Our little David of the Republicans has killed the Goliath of Federalism, and for this I am willing to reward him.'"—See *Life of William Plumer*, by his son, page 328.

ly. Every legitimate avenue to a retrieval of his character and fortune seemed to be closed, and he became desperate. His ambition was as intense as ever, and he sought new fields for the exercise of his powers. He spent the ensuing summer in the West. It was for him a season of wide observation of men and things, having a bearing upon some grand enterprise which he had conceived. As he went leisurely down the Ohio he visited Harman Blennerhassett, a wealthy and cultivated Irishman, who, with a beautiful and equally cultivated wife, had formed for themselves a sort of terrestrial paradise upon an island in the Ohio River a short distance below the mouth of the Muskingum. Husband and wife were equally charmed by Burr. He fired their imaginations with glimpses of his schemes of personal grandeur for all who should co-operate with him. He filled their minds with dreams of immense wealth and power; and when he left their home the sunshine of their sweet domestic felicity had departed forever. Blennerhassett was a changed man. He had placed his wealth and reputation in the keeping of an unprincipled profligate, and lost both.[1]

At that time the brave and incorruptible Andrew Jackson was in command of the Tennessee militia. In May[a] Burr appeared at the door of his mansion, a few miles from Nashville, and was received as an honored guest. To that stern patriot he talked of the establishment of a splendid empire in the Southwest, where the Spaniards then ruled; and, before he departed, he had won Jackson's confidence, and his promises of co-operation. He met Wilkinson at St. Louis, and divulged some of his schemes to that weak man. He won the friendship of other influential persons, among them General Adair, of Kentucky; and in the autumn he returned to Washington, and sought to win to his service dissatisfied military and naval officers. He talked enigmatically, and, to the

[a] 1806.

BLENNERHASSETT'S RESIDENCE.

[1] Blennerhassett's was indeed a beautiful and happy home. It was the creation of wealth, taste, and love. The mansion was elegant. The gardens were laid out and planted with care. Conservatories were rich in exotics. Science, music, painting, farm culture, and social pleasures made up a great portion of the sum of daily life in that elegant retreat. It became the resort of the best minds west of the mountains. The lately rude island smiled with perpetual beauty. To the simple settlers upon the neighboring shore the house seemed like a palace, and the way of living there like that of a prince. Into that paradise the wily serpent crept, and polluted it with its slime.

Harman Blennerhassett was a descendant of an ancient Irish family, whose seat was Castle Conway, in Kerry. His education was thoroughly given at Trinity College, in Dublin, and he graduated at the same time with his friend and kinsman, Thomas Addis Emmett. He loved and studied science. On the death of his father in 1798 he inherited a large fortune. Having become involved in political troubles, he sold his estate, went to England, and married the beautiful and accomplished Miss Agnew, granddaughter of one of the British generals killed at the battle at Germantown, near Philadelphia. They came to America, journeyed to the West, purchased the island in the Ohio which still bears his name, made their home there, and for five years before Burr's appearance they had enjoyed perfect happiness and repose. A fine library, pictures, scientific apparatus gave them implements for mental culture, and they improved the opportunity. When Burr's mad schemes failed Blennerhassett's paradise was laid waste. He became a cotton-planter in Mississippi, but finally lost his fortune. He and his wife finally returned to England, where he died at the age of sixty-one years. His widow came to America to seek from Congress some remuneration for his losses. While the matter was pending she sickened and died in poverty in New York, in August, 1842, and was buried by the Sisters of Charity.

ears of some, disloyally. Now he spoke of an expedition against Mexico, then of a union of the Western States and Territories into a glorious independent government. To General Eaton he talked of usurpation—of taking possession, by the instrumentality of a revolution, of the national capital and archives, and, Cromwell-like, assuming for himself the character of a protector of an energetic government.[1] The President was apprised of these things, but he regarded Burr's language and schemes as those of a desperate politician too weak to be dangerous.[2]

In the summer of 1806 Burr was again in the West, engaged in his grand scheme, into the inner secrets of which he had not allowed any man to penetrate. Blennerhassett's home was his head-quarters, and a military organization was his work. A flotilla was formed at Marietta, on the Ohio, laden with provisions and military stores; and large numbers of leading men in the West, ignorant of the real designs of Burr, but believing the great central plan to be the construction of a magnificent Anglo-Saxon empire in Mexico, in whose glories they all might share, joined in the enterprise. Wilkinson was made the arch-conspirator's willing tool. Having been engaged in intrigues with the Spaniards in a scheme that would have dismembered the Union, he was now a fitting instrument for Burr's disloyal designs.

But in Kentucky there was a man not to be deceived by Aaron Burr. It was that remarkable character, Colonel Joe Daviess, who gave his life to his country on the field of Tippecanoe. He was then the United States District Attorney for Kentucky. He believed Burr to be engaged in treasonable plans, and procured his arrest. Young Henry Clay defended the prisoner, and he was acquitted; but Daviess never doubted his guilt. Jackson too had become convinced that Burr was preparing to separate the West from the rest of the Union, and he denounced him. "I hate the Dons," he wrote to Governor Claiborne,[a] "and would delight to see Mexico reduced; but I would die in the last ditch before I would see the Union disunited!" Wilkinson, alarmed at the aspect of affairs, turned traitor to Burr, and also denounced him.

[a] November 12, 1806.

Meanwhile the government had become alarmed. The whole West, and indeed the whole country, was agitated by Burr's operations; and the magnitude of his preparations, the persons involved in his toils, and the known disposition of unscrupulous politicians west of the mountains to set up for independency, caused the President to take measures to arrest what seemed to be treason, in the bud. Jefferson did not choose to give it that complexion, and, in a proclamation for the arrest of Burr's designs, whatever they might be, he warned all persons against participating in a scheme for "invading the Spanish dominions."

Boats at Marietta, on the Ohio, loaded for New Orleans with materials for the expedition, were seized, and Blennerhassett's Island was occupied by United States troops. In February, 1807,[b] Burr was arrested near Fort Stoddart, on the Tombigbee River, in the present State of Alabama, by Lieutenant (afterward Major General) E. P. Gaines. He was taken to Richmond, in Virginia, and there tried on a charge of treason. Chief Justice Marshall presided over the court. Burr was acquitted; but, from that day to this, no intelligent student of the history of events in the West during the years 1805 and 1806, doubts that he was engaged in a wicked conspiracy to dissever the Union, and establish a government over which, in some form, he should be the ruler. His escape from conviction was so narrow, and his fears of farther prosecution were so great, that, after remaining concealed for several weeks among his friends, he sailed for Europe under the name of G. H. Edwards. He remained in exile and poverty for several years.

[b] February 19.

---

[1] "He said if he could gain over the marine corps, and secure the naval commanders Truxtun, Preble, Decatur, and others, he would turn Congress neck and heels out of doors, assassinate the President, seize on the treasury and navy, and declare himself the protector of an energetic government."—Deposition of General William Eaton. See *Life of Eaton*, page 396–400, inclusive.   [2] The same, page 401.

The "Rule of 1756" modified.   Commercial Thrift in the United States.   The Jealousy of British Merchants aroused.

While the people of the United States were violently agitated by these events in the West the war in Europe was progressing, and France and England had commenced their desperate game for supremacy at the expense of the commercial prosperity of the world.

For a long time the commercial thrift of the United States, fostered by a modification of the British "rule of 1756,"[1] had been the envy of English merchants. That modification had been made solely for the supposed benefit of British commercial interests. Relying upon the faith of that government, tacitly pledged in the formal exposition of the terms of that modification by the law officer of the crown, the American ship-owners commenced and carried on a most extensive and profitable trade.[2] American vessels became the chief carriers of the products of the colonies of France and Holland; also of Spain after her accession to the French alliance. Sweden, Denmark, and the Hanse Towns[3] were then the only neutral maritime powers, and these, in common with the United States, were fast growing rich.[4]

First the envious British merchants complained; then the privateersmen and navy officers, who declared that, as there were no more prizes to take, their occupation was

---

[1] See note 1, page 84.

[2] On the accession of Alexander to the throne of Russia, after the assassination of the Emperor Paul in March, 1801, the most friendly relations were established between that country and Great Britain. On the 17th of June, 1801, a treaty was concluded between the two governments "to settle," as the preamble expressed it, "an invariable determination of the principles of the two governments upon the rights of neutrality." In that treaty not only the "rule of 1756" was not recognized, but the right of the neutral to trade with the colonies of belligerents, and from his own country in the produce of those colonies to the mother country, was expressly stipulated. As this was avowedly the "settled principle" of the government of Great Britain, American commerce had no more fears. But its sense of security was soon disturbed, but immediately quieted by the prompt action of Mr. King, the American minister at the British court. Early in 1801 he was informed that a decree of the Vice-Admiralty Court at Nassau, New Providence, had condemned the cargo of an American ship going from the United States to a port in the Spanish colonies, the cargo consisting of articles the growth of old Spain. Mr. King immediately presented a respectful remonstrance to the British government against this infringement of the rights of neutrals. The matter was referred to the king's advocate general (Lord Hawkesbury), who reported, on the 16th of March, 1801, in the following words, the doctrine of England *at that time** concerning the rights of neutrals:

"It is now distinctly understood, and has been repeatedly so decided by the High Court of Appeals, that *the produce of the colonies of the enemy may be imported by a neutral into his own country, and may be exported from thence, even to the mother country of such colony; and, in like manner, the produce and manufactures of the mother country may, in this circuitous mode, legally find their way to the colonies.* The direct trade, however, between the mother country and its colonies has not, I apprehend, been recognized as legal, either by his majesty's government or by his tribunals." He then explained what rule should govern the carrying of goods to cause them to avoid a fair definition of "direct trade" and be in conformity to the modification of the "rule of 1756," above mentioned, by saying, "that landing the goods and paying the duties in the neutral country breaks the continuity of the voyage, and is such an importation as legalizes the trade, although the goods be reshipped in the same vessel, and on account of the same neutral proprietors, and be forwarded for sale to the mother country or the colonies."

On the 30th of March the Duke of Portland (the principal Secretary of State) sent the above extracts from the report of the advocate to the Lords Commissioners of the Admiralty, with a letter in which he said, "I have the honor to signify to your lordships the king's pleasure that a communication of the doctrine laid down in the said report should be immediately made by your lordships to the several judges presiding in them, setting forth what is held to be the law upon the subject by the superior tribunals for their future guidance and direction."—Letters from Messrs. Monroe and Pinckney to Lord Howick, August 20, 1806.

[3] Lubeck, Hamburg, and Bremen. These are all that remain of the ancient Hanseatic League, a commercial union of a number of German port-towns in support of each other against the piracies of the Swedes and Danes, formed in 1164, and formally signed in 1241. At one time the league comprised sixty-six cities, and possessed great political power. They were reduced by various causes to their present number more than two hundred years ago. The Congress at Vienna in 1815 guaranteed the freedom of these cities.

[4] The following table exhibits the export trade of the United States for four years:

YEARS.	FOREIGN.	DOMESTIC.	TOTAL.
1803	13,594,000	42,206,000	55,800,000
1804	36,231,000	41,468,000	77,699,000
1805	53,179,000	42,387,000	95,566,000
1806	60,283,000	41,253,000	101,536,000
	163,287,000	167,314,000	330,601,000

This exhibit was made peculiarly annoying to the English, because the foreign articles were principally productions of the colonies of the enemies of Great Britain.

---

* Montesquieu, writing ten years before the English "rule of 1756" in regard to the rights of neutrals was promulgated, said, concerning the spirit of that people, "Supremely jealous with respect to trade, they bind themselves but little by treaties, and depend only on their own laws. Other nations have made the interests of commerce yield to those of politics; the English, on the contrary, have ever made their political interests give way to those of commerce."—See *The Spirit of Laws*, ii., 8.

greatly interfered with. The enemies of Great Britain, having full use of neutral merchant vessels, had none of their own on the ocean. Armed ships, protected by the neutral flag, performed all the duties of practical commerce, and the trade of the maritime foes of England was but little interrupted by existing war. The "rule of 1756," it was alleged, was wholly evaded.

These complaints were heeded. The Courts of Admiralty began to listen willingly to suggestions that this allegation of neutral property was in many, if not in most cases, a mere fraud, intended to give to belligerent goods a neutral character; and early in the summer of 1805 the "rule of 1756" was revived in full force.[1] Like kindred measures on previous occasions,[2] it was put into operation secretly; and the first intimation that the maritime law laid down by the king's advocate in 1801, was abrogated, was the seizure by British cruisers and condemnation by British Admiralty Courts of American vessels and their cargoes. At the same time English public writers put forth specious defenses of the action of their government in its revival of the old practice. One of these was James Stephens, a lawyer of ability, supposed to have been employed for the purpose by the government. He wrote[a] an able and elaborate essay, under the title of "War in Disguise, or the Frauds of the Neutral Flags," in which, taking the "rule of 1756" as the law of nations, "to which," he said, "the neutral powers have all assented, in point of principle, by submitting to its partial application,"[3] he argued that the immense trade carried on with the enemies of England under the American flag was essentially war against Great Britain.

[a] October, 1805.

"War in Disguise" was "written in the spirit of a lawyer stimulated by that of a merchant,"[4] and was full of dogmatic assertions and bold sophistries. It was ably answered in England by Alexander Baring,[5] and in America by James Madison, then

---

[1] In May, 1805, the decision of the Lords of Appeal on the case of the cargo of the American ship *Essex* unchained the chafing English cruisers. It was necessary, for the sake of decency, to give to the world a fair excuse for that decision. It had already been decided that when goods had been made a common stock of America by a fair importation and *the payment of duties*, they might be re-exported from thence to any part of the world. To evade this decision, the Court of Appeals, in the case above alluded to, established the illegality of the neutral trade, "founded on a discovery," says Alexander Baring (see note 5, below), "now made for the first time, that the duties on the cargo imported had not actually been paid *in money*, but by bond of the importer." This decision contracted the whole foreign trade of America excepting that in her own produce. "It circulated rapidly among our cruisers and privateers," continues Mr. Baring, "and in the course of a fortnight the seas were cleared of every American ship they could find, which now crowded our ports for trial."—See Baring's *Inquiry into the Causes and Consequences of the Orders in Council*, pages 81, 82.

[2] See page 84.

[3] This assumption was characteristic. England, on her own motion, promulgated the "rule of 1756" as a "law of nations;" and having the power to enforce it for half a century in the face of the most vehement protests of every respectable maritime nation—even armed protests—her statesmen and publicists agreed that those nations had "assented to it;" as if a *wrong unresented* on account of the weakness of the sufferers became a *right!* It was never assented to. The "Armed Neutrality" of 1780 and 1800 were marked protests against it, and the American principle and policy always opposed the assumption. From the first protest against it in 1793 until the close of 1861, when Secretary Seward, in a letter to Lord Lyons, the British minister at Washington, in the case of the *San Jacinto* and *Trent*, reiterated the American doctrine concerning the protecting powers of a neutral flag, the Americans have opposed the "rule of 1756." For a full account of the case of the *San Jacinto* and *Trent*, see Lossing's *Pictorial History of the Civil War*.

[4] Madison.

[5] The eminent English merchant, Alexander Baring (afterward Lord Ashburton, and at that time a member of Parliament), put forth a pamphlet in February, 1808, entitled *An Inquiry into the Causes and Consequences of the Orders in Council*, etc. It was published in February, 1808, and contains a most searching exposure of the mischievous exaggerations and sophisms of this essay. It is not extravagant to say that that essay, in its injurious influence, was one of the most potent causes of the war between the United States and Great Britain in 1812, because it justified in a semi-official manner the outrages of the British government, through its navy, on the commerce of the United States, under the sanction of orders in council, and deluded the English mind with a semblance of justice. Speaking of some of the statements of the author of *War in Disguise*, Mr. Baring said, "He appears ignorant of every thing relative to American trade to a degree incredible."

War in Disguise was followed by other pamphlets of lesser note on the same side. Among the most noted of these was one entitled *The Present Claims and Complaints of America Briefly and Fairly Considered*. It was an echo of *War in Disguise*, and was published in London at the close of May, 1806. On the back of the title-page of the copy in my possession is the following memorandum in manuscript by Brooke Watson, who was an eminent Canadian merchant when the Revolution broke out in 1775, and was a violent partisan of the crown:

"June 5th, 6th, 7th, and 8th, 1806. Read this pamphlet with all the attention in my power to give it, and under all the consideration of my capacity, accompanied with as much disinterestedness as the nature of the subject will permit to exercise. I am of opinion that, should this country give way to the solicitations of the American States, and much less to their hostile threats, they will, by so doing, that is, by allowing the Americans to be the carriers of the produce of the French colonies to the mother country, sacrifice the deepest interest of this nation to the views of France and the growing insolence of the Americans.—East Sheen, 8th June, 1806. BROOKE WATSON.

"Read 'War in Disguise,' Lord Sheffield, etc."

the Secretary of State. In that answer, referring to menaces in Mr. Stephens's essay, Madison uttered the following noble words, prophetic of soon-coming deeds that vindicated the power behind them: "The blessing of God on our first contest in arms made this nation sovereign, free, and independent. Our citizens feel their honorable condition, and, whatever may be their opinion on questions of national policy, *will firmly support the national rights.* Our government must therefore be permitted to judge for itself. No minister, however splendid his talents, no prince, however great his power, must dictate to the President of the United States."[1]

The foreign relations of the United States at the opening of the year 1806 were unpromising. The conduct of the Spanish government in reference to Louisiana seemed to render war with that nation inevitable. Forbearance on the part of the Americans was exhausted, and a select committee of Congress reported[a] that the aggressions of Spain afforded ample cause for war. But as the policy of the country was always a peaceful one, it was proposed, while preparing for hostilities, to endeavor to avert them, and settle all matters in dispute by the purchase of a part or the whole of the Floridas from Spain. Action to that end was taken, but the war-cloud soon passed away.

[a] January 3, 1806.

Not so with the harbingers of a storm that was evidently brewing between the United States and Great Britain. The depredations of British cruisers and privateers on American commerce, commenced under the most absurd and frivolous pretexts,[2] and fully sanctioned by the British government, produced the most intense indignation throughout the country; and when the Ninth Congress had assembled at Washington in December, 1805, the subject was speedily presented to their notice. Mr. Jefferson had been re-elected President of the United States, and the Democratic party, of which he was the founder and head, had an overwhelming majority in the National Legislature. Its power became somewhat weakened by the defection of John Randolph, of Roanoke, one of its leaders, a quarrelsome and ambitious man, of varied but not solid attainments, who carried with him several of his Virginia colleagues, and filled the halls of legislation during the entire session with unprofitable bickerings.

On account of British depredations, memorials from the merchants of nearly all of the maritime towns of the United States north of the Potomac, argumentative and denunciatory in substance, and numerously signed, were presented to the President; and on the 17th of January these, with a special message on the subject, were laid before Congress by Mr. Jefferson, together with parts of the diplomatic corre-

---

[1] This reply to Mr. Stephens was published anonymously in February, 1806, with the title of *An Answer to "War in Disguise;" or, Remarks on the New Doctrine of England concerning Neutral Trade.*

After the capture of the *Macedonian* by Decatur in the autumn of 1812, the following epigram appeared in Cobbett's *Political Register*, an English publication:

"WAR IN DISGUISE; OR,
AN APOLOGY FOR HIS MAJESTY'S NAVY.

"One Stephens, a lawyer, and once a reporter,
Of war and of taxes a gallant supporter,
In some way or other to Wilberforce kin,
And a member, like him, of a borough bought in,
Who a Master in Chancery since has been made,
Wrote a pamphlet to show that Jonathan's TRADE
Was a 'WAR IN DISGUISE;' which, though strange at first sight,
Events have since proved may have been but too right;
For when Carden the ship of the Yankee Decatur
Attacked, without doubting to take her or beat her,
A FRIGATE she seemed to his glass and his eyes;
But when *taken himself*, how great his surprise
To find her a SEVENTY-FOUR IN DISGUISE!

"If Jonathan thus has the art of disguising,
That he captures our ships is by no means surprising;
And it can't be disgraceful to strike to an elf
Who is more than a match for the devil himself.—PUSS."

[2] Baring's *Inquiry*, etc., page 96.

spondence on the same topic by Mr. Monroe, the United States minister at the British court. The President assured Congress that Mr. Monroe had been instructed "to insist on rights too evident and too important to be surrendered.[1]

The memorials from the merchants were generally drawn with great ability; and it is a notable fact that these men, who, as a class, naturally deprecate war because it is destructive to commerce, and are willing to make great concessions to avoid it, called earnestly upon the government to put forth the strong powers of the army and navy, if necessary, in defense of the rights of neutrals and the protection of American interests.

There were memorials from Boston, Salem, Newburyport, New Haven, New York, Philadelphia, and Baltimore, and all called loudly for redress, under the evident expectation that to insist upon it would cause war.

The Boston merchants said that they fully relied that "such measures would be promptly adopted as would tend to disembarrass commerce, *assert our rights, and support the dignity of the United States.*"

The merchants of Salem said, "If, however, conciliation can not effect the purpose, and an appeal to arms be the last and necessary protection of honor, they feel no disposition to decline the common danger or shrink from the common contribution. Relying on the wisdom and firmness of the general government on this behalf, they feel no hesitation to *pledge their lives and properties in the support of the measures which may be adopted to vindicate the public rights and redress the public wrongs.*"

The merchants of Newburyport relied "with confidence on the firmness and justice of the government to obtain for them compensation and protection;" and those of New Haven called upon that government "firmly to resist every encroachment upon the rights of neutral nations." They tendered "assurances of their disposition to give aid and support to every measure calculated to accomplish this important object."

The New York merchants declared their firm "reliance upon the government of their country that their rights would not be abandoned, and (referring to the assumption of the author of "War in Disguise," see page 139) that no argument in favor of a usurpation would ever be derived from their acquiescence." They concluded by saying, "We pledge our united support in favor of all the measures adopted to vindicate and secure the just rights of our country."

The merchants of Philadelphia suggested that when every peaceable means consistent with honor had been tried to recover redress, and failed, that a resort to arms might be necessary. "If such measures should prove ineffectual," they said, "whatever may be the sacrifice on their part, it would be met with submission."

These memorials were signed by merchants of every shade of politics, and by foreigners doing business in these ports. For more than ten years they had suffered greatly from the varying but always aggressive policy of Great Britain, a policy now greatly aggravated by the latitude tacitly given to the British cruisers in respect to American commerce. These were in little danger of being made answerable for any errors, and were consequently not disposed to make nice distinctions. They detained and sent in every vessel they met under the most frivolous pretenses, in which they were encouraged by the expectation of actual war. They captured American vessels with cargoes wholly of American produce; and the owners of privateers were in the daily practice of taking in valuable cargoes and offering immediately to release them for one or two hundred guineas, and sometimes a larger sum. "In these instances," says Mr. Baring, "the judge decreed the restitution of the ship and cargo, and costs against the captors, with expressions of indignation which so lawless an outrage necessarily excited. The latter had, in the face of this censure, the audacity to enter ap-

---

[1] *Statesman's Manual,* i., 278.

peals, and the American was obliged either to compromise or leave to the captor the option of bringing forward his appeal within a twelve-month, with the possible advantage of an intervening war securing to him his prize.[1] The London merchant," he said, "is either obliged to acquiesce in this iniquitous robbery, or let his correspondent suffer the more expensive vexations which it is, unfortunately, in the power of these people to inflict. If these are the maritime rights," exclaims the honest and indignant Englishman, "for which, we are told, with a pompous ambiguity that always avoids coming to the point, 'our ancestors fought and bled,' and for which 'we crushed the Northern Confederacy,'[2] I am strangely mistaken."[3]

Another and most serious subject of complaint against Great Britain was now considered in connection with the depredations upon American commerce. It was the impressment into the British naval service of seamen taken without leave from American vessels, and who were sailing under the protection of the American flag. To this subject we have already referred.[4] It had been a topic of complaint and negotiation from the beginning of the national government in 1789, and impressment in general was a system against which humane British publicists and statesmen had declaimed. But the British government, not always the exponent of the English mind and heart, governed by expediency rather than justice, and having the precedents of more than four hundred years to support its policy in this respect,[5] had then for half a century chosen to exercise that power in procuring seamen for its navy, and to utterly disregard other hoary precedents which would have justified it in abolishing the nefarious system.[6] It was too useful in time of war, in the replenishment of the navy, to be relinquished. Upon it had been ingrafted another more universally offensive. It was that of *searching neutral vessels* for British seamen, and, seizing them without other criteria of their nationality than the presumptive evidence which similarity of language afforded, impressing them into the British naval service. In the course of fifteen years thousands of native Americans had thus been made to serve a master whom they detested. There being no maritime power strong enough to resist these aggressions, it was assumed by Great Britain, as in the case of the "rule of 1756," that it was for her an established "maritime right."

From the beginning of its career the government of the United States protested against the right of search and the impressment of seamen taken from under the American flag. In his instructions to the United States minister in London, in the summer of 1792, Mr. Jefferson directed him to call the attention of the British ministry to the subject. That government not denying that American seamen had been impressed, had made the degrading proposition that, for their protection against such "accidents," such seamen should carry with them a certificate of citizenship! "This is a condition," said Mr. Jefferson, "never yet submitted to by any nation."[7] The right to enter an American vessel without leave, *for any pretense*, was then, and always has been, strongly denied by the government of the United States. The War of 1812 with England was a solemn protest against the assumption of that right by the British government; and such a requirement of American sailors would operate practically as a warrant to British cruisers for stripping almost every American vessel of its seamen, for the habits, calling, and vicissitudes of the sailor are such that most of them would soon lose their "certificates." The proposition had been unhesitatingly rejected as inadmissible by an independent nation.

In October of the same year Mr. Jefferson again called the attention of the embassador to the subject, "so many instances" of impressment having been complained

---

[1] *Inquiry*, etc., page 94.   [2] Armed Neutrality. See note 2, page 83.   [3] Baring's *Inquiry*, pages 95, 96, 97.
[4] See page 85.
[5] The statute of 2 Richard II. speaks of impressment being well known as early as 1378.
[6] Impressment was declared to be illegal by the British government in 1641.
[7] Mr. Jefferson to Mr. Pinckney, June 11, 1792.

of;[1] and in November he expressed to Mr. Pinckney the hope that he might "be able to make the British ministry sensible of the necessity of punishing the past and preventing the future."[2]

In 1796 Timothy Pickering, then Secretary of State, in his instructions to Mr. King, American minister at the Court of London,[3] spoke of "the long and fruitless attempts that have been made to protect American seamen from British impress," and directed him to do all in his power to enable the American flag to "protect those of whatever nation who sail under it."[4] In another dispatch the same year he alludes to the fact that the British government had gone so far as not to "permit inquiry on board their ships for American seamen," and therefore "their doom is fixed for the war. Thus," he said, "the rights of an independent nation are to be sacrificed to British dignity. Justice requires that such inquiries and examinations be made, because, otherwise, the liberation of our seamen will be impossible. For the British government then to make professions of respect to the rights of our citizens, and willingness to release them, and yet deny the only means of ascertaining those rights, is an insulting tantalism. If the British government have any regard to our rights, any respect for our nation, and place any value on our friendship, they will even facilitate to us the means of releasing our oppressed citizens."[5]

A little later he wrote, "The British naval officers often impress Swedes, Danes, and other foreigners from the vessels of the United States. They have even sometimes impressed Frenchmen! . . . They can not pretend an inability to distinguish these foreigners from their own subjects. They may with as much reason rob the American vessels of the property or merchandise of the Swedes, Danes, or Portuguese, as seize and detain in their service the subjects of those nations found on board American vessels."[6]

During the following year very many complaints concerning impressed American seamen were made to the government of the United States, and cases of absolute

---

[1] Mr. Jefferson to Mr. Pinckney, October 12, 1792.
[2] The same to the same, November 6, 1792.
[3] Rufus King was born in Scarborough, Maine, in the year 1755. He was a student in Harvard College in 1775, when the breaking out of the war for independence suspended that institution. He chose the law for his profession, and became an able practitioner. He was in Sullivan's army in Rhode Island in 1778, and was admitted to the bar in 1780. His first appearance was in opposition to his great instructor, Theophilus Parsons, of Newburyport. His oratorical talents soon became known and appreciated, and in 1784 he was elected to a seat in the Legislature of Massachusetts. In the National Convention of 1787 he was an efficient member, and nobly advocated the ratification of the Constitution there adopted. Having married the daughter of an opulent merchant of New York, Mr. King made that city his residence in 1788, and the next year was elected to a seat in the Legislature of New York. He was one of the first United States senators from New York, and in 1796 was appointed minister to Great Britain. He returned home in 1803. From 1813 to 1826 he was a member of the United States Senate. At the close of his term he was sent to England as minister plenipotentiary, but ill health compelled him to relinquish his post and return home after a residence of about a year there. He died at his home near Jamaica, Long Island, on the 29th of April, 1827, at the age of seventy-two years.
[4] Mr. Pickering to Mr. King, June 8, 1796.
[5] The same to the same, September 10, 1796.
[6] The same to the same, October 26, 1796.

cruelty exercised toward and hardships endured by American seamen thus impressed were reported.[1]

The United States government, always inclined to peace, frequently urged upon that of Great Britain the necessity of a convention which should settle the questions of impress and neutrality, but without success, for the British government practically assumed the right to be a law unto itself. Early in 1799 Mr. King made an earnest representation on the subject to Lord Grenville, denying, as he had on former conferences, any right of the kind on the part of Great Britain, and suggesting that American ships of war, by permission of their government, might with equal right pursue the same practice toward British merchantmen. He protested against the indiscriminate seizure on board of American vessels of seamen of several nations, and pressed him for some definite assurance of a change. But Grenville, as usual, was evasive, and the conference ended without a prospect of satisfaction. Grenville assured Mr. King that all Americans so impressed should be discharged on application for that purpose; but the American minister very properly considered that offer far short of satisfaction. "Indeed," he said, "to acquiesce in it is to give up the right."[2]

Late in the year 1800, John Marshall, then Secretary of State, wrote an able and eloquent letter to Mr. King in London on the subject of the impress. "The impressment of our seamen," he said, "is an injury of very serious magnitude, which deeply affects the feelings and the honor of the nation. . . . They are dragged on board British ships of war with evidences of citizenship in their hands, and forced by violence there to serve until conclusive testimonials of their birth can be obtained. . . . Although the Lords of the Admiralty uniformly direct their discharge on the produc-

---

[1] Investigation revealed the following facts: on the 4th of July, 1794, Captain Silas Talbot, of the United States Navy, wrote from Kingston, Jamaica, to Secretary Pickering, that Admiral Sir Hyde Parker had "issued a general order to all captains and commanders of ships and vessels of war, directing them not to obey any writ of *habeas corpus*, nor suffer any men to leave their ships in consequence of such writ." This order was issued because Talbot had made successful applications to the civil authorities on that island for the release of enslaved Americans on board British vessels. Talbot, however, persevered in his humane efforts, and he wrote that, while all the writs which he had obtained were served, none of them were obeyed. The naval officers on that station set the civil authority at defiance, and Talbot wrote, "The laws in this island, it seems, can not be administered for the relief of American citizens who are held in British slavery, many of whom, as they write me from on board Captain Otway's ship, *have been brought to the gangway and whipped for writing to their agent to get them discharged!*"

William Cobbett, an Englishman, wrote afterward in his *Political Register*, saying, "Our ships of war, when they meet an American vessel at sea, board her and take out of her by force any seamen whom our officers assert to be British subjects. *There is no rule by which they are bound. They act at discretion;* and the consequence is that great numbers of native Americans have been impressed, and great numbers of them are now in our navy. . . . That many of these men have died on board our ships, that many have been wounded, that many have been killed in action, and that many have been worn out in the service there can be no doubt. Some obtain their release through the application of the American consul here; and of these the sufferings have in many instances been very great. There have been instances where men have thus got free *after having been flogged through the fleet for desertion.** But it has been asked whether we are not to take our sailors where we find them? To which America answers, 'Yes.'. . . She wishes not to have in her ships any British sailors, and she is willing to give them up whenever the fact of their being British sailors can be proved; but let not men be seized in her ships upon the high seas (and sometimes at the mouths of her own rivers), where there is nobody to judge between the parties, and where the British officer going on board is at once ACCUSER, WITNESS, JUDGE, and CAPTOR!"

[2] Mr. King to Mr. Pickering, March 15, 1799.

---

* There is ample testimony to prove the cruel treatment experienced by impressed American seamen on board British vessels. Richard Thompson, a native of New Paltz, Ulster County, New York, testified at Poughkeepsie on the 17th of April, 1793, that, while on the sea in a merchant vessel, he was impressed on board the British vessel of war *Peacock* in 1810. He was not allowed to write to his friends. When he and two other impressed American seamen heard of the declaration of war in 1812, they claimed to be considered prisoners of war, and refused to do duty any longer. They were ordered to the quarter-deck, put in irons for twenty-four hours, then taken to the gangway, stripped naked, "tied and whipped, each one dozen and a half lashes, and put to duty." When the *Peacock* went into action with the *Hornet* they asked the captain to be sent below, that they might not fight against their countrymen. The captain called a midshipman and told him to "do his duty." That duty was to hold a pistol at the head of Thompson and threaten to blow his brains out if he and his companions did not do service. They were liberated on the capture of the *Peacock* by the *Hornet*. Another seaman from Ulster County, named James Tompkins, testified to greater cruelties inflicted on himself and three others, who were impressed on board the British ship *Acteon* in April, 1812. When they refused to do duty they were whipped "five dozen lashes each." Two days afterward they received four dozen lashes each. They still refused to do duty, and, after the lapse of another two days, they received two dozen lashes each. They still refused, and, after being whipped again, they were put in irons, where they were kept three months. On their arrival in London they heard of the capture of the *Guerriere*. With a shirt and handkerchiefs they made stripes and stars for American colors, hung it over a gun, and gave three cheers for the victory. For this outburst of patriotism they received two dozen lashes each.

tion of this testimony, yet many must perish unrelieved, and all are detained a considerable time in lawless and injurious confinement. It is the duty as well as a right of a friendly nation to require that measures be taken by the British government to prevent the continued repetition of such violence by its agents. . . . The mere release of the injured, after a long course of serving and suffering, is no compensation for the past, and no security for the future. . . . The United States, therefore, require positively that their seamen who are not British subjects, whether born in America or elsewhere, shall be exempt from impressment. The case of British subjects, whether naturalized or not, is more questionable; but the right even to impress *them* is denied. . . . Alien seamen, not British subjects, engaged in our merchant service, ought to be equally exempt with citizens from impressments. We have a right to engage them, and have a right to and an interest in their persons to the extent of the service contracted to be performed. Britain has not a pretext of right to their persons or their service. To tear them, then, from our possession is at the same time an insult and an injury. It is an act of violence for which there exists no palliative." After alluding to the fact that the principles of the United States government would not allow retaliation by impressments from the British merchant ships, and suggesting that something in that way might be done by *recruiting* from that service, Mr. Marshall concludes by saying, "Is it not more advisable to desist from, and to take effectual measures to prevent an acknowledged wrong, than, by perseverance in that wrong, to excite against themselves the well-founded resentment of America, and force our government into measures which may possibly terminate in open rupture?"[1]

These suggestions were all submitted to the British ministry, but without the slightest visible effect. While the war continued, the nefarious practice was carried on vigorously; but when the general pacification of Europe took place in 1801, and the Peace of Amiens gave a respite to British ships of war—when their seamen were in excess of the demand—impressments ceased, and the American minister in London, untaught by past experience and observation, wrote, "I am in hopes that Lord St. Vincent will be inclined to attend to our reiterated remonstrances against the impressment of our seamen and the vexations of our trade."[2] Vain expectation!

Early in the year 1800[a] Mr. Liston, the British minister in the United States, submitted to President Adams a proposition for the reciprocal delivery of deserters, so worded as to sanction impressment on board of *private* vessels, but to except "public ships of war." It was rejected. Pickering, the Secretary of State, said, "It appears utterly inadmissible, unless it would put an end to impressments."[3] The Secretary of the Navy said, "It is better to have no article, and meet all consequences, than not to enumerate merchant vessels on the high seas among the things not to be entered in search of deserters."[4] The Secretary of the Treasury objected to it because it did not "provide against the impressment of American seamen."[5] The Secretary of War objected to it on the same ground, saying, "If this article [the seventh in Mr. Liston's proposition] means what it is apprehended it does, it is utterly inadmissible."[6] The President and his Cabinet, thus planting themselves upon the broad principles of neutral rights and the sanctity of the national flag laid down at the beginning, would listen to nothing short of a recognition of those rights and of that sanctity.[7]

[a] February 4.

When hostilities between Great Britain and France were revived in 1803, the im-

---

[1] Marshall to King, September 20, 1800.   [2] Mr. King to the Secretary of State, February 23, 1801.
[3] Pickering to the President, February 20, 1800.   [4] Benjamin Stoddert to the President, February 26, 1800.
[5] Oliver Wolcott to the President, April 26, 1800.   [6] James M'Henry to the President, April 16, 1800.

[7] From June, 1797, until the beginning of 1801, no less than 2059 applications for seamen impressed, including many made previously by Mr. King and Mr. Pinckney, were made. Of these, only 102 were British subjects—less than one twentieth of the whole impressed. Eleven hundred and forty-two were discharged as not being British subjects, and 805, more than one half, were held for farther proof, while there existed strong presumption that the whole, or a greater part, at least, were aliens.—LYMAN's *Diplomacy of the United States*, ii., 15, note.

press was again put into active operation. The American minister in London, Mr. Monroe, following up previous efforts made by Mr. King when that gentleman perceived that war was inevitable,[1] used every lawful endeavor to make a mutually satisfactory arrangement concerning it. In a letter of instructions to that minister early in 1804,[a] Mr. Madison, then Secretary of State, ably and lucidly reviewed the whole subject of the impress and the rights of neutrals. His letter opened with the following clear enunciation of the doctrines of the two nations:

[a] January 5.

"We consider a *neutral flag on the high seas as a safeguard to those sailing under it*. Great Britain, on the contrary, asserts a right to search for and seize her own subjects ; and under that cover, as can not but happen, are often seized and taken off citizens of the United States, and citizens or subjects of other neutral countries navigating the high seas under the protection of the American flag."

After brief and cogent argument, Mr. Madison said, "Were it allowable that British subjects should be taken out of American vessels on the high seas, it might at least be required that the proof of their allegiance should lie on the British side. This obvious and just rule is, however, reversed. And any seaman on board, though going from an American port, sailing under an American flag, and sometimes even speaking an idiom proving him not to be a British subject, is presumed to be such *unless proved to be an American citizen.* It may be safely affirmed that this is an outrage which has no precedent, and which Great Britain would be among the last nations in the world to suffer, if offered to her own subjects and her own flag.[2]

* * * * * * * * * *

"Great Britain has the less to say on the subject, as it is in direct contradiction to the principles on which she proceeds in other cases. While she claims and seizes on the high seas her own subjects voluntarily serving in American vessels, she has constantly given, when she could give, as a reason for not discharging from her service American citizens, that they had voluntarily engaged in it. Nay, more; while she impresses her own subjects from the American service, although they have been settled, and married, and naturalized in the United States, she constantly refuses to release from hers American seamen pressed into it whenever she can give for a reason that they are either settled or married within her dominions. Thus, when the voluntary consent of the individual favors her pretensions, she pleads the validity of that consent. When the voluntary consent of the individual stands in the way of her pretensions, it goes for nothing. When marriage or residence can be pleaded in her favor, she avails herself of the plea. When marriage, residence, and naturalization are against her, no respect whatever is paid to either. She takes by force her own subjects voluntarily serving in our vessels. She keeps by force American citizens involuntarily serving in hers. More flagrant inconsistencies can not be imagined."

No arguments, no remonstrances, no appeals to justice or the demands of international comity, could induce the British government at that time, when waging war with all its powers, to relinquish so great an advantage.

---

[1] In the spring of 1803 Mr. King made a determined effort to prevent a revival of the practice of impressment. On the 7th of May he submitted the following article to the British ministry: "No person shall be impressed or taken on the high seas out of any ship or vessel belonging to the subjects or citizens of one of the parties by the public or private armed ships or men-of-war belonging to or in the service of the other party." Lord St. Vincent, the First Lord of the Admiralty, and Lord Hawkesbury, the Secretary of State for Foreign Affairs, at first assented to this article; but, after consultation with Sir William Scott, an exception was required in favor of the *narrow seas*. This proposal was rejected by Mr. King. It was regarded as a subterfuge. The government, at the opening of another war, was determined not to relinquish the practice of impressments from American vessels, and this revival of an obsolete claim of England to exclusive jurisdiction over the seas surrounding the British Isles as far south as Cape Finisterre and north to a point on the coast of Norway, which it was known the Americans would reject, was done as an excuse for terminating the negotiation on the practice of the impress.

[2] Cooper, in his *Naval History of the United States,* ii., 84, says: "On the 12th of June [1805] No. 7 [gun-boat] fell in with the fleet of Admiral Collingwood off Cadiz, and, while Mr. Lawrence was on board one of the British ships, a boat was sent and took three men out of No. 7, under the pretense that they were Englishmen. On his return to his own vessel Mr. Lawrence hauled down his ensign, but no notice was taken of the proceeding by the British. It is a fitting commentary on this transaction that in the published letters of Lord Collingwood, when he speaks of the impressment of Americans, he says that England would not submit to such an aggression for an hour."

National Independence and Honor imperiled.   Memorials to Congress for decided Action.   Hesitation of Congress.

Day after day proofs were received of the sufferings of American citizens on account of the impress; and so flagrant and frequent were these outrages toward the close of 1805, that, in the memorials presented to Congress on the subject of British depredations upon American commerce, already alluded to, the impressment of American seamen was a prominent topic.[1]

Action in Congress on these subjects, so vital to the interests of the people and the dignity of the nation, was prompt. It was felt that a crisis was reached when the independence of the United States must be vindicated, or the national honor be imperiled. There was ample cause for most vigorous retaliatory measures toward Great Britain, ay, even for war. But the administration itself, and the host of its opponents, were willing to bear a little longer than take the responsibility of an open rupture with Great Britain. A resolution offered in the United States Senate, declaring that the depredations upon American commerce under the sanction of the British government were "unprovoked aggressions upon the property of the citizens of the United States, violations of their neutral rights, and encroachments upon their national independence," was adopted by unanimous vote;[a] but when, four days afterward,[b] another resolution was offered requesting the President to "demand the restoration of the property of those citizens captured and condemned on the pretext of its being employed in a trade with the enemies of Great Britain, indemnification for past losses, and some arrangement concerning the impressment of seamen," there was hesitation. To obtain the redress sought, there were only four modes—namely, negotiation, non-intercourse, embargo, and war. The first had been tried in vain; the second and third would be menacing and offensive; and the fourth, all parties at that time deprecated. There was a division in the vote. There was unanimity in denunciation, but differences when the test of positive action was applied. There were twenty votes in the affirmative, and six in the negative.

[a] February 10, 1806.
[b] February 14.

It was resolved to try negotiations once more. William Pinkney,[2] of Maryland, who had considerable diplomatic experience, was finally appointed a minister extraordinary to England,[c] to become associated with Monroe, the resident

[c] May.

---

[1] "The impressment of our seamen, notwithstanding clear proofs of citizenship, the violation of our jurisdiction by captures at the mouths of our harbors,* and insulting treatment of our ships on the ocean, are subjects worthy the serious consideration of our national councils."—*Salem Memorial.*

"The constancy and valor of the seamen of the United States are justly themes of patriotic exultation. From their connection with us, we consider their cause as our cause, their rights as our rights, their interests as our interests. Our feelings are indignant at the recital of their wrongs."—*New York Memorial,* signed by John Jacob Astor and others.

"That our seamen should be exposed to meanest insults and most wanton cruelties, and the fruits of their industry and enterprise fall a prey to the profligate, can not but excite both feeling and indignation, and call loudly for the aid and protection of government."—*Philadelphia Memorial.* The New Haven and Baltimore memorials expressed similar sentiments.

[2] William Pinkney was born at Annapolis, Maryland, on the 17th of March, 1764. His father was a Loyalist, but William, as he approached manhood, toward the close of the Revolution, espoused the cause of his country. At the age of twenty-two years he was admitted to the bar, and commenced the practice of his profession in Harford County, Maryland, where he married the sister of (afterward) Commodore Rodgers. He was a member of the Executive Council of Maryland in 1792, and in 1795 was chosen to the Legislature. The next year he was appointed one of the commissioners under the provisions of Jay's treaty, and proceeded to England. He remained there until 1805, when he returned, and made Baltimore his residence. He was distinguished for his legal learning and eloquence, and was immediately appointed Attorney General of Maryland. He was sent to England for the object mentioned in the text, in 1806, where he remained until 1811, when he returned home. He fought bravely in the battle near Bladensburg in 1814, and was soon afterward elected to Congress. In 1816 he was appointed minister to Russia. He remained there until 1820, when he returned, and was chosen to a seat in the Senate of the United States. In that body, and in the United States Courts, he labored intensely until 1821, when his health suddenly gave way. He died on the 25th of February, 1822, in the fifty-ninth year of his age.

---

* This had been done repeatedly. The American waters were almost continually plowed by British cruisers at this time. A few weeks later an event occurred which aroused the greatest indignation throughout the country. A small coasting vessel, navigated by Captain John Pearce, of New York, running for Sandy Hook, was fired into by the British cruiser *Leander,* Captain Whitby. Captain Pearce was killed. It was, morally, a gross act of piracy. The act itself called forth bitter denunciations at a meeting held at the Tontine Coffee-house, in New York, on the following day (April 26, 1806). A resolution proposed by a committee, of which Rufus King, late minister to England, was chairman, declared that an administration that would suffer foreign armed ships to "impress, wound, and murder citizens" was "not entitled to the confidence of a brave and free people." The public indignation was increased when it became known that Captain Whitby, who was brought to trial in England for the murder of Captain Pearce, and his guilt fairly proven by evidence dispatched thither by the United States government, was *honorably acquitted!*

minister, in negotiating a treaty that should settle all disputes between the two governments. It was thought expedient, at the same time, to use the second method prospectively, as an auxiliary to the American ministers, for it would appeal potentially to the commercial interest of Great Britain, then, as ever, the ruling power in the state. Accordingly, after long and earnest debates, the House of Representatives passed an act[a] prohibiting the importation into the United States of a great variety of the most important manufactures of Great Britain. It passed the Senate on the 16th of April, and on the 18th became a law.[1] To give time for the negotiations, the commencement of the prohibition was postponed until the middle of the following November.

[a] March 28, 1806.

In the debate upon the Non-importation Act in Congress, and in its discussion among the people, the old party lines, which, to some extent, had appeared faint when great national questions were fairly discussed, became perfectly distinct. The measure was regarded by the jealous opponents of Jefferson and his Cabinet as a display of that hostility to Great Britain because of love for France, which the President and his Secretary had so frequently manifested during the administrations of Washington and Adams. It was regarded as a measure calculated to lead the country into a war with Great Britain. The administration party, on the contrary, charged the Federalists, because they were unwilling to support the measure, with being friendly to their country's oppressor. The old political war-cries were sounded, and "French party" and "British party" became familiar words again on the lips of partisans. The Federalists affected to regard Great Britain in her wars with France, and especially in the current one with Napoleon, as the champion of the liberties of the world against an audacious aspirant for universal empire; while the Democrats affected to consider the Emperor of the French as a great regenerator, who was destined to benefit the world by prostrating tottering thrones, effacing corrupt dynasties, purifying the political atmosphere of Europe, and giving new life and vigor to the people. Such were the antagonistic ideas then distinctly developed. The Non-importation Act was passed by a strictly party vote—ninety-three Democrats, against thirty-two Federalists and "Quids," as John Randolph and his six secessionists were called. The heat of that debate in the first session of the Ninth Congress developed the germ of the *War* and *Anti-war* parties, so strong and implacable just previous to and during the WAR OF 1812.

---

[1] The following is a list of articles prohibited: All articles of which leather, silk, hemp or flax, and tin and brass (tin sheets excepted) were the materials of chief value; woolen cloths whose invoice prices should exceed five shillings sterling a yard; woolen hosiery of all kinds; window-glass, and all the manufactures of glass; silver and plated ware; paper of every description; nails and spikes; mats, and clothing ready made; millinery of all kinds; playing-cards; beer, ale, and porter; and pictures and prints.

Hopes created by a new British Ministry.   Disappointment.   Negotiations reopened.   Charles James Fox.

CHAPTER VIII.

> " You all remember well, I guess,
>   The *Chesapeake* disaster,
> When Britons dared to kill and press,
>   To please their royal master."
> Song—Rodgers and Victory.

> " From the deep we withdraw till the tempest be past,
>   Till our flag can protect each American cargo;
> While British ambition's dominion shall last,
>   Let us join, heart and hand, to support the Embargo:
>   For Embargo and Peace
>   Will promote our increase;
> Then embargoed we'll live till injustice shall cease:
>   For ne'er, till old Ocean retires from his bed,
> Will Columbia by Europe's proud tyrants be led."
> Song—Embargo and Peace.

HILE the debate on the Non-importation Act was at its height in Congress, intelligence came of a change in the British ministry that promised a speedy adjustment of all matters in dispute between the two countries. William Pitt died in January,[a] and at the beginning of February a new Cabinet was formed, known in English history as "All-the-talents Ministry," of which the peaceful, humane, and liberal Charles James Fox was the most influential member,[1] as Secretary of State for Foreign Affairs.

[a] January 23, 1806.

Under the impression that the new ministry would be more ready to act justly toward the Americans than the old one, Mr. Pinkney sailed for England. He was soon undeceived. England's policy in the conduct of the tremendous war in which she was engaged was too firmly established to be disturbed by the private opinions and wishes of individuals, and Mr. Fox appears to have imbibed the views of his predecessors in office concerning the complaints of the Americans on the subject of the impress and neutral rights.

Before Pinkney's arrival Fox had expressed to Monroe some sensibility at the passage of the Non-importation Act. He declared that it embarrassed him, because it would place him in the position of treating under seeming compulsion. Monroe gave a satisfactory explanation, and, on the arrival of Pinkney, Lords Holland and Auckland were appointed to negotiate with the American envoys.

The negotiations commenced in August.[b] As the American commissioners were instructed to make no treaty which did not secure the vessels of their countrymen on the high seas against visitations from press-gangs, this topic naturally occupied the early and earnest attention of the negotiators. The American commissioners, under instructions, contended that the right of impressment existing by municipal law could not be exercised out of the jurisdiction of Great Britain, and, consequently, upon the high seas. In reply, the British commissioners recited the old

[b] August 2.

---

[1] Fox and Burke stood side by side in the opposition to Lord North in the long struggle before and during the American Revolution. He was always on the liberal side in politics, of the Whig school, and was intensely hated by the king. At one time, at the close of the Revolution, the nation appeared to be divided into parties, one known as the king's, and the other as Fox's. On one occasion Dr. Johnson said, "Fox is an extraordinary man; here is a man who has divided a kingdom with Cæsar, so that it was a doubt which the nation should be ruled by—the sceptre of George III. or the tongue of Fox." He was always an advocate for a peace policy, and his accession to power in 1806 gave the thinking men of England hopes of a cessation of the wasting war with the all-conquering Napoleon. To that end he labored, and had well-nigh accomplished measures for pacification when, on the 13th of September, 1806, he died.

doctrine that no subject of the king could expatriate himself—"once an Englishman, always an Englishman"—and argued that to give up that right would make every American vessel an asylum for British seamen wishing to evade their country's service, and even for deserters from British ships of war. They were sustained in this view by the law officers of the crown and the Board of Admiralty, and would not yield the point. Here the American commissioners might have terminated the negotiation, because the vital object of their appointment could not be obtained.

At length this impressment question was placed in an attitude to allow negotiations upon other topics to go on. While the British commissioners declared that their government would not relinquish by formal treaty the right of impressment on the high seas, they agreed that special instructions should be given and enforced for the observance of great caution against subjecting any American-born citizens to molestation or injury. They gave the American commissioners to understand, although it was not expressed in terms, that the intention of the British government was not to allow impressments from American vessels on the high seas except under extraordinary circumstances, such as having on board known deserters from the British navy, and thus gradually to abandon the practice. This proposition was put in writing,[a] and the negotiations on other topics proceeded.

[a] November 8, 1806.

The terms of a treaty considered in many respects more favorable to the Americans than that of Jay in 1794, to continue for ten years, were soon agreed to. The trade between the United States and the European possessions of Great Britain were placed on a footing of perfect reciprocity, but no concessions could be obtained as to the trade of the West Indies; while in the matter of the East India trade terms as favorable to the Americans as those of Jay's would not be granted. The provisions in that treaty concerning blockades and contraband were adopted, with an additional provision that no American vessels were to be visited or seized within five miles of the coast of the United States.

In regard to the carrying-trade, in which American vessels were so largely concerned, the modification of the "rule of 1756" (stipulated in the treaty with Russia in 1801, already alluded to)[1] was agreed to, but to operate only during the current war, by which such vessels could transport to any belligerent colony not blockaded by a British force, any European goods not contraband of war, providing such goods were American property, and the continuity of the voyage had been broken by their having been previously landed in the United States, and a duty paid of at least one per cent. above the amount drawn back on re-exportation. In like manner the produce of the colony might be carried back, and taken into any port in Europe not blockaded.

At this point in the negotiation, intelligence of the issue of the Berlin Decree,[2] which we shall consider presently, reached the commissioners. It produced hesitation on the part of the British negotiators. They required assurances that the United States would not allow their trade with Great Britain, and in British merchandise, to be interrupted and interfered with by France without taking measures to resent it. This assurance the American commissioners refused to give, as they were not inclined to pledge their government to quarrel with France for the benefit of English trade. Holland and Auckland waived the point and signed the treaty, at the same time presenting a written protest against the Berlin Decree, reserving to the British government the right, should that decree be actually carried into force as against neutrals, and be submitted to by them, to take such measures of retaliation as might be deemed expedient.

Had this treaty not been based in a degree upon contingencies and promises, leaving American commence still, in the absence of positive treaty stipulations, at the

---

[1] See note 2, page 138. [2] See page 129.

mercy of British policy, it might have been considered so advantageous to the merchants of the United States, being an advance in the right direction, as to have received the favor of the administration. But it was too loose in its actual guarantees, and the experience of the past was too admonitory to allow such a treaty to be accepted as a satisfactory settlement of difficulties between the two governments. It also failed to secure the most vital advantages contemplated in the appointment of the commission, namely, the abolition of the impress from American vessels and relinquishment on the part of Great Britain of its claims to a right of search. Such being its character, the President, at the risk of being charged with usurpation, did not even lay the treaty before the Senate, but, on his own responsibility, seconded by the co-operation of Mr. Madison, his Secretary of State, he refused to ratify it. That refusal destroyed all hope of negotiating another treaty so favorable to the Americans, for, long before it reached the British government in official form, the Fox and Grenville ministry had disappeared. It had been superseded[a] by one in which Liverpool, Percival, and Canning, all disciples of the more warlike Pitt, were the leading spirits. The remains of Fox had lain in Westminster Abbey six months when this change in the administration took place.[1]   [a] March, 1807.

As might have been expected, Jefferson was vehemently assailed by the opposition; and the merchants, as a class, misled by the deceptive clamor of politicians, swelled the voice of denunciation. The Federalists, ever suspicious of the President, their arch-enemy in former crises of the government, charged him with insincerity when he protested his earnest desire for an honorable adjustment with England; and they were inclined to regard the rejection of the treaty as a deliberate manœuvre to cherish popular passion, and thus to strengthen the party hold of the President and his destined successor, Mr. Madison.[2]

The war against the administration was waged unrelentingly. Another great struggle between the Democrats and Federalists for the prize of the Presidency and national rule now commenced, and some leading men of the opposition who, when in power, had bitterly denounced the course of the British government because of its course on the impress and neutral rights, now became either silent spectators or virtual apologists for England. Yet the Democratic party steadily gained in numbers and influence even in New England, and the war feeling became more and more intense and positive among the people.

We have already alluded to the seizure of Hanover by the Prussians at the instigation of Napoleon.[3] This offense against the Crown of England was immediately resented; or, rather, it was made the pretext for employing against France a measure which, as in 1756 and 1792, was calculated to starve the empire. By orders in Council, issued on the 16th of May, 1806, the whole coast of Europe from the Elbe, in Germany, to Brest, in France, a distance of about eight hundred miles, was declared in a state of blockade, when, at the same time, the British navy could not spare from its other fields of service vessels enough to enforce the blockade over a third of the prescribed coast. It was essentially a "paper blockade," then valid according to English "laws of nations"—laws of her own enactment, and enforced by her own material power. The almost entire destruction of the French and Spanish fleets off Trafalgar, a few months before,[b] had annihilated her rivals for the sovereignty of the seas, and she now resolved to control the trade of the world, by which she might procure pecuniary means to carry on the war.   [b] October 21, 1805.

The British orders in Council somewhat startled American commerce, and by some was considered, so far as that commerce was concerned, as not only a countervailing measure in view of the Non-importation Act of the American Congress, but a positively belligerent one. But its effects were slight in comparison with the pros-

---
[1] See page 128.
[2] Hildreth's *History of the United States*, Second Series, ii., 663.
[3] See page 128.

trating blow inflicted upon the American shipping interest when, from the "Imperial Camp at Berlin" on the 21st of November, 1806, Napoleon issued the famous decree which declared the British Islands in a state of blockade, forbade all correspondence or trade with England, defined all articles of English manufacture or produce as contraband, and the property of all British subjects as lawful prize of war.[1]

Resting for moral support upon England's cherished "law of nations," Napoleon made this declaration of a practically universal blockade when he had scarcely a ship at his command to enforce it; for Lord Nelson, as we have just observed, had almost demolished the whole French and part of the Spanish fleet off Trafalgar just thirteen months before.[a]

[a] October 21, 1805.

On land the power of Napoleon was scarcely bounded by any river in Europe. Within his grasp was seemingly the sceptre of universal empire, of which he dreamed with the ambition of an Alexander. State after state had been added to his dominions, and brother after brother had been placed upon thrones of his own construction, amid the ruins of old dynasties. He now endeavored, by the practice of England's logic, to dispute with her in a peculiar way the sceptre of the seas.[2]

This was the beginning of what was afterward called the *Continental System*, commenced avowedly as a retaliatory measure, and designed primarily to injure and, if possible, to destroy the commercial prosperity of England. Napoleon adhered to it for several years as a favorite scheme, to the delight and profit of smugglers created by the system, and the immense injury of the commerce of the world. He compelled most of the states of Europe to become partners in the league against Great Britain. A refusal to join it was considered a just cause for war. Yet England, with such powers against her, and such an injurious system impinging heavily upon her maritime and trading interests, defied Napoleon and his allies, and exhibited a moral and material energy which commands our wonder and highest respect.

America was at this time really the only neutral in the civilized world. Her isolation enabled her to maintain that position, and enjoy prosperity while Europe was resonant with the din of battle, clouded with the smoke of camps and ruined towns, and wasted by the terrible demands of moving armies. But her security and prosperity were likely to be disturbed by this unrighteous decree from the "Imperial Camp." It was so broad in its application, that it would be equally injurious to neutrals and belligerents. The commercial world perceived this with its keen eye, and American commerce was convulsed by a thrill of apprehension. Rates of insurance ran up to ruinous heights at the beginning of 1807, and commercial enterprises of every kind were suspended.

This panic was somewhat allayed by a letter from John Armstrong, American minister at Paris, who believed the operations of the decree would be only municipal, and was assured by the French Minister of Marine that the existing commercial relations of the United States and the French Empire, as settled by the Convention of 1800,[3] would not be disturbed.[4] This assurance was subsequently strengthened by the fact that the decree was not enforced against American vessels until about a year afterward,[5] Napoleon doubtless hoping the United States, growing every day more and more hostile toward England because of her injustice, would be induced to join the league against that power. The Americans were also taught to rely upon the traditional policy of France concerning the rights of neutrals, so plainly avowed in the Armed Neutrality Treaty in 1780, earnestly proclaimed ever since by the French

---

[1] See note 1, page 129.
[2] Napoleon at this time had been compelled to abandon his schemes for the invasion of England. He had lost St. Domingo, and all prestige in the West Indies, and had no means of annoying his most potent enemy, on the sea.
[3] See twelfth and fourteenth articles of that Convention in *Statesman's Manual*, iv., 342, 343.
[4] On the 10th of December, Minister Armstrong asked for an explanation of the Berlin Decree. Monsieur Decres, the Minister of Marine, replied on the 24th that he considered the decree as in no way modifying "the regulations at present observed in France with regard to neutral navigators, nor, consequently, of the Convention of the 30th of September, 1800, with the United States of America."
[5] Baring's *Inquiry*, etc., page 116, cited in note 1, page 129.

rulers, and reiterated in the charges against England in the preamble to the famous decree under consideration.

The promises of security to American commerce from the operations of the Berlin Decree were soon broken. The powers of that decree were put forth in the autumn of 1807. The Peace of Tilsit[1] had released a large number of French soldiers from duties in the camp and field, and these were employed at various ports along the coasts of Europe in strictly enforcing the blockade and putting the Continental System into active operation. Even American commerce did not remain undisturbed; on the contrary, it was directly threatened by a decision of Regnier, the French Minister of Justice, who declared that all merchandise derived from England and her colonies, by whomsoever owned, was liable to seizure even on board neutral vessels.[2] As Americans were then the only neutrals, this decision was aimed directly at them, with the intention, no doubt, of forcing the United States into at least a passive co-operation with Bonaparte in his deadly designs against British commerce and the liberties of that people. When Minister Armstrong made inquiries concerning this interpretation of the Berlin Decree, Champagny, the French Minister for Foreign Affairs, coolly replied that the principal powers of Europe for eleven months had not only not issued any protest against the decree, but had agreed to enforce it, and that to make it effectual its execution must be complete. He disposed of the treaty obligations in the matter by saying that, since England had disregarded the rights of all maritime powers, the interests of those powers were common, and they were bound to make common cause against her;[3] that is to say, any nation that would not join Napoleon in enforcing his iniquitous Continental System, ostensibly against England, but really against the commerce of the world, forfeited its claim to have its treaty stipulations regarded! This doctrine was speedily followed up by practice, when the American ship *Horizon*, stranded upon the French coast, was, with her cargo, in violation of every principle of humanity, confiscated in the French prize court, acting under Regnier's decision,[a] on the ground that that cargo consisted of merchandise of British origin. This decision and confiscation became a precedent for the speedy seizure and sequestration of a large amount of American property.

[a] November 10, 1807.

Almost simultaneously with this practical illustration of Regnier's interpretation of the Berlin Decree in the case of the *Horizon*,[b] Great Britain made a more destructive assault on the rights of neutrals than any yet attempted by either party. By orders in council, adopted on the 11th and promulgated on the 17th of November, all neutral trade was prohibited with France or her allies unless through Great Britain.[4] This avowed measure of retaliation for the issue of

[b] November 10.

---

[1] This was a treaty of peace concluded between France and Russia on the 7th of June, 1807, when Napoleon restored to the Prussian monarch one half of his territories, and Russia recognized the Confederation of the Rhine, and the elevation of Napoleon's three brothers, Joseph, Louis, and Jerome, to the thrones respectively of Naples, Holland, and Westphalia.

[2] Letter to the Imperial Attorney General for the Council of Prizes, September 18, 1807.

[3] "All the difficulties which have given rise to your reclamations," said Champagny to Armstrong, "would be removed with ease if the government of the United States, after complaining in vain of the injustice and violations of England, took, with the whole Continent, the part of guaranteeing itself therefrom. England has introduced into the maritime war an entire disregard for the rights of nations: it is only in forcing her to a peace that it is possible to recover them. On this point the interest of all nations is the same. All have their honor and independence to defend."—LYMAN'S *Diplomacy of the United States*, i., 411.

This was all very true, but the terms on which the United States were invited to join that Continental league were entirely inconsistent with their principles concerning blockades—principles identical with those of the Armed Neutrality of 1780. The Berlin Decree asserted principles the very reverse of these, and in an extreme degree—principles against which the Americans had ever protested—principles which the French minister, only a year before, had pronounced "monstrous and indefensible."

[4] Mr. Baring, in his able *Inquiry into the Causes and Consequences of the Orders in Council*, gives the following analysis of the extremely lengthy document:

"All trade directly from America to every port and country of Europe at war with Great Britain, or from which the British flag is excluded, is totally prohibited. In this general prohibition every part of Europe, with the exception at present of Sardinia, is included, and no distinction whatever is made between the domestic produce of America and that of the colonies re-exported from thence.

the Berlin Decree was only a pretext for pampering the greed of the British colonial merchants and ship-owners. As the Americans were the only neutrals, it was a direct blow against their commerce, of which, for ten years, the British had been exceedingly jealous. The effect was to deprive American vessels of all the advantages of neutrality.

In retaliation for the issuing of these orders, Bonaparte promulgated another decree, dated "At our Palace at Milan, December 17, 1807," which extended and made more vigorous that issued from Berlin. It declared every vessel which should submit to be searched by British cruisers, or should pay any tax, duty, or license-money to the British government, or should be found on the high seas or elsewhere bound to or from any British port, denationalized and forfeit.[1] With their usual servility to the dictates of the conqueror, Spain and Holland immediately issued similar decrees. Thus, within a few months, the commerce of the United States, carried on in strict accordance with the acknowledged laws of civilized nations, was swept from the ocean. Utterly unable, by any power it then possessed, to resist the robbers upon the great highway of nations, the independence of the republic had no actual record. It had been theoretically declared on parchment a quarter of a century before, but the nation and its interests were now as much subservient to British orders in council and French imperial decrees as when George the Third sent governors to the colonies of which it was composed, and Beaumarchais, in behalf of Louis the Sixteenth, supplied their feeble, rebellious hands with weapons wherewith to fight for liberty and independence.

While the commerce of the world was thus becoming the sport of France and England—traditionary enemies and implacable duelists for a thousand years—unscrupulous gamesters for power—an event occurred which excited in the United States the most intense animosity toward Great Britain, and created a powerful war party among legislators and people.

To give efficiency to the Orders in Council, the British government kept a naval force continually hovering along the American coast. They frequently intruded into American waters, and were a great vexation and annoyance to navigators and merchants. They were regarded as legalized plunderers employed by a strong nation to despoil a weaker one.[2] Every American vessel was liable, on leaving port, to be arrested and seized by this marine police, sometimes under the most untenable pretexts, and sent to England as a prize. The experience of the *Leander*, already mentioned (see page 147), was the experience of hundreds of vessels, excepting the murder of their commanders; and, as we have seen, remonstrances and negotiations were of no avail. A crisis was at length reached in the summer of 1807.

"The trade from America to the colonies of all nations remains unaltered by the present orders. America may export the produce of her own country, but that of no other, directly to Sweden.

"With the above exception, all articles, whether of domestic or colonial produce, exported by America to Europe, must be landed in this country [England], from whence it is intended to permit their re-exportation under such regulations as may hereafter be determined.

"By these regulations it is understood that duties are to be imposed on all articles so re-exported; but it is intimated that an exception will be made in favor of such as are the produce of the United States, that of cotton excepted.

"Any vessel the cargo whereof shall be accompanied with certificates of French consuls abroad of its origin, shall, together with the cargo, be liable to seizure and confiscation.

"Proper care shall be taken that the operation of the orders shall not commence until time is afforded for their being known to the parties interested."—See *Inquiry*, etc., page 15.

When introducing this analysis of the orders of the 11th of November, Mr. Baring remarks that "they are so much enveloped in official jargon as to be hardly intelligible out of Doctors' Commons, and not perfectly so there." In a note he says, "I beg to disclaim any intention to expound the ritual text; it seems purposely intended that no person should profane it with his comprehension without paying two guineas for an opinion, with an additional benefit of being able to obtain one directly opposed to it for two more."

[1] "These measures," said the fourth article of the Milan Decree, "which are resorted to only in just retaliation of the barbarous system adopted by England, which assimilates in its legislation to that of Algiers, shall cease to have any effect with respect to all nations who shall have the firmness to compel the English government to respect their flag." It declared that the provisions of the present decree should be null as soon as England should "abide again by the principles of the law of nations which regulate the relations of civilized states in a state of war."

[2] Privateers with French commissions were guilty of depredations upon American commerce, but the occasions were rare.

| Reorganization of the Naval Service. | The "Gun-boat Policy." | Deserters from British Ships. |

Notwithstanding the many depredations upon American commerce and the increasing menaces of the belligerents in Europe, very little had been done to increase the efficiency of the navy of the United States since its reduction at the close of the war with the Barbary States. The squadron in the Mediterranean had been gradually reduced, but several small vessels had been built. Two of these, the ship *Wasp*, 18, and brig *Hornet*, 18, constructed after French models, and ranking as sloops-of-war, were beautiful, stanch, and fast-sailing craft.

In the spring of 1806 the naval service was reorganized,[1] yet nothing of great importance was contemplated to increase its material strength excepting the construction of gun-boats.[2] The President had imbibed very strong prejudices in favor of these vessels. A flotilla of them, obtained from Naples, had been used effectively in the war with Tripoli in 1804, and they were favorites in the service because they afforded commands for enterprising young officers. A few were built in the United States in 1805, their chief contemplated use being the defense and protection of harbors and rivers. Then was inaugurated the "gun-boat policy" of the government, so much discussed for three or four years afterward.

Toward the close of 1806 the President officially announced that the gun-boats (fifty in number) "authorized by an act of the last session" were so far advanced that they might be put in commission the following season.[3] Yet only in the Mediterranean Sea was there a foreign station of the navy of the United States where an American cruiser might be seen at the beginning of 1807, notwithstanding American merchant vessels to the amount of 1,200,000 tons were afloat. Nor was there a home squadron worthy of the name; while British and French cruisers were swarming on our coasts, and British orders and French decrees were wielding the besom of destruction against our commerce.

In the spring of 1807 a squadron of British ships of war, whose rendezvous was Lynnhaven Bay,[4] just within Cape Henry, in Virginia, were watching some French frigates which had been for some time blockaded at Annapolis, in Maryland. One of the British vessels was the *Melampus*, 38. Three of her men deserted, and enlisted among the crew of the United States frigate *Chesapeake*, then being fitted for sea at the navy yard at Washington to join the Mediterranean squadron. Mr. Erskine, the British minister, who had been sent to Washington by Fox to supersede Merry, the successor of Liston, made a formal request of the President for their surrender, but without any warrant found in the laws of nations, or in any agreement between the two governments. A proposition to deliver up British deserters had been made by Monroe and Pinkney during the late negotiations, as an inducement for the British to abandon the practice of impressment, but nothing on that point had been accomplished.

The United States government, willing to be just, and anxious for honorable peace, instituted inquiries concerning the deserters. They were actually enlisted for service

---

[1] By an act of Congress in April, 1806, the President was authorized to employ as many of the public vessels as he might deem necessary, but limiting the number of officers and seamen. The list of captains was increased by the act to thirteen, that of the masters and commanders to nine, and that of the lieutenants to seventy-two. In consequence of deaths and resignations there were many promotions, and sixty-nine midshipmen were raised to the rank of lieutenant.

The names of the captains under the new law were as follows: Samuel Nicholson, Alexander Murray, Samuel Barron, John Rodgers, Edward Preble, James Barron, William Bainbridge, Hugh G. Campbell, Stephen Decatur, Thomas Tingey, Charles Stewart, Isaac Hull, John Shaw, and Isaac Chauncey. Of these Commodore Stewart is now (1867) the only survivor.

The names of the masters and commanders were as follows: John Smith, George Cox, John H. Dent, Thomas Robinson, David Porter, John Carson, Samuel Evans, and Charles Gordon. Not one survives.

[2] The act of Congress for "fortifying the Ports and Harbors of the United States and for building Gun-boats" was approved on the 21st of April, 1806. It provided for the construction of fifty gun-boats.

[3] Annual message, December 2, 1806.—See *Statesman's Manual*, i., 282.

[4] Here the French fleet under the Count de Grasse lay early in September, 1781, when the English fleet under Admiral Graves appeared off Cape Charles, entering the Chesapeake Bay. The French prepared for conflict, and put to sea. The British bore down upon them, and on the afternoon of the 5th of September a partial action took place. The two fleets were within sight of each other for five consecutive days, but had no other engagement. For an account of these events and a diagram, see Lossing's *Field-book of the Revolution*, ii., 306, latest edition.

LYNNHAVEN BAY.

on board the *Chesapeake;* but it was established by competent testimony that one was a native of the Eastern Shore of Maryland, that another was a colored man and a native of Massachusetts, and in the case of the third there was strong circumstantial evidence of his being a native-born citizen of Maryland.[1] Under these circumstances, as the claims of British citizenship could not be established, and as the government was not disposed to surrender any seamen who claimed its protection, a refusal in respectful terms was communicated to Mr. Erskine. No more was said upon the subject; but it appears to have stimulated Vice-Admiral Berkeley, on the Halifax station, under whose command was the squadron in Lynnhaven Bay, to the assumption of authority which led to much trouble.

At about the beginning of June the *Chesapeake* sailed from Washington to Norfolk, and on the 19th she was reported to Commodore James Barron, the appointed flag-officer of the Mediterranean squadron, as ready for sea. She dropped down to Hampton Roads, and on the morning of the 22d of June—a bright, beautiful, hot morning—at about eight o'clock, she weighed anchor, under the command of Captain Gordon, and bearing the broad pennant of Commodore Barron. She was armed with twenty-eight 18-pounders on her gun-deck, and twelve carronades[2] above, making a total of forty guns. She was a vessel of ordinary character, and bore a crew numbering three hundred and seventy-five.

On the evening of the 21st,[a] the British squadron in Lynnhaven Bay, charged with the double duty, it seems, of watching the French frigates and the *Chesapeake*, consisted of the *Bellona*, 74; the *Melampus*, 38; the *Leopard*, 50; and another whose name was not mentioned. The *Leopard*, Captain Humphreys, was charged with the duty of intercepting the *Chesapeake*. She was a small two-decker, and is said to have mounted fifty-six guns. She preceded the *Chesapeake* to sea several miles, her sails bent by a gentle northwest breeze.

[a] June, 1807.

The *Leopard* kept in sight of the *Chesapeake* until three o'clock in the afternoon, when the former bore down upon the latter and hailed, informing Commodore Barron that she had a dispatch for him. The *Chesapeake* responded by lying-to, when some of her officers discovered that the *Leopard's* ports were triced up—an evidence of belligerent intent—but they did not mention the fact to Captain Gordon or the com-

---

[1] The names of the deserters were William Ware, who had been pressed from an American vessel on board the *Melampus* in the Bay of Biscay; Daniel Martin, colored, pressed at the same time and place; and John Strachan, pressed on board the same vessel from an English Guineaman off Cape Finisterre. Ware and Strachan had protections, but Martin had lost his.—See Commodore Barron's Letter to the Secretary of the Navy, dated April 2, 1807. It is proper to state that Mr. Hamilton, the British consul at Norfolk, made repeated official demands for these three seamen and another, and was as often refused by the officers of the *Chesapeake*, acting under government orders.

[2] A carronade is a short piece of ordnance, having a large calibre, and a chamber for the powder like a mortar. It derives its name from Carron, in Scotland, where it was first made.—*Webster.*

modore. A British boat came alongside, and the lieutenant in command was politely received by Barron in the cabin of the *Chesapeake*. He informed the commodore that he was in search of deserters, and, giving their names, he demanded their release, on the authority of instructions issued at Halifax on the 1st of June by Vice-Admiral Berkeley. Those instructions directed all captains under his command, should they fall in with the *Chesapeake* out of the waters of the United States, to show their orders, and "to proceed and search" for such deserters; at the same time, should the commander of the *Chesapeake* make a similar demand, they were to allow him to search for deserters from the American service, "according to the usages of civilized nations on terms of peace and amity with each other."[1] He also presented a note from Captain Humphreys of the *Leopard*, expressing a hope that every circumstance respecting the deserters might "be adjusted in a manner that the harmony subsisting between the two countries might remain undisturbed."

Barron was justly astonished at the impertinence of Humphreys and the assumptions of Berkeley. The "customs and usages" referred to by the latter were confined to the British navy, and were subjects for *complaint* by "civilized nations." The practice had been advocated only in the British Parliament and by the British press; and twice already the "usage" had been applied to American vessels by British cruisers and denounced as outrageous.[2] Barron knew well that the first outrage of the kind had caused the issuing of a standing order from his government to the commanders of national vessels never to allow their crews to be mustered except by their own officers. He therefore made a short reply to Humphreys, telling him he knew of no deserters on board the *Chesapeake*, that he had instructed his recruiting officers not to enlist British deserters, and explicitly assuring him that his crew should not be mustered except by their own officers.

While the lieutenant was waiting for Barron's answer, the officers of the *Chesapeake*, suspicious of some mischief brewing, were busy in clearing the ship for action. She had left port all unprepared for conflict. Without the least expectation of encountering an enemy, she had gone to sea without preparation for hostile service, either in the drilling of her men or in perfecting her equipments. She was littered and lumbered by various objects, and her crew had been mustered only three times.

When the lieutenant left, Barron seems to have imagined that some hostile demonstration might follow his refusal to allow a search for deserters. His men were silently called to quarters, and the ship was regularly prepared for action. He soon received a trumpet message from Humphreys, saying, "Commodore Barron must be aware that the orders of the vice-admiral must be obeyed." Barron replied that he did not understand. The hail was several times repeated, and then a shot was sent from the *Leopard* athwart the bows of the *Chesapeake*. This was speedily followed by another, and as quickly the remainder of the broadside was poured into the almost helpless frigate. Owing to obstructions it was difficult to get her batteries ready; and when one broadside was ready for action there was no priming-powder. When a small quantity was brought, there were no matches, locks, nor loggerheads, and not a shot could be returned. Meanwhile the *Leopard*, at not more than pistol-shot distance, and in smooth water, poured several broadsides upon the unresisting ship, killing three men and wounding eighteen. Barron and his aid (Mr. Broome), who were standing in the gangway watching the assailant, were slightly hurt. The commodore frequently expressed a desire that one gun, at least, might be fired before he should

---

[1] Vice-Admiral Berkeley's circular order recited that many seamen, subjects of his Britannic majesty, and serving in the British Navy, had deserted from several British ships, which he named, and had enlisted on board the frigate *Chesapeake*, and had openly paraded the streets of Norfolk, in sight of their officers, under the American colors, protected by the magistrates of the town and the recruiting officer, who refused to give them up, either on demand of the commanders of the ships to which they belonged or on that of the British consul.

[2] See the account of outrage in case of the *Baltimore*, Captain Phillips, on page 102, and that of the American gunboat overhauled by one of Admiral Collingwood's vessels in the Mediterranean, note 2, page 146. An apology was made for the former outrage, but the latter was passed by.

strike his flag, for he perceived that a surrender would be necessary to save the ship from utter destruction. He was gratified. Just as the colors in their descent touched the taffrail, Lieutenant Allen, who had made ineffectual attempts to use a loggerhead,[1] ran with a live coal between his fingers and touched off one of the guns of the second division of the ship, of which he was commander.

The *Leopard* had kept up her cannonade, without any response, for about twelve minutes. Twenty-one of her round shot had hulled the *Chesapeake*, and her grape had made considerable havoc with the victim's sails and rigging. When the American ensign was lowered, two British lieutenants and several midshipmen went on board, mustered the crew, arrested the three deserters from the *Melampus*, dragged from his concealment in the coal-hole the fourth, named John Wilson, who had deserted from the *Halifax*, and bore them all away to the *Leopard*. Barron, meanwhile, had informed Humphreys by note[2] that the *Chesapeake* was his prize; but that commander refused to receive her, saying, "My instructions have been obeyed, and I desire nothing more." He then expressed regret because of the loss of life, and offered any assistance the crippled ship might require. His proffered sympathies and aid were indignantly rejected; and the *Chesapeake*, with mortified officers and crew, made her way sullenly back to Norfolk.

The unfortunate deserters were taken to Halifax, tried by a court-martial, and sentenced to be hung. The three Americans were reprieved on condition that they should re-enter the British service, but Wilson, the English subject, was hanged.

When Canning, the British Minister for Foreign Affairs, heard of the outrage, he expressly disavowed the act in behalf of his government, and informed Monroe and Pinkney that orders had been sent out for the recall of Berkeley from his command. Humphreys also suffered the displeasure of his government because he had exceeded his instructions, and he was never again employed in service afloat. One of the Americans remanded to slavery in the British navy died in captivity; the others, after five years of hard service, were restored[a] to the deck of the ship from which they had been taken. Provision was also made for the families of the slain.

[a] June 13, 1812.

The attack on the *Chesapeake* created the most intense excitement and indignation throughout the United States, and for a time all local politics were forgotten, and all parties, Federalists and Democrats, natives and foreigners, were united in a firm resolve that Great Britain should make reparation for the wrong, or be made to feel the indignation of the insulted republic in the power of war. Public meetings were held in all the principal cities from Boston to Norfolk,[3] in which the feelings of the people were vehemently expressed. "It is an act of such consummate violence and wrong," said the citizens of Philadelphia,[4] "and of so barbarous and murderous character, that it would debase and degrade any nation, and much more so a nation of freemen, to submit to it." Such were the sentiments every where expressed, and there

---

[1] A loggerhead is a spherical mass of iron heated and used in place of a match in firing cannon in the navy.

[2] Barron's dispatch to the Secretary of the Navy, June 23, 1807; Cooper's *Naval History of the United States*, ii., 97-104; Hildreth's *History of the United States*, Second Series, ii., 678; Perkins's *History of the Late War*, page 22.

[3] On the return of the *Chesapeake* to Norfolk a public meeting was held there, when it was resolved that no intercourse of any kind should be held with the British squadron in the vicinity until the pleasure of the President should be known. Captain Douglas, the commander of the squadron, made some insolent threats, when Cabell, Governor of Virginia, ordered detachments of militia to Norfolk and Hampton. Douglas, finding his threats to be working mischief for himself, became as obsequious as he was before insolent, and withdrew from a menacing position in Hampton Roads to Lynnhaven Bay. Decatur, then in command of the American naval force at Norfolk, was ordered not to molest him while he remained there. Some rather spicy correspondence with Erskine, the British minister, ensued, in the course of which he asked indemnification for some water-casks belonging to the British fleet destroyed by the indignant people of Hampton after the return of the *Chesapeake!* In a letter to the Secretary of State from Monticello, concerning this demand under such circumstances, President Jefferson wrote: "It will be very difficult to answer Mr. Erskine's demand respecting the water-casks in a tone proper for such a demand. I have heard of one who, having broken his cane over the head of another, demanded payment for his cane. This demand might well enough have made part of an offer to pay the damages done to the *Chesapeake*, and to deliver up the authors of the murders committed on board her."

[4] July 1, 1807. The secretary of the meeting, who drafted the resolutions, was Joseph Hopkinson, Esq., a leading Federalist, and author of *Hail, Columbia!*

was a general desire for an immediate declaration of war against Great Britain to redress all wrongs and grievances. But the President and his Cabinet, averse to war, preferred a pacific course, and determined to allow Great Britain an opportunity for a disavowal of the act, and to make reparation of the wrong. The former, as we have observed, was promptly done by Mr. Canning; the latter, embarrassed by intricate negotiations, was accomplished more tardily.

In response and submission to the popular will, the President issued a proclamation on the 2d of July, in which he complained of the habitual insolence of the British cruisers, expressed his belief that the present outrage was unauthorized, and ordered all British armed vessels to leave the waters of the United States immediately. As his government possessed no power to compel compliance with this order, he directed that, in case of their refusal to leave, all intercourse with them, their officers and crews, should be at once suspended. He forbade all persons affording such vessels aid of any kind, unless in the case of a ship in distress or charged with public dispatches. Preparations for defense were also made. Most of the gun-boats in commission were ordered to New York, Charleston, and New Orleans; military stores were purchased; one hundred thousand militia were ordered to be detached by the different states, but without pay, and volunteers were invited to enroll themselves.

Commodore Barron was made to feel the nation's indignation most severely. He was accused of neglect of duty, and was tried by a court-martial on specific charges of that nature. The navy, government, and nation appear to have predetermined his guilt. The wounded national pride needed a palliative, and it was found in the supposed delinquencies of the unfortunate commodore. He was found guilty, and sentenced to five years' suspension from the service, without pay or emoluments.[1] Captain Gordon was tried on the same charge, but his offense was so slight that he was only privately reprimanded. Such also was the fate of Captain Hall, of the marines; while the gunner, for neglect in having priming-powder sufficient, was cashiered.

It was the opinion of Mr. Cooper that these officers were made the

---

[1] James Barron was born in Virginia in 1768, and commenced his services in the navy under his father, who was "commodore of all the armed vessels of the Commonwealth of Virginia" during the Revolution and the Confederation. He was commissioned a lieutenant under Barry in 1798, and the following year was promoted to the highest grade then known to the navy, namely, *captain*. With, and subordinate to his brother Samuel, he sailed to the Mediterranean that year, where he soon acquired fame for his skill in seamanship. He was one of the best officers and disciplinarians in the navy. The affair of the *Chesapeake* and its effects upon himself cast a shadow over his future life. He was restored to official position, but, somewhat broken in spirit, he never afterward entered the service afloat. In 1820 he and Decatur had a correspondence on the affair of the *Chesapeake*, which resulted in a duel, the particulars of which will be given hereafter. The duel was fought near Bladensburg, four miles from Washington City. Both were badly wounded. Decatur died; Barron recovered after months of intense suffering.

Barron held several important commands in the service on shore, and at the time of his death, on the 21st of April, 1851, he was the senior officer of the United States Navy. He died at Norfolk, in Virginia, and was buried in St. Paul's Church-yard there, with military and civic honors, on the morning of the 23d of April. A funeral sermon was preached in the venerable and venerated church by Rev. William Jackson. It was a beautiful tribute to the worth of a brave and ill-requited patriot.

scape-goats of the government, where divided power is too often not only irresponsible but inefficient. "It may well be questioned," he says, "if any impartial person, who coolly examines the subject, will not arrive at the conclusion that the real delinquents were never put on their trial." He then adverts to the fact that four months had been consumed in fitting this single vessel for sea, under the immediate eye of the government, at a time when there was pressing necessity for her service; that she did not receive all her guns until a few days before she sailed; that her crew were coming on board until the last hour before her departure; that her people had been quartered only three days before she put to sea, and that she was totally unfitted for active service when she was ordered to leave port. "When it was found that the nation had been disgraced," continues Mr. Cooper, "so unsound was the state of popular feeling that the real delinquents were overlooked, while their victims became objects of popular censure."[1]

The President's proclamation was followed by the dispatch of the armed schooner *Revenge* to England with instructions to the American ministers (Monroe and Pinkney) to demand reparation for insults and injuries in the case of the *Chesapeake*, and to suspend all other negotiations until it should be granted. Unfortunately for the success of the special negotiations, these instructions also directed them, in addition to a demand for an apology and indemnity to the families of the killed, to insist, by way of security for the future, that the visitation of American vessels in search of British subjects should be totally relinquished. This was inadmissible. The British government refused to treat upon any other subject than that of reparation. A disavowal of the act had already been made, and every disposition to be just and friendly had been shown. The ministry even placed their government in the position of an injured party, inasmuch as the proclamation concerning British ships of war in American waters was evidently an act of retaliation before a demand for reparation had been made, or the disposition of the British Cabinet had been ascertained.

Monroe and Pinkney had already proposed to reopen negotiations for a treaty on the basis of the one returned from their government unratified,[2] and, with these new instructions, they pursued the subject with so much assiduity that Mr. Canning made to them a formal and final reply[a] that, while he was ready to listen to any suggestions with a view to the settlement of existing difficulties, he would not negotiate anew on the basis of a treaty concluded and signed, and already rejected by one of the parties. Indeed there was a decided aversion to treating at all on the subject of impressments; and the views of the government on that topic were plainly manifested when, by royal proclamation,[b] all British mariners, in whatever service engaged, were required to leave it forthwith and hasten to the aid of their native country, then menaced and imperiled, and her "maritime rights" called in question. It authorized all commanders of foreign ships of war to seize British seamen on board foreign merchant vessels (but without undue violence), and take them to any British port. It also demanded from all foreign ships of war the delivery of all British mariners on board of them; and that in case of a refusal to give them up, proper notice should be communicated to the British minister resident of the nation to which such contumacious vessel and commander might belong, that measures for redress might be employed.

[a] October 22, 1807.

[b] October 17.

Mr. Monroe formally objected to this proclamation, as shutting the door against all future negotiations on the subject of impressments.[3] Canning replied that it was

---

[1] Cooper's *Naval History of the United States*, ii., 110. [2] See page 151.
[3] James Monroe was born in Westmoreland County, in Virginia, on the 2d of April, 1759. His youth was spent among political excitements when the old war for independence was kindling. He left the College of William and Mary for the camp, and enrolled himself a soldier for freedom. He was severely wounded in the van of battle at Trenton, and was promoted to captain. In other battles he was conspicuous for bravery; and after that of Monmouth he left the army, and commenced the study of law with Mr. Jefferson. When Arnold and Cornwallis invaded Virginia in 1781, he again took up arms as a volunteer. He was elected a member of the Virginia Legislature in 1782. He was promoted to the Executive Council, and at the age of twenty-five was elected to a seat in the National Congress. He remained in public

only a declaration of existing law, and necessary for the information of British commanders who might be placed in a situation similar to that of Captain Humphreys, of the *Leopard*.

It was evident to both parties that the topic of that outrage could not be satisfactorily treated in London, because the American ministers could not separate it from that of impressment. The British government resolved therefore to send a special

minister to Washington, provided with instructions to bring the unhappy dispute to an honorable conclusion. H. G. Rose, a son of one of the ministers, was appointed for the delicate duty, and arrived at Annapolis in January, 1808. His mission was fruitless. He was instructed not to treat of the affair of the *Chesapeake* while the recent proclamation of the President was in force, nor to connect the subject with that of impressments from private vessels. As the proclamation had reference to the conduct of British armed vessels in American waters from the beginning of the current European war, the President refused to withdraw the document, and Rose returned in the same vessel that bore him to our shores. Meanwhile Monroe had returned home, leaving Pinkney resident minister in London. All hopes of settling existing difficulties with England were at an end, and from the beginning of 1808 the political relations between the two governments foreboded inevitable hostilities at no distant day.

The critical condition of foreign relations induced the President to call the Tenth Congress together as early as the 25th of October. The administration party had an overwhelming majority in that body, and was daily increasing in strength throughout the country. The confidence of the Democrats in Jefferson's wisdom, sagacity, and patriotism was unbounded. In the United States Senate there were only six Federalists, and one of them, John Quincy Adams, soon left their ranks and joined those of the dominant party.[1] A new Democratic member appeared at about the same time, and began a career as a national legislator which forms a wonderful chapter in the history of the government. It was Henry Clay,[2] who had been appointed to fill, for a single session, the seat made vacant by the resignation of General John

---

life, and, with Patrick Henry and others of his state, he opposed the ratification of the National Constitution. He was one of the first United States senators from Virginia under it. He was sent to France as embassador in 1794, and was recalled by Washington in 1796. In 1798 he was elected Governor of Virginia, and three years afterward Mr. Jefferson sent him to Paris to assist in negotiations for the purchase of Louisiana. He was then transferred to the British court as co-laborer in diplomacy with Mr. Pinkney. In 1811 he was again elected Governor of Virginia, but was soon called to the Cabinet of Mr. Madison as Secretary of War. In 1816 he was elected President of the United States, and held that office eight years, when he retired from public life. He lived in Virginia until 1831, when he took up his residence with his son-in-law in the city of New York. He died there on the 4th of July of that year, at the age of little more than seventy-one years.

[1] Mr. Adams was then forty years of age, and had been in the Senate since 1803. "He is a man of much information," wrote his contemporary and friend, Senator Plumer, of New Hampshire, in April, 1806, "a correct and animated speaker, of strong passions, and of course subject to strong prejudices, but a man of strict, undeviating integrity. He is not the slave of party, nor influenced by names, but free, independent, and occasionally eccentric."

[2] "This day [December 29, 1806]", wrote Senator Plumer, "Henry Clay, the successor of John Adair, was qualified, and took his seat in the Senate. He is a young lawyer. His stature is tall and slender. I had much conversation with him, and it afforded me much pleasure. He is intelligent, and appears frank and candid. His address is good, and his manners easy."—*Life of Plumer*, page 351.

Political Complexion of the Tenth Congress.   The President's Message.   An Embargo established.

Adair, then under a cloud because of his recent participation with Aaron Burr in his schemes in the Valley of the Mississippi.

In the House of Representatives the Democratic party had about the same average majority as in the Senate. The opposition, even with the "Quids"—John Randolph and his Virginia seceders—could not command at any time more than twenty-eight votes. Their chief leaders were Samuel W. Dana, of Connecticut, who had been a member since 1796; the late Josiah Quincy, of Massachusetts, who took his seat in 1805; Barent Gardinier, of New York, and Philip Barton Key, of Maryland. Among the new administration members was Richard M. Johnson, of Kentucky. Thus sustained by the National Legislature and the people, the policy of the President and his Cabinet became the policy of the country.

In his seventh annual message[a] the President called the attention of Congress to several very important subjects. He gave a narrative of unsuccessful efforts to settle with Great Britain all difficulties concerning search and impressments; considered the affair of the *Chesapeake*, the refusal of the British commanders to obey the orders of his proclamation to leave American waters, the orders in Council and Decrees, the subject of national defenses, the uneasiness of the Indians on the frontiers, and the relations with other foreign governments. He also expressed great dissatisfaction at the acquittal of Burr, through erroneous, if not mischievous interpretation of law, as he evidently believed; and he pressed upon the attention of Congress the propriety of so amending the law as to prevent the destruction of the government by treason.[1]

[a] October 27, 1807.

Having been officially informed[b] of the new interpretation of the Berlin Decree,[2] and unofficially apprised of the almost simultaneously issued British orders in Council, the President communicated to Congress[c] the facts in his possession, and recommended the passage of an Embargo Act—"an inhibition of the departure of our vessels from the ports of the United States."[3] The Senate, with closed doors, proceeded to the consideration of the subject, and, after a session of four hours and a departure from ordinary rules, passed a bill[d] laying an embargo on all shipping, foreign and domestic, in the ports of the United States, with specific exceptions. The minority made a feeble opposition to the measure.[4] They asked for delay, but it was not granted, and the act was passed by a strictly party vote—ayes twenty-two, noes six. John Quincy Adams thus signified his adherence to the dominant party by voting with them. In the House, which also sat with closed doors, the passage of the act was pressed with equal zeal by the friends of the administration, and was as warmly opposed by the Federalists and "Quids." The bill was debated for three days in Committee of the Whole, the sittings continuing far into each night. The bill was passed on Monday, the 21st, at almost midnight, by a vote of eighty-two to forty-four, and became a law by receiving the signature of the President on the following day. It prohibited all vessels in the ports of the United States from sailing for any foreign port, except foreign ships in ballast, or with cargoes taken on board before notification of the act; and coastwise vessels were required to give heavy bonds to land their cargoes in the

[b] December 11.
[c] December 18.
[d] December 18.

---

[1] "The framers of our Constitution," said the President, "certainly supposed they had guarded as well their government against destruction by treason, as their citizens against oppression under pretense of it; and if these ends are not attained, it is of importance to inquire by what means more effectual they may be secured."—*Statesman's Manual*, i., 297. Jefferson, like many other sagacious men, felt at that time that the Union had barely escaped dissolution from the infamous machinations of Burr and his dupes.

[2] See page 129.   [3] Special Message to Congress, December 18, 1807.

[4] The President was charged with having recommended an embargo before receiving positive information of the Berlin Decree and the Orders in Council. This was a mistake. Of the former he had been informed for a week previously to his communication to Congress on the subject by an official letter from Mr. Armstrong; and on the morning of the day on which the message was sent in, the *National Intelligencer*, of Washington City, contained a paragraph from a London paper of the 10th of November, announcing the Orders in Council "awaiting his majesty's signature." Private letters had also reached him, by which he was satisfied that, by the combined action of the belligerents, the foreign commerce of the United States was utterly destroyed.

United States. What little life was left in American commerce under the pressure of the orders and decrees of the belligerents was utterly crushed out by this act.

The Embargo Act, universal in its application and unlimited in its duration, was an experiment never before tried by any nation—an attempt, by withholding intercourse from *all the world*, to so operate upon two belligerent nations as to compel them to respect the rights and accede to the claims of an injured neutral. Its professed objects were to induce France and England to relax their practical hostility to neutral commerce, and to preserve and develop the resources of the United States. But it accomplished neither. The French government viewed it as timely aid to their Continental System, and far more injurious in its effects upon Great Britain than upon France; while England, feeling that her national character and honor were at stake, and believing that she could endure the privations which the measure would inflict in both countries longer than America, proudly refused to yield a single point under the pressure of this new method of coercion. The words of Josiah Quincy became prophetic. "Let us once declare to the world," he said, "that, before our embargo policy be abandoned, the French decrees and the British orders must be revoked, and we league against us whatever spirit of honor and pride exists in both those nations. . . . No nation will be easily brought to acknowledge such a dependence on another as to be made to abandon, by a withholding of intercourse, a settled line of policy."[1]

Opposition to the measure, in and out of Congress, was violent and incessant. The topic was made a strong battery from which the Federalists hurled their hottest denunciatory shot against the administration. Old party cries were again heard, and the people were startled by the bugbear of French influence in the councils of the nation. The President was charged with secret intrigues with Bonaparte for an alliance of the United States and France against Great Britain, the traditional object of hatred by the Democratic party. The suggestion alarmed intelligent men, for the history of six years had taught them that the allies of the Corsican soon became his subjects.[2] The New England people were taught to believe that the Embargo was the result of a combination of Western and Southern states to ruin the Eastern commonwealths; and every art which party tactics could command was brought to bear in the service of the opposition, who, as politicians, hoped, by means of the alarm, distraction, and real distress which then prevailed, to array such numbers against the dominant party that, in the election for President of the United States to be held a few months later, they might fill the Executive chair with one of their own number.

---

[1] Speech in Congress on the supplementary Embargo Act, February, 1808.

[2] In the course of debate on a supplementary Embargo Act in Congress, on the 20th of February, Gardinier denounced the whole affair as a sly, cunning measure to aid France. "Is the nation prepared for this?" he vehemently exclaimed. "To settle that point," he said to the defenders of the measure, "tell the people what your object is; tell them that you mean to take part with the 'Great Pacificator.' Else stop your present course. Do not go on forging chains to fasten us to the car of the imperial conqueror!"

"The commercial portion of the United States (I mean from Pennsylvania to New Hampshire"), wrote Timothy Pickering on the 26th of January, 1808, "are in general yet patient, because, from their unlimited confidence in the President's wisdom and patriotism, they believe that some mighty state secret induced him to recommend the Embargo. If they supposed, as I do, that it originated in the influence of France—perhaps in a concert with that government, the sooner to pull down the power of Britain—the public indignation would be roused, and our country saved from becoming the provinces of the 'emperor and king.'

"I greatly regret the retaliating order of Great Britain; for, though it really furnishes no ground for the Embargo, it will yet be urged by the President's friends to justify it. The path of interest and common policy was plain. We should have pursued our ordinary commerce with all the British dominions, and armed our vessels against French cruisers. This would have offended Bonaparte. No matter. *While Britain maintains her own independence ours will be safe.* If she fall (which I do not believe will happen), our condition would not be worse. With arms in our hands, and a manly military spirit pervading our country, we should be respected by the conqueror; but tamely crouching, without any resistance, we should be treated, as we should deserve, with contempt, and all the indignities due to voluntary slaves."—*MS. Letter to General Ebenezer Stevens,* dated "City of Washington, January 26, 1808."

This remarkable letter, now before me, from a senator of the United States to a leading merchant of the city of New York, is cited to show, first, how powerfully partisan feelings may operate upon the opinions and judgment of a true patriot, and, secondly, how much the leading men of the country at that time considered the United States a dependent on Great Britain. "While Britain maintains her *own* independence *ours* will be safe!" The war that speedily followed dispelled that servile spirit.

That section of the Federalists known as the "Essex Junto" were the most uncompromising opponents of the administration and the Embargo; and many of those who, only two years before, had vehemently denounced Great Britain because of her persistent assaults upon the rights of neutrals, were now, in the heat of party zeal, the apologists of, and sympathizers with that government, whose aggressions had constantly increased. In the very month[a] when that eminent British merchant, Alexander Baring, declared before the world that "it would be no exaggeration to say that upward of three fourths of all the merchants, seamen, etc., engaged in commerce or navigation in America, have, at some time or other, suffered from acts of our [British] cruisers,"[1] a leading Federal politician (who, two years before,[b] declared, by his vote in the National Senate, that the conduct of Great Britain was "an unprovoked aggression upon the property of the citizens of the United States, a violation of their neutral rights, and an encroachment upon their national independence"), wrote to a friend that, "although England, with her thousand ships of war, could have destroyed our commerce, *she has really done it no essential injury.*"[2]

[a] February, 1808.

[b] February 10, 1806.

It was soon discovered that the Embargo Act was frequently violated by enrolled coasting vessels carrying cargoes to the West Indies, and it became necessary to pass supplementary acts to prevent such evasions of the law. It was chiefly in the debates upon these acts that the acrimony already noticed appeared. Gardinier, of New York, made the most sweeping charges of corruption, and affiliation with the "French usurper" against the majority in Congress. His violence and abuse elicited some personal attacks, and one of them so incensed him that he challenged his assailant (Campbell) to mortal combat. They met at Bladensburg. Gardinier was shot through one side of his body, but, after weeks of suffering, he recovered and came back to Congress, not a whit subdued. Disputes ran high throughout the country, and public speeches, newspapers, and pamphlets teemed with the most vehement assaults upon the dominant party.[3] Many men, dreading the horrors of a war with

---

[1] Baring's *Inquiry*, etc.

[2] Timothy Pickering to James Sullivan, Governor of New Hampshire, February 16, 1808.

[3] Among the few political pamphlets of that period, now extant, is a remarkable one before me, entitled *The Embargo; or, Sketches of the Times: a Satire*. It is a poem, and was written by WILLIAM CULLEN BRYANT, then a lad only about thirteen years of age, who is still (1867) in active political life, and holds a front rank among the literary celebrities of the age. In rhythm, vigor of thought, and force of expression, this production of his early years gave ample assurance of the future distinction of the author as a poet and political writer.* But politics were seldom the theme for his muse after this early effusion of that nature.

In the preface he spoke of the "terrapin policy" of the administration—the policy designed by the Embargo of shutting the nation up in its own shell, as it were, like the terrapin. His epigraph, from Pope's *Essay on Satire*, contained the significant line,

"When private faith and public trust are sold."

He assailed the President and his supporters as vigorously as if his weapon had been wielded by the hand of long experience. Seriously believing that his country was in great peril, he wrote—

"Ill-fated clime! condemned to feel th' extremes
Of a weak ruler's philosophic dreams;
Driven headlong on to ruin's fateful brink,
When will thy country feel, when will she think?"

Of the Embargo he wrote—

"Curse of our nation, source of countless woes,
From whose dark womb unreckoned misery flows,
Th' Embargo rages, like a sweeping wind—
Fear lowers before, and Famine stalks behind."

Influenced by the common opinion of the opposition, he said to his countrymen—

"How foul a blot Columbia's glory stains!
How dark the scene! Infatuation reigns!
For French intrigue, which wheedles to devour,
Threatens to fix us in Napoleon's power."

. . . .

* In a notice of the second edition, with other poems, printed in 1809, the *Monthly Anthology* for June of that year said, "If the young bard has met with no assistance in the composition of this poem, he certainly bids fair, should he continue to cultivate his talent, to gain a respectable station on the Parnassian Mount, and to reflect credit on the literature of his country."

England, which they believed the Embargo Act would evoke, preferred to give freedom to the commerce of the country, and let it provide itself against the risks that menaced it, rather than to kill it outright. Such was the feeling of many merchants; but patriotic statesmen, holding the dignity and the independence of the United States as of far more consequence than the temporary interests of trade, advocated the most stringent execution of the Embargo Act, and at the middle of March[a] the supplementary enactments became law.

[a] March 12, 1808.

At about the same time the British Parliament, with an air of condescension, passed an act,[b] as a favor to neutrals, permitting them (United States and Sweden) to trade with France and her dependencies, on the condition that vessels engaged in such trade should first enter some British port, *pay a transit duty, and take out a license!*[1] In other words, the United States were told by England, with as much insolence and *hauteur* in fact as the Dey of Algiers ever exhibited, "Pay me tribute, and my cruisers (or corsairs) will be instructed not to plunder you." This was properly regarded as a flagrant insult—one which the British government would never have offered except to a nation supposed to be incapable of efficiently resenting it. When to this insult was added a positive injury, a few weeks later,[c] in the form of instructions issued by ministers, in the name of the half-demented king, to the British naval commanders, expressly intended to induce Americans engaged in commercial pursuits to violate the blockade, the administration resolved to plant itself firmly upon that dignity and independence which a free people ought always to assert. Those instructions, so disgraceful to the British ministers, were severely condemned by every honest man in the British realm.[2]

[b] March 25.

[c] April 11.

Evasions of the Embargo continued, and another supplementary act, applying to the navigation of rivers, lakes, and bays, increased its stringency, and awakened new and more bitter denunciations of the measure. But the government was immovable.

> Oh ne'er consent, obsequious, to advance
> The *willing vassal* of imperious France!
> Correct that suffrage you misused before,
> And lift your voice above a Congress roar.
> . . . .
> Rise, then, Columbia! heed not France's wiles,
> Her bullying mandates, her seductive smiles;
> Send home Napoleon's slave, and by him say
> No art can lure us, and no threats dismay;
> Determined yet to war with whom we will,
> Choose our allies, or dare be neutral still."

I have cited the above as an example of the intensity of feeling against the administration at that time among those politically opposed to Jefferson and his party—a feeling that made even boys politicians.

[1] This was essentially a *tribute* in the form of a *duty*, more odious in principle and application than the stamp tax that aroused the American colonists in 1765. The effect may be illustrated by showing the amount of tribute which American commerce was required by the act to pay upon only two of the many articles specified, with the percentage of the tariff, namely, cotton and tobacco. The amount on a cargo of cotton, at the then current prices, costing at New Orleans $43,500, would be subjected to a tax in some English port, before it would be allowed to depart for a French port, of $6500. To this would be added about $2000 more on account of other charges. A cargo of tobacco of four hundred hogsheads would be subjected to a tribute of about $13,000. The estimated annual tribute upon tobacco alone was $2,338,000. It was proposed to tax a great variety of American productions in the same way.

[2] The following is a copy of the instructions:

"George R.: Instructions to the commanders of our ships of war and privateers. Given at our Court at Windsor, the 11th day of April, 1808, in the 48th year of our reign:

"Our will and pleasure is that you do not interrupt any neutral vessel laden with lumber and provisions, and going to any of our colonies, islands, or settlements in the West Indies or South America, *to whomsoever the property may appear to belong, and notwithstanding such vessel may not have regular clearances and documents on board.* And in case any vessel shall be met with, and being on her due course to the alleged port of destination, an indorsement shall be made on one or more of the principal papers of such vessel, specifying the destination alleged and the place where the vessel was so visited. And in case any vessel so laden shall arrive and deliver her cargo at any of our colonies, islands, or settlements aforesaid, such vessel shall be permitted to receive her freight and to depart, either in ballast or with any goods that may be legally exported in such vessel, and to proceed to any unblockaded port, notwithstanding the present hostilities, or any future hostilities which may take place. *And a passport for such vessel may be granted by the governor, or other person having the chief civil command of such colony, island, or settlement.*"

A British-born writer of the day, after declaring that this order was a sufficient cause of war, said, "What! one of the most potent monarchs in the world, rather than do justice to an unoffending nation, on which, for fourteen years, his ministers had perpetrated the most flagrant outrages, invites, and tempts, and affords facilities to its citizens to violate the laws of their country, and openly pursue the infamous trade of smuggling."—*Mathew Carey.*

It was deaf to the prayers for a repeal made in petition after petition that poured into Congress, especially from New England. A proposition for repeal, and to allow merchant vessels to arm and take care of themselves, was voted down by a large majority; and the only glimpse of light was seen through an authorization given to the President to suspend the Embargo Act, according to his discretion, in case of peace in Europe, or such changes in the policy of the belligerents as might, in his judgment, make the navigation of the seas safe to American vessels. It was in the debate on this proposition that Josiah Quincy, who had then taken a place among the acknowledged leaders of the Federal party, used the language already quoted on page 163. He denounced the whole policy as fallacious and mischievous. "The language of that policy is," he said, "'Rescind your decrees and your orders, or we will, in our wrath, abandon the ocean!' And suppose Great Britain, governed by the spirit of mercantile calculation, should reply, 'If such be your mode of vengeance, indulge it to your heart's content! It is the very thing we wish. You are our commercial rivals, and, by driving you out of the market, we shall gain more than we can lose by your retirement.' . . .

"It is to be feared," continued Mr. Quincy, "that, having grown giddy with good-fortune, attributing the greatness of our prosperity to our own wisdom, rather than to a course of events over which we have had no influence, we are now entering that school of adversity, the first blessings of which is to chastise our overweening conceit of ourselves. A nation mistakes its relative importance and consequence in thinking that its countenance, or its intercourse, or its existence is all-important to the rest of mankind. An individual who should retire from intercourse with the world for the purpose of taking vengeance on it for some real or imaginary wrong, would, notwithstanding the delusions of self-flattery, be certainly taught that the world moved along just as well after his dignified retirement as before. Nor would the case of a nation which should make a similar trial of its consequence be very different. The intercourse of human life has its basis in a natural reciprocity, which always exists, however national or personal vanity may often suggest to inflated fancies that, in the intercourse of friendship, civilities, or business, they give more than they receive."

These were words of wisdom—words as wise and significant now as they were then. They combated a great error—an error fully exemplified in our day in the assumption of a single class of our citizens, namely, the cotton-growers. These, knowing the value of their great staple and its consequence to the civilized world, believed or asserted, before the late Civil War, that it gave them power to dictate certain lines of policy to the governments of the earth. In the madness of their error they proclaimed cotton a KING too potent for all other kings. Believing that the producers of the raw material have the consumers of it always in their power, and may bring the latter to terms at any time by cutting off the supply, they forgot the great fact that dependence is reciprocal, and that, in commercial conflicts, the producer, being the poorer party, is always the first to succumb. The events and results of the late Civil War laid bare that radical error to the full comprehension of all, as well as to acute political economists.

So it was with the Embargo. Those who expected to see great national triumphs follow that measure, which was expected to starve the English manufacturing operatives and the West India slaves, were bitterly disappointed. The evils brought upon their own national industry in various forms were far greater than those inflicted upon England or France. It had one good effect, namely, the encouragement and establishment of various manufactures in the United States, which have ever been important elements of our national independence.[1]

---

[1] When war was declared against Great Britain in 1812, the manufacture of cotton was carried on extensively in Rhode Island. A writer in 1813 estimated the number of cotton factories built and in course of erection at that time, eastward of the Delaware River, at five hundred.

CHAPTER IX.

> "Let traitors, who feel not the patriot's flame,
> Talk of yielding our honor to Englishmen's sway;
> No such blemish shall sully our country's fair fame:
> We've no claims to surrender, nor tribute to pay.
> Then, though foes gather round,
> We're on Liberty's ground,
> Both too wise to be trapp'd, and too strong to be bound."
>
> SONG—EMBARGO AND PEACE.

> "Where are you from?" bold Rodgers cried,
> Which made the British wonder:
> Then with a gun they quick replied,
> Which made a noise like thunder.
> Like lightning we returned the joke,
> Our matches were so handy;
> The Yankee bull-dogs nobly spoke
> The tune of Doodle Dandy."
>
> SONG—RODGERS AND VICTORY.

PRESIDENT Jefferson's policy had been to keep the army and navy upon the cheapest footing compatible with a due regard to the public good. It was now evident that these arms of the public service must be materially strengthened, in order to secure the national safety, and the President asked Congress to augment the number and efficiency of the regular army. They did so. The measure was opposed by the Federalists, but a bill to raise seven regiments passed by a vote of ninety-eight to sixteen. Other provisions for war followed. The sum of $1,000,000 was placed at the disposal of the President for the erection of coast and harbor defenses. Another sum of $300,000 was appropriated for the purchase of arms, and $150,000 for saltpetre. The President was also authorized to call upon the governors of the several states to form an army, in the aggregate, of one hundred thousand militia, to be immediately organized, equipped, and "held in readiness to march at a moment's warning" when called for by the Chief Magistrate. He was also authorized to construct arsenals and armories at his discretion; the sum of $200,000 was placed at his disposal for providing arms and military equipments for the whole body of the militia of the republic; and about a million of dollars were appropriated to pay the first year's expenses of the seven new regiments. The government appropriated altogether about $5,000,000 for war purposes.[1]

Efforts were made to increase the efficiency of the navy by adding to the few seamen already in the service twelve hundred and seventy-two additional men, to put on board the gun-boats then completed or in process of construction. In December[a] the President had been authorized to procure one hundred and eighty-eight additional gun-boats by purchase or construction, making, in all, two hundred and fifty-seven.[2] Mr. Jefferson's idea appears to have been to have these

[a] 1807.

---

[1] The formation of new regiments brought into the service several men who became conspicuous in the War of 1812. Among them was Wade Hampton, of South Carolina, who had been in the army of the Revolution, and was now made a brigadier general. Among the colonels were Smythe and Parker, of Virginia, and Boyd, of Massachusetts. Peter Gansevoort, of New York, also of the Continental army, was made a brigadier. Zebulon Pike was promoted to major, and Winfield Scott and Zachary Taylor both took offices in the army, the former as a captain, and the latter as a lieutenant.

[2] The engraving on the following page shows the different forms of the gun-boats at that time. The group is made from drawings presented to me when visiting the navy yard at Gosport, opposite Norfolk, in Virginia, in the spring of

boats in readiness, properly distributed, but not actually manned until necessity should call for their being put into commission. This proposition excited much ridicule, not only among naval officers, but among the people at large.[1] The whole gun-boat system was denounced as "wasteful imbecility, called by the name of economy," and Jefferson was pointed at as a dreaming philosopher without a whit of military knowledge, as evinced when Governor of Virginia in 1781.[2]

There seemed to be, for reasons quite inexplicable, a most violent hostility to a navy, especially at the South. A member (Mr. Williams) from South Carolina said that he "was at a loss to find terms sufficiently expressive of his abhorrence of a navy. He would go a great deal farther to see it burned than to extinguish the fire. It was a curse to the country, and had never been any thing else. Navies had deceived the hopes of every country which had relied upon them." He affirmed that the people were willing to give commerce all the protection in their power, "but they could not provide a navy for that purpose." Others opposed a navy because it might be a measure for increasing Executive patronage; and no act was passed or appropriation

GUN-BOATS.

made, either for the employment of more men, or for the placing in commission any additional vessels, until January, 1809, when the President was directed to equip the

---

1853. I am indebted to Mr. James Jarvis for them. The drawings were made by one who assisted in their construction, and who was then engaged in service at Gosport.

[1] Among those who ridiculed the gun-boat system was Colonel John Trumbull, the artist. According to that system, he said, "Whenever danger shall menace any harbor, or any foreign ship shall insult us, somebody is to inform the governor, and the governor is to desire the marshal to call upon the captains of militia to call upon the drummers to beat to arms and call the militia-men together, from whom are to be *drafted* (not impressed) a sufficient number to go on board the gun-boats and drive the hostile stranger away, unless, during this long ceremonial, he should have taken himself off.—TRUMBULL'S *Reminiscences of his own Times*, page 252.

[2] In the political poem quoted from on page 164, the author thus alludes to Mr. Jefferson at that time:

"And thou, the scorn of every patriot name,
 Thy country's ruin, and her councils' shame!
Poor, servile thing! derision of the brave!
Who erst from Tarleton fled to Carter's cave;
Thou, who, when menaced by perfidious Gaul,
Didst prostrate to her whiskered minion fall;
And when our cash his empty bags supplied,
Did meanly strive the foul disgrace to hide.
Go, wretch, resign the Presidential chair,
Disclose thy secret measures, foul or fair;
Go search with curious eye for horned frogs
'Mid the wild wastes of Louisiana bogs;
Or where Ohio rolls his turbid stream,
Dig for huge bones, thy glory and thy theme."

United States, 44, *President*, 44, *Essex*, 32, and *John Adams*, 24, the latter vessel having been cut down from a frigate to a sloop of war.¹

The country was now agitated by an approaching election for President and Vice-President of the United States, and for a time the political caldron seethed violently. Early in 1808 a Democratic caucus of members of Congress nominated James Madison for President, and George Clinton for Vice-President of the republic. There was then a schism in the Democratic party, caused by the ambition of leaders. Madison, Monroe, and Clinton were each candidates for the Chief Magistrate's chair; and the Federalists, perceiving, as they thought, some chance for success in the canvass, nominated C. C. Pinckney, of South Carolina, for President, and Rufus King, of New York, for Vice-President. The result was the election of Madison and Clinton.

Meanwhile events were transpiring on both sides of the Atlantic, apparently tending to a general abandonment of the policy of the Orders, Decrees, and Embargo. The able *Inquiry* of Mr. Baring concerning the orders in Council, already cited, made a powerful impression upon the mercantile classes of England. He had fully exposed the inexpediency and injustice of the measures, and nobly vindicated the character and conduct of the Americans. Some of the late Cabinet associates of Mr. Fox denounced those orders as both inexpedient and unjust; and petitions for their repeal, numerously signed by the merchants and manufacturers of Hull, Manchester, Liverpool, and London, were presented to the House of Lords on the 17th and 21st of March,ᵃ while a bill affirming the action of the Privy Council in the matter was pending. Henry Brougham, an eminent barrister, was the advocate of the petitioners, and was heard with profound attention, on the 6th of April, in that body of peers of the realm of which, a little more than twenty years afterward, he became a distinguished member.² Already, in the month of March, resolutions moved against them by Lords Erskine, St. John, Holland, and Lauderdale, and a protest signed by the Earls of Lauderdale, King, and Albermarle, had prepared the way for Brougham's argument. These documents contained, within their brief limits, close and sound arguments on the whole subject. The motion of Erskine discussed the illegality of the new system in a constitutional view. Lord St. John's treated of its repugnance to the law of nations. Lord Holland's set forth with great clearness its effects upon British intercourse with foreign nations; and Lord Lauderdale's motion showed its prejudicial tendency to British commerce in general. The protest of the three peers named discussed more particularly the consequences on the cotton trade.³ But the efforts of these statesmen and the array of facts set forth in the minutes of evidence taken at the bar of the House of Lords, before a Committee of the whole House, on the subject of the orders,⁴ were insufficient to move the majority, and the ministry triumphed. The bill affirming the action of the Council and making it permanent was passed, and Parliament fixed the amount of *tribute* in the form of "transit duties,"

ᵃ 1808.

---

¹ This vessel was built as a small frigate of 24 in Charleston, South Carolina. She was cut down to a sloop, then raised to a frigate; finally cut down to a sloop again, and, about the year 1830, was entirely rebuilt as a first-class ship.—Cooper's *Naval History of the United States*, ii., 116.

² This was the now (1867) venerable Lord Brougham. He had recently made London his residence, having practiced law in his native city of Edinburg until 1807. He entered Parliament as a Whig in 1810, and was a coworker with Clarkson, Wilberforce, and Granville Sharpe in favor of the negro slave. He was the vindicator of Queen Caroline against the persecution of her infamous husband, King George the Fourth. His voice and pen were ever on the side of reform and humanity. In 1830 he became a peer, and Lord Chancellor of England. He has ever held a high place in literature, his first contributions having appeared in the *Edinburg Review*, at its commencement in 1802. In his several departments of labor as philosopher, law reformer, statesman, and critic, he has ever stood pre-eminent. He has resided much at Cannes, in France, during his later years, on account of ill health.

During the late Civil War in America, Lord Brougham wrote and spoke in favor of the insurgents, who were fighting for the perpetuation of the slave system which he had opposed all his life, and against the government whose most zealous adherents were avowed Abolitionists.

³ According to the statement of that protest, the amount of cotton wool exported to England from the United States in 1807 was "250,000 bags, amounting, at £12 per bag, to the value of £3,000,000."

⁴ Printed, with the motions and protest alluded to, and an abstract of Brougham's speech, in a thin volume of about two hundred pages.

just referred to, which neutrals must pay to England for permission to navigate the ocean without fear of sea-robbers.

Napoleon, inspired by the keenest sagacity, expressed his approbation of the Embargo. He was then in Spain, ostensibly for the purpose of crushing royal intrigues for the good of the people, but really in preparing a throne for his brother Joseph. Murat, with a competent force, occupied Madrid in March,[a] and in June Joseph was declared by the Emperor to be King of Spain. From Bayonne, in March, Napoleon issued a decree directing the seizure and confiscation of all American vessels in France, or which might arrive there; and when Minister Armstrong remonstrated, he was given to understand that the Emperor expected the Embargo to be *full and perfect.* "No American vessel," said the French minister craftily, "can be *lawfully* abroad since the passage of the Embargo Act; and those pretending to be such must be either English, or, if American, vessels which come under the ban of the Milan Decree because of subserviency to the British orders. The Emperor well knew that there were a large number of American vessels afloat which, under the temptation of immense profits, were sailing under British licenses; and others were evading French prohibitions by forged documents, which indicated that they had come directly from America. This leak in his Continental System Napoleon was determined to stop, and for that purpose his Bayonne Decree was effectual.

[a] 1808.

The Spaniards resisted the attempts of Napoleon to place his brother on their throne, and there was a general uprising of the Dons. The whole Spanish Peninsula and the Spanish colonies in Central and South America were thrown open to British commerce, and by so much weakened the effect of the American Embargo on that commerce. A repeal of the orders in Council as they related to Spain, and also to Portugal, whose royal family had lately fled to Brazil and opened a vast country there, immediately followed. On the receipt of intelligence concerning these facts, petitions from several maritime towns in the United States were sent to the President, praying for a suspension of the Embargo Act as to Spain and Portugal; but he declined, saying, "To have submitted our rightful commerce to prohibitions and tributary exactions from others would have been to surrender our independence. To resist them by arms was war, without consulting the state of things or the choice of the nation." He contended that the Embargo, "besides saving to our citizens their property, and our mariners to their country," gave time for the belligerent nations to revise a conduct as contrary to their interests as it was to our rights. As to Spain, he wisely suggested that her resistance might not prove (as it did not) effectual.

But the President had already taken some measures in the direction of repeal. As early as the close of April[b] he had sent instructions to Pinkney in London, and Armstrong in Paris, authorizing them to offer a repeal of the Embargo on certain conditions. To England such repeal was offered on condition of her recalling her orders in Council. To France Armstrong appears to have offered, in addition to a repeal of the Embargo Act, a declaration of war against Great Britain in the event of her not recalling her offensive orders after the Emperor should have withdrawn his Berlin, Milan, and Bayonne decrees.[1]

[b] April 31.

Canning spoke for his government in a very courteous but extremely sarcastic note, assuring Mr. Pinkney of the kindly feeling of his majesty toward the United States, but expressing his unwillingness to change the policy involved in those orders, under the present aspect of the case. He could not see the impartiality of the Em-

---

[1] Armstrong's instructions said, "Should she [France] set the example of revocation, Great Britain would be obliged, either by following it, to restore to France the full benefit of neutral trade, which she needs, or, by persevering in her obnoxious orders after the pretext for them had ceased, to render collision with the United States inevitable."
Pinkney's instructions said, "Should the French government revoke so much of its decrees as violate our neutral rights, or give explanations and assurances having the like effect, and entitling it, therefore, to a removal of the Embargo as it applies to France, it will be impossible to view a perseverance of Great Britain in her retaliatory orders in any other light than that of war, without even the pretext now assumed by her."

bargo which Mr. Pinkney claimed;[1] nor did his majesty feel inclined to recall his orders while the proclamation of the President concerning the interdiction of British ships of war in American waters remained in full force.[2] He alluded to the timeliness of the Embargo in assisting France in her blockade of Europe, but expressed an unwillingness to believe that the Americans intended, or could have any interest in "the subversion of the British power."[3] The letter concluded with a hope that a perfect understanding between the two governments might be maintained. But its tone was so ironical—so disingenuous and uncandid—so full of the spirit of a selfish strong man in his dealings with a weak one, that it irritated the American minister to whom it was addressed, and the administration that made the overture, not a little.

Mr. Pinkney expressed his views strongly against a repeal of the Embargo Act in a letter to Mr. Madison. "The spirit of monopoly," he said, "has seized the people and government of this country. We shall not, under any circumstances, be tolerated as rivals in navigation and trade. . . . If we persevere we must gain our purpose at last. By complying with the policy of the moment we shall be lost. By a quiet and systematic adherence to principle we shall find the end of our difficulties. The Embargo and the loss of our trade are deeply felt here, and will be felt with more severity every day. The wheat harvest is likely to be alarmingly short, and the state of the Continent will augment the evil. The discontents among their manufacturers are only quieted for a moment by temporary causes. Cotton is rising, and will soon be scarce. Unfavorable events on the Continent will subdue the temper, unfriendly to wisdom and justice, which now prevails here. But, above all, the world will, I trust, be convinced that our firmness is not to be shaken. Our measures have not been without effect. They have not been decisive, because we have not been thought capable of persevering in self-denial—if that can be called *self-denial* which is no more than prudent abstinence from destruction and dishonor."

The French Emperor maintained an ominous silence on the subject. He made no response to Armstrong's proposition, and this reticence was quite as offensive as Canning's irony. "We have somewhat overrated our means of coercion," Armstrong wrote to the Secretary of State.[a] "Here it is not felt; and in England, amid the more recent and interesting events of the day, it is forgotten. I hope, unless France shall do us justice, we shall raise the Embargo, and make, in its stead, the experiment of an armed commerce. Should she adhere to her wicked and foolish measures, there is much more besides that we can do; and we ought not to omit doing all we can, because it is believed here that we can not do much, and even that we will not do what little we can."

[a] August 31, 1808.

At home the Embargo Act met with the most violent opposition in various forms. It was talked against and acted against, especially by the leaders of the opposition in the Eastern States. They excited a very strong sectional feeling by calling it

---

[1] "If considered as a measure of impartial hostility against both belligerents," wrote Mr. Canning, "the Embargo appears to his majesty to have been manifestly unjust, as, according to every principle of justice, the redress ought to have been first sought from the party originating the wrong. And his majesty can not consent to buy off that hostility, which America ought not to have extended to him, at the expense of a concession made, not to America, but to France."

[2] Alluding to the failure of Rose's mission in regard to the affair of the *Chesapeake*, Mr. Canning, with singular unfairness, remarked, speaking of the President's proclamation which that affair drew forth concerning British vessels of war, "The continuance of an interdiction which, under such circumstances, amounts so nearly to direct hostility, after the willingness professed, and the attempt made by his majesty to remove the cause on which that measure had been originally founded, would afford but an inauspicious omen for the commencement of a system of mutual conciliation; and the omission of any notice of that measure in the proposal which Mr. Pinkney has been instructed to bring forward, would have been of itself a material defect in the overture of the President."

[3] "By some unfortunate concurrence of circumstances," said Mr. Canning sarcastically, "without any hostile intention, the American Embargo *did* come in aid of the 'blockade of the European Continent' precisely at the very moment when, if that blockade could have succeeded at all, this interposition of the American government would most effectually have contributed to its success."

These words of Canning were caught up by the opposition in America as additional evidence that the administration were playing into the hands of Napoleon, and the old cry of "French party" was vigorously revived for a while.

sometimes a "Virginia measure," at others a "Southern measure," and at all times a "subserviency to French dictation." They declared that it was a blow aimed intentionally at the prosperity of New England, she having greatly the preponderance in commercial and navigating interests; and that, while the whole country felt the injury inflicted by the Embargo Act more than England or France, that injury fell mostly upon the Eastern States. This deceptive statement, made chiefly for political effect, was contradicted by the commercial statistics of the United States.[1]

Infractions of the Embargo were open and frequent all along the New England coast, for the magistrates winked at them; and smuggling became so general, especially by way of Lake Champlain, that the first active services of the newly-created army were enforcements of the laws on the Northern frontier, under the direction of Wilkinson, while gun-boats were sent into several of the Eastern ports for the same purpose. The leaders of the opposition, hoping to break down the Democratic party, made the Embargo Law as odious as possible, cast obstacles in the way of its execution, and used every means to induce England to believe that it was so unpopular that it would be speedily repealed in the face of the continuance of her orders in Council. "They are now playing a game," the President wrote, " of the most mischievous tendency, without perhaps being themselves aware of it. They are endeavoring to convince England that we suffer more from the Embargo than they do, and if they will but hold out a while we must abandon it. It is true, the time will come when we must abandon it. But if this is before the repeal of the orders in Council, we must abandon it only for a state of war. The day is not distant when that will be preferable to a longer continuance of the Embargo. But we can never remove that, and let our vessels go out and be taken under these orders, without making reprisals. Yet this is the very state of things which these Federal monarchists are endeavoring to bring about; and in this it is but too possible they may succeed. But the fact is, if we have war with England, it will be solely produced by these manœuvres."[2]

An "Anglican party," a mere political myth in former years, was now a practical reality.[3]

Another form of opposition to the Embargo was a declaration of several eminent lawyers of Massachusetts that it was unconstitutional; and very soon the doctrine of the Virginia nullifiers, as put forth in the Kentucky and Virginia resolutions of 1798, so decidedly condemned by the Federalists as tending directly to disunion, was speedily proclaimed by that same party all over New England as being orthodox. When it was known that the party was defeated, and that Madison was elected President, the unpatriotic cry of disunion was heard throughout New England, in the deceptive accents of proclamations that a state, as such, has a right to declare void any act of the National Congress that might be deemed unconstitutional. That doctrine was as boldly proclaimed in the Eastern States as it had been in Virginia and the South ten years before.[4] The arguments used by the Virginia nullifiers and secessionists in

---

[1] According to official tables, the value of the exports of the United States from 1791 to 1813 was $1,343,047,000. Of this amount the exports of the Eastern, Middle, and Southern States were in value as follows:

Five Eastern States $299,192,000
Four Middle States................................. 534,766,000
Six Southern States and District of Columbia....... 509,089,000

or for the New England States less than one fourth of the whole amount.

[2] Jefferson to Dr. Lieb, of Philadelphia, June 23, 1808.

[3] The following clause in a resolution adopted at a public meeting in Topsfield, Massachusetts, on the 15th of January, 1807, expressed the sentiments, and illustrated the actions of a large class of Americans at that time: "This assembly can not refrain from expressing its conviction that neither the honor nor the permanent interests of the United States require that we should drive Great Britain, if it were in our power, to the surrender of those claims [right of search, impress, and confiscation] so essential to her in the mighty conflict in which she is at present engaged—a conflict interesting to humanity, to morals, to religion, and the last struggle of liberty."

[4] A memorial from the town of Bath, in Maine, to the Massachusetts Legislature, dated December 27, 1808, contained the following resolution: "That a respectful address be forwarded in the name of the people of this town to the Legislature of this commonwealth, stating to them the wrongs and grievances we already suffer, and the painful apprehen-

1798 against the Alien and Sedition laws were used in New England in 1808 against the Embargo laws. Happily we are far enough removed from the din of that old conflict of parties to view the contest dispassionately, and perceive that we can, with just charity, declare that these New England leaders were no more real disunionists at heart than were Jefferson and Madison, and that both parties, having confidence in the people, ventured to use dangerous weapons in their partisan strife for the supremacy, feeling, as Jefferson said in his inaugural address, already cited, that there was safety in tolerating a great error " when reason is left free to combat it."

The second session of the Tenth Congress was commenced on the 7th of November,[a] and, at the earliest possible moment after the organization, the opposition opened their batteries upon the Embargo in various forms. In both houses motions for a repeal or modification of the act were presented, and long and warm debates ensued. But in both houses there was a decided majority in favor of sustaining the measure, and these were supported by resolutions in favor of the Embargo passed by the Legislatures of New Hampshire, Pennsylvania, Ohio, Kentucky, Virginia, the Carolinas, and Georgia. The whole country was agitated by the discussion of the question, and in private and public assemblies the great incubus upon commerce was the topic which occupied all minds, and shaped the tenor of general conversation.

[a] 1808.

The history of parties, their tactics and manœuvres, their struggles and animosities at that time, bearing as they do, more or less directly, upon the subject of this volume, form a very interesting chapter in the chronicles of the nation for the student of our history. Our plan and space do not admit of even an outline narrative of those purely partisan conflicts, and we must pass on to a rapid consideration of events which speedily caused war between the United States and Great Britain.

The policy of the administration being fully sustained, more stringent measures for enforcing the Embargo were adopted. The Enforcing Act, as it was called, caused such opposition and exasperation in New England, that action among the people and in State Legislatures assumed the aspect of incipient rebellion. Then it was that disunion sentiments, just alluded to, were freely uttered in nearly all the region eastward of the longitude of the Hudson River. Many wise men began to regard civil war as possible, if not inevitable. Some weak-kneed members of the administration party in Congress were disturbed by the mutterings of the thunder indicating an approaching

---

sions we experience of speedily having our calamity increased by the addition of still more restrictive and arbitrary laws; expressing to them our approbation of the measures they have already adopted upon the subject, and requesting them to take such other immediate steps for relieving the people, either by themselves alone or in concert with other commercial states, as the extraordinary circumstances of our situation require."

In Gloucester, Massachusetts, a town meeting resolved, on the 12th of January, 1809, "that to our *state government* we look for counsel, protection, and relief at this awful period of general calamity."

The people of Boston, in a memorial dated January 25, 1809, said: "Our hope and consolation rest with the Legislature of our state, to whom it is competent to devise means of relief against the unconstitutional measures of the general government; that your power is adequate to this object is evident from the organization of the confederacy."

The opposition press uttered many violent and inflammatory appeals to the people. A hand-bill was circulated in Newburyport which contained the following sentences: "Let every man who holds the name of America dear to him stretch forth his hand and put this accursed thing, the EMBARGO, from him. Be resolute; act like the sons of liberty, of GOD, and of your country; nerve your arms with VENGEANCE against the DESPOT who would wrest the inestimable gem of your independence from you, and you shall be *conquerors!*"

"We know," said the *Boston Repertory*, "if the Embargo be not removed, our citizens will ere long set its penalties and restrictions at defiance. It behooves us to *speak*, for *strike* we must if speaking does not answer."

"It is better to suffer the amputation of a limb [meaning the severance of New England from the Union"], said the *Boston Gazette*, "than to lose the whole body. We must prepare for the operation. Wherefore, then, is New England asleep? Wherefore does she *submit to the oppression of enemies in the South?* Have we no Moses who is inspired by the God of our fathers, and will *lead us out of Egypt?*"

"This perpetual Embargo," said Russell, in the *Boston Centinel*, "being unconstitutional, every man will perceive that *he is not bound to regard it, but may send his produce or merchandise to a foreign market in the same manner as if the government had never undertaken to prohibit it.* If the petitions do not produce a relaxation or removal of the Embargo, the people ought to immediately assume a higher tone. The government of Massachusetts has also a duty to perform. The state is *still sovereign and independent.*"

The above passages have been cited to give an idea of the state of public feeling under the pressure of the Embargo. Never had the patriotism of the people greater temptations than at the gloomy period of utter commercial stagnation or ruinous fluctuation from 1808 to 1812, inclusive of those years.

tempest, and, for the purpose of pacifying the discontented people, the majority passed an act[a] appointing the last Monday in May following as the time for the assembling of the new Congress, when a repeal of the Embargo would occur, and the alternative of war with Great Britain be accepted.

[a] January 19, 1809.

Josiah Quincy

This postponement of the repeal and the expressed intention of going to war called forth from Quincy,[1] the Federal leader in the lower House, a most withering, denunciatory speech — a speech that stung the dominant party to the quick, and rankled like a thorn for a long time. He treated their assertion that war would be the alternative of repeal with the most bitter scorn. He had heard enough of that "eternal clamor," he said, and, if he could help it, the old women of the country should no longer be frightened by the unsubstantial bugbear. He taunted them with cowardice, and declared his conviction that no insult, however gross, that might be offered by France or Great Britain, could force the majority into a declaration of war. "To use a coarse but common expression," he said, "they could not be kicked into a war." He declared that all the officers for the new army were partisans of the administration. "If the intention had been," he said, "to unite the nation as one man against a foreign enemy, is not this the last policy which any administration ought ever to have adopted? Is not a party army the most dreadful and detestable of all engines, the most likely to awaken suspicions and to inspire discontent?" He then sneered at the idea of going to war with England—the great maritime power of the world—with "but one frigate and five sloops in commission," while the administration had not "resolution enough to meet the expenses of the paltry little navy rotting in the Potomac!"

Quincy's lash stirred up a strong war feeling throughout the Democratic party, and stimulated the administration to more vigorous efforts for increasing the army and navy. The Southern members, with Williams, of South Carolina, at their head,

---

[1] Josiah Quincy was born in Boston, Massachusetts, on the 4th of February, 1772. He was educated at Harvard University, in Cambridge, where he was graduated in 1790. He entered upon the practice of the law in Boston. In 1804 he was elected to a seat in the National Congress, and held that position eight successive years. In 1813 he declined a re-election. He was chosen a senator from Suffolk, and was a representative in the upper House of the Legislature of Massachusetts for four successive years. He was speaker of the lower House in 1820, and the following year was appointed judge of the Municipal Court of Boston. In 1823 he was chosen mayor of that city, and held the office six consecutive years, when he declined a re-election. He was chosen President of Harvard University in 1829, and held that honorable position until his resignation in 1845, from which time he enjoyed leisure in private life, but always actively alive to events around.

Mr. Quincy was an author of reputation, his most considerable works being *A History of Harvard University*, in two volumes, with illustrations by his daughter; *Memoir* of his father (Josiah Quincy) and others; *A Memorial History of Boston*, etc. Mr. Quincy lived until the 2d day of July, 1864, when he died at his country seat in Quincy, Massachusetts, in the ninety-third year of his age. He and the late Lord Lyndhurst (son of Copley, the painter) were born in Boston on the same night, and the same physician attended both mothers.

The writer visited him when he was in his nineteeth year, and had the pleasure and profit of his conversation concerning past days; and when he spoke of having a distinct recollection of being carried out of Boston by way of the British fortifications on the Neck in 1775, and undergoing a purification by sulphur vapor on account of small-pox in the city, I seemed to be talking with a patriarch indeed—a man whose memory embraced the stirring events of much of the two centuries. He was born at the opening of the just rebellion of a great people against real tyranny, and lived to speak patriotic words in condemnation of a most unrighteous rebellion of a few demagogues against, as one of their number had but recently said, "the most beneficent government on the face of the earth."

Cotton supposed to be King of Commerce.   *Non-intercourse Act.*   *Signs of Reconciliation.*

vehemently opposed every expenditure for the navy. That violent sectionalist, with the shallowness and selfishness of his class, could perceive no other American interest but that of *cotton* worth fighting for or preserving. The "transit duty" imposed upon neutral merchandise by a late action of the British government was the chief object of his ire and assault, and because of that measure he was eager to go to war. Dazzled by the increase of the cotton trade, he believed that product of Carolina to be the King of Commerce, around which all other interests should revolve as satellites or courtiers. "The great staple," he said, "of the country—cotton—worth more than any two others, is coerced into Great Britain, and is absolutely prohibited from re-exportation altogether. . . . You are to raise cotton to carry to the British dominions, and nowhere else! What does this amount to? Any thing short of the assumption of the sovereignty of the soil? And yet gentlemen can not see any cause of war! All the objections made to war with Great Britain—want of revenue, want of ships, want of objects of attack, destruction of commerce, danger to our liberties from standing armies—are nothing but disguises for want of patriotism, and contemptible cowardice."

Yet, when Joseph Story, the afterward eminent jurist, with a broader statesmanship, a wiser forecast, and a true national patriotism, suggested a fleet of fifty fast-sailing frigates for the protection of *all* the industrial interests of the United States, and the support of the dignity and independence of the government, scarcely a man was to be found from the region southward of the Delaware to second his views; and Williams declared that if the rights of America were only so to be saved, he was for abandoning them at once. "Impatient as he was to fight for the rights of the cotton-growers, he had not the least idea of going to war for the rights of ship-owners. While urging the navigating interest to submit quietly to destruction, in hopes of forcing a wider market for cotton, he declaimed with the most perfect unconsciousness about the *self-sacrifice of the South and the selfishness of the North!*"[1]—a most untruthful and ungenerous assertion, which has been constantly repeated ever since by unscrupulous demagogues for selfish purposes, to the material injury of the whole country, and especially of the slave-labor states.

The outside pressure upon the administration against the Embargo Act became too great for resistance, and on the 1st of March, 1809, it was repealed. As a pacific countervailing measure, to induce the European belligerents to respect the rights of neutrals, a Non-intercourse Act was passed, by which the commerce of America was opened to all the world except to England and France, and British and French ships of war were equally excluded prospectively from American ports. This measure was denounced by the opposition with more bitterness, if possible, than the Embargo Act. It was declared to be actual war in disguise—a cowardly obedience to French mandates—an attempt to produce hostilities with Great Britain at the instigation and for the benefit of Napoleon. Strange as it may appear to us, this foolish bugbear—this Gallic mask of demagogues for disturbing the nerves of the timid—was still effective, and the country was so agitated by the alarmists that the paralysis of industry continued. The wings of partially-released commerce fluttered timidly in harbors, because its imagination pictured whole bevies of war-hawks abroad.

Relief soon came, and the doves of peace whitened the horizon. For some time the administration, persuaded of the incompetence of the Embargo to effect its intended purposes, had been unofficially negotiating with Mr. Erskine, the British minister resident at Washington, for a settlement of the disputes between the two governments, and Mr. Madison took the Presidential chair on the 4th of March, vacated by Mr. Jefferson, with a sanguine expectation that the beginning of his administration would be signalized by some promise of peace and prosperity for his country.

---

[1] Hildreth's *History of the United States*, Second Series, iii., 126.

James Madison [signature]

Mr. Erskine had made such representations to his government that Mr. Canning instructed him to offer to propose to the Americans a reciprocal repeal of all the prohibitory laws upon certain conditions. But these conditions were so partial to England—requiring the Americans to submit to the detested "rule of 1756," and to allow British cruisers to capture all American vessels attempting to trade with France—that they were rejected. But an arrangement was speedily made, by which, upon the orders in Council being recalled, the President should issue a proclamation declaring a restoration of commercial intercourse with Great Britain, but leaving all restrictive laws against France in full force. Mr. Erskine offered, in addition, reparation for the insult and injury in the case of the *Chesapeake*, and also assured the American government that Great Britain would immediately send over an envoy extraordinary "invested with full powers to conclude a treaty on all points of the relations between the two governments." This arrangement was completed on the 18th of April.[a] On the following day the Secretary of State received a note from Mr. Erskine, saying, "I am authorized to declare that his majesty's orders in Council of January and November, 1807, will have been withdrawn, as respects the United States, on the tenth day of June next." On the same day President Madison (only forty-four days after his inauguration) issued a proclamation[b] declaring that trade with Great Britain might be renewed after the tenth day of the following June.[1]

[a] 1809.
[b] April 19.

This proclamation was hailed with the greatest joy throughout the United States as an omen of brighter days. The voice of partisan strife was hushed, and President Madison was lauded as the representative of the whole American people, and not of a party only. He was toasted and praised by the Federalists, invited to their feasts, and hailed as a Washingtonian worthy of all confidence. The foolish idea of "French influence" was dispelled, and every body indulged in millennial anticipations. England was lauded for her generosity and magnanimity, and in the House of Representatives John Randolph offered the following resolution on the 2d of May: "*Resolved*, That the promptitude and frankness with which the President of the United States has met the overtures of the government of Great Britain toward a restoration of harmony and freer commercial intercourse between the two nations meet the approbation of this House." The warmest Federalists supported the resolution, and a contemporary says that the praise of the President by his former political enemies was so universal that "the Democrats grew jealous. They were afraid of losing the attachment of the President, whose election they had made such exertions to secure."

The joy of the Americans was brief. On the 31st of July Mr. Erskine communicated to the President the mortifying fact that his government had refused to affirm his arrangement. This refusal was made ostensibly because the minister had exceed-

---

[1] After the usual preamble citing the action between the government and "the Honorable David Montague Erskine, his majesty's envoy extraordinary," he said, "Now, therefore, I, James Madison, President of the United States, do hereby proclaim, that the orders in Council aforesaid will have been withdrawn on the said tenth day of June next; after which day the trade of the United States with Great Britain, as suspended by the act of Congress above mentioned, an act laying an embargo on all ships and vessels in the ports and harbors of the United States, and the several acts supplementary thereto, may be renewed."

ed his instructions, and was not authorized to make any such arrangement. It was charged that this was not the true reason, because the arrangement as made was perfectly just to both parties, and more favorable to England than to the United States. To America it offered simply a repeal of the orders in Council and atonement for the outrage on the *Chesapeake;* to England it offered a restoration of all the advantages of a vast and valuable commerce, and a continuance of non-intercourse between the United States and France. The most plausible conjectures for the disavowal of an arrangement so desirable were, first, that the implied censure of the British government respecting the conduct of Admiral Berkeley, contained in one of the letters of the Secretary of State to Mr. Erskine,[1] so irritated the old monarch, who had always hated the Americans, that he refused his assent; secondly, that the recent violent proceedings in New England in relation to the enforcement of the Embargo Act deceived the British ministry into the belief that the American government would be compelled by popular clamor to repeal the Embargo, and leave England's restrictive policy unimpaired. To the comprehension of the writer, the true reason for the rejection may be found in the fact that such an arrangement would interfere in a deep-laid scheme to break up the American Union, by fomenting sectional antagonisms based chiefly upon the clashing of apparently diverse interests. Two years later it was discovered that the British authorities in Canada had an accredited agent in Boston for that purpose, the British government ignorantly supposing the opposition of the Federalists to be real disloyalty.[2] Whatever may have been the true reason for the rejection, the historical fact remains that England spurned the olive-branch so confidingly offered. The orders in Council stood unrepealed, Mr. Erskine was recalled,[3] and a proclamation of the President of the United States, dated 9th of August, 1809, declared the Non-intercourse Act to be again in full force in regard to Great Britain. The British government also issued orders to protect from capture such American vessels as had left the United States in consequence of the President's proclamation of April preceding.

The blessings of the opposition, so freely showered upon the administration when the blossoms of May and the leaves of June were unfolding, returned to their bosoms, and at the season of the harvest-moon curses flowed out as freely. It was charged that Madison and his Cabinet were acquainted with Canning's instructions to Erskine; that they knew the latter had exceeded his instructions, and that there was no expectation of the arrangement being confirmed by the British government; and that the whole affair was a pitiful trick of the administration to cast the odium of continued restrictions upon commerce from their own shoulders upon that of the British ministry. The partisan war was soon revived in all its rancor.

Francis James Jackson, who had been the British minister at Copenhagen in 1807, succeeded Mr. Erskine. He was an unscrupulous diplomat, and, because of his complicity in the unwarrantable attack by British land and naval forces upon the capital of Denmark in early September, 1807, he was known as "Copenhagen Jackson."[4] The

---

[1] Secretary Robert Smith, in a letter to Mr. Erskine on the 17th of April, said, "I have it in express charge from the President to state that, while he forbears to insist on a farther punishment of the offending officer, he is not the less sensible of the justice and utility of such an example, nor the less persuaded that it would best comport with what is due from his Britannic majesty to his own honor."

[2] For an account of this matter, see Chapter XI. of this work.

[3] Mr. Erskine was the eldest son of the celebrated English orator and lord chancellor. In the year 1800 he married the daughter of General John Cadwalader, of Philadelphia, with whom he lived until 1843, when she died. His eldest son he named Thomas Americus, and is still living, I believe, the successor to his father's title. In 1848 Lord Erskine married again. This wife died in April, 1851, and he again married in December, 1852. His last wife was the widow of Thomas Calderwood Durham, Esq., of Largo and Palton. He had children only by his first wife. He succeeded to his father's titles in 1823. He was educated for the law at Trinity College, Cambridge, but was much of his life in diplomatic service. He was British envoy at Washington from 1806 to 1810, and afterward represented his country at the courts of Wurtemberg and Bavaria. In 1843 he retired from public life, and died on the 19th of March, 1855.

[4] The British government strongly suspected that Denmark would acquiesce in the dictates of the French emperor, and become the ally of the conqueror. If so, the Danish fleet would fall into his hands, and England's life might be imperiled. She therefore sent a formidable armament to the Baltic, accompanied by Jackson as envoy extraordinary, to negotiate with the Danish government, the basis of which was an English protectorate of Danish neutrality, on condi-

"Copenhagen Jackson" and his Misconduct.   Proposed Revocation of the French Decrees.   Napoleon on Armstrong.

infamy of that affair made every person connected with it odious to the people of the United States. It was a foul blot upon the boasted civilization and Christianity of Great Britain; and the sending of Jackson, who had been a conspicuous actor in the tragedy, as minister to Washington while causes for serious irritation between the two governments existed, was regarded as a meditated insult by the extreme members of the dominant party.

Jackson was received with cool courtesy, but his deportment soon excited the thorough dislike of those with whom he came in contact. He was insolent, irritable, and quarrelsome. He had an unbounded admiration of the greatness of the people he represented, and a corresponding contempt for the people he had been sent to. He regarded the Americans as an inferior people, and treated the officers of government with the *hauteur* which he had practiced toward weak and bleeding Denmark when he negotiated with her at the mouths of British cannon. His manners were so offensive that, after the second verbal conference with him, Secretary Smith refused any farther correspondence except in writing. The insolent diplomat was offended, and wrote an impudent letter to the secretary. He was soon informed that no farther communications would be received from him. Disappointed and angry, he left Washington, with every member of his diplomatic family, and retired to New York.[1] The American government requested his recall, and early in 1810 he was summoned back to England. But his government manifested the greatest indifference as to its relations with the United States. The request for his recall was received with the most perfect coolness, and no other minister was sent to Washington until early in 1811.

In the early part of 1810,[a] the President received intimations from abroad that a way was probably opened for a repeal of the restrictive orders and decrees. M. de Champagny (Duke de Cadore), the French Minister of Foreign Affairs, in a letter to Minister Armstrong, said that if England would revoke her blockade against France, the latter would revoke her Berlin Decree.[2] Minister Pinkney, still in London, on receiving this information, approached the British ministry on the subject, and he expressed to his own government his hope that the restrictive measures of the belligerents would be speedily removed.[3] To aid in negotiations to that effect, Congress, on the 1st of May, 1810, repealed the Non-intercourse and Non-importation laws, and substituted an act excluding both British and French armed vessels from the waters of the United States. It farther provided that, in case either Great Britain or France should so revoke or modify its acts before the 3d of March,

[a] March.

---

tion that its fleet should be deposited in British ports until the termination of the war with France. The Danish government rejected this degrading proposal, and claimed the rights of a neutral, independent nation, whereupon the British armament of twenty-seven sail of the line, and twenty thousand land troops, under the respective commands of Admiral Gambier and Lord Cathcart, attacked Copenhagen. The splendid cathedral, many public buildings and private houses, were destroyed, and with them two thousand lives. The city was on fire from the 2d until the 5th of September. A great part of the city was consumed, when a flag of truce was displayed by the Danish commander. The Danish fleet and a large quantity of naval stores were surrendered. But the indignant Danish government refused to ratify the capitulation, and issued a declaration of war against England. Russia, indignant at the shameful treatment of Denmark, also declared war against England, and issued a manifesto on the 30th of October ordering the destruction of all British ships and property.

[1] Jackson found a residence in the city too uncomfortable, on account of the detestation in which he was held, and he took up his abode at Claremont, the seat of the Post family, at the present Manhattanville, now Jones's Hotel, a fashionable place of resort.

[2] See letter of Armstrong to the Secretary of State, January, 1810, in *American State Papers*. The manner of the correspondence of Minister Armstrong with the French government at this time appears to have excited the hot displeasure of the Emperor, who wrote to M. de Champagny on the 19th of January, 1810, as follows:

"MONSIEUR DUKE DE CADORE,—You must see the minister from America. It is beyond all ridiculous that he writes of things that one does not comprehend. I prefer that he should write in English, but at length, and in a manner that we can understand. How is it that in affairs so important he contents himself with writing letters of four lines? Speak to the secretary who is here; speak also to the secretary who is about arriving from America. Send by a courier extraordinary a dispatch in cipher to make them understand that that government is not represented here; that its minister don't understand French—is a morose man, with whom one can not deal; that all obstacles would be removed if we had an envoy to talk with. Write in detail on the matter. Let me know what effect the letter from Altenburg has had in the United States—what has been done, and what is proposed. Write to America in such manner that the President may know what a fool has been sent here.   NAPOLEON."

[3] Letter of Pinkney to the Secretary of State, February 28, 1810, in *American State Papers*.

1811, as that they should cease to violate the neutral commerce of the United States, and if the other nation should not, within three months thereafter, in like manner revoke or modify its edicts, the provisions of the Non-intercourse and Non-importation laws should, at the expiration of the three months, be revived against the nation neglecting or refusing to comply.

When this act was communicated to the French government, M. de Champagny addressed a note to Minister Armstrong, dated 5th of August, 1810, officially declaring that "the decrees of Berlin and Milan are revoked, and that after the first day of the following November they will cease to have effect; it being understood that, in consequence of this declaration, the English shall revoke their orders in Council, and renounce the new principles of blockade which they have wished to establish, or that the United States, conformably to their law, will cause their rights to be respected by the English." This was explicit, and the President doubted not it was sincere. Therefore, in accordance with the provisions of the act of the 1st of May, he issued a proclamation on the 2d of November announcing this revocation of the French decrees, and declaring the discontinuance, on the part of the United States, of all commercial restrictions in relation to France and her dependencies. On the same day the Secretary of the Treasury issued an order to all collectors of the customs to act in conformity with the President's proclamation, but to enforce against English war vessels, and against her commerce, the law of May[a] after the 2d of the following February, unless, meanwhile, information should be received by the President of the revocation of her orders in Council. [a] May 1, 1810.

. The United States had been made to doubt Gallic faith. Professing to be indignant at what seemed to be partiality shown to England by the Americans in their restrictive acts, Bonaparte had caused the seizure and confiscation of many American vessels and their cargoes. Armstrong remonstrated from time to time, and finally, when notified that a large number of these vessels were to be sold, he presented a vigorous protest,[b] and recapitulated the many aggressions which American commerce had suffered from French cruisers. This just remonstrance was ungenerously responded to by a decree, issued by the Emperor from Rambouillet on the 23d of March, 1810, which declared that "all American vessels which should enter French ports, or ports occupied by French troops, should be seized and sequestered." Under this decree, many American vessels and millions of American property were seized. But it was supposed that the proclamation of the President on the 2d of November would annul these hostile proceedings, and release the vessels. On the contrary, the French government simply suspended the causes in the Council of Prizes[c] until February, 1811, in order to ascertain whether the United States would enforce the proclamation of November against Great Britain. At the same time the French government abstained from furnishing the American government with formal official evidence of any decree relating to the revocation of former edicts, and the whole matter rested upon the simple letter of the Duke of Cadore (Champagny) to Mr. Armstrong.[d] [b] March 10. [c] December 25. [d] August 5.

Great Britain took advantage of this fact, and resisted the application to rescind her orders, on the ground that she was furnished with no evidence that the decrees had been rescinded, because the French government had never promulgated any edict for this revocation. But she had the evidence of the French minister's explicit declaration, on which the action of the United States government was based, as well as a general order of the French government to the Director General of Customs[e] not to apply the Berlin and Milan Decrees to American vessels entering French ports after the 1st of November, 1810. These official declarations of the French government were sufficient for the United States, and should have been for Great Britain, for, if faith could not have been placed in them, decrees from the same source would have had little value. But France and England [e] December 25.

were playing such a desperate game, that they not only rightfully suspected each other of duplicity continually, but doubted the sincerity of the United States, although that government had never, in the smallest degree, broken its faith with either. England refused to recall her orders in Council; Bonaparte refused to make any indemnity for the seizures under the Bayonne and Rambouillet Decrees, and American commerce was left in a state of the most painful suspense.

Having exhausted all arguments in endeavoring to convince the British ministry of the reality of the French revocation,[1] and to effect a recall of the orders, Mr. Pinkney left England and returned home, satisfied that, while she could sustain herself in the prosecution of the war, she would never yield an iota of her power to oppress the weak. At this very time, spurned as they had been, the United States proceeded to open another door of reconciliation, by an act of Congress providing that, in case at any time " Great Britain should revoke or modify her edicts, as that they shall cease to violate the neutral commerce of the United States, the President of the United States should declare the fact by proclamation, and that the restrictions previously imposed should, from the date of such proclamation, cease and be discontinued."[2]

To this friendly proposition England was deaf. She would listen to no appeals to her justice or her magnanimity. For long years she had been the aggressor and the oppressor, and yet she refused to heed the kindly voice of her best friend when it pleaded for simple justice. At that very time she was exercising, by the might of her navy, the most despotic sway upon the ocean, and committing incessant injuries upon a friendly power. She had, at that time, impressed from the crews of American merchant vessels, peaceably navigating the high seas, not less than SIX THOUSAND MARINERS who claimed to be citizens of the United States, and who were denied all opportunity to verify their claims. She had seized and confiscated the commercial property of American citizens to an incalculable amount. She had united in the enormities of France in declaring a great proportion of the terraqueous globe in a state of blockade, effectually chasing the American merchant from the ocean. She had contemptuously disregarded the neutrality of the American territory, and the jurisdiction of the American laws within the waters and harbors of the United States. She was enjoying the emoluments of a surreptitious trade, stained with every species of fraud and corrruption, which gave to the belligerent powers the advantage of a peace, while the neutral powers were involved in the evils of war. She had, in short, usurped and exercised on the water a tyranny similar to that which her great antagonist had usurped and exercised on the land. And, amid all these proofs of ambition and avarice, she demanded that the victims of her usurpations and her violence should revere her as the sole defender of the rights and liberties of mankind ![3]

At about the time when Mr. Pinkney left England, Augustus J. Foster, who had been secretary to the British legation at Washington, was appointed[a] envoy extraordinary to the United States, charged with the settlement of the affair of the *Chesapeake* and other matters in dispute between the two governments.[4] He had just fairly entered upon the duties of his peaceful mission, when an event occurred that produced great complications and ill feelings.

[a] February 15, 1811.

---

[1] The British ministry, in their refusal to rescind the orders, made a strong point of the fact that one of the conditions in Champagny's letter was the renouncing by the English what were called the "new British principles of blockade," namely, the blockading of all commercial unfortified towns, coasts, harbors, and mouths of rivers. Bonaparte claimed that it ought to be confined to fortified places. Great Britain would not relax an iota of her pretensions in this matter.
[2] Act of Congress, passed 2d of March, 1811.
[3] See Dallas's *Exposition of the Causes and Character of the late War*.
[4] In announcing this appointment, the British ministry assured Mr. Pinkney of the most pacific feelings of their government toward that of his own, and that the delay in filling the place caused by the recall of Jackson was not because of any indisposition to keep up friendly diplomatic relations, but from a desire to make a satisfactory appointment, and also from late interruptions to official business owing to the mental disability of the king and the establishment of a regency. The king had shown signs of insanity in 1788, and a Regency Bill was submitted to Parliament in December of that year. The king recovered, and in February following it was withdrawn. In 1810 the physicians of the king announced his confirmed insanity, and on the 5th of February, 1811, his son, the Prince of Wales, afterward George the

| Outrage by a British Cruiser. | Commodore Rodgers. | The Frigate *President* ordered to Sea. |

Since the favorable arrangement with France, British cruisers hovering upon the American coast had become more and more annoying to commerce. A richly-laden American vessel bound to France had been captured within thirty miles of New York;[1] and early in the month of May a British frigate, supposed to be the *Guerriere*, Captain Dacres, stopped an American brig only eighteen miles from New York, and a young man, known to be a native of Maine, was taken from her and impressed into the British service.[2] Similar instances had lately occurred, and the government resolved to send out one or two of the new frigates[3] immediately for the protection of the coast trade from the depredators.

The *President*, Captain Ludlow, was then anchored off Fort Severn,[4] at Annapolis,

FORT OR BATTERY SEVERN, AT ANNAPOLIS.

bearing the broad pennant of Commodore Rodgers, the senior officer of the navy. The commodore was with his family at Havre de Grace, seventy miles distant;[5] the *President's* sailing-master was at Baltimore, forty miles distant; her purser and chaplain were at Washington, an equal distance from their posts, and all was listlessness on board the frigate, for no sounds of war were in the air. Suddenly, at three o'clock in the afternoon of the 7th of May, while Captain Ludlow was dining on board the sloop-of-war *Argus*, lying near the *President*, the gig was seen, about five miles distant, sailing at the rate of ten miles an hour, with the commodore's broad pennant flying, denoting that he was on board.[6] Rodgers was soon on the *President's* quarter-deck. He had received orders[a] from his government to put to sea at once in search of the offending British vessel, and on the 10th he weighed anchor [a] May 6, 1811.

Fourth, went before the Privy Council in great state, and was sworn in as regent of the kingdom. He held that office until the death of his father in 1820, when he became king.

[1] Hildreth, Second Series, iii., 245.

[2] Although the sea was running high, the captain of the *Spitfire* (the arrested brig) went with the young man on board the frigate, and assured the commander that he had known him from boyhood as a native of Maine. The insolent reply was, "All that may be so, but he has no protection, and that is enough for me."—*New York Herald*, May 11, 1811.

[3] The American navy then in active service consisted of the *President, Constitution*, and *United States*, 44 each; the *Essex*, 32; *John Adams*, 24; *Wasp* and *Hornet*, 18 each; *Argus* and *Siren*, 16 each; *Nautilus, Enterprise*, and *Vixen*, 12 each; and a large flotilla of gun-boats, commanded principally by sailing-masters selected from the officers of merchant vessels.—Cooper, ii., 118.

[4] The present Fort or Battery Severn, composed of a circular base and hexagonal tower, is upon the site of a fort of the same name, erected, with other fortifications, in 1776. It was then little more than a group of breast-works. These were strengthened at the beginning of the war in 1812. The present fort, seen in the picture, is rather a naval than a military work, its principal use being for a practice-battery for the students in the Naval Academy there, and for the defense of the naval arsenal, school, and officers' quarters. That academy (which was removed to Newport, Rhode Island, on the breaking out of the civil war in the spring of 1861, and its buildings at Annapolis used for hospital purposes during the conflict) was to the navy what the West Point Academy is to the army. The grounds about Fort Severn are very beautiful, and delight the eyes of all visitors. In addition to the Naval Monument there, already mentioned (page 124), are others, both elegant and expensive.

[5] The residence of Commodore Rodgers at Havre de Grace, at that time, was yet standing when I visited that town in November, 1861. It stood at near the junction of Washington and St. John Streets, and was occupied by William Poplar. It was a two-story brick house, substantially built, and well preserved, as seen in the engraving on the next page. It will be referred to again, in an account of my visit to Havre de Grace above alluded to.

[6] Letter from an officer on board the *President* in the *New York Herald*, June 3, 1811.

COMMODORE RODGERS'S RESIDENCE.

and proceeded down the Chesapeake, with the intention of cruising off New York as an inquirer concerning the impressment. He stopped on his way down the bay for munitions, and on the 14th passed the Virginia capes out upon the broad ocean. He lingered there as an observer for a day or two, and at about noon on the 16th, Cape Henry bearing southwest, and distant about forty miles, he discovered a strange sail on the eastern horizon. The squareness of her yards and symmetry of her sails proclaimed her a war vessel. She was bearing toward the *President* under a heavy press of sail. Thinking she might be the offender, the *President* stood for the stranger, and at two o'clock displayed her broad pennant[1] and ensign. The stranger made several signals. These were unanswered, and she bore away southward.[2]

---

[1] A pennant is a streamer made of a long, narrow piece of bunting, worn at the mast-heads of vessels of war. A *broad pennant* is a square piece of the same material, placed at the mast-head of the commodore's flag-ship. It is sometimes spelled *pendant* and *pennon*. The latter is not, strictly, a streamer. It is a shorter flag, split at the end, and used on merchant vessels. In the Middle Ages it was carried by knights at the heads of their lances. It is sometimes used poetically for a streamer or banner.

[2] "Made the signal 275, and finding it not answered, concluded she was an American frigate," wrote the commander of that vessel to his superior on the 21st of May. Each nation has a system of naval signals of its own, unknown to all others, and changed frequently, and for that reason Commodore Rodgers could not answer. These signals comprise a system of telegraphic signs, by which ships communicate with each other at a distance and convey information, or make known their wants. This is done by means of a certain number of flags and pennants of different colors, peculiarly arranged, which indicate the different numerals from 1 to 0. Particular flags or pennants are also used for specific purposes; for example, one pennant is called the *interrogative*, and, when hoisted, signifies that a question is asked; while another flag signifies affirmative, negative, etc. To correspond with the flags, signal-books are formed, with sentences or words which these flags represent. These books contain a list of the most common words in the language, with a table of such geographical names as are likely to be needed at sea, and also a list of the ships belonging to the navy of the country.*—*New American Cyclopædia*, article SIGNALS.

To give the reader a practical idea of the working of naval signals, I introduce graphic and explanatory descriptions from Rodgers and Black's *Semaphoric Signal-book*, approved by the Secretary of the Navy, J. Y. Mason, in 1847. These signals are composed of nine flags and five short pennants, capable of making 100,000 signals. These flags and pennants are seen in the engraving, No. 1. There are three colors, namely, red, white, and blue. The red and blue are represented by shading, the lines of the former being perpendicular, and of the latter horizontal. Each of the flags has the same signification as the number above it.

The pennants are used for duplicating or repeating. They are intended as substitutes for the numbers of such flags as are already in use; for example, in the signal number 2325 the figure 2 occurs twice. Having but *one* flag to represent that figure, another is substituted to answer its purpose, and this is done by using a pennant termed duplicate. The four pennants in the lower section of engraving No. 1 represent 1st, 2d, 3d, and 4th duplicates in the order of common enumeration. The first duplicate always repeats the number of the upper or *first* flag (the counting is always downward) of the signal with which it is hoist-

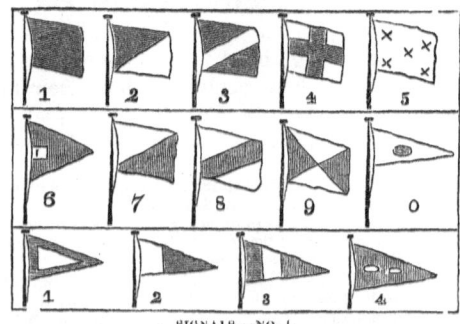

SIGNALS.—NO. 1.

SIGNAL-BOOK.

* These signal-books, when prepared for actual service at sea, are covered with canvas, containing a plate of lead on each side sufficient to sink them. This is for the purpose of destroying them, by throwing them into the sea when a vessel is compelled to strike her colors, to prevent their falling into the hands of the enemy. The annexed picture of a signal-book so covered and leaded is from a drawing of one before me which was used by Commodore Barney. It is about nine inches in length. The lead is stitched into the canvas cover. It was found among Barney's papers, which that indefatigable antiquary of Philadelphia, John A. M'Allister, secured from destruction, and deposited for safe keeping with the collections of the Pennsylvania Historical Society. Those papers were kindly placed at my disposal by Mr. M'Allister, and from them I gleaned much valuable material used in the preparation of a portion of this work.

Anxious to speak with her, Rodgers gave chase. The *President* gained upon her, and at three in the afternoon was so near that her hull was seen upon the horizon;

ed; the 2d duplicate repeats the *second* flag, and so on. The first duplicate, hoisted singly, is *answering pennant;* the 2d, hoisted singly, is *No;* the 3d, hoisted singly, is *Yes;* and the 4th, hoisted singly, is *numeral signal.* 0, or cipher pennant, hoisted singly, is *alphabetical signal.*

Engraving No. 2 shows four examples of the use of the signals, in all of which the duplicates are used. By attention to the above explanations, the operation will be readily understood. The first section of the engraving No. 2 represents the number 2295, opposite which, in the signal-book, will be found the words, "The commodore wishes to see you." The second section represents the number 2329 — "Can you spare a compass?" In these two the 1st duplicate is used, repeating the number of the first or upper flag. In the third section is represented number 6404 — "Prepare for action."

SIGNALS.—NO. 2.

In the fourth section, number 7226—"Strange sail on the starboard." In these two the second duplicate repeats the number of the second flag hoisted. The recipient of the information conveyed by the signals writes down the numbers on a slate, and then readily finds the meaning by referring to the corresponding number in the signal-book.

In a calm the signals are displayed on a more horizontal line, as seen in engraving No. 3, which represents number 1307 — "Is becalmed, and requires a steam-boat to tow."

The same flags and pennants are also used for alphabetical signals, to spell a word or name. The 0, or cipher signal, is hoisted singly, as the preparatory signal, after which the 0 or cipher signal is placed above or below the flags where required, as seen in engraving No. 4, and indicated in the alphabet below.

During the autumn and winter of 1811 and 1812, when war with England seemed to be inevitable, the attention of Commodore Rodgers was much occupied with the subject of land telegraphs for army purposes, and naval signals. He invented a telegraph which was adopted. On the 31st of April, 1812, he wrote to the Secretary of the Navy from the *President*, then lying in Hampton Roads, recommending a change in the naval signals, several years having elapsed since the system of day signals then in use had been introduced. He thought it had become known to the British navy. In that letter, preserved in the Department at Washington, he sent a drawing made in accordance with the proposed change. His suggestions were adopted, and the signals delineated in the engraving No. 5, on the next page, copied from Rodgers's manuscripts, were those used during the War of 1812.

SIGNALS.—NO. 3.

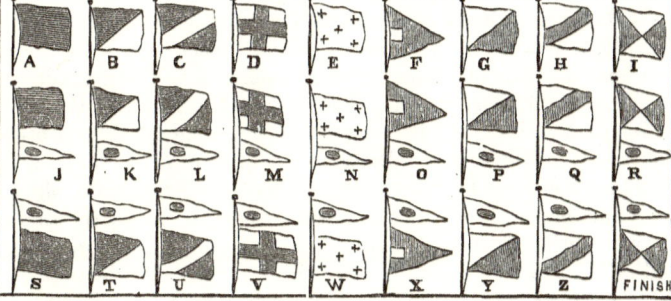

SIGNALS.—NO. 4.

A frequent change in the arrangement of the signal flags is necessary, for obvious reasons. The code of signals used in the United States Navy just previous to the late civil war was prepared by a board of officers consisting of Commodores M'Cauley and Lavalette, and Commanders Marchand and Steedman. It was adopted by the Navy Department in 1857. In 1859 another board of officers tested and approved a system of night signals invented by B. F. Coston, of the United States Navy. In October, 1861, they were adopted in the United States army. A new system of signals for both the army and navy was arranged by Major (afterward Colonel) Albert J. Myer, which was used throughout the war. Major Myer was the chief signal officer during all that time, and is now (1867) at the head of the signal department of the army.

1	2	3	4	5	6	7	,8	9
A	**B**	**C**	**D**	**E**	**F**	**G**	**H**	**I**
10	20	30	40	50	60	70	80	90
J	**K**	**L**	**M**	**N**	**O**	**P**	**Q**	**R**
01	02	03	04	05	06	07	08	09
S	**T**	**U**	**V**	**W**	**X**	**Y**	**Z**	Finish

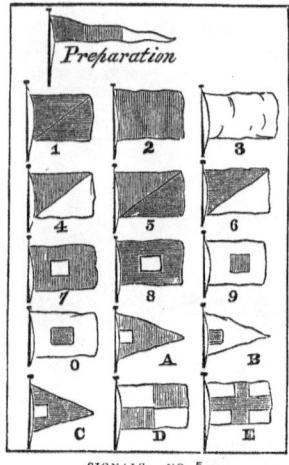

SIGNALS.—NO. 5.

but the breeze slackened, and night fell upon the waters before the two vessels were near enough to each other to discern their respective characters.

At twenty minutes past eight in the evening the *President* brought-to on the weather-bow, or a little forward of the beam of the stranger, and, when within about a hundred yards of her, Rodgers hailed, and asked "What ship is that?" No answer was given, but the question was repeated from the stranger, word for word. After a pause of fifteen or twenty seconds Rodgers reiterated his inquiry, and, before he could take his trumpet from his mouth, was answered by a shot that cut off one of the main-top-backstays of his vessel, and lodged in her mainmast. He was about to order a shot in return, when a gun from the second division of his ship was fired.[1] At almost the same instant the antagonist of the *President* fired three guns in quick succession, and then the rest of her broadside, with musketry. This provocation caused the *President* to respond by a broadside. "Equally determined," said Rodgers, "not to be the aggressor, or suffer the flag of my country to be insulted with impunity, I gave a general order to fire."[2] In the course of five or six minutes his antagonist was silenced, and the guns of the *President* ceased firing, the commander having discovered that his assumed enemy was a feeble one in size and armament. But, to the surprise of the Americans, the stranger opened her fire anew in less than five minutes. This was again silenced by the guns of the *President*, when Rodgers again demanded "What ship is that?" The wind was blowing freshly at the time, and he was able to hear only the words, "His majesty's ship—" but the name he could not understand. He immediately gave the name of his own vessel, displayed many lights to show his whereabouts in case the disabled ship should need assistance, and bore away.

At dawn the *President* discovered her antagonist several miles to the leeward, and immediately bore down upon her to offer assistance. Lieutenant Creighton was sent in a boat to learn the names of the vessel and her commander, to ascertain the extent of damage, offer assistance, and to express the regret of the commodore that necessity on his part had led to such results. Lieutenant Creighton brought back the information that the ship was the British sloop-of-war *Little Belt*, 18, Captain A. B. Bingham, who had been sent to the waters off Charleston, South Carolina, in search of the *Guerriere*, and, not finding her, was cruising northward for the same purpose, according to his instructions.[3] Captain Bingham politely refused aid, because he did not need it, and sailed away to Halifax, where he reported to "Herbert Sawyer, Esq., Rear-admiral of the Red," the commander-in-chief on the American station.[4] The *President* proceeded on her voyage toward New York, and "off Sandy Hook," on the 23d,[a] Commodore Rodgers wrote the dispatch to the Secretary of the Navy from which the foregoing facts have been drawn.

[a] May, 1811.

The reports of the occurrence by Rodgers and Bingham were utterly contradictory

---

[1] Two English seamen, who professed to have been deserters from the *President*, testified at Halifax that this gun was discharged by accident.—*London Times*, December 7, 1811.
[2] Rodgers's dispatch to the Secretary of the Navy, May 23, 1811.
[3] These instructions were dated at "Bermuda, this 19th day of April, 1811," signed by H. N. Somerville, by command of Admiral Sawyer, and addressed to "Arthur Batt Bingham, Esq., commander of his majesty's sloop *Little Belt*." In the instructions he was enjoined to be "particularly careful not to give any just cause of offence to the government or subjects of the United States of America; and to give very particular orders to this effect to the officers you may have occasion *to send on board ships under the American flag*."
[4] Bingham reported his vessel much damaged in her masts, sails, rigging, and hull; many shot through between wind and water, and many shot imbedded in her side and all her upper works, with the starboard pump shot away. He told Creighton that he had all necessary materials on board for making sufficient repairs to enable him to reach Halifax.

in respect to the most essential fact, namely, as to the aggressor. Rodgers stated positively that he hailed twice, and his words were repeated by the stranger; that she first fired one shot, which struck his vessel, then three shots, and immediately

afterward the remainder of her broadside, before he opened his guns upon her, except the single one which one of the deserters declared was discharged by accident. This account was fully corroborated, before a court of inquiry, by every officer and some of the subordinates who were on board the *President*, under oath. On the contrary, Captain Bingham reported that *he* hailed first, and that *his* words were twice repeated from the *President*, when that vessel fired a broadside, which the *Little Belt* immediately returned. This statement was fully corroborated before a court of inquiry, held at Halifax on the 29th of May,[a] by the officers of the *Little Belt*, and two deserters from the *President*, under oath. Bingham and his supporting deponents declared that the action lasted from forty-five minutes to one hour; while Rodgers declared that it lasted altogether, including the intermissions, not more than fifteen min-

[a] 1811.

utes.[1] Bingham also intimated in his dispatch that he had gained the advantage in the contest.[2]

When intelligence of this affair went over the land it produced intense excitement. Desires for and dread of war with England were stimulated to vehement action, and conflicting views and expressions, intensified by party hate, awoke spirited contentions and discussions in every community. The contradictions of the two commanders were in due time made known, and added fuel to the fires of party strife. Each government naturally accepted the report of its own servant as the true one. Not so with all the people of the United States. The opposition politicians and newspapers, with a partisanship more powerful for a while than patriotism, took sides with the British; and, eager to convict the administration of belligerent intentions, while at the same time they inconsistently assailed it because of its alleged imbecility and want of patriotism in not resisting and resenting the outrages and insults of Great

---

[1] John Rodgers was born at Havre de Grace, in Maryland, in 1771. He entered the navy as lieutenant, on the 9th of March, 1798, and was the executive officer of the *Constellation*, under Commodore Truxtun, when the *Insurgente* was taken. See page 103. He was appointed captain in March, 1799, and he was in active service during the naval operations in the Mediterranean until 1805. He was the oldest officer in rank in the navy at the time of the occurrence narrated in the text. He was the first to start on a cruise with a squadron after the declaration of war in 1812. His efficient services during that war will be found detailed in future pages. From April, 1815, until December, 1824, he served as president of the board of Navy Commissioners, and from 1824 until 1827 he was in command of a squadron in the Mediterranean. On his return in 1827 he resumed his place at the board, and held it for ten years, when he relinquished it on account of failing health. He died at Philadelphia in August, 1838. The portrait above given was copied from an original painting in the Navy Department at Washington.

[2] "The action then became general, and continued so for about three quarters of an hour, when he [the American] ceased firing, and appeared to be on fire about the main hatchway. He then filled. I was obliged to desist from firing, as the ship falling off, no gun would bear, and had no after-sail to keep her to."—Dispatch to Admiral Sawyer, May 21, 1811.

Britain, or making efficient preparations for such resistance and resentment, circulated a report, with the fiercest denunciations, that Rodgers had sailed with orders from Washington to rescue by force the young man lately impressed from a Portland brig.[1] They exultingly drew a comparison between the late and present Democratic administration, the former denying the right of the *Leopard* to take a seaman by force from the *Chesapeake*, the latter ordering Rodgers to do what Captain Humphreys had been condemned by the Americans and punished by his own government for doing. Rodgers himself, who had behaved most prudently, gallantly, and magnanimously in the matter, received his full share of personal abuse from the opponents of the administration; and, strange as it may seem, when the question was reduced to one of simple veracity on the part of the two commanders, a large number of his countrymen, even with the overwhelming testimony of all the officers and many of the subordinates of the *President* against that of five officers and two deserters produced by Captain Bingham, were so misled by party zeal as to express their belief that the British commander uttered nothing but truth, and that Rodgers and his people all committed perjury! But these ungenerous and unpatriotic assaults soon lost their chief sustenance when the Secretary of State officially declared that no orders had been given for a forcible rescue of the impressed American; and the satisfaction of Mr. Foster, the British minister at Washington (who had requested an inquiry into the conduct of Rodgers), that the statements of that commander were substantially true, was manifested by the fact that the subject was dropped in diplomatic circles, was never revived there, and the affair of the *Chesapeake* was settled in accordance with the demands of the government of the United States.

But while the two governments tacitly agreed to bury the matter in official oblivion, the people of the respective countries, highly excited by the event, would not let it drop. It increased the feeling of mutual animosity which had been growing rapidly of late, and widened the gulf of separation, which every day became more and more difficult of passage by kindly international sentiments; and when the Twelfth Congress assembled, a month earlier than usual,[a] the administration party in and out of that body was found to be decidedly a war party, while the Federalists, growing weaker in numbers every day, were as decidedly opposed to war.

[a] November 4, 1811.

---

[1] The charge was apparently justified by the tenor of a letter, already referred to, purporting to have been written by an officer on board the *President* on the 14th of May, but whose name was never given. He wrote: "By the officers who came from Washington we learn that we are sent in pursuit of the British frigate who had impressed a passenger from a coaster. Yesterday, while beating down the bay, we spoke a brig coming up, who informed us that she saw the British frigate the day before off the very place where we now are; but she is not now in sight. We have made the most complete preparations for battle. Every one wishes it. She is exactly our force, but we have the *Argus* with us, which none of us are pleased with, as we wish a fair trial of courage and skill. Should we see her, I have not the least doubt of an engagement. The commodore will demand the person impressed; the demand will doubtless be refused, and the battle will instantly commence.... The commodore has called in the boatswain, gunner, and carpenter, informed them of all circumstances, and asked if they were ready for action. Ready was the reply of each."—*New York Herald*, June 3, 1811.

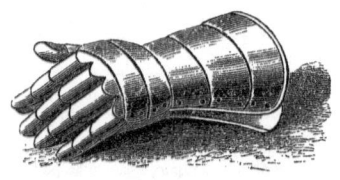

CHAPTER X.

"On Wabash, when the sun withdrew,
And chill November's tempest blew,
Dark rolled thy waves, Tippecanoe,
Amidst that lonely solitude.

. . . .

But Wabash saw another sight;
A martial host, in armor bright,
Encamped upon the shore that night,
And lighted up her scenery."

SONG—TIPPECANOE.

"Bold Boyd led on his steady band,
With bristling bayonets burnished bright.
What could their dauntless charge withstand?
What stay the warriors' matchless might?
Rushing amain, they cleared the field;
The savage foe constrained to yield
To Harrison, who, near and far,
Gave form and spirit to the war."

BATTLE OF TIPPECANOE.

WHILE the nation was agitated by political contentions, and the low mutterings of the thunder of an oncoming tempest of war were heard, heavy, dark, and ominous clouds of trouble were seen gathering in the northwestern horizon, where the Indians were still numerous, and discontents had made them restless.

In the year 1800, as we have seen (page 130), the Indiana Territory (then including the present States of Indiana, Illinois, and Wisconsin) was established, and the late President Harrison, then an energetic young man of less than thirty years of age, was appointed governor. He had resigned his commission of captain in the United States army, and for a few years had been employed in civil life. In the year 1805 a Territorial Legislature was organized, much to the discontent of the French settlers on the Wabash, and Vincennes, an old town already spoken of (page 40), was made the capital. Harrison was popular among all classes, and particularly with the Indians; and he managed the public affairs of the Territory with prudence and energy in the midst of many difficulties arising out of land speculations, land titles, treaties with the Indians, and the machinations of traders and the English in Canada. He had much to contend against in the demoralization of the Indians by immediate contact with the white people, especially effected by whisky and other spirituous liquors.[1]

By a succession of treaties, Governor Harrison, at the close of 1805, had extinguished Indian titles to forty-six thousand acres of land within the domain of Indiana. Every thing had been done in accordance with the principles of exact justice, and, had the governor's instructions been fully carried out, the Indians would never have had cause to complain. But settlers and speculators came, bringing with them, in many cases, the peculiar vices of civilized society, which, when copied by the Indians, were intensified fourfold. Regarding the natives as little better than the wild beasts of the forest, they defrauded them, encroached upon their reserved domain, and treated them with contempt and inhumanity. "You call us your children," said an old chief to Harrison one day, in bitterness of spirit—" you call us your children

---

[1] "I do not believe," wrote General Harrison in 1805, "that there are more than six hundred warriors on the Wabash, and yet the quantity of whisky brought here annually for their consumption is said to amount to six thousand gallons."

—why do you not make us happy, as our fathers, the French, did? They never took from us our lands; indeed, they were common between us. They planted where they pleased, and they cut wood where they pleased, and so did we. But now, if a poor Indian attempts to take a little bark from a tree to cover him from rain, up comes a white man and threatens to shoot him, claiming the tree as his own."[1] And so, with ample reason, they murmured on. Emissaries sent out by the British authorities in Canada fanned the flame of discontent; and Elliott, the old enemy of the Americans, still living near Malden, observing symptoms of impending war between the United States and Great Britain, was again wielding a potent influence over the chiefs of the tribes in the Northwest. Their resources, as well as privileges, were curtailed. Napoleon's Continental System touched even the savage of the wilderness. It clogged and almost closed the chief markets for his furs, and the prices were so low that Indian hunters found it difficult to purchase their usual necessaries from the traders. At the beginning of 1811 the Indians were ripe for any enterprise that promised them relief and independence.

A powerful warrior had lately become conspicuous, who, like Metacomet, the Wampanoag, and Pontiac, the Ottawa, essayed to be the savior of his people from the crushing footsteps of the advancing white man. He was one of three sons born of a Creek mother (Methoataske) at the same time, in a cabin built of sapling logs unhewn, and chinked with sticks and mud, near the banks of the Mad River, a few miles from Springfield, Ohio. They were named respectively Tecumtha, Elkswatawa, and Kamskaka. Tecumtha[2] was the warrior alluded to. His name signifies, in the Shawnoese dialect, "a flying tiger," or "a wild-cat springing on its prey." He was a well-built man, about five feet ten inches in height.[3] Elkswatawa, "the loud voice," also became famous,

BIRTHPLACE OF TECUMTHA AND HIS BROTHERS.

or, more properly speaking, notorious; but Kamskaka lived a quiet, retired life, and died in ignoble obscurity.

As early as 1805, Elkswatawa, pretending to have had a vision, assumed to be a prophet, and took the name of Pemsquatawah, or "open door." Up to that period he had been remarkable for nothing but stupidity and intoxication. He was a cunning, unprincipled man, whose countenance was disfigured by the loss of an

---

[1] Governor Harrison to the Secretary of War.
[2] The late Colonel John Johnston, of Dayton, Ohio, who was Indian Agent among the Shawnoese and neighboring tribes for many years, and knew Tecumtha well, informed me that the proper way to spell that warrior's name, according to the native pronunciation, is as I have given it. On such authority I have adopted the orthography in the text. From Colonel Johnston, whose name will be frequently mentioned in the course of our narrative, I obtained much valuable information concerning the Indians of the Northwest from the year 1800 to 1812, during a visit with him in the autumn of 1860.

The birthplace of Tecumtha and his brothers was at the Piqua village, about five miles west from Springfield.* The engraving, copied by permission from Howe's *Historical Collections of Ohio*, shows the place of his birth as it appeared a few years ago. It is on the north side of the Mad River. A small hamlet, called West Boston, now occupies the site of the Piqua village. The Indian fort at that place, consisting of a rude log hut surrounded by pickets, stood upon the hill seen on the left of the picture. [3] Colonel Johnston.

* This was ancient Piqua, the seat of the Piqua clan of the Shawnoese, a name which signifies "a man formed out of the ashes," and significant of their alleged origin. See Howe's *Historical Collections of Ohio*, page 362. Modern Piqua, oftentimes confounded with that of the ancient one in speaking of Tecumtha, is a flourishing village on the Great Miami River, Miami County. Upper Piqua, three miles above the village, is a place of considerable historical interest. The reader is referred to Mr. Howe's valuable work for interesting details concerning the events which made it famous.

eye.[1] While lighting his pipe one day, he fell to the earth, as if dead. Preparations were made for his burial. When his friends were about to remove him, he opened his eyes and said, "Be not fearful. I have been in the Land of the Blessed. Call the nation together, that I may tell them what I have seen and heard." His people were speedily assembled, and again he spoke, saying, "Two beautiful young men were sent to me by the Great Spirit, who said, The Master of Life is angry with you all. He will destroy you unless you refrain from drunkenness, lying, stealing, and witchcraft, and turn yourselves to him. Unless the red men shall do this, they shall never see the beautiful place you are now to behold." He was then taken to a gate which opened into the spiritland, but he was not permitted to enter.[2]

THE PROPHET.

Such was the prophet's story. He immediately entered upon his mission as a professed preacher of righteousness. He inveighed against drunkenness and witchcraft, and warned his people to have nothing to do with the pale-faces, their religion, their customs, their arms, or their arts, for every imitation of the intruders was offensive to the great Master of Life. Tecumtha, possessed of a master mind and a statesman's sagacity, was the moving spirit in all this imposture. It was a part of his grand scheme for obtaining influence over the Northwestern tribes for political purposes, and he went from tribe to tribe publishing the wonders of his brother's divine mission.

The Prophet's harangues excited the latent superstition of the Indians to the highest degree, and for a while his sway over the minds of the savages in the Northwest was almost omnipotent. The chiefs and leading men of his own tribe denounced him, but the people sustained him. Success made him bold, and he used his newly-acquired power for the gratification of private and public resentments. He was accuser and judge, and he caused the execution of several hostile Delaware chiefs on a charge of witchcraft. A terrorism began to prevail all over the region where his divine mission was recognized. The credulous—men, women, and children—came long distances to see the oracle of the Great Spirit, who, they believed, wrought miracles.[3] Their numbers became legion, and the white settlers were alarmed.

Tecumtha's deep scheme worked admirably. In the great congregation were lead-

---

[1] The portrait of the Prophet is from a pencil sketch made by Pierre Le Dru, a young French trader, at Vincennes, in 1808. He made a sketch of Tecumtha at about the same time, both of which I found in possession of his son at Quebec in 1848, and by whom I was kindly permitted to copy them. That of Tecumtha will be found in Chapter XIV. Owing partly to his excessive dissipation, the Prophet appeared much the elder of Tecumtha.

[2] Drake's *Book of the Indians*, page 624.

[3] The Prophet was without honor in his own country, and he left Piqua and settled in a village of his own at Greenville, in Ohio, where Wayne held his great treaty in 1795, on lands already ceded to the United States. At the instigation of Tecumtha, no doubt, he sent emissaries to the tribes on the Lakes and on the Upper Mississippi, to declare his prophecy that the earth was about to be destroyed, except in the immediate residence of the Prophet at Greenville. Alarm caused many to flock thither as a place of refuge, and this gave Tecumtha an opportunity to divulge with ease to a large number, his plans for a confederacy. The Prophet made many predictions concerning the future glory of the Indians. His disciples spread the most absurd tales about his wonderful power—that he could make pumpkins spring out of the ground as large as wigwams, and that his corn grew so large that one ear would feed a dozen men. They spread a belief that the body of the Prophet was invulnerable, and that he had all knowledge, past, present, and future. It is said that so great a number flocked to Greenville to see him, that the southern shores of Lakes Superior and Michigan were quite depopulated. The traders were obliged to abandon their business. Of these deluded fanatics not more than one third ever returned, having died in consequence of the privations of hunger, cold, and fatigue. They perished by scores upon their weary pilgrimage.—*MS. Life and Times of Tecumseh*, by Henry Onderdonk, Jr., 1842.

ing men from all the surrounding tribes, even from the Upper Mississippi, and he had a rare opportunity to confer with them together on the subject of his darling project, a grand confederation of all the tribes in the Northwest to drive the white man across the Ohio, and reclaim their lands which they had lost by treaties. He declared to assembled warriors and sachems, whenever opportunity offered, that the treaties concerning those lands northward of the Ohio were fraudulent, and therefore void; and he always assured his auditors that he and his brother, the Prophet, would resent any farther attempts at settlement in that direction by the white people.

Governor Harrison perceived danger in these movements, and early in 1808 he addressed a speech to the chiefs and head men of the Shawnoese tribe, in which he denounced the Prophet as an impostor. "My children," he said, "this business must be stopped. I will no longer suffer it. You have called a number of men from the most distant tribes to listen to a fool, who speaks not the words of the Great Spirit, but those of the Evil Spirit and of the British agents. My children, your conduct has much alarmed the white settlers near you. They desire that you will send away those people; and if they wish to have the impostor with them they can carry him. Let him go to the Lakes; he can hear the British more distinctly."

This speech exasperated and alarmed the brothers. The Prophet and his followers, frowned upon by the Shawnoese in general, who listened to the governor, took up their abode in the spring of 1808 on the banks of the Wabash, near the mouth of the Tippecanoe River. Tecumtha was there too, when not on his political journeys among the neighboring tribes, but he was cautious and silent. The Prophet, more directly aimed at in Harrison's speech, hastened to deny any complicity with the British agents, or having hostile designs. He visited Vincennes in August to confer in person with the governor, and to give him renewed and solemn assurances that he and his followers wished to live in harmony with the white people. So specious were the words of the wily savage, that Harrison suspected he had misjudged the man, and he dismissed the Prophet with friendly assurances.

The governor soon had reason to doubt the fidelity of the oracle. There were reported movements at the Prophet's town on the Wabash, half religious and half warlike, that made him suspect the brothers of unfriendly designs toward the Americans. He charged them with having made secret arrangements with British agents for hostile purposes, and pressed the matter so closely that, at a conference between the governor and the Prophet at Vincennes in the summer of 1809, the latter acknowledged that he had received invitations from the British in Canada to engage in a war with the United States, but declared that he had rejected them. He renewed his vows of friendship, but Harrison no longer believed him to be sincere.

Soon after this interview Harrison concluded a treaty at Fort Wayne[a] with Delaware, Pottawatomie, Miami, Kickapoo, Wea, and Eel River Indians, by which, in consideration of $8200 paid down, and annuities to the amount of $2350 in the aggregate, he obtained a cession of nearly three millions of acres of land extending up the Wabash beyond Terre Haute, and including the middle waters of the White River.[1] Neither Tecumtha, nor his brother, nor any of their tribe had any claim to these lands, yet they denounced those who sold them, declared the treaty void, and threatened to kill every chief concerned in it. Tecumtha grew bolder and bolder, for he was sanguine of success in his great scheme of a confederation, and the arrest of the white man's progress. He had already announced the doctrine, opposed to state or tribal rights, that the domain of all the Indians belonged to all in common, and that no part of the territory could be sold or alienated without the consent of all. This was the ground of the denunciations of the treaty by Tecumtha and his brother, and the justification of their threats against the offending chiefs—threats the

[a] September 30, 1809.

---

[1] The Weas and Kickapoos were not represented at the council, but the former, in October, and the latter, in December, confirmed the treaty at Fort Wayne.

more alarming, because the warlike Wyandots, on the southern shores of Lake Erie, whom all the tribes so feared and respected that they called them uncles, had lately become the allies of these Shawanoese brothers.

In the spring of 1810 the Indians at the Prophet's town gave unmistakable signs of hostility. They refused to receive the "annuity salt," and insulted the boatmen who took it to them by calling them "American dogs." These and other indications of hostility caused Harrison to send frequent messengers to the Prophet and his brother. Finally, in July, he sent a letter to them by Joseph Barron, a Frenchman, known to and respected by all the Indian tribes in that region as a faithful and kind-

JOSEPH BARRON.

hearted interpreter. He was instructed to invite the brothers to meet the governor in council at Vincennes, and lay their alleged grievances before him. Barron was received by the Prophet in a most unfriendly spirit. The oracle was surrounded by several Indians, and when the interpreter was formally presented his single eye kindled and gleamed with fiercest anger. Gazing upon the visitor intently for several minutes without speaking, he suddenly exclaimed, "For what purpose do *you* come here? Brouillette was here; he was a spy. Dubois was here; he was a spy. Now *you* have come. You, too, are a spy." Then, pointing to the ground, he said, vehemently, "There is your grave, look on it!" At that moment Tecumtha appeared, assured Barron of his personal safety, heard the letter of Governor Harrison, and promised to visit Vincennes in the course of a few days.[1]

On the morning of the 12th of August Tecumtha appeared at Vincennes. He had been requested to bring not more than thirty warriors with him; he came with four hundred fully armed, and encamped in a grove on the outskirts of the town. The inhabitants, most of whom were unarmed, were startled by this unexpected demonstration of savage strength, and, partly on

---

[1] Statement of Mr. Barron, quoted by Dillon in his *History of Indiana*, page 441. Mr. Barron was a native of Detroit. He was employed by Harrison as interpreter about eighteen years. He was an uneducated man, of much natural ability, and very interesting in conversation. He was slender in form, about a medium height, had black eyes, sallow complexion, a prominent nose, small mouth, and wore his hair in a cue, *à la aborigine*, with a long black ribbon dangling down his back. He was a facetious, pleasant, social, and entertaining man, full of anecdotes and *bon mots*. He was fond of music, and played the Indian flutes with skill. Barron was acquainted with most of the Indian dialects east of the Mississippi. In 1837 he accompanied emigrating Pottawatomies to the West. He also accompanied another party of the same tribe in 1838 to their lands beyond the Mississippi. He afterward returned to the Wabash, and, after a protracted illness, died on the 31st of July, 1843, at an advanced age, at the residence of his son on the Wabash, near its confluence with the Eel River.

Mr. Barron was at the battle of Tippecanoe with Harrison, and this circumstance greatly exasperated the Indians against him. They were very anxious to capture and torture him. So important did they consider him, that they made rude sketches of his features on the barks of trees, and sent them among the various tribes, that they might know and catch him. One of these was for some time in possession of Mr. Compret, of Fort Wayne. It was carried to Germany by a Catholic priest as a great curiosity. Another, on a piece of beech bark, was preserved a long time at Fort Dearborn, and in 1836 was in possession of James Hertz, a private soldier at Mackinaw, from whom a friend procured it, and in the autumn of 1861 sent me a tracing of it. The sketch is a fac-simile on a reduced scale.

George Winter, Esq., an artist of Lafayette, Indiana, painted a portrait of Mr. Barron in 1837. He kindly furnished me the copy from which the above engraving was made; also with the information concerning the famous interpreter contained in this note. Mr. Winter was the painter of the portrait of Frances Slocum, the lost child of Wyoming.—See Lossing's *Field-book of the Revolution*, i., 369.

Brouillette and Dubois, mentioned above, with Francis Vigo, Pierre La Plante, John Conner, and William Prince, were influential men, and were frequently employed by Harrison as messengers to the Indians.

INDIAN DETECTER.

account of their fears, and partly because of the fame of Tecumtha as an orator, they flocked to the governor's house. Seats had been prepared for those who were to participate in the council under the portico of the governor's residence; but when Tecumtha, after placing the great body of his warriors in camp in the shade of a grove near by, advanced with about thirty of his followers, he refused to enter the area with the white people, saying, "Houses were built for you to hold councils in; Indians hold theirs in the open air." He then took a position under some trees in front of the house, and, unabashed by the large concourse of people before him, opened the business with a speech marked by great dignity and native eloquence. When he had concluded, one of the governor's aids, through Barron the interpreter, said to the chief, pointing to a chair, "Your father requests you to take a seat by his side." The chief drew his mantle around him, and, standing erect, said, with scornful tone, "My father! The sun is my father, and the earth is my mother; on her bosom I will repose," and then seated himself upon the ground.

Tecumtha's speeches at this council were bold, arrogant, and sometimes insolent. He avowed the intention of himself and brother to establish, by a confederacy of the tribes, the principle of common interest in the domain as intended by the Great Spirit, and to not only prevent any other sale or cession of lands, but to recover what had been lately ceded by the treaty at Fort Wayne. He declared his intention to kill all the "village chiefs" who had made the sale if the lands were not returned, because he was authorized, he said, by all the tribes to do so. "Return those lands," he said, "and Tecumtha will be the friend of the Americans. He likes not the English, who are continually setting the Indians on the Americans."[1]

Governor Harrison, in his reply, ridiculed the idea that the Great Spirit had intended the Indians to be one people. "If such had been his intention," he said, "he would not have put six different tongues into their heads, but would have taught them all to speak one language." As to the lands in dispute, the Shawnoese had nothing to do with it. The Miamis owned it when the Shawnoese were living in Georgia, out of which they had been driven by the Creeks. The lands had been purchased from the Miamis, who were the true owners of it, and it was none of the Shawnoese's business. When these asseverations were interpreted, Tecumtha's eyes flashed with anger. He cast off his blanket, and, with violent gesticulations, pronounced the governor's words to be false. He accused the United States of cheating and imposing upon the Indians. His warriors, receiving a sign from him, sprang to their feet, seized their war-clubs, and began to brandish their tomahawks. The governor started from his chair and drew his sword, while the citizens seized any missile in their way. It was a moment of imminent danger. A military guard of twelve men, who were under some trees a short distance off, were ordered up. A friendly Indian cocked his pistol, which he had loaded stealthily while Tecumtha was speaking, and Mr. Winans, a Methodist minister, ran to the governor's house, seized a gun, and placed himself in the door to defend the family. The guard were about to fire, when Harrison, perfectly collected, restrained them, and a bloody encounter was prevented. When the interpreter told him the cause of the excitement, he pronounced Tecumtha a bad man, and ordered him to leave the neighborhood immediately. Tecumtha retired to his camp, the council was broken up,[a] and no sleep came to the eyelids of the people of Vincennes that night, as they expected an attack from the savages.

[a] August 20, 1810.

On the following morning, Tecumtha, with seeming sincerity, expressed his regret because of the violence into which he had been betrayed. He found in Harrison a man not to be awed by menaces nor swayed by turbulence. With respectful words he asked to have the council resumed. The governor consented, and then placed two companies of well-armed militia in the village, for the protection and encouragement of the inhabitants. Tecumtha, always dignified, laid aside his insolent manner, and

---

[1] Onderdonk's MS. *Life of Tecumseh.*

publicly disavowed any intention of attacking the governor and his friends on the preceding day. When asked whether he intended to persist in his opposition to the late treaty, he replied firmly that he should "adhere to the old boundary." Chiefs from five different tribes immediately arose, and declared their intention to support Tecumtha in the stand he had taken, and their determination to establish the proposed confederacy.

Harrison well knew the great ability and influence of Tecumtha, and was very anxious to conciliate him. On the following day, accompanied only by Mr. Barron, he visited the warrior in his camp, and had a long and friendly interview with him. He told Tecumtha that his principles and his claims would not be allowed by the President of the United States, and advised him to relinquish them. "Well," said the warrior, "as the Great Chief is to determine the matter, I hope the Great Spirit will put sense enough into his head to induce him to direct you to give up this land. It is true, he is so far off he will not be injured by the war. He may sit still in his town and drink his wine, while you and I will have to fight it out."[1] The conference ended by the governor's promising to lay the matter before the President.

War with the followers of Tecumtha and the Prophet now seemed probable, and Harrison commenced measures to meet it. A small detachment of United States troops, under Captain Cross, stationed at Newport, Kentucky, were ordered to Vincennes, there to join three companies of militia infantry and a company of Knox County dragoons, in the event of an attack from the savages. The governor had paid particular attention to drilling the militia, and now, when their services were likely to be needed, they felt much confidence on account of their discipline.

The Indians on the Wabash, grown bold by the teachings of their great military leader, the oracular revelations of the Prophet, and the active encouragement of the British in Canada, began to roam in small marauding parties over the Wabash region in the spring of 1811, plundering the houses of settlers and the wigwams of friendly Indians, stealing horses, and creating general alarm. Tecumtha was exceedingly active, at the same time, in efforts to perfect his confederacy and inciting the tribes to war; and, early in the summer, the movements of the Indians were so menacing that Governor Harrison sent Captain Walter Wilson, accompanied by Mr. Barron, with an energetic letter to the Shawnoe brothers.[a] He assured them that he was fully prepared to encounter all the tribes combined, and that if they did not put a stop to the outrages complained of, and cease their warlike movements, he should attack them. [a June 24, 1811.]

Tecumtha was alarmed. He received the messengers very courteously, and promised to see the governor in person very soon, when he would convince him that he had no desire to make war upon the Americans. He accordingly appeared at Vincennes on the 27th of July, accompanied by about three hundred Indians, twenty of them women. The inhabitants were alarmed. It was believed that the wily savage had intended, with these warriors at hand, to compel the governor to give up the Wabash lands. But when, on the day of his arrival, he saw seven hundred and fifty well-armed militia reviewed by the governor, he exhibited no haughtiness of tone and manner. He was evidently uneasy. He made the most solemn protestations of his friendly intentions and desires to restrain the Indians from hostilities, yet he earnestly but modestly insisted upon a return of the lands ceded by the treaty at Fort Wayne. His duplicity was perfect. He left Vincennes a few days afterward with twenty warriors, went down the Wabash, and, as was afterward ascertained, visited the Southern Indians—Creeks, Choctaws, and Chickasaws—and endeavored to bring them into his league against the white people. The remainder of his followers from the Prophet's town, astonished at the military display at Vincennes, returned to their rendezvous on the Tippecanoe, filled with doubt and alarm.

---

[1] Dawson's *Life of Harrison*, page 59; Drake's *Book of the North American Indians.*

The government had suggested to Harrison the propriety of seizing Tecumtha and the Prophet, and holding them as hostages for the good behavior of their followers. The governor, in turn, suggested, as a better method of obtaining peace and security, an increase of the military resources of the Territory, and the establishment of a military post high up the Wabash toward the Prophet's town. The wisdom of this suggestion was conceded. The Fourth Regiment of United States Infantry, under Colonel John P. Boyd,[1] was ordered from Pittsburg to the Falls of the Ohio, now Louisville; and Governor Harrison was authorized[a] to employ these troops and call out the militia of the Territory for the purpose of attacking the hostile savages on the Tippecanoe, if he should deem it advisable. This authorization gave the inhabitants about Vincennes great relief. They had already, before the arrival of the order, appointed a committee at a public meeting[b] to ask the government to direct the dispersion of the hostile bands at the Prophet's town.[2]

[a] July 17, 1811.

[b] July 31.

The government was anxious to preserve peace with the Indians, and Harrison's orders gave him very little discretionary powers in the matter of levying war upon the savages. They were sufficient for his purpose. He determined to push forward, build a fort on the Wabash, make peaceful overtures, and if they were rejected, open war vigorously. He called Colonel Boyd to Vincennes with his detachment, consisting of a part of the Fourth Regiment and some riflemen, and asked for volunteers. The response was quick and ample. Revenge because of wrongs suffered at the hands of the Indians north of the Ohio slumbered in many bosoms, especially in Kentucky; and when the voice of the popular Harrison called for aid, it was like the sound of the trumpet. Old Indian warriors in Kentucky like General Samuel Wells

---

[1] John Parke Boyd was born in Newburyport, Massachusetts, December 21, 1764. His father was from Scotland, and his mother was a descendant of Tristam Coffin, the first of that family who emigrated to America. He entered the army in 1786, as ensign in the Second Regiment. With a spirit of adventure, he went to India in 1789, having first touched at the Isle of France. In a letter to his father from Madras, in June, 1790, he says, "Having procured recommendatory letters to the English consul residing at the court of his highness, the Nizam, I proceeded to his capital, Hydrabad, 450 miles from Madras. On my arrival, I was presented to his highness in form by the English consul. My reception was as favorable as my most sanguine wishes had anticipated. After the usual ceremony was over, he presented me with the command of two kansolars of infantry, each of which consists of 500 men." His commission and pay were in accordance with his command. He describes the army of the Nizam, which had taken the field against Tippoo Sultan. It consisted of 150,000 infantry, 60,000 cavalry, and 500 elephants, each elephant supporting a "castle" containing a nabob and servants. He remained in India several years, in a sort of guerrilla service, and obtained much favor. He was in Paris early in 1808, and at home in the autumn of that year, when he was appointed (October 2) colonel of the Fourth Regiment of the U. S. Army. He was in the battle of Tippecanoe in November, 1811, and on the commencement of war with Great Britain he was appointed (August 26) a brigadier general. He held that rank throughout the war. He was at the capture of Fort George, and in the battle of Chrysler's Field, or Williamsburg, in Canada. He left the army in 1815, and the following year he went to England to obtain indemnity for the loss of a valuable cargo of saltpetre, captured by an English cruiser while on its way from the East Indies. He procured only a single installment of $30,000. President Jackson appointed him Naval Officer at Boston in 1830. He died there the same year, on the 4th of October, at the age of sixty-six years.

General Boyd was a tall, well-formed, and handsome man; kind, courteous, and generous. I am indebted to the courtesy of the Hon. William Willis, of Portland, Maine, for the materials of the above brief sketch and the profile of the general.

[2] The committee consisted of Samuel T. Scott, Alexander Devin, Luke Decker, Ephraim Jordan, Daniel M'Clure, Walter Wilson, and Francis Vigo. In a letter dated August 3, 1811, and addressed to the President, they said, "In this part of the country we have not, as yet, lost any of our fellow-citizens by the Indians; but depredations upon the property of those who live upon the frontiers, and insults to the families that are left unprotected, almost daily occur."--Dillon's *History of Indiana*, page 456.

and Colonel Owen instantly obeyed. They hastened to the field, accompanied by the eloquent Kentucky lawyer, Joseph Hamilton Daviess, Colonel Frederick Geiger, Captain Peter Funk[1] at the head of a company of cavalry, and Croghan, O'Fallon, Shipp, Chum, Edwards, and other subalterns, who had been mustered by Geiger near Louisville. All of these have praisers for bravery in the annals of their country.

On the 26th of September Governor Harrison left Fort Knox,[2] at Vincennes, with about nine hundred effective men, marched up the Wabash Valley, and on the 3d of October halted on the eastern bank of the river, about two miles above an old Wea village, where the town of Terre Haute, Indiana, now stands. It was a spot famous in Indian tradition as the scene of a desperate battle, at some time far in the past, between tribes of the Illinois and Iroquois. On this account the old French settlers had named the spot "Battaille des Illinois." There they immediately commenced the erection of a quadrangular stockaded fort, with a block-house at three of the angles; and there the governor received deputations from friendly Delaware and Miami Indians, who assured him that the hostility and strength of the Prophet was increasing. In war-speeches to them he had declared that the hatchet was lifted up against the Americans; and this information was affirmed on the night of the 10th of October, when some prowling Shawnoese, who had come down the Wabash, wounded one of the sentinels. Harrison sent a deputation of Miamis to the Prophet's town with a message to the impostor, requiring the Indians on the Tippecanoe to disperse immediately to their respective tribes. It also required the Prophet to restore all the stolen horses in his possession, and surrender the men who had murdered white people on the Indiana and Illinois frontiers. The messengers never returned with an answer.

The fort was completed on the 28th of October. It was built upon a bluff thirty or forty feet above the Wabash, and covered about an acre of ground. On the day of its completion it was named, by the unanimous request of the officers present, FORT HARRISON, in honor of the governor. Colonel Daviess made a speech on the occasion. Standing over the gate, and holding a bottle of whisky in his hand, he said, in conclusion, "In the name of the United States, and by the authority of the same, I christen this Fort Harrison." He then broke the bottle over the gate, when a whisky-loving soldier, standing near, exclaimed, with the usual expletive, "It is too bad to waste whisky in that way—water would have done just as well." Less than a year afterward that little fort became the theatre of heroic exploits under Captain Zachary Taylor, which we shall consider hereafter.

I visited Terre Haute and the site of Fort Harrison late in September, 1860.[a]   I had spent the previous day at Fort Wayne, in visiting and sketching the grave of Little Turtle, the great Miami chief, and other places of interest about that historic city. A storm had just ended, and the sky was still murky

[a] September 26.

---

[1] I am indebted to Mr. D. R. Poignard, of Taylorsville, Kentucky, for a very interesting narrative of this campaign, taken by him from the lips of Captain Funk in 1862, then aged eighty years, and enjoying good health of mind and body on his fertile farm eight miles from Louisville. Mr. Funk was a native of Maryland, where he was born in 1782. He was of German descent. His narrative is clear, and exceedingly interesting, and I have availed myself of its valuable information in compiling the account of this memorable campaign.

Captain Funk says that Governor Harrison was in Louisville in August, 1811, when the narrator was in command of a company of militia cavalry there. At Harrison's personal request he hastened to Governor Scott, and obtained permission to raise a company of cavalry to join the forces of the Governor of Indiana at Vincennes, for an expedition up the Wabash. Harrison also called for a company of infantry, to be raised by Captain James Hunter, who was afterward second in command, under Colonel Croghan, at Fort Stephenson, on the Sandusky; but, before leaving Louisville, he concluded that Funk's cavalry would be quite sufficient. Captain Funk raised his company in the course of a few days, and early in September joined Colonel Bartholomew's regiment, then marching on Vincennes. At this place they found Colonel Joseph H. Daviess, with two other volunteers (James Mead and Ben. Saunders) from Lexington, the colonel's then place of residence. There were with him, also, four young gentlemen from Louisville, namely, George Croghan, John O'Fallon, a *millionaire* of St. Louis in 1862, —— Moore, afterward a captain in the U. S. Army, and —— Hynes.

The signature of Captain Funk (then bearing the title of Major), above given, is copied from a note to me from him, written in September, 1861.

[2] Fort Knox was erected by Major Hamtramck in 1787, and named in honor of General Henry Knox, the Secretary of War.

when we left, at two in the afternoon, for Indianapolis. We arrived at Peru, a little village on the Wabash fifty-six miles west of Fort Wayne, at sunset. The dull clouds had lifted the space of a degree from the horizon, and allowed the last rays of the sun to give glory to the thoroughly saturated country for a few minutes, before the luminary disappeared behind the forests that skirted a wide prairie on the west.

At Peru, a railway leading southward to the capital of Indiana connects with the Toledo and Wabash Road, over which we had traveled. But there was no evening connection, and we were compelled to remain among the Peruvians until morning. Theirs is a small village. Town and taverns were filled with people, drawn thither by the two-fold attraction of a county fair and a desire to go to Indianapolis in the morning, where the late Judge Douglas, one of the candidates for the Presidency of the United States, was to speak. I found a crowd of railway passengers around the register of the inn where I stopped, all anxious to secure good lodgings for the night. The applicants were many, and the beds proportionately few. I was fortunate enough to have for my room-companion for the night, Judge Davis, of Bloomington, Illinois, a gentleman of great weight in the West, and an ardent personal friend of the late President Lincoln. He declared that, if his friend should be elected, he would be found to be "the right man in the right place." Judge Davis is now (1867) one of the Associate Justices of the Supreme Court of the United States.

Having half an hour to spare before supper and the approaching darkness, I strolled around the village, that lies upon a rolling plain and along the banks of the beautiful Wabash—beautiful, indeed, because of variety in outline, greenness of verdure, and its fringes of graceful trees and shrubbery. Many of the trees were more ancient than the dominion of the white man there, and others were as young as the town near by, so lately sprung up from the shadows of the wilderness. A canal, with muddy banks, dug along the margin of the river, somewhat marred the beauty of the scene. It was quite dark when I retired to the inn, having called on the way at the house of Mr. Grigg, whose wife is a daughter of the Little Turtle. They were absent, and I missed the anticipated pleasure of an interview with one whose father bore such a conspicuous part in the history of the Northwest.

I left Peru, in company with Judge Davis, at six o'clock the following morning, and reached Indianapolis at ten. It was a sunny day. The town was rapidly filling with people pouring in by railways and common roads from all directions. Flags were flying, drums were beating, marshals were hurrying to and fro, and the crowds were flowing toward the "Bates House," the common centre of attraction, where Judge Douglas was receiving his friends in a private parlor, and waiting for the appointed hour when he should go out and speak to the people on the political topics of the day. Over the broad street a splendid triumphal arch was thrown, and every avenue to the hotel was densely thronged with eager expectants. I made my way through the living sea, and registered my name for dinner at the "Bates," expecting to leave for Terre Haute at evening. After spending an hour with Mr. Dillon, author of the latest history of Indiana, I was informed that a train would leave for the West at meridian. So I again elbowed my way through the crowd just as Judge Douglas was entering his carriage, and, with the shouts of twenty thousand voices ringing in my ears, I escaped to the empty streets, and reached the railway station just in time for the midday train. I was soon reminded that I had involuntarily made a liberal contribution to some light-fingered follower of the itinerant candidate for the crown of civic victory. I had been relieved of the present care of that subtle magician thus apostrophized by Byron:

> "Thou more than stone of the philosopher!
> Thou touchstone of Philosophy herself!
> Thou bright eye of the mine! thou loadstar of
> The soul! thou true magnetic pole, to which
> All hearts point duly north, like trembling needles!"

Visit to Terre Haute and the Site of Fort Harrison.   Sketch of the Fort.   A Traveler in Trouble.

Terre Haute (high land) is seventy-three miles westward of Indianapolis. It is a pleasant village, and the capital of Vigo County. It then contained less than two thousand inhabitants. It is on a high plain on the left bank of the Wabash, and is one of the most delightful summer residences in all that region. We arrived there at four o'clock in the afternoon. Hoping to visit the site of Fort Harrison that evening, so as to leave in the morning, I immediately sought a gentleman in the village to whom I had a letter of introduction. The town was almost depopulated by the attractions of a county fair in its neighborhood. The afternoon was so pleasant that men, women, and children had all gone to the exhibition, and not a vehicle of any kind could be found to convey me to the fort, over two miles distant. After wasting more than an hour in fruitless attempts to procure one, I fell back on my unfailing reserve, and started off on foot. It was twilight when I reached the spot—twilight too dim to make a sketch of the locality. The old sycamore and elm trees that were there in their early maturity when the fort was built yet stand along the bank between the canal and the ruin, and on the western shore of the Wabash opposite may still be seen the fine old timber upon the low and frequently-overflowed bottom; but nothing of the fort remained excepting the logs of one of the block-houses, which then (1860) formed the dwelling of Cornelius Smock within the area of the old stockade. I had the good-fortune to meet an old man (in my haste I forgot to inquire his name), when near the site of the fort, who was there in 1813, soon after Captain Taylor's defense of it. He pointed out the exact locality, and gave me such a minute description of the structure, that I made a rough outline of it on the spot, a finished copy of which is seen in the picture. He pronounced it perfect according to his recollection. Its truthfulness was confirmed on my return to the Terre Haute House by a picture, made in like manner a few years ago from the recollections of old people, and lithographed.[1] It was placed in my hands by Mr. Ralston, of the gas-works; and I was surprised to find such a perfect agreement, even in detail. I have no doubt the engraving here given is a truthful representation of Fort Harrison and its surroundings in 1813.

FORT HARRISON.

I left Terre Haute for Crawfordsville, Indiana, at three o'clock in the morning,[a] checking my luggage (as I thought) to the Junction near Greencastle, the capital of Putnam County, where the Louisville, New Albany, and Chicago Railway crosses that of the Terre Haute and Richmond. By mistake my trunk was checked for Philadelphia, and was not left at the Junction. I found the telegraph operator in his bed half a mile from the station, but he could not send a message with effect before seven o'clock, at which time my luggage would be beyond Indianapolis, making its way toward Philadelphia at the rate of twenty-five miles an hour. The winged electricity was more fleet than the harnessed steam. It headed the fugitive at Richmond, a hundred miles distant, and at two o'clock in the afternoon it was brought back a prisoner to Greencastle Station, much to my relief. I

[a] September 27, 1860.

---

[1] Published by Modesitt and Hager in the year 1848.

think I never saw so much beauty in an old black leather trunk before nor since. Meanwhile I had pretty thoroughly explored Greencastle, chiefly before daylight, when trying to find my way back to the station from the telegraphist's lodgings. Every street appeared to end at a vacant lot. At length, just at dawn, I received directions from an Irishman, with an axe on his shoulder, more explicit than clear. "Is it the dapo' you want?" he inquired. "Yes." "Will, thin," he said, "jist turn down to the lift of the Prisbyterian Church that's *not* finished, and go by the way of the church that *is* finished; turn right and lift as many times as ye plaze, and bedad ye'll be there." Perfectly satisfied I walked on, found the station by accident, waited patiently for the telegraphist, and then went to the village, half a mile distant, to breakfast.

Greencastle is pleasantly situated upon a high table-land, sloping every way, about a mile east of the Walnut Fork of the Eel Run, and then contained between two thousand and three thousand inhabitants. I remained there until three o'clock in the afternoon, when I left for Crawfordsville, twenty-eight miles northward, where I met my family and remained a few days, the guest of the Honorable (afterward Major General) Lewis Wallace, the gallant commander first of the celebrated Eleventh Indiana Regiment in Western Virginia, and afterward of loyal brigades and divisions in Kentucky, Tennessee, and Northern Mississippi, in the late Civil War.[1] There I met the Honorable Isaac Naylor, who was with Harrison at the battle of Tippecanoe. He had been a resident of Crawfordsville since 1833, and for fifteen years was Judge of the Circuit Court. From him I obtained much valuable information concerning the incidents of the battle of Tippecanoe and the preceding march of the army from Vincennes.[2]

J Naylor

I also visited, at Crawfordsville, the late venerable Major Ambrose Whitlock, one of the last survivors of General Wayne's army in the Northwest. He was first under the immediate command of Hamtramck, and afterward served as aid to Wayne, and became lieutenant in the company of which Harrison was captain. Major Whitlock was the founder of Crawfordsville. He was at the head of the Land-office in Indiana, as receiver of the public moneys of the United States, for eight years. William H. Crawford, Monroe's Secretary of the Treasury, appointed him to that station. The office was at Terre Haute. It was finally determined to establish an office in another part of the Territory for the convenience of the settlers, and the selection of the locality was left to the judgment of Major Whitlock. He found in the wilderness near Sugar Creek, in a thickly-wooded dell, a spring of excellent water, and resolved to establish the new Land-office near that desirable fountain. Settlers came. He laid out a village, and named it Crawfordsville, in honor of his friend of the Treasury Department. He resided there ever afterward. His house was upon a gentle eminence eastward of the railway, and the wooded dell and the ever-flowing spring of sweet water formed a part of his premises on the eastern borders of the village. Major Whitlock[3] was ninety-one years of age at the time of my visit, yet his mental faculties

---

[1] For an account of General Wallace's military services, see Lossing's *Pictorial History of the Civil War.*

[2] Judge Naylor was born in Rockingham County, Virginia, on the 30th of July, 1790, and at the age of three years was taken by his family to a settlement near Ruddle's Station, Bourbon County, Kentucky. He removed to Clarke County, Indiana, in 1805, and in 1810 made a voyage to New Orleans on a flat-boat. He repeated it next year, and soon after his return, and while preparing for college, he joined Harrison's army at Vincennes as a volunteer in Captain James Bigger's company. He assisted in the construction of Fort Harrison, participated in the battle of Tippecanoe soon afterward, and, at different times during the war with Great Britain that ensued, served as a volunteer, but was not in any other battle. In 1860 he was elected Judge of the Common Pleas of Montgomery County.

[3] Ambrose Whitlock was born at Bowling Green, Caroline County, Virginia, on the 25th of April, 1769. At an early age he went to Kentucky. He enlisted in Wayne's army, and was with him throughout his Indian campaigns. At one time he was his aid. He was five years in garrison at Fort Washington (Cincinnati) as sergeant. President Adams commissioned him lieutenant in 1800. In 1802 he was appointed assistant military agent at Vincennes, and also assistant paymaster. He became district paymaster in 1805, a first lieutenant in the regular army in 1807, and a captain in 1812.

were quite vigorous. Unlike many soldiers of the past, a large portion of his life was blessed with an affluence of health and fortune.

On the evening of a sultry day, the last one of September, we left Crawfordsville for Lafayette, Indiana, twenty-eight miles northward, with the intention of visiting the Tippecanoe battle-ground the next morning. The country through which we passed for the first few miles was hilly, and heavily timbered, and the foliage was beginning to assume the gorgeous hues of autumn. It was the first evidence we had seen of the actual departure of summer, for nearly all September had been more like August in temperature, than itself. We soon reached a small prairie, the first we had seen, and at eight o'clock arrived at Lafayette. The town, containing full ten thousand inhabitants, was all alive with

political excitement, the "Douglas Democrats" and the "Republicans"[1] both holding public meetings there. The former, convened at a hotel, was addressed by Herschel V. Johnson, of Georgia, the "Douglas" candidate for the Vice-Presidency of the United States; the latter, held in the court-house, was addressed by Mr. Howard, member of Congress from Michigan, whom I had met a few days before at the table of Senator Lane, of Crawfordsville. Torch-light processions of the "Wide-awakes" and the "Little Giants"[2] followed the speeches; and as they marched and countermarched in the same streets at the same time, they became so entangled to the eye of the spectator that it was difficult for a partisan to recognize his own political representative in the moving illumination. This was followed by drum-beatings and huzzas, which were kept up until midnight.

He relinquished his rank in the line in June, 1814, and in May, 1815, was appointed deputy paymaster general of the district composed of Kentucky, Illinois, and Indiana. He was disbanded in 1816, having served in the army twenty-three years and a half, and attained to the rank of major. He was never in military service afterward. After serving eight years as receiver of the public moneys in Indiana, he was dismissed by General Jackson to make room for some one else. It is supposed that not half a dozen soldiers of Wayne's army now (1867) survive. In the possession of Mr. Dillon at Indianapolis I saw a daguerreotype of Martin Huckleberry, one of Wayne's army, then (September, 1860) just taken from life; and in Bangor, Maine, I saw in November, 1860, Henry Van Meter, a colored man, over ninety years of age, who was also in "Mad Anthony's" army. I am indebted to General Wallace for the portrait of Major Whitlock, from which this engraving was made. It was taken when he was in his ninety-first year. He died at his residence in Crawfordsville on the 26th of June, 1863, when over ninety-four years of age.

[1] There was a schism in the great Democratic party, so-called, in the spring of 1860, when one portion nominated Stephen A. Douglas, of Illinois, for the Presidency, and were called the "Douglas Democrats," and the other portion nominated John C. Breckinridge, of Kentucky, then the Vice-President of the United States, and were known as the "Breckinridge Democrats." Opposed to the entire Democratic party was the Republican, a political organization of a few years' standing, composed of men of all the old parties, whose leading distinctive object was the prevention of the extension of slavery beyond the states and Territories in which it already existed. This party had nominated Abraham Lincoln, of Illinois, for President. A fourth party, professedly conservative, and calling themselves the Union party, nominated John Bell, of Tennessee, for President, and Edward Everett, of Massachusetts, for Vice-President. They were frequently called the Bell-Everett party. At the election in November, 1860, these four candidates were supported by their respective friends. Mr. Lincoln was elected. Mr. Douglas died in the city of Chicago early in the following June. Mr. Bell had already declared his affiliation with rebels in arms against the government; while Mr. Breckinridge, a lately-chosen senator from Kentucky, only waited for the close of the extraordinary session of Congress, held in July, and the payment of his salary from the Treasury of the United States, to openly declare himself an enemy to that country, and become a traitor by taking up arms to overthrow the government.

[2] Republican associations, pledged to the support of the candidates of that party, were formed all over the free-labor states in 1860. They wore round capes, and oftentimes lights on their hats, and assumed the name of "Wide-awakes." They formed the staple of Republican torch-light processions in the autumn of 1860. Mr. Douglas was a short, powerful man. In allusion to his mental strength and shortness in stature, he was called by his admirers the Little Giant. The young men of his party formed associations like the "Wide-awakes," called themselves "Little Giants," and formed the staple of the torch-light processions of the Douglas party in the autumn of 1860.

At Lafayette I met Mr. George Winter, an English artist who has resided many years in Indiana, and had the pleasure of inspecting his fine collection of Indian portraits and scenes painted by him from nature. His collection possesses much historical and ethnological value, and ought to be in the possession of some institution where it might be preserved and the individuals never separated. He was intimately acquainted with many of the characters whose features he has delineated, and he has collected stores of anecdotes and traditions of the aboriginals of the Northwest. The memory of Mr. Winter's kind attentions while we were in Lafayette is very pleasant.

The first day of October dawned brightly, and the temperature of the air was like that of early June. Before sunrise we visited the artesian well of sulphur-water in the public square, the result of a deep search for pure water. A neat pavilion covers it; cups are furnished for the thirsty, and not far off are baths of it for invalids and others.

At an early hour we departed for the battle-ground of Tippecanoe, seven miles northward. We passed over a level and pleasant country most of the way, crossing the railway several times. Within three miles of the battle-ground we crossed the Wabash on a cable-bateau,[1] and watched with interest the perilous fording of the stream just above, near the railway bridge, by a man and woman in a light wagon. Twice they came near being submerged in deep channels, but finally reached the shore with only wet feet. The man saved the ferriage fee of twelve cents.

We arrived at the Battle-ground House at ten o'clock, passing the scene of the conflict just before reaching it. Resting in the cool shadows of the stately trees that still cover the spot, let us turn to the chronicle of the Past and study the events which have made this gentle elevation, overlooking a "wet prairie," classic ground.

Fort Harrison, as we have seen, was completed on the 28th of October. It was garrisoned by a small detachment under Lieutenant-colonel Miller—the "I'll try, sir!" hero of the battle of Niagara, three years later. The main body of the army moved forward the next day,[a] and on the 31st, soon after passing the Big Raccoon Creek, crossed to the western side of the Wabash, near the site of the present village of Montezuma, in Parke County.[2]

[a] October 29, 1811.

There the troops were joined by some of the Kentucky volunteers, under Wells, Owen, and Geiger.[3] Harrison was commander-in-chief by virtue of his office as gov-

---

[1] These were large flat-boats for conveying passengers, teams, and freight. They are pushed across by poles at low water, and at high water are secured and assisted in the passage by a huge cable stretched from shore to shore.

[2] Dillon's *History of Indiana*, page 462.

[3] Having been informed that the Indians were more numerous in his front than he had anticipated, Governor Harrison had sent Colonel Daviess and one or two others to Kentucky to apply for a re-enforcement of five hundred men. Brigadier General Wells immediately ordered out his brigade and beat up for volunteers. The privates hanging back, Wells and several of his officers stepped out, and being joined by some of the file, the volunteers mustered thirty-two men. They elected Colonel F. Geiger as their captain. The reluctance of the men to turn out was owing in part to their scruples, the brigade having been ordered out without orders from the Governor of Kentucky. The governor being at Frankfort, there was no time to consult him.—*Funk's Narrative.*

ernor of the Territory, and Boyd was his next in command. The whole force consisted of nine hundred and ten men, and was composed of two hundred and fifty regulars under Boyd, sixty volunteers from Kentucky, and six hundred Indiana militia. The mounted men, consisting of dragoons and riflemen, amounted to about two hundred and seventy. The command of the dragoons was given to Colonel Daviess, and of the riflemen to General Wells, both having the relative rank of major.

The army was near the Vermilion River on the 2d of November, and there, on the western bank of the Wabash, built a block-house twenty-five feet square, in which eight men were placed, to protect the boats employed in bringing up provisions for the army. On the following day[a] the army moved forward, and on the 5th encamped within eleven miles of the Prophet's town. Harrison had been careful, on the preceding day, to avoid the dangerous passes of Pine Creek, whose banks, for fifteen or twenty miles from its mouth, were immense cliffs of rock, where a few men might dispute the passage of large numbers.[1] [a] November 3, 1811.

From their encampment on the 5th, looking northward, stretched an immense prairie, extending far beyond the limits of vision. It reached to the Illinois at Chicago, the guides asserted. It filled the troops, who had never been on the northwest side of the Wabash, with the greatest astonishment; but their attention was soon drawn from the contemplation of nature to watchfulness against the wiles of their own species. Until now they had seen no Indians, though often discovering their trails. On the following day,[b] when within five or six miles of the Prophet's town, they were seen hovering around the army on every side. The approach [b] November 6. of the troops had become known to the Prophet, and his scouts, numerous and sagacious, watched every step of the invaders. Great caution was now necessary, and the same order of march which Harrison, as Wayne's aid, had planned for that general in 1794,[2] he now adopted. The infantry marched in two columns on both sides of the path, and the dragoons and mounted riflemen in front, rear, and on the flanks. To facilitate the march, and keep the troops in position for a quick and precise formation into battle order in the event of an ambuscade, they were broken into short columns of companies. They had now left the open prairie, and were marching most of the time through open woods, the ground furrowed by ravines. Parties of Indians were continually making their appearance, and Barron and other interpreters tried, but in vain, to speak to their leaders. Finally, when within a mile and a half of the Prophet's town, Toussaint Dubois, of Vincennes, offered to take a message to the mongrel warrior-pontiff. The menaces of the savages were so alarming that he soon turned back, and the army pressed forward toward the Tippecanoe.

The alarmed savages now asked for a parley. It was granted. They assured Harrison that the Prophet had sent back a friendly message by the Delaware and Miami couriers, but that they had gone down the eastern bank, and missed him on his march. They were surprised at his coming so soon, and hoped he would not disturb and frighten their women and children by occupying their town. Harrison assured them that he was ready to have a friendly talk with them, and desired a good place for an encampment. They pointed to a suitable spot back from the Wabash, on the borders of a creek less than a mile northwest from the Prophet's town. Two officers (Majors Taylor and Clarke) were sent with Quarter-master Piatt to examine it. They reported that the situation was excellent. Harrison then parted with the chiefs who had come out to meet him, after an interchange of promises that no hostilities should be commenced until an interview should be held the following day. "I found the ground destined for the encampment," Harrison wrote, " not altogether such as I could wish

---

[1] It was believed that the Indians might make a stand there, as they did in 1780, when General George Rogers Clarke undertook a campaign against the Wabash Indians, and again, in 1790, when Major Hamtramck penetrated that region with a small force as high as the Vermillion River, to make a diversion in favor of General Harmar's expedition on the Maumee. [2] See page 54.

it. It was, indeed, admirably calculated for the encampment of regular troops that were opposed to regulars, but it afforded great facility to the approach of savages. It was a piece of dry oak land, rising about ten feet above the level of a marshy prairie in front (toward the Prophet's town), and nearly twice that height above a similar prairie in the rear, through which, and near to this bank, ran a small stream clothed with willows and other brushwood. Toward the left flank this bench of land widened considerably, but became gradually narrower in the opposite direction, and at the distance of one hundred and fifty yards from the right flank terminated in an abrupt point."[1] No doubt the wily savages recommended this position that they might employ their peculiar mode of warfare advantageously.

The above is a good description of the locality as it appeared when I visited it in the autumn of 1860. It was still covered with the same oaks; on "the front," toward Wabash and Tippecanoe Creek, stretched the same "wet" or frequently overflowed prairie; in "the rear" was the same higher bank, and prairie, and Burnet's Creek; and at the "abrupt point" the Louisville, New Albany, and Chicago Railway strikes the "bench of land," and runs parallel with the common wagon-road along the bank overlooking the "wet prairie." In the annexed sketch, taken from "the abrupt point," looking northeast over the camp-ground, is seen the southern portion of the inclosure of the battle-field, near which Spencer's riflemen were posted, indicated on the plan of the encampment on page 205. The horseman denotes the direction of the wet prairie toward the Prophet's town, and the steep bank seen on the left of the picture has Burnet's Creek flowing at its base, and was still "clothed with willows," shrubbery, and vines.

VIEW AT TIPPECANOE BATTLE-GROUND.

Harrison arranged his camp with care on the afternoon of the 6th of November, in the form of an irregular parallelogram, on account of the slope of the ground. On the front was a battalion of United States infantry, under Major George Rogers Clarke Floyd,[2] flanked on the left by one company, and on the right by two companies of Indiana militia, under Colonel Joseph Bartholomew.[3] In the rear was a battalion of United States infantry, under Captain William C. Baen,[4] acting as major, with Captain Robert C. Barton,[5] of the regulars, in immediate command. These were supported on the right by four companies of Indiana militia, led respectively by Captains

---

[1] Harrison's dispatch to the Secretary of War from Vincennes, November 18, 1811.
[2] Was appointed Captain of the Seventh Infantry in 1808, and Major of the Fourth Infantry in 1810. In August, 1812, he was promoted to Lieutenant Colonel of Seventh Infantry, and resigned in April, 1813.
[3] Afterward Lieutenant Colonel of Indiana Volunteers under General Harrison. He was appointed United States Major General of the Indiana Territory in 1816.
[4] Appointed Captain of the Fourth Infantry in 1808, and died of his wounds received in the battle of Tippecanoe on the 9th of November, 1811.
[5] First Lieutenant in Fourth Infantry in 1808, promoted to captain in 1809, and resigned in September, 1812.

| Harrison's Instructions. | The Camp in Repose. | The Indians in Commotion. | The Prophet's Treachery. |

Josiah Snelling, Jr.,[1] John Posey, Thomas Scott, and Jacob Warrick, the whole commanded by Lieutenant Colonel Luke Decker. The right flank, eighty yards wide, was filled with mounted riflemen, under Captain Spear Spencer. The left, about one hundred and fifty yards in extent, was composed of mounted riflemen, under Major General Samuel Wells,[2] commanding as major, and led by Colonels Frederick Geiger[3] and David Robb, as captains. Two troops of dragoons, under Colonel Joseph H. Daviess, acting as major, were stationed in the rear of the front line near the left flank; and at a right angle with these companies, in the rear of the left flank, was a troop of cavalry as a reserve, under Captain Benjamin Parke.[4] Wagons, baggage, officers' tents, etc., were in the centre.

Having completed the arrangement of his camp and supped, Harrison summoned the field-officers to his tent by a signal, and gave them instructions. He ordered that each corps that formed the exterior line of the camp should hold its ground, in case of an attack, until relieved. In the event of a night attack, the cavalry were to parade dismounted, with their pistols in their belts, and act as a *corps de reserve*. Two captains' guards, of forty-two privates each, and two subalterns', of twenty each, were detailed to defend the camp. The whole were commanded by the field-officer of the day. Thus prepared, the whole camp, except the sentinels and guards, were soon soundly sleeping. There was a slight drizzle of rain at intervals, and the darkness was intense, except occasionally when the clouds parted and faint moonlight came through.

Quite different was the condition of affairs in the Indian camp. There was no sleep there. Both parties had agreed to parley before fighting, and there should have been no excitement; but the dusky foe of the white man had no respect for truces. The unprincipled Prophet, surrounded by his dupes, prepared for treachery and murder as soon as the curtain of night had fallen upon the land.[5] He brought out the Magic Bowl. In one hand he held the sacred torch, or "Medean fire," in the other a string of beans which he called holy, and were accounted to be miraculous in their effect when touched. His followers were all required to touch this talisman and be made invulnerable, and then to take an oath to exterminate the pale-faces. When this was accomplished, the Prophet went through a long series of incantations and mystical movements; then turning to his highly-excited band, about seven hundred in number, he told them that the time to attack the white men had come. "They are in your power," he said, holding up the holy beans as a reminder of their oath. "They sleep now, and will never awake. The Great Spirit will give light to us, and darkness to the white men. Their bullets shall not harm us; your weapons shall be al-

---

[1] First Lieutenant in Fourth Infantry in 1808, regimental paymaster in April, 1809, and promoted to captain in June the same year. He was breveted a major for gallantry at Brownstown, in August, 1812. In April, 1813, was appointed assistant inspector general, with the rank of major, and in February, 1814, was commissioned Lieutenant Colonel of the Fourth Regiment of Riflemen. In April he received the commission of inspector general, with the rank of colonel. He was distinguished at Lyon's Creek, on the Chippewa, under General Bissell; and when the army was placed on a peace footing in 1815 he was retained as Lieutenant Colonel of the Sixth Infantry. He was promoted to Colonel of the Fifth in 1819. He died at Washington City on the 20th of August, 1828.

[2] He was a major in Adair's battalion of mounted riflemen, General Charles Scott's division of Kentucky Volunteers, in 1793. He was afterward made Major General of the Kentucky Militia. He was appointed Colonel of the Seventeenth Regiment of Infantry in March, 1812, and was disbanded in May, 1814.

[3] He afterward commanded a company of Louisville Volunteers under Major General Harrison.

[4] Parke was promoted to major on this field of action by Governor Harrison for his gallant conduct. His company was discharged in November, 1812.

[5] It is believed that the treachery of the Indians did not take the shape of an attack on Harrison's camp until late that evening, it having been primarily arranged that they should meet the governor in council, and appear to agree to his terms. At the close the chiefs were to retire to their warriors, when two Winnebagoes, selected for the purpose, were to kill the governor, and give the signal for the uprising of the Indians.—See *Indian Biography*, by Samuel G. Drake, 1832; 12mo, page 337.

ways fatal." Then followed war-songs and dances, until the Indians, wrought up to a perfect frenzy, rushed forth to attack Harrison's camp without any leaders. Stealthily they crept through the long grass of the prairie in the deep gloom, intending to surround their enemy's position, kill the sentinels, rush into the camp, and massacre all.[1]

Harrison was in the habit of rising at four o'clock in the morning, calling his troops to arms, and keeping them so until broad daylight. On the morning of the 7th of November he was just pulling on his boots at the usual hour, when a single gun was fired by a sentinel at the northwest angle of the camp, near the bank of Burnet's Creek. This was instantly followed by the horrid yells of numerous savages in that quarter, who opened a murderous fire upon the companies of Baen and Geiger that formed that angle. The foe had been creeping up stealthily to tomahawk the sentinels, but the sharp eyes of one of them had detected the moving savage in the gloom, and fired upon him with fatal effect.[2] Their assault was furious, and in their frenzy several Indians penetrated through the lines, but never to return.

The whole camp was soon awakened by demon yells and a cry to arms, and the officers, with all possible speed and precision, in the faint light of smouldering fires, placed their men in battle order. These fires were then extinguished, for they were more useful to the assailants than to the assailed. Nineteen twentieths of the troops had never been in battle, yet, considering the alarming circumstances of the attack, their conduct was cool and gallant, and very little noise or confusion followed such a sudden awaking from sleep and call to defend life. The most of them were in line before they were fired upon, but some were compelled to fight defensively at the doors of their tents.

Harrison called for his horse—a fine white charger—but in affright the animal had pulled up the stake that held his tether, and could not be found. The governor immediately mounted a fine bay horse that stood snorting near, and with his aid, Colonel Owen, hastened to the angle of the camp where the attack was first made.[3] He found that Barton's company had suffered severely, and the left of Geiger's was entirely broken. He immediately ordered Cook's company and that of the late Captain Wentworth, under Lieutenant Peters, to be brought up from the centre of the rear line, where the ground was much more defensible, and form across the angle in support of Barton and Geiger. At that moment the governor's attention was directed to firing at the northeast angle of the camp, where a small company of United States riflemen, armed with muskets, and the companies of Baen, Snelling, and Prescott, of the Fourth Regiment, were stationed. There he found Major Daviess forming the dragoons in the rear of those companies. Observing heavy firing from some trees about twenty paces in front of them, he directed the major to dislodge them with a part of his dragoons. "Unfortunately," says Harrison in his dispatch to the Secretary of War, "the major's gallantry determined him to execute the order with a smaller force than was sufficient, which enabled the enemy to avoid him in front and

---

[1] During the night a negro camp follower who had been missed from duty was found lurking near the governor's marquee, and arrested. He was tried after the battle by a drum-head court-martial, and was convicted of having deserted to the enemy, and returned for the purpose of murdering the governor. He was sentenced to be hung immediately, but was saved in consequence of the kindness of heart of the governor. His imploring eyes touched Harrison's tender feelings, and he referred the matter to the commissioned officers present. Some were for his immediate execution, when Snelling said, "Brave comrades, let us save him. The wretch deserves to die; but as our commander, whose life was more particularly his object, is willing to spare him, let us also forgive him. I hope, at least, that every officer of the Fourth Regiment will be on the side of mercy." Ben was saved.—Harrison's letter to Governor Scott, of Kentucky, cited by Hall, page 149. Captain Funk, in his narrative, says the negro was the driver of Governor Harrison's cart, and that he informed the Indians that the white people had no cannon with them. Cannon were the dread of the savages. Doubtless this information caused a change in the policy mentioned in note 5, page 203, and caused the savages to conclude to attack the pale-faces.

[2] Judge Naylor, of Crawfordsville, already mentioned as a participant in the battle, informed me that the name of the sentinel who first fired and gave the alarm was Stephen Mars, of Kentucky. He fired, and fled to the camp, but was shot before reaching it.

[3] Statement of Judge Naylor. Captain Funk says that Harrison's own white horse was ridden by Major Taylor, the general's aid, against his wishes.

attack him on his flanks. The major was mortally wounded,[1] and his party driven back."[2] Harrison immediately promoted Captain Parke to Daviess's rank just as intelligence was brought to him that Captain Snelling, with his company of regulars, had driven the savages from their murderous position with heavy loss.

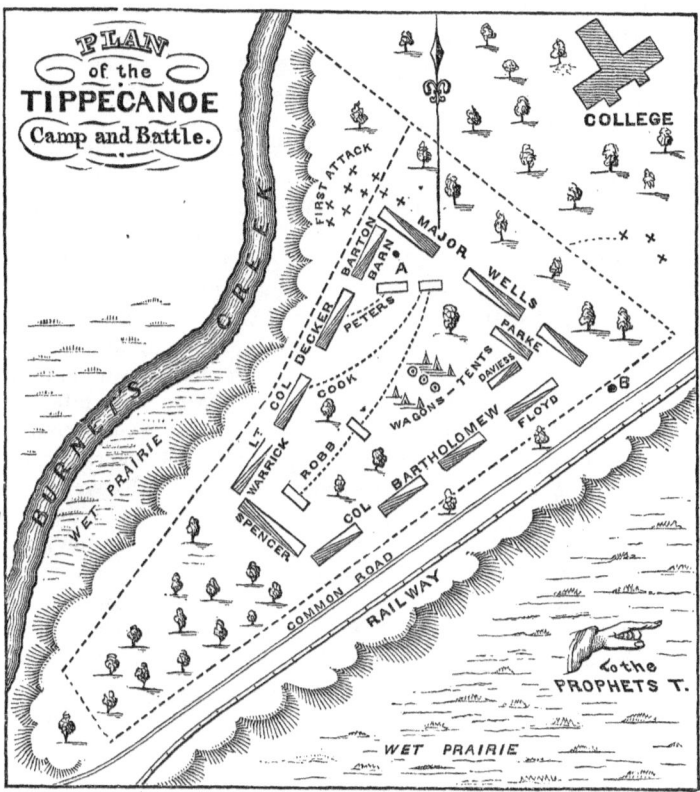

The battle now became more general. The Indians attacked the camp on the whole front and both flanks, and a portion of the rear line. They fell with great severity upon Spencer's mounted riflemen on the right and the right section of Warrick's company, which formed the southwest angle of the encampment. Spencer and his lieutenant were killed, and Warrick was mortally wounded, and yet their men gallantly maintained their position. They were speedily re-enforced by Robb's riflemen, who had been driven or ordered by mistake from their position on the left flank toward the centre of the camp, and at the same time Prescott's company of the Fourth Regiment was ordered to fill the space vacated by the riflemen, the grand object being to maintain the lines of the camp unbroken until daylight, when the as-

[1] The letter B in the plan marks the spot where Daviess fell. It was near an oak whose top was blown off in a gale a few years ago. It is seen in the sketch of the battle-ground as it appeared in 1860, printed on page 209.
[2] Daviess was gallant and impatient of restraint. One of his party was General Washington Johns, of Vincennes, a quarter-master of the dragoons, who was intimate with Harrison. Daviess sent him to the governor when the Indians first made the attack at this point, asking permission to go out on foot and charge the foe. "Tell Major Daviess to be patient; he shall have an honorable station before the battle is over," Harrison replied. In a few moments Daviess repeated the request, and the governor made the same reply. Again he repeated it, when Harrison said, "Tell Major Daviess he has heard my opinion twice; he may now use his own discretion." The gallant major, with only twenty picked men, instantly charged beyond the lines on foot, and was mortally wounded. He was a conspicuous mark in the gloom, because he wore a white blanket coat.—Statements of Judge Naylor and Captain Funk. The latter says Colonel Daviess's horse was a roan bought of Frank Moore, of Louisville. The Indians were masked by some fallen timber. Captain Funk attended him at about nine o'clock; assisted in changing his clothes, and dressing his wounds. He was shot between the right hip and ribs, and it was believed that the fatal bullet proceeded from the ranks of his friends firing in the gloom. Daviess was afraid the expedition might be driven away hastily, and leave those wounded behind. He exacted a promise from Captain Funk that in no event would he leave him to fall into the hands of the savages.

sailed would be able to make a general charge upon a visible foe. To do this required great activity on the part of the commander. Harrison was constantly riding from point to point within the camp, and kept the assailed positions re-enforced. Finally, when the day dawned, he discovered the larger portion of the Indians to be on the two flanks. He accordingly strengthened these, and was about to order the cavalry, under Parke, to charge upon the foe on the left, when Major Wells, not understanding Harrison's intentions, led the infantry to perform that duty. It was executed gallantly and effectually. The Indians were driven at the point of the bayonet, and the dragoons pursued them into the wet prairies on both sides of the ridge on which the battle was fought. The ground was too soft for the horsemen to pursue, and the savages escaped. Meanwhile the Indians had been charged and put to flight on the right flank, and had also taken refuge in the marshy ground, chiefly on the side of Burnet's Creek, where they were sheltered from view.[1]

Looking eastward from the site of the battle-ground over the "wet prairie" (now a fenced and cultivated plain) toward the Wabash, the visitor will see a range of very gentle hills, covered with woods. On one of these the Prophet stood while the battle was raging on that dark November morning, at a safe distance from danger, singing a war-song and performing some protracted religious mummeries. When told that his followers were falling before the bullets of the white men, he said, "Fight on, it will soon be as I told you." When at last the fugitive warriors of many tribes—Shawnoese, Wyandots, Kickapoos, Ottawas, Chippewas, Pottawatomies, Winnebagoes, Sacs, and a few Miamis—lost their faith, and covered the Prophet with reproaches, he cunningly told them that his predictions had failed because, during his incantations, his wife touched the sacred vessels and broke the charm! Even Indian superstition and credulity could not accept that transparent falsehood for an excuse, and the impostor was deserted by his disappointed followers, and compelled to take refuge with a small band of Wyandots on Wild-cat Creek. The foe had scattered in all directions into places where the white man could not well follow.

> "Sound, sound the charge! spur, spur the steed,
> And swift the fugitives pursue:
> 'Tis vain; rein in—your utmost speed
> Could not o'ertake the recreant crew.
> In lowland marsh, in dell or cave,
> Each Indian sought his life to save;
> Whence peering forth, with fear and ire,
> He saw his Prophet's town on fire."

When, on the day after the battle,[a] Harrison and his army advanced upon the Prophet's town, they found it deserted. After getting all the copper kettles they could find, and as much beans and corn as they could carry away, they applied the torch, and the village and a large quantity of corn were speedily reduced to ashes. Six days afterward the army, bearing the wounded in twenty-two wagons, reached Fort Harrison on its return to Vincennes. Captain Snelling, with his company of regulars, was left to garrison the fort, and, on the 18th of the month, the remainder of the army, excepting some volunteers disbanded the day before, were at Fort Knox, in the capital of the Indiana Territory. The immediate result of the expedition was to scatter the Prophet's warriors on the Wabash, frustrate the scheme of Tecumtha, and give temporary relief to the settlers in Indiana.

Tecumtha, who was really a great man (while the Prophet was a cunning demagogue and cheat—a tool in the hands of his brother), was absent among the South-

[a] November 8, 1811.

---

[1] Harrison's dispatch to Dr. Eustis, Secretary of War, November 18, 1811; M'Afee's *History of the Late War in the Western Country*, pages 22–30; Onderdonk's MS. *Life of Tecumseh*; Drake's *Indian Biography*; Hall's *Life of Harrison*, pages 132–146; Dillon's *History of Indiana*, pages 447–472; statements to the author by Judge Naylor, of Crawfordsville, Indiana, and Major Funk, of Kentucky.

The 7th was passed in burying the dead and strengthening the encampment, for rumors were plenty that Tecumtha was coming to the aid of his brother with a thousand warriors. "Night," says Captain Funk, "found every man mounting guard, without food, fire, or light, and in a drizzly rain. The Indian dogs, during the dark hours, produced frequent alarms by prowling in search of carrion about the sentinels."

ern Indians when the battle of Tippecanoe occurred. He returned soon afterward, and found all his schemes frustrated by the folly of the Prophet. The sudden unpopularity of the impostor deprived him of a strong instrument in the construction of his confederacy, to which his life and labors had been long directed with the zeal of a true patriot. He saw his brightest visions dissipated in a moment. Mortified, vexed, and exasperated, and failing to obtain the acquiescence of Governor Harrison in his proposition to visit the President with a deputation of chiefs, he abandoned all thoughts of peace, and became a firm ally of the British.[1]

In the battle of Tippecanoe Harrison lost, in killed and wounded, one hundred and eighty-eight.[2] It was a hard-fought and well-fought battle, and attested both the skill and bravery of Harrison.[3] The expediency and conduct of the campaign were topics for much discussion, and elicited not a little severity of censure from the opponents of the administration and of war. Harrison was a personal and political friend of President Madison, and this gave license to the opposition to make him a target for denunciatory volleys. His prudence, his patriotism, his military skill, his courage, were all brought in question; and some claimed the chaplet of fame for the victory gained, for the brow of Colonel Boyd.[4] But time, the great healer of dissen-

[1] Elkswatawa (the Prophet) now started on a recruiting-tour among the various tribes on the Upper Lakes and Mississippi, all of which he visited with astonishing success. He entered the villages of his most inveterate enemies, and of others who had not even heard his name, and so manœuvred as to make his mystery-fire and sacred string of beans a safe passport through all their settlements. He enlisted some eight or ten thousand warriors to fight the battles of his brother. He carried into every wigwam an image of a dead person the size of life, which was ingeniously made of some light material, and kept concealed under bandages of thin white muslin, and not to be opened to public scrutiny. Of this he made great mystery, and got his recruits to swear by touching the string of white beans attached to its neck. By his extraordinary cunning he carried terror wherever he went. If they did not obey him he threatened to make the earth tremble to its centre and darken the light of the sun. Nature seemed to conspire with the Prophet, for at this very time an earthquake extended along the Mississippi, demolishing houses and settling the ground. A comet, too, appeared in the north with fearful length of tail, and seemed a harbinger to the fulfillment of the predictions of the Prophet. The sun was eclipsed, to the great terror of the savages, but, as the Prophet declared, it resumed its wonted brightness because of his intercession. But while in the full tide of success, two rival chiefs of his own tribe dogged the footsteps of the Prophet, denounced him as an impostor, and exposed his tricks.—Onderdonk's MS. *Life of Tecumseh.*

[2] He lost, in killed and wounded, ten officers, namely, one aid-de-camp, one major, three captains, two subalterns, one sergeant, and two corporals. Judge Naylor told me that the sergeant and himself were asleep at the same fire when the attack commenced, and that a bullet from an Indian's musket killed him as he was springing to his feet. Colonel Abraham Owen, Harrison's aid-de-camp, was killed early in the engagement, when he and the governor rode to the point of first attack. Letter A in the plan on page 205 marks the spot where he fell. He rode a white horse, and this made him a mark for the Indians. The enemies of Harrison afterward asserted that the latter, to conceal himself, had exchanged horses with Owen. The fact was as I have stated—his own horse had scampered away in a fright, and he had mounted the first one near, which happened to be a dark-colored one. The horse Owen rode was his own. That officer had joined him as a private of Geiger's company, and had been accepted as his volunteer aid. He was a good citizen and a brave soldier, and had been a member of the Kentucky Legislature.

Among the mortally wounded, and who died before Harrison made his report, was Major Daviess, and Captains Baen and Warrick. Daviess, commonly called "Joe Daviess," was the most brilliant man in that little army, and was as brave as he was brilliant. He was a Virginian by birth, and at the time of his death was only thirty-seven years of age. He took a leading part against Aaron Burr in the West in 1806. Previous to that he had been a successful opponent of the Nicholases in political movements, they being Republicans and he a Federalist. He was a great student, very abstemious, used a hewn block for a pillow, and a bed nearly as hard. His oratory was powerful, and Wilson C. Nicholas, the leader of that art in Kentucky at the close of the last century, was often compelled to bend to his young rival. Alluding to this power, a Tennessee poet (Robert Mack) wrote as follows, in a rhyming eulogy, after his death:

"Emerging from his studious shed,
   Behold, behold him rise!
All Henry bursting from his tongue,
   And Marshall from his eyes.
Chained by the magic of his voice,
   Fierce party spirit stood;
E'en prejudice almost gave way,
   While with resistless reasoning's sway
O'er far-famed Nicholas he rolled
   The oratorial flood."

In 1801, '02 Mr. Daviess went to Washington City on professional business, and was the first Western lawyer who ever appeared in the Supreme Court of the United States. Mr. Jefferson made him Attorney of the United States for the District of Kentucky. He married a sister of Chief Justice Marshall, and always held a front rank in his profession. Daviess County, Kentucky, was named in his honor. He was wounded at about five o'clock in the morning of the 7th of November, and survived until one o'clock in the afternoon of the same day. He was nearly six feet high, vigorous and athletic. He was born in Bedford County, Virginia, on the 4th of March, 1774.

[3] Harrison was continually exposed during the action, but escaped unhurt. A bullet passed through his hat. Major Henry Hurst, who was one of his aids-de-camp (and an active one) in this battle, and was the only lawyer who resided in Indiana while it was a Territory, died at Jeffersonville, on the Ohio, opposite Louisville, where he had lived forty years, on the 1st of January, 1855, in the eighty-fifth year of his age.

[4] In his dispatch to the Secretary of War, Harrison said of Colonel Boyd: "The whole of the infantry formed a small

sions, corrector of errors, and destroyer of party and personal animosities, has long since silenced the voice of detraction; and the verdict of his countrymen to-day, as they study the record dispassionately, is coincident with that of his soldiers at the time, and of the Kentucky Legislature shortly afterward, who, on motion of the late venerable member of Congress, John J. Crittenden, resolved, "That in the late campaign against the Indians on the Wabash, Governor W. H. Harrison has, in the opinion of this Legislature, behaved like a hero, a patriot, and a general; and that for his cool, deliberate, skillful, and gallant conduct in the late battle of Tippecanoe, he deserves the warmest thanks of the nation." History, art, and song[1] made that event the theme for pen, pencil, and voice; and when, thirty years afterward, the leader of the fray was a candidate for the Presidency of the United States, he was every where known by the familiar title of Old Tippecanoe. His partisans erected log-cabins in towns and cities, and in them sang in chorus,

> "Hurrah for the father of all the green West,
> For the Buckeye who follows the plow!
> The foemen in terror his valor confessed,
> And we'll honor the conqueror now.
> His country assailed in the darkest of days,
> To her rescue impatient he flew;
> The war-whoop's fell blast, and the rifle's red blaze,
> But awakened Old Tippecanoe."

The battle-field of Tippecanoe has become classic ground. It belonged to the State of Indiana, and had been inclosed with a rude wooden fence for several years, which, we were told, was soon to give place to an iron one. The inclosure comprised seven acres. It was a beautiful spot. The ground, gently undulating, and sloping from *Battle-ground City*[2] (an infant in years and size), was still covered with the noble oaks. In the sketch here given, made when I visited it in October, 1860, the spectator is supposed to be standing just northward of the place where Major Wells's line, on the left flank, was formed (see a plan of the camp on page 205), and looking southwest over the once wet prairie toward the Wabash. On the extreme left, in the distance, is seen the gentle eminence on which the Prophet stood during the battle, singing his war-songs. Farther to the right, near the row of posts, is a large tree with the top broken off. It marks the spot near which Daviess fell. There is only space enough between it and the verge of the prairie below for the common road and the railway.

---

brigade, under the immediate orders of Colonel Boyd. The colonel throughout the action manifested equal zeal and bravery in carrying into execution my orders, in keeping the men to their posts, and exhorting them to fight with valor." Judge Naylor informed me that he heard Colonel Boyd frequently cry out, "Huzzah! my sons of gold, the day is ours!"

[1] Among the many "verses composed on the occasion of the battle of Tippecanoe," none were more popular in the West, for a long time, than a string of solemn doggerel, printed on a small broadside of rough paper, at Frankfort, Kentucky. A copy lies before me. It is entitled, "A Bloody Battle between the United States Troops, under the command of Governor Harrison, and several Tribes of Indians, near the Prophet's Town, November 7, 1811." At the head is a rude wood-cut, evidently made by an amateur for some other scene, for a camp exhibits two cannon. A little distance off are seen three Indians. I give a fac-simile of this remarkable "illustration" (of reduced size), as a specimen of the art in the West at that time. The following specimen of the "poetry" shows a "fitness of things" between the rhyme and the picture:

> "Harrison, a commander of great renown,
> Led on our troops near by the Prophet's town;
> After evils o'ercome and obstructions past,
> Near this savage town they encamped at last."

Readers anxious to peruse the other seven verses will find the whole "poem" in the third volume of M'Carty's *National Song-book*, page 440.

[2] This village is the child of a college located there, called *The Battle-ground Institute*, devoted to the education of both sexes. It was founded in 1858, and the village was soon afterward laid out. Both college and "city" are flourishing. The former was under the charge of Rev. E. H. Staley when I was there, and contained almost three hundred pupils. The college is situated in a grove of oaks on the upper border of the battle-ground, and the shaded inclosure forms a delightful promenade and place for out-of-door study. Several students, with their books, were seen under the trees when we were there.

TIPPECANOE BATTLE-GROUND IN 1860.

We dined at the Battle-ground House, and departed for Chicago, one hundred and forty miles distant, at three o'clock in the afternoon. The journey was one of real pleasure. Soon after leaving, we entered a prairie, and traversed its dead level for seventy miles, passing some little villages on the way. It was rich with verdure and late prairie-flowers, and the broad expanse was dotted here and there in every direction, as far as the eye could comprehend, with clumps of tall trees and shrubbery, which appeared like islands in the midst of a vast green sea. Toward evening heavy black clouds gathered in the northwestern sky, and when we approached Michigan City that stands among the sand dunes at the head of Lake Michigan, just at sunset, we ran into a heavy thunder-shower that was sweeping around the majestic southern curve of that inland sea. Darkness soon came on, and as we approached Chicago, late in the evening, we encountered another shower. On lake and prairie the lightning descended in frequent streams, and the thunder roared fearfully above the din of the dashing railway train. But all was serene when we arrived at Chicago. The stars were beaming brightly, and a young moon was just dipping its horn below the great prairie on the west. It had been a day of exciting pleasure as well as fatigue, and the night at the Richmond House was one of sweet repose for us all.

O

CHAPTER XI.

"Hark! the peal of war is rung;
Hark! the song for battle's sung;
Firm be every bosom strung,
And every soldier ready.
On to Quebec's embattled halls!
Who will pause when glory calls?
Charge, soldiers! charge its lofty walls,
And storm its strong artillery!
Firm as our native hills we'll stand,
And should the lords of Europe land,
We'll meet them on the farthest strand;
We'll conquer or we'll die!"

FROM THE TRENTON TRUE AMERICAN.

INTELLIGENCE of the battle of Tippecanoe reached Washington City soon after the Twelfth Congress had assembled, and produced a profound sensation in that body. They had been convened by proclamation a month earlier[a] than the regular day of meeting. The affairs of the country were approaching a crisis, and this session was to be the most important of any since the establishment of the nation. Both political parties came fully armed and well prepared for a desperate conflict. The Federalists were in a hopeless minority in both houses, but were strong in materials. They had but six members in the Senate, where even Massachusetts, the home of the "Essex Junto," was represented by a Democrat in the person of the veteran Joseph B. Varnum, the speaker of the last House, who had been chosen to supersede Timothy Pickering.[1] Giles, of Virginia, having joined a faction similar to Randolph's "Quids" in its relations to the administration, Wm. H. Crawford, of Georgia, became the leader in the Senate of the dominant party proper, and was ably supported by Campbell, of Tennessee.

In the lower House the Federalists had but thirty-six members, whose great leader was Quincy, of Massachusetts, ably supported by Key, of Maryland, Chittenden, of Vermont, and Emott, of New York. Connecticut and Rhode Island were still numbered among the Federal states; but in the remainder of New England and the State of New York the Democrats had a decided majority. There were but ten Federalists for all the states south of Pennsylvania and Delaware. The more radical members of the last Congress had been re-elected; and in Cheves, Calhoun and Lowndes, of South Carolina, Clay, of Kentucky, and Grundy, of Tennessee—all young men and full of vigor—appeared not only Democratic members of ability, but enthusiastic champions of war with Great Britain. With these came the veteran Sevier, the hero

[a] November 4, 1811.

---

[1] The contest for power between the Federalists and Democrats of Massachusetts had been long and bitter. In 1811 the latter succeeded in electing their candidate for governor (Elbridge Gerry), and a majority of both houses of the Legislature. In order to secure the election of United States senators in the future, it was important to perpetuate this possession of power, and measures were taken to retain a Democratic majority in the State Senate in all future years. The senatorial districts had been formed without any division of counties. This arrangement, for the purpose alluded to, was now disturbed. The Legislature proceeded to rearrange the senatorial districts of the state. They divided counties in opposition to the protests and strong constitutional arguments of the Federalists; and those of Essex and Worcester were so divided as to form a Democratic district in each of those Federal counties, without any apparent regard to convenience or propriety. The work was sanctioned, and became law by the signature of Governor Gerry. He probably had no other hand in the matter, yet he received most severe castigations from the opposition.

In Essex County, the arrangement of the district in its relation to the towns was singular and absurd. Russell, the veteran editor of the *Boston Centinel*, who had fought against the scheme valiantly, took a map of that county and des-

Henry Clay chosen Speaker.   The President's feeble War-trumpet.   History of the Gerry-mander.

of King's Mountain, and first Governor of Tennessee—"stiff and grim as an Indian arrow; not speaking, but looking daggers."[1] The young and ardent members, with the imperious Clay at their head, immediately took the lead; and the warlike temper of the House was manifested by the election of Mr. Clay to the speakershp by the decided vote of seventy-five, against thirty-eight given for William Bibb, the peace candidate, and a dozen scattering votes.[2] A determination that inactivity and indecision should no longer be the policy of the administration was soon manifested, and the timid President Madison found himself, as the standard-bearer of his party, surrounded, like a cautious sachem, with irrepressible young warriors eager for a fray.

The President, in his annual message,[a] sounded a war-trumpet, though rather feebly. After alluding to the condition of the national defenses, he said, "I must now add, that the period has arrived which claims from the legislative guardians of the national rights a system of more ample provision for maintaining them. Notwithstanding the scrupulous justice, the protracted moderation, and the multiplied efforts on the part of the United States, to substitute for the accumulating dangers to the peace of

[a] November 5, 1811.

THE GERRY-MANDER.

ignated by particular coloring the towns thus selected, and hung it on the wall of his editorial room. One day Gilbert Stuart, the eminent painter, looked at the map, and said the towns which Russell had thus distinguished resembled some monstrous animal. He took a pencil, and with a few touches added what might represent a head, wings, claws, and tail. "There," Stuart said, "that will do for a salamander." Russell, who was busy with his pen, looked up at the hideous figure, and exclaimed, "Salamander! call it *Gerrymander!* The word was immediately adopted into the political vocabulary as a term of reproach to the Democratic Legislature.—See *Specimens of Newspaper Literature, with Personal Memoirs, Anecdotes, and Reminiscences,* by Joseph T. Buckingham, ii., 91.

Stuart's monstrous figure of the *Gerry-mander* was presented upon a broadside containing a natural and political history of the animal, and hawked about the country. From one of these before me, kindly placed in my possession by the late Edward Everett, I copied the picture given in this note, which is about one half the size of the original.

After giving some ludicrous guesses as to its character and origin—whether it was the genuine *Basilisk,* the *Serpens Monocephalus* of Pliny, the *Griffin* of romance, the *Great Red Dragon* or *Apollyon* of Bunyan, or the *Monstrum Horrendum* of Virgil—the writer of the natural history of the Gerry-mander says that the learned Dr. Watergruel proved it to be a species of salamander, engendered partly by the devil in the fervid heats of party strife. "But," he says, "as this creature has been engendered and brought forth under the sublimest auspices, the doctor proposes that a name should be given to it expressive of its genus, at the same time conveying an elegant and very appropriate compliment to his excellency the governor, who is known to be the zealous patron of whatever is new, astonishing, and erratic, especially of domestic growth and manufacture. For these reasons, and other valuable considerations, the doctor has decreed this monster shall be denominated a GERRY-MANDER."   [1] Hildreth.

[2] Mr. Clay was elected on the first ballot. The vote stood—for Clay, 75; for Bibb, 38; for Bassett, of Virginia, 1; for Nelson, of Virginia, 2; and for Macon, of North Carolina, 3. Mr. Clay was declared duly elected speaker. A corre-

the two countries all the mutual advantages of re-established friendship and confidence, we have seen that the British Cabinet perseveres not only in withholding a remedy for other wrongs, so long and so loudly calling for it, but in the execution, brought home to the threshold of our territory, of measures which, under existing circumstances, have the character as well as the effects of war on our lawful commerce. With this evidence of hostile inflexibility in trampling on rights which no independent nation can relinquish, Congress will feel the duty of putting the United States into an armor and an attitude demanded by the crisis, and corresponding with the national spirit and expectations." Yet Mr. Madison, like Mr. Jefferson, was anxious to avoid war, if possible.

A war-note in a higher key was speedily sounded by the Committee on Foreign Relations, of which Peter P. Porter, of New York, was chairman. They made a short but energetic report on the 29th of November.[a] They referred in severe terms to the wrongs which for more than five years the commerce of the United States had suffered from the operations of the conflict for power between England and France—wrongs inaugurated by British orders in Council, and imitated, in retaliation, by French decrees. They charged Great Britain with the crime of persisting in the infliction of these wrongs after France, by abandoning her decrees, so far as the United States were concerned, had led the way toward justice to neutrals. They then arraigned Great Britain upon a more serious charge—that of continued impressment of American seamen into the British service. While they pleaded for the protection of commerce, they were not, they said, "of that sect whose worship is at the shrine of a calculating avarice. . . . . Although the groans of those victims of barbarity for the loss of (what should be dearer to Americans than life) their liberty—although the cries of their wives and children, in the privation of protectors and parents, have of late been drowned in the louder clamors of the loss of property, yet is the practice of forcing our mariners into the British navy, in violation of the rights of our flag, carried on with unabated rigor and severity. If it be our duty to encourage the fair and legitimate commerce of this country by protecting the property of the merchant, then, indeed, by as much as life and liberty are more estimable than ships and goods, so much more impressive is the duty to shield the persons of our seamen, whose hard and honest services are employed, equally with those of the merchants, in advancing, under the mantle of its laws, the interests of their country. To sum up, in a word, the great cause of complaint against Great Britain, your committee need only say, that the United States, as a sovereign and independent power, claim the right to use the ocean, which is the common and acknowledged highway of nations, for the purposes of transporting, in their own vessels, the products of their own soils and the acquisitions of their own industry to a market in the ports of friendly nations, and to bring home, in return, such articles as their necessities or convenience may require, always regarding the rights of belligerents as defined by the established laws of nations. Great Britain, in defiance of this incontestable right, captures every American vessel bound to or returning from a port where her commerce is not favored; enslaves our seamen, and, in spite of our remonstrances, perseveres in these aggressions. To wrongs so daring in character and so disgraceful in their execution, it is impossible that the people of the United States should remain indifferent. We must now tamely and quietly submit, or we must resist by those means which God has placed within our reach.

[a] 1811.

spondent of the New York *Evening Post* wrote: "He made a short address to the House on taking his seat, which, from the lowness of his voice at that time, could not be distinctly heard." In the same letter the writer said, "It is believed Clay was not thought of for Speaker till Sunday; he certainly was not publicly mentioned. The Democrats had a caucus Sunday evening, and fixed on Clay. This was done to prevent the election of Macon, who has too much honesty and independence for the leading administration men."

Mr. Clay was then thirty-four years of age, and this was his first appearance as a member in the House of Representatives. He was in the Senate previously, as we have observed. The portrait given on the previous page is from a painting from life by the late Mr. Ranney, when Mr. Clay was nearly sixty years of age.

"Your committee would not cast a shade over the American name by the expression of a doubt which branch of this alternative will be embraced. The occasion is now presented when the national character, misunderstood and traduced for a time by foreign and domestic enemies, should be vindicated. If we have not rushed to the field of battle like the nations who are led by the mad ambition of a single chief in the avarice of a corrupted court, it has not proceeded from the fear of war, but from our love of justice and humanity. That proud spirit of liberty and independence which sustained our fathers in the successful assertion of rights against foreign aggression is not yet sunk. The patriotic fire of the Revolution still lives in the American breast with a holy and unextinguishable flame, and will conduct this nation to those high destinies which are not less the reward of dignified moderation than of exalted valor. But we have borne with injury until forbearance has ceased to be a virtue. The sovereignty and independence of these states, purchased and sanctified by the blood of our fathers, from whom we received them, not for ourselves only, but as the inheritance of our posterity, are deliberately and systematically violated. And the period has arrived when, in the opinion of your committee, it is the sacred duty of Congress to call forth the patriotism and resources of the country. By the aid of these, and with the blessing of God, we confidently trust we shall be able to procure that redress which has been sought for by justice, by remonstrance, and forbearance in vain."

The committee, "reserving for a future report those ulterior measures which, in their opinion, ought to be pursued," earnestly recommended Congress to second the proposition of the President by immediately putting the United States "into an armor and attitude demanded by the crisis, and corresponding with the national spirit and expectations." In a series of resolutions they recommended the immediate completion of the military establishment as authorized by law, by filling up the ranks and prolonging the enlistments; the authorization of an additional force of ten thousand regular troops to serve for three years, and the acceptance by the President, under proper regulations, of any number of volunteers not exceeding fifty thousand, to be organized, trained, and held in readiness; giving the President authority to order out detachments of militia when the interests of the country should require; the immediate repairing of all national vessels and fitting them for service, and the allowing merchant ships to arm in their own defense.[1]

This report, spread upon the wings of the press, went over the country swiftly—not so swiftly as now, for railways and telegraphs were unknown[2]—and produced a

---

[1] Niles's *Weekly Register*, i., 253.

[2] The first trip made by a locomotive on this continent was thus described a few years ago in a speech at an Erie Railway festival, by Horatio Allen, the eminent engineer:

"When was it? Who was it? And who awakened its energies and directed its movements? It was in the year 1828, on the banks of the Lackawaxen, at the commencement of the railroads connecting the canal of the Delaware and Hudson Canal Company with their coal mines, and he who addresses you was the only person on that locomotive. The circumstances which led to my being alone on the engine were these: The road had been built in the summer; the structure was of hemlock timber, and rails of large dimensions notched on caps placed far apart. The timber had cracked and warped from exposure to the sun. After about three hundred feet of straight line, the road crossed the Lackawaxen Creek on trestle-work about thirty feet high, with a curve of three hundred and fifty-five to four hundred feet radius. The impression was very general that the iron monster would either break down the road, or it would leave the track at the curve and plunge into the creek. My reply to such apprehensions was that it was too late to consider the probability of such occurrences; there was no other course than to have a trial made of the strange animal, which had been brought here at a great expense, but that it was not necessary that more than one should be involved in its fate; that I would take the first ride alone, and the time would come when I should look back to the incident with great interest. As I placed my hand on the throttle-valve handle, I was undecided whether I would move slowly or with a fair degree of speed; but, believing that the road would prove safe, and preferring, if we did go down, to go handsomely, and without any evidence of timidity, I started with considerable velocity, passed the curve over the creek safely, and was soon out of hearing of the vast assemblage. At the end of two or three miles I reversed the valve and returned without accident, having thus made the first railroad trip by locomotive on the Western hemisphere."

The first regular telegraphic dispatch, for the public eye and ear, was sent from Washington City to Baltimore by Professor Samuel F. B. Morse, the inventor of the electro-telegraphic system of intellectual communication, in May, 1844. The dispatch, furnished to Professor Morse, according to promise, by Miss Anna Ellsworth, daughter of the then Commissioner of Patents, who had taken great interest in Mr. Morse's experiments, was worthy of the occasion: it was the expression of Balaam—"WHAT HATH GOD WROUGHT!" That first dispatch, in the telegraphic language, may be found in the archives of the Connecticut Historical Society.

powerful impression upon the American mind and heart. No one could deny the truthfulness of its statements, and few well-informed persons doubted the wisdom and justice of its conclusions. While great indignation was felt toward France for her past and present aggressions upon the rights of neutrals, much stronger was the feeling against Great Britain, because it had been her settled policy and her practice for more than half a century, and had been used with cruel rigor long before France, in retaliation, adopted the same instrument for warfare. This indignation was more vehement because England, with haughty persistence, and in violation of the sovereignty and independence of the United States, continued her nefarious practice of impressing American seamen into the British naval service. Upon such burning feelings throughout the land, just then stimulated to great intensity by the intelligence from the Indian country, fell the fuel of this trumpet-toned report. It was short, perspicuous, and pungent. It was read by every body; and every measure proposed in Congress, looking to hostilities with Great Britain, was applauded by a large majority of the people.

In Congress warm debates followed on the resolutions appended to the report. It was admitted that the United States could not meet Great Britain on the ocean fleet to fleet, but it was believed that when an army from the States should appear on the soil of Canada, or of the other British provinces in the farther East, the people, then tired of being ruled as colonies, would gladly join fortunes with the young Giant of the West. It was believed that their bosoms swelled with desires since embodied in these words of an English poet:

> "There's a star in the West that shall never go down
> 'Till the records of valor decay;
> We must worship its light, though 'tis not our own,
> For liberty bursts in its ray."

It was also believed that American privateers would speedily ruin British commerce and fisheries, and that, by sea and land expeditions, the people of the United States would be remunerated tenfold for all the spoliations inflicted on their commerce, and thus compel the British government to act justly and respectfully.[1]

Most of the Southern and Western members were in favor of war. But John Randolph, always happy in his element of universal opposition, battled against the men of his own section in his peculiar way, sometimes with ability, always discursorily, and frequently with the keenest satire. He endeavored to excite the fears of the members of the slave-labor states by warning them that an invasion of Canada might be retorted upon Southern soil with fearful effect. He declared that the slaves had already become polluted by that French democracy which animated the administration party, who were so eager to go to war with the enemy of Napoleon, whom he ranked, as a scourge of mankind, with Tamerlane and Genghis Khan—"malefactors of the human race, who grind down men into mere material of their impious and bloody ambition." He said the negroes were rapidly gaining notions of freedom, destructive alike to their own happiness and the safety and interests of their masters. He denounced as a "butcher" a member of Congress who had proposed the abolition of slavery in the District of Columbia. He said men had broached on that very floor the doctrine of imprescriptible rights to a crowded audience of blacks in the galleries, teaching them that they were equal to their masters. "Similar doctrines," he said, "are spread throughout the South by Yankee peddlers; and there are even owners of slaves so infatuated as, by the general tenor of their conversation, by contempt of order, morality, religion, unthinkingly to cherish these seeds of destruction. And what has been the consequence? Within the last ten years repeated alarms of slave-insurrections, some of them awful indeed. By the spreading of this infernal doctrine the whole South has been thrown into a state of insecurity. . . . . You have de-

---
[1] Porter's Speech.

prived the slave of all moral restraint," he continued, addressing the Democratic members; "you have tempted him to eat of the tree of knowledge just enough to perfect him in wickedness; you have opened his eyes to his nakedness. . . . . God forbid that the Southern States should ever see an enemy on these shores with their infernal principles of French fraternity in the van! While talking of Canada, we have too much reason to shudder for our own safety at home. I speak from facts when I say that the night-bell never tolls for fire in Richmond that the frightened mother does not hug her infant the more closely to her bosom, not knowing what may have happened. I have myself witnessed some of these alarms in the capital of Virginia."

Randolph[1] then gave the Democrats some severe words concerning the adverse policy advocated by their party in 1798, when the Federal administration was preparing for a war with France. He taunted them with being preachers of reform and economy heretofore, but now, in their blind zeal to serve their French master, were willing to create a heavy national debt by rushing into an unnecessary and wicked war with a fraternal people—fraternal in blood, language, religion, laws, arts, and literature.[2]

Randolph's speech had but little effect upon his auditors other than to irritate the more sensitive and amuse the more philosophic. A few members, at the risk of poisoned arrows from his tongue, ventured to give him some home thrusts, while Calhoun, then less than thirty years of age, made this the occasion of his first oratorical effort in that great theatre of legislative strife wherein he so long and so valiantly contested.[3] With that dexterous use of subtle logic which never failed to give him

---

[1] John Randolph claimed to be seventh in descent from Pocahontas, the famous Indian princess. He was born three miles from Petersburg, in Virginia, on the 2d of June, 1773. He was educated at Princeton College, New Jersey, Columbia College, New York, and William and Mary College, in Virginia. From infancy he suffered from ill health. He studied law, but never practiced it. His first appearance in public life was in 1799, when he was elected to a seat in the National Congress, and for thirty years, with an interval of two years each, he held a seat in that body. He became insane for a time in 1811, and had returns of his malady at intervals during the remainder of his life. He strenuously opposed the war with Great Britain in 1812, and after that event his political career was very erratic. He was the warm friend of General Jackson in 1828, and in 1830 that gentleman appointed him United States Minister to Russia. He could not endure the winter on the Neva, and his stay in Russia was short. He resided in England for a while, and after his return his constituents elected him to Congress. But he did not take his seat. Consumption laid its hand upon him, and he died in a hotel in Philadelphia, on the 23d of May, 1833, while on his way to New York to embark for Europe.

[2] Speech in the House of Representatives, December 10, 1811.—Niles's *Register*, i., 315.

[3] John Caldwell Calhoun was born in Abbeville District, South Carolina, on the 18th of March, 1782. His mother was a native of Virginia. He entered Yale College as a student in 1802, where he was marked as a young man of genius and great promise. He was graduated in 1804 with the highest honors of the institution. He studied law in Litchfield, Connecticut, and entered upon its practice in his native district. He was elected to a seat in the Legislature of South Carolina in 1808, and in 1811 he took his seat as member of the National Congress as a stanch Republican or Democrat. He ably supported Mr. Madison's administration, and in 1817 President Monroe called him to his Cabinet as Secretary of War. He was elected Vice-President of the United States in 1825, and was re-elected with Jackson in 1828. He succeeded Hayne in the Senate of the United States in 1831, and became the leader in the disloyal movement of his native state known in history under the general title of Nullification, in 1832-'33. President Tyler called him to his Cabinet as Secretary of State in 1843, and he again entered the Senate as the representative of his state in 1845. He held that position until his death, which occurred at Washington City on the 31st of March, 1850, when he was just past sixty-eight years of age. Our portrait of Mr. Calhoun, on the next page, is from one taken from life about the year 1830, when he was forty-eight years of age.

ingenious arguments in favor of any views he might desire to enforce, he replied to Randolph at some length, insisting that it was a principle as applicable to nations as to individuals to repel a first insult, and thus command the respect, if not the fear of the assailant. "Sir," he said, "I might prove the war, should it ensue, justifiable by the express admission of the gentleman from Virginia; and necessary, by facts undoubted and universally admitted, such as that gentleman did not pretend to controvert. The extent, duration, and character of the injuries received; the failure of those peaceful means heretofore resorted to for the redress of our wrongs, is my proof that it is necessary. Why should I mention the impressment of our seamen; depredation on every branch of our commerce, including the direct export trade, continued for years, and made under laws which professedly undertake to regulate our trade with other nations;[1] negotiation resorted to time after time till it became hopeless; the restrictive systems persisted in to avoid war and in the vain expectation of returning justice? The evil still grows, and in each succeeding year swells in extent and pretension beyond the preceding. The question, even in the opinion and admission of our opponents, is reduced to this single point, Which shall we do, abandon or defend our own commercial and maritime rights, and the personal liberties of our citizens in exercising them? These rights are essentially attacked, and war is the only means of redress. The gentleman from Virginia has suggested none, unless we consider the whole of his speech as recommending patient and resigned submission as the best remedy. Sir, which alternative this House ought to sustain is not for me to say. I hope the decision is made already by a higher authority than the voice of any man. It is not for the human tongue to instill the sense of independence and honor. This is the work of nature—a generous nature that disdains tame submission to wrongs. This part of the subject is so imposing as to enforce silence even on the gentleman from Virginia. He dared not deny his country's wrongs, or vindicate the conduct of her enemy."

In this dignified strain Mr. Calhoun charmed his listeners, steadying the vacillating, convincing the doubting, and commanding the respectful attention of the opponents of the resolutions. He treated Randolph's bugbear of slave insurrection with lofty contempt. "However the gentleman may frighten himself," he said, "with the disorganizing effects of French principles, I can not think our ignorant blacks have felt much of their baleful influence. I dare say more than one half of them never heard of the French Revolution."[2]

The Federalists said very little on this occasion. It had always been their policy to be prepared for war. The resolutions appended to the report of the Committee on Foreign Relations were adopted,[a] and bills were speedily prepared and passed for augmenting the army. Additional regulars to the num-

[a] December 16, 1811.

---

[1] See page 165.
[2] *Abridgment of the Debates of Congress from* 1789 *to* 1856, by Thomas H. Benton, iv., 449.

Augmentation of the Army.   Patriotism of leading Federalists.   Reasons of Quincy and Emott for their Course.

ber of twenty-five thousand were authorized by a vote of the House early in January.ᵃ The bill also provided for the appointment of two major generals and five additional brigadiers; also for a bounty to new recruits of sixteen dollars, and, at the time of discharge, three months' extra pay and a certificate for one hundred and sixty acres of land.[1] On the 14th of the month another act was passed, appropriating a million of dollars for the purchase of arms, ordnance, camp equipage, and quarter-master's stores; and four hundred thousand dollars for powder, ordnance, and small-arms for the navy. Thus, in a brief space of time, the little army of the peace establishment, which had been comparatively inactive, was swelled in prospective from about three thousand men to more than seventy thousand regulars and volunteers. The President was authorized to call upon the governors of states

ᵃ January 4, 1812.

---

[1] Seven of the thirty-seven Federalists in the House voted for these measures. These were Quincy and Reed, of *Massachusetts*; Emott, Bleecker, Gold, and Livingston, of *New York*; and Milnor, of *Pennsylvania*. The latter was the late James Milnor, D.D., Rector of St. George's Church, New York. It was during this session of Congress that he became deeply impressed with religious sentiments, and felt himself called to the Gospel ministry. He abandoned the lucrative profession of the law and the turbulent field of politics, and took orders in the Protestant Episcopal Church, of which, until his death, in the spring of 1844, he was "a bright and shining light."

The position taken by these leading Federalists at that critical time, in opposition to the great body of their colleagues in Congress and of the party in New England, was patriotic in the highest degree, and yet, so doubtful were they of the verdict which posterity might pass upon their actions, that two of them (Quincy and Emott) prepared quite an elaborate defense, in which the reasons for their course were ably set forth. It was drawn up by Emott, slightly amended by Quincy, and signed by both. It was left in Emott's hands, to be used at any future time by him or his descendants in vindication of their course. Posterity—even contemporaries—have pronounced their course wise and patriotic. The original manuscript, in the possession of the Hon. James Emott, of Poughkeepsie, New York, a son of one of the signers, is before me while I write. It is in the delicate and neat handwriting of the elder Emott,* and dated January 1, 1812. After clearly stating the position of public affairs, they say: "We thought it therefore worthy of an experiment to allow the administration to make out their case before the great bar of the public without, as heretofore, aiding it by an early opposition; and we hoped, and yet hope, that by withdrawing the aliment of party rancor it will cease to exist, and that the people will see the precipice to which they have been drawn, and the danger which awaits the country unless there is a speedy and radical change of men or measures. . . . By leaving the government in the first instance unmolested, in its measures the people may receive a distinct impression of its objects. If they are really of that high and commanding character as to effectuate what their friends promised, relief to our country, it is of little consequence from whose hands so desirable a blessing is received. But if the character of the plans of the administration continues time-serving, self-oppressive, and hypocritical, on it and its supporters would fall the responsibility, without the possibility of transferring it to those who had neither shared nor opposed their purposes."

These gentlemen then allude to the prevalent opinion that if the Federalists should withhold their opposition, the British government, hopeless of a party in its favor in the United States, would relax its restrictive measures. They then declare that if the British government or people believe that opposition of the Federalists arises from any unpatriotic motives, "bottomed on a desire for power to be obtained at the expense of the interests of the nation," there has been an essential and lamentable mistake.

In reference to the measures proposed for putting the country in a state of adequate strength in the event of war, for which these gentlemen voted four days after the date of the paper under action, they remarked: "In re-estimating our duties upon this occasion, we have not deemed it necessary to take into consideration the causes which have led to our present embarrassments. We certainly do not entertain the opinion that the course which has been pursued by the administration is either correct or to be justified; but we can not but perceive that our present difficulties are not so apparently and exclusively attributable to the American government as to justify a resort to a policy which would leave the nation unprotected and defenseless. . . . It is because we wish for peace with security that we are willing to add to the present military establishment. . . . Our country and our firesides are dear to us. We think they are in danger, and we wish to protect them. . . . When, by measures in which we have had no agency, and for which we do not hold ourselves responsible in whole or in part, we discover that a necessity has been produced for defensive preparations, we can not permit ourselves to resist such preparations from motives of general opposition to the administration, or from a desire to render it odious to the country."

---

* James Emott was born at Poughkeepsie, New York, on the 14th of March, 1771. He chose the profession of law as his vocation, and commenced its practice at Ballston Centre, New York, a growing village a few miles from Ballston Spa. In 1797 he was appointed a commissioner, with Robert Yates and Vincent Mathews, to settle disputes concerning titles to lands in the military tract of Onondaga County. The commissioners held their sittings at Albany, and to that city Mr. Emott removed about the year 1800. In 1804 he was chosen to represent Albany County in the State Legislature. He soon afterward removed to the city of New York, and after practicing law there for a while he returned to Poughkeepsie, and was elected to represent the Duchess District in the National Congress. He took his seat in 1809, and continued in possession of it by re-election until 1813. In politics he was a Federalist, and was one of the prominent leaders, yet his patriotism was never in subjection to the behests of party. He was representative of Duchess County in the New York Assembly in 1814, and was Speaker of the House. He was a member of that body four consecutive years. In 1817 he was appointed first judge of Duchess County, and held the office until 1823, when, for political reasons, he was removed to make room for the late Maturin Livingston. He was appointed judge of the second circuit by Governor Clinton in 1827, and held it until 1831, when he was sixty years of age. Judge Emott then retired from active life. He died at Poughkeepsie, New York, on the 10th of April, 1850, aged seventy-nine years.

each to furnish his respective quota of one hundred thousand militia, to be held in readiness to instantly obey the call of the chief magistrate. For the expense of this reserve one million of dollars were appropriated.

The State Legislatures, meanwhile, spoke out emphatically for war if necessary. New Jersey, Pennsylvania, Virginia, Georgia, Kentucky, and Ohio, resolved to stand by the general government when decisive measures should be adopted; and, in their reply to the annual message of Governor Gerry, the House of Representatives of Massachusetts exhibited the same sentiments, denouncing Great Britain as a "piratical state," and her practice of impressment "man-stealing."

The navy, important as it proved to be in the war that followed, was neglected. Cheves, of South Carolina, made a report in favor of its augmentation; and he and Lowndes, in supporting speeches, hinted at the expediency of constructing forty frigates and twenty-five ships of the line. It was urged by these members, in direct opposition to the narrow views of Williams from the same state a year before, that "protection to commerce was protection to agriculture." Quincy also argued that protection to commerce was essential to the preservation of the Union, and, with a covert but significant threat, he gave as a reason that the commercial states could not be expected to submit to the deliberate and systematic sacrifice of their most important interests.[1] Their pleas were in vain. A bill, containing only an appropriation of four hundred and eighty thousand dollars for repairing three frigates—*Constellation*, *Chesapeake*, and *Adams*—and two hundred thousand dollars annually for three years, to purchase timber for the purpose of refitting three others, was passed, and sent to the Senate, where Lloyd, of Massachusetts, moved to insert an appropriation for thirty new frigates.[a] "Let us have the frigates," he said; "powerful as Great Britain is, she could not blockade them. With our hazardous shores and tempestuous northwesterly gales from November to March, all the navies in the world could not blockade them. Divide them into six squadrons. Place those squadrons in the northern ports ready for sea, and at favorable moments we would pounce upon her West India Islands, repeating the game of De Grasse and D'Estaing in '79 and '80. By the time she was ready to meet us there, we would be round Cape Horn cutting up her whalemen. Pursued thither, we would skim away to the Indian Seas, and would give an account of her China and India ships very different from that of the French cruisers. Now we would follow her Quebec, now her Jamaica convoys; sometimes make our appearance in the chops of the Channel, and even sometimes wind north almost into the Baltic. It would require a hundred British frigates to watch the movements of these thirty. Such are the means by which I would bring Great Britain to her senses. By harassing her commerce with this fleet, we could make the people ask the government why they continued to violate our rights."

[a] January 17, 1812.

Crawford, of Georgia, replied at some length, and the Senate, unmoved by the glowing pictures of naval achievements drawn by the senator from Massachusetts, not only refused to sanction Lloyd's amendment, but reduced the appropriation for repairs to three hundred thousand dollars.

While the war party, strong in Congress and throughout the country, were energetic in action and impatient of delay, Mr. Madison showed great timidity. It was owing, doubtless, in a great degree, to the character of his Cabinet, which unfortunately surrounded him at that momentous crisis. Mr. Monroe, the Secretary of State, was the only member who had any military taste and experience, and he had seen only limited service in the Revolution. Gallatin, the Secretary of the Treasury, was a civilian, and was avowedly opposed to the war with Great Britain. Eustis, the Secretary of War, knew very little about military affairs. Hamilton, the Secretary of the Navy, had no practical knowledge of naval affairs to qualify him for the station;

---

[1] Hildreth, Second Series, iii., 277.

Madison threatened with Desertion by the War Party.   He recommends an Embargo.   A British Plot discovered.

and Mr. Madison himself was utterly unable, though by virtue of his office commander-in-chief of the army and navy of the United States, to grasp with vigor the conduct of public affairs in a time of war. Consciousness of this made him timid and vacillating.

The administration members of Congress at length resolved to take a bold and decided stand with the President. His first term of office was drawing to a close, and it was known that he was anxious for re-election. The leading Democrats in the State of New York, whose voices were potential in the matter at that time, dissatisfied with Mr. Madison's weak course, contemplated nominating De Witt Clinton, then mayor of the city of New York, for the Presidency of the United States. His pretensions were sustained by Gideon Granger, the postmaster general, who doubted the propriety of a war with Madison as leader. Other influential Democrats in different parts of the country held similar views.

In this state of things, Mr. Madison was waited upon[a] by several of the leading Democratic members of Congress, and informed, in substance, that war with England was now resolved upon by the dominant party, the supporters of his administration; that the people would no longer consent to a dilatory and inefficient course on the part of the national government; that, unless a declaration of war took place previous to the Presidential election, the success of the Democratic party might be endangered, and the government thrown into the hands of the Federalists; that, unless Mr. Madison consented to act with his friends, and accede to a declaration of war with Great Britain, neither his nomination nor his re-election to the Presidency could be relied on. Thus situated, Mr. Madison concluded to waive his own objections to the course determined on by his political friends, and to do all he could for the prosecution of a war for which he had neither taste nor practical ability.[1]

[a] March 2, 1812.

Mr. Madison's first step in the prescribed direction after this interview was in the form of a confidential message to Congress on the 1st of April, recommending, as preliminary to a declaration of war, the immediate passage of a law laying a general embargo on all vessels then in the ports of the United States, or that might thereafter enter, for the period of sixty days. Meanwhile another subject had produced very great excitement throughout the country. An Irishman, named John Henry, who had become a naturalized citizen of the United States, and had lived several years in Canada, appeared at the Presidential mansion one dark and stormy evening early in February,[b] 1812. He bore a letter of introduction to Mr. Madison from Governor Gerry, of Massachusetts, who seemed to be impressed with the truthfulness of Henry, and the great importance of the information which he proposed to lay before the President.[2] An interview was arranged for the following evening, when Henry divulged to the President what appeared to be most astounding secrets concerning efforts that had been in progress for two years on the part of the British authorities in Canada, sanctioned by the home government, to effect a separation of the Eastern States from the Union, and to attach them to Great Britain. He told Mr. Madison that, up to the year 1809, he had been living for five

[b] February 2.

---

[1] Statement of James Fisk, a Democratic member of Congress from Vermont, who was one of the committee, cited in the *Statesman's Manual*, i., 444. The feeling against Mr. Madison on account of his timid policy had begun to manifest itself very strongly among his political friends in Congress before the close of 1811. The New York *Evening Post*, of January 6, 1812, says: "The Houses of Congress refused to adjourn on the 1st of January in order to wait on the chief magistrate. It was an intended insult."

Henry Dearborn, an officer of the Revolution, then in Washington, and who had lately been appointed a major general in the national army, wrote to his daughter, saying: "You may tell your neighbors they may prepare for war; we shall have it by the time they are ready. I know that war will be very unwelcome news to you, but I also know that you possess too much Spartan patriotism to wish your father to decline a command for the defense of the honor of our beloved country. You would, if necessary, urge him to the field rather than a speck of dishonor should attach to him for declining such a command."

[2] Henry had spent a week in Baltimore. He left that city for Washington on the morning of the 1st of February.—Letter in Niles's *Register*, ii., 46.

years on his farm in Vermont, near the Canada line, and amused himself in writing essays for the newspapers against republican governments, which he detested. Those essays, he said, had arrested the attention of Sir James Craig, then Governor General of Canada, who invited him to Montreal at the close of 1808. At that time the violent demonstrations of the Federalists in New England against the embargo induced the English to believe that there was deep-seated disaffection to the government of the United States on the part of the people of that section. Under that impression Henry was commissioned by Sir James Craig to proceed to Boston, and ascertain the true state of affairs there, and the temper of the people in that part of the Union. His instructions directed him especially to ascertain whether the Federalists of Massachusetts would, in the event of their success at the approaching election, be disposed to separate from the Union, or enter into any connection with England. "The earliest information on this subject," said Sir James, "may be of great consequence to our government; as it may also be, that it should be informed how far, in such an event, they would look to England for assistance, or be disposed to enter into a connection with us."¹ Henry was authorized to intimate to the Federalist leaders, if the supposed state of things should be found to exist, that they might communicate to the British government through him.²

According to Henry's statement, he passed through Vermont after receiving these instructions, and arrived at Boston on the 5th of March. There he remained about three months, spending his time in coffee-houses and disreputable places, until Erskine's arrangement and a recall by Ryland,ᵃ Craig's Secretary, put an end to his mission. During that time Henry had addressed fourteen letters to Sir James over the initials "A. B.," most of them written at Boston. The earlier ones were filled with the most encouraging accounts of the extreme disaffection of the Eastern people, especially those of Massachusetts, on account of the commercial restrictions. He expressed his belief that, in the event of a declaration of war against Great Britain by the United States, the Legislature of Massachusetts would take the lead in establishing a separate Northern Confederacy, which might, in some way, end in a political connection with Great Britain. The grand idea of destroying the Union was the theme of all the letters, expressed or implied. "If a war between America and France," he wrote, "be a grand desideratum, something more must be done; an indulgent, conciliating policy must be adopted.... To bring about a separation of the states under distinct and independent governments is an affair of more uncertainty, and, however desirable, can not be effected but by a series of acts and long-continued policy tending to irritate the Southern and conciliate the Northern people.... This, I am aware, is an object of much interest in Great Britain, as it would forever insure the integrity of his majesty's possessions on this continent, and make the two goverments, or whatever member the present confederacy might join with, as useful and as much subject to the influence of Great Britain as her colonies can be rendered."³

ᵃ May 4, 1809.

---

¹ Sir James Craig's Instructions to John Henry, dated at Quebec, 6th February, 1809.
² Henry was furnished with the following credentials, to be used if circumstances should require:
"The bearer, Mr. John Henry, is employed by me, and full confidence may be placed in him for any communication which any person may wish to make to me on the business committed to him. In faith of which I have given him this, under my hand and seal, at Quebec, the 6th day of February, 1809. J. H. CRAIG."
Henry was also furnished with a cipher to be used in his correspondence.
³ Henry to Sir James Craig, 13th of March, 1809. Mr. Erskine's arrangement greatly disappointed the British authorities in Canada, who doubtless expected to reap great rewards from the home government by a successful effort to disrupt the American Union. For twenty years they had been inciting the Indians on the Northwestern frontiers to war upon the Americans, and now they hoped, by a successful movement among those whom they supposed to be as mer-

Henry's Correspondence in Madison's Possession.   The President's Message on the Subject.

Henry soon perceived that his estimate of New England disloyalty was simply absurd, and he came to the conclusion that the idea of a withdrawal from the Union was unpopular; that, as matters stood, the Federalists would confine themselves to the ordinary resistance of political opposition. "Weak men," he wrote, "are sure to temporize when great events call upon them for decision."

Henry's performances seem to have pleased Sir James Craig, who promised him employment in Canada worth at least a thousand pounds ($5000) per annum. Henry waited long for the fulfillment of that promise, and finally Sir James died. In June, 1811, the British spy was in London humbly petitioning the government for remuneration for his services in Boston. There he was at first treated with great consideration by the government. "I was received in the highest circles," he said to his friend, the Count Edward de Crillon. "I was complimented with a ticket as member of the PITT CLUB without being balloted for."[1] But when he had spent all his money, and presented his claims for retribution, the government attempted to cheapen his services. He claimed thirty thousand pounds, but speedily lowered his demands. He would be content, he said, with the office of Judge Advocate of Lower Canada, with a salary of five hundred pounds a year, or a consulate in the United States. Robert Peel, the Earl of Liverpool's under secretary, in behalf of that official, politely referred Henry to Sir James Craig's successor in Canada, Sir George Prevost. The spy was exasperated, and sailed for Boston instead of for Quebec, full of wrath, and a determination to be revenged by divulging the whole secret of his mission to the United States government, and, if possible, receive from it the remuneration which he had vainly sought in England. He was successful. Mr. Madison was satisfied of the great value of Henry's disclosures at that crisis, when war against England was about to be declared. They gave overwhelming proof of the secret designs of the British government to destroy the new republic in the West. Out of the secret service fund in his possession he gave Henry fifty thousand dollars for the entire correspondence of the parties to the affair in this country and in England.

After receiving the money[2] Henry went to Philadelphia, where he wrote a letter to the President[a] as a preface to his disclosures. On the 9th of March the United States sloop-of-war *Wasp*, Captain Jones, sailed from Sandy Hook with dispatches for Mr. Barlow, the American minister at Paris, bearing away Henry to sunny France, where he would be safe from British vengeance. On the same day the President laid the Henry documents[3] before Congress, with a message, in which he said, "They prove that at a recent period, while the United States, notwithstanding the wrongs sustained by them, ceased not to observe the laws of neutrality toward Great Britain, and in the midst of amicable professions and negotiations on the part of the British government through its public minister here [Mr. Erskine], a secret agent of that government was employed in certain states—more especially at the seat of government in Massachusetts—in fomenting disaffection to the constituted authorities of the nation, and in intrigues with the disaffected for the purpose of bringing about resistance to the laws, and eventually, in concert with

[a] February 20, 1812.

---

cenary as themselves, to reduce the United States to virtual vassalage. Ryland, Governor Craig's secretary, in a letter to Henry on the 1st of May (four days before his official letter summoning him to Montreal), exhibited that disappointment. He concluded his letter in these petulant words: "I am cruelly out of spirits at the idea of Old England truckling to such a debased and accursed government as that of the United States."

[1] De Crillon's deposition before the Committee on Foreign Relations, submitted to Congress March 13, 1811.

[2] This was paid out of the Treasury of the United States in two sums, on the draft of Albert Gallatin, Secretary of the Treasury, to the order of James Graham, the United States Treasurer, one for forty-nine thousand dollars, and the other for one thousand dollars, dated 10th of February, 1812. Henry was probably swindled out of his money. He had landed at Boston with a Frenchman calling himself the Count de Crillon, and a great intimacy grew up between them. They went to Washington together. When Henry returned to Baltimore he had a deed from the "count" for an estate in Languedoc, the consideration being four hundred thousand francs. It is probable the count received the forty-nine thousand dollars, and Mr. Henry the one thousand dollars, the latter being sufficient to enable him to reach his valuable French estate. The "count," who became a witness in the government investigation of Henry's disclosures, proved to be an arrant knave and impostor.

[3] These may be found in Benton's *Abridgment of the Debates in Congress*, iv., 506 to 514 inclusive.

a British force, of destroying the Union, and forming the eastern part thereof into a political connection with Great Britain."

The indignation against Great Britain was intensified by these disclosures, and the inhabitants of New England felt deeply annoyed by this implied disparagement of the patriotism of their section. Both political parties endeavored to make capital out of the affair. The Democrats vehemently reiterated the charge that the Federalists were a "British party," and "disunionists;"[1] while the opposition alleged that the affair was a political trick of the administration to damage their party, insure the re-election of Madison, and to offer an excuse for war. The feeling excited in New England against the administration was intense, and the indignation of the people was almost equally divided between the President and the British sovereign. It was charged that the whole matter was a fraud; that Monroe wrote the letter purporting to have been sent by Henry from Philadelphia to the government, and that the paper on which Lord Liverpool's communication to Henry, through Robert Peel, was written, bore the mark of a Philadelphia paper manufacturer.

These charges were all untrue. Every thing about the matter was genuine. The British minister at Washington (Mr. Foster), two days after the President's message was published, declared in the public prints[a] his entire ignorance of any transaction of the kind, and asked the United States government to consider the character of the individual[2] who had made these disclosures, and to "suspend any farther judgment on its merits until the circumstances shall have been made known to his majesty's government." That government was called upon for an explanation, early in May, by Lord Holland, who gave notice[b] that he should make a motion to call for the correspondence in relation to the intrigue. Ministers were alarmed, and their guilt was apparent in their efforts to suppress inquiry. Every pretext was brought to bear to oppose the motion. When they could no longer deny the facts, they endeavored to throw the obloquy of the act upon the dead Sir James Craig. The ministerial party in the House of Lords, when the motion was made, prevailed, and, by a vote of seventy-three against twenty-seven, refused to have the correspondence produced. Lord Holland declared in his closing speech that, until such investigation should be had, the fact that Great Britain had entered into a dishonorable and atrocious intrigue against a friendly power would stand unrefuted. And it does stand unrefuted to this day. It was so palpable, that Madison, in his war message on the 1st of June, made this intrigue one of the serious charges against Great Britain as justifying war.

The President, as we have observed, sent a confidential message to Congress on the 1st of April, recommending the laying of an embargo for sixty days. It was avowedly a precursor of war; and Mr. Calhoun immediately presented a bill in Com-

[a] March 11, 1812.
[b] May 5.

---

[1] They called up in formidable array the proceedings of the New England people against the Embargo Laws during the past two or three years, and in an especial manner they arraigned Mr. Quincy, the great opposition leader of the House, who, a year before (January 14, 1811), in the debate on the bill to enable the people of the Territory of Orleans to form a State Constitution preparatory to their admission into the Union, had declared that the passage of the bill would "justify a revolution in this country." "Look," they said, "to the signification of this passage in Mr. Quincy's speech —a passage which, when called to order, he reduced to writing: "I am compelled to declare it as my deliberate opinion that, if this bill passes, the bonds of the Union are virtually dissolved; that the states which compose it are free from their moral obligations, and that, as it will be the right of all, so it will be the duty of some to prepare definitely for a separation, amicably if they can, violently if they must." For an abstract of Mr. Quincy's speech on that occasion, see Benton's *Abridgment of the Debates in Congress*, iv., 327.

The Senate, by resolution, asked for the names of persons in Boston or elsewhere who were concerned in the plot with Henry. By Secretary Monroe's reply, it seems that the spy never mentioned the name of any individual.

[2] John Henry was a native of Ireland. He appeared in Philadelphia about the year 1793 or 1794, having come over as a steerage passenger. He possessed considerable literary ability, and became editor of Brown's *Philadelphia Gazette*. He afterward kept a grocery, and married in that city. Having become naturalized, and obtained a commission in the army in the time of the expected war with France, he had command of an artillery corps under General Ebenezer Stevens, of New York, and was superior officer at Fort Jay, on Governor's Island, for more than a year. He afterward had a command at Newport, where he quitted the service, settled upon a farm in Northern Vermont, studied law, and after five years entered upon the service recorded in the text. "He was a handsome, well-behaved man," says Sullivan, "and was received in some respectable families in Boston."

| Efforts to alarm the People. | War predicted. | The Sins of France. | Embargo Act passed. |

mittee of the Whole in accordance with the recommendation.[1] The opposition sounded an alarm. The weakness of the country, and its utter want of preparation for war, became the themes of impassioned appeals to the fears of the people. The continued aggressions of France—equal, they said, to those of England[2]—were pointed to as causes for war with that nation, and it might be necessary to encounter both at the same time.

To these alarmists Clay vehemently responded. He charged them with having cast obstacles in the way of preparation, and now made that lack of preparation an excuse for longer submission to great wrongs. Weak as we are, he said, we could fight France too, if necessary, in a good cause—the cause of honor and independence. He had no doubt that the late Indian war on the Wabash had been excited by the British;[3] and he alluded to the employment of Henry, as a spy and fomentor of disunion, as another gross offense. "We have complete proof," he said, "that England would do every thing to destroy us. Resolution and spirit are our only security." He viewed the Embargo as a war measure, and " war we shall have in sixty days," he said.

John Randolph implored the House to act with great caution. He said the President dared not plunge the country into a war while in its present unprepared state. There would be no war within sixty days. He believed the spirit of the people was not up to war, or the provocation of an Embargo Act would not be needed.

Other remarks were heard from both sides. The bill, by the aid of the previous question, was passed that evening[a] by a vote of seventy against forty-one. It was sent to the Senate the next morning. That body suspended the rules, took up the bill, and carried it through all the stages but the last, with an amendment increasing the time to ninety days. It was sent back to the House the next morning,[b] where it was concurred in, and on Saturday, the 4th of April, it became a law by the signature of the President. It had been violently assailed by Quincy, when it came back from the Senate, as an attempt to escape war, not as a preliminary to it. It was absurd to think of creating a sufficient army and navy in ninety days to commence war. He coincided with Randolph in the belief that the Embargo was only intended to aid Bonaparte, by stopping the shipment of

[a] April 1, 1812.

[b] April 3.

---

[1] When the Embargo project was first suggested in the Committee on Foreign Relations, it was proposed to discuss it under a pledge of secrecy. John Randolph refused to be bound by any such pledge, denying the committee's authority to impose it. Mr. Calhoun, with frank generosity, on the ground that all should have an equal chance, communicated to Mr. Quincy the fact that an embargo was to be laid the day before the committee's report to that effect was made. Quincy, Lloyd, and Emott immediately sent expresses with the information to Philadelphia, New York, and Boston. Emott's message appeared in the New York *Evening Post* on the 31st of March, the day before the President's message was sent in. In consequence of this information, several vessels at these respective ports loaded and escaped to sea before the Embargo was laid.

[2] These assertions contained much truth. According to a report laid before Congress on the 6th of July, 1812, it appeared that the whole number of British seizures and captures of American vessels since the commencement of the Continental War was 917. Of these, 528 had occurred previously to the orders in Council of November, 1807, and 389 afterward. The French seizures and captures were 558 ; of these, 206 were before the Berlin and Milan decrees, 317 afterward, and 45 since their alleged repeal. Recent Danish captures amounted to 70, and Neapolitan to 47. Besides these there had been extensive Dutch and Spanish seizures, which, it was alleged, should properly be placed to the French account, as those countries were under the control of Napoleon. It was also stated that more than half the captures by British cruisers had been declared invalid, and restoration ordered, while in France only a quarter of the vessels seized were so treated. It must be confessed that France was guilty of direct and indirect spoliation of American commerce to an extent equal, if not exceeding that inflicted by Great Britain.

[3] On the 11th of June the Secretary of War laid before Congress numerous letters from military and civil officers of the government from various portions of the Northwestern, Western, and Southwestern frontiers, dating back as far as 1807, and giving overwhelming evidence of the continual efforts of British emissaries to stir up the Indians to hostilities against the United States, and to win them to the British interest in expectation of war between the two countries. I will quote as a matter of fact, not speculation, from a speech of Red Jacket, the great Seneca chief, in behalf of himself and other deputies of the Six Nations, in February, 1810:

"Brother,—Since you have had some disputes with the British government, their agents in Canada have not only endeavored to make the Indians at the westward your enemies, but they have sent the war-belt among our warriors [in Western New York], to poison their minds and make them break their faith with you. At the same time we had information that the British had circulated war-belts among the Western Indians, and within your territory."

Copious extracts from the letters above mentioned as having been laid before the Secretary of War may be found in Niles's *Weekly Register*, ii., 342.

provisions to Spain, where the British armies were then beginning to win victories.[1] It was called, in ridicule, "a Terrapin War."[2]

The Embargo Act (which prohibited the sailing of any vessel for any foreign port, except foreign vessels, with such cargoes as they had on board when notified of the act) was speedily followed by a supplement[a] prohibiting exportations by land, whether of goods or specie.[3] Farther provision was also made for the immediate strengthening of the army.

[a] April 14, 1812.

These belligerent measures were hailed with joy throughout the country by the war party, who were dominant and determined. They alarmed those who wished for peace; yet these, unwilling to believe that the administration would push matters to the extreme of actual hostility, acquiesced in the embargo because of a delusive hope that it might be the means of causing Great Britain to modify its system concerning neutrals, and thereby avert war. It was, indeed, a *delusive* hope. The letters of Jonathan Russell (who had succeeded Mr. Pinkney as minister to England) at this time gave no encouragement for it. On the contrary, they were discouraging. To Mr. Monroe he wrote, after attending discussions on the orders in Council in Parliament: "If any thing was wanting to prove the inflexible determination of the present ministry to persevere in the orders in Council, without modification or relaxation, the declarations of leading members of the administration on these measures must place it beyond the possibility of a doubt. I no longer entertain a hope that we can honorably avoid war."[4]

---

[1] One great object of the Embargo appears to have been to detain at home as many merchant ships as possible, for the twofold purpose, in view of approaching war, to keep them from British privateers, and to engage them for that service on the part of the Americans. Mr. Alison, the British historian, suggests only part of the truth in saying that it was to prevent intelligence of the proceedings of the Americans in their preparations for war reaching England, and to furnish them with means, from their extensive commercial navy, of manning their vessels of war. To do this, cost the nation a great sacrifice. A writer in the *American Review* of April, 1812, estimated the loss as follows:

Mercantile loss	$24,814,249
Deteriorated value of surplus produce and waste	40,196,028
Loss sustained by the revenue	9,000,000
Total national loss	$74,010,277, or $6,167,523 a month.

[2] See note 3, page 164. Argument, ridicule, satire were all employed against the "Terrapin War." During the late spring and early summer of 1812, the subjoined song was sung at all gatherings of the Federalists, and was very popular:

"Huzza for our liberty, boys,
These are the days of our glory—
The days of true national joys,
When terrapins gallop before ye!
There's Porter, and Grundy, and Rhea,
In Congress who manfully vapor,
Who draw their six dollars a day,
And fight bloody battles *on paper!*
Ah! this is true Terrapin war.

"Poor Madison the tremors has got,
'Bout this same arming the nation·
Too far to retract, he can not
Go on—and he loses his station.

Then bring up your 'regulars,' lads,
In 'attitude' nothing ye lack, sirs,
Ye'll frighten to death the Danads,
With fire-coals blazing aback, sirs!
Oh, this is true Terrapin war!

"As to powder, and bullet, and swords,
For, as they were never intended,
They're a parcel of high-sounding words,
But never to *action* extended.
Ye must *frighten* the rascals away,
In '*rapid descent*' on their quarters!"
Then the plunder divide as ye may,
And drive them headlong in the waters.
Oh, this is *great* Terrapin war!"

FAC-SIMILE OF A NEWSPAPER CUT.

[3] The opposition speakers and newspapers denounced the Embargo (especially the "Land Embargo," as the supplementary act was called) in unmeasured terms. The land trade with Canada, so suddenly arrested and thrown into confusion by it, was represented by a bewildered serpent, which had been suddenly stopped in its movements by two trees, marked respectively EMBARGO and NON-INTERCOURSE. The wondering snake is puzzled to know what has happened, and the head cries out, "What is the matter, tail?" The latter answers, "I can't get out." A cock (in allusion to France) stands by, crowing joyfully.

[4] Letter to Secretary Monroe, March 4, 1812. Mr. Percival, one of the Cabinet, and a leading administration member, said, in the course of debate: "As England is contending for the defense of her maritime rights, and for the preservation of her national existence, which essentially depends on the maintenance of these rights, she could not be expected, in the prosecution of this great and primary interest, to arrest or vary her course *to listen to the pretensions of neutral nations, or to remove the evils, however they might be regretted, which the uniform policy of the times indirectly or unintentionally extended to them.*"

| British Orders and French Decrees unrepealed. | A preliminary War Measure. | Madison renominated. |

The determination of the British government not to relax the rigor of the orders in Council was explicitly stated a few weeks later,[a] when Mr. Foster, the British minister at Washington, in a letter to Mr. Monroe, after reviewing the whole ground of controversy between the two countries, said: "Great Britain can not admit, as a true declaration of public law, that free ships make free goods. She can not admit, as a principle of public law, that arms and military stores are alone contraband of war, and that ship-timber and naval stores are excluded from that description; and she feels that to relinquish her just measures of self-defense and retaliation would be to surrender the best means of her own preservation and rights, and with them the rights of other nations, so long as France maintains and acts upon such principles."

[a] 30th May, 1812.

The conduct of France now became a subject for just animadversion, and cast obstacles in the way of the arguments of the war party concerning the orders in Council. Joel Barlow had been sent to France as the successor of minister Armstrong. He strove in vain to procure from the French government any promise of indemnity for past spoliations, or of a relaxation of restrictive measures in future. The President and his Cabinet had earnestly hoped that the Berlin and Milan decrees would be repealed, thereby compelling Great Britain to withdraw her orders in Council, or stand before the world as a willful violator of the rights of nations. In this they hoped for a door of escape from war. It was certain that, while the decrees stood absolutely unrepealed in form, Great Britain would not relax her restrictive system one iota. Dispatches from Barlow late in March gave no hope of a change. Indeed, the French Minister for Foreign Affairs had laid before the Conservative Senate[b] a report in which those decrees were spoken of as embodying the settled policy of the emperor, to be enforced against all nations who should suffer their flags to be "denationalized" by submitting to the pretensions of the British to seize enemies' goods in neutral vessels, to treat timber and naval stores as contraband, or to blockade a port not also invested by land.

[b] March 10

Thus matters stood on the 1st of June, when Mr. Madison sent into Congress, after previous arrangement with the Committee on Foreign Affairs, a most important confidential message, by which he was fairly committed to the war policy. He had hesitated somewhat. He was willing to sign a bill declaring war against Great Britain, but he did not wish to appear as a leader in the measure. His new political masters would consent to no flinching. They resolved that the President should share the fearful responsibility with themselves. A Congressional caucus was about to be held to nominate a Democratic candidate for the Presidency, and a committee, with the imperious Clay at their head, waited on Mr. Madison, and told him plainly that he must move in a declaration of war, or they would not support him for re-election. He yielded. The caucus was held. Eighty members were present. Varnum, of Massachusetts, was president, and Richard M. Johnson, of Kentucky, was secretary. The entire vote was given to Mr. Madison. George Clinton, the Vice-President, whom they had intended to nominate for re-election, had died a few

A little later a London ministerial paper used the following language, which exposed the animus of the men in power and the aristocratic and mercantile classes: "As Great Britain has got possession of the ocean, it must have the right to enact laws for the regulation *of its own element, and to confine the tracks of neutrals* within such boundaries *as its own rights and interests require to be drawn.*"—*London Courier*, April, 1812.

weeks before,[1] and the aged Elbridge Gerry, lately defeated as a candidate for reelection to the governorship of Massachusetts, was placed on the ticket for Vice-President. This matter disposed of, and the continued claims of De Witt Clinton, of New York, to a nomination for President being considered as of little moment, the war party, led by Clay and Calhoun, put forth vigorous exertions for the full accomplishment of their purposes.

In his message to Congress on the 1st of June the President recapitulated the wrongs which the people of the United States had suffered at the hands of Great Britain—wrongs already noticed in preceding pages, and need not be repeated here. He declared that her conduct, taken together, was positively belligerent. "We behold in fine," he said, "on the side of Great Britain, a state of war against the United States, and on the side of the United States a state of peace toward Great Britain."[2] He warned his countrymen to avoid entanglements "in the contests and views of other powers"—meaning France—and called their attention to the fact that the French government, since the revocation of her decrees as applied to American commerce, had authorized illegal captures by her privateers; but he abstained at that time from offering any suggestions concerning definitive measures with respect to that nation.

The message was referred to the Committee on Foreign Relations,[3] and on the 3d of June Mr. Calhoun, its then chairman, presented a report, in which the causes and reasons for war were more fully stated—more in historical order and detail—than in the President's message. In concluding the review of British aggressions, the report declared that the hostility of the government of Great Britain was evidently based

CLINTON'S TOMB.

[1] George Clinton was born in Ulster County, New York, in 1739. He chose the profession of the law for his avocation. In 1768 he was elected to a seat in the Colonial Legislature, and was a member of the Continental Congress in 1775. He was appointed a brigadier in the army of the United States in 1776, and during the whole war was active in military affairs in New York. In April, 1777, he was elected governor and lieutenant governor, under the new Republican Constitution of the state, and was continued in the former office eighteen years. He was president of the Convention assembled at Poughkeepsie to consider the Federal Constitution in 1788. He was again chosen governor of the state in 1801, and three years afterward he was elected Vice-President of the United States. He occupied that elevated position at the time of his death, which occurred at Washington City on the 20th of April, 1812.

Mr. Clinton expired about nine o'clock in the morning. He had been ill for some time, and his death was not unexpected. His funeral took place on the afternoon of the 21st. The corpse was removed from his lodgings to the Capitol, escorted by a troop of horse. There it remained until four o'clock, when the procession, composed of cavalry and the marine corps, clergymen, physicians, mourners, the President of the United States, members of both houses of Congress, heads of departments, etc., moved to the Congressional burying-ground, situated on the Eastern Branch of the Potomac, about a mile eastward of the Capitol. Over his grave a monument of white marble was erected. The annexed sketch of it was made when I visited that resting-place of many of the American worthies, in the autumn of 1861. It is about fifteen feet in height. The tablet for the inscription, and a profile in high relief on the obelisk, are of statuary marble. On the east side (in shadow in the picture) is the inscription; on the north side the fasces; on the west side a serpent on a staff; and on the south side the winged caduceus of Mercury. On the west side of the obelisk is a Roman sword, crossed by a saber, and tied together by a scarf. The following is a copy of the inscription:

"To the memory of GEORGE CLINTON. He was born in the State of New York on the 26th of July, 1739, and died at Washington on the 20th of April, 1812, in the 73d year of his age. He was a soldier and statesman of the Revolution, eminent in council, distinguished in war. He filled, with unexampled usefulness, purity, and ability, among many other high offices, those of governor of his native state, and of Vice-President of the United States. While he lived, his virtue, wisdom, and valor were the pride, the ornament, and the security of his country; and when he died he left an illustrious example of a well-spent life, worthy of all imitation. This monument is affectionately dedicated by his children."

[2] For the message in full, see *Statesman's Manual*, i., 387.

[3] The committee was composed of John C. Calhoun, of South Carolina; Felix Grundy, of Tennessee; John Smillie, of Pennsylvania; John A. Harper, of New Hampshire; Joseph Desha, of Kentucky; and Ebenezer Seaver, of Massachusetts.

Action of the House of Representatives in Secret Session.   Action of the Senate on a Declaration of War.

on the fact that the United States were considered by it as its commercial rival, and that their prosperity and growth were incompatible with its welfare. "Your committee," said the report, "will not enlarge on any of the injuries, however great, which have a transitory effect. They wish to call the attention of the House to those of a permanent nature only, which intrench so deeply on our most important rights, and wound so extensively and vitally our best interests, as could not fail to deprive the United States of the principal advantages of their Revolution, if submitted to. The control of our commerce by Great Britain, in regulating at pleasure and expelling it almost from the ocean; the oppressive manner in which these regulations have been carried into effect, by seizing and confiscating such of our vessels, with their cargoes, as were said to have violated her edicts, often without previous warning of their danger; the impressment of our citizens from on board our own vessels on the high seas and elsewhere, and holding them in bondage till it suited the convenience of their oppressors to deliver them up, are encroachments of that high and dangerous tendency which could not fail to produce that pernicious effect; nor would these be the only consequences that would result from it. The British government might, for a while, be satisfied with the ascendency thus gained over us, but its pretensions would soon increase. The proof which so complete and disgraceful a submission to its authority would afford of our degeneracy, could not fail to inspire confidence that there was no limit to which its usurpations and our degradation might not be carried."

On the presentation of this report the doors were closed, and a motion to open them was denied by a vote of seventy-seven against forty-nine. Mr. Calhoun then presented a bill, as part of the report, declaring war between Great Britain and her dependencies and the United States and its Territories. Amendments were offered. Ten votes were given for a proposition by M'Kee, of Kentucky, to include France in the declaration. Mr. Quincy endeavored, by an addition to the bill, to provide for the repeal of all restrictive laws bearing upon commerce; and Randolph moved to postpone the whole matter until the following October. All were rejected, and the bill, as Calhoun presented it, was passed on the 4th day of June by a vote of seventy-nine for it and forty-nine against it.

When the bill reached the Senate[a] it was referred to a committee already appointed to consider the President's message. It remained under discussion twelve days. Meanwhile the people throughout the country were fearfully excited by conflicting emotions. A memorial against the war went from the Legislature of Massachusetts; and another from the merchants of New York, led by John Jacob Astor, recommending restrictive measures as better than war. War-meetings were held in various places, and the whole country was in a tumult of excitement. Finally, on the 17th of June—the anniversary of the battle of Bunker Hill—the bill, with some amendments, was passed by a vote of nineteen against thirteen. It was sent back to the House on the morning of the 18th, where the amendments were concurred in. The bill was engrossed on parchment, and at three o'clock on the afternoon of that day became a law by the signature of the President.[1] In the House, the members from Pennsylvania, and the states South and West, gave sixty-two votes for it

[a] June 5, 1812.

---

[1] The act declaring war was drawn up by William Pinkney, late minister to England, and then Attorney General of the United States. It is as follows: "That war be, and the same is hereby declared to exist between the United Kingdom of Great Britain and Ireland and the dependencies thereof and the United States of America and their Territories; and that the President of the United States is hereby authorized to use the whole land and naval force of the United States to carry the same into effect, and to issue to private armed vessels of the United States commissions, or letters of marque and general reprisal,* in such form as he shall think proper, and under the seal of the United States, against the vessels, goods, and effects of the government of the said United Kingdom of Great Britain and Ireland and the subjects thereof."

* *Letters of marque and reprisal*, or commissions to seize the goods of an enemy in time of war and not incur the penalty of robbery or piracy, were issued in England as early as Edward the First. It has ever been a powerful belligerent arm in warfare against commercial nations, and the system was of great service to the Americans during their war with Great Britain in 1812–'15. Efforts have recently been made to abolish the system among nations. It should be, for, after all, it is only legalized piracy.

to seventeen against it. In the Senate the same states gave fourteen for it to five against it. "Thus," says a late writer, "the war may be said to have been a measure of the South and West to take care of the interests of the North, much against the will of the latter."[1]

When the War Act became law, the injunction of secrecy was removed, and on the following day[a] the President issued a proclamation announcing the fact, and calling upon the people of the United States to sustain the public authorities in the measures to be adopted for obtaining a speedy, just, and honorable peace. "I exhort all the good people of the United States," he said, "as they love their country; as they value the precious heritage derived from the virtue and valor of their fathers; as they feel the wrongs which have forced on them the last resort of injured nations; and as they consult the best means, under the blessing of divine Providence, of abridging its calamities, that they exert themselves in preserving order, in promoting concord, in maintaining the authority and the efficiency of the laws, and in supporting and invigorating all the measures which may be adopted by the constituted authorities."

[a] June 19, 1812.

This was soon followed by an able protest against the measure. It was chiefly written by Mr. Quincy, who then stood at the head of the opposition, not only in Congress, but throughout the country. The prestige of his father's name as a leading patriot of the Revolution; his own long services in the National Legislature; his family connections and influence; his sterling worth in private life; his withering sarcasm of tongue and pen; his fluency of speech in declamation or debate, and his handsome and commanding presence, all combined to make him peerless as a leader. He was consequently assailed with the greatest bitterness by the friends of the administration; and squibs, and epigrams, and caricatures[2] frequently attested the general acknowledgment of his commanding position. Mr. Quincy outlived all of his contemporaries. Not one of the members of the Twelfth Congress — the Congress that declared war against Great Britain in 1812 — was living at the time of his death. He was born with the nation, whose full independence was only achieved at the close of that

JOSIAH the FIRST.

[1] Edwin Williams, in the *Statesman's Manual*, i., 450.
[2] One of the caricatures of Mr. Quincy is before me. It was engraved and published by William Charles,[*] of Philadelphia, and is entitled "Josiah the First." He is represented as a king, in reference to his political domination. On

[*] Of William Charles, the engraver above mentioned, who published several caricatures during the War of 1812–'15, very little is remembered. The venerable Doctor Alexander Anderson, of New York, the father of wood engraving in America, and yet (1867) a practitioner of the art at the age of ninety-two years, informed the writer that he knew Charles when he first came to America, about the year 1801. He was a native of Edinburg, Scotland. He caricatured one or more of the magistrates of that city, and, to avoid the consequences of prosecution, he left and came to the United States. He practiced his art in New York for a number of years without success, and then went to Philadelphia. The venerable John M'Allister, of Philadelphia, now (1867) more than eighty years of age, writes me that he remembers Charles and his small book-store and print-shop, which he opened in Philadelphia just before the War of 1812. After the suspension of specie payments by the banks in 1814, he engraved, printed, and vended a great quantity of notes for fractions of dollars, commonly known as "shinplasters." He died in Philadelphia in the year 1821, and his widow continued his bookselling and stationery business. I am indebted to Mr. M'Allister for the caricature of Mr. Quincy above given.

war, and lived to see it, in sturdy maturity, not only resist a most dangerous internal and inherited disease that threatened to destroy its life, but to rise from the attack purified and strengthened, with every promise of long and vigorous existence impressed upon every fibre of its being.[1]

Mr. Quincy, it has been observed, wrote the most of the minority's protest against the war. He was aided by Mr. Bayard, of Delaware, and some suggestions were made by others. It was signed by all the minority members of the House of Representatives, and was issued in the form of an address to their constituents, in which their conduct in voting against the war was vindicated.[2] They set forth perspicuously the state of the country, and the course of the administration and its supporters in Congress. They professed to believe that a war with Great Britain would necessarily lead to a political connection with France, then waging bitter hostilities against her—a connection which would be extremely hazardous to the liberties of the United States. They professed to regard France as the greater aggressor of the two, and looked upon her commerce as not worth contending for. Notwithstanding the French edicts, a profitable trade might be carried on with England, for France had not the power to enforce their edicts to a very great extent. Indeed, a large portion of the world where American commerce might be made profitable was not affected by the actions of either of the belligerents. They would, therefore, authorize the American merchantmen to arm in their own defense, become their own protectors, and go wherever they chose to risk themselves. As to the invasion and seizure of Canada, which was a part of the programme of the war party, they considered an attempt to carry out that measure as unjust and impolitic in itself, very uncertain in the issue, and unpromising as to any good results. They pointed to the unprepared state of the country as vehemently forbidding a declaration of war. "With a navy comparatively nominal, we are about to enter into the lists against the greatest marine on the globe. With a commerce unprotected and spread over every ocean, we propose to make profit by privateering, and for this endanger the wealth of which we are honest proprietors. An invasion is threatened of the colonies of a power which, without putting a new ship into commission, or taking another soldier into pay, can spread alarm or desolation along the extensive range of our seaboard. Before adequate fortifications are prepared for domestic defense, before men or money are provided for a war of attack, why hasten into the midst of this awful contest, which is laying waste Europe? It can not be concealed that to engage in the present war against England is to place ourselves on the side of France, and

---

his head is a crown. His coat is scarlet, his waistcoat brown, his breeches light green, and his stockings white silk. In one hand he holds a sceptre, and in the space near his head (omitted in our reduced copy) are the words: "I, Josiah the First, do, by this royal proclamation, announce myself King of New England, Nova Scotia, and Passamaquoddy; Grand Master of the noble Order of the Two Codfishes." On his left breast are seen two codfishes crossed, forming the order, and in the sea behind him that kind of fish is seen sporting in the water. These were probably introduced in allusion to his defense on the floor of Congress of the rights of the New England fishermen; or possibly because of the fact that the representation of a codfish has hung in the Representatives' Hall in the State-house at Boston since the year 1784, "as a memorial," in the language of John Rowe, who that year moved that it be placed there, "of the importance of the codfishery to the welfare of the commonwealth of Massachusetts."

[1] On the 29th of June, 1861, Mr. Quincy made a speech to the officers and soldiers of Captain Forbes's *Coast Guard* at Quincy, Massachusetts. He was then in his ninetieth year. In the course of his remarks on the great uprising of the people of the Northern section of the Union to put down the demagogues' rebellion in the Southern section, he remarked: "With what pride and joy would the founders of this republic have hailed the events of our day—a whole people rising as one man, with one mind and one heart, in support of the Constitution and the Union; upspringing from the East, the North, and the West, the farmer from the field, the mechanic from the work-bench—all classes and all professions—forgetting their gains, and ready to make sacrifices with one thought and one will to protect, to preserve, and to render the union of these states immortal. These are the true glories of a republic, evidencing that the masses which compose it understand the value of their liberties, and are prepared to sacrifice property and life in their defense."

[2] The following are the names of the signers of the protest:

George Sullivan, William Reid, Epaphroditus Champion, Benjamin Tallmadge, H. M. Ridgeley, Joseph Lewis, Jr., Elijah Brigham, Leonard White, Jonathan O. Moseley, Asa Fitch, Philip Stuart, Thomas Wilson, Abijah Bigelow, Laban Wheaton, Lyman Law, James Emott, Philip B. Key, A. M'Bryde, Josiah Quincy, Elisha R. Potter, Lewis B. Sturges, James Milnor, James Breckinridge, Joseph Pearson, William Ely, Richard Jackson, Jr., Timothy Pitkin, Jr., Thomas R. Gould, John Baker, Martin Chittenden, Samuel Taggart, John Davenport, Jr., H. Bleecker, C. Goldsburgh. The protest was printed in newspapers and on broadsides, and widely circulated.

expose us to the vassalage of states serving under the banners of the French emperor."

"It is said," they remarked, "that war is demanded by honor. Is national honor a principle which thirsts after vengeance, and is appeased only by blood; which, trampling on the hopes of man and spurning the law of God, untaught by what is past and careless of what is to come, precipitates itself into any folly or madness to gratify a selfish vanity or to satiate some unhallowed rage? If honor demands a war with England, what opiate lulls that honor to sleep over the wrongs done us by France?"

"What are the United States to gain by this war?" they asked. "Will the gratification of some privateersmen compensate the nation for that sweep of our legitimate commerce by the extended marine of our enemy which this desperate act invites? Will Canada compensate the Middle States for New York, or the Western States for New Orleans? Let us not be deceived. A war of invasion may invite a retort of invasion. When we visit the peaceable, and, as to us, innocent colonies of Great Britain[1] with the horrors of war, can we be assured that our own coast will not be visited with like horrors? At a crisis of the world, such as the present, and under impressions such as these, the undersigned can not consider the war into which the United States have in secret been precipitated as necessary, or required by any moral or political expediency."

Thus the issue was fairly placed before the country. The time for discussion was ended; the time for action had arrived. While one portion of the people—the vast majority—were nobly responding to the call of the President to sustain the government by word and deed, another portion were preparing to cast obstacles in the way of its success. An organization was soon visible, called the *Peace Party*, composed chiefly of the more violent opponents of the administration and disaffected Democrats, whose party-spirit held their patriotism in complete subordination. Lacking the sincerity or the integrity of those patriotic members of the Congressional minority, whose protest was the voice of their consciences made audible, they endeavored, by attempting to injure the public credit, preventing enlistments into the armies, spreading false stories concerning the strength of the British and weakness of the Americans, and by public speeches, sermons, pamphlets, and newspaper essays, to compel the government to sheathe the sword and hold out the olive-branch of peace at the cost of national honor and independence. These machinations were kept up during the whole war to the great embarrassment of the government and the injury of the country. To this unpatriotic *Peace Party* a large number of the leading Federalists gave no countenance, but, with a clear perception of duty to their country, and in accordance with the principles of the true spirit of republicanism, many of them, bound to the expressed will of the majority, yielded their private views to the necessities of the hour, and lent their aid, as the President desired all good citizens to do, "to the constituted authorities for obtaining a speedy, a just, and an honorable peace."

Having resolved on war, the next important labor for Congress to perform was making adequate provisions for prosecuting it. One of the most important considerations was finance, for money has been justly styled the "sinews of war." In February[a] the Committee of Ways and Means reported a system of finance adapted to a state of war for three years. Its chief features contemplated the support of war expenses wholly by loans; and the ordinary expenses of the government, including the interest on the national debt, by revenues. They estimated the war expenses at $11,000,000 for the first year. Aware that a state of

[a] February 17, 1812.

---

[1] The House of Representatives resolved that, in the event of a determination to invade Canada or other British provinces, the President should be authorized to issue a proclamation assuring the inhabitants thereof that all their rights, of every kind, should be respected if their territory should become a part of the United States.

war would diminish the revenue, they proposed a tariff by which the imposts should be doubled, foreign tonnage raised to a dollar and a half, a direct tax of $3,000,000, and an extensive system of internal duties and excise.[1] Congress adopted this financial scheme generally, and authorized[a] a loan of $11,000,000, at an interest not exceeding six per cent. a year, and reimbursable in twelve years. The Secretary of the Treasury directed subscriptions to be opened at the principal banks in the United States on the first and second days of May;[b] and, to induce the banks to subscribe, it was agreed that their subscriptions should remain as deposits until called for by the wants of the Treasury.

[a] March 14, 1812.
[b] 1812.

When war was declared, it was found, by the returns of the subscriptions to the $11,000,000 loan, that the banks had subscribed only $4,190,000, and individuals $1,928,000, leaving a deficiency of $4,882,000. To supply that deficiency, the President was authorized to issue Treasury notes, payable in one year, and bearing an annual interest of five and two fifths per cent., to be receivable in all payments at the Treasury. This was intended to pass as currency, and supersede, to a certain extent, the circulation of bank-notes. It was estimated that the entire expenses of the country for the fiscal year of 1812–'13, including the $11,000,000 for war purposes, and the interest on $45,154,000 (the amount of the public debt), would be $26,616,619.[2]

On the 26th of June Congress passed an act respecting the issue of letters of marque and reprisal, and another for the consolidation of the old army and the new levies; the regular force to consist of twenty regiments of foot, four of artillery, two of dragoons, and one of riflemen, which, with engineers and artificers, would make a force of thirty-six thousand seven hundred men. The actual regular force—experienced, disciplined, and effective—was only about three thousand men. The regular force under arms at that time was about ten thousand men, but more than half of them were raw recruits. Little reliance could be placed on the militia except for garrison duty, notwithstanding they were eight hundred thousand strong in a population of eight millions. They were not compelled by law to serve more than three years, nor go beyond the limits of their respective states. To volunteers the government and the country looked for numbers, and the President was authorized to place them on a footing with the regular army, and, with their consent, to appoint their officers.

The navy consisted of only three frigates of forty-four guns each, three of thirty-eight, one of thirty-six, one of thirty-two, three of twenty-eight, nine smaller vessels ranging from twelve to eighteen, and one hundred and sixty-five gun-boats.

Congress adjourned on the 6th of July. They had requested the President to recommend a day of public humiliation and prayer to be observed by the people of the United States for the purpose of publicly invoking the blessing of the Almighty on their cause, and the speedy restoration of peace. In accordance with this request, the President issued a proclamation on the 9th of July, recommending the setting apart of the third Thursday of August following[c] for that purpose. That day was generally observed throughout the Union; in most places in accordance with the spirit of the Congressional resolutions and the proclamation of the President, while from several New England pulpits went forth denunciations of the

[c] August 20.

---

[1] As an excise duty on liquors was proposed by Mr. Gallatin, the Secretary of the Treasury, who was one of the leaders in the famous "Whisky Insurrection" in Western Pennsylvania a few years before (see page 88), which was produced by a similar duty, he was severely handled by the opposition. Smilie, a Pennsylvania member of Congress, who was much more deeply implicated in wrong-doing in connection with that insurrection than Mr. Gallatin, and who now voted against the excise on liquors, was assailed with ridicule. On account of his defective education and his use of bad grammar in his Congressional speeches, the following epigram, which appeared in a leading Federal paper in March, 1812, was pointed:—

"A tax on *whisky* is a tax on *sin:*
Why then should Smilie hate the home-made gin-tax?
Because he is, and he has ever been,
A most invet'rate enemy to *syn*-tax."

[2] *History of the Political and Military Events of the late War between the United States and Great Britain,* by Samuel Perkins, page 53.

war, and the alleged authors and abettors of it.[1] The national anniversary that year was also made the occasion for political speeches, songs, and toasts condemnatory of the measures of the administration. Some of these were fierce, others were mild, and still others were dignified and patriotic—firm, outspoken, manly arguments against the necessity, the wisdom, or the justice of the war, but evincing a love of country more potent than love of party or opinions.[2]

---

[1] Already the governor of Massachusetts had appointed the 23d of July as a day of humiliation, fasting, and prayer. It was made the occasion for plain speaking from the pulpit against the war. Sometimes there was bitterness in the words, but generally these sermons breathed a spirit of sorrow because of the calamities threatened by the war. Among others, William Ellery Channing, of Boston, on both the state and the national fast-days, spoke out plainly, but with that charitable and sweet Christian spirit which characterized his whole life. "The cry has been," he said, "that war is declared, and all opposition should therefore be hushed. A sentiment more unworthy of a free country can hardly be propagated. If this doctrine be admitted, rulers have only to declare war, and they are screened at once from scrutiny. At the very time when they have armies at command, when their patronage is most extended, and their power most formidable, not a word of warning, of censure, of alarm must be heard. The press, which is to expose inferior abuses, must not utter one rebuke, one indignant complaint, although our best interests and most valuable rights are put to hazard by an unnecessary war. The sum of my remarks," he said, in concluding his discourse on the state fast-day, "is this: It is your duty to hold fast, and to assert with firmness those truths and principles on which the welfare of your country seems to depend; but do this with calmness, with a love of peace, without ill-will and revenge. Improve every opportunity of allaying animosities. Strive to make converts of those whom you think in error. Discourage, in decided and open language, that rancor, malignity, and unfeeling abuse which so often find their way into our public prints, and which only tend to increase the already alarming irritation of our country." "Our duties to our rulers," he said, on the national fast-day, "are not so easily presented. It is our duty toward them to avoid all language and conduct which will produce a spirit of insubordination, a contempt of laws and just authority. At the same time, we must not be tame, abject, and see, without sensibility, without remonstrance, our rights violated and our best blessings thrown away. Our elective form of government makes it our duty to expose bad rulers, to strip them of unmerited confidence and of abused power. This is never more clearly our duty than when our rulers have plunged us into an unjustifiable and ruinous war—a war which is leading us down to poverty, vice, and slavery. To reduce such men to a private station no fair and upright means should be spared, and, let me add, no other means should be employed. Nothing can justify falsehood, malignity, or wild, ungoverned passion. Be firm, but deliberate; in earnest, yet honest and just."

[2] In the New York *Evening Post*, July 21, 1812, may be found the following notice of a speech by the afterward eminent Daniel Webster, who had not yet appeared prominently in public life. He entered Congress the next year.

"WEBSTER'S ORATION.—A gentleman of this name, distinguished in the State of New Hampshire for the superiority of his talents, delivered an oration to the Washington Society at Portsmouth on the 4th of July. The following extracts will be read with pleasure:

"'With respect to the war in which we are now involved, the course which our principles require us to pursue can not be doubtful. It is now the law of the land, and as such we are bound to regard it. Resistance and insurrection form no parts of our creed. The disciples of *Washington* are neither tyrants *in* power nor rebels *out*. If we are taxed to carry on this war, we shall disregard certain distinguished examples, and shall pay. If our personal services are required, we shall yield them to the precise extent of our constitutional liability. At the same time, the world may be assured that we know our *rights*, and shall exercise them. We shall express our opinions on this, as on every measure of government, I trust without passion, I am certain without *fear*. We have yet to learn that the extravagant progress of pernicious measures abrogates the duty of opposition, or that the interest of our native land is to be abandoned by us in the hour of the thickest danger and sorest necessity. By the exercise of our constitutional right of suffrage, by the peaceable remedy of election, we shall seek to restore wisdom to our councils and *peace* to our country.'"

Those who remember Mr. Webster's patriotic course in the Senate of the United States in voting for the "Force Bill," to crush incipient treason and rebellion in South Carolina in 1833, will perceive in the above extract the visible germ of that stanch patriotism which distinguished him through life. On the occasion referred to he said, with the spirit that animated him in 1812, "I am opposed to this administration; but the country is in danger, and I will take my share of the responsibility in the measure before us."

The *Evening Post* of the same date contains an "Ode for the Fourth of July," written by William Cullen Bryant, then seventeen years of age. He is now (1867), after a lapse of fifty-five years, one of the proprietors and the editor in chief of that journal, which he has ably conducted for a very long period. The following stanzas selected from that Ode give a specimen of its character which made it very popular at the time:

"Lo! where our ardent rulers
  For fierce assault prepare,
While eager "*Ate*" awaits their beck
  To "slip the dogs of war."
In vain against the dire design
  Exclaims the indignant land;
The unbidden blade they haste to bare,
  And light the unhallowed brand.
Proceed! another year shall wrest
  The sceptre from your hand.

"The same ennobling spirit
  That kindles valor's flame,
That nerves us to a war of right,
  Forbids a war of *shame*.
For not in *Conquest's* impious train
  Shall Freedom's children stand;
Nor shall in guilty fray be raised
  The high-souled warrior's hand;
Nor shall the *Patriot* draw his sword
  At Gallia's proud command."

CHAPTER XII.

> "The tocsin has sounded—the bugle has blown,
> And rapid as lightning the rumor has flown,
> That, prepared to defend our heaven-blessed soil,
> Our country to save and proud tyrants to foil,
> We submit without murmur to danger and toil."
>   SONG—THE TOCSIN HAS SOUNDED.

EFORE entering upon a description of the stirring scenes of actual conflict of arms during the war, let us make brief notes of the position of the belligerents in relation to the struggle.

The Prince of Wales (afterward George the Fourth) had become actual sovereign of Great Britain by the removal of the restrictions of the bill which created him regent of the realm. The court physicians had pronounced the insanity of the old king to be incurable. This change in the practical relations of the prince to the government took place in February, 1812, and in May following a radical change in the Cabinet occurred, on account of the murder of Mr. Perceval, the Chancellor of the Exchequer, by Bellamy, a Liverpool ship-broker, who charged his commercial losses upon the government, and sought revenge in slaying one of its chief servants. Lord Sidmouth was appointed Secretary of State, the Earl of Harrowby Lord President of the Council, and Mr. Vansittart Chancellor of the Exchequer. Lord Castlereagh was Secretary for Foreign Affairs.

THE PRINCE REGENT—GEORGE IV.

Great Britain was still waging a tremendous war against Napoleon. Wellington was at the head of her armies in the Spanish Peninsula, and her forces by land and sea were generally successful. Her inherent energy was wonderful. Russia refused to bow the knee to the Corsican, and he threatened her with invasion. Great Britain became her ally, and the summer and autumn of 1812 saw the hopes of the ambitious emperor of obtaining universal dominion clouded with fearful doubts. Six days after the United States declared war against Great Britain, the victorious Napoleon, with an immense and splendid army, crossed the Niemen[a] in the face of three hundred thousand Russians, and pushed on toward Moscow. At Borodino the retreating Muscovites confronted their invaders,[b] and when the curtain of night fell upon the battle-field, ninety thousand killed and wounded soldiers lay there. The French entered Moscow in triumph, but it was soon a heap of ashes. Late in October, with one hundred and twenty thousand men, the emperor commenced a retreat toward France. Six months from the time of his entering Russian territory he had lost, in slain, wounded, starved, frozen, and prisoners, four hundred and fifty thou-

[a] June 24, 1812.
[b] Sept. 6.

sand men, and yet he had scarcely reached Paris before he issued orders for new conscriptions with which to prosecute the war! The sun of his glory was low in the west, yet it blazed out brilliantly before it set. In 1812, Great Britain, Russia, Sweden, and Spain were allied in arms against France, Prussia, Italy, Austria, and Poland.

The British navy at that time consisted of two hundred and fifty-four ships-of-the-line, of 74 guns and upward; thirty-five 50's and 44's; two hundred and forty-seven frigates; and five hundred and six smaller vessels of war; making a total of one thousand and thirty-six. Of these there were five ships-of-the-line, nineteen frigates, forty-one brigs, and sixteen schooners on the American station; that is to say, at Halifax and Newfoundland, Jamaica and the Leeward Islands.[1] They had also four armed vessels on Lake Ontario, namely, *Royal George*, 22; *Earl of Moira*, 16; *Prince Regent*, 14; and *Duke of Gloucester*, 8. They also had several smaller vessels nearly ready for service.

The British regular land force in Upper Canada when war was declared did not exceed fifteen hundred men;[2] but the aggregate of that in Lower Canada, and in the contiguous British provinces was estimated at six thousand regular troops. The population of all the North American British colonies was estimated at 400,000, and their militia at 40,000. They had an immense assailable frontier, stretching along a series of great lakes, and the Rivers St. Mary's, St. Clair, Detroit, Niagara, and St. Lawrence, commencing at Lake Superior on the west, and terminating far below Quebec on the east, along a line of about 1700 miles. Out of Lake Superior flows a rapid current, over immense masses of rock, through a channel for twenty-seven miles called the St. Mary's River, and enters Lake Huron, at the head of which is the British island of St. Joseph. On that island was then a small fort and garrison. It is distant above Detroit about three hundred and thirty miles by water. The shores of Lake Huron at that time were uninhabited except by Indians and a few traders. At its western angle is a short and wide strait, connecting it with Lake Michigan, in the centre of which is the island of Michilimackinack, which is about nine miles in circumference. On this island the Americans had a small fort and garrison. The waters flow out of Lake Huron through the rivers and Lake St. Clair, and then through the Detroit River into Lake Erie. On the latter river, at Amherstburg, the British had a fort and small garrison, where ships for service on Lake Erie were built. The British had no harbor or military post on Lake Erie. At its foot, at the head of the Niagara River, was Fort Erie, a distance of five hundred and sixty-five miles from Quebec. Just above Niagara Falls, at the mouth of the Chippewa River, there was a small stockade, called Fort Chippewa. Near the mouth of the Niagara River, not quite seven miles below Queenstown, was Fort George, constructed of earthen ramparts and cedar palisades, mounting some guns not heavier than nine-pounders. Half a mile below the fort, at the mouth of the Niagara River, was a pretty little village called Newark, now Niagara. On the north side of Lake Ontario is York, or Toronto Harbor, where was an old fort and a block-house. York was then the capital of Upper Canada. On the eastern extremity of the lake is Kingston, with a fine harbor, and was defended by a small battery of nine-pounders on Point Frederick. It was the most populous town in the Upper Province at that time, and formed the principal naval dépôt of the British on Lake Ontario. There were some military works at Montreal, and very strong ones at Quebec.

At the time when war was declared the United States were at peace with all the world, and had very little commerce exposed upon the ocean, owing to restrictions

---

[1] Steele's List, 1812.
[2] These consisted of the Forty-first Regiment, 900 men; Tenth Veterans, 250; Newfoundland Regiment, 250; Royal Artillery, 50; Provincial Seamen, 50. These forces had to occupy the Forts St. Joseph, Amherstburg, Chippewa, Erie, George, York (Toronto), and Kingston, and to defend an assailable frontier of nearly thirteen hundred miles.—*Life and Correspondence of Major General Sir Isaac Brock, K.B.*, by Ferdinand Brock Tupper, p. 168.

and dangers which had prevailed for a few years. Of the land and naval forces at that time we have spoken in the last chapter. In addition to full twelve hundred miles of frontier along the British provinces, there was a sea-coast of a thousand miles to defend against the most powerful maritime nation in the world.

The subject of sea-coast, harbor, and frontier defenses attracted the attention of the government at an early period. A school for military instruction, especially for the education of engineers, to be established at West Point, on the Hudson, was authorized by Congress in the spring of 1802;[a1] and from to time to time appropriations had been made for fortifications, and works had been erected. The corps of engineers, authorized by the law just named, commenced their functions as constructors of new forts or repairers of old ones in the year 1808, when a war with England was confidently expected; and that body of young men continued thus employed, in a moderate way, until the breaking out of the war in 1812, when they were sent to the field, and all won military distinction.[2] The forts completed previous to 1809 were the only fortifications for the defense of the sea-coast of the United States at the commencement of the war in 1812.[3]

[a] March 16, 1802.

---

[1] Washington recommended the establishment of a military academy at West Point so early as 1783, when, on the approach of peace, his thoughts were turned to the future military condition of his country. Soon after he became President of the United States, he again called the attention of his countrymen to the importance of a military academy, and again indicated West Point as the proper place. In 1794, Colonel Rochefontaine, a French officer in the service of the United States, and other officers of artillery, were stationed at West Point for the purpose of establishing a military school there. They rebuilt the front of Fort Putnam, on the mountains in the rear, in 1795, and constructed five or six small casemates, or bomb-proofs. Fort Clinton, on the Point, was then partly in ruins. Its magazine, twenty-five by two hundred feet in size, built of stone and lined with plank, and trenches, was quite perfect. Several buildings were erected, and the whole post was under the charge of Major Jonathan Williams. The library and apparatus were commenced, but the school was soon suspended. It was revived in 1801 by Mr. Jefferson, and in the spring of the following year Congress, as we have observed in the text, authorized the establishment of a military academy there. Meanwhile the harbors on the coast were defended only by small redoubts. They were insignificant affairs. "It is worthy of remembrance," observed the late venerable General J. G. Swift, in a letter to the author in February, 1860, "that the sites upon which these small works were built were those selected in the Revolutionary struggle, and they remain to this day the best for their purpose."

[2] Letter of General Swift to the author, February 13, 1860. In November, 1802, the engineers at West Point formed a *Military and Philosophical Society*, the object of which was the promotion of military science. The following are the names of the original members: Jonathan Williams, Decius Wadsworth, William A. Barron, Jared Mansfield, James Wilson, Alexander Macomb, Jr., Joseph G. Swift, Simon M. Leroy, Walter K. Armistead, and Joseph G. Totten. These were the members present at the first meeting. Swift and Totten were the latest survivors of this little company. The former died in the summer of 1865, and the latter in the spring of 1864. Their portraits will be found in this work. Totten was the chief military engineer of the United States at the time of his death. The society consisted of many persons besides military men. Its membership, during its ten years' existence, comprised most of the leading men in the country, especially of the army and navy. The MS. records of the society, in four folio volumes, are in the New York Historical Society.

[3] The following statement of the names, locations, and conditions of the coast fortifications previous to 1808, I have compiled from a manuscript general return of such works by Colonel Jonathan Williams* and Captain Alexander Macomb, which I found among the minutes of the *Military and Philosophical Society* of West Point, mentioned in a preceding note. Some of these forts were somewhat strengthened before the declaration of war in 1812, but the change in their general condition was not very great.

Fort Sumner, Portland, Maine.—A square block-house.

Fort William and Mary, Portsmouth, New Hampshire.—A ruin.

Fort Lily, Gloucester, Cape Ann.—Three sides of an unfinished figure, being one front and two diverging lines. A square block-house in the rear.

Fort Pickering, at Salem, Massachusetts.—Three sides of a rectangular figure, without bastions, flanks, or any prominence whatever. The lower part of the sides is stone-work, with parapets of earth. Closed in the rear by barracks, a

---

* Jonathan Williams was born in Boston in 1750. He was appointed Major of the Second Artillery and Engineers in February, 1801, and in December following Inspector of Fortifications and Superintendent of the Military Academy at West Point. In July, 1802, he was promoted to Lieutenant Colonel of Engineers, and resigned in June the following year. In April, 1805, he resumed the service among the Engineers, with the same rank, and in February, 1808, was promoted to colonel; he resigned in July, 1812. In 1814 he was elected to a seat in Congress from Philadelphia, but never occupied it. He died on the 20th of May, 1815, at the age of sixty-five years.—Gardner's *Dictionary of the Army*, 487. Colonel Williams was the author of *A Memoir of the Thermometer in Navigation*, and *Elements of Fortification*.

236   PICTORIAL FIELD-BOOK

The Coast Defenses of the United States in the year 1812.

A new system of naval warfare had lately been suggested by Robert Fulton, who
had been a long time abroad, and who had recently returned home[a] to
achieve an immortal triumph in science and art, and the beginning of a

[a] December, 1806.

brick wall, and gate. A square block-house in the centre, and an old stone building in the rear and on the left, without
the lines. A sketch of its appearance in 1860 may be found in another part of this volume.

Fort Sewall, at Marblehead, Massachusetts, is an irregular oblong figure, with a square block-house. It is founded, on
one side, on a rock, and on the opposite side has a wall and arches, forming a magazine below. One stone house within
the lines. A sketch of this old fort as it appeared in 1860 may be found in another part of this work.

Fort Independence, in Boston Harbor.—New work. An irregular pentagon and well fortified, with five bastions. Three
bastions and one curtain finished. This fort (whose present appearance is seen in the engraving) is on Castle Island,

FORT INDEPENDENCE.

on the site of a fortification erected during the early years of the Massachusetts colony. It was rebuilt in 1644, and
burned in 1673. A new fort of stone was then erected, and other works, and it became the shelter of the British during
the years preceding the Revolution. After the Revolution it was called Fort Adams. In 1799 Castle Island was ceded
to the United States, and President Adams named the works Fort Independence. The present structure was erected in
1801, '2, and '3. It and Fort Warren, on an island opposite, command the entrance to Boston Harbor. The fort may
contain a thousand men in time of war.

Fort Wolcott, near Newport, Rhode Island.—Built of stone cemented with lime. Had a brick and stone magazine, a
sally-port and ditch, reverberatory furnace. Supported by two wings or bastions, both facing the harbor. Revetments
in stone laid in lime cement; parapets supplied with sod-work; the batteries intended for ten pieces of cannon. Had
five pieces, 32-pounders each. Barracks two stories high, composed of brick, and bomb-proof.

Fort Adams, Newport Harbor.—Form similar to Fort Wolcott. Situated on Brenton's Point, nearly opposite the
Dumplings Fort on Canonicut Island. Similar in all its arrangement and construction to Fort Wolcott. It was then
unfinished.

Fort Hamilton, Narraganset Bay, near Newport, a mile northwest of Fort Wolcott, on Rose Island.—Extensive fortifications, commenced in 1802. Quadrilateral in form, presenting two regular and two tower bastions. Works suspended in 1803. It was intended to be wholly constructed of stone, brick, and sod-work. The barracks were completed, and
were considered the finest in America at that time. It was intended to mount seventy cannon. About half completed
when the war broke out.

North Battery, Rhode Island, about three fourths of a mile northeast of Fort Wolcott, on a point of land nearer Newport.—Semicircular, and calculated for about eight guns. It was unfinished.

Dumplings Fort.—Entrance to Narraganset Bay, nearly opposite Fort Adams. A round tower bastion, built in 1804,
of stone well cemented. It was about eighty feet above the water, and rose fifteen to twenty feet above the rock on
which it was built. It contained a good magazine, and three other bomb-proof rooms for the men. No cannon were
mounted. The platforms were not completed. Calculated for seven pieces, exclusive of howitzers and mortars. It was
believed that thirty men might defend it.

Towering Hill, near Newport, Rhode Island, one mile east of the North Battery, and due north from the city.—It commanded the whole town, the country around, and a part of the harbor. Remains of Revolutionary works there. A small
block-house built in 1799 or 1800 was entire.

Fort Trumbull, New London, Connecticut, on a rocky point of land projecting into the River Thames.—Form irregular. The walls fronting the water built of solid stone, elevated to the usual height, and finished with turf and gravel.
Badly situated against an enemy on land, as the hills around it and across the river are higher than the fort. It had a
small magazine and stone block-house, and fourteen guns mounted. A view of this fort may be seen in another part
of this work.

Fort Jay, on Governor's Island, New York Harbor,* thirteen hundred yards south of the Battery, at the lower extremity of the city of New York.—It was a regular fort, with bastions, quite strong, but then unfinished. It had a handsome
gateway, with a corps de garde draw-bridge. In the centre of the fort was a square block-house of timber, two stories
high, but probably not cannon-proof; under it was a well. It had two detached batteries, one mounting four 18-pound-
ers and an 8-inch French mortar, with platforms for four others; and the other ten pieces, 18 and 24 pounders; origin-

* Governor's Island was called Pag-ganck by the Indians, and Nutten Island by the Dutch. It was purchased, as a
public domain, by Governor Van Twiller, in the early days of the Dutch rule in New York. In the settlement of the
accounts of the Revolutionary debt, New York agreed to erect fortifications in the harbor in front of the city of New
York, in payment of the quota required from that state. In accordance with an act passed by the State Legislature in
March, 1794, the sum of one hundred and fifty thousand dollars was expended, under the direction of a committee, in
constructing fortifications. The committee consisted of George Clinton, Matthew Clarkson, James Watson, Richard
Varick, Nicholas Fish, Ebenezer Stevens, and Abijah Hammond. A further sum of one hundred thousand dollars was
granted on the 6th of April, 1795, to complete the works on that and Oyster (now Ellis's) Island. Fort Jay was built,
and in February, 1800, the island and all its appurtenances were ceded to the United States. The island contains seventy-two acres of land.

wonderful revolution in commerce, by the successful introduction of navigation by steam.[a] While abroad, Mr. Fulton had conceived the idea of destroying ships by introducing floating mines under their bottoms in submarine boats, and ex-

[a] 1807.

CASTLE WILLIAMS.

ally intended for thirteen guns. The parapet had fifty-one embrasures, and it would take one thousand men to man the parapet. The fort, being commanded by hills on the Long Island shore, was not constructed to withstand a siege, but as a guard to the entrance to the East River, and to operate against an enemy in the harbor or in the city.

Ellis's and *Bedloe's* Islands both had fortifications on them. The former, lying a little more than two thousand yards southwest from the Battery, had a semicircular battery calculated for thirteen guns. The parapet, of timbers, was unfinished. Twelve 12-pounders lay there, but no guns were mounted. It was commanded by Bedloe's Island, twelve hundred yards distant; also by Paulus's Hook (Jersey City), lying north of it. There were good quarters for officers and men. It was an excellent position to defend the harbor from an enemy coming in at the Narrows. Only a part of the island then belonged to the United States.

On *Bedloe's Island* a battery had been commenced, and brick buildings for quarters. No cannon were mounted excepting two field-pieces that belonged to Fort Jay. A dismounted 24-pounder lay upon the island. It was almost useless, as a defensive work. Major Decius Wadsworth was then in command of the District of New York, and these works were under his supervision. Of the islands in New York Harbor, and the modern fortifications upon them, I shall have occasion to write hereafter.

Fort Mifflin, on the southeast extremity of Mud Island, in the Delaware, just below Philadelphia, was an irregular oval. It was the old British fort of the Revolution. It had been strengthened, and was a very important work. It was constructed of stone, brick, and earth, with heavy guns mounted. A long account of it is given in the MS. records of the *Military and Philosophical Society* (New York Historical Society), vol. iv.

Fort M'Henry, at Baltimore, was a new work situated on a point of land between the Patapsco River and the harbor. It was a regular pentagon, with a well-executed revetment; also a magazine, and barracks sufficient for one company. The counterscarp, covert, and glacis were yet to be made. On the water side was the wall of a battery, but not yet inclosed. It is a well-chosen position to prevent ships reaching Baltimore, and is about two and a half miles from the city. At the time we are considering, a large house belonging to a citizen stood in front of the battery, next the extreme point, and, in the event of a ship's passing, would have to be battered down, as it would cover the vessel. A picture of the fort as it appeared in 1861 may be found in another part of this work.

Fort Severn, at Annapolis, has already been noticed. See note 4, on page 181.

Forts Norfolk and *Nelson*, one on each side of the Elizabeth River, near Norfolk, Virginia, were of some importance. The former, on the Norfolk side of the river, a mile and a half below the town, was an oblong square, with two bastions, built chiefly of earth, and a ditch on three sides of it. Within it was one frame house and eight small log huts, all in bad condition. Two 12, four 9, and thirteen 6 pounders, two brass 8-inch howitzers, and seven carronades, all dismounted, were lying there. The fort was on the site of some works thrown up during the Revolution.

Fort Nelson was about a mile below the town, on the opposite side of the river. Its form was triangular, but irregular, the works of the Revolutionary era having been used. It covered nearly two acres of ground. It was built of earth. It had two batteries with embrasures, lined with brick inside. In it were one large two-story house, two rooms on a floor, a kitchen, and smoke-house. There were thirteen 24-pounders and one 12-pounder mounted; the carriages were rotten, and unfit for service. This fort, like the one opposite, was intended to guard the approach to the town by water. On the land side the walls were not more than three feet high. The magazine was too damp for use.

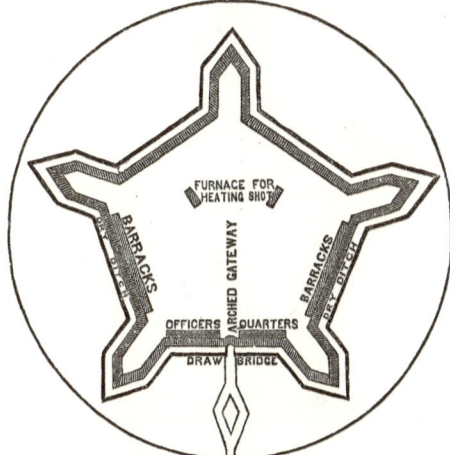

PLAN OF FORT M'HENRY.

ploding them there. He was filled with the benevolent idea that the introduction of such secret and destructive agencies would have a tendency to do away with naval warfare, and thus would be established what he called the *Liberty of the Seas*. Impelled by this grand idea, he left France, where he had been residing several years, and went over to England in 1804, for the purpose of offering his invention to the British government.[1] He finally obtained permission to make a public experiment of his TORPEDO, as he called his "infernal machine," and he was furnished

---

For the protection of Charleston Harbor there were several works, some of them as old as the Revolution. *Fort Johnson*, on James's Island, was enlarged and strengthened in 1793, and afterward repaired and patched at various times. The chief works were of brick. The barracks were of wood, one-story high; there was also a block-house. A large portion of the fort was carried away by a hurricane in 1804, and the remainder was inundated, sapped, and destroyed. *Fort Pinckney*, built in 1798, stood upon a marsh in front of Charleston called Shute's Folly. Built entirely of brick. It mounted eight 26-pounders *en barbette*. At the best it was an inefficient work, and in 1804 it too was sapped during the great hurricane, and rendered almost useless. *Fort Moultrie* was built on the site of the fort of that name in the Revolution. It was constructed in 1798, chiefly of brick and palmetto logs. It mounted on the ramparts ten 26-pounders *en barbette*, on double sea-coast carriages; one mortar, and six 12-pounders and a howitzer in the ditch. This fort was also greatly damaged by the hurricane. The counterscarp and glacis were entirely swept away; no ditch remained; every traverse, and gun, and the reverberatory furnace were washed away and buried in the sand. All the wood-work of the fort was rotten, yet the fort was in a condition to be repaired. At the south end of the city of Charleston were the remains of *Fort Mechanic*, a redoubt in utter ruin.

Such was the general condition of the sea-coast defenses of the United States when war was declared in 1812.

On the Northern and Northwestern frontiers were some military posts and fortifications. First was the fort on the island of Michillimackinack, in the strait between Lakes Huron and Michigan. At Chicago, on Lake Michigan, was *Fort Dearborn*; at the head of the Maumee, *Fort Wayne*; a strong fort at Detroit; a battery and block-house at Erie; a battery at Black Rock, just below Buffalo; *Fort Niagara*, a strong work built by the French, at the mouth of the Niagara River; another considerable fort at Oswego, and a military post and a battery, called *Fort Tompkins*, at Sackett's Harbor. All of these will be noticed in the course of our narrative.

[1] Mr. Fulton took up his residence in Paris with Joel Barlow, and remained with him seven years. It was during that time that he planned his submarine boat, which he called a nautilus, and the machines attached to which he styled submarine bombs. He offered his invention several times to the French government, and once to the Dutch embassador at Paris, but did not excite the favorable attention of either. He then opened negotiations with the British government, and went to London in 1804. There he held interviews with Mr. Pitt and Lord Melville, and explained the nature of his invention to them. Pitt was convinced of its great value, but Melville condemned it. In the course of a month a committee was appointed to examine, whose chairman was Sir Joseph Banks. They reported the submarine boat to be impracticable, when Mr. Fulton abandoned the idea of employing a submarine vessel, and turned his attention to the arrangement of his bombs, so that they might be employed without submerged boats. These he called TORPEDOES, and, in a memorial afterward presented to the American Congress,* he thus describes their construction, and method of operation:

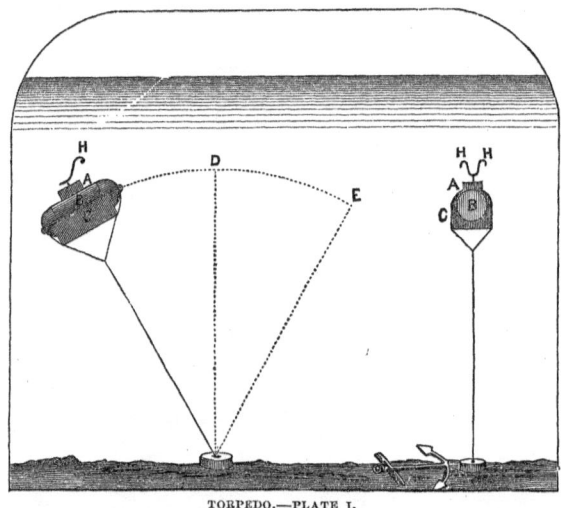

TORPEDO.—PLATE I.

PLATE I. This shows the torpedo anchored, and so arranged as to blow up a vessel that should strike it. B is a copper case, two feet long and twelve inches in diameter, capable of containing one hundred pounds of gunpowder. A, a brass box, in which is a lock, similar to a common gun-lock, with a barrel two inches long, and holding a musket-charge of powder. The box, with the lock cocked and barrel charged, is screwed to the copper case B. H is a lever, having a communication with the cock inside the box A, holding the lock cocked, and ready to fire. C, a deal box filled with cork and tied to the case B, so as to make the torpedo fifteen to twenty pounds lighter than the water specifically, so as to give it buoyancy. It is held down to a given depth by a weight. A small anchor is attached to the weight to prevent its being moved by the tides. The torpedo was sunk not so deep as the usual draft of vessels to be acted upon. In flood-tide it would be oblique to the weight, at slack water perpendicular at D, and during the ebb again oblique at E. At ten feet below the surface the tide would not be likely to disturb it seriously. When a ship in sailing should strike the lever H, an instantaneous explosion would take place, and the utter destruction of the vessel would follow. Fulton proposed to anchor a hundred of these in the Narrows, approaching the harbor of New York, in the event of war. The figure on the right shows an end view of the torpedo, with a forked link, by which the chances of being struck by a vessel were increased.

---

* Mr. Fulton's memorial, published in pamphlet form in 1810, by William Elliott, 114 Water Street, New York, bears the following title: TORPEDO WAR *and* SUBMARINE EXPLOSION, *by* ROBERT FULTON, *Fellow of the American Philosophical Society, and of the United States Military and Philosophical Society*. Its motto—*The Liberty of the Seas will be the Happiness of the Earth*.

with a Danish brig, named *Dorothea*, and two boats, with eight men each, for the purpose. On the 15th of October, 1805, the *Dorothea* was anchored in Walmer

PLATE II. This represents another kind of torpedo—a clock-work torpedo*—intended to attack a vessel while lying at anchor or under sail, by harpooning her on her larboard or starboard bow. B, a copper case containing one hundred pounds or more of gunpowder. C, a cork cushion, to give buoyancy to the whole. A, a cylindrical brass box, about seven inches in diameter and two deep, in which is a gun-lock, with a barrel two inches long to receive a charge of powder and wad, which charge is fired with the powder of the case B. In the brass box A there is also a piece of clock-work, moved by a coiled spring, which being wound up and set, will let the lock strike fire in any number of minutes which may be determined, within an hour. K is a small line fixed to a pin, which holds the clock-work inactive. The instant the pin is withdrawn the clock-work begins to move, and the explosion will take place in one, two, three, or any number of minutes for which it has been set. The whole is made perfectly water-tight. D is a pine box, two feet long and six or eight inches square, filled with cork to give it buoyancy, as in Plate I., although in this case it floats on the surface, no weights for submergence being used. To this the torpedo is suspended. The line of suspension should be long enough to bring the torpedo well back toward the stern of the vessel. From the torpedo and float D are two lines, each twenty feet long, united at E. From these a single line, about fifty feet in length, is attached to a harpoon. This, when the vessel is harpooned in the bow, will bring the torpedo under the bottom, at about midships, of a man-of-war. The harpoon I is a round piece of iron, half an inch in diameter, two feet long, with a butt of one inch, which is the exact calibre of the gun from which it is to be projected. In the head of the barbed harpoon is an eye; the point about six inches long. Into the eye the line of the harpoon is spliced, and a small iron or tough copper link runs on the shaft of the harpoon. To this link the line is attached at such length as to form the loop H when the harpoon is in the gun. When fired, the link will slide along to the butt of the harpoon, and, holding the rope and the harpoon parallel to each other, the rope will act like a tail or rod to a rocket, and guide it straight. F is the harpoon gun, acting upon a swivel fixed in the stern-sheets of a boat. The harpoon is fixed in the vessel's bow, with the line from the torpedo attached; the torpedo clock-work is set in motion, the machine is thrown overboard, and the tide, on the motion of the vessel, quickly places it under the ship.

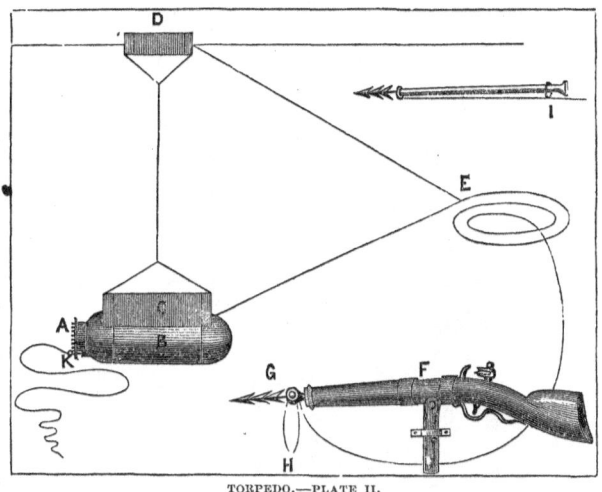

TORPEDO.—PLATE II.

PLATE III. The upper portion of the plate represents the stern of a row-boat, with the harpoon-gun and torpedo just described. A platform, four feet long and three feet wide, is made on the stern, level with the gunwale, and projecting over the stern fifteen or eighteen inches, so that the torpedo, in falling into the water, may clear the rudder. The ropes are carefully disposed so that there may be no entanglement. The letters in this figure (A, B, and C) denote the parts, as in the last plate. The pin D, which restrains the clock-work, is drawn, when the torpedo is cast off, by the line attached to the boat at E. The harpooner, stationed at the gun,

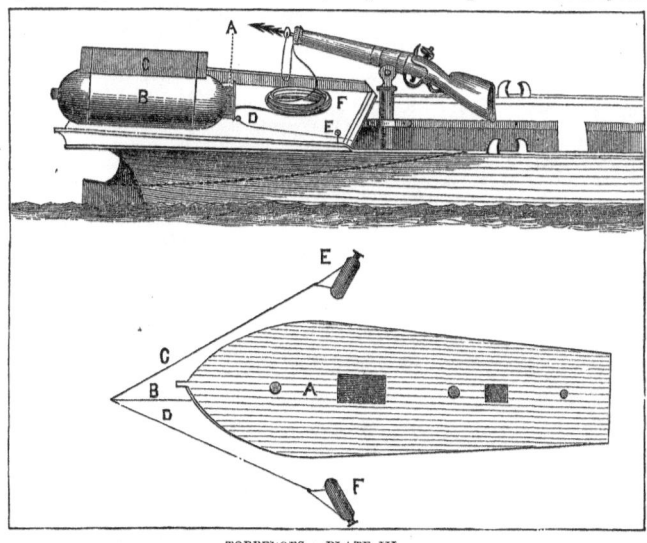

TORPEDOES.—PLATE III.

---

* The late Henry Frasse, who for many years kept a shop in Fulton Street, New York, for the sale of watch-maker's materials, made the clock-work for Mr. Fulton. In his account-book before me is the following entry at the time we are considering:

"Dt. Mr. Fulton a H'y Frasse:

"26th May, 1810.—a Fulton repare un turpedos, le grand ressort, volant et roue, 4.50."

Mr. Frasse was then the only machinist of note in the city of New York. He died in February, 1849, at the age of sixty-eight years.

Road, not far from Deal, and in sight of Walmer Castle, the residence of William Pitt, the English prime minister, and there, in the presence of a large number of naval officers and others,[1] he made a successful exhibition. He first practiced the boatmen with empty torpedoes. One was placed in each boat, and connected by a small rope eighty feet long. The *Dorothea* drew twelve feet of water, and the torpedoes were suspended fifteen feet under water when cast from the boats, at the distance of seventy-five feet apart. They floated toward the brig with the tide, one on each side of her. When the connecting-line struck the hawser of the brig, both torpedoes were brought by the tide under her bottom.

Having exercised the men sufficiently, Fulton filled one of the torpedoes with one hundred and eighty pounds of gunpowder, set its clock-work (explained in note 1, page 238) to eighteen minutes, and then went through with the same manœuvres as before, the filled and the empty torpedo being united by a rope. At the expiration of eighteen minutes from the time the torpedoes were cast overboard, and were carried toward the *Dorothea*, a dull explosion was heard, and the brig was raised bodily about six feet,[2] and separated in the middle; and in twenty minutes nothing was seen of her but some floating fragments. The pumps and foremasts were blown out of her; the fore-topsail-yards were thrown up to the cross-trees; the fore-chain plates, with their bolts, were torn from her sides, and her mizzen-mast was broken off in two places. The experiment was perfectly satisfactory; but the British government refused to purchase and use the invention, because it was thought to be inexpedient

DESTRUCTION OF THE DOROTHEA.

also steers the boat, and fires according to his judgment. If the harpoon sticks into the bow of the vessel, the boat is immediately moved away, the torpedo cast out of the boat, and the clock-work set in motion. If the harpoon misses the ship, the torpedo may be saved, and another attack be made. Fulton proposed to have twelve men in each boat, all armed for their protection or offensive movements, if necessary. The figure in the lower part of the plate is a bird's-eye view of a vessel (A) at anchor. B, her cable; E F, two torpedoes; C D, their coupling lines, twelve feet long. It is touching the vessel's cable, and the torpedoes being driven under her by the tide. In this way the *Dorothea*, mentioned in the text, was attacked. Those were clock-work torpedoes.

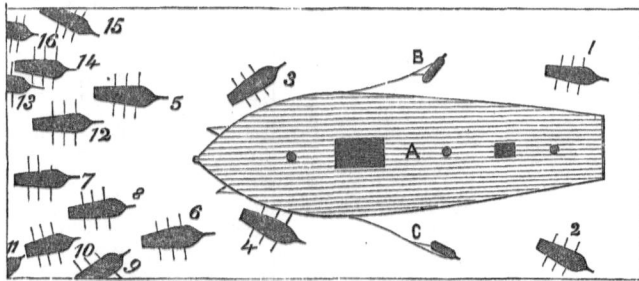

TORPEDOES.—PLATE IV.

PLATE IV. represents a bird's-eye view of a vessel at anchor, or under weigh, attacked by a flotilla of mortar-boats. A is the vessel, and B C two torpedoes operating by means of the harpoon movement. When it was objected that these boats would be exposed to grape, canister, and musket balls from the vessel, Fulton estimated that the time of danger, by expert movements, would not exceed four minutes—two in approaching near enough to fire the harpoon, and two for retreating. He entered into a calculation of the greater efficiency and less exposure of the torpedo system, in harbor defense, than ships of war. I have given this description of the torpedo as illustrative of a part of the history of the times we are considering. Science and mechanical skill have since produced far more destructive engines of war, and yet Fulton's dream of establishing the *liberty of the seas* by means of the torpedo, or any other instrumentality, remains unaccomplished. A *Monitor* of to-day is worth a million of torpedoes for harbor defense.

[1] Admiral Holloway, Sir Sidney Smith, Captain Owen, Captain Kingston, Colonel Congreve, and a greater portion of the officers of the fleet under Lord Keith were present. Pitt was in London, and did not see the exhibition. Colonel Congreve was the inventor of the rocket, or "pyrotechnic arrow," as Fulton called it, bearing his name.

[2] The engraving is from a drawing by Fulton, appended to his memorial to Congress in 1810.

for the mistress of the seas to introduce into naval warfare a system that would give great advantages to weaker maritime nations. The Earl St. Vincent said Pitt was a fool to encourage a mode of warfare which they, who commanded the seas, did not want, and which, if successful, would deprive them of it.[1]

At the beginning of 1807 Mr. Fulton was in Washington with his drawings, models, and plans for a "torpedo war." He was favorably listened to then, but his plans were regarded with more interest after the affair of the *Leopard* and *Chesapeake*, a few months later. That affair caused much public discussion about harbor defenses, and able practical writers, like Colonel Williams and John Stevens, favored the use of Fulton's torpedoes. It was believed that measures would be taken to drive British vessels of war from American harbors, and on the 6th of July Fulton again brought his torpedoes to the notice of the Secretary of the Navy. Congress made a small appropriation for experiments, and on the 20th of July, by the direction of the President, Fulton performed a feat in the harbor of New York similar to that of the destruction of the *Dorothea* in Walmer Road. He utterly destroyed a vessel of two hundred tons burden, and convinced the spectators that any ship might be so demolished.[2] The experiment created quite a sensation in England. The Earl of Stanhope, Fulton's early friend, alluded to it in Parliament, and reproached the government, by implication, for suffering such an invention to go to America, when, for three thousand pounds, they might have possessed it. Nothing farther of importance was done in the matter, for Fulton was then deeply engaged in bringing to a successful issue his experiments in navigating by steam as a motor. But when those experiments resulted in absolute and brilliant success, and men's minds were filled with speculations concerning the future of this new aid to commerce, he believed that his torpedo system would be of far more benefit to mankind than navigation by steam. In a letter to a friend, giving him an account of his first voyage to Albany and back by steam—the first achievement of the kind—he said: "However, I will not admit that it is *half so important* as the torpedo system of defense and attack, for out of it will grow the liberty of the seas, an object of infinite importance to the welfare of America and every civilized country. But thousands of witnesses have now seen the steam-boat in rapid movement, and believe; they have not seen a ship-of-war destroyed by a torpedo, and they do not believe."[3]

How utterly impotent is the finite mind when it attempts to understand the future. It is like a bewildered traveler in a dark night attempting to comprehend an almost illimitable prairie before him by the aid of a "fire-fly lamp." The torpedo is forgotten; the steam-boat, in *Monitor*[4] form, is now (1867) the great champion for the "liberty of the seas."

In January, 1810, Fulton again visited Washington, and at Kalorama, the seat of his good friend Barlow, near Georgetown, in the presence of President Jefferson, Secretary Madison, and a large number of members of Congress, he exhibited and explained the plans and models of improved torpedoes, such as are described in note 1,

---

[1] Letter from Robert Fulton to Joel Barlow.

[2] Mr. Fulton invited the Governor of the State of New York, the Corporation of the city, and many others, to witness his experiments. They assembled at Fort Jay, on Governor's Island, on the 20th of July, and in the shadow of the great gateway he lectured on the subject of his torpedoes. He had a blank one for his explanations, and his numerous auditors gathered close around him, with great eagerness, to catch every word from his lips, and see every part of the machine. At length he turned to one of the torpedoes lying near, under the gateway of the fort, to which his clock-work was attached, and drawing out the plug, and setting it in motion, he said: "Gentlemen, this is a charged torpedo, with which, precisely in its present state, I mean to blow up a vessel. It contains one hundred and seventy pounds of gunpowder, and if I were to suffer the clock-work to run fifteen minutes, I have no doubt that it would blow this fortification to atoms." The circle of the audience around Mr. Fulton immediately widened, and, before five of the fifteen minutes had elapsed, all but two or three had disappeared from the gateway, and retired to as great a distance as possible with the utmost speed. Fulton, entirely confident in his machine, was perfectly calm. "How frequently fear arises from ignorance," he said.—Colden's *Life of Fulton*, page 78.

[3] Letter to Joel Barlow from New York, dated August 22, 1807.

[4] For a description of the *Monitor*, a new style of vessel of war, first made known to the world by a terrible encounter with the *Merrimack*, another efficient vessel of war, in Hampton Roads, Virginia, in March, 1862, see Lossing's *Pictorial History of the Civil War*.

page 238. They were deeply impressed with the value of the invention, and in March Congress appropriated five thousand dollars for farther experiments, to be publicly made in the harbor of New York, under the direct superintendence of Commodore Rodgers and Captain Chauncey. The sloop-of-war *Argus* was prepared to defend herself against Fulton's torpedo attacks.[1] The experiments were tried in the autumn.[a] They failed, so far as attacks upon the *Argus* were concerned, and Rodgers reported the scheme to be wholly impracticable. Commissioners, among whom were Chancellor Livingston, Morgan Lewis, and Cadwallader Colden, reported in its favor. But Fulton, then still deeply engaged in steam-boat matters, made no farther efforts to induce the government to adopt his torpedo system; yet his faith in its value was not abated.

[a] September and October, 1810.

When war was declared in 1812, Fulton revived his torpedo scheme, but could not win the countenance of the government. Several attempts to put it in execution were made by inexperienced persons, and failed, and torpedoes did not enter into the system of warfare carried on at that time. But while they were not actually used, except in a few isolated cases, against the British vessels of war, a wholesome fear of them was abroad in the British navy. There was great anxiety manifested on the part of the British naval commanders, when they approached our coasts, to know where Mr. Fulton[2] was; and, such was their caution, they seldom attempted to enter the harbors of the United States during the war. No doubt the fear of Fulton's torpedoes

FULTON'S BIRTH-PLACE.

[1] Fulton had also invented a submarine machine for cutting the cables of ships at anchor. Experiments with this were tried at the same time.

[2] Robert Fulton was born at Little Britain, Lancaster County, Pennsylvania, in 1765. His parents were from Ireland. His early education was meagre. At the age of seventeen he was painting miniatures* at Philadelphia, and indulging his taste for mechanics in the work-shops of that city. His friends sent him to London, to receive instructions in painting, when he was twenty-one years of age. The celebrated West was his instructor. The Earl of Stanhope, who took great interest in mechanics, became his friend, and encouraged his taste for the useful arts. He heard of the experiments of Fitch and Evans in the use of steam for navigation, and his active mind began to speculate on the subject, and have glorious perceptions of future achievements. He left painting, and became an engineer. He entered the family of Joel Barlow, at Paris, in 1797, and there he became acquainted with Chancellor Livingston, with whom he carried on experiments in navigation by steam. They saw wealth and honor as the reward of success in that line on the inland waters of the United States. They came home, and were successful. The first voyage from Albany to New York silenced all doubt. In

* In White's *Philadelphia Directory*, 1785, is the following: "Robert Fulton, miniature painter, corner of Second and Walnut Streets."

saved several of our sea-port towns from destruction. Fulton's steam-frigate, launched in 1814, will be noticed hereafter.

Notwithstanding war had been declared by a large majority in Congress, and was approved by an equally large majority of the people of the United States, the administration was anxious for some honorable means for averting it. Indeed, both governments at the last moment seemed to hesitate. In the United States there was a large and powerful party utterly opposed to hostilities. There was a smaller organization, called the "Peace party," who were pledged to cast obstacles in the way of the government while hostilities should last. The authorities of several of the states took ground early against affording aid to the government; and it was very soon perceived that the Canadians, whose willingness to cast off the yoke of the imperial government had not been doubted, were generally loyal, and ready to take up arms against the United States. The Governors of Massachusetts, Rhode Island, and Connecticut refused to comply with the requisition made upon them for militia immediately after the declaration of war was promulgated. They planted themselves upon the Constitution, and the act of Congress authorizing the President to make a requisition for the militia, which contemplated the exigency of expected invasion. No evidence of any danger of invasion, they said, existed; and, supported by the judiciary and Legislatures of their respective states, they set the President at defiance. The Legislature of New Jersey denounced the war as "inexpedient, ill-timed, and most dangerously impolitic, sacrificing at once countless blessings." The Maryland House of Delegates passed resolutions commending the action of the Governors of Massachusetts, Rhode Island, and Connecticut, and disapproving of the war; while in the Senate opposite views were expressed. The Legislature of Pennsylvania rebuked the action of the three New England governors, and called it "an alarming and unexpected occurrence." They resolved that "the declaration of war was the result of solemn deliberation, sound wisdom, and imperious necessity." The Legislature of Ohio declared that the United States had been driven into the war by the aggressions of Great Britain, and said, "The man who would desert a just cause is unworthy to defend it." The Governor of New York exhorted a hearty concurrence in support of the national government; and the new State of Louisiana, just admitted into the Union, said, by the voice of its governor, "If ever war was justifiable, the one which our country has declared is that war. If ever a people had cause to repose in the confidence of their government, we are that people."

These conflicting views produced corresponding conflict of action. Party spirit was aroused in all its fierceness. Personal collisions became frequent occurrences, and in the city of Baltimore a most fearful riot occurred, the result of which was murder and maiming.[1]

1809 he obtained his first patent. His torpedo scheme failing, he turned his attention to submarine batteries. In 1814 he was directed by Congress to construct a war steamer. She was launched, and called *Fulton*. He died seven months afterward (February 24, 1815), at the age of fifty years. Our engraving of Mr. Fulton is from a portrait by Benjamin West, painted in 1805. The view of his residence is from a sketch by E. B. Cope, Esq. It gives its present appearance.

[1] There was a violent opposition newspaper called *The Federal Republican*, edited by a young man only twenty-six years of age. Baltimore was then a flourishing commercial city, and this paper was the organ of the mercantile interest, which had suffered from the restrictive commercial measures, and was now prostrated by the impending war. The *Republican* denounced the declaration of war, and, in defiance of intimations that had been made in Congress that when that declaration was once made all opposition to the war must cease, the editor announced his determination to speak as freely against the administration and its measures as before, thereby reversing the policy of his party in 1708 in the matter of the Alien and Sedition Laws. "We mean," he said, "to represent, in as strong colors as we are capable, that the war is unnecessary, inexpedient, and entered into from partial, personal, and, as we believe, motives bearing upon their front marks of undisguised foreign influence which can not be mistaken." This announcement was made on Saturday, June 20th, and on Monday evening, the 22d, a mob, headed by a French apothecary, proceeded to the office of that paper and demolished it. Having thus commenced violence, they proceeded to the wharves and dismantled some vessels, and committed other heinous acts. The publisher of the *Federal Republican* determined to re-establish the office. The lower portion of the house of one of the proprietors was used for the purpose. The paper was printed in Georgetown, but published then in Baltimore after a silence of five weeks. According to expectation, the publishing office was attacked. The magistrates of the city seemed to have used no means to quell the riot in June, and were not expected to do so now. General Henry Lee, then a resident of Baltimore, furnished the proprietors with a regular plan of defense, and offered to superintend the execution of it. General Lingan, another soldier of the Revolution, and also

The people of Canada, whose soil was about to be invaded, were filled with feelings of doubt and alarm, especially in the Upper Province. A large number of the inhabitants in that section were natives of the United States who had emigrated thither to better their condition. Many of them still felt a lingering affection for the land of their birth, and were unwilling to take up arms against it; but there was another class of emigrants—Loyalists, or the children of Loyalists of the Revolution—political exiles—occupying a large tract of land lying between Lakes Erie and Ontario, and westward, who were indebted to the liberality of the British government for the soil they were cultivating, and to their own industry for the roofs that sheltered them. These retained bitter feelings toward the United States, and took up arms with alacrity against a people whom they regarded as their oppressors. When war was actually commenced—when American troops were actually encamped on Canadian territory, these old Loyalists formed a most energetic and active element in the firm opposition which the invasion encountered. To these the Legislature of Upper Canada, whose loyalty was at first considered somewhat doubtful, addressed a most stirring appeal, soon after the American declaration of war was known, to the delight of the governor and the English party. "Already," they said, "have we the joy to remark that the spirit of loyalty has burst forth in all its ancient splendor. The militia in all parts of the province have volunteered their services with acclamation, and displayed a degree of energy worthy of the British name. They do not forget the blessings and privileges which they enjoy under the protective and fostering care of the British empire, whose government is only felt in this country by acts of the purest justice, and most pleasing and efficacious benevolence. When men are called upon to defend every thing they call precious, their wives and children, their friends and possessions, they ought to be inspired with the noblest resolutions, and they will not be easily frightened by menaces, or conquered by force; and beholding, as we do, the flame of patriotism burning from one end of the Canadas to the other, we can not but entertain the most pleasing anticipations. Our enemies have, indeed, said that they can subdue this country by a proclamation; but it is our part to prove to them that they are sadly mistaken; that the population is determinately hostile, and that the few who might be otherwise inclined will find it their safety to be faithful."

The address then proceeded to warn the people that, "in imitation of their European master (Napoleon)," the United States would "trust more to treachery than to

---

a Federalist, joined him, and about twenty others made up the defensive party. They were well-armed and provisioned for a siege. On the evening of the 26th of July (the evening of the day on which the revived newspaper first appeared) the mob assembled. After assailing the building with stones for some time, they forced open the door, and when ascending the stairs they were fired upon. One of the ringleaders was killed and several were wounded. After much solicitude, two magistrates, by virtue of their authority, ordered out two companies of militia, under General Stricker, to quell the mob. A single troop of horse soon appeared, and at about daylight the mayor and General Stricker appeared. A truce was obtained, and it was agreed that the defenders, some of whom were hurt, and who were all charged with murder, should be conducted to prison to answer that charge. They were promised not only personal safety, but protection of the premises by a military guard. On their way to prison the band played the rogue's march. The mob immediately sacked the house. Only a few more of the military could be persuaded to come out, and the mob had its own way to a great extent. At night they gathered around the prison, and the turnkey was so terrified that he allowed them to enter. The prisoners extinguished their lights and rushed out. They mingled with the mob, and thus several escaped. Some were dreadfully beaten, and three were tortured by the furious men. General Lee was made a cripple for life, and General Lingan, then seventy years of age, distinguished for his services in the field during the old war for independence, expired in the hands of the mob.* In the treatment of their unfortunate prisoners the most intense savagism was displayed. The riot was at length quelled, and the city magistrates, on investigation, placed the entire blame on the publishers of the obnoxious newspaper. It was decided that in a time of war no man has a right to cast obstacles in the way of the success of his country's undertakings. The course of the *Federal Republican* was condemned as treasonable—as giving aid and comfort to the enemy; and its fate was not mourned outside of the circle of its political supporters. While all right-minded men deprecated a mob, and condemned, in unmeasured terms, its atrocities, they as loudly condemned the unpatriotic course of the offending newspaper.

* Funeral honors were paid to General Lingan, at Georgetown, on the 1st of September following, by a great procession, and an oration by the late George Washington Parke Custis, the adopted son of Washington. His oration was extemporaneous, and was an eloquent and impassioned appeal to the feelings of his auditors. Only three years and six months after the death of the orator, the blood of other patriots, not engaged in the immediate defense of the liberty of the press, but hurrying to the national capital to save it from the grasp of fratricides, were slain in the streets of Baltimore by a mob (April 19, 1861), who, as in 1812, were tenderly dealt with, if not encouraged, by the magistrates of the city.

force;" that they would be falsely told that armies come to give them freedom and peace; that emissaries "of the most contemptible faction that ever distracted the affairs of any nation—the minions of the very sycophants who lick the dust from the feet of Bonaparte," would endeavor to seduce them from their loyalty.

This address had a powerful effect. The prudence and sagacity of Sir George Prevost, the governor general of Canada, had allayed the political agitations in the Lower Province, which had assumed a threatening aspect during the administration of his predecessor, Sir James H. Craig. Now, when war seemed impending, the Legislature of the Lower Province, laying aside their political bickerings, voted to furnish two thousand unmarried men to serve for three months during two successive summers. Besides these, a corps, called the Glengary Light Infantry, numbering, on the 1st of May, 1812, four hundred rank and file, and drawn chiefly from the Lower Province, was organized. Its officers promised to double that number. At the same time, enlistments were made in Acadia and Nova Scotia, while Lieutenant M'Donell gathered under his banner a large number of Highlanders, settled upon the Lower St. Lawrence and the Gulf.[1] It was soon made evident to the Americans that no dependence could be placed upon disloyalty among the Canadians, and that, instead of finding friends and allies north of the lakes, they would find active foes.

While these events were transpiring in America, there were movements abroad which faintly promised an adjustment of difficulties between the two governments without a resort to arms. Immediately after the declaration of war, President Madison, through Secretary Monroe, sent a dispatch[a] to Mr. Russell, the American minister at the British court, by Mr. Foster, the English minister retiring from Washington,[2] instructing him to offer an armistice preliminary to a definite arrangement of all differences, on condition of the absolute repeal of the obnoxious orders in Council, the discontinuance of impressment, and the return of all American seamen who had been impressed and were still in the British service. He was authorized to promise, on the part of the United States, a positive prohibition of employment for British seamen in the American service, public or private, on condition of a reciprocity in kind on the part of the British government. He made still more liberal advances toward reconciliation in a subsequent dispatch,[b] offering to agree to an armistice on a tacit understanding, instead of a positive stipulation, that no more American seamen should be impressed into the British service.

[a] June 26, 1812.

[b] August 24.

The British government had already taken action on the orders in Council. We have noticed the effect of Brougham's efforts in Parliament, and Baring's potent *Inquiry* on the subject of those orders. In the spring of 1812 a new order was issued, declaring that if at any time the Berlin and Milan Decrees should, by some authoritative act of the French government publicly promulgated, be withdrawn, the orders in Council of January, 1807, and of April, 1809, should be at once repealed. Mr. Barlow, the American minister at Paris, immediately after receiving information of this new order, pressed the French government to make a public announcement that those decrees had ceased to operate, as against the United States, since November, 1810. The Duke of Bassano exhibited great reluctance to do so, but finally, persuaded that the Americans would resume trade with Great Britain in defiance of the few French cruisers afloat, and that the two governments might form an alliance against the emperor, produced a decree, dated April 28, 1811, directing that, in consideration of the resistance of the United States "to the arbitrary pretensions advanced by the British orders in Council, and a formal refusal to sanction a system hostile to the independ-

---

[1] *A History of the War between Great Britain and the United States of America during the Years* 1812, 1813, *and* 1814, by G. Auchinleck, pages 46–48 inclusive.

[2] Mr. Foster sailed from New York for Halifax in the brig *Colibri*, on Sunday, July 12, accompanied by Mr. Barclay, the British consul at New York.

ence of neutral powers, the Berlin and Milan Decrees were to be considered as not having existed, as to American vessels, since November 1, 1810."[1] Barlow perceived, by the date of this document, that there was dissimulation and lack of candor in the whole matter, and, by pressing the duke with questions, caused that minister to utter what were doubtless absolute falsehoods.[2] In truth, the French had, throughout this whole matter of decrees, and the enforcement of the Continental System, been guilty of deception and injustice to a degree that would have justified an honest nation in suspending all diplomatic relations with them.

On receiving a copy of this decree Barlow dispatched it to London by the *Wasp*, for Mr. Russell's use. It reached there just in time to co-operate with the British manufacturers, who had procured the appointment of a committee of the House of Commons to inquire into the effects of the orders in Council on the commercial interests of the nation.[3] Castlereagh, to whom Russell presented the decree, considered it too limited to induce the British government to make any change in its policy. But he and his colleagues were compelled to yield. The new ministry, who came in after Mr. Perceval's death,[4] were very strongly pressed by Brougham, Baring, and others, and menaced with the desertion of their supporters in the manufacturing districts. Finally, on the 16th of June,[a] Brougham, after a minute statement of facts brought out by the inquiry of the Commons' committee, and an eloquent exposition of the absurd policy pursued by the government,[5] moved an address to the Prince Regent, beseeching him to recall or suspend the orders in Council, and to adopt such other measures as might tend to conciliate neutral powers, without sacrificing the rights and dignity of his majesty's crown. Castlereagh deprecated this "hasty action," as he called it, and stated that it was the intention of the government to make a conciliatory proposition to the Cabinet at Washington. On an intimation that this definite proposition was decided upon in the Cabinet, and would appear in the next *Gazette*, Brougham withdrew his motion. On the 23d[b] a declaration from the Prince Regent in Council was published, absolutely revoking all orders as far as they regarded America. It was accompanied by a proviso that the present order should have no effect unless the United States should revoke their Non-intercourse Act, and place Great Britain on the same relative footing as France. The order also provided that the Prince Regent should not be precluded, if circumstances should require it, from restoring the orders in Council, or from taking such other measures of retaliation against the French as might appear to his royal highness just and necessary.[6]

[a] 1812.
[b] June.

Intelligence of this conditional revocation of the orders in Council reached Mr. Foster before he sailed from Halifax, and he obtained from the naval commander on that station (Admiral Sir John Borlase Warren) consent to a mutual suspension of pro-

---

[1] The new decree was dated "Palace of St. Cloud, April 28, 1811," and signed by Napoleon as "Emperor of the French, King of Italy, Protector of the Confederation of the Rhine, and Mediator of the Swiss Confederacy."

[2] Barlow asked Bassano if the decree, apparently a year old, had ever been published. He was answered no, adding that it had been shown to Mr. Russell, when Chargé d'Affaires at Paris, and had been sent to Serrurier, at Washington, to be communicated to the American government. The records on both sides of the Atlantic proved this statement to be untrue. The decree was a fresh one, antedated for diplomatic effect.

[3] The examination of this committee, who were authorized to summon persons and papers, commenced on the 29th of April, and continued until the 13th of June. Witnesses from almost every part of Great Britain were examined, and in every case the transcendent importance of American commerce to the welfare of England was made manifest by testimony. The folly, wickedness, and stupidity of the orders in Council were fully exposed; and in the volume of almost seven hundred pages, filled with the minutes of that examination, an awful picture is given of the calamities to trade which those orders had produced. [4] See page 233.

[5] He decried the sort of half-piratical commerce which England was then pursuing in unmeasured terms. "It is this miserable, shifting, doubtful, hateful traffic that we prefer to the sure, regular, increasing, honest gains of American commerce—to a trade which is placed beyond the enemy's reach; which, besides enriching ourselves in peace and honor, only benefits those who are our natural friends, over whom he has no control; which supports at once all that remains of liberty beyond the seas, and gives life and vigor to its main pillar within the nation—the manufactures and commerce of England. . . . That commerce is the whole American market, a branch of trade in comparison of which, whether you regard its extent, its certainty, or its progressive increase, every other sinks into insignificance. It is a market which in ordinary times may take off about thirteen millions [$65,000,000] worth of our manufactures, and in steadiness and regularity it is unrivaled." [6] *American State Papers*, ix., 83.

ceedings against captured vessels. This fact was communicated to Mr. Boker, the British secretary of legation left at Washington, to be laid before the President. Foster also stated that he had advised Sir George Prevost, Governor General of Canada, to propose a suspension of hostilities on land. This was done, and General Dearborn, the commander of the American forces on the Northern frontier, provisionally agreed to an armistice.[1] Joy filled many hearts at these promises of peace and returning prosperity; but it was of short duration. The United States government refused to ratify this armistice, or to accept the other propositions of the ex-minister, because the President doubted his authority to suspend the proceedings of prize courts; was uncertain how far these arrangements would be respected by the British officers themselves; saw no security against the Indian allies of the English, then hovering like a dark cloud on the Northwestern frontier; and considered the arrangement unequal, as it would afford an opportunity to re-enforce Canada during the armistice. The President was also apprehensive that a suspension of hostilities previous to receiving an answer from the British government on the subject of impressment might appear like waiving that point.

When Mr. Russell presented his instructions[a] to Castlereagh on the subject of an armistice, that minister replied[b] that the orders in Council had been already provisionally repealed, and that instructions had been sent to Admiral Warren, on the Halifax station, to propose a suspension of hostilities on that basis. At the same time the British minister declined any discussion of the vital subject of impressment, and the release of impressed seamen. He even expressed surprise that, "as a condition preliminary even to a suspension of hostilities, the government of the United States should have thought fit to demand that the British government should desist from its *ancient and accustomed practice of impressing British seamen from the merchant ships of a foreign state*, simply on the assurance that a law shall hereafter be passed to prohibit the employment of British seamen in the public or commercial service of that state." He said that his government was willing to discuss any proposition concerning abuses in the practice of impressment, or the substitution of some method of accomplishing the same object with less vexation in practice; "but they can not consent," he said, "to suspend the exercise of a *right upon which the naval strength of the empire mainly depends*," unless assured that the object might be attained in some other way.[2]

[a] August 24, 1812.
[b] August 29.

Of all the grievances complained of by the Americans, that of impressment was the most serious. It was a practical violation of the sovereignty and independence of the United States, and was of more consequence to the character of the nation than all blockades or other obstructions to commerce. It offended, in the highest degree, the patriotism of every true American; and it touched not only the political sensibilities of a free people at a most tender point, but it impressed them keenly with a sense of social wrong. At that very time there were upward of six thousand cases of impressment of American seamen on the records of the State Department, and it was believed that as many more, never reported to the government, had occurred. Castlereagh admitted, on the floor of the British Parliament, that there were three thousand five hundred impressed servants in the British navy, claiming to be American seamen, but said that they might be discharged on proving their citizenship. American citizens, kidnapped from the decks of American vessels by British cruisers, and made slaves in British ships, were offered freedom only on condition of proving

---

[1] General Dearborn's head-quarters at this time were at Greenbush, opposite Albany, in New York. Thither Sir George Prevost sent his adjutant general, Baynes, to propose an armistice, and clothed with power to conclude one. Dearborn and Baynes signed it on the 9th of August. The agreement was to affect only Dearborn and the frontiers of New York, and the armies of the British along the opposite and corresponding line.

[2] *American State Papers*, ix., 73.

themselves to be American citizens! Ay, more, subjected, at the same time, as we have seen, to the liability of receiving degrading punishment for attempting to secure that freedom![1]

Perceiving no hope of an adjustment of difficulties with the rulers of England, Mr. Russell obtained his passports,[a] and, leaving Mr. Reuben Guant Beaseley as agent for prisoners of war in London, he returned home, intimating by his departure that diplomacy between the two goverments had ended, and that the war, already begun on land and sea, must proceed. On the 12th of October the English government issued letters of marque and reprisal against the Americans.[2] The armistice on the Canada frontier had been ended for some weeks, and the war went on.

[a] September 2, 1812.

History has no record of a people more righteous in persisting in war than were the Americans at this time, when their plea for simple justice was so insolently spurned by the men who then unfortunately governed the British nation. They had tried every peaceful measure consistent with national honor for obtaining a redress of grievances, as they did for ten long and weary years, exposed to insult and oppression from the same government, before the Revolution. They were now determined to secure fully and forever that dignity and independence in the family of nations to which their strength and importance entitled them. "It was a war," says a late historian[3] (whose sympathies with the Federalists is manifested on every page of his narrative), "for the rights of personal freedom—the freedom, suppose, of Britons and other foreigners, as well as Americans,[4] from the domineering insolence of British press-gangs—an idea congenial to every manly soul, and giving to the contest a strong hold on the hearts of the masses; in fact, a just title to the character of a democratic war, in the best sense of that very ambiguous epithet, and even to be called a second war for independence, as its advocates delighted to describe it."

With these facts before them, writers and speakers of American birth, at that time, for party purposes, magnified the generosity of Great Britain, its Christian desire for peace, its magnanimous offers of reconciliation; and declaimed most piteously about the cruelty of waging war against a nation kindred in blood, language, and religion, in the hour of its great extremity, when a desperate adventurer was seeking to destroy it. Even at this late day, a Scotch Canadian writer, with all the facts of history in his possession, has ungenerously declared that "the war—the grand provocation having been thus [by conditional repeal of the orders in Council] removed—was persisted in, for want of a better excuse, on the ground of the 'impressment question,'" and adds, "The government of the United States stand, then, self-condemned of wanton aggression on the North American colonies of Great Britain, and of prosecuting the war on grounds different from those which they were accustomed to assign."[5]

Thus it has ever been with British writers and statesmen of a certain class, who represent the great leading idea of the boasted Mistress of the Seas when she was less enlightened than now. We have already quoted the following words of Montesquieu concerning English politics a hundred years ago—"the English have ever made their political interests give way to those of commerce."[6] These words bear

---

[1] See note, page 144.
[2] Subsequently to this act, the British government, pressed by the necessities of their army in Spain, freely granted licenses or protections to American vessels engaged in carrying flour to the ports of that country. This traffic was subjected to heavy penalties by Congress, yet it was largely indulged in, because it afforded immense profits—profits more than equal to the risks. These licenses were cited by the opponents of the war then, and by British writers since, as evidences of the great forbearance of the British government, for which the Americans should have been profoundly thankful!
[3] Hildreth's *History of the United States*, Second Series, iii., 352.
[4] The Americans justly contended that the flag should protect every man who was innocent of crime, who sought security under its folds, wherever his birth-place might have been. It represented the sovereignty of the nation, and, as such, claimed full respect.
[5] Auchinleck's *History of the War of* 1812, page 38.   [6] See sub-note *, page 138.

repetition in this connection. In estimating the character of other nations, men of the class alluded to are always governed by the *commercial* idea, and can not comprehend the fact, frequently illustrated in history (even slightly in their own), that a people may contend for something more noble than pounds, shillings, and pence. That class of writers and statesmen, who governed England about a century ago, believed that a slight remission of taxes on tea would purchase the allegiance and abject submission of the Americans. The same class of writers and statesmen, of the Stephen and Castlereagh stamp, who governed England in 1812, believed that a concession to American commerce would be an equivalent for national honor and independence; and the same class of writers and statesmen who governed England in 1861 could not comprehehend the great fact that the American government was struggling for its life against household assassins, without counting the cost in pounds, shillings, and pence. They are a class who never learn, and are prominent only as national mischief-makers.

The door of reconciliation, as we have seen, was shut in the autumn of 1812. The war had been already commenced on sea and land. Provision had been made by Congress for the organization of an adequate army. One of the most important measures was the appointment of officers to command the troops. A greater portion of the most distinguished and meritorious officers of the Revolution had passed away, and there were none of experience left who had held a commission above colonel in the Continental army. A long season of peace, except during difficulties with the Indians, had deprived the younger army officers in the service of the opportunity of real experience in the practical art of war.

HENRY DEARBORN.

Notwithstanding the surviving soldiers of the old war had advanced far in the journey of life, and most of them had been long enjoying the quietude of civil pursuits, it was thought to be most prudent to call them to the head of the new army, with their small experience of actual field duty, than to trust to those who had never been under fire. The collector of the port of Boston, Henry Dearborn, late Secretary of War, an active Democrat, and then sixty-one years of age, was appointed[a] first major general, or acting commander-in-chief, having the Northern Department under his immediate control.[1] Thomas Pinckney, of South Carolina, was appointed[b] second major gen-

[a] February, 1812.
[b] March.

---

[1] Henry Dearborn was born in Hampton, New Hampshire, in March, 1751. At Portsmouth he studied the science of medicine with Dr. Jackson Jackson, and commenced its practice there in 1772. When the old war for independence was impending, he took an active part in politics on the popular side, and gave as much attention as his engagements would allow to military matters. On the day after the skirmish at Lexington, in April, 1775, he marched toward Cambridge at the head of sixty men. He then returned to New Hampshire, was commissioned a captain in Colonel Stark's regiment, and by the middle of May was back to Cambridge with a full company. He was in the battle of Bunker's Hill, and accompanied General Arnold in his perilous expedition through the wilderness of Maine to Quebec in the autumn of that year. He suffered dreadfully from privations and a fever, but was sufficiently recovered to participate in the assault on Quebec at the close of the year, when he was made a prisoner. He was not exchanged until March, 1777, when he was appointed a major in Scammell's regiment. He was in the campaign opposed to Burgoyne, and behaved gallantly on the field of Saratoga, where he was promoted to lieutenant colonel. He was at Monmouth, in Sullivan's campaign, and in the siege of Yorktown. In 1784 he settled on the banks of the Kennebec as a farmer. Washington appointed him marshal of the District of Maine in 1789, and he was elected to Congress from that Territory. He was called to Jefferson's Cabinet, as Secretary of War, in 1801, which position he filled for eight years. Mr. Madison appointed him collector of the port of Boston in 1809; and in February, 1812, he was commissioned a major general in the United States army. Ill health compelled him to relinquish that position, and he assumed command of the military district of New York City. He retired to private life in 1815. In 1822 President Monroe appointed him minister to Portugal, where he

eral, and placed in command of the Southern Department. Joseph Bloomfield, Governor of New Jersey,[1] James Winchester, of Tennessee, J. P. Boyd, of Massachusetts, and William Hull, Governor of the Territory of Michigan, were commissioned briga-
[a] April 8, 1812. diers.[a] The same commission was given[b] to Thomas Flournoy, of Geor-
[b] June.
[c] July 4. gia. John Armstrong, of New York, also received the commission[c] of a
[d] July 2. brigadier, to fill the vacancy caused by the recent death[d] of General Pe-
[e] July 8. ter Gansevoort. This was soon followed by a like commission[e] for John Chandler, of Maine. Morgan Lewis, of New York, was appointed quarter-master gen-
[f] April 3. eral,[f] and Alexander Smyth, of Virginia, late Colonel of the Rifles, was
[g] March 30. appointed inspector general,[g] each bearing the commission of brigadier. Thomas H. Cushing,[2] of Massachusetts, then Colonel of the Second Regiment, was appointed adjutant general, with the rank of brigadier. James Wilkinson, of Maryland, the senior brigadier in the army, was sent to New Orleans to relieve Wade Hampton, now a brigadier, and a meritorious subaltern officer in South Carolina during the Revolution. Alexander Macomb, of the Engineers, was promoted to colonel; and Winfield Scott and Edmund Pendleton Gaines, of Virginia, and Eleazer W. Ripley, of Maine, were commissioned colonels.

GENERAL DEARBORN'S RESIDENCE.

remained two years. He died at the house of his son in Roxbury, Massachusetts, on the 6th of June, 1829, at the age of seventy-eight years. He had been living with his son some time. The house in which he died is yet (1867) standing on Washington Street, Roxbury. It is a fine old mansion, surrounded by trees, many of them rare. It was occupied, when I made the sketch in 1860, as a summer boarding-house by Mrs. Shepard. Not far from it, at the junction of Washington and Centre Streets, or of the Cambridge and the Dedham and Rhode Island Roads, was a rude stone, in which was inserted an iron shaft and fork for the support of a street lamp. It is called the Parting Stone. On one side

THE PARTING STONE.

is the inscription, *The Parting Stone*, 1744, *P. Dudley*; on another, *Dedham and Rhode Island*; and on a third, *Cambridge*. It appears to have been erected by Mr. Dudley, at the parting of the ways, as a sort of guide-post, and there it had remained for a hundred and sixteen years.

[1] General Bloomfield was in New York when war was declared. He had arrived on the 2d of June, to take charge of the fortifications there. He was the first to announce the declaration of war to troops in a formal manner. This he did in the following brief order, issued on the 20th of June:

"General Bloomfield announces to the troops that *war is declared by the United States against Great Britain.*
"By order, R. H. M'PHERSON, A. D. C."

Government expresses had passed through New York City for Albany and Boston with the news at ten o'clock that morning.

The first prisoner taken after the declaration of war was Captain Wilkinson, of the Royal Marines, who excited the suspicions of the people of Norfolk, Virginia, that he was about to communicate the fact that war was declared, to a British man-of-war known to be hovering on the coast. He was seen making his way rapidly from the house of the British consul through back streets to a mail-boat about to start for Hampton. He darted on board the boat, and attempted to conceal himself. A boat from the navy yard, and another from Fort Norfolk, were dispatched after the mail-boat. Captain Wilkinson was brought back, and conveyed to the navy yard as a prisoner.

[2] Thomas H. Cushing was appointed captain of infantry in 1791. He was in the Sub-legion in 1792. In 1797 he was appointed inspector of the army; and in April, 1802, he was made adjutant and inspector, with the rank of lieutenant colonel. He was promoted to colonel in 1805, and commissioned adjutant general in 1812, with the rank of brigadier. He was disbanded in 1815, and the following year was appointed collector of the port of New London. He died on the 19th of October, 1822.—*Gardner's Dictionary of the Army.*

CHAPTER XIII.

"Let Feds, Quids, and Demos together unite,
For our country, our laws, and our altars to fight;
While our tars guard the seaboard, our troops line the shore,
Let our enemies face us, we'll ask for no more.
While our hand grasps the sword well prepared for the fight,
On Washington's glory we dwell with delight;
His spirit our guide, we can feel no alarms;
While for Freedom we fight, we're victorious in arms!"

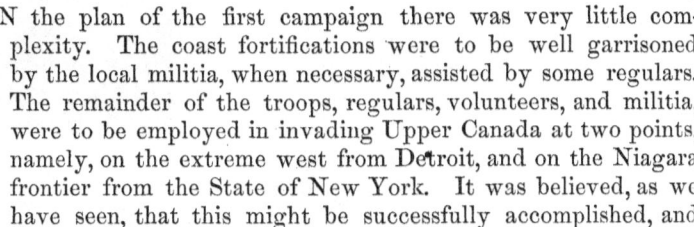

IN the plan of the first campaign there was very little complexity. The coast fortifications were to be well garrisoned by the local militia, when necessary, assisted by some regulars. The remainder of the troops, regulars, volunteers, and militia, were to be employed in invading Upper Canada at two points, namely, on the extreme west from Detroit, and on the Niagara frontier from the State of New York. It was believed, as we have seen, that this might be successfully accomplished, and that Canadian sympathy would complete and make permanent the easy conquest. This achieved, a victorious army, in a friendly country, might go down the St. Lawrence to Montreal and Quebec, and liberate the Lower Province from British rule, while Nova Scotia and New Brunswick (according to the opinions of the more sanguine), sympathizing with the movement, would welcome the invaders, and British rule in North America would cease forever. The Americans, remunerated by their conquests for commercial spoliations, would soon find British statesmen in power ready to do justice to an injured nation. The originators of this campaign seem to have forgotten the costly and disastrous lessons of 1775–'76, when a similar attempt to invade, conquer, and liberate Canada was made, and similar expectations of welcome were indulged.

Governor Hull, of Michigan, was in Washington City during a part of the winter and spring of 1812, while legislative preparations for war were in progress. The invasion of Canada was freely spoken of in official circles, but his voice was heard against it. He knew that the British authorities in that country had sent messengers to all the principal Indian tribes in the Northwest, with arms and presents, exhorting them to become the allies of Great Britain in the event of war. He knew that his Territory was threatened with desolation by these savages, and that, without a fleet on Lake Erie, where the British had full sway, and with the inadequate preparations even for a defense of the Territory which then existed, the idea of a successful invasion of the neighboring province was preposterous. He therefore urged the President to increase the military force in his Territory simply for its defense; and, for the third time, he called attention to the positive necessity of a small American fleet on the lake.[1]

President Madison listened to the advice of Hull to some extent. Commander Stewart was ordered to Washington to receive the appointment of agent on Lake Erie, and also orders concerning the building of a fleet on those waters. The Presi-

---
[1] Immediately after the battle of Tippecanoe, the principal inhabitants of Detroit, alarmed at the aspect of affairs around them, petitioned Congress to strengthen their defenses. The Territory was too sparsely populated to present much resistance to the savages. The whole white population of Michigan was only about four thousand eight hundred, and of this number four fifths were Canadian French. The remainder were chiefly Americans, with a few English and Scotch.—Lanman's *History of Michigan*, page 193.

dent made a requisition upon Governor Meigs, of Ohio, for twelve hundred militia, to be detached, drilled, and prepared to march to Detroit; and he requested Hull to accept the commission of a brigadier general, and take command of them. Hull declined the proposed honor and service, expressing a wish not to engage in military employment. He was finally persuaded to accept the appointment, but with no other object, he said, than to aid in the protection of the inhabitants of Michigan against the savages. He retained his office of governor of the Territory, and returned to the Northwest, prepared for any duty in that region, civil or military, to which his government might call him.

[a] April 6, 1812. Governor Meigs's call[a] for troops to assemble at Dayton, at the mouth of the Mad River, on the Great Miami,[1] was heartily responded to. At the close of April, the time appointed for the rendezvous, more than the required number had flocked to the camp. The Indian wars and depredations, which had been instigated by British emissaries, had greatly exasperated the settlers north of the Ohio, and they were anxious to strike an avenging blow. Many of the best citizens sought this opportunity to serve their country, and these were found at the place of rendezvous, enduring all the privations of camp life, without tents or other conveniences, for more than a fortnight. It was the middle of May before blankets and camp equipage arrived from Pittsburg by way of Cincinnati. But the troops had not been idle. They had organized three regiments, and elected their field officers; and when General Hull arrived there on the 25th of May, and took formal command, they were nearly ready for a forward movement. Duncan M'Arthur was chosen colonel of the First Regiment, and James Denny and William Trimble were elected majors; James Findlay was chosen colonel, and Thomas Moore and Thomas Van Horn majors of the Second Regiment; and the late Lewis Cass, of Detroit, then thirty years of age, was chosen colonel of the Third Regiment, with Robert Morrison and J. R. Munson as majors. The veteran Fourth Regiment of regulars, stationed at Fort Vincennes, and commanded by Lieutenant Colonel James Miller, since the promotion of Boyd, had been ordered to join the militia at Dayton.

[b] April 6. Governor Meigs, under the same date,[b] ordered Major General Elijah Wadsworth, commanding the fourth division of the Ohio militia, to raise, without delay, three companies of men. Wadsworth obeyed with alacrity, and the requisite number were soon in the field, selected from the brigades of Generals Miller, Beale, Perkins, and Paine, which composed the fourth division.[2]

---

[1] The present fine city of Dayton, the county seat of Montgomery County, then contained about four hundred souls. It derives its name from General Jonathan Dayton, of New Jersey, who, with Generals St. Clair and Wilkinson, and Colonel Israel Ludlow, purchased a large tract of land in that section of the state.

[2] The following incident connected with the volunteering was communicated to the author by the late venerable Elisha Whittlesey, then (1862) First Auditor of the Treasury Department at Washington, who was one of General Wadsworth's aids: Colonel John Campbell, of Paine's brigade, called out his corps at Ravenna on the 23d of May. After some stirring music, he placed himself in front of his regiment, and requested all who were willing to volunteer to step forward. Many complied, but far too few to make the proper number for a company. Finally, Colonel Campbell was compelled to stimulate them by threatening to resort to a draft. Their colonel had volunteered. It was a bright, sunny day, and he saw, high in the heavens, a brilliant star. He told his men that it was a good omen. One, who had

Rendezvous of Ohio Volunteers.   A Visit to Colonel John Johnston.   Sketch of his Life.

The place of the early rendezvous of the Ohio Volunteers was on the north side of the Mad River, upon a beautiful plain about two miles above Dayton. I visited the spot late in September, 1860, just as the heavy clouds of a cold northeast storm were passing away. We reached the valley of the Great Miami at Hamilton, the site of Fort Hamilton, twenty-five miles above Cincinnati, at twilight, and then traversed that beautiful region, thirty-five miles farther to Dayton, where we arrived at a little past eight o'clock. At an early hour the next morning I started for the place of the gathering of Hull's army, but a storm, that had begun during the night, was too fierce to allow a comfortable ramble over the fields, so I rode to the pleasant mansion of Colonel Jefferson Patterson, a mile or more from the town, to visit the venerable Colonel John Johnston, who had been in that country as Indian agent, and in the performance of other government business, for more than half a century. I found him in the apparent enjoyment of all his faculties, mental and physical, although the number of his years was eighty-five. He was over six feet in height, and not at all bent by the burden of years. Under the hospitable roof of Colonel Patterson, his son-in-law, I spent nearly the whole day, and listened, with the greatest satisfaction and profit, to the narration of the venerable pioneer's long experience in frontier life. He had been well acquainted with most of the leading men in that region, white and red, since the beginning of the century. His residence as Indian agent was mostly with the Shawnoese. He knew Tecumtha and the Prophet well, and had entertained the Little Turtle at his table. He informed me that he was writing a memoir of his Life and Times, and hoped to be spared to complete it. He exhibited every promise of centenary honors in action and speech, but death has since borne him to the grave.[1]

held back, declared that if he could see the star he would volunteer. He saw it and kept his promise. Others followed, and the company was soon filled. They all signed a volunteer roll. They then elected Colonel Campbell their captain.

[1] The accompanying likeness of Colonel Johnston is from a plate published in Moore's *Masonic Review*. On the back of a daguerreotype of him, which he showed me at the time of my visit, was the following, in his own firm and plain hand-writing:

"Born near Ballyshannon, Ireland, March 25, 1775. Emigrated to the United States with his parents in 1786, and settled in Cumberland County, Pennsylvania. Was with Wayne's army on the Ohio, at Cincinnati, in the winter of 1792 and '93. A captain in Philadelphia in 1798; a clerk in the War Department; agent for Indian Affairs in the Northwest thirty-one years; a canal commissioner of Ohio eleven years; paymaster and quartermaster in the War of 1812; a commissioner for treating with the Indians in 1841-'2 [for their removal westward].

Presented to my beloved daughter, Julia Johnston Patterson, and her family, by her most affectionate father, JOHN JOHNSTON."

Colonel Johnston was an active member of the masonic fraternity. He was admitted to its mysteries at Bourbon Court-house (now Paris), Kentucky, in the winter of 1794-'5. As secretary of a lodge in Philadelphia, he walked in the funeral procession in honor of the deceased Washington, in 1800, when General Lee pronounced his famous oration. A brother member from Ireland, who walked by his side, came to Cincinnati fifty years afterward, and was welcomed to a lodge there by Colonel Johnston. — Moore's *Masonic Review*, xvi., 1. When, in the summer of 1845, the remains of Daniel Boone and his wife were taken from Missouri and buried in the public cemetery at Frankfort, Kentucky, Colonel Johnston was one of the pall-bearers. He was president of the Historical and Philosophical Society of Ohio, and member of several kindred societies in other parts of the Union. Colonel Johnston died at Washington City on the 19th of April, 1861, at the age of eighty-six years. He visited the national capital for the twofold purpose of settling some accounts with the government and soliciting the appointment of a grandson to a cadetship at West Point. He was disappointed in his efforts. The great rebellion was then menacing the existence of the republic he loved so well and had served so faithfully. Sumter had fallen before its fury, and the fratricidal

It was late in the afternoon when I left Colonel Johnston, and rode to the place of the gathering of the Ohio militia. We crossed the Mad River at Dayton, rode up the turnpike a short distance beyond the toll-gate, and, turning into a road on the right, found the place about half a mile farther in that direction. It is a low prairie, and when I visited it[a] it was covered with Indian corn, some standing and some of it harvested. The distant trees in the little sketch show the line of the Mad River.

PLACE OF RENDEZVOUS, NEAR DAYTON, AS IT APPEARED IN 1830.

[a] September 20, 1860.

I returned to Dayton in time to take the cars for Sandusky at six o'clock. As we left the station, an immense deep blue-black cloud came rolling up from the west. In a few moments large drops of rain fell with the sound of hail on the car roof. Suddenly a flash of vivid lightning broke from the cloud, and a crashing thunder-peal rolled over the land. A shower of cold rain followed. Before it ceased the sun beamed out brilliantly in the west, and we seemed to be enveloped in a falling flood of glittering gold. Then from many lips in the car were heard the exclamations, "How beautiful! how glorious!" and all eyes were turned eagerly toward the east, where,

"In pomp transcendent, robed in heavenly dyes,
Arch'd the clear rainbow round the orient skies."

Twilight soon followed, and while moving at a moderate speed, near Cross's Station, eighteen miles above Dayton, a "switch" in wrong position threw our train off the track, but with no other serious effect than producing a detention for three hours in a most dreary place. There was a hamlet of a few houses near, and some of us went out in the chilly night air to search for food and drink. In every house but one nearly all the inmates were sick with fever and ague, and only at the dwelling of a pleasant-spoken and kindly-acting German woman could any thing be procured. There I obtained some fresh bread and milk, and was offered coffee. I laid in stores sufficient for a night's campaign, hardly expecting to see Springfield, six miles beyond, before morning. We were agreeably disappointed. Through the exertions of the mail agent and others, we were in the enjoyment of comfortable quarters at the "Willis House," in Springfield, before midnight.

The morning dawned brilliantly. The sky was cloudless and the air was cool, and at about eleven o'clock I departed for Sandusky. From Springfield northward the poverty of the soil became more and more apparent, until we reached the high swampy land of the summit near Kenton. The road lay much of the way through forests or recent clearings. About a mile north of Hudsonville Station (six miles south of Kenton) we crossed diagonally the road made by Hull in his march from the Mad River to the Maumee. It was visible on each side, as far as the eye could comprehend it, as a broad avenue through the forest, running from southeast to northwest, now filled with a delicate second growth of timber.

From Kenton[1] to Tiffin,[2] on the Lake Erie slope, a distance of forty miles, the country was newly cleared of the woods most of the way. Few other than log houses

---

assassin was at the doors of the capital. His clear and active mind comprehended the danger to the liberties of his country. He sickened, but, it was believed, not seriously. He kept his room; and, in the absence of his attendant, laid down upon his bed and expired. His body was buried at Piqua, with the remains of his wife and eight children.

[1] Named in honor of Simon Kenton, a noted pioneer.
[2] Named in honor of Edward Tiffin, who was president of the Convention that framed the Constitution of the State of Ohio, and first governor of that state.

OF THE WAR OF 1812.   255

Arrival at Sandusky.   Hull takes Command of Ohio Volunteers.   He Addresses the Troops.

were seen. Tiffin is the capital of Hardin County. It is quite a large town, spread over a considerable surface of a gentle eminence on the east bank of the Sandusky River. On the lower ground opposite is the little straggling village of Fort Ball, the site of a stockade of that name, which the Ohio Volunteers erected there during the early part of the war of 1812. It occupied about a third of an acre of ground, and was named in honor of Lieutenant Colonel James V. Ball, commander of a squadron of cavalry under General Harrison, whose exploits will be mentioned in connection with events at Lower Sandusky (now Fremont), nearer the lake. We passed Tiffin and Fort Ball at five o'clock, and reached Sandusky City, on Sandusky Bay, a little after sunset. There I sojourned two or three days at the house of an esteemed kinswoman.

The command of the little army of volunteers near Dayton was surrendered to General Hull by Governor Meigs[1] on the morning of the 25th of May.[a] The governor made a stirring speech on the occasion, and congratulated the soldiers on their good fortune in being placed under the command of an experienced officer who had fought for freedom in the War of the Revolution. Colonel Cass also addressed the troops with eloquent words, which were loudly applauded. General Hull then came forward, took formal command, and, in a patriotic speech of some length, he stirred the blood of the volunteers, and made them eager to meet the dusky foe on the distant frontier. "In marching through a wilderness," he said, "memorable for savage barbarity, you will remember the causes by which that barbarity has been heretofore excited. In viewing the ground stained with the blood of your fellow-citizens, it will be impossible to suppress the feelings of indignation. Passing by the ruins of a fortress,[2] erected in our territory by a foreign nation in times of profound peace, and for the express purpose of exciting the savages to hostility, and supplying them with the means of conducting a barbarous war, must remind you of that system of oppression and injustice which that nation has continually practiced, and which the spirit of an indignant people can no longer endure."[3]

[a] 1812.

This speech touched sharply a tender chord of feeling in every bosom, and they gave their general their fullest confidence. Most of them had never seen him before. His manner was pleasing; his general deportment was familiar, yet not undignified; and his gray locks commanded reverence and respect. There were some, who professed to know him well, who doubted the wisdom of the government in choosing him to fill so important a station at a time so critical, yet they generally kept silent,

---

[1] Return Jonathan Meigs was born at Middletown, Connecticut, in 1765, and was graduated at Yale College. He chose the law as a profession, and commenced its practice in his native town. He was chosen chief justice of the Supreme Court of Connecticut in the winter of 1802–'3. In the following year President Jefferson appointed him commandant of United States troops and militia in Upper Louisiana, and soon afterward he became one of the judges of that Territory. He was commissioned a judge of Michigan Territory in 1807. He resigned the following year, and was elected governor of Ohio. His election was unconstitutional because of non-residence, not having lived four years in Ohio prior to the election. He was appointed United States senator for Ohio in 1808. That office he resigned, and was elected governor of that state in 1810. He was governor during the greater part of the War of 1812, and was one of the most energetic men of the West in the prosecution of that war. He was appointed postmaster general in March, 1814, and managed that important department of the government with great ability until 1823. He died at Marietta, Ohio, on the 29th of March, 1825. Governor Meigs was a tall and finely-formed man, and in deportment was dignified, yet urbane in the extreme.

The singular name of Governor Meigs suggests inquiry as to its origin. The answer may thus be briefly given: A bright-eyed Connecticut girl was disposed to coquette with her lover, Jonathan Meigs; and on one occasion, when he had pressed his suit with great earnestness, and asked for a positive answer, she feigned coolness, and would give him no satisfaction. The lover resolved to be trifled with no longer, and bade her farewell forever. She perceived her error, but he was allowed to go far down the lane before her pride would yield to the more tender emotions of her heart. Then she ran to the gate and cried, "Return, Jonathan! return, Jonathan!" He did return; they were joined in wedlock, and, in commemoration of these happy words, they named their first child Return Jonathan. He was born in 1740; was the heroic Colonel Meigs of which history says so much, and was the father of the governor of Ohio, who bore his name.   [2] Fort Miami, on the Lower Maumee, just below the Falls.

[3] *History of the late War in the Western Country*, by Robert B. M'Afee, p. 51.

Hull's Troops joined by Regulars. — Honors paid to the latter. — The Army in the Wilderness.

wishing to give him every opportunity to disappoint their expectations, win success for his country, and honors for himself.

On the 1st of June[a] the little army commenced its march up the Miami. General Hull had appointed his son, Captain A. F. Hull, and Robert Wallace, Jr., his aids-de-camp; Lieutenant Thomas S. Jesup, of Kentucky, his brigade major; Dr. Abraham Edwards his hospital surgeon; and General James Taylor, of Kentucky, his quartermaster general.[1] He proceeded to Staunton, a small village on the east bank of the Miami, and thence moved on to Urbana,[2] where the volunteers were joined by the Fourth Regiment of regulars under Lieutenant Colonel James Miller.[3] They were met about a mile from the village by Colonels M'Arthur, Cass, and Findlay, at the head of their respective regiments, by whom they were escorted into camp. They were led under a triumphal arch of evergreens, decked with flowers, surmounted with an eagle, and inscribed with the words, in large letters, "TIPPECANOE—GLORY."[4] On their arrival, General Hull issued an order complimentary to the regulars and congratulatory to the volunteers. "The general is persuaded," he said, "that there will be no other contention in this army but who will most excel in discipline and bravery.... The patriots of Ohio, who yield to none in spirit and patriotism, will not be willing to yield to any in discipline and valor."

[a] 1812.

The troops were now at a frontier town. Between them and Detroit, two hundred miles distant, lay an almost unbroken wilderness, a part of it the broad morasses of the watershed between the Ohio and the lakes, and beyond these the terrible Black Swamp in the present counties of Henry, Wood, and Sandusky. There was no pathway for the army, not even an Indian trail. They were compelled to cut a road, and for this purpose M'Arthur's regiment was detached. The difficulties and labors were very great, for heavy timber had to be felled, causeways to be laid across morasses, and bridges to be constructed over considerable streams. They also erected block-houses for the protection of the sick, and of provision trains moving forward with supplies for the army. Industry and perseverance overcame all obstacles, and, on the 16th of June, the road was opened to the scouts at a point in Hardin County, not far from Kenton. Two block-houses were built on the south bank of that stream, stockaded, and the whole work named Fort M'Arthur. The fortifications did not inclose more than half an acre. There were log huts for the garrison, and log corn-cribs for the food. It was a post of great danger. Hostile Indians, and especially the warlike Wyandots, filled the forest, and were watching every movement with vigilant eyes and malignant hearts.

The army halted at Fort M'Arthur on the 19th, and Colonel Findlay was detached with his regiment to continue the road to Blanchard's Fork of the Au Glaize, a tributary of the Maumee. Three days afterward the whole army followed, excepting a small garrison for Fort M'Arthur, under Captain Dill, left to keep the post and take care of the sick. Heavy rains now fell, and the little army was placed in a perilous position. They had reached the broad morasses of the summit, and had marched only sixteen miles, when the deep mud impelled them to halt. They could go no farther. The black flies and musquitoes were becoming a terrible scourge. The cattle were placed on short allowance, and preparations were made to transport the bag-

---

[1] General Taylor was yet living, at the age of seventy-nine, in 1848, at Newport, Kentucky.

[2] Urbana is the capital of Champaign County, Ohio. It was laid out by Colonel William Ward, a Virginian, in 1805. The army of General Hull encamped in the eastern part of the village. This being a frontier town, it was afterward used as a place of rendezvous and departure for troops going to the frontier. The old court-house, built in 1807, was used as a hospital.

[3] These troops came from Vincennes. They had come by the way of Louisville, through Kentucky, and had been every where received with honors. Their services at Tippecanoe were duly appreciated. At Cincinnati the shore was lined with the inhabitants waiting to receive them as they crossed the Ohio from Newport. A triumphal arch had been built, over which, in large letters, were the words, "THE HEROES OF TIPPECANOE." They were received with cheers and a salute of seventeen guns (the number of the states at that time), and they, only, passed under the arch. Food and liquor in great abundance were sent to their camp.—*Lieutenant Colonel Miller to his Wife*, June 12, 1812—*Autograph Letter.*

[4] Lieutenant Colonel Miller to his Wife, June 12, 1812—Autograph Letter.

gage and stores on pack-horses. They built a fort, which, in allusion to the circumstances, they called Fort Necessity.

Here Hull was met by two messengers from Detroit—General Robert Lucas and William Denny—whom he had sent from Dayton to that post with dispatches for acting Governor Atwater. Their report was disheartening. General Lucas had been present at a council of the chiefs of several tribes at Brownstown—Ottawas, Ojibwas or Chippewas, Wyandots, and others. All but Walk-in-the-Water, principal chief of the Wyandots, made peaceful professions. The latter spoke many bold and unfriendly words. The British, too, were making hostile manifestations. They had collected a considerable body of Indians at Malden, where they were fed, and armed, and well supplied with blankets and ammunition. Kind and generous treatment made them fast friends of the British, and eager to go out upon the war-path against the Americans. Tecumtha was also wielding his great influence in the same direction; and to Hull and his friends the situation of Detroit, with its weak defenses, seemed, as it really was, in great peril. The danger made him impatient to push forward. At length the rain ceased, the earth became more firm, the army marched under the guidance of Zane, M'Pherson, and Armstrong (three men well acquainted with wood-craft), and at the end of three days were on Blanchard's Fork, where Colonel Findlay had erected a stockade fort, which was called by his name. It was about fifty yards square, with a block-house at each corner, and a ditch in front. It was on the southwest side of the stream, where the village of Findlay now stands. The fort stood at the end of the present bridge.[1]

At Fort Findlay General Hull received a dispatch[a] from the War Department directing him to hasten to Detroit, and there await farther orders. It was dated on the morning of the day when war was declared, but contained not a word concerning that measure.[2] This will be mentioned again presently.

[a] June 24, 1812.

Hull ordered all the camp equipage to be left at the fort, and made preparations for an immediate advance. Colonel Cass was sent forward with his regiment to open a road to the Rapids of the Maumee;[3] and a few days afterward the whole army, excepting detachments left in the forts, were encamped upon a plain on the eastern bank of that stream, opposite Wayne's battle-ground of 1794. There the wearied troops had the first glimpse of civilization since they left Urbana. They were taken across the stream, and marched down its left bank, through a small village at the foot of the Rapids,[4] to a level spot near the ruins of the old British fort Miami, where they encamped.

So wearied and worn were Hull's beasts of burden when he reached navigable waters connecting with his destination that he resolved to relieve them as much as possible. He accordingly dispatched, from the foot of the Rapids, the schooner *Cuyahoga* for Detroit with his own baggage and that of most of his officers; also all of the hospital stores, intrenching tools, and a trunk containing his commission, his instructions from the War Department, and complete muster-rolls of the whole army.[5] The wives of three of the officers, Lieutenant Dent, and Lieutenant Goodwin, with thirty soldiers as protectors of the schooner, also embarked in her. A smaller vessel, under the charge of Surgeon's Mate James Reynolds, was dispatched with the *Cuyahoga* for the conveyance of the army invalids, and both sailed into Maumee

---

[1] Howe's *Historical Collections of Ohio*, page 238.
[2] Armstrong's *Notices of the War of 1812*, i., 48. Hull's *Memoir of the Campaign of the Northwestern Army*, page 36.
[3] Miami and Maumee mean the same thing. The latter method of spelling more nearly indicates the pronunciation to an English ear than the former. The Indians pronounced it as if spelled Me-aw-me. So the French spelt it, according to their pronunciation of *i* and *a*, Mi-a-mi. To distinguish this stream from the two of the same name (Great and Little Miami) that empty into the Ohio, this was frequently called the Miami of the Lakes.
[4] Now Maumee City, nearly opposite Perrysburg, the capital of Wyandotte County.
[5] Robert Wallace, one of General Hull's aids-de-camp, in a letter published in a newspaper at Covington, Kentucky, in 1842, and quoted in the Appendix to General Hull's *Military and Civil Life*, page 443, says, "His son, Captain Hull (who was also an aid), in executing this order, unfortunately shipped a small trunk containing the papers and reports of the army, for which he was afterward severely reprimanded by his father."

R

Bay, where Toledo now stands, on the evening of the 1st of July. On the same day the army moved toward Detroit through the beautiful open country, by the way of Frenchtown, on the River Raisin, now the pleasant city of Monroe, in Michigan.

[a] July, 1812. When approaching Frenchtown toward the evening of the 2d,[a] Hull was overtaken by a courier, sent by the vigilant postmaster at Cleveland, with a dispatch from the War Department, which read as follows:

"SIR,—War is declared against Great Britain. You will be on your guard. Proceed to your post with all possible expedition; make such arrangements for the defense of the country as in your judgment may be necessary, and wait for farther orders."

This dispatch was explicit and easily understood, but its date, and the time and manner of its reception, perplexed the general. It bore the same date as the one received a week earlier at Fort Findlay, in which there was no intimation of a declaration of war. *That* had been sent by a special courier from the seat of government; *this* had been sent by mail to Cleveland, to be there intrusted to such conveyance as "accident might supply," through one hundred miles of wilderness.[1] The former contained an important order; the latter contained information more important. This fact was inexplicable to Hull, and remains unexplained to this day. The circumstance made him feel serious apprehensions for the safety of the schooner and her consort. The question pressed heavily upon his mind whether the British commander at Malden, past which the vessels must sail, might not already have heard of the declaration of war. In that event they might be seized, and valuable plunder as well as valuable information would fall into his hands. Moved by these considerations, he dispatched an officer with some men to the mouth of the Raisin to stop the schooner, but their arrival was too late. With a fair wind she had passed that point.

A few hours afterward Hull's apprehensions were justified by events, for he learned, on the morning after his arrival at Frenchtown, that the *Cuyahoga* had been captured. While sailing past Malden, unconscious of danger, at ten o'clock on the morning of the 2d, she was brought to by a gun from the shore. The British armed vessel *Hunter* went alongside of her, and schooner and cargo became a prize. The troops and crew were made prisoners of war. The vessel with the invalids, being behind the schooner, passed up the more shallow channel on the west side of Bois Blanc Island, and reached Detroit in the afternoon of the next day[b] in safety.[2]

[b] July 3. The British commander at Malden, and those of other posts, *had* been notified of the declaration of war through the vigilance of British subjects in New York. Sir George Prevost, the governor general of Canada, was informed of the fact on the 24th of June by an express from New York to the Northwest Fur Company, which left that city on the 20th, the day when intelligence of the declaration of war reached there. On the 25th, Sir George sent a courier with a letter to Sir Isaac Brock, the lieutenant governor at York (now Toronto), but it did not reach him until the 3d of

---

[1] I am indebted to the Hon. Elisha Whittlesey, of Ohio, late First Auditor of the United States Treasury, for the following interesting account of the transmission of this dispatch from Cleveland to the camp. Mr. Walworth, the postmaster at Cleveland, was requested by the postmaster general to send the dispatch by express. Charles Shaler, Esq., a young lawyer, then in Cleveland (brother-in-law of Commodore M'Donough), was persuaded to become the bearer, certainly as far as the Rapids of the Maumee, and possibly to Detroit. The compensation agreed upon was thirty-five dollars. On searching the mail the dispatch could not be found. It was suggested to Mr. Walworth that it might be in the Detroit mail. Having been informed by letter of the declaration of war, and believing the dispatch to be of great importance, he considered it his duty to open the Detroit mail. He did so, but with reluctance, and found the dispatch. At about noon on the 28th of June Mr. Shaler started from Cleveland on horseback. He was obliged to swim all the streams excepting the Cuyahoga at Cleveland. No relays of horses could be obtained. He reached the Rapids on the night of the 1st of July. There he was informed that the army was moving rapidly toward Detroit. He pursued and overtook it not far from the Raisin, at two o'clock in the morning of the 2d, just as the moon was rising. After some formality he was ushered into the presence of Hull, who was dressing. He was requested to be silent in the presence of camp listeners. A council of officers was immediately summoned. The army was put in motion at dawn. He accompanied it to Detroit, where his horse died from the effects of the rapid journey through the wilderness. Mr. Shaler remained in Detroit until he saw the flag of his country raised over the soil of Canada. He returned to Cleveland partly on foot, and partly on hired and borrowed horses. [2] Letter of Dr. Reynolds, dated at Detroit, July 7, 1812.

How British Officers in Canada were informed of the Declaration of War. Hull's Army at Detroit.

July, when he was at Fort George, on the Niagara frontier. He had been informed of the event by express from New York as early as the 27th of June.[1] Colonel St. George, at Malden, was informed of it by letter on the 30th, two days before it reached Hull; and Captain Roberts, in command of the British post on the island of St. Joseph, at the head of Lake Huron, was notified by letter also on the 8th of July. The letters to the last two named commanders were in envelopes franked by the American Secretary of the Treasury.[2] How these were obtained remains a mystery, for no man believes that Mr. Gallatin would have lent such assistance to any known enemy of his country. The fact that he was opposed to the war gave currency to a report that he was willing to cast obstacles in the way of the invasion of Canada, a scheme which many even of the war-party regarded as unwise. Mr. Madison was also charged with having, under the influence of Virginia politicians and the wily Calhoun, withheld aid from Hull, that the conquest of Canada might not be effected, as it would, by annexation to the United States, materially increase the area and political influence of free-labor territory, and more speedily snatch the sceptre of dominion in the affairs of the government from the slave-labor states. Assertions of this kind were prevalent at that day, and have been revived in our time.[3]

Hull's army rested a day at Frenchtown, and spent the 4th of July in constructing a bridge across the Huron River, near Brownstown, twenty-five miles from Detroit. They had passed a hostile Wyandotte village, and observed a large vessel with troops on board at Malden. Expecting an attack by a combined force of British and Indians, Hull's troops slept upon their arms that night.[4] They marched early the next morning; and at evening, having passed the Rivers Aux Ecorces and Rouge, encamped at Spring Wells,[5] at the lower end of the Detroit settlement, opposite Sandwich in Canada, where a British force was stationed, and not far from which, up the river opposite Detroit, they were throwing up fortifications. The camp was upon a pleasant eminence, eligible for a commanding fortification. From its crown they hurled a few heavy shot across the river, "which cleared out a number of inhabitants

---

[1] The late Honorable William Hamilton Merritt, of St. Catharine's, Canada West, who was a member of the Canadian Parliament, was an active officer of dragoons during the early portion of the war on the Canadian Peninsula. He left a very valuable narrative of the events of the war in that section, in manuscript, which his family kindly placed in my hands. In that narrative I find the following statement: "We received intelligence of the declaration of war by the United States on the 27th of June, 1812, from a messenger sent by the late John Jacob Astor to Thomas Clark, Esq., of Niagara Falls. The express was immediately sent to President General Brock, who was at York."

[2] Letter of General Jesup to General Armstrong, cited in the latter's *Notices of the War of 1812*, i., 195.

[3] It is said that when (as we shall hereafter notice) General John Armstrong and President Madison quarreled, the former, in a pamphlet, boldly made the charge alluded to in the text. They became reconciled, and the pamphlet was withdrawn, and the whole issue, as far as practicable, was destroyed. One of these pamphlets was, it is said, in possession of the late Alvan Stewart. In a letter of that gentleman to "The Liberty Party" in 1846, he alluded to this matter as follows: After noticing the points on the frontier to which General Smyth, of Virginia, General Winder, of Maryland, Generals Wilkinson and Hampton, then of Louisiana, were stationed with their troops, he says, "Four slave-holding generals, with their four armies, were stretched out on our northern frontier, not to *take* Canada, but to prevent its being taken by the men of New England and New York, in 1812, '13, and '14, lest we should make some six or eight free states from Canada, if conquered. This was treason against Northern interests, Northern blood, and Northern honor. But the South furnished the President and the Cabinet. This revelation could have been proved by General John Armstrong, then Secretary of War, after he and Mr. Madison had quarreled."— *Writings and Speeches of Alvan Stewart on Slavery*, edited by his son-in-law, Luther R. Marsh, Esq., page 47.

We have seen that Commander Stewart (now the venerable admiral bearing the title of Old Ironsides) was called to Washington City on public business. At that time, while in conversation with Mr. Calhoun upon public matters, the latter declared to the former that whenever the control of the national government should pass out of the hands of the Southern politicians (he spoke for them, and not for the people), they would "resort to a dissolution of the Union."—See Letter of Commodore Stewart to G. W. Childs, May 24, 1861.

[4] It was the intention of the British to attack Hull in the swamps of the Huron River. It was prevented by a deceptive communication to the commander at Malden by a resident there, and a friend of Hull's. He informed Colonel St. George that Hull had sent for cannon at Detroit, and intended to cross the river and attack Fort Malden. This caused the British commander to concentrate his troops for the defense of the fort. Meanwhile Hull moved on toward Detroit. Speaking of this event in the march, Robert Wallace, one of General Hull's aids, writing in 1842 to the *Licking Valley Register*, Covington, Kentucky, says, "During that day it was remarked to me by several officers that General Hull appeared to have no sense of personal danger, and that he would certainly be killed if a contest commenced. This was said to prepare me for taking orders from the next in rank."

[5] This locality was sometimes called The Sand Hills. Out of these, on the river side, many springs of pure water formerly gushed out, and these gave the name by which the place was generally known. For the same reason the French called it Belle Fontaine. The sand-hills, three in number, were Indian burial-places.

very quick."[1] There, and near Fort Detroit, Hull allowed his troops to wash their clothes and have their arms repaired, while he was awaiting farther orders from his government.[2]

Officers and men, anxious to invade Canada, were impatient, and even a mutinous spirit was manifested by some of the Ohio Volunteers. They burned with a desire to cross the river and attack the foe. The sight of growing fortifications, that would endanger the town and fort of Detroit, and soon become too formidable to face in crossing the river, maddened them, and it was with great difficulty that their officers restrained them.[3] To quiet their tumultuous impulses, Hull called a council of the field officers. He assured them that he had no authority to invade Canada. They insisted that it was expedient to do so immediately, and drive off the fort-builders. "While I have command," he said, firmly, "I will obey the orders of my government. I will not cross the Detroit until I hear from Washington." The young officers heard this announcement with compressed lips, and doubtless many a rebellious heart—rebellious toward the commander—beat quickly, with deep emotion, for hours after the council was dismissed. The general was perplexed; but, happily for all concerned, a letter came from the Secretary of War that evening, directing him to "commence operations immediately," and that, should the force under his command be equal to the enterprise, and "consistent with the safety of the American posts," he should take possession of Fort Malden at Amherstburg, and extend his conquests as circumstances might justify.[4] He was also directed to give assurance to the inhabitants of the province about to be invaded, of protection to their persons and property. With such official warrant in his hands, Hull determined to cross into Canada at once, to the delight of his army, both officers and privates.[5]

Detroit at that time stretched along the river at a convenient distance back, and the present Jefferson Avenue was the principal street. It contained one hundred and sixty houses, and about eight hundred souls. The inhabitants were chiefly of French descent. Only seven years before, every building but one in the village was destroyed by fire.[6] On the hill, in the rear, about two hundred and fifty yards from the river, stood Fort Detroit, built by the English after the conquest of Canada a hundred years ago. It was quadrangular in form, with bastions and barracks, and

---

[1] Lieutenant Colonel Miller to his Wife, July 7, 1812—Autograph Letter.

[2] Colonel William Stanley Hatch, of "River Home," near Cincinnati, kindly placed in my hands a chapter of his unpublished "*Memoirs of the War of 1812 in the Northwest*," containing a minute account of events which came under his own observation during the campaign of General Hull from May until the middle of August. Colonel Hatch was a volunteer in the Cincinnati Light Infantry, commanded by Captain John F. Mansfield of that city, and from the invasion of Canada to the surrender of the army he was acting assistant quartermaster general. To his narrative I am indebted for a number of facts given in this sketch not found recorded in history. He says that on Monday, the 6th of July, the fourth regiment of regulars marched to the fort, and that the next day the volunteers marched thither, and took up their position near the fort, south, west, and north of it.

[3] General Hull had been subjected to much annoyance from the Ohio Volunteers from the beginning of the march. They were militia just called into the field, and had never been restricted by military discipline. They were frequently quite insubordinate. This fact was brought out on Hull's trial. "One evening," says Lieutenant Baron, of the Fourth Regiment, in his testimony at the trial of General Hull, "while at Urbana, I saw a multitude, and heard a noise, and was informed that a company of Ohio Volunteers were riding one of their officers on a rail. In saying that the Ohio Volunteers were insubordinate, witness means that they were only as much so as undisciplined militia generally are. Some thirty or forty of the Ohio militia refused to cross into Canada at one time, and thinks he saw one hundred who refused to cross when the troops were at Urbana."—Forbes's *Report of the Court-martial*, page 124. The same witness testified to the manifestation of a mutinous spirit at other times. On one occasion, he says, General Hull rode up and said to Colonel Miller, "Your regiment is a powerful argument; without them I could not march these men to Detroit."

[4] Dispatch of William Eustis, Secretary of War, to General Hull, dated June 24, 1812.

[5] On the morning of the 6th Colonel Cass was sent to Malden with a flag of truce, to demand the baggage and prisoners taken from the schooner. On his approach he was blindfolded, and in this condition was taken before Colonel St. George. He was treated courteously. The demand was unheeded, and, being again blindfolded, he was led out of the fort. He returned to camp with Captain Burbanks, of the British army.—*M'Afee*.

[6] The city of Detroit is about nine miles below Lake St. Clair. The river, or strait, between St. Clair and Lake Erie gave it its name, *de troit* being the French name of a strait. The Indians called it *Wa-wa-o-te-wong*. It was a trading-post of the French as early as 1620, before any of the French missionaries had penetrated the distant wilderness from Quebec and Montreal. It was established as a settlement in 1701, when Antoine de la Motte Cadillac, lord of Bouaget, Moun Desert, having received a grant of fifteen miles square from Louis XIV., reached the site of Detroit with a Jesuit missionary and one hundred men, and planted the first settlement in Michigan.—*Charlevoix*. The name of the old Indian village on its site was called by the Ottawas Teuchsa Grondie.—*Colden*, cited by Lanman in his *History of Michigan*, page 61.

covered about two acres of ground. The embankments were nearly twenty feet in height, with a deep dry ditch, and were surrounded by a double row of pickets. The outside row was in the centre of the ditch, and the other row projected from the bank, forming what is technically called a *fraise*. There was a work, called the Citadel Fort, that stood on the site of the present Arsenal, or Temperance Hotel, in Jefferson Avenue. The fort was garrisoned when Hull arrived by ninety-four men. Its position was one of considerable strength, but, unfortunately, it did not command the river, and could not damage the armed vessels which the British at that time employed in those waters.[1] The town was surrounded by strong pickets, fourteen feet high, with loop-holes to shoot through. The pickets commenced at the river, on the line of the Brush farm, and followed it to about Congress Street; thence westerly, along or near Michigan Avenue, back of the old fort, to the east line of the Cass farm, and followed that line to the river. On Jefferson Avenue, at the Cass line, and on Atwater Street, on the Brush farm, massive gates were placed. These pickets, which had been erected as defenses against Indian incursions, were yet well preserved in 1812.[2]

The fortifications which the British were erecting on the opposite side of the river (then about three fourths of a mile wide) would, if completed, not only command the town, but seriously menace the fort; so, with all possible expedition, Hull prepared to cross and drive the British toward Malden. His force at that time, including the Michigan militia, under Colonel Elijah Brush, who had joined those from Ohio, numbered about twenty-two hundred effective men.[3]

After great exertions, Hull collected boats and canoes sufficient to carry about four hundred men at a time. These would be too few to cross in the face of the enemy behind his breastworks, and he resorted to strategy. Toward the evening of the 11th, all the boats were sent down the river to Spring Wells, in full view of the British, and at the same time Colonel M'Arthur, with his regiment, marched to the same point. The British prepared to dispute their passage. After dark, troops and boats moved silently up the river to Bloody Bridge, a mile and a half above Fort Detroit, and prepared to cross there. Finding all silent at Spring Wells, the deceived British believed that the Americans had gone stealthily down the river to attack Malden. Under this impression, they left Sandwich, and in the morning the Americans had no one to op-

VIEW AT BLOODY BRIDGE IN 1860.[4]

---

[1] At that time the Americans had a small frigate, named the *Adams*, nearly completed, at the ship-yard on the Rouge River.   [2] Judge Witherell's *Reminiscences of Detroit*.   [3] Lieutenant Colonel Miller—Autograph Letter.
[4] This view is from the bridge that was over Bloody Run, in Jefferson Avenue, in 1860. Bloody Bridge was nearer the Detroit River, seen in the distance. It was near the second fence from the river, running from the left in the picture, and at the most distant point where the stream of water is seen. That stream is Bloody Run. The large tree in the foreground was a whitewood. It was sixteen feet in circumference; and scars of the bullets received into it during a battle a hundred years ago might still be seen in its huge trunk.

[a] July 12, 1812. pose their landing. At dawn[a] the regular troops and the Ohio Volunteers crossed to the Canadian shore to a point opposite the lower end of Hog Island. They looked with suspicious eye upon a stone wind-mill on the shore, for it appeared like an excellent place for a concealed battery.[1] But there was no resistance,[2] and the little army first touched Canada just above the present town of Windsor. It was a bright and lovely Sabbath morning, with a gentle breeze from the southwest. The American flag was immediately hoisted by Colonel Cass and a subaltern[3] over Canadian soil, and was greeted by cheers from the invaders, the spectators of the passage of the Detroit at Bloody Bridge, and from the fort and town. They were also cordially received by the French Canadians. The Americans encamped

COLONEL BABIE'S RESIDENCE.

on the farm of Colonel Francis Babie,[4] a French Canadian and British officer, with his fine brick mansion (then unfinished, and yet standing in Windsor) in the centre of the camp. This was taken possession of by General Hull, and used as head-quarters for himself and principal officers. The little village of Sandwich, a short distance below, gave its name to this locality, and Hull's dispatches from his head-quarters were always dated at "Sandwich."

[b] July 12. On the day of the invasion,[b] the commanding general issued a stirring proclamation to the inhabitants of Canada, which was written by Colonel Lewis Cass. "After thirty years of peace and prosperity," he said, "the United States have been driven to arms. The injuries and aggressions, the insults and indignities of Great Britain, have once more left them no alternative but manly resistance or unconditional submission." He then declared that he came as a friend, and as their liberator from British tyranny, and not as an enemy or mere conquering invader. "I tender you," he said, "the invaluable blessings of civil, political, and religious liberty, and their necessary results, individual and general prosperity. . . . Remain at your homes; pursue your peaceful and accustomed avocations; raise not your hands against your brethren." He assured them that the persons and property of all peaceful citizens should be perfectly secure. He did not ask them to join his army. "I come prepared," he said, "for any contingency. I have a force which will look down all opposition, and that force is but the vanguard of a much greater." All that he asked of them was to remain peacefully at their homes. At the same time, knowing that the British had in their service hordes of merciless savages, whose mode of warfare was indiscriminate slaughter of men, women, and children, or the

---

[1] "Expecting, of course, that the enemy would contest our landing, we were thinking, as we left the shore, of the amusing fact that we should doubtless commence our active campaign by attacking a wind-mill."—*Colonel Hatch's Narrative.* The invasion proved to be about as ridiculous and bootless as Quixotte's attack on the wind-mills. This building was yet standing when I visited the spot in the autumn of 1860.

[2] "As we were crossing the river we saw two British officers ride up very fast opposite where we intended landing, but they went back faster than they came. They were Colonel St. George, the commanding officer at Malden, and one of his captains."—Lieutenant Colonel Miller to his Wife, July 14, 1812—Autograph Letter.

[3] "Tell our much-beloved Father Flint that his son James had the honor and gratification, as commanding officer, to plant, with his own hands, assisted by Colonel Cass, the first United States standard on the pleasant bank of the Detroit River, in King George's province of Upper Canada."—Lieutenant Colonel Miller to his Wife, July 14, 1812—Autograph Letter.

[4] Pronounced as if spelt Baw-bee. The house was about eight rods back from Sandwich Street, Windsor, with shops and mean buildings in front of it. It was a brick house, stuccoed in front, and made to represent blocks of stone. Before it was a garden, the remnant of a more spacious and beautiful one, that extended to the river bank. The house belonged to a son of Colonel Babie. When Hull took possession of it the floors were laid and the windows were in, but the partitions were not built. These were immediately made of rough boards. The general and his aids, according to Colonel Hatch's narrative, occupied the north half of the house, or the portion seen over the heads of the two figures in the picture. The councils of war were held in the second story, over the rooms occupied by the general. General James Taylor, of Kentucky, the quartermaster general, occupied a part of the house as his head-quarters, but, being unwell, he lodged in Detroit.

Effect of Hull's Proclamation.   A Reconnoissance toward Malden.   Foraging Expedition to the Thames.

torture of prisoners, he warned the inhabitants that no quarter would be shown to them if found fighting by the side of the Indians. "The first stroke of the tomahawk, the first attempt with the scalping-knife," he said, "will be the signal for an indiscriminate scene of desolation. No white man found fighting by the side of an Indian will be taken prisoner. Instant destruction will be his lot."

This proclamation, the presence of a considerable army, and the sight of the American flag flying on both sides of the Detroit, produced a powerful effect. Many of the Canadian militia deserted the British standard. Some joined the Americans, and others returned to their farms. A large number of families, terrified by the tales of British officers concerning the savagism of the invaders, had fled to the depths of the forests. These were soon assured, and most of them accepted Hull's promised protection, and returned to their homes.[1]

On the morning of the 13th[a] Hull sent a reconnoitring party toward Fort Malden, at the little village of Amherstburg, eighteen miles below his headquarters, a spot associated in the minds of the people of the West with every thing hideous in the annals of their sufferings from Indian depredations, for there the raids of the savages upon the frontier settlements had been arranged by Elliott, M'Kee, Girty, and others. The troops were anxious to break up that nest of vultures; and the reconnoitring party, under Captain Henry Ulery, of Colonel Findlay's regiment, went upon duty with great alacrity. They returned toward evening with intelligence that at Turkey Creek, nine miles below the camp, they had been informed that about two hundred Indians, under Tecumtha (then in the British service), had been lying in ambush at the southern end of the bridge over that stream, and that the forest was full of prowling savages. Hull immediately ordered his camp to be fortified on the land side, and what cannon he had to be placed in battery on the bank of the river, for vague rumors came that the British were about to send a small fleet up to co-operate with a land force in an attack upon the Americans. Rumors also came of Indians up the river, and a detachment of Sloan's cavalry were sent in that direction. They sent word back that they had discovered a party of savages. At eight o'clock the same evening, Colonel M'Arthur, with one hundred men, went in pursuit. The chase was vigorous, and at Ruscum River the pursuers fell upon the rear of the fugitives, who dispersed, fled to the woods, and escaped. M'Arthur was about to return, when Captain Smith, of the Detroit Dragoons, overtook him with orders to push forward to the settlements on the Thames in search of provisions. He instantly obeyed, penetrated as far as the Moravian towns, sixty miles from its mouth, near which the battle of the Thames occurred in 1813, and found many farmhouses and cultivated fields along the picturesque borders of the river. Among the homes near its mouth was that of Isaac Hull, a nephew of the general. The owner had fled. The house was guarded by a file of British soldiers. These were disarmed and paroled. Boats along the stream were seized, and loaded with the winnings of the expedition; and on the 17th M'Arthur returned to camp with about two hundred barrels of flour, four hundred blankets, and quite a large quantity of military stores. These were chiefly public property, collected for the British troops at Malden, and yet Hull gave a receipt for the whole, public and private.

[a] July, 1812.

Meanwhile small expeditions had been sent toward Malden. Colonel Cass, with

---

[1] Hull sent a copy of his proclamation to the Secretary of War, with a letter in which he expressed a hope that it would be "approved by the government." To this Secretary Eustis replied, on the 1st of August, saying, "Your letters of the 13th and 14th, together with your proclamation, have been received. Your operations are approved by the government." Such is the record; and yet, for more than fifty years, writers on the subject of this campaign have asserted that the proclamation was unauthorized and disapproved by the government. The American commissioners, at the treaty of Ghent, in the face of Secretary Eustis's letter to the contrary, made the same assertion; and this proclamation has been always cited as one of the sins of the unfortunate General Hull. The British complained of it as an attempt to seduce the Canadians from their loyalty, and the enemies of Hull have stigmatized it as a "pompous and vaporing proclamation." As Brackenridge remarks, "Had he been eventually successful, there is no doubt that it would have been regarded as an eloquent production."

two hundred and eighty men, accompanied by Lieutenant Colonel Miller, of the regulars, pushed forward to the Ta-ron-tee, as the Wyandots called it, or *Riviere Aux Canards*, as it was named by the French, a wide and deep stream that passes through

VIEW AT THE RIVIERE AUX CANARDS.

broad marshes into the Detroit River, about four miles above Malden. On the southern side of this stream, at the end of a bridge, was a British picket, composed of some of the Forty-first regiment, Canadian militia, and Indians under Tecumtha.[1] Leaving a rifle company of forty men in ambush, Cass marched three or four miles up the stream to a ford, came down on the south side, wading across streams armpit deep, and confronted the enemy at sunset. There he was checked by a deep tributary of the *Aux Canards*, and compelled to make a circuit of more than a mile to gain the shore next to the enemy. This was soon accomplished. Forming with his riflemen on each wing, Cass dashed upon the foe with great impetuosity, who fled at the first fire. He had been re-enforced; and three times he rallied, changed front, and fired upon the pursuers. Cass chased the fugitives about half a mile, the drums beating Yankee Doodle; when night fell, the pursuit was relinquished, and the attacking party returned to the bridge. A courier was sent to head-quarters to ask permission to hold the bridge, as it would be of great importance in the march of the army toward Malden. Hull refused to grant it. It was too near the enemy, he said, to be held with safety by a small detachment; and, not having received his heavy cannon from Detroit, he was not prepared to attack strong Fort Malden at Amherstburg.[2] The impatient officers and soldiers were irritated by the refusal, and murmured loudly, but Hull was unyielding. This was the first battle and victory in the second war for independence. It was hailed throughout the United States as an omen of success, and Colonel Cass was called the "Hero of Ta-ron-tee." He took two prisoners; and from deserters he learned that some of the enemy were killed, and nine or ten wounded, while he did not lose a man.

That the Americans might have taken Malden with the means at their command when they first crossed into Canada there can be no doubt. Why Hull did not attempt it is a question not easily answered to-day, unless we look for a solution in the fact that the Americans had no reliable information concerning the real strength of

---

[1] On the morning of the 17th a re-enforcement of troops arrived at the bridge, consisting of the remainder of the Fourth United States regiment, and a piece of artillery, under Captain Eastman. A council of officers was convened. A majority of them insisted on leaving the bridge, while Colonel Cass and Captain Snelling insisted on holding it, as it would be of the utmost importance in marching upon Malden. The overruling of their opinion, and the refusal of Hull to allow the bridge to be held, caused its abandonment. This was one of the most fatal of the delays of Hull in the early movements of this Canadian invasion.

[2] "This determination," says Wallace (*Licking Valley Register*, 1842), "occasioned a delay of nearly three weeks, which proved most fatal to the results of the campaign. Had we been prepared for an immediate attack on Malden, our campaign would have been as glorious as it was otherwise disastrous, and the name of General Hull would have been exalted to the skies."

the fort and garrison. The fort itself was weak, and the garrison was weaker. The militia and Indians were constantly deserting. The fort consisted of four bastions flanking a dry ditch, with a single interior defense of picketing, perforated with loop-holes for musketry. All the buildings were of wood, roofed with shingles. A few shells would have destroyed the works. The garrison was composed of about two hundred men of the first battalion of the Forty-first Regiment, commanded by Captain Muir; a very weak detachment of the Royal Newfoundland Fencibles; and a subaltern command of artillery under Lieutenant Troughton.[1] The exact number of Indians there at that time is not known. Colonel St. George, the commander of the post, was so well convinced of his inability to hold it against a respectable force, that orders were given to the garrison to be ready at a moment's notice to leave the works. He preferred to risk a battle in the open field to incurring the dangers of a siege in a fortification so untenable.

But Hull did not advance upon Malden, and the post was saved and speedily strengthened. Little enterprises like that in which Colonel Cass was engaged (though none were so important in their actual or promised results) broke the monotony of camp life, while most precious time was passing away—"wasting," the young officers said. "I can scarcely restrain my indignation sufficiently while writing to describe the event in deliberate terms," said one of them in 1817.[2] "The officers," he says, "from this occurrence, began to distrust the views of the general, and their opinion of his abilities began to dwindle into contempt."

A report reached the camp, on the evening of the 17th,[a] that the *Queen Charlotte*, a British armed vessel of eighteen guns, at Malden, was sailing up the river, and committing depredations on the American side. Colonel Findlay was immediately detached with a small reconnoitring party toward the Aux Canards. He found the planks of the bridge torn up, the timbers formed into a breast-work on the south side of the stream, and the *Queen Charlotte* lying at the mouth of the river within easy supporting distance.[3] The great advantage acquired by Colonel Cass in taking possession of that bridge was utterly lost. On the following day, a small party, under Captain Snelling, went down as a corps of observation; and, to the delight of the whole army, Hull issued an order[b] for its movement, which gave implied assurance of an immediate march on Malden. Under the direction of that order, Colonel M'Arthur, the senior officer, marched down the river, on the morning of the 19th, with a detachment of his regiment, one hundred and fifty strong, and joined Captain Snelling at the Petit Côte settlement, about a mile above the bridge.

[a] July, 1812.

[b] July 18.

M'Arthur was instructed to ascertain the situation of affairs at the Aux Canards, but not to go within reach of the guns of the *Queen Charlotte*. With his adjutant and a few riflemen he went to the top of a ridge, about three hundred yards from the river, to reconnoitre. He ascertained that the battery on the south side of the stream was supported by about sixty regulars, one hundred and fifty Canadian militia, twenty-five dragoons, and fifty Indians. Some little skirmishing ensued between the Indians, who had crossed on the timbers of the bridge, and the American riflemen; and Colonel M'Arthur was fired upon by a gun-boat, until then undiscovered, under the bank of the river, while he was reconnoitring the position of the *Queen Charlotte*. He also came near being cut off by the Indians. Soon after this the whole detachment engaged in two skirmishes with the Indians. In the last the latter were commanded by Tecumtha. The ammunition of the Americans becom-

---

[1] Auchinleck's *History of the War of 1812*, page 51.
[2] Robert B. M'Afee.—*History of the late War in the Western Country*, page 65.
[3] A short distance up the Rouge River, and not far from Detroit, was a ship-yard (see the map), where a small brig, called the *Adams*, was being fitted for service at this time, under the direction of H. H. Brevoort, of the navy, who was called "Commodore" in Hull's orders. From the 12th to the 20th of July great exertions were made to perfect her preparations.

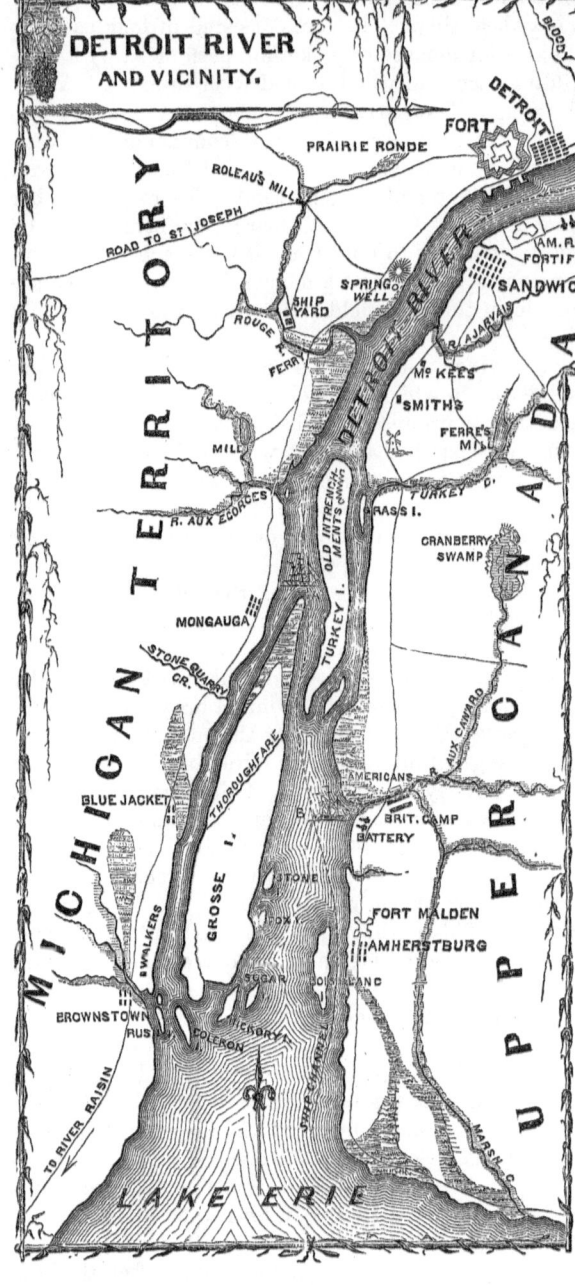

ing scarce, they fell back, and M'Arthur sent an express to camp for re-enforcements. On the arrival of the messenger, Colonel Cass hastened down with one hundred and fifty men and a six-pounder. He met the retreating detachment at Turkey Creek Bridge, when the united forces pushed on to Petit Côte, and there encamped for the night. The enemy had been re-enforced in the mean time with both men and artillery. Cass was anxious to attack them, and, at his request, M'Arthur ordered the whole force toward the bridge. A few shots of the six-pounder were exchanged with the artillery of the enemy, but with little effect; and toward evening the whole detachment marched back to camp fatigued and dispirited, and bereft of all confidence in the commanding general. All accused him of incapacity; many of them denounced him in private conversation as a coward, and a few expressed the belief that he was treacherous. These suspicions were confirmed to their minds by his leaving his army on the 21st of July, and remaining at Detroit four days, without, as they alleged, any but frivolous pretexts.[1]

During the absence of Hull, the command of the troops in Canada devolved on Colonel M'Arthur,[2] who resolved to make an effort to attack Malden. He dispatched

---

[1] M'Afee, pages 66 to 68.
[2] A biographical sketch of M'Arthur will be found in another part of this work. See Index.

Captain M'Cullough, with Rangers, to seek a passage for artillery across the Canards above the bridge, so as to avoid the guns of the battery and the *Queen Charlotte*. He found it impracticable, on account of the deep morasses that bordered the stream for several miles. Informed that the Indians had been seen between the Aux Canards and Turkey Creek, M'Arthur sent Major Denny and one hundred and seventeen men, all militia, to drive them back. The major marched on the night of the 24th, and early next morning found an Indian ambuscade in the Petit Côte settlement, where he captured a French captain of a militia company then at Malden. During the day he had skirmishes with the savages. In the last a part of his line gave way, and he was compelled to retreat in confusion, pursued for two miles and a half by the Indians.[1] Near Turkey Creek Bridge the major endeavored to rally his men, but in vain. They crossed the bridge, and met General Lucas with re-enforcements, when the whole party returned to camp.[2] Denny had lost six killed and two wounded. This was the FIRST BLOOD SHED IN THE WAR.[3]

While the little invading army were perplexed with doubts and fears, and startled by dreadful suspicions concerning their commander-in-chief, alarming intelligence came from the north—the far distant and mysterious region of the upper lakes, which was considered the great hive of the savages. In the bosom of the clear, cold, deep waters of the strait between Lakes Huron and Michigan—a strait forty miles in length and four in breadth — stands a limestone rock, about seven miles in circumference, rising in its centre to an altitude of nearly three hundred feet, and covered with a rough and generous soil, out of which springs heavy timber. The Indians,

MACKINACK, FROM ROUND ISLAND.[4]

speaking the Algonquin tongue, impressed with its shape, called it Michillimackinack, which signifies The Great Turtle. On the opposite shore, which is the most north-

---

[1] British authorities say that there were only twenty-two Indians, of the Minoumin tribe, in this engagement.—See Auchinleck, page 52.
[2] Major Denny, at his own request, was subjected to the scrutiny of a court of inquiry, over which Colonel M'Arthur presided. He was acquitted of all blame.
[3] The check given to the Americans at the Aux Canards was made the subject of congratulation in a general order issued by General Brock on the 6th of August.
[4] On the right is seen the projecting crag called Robinson's Folly; on the left the Lover's Leap; and in the centre Fort Mackinack, with the village of Mackinack below it. Old Fort Holmes, now a ruin, is on the higher ground in the rear. This view is from a sketch by C. F. Davis, made in August in 1839 from Round Island, and is pronounced by those who have visited Mackinack to be faithful.

erly point of the peninsula of Michigan, the French Jesuit missionaries planted the symbol of Christianity as early as 1671, and called the Head-land Point of Ignatius. La Salle, the discoverer of the Mississippi, with Father Hennepin and others, were there in 1679; and by the side of the standard of the Prince of Peace they erected a strong-hold of war, and called it Fort Michillimackinack. The name was abbreviated to Mackinack (pronounced Mackinaw), and that orthography we will adopt.

When, on the conquest of Canada from the French, this post fell into the hands of the English, the savages that filled the country remained hostile to their new masters. "You have conquered the French," they said, "but you have not conquered us." The mighty Pontiac, the Ottawa chief, was then forming his giant confederacy in the Northwest for the extermination of the English westward of the Niagara. The principal tribes of that region were the Ottawas and Ojibwas, or Chippewas. The latter were the most powerful. Their most important village was upon the back of Michillimackinack, The Great Turtle, in the strait, where a hundred warriors resided.

[a] June 4.   On the morning of the king's birthday,[a] 1763, the forests and Fort Mackinack was filled with the Ojibwas. They professed warm friendship for the English, and invited the garrison out to see their great game of ball, the favorite amusement of the Indians. It was a gay and exciting scene. At length a ball went up from the midst of the players in a lofty curve, and fell near the pickets of the fort. It was a preconcerted signal. The warriors rushed toward the fort as if in quest of the ball. Their hands were soon filled with gleaming hatchets, which the squaws had concealed beneath their blankets. A bloody massacre ensued. After a saturnalia of several days, the Indians, alarmed by rumors of the approach of a strong English force, took refuge on the island—three hundred and fifty warriors, with their families and household effects—carrying with them Alexander Henry, an English trader, who had been saved from the massacre by the hands of friendly Indians. The following year Fort Mackinack was garrisoned by the English. The Indians had fled from the island, and settlements upon it immediately commenced. It is a most delightful spot. As seen from the water, it presents a most striking picture of white cliffs, contrasting beautifully with the green foliage that half covers them. In the centre the land rises in wooded heights, in some places three hundred feet above the lake. The rocks form fantastic shapes. Here may be seen a cave, there a towering pinnacle, and in other places gorges are spanned by natural bridges. One of the most noted of these is the Arch Rock, second only in picturesqueness to the famous Natural Bridge in Virginia. The crown is over one hundred feet above the water, and almost forty above the ground. It was formed by the falling out of great masses of stone. The Rabbit's Peak, the Sugar-loaf, Plutonic Cave, Devil's Kitchen, Giant's Causeway, and the Lover's Leap, are all famous places, and clustered with stirring legends connected with the French and English occupation, or running back to the dim old traditions of the Children of the Forest. But I will not occupy more space in describing this now famous summer resort for tourists and sportsmen—a place I have never visited. I was about to

ARCH ROCK, MACKINACK.

take passage at Chicago for the strait in the autumn of 1860, when I heard that snows had fallen there, and that the sceptre of Boreas was omnipotent over all those north-

FORT MACKINACK.

ern waters. So I turned my face homeward, content to rely upon others for all needful information. At Detroit I found the sketch of a distant view of Mackinack Island, printed on page 267; and from Ballou's Drawing-room Companion I have copied the Arch Rock, and a near view of Mackinaw village and fort, sketched by an officer of the United States Army.

Mackinack came into the possession of the United States in 1796, when the Western military posts were finally surrendered by the British; and in 1812, Fort Holmes,[1] on the high southwest bluff of the island overlooking the fine harbor, was garrisoned by fifty-seven men, rank and file, under the command of Lieutenant Porter Hancks, of the United States Artillery. The post was a very important one as a defense to the fur-traders, and a check upon the Indians. The fort stood upon a bluff overlooking the fine semicircular harbor, a mile in extent, with an uninterrupted view into Lake Huron to the northeast, and Lake Michigan on the west. It was entirely commanded by the higher ground in the rear, on which was a stockade defended by two block-houses, in each of which a brass six-pounder was mounted. On a battery in front were two long nine-pounders, two howitzers, and a brass three-pounder. These commanded the approach to the gate. The magazine was bomb-proof, but without much ammunition or many implements of war.[2]

Such was the American post in the far off wilderness, isolated from the haunts of civilized life more than one half of the year by ice and snow, surrounded by hordes of savages ready to raise the hatchet in the pay of those who might seem to be the stronger party, and liable, in the event of war, to assault by allied British and Indians from Fort St. Joseph, on an island of that name about forty miles northeast from Mackinack, in command of Captain Charles Roberts, and garrisoned with a detachment of the Tenth Royal Veteran Battalion, forty-six in number. This fort had been erected in the spring of 1812 by order of the vigilant General Brock, and that circumstance had given some uneasiness to Lieutenant Hancks. Rumors of expected hostilities had already been conveyed to him by traders, but the first knowledge that he received of the actual declaration of war was from Captain Roberts, who, on the morning of the 17th of July, appeared at Mackinack with his garrison of British regulars, two hundred and sixty Canadian militia, and seven hundred and fifteen Indians, chiefly of the tribes of the Sioux, Ottawas, Winnebagoes, and Ojibwas (Chippewas), and demanded the surrender of the post.

Captain Roberts was a vigilant and energetic officer. As soon as Sir Isaac Brock was apprised, at Fort George, on the Niagara frontier, of the declaration of war, he

---

[1] Named in honor of Lieutenant Holmes, of Rodgers's Rangers, so celebrated in the French and Indian war. He was in command of Fort Miami, on the Maumee River, in 1763. He was murdered there on the 27th of May, 1763, through the treachery of a young Indian girl who lived with him. She represented to him that a squaw lay dangerously ill in a wigwam not far off, and desired him to bleed her. He went out for the purpose, and was shot. The sergeant who went out to learn the cause was made a prisoner, and the fort was captured.

[2] *History of the Second War between the United States of America and Great Britain*, by Charles J. Ingersoll, i., 80.

^a June 26, 1812. dispatched an express^a to Captain Roberts with the important intelligence. A letter from another hand, as we have observed, had already given that information to Roberts. Brock ordered him to attack Mackinack immediately, if practicable; or, in the event of his being attacked by the Americans, to defend his post to the last extremity. Another order, issued two days later,^b directed ^b June 28. him to summon to his assistance the neighboring Indian tribes, British and American, and to solicit the co-operation of the employes of the Northwest Fur Company in that vicinity. Still another was issued, giving Captain Roberts discretionary powers.

Mr. Pothier, the agent of the Northwest Company, was then at St. Joseph's, and Roberts laid before him his plan of operations. Pothier approved of them, and placed all the resources of the company at that point at his disposal; and he offered to command in person one hundred and fifty Canadian *voyageurs*, then employed in the company's service, and within call.

On the morning of the 16th of July—a bright and beautiful morning—the wind blowing gently from the northwest, Captain Roberts embarked with his whole force, civilized, semi-civilized, and savage, for Mackinack, in boats, bateaux, and canoes, accompanied by two six-pounders, and convoyed by the brig *Caledonia*, belonging to the Northwest Fur Company, which was laden with provisions and stores. Meanwhile the doomed garrison at Mackinack was ignorant of the declaration of war and the impending blow. Lieutenant Hancks had observed with some uneasiness the sudden coolness of Ottawa and Ojibwa chiefs, who had professed great friendship only a few days before; and on the morning when Roberts sailed from St. Joseph's, the Indian interpreter at Mackinack told Hancks that he had been assured that the Indians, who had just assembled in great numbers at St. Joseph's, were about to attack Fort Holmes. Hancks immediately summoned the American gentlemen on the island to a conference. It was thought by them expedient to send a confidential agent to St. Joseph's to ascertain, if possible, the temper of the commandant of the garrison, and to watch the movements of the Indians. Captain Daurman was sent on that errand. He embarked at about sunset on the 16th.^c The moon was ^c July. at its full, and when night fell upon the waters they were softly illuminated by its dim effulgence.

Captain Daurman had accomplished fifteen miles of his voyage when he met the hostile flotilla, and was made a prisoner. He was paroled on the condition that he should land on Mackinaw in advance of the invaders, summon the inhabitants to its west side to receive the protection of a British guard for their persons and property, and not to give any information to Hancks of the approach of the expedition. He was also instructed to warn the inhabitants that all who should go to the fort would be subject to a general massacre!

Daurman was landed just at dawn, and fulfilled the provisions of his parole to the very letter. But, while the inhabitants were flying from the village to seek British protection from the blood-thirsty savages, Dr. Day, an American gentleman, more courageous than the rest, hastened to the fort and gave the alarm. This was the first intimation that reached Hancks of the approach of an enemy. That enemy had already landed, and taken one of his two heavy guns, in the gray morning twilight of the 17th, to the crown of the island, in the rear of the fort, and placed it in battery so as to command the American works at their weakest point. It was too late for Hancks to prepare for defense. By nine o'clock in the morning Roberts had possession of the heights, and the woods back of the fort seemed to be swarming with painted savages. At half past eleven a summons was made for the immediate surrender of the fort, garrison, and island "to the forces of his Britannic majesty." "This," said Hancks, in his report to the government, "was the first intimation I had of the declaration of war." Hancks held a consultation with his officers and the

American gentlemen in the fort, and it was agreed that the overwhelming force, and the character of the assailants, made it expedient to surrender.[1] Honorable terms were allowed by capitulation, and at meridian the American colors were taken down, and those of Great Britain were put in their place. The garrison marched out with the honors of war. The prisoners were all paroled, and those who decided to leave Mackinaw were conveyed in a British cartel to Detroit. An order was then issued warning all those upon Mackinack who would not take an oath of allegiance to the British government to leave the island within a month from the date of the capitulation. All private property was held sacred, and the Indians were thoroughly restrained. "It was a fortunate circumstance," wrote John Askin, Jr.,[a] of the British Store-keeper's Department, to Colonel William Claus at Fort George, "that the fort surrendered without firing a single gun, for had they done so I firmly believe not a soul of them would have been saved." This admission on the part of a British officer connected with the expedition, and who commanded two hundred and eighty of the savages, stains indelibly the character of the government that employed such instrumentalities—a practice which the great Earl of Chatham had vehemently denounced on the floor of the British Parliament more than thirty years before.[2]

[a] July 18, 1812.

The capture of Mackinack was of the highest importance to the British interests, immediate and prospective. Valuable stores and seven hundred packages of costly furs were among the spoils of victory. The key to the fur-trade of a vast region was placed in the possession of the enemies of the United States. The command of the Upper Lakes, with all its vast advantages, was transferred to that enemy. The prison bar that kept back the savages of that region and secured their neutrality was drawn, and Detroit was exposed to fearful raids by those fierce barbarians of the wilderness, whose numbers were unknown, and the dread of whom made all the frontier settlements shudder with horror.

Such was another result of the criminal remissness, willful neglect, or imbecility of the Secretary of War. Hancks might have been apprised of the declaration of hostilities nearly a week earlier than the information reached Roberts. American instead of British efforts might have been successful, and the captured fortress might have been a British instead of an American post.

---

[1] "Three American gentlemen, who were prisoners, were permitted to accompany the flag; from them I ascertained the strength of the enemy to be from nine hundred to one thousand strong. . . . The following particulars relating to the British force were obtained after the capitulation from a source that admits of no doubt: Regular troops, 46, including four officers; Canadian militia, 260. Total, 306. *Savages*—Sioux, 56; Winnebagoes, 48; Tallesawains, 39; Chippewas and Ottawas, 572. Total, 1021. It may be remarked that one hundred and fifty Chippewas and Ottawas joined the British two days after the capitulation."—Lieutenant Hancks's Letter to the Secretary of War, August 4, 1812.

[2] In the course of a debate in 1777 concerning the employment of Indians, a member of the House of Lords justified their employment by saying that the British had a right to use the means "which God and Nature had given them." Pitt (Earl of Chatham) scornfully repeated these words. "God and Nature! Those abominable principles, and this most abominable avowal of them, demands most decisive indignation. I call upon that right reverend bench (pointing to the bishops), those holy ministers of the Gospel and pious pastors of the Church—I conjure them to join in the holy work, and to vindicate the religion of their God." His appeal to the bishops was vain. Every man of them voted for the employment of the savages in a war against their brethren in America, then struggling for their freedom.

During the war of 1812 British publicists continually insisted upon the necessity of conciliating the Indians, making them allies, and using them as terrible instruments of warfare. One of them, in the British *Quarterly Review*, No. 4, called piteously upon the British government to look after the interests of the savages. "The aboriginal natives," he said, "had been our faithful allies during the whole of the American rebellion, yet not a single stipulation was made in their favor. . . . We dare assert, and recent facts [the aid given by the Indians in the vicinity of Detroit] have gone far in establishing the truth of the proposition, that the Canadas *can not be effectually and durably defended without the friendship of the Indians!*"

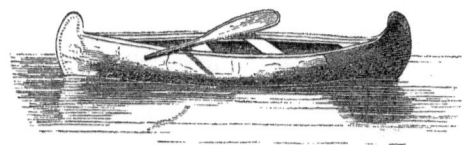

CHAPTER XIV.

"They who have nothing more to fear may well
Indulge a smile at that which once appall'd,
As children at discovered bugbears."
BYRON: *Sardanapalus*.

DISASTROUS in the highest degree to the American cause was the fall of Mackinack, and the prospect which it presented to Hull was justly appalling. His uneasiness was increased by intelligence that came almost hourly of the web of extreme difficulties fast weaving around him. He had sent to the Governors of Ohio and Kentucky for re-enforcements and supplies, but he had, as yet, no positive tidings of their approach. From the north came sounds of dreadful import to a handful of isolated soldiers. The savage chiefs in alliance with the British at Mackinack had sent couriers to all the villages south as far as the Maumee, informing their warriors of that alliance, of the fall of Mackinack, of the investment of Chicago, and of their active preparations to proceed to Malden in great force, to join other warriors there, and attack Detroit. From the east came a rumor that the Canadians and savages in that direction were also hasting toward Malden, and that a detachment of British soldiers, with artillery, under the command of Major Chambers, had landed at the west end of Lake Ontario, penetrated in the direction of Detroit as far as the River Trench, or Thames, and were receiving great accessions of militia and Indians on their march. The alarm created by these facts and rumors was immediately intensified by farther reports[a] that Colonel Proctor, of the British army, had arrived at Malden from Fort Erie with re-enforcements.[1] Then came over from Sandwich an intercepted letter from a member of the Northwest Company at Fort William, dated two days after the fall of Mackinack, saying that, on the receipt of the declaration of war, their agents ordered a general muster of their forces, which amounted to twelve hundred men, exclusive of several hundreds of the natives. "We are equal, in all," he said, "to sixteen or seventeen hundred strong. One of our gentlemen started on the 17th with several light canoes for the interior country to rouse the natives to activity, which is not hard to do on the present occasion. We likewise dispatched messengers in all directions with the news. I have not the least doubt but our force two days hence will amount to five thousand effective men. Our young gentlemen and engagees offered most handsomely to march immediately for Michillimackinack. Our chief, Mr. Shaw, expressed his gratitude, and drafted one hundred. They are to proceed this evening for St. Joseph's. He takes about as many Indians. Could the vessel contain them, he might have had four thousand more. It now depends on what accounts we receive from St. Joseph's, whether these numerous tribes from the interior will proceed to St. Joseph's or not."[2]

[a] August 4, 1812.

In addition to these causes for alarm, Hull discovered a spirit of mutiny in his own camp which gave him more uneasiness still—a spirit, he said, "which before had manifested itself in whispers, increased and became more open. It was evident it was now fostered and encouraged by the principal officers of the militia, and was

---

[1] Hull's *Campaign of* 1812, page 58.
[2] Letter of Mr. M'Kenzie, of the Northwest Company, at Fort William, to Mr. M'Intosh, of Sandwich, July 19, 1812, cited by Hull in his *Campaign of* 1812, page 59.

fast rising into an avowed conspiracy."¹ This mutinous spirit we shall consider presently.

Such was the situation of General Hull and his army at the middle of the first week in August, when the cheering intelligence reached them that Captain Henry Brush, of Chillicothe, Ohio, with two hundred and thirty volunteers, one hundred beef cattle and other provisions, and a mail, were at the crossing of the River Raisin, thirty-five miles distant.

The energy and vigilance of Major General Brock, and the lack of these qualities at this time in General Hull, saved Upper Canada from a disastrous invasion. The amiable Sir George Prevost, the governor general, was spending precious time at Quebec in absolute unbelief of impending war, while Brock, who, in October,[a] 1811, had been made "president and administrator of the government of Upper Canada"—that is to say, lieutenant governor—perceived, from the moment of his arrival at his post, that war was inevitable, and made preparations accordingly. He was vigilant, active, sagacious, and brave, and made the most of his inadequate resources to repel the invasion of Hull. From the beginning he was opposed to the employment of the Indians, and discountenanced the attempts to arouse their resentment against the Americans before war was declared; but necessity compelled him to accept their services.² He endeavored to strengthen the remote military posts. When navigation opened in the spring of 1812, he sent a supply of ordnance and stores to St. Joseph's and to Amherstburg. He visited the latter post early in June, taking with him a re-enforcement of one hundred men of the Forty-first Regiment. But in all his movements he was restrained by his superior. As late as his departure for Amherstburg, Sir George Prevost, not believing hostilities to be near, recommended him to employ the most rigid economy in the public expenditure, and to avoid all expenses not absolutely necessary, because of the great difficulty of raising money.

[a] October 9.

When intelligence of the declaration of war reached Brock he was at York, now Toronto, the capital of his province. He had just been offered a company of farmers' sons, with their draught-horses, for the equipment of a car brigade, under Captain Holcroft, of the Royal Artillery. He was considering this generous offer of the yeomanry when the startling news arrived. It was immediately accepted. An extraordinary session of the Legislature was summoned; and with Evans, his brigade major, and his aid-de-camp, Captain Glegg, he hastened to Fort George, on the Niagara frontier, and there established his military head-quarters. His intention was to cross the Niagara River immediately and capture the American fort of that name, but he shrank from the responsibility of taking such an important step without instructions, at the same time assuring his superior that it might be "demolished, when found necessary, in half an hour."³ He contented himself with making preparations for offensive or defensive movements, as circumstances might require. The militia of the peninsula between Lakes Erie and Ontario being summoned to his standard, eight hundred men responded by their presence. Yielding to necessity, he called upon the Indians on the Grand River for aid, and a hundred came, under John Brant, bringing promise of the speedy appearance of the remainder.⁴

By the 3d of July the "car brigade" was completed, with horses belonging to gentlemen "who spared them free of expense." Meanwhile the Americans had gathered a considerable force on the east side of the river, scattered at different points

---

¹ Hull's *Campaign of* 1812, page 60. See note 3, page 260 of this work.
² In a letter to Sir George Prevost, written December 3, 1811, after hearing of the Tippecanoe affair, he said: "My first care, on my arrival in this province, was to direct the officers of the Indian Department at Amherstburg to exert their whole influence with the Indians to prevent the attack which I understood a few tribes meditated against the American frontier."
³ Letters to Sir George Prevost, July 3 and 25, 1812, cited by Tupper in his *Life of Brock*, pages 171 and 198.
⁴ Letter of Brock to Sir George Prevost, July 3, 1812.

S

FORT NIAGARA, FROM FORT GEORGE.

along a line of thirty miles from Buffalo to Fort Niagara, and estimated by General Brock to be twelve hundred strong.[1]

On the 20th of July Brock received intelligence of Hull's invasion; also a copy of his proclamation, with hints of its effect. Those hints, and a knowledge of the weakness of Fort Malden, alarmed him.[2] The Legislature, about to meet at York, would require his presence, and he could not leave for the field in the West, as he desired to do. Divided duties perplexed him. He instantly recalled a portion of the militia whom he had permitted to go home to gather in the grain harvest, and they murmured. He dispatched Colonel Proctor, of the Forty-first Regiment, with such re-enforcements as he could spare, to assume command at Amherstburg, and the inhabitants of the Niagara border felt themselves abandoned. He issued a counter-proclamation[a] to neutralize the effect of Hull's, and hope revived.

a July 22, 1812.

Leaving the military along the Niagara frontier in charge of Lieutenant Colonel Myers, Brock hastened to York, and, with much parade, opened the Legislature in person. His address was cordially responded to; but he soon found that the Legislature partook, in a large degree, of the despondency of a great portion of the people of Upper Canada, which Hull's menacing proclamation and actual invasion had produced. Five hundred militia in the Western District had already sought Hull's protection; the Norfolk militia, most of them connected by blood with the inhabitants of the United States, peremptorily refused to take up arms; and the Indians on the Grand River, in the heart of the province, after some of their chiefs returned from a visit to Hull, refused, with few exceptions, to join the British standard, declaring their intention to remain neutral. With such promises of failure and disaster before them if resistance should be made, a majority of the Assembly were more disposed to sub-

---

[1] Brock was very anxious to capture Fort Niagara, but was restrained by his superior. Sir George Prevost believed it to be a party war, and was unwilling to do that which might rouse the national spirit of the Americans, and unite both parties against the British. He believed that the war party could not carry on hostilities long. He therefore commanded Brock to act strictly on the defensive.

[2] Hull, as we have seen, invaded Canada and issued his proclamation on the 12th of July, but it was not until the 15th that Lieutenant Colonel St. George wrote to General Brock on the subject. "It is strange," said the latter, "that three days should be allowed to elapse before sending to acquaint me of this important fact. Hull's insidious proclamation,"* he continued, "herewith inclosed, has already been productive of considerable effect on the minds of the people. In fact, a general sentiment prevails that, with the present force, resistance is unavailing. I shall continue to exert myself to the utmost to overcome every difficulty."—Brock to Prevost, Fort George, July 20, 1812.

* The editor of the *Life and Correspondence of Sir Isaac Brock*, speaking of the invasion, says, "Brigadier General Hull issued on that day the following insidious but able proclamation, which was doubtless written at Washington."—See *Life*, etc., page 185.

Symptoms of Disloyalty in Canada. Brock's Influence. His Proclamation. Volunteer Militia.

mit, and to court the favor of the invaders, than to stand up boldly in defense of their province. Mr. Wilcox, a prominent politician of York or Toronto, and editor of a leading newspaper, took strong ground in favor of the Americans, but he was finally overawed by the energy and influence of Brock, and induced to offer him the use of his pen and services. Wilcox was not a hearty supporter of the British, and afterward joined the American army, in the service of which he was killed at Fort Erie. Perceiving this alarming symptom of disloyalty, and apprehending more evil than good from the presence, in a body, at the capital of these timid representatives of the people, Brock prorogued the Assembly as soon as it had passed the necessary supply bills.[1] He had sought in vain for its leave to suspend the *Habeas Corpus Act* or to declare martial law when necessary; but, after consultation with his council, Brock resolved to do both, should certain exigencies occur.[2]

Brock's confident tone in his speech at the opening of the Legislature, and the spirit and power of his counter-proclamation, produced a marked change;[3] and when, very speedily, the fall of Mackinack and the American reverses on the Detroit frontier became known, a reversal of public sentiment was so manifest that Brock was enabled to write to Sir George Prevost from York, saying, "The militia stationed here volunteered their services this morning[a] to any part of the province without the least hesitation. I have selected one hundred, whom I have directed to proceed without delay to Long Point, where I propose collecting a force for the relief of Amherstburg. This example, I hope, will be followed by as many as may be required.[4]

[a] July 29, 1812.

We have observed that the Americans on the banks of the Detroit were cheered by the approach of Captain Brush to the Raisin with men, cattle, provisions, and a mail, all sent forward by the vigilant and untiring Governor Meigs, of Ohio. A messenger soon bore from him to General Hull the information that a party of Indians, under Tecumtha, and possibly some British regulars, had crossed the Detroit from Malden, and were lying near Brownstown, at the mouth of the Huron River, twenty-five miles below Fort Detroit, for the purpose of seizing the treasures in charge of

---

[1] Tupper's *Life and Correspondence of Brock*, page 203.
[2] Sir George Prevost seemed to have had similar difficulties in the lower province. On the 31st of July he wrote to General Brock, saying, "I believe you are authorized by the commission under which you administer the government of Upper Canada to declare martial law, in the event of invasion or insurrection; it is therefore for you to consider whether you can obtain any thing equivalent to that power from your Legislature. I have not succeeded in obtaining a modification of it in Lower Canada, and must, therefore, upon the occurrence of either of those calamities, declare the law martial unqualified, and, of course, shut the doors of the courts of civil law."
[3] Brock's proclamation, issued from Fort George, was calculated to arouse both the pride and the resentment of those Canadians who were of the American refugee families. In allusion to Hull, he said, "He has thought proper to invite his majesty's subjects not only to a quiet and unresisting submission, but insults them with a call to seek voluntarily the protection of his government." Referring to Hull's assertion of the tyranny of the British government, Brock asked, "Where is the Canadian subject who can truly affirm to himself that he has been injured by the government in his person, his property, or his liberty? Where is to be found, in any part of the world, a growth so rapid in prosperity and wealth as this colony exhibits? Settled not thirty years, by a band of veterans exiled from their former possessions on account of their loyalty, not a descendant of these brave people is to be found who, under the fostering liberality of their sovereign, has not acquired a property and means of enjoyment superior to what were possessed by their ancestors." He then warned them of the immense advantages which they would lose by a separation from Great Britain, the greatest maritime nation on the globe, their exclusion from the ocean by being a Territory of the United States, and the danger of becoming reannexed to France when once estranged from the protection of Great Britain. "Are you prepared," he said, "inhabitants of Canada, to become willing subjects, or, rather, slaves to the despot who rules the nations of Continental Europe with a rod of iron? If not, arise in a body; exert your energies; co-operate cordially with the king's regular forces to repel the invader; and do not give cause to your children, when groaning under the oppression of a foreign master, to reproach you with having so easily parted with the richest inheritance of this earth—a participation in the name, character, and freedom of Britons!" He assured them that if, by this sudden war, and a lack of aid, his majesty's arms should be obliged to yield, the province would not be abandoned, and that no peace would be made with the United States of which the restoration of the Canadas to Great Britain should not make the most prominent condition. He then alluded to Hull's threat of "no quarter" for those who should be found fighting with the Indians. He pointed to the aborigines, whose property, like that of the white people, was in danger. "By what new principle," he said, "are they to be prohibited from defending their property? If their warfare, from being different from that of the white people, be more terrific than the enemy, let him retrace his steps. They seek him not, and can not expect to find women and children in an invading army." Hull's threat was denounced as inhuman; and assurance was given that its execution would be considered "as deliberate murder, for which every subject of the offending power must make expiation."
[4] Tupper's *Life and Correspondence of Brock*, page 207.

Brush, so precious to the little army. Brush was unwilling to risk those treasures and his small force without an escort, and he appealed to Hull to send him a detachment of men for that purpose. The general hesitated, and, when the Ohio colonels joined in a request that an escort should be sent, he flatly refused compliance. At length better counsels prevailed, and, after much persuasion, he ordered Major Thomas B. Van Horne, of Colonel Findlay's Ohio regiment, to proceed to the Raisin with a detachment of two hundred men from that corps, to join Brush, and afford a safe convoy for the cattle, provisions, and mail. The major obeyed with alacrity. He crossed the Detroit with his command on the 4th of August, and encamped that night on the banks of the Ecorces River, where the soldiers slept on their arms. They resumed their march early on the following morning. A light fog veiled the flat country along the borders of the river. The air was still and sultry. Four spies, under Captain William M'Cullough, preceded the troops, to watch for the enemy. They lost their way, and, while passing around a corn-field in bloom, they were fired upon by a dozen Indians who lay in ambush there. M'Cullough fell from his horse severely wounded, and, before the detachment could reach the spot, the savages had scalped him and bore away his shining locks in triumph. His country was thus bereaved of one of the bravest and most devoted of its defenders, and the whole army sincerely mourned a real loss.

The detachment was moving very cautiously half an hour after this sad occurrence, when it was joined by some mounted militia, and a few gentlemen who had taken this opportunity to travel in safety to the Raisin. These, with Major Van Horne, stopped at the house of a Frenchman for water, and were informed by him that several hundred Indians and British soldiers were lying in ambush, near Brownstown, for the purpose of intercepting the party. Van Horne had become accustomed to alarmists, and did not credit the story. He marched on in fancied security, his front guard of twenty-four men in two columns, each column preceded by three dragoons, and the main body in the same order. The mail, with a mounted escort, was placed in the centre. Where the ground would permit, the columns marched a hundred yards apart. As they approached Brownstown the road passed through a narrow prairie skirted with thick woods, and a creek on the right. The woods on the creek came to a point toward the town, through which the road passed to the ford. On the left were corn-fields and thickets of thorn bushes; and near the creek the columns were compelled to approach each other on account of the narrowness of the way. Just as they reached its margin, and were entering upon the open ground around the village, near the house of Adam Brown, a heavy fire, at only fifty yards' distance, was opened upon them from both sides by a large body of Indians who lay in ambush in the thickets and the woods. The attack was sudden, sharp, and deadly, and the troops were thrown into confusion. Apprehensive that he might be surrounded, Major Van Horne immediately ordered a retreat. This movement was conducted with much confusion. The Indians pursued, and a running fight was kept up for a considerable distance, the retreating Americans frequently turning upon the savage foe, and giving him deadly volleys. The retreat

THOMAS B. VAN HORNE.

Perils of a Supply-train.   Loud Complaints against Hull.   Cheering Orders.   A grievous Disappointment.

continued to the Ecorces, but the Indians, restrained by the prudent Tecumtha, only followed about half that distance.[1] The mail was lost, and passed into the hands of the British authorities, by which most valuable information concerning the weakness and disaffection of Hull's army was made manifest, for the officers and soldiers had written freely to their friends at home on the subject.[2] The detachment also lost seventeen killed and several wounded, who were left behind.[3]

Hull was greatly disconcerted by the news of Van Horne's repulse and loss. His colonels urged the employment of immediate and efficient measures for retrieval, and begged him to send a sufficient force to overcome any obstacles likely to be met between Detroit and the Raisin. Brush was in danger, and the army would soon need the supplies in his charge. The way between the army and Ohio must be kept open, and no time was to be lost in securing these important ends. "Send five hundred men at once," they said, "to escort Brush to Detroit." "I can spare only one hundred men," was the general's disheartening reply. These were too few, and the enterprise was abandoned for the moment. Brush was left to the mercy of Tecumtha and his savage followers, and the needed supplies for the army were placed in imminent peril. Indignation and alarm stirred the blood of the officers.

The mutinous spirit, of which Hull afterward wrote, was now vehemently exhibited. There was plain and loud talk at head-quarters—talk which startled the general, and caused him to call a council of field officers,[a] the result of which was an agreement to march immediately upon Malden. Orders were issued for the medical and surgical departments to prepare for active duties in the field; for the securing of boats at Detroit; for leaving the convalescents under an officer at Sandwich, with means for crossing the river, if desired; for a raft of timber and planks for a bridge to be floated down the river; for drawing, on the morning of the 8th, by the whole army, cooked rations for three days; and for the return of "all artificers, and all men on any kind of extra duty," to their regiments immediately.

[a] August 7, 1812.

This order diffused joy throughout the little army. They believed that the hour for energetic action had come. Every man was busy in preparation; and a long summer's day was drawing to a close, when another order from the commanding general cast a cloud of disappointment over the camp more sombre than the curtain of night that speedily fell upon it. It was an order for the army *to recross the river to Detroit!*—an order to abandon Canada, and leave to the vengeance of their own government the inhabitants who, confiding in Hull's promises of protection, had refused to take up arms in defense of their invaded territory. This order was in consequence of intelligence just received that a considerable force of British regulars, militia, and Indians were coming to attack the Americans in the rear, under General Brock.

But Canada was not to be wholly abandoned. Major Denny, with one hundred and thirty convalescents and a corps of artillerists, under Lieutenant Anderson, was left "to hold possession of that part of Canada, and afford all possible protection to the well-disposed inhabitants." A strong house, belonging to one Gowris, had been stockaded, and called Fort Gowris. In this, and in a long stone building yet standing in Sandwich,[4] which the American soldiers had used as barracks, the con-

---

[1] For his gallantry in this campaign, Major Van Horne, while a prisoner on parole, was promoted to Lieutenant Colonel in the Twenty-sixth Regular Infantry, and was transferred to the Nineteenth in 1814. He was disbanded in June, 1815.

[2] The battle-ground was about five miles below the present village of Trenton, in Michigan.

[3] Among the killed were Captains William M'Cullough, Robert Gilchrist, Henry Ulery, and Jacob Boerstler; Lieutenant Jacob Pentz, and Surgeons Edward Roby and Andrew Allison.—M'Afee, page 74. Hull's Letter to the Secretary of War, dated Sandwich, August 7, 1812.

[4] This building was erected for a school in 1807 or 1808. It was in a dilapidated state when I sketched it in the autumn of 1860. It occupies an open space in the village of Sandwich. Several poor families occupied it. The place known as Spring Wells is opposite, and indicated in our little sketch by the buildings with tall chimneys, from which columns of smoke are rising. These compose the copper smelting-works at Spring Wells. A long wharf on the Sand-

BARRACKS AT SANDWICH.

valescents were placed, and Denny was ordered to defend the post to the last extremity against musketry, but to leave it in the event of artillery being brought against it so powerfully as to make it untenable.[1]

Sullenly that humiliated army obeyed their overcautious commander, and during the night of the 7th and morning of the 8th[a] they crossed the deep, dark, rapidly-flowing river in sadness, and encamped upon the rolling plain behind Fort Detroit. Hull's reason for this mortifying termination of his invasion of Canada was the receipt of intelligence, as we have observed, that General Brock was hasting toward Amherstburg with re-enforcements, and the necessity of securing a permanent communication between his army and the sources of its supplies in the Ohio settlements. He accordingly dispatched six hundred men, under Lieutenant Colonel James Miller, on the afternoon of the 8th, to open a communication with the Raisin and escort Brush to Detroit. The detachment consisted of the Fourth Regiment of regulars; two small corps of the First Regiment, under Lieutenant Dixon Stansbury and Ensign Robert A. M'Cabe; detachments from the Ohio and Michigan volunteers—the latter, sixty in number, from the "Michigan Legion,"[2] mostly French, under Captain Antoine Dequindre; a corps of Captain Dyson's artillerists, then stationed at the fort with a six-pounder, under Lieutenant John L. Eastman (who was Miller's brigade major on this occasion), and a howitzer, under Lieutenant James Daliba; and a part of Captains Smith and Sloan's cavalry, under the latter. Majors Van Horne and Morrison were associated with Lieutenant Colonel Miller as field officers. "Commodore" Brevoort, who was a captain of infantry, and appointed commander of any government vessels that might be placed on the lakes, and Captain A. F. Hull, the general's son, who was afterward killed at the Battle of Niagara Falls, volunteered as aids to Lieutenant Colonel Miller.[3]

The troops paraded on the north side of Jefferson Avenue, in Detroit, nearly opposite where the Exchange now stands. When placed in marching order, Lieutenant Colonel Miller rode up in front of them, and in his clear, loud voice, said to the volunteers and militia, "Soldiers, we are now going to meet the enemy, and to *beat* them. The reverse of the 5th (Van Horne's) must be repaired. The blood of our brethren, spilt by the savages, must be avenged. I shall lead you. You shall not disgrace yourselves nor me. Every man who shall leave the ranks or fall back without orders will be instantly put to death. I charge the officers to execute this order." Then, turning to the veteran Fourth Regiment of regulars, he said, "My brave soldiers, you will add another victory to that of Tippecanoe—another laurel to that gained on the Wabash last fall. If there is now any man in the ranks of the detachment who fears to meet the enemy, let him fall out and stay behind." A loud

[a] August, 1812.

---

wich side of the river is seen toward the right of the position. The British picketed this building, and used it for barracks in 1813. [1] M'Afee, page 77.

[2] This "Legion" had been organized during the winter of 1811-'12, as a home guard against the Indians, who were then menacing the Michigan settlers. They were mustered into the volunteer service under the act of February 6, 1812. The "Legion" was composed of one company of dragoons, commanded by Captain Richard Smythe, and three companies of infantry, commanded respectively by Captains Antoine Dequindre, Stephen Mack, and Hubert la Croix.

[3] Hull's letter to the Secretary of War, August 13, 1812; Judge Witherell's paper on the Battle of Monguagen, read before the Michigan Historical Society in the spring of 1859.

huzza went up from the entire corps, and "I'll not stay! I'll not stay!" broke from every lip.[1]

Miller led his detachment to the River Rouge that night, crossed it in two scows, and bivouacked on its southern shore. The march was resumed early in the morning. Major Thompson Maxwell,[2] with the spies, led the way, followed by a vanguard of forty-men, under the high-souled Captain Snelling, of the Fourth Regulars. The infantry marched in two columns, about two hundred yards apart. The cavalry kept the road in the centre in double file. The artillery followed, and flank-guards of riflemen marched at proper distances. In this order a line of battle might be instantly formed. The march was very slow, owing to the difficulty of moving cannon over marshy ground.

At about nine in the morning—a sultry Sabbath morning—the sky overcast with clouds, and not a leaf stirring upon the trees, it became evident that an enemy was near. Several Indians, fleet of foot, were seen flying in the distance. But nothing of much interest occurred until, in the afternoon, they approached the Indian village of Maguaga, fourteen miles below Detroit, where a man named White, who, with his young son, accompanied the expedition as an amateur soldier, and in his eagerness had outstripped the spies, was shot from his horse near the cabin of the chief Walk-in-the-Water, behind which some Indians were concealed.[3] He was scalped before the advance-guard could reach the spot.

It was between three and four o'clock in the afternoon when Snelling and his men reached the Oak Woods, near Maguaga. They had just entered a clearing, surrounded with an oak forest and thick bushes, near the bank of the Detroit River, when they received a terrible volley from a line of British and Indians, the former under Major Muir, of the Forty-first Regiment, and the latter under Tecumtha. This was a detachment which Proctor had sent over from Fort Malden, at Amherstburg, to Brownstown, to repeat the tragedy of the 5th (Van Horne's defeat), cut off communication between the Raisin and Detroit, and capture the stores in charge of Captain Brush. The party consisted of about one hundred of the Forty-first Regiment, as many Canadian militia, and between two and three hundred Indians. Among the leaders of the latter were Tecumtha, Walk-in-the-Water, Lame-Hand, and Split-Log —all chiefs of note.

The flying savages, seen by the Americans in the morning, and who had been scouting for Muir, had entered the little British camp at Brownstown in hot haste, uttering the peculiar news-cry, and warning the soldiers that the enemy, strong in numbers, was advancing upon them. The camp was immediately broken up, and Muir and Tecumtha, with their followers, pressed forward to Maguaga, and formed an ambush in the Oak Woods. There they lay for several hours, awaiting the slowly-approaching Americans, and were joined by a fresh detachment from Malden, under Lieutenant Bullock, of the Forty-first Grenadiers, who had been sent by General

---

[1] Judge Witherell.

[2] Major Maxwell was well known in Detroit. He had been a soldier in the French and Indian War, and was one of the survivors of the battle at Bloody Bridge, just above Detroit, in "Pontiac's War." He was a brave soldier in the Revolution. He was with Wayne on his campaigns, and followed Miller upon the heights at the battle of Niagara Falls (Lundy's Lane) when he took the British battery on the crown. He died on the River Rouge about the year 1834.—Judge Witherell.

[3] Walk-in-the-Water's residence at Maguaga was on the land afterward owned by Major Biddle, and on which he built his farm-houses. Judge Witherell says, "I knew him well in my boyhood. He was then a man past middle age, with a fine, commanding person, near six feet in height and well-proportioned, and as straight as an arrow. He was mild and pleasant in his deportment." The chief was friendly to the United States, and desired to join them at the beginning of the war; but the instructions of his government not to employ savages and his own humane impulses would not allow Hull to accept his services. They were soon exposed to the attacks of the British and their savage allies; and as the United States could give them no protection, Walk-in-the-Water and his band of Wyandots joined the British at Malden. Their hands were in that service, but the heart of the chief was not there. Walk-in-the-Water died about the year 1817. His *totem* or arms was a *turtle*.

Walk-in-the-Water was a Huron, of the Wyandot tribe. His Indian name was My-ee-rah, and he was among the most active of the chiefs with Tecumtha in the War of 1812. Far-he, or King Crane, the grand chief of the Wyandots, resided at Sandusky. We shall meet Walk-in-the-Water again, at the River Raisin and the Thames.

Brock from Fort George.¹ He had reached Malden the previous day, and was sent over to assist Muir and his savage allies. He took with him twenty of his grenadiers, twenty light infantry, and twenty battalion-men. The Indians occupied the left of the line.²

A single shot on the left of the foe, then the terrible yells of scores of savages, and then a heavy volley of musketry from the whole British line, were the first intimations given to Snelling of the presence of the concealed enemy. He received and returned the fire gallantly, and maintained his position until joined by the main body. Miller's quick ear caught the first sound of battle, and, ordering his men forward at double quick, he rode at full speed toward the field of conflict. As his troops came up and formed in battle order, he waved his sword aloft, and cried, "Charge! boys, charge!"³ The order was instantly, gallantly, and effectually obeyed; and, at the same time, a six-pounder poured in a storm of grape-shot that made sad havoc. A body of Indians, that had been detached to the left of the foe, and near the river, was driven back by an impetuous charge by Major Dequindre and his Michigan and Ohio Volunteers,⁴ and fled. Their white auxiliaries, who performed but little fighting in this engagement, mistaking them for Indian allies of the Americans, fired upon them. The savages returned it with spirit, and for a few moments these friends in the same service seemed determined to annihilate each other.

The battle had now become general. This sudden blow upon the right wing, and the confusion produced by the mistake just mentioned, alarmed the centre, and the whole British line, civilized and savage, wavered. Closely pressed in front, and expecting an attack in the rear, the British regulars and Canadians broke and fled in confusion, leaving Tecumtha and his savages to bear the brunt of the battle, which they did with great obstinacy.⁵ Muir rallied his men, in a good position, a quarter of a mile in rear of the battle-ground, when, becoming alarmed by firing in the woods on the left, they retreated "at the double-quick," as Major Richardson said, gained their boats as speedily as possible, and sped across the river to Malden as fast as strong arms and stout oars could take them. The savages finally broke and fled, and Miller ordered Sloan to pursue them with his cavalry. That officer's courage seemed to

---

¹ The entire British force at Monguaga, including the Indians, has been differently estimated by different writers. It was probably about equal to that of the Americans.

² Major Richardson, of the Forty-first, gives the following description of the appearance of the Indian warriors on the march from Brownstown to Monguaga: "No other sound than the measured step of the troops interrupted the solitude of the scene, rendered more imposing by the wild appearance of the warriors, whose bodies, stained and painted in the most frightful manner for the occasion, glided by us with almost noiseless velocity, without order and without a chief; some painted white, some black, others half black and half red, half black and half white; all with their hair plastered in such a way as to resemble the bristling quills of the porcupine, with no other covering than a cloth around their loins, yet armed to the teeth with rifles, tomahawks, war-clubs, spears, bows and arrows, and scalping-knives. Uttering no sound, and intent on reaching the enemy unperceived, they might have passed for the spectres of those wilds—the ruthless demons which war had unchained for the punishment and oppression of men." Major Richardson, perceiving the necessity of an apology for being found fighting Christian men side by side with these savage pagans as brethren in arms, says, but without warrant, "The natives must have been our friends or our foes. Had we not employed them the Americans would; and, although humanity must deplore the necessity imposed by the very invader himself of counting them among our allies, and combating at their sides, the law of self-preservation was our guide, and scrupulous, indeed, must be the power that would have hesitated at such a moment in its choice."—*War of 1812. First Series, containing a full and detailed Narrative of the Operation of the Right Division of the Canadian Army*, by Major Richardson, K. S. F.—Pamphlet, page 52.

Auchinleck, without the shadow of justification, says (page 55), that "every possible exertion was employed by agents of the United States government to detach the Indians from us, and to effect an alliance with them on the part of the States." Every honorable exertion *was* used by the United States to detach the Indians from the British interest and persuade them to remain *neutral*, but the government never consented to an alliance with the savages until the practice of the British made it necessary, as in the old struggle for independence, when Washington said "we must fight Indians with Indians."

³ Miller was thrown from his horse. He was supposed to be shot, and the savages rushed forward to scalp him. They were driven back, and in a few moments he was remounted.—Judge Witherell. M'Afee says he remained on foot through the remainder of the battle, and that the most active part devolved upon Majors Van Horne and Morrison.

⁴ Among those who performed gallant service in this charge was Sergeant Nathan Champe, son of Sergeant Champe, famous in the Revolution as the one employed by Washington to seize Arnold in the city of New York. Lieutenant George Johnston, who died at Green Bay in 1850, commanded the Michigan Cavalry on this occasion, and was called the Murat of that corps.—Judge Witherell.

⁵ For his services on this occasion Tecumtha was rewarded by the British government with the commission of a brigadier general.

have been paralyzed for the moment. He stood still. The impetuous Snelling perceived it, and, rushing up to him, peremptorily ordered him to dismount, leaped upon the horse himself, and, at the head of his troops, bareheaded (his hat having been shot away in the battle), his red hair streaming in the wind, he dashed after the fugitives, and pursued them more than two miles, when the danger of an ambuscade, the necessary care of the wounded, and the approach of night, induced Lieutenant Colonel Miller to order a suspension of the chase. The rout and victory were complete. According to the British account, the loss of their regulars was twenty-four, only one of whom was killed.[2] That of the militia and Indians were never reported. Our troops found forty of the latter dead on the field. The loss of the Americans was eighteen killed and fifty-seven wounded.[3]

MAGUAGA BATTLE-GROUND.[1]

Miller was anxious to follow up his advantage gained, and push on to the Raisin; and at sunset he dispatched a messenger to Hull reporting his success, and asking for a supply of provisions. Hull ordered Colonel M'Arthur to take one hundred men of his regiment, and six hundred rations, and go down the river in boats for the relief of Miller. M'Arthur embarked at a little past two in the morning,[a] in nine boats, and, under the cover of darkness and a drenching rain, he passed the *Queen Charlotte* and the *Hunter*, and reached his destination in safety. The wounded were immediately conveyed to the boats, but, in attempting to return by daylight, M'Arthur found himself intercepted by the British vessels. He hastened to the shore, left the boats, conveyed the wounded through the woods to the road, and sent them to Detroit in wagons, which, with proper forecast, he had ordered down, because he anticipated this very difficulty. Colonel Cass had come down in the mean time, and attempted to secure the boats, but before he reached the shore they were seized by the British and lost.

[a] August 10, 1812.

Miller was injured by the fall from his horse at the beginning of the battle, and was so ill that he could not proceed toward the Raisin immediately. He sent to Hull for more provisions. His messenger met Cass below the River Aux Ecorces, and

---

[1] This is from a pencil sketch made by an officer of the United States Army in 1816. Beyond the opening out of the Oak Woods, mentioned in the text, is seen the Detroit River, with Grosse Isle in the distance. The Indian village near which this battle was fought is spelled sometimes *Maguaga*, according to the orthography of the official dispatches; *Mongenaga*, according to Mellish's Military Atlas, from which our map on page 266 was copied; and *Monguagon*, according to Judge Witherell and other local writers. I have adopted the orthography of the dispatches. The battle-ground was at or near the present village of Trenton, in Michigan.

[2] Hull's Letter to the Secretary of War, August 13, 1812; Major Richardson, quoted by Auchinleck, pages 53 and 54; M'Afee, pages 78 and 79; Judge Witherell's Paper, read before the Michigan Historical Society in the Spring of 1857; Lieutenant Colonel Miller to his Wife, August 27, 1812—Autograph Letter.

[3] Major Muir and Lieutenant Sutherland were the only British officers wounded. Tecumtha was also slightly wounded in the neck by a buck-shot.

acquainted him with the delay. Cass knew that time was precious, for Proctor, relieved of all apprehensions of an attack upon Malden, would doubtless send over a larger force of Europeans and savages to bar the way to the Raisin, and attack Brush there. He therefore sent this laconic dispatch to Hull: "SIR,—Colonel Miller is sick; may I relieve him?—L. CASS." Receiving no reply, he returned to Detroit, meeting on his way an express bearing to Miller positive orders for the whole detachment to return to head-quarters. Thus another favorable moment for achieving great good was lost by what seemed the timidity and instability of the commanding general. Miller was only twenty-two miles from the Raisin. Dispirited in the extreme, he and his troops left their camp at noon on the day after the battle, and made their way slowly back to Detroit.

Hull's shortcomings were freely spoken of, and the belief was inculcated among the troops that he was either traitorously inclined, or had become an imbecile. At times he would be shut up in his room[1] for hours, inaccessible to all but his son, who was his aid-de-camp; at others he appeared abstracted and confused—"sullen in deportment, and wavering in his orders."[2] His incompetency to meet the crisis at hand was felt by all, and his officers of every grade, after consultation, came to the conclusion that the salvation of the little army would only be found in depriving him of the command and giving it to another.[3] Lieutenant Colonel Miller was invited to accept it. He declined, but expressed his willingness to unite with them in giving the command to M'Arthur, the senior officer of the volunteers, and one of the most vigilant and active soldiers in the army. It would be a bold step for subordinates to strip a commanding general of his sword and epaulets while at the head of his army, and, when they were ready to act, they naturally hesitated. Relief might speedily come from Ohio. Governor Meigs, it was suggested, might accompany it in person, and upon him the honor might properly be laid. Colonel Cass acted promptly on this suggestion, and wrote[a] an energetic letter to the governor, urging him to press forward with re-enforcements and supplies. He informed him that the army had been reduced to a critical situation "from causes not fit to be put on paper." He told him that the golden opportunity for success had passed by, and mildly remarked that, unfortunately, the general and the principal officers could not view the situation and prospect of affairs in the same light. "That Malden," he said, "might easily have been reduced, I have no doubt. . . . But instead of looking back, we must now look forward. . . . Our supplies must come from our state." He called for two thousand men at least, and added, "It is the unanimous wish of the army that you should accompany them."

[a] August 12, 1812.

Before this letter was shown to the other officers a change in affairs had taken place. The British were congregating in force at Sandwich, and, in view of this menace, the following postscript was added to the letter: "Since the other side of this letter was written, new circumstances have arisen. The British force is opposite, and our situation has nearly reached its crisis. Believe all the bearer will tell you. Believe it, however it may astonish you, as much as if told by one of us. Even a c**** is talked of by the *****. The bearer will supply the vacancy.[4] On you we

---

[1] "In my boyhood," says Judge Witherell, "I knew him well. His appearance was venerable and dignified; his heart was the seat of kindness; he was unquestionably an honest man. The general had a most excellent family. Mrs. Hull, a portly, fine-looking woman, made it the principal business of her life to visit the sick and provide for the destitute poor." [2] M'Afee, page 82.
[3] Colonel Hatch says, "On a private consultation on the 12th of August with those known to be the most active of the subordinate officers and men of the volunteer regiments, it was decided to get up a Round Robin* (so called), addressed to the three colonels, requesting the arrest or displacement of the general from his command, and vesting, by common consent, the eldest colonel, M'Arthur, with all the powers incidental to chief command.
[4] "The doubtful fate of this letter rendered it necessary to use circumspection in its details, and therefore the blanks were left. The word 'capitulation' will fill the first, and 'commanding general' the other."—Colonel Cass to the Secretary of War, Washington City, September 10, 1812.

* A phrase (rond ruban) originally derived from a custom of the French officers, who, on signing a remonstrance or petition to their superiors, wrote their names in a circular form, so that it might be impossible to ascertain who had headed the list.

depend." This was signed by Cass, Findlay, M'Arthur, Taylor, and Colonel Elijah Brush, of the Michigan militia.

General Brock joined Proctor at Amherstburg or Malden on the night of the 13th.[a] Relieved from civil duties on the 6th, he procured pecuniary aid from an association of gentlemen, and, with two hundred volunteers, he sailed from York for Burlington Bay, at the west end of Lake Ontario. He had been called upon to repel a formidable invasion with few troops, and without a money-chest, provisions, blankets, or even shoes for the militia whom he expected to muster into the service. Those gentlemen known as "The Niagara and Queenston Association" supplied him with several thousand pounds sterling in the form of bank-notes, which were afterward redeemed with army bills. He had sent forty of the Forty-first Regiment to Long Point, on Lake Erie, to gather the militia there, and fifty more of the same regiment were sent to the Indians in the interior, to induce them to engage in the expedition. On his way across the country he held a council[b] at the Mohawk settlement on the Grand River, and sixty warriors promised to join him on the 10th.

[a] August, 1812.
[b] August 7.

With his few regulars and three hundred militia, Brock embarked in boats, batteaux, and canoes (supplied by the neighboring farmers) at Long Point,[c] and, after a rough voyage of five days and nights, nearly two hundred miles in extent, he reached Amherstburg a little before midnight of the 13th.[d] The patient endurance of his troops delighted him. He was welcomed by a *feu de joie* of musketry from Tecumtha and his band on Bois Blanc Island, before Amherstburg. Half an hour afterward that warrior was

[c] August 8.

TECUMTHA.

brought over by Colonel Elliot, the Indian agent whom we have already spoken of (who lived near Amherstburg), and Brock was introduced to the great chief of the Shawnoese.[1] It being late, the conference was short, and they parted with the understanding that a council would be called immediately.

Brock held a conference with the Indians on the morning of the 14th. About one thousand were present. The general opened the interview by informing

---

[1] Captain J. B. Glegg, Brock's aid-de-camp, has left on record the following description of Tecumtha at that interview: "Tecumseh's appearance was very prepossessing: his figure light, and finely proportioned; his age I imagined to be about five-and-thirty [he was about forty]; in height, five feet nine or ten inches; his complexion light copper; countenance oval, with bright hazel eyes, bearing cheerfulness, energy, and decision. Three small silver crosses or coronets were suspended from the lower cartilage of his aquiline nose, and a large silver medallion of George the Third, which I believe his ancestor had received from Lord Dorchester when Governor General of Canada, was attached to a mixed-colored wampum string and hung round his neck. His dress consisted of a plain, neat uniform, tanned deer-skin jacket, with long trowsers of the same material, the seams of both being covered with neatly-cut fringe, and he had on his feet leather moccasins, much ornamented with work made from the dyed quills of the porcupine."

The portrait of Tecumtha above given is from a pencil sketch by Pierre le Dru, mentioned in note 1, page 189. In this I have given only the *head* by Le Dru. The cap was red, the band ornamented with colored porcupines' quills, and in front was a single eagle's feather, black, with a white tip. The sketch of his dress (and the medal above described), in which he appears as a brigadier general of the British army, is from a rough drawing which I saw in Montreal in the summer of 1858, made at Malden soon after the surrender of Detroit, where the Indians celebrated that event by a grand feast. It was only on gala occasions that Tecumtha was seen in full dress. The sketch did not pretend to give a true likeness of the chief, and was valuable only as a delineation of his costume. From the two we are enabled to give a pretty faithful picture of the great Shawnoese warrior and statesman as he appeared in his best mood. When in full dress he wore a cocked hat and plume, but would not give up his blue breech-cloth, red leggins fringed with buckskin, and buckskin moccasins.

them that he had come to assist them in driving the Americans from Detroit and their rightful hunting-grounds north of the Ohio. His speech was highly applauded by Tecumtha, who replied in an eloquent and sagacious manner, and gave Brock a high opinion of his genius.[1] Not deeming it prudent to reveal too much of his plan of operations to the assembled savages, the latter invited Tecumtha, with a few old chiefs, to Colonel Elliott's quarters, and there he laid the whole matter before them. The chiefs listened with great attention, and assured Brock that he should have their cordial co-operation. In reply to his question whether the warriors could be restrained from drinking whisky, Tecumtha replied that, before leaving their country on the Wabash, they had promised him that they would not taste a drop of the fire-water until they had humbled the *big-knives*—the Americans—and that they might be relied on.[2]

Brock had issued a general order early in the morning of the 14th, in which he calmed the fears of those inhabitants who had deserted from the British army, or had taken protections from Hull, by expressing his willingness to believe that their conduct proceeded more from their anxiety to get in their harvests than from "any predilection for the principles and government of the United States." This ingenious offer of amnesty by implication was sent out upon the roads northward, and was accepted by the great body of the inhabitants, who were alarmed and exasperated by Hull's desertion of them; and when, on the same day, Brock marched from Malden to Sandwich, he passed through a country of friends.

[a] August 11, 1812. Major Denny had already evacuated Fort Gowris,[a] and, with the convalescents and troops under his command, had crossed the river to Detroit. The American camp at Sandwich and vicinity was immediately taken possession of by British troops, under Captain Dixon, of the Royal Engineers (whom we shall meet at Fort Stephenson), and a battery was planted so as to command Detroit. The American artillerists begged permission to open upon them from the fort with twenty-four pounders,[3] but Hull would not grant it, and the enemy was allowed to complete his preparations for reducing the fort without molestation. The brave Captain Snelling asked permission to go over in the night and take the works, but Hull would listen to no propositions of the kind. He seemed unwilling to injure or exasperate the enemy.

That General Hull had determined to surrender Detroit, under certain contingencies, rather than risk an engagement with, or a protracted siege by the British and Indians, at least two or three days before that deed was accomplished, the careful student of the history of that affair can not doubt. All of his movements indicate this, according to the positive testimony given by M'Afee, and of Colonel Stanley Hatch's narrative, already cited. Hatch was Hull's assistant quartermaster general. Hull seemed convinced that, under all the circumstances, the post would be untenable against such a force as the enemy might bring to bear upon it, unless his communication with Ohio might be kept up. Dearborn had failed to make any diversions in his favor on the Niagara or at Kingston, as he had been directed to do.[4] His communication with Ohio (his only source of supply), lying beyond a trackless wilder-

---

[1] Brock wrote of Tecumtha as follows: "A more sagacious or a more gallant warrior does not, I believe, exist. He was the admiration of every one who conversed with him. From a life of dissipation he has not only become, in every respect, abstemious, but he has likewise prevailed on all his native, and many of the other tribes, to follow his example." [2] Tupper's Life of Brock, page 220.
[3] The execution of heavy guns at long distances at that time was feeble when compared to that of the rifled cannon and conical balls used at the present day. In the year 1812, the late Ichabod Price, of New York (who died in that city on the 1st of March, 1862, at the age of eighty-one years), suggested to the War Department both rifled cannon and conical balls. He was then a sergeant of an artillery corps of the State of New York, who volunteered for the defense of the state. The department would not listen to Price's proposition; but his genius was so well attested in the presence of President Madison that he commissioned him a lieutenant in the regular army of the United States.
[4] Letter of the Secretary of War to General Dearborn, August 1, 1812. Of the position of affairs on the Niagara frontier at this time much will be said hereafter. Suffice it to say now that General Dearborn agreed to a conditional armistice with Sir George Prevost, an arrangement which the government of the United States subsequently repudiated.

ness two hundred miles away, was cut off. His provisions, he thought, were becoming too scarce to warrant the risk of a protracted siege, and an intercepted letter from Proctor to Roberts at Mackinack threatened a descent of five thousand Indians from that region. Hemmed in on every side, and his force wasting with disease, disappointment, and death, his kindness of heart, and the growing caution incident to old age, made him timid and fearful. He did not know that the letter from Proctor at Malden had been sent for the purpose of interception to alarm him.[1] He did not know that a large portion of Brock's troops, reported to him as regulars, were only the militia of Long Point and vicinity, dressed in scarlet uniforms to deceive him.[2] He was too honest (whatever may be said of his military sagacity) to suspect deceptions of this kind, and he sincerely believed that his little army would be exterminated by the savages should he exasperate them by shedding their blood. "A man of another mould, full of resolution and resource," says Ingersoll, "might have triumphed over the time-serving negligence of his own government, and the bold resistance of an enemy who could not fail to perceive that he had a feeble and dismayed antagonist to deal with."[3]

On the 14th General Hull sent a message to Captain Brush informing him that a sufficient detachment to escort him to head-quarters could not then be spared, and directing him to remain where he was until farther orders, or, if he thought best, to attempt a forward movement by a circuitous and more inland route, after consulting with Colonel Anderson and Captain Jobard, the bearers of the letter.[4] Toward the evening of the same day, he changed his mind, and concluded to send a detachment to escort Brush to Detroit. He communicated his plan to Colonels M'Arthur and Cass, who not only approved of it, but volunteered to perform the duty. They were permitted to choose three hundred and fifty men from their respective regiments. M'Arthur, as senior officer, took the command; and they left in haste in the evening without a sufficient supply of provisions for a protracted absence, or even of blankets for repose in resting, for they were assured that they would doubtless meet Brush between the Rouge and Huron, and not more than twelve miles distant. When they remonstrated because they were dispatched with a scanty supply of provisions, Hull promised to send more after them on pack-horses. But Brush's orders left it optional with him to remain or move forward. He was *not* found on the way, nor were provisions received from Hull as promised.

The detachment under M'Arthur and Cass crossed the Rouge that evening,[a] and the next day pushed forward by a circuitous route toward the head waters of the Huron, twenty-four miles from Detroit, when they became entangled in a swamp, and could proceed no farther. Half famished and greatly fatigued by their march through the forest, they had prepared to bivouac for the night, when, just as the evening twilight was fading away, a courier arrived with a summons from Hull to return immediately to Detroit.[5] The order was obeyed, and they

[a] August 14, 1812.

---

[1] I was informed by the venerable Robert Reynolds, of Amherstburg, who was a deputy assistant commissary general in the British army in Canada during the war, that Proctor sent a letter to Captain Roberts telling him that his force was considerable, and that he need not send down more than five thousand Indians. This letter, according to instructions, was intercepted, and placed in the hands of Hull, who had visions immediately of an overwhelming force coming down upon his rear, while a superior army should attack him in front.

[2] I visited the Long Point region at Norwichville in the autumn of 1860, where early settlers were yet living. There I was informed, from the lips of Adam Yeigh, of Burford, who was one of the volunteers, that all of the recruits from his neighborhood were dressed in scarlet uniform at the public expense. When they approached Sandwich he said these raw recruits were mixed with the regulars, each volunteer being placed between two regulars. By this stratagem Hull was deceived into the belief that a large British force was marching against him. Yeigh was an energetic young man, and soon won the confidence of Brock, who gave him the following directions on the day that they marched upon Sandwich from Amherstburg: If your lieutenant falls, take his place; if your captain falls, take his place; if your colonel falls, take his place. As no blood was shed on the occasion, and nobody fell, Yeigh failed of promotion. He cited this circumstance to show how nearly he came to being a British colonel.

[3] *Historical Sketches of the Second War*, etc., i., 81.
[4] Hull's *Memoir of the Campaign of 1812*, page 73.
[5] Letter of Colonel Cass to the Secretary of War, September 10, 1812.

approached head-quarters the next day at about ten o'clock in the morning. Meanwhile affairs at Detroit had reached a crisis.

On the morning of the 15th of August, General Hull pitched his marquee in the centre of his camp, near the fort. It was the first time since the 4th of July that it had made its appearance, and much attention and remark was elicited by it, especially because its top was ornamented with red and blue stripes, which made it conspicuous among the tents.[1] The British had been in considerable force on the opposite shore since the 13th, and had been permitted to throw up intrenchments, and to plant a battery for two eighteen-pounders and an eight-inch howitzer in a position to command the town and fort, notwithstanding the latter was armed with twenty-eight pieces of heavy ordnance, which the artillerists were anxious to use in driving the enemy from his works. When his preparations for attack were completed, General Brock, at little past meridian on the 15th, sent Lieutenant Colonel M'Donell and Major Glegg from Sandwich, with a flag, to bear to General Hull a summons for the unconditional surrender of the post. "The force at my disposal," said Brock, "authorizes me to require of you the surrender of Detroit. It is far from my inclination to join in a war of extermination, but you must be aware that the numerous body of Indians who have attached themselves to my troops will be beyond my control the moment the contest commences."[2]

This covert threat of letting loose the blood-thirsty savages upon the town and garrison of Detroit deeply impressed the commanding general with contending emotions. His pride of character, and his patriotism, for which all venerated him, bade him fight; his fear of the consequences to the army and the inhabitants under his charge bade him surrender. His whole effective force then at his disposal did not exceed one thousand men,[3] and the fort was thronged with trembling women, and children, and decrepit old men of the town and surrounding country, who had fled thither to escape the blow of the tomahawk and the keen blade of the scalping-knife. For full two hours he kept the flag waiting while revolving in his mind what to do. His troops were confident in their ability to successfully confront the enemy, and were eager to measure strength with him; and at length Hull mustered resolution sufficient to say to Brock, "I have no other reply to make than to inform you that I am ready to meet any force which may be at your disposal, and any consequences which may result from its execution in any way you may think proper to use it." He added, apologetically, that a certain flag of truce, sent to Malden at about the time Colonel Cass fell upon the British and Indians at the Aux Canards, proceeded contrary to his orders; and that the destruction of Gowris's house at Sandwich was also contrary to his orders.[4]

Hull's response to Brock, when made known, was welcomed by the troops with the most lively satisfaction; and when the flag touched the Canada shore, the bearers were startled by a loud huzza from the fort at Detroit and the adjacent camp. The time for trial, and, as Hull's little army believed, of victory for them, was at hand, and the most active preparations to meet the foe was seen on every side. Major Jesup rode down to Spring Wells to reconnoitre the enemy at Sandwich. He was satisfied, from the position which the *Queen Charlotte* had taken, that the British intended to land at that place under cover of her guns. Having selected a commanding point for a battery from which that vessel might possibly be driven away, he hastened back to head-quarters, and requested Hull to send down a twenty-pounder for the purpose. Hull refused. Jesup returned to Spring Wells, where he found Captain

---

[1] M'Afee, page 85. [2] Brock to Hull, dated Sandwich, August 15, 1812.
[3] Hull, in his report to the Secretary of War, August 26, 1812, said he "did not exceed eight hundred men." Colonel Cass, in a letter to the same Cabinet minister, on the 10th of September, said that the morning report of the 15th "made our effective men present fit for duty 1060." Major Jesup estimated them at 950.
[4] When Major Denny evacuated Fort Gowris he set fire to the picket and other works used for strengthening it, when the flames accidentally seized the house and destroyed it.

Snelling, with a few men and a six-pounder, occupying the place he had selected for his battery. They perceived that the greater part of the British forces were at Sandwich, and both hastened to head-quarters. Jesup now asked for one hundred and fifty men to go over and spike the enemy's guns opposite Detroit. Hull said he could not spare so many. "Give me one hundred, then," said the brave Jesup. "Only one hundred," said Snelling, imploringly. "I will think of it," was Hull's reply; and soon afterward he took refuge in the fort, for at four o'clock in the afternoon the British battery of five guns opposite, under the direction of Captain Dixon, of the Royal Engineers, opened upon the town, the fort, and the camp, with shot and shell. All the troops, except Findlay's regiment, which was stationed three hundred yards northwest of the fort, were ordered within the walls, crowding the work far beyond its capacity.[1]

The British kept up their cannonade and bombardment until toward midnight.[2] The fire was returned with great spirit, and two of the enemy's guns were silenced and disabled.[3] At evening twilight it was suggested to Hull that as the fort did not command the river, a strong battery might be placed near the margin of the stream, so as to destroy the enemy as fast as they should attempt to land. An eligible point for the purpose, in the direction of Spring Wells, was selected, but the general, whose mind seemed to have been benumbed from the moment the enemy's battery was opened, would listen to no suggestions of the kind; and when that enemy, in full force, crossed the river during the early morning of the 16th—a calm and beautiful Sabbath morning—completing the passage in the matin twilight, they were allowed to land without the least molestation from ball or bullet. Colonels Elliott and M'Kee, with Tecumtha, had crossed during the night two miles below, with six hundred Indians, and taken position in the woods to attack the Americans on flank and rear, should they attempt to dispute the debarkation of the regulars and militia, who numbered seven hundred and seventy men, with five pieces of light artillery.[4] When all had breakfasted, the invaders moved toward the fort; the white troops in a single column, their left flank covered by the Indians, who kept in the woods a mile and a half distant. Their right rested on the Detroit River, and was covered by the guns of the *Queen Charlotte.*

Lieutenant Colonel Miller, with the 4th Regiment, was now in the fort; and the Ohio Volunteers and part of the Michigan militia were posted behind the town palisades, so as to annoy the enemy's whole left flank. The remainder of the militia were stationed in the upper part of the town, to resist the incursions of the Indians,

---

[1] *Historical Sketches of the late War*, by John Lewis Thomson, page 30.

[2] During the evening a large shell was thrown from a battery opposite where Woodward Avenue now is. It passed over the present Jefferson Avenue, then the principal street of the town, and fell upon the roof of Augustus Langdon, which stood on what is now the southerly corner of Woodward Avenue and Congress Street. Coming down through the house, which was two stories in height, it fell upon a table around which the family were seated, and went through to the cellar. The family had just time to flee from the house, when the shell exploded, almost wrecking the building. —*Judge Witherell.*

[3] The battery that did the greatest execution was placed, according to Judge Witherell, in the rear of the spot where the United States Court-house now stands. It was commanded by Lieutenant Daliba, of Dyson's Artillery Corps. He was a brave soldier. During the cannonade he stood in the ramparts, and when he saw the smoke or flash of the enemy's cannon, he would call out to his men "Down!" when they would drop behind the parapet until the shot had struck. A large pear-tree stood near the battery and was somewhat in the way. Colonel Mack, of the Michigan militia, ordered a young volunteer named John Miller to cut it down. John obeyed with alacrity. Seizing an axe, he hewed away diligently until he had about half severed the trunk, when a cannon ball from the enemy cut away nearly all of the remainder. The young man coolly turned toward the enemy and called out, "Send us another, John Bull; you can cut faster than I can."

It is related that a negro was seen, on the morning of the 16th, when the shot were striking thick and fast around the fort, behind a chimney on the roof of one of the barracks in the fort. He watched the smoke of the cannon across the river, and would then dodge behind the chimney. At length an eight-pound ball struck the chimney just over his head, demolished it, and covered the skulker with brick and mortar. Clearing himself from the rubbish, and scratching his woolly head, he exclaimed, "What de debble you doin up dar!" He fled to a safer place.

[4] According to Brock's official account, the number of troops which he marched against the fort was a little over thirteen hundred, as follows: 30 artillery; 250 of the 41st Regiment; 50 Royal Newfoundland Regiment; 400 militia, and about 600 Indians. His artillery consisted of three 6-pounders and two 3-pounders.—Tupper's Life of Brock, page 250. The number of Indians was probably greater than here stated, as 1000 warriors attended a council a few days before.

whose chief motive in joining the British standard was plunder, and the free and safe indulgence of their ferocity. Two twenty-four-pounders had been placed in battery on an eminence from which they could sweep the advancing column.[1] The American force was considerably less than that of the British, white and red combined, but their position was much superior. They had four hundred rounds of twenty-four-pound shot fixed; about one hundred thousand cartridges prepared; ample provisions for fifteen days and more approaching, and no lack of arms and loose ammunition.[2]

The invaders advanced cautiously, and had reached a point within five hundred yards of the American line, near the site of Governor Woodbridge's residence, at the crossing of the Central Railroad, when General Hull sent a peremptory order for his soldiers to retreat into the fort. The troops were astounded and bewildered. Confident in their ability to repulse and probably capture the invaders, they were eager for the order to begin the contest. "Not a sign of discontent broke upon the ear; not a look of cowardice met the eye. Every man expected a proud day for his country, and each was anxious that his individual exertion should contribute to the general result."[3] Like true soldiers they obeyed, but not without loud and fearless expression of their indignation, and their contempt for the commanding general. Many of them, high-spirited young men from the best families in Ohio, showed symptoms of positive mutiny at first; and the twenty-four-pounder would have poured a destructive storm of grape-shot upon the advancing column, notwithstanding the humiliating order, had not Lieutenant Anderson, who commanded the guns, acting under the general's direction, forcibly restrained them. He was anxious to reserve his fire until the approaching column should be in the best position to receive the most destructive volleys. The guns were heavily charged with grape-shot, and would have sent terrible messengers to many of the "red-coats," as the scarlet-dressed British were generally termed. The eager artillerists were about to apply the match too soon, when Anderson sprang forward, with drawn sword, and threatened to cut down the first man who should disobey his orders.

The infuriated soldiers entered the already over-crowded fort, while the enemy, after reconnoitring the fort and discovering the weakness of the fortification on the land side, prepared to storm it. But, before they could form for the purpose, the occasion had ceased. The fire from the battery on the Canada shore, kept up slowly since dawn, had become very vigorous. Up to this time no casualty had resulted from it within the fort. Now a ball came bounding over the fort wall, dealing death in its passage. A group standing at the door of one of the officers' quarters were almost annihilated. Captain Hancks, of Mackinaw, Lieutenant Sibley, and Dr. Reynolds, who accompanied Hull's invalids from the Maumee to Detroit, were instantly killed, and Dr. Blood was severely wounded. Two other soldiers were killed almost immediately afterward by another ball; and still two others on the outside of the fort were slain.

Many women and children were in the house where the officers were slain. Among them were General Hull's daughter and her children. Some of the women were petrified with affright, and were carried senseless to the bomb-proof vault for safety. Several of them were bespattered with blood; and the general, who saw the effects of the ball from a distance, knew not whether his own child was slain or not. These casualties, the precursors of future calamities, almost unmanned him, and he paced the parade backward and forward in the most anxious frame of mind. At that moment an officer from the Michigan militia in the town, who had observed the steady approach of the enemy without a gun being fired from the fort or the twenty-four

---

[1] This was in Jefferson Avenue, in front of the Cass farm, before the hill was cut down. The elevation was then about the same as it is now at the intersection of Woodward Avenue. These guns were placed there by Lieutenant Anderson, of the United States Engineers. Although the landing-place of the enemy at Spring Wells was about three miles off, Anderson opened upon the foe while they were crossing, but without doing much damage.

[2] Colonel Cass to the Secretary of War, September 10th, 1812.   [3] The same to the same.

pounders outside, came in haste to inquire whether it was the intention of the general to allow that body alone to defend the place; also to inform him that the British and Indians were at the tan-yard, close upon the town. The general made no reply, but, stepping into a room in the barracks, he prepared a note hastily, handed it to his son, Captain Hull, and directed him to display a white flag immediately from the walls of the fort,[1] where it might be seen by Captain Dixon over the river.[2] This was done. The firing soon ceased, and in a few minutes Captain Hull was "unexpectedly seen emerging from the fort"[3] with a flag of truce. At the same time, a boat, with a flag, was dispatched to the commander of the battery on the Canada shore.

Captain Hull bore proposals for an immediate capitulation. He soon returned with Lieutenant Colonel M'Donell and Major Glegg, who were authorized by Brock to negotiate the terms of surrender. The white flag upon the walls had awakened painful suspicions; the arrival of these officers announced the virtual betrayal of the garrison. Hull had asked no man's advice, nor suggested to any the possibility of a surrender.[4] His act was quick, and as unexpected as a thunderbolt from a clear sky. Not a shot had been fired upon the enemy—not an effort to stay his course had been made. For a moment nothing but reverence for gray hairs, and veneration for a soldier of the Revolution, saved the commander from personal violence at the hands of his incensed people. Many of the soldiers, it is said, shed tears of mortification and disappointment.

The terms of capitulation were soon agreed to,[5] and the American commander issued a general order saying that it was "with pain and anxiety" that he announced to the Northwest Army that he had been compelled, from a sense of duty, to agree to articles of capitulation, which were appended to the averment. He then sent a

---

[1] "Leonard Harrison, of Dearborn, told me that soon after a white flag was hoisted at the fort he happened to be standing near Colonel Findlay, of the Ohio Volunteers, and Lieutenant Colonel Miller, of the Fourth Infantry. Colonel Findlay said, 'Colonel Miller, the general talks of a surrender; let us put him under arrest.' Miller replied, 'Colonel Findlay, I am a soldier; I shall obey my superior officer,' intimating that if Findlay would assume the command of the army he would obey him. Had the stern old M'Arthur, or the younger and more impetuous Cass been present, either of them would have taken the responsibility."—*Judge Witherell.*

Miller's true soldierly qualities of obedience and acquiescence is shown in the careful manner in which, to his wife, he wrote concerning the surrender, from his prison at Fort George, on the 27th day of August, 1812. "Only one week after I, with six hundred men, completely conquered almost the whole force which they then had, they came out and took Fort Detroit, and made nearly two thousand of us prisoners, on Sunday, the 16th instant. There being no operations going on below us [meaning Niagara frontier] gave them an opportunity to re-enforce. The number brought against us is yet unknown; but my humble opinion is we could have defeated them, without a doubt, had we attempted it. But General Hull thought differently, and surrendered without making any terms of capitulation. Colonel Brush and I made the best terms we could after the surrender, which were but poor."—*Manuscript Letter.*

[2] The white "flag" was a table-cloth. It was waved from one of the bastions by Captain Burton, of the Fourth Regiment, by order of General Hull.   [3] Tupper's Life of Brock, page 232.

[4] In his dispatch to the Secretary of War, dated at Fort George, August 26, 1812, General Hull generously said: "I well know the high responsibility of the measure, and *take the whole of it on myself.* It was dictated by a sense of duty, and a full conviction of its expediency. The bands of savages which had then joined the British force were numerous beyond any former example. Their numbers have since increased; and the history of the barbarians of the north of Europe does not furnish examples of more greedy violence than these savages have exhibited. A large portion of the brave and gallant officers and men I commanded would cheerfully have contested until the last cartridge had been expended and the bayonets worn to the sockets. I could not consent to the useless sacrifice of such brave men when I knew it was impossible for me to sustain my situation. It was impossible, in the nature of things, that an army could have been furnished with the necessary supplies of provisions, military stores, clothing, and comforts for the sick, on pack-horses, through a wilderness of two hundred miles, filled with hostile savages. It was impossible, sir, that this little army, worn down by fatigue, by sickness, by wounds, and deaths, could have supported itself not only against the collected force of all the Northern nations of Indians, but against the united strength of Upper Canada, whose population consists of more than twenty times the number contained in the Territory of Michigan, aided by the principal part of the regular forces of the province, and the wealth and influence of the Northwest and other trading establishments among the Indians, which have in their employment more than two thousand white men."

After alluding to Colonels M'Arthur, Findlay, Cass, and Miller in commendatory terms, he said: "If aught has taken place during the campaign which is honorable to the army, these officers are entitled to a large share of it. If the last act should be disapproved, no part of the censure belongs to them." He closed his dispatch by soliciting an early investigation of his conduct, and requesting the government not to be unmindful of his associates in captivity, and of the families of the brave men who had fallen in the contest.

[5] It was stipulated that the fort at Detroit, with all its dependencies, and the troops there, excepting such of the militia of Michigan Territory who had not joined the army, should be surrendered, with all public property of every kind. The command of Captain Brush at the River Raisin, and M'Arthur's then away from Detroit, were, at the request of Hull, included in the capitulation, while the Ohio militia, who had not yet joined the army, were paroled on condition that they should return home, and not serve during the war.

T

messenger with a note to Colonel M'Arthur (who, with Colonel Cass and the detachment sent toward the Raisin, were, as we have seen, hastening back to Detroit) informing him of the surrender, and that he and his command were included in the capitulation as prisoners of war.[1] They had arrived in sight of Detroit at about the time when the American white flags had silenced the British cannon,[2] thoroughly exhausted by rapid and fatiguing marches and lack of food, for they had tasted nothing for more than forty-eight hours, excepting some green pumpkins and potatoes found in the fields. They had observed the enemy, and the ease with which, in connection with the army at Detroit, they might capture him by falling upon his rear. But all was silent. That fact was a sealed enigma. There were two armies within half cannon-shot of each other, and yet, to the ears of these listeners, they both seemed as silent as the grave. Had there been firing, or any signs of resistance, M'Arthur would have fallen upon the rear of the invaders even without orders. But all was mystery until the arrival of Hull's courier with the unwelcome tidings.

M'Arthur attempted to communicate with Hull, but failed. He sent a message to Captain Brush with Hull's note, saying, "By the within letter you will see that the army under General Hull has been surrendered. By the articles you will see that provision has been made for the detachment under your command; you will therefore, I hope, return to Ohio with us."[3]

At sunset Colonel Elliott came to M'Arthur from the fort with the articles of capitulation, and with authority from Brock to receive tokens of the submission of the detachment. The dark, lustrous eyes of M'Arthur flashed with indignation at the demand. As they filled with tears of deepest mortification, he thrust his sword into the ground, and broke it in pieces, and then tore his epaulettes from his shoulders. This paroxysm of feeling was soon succeeded by dignified calmness; and in the dim twilight M'Arthur and Cass, with their whole detachment, were marched into the fort, where the arms of the soldiers were stacked. Before the curtain of night had been fairly drawn over the humiliating scene the act of capitulation and surrender was completed—an act which produced universal mortification and intense indignation throughout the country.[4] In less than two months after war was declared, and the favorite scheme of an invasion of the enemy's provinces had been set in motion, a strong military post, a spirited army, and a magnificent territory, with all its inhabitants,[5] had been given up without an effort to save them, or a moment's waiting for the arrival of powerful re-enforcements and ample supplies, then on their way from the southward. About two thousand men in all[6] became prisoners of war.

---

[1] "Such part of the Ohio militia," he said, "as have not joined the army [meaning Brush's detachment at the Raisin] will be permitted to return to their homes, on condition that they will not serve during the war. Their arms, however, will be delivered up, if belonging to the public."

[2] They had been discovered by Brock's scouts, and their presence in the rear caused the British general to move to the attack sooner than he intended to. "Hearing," says Brock, in his official dispatch, "that his [M'Arthur's] cavalry had been seen that morning three miles in our rear, I decided on an immediate attack."

[3] On the evening of the 17th, Captain Elliott, son of Colonel Elliott, with a Frenchman and Wyandot Indian, approached Brush's encampment at the Raisin bearing a flag of truce, a copy of the capitulation at Detroit, and authority to receive the surrender of Brush and his command. Lieutenant Couthier, of the Raisin, the officer of the day, blindfolded Elliott, and led him to the block-house. Brush was not satisfied that his visit was by authority, or that the document was genuine, so he ordered Elliott's arrest and confinement. M'Arthur's letter testified to the genuineness of Elliott's document and authority, when Brush hastily packed up the public property at the Raisin, and, with his whole command and his cattle, started for Ohio, directing Elliott to be released the next day. The angry Elliott sent for Tecumtha to pursue Brush. It was too late.—Statement of Peter Navarre (who was an eye-witness) to the Author in September, 1860; Letter to the Author from the Hon. Elisha Whittlesey, of Ohio.

[4] Among other demonstrations in different parts of the country, the newspapers of the day noticed that at Greensborough, North Carolina, General Hull was hung and burnt in effigy, "in accordance with the prescription of a public meeting."

[5] The whole white population of Michigan at that time was between four and five thousand. The greater part were Canadians. Their settlements were chiefly on the Maumee, Raisin, Ecorce, Rouge, Detroit River, Lake St. Clair, and the island of Mackinack. They paid very little attention to agriculture, being engaged chiefly in hunting, fishing, and trading with the Indians. They did not produce sufficient from the earth to give themselves sustenance; and their beef, pork, corn, and flour were brought from a distance.

[6] Estimates of the number actually included in the capitulation vary from 1800 to 2500. I have examined all, and think the number was not far from 2000.

These consisted of two squadrons of cavalry, one company of artillery, the 4th United States Regiment, and detachments from the 1st and 3d; three regiments of Ohio Volunteers, and one regiment of the Michigan militia. The British obtained by this capitulation (for it was not a victory) a large amount of arms, ammunition, and stores, all of which, especially arms, were greatly needed in Upper Canada.[1] It was a godsend to the provinces in every aspect. The surrender caused months of delay before another invading army could be brought into the field, and thus gave the British time for preparation; and it secured the friendship and alliance of savage tribes, who, as usual, were ready to join whatever side seemed to be the stronger party, and safest as an ally.

The formal surrender of the fort and garrison took place at meridian, on the 16th.[2] At the same hour the next day (Monday, the 17th) General Brock and his staff, with other officers, appeared in full uniform, and in their presence a salute was fired from the esplanade in front of the fort, with one of the brass cannon included in the capitulation. It bore the following inscription: "TAKEN AT SARATOGA ON THE 17TH OF OCTOBER, 1777." When the British officers saw this, they were so delighted that some of them greeted the old British captive, now released, with kisses; and one of them remarked to Colonel Hatch, from whose manuscript narrative I have gained the facts, "we must have an addition put to that inscription, namely, 'RETAKEN AT DETROIT AUGUST 16, 1812.'"[3] The salute was answered by Dixon's battery on the Canada shore, and by the *Queen Charlotte*, which came sweeping up the middle of the river from the waters between Spring Wells and Sandwich, and took position directly in front of the town.[4]

It was on this occasion that General Brock paid marked respect to Tecumtha. He took off his own rich crimson silk sash and publicly placed it round the waist of the chief. Tecumtha received it with dignity and great satisfaction; but the following day he appeared without the badge of honor. Brock apprehended that some offense had been given to the chief, but, on inquiry, he found that Tecumtha, with great modesty and with the most delicate exhibition of praise, had placed the sash upon the body of Round Head, a celebrated and remarkable Wyandot warrior, saying, "I do not want to wear such a mark of distinction, when an older and abler warrior than myself is present."

The volunteers and militia who were made prisoners, and some minor regular officers, were permitted to return home on parole. Those of Michigan were discharged at Detroit, and the Ohio Volunteers were borne in vessels to Cleveland, from which point they made their way home. General Hull and the regulars were held as prisoners of war, and sent to Montreal. They were taken to Malden, and there embarked on board the *Queen Charlotte, Hunter*, and other public vessels, and conveyed to Fort Erie, opposite Buffalo. From that point they were marched to Fort George, where they were again placed in vessels and sent to Kingston. From that post they were escorted by land to Montreal.

General Hull and his fellow-prisoners reached Fort George, on the Niagara, on the 26th of August, when the commander immediately wrote a lengthy report of the surrender and attendant events, but was not permitted to forward it, until his arrival at Montreal.[5] Information of the disaster had already reached General Van

---

[1] The spoils were 2500 stand of arms; twenty-five iron, and eight brass pieces of ordnance; forty barrels of gunpowder, a stand of colors, and a great quantity and variety of military stores. The armed brig *Adams* also became a prize. She was immediately put in complete order, and her name changed to *Detroit*, under which title we shall meet her hereafter, in the British service.

[2] The garrison flag surrendered on that occasion was taken to Montreal by Captain Glegg, Brock's aid-de-camp.

[3] This cannon was retaken from the British at the battle of the Thames, in October, 1813. I saw it in the state arsenal at Frankfort, Kentucky, when I visited that city in April, 1861. It is a small three-pounder, three feet four inches in length. It has the British mark of the broad arrow upon it, and the date of "1775."

[4] After the surrender, General Hull returned to his own house, where he had resided as Governor of Michigan. It was then occupied by Mr. Hickman, his son-in-law. A British guard attended him.—*Wallace*.

[5] It was Hull's intention to forward his dispatch from Fort George by Major Witherell, of the Michigan Volunteers;

Rensselaer, at Lewiston, and he had promptly sent the news by express to General Dearborn, the senior commander in the army, whose head-quarters at that time were at Greenbush, opposite Albany, on the Hudson River. For this important errand Van Rensselaer employed Captain Darby Noon, the leader of a fine company of Albany Volunteers, who were then stationed at or near Fort Niagara. Captain Noon was a man of great energy, and he performed the service in an incredibly short space of time. He rode express all the way, changing his horses by impressing them when necessary, assuring the owners of remuneration from the government. He neither slept on the way, nor tasted food, excepting what he ate on horseback. When he arrived at Greenbush, he was so much exhausted that he had to be lifted from his horse, and he was compelled to remain in his bed for several days.[1]

[a] August 16, 1812.

On the day of the surrender,[a] General Brock issued a proclamation to the inhabitants of Michigan, in which they were assured of protection in life, property, and religious observances, and were called upon to give up all public property in the Territory. Having made arrangements for the civil and military occupation of the Territory, and leaving Colonel Proctor in command of a garrison of two hundred and fifty men at Detroit, he hastened back to York, where he arrived on the 27th,[b] and was received with the greatest enthusiasm by the people,

[b] August.

who regarded him as the savior of the province. In the short space of nineteen days he had met the Legislature, arranged the public affairs of the province, traveled about three hundred miles to confront an invader, and returned the possessor of that invader's whole army and a vast territory, about equal in area to Upper Canada. Henceforth, during his brief career, he was the idol of the Canadians, and the Prince Regent, representing the majesty of Great Britain, created him a baronet.[c2]

[c] October 10.

While General Hull was on his way toward Montreal, Colonel Cass, at the request of Colonel M'Arthur, was hasting to Washington City, " for the purpose," as he said, " of communicating to the government such particulars respecting the expedition lately commanded by Brigadier General Hull, and its disastrous results, as might enable them correctly to appreciate the conduct of the officers and men, and to develop the causes which produced so foul a stain upon the national character."[3] This com-

---

but Brock having gone directly to York, the commander of the post would not take the responsibility of allowing his prisoner to correspond with his government. From Montreal he sent his dispatch, dated August 26th, by Lieutenant Anderson, of the Artillery, to the Secretary of War.—Hull's *Letter to the Secretary of War*, Montreal, September 8, 1812.

[1] Darby Noon was a native of Ireland, and a man of great personal worth. He raised and equipped a volunteer company at Albany, almost entirely at his own expense, and in 1813 was commissioned a major in the 41st Regiment of New York State Militia. His wife was Caroline Broome, daughter of Lieutenant Governor Broome, of New York. Major Noon survived the war only eight years, dying in September, 1823. From his widow, who died in 1861, I received the above portrait of the gallant officer.

[2] General Brock's dispatches and the colors of the United States 4th Regiment reached London on the 6th of October, the anniversary of his birth, where, in honor of his achievement at Detroit, the Park and Town guns were fired. Only a week later, and the gallant general was no more.

[3] Ex-Governor Samuel Huntington was at Cleveland, a volunteer, when Colonel Cass arrived there on his way to the

munication was made in writing on the 10th of September, in which was given an outline history of events near Detroit, from the landing in Canada until the surrender. It exhibited much warmth of feeling, and its circulation in print prejudiced the public mind against Hull, and intensified the indignant reproaches which the first intelligence of the surrender had caused to be hurled at the head of the unfortunate general. It also diverted public attention for the moment from the palpable inefficiency of the War Department,[1] the effects of the armistice, and the injurious delays of General Dearborn,[2] to which much of the disaster should properly be charged. Colonel Cass's *opinions*, as well as *facts*, were eagerly accepted by the excited public as veritable history, and few had words of palliation to offer for the captive veteran when they read the following glowing, dogmatic words at the conclusion of the young colonel's letter: "To see the whole of our men, flushed with the hope of victory, eagerly awaiting the approaching contest—to see them afterward dispirited, hopeless, and desponding, at least five hundred shedding tears, because they were not allowed to meet their country's foe and to fight their country's battles, excited sensations which no American has ever before had cause to feel, and which, I trust in God, will never again be felt while our men remain to defend the standard of the Union. . . . . . Confident I am that, had the courage and conduct of the general been equal to the spirit and zeal of the troops, the event would have been as brilliant and successful as it is disastrous and dishonorable.[3]

General Hull and his fellow-captives arrived at Montreal on Sunday afternoon, the 6th of September, and attracted much attention. The prisoners numbered, rank and file, three hundred and fifty. They were escorted from Kingston by one hundred and thirty men, under Major Heathcote, of the Newfoundland Regiment. At Cornwall, opposite St. Regis, they were met by Captain Gray, of the Quarter-master's department, who took formal charge of the prisoners. They had other escorts of troops until

---

seat of government. Huntington accompanied him to Washington, at the request of General Wadsworth. When within two days ride of the national capital, Cass was prostrated by sickness. Huntington pressed forward, and was the first to give positive information of Hull's surrender, to the Secretary of War. This made Dr. Eustis impatient for the arrival of Cass. "The Secretary at War," wrote Huntington, "was very desirous to see him, and requested me to go after him in a carriage. I met him the first day, about thirty-five miles from this. He had recovered sufficiently to pursue the journey."—Autograph Letter of Governor Huntington to General Meigs, Washington City, September 12, 1812.

[1] Secretary Eustis seems to have been so conscious of his fatal mistake in not sending his letter to Hull, announcing the declaration of war, by which his vessel and its precious contents, captured at Malden at the beginning of July, might have been saved, that, as late as the 18th of December, four months after the surrender of Detroit, he gave evidence of his belief that public opinion would lay the responsibility of the disaster upon him. In a letter to General Dearborn of that date, he said: "Fortunately for you, the want of success which has attended the campaign will be attributed to the Secretary of War. So long as you enjoy the confidence of the government, the clamor of the discontented should not be regarded." Governor Huntington, in his letter to Governor Meigs, mentioned in the preceding note, said: "The whole blame is laid at the door of the present administration, and we are told that if De Witt Clinton had been our president, the campaign would have been short and glorious—it would have been short, no doubt, and terminated by an inglorious peace."—Autograph Letter, Washington City, September 12, 1812.

[2] General Dearborn, early in August, signed an armistice, entered into between himself and Sir George Prevost, for a cessation of hostilities until the will of the United States government should be known, there then being, it was supposed, propositions for peace on the part of Great Britain before the Cabinet at Washington. On this account Sir George had issued positive instructions for a cessation of hostilities. Dearborn signed the armistice on the 9th of August. Had he sent a notice of it by express to Hull, as that officer did of his surrender to Dearborn, Detroit might have been saved, for it would have reached Hull before the 15th of August, and the imperative commands of Prevost would have prevented Brock's acting on the offensive. Meanwhile Hull's supplies and re-enforcements would have arrived from Ohio, and made him strong enough to invade Canada again at the conclusion of the armistice. But instead of sending a notice of the armistice to Hull by express, Dearborn, like the Secretary of War with his more important dispatches, intrusted his letter to the irregular mails, and it was actually *nine days* going from Albany to Buffalo! The first intimation of an armistice which Hull received was while on his way toward the Niagara as a prisoner of war.

[3] Lewis Cass was born at Exeter, New Hampshire, on the 9th of October, 1782. At the age of seventeen years he crossed the Alleghany Mountains on foot, and settled in Marietta, Ohio, where he studied law, and was active in proceedings against Aaron Burr. Jefferson appointed him Marshal of Ohio in 1807. He took an active part in the war of 1812 in the West, and, late in 1813, President Madison appointed him Governor of the Territory of Michigan. He held that position till 1831, when he was called to the Cabinet of President Jackson as Secretary of War. In 1836 he went to France as American Minister at the Court of St. Cloud. He returned home in 1842. He was elected United States Senator by the Legislature of Michigan in 1845, and he held that position until called to Buchanan's Cabinet in 1857. He resigned that position at near the close of 1860, because he could not remain associated with the President's confidential advisers, who, he was satisfied, were plotting treason against his country. He retired from public life, and died at Detroit on the 17th of June, 1866, at the age of eighty-four years.

they reached the vicinity of Montreal, when they were left in charge of the militia until preparations could be made for the formal entrance into the city. This was not accomplished until quite late in the evening, when they were marched in in the presence of a great concourse of rejoicing people, who had illuminated the streets through which the triumphal procession passed. General Hull was received with great politeness by Sir George Prevost, the Governor General and Commander-in-chief, and invited to make his residence at his mansion during his stay in Montreal. On Thursday following,[a] General Hull and eight of his officers set out for the United States on their parole.

[a] September 10, 1812.

General Hull retired to his farm at Newton, Massachusetts, from which he was summoned to appear before a court-martial at Philadelphia on the 25th of February, 1813, of which General Wade Hampton was appointed president. The members appointed consisted of three brigadier generals, nine colonels, and three lieutenant colonels; and the eminent A. J. Dallas, of Pennsylvania, was judge advocate. This court was dissolved by the President without giving a reason for the act; and, almost a year afterward, Hull was summoned to appear before another, to convene at Albany, New York. It met on the 3d of January, 1814. General Dearborn was the president, and he was assisted by three brigadier generals, four colonels, and five lieutenant colonels.[1] Again Mr. Dallas was judge advocate. As Hull blamed Dearborn for his negligence, and as his own acquittal would condemn that officer, he might very properly have objected to the appointed president of the court; but he was anxious for a trial, and he waived all feeling. He was charged with treason, cowardice, and neglect of duty and unofficer-like conduct from the 9th of April to the 16th of August, 1812.[2] General Hull objected to the jurisdiction of the court on the first charge—*treason*—as a matter of civil cognizance only. The court concurred in this view, and he was tried only on the other charges. After a session of eighty days, the court decided[b] that he was not guilty of treason,[3] but found him guilty of the second and third charges, namely, cowardice, and neglect of duty and unofficer-like conduct. He was sentenced to be shot dead, and his name to be struck from the rolls of the army.[4]

[b] March 26.

---

[1] Generals Bloomfield, Parker, and Covington; Colonels Fenwick, Carberry, Little, and Irvine; and Lieutenant Colonels Dennis, Connor, Davis, Scott, and Stewart.

[2] The specifications under the charge of TREASON were, 1st. "Hiring the vessel to transport his sick men and baggage from the Miami to Detroit." 2d. "Not attacking the enemy's fort at Malden, and retreating to Detroit." 3d. "Not strengthening the fort of Detroit, and surrendering."
The specifications under the charge of COWARDICE were, 1st. "Not attacking Malden, and retreating to Detroit." 2d. "Appearances of alarm during the cannonade." 3d. "Appearances of alarm on the day of the surrender." 4th. "Surrendering of Detroit." The specifications under the third charge were similar to those under the second.

[3] It is perhaps not technically true that the court decided that he was not guilty of treason. They determined that they could not try him on that charge, but said "the evidence on the subject having been publicly given, the court deem it proper, in justice to the accused, to say that they do not believe, from any thing that has appeared before them, that General William Hull has committed treason against the United States."

[4] The President approved the sentence on the 25th of April, and on the same day the following general order was issued:

| Hull pardoned by the President. | A Consideration of Hull's public Character. | His own Defense. |

The court strongly recommended him to the mercy of the President, on account of his age and his revolutionary services. Mr. Madison pardoned him, and he retired to his farm, to live in comparative obscurity, under a cloud of almost universal reproach, for about twelve years. He wrote a vindication of his conduct in the campaign of 1812, in a series of letters, published in the *American Statesman* newspaper in Boston,[1] and on his dying bed he declared his belief that he was right, as a soldier and a man, in surrendering Detroit. He had the consolation of feeling, before his death, a growing sympathy for him in the partially disabused public mind, which prophesied of future vindication and just appreciation.[2]

I have given, in this and the preceding chapter, as faithful a general history of Hull's campaign as a careful and dispassionate study of documentary and other contemporaneous narratives, written and verbal, have enabled me to do. I have recorded what I believe to be undoubted facts. As they stand in the narrative, unattended by analysis, comparison, or argument, they present General Hull in his conduct of the campaign in some instances in an unfavorable light: not as a traitor—not as an actual coward, but as bearing to the superficial reader the semblance of both. But, after weighing and estimating the value of these facts in connection with current circumstances to which they bore positive relationship—after observing the composition of the court-martial, the peculiar relations of the court and the witnesses to the accused, and the testimony in detail, the writer is constrained to believe that General Hull was actuated throughout the campaign by the purest impulses of patriotism and humanity. That he was *weak*, we may allow; that he was *wicked*, we can not believe. His weakness, evinced at times by vacillation, was not the child of cowardice, but of excessive prudence and caution, born of the noblest sentiments of the human heart. These, in his case, were doubtless enhanced by the disabilities of waning physical vigor.[3] He was thus far down the western slope of life, when men *counsel* more than *act*. The perils and fatigues of the journey from Dayton to Detroit had affected him, and the anxieties arising from his responsibilities bore heavily upon his judgment. These difficulties his young, vigorous, ambitious, daring officers could not understand; and while they were cursing him, they should have been kindly cherishing him. When he could perceive no alternative but surrender or destruction, he bravely determined to choose the most courageous and humane course; so he faced the taunts of his soldiers, and the expected scorn of his countrymen, rather than fill the beautiful land of the Ohio, and the settlements of Michigan, with mourning.

Hull had warned the government of the folly of attempting the conquest of Can-

---

"Washington City, April 25, 1814.

"The rolls of the army are to be no longer disgraced by having upon them the name of Brigadier General William Hull. The general court-martial, of which General Dearborn is president, is hereby dissolved.

"By order, "J. B. WALBACH, Adjutant General."

[1] These were published in a volume of three hundred and ten pages, entitled, *Memoirs of the Campaign of the Northwestern Army of the United States. A.D. 1812.* General Hull's long silence was owing to the fact that his papers were burnt in the vessel in which they were sent from Detroit to Buffalo, after the surrender, and that during two administrations he vainly applied to the War Department at Washington for copies of papers necessary for his defense. It was not until John C. Calhoun became Secretary of War that any notice was taken of his application. That officer promptly caused copies to be made of all papers that General Hull desired, when he commenced his vindication in his memoir just mentioned.

[2] He was always calm, tranquil, and happy. He knew that his country would one day also understand him, and that history would at last do him justice. He was asked, on his death-bed, whether he still believed he had done right in the surrender of Detroit, and he replied that he did, and was thankful that he had been enabled to do it.—*History of the Campaign of 1812*, by his grandson, James Freeman Clark, page 365. Mr. Wallace, one of his aids, says that when he parted with the general at Detroit to return home, the white-haired veteran said, "God bless you, my young friend! You return to your family without a stain; as for myself, I have sacrificed a reputation dearer to me than life, but I have saved the inhabitants of Detroit, and my heart approves the act."

[3] Mr. Wallace, one of Hull's aids, whose testimony we have before alluded to, says: "General Cass has since declared to me that he thought the main defect of General Hull was the 'imbecility of age,' and it was the defect of all the old veterans who took the field in the late war. A peaceful government like ours must always labor under similar disadvantages. Our superannuated officers must be called into service, or men without experience must command our armies."

ada without better preparation. But the young hot-bloods of the administration—Clay, and others—could not wait; and the President and his Cabinet, lacking all the essential knowledge for planning a campaign, had sent him on an errand of vast importance and difficulty without seeming to comprehend its vastness, or estimating the means necessary for its accomplishment. The conception of the campaign was a huge blunder, and Hull saw it; and the failure to put in vigorous motion for his support auxiliary and co-operative forces, was criminal neglect. When the result was found to be failure and humiliation, the administration perceived this, and sought a refuge. Public indignation must be appeased—the lightning of the public wrath must be averted. General Hull was made the chosen victim for the peace-offering—the sin-bearing scape-goat; and on his head the fiery thunderbolts were hurled. The grass has grown greenly upon his grave for more than forty years. Let his faults (for, like all men, he was not immaculate) also be covered with the verdure of blind Charity.[1] Two generations have passed away since the dark cloud first brooded over his fair fame. We may all see, if we will, with eyes unfilmed by prejudice, the silver edging which tells of the brightness of good intentions behind it, and prophesies of evanishment and a clear sky. Let History be just, in spite of the clamors of hoary Error.

> "'Tis strange how many unimagined charges
> Can swarm upon a man, when once the lid
> Of the Pandora-box of contumely
> Is open'd o'er his head."—SHAKSPEARE.

---

[1] William Hull was born in Derby, Connecticut, on the 24th of June, 1753. He was graduated with honor at Yale College when he was nineteen years of age. He first studied divinity, but left it for the law. He was a meritorious soldier and officer throughout the Revolution, and participated in nine battles. He went to Canada on an Indian commission in 1792. He held judicial and representative offices in Massachusetts, and, as we have seen, was placed in a responsible military and civil station at the beginning of the War of 1812. He died at Newton, Massachusetts, in November, 1825. I am indebted to General Hull's granddaughter, Miss Sarah A. Clarke, of Newport, Rhode Island, for a copy of his portrait, painted by Stuart, from which our engraving was made. The signature is copied from a letter in my possession, written at White Plains, New York, in the autumn of 1778.

CHAPTER XV.

> "And who supplies the murderous steel?
> And who prepares the base reward
> That wakes to deeds of desperate zeal
> The fury of each slumbering horde?
> From Britain comes each fatal blow;
> From Britain, still our deadliest foe."
>
> THE KENTUCKY VOLUNTEER; BY A LADY.

IT was a beautiful, clear, breezy morning, early in October, 1860, when the writer left Chicago, with his family, to visit the theatre of events described in the two preceding chapters. We took the Michigan Central train for Detroit, and soon lost sight of the marvelous metropolis of Illinois, and Lake Michigan, on which it stands.[1] We swept rapidly around the magnificent curve of the head of the lake, and after leaving the sand dunes of Michigan City, and the withered bud of a prospective great mart of commerce at New Buffalo, traversed a beautiful and fertile country in the western half of the lower part of the peninsula and State of Michigan. Large streams of water, mills, neat villages, broad fields covered with ripe corn, spacious barns, and hardy people, seen all along the way to Marshall, where we dined, and beyond, proclaimed general prosperity. Among the most considerable streams crossed during the day were the St. Joseph, Kalamazoo, Battle Creek, and Huron. Over the latter, in its crooked course, we passed several times when approaching the metropolis (Lansing is the capital) of Michigan. It was the dusk of mere starlight when we traveled over that section of the route, and it was late in the evening when we reached Detroit, and found a pleasant home at the Russell House for the few days of our sojourn in that neighborhood.

The following day was the Sabbath. The air was as warm as in early June. A drizzling rain moistened all the streets and caused small congregations in the churches. We listened to the full, powerful voice of Bishop M'Coskry in the morning, and in the afternoon strolled with a friend far down beautiful Fort Street,[2] and enjoyed the prospect of fine residences and ornamental gardens. The sun shone brightly all the afternoon, but in the evening heavy clouds came rolling up from the southwest. At nine o'clock a thunder-storm burst over the city, which sent down lightning and rain until past midnight. No traces of this elemental tumult were seen above in the morning—

> "The thunder, tramping deep and loud,
> Had left no foot-marks there."

The sky was cloudless, and a cool breeze from the northwest—cooler than any we had felt since the dog-days—reminded us that autumn had succeeded summer. It came from the far-off region beyond Mackinack, where snow had already whitened the hills.

At an early hour I started for Monroe, on the site of old Frenchtown, on the river

---

[1] This is the largest of the lakes that lie wholly within the United States. It is 330 miles long, and has an average width of 60 miles. It contains 16,981 square miles, or 10,868,000 acres. Its average depth is about 900 feet, and its elevation above tide water is about 300 feet.

[2] The residence of the late General Cass was on this street. It was a spacious but very modest wooden building, on the corner of Fort and Cass Streets, a little westward of the site of the old fort. His former residence—a small, low, one-storied building, with four dormer windows—was yet standing, on the west side of Larned Street, near the corner of Second Street.

Raisin, to visit the places of historic interest in that vicinity, where I spent the day pleasantly and profitably. Of the events of that day I shall write hereafter. On the following morning[a] I procured a horse and light wagon, crossed the ferry to the Canada shore at Windsor, and started for Amherstburg, eighteen miles down the stream toward Lake Erie. In the lower part of Windsor I sketched Colonel Babie's house, delineated on page 262, and then rode on to Sandwich, two miles below, where I met one of that famous class known as "the oldest inhabitants" in the person of Mr. John B. Laughton, who was born in Detroit, but who has been a British subject from his early years. When, in 1796, the post of Detroit was evacuated by the British, according to the provisions of the treaty of 1783, many residents of English, Irish, and Scottish lineage, preferring "not to be Yankees," as Mr. Laughton said, crossed the river and settled along its Canada shore. Mr. Laughton was a member of the Kent militia in 1812; and from Sandwich he saw the white flag that proclaimed the surrender of Detroit. He was then a young man twenty-two years of age. He was afterward in the affair known as the battle of the Long Woods, in Canada; also at the battle of Chippewa, where he lost a brother killed; and at that of Niagara, where he lost his own liberty, and was sent a prisoner to Greenbush, opposite Albany. He related many interesting circumstances connected with the surrender. He spoke of the Canadian Volunteers in the uniforms of regulars, by which Hull was deceived; and said that among the Indians who followed Brock into the fort at Detroit were several Canadians, painted and dressed like the savages, who each held up a white arm to show Hull that they had defied the menace in his proclamation respecting the treatment of such offenders.

[a] October 6, 1860.

Sandwich was an exceedingly pleasant village. Around it were orchards of pear and apple trees of great size, which attested the fact that it is one of the oldest settlements in Canada. Here the disbanded French soldiers settled after the peace of Paris in 1763. The houses had pleasant gardens attached to them; and as the town was the capital of Essex County, it contained a jail and court-house, and the residence of the county officers.

I left Sandwich toward noon, and a little past meridian crossed Turkey Creek. For several miles below Sandwich the banks of Detroit are low and sandy. The road, lying much of the way in sight of the river, was in excellent condition, and with the picturesque and interesting scenery forms a most attractive drive in pleasant weather. Passing through the Petit Côte settlement, I arrived at a neat little tavern near the northern bank of the *Aux Canards*, where I met an old French Canadian who was present when Cass, and Findlay, and M'Arthur, and Snelling made their military visits there in 1812. He was loyal then, but quiet; and when it was safe to do so, in the absence of the Americans, he furnished the *Queen Charlotte* with vegetables. He pointed out the ridge from which M'Arthur reconnoitred the whole position, and also the spot where Colonel Cass planted his six-pounder, and "blazed away" at the enemy on the southern shore of the stream. The bridge seen in the centre of the picture on page 264 was upon the site of the old one, and, like it, was reached by a causeway at both ends. I sketched the scene, then crossed the *Aux Canards* over the causeway and the bridge, and hastened on to Amherstburg, for the day was rapidly wearing away. Most of the way from *Aux Canards*, or Taron-tee, to Amherstburg, the river bank is high, and the road passing along its margin was thickly settled, for the farms were narrow. Most of the houses were large, with fine gardens around them. Among the most attractive of these was "Rosebank," the residence of Mr. James Dougall, an eminent horticulturist, about three miles from Amherstburg.

It was nearly three o'clock when the steeples of Amherstburg announced its presence. I soon crossed a beautiful open plain, whereon cattle were grazing, bounded on the left by streets of neat log cottages, whitewashed and embowered, each a story in height, with two acres of land attached. The plain was a military reserve of one hundred and thirty acres, and the cottages were the dwellings of pensioners—superannuated British soldiers—who were well cared for by their government. On the right of the road, in the upper part of Amherstburg, within a high picket inclosure, was Fort Malden; its chief building (barracks) were then devoted to more humane purposes than war. It was used for the insane in Canada West, as a branch of a parent asylum for such unfortunates situated at Toronto. No part of the old fort remained. The new one was constructed during the excitement incident to the "Patriot War," or "Rebellion," as men of different bias respectively call an outbreak in the Canadas in 1838. It was constructed in 1839.

Amherstburg had an antiquated appearance, the houses having been chiefly built by the French. The streets were narrow, and the side-walks were mostly paved with irregular stones. I had but little time to devote to an inspection of the place. After ordering dinner at Salmoni's, I went out with an intelligent lad, and visited the fort and other places of interest along the shore. The ship-yard, where a part of Barclay's fleet on Lake Erie was built, was a few rods above Salmoni's; and from the corner of a large red stone house, overlooking the whole locality, and commanding quite an ex-

VIEW OF MALDEN, WHERE THE BRITISH SHIPS WERE BUILT.

tensive view of the river southward, with Elliott's Point on the left and Bois Blanc Island on the right, I made the accompanying sketch. The wharf, then used chiefly for wood, was precisely where the British vessels were launched. In the direction of the ship under sail (seen in the picture), just off Elliott's Point on the left, is seen Lake Erie. Looking a little farther to the right, on Bois Blanc Island, is seen the lighthouse, near which was a block-house and battery in 1812; and on each side of the group of sails at the wharf is seen a block-house, both erected in 1838. There was a block-house on the right of Salmoni's Hotel, and another at the upper end of the ship-yard, near the fort, in 1812.

After dinner I visited the venerable Robert Reynolds, living in a fine brick mansion, surrounded by charming grounds, on the bank of the river, just below Amherstburg. From his grounds there is a view of Elliott's Point, where Colonel Elliott, already mentioned frequently, resided. Just below it, three or four miles from Amherstburg, is Hartley's Point, where General Harrison landed when he invaded Canada in 1813. Mr. Reynolds was in the eightieth year of his age when I visited him. His sister, but little his junior, lived with him. They were born in Detroit. He was deputy assistant commissary general in the British army in the War of 1812, and was at the taking of Detroit. He was also at Dol-

sen's on the day of the battle of the Thames. From that time until the peace he was stationed at Burlington Heights, at the west end of Lake Ontario. His sister told me that she distinctly heard the firing between the fleets of Perry and Barclay in the memorable battle of Lake Erie, in September, 1813; and that she also saw from her residence the vessels conveying Harrison's army from the Raisin to the Canada shore. Mr. Reynolds knew Proctor and Tecumtha well, and seemed to have a very unfavorable opinion of the former as a commander. He spoke of his conduct at the Thames as "shameful," and justified the strictures of Tecumtha.

It was sunset when I left Amherstburg for Detroit. In the western sky, as I looked over the fields where Van Horne and Miller had wrestled with the mongrel foe, when the country was almost a wilderness, were seen gorgeous cloud-bars of crimson and gold. These faded into dull lead; and just as daylight yielded the sceptre to starlight, I crossed the sluggish Ta-ron-tee. It was a summer-like evening, and before I reached the slope of the highway leading up to Sandwich, the lights of Detroit gave pleasant indications that the end of the journey was near. It was nine o'clock when I entered Windsor, and on inquiring of a man, standing on the piazza of a large wooden building, for the proper turn to the Ferry, I was told that the boat had ceased running for the night. For a moment I was perplexed. I did not wish to remain all night in Windsor when Detroit was so near. "Where can I leave my horse and wagon in safety," I inquired. "At this house," the man replied. "What is the name of it?" I asked. "Windsor Castle," he answered. The name and the building were in ludicrous contrast. But my business was not to criticise; so I left the horse in care of the groom of the stables of Windsor Castle, crossed the dark and swift-flowing waters to Detroit in a light skiff hired for the occasion, and wondered all the way at my confidence in a stranger whose face I could not see in the darkness. But horse and wagon were found the next morning well cared for at "Windsor Castle."

I spent Wednesday, the 7th of October, in visiting places of interest in Detroit under the kind guidance of Mr. Moore, of that city. We first went to the wharves in rear of the warehouses of Messrs. Mooney and Foote, and Sheldon, to see three iron cannon that were captured from the British in the naval battle on Lake Erie, where Perry was victorious. They were then put to the more commendable use of posts for fastening vessels to the wharves. One of them was a long twenty-four-pounder, and the other two were thirty-two-pound carronades. After visiting the rooms of the Michigan Historical Society, where I found nothing of interest connected with the subject of my researches, we rode out on the noble Jefferson Avenue to Bloody Run, stopping on the way for a brief interview with the late Honorable B. F. H. Witherell, from whose local sketches quotations have been made in preceding chapters. Judge Witherell kindly placed in my hands much valuable historical material, the fruit of his own researches.

BRITISH CANNON AT DETROIT.

Siege of Detroit by Pontiac.   Fight at Bloody Run.   Origin of the Name.   Elmwood Cemetery.

Bloody Run, as a little stream that comes down gently to the great avenue, after beautifying Elmwood Cemetery, is called, holds a conspicuous place in the annals of Indian wars. The event which gave it its present name (it was formerly known as Parent's Creek) may be thus briefly stated: We have already alluded to the conspiracy of Pontiac in 1763. He had said to some Canadians in council: "I have told you before, and I now tell you again, that when I took up the hatchet it was for your good. This year the English must all perish throughout Canada. The Master of Life commands it." He then told them that they must act with him, or he would be their enemy. They cited the capitulation at Montreal, which transferred Canada to the English, and refused to join him. He pressed forward in his conspiracy without them, and finally invested Detroit with a formidable force.

In July, 1763, Pontiac was encamped behind a swamp, about two miles north of the fort at Detroit. Captain Dalyell,[1] who had ranged with Putnam in Northern New York, arrived with re-enforcements for the fort at the close of the month, and obtained permission of the commandant to attack Pontiac at once. A perfidious Canadian, possessed of the fact, communicated it to Pontiac, and he made ready for an attack.

At a little past midnight,[a] Dalyell marched to Parent's Creek. The darkness, owing to a storm, was intense. Pontiac, forewarned, had posted his warriors all along the route for a mile in front of his camp, so that a thousand eager ears were listening for the approach of the white men. Five hundred dusky warriors were lurking near the rude log bridge, at the mouth of the wild ravine, through which Parent's Creek flowed. Dalyell's advance was just crossing the bridge when terrific yells in front, and a blaze of musketry on the left flank, revealed the presence of the wily foe. One half of the advanced party were slain, and the remainder shrank back appalled. The main body advancing also recoiled. Then came another volley, when the voice of Dalyell in the van inspired his men. With his followers he pushed across the bridge, and charged up the hill; but in the blackness the skulking enemy could not be seen, and his presence was known only by the flash of his guns.

[a] July 31, 1763.

Word now reached Dalyell that the Indians, in large numbers, had gone to cut off his communication with the fort. He sounded a retreat, and in good order pressed toward Detroit, exposed to a most perilous enfilading fire. Day dawned with a thick fog enveloping all objects, and now, for the first time, dim glimpses of the enemy were obtained. They came darting through the mist on flank and rear, and as suddenly disappeared after firing deadly shots upon the English. One of these slew Captain Dalyell while he was attempting to bear off a wounded sergeant. The detachment finally reached the fort, having lost sixty-one of their number in killed and wounded. Most of the slain fell at the bridge. Parent's Creek has ever since been called, from that circumstance, Bloody Run, and the old structure was always called Bloody Bridge. That bridge, as we have before remarked, was much nearer the Detroit than Jefferson Avenue. At the culvert where that avenue crosses Bloody Run stands a huge whitewood tree, delineated on page 261, yet, as we have observed, scarred by the bullets that were fired in that sanguinary encounter more than a hundred years ago.

On leaving Bloody Run we rode up to the Elmwood Cemetery, and made the tour of those hallowed grounds, where taste and industry, aided by natural advantages, have produced one of the most charming places for the repose of mortality with which our country begins to abound. We lingered there for more than an hour, and returned to the city in time for a late dinner, and a visit to the grave of Colonel

---

[1] This name is frequently written Dalzell. James Dalyell had been appointed a lieutenant in the Sixtieth Regiment of Royal Americans in 1756, and obtained the command of a company in the second battalion of the First Regiment of Foot. He was a brave and efficient officer, and had performed important services during the French and Indian war.

Hamtramck, with Mr. R. M. Lyon,[1] to whose kind attentions while in Detroit I was much indebted. The monument that covered that brave soldier's grave is delineated on page 56.

At twilight I called upon the Hon. C. Moran, who, though only a lad of sixteen years, was performing sentinel duty in the fort at Detroit when it was surrendered. He *C. Moran* said he saw General Hull during the heavy cannonading, just before the white flag was run up, sitting upon the grass within the fort apparently unmoved by the terrors of the scene. He related many interesting particulars of occurrences within the fort at that time, and it was with real regret that I felt compelled to make the interview short, for I had made an engagement to call on Mr. Robert M. Eberts, a native of Detroit, and a resident of that place since his birth in 1804. Mr. Eberts was full of interesting reminiscences, and the half hour passed with him was one of real pleasure and profit.[2] Late in the evening I returned to the Russell House, copied the picture of Mackinack on page 267, and early the following morning—a cold, blustering, genuine late-November kind of morning—crossed the Detroit, and proceeded by railway along the borders of Lake St. Clair to Chatham, for the purpose of visiting the battle-ground of the Thames or Moravian Towns. Of that visit I shall write hereafter.

I have said that we went from Chicago to Detroit. These cities bear an intimate relation in the history of the period we are considering, for on the very day[a] when Brock demanded the surrender of Detroit, the little garrison of Fort Dearborn, at Chicago, compelled to leave that post, set out upon their fatal march toward Fort Wayne.

[a] August 15, 1812.

The site of Chicago (spelt by the early settlers Chigagua, Chikakou, and Chikako) was first visited by a white man in 1674, when Father Marquette, a French Jesuit priest, built a cabin there, planted a missionary station, and deposited the seed of the present great city. It lay in the path of explorations by commercial and religious adventurers, one seeking trade, the other desiring to give the light of the Gospel to the heathen of the New World. It was visited in turn by Marquette, Allouez, La Salle, Durantaye, La Hontan, De St. Come, Gravier, Charlevoix, and others of less note. In 1685 Durantaye built a fort where, eleven years before, Marquette erected his cabin. How long it remained a missionary station it is difficult now to determine.[3]

"The first white man who settled here was a negro," the Indians of Chicago said, with great simplicity. He was a mulatto from St. Domingo, named Jean Baptiste Point au Sable, who found his way to that far-off wilderness in the year 1796. He did not remain long, and the improvements which he had commenced fell into the hands of John Kinzie, a native of Quebec, and for nearly twenty years the only white inhabitant of Northern Illinois, with the exception of a few American soldiers. He was an enterprising trader with the Indians, and in 1804 made Chicago his home.

---

[1] Mr. Lyon was a Pension and Bounty Land Agent in Detroit. He informed me that he had in his possession complete copies of all army rolls of the War of 1812 for Michigan, Ohio, New York, and other states, besides other record evidence of service. He had also in his possession muster-rolls of the Black Hawk, Patriot, and Mexican wars. He was probably better prepared, by the amount of positive information in his possession, and the devotion of undivided attention to the subject, to serve claimants for pensions and bounties than any other man west of Lake Erie.

[2] Positive statements made to me by Mr. Eberts and Judge Moran, when combined, form a curious subject for speculation. Mr. Eberts assured me that General Brock sent a hollow silver bullet (repeating Sir Henry Clinton's famous act in 1777) from Fort George to Major Muir at Fort Malden, containing a message, and that the major sent it by Richard Eberts (whom I saw at Chatham), brother of my informant, to Colonel Askin, a British officer residing at Strahan in Canada. Askin's son-in-law, Colonel Brush, was then one of General Hull's aids-de-camp, and it was believed, after the surrender, that the bullet contained a communication from Brock to Brush. Judge Moran told me that on one occasion his uncle was sent by Colonel Brush to Askin, his father-in-law, with a package, and that he was made a prisoner, and detained in Canada for some time. The bullet and the package seem to have some connection in the matter.

[3] Chicagou was the Indian name of the Illinois River, at the mouth of which the city stands. In the language of the Pottawatomies, who inhabited that region, the name signifies a skunk or pole-cat—some say the wild onion, both of which emit unpleasant odors, and were abundant there. It is said that the Pottawatomies wore garters of the dried skunk's skin.—*Sketch of the Early History of Chicago,* by John Gilmartin Shea.

During the two previous years the United States government had erected a stockade there, and on the 4th of July of that year it was formally named Fort Dearborn, in honor of the then Secretary of War. It had a block-house at each of two angles on the southern side, a sally-port and covered way on the north side, that led down to the river, for the double purpose of providing a means of escape and for receiving water during a siege, and was strongly picketed.[1] It stood upon a little rise of

KINZIE MANSION AND FORT DEARBORN.

ground on the south bank of the Chicago River, about half a mile from its mouth. On the north bank of that stream, directly opposite the fort, Mr. Kinzie enlarged into a spacious but very modest mansion the house built by Jean Baptiste and his immediate successor, Le Mai. Within an inclosed green in front he planted some Lombardy poplars, and in the rear was a fine garden and growing orchard. There he lived with his young family for eight years, isolated from society excepting that of the military, but enjoying great peace, with every necessary and many of the luxuries of life, and possessing the confidence and esteem of the surrounding Indians.

The peacefulness of the current of life at Chicago was interrupted in the spring of 1812. The garrison was commanded by Captain Nathan Heald,[2] assisted by Lieutenant Linai T. Helm,[3] a son-in-law of Mrs. Kinzie, and Ensign George Ronan. The surgeon was Dr. Van Voorhees. The garrison consisted of fifty-four men. The only other residents of the post, at the time of the events we are about to consider, were Mr. Kinzie and his family, the wives of Captain Heald and Lieutenant Helm and of some of the soldiers, and a few Canadian *voyageurs*, with their wives and children. The officers and their troops, like Mr. Kinzie, were on the most friendly terms with

---

[1] Fort Dearborn was erected under the superintendence of Major John Whistler, who was also the overseer of the construction of Fort Wayne, at the forks of the Maumee. Major Whistler was an Englishman. He was taken prisoner with Burgoyne at Saratoga in 1777, and remained in the United States. He settled in Maryland, and in 1790-91 joined the troops under General St. Clair, and was with him at his defeat on the Miami in November, 1791, where he was acting as adjutant and was wounded. He was commissioned an ensign of the First Infantry in the spring of 1792, and in the autumn was made a lieutenant in the first sub-legion. He passed through other grades of service until, on the 10th of July, 1812, he was breveted a major. He was disbanded in 1815, and three years afterward became military storekeeper at St. Louis. He died at Belle Fontaine, Missouri, in 1827.

In building Fort Dearborn, Major Whistler had no oxen, and the timber was all dragged to the spot by the soldiers. He worked so economically that the fort, Colonel Johnston, of Dayton (who furnished him with some materials from Fort Wayne), told me, did not cost the government over fifty dollars. For a while the garrison could get no corn, and Whistler and his men subsisted on acorns.

[2] Heald, who was a native of Massachusetts, joined the army as ensign in the spring of 1799. He became a first lieutenant in November of the same year. In January, 1807, he was commissioned a captain, and held that office until the 26th of August, 1812, when, on account of his good conduct at Chicago, he was promoted to major. He was disbanded in 1815.

[3] Helm, of Kentucky, entered the army as ensign in December, 1807, and became second lieutenant the following year. He was promoted to first lieutenant in January, 1813, and to captain in April, 1814. He resigned in September following.

the Pottawatomies and Winnebagoes, the principal tribes in that neighborhood; yet they could not win them from their decided attachment to the British, from whom, at Fort Malden, they annually received large presents as bribes to secure their alliance. After the battle of Tippecanoe, the previous autumn,[a] in which portions of their tribes were engaged, it had been observed that the leading chiefs became sullen, and suspicions of contemplated hostility sometimes clouded the minds of Heald and his command. One day in the spring of 1812, Nau-non-gee and a companion, both of the Calumet band, were at Fort Dearborn. When passing through the quarters, they observed Mrs. Heald[1] and Mrs. Helm[2] playing at battledore. Turning to Mr. Griffith, the interpreter, Nau-non-gee said: "The white chiefs' wives are amusing themselves very much; it will not be long before they are living in our corn-fields." The terrible significance of these words, then hidden, was made apparent a few weeks later.

[a] November, 1811.

On the evening of the 7th of April, 1812, Mr. Kinzie's children were dancing before the fire to the music of their father's violin, when their mother came rushing wildly in, pale with terror, and exclaiming, "The Indians! the Indians!" "What? where?" exclaimed Mr. Kinzie, in response. "Up at Lee's, killing and scalping!" gasped the affrighted mother. It seems that the alarm had been given by a man and boy,[3] who had been fleeing from destruction down the opposite side of the river, and had shouted the terrible fact to the family of Mr. Burns, half a mile above the fort, where Mrs. Kinzie was in attendance upon a newly-made mother. Not a moment was to be lost. Mr. Kinzie immediately hurried his family into two old *pirogues*[4] moored in front of his house, and conveyed them across the river to the fort. At the same time the intrepid Ensign Ronan, with six men, started up the river in a scow to save the Burns family; and a cannon was fired to give notice of danger to a party of soldiers who had gone up the river to catch fish. Mrs. Burns, with an infant not a day old,[5] and the rest of her family, were taken in safety to the fort; and the absent soldiers, who were two miles above Lee's, made their way back in the darkness, discovering on their way the bodies of murdered and scalped persons at Lee's Place. These were obtained the next day, and were buried near the fort. It was afterward ascertained that the savage scalping-party were Winnebagoes, from Rock River, who had come with the intention of destroying every white person outside of the fort. The noise of the cannon frightened them, and they fled back to their homes.

---

[1] Rebecca Heald was a daughter of General Samuel Wells, of Kentucky (one of the heroes of Tippecanoe), and niece of Captain William Wells, who will appear prominently in our narrative. She was with her uncle at Fort Wayne two or three years before the war, where Captain Heald became acquainted with her. Their acquaintance ripened into mutual attachment. He taught her the use of the rifle, in which she became very expert. They were married in 1810 or 1811, and she accompanied her husband to Fort Dearborn.

[2] Mrs. Helm was a daughter of Colonel M'Killup, a British officer attached to one of the companies who were stationed at Fort Miami, on the Maumee, at the time of Wayne's appearance there in 1794. While reconnoitring one night, he was mistaken for an enemy, and mortally wounded. His widow married Mr. Kinzie, with whom, and this daughter, she removed to Chicago in 1803. Here the daughter, at the age of eighteen years, married Lieutenant Helm, of Kentucky, in 1811. She died suddenly at Waterville, in Michigan, in 1844.—*Pioneer Women of the West*, by Mrs. E. F. Ellet.

[3] These were a discharged soldier and a son of Mr. Lee, who lived near the fort, and cultivated a farm about three miles up the south branch of the Chicago River, in the vicinity of the point where Halstead Street now crosses that stream. See map on page 266. This was known as Lee's Place. Lee and all his family, except Mrs. Lee and her infant, perished in the massacre at Chicago on the 15th of August.

[4] *Pirogue*, or *piragua*, originally meant a canoe formed out of the trunk of a tree, or two canoes united. A vessel used in this country as a narrow ferry-boat, carrying two masts and a lee-board, is called *piragua*.

[5] The main facts of this narrative of affairs at Chicago, in 1812, are derived from a most interesting account from the pen of Mrs. John H. Kinzie, of Chicago, published in pamphlet form in 1844, and repeated substantially in a charming history of personal adventures on the northwestern frontier, by the same accomplished lady, in a volume published in 1856, entitled, *Wau-bun, the "Early Day" in the Northwest*. Mrs. Kinzie is a daughter-in-law of Mr. John Kinzie, the trader just mentioned, and much of the narrative of the events which we are considering she received from Mrs. Helm, an actor in the events. Of this infant of Mrs. Burns she gives a few words of interesting narrative. The mother and child were made prisoners at Chicago by a chief, and carried to his village. His attentions to them aroused the jealousy of his spouse, and one day she spitefully struck the infant with a tomahawk with the intention of killing it. The blow took off some of the scalp. "Thirty-two years after this," says Mrs. Kinzie, "as I was on a journey to Chicago in the steamer Uncle Sam, a young woman, hearing my name, introduced herself to me, and, raising the hair from her forehead, showed me the mark of the tomahawk which had so nearly been fatal to her."—*Wau-bun*, page 244.

| Order for the Evacuation of Chicago. | Danger in the Movement. | The Commandant warned against it. |

All of the inhabitants of Chicago not belonging to the garrison now took refuge in the Agency House, which stood upon the esplanade, about twenty rods west from the fort, on the site of the present light-house, and there intrenched themselves. This was an old-fashioned log house, with a passage running through the centre, and piazzas extending the whole length of the building, front and rear. These were planked up. Port-holes were cut in the barricade, and sentinels were posted there every night. For some time hostile Indians hovered around the post and committed depredations; but at last they disappeared, and for several weeks the dwellers at Chicago experienced no alarm.

Toward the evening of the 7th of August,[a] Win-ne-meg, or The Catfish, a friendly Pottawatomie chief, who was intimate with Mr. Kinzie, came to Chicago from Fort Wayne as the bearer of a dispatch from General Hull to Captain Heald, in which the former announced his arrival at Detroit with an army, the declaration of war, the invasion of Canada, and the loss of Mackinack. It also conveyed an order to Captain Heald to evacuate Fort Dearborn, if practicable, and to distribute, in that event, "all the United States property contained in the fort, and in the government factory or agency, among the Indians in the neighborhood." This was doubtless intended to be a peace-offering to the savages, to prevent their joining the British, then menacing Detroit. [a] 1812.

Win-ne-meg, who knew the purport of the order, begged Mr. Kinzie to advise Captain Heald not to evacuate the fort, or the movement would be difficult and dangerous. The Indians had already received information from Tecumtha of the disasters to the American arms, and the withdrawal of Hull's army from Canada, and were becoming daily more restless and insolent. Heald had an ample supply of ammunition and provisions for six months; why not hold out until relief could be sent from the southward? Win-ne-meg farther urged that, if Captain Heald should resolve to evacuate, it should be done immediately, before the Indians should be informed of the order, or could prepare for formidable resistance. "Leave the fort and stores as they are," he said, "and let them make distributions for themselves; and while the Indians are engaged in that business, the white people may make their way in safety to Fort Wayne."

Mr. Kinzie readily perceived the wisdom of Win-ne-meg's advice, and so did Captain Heald's officers, but the commander resolved to obey Hull's order strictly as to evacuation and the distribution of the public property. He caused that order to be read to the troops on the morning of the 8th,[b] and then assumed the whole responsibility. His officers expected to be summoned to a council, but were disappointed. Toward evening they called upon the commander, and, when informed of his determination, they remonstrated with him. The march, they said, must necessarily be slow, on account of the women and children and infirm persons, and therefore, under the circumstances, extremely perilous. Hull's order, they said, left it to the discretion of the commander to go or to stay; and they thought it much better to strengthen the fort, defy the savages, and endure a siege until relief should reach them. Heald argued in reply that special orders had been issued by the War Department that no post should be surrendered without battle having been given by the assailed, and that his force was totally inadequate to an engagement with the Indians. He should expect the censure of his government, he said, if he remained; and having full confidence in the professions of friendship of many of the chiefs about him, he should call them together, make the required distribution, and take up his march for Fort Wayne. After that his officers had no more communications with him on the subject. The Indians became more unruly every hour, and yet Heald, with fatal procrastination, postponed the assembling of the savages for two or three days. They finally met near the fort on the afternoon of the 12th,[c] and there the commander held a farewell council with them. [b] August. [c] August.

U

Heald invited the officers to join him in the council, but they refused. They had received intimations that treachery was designed—that the Indians intended to murder them in the council-circle, and then destroy the inmates of the fort. The officers remained within the pickets, and, opening the port of one of the block-houses so as to expose the cannon pointed directly upon the group in council, they secured the safety of Captain Heald. The Indians were intimidated by the menacing monster, and accepted Heald's offers with many protestations of friendship. He agreed to distribute among them not only the goods in the public store—blankets, broadcloths, calicoes, paints, etc.—but also the arms, ammunition, and provisions not necessary for the use of the garrison on its march. It was stipulated that the distribution should take place the next day, soon after which the garrison and white inhabitants would leave the works. The Pottawatomies agreed, on their part, to furnish a proper escort for them through the wilderness to Fort Wayne, on condition of being liberally rewarded on their arrival there.

When the result of the council was made known, Mr. Kinzie warmly remonstrated with Captain Heald. He knew the Indians well, and their weakness in the presence of great temptations to do wrong. He begged the commander not to confide in their promises at a moment so inauspicious for faithfulness to treaties. He especially entreated him not to place in their hands arms and ammunition, for it would fearfully increase their power to carry on those murderous raids which for months had spread terror throughout the frontier settlements. Heald perceived his folly, and resolved to violate the treaty so far as arms and ammunition were concerned.

On that very evening, when the chiefs of the council seemed most friendly, a circumstance occurred which should have made Captain Heald shut his gates to his dusky neighbors, and resolve not to leave the fort. Black Partridge, a hitherto friendly chief, and a man of much influence, came quietly to the commander and said: "Father, I come to deliver to you the medal I wear. It was given me by the Americans,

THE BLACK PARTRIDGE'S MEDAL.

and I have long worn it in token of our mutual friendship. But our young men are resolved to imbrue their hands in the blood of the white people. I can not restrain them, and I will not wear a token of peace while I am compelled to act as an enemy."[1] This solemn and authentic warning was strangely unheeded.

---

[1] This medal, as I have been informed, was received by the Black Partridge at the treaty of Fort Wayne, on the 30th of September, 1809, mentioned on page 190. It was of silver. The engraving is the exact size of the original. It was copied from one in the possession of the widow of General Jacob Brown, of Brownsville, New York, where I saw it in

Another Warning.   Arms, Powder, and Whisky destroyed.   Arrival of Re-enforcements.   Too late.

The morning of the 13th was bright and cool. The Indians assembled in great numbers to receive their presents. Nothing but the goods in the store were distributed that day; and in the evening the Black Partridge said to Mr. Griffith, the interpreter, "Linden birds have been singing in my ears to-day; be careful on the march you are going to take." This was another solemn warning, and it was communicated to Captain Heald. It, too, was unheeded; and at midnight, when the sentinels were all posted and the Indians were in their camps, a portion of the powder and liquor in the fort was cast into a well near the sally-port, and the remainder into a canal that came up from the river far under the covered way. The muskets not reserved for the garrison were broken up, and these, with shot, bullets, flints, gun-screws, and every thing else pertaining to fire-arms, were also thrown into the well. A large quantity of alcohol belonging to Mr. Kinzie was poured into the river, and before morning the destruction was complete. But the work had not been done in secret. The night was dark, and vigilant Indians had crept to the fort as noiselessly as serpents, and their quick senses had perceived the destruction of what, under the treaty, they claimed as their own. In the morning the work of the night was made more manifest. The powder was seen floating upon the surface of the river, and the sluggish water had been converted by the whisky and the alcohol into "strong grog," as an eye-witness remarked. Complaints and threatenings were loud among the savages because of this breach of faith;[1] and the dwellers in the fort were impressed with a dreadful sense of impending destruction, when the brave Captain Wells, Mrs. Heald's uncle, and adopted son of the Little Turtle, was discovered upon the Indian trail near the Sand Hills, on the border of the lake not far distant, with a band of mounted Miamis, of whose tribe he was a chief.[2] He had heard at Fort Wayne of the orders of Hull to evacuate Fort Dearborn, and, being fully aware of the hostilities of the Pottawatomies, he had made a rapid march across the country to re-enforce Captain Heald, assist in defending the fort, or prevent his exposure to certain destruction by an attempt to reach the head of the Maumee. But he was too late. All means for maintaining a siege had been destroyed a few hours before, and every preparation had been made for leaving the post the next day.

When the morning of the 15th arrived, there were positive indications that the Indians intended to massacre all the white people. They were overwhelming in numbers, and held the fate of the devoted band in their grasp. When, at nine o'clock, the appointed hour, the gate was thrown open, and the march commenced, it was like a funeral procession. The band struck up the Dead March in Saul. Captain Wells,

---

the summer of 1860. She also had a smaller medal of the same kind, struck for the same occasion. These were distributed among the inferior chiefs.

[1] The celebrated chief Black Hawk, who was among the Indians at the time of the massacre at Chicago, declared that, had the treaty been fully carried out, the white people would not have been attacked. And such has been the general impression of students. But the conduct of Black Partridge before the powder and liquor were destroyed disproves this. No doubt the massacre had been determined on as soon as the order for the evacuation was made known to the Indians.

[2] When in Toledo, Ohio, in the autumn of 1860, I spent an hour pleasantly and profitably with General John E. Hunt, a brother-in-law of General Cass, whose early life was spent among the stirring scenes of the frontier. He was in the fort at Detroit when it was surrendered. He knew Captain William Wells, and from his lips the substance of the following brief notice was communicated: When a child, Wells was living with his relative, Hon. Nathaniel Pope, of Kentucky, where he was stolen by a band of Miami Indians and taken to the Maumee country. He was adopted by Little Turtle, the eminent Miami chief. He was rescued by his relatives, but had become so attached to his Indian friends and their mode of life that he returned to them. He was compelled to go upon the war-path when Harrison invaded that region, and was with the Indians who defeated St. Clair. No doubt he swayed the mind of Little Turtle when Wayne appeared in that region, for that chief was favorable to peace with the great Blacksnake, as they called him. Wells saw clearly the weakness of the Indians; and one day, while in the woods, he suddenly informed his foster-father that he should leave him, to join the army of Wayne. "I now leave your nation for my own people," said Wells. "We have long been friends. We are friends yet, until the sun reaches there," pointing to a place in the heavens. "From that time we are enemies. Then, if you wish to kill me, you may; if I want to kill you, I may." At the hour named, Wells crossed the Maumee, and, asking the direction toward Wayne's army, disappeared in the forest. In Wayne's army he commanded a company of the spies. When peace was restored, after the treaty of Greenville, in 1795, he and the Little Turtle became good friends. He married the Little Turtle's sister, a Miami girl, and became a chief of that nation. One of his daughters was the wife of Judge Wolcott, of Maumee City, Ohio. Wells was Indian Agent at Fort Wayne when the War of 1812 broke out. He had lived there since 1804.

with his face blackened with wet gunpowder in token of his impending fate, took the lead with his friendly Miamis, followed by Captain Heald, and his heroic wife by his side. Mr. Kinzie accompanied them, hoping, by his personal influence, to soften, if he could not avert, the impending blow. His family were left in a boat, in charge of a friendly Indian, to be conveyed around the head of the lake to Kinzie's trading station, on the site of the present village of Niles, in Michigan.

Slowly the procession moved along the lake shore until they came to the Sand Hills, between the prairie and the beach, when the escort of Pottawatomies, about five hundred in number, under The Black-bird, filed to the right, and placed those hills between themselves and the white people. Wells and his Miamis had kept in the advance; suddenly they came dashing back, the leader shouting, "They are about to attack us: form, instantly!" These startling words were scarcely uttered when a storm of bullets came from the Sand Hills, but without serious effect. The treacherous and cowardly Pottawatomies had made those hillocks their cover for a murderous attack. The troops, hastily brought into line, charged up the bank, when one of their number, a white-haired man of seventy years, fell dead from his horse, the first victim. The Indians were driven back, and the battle was waged on the open prairie between fifty-four soldiers, twelve civilians, and three or four women, against about five hundred Indian warriors. Of course, the conflict was hopeless on the part of the white people; but they resolved to make the butchers pay dearly for every life which they destroyed.[1]

The cowardly Miamis fled at the first onset. Their chief rode up to the Pottawatomies, charged them with perfidy, and, brandishing his glittering tomahawk, declared that he would be the first to lead Americans to punish them. He then wheeled and dashed after his fugitive companions, who were scurrying over the prairie as if the Evil Spirit was at their heels.

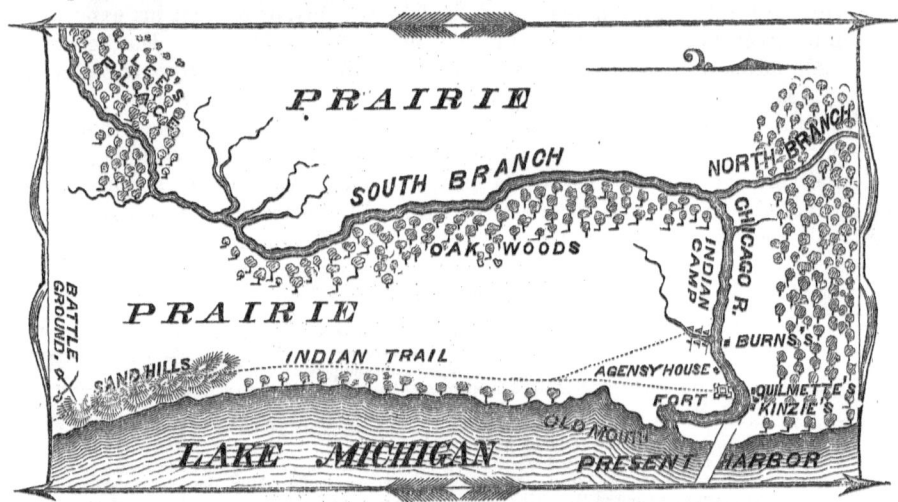

SITE OF CHICAGO AND OF EVENTS THERE IN 1812.

The conflict was short, desperate, and bloody. Two thirds of the white people were slain or wounded, and all the horses, provisions, and baggage were lost. Only twenty-eight strong men remained to brave the fury of about five hundred Indians, who had lost but fifteen in the conflict. The devoted band had succeeded in breaking through the ranks of the assassins, who gave way in front and rallied on the flank,

---

[1] The place of conflict at the Sand Hills was on the site of a lot (vacant when I visited it in 1860) in the rear of the house of the late Widow Clark, between Indiana and Michigan Avenues, just south of North Street, and about fifty rods from the lake.

and gained a slight eminence on the prairie near a grove called The Oak Woods. The savages did not pursue. They gathered upon the Sand Hills in consultation, and gave signs of willingness to parley. Farther conflict with them would be rashness; so Captain Heald, accompanied by Perish Le Clerc, a half-breed boy in Mr. Kinzie's service, went forward, met Black-bird on the open prairie, and arranged terms for a surrender. It was agreed that all the arms should be given up to Black-bird, and that the survivors should become prisoners of war, to be exchanged for ransoms as soon as practicable. With this understanding, captured and captors all started for the Indian encampment near the fort.[1]

So overwhelming was the savage force at the Sand Hills, that the conflict, after the first desperate charge, became an exhibition of individual prowess—a life-and-death struggle, in which no one could render any assistance to his neighbor, for all were principals. In this conflict women bore a conspicuous part. All fought gallantly so long as strength permitted them. The brave Ensign Ronan wielded his weapon even when falling upon his knees because of loss of blood.[2] Captain Wells displayed the greatest coolness and gallantry. He was by the side of his niece when the conflict began. "We have not the slightest chance for life," he said. "We must part, to meet no more in this world; God bless you." With these words, he dashed forward with the rest. In the midst of the fight he saw a young warrior, painted like a demon, climb into a wagon in which were twelve children of the white people, and tomahawk them all! Forgetting his own immediate danger, Wells exclaimed, "If that is their game, butchering women and children, I'll kill too." He instantly dashed toward the Indian camp, where they had left their squaws and little ones, hotly pursued by swift-footed young warriors, who sent many a rifle ball after him. He lay close to his horse's neck, and turned and fired occasionally upon his pursuers. When he had got almost beyond the range of their rifles, a ball killed his horse and wounded himself severely in the leg. The young savages rushed forward with a demoniac yell to make him a prisoner and reserve him for the torture, for he was to them an arch offender. His friends Win-ne-meg and Wau-ban-see vainly attempted to save him from his fate. He knew the temper and the practices of the savages well, and resolved not to be made a captive. He taunted them with the most insulting epithets to provoke them to kill him instantly. At length he called one of the fiery young warriors (Per-so-tum) a *squaw*, which so enraged him that he killed Wells instantly with a tomahawk, jumped upon his body, cut out his heart, and ate a portion of the warm and half-palpitating morsel with savage delight.[3]

The wife of Captain Heald, who was expert with the rifle and an excellent equestrian, deported herself bravely. She received severe wounds. Faint and bleeding, she managed to keep the saddle. A savage raised his tomahawk to kill her, when she looked him full in the face, and, with a sweet, melancholy smile, said, in the Indian tongue, "Surely you will not kill a squaw!" The appeal was effectual. The arm of the savage fell, and the life of the heroic woman was saved. Mrs. Helm, the stepdaughter of Mr. Kinzie, had a severe personal encounter with a stalwart young Indian, who attempted to tomahawk her. She sprang on one side, and received the blow intended for her head upon her shoulder, and at the same instant she seized the savage around the neck, and endeavored to get hold of his scalping-knife, which hung in a sheath upon his breast. While thus struggling, she was dragged from her antag-

---

[1] Captain Heald's dispatch to Adjutant General Cushing, October 23, 1812.
[2] Mrs. Helm speaks of the terror of Dr. Van Voorhees at that time. He was badly wounded. His horse had been shot under him. "Do you think," he said to Mrs. Helm, "they will take our lives?" and then talked of offering a large ransom for existence. She advised him not to think of life, but of inevitable death. "Oh!" he exclaimed, "I can not die. I am not fit to die. If I had only a short time to prepare for it—death is awful!" She pointed to the falling Ronan, and said, "Look at that man! at least he dies like a soldier." "Yes," gasped the terrified surgeon, "but he has no terror of the future—he is an unbeliever!" At that moment Mrs. Helm had a deadly struggle with a young Indian, and a moment afterward she saw the dead body of the surgeon. He had been slain by a tomahawk.
[3] Statement of Colonel John Johnston, of Dayton, to the author.

onist by another Indian, who bore her, spite of her desperate resistance, to the margin of the lake, and plunged her in, at the same time, to her astonishment, holding her so that she would not drown. She soon perceived that she was held by a friendly hand. It was that of the Black Partridge who had saved her. When the firing ceased and the capitulation was concluded, he conducted her to the prairie, where she met her father, and heard that her husband was safe. Bleeding and suffering, she was conducted to the Indian camp by the Black Partridge and Per-so-tum, the latter carrying in his hand a scalp which she knew to be that of Captain Wells by the black ribbon that bound the queue.

The wife of a soldier named Corbord, believing that all prisoners were reserved for torture, fought desperately, and suffered herself to be literally cut in pieces rather than surrender. The wife of Sergeant Holt, who was badly wounded in his neck at the beginning of the engagement, received from him his sword, and behaved as bravely as an Amazon. She was a large and powerful woman, and rode a fine, high-spirited horse, which the Indians coveted. Several of them attacked her with the butts of their guns, for the purpose of dismounting her, but she used her sword so skillfully that she foiled them. She suddenly wheeled her horse and dashed over the prairie, followed by a large number, who shouted, "The brave woman! the brave woman! don't hurt her!" They finally overtook her, and, while two or three were engaging her in front, a powerful savage seized her by her neck, and dragged her backward to the ground. The horse and woman became prizes. The latter was afterward ransomed.

When the captives were taken to the Indian camp a new scene of horrors was opened. The wounded, according to the Indians' interpretation of the capitulation, were not included in the terms of the surrender. Proctor had offered a liberal sum for scalps delivered at Malden; so, nearly all the wounded men were killed, and the value of British bounty, such as is sometimes offered for the destruction of wolves, was taken from each head.[1] In this tragedy Mrs. Heald played a part, but fortunately escaped scalping. In order to save her fine horse, the Indians had aimed at the rider. Seven bullets took effect upon her person. Her captor, who was about to slay her upon the battle-field, as we have seen, left her in the saddle, and led the horse toward the camp. When in sight of the fort his acquisitiveness overpowered his gallantry, and he was taking her bonnet from her head in order to scalp her, when she was discovered by Mrs. Kinzie, who was yet sitting in the boat, and who had heard the tumult of the conflict, but without any intimation of the result until she saw the wounded woman in the hands of her savage captive. "Run! run, Chandonnai!" exclaimed Mrs. Kinzie to one of her husband's clerks, who was standing on the beach. "That is Mrs. Heald. He is going to kill her! Take that mule, and offer it as a ransom." Chandonnai promptly obeyed, and increased the bribe by offering in addition two bottles of whisky. These were worth more than Proctor's bounty, and Mrs. Heald was released. She was placed in Mrs. Kinzie's boat, and there concealed from the prying eyes of other scalp-hunters.

Toward evening the family of Mr. Kinzie[2] were allowed to return to their own

---

[1] A writer, signing his communication "*An Officer*," under date of "Buffalo, March 8, 1813," speaks of the arrival there of Mrs. Helm, and her narrative of sufferings at and after the massacre at Chicago. "She knows the fact," he says, "that Colonel Proctor, the British commander at Malden, bought the scalps of our murdered garrison at Chicago, and, thanks to her noble spirit, she boldly charged him with the infamy in his own house." This independence was probably the cause of the cruel treatment which she and her husband received at the hands of Proctor. She and her husband, after several weeks of captivity among the Indians, were united at Detroit, where Proctor caused them both to be arrested, and sent on horseback, in the dead of a Canadian winter, across the wilderness to Fort George, on the Niagara frontier. The writer farther says concerning the statements of Mrs. Heald, "She knows, from the tribe with whom she was a prisoner, and who were the perpetrators of those murders, that they intended to remain true, but that *they received orders* from the British to cut off our garrison whom they were to escort."—Niles's *Weekly Register*, April 3, 1813.

[2] John Kinzie, who bore so conspicuous a part in the events we are considering, was born in Quebec, in 1763, and was the only offspring of his mother's second marriage. His father died while he was an infant, and his mother married a third time, and with her husband (Mr. Forsythe) removed to the city of New York. At the age of ten years

house, where they were greeted by the friendly Black Partridge. Mrs. Helm was placed in the house of Ouilmette, a Frenchman, by the same friendly hand. But these and all the other prisoners were exposed to great jeopardy by the arrival of a band of fierce Pottawatomies from the Wabash, who yearned for blood and plunder. They searched the houses for prisoners with keen vision, and when no farther concealment and safety seemed possible, some friendly Indians arrived, and so turned the tide of affairs that the Wabash savages were ashamed to own their blood-thirsty intentions.[1]

In this terrible tragedy in the wilderness fifty-five years ago, twelve children, all the masculine civilians but Mr. Kinzie and his sons, Captain Wells, Surgeon Van Voorhees,[2] Ensign Ronan, and twenty-six private soldiers, were murdered. The prisoners were divided among the captors,[3] and were finally reunited, or restored to their friends and families. A few of them have survived until our day. Mrs. Rebecca Heald died at the St. Charles Mission, in Missouri, in the year 1860. Major John H. Kinzie, of Chicago (husband of the writer of "Wau-bun"), his brother Major Robert A. Kinzie, and Mrs. Hunter, wife of General David Hunter, of the National Army, are [1867] surviving children of Mr. Kinzie, and were with their mother in the boat. The brothers were both officers of Volunteers during the late Civil War; and a most promising son of John Kinzie became a martyr for his country in that war. Paul de Garmo, another survivor, was living at Maumee City, Ohio, when I visited that place in 1860, but I was not aware of the fact until after I had left. Jack Smith, a sailor on the lakes, who was a drummer-boy at the time, was alive within the last two or three years. It is believed that no other survivors of the massacre are now [1867] living.

On the morning after the massacre the fort was burned by the Indians, and Chicago remained a desolation for about four years. In 1816 the Pottawatomies ceded to the United States all the land on which Chicago now stands, when the fort was rebuilt on a somewhat more extended scale, and the bones of the massacred were collected and buried. One of the block-houses of the new fort remained, near the bank of the river, until 1856, when it was demolished. The view here given (by whom

---

young Kinzie was placed in a school in Williamsburg, near Long Island. One day he made his way to the North River, got on board of an Albany sloop, and started for Quebec. Fortunately for him, he found a passenger who was on his way to that city, who took charge of him. At Quebec the boy apprenticed himself to a silversmith. Three years afterward, his family, having returned to Canada for the purpose of moving to Detroit, discovered him. They had supposed him lost forever. When he grew up he loved the wilds. He became a trader, and lived most of the time on the frontier and among the Indians. He established trading-houses. He married the widow of a British officer in 1800, and settled at Chicago in 1804. There he became a captain in 1812, and in January, 1813, joined his family at Detroit. There he was badly treated by General Proctor, who cast him into prison at Malden. He was finally sent to Quebec, to be forwarded to England, for what purpose was never known. The vessel in which he sailed was compelled to put back, when he was released and returned to Detroit, where he found General Harris in possession. He and his family returned to Chicago in 1816, when the fort was rebuilt. Mr. Kinzie died there on the 6th of January, 1828, at the age of sixty-five years. This was two years before the town of Chicago was laid out into lots by commissioners appointed by the state.

[1] The leader of the friendly party was Billy Caldwell, a half-breed and a chief. The Black Partridge told him of the evident intentions of the Wabash Indians. They had blackened their faces, and were then seated sullenly in Mr. Kinzie's parlor, preparatory to a general massacre of all the remaining white people. Billy went in, took off his accoutrements, and said, in a careless way, "How now, my friends! A good day to you. I was told there were enemies here, but I am glad to find only friends. Why have you blackened your faces? Is it that you are mourning for your friends lost in battle? Or is it that you are fasting? If so, ask our friend here (Mr. Kinzie), and he will give you to eat. He is the Indian's friend, and never yet refused them what they had need of." The hostile savages were surprised and overwhelmed with shame.—Mrs. Kinzie's *Wau-bun*, page 238.

[2] John Cooper, M.D., of Poughkeepsie, New York, was the immediate predecessor of Doctor Van Voorhees at Fort Dearborn. They were natives of the same town (Fishkill, Dutchess County, New York) and class-mates. Van Voorhees was a young man of great powers. Dr. Cooper left the fort in 1811, tendered his resignation, and left the army. He died at Poughkeepsie in 1863, where he had been for many years the oldest medical practitioner in the place.

[3] Captain Heald was quite severely wounded and made a prisoner by an Indian from the Kankakee, who had a strong personal regard for him, but who, on seeing the feeble state of Mrs. Heald, released him and allowed him to accompany her to the mouth of the St. Joseph's, in Michigan. On returning to his village, the Indian found himself an object of great dissatisfaction because he had released his prisoner; so he resolved to go to St. Joseph and reclaim him. Friendly Indians gave Heald warning, and he and his wife went to far-off Mackinack in an open boat, and surrendered themselves to the British commander there as prisoners of war. This kept them out of the hands of the savages.—*Wau-bun*, page 243.

BLOCK-HOUSE AT CHICAGO.

sketched I know not) was drawn not long before the demolition. On the left of the picture is seen the light-house and a steam-boat in the Chicago River, above the Rush Street bridge, at the termination and junction of Wabash Avenue and River Street. On the right, across the river, not far from the site of the Kinzie mansion, is seen the hotel called the Lake House, and in the foreground, on the right, is seen two venerable trees, one of which was standing on the vacant lot where the block-house was when I visited Chicago in 1860. At that time I had the pleasure of meeting Mrs. John H. Kinzie, the author of *Wau-bun*, at her own house, and heard from her own lips interesting reminiscences of Chicago in 1831, the year after state commissioners laid it out into town lots. To Mrs. Kinzie's skillful pencil we are indebted for the sketch of Fort Dearborn and the Kinzie mansion printed on page 303; also for the map on page 308. Although she was a woman of about middle age, she and her husband were the "oldest inhabitants" of Chicago. They are the only persons now [1867] living there who were residents of Chicago in 1831, within the present city limits. There were two settlers living without the city limits in 1860 who resided on the same spot in 1831. These were Archie Clybourn and John Clack, the latter generally known as "Old Hunter Clack." They were originally from the Kanawha Valley, in Virginia. These had been witnesses of its marvelous growth from a stockade fort in the wilderness, and a few rude houses, to a city of almost two hundred thousand inhabitants in the course of only thirty-six years! Chicago is now the great entrepôt for the grain of the teeming Northwest—the central point to which about a dozen important railways converge[1]—and yet there, only thirty-six years ago, Mrs. Kinzie and her family, during a whole winter, were compelled to use the greatest economy for fear they might exhaust their slender stock of flour and meal before it could be replenished from "below!" At the same time, the Indians of that neighborhood were famishing—"dying in companies from mere destitution. . . . . . Soup made from the bark of the slippery elm, or stewed acorns, was the only food that many had subsisted on for weeks."[2]

---

[1] The Michigan Central; the Michigan Southern and Northern Indiana; the Pittsburg, Fort Wayne, and Chicago; the Chicago branch of the Illinois Central; the St. Louis, Alton, and Chicago; the Chicago and Rock Island; the Illinois Grand Trunk; the Chicago, Fulton, and Iowa; the Galena, Chicago, and Union; the Chicago and Northwestern; and the Chicago and Milwaukee, with numerous tributaries.

[2] For a full description of Chicago in 1831, the reader is referred to the seventeenth chapter of Mrs. Kenzie's *Wau-bun*.

Chicago a Generation ago.   Its historical Localities.   Tecumtha's Hopes revived.   Designs against Fort Wayne.

The city of Chicago now covers the entire theatre of the events just described. The old channel of the river, from the fort to its mouth, has been filled or covered, and the present harbor constructed. The Sand Hills have been leveled; and where the battle on the prairie—the struggles of brave warriors, and the chase and murder of Wells—occurred, populated streets now lie. It was while passing along one of these (Michigan Avenue)—the finest in point of beauty, taste, and prospect in all the West, when on our way out to the pleasant suburban village of Hyde Park, on the lake shore, to visit some old friends, that we were directed to the site of the Sand Hills, the Oak Woods, and Lee's Place. Very near the spot where the Kinzie mansion stood—where food was so scarce only thirty years ago, immense "elevators"—the largest in the world—receive, weigh, and send off annually millions of bushels of the *surplus* grain of the Northwest! This transformation is the work of a single generation. It seems like a magic product evolved by the attrition of Aladdin's lamp.[1]

When the work of destruction, and the final disposition of the prisoners at Chicago were completed, The Black-bird and his savage horde pressed toward Fort Wayne. The fall of Mackinack and Detroit, and the destruction of the military post at Chicago, so completely broke the power of the United States in the Northwest for the moment, that the Indians, believing that there would be perfect safety in openly joining the British, did so. Tecumtha's hopes of establishing a confederacy of the Indians to drive the white people from the country north of the Ohio revived. The prospect of success seemed brighter than ever, and, with the energy of a patriot and enthusiast, he sent emissaries among all the tribes to invite them to take the war-path, with the sole intent of complete expulsion or utter extermination. The Winnebagoes, Pottawatomies, Kickapoos, Ottawas, Shawnoese, and less powerful tribes, gladly listened; and all over the region south of Lake Erie, far toward the Ohio, the young men were speedily engaged in the war-dance.

Proctor and Tecumtha resolved to reduce Forts Wayne and Harrison immediately. The former, as we have seen, was at the head of the Maumee,[2] and the latter on the Wabash.[3] Major Muir, with British regulars and Indians, were to proceed from Malden up the Maumee Valley to co-operate with the Indians; and the 1st of September was appointed as the day when Fort Wayne should be invested by them. The garrison consisted of only seventy men, under Captain James Rhea,[4] with four small field-pieces. The savages were there as early as the 28th of August,[a] and at about the same time hostile bands, for the purpose of diverting attention from Forts Wayne and Harrison, and preventing their garrisons being re-enforced, were directed to prosecute warfare at distant points in their usual mode—murdering isolated settlers, with their women and children. Pursuant to these instructions, a scalping-party of Shawnoese fell upon "The Pigeon Roost Settlement," on a tribu-

[a] 1812.

---

[1] I am indebted to the accurate knowledge and kind courtesy of Mrs. Kinzie for the following information respecting the localities of acts in the events we have just recorded, as indicated by places to-day:

The "Kinzie mansion" was on the north side of the Chicago River, at the intersection of Pine and North Water Streets, as they now are in "Kinzie's addition," and about eighty feet east of the Lake House.

The house of Ouilmette was between what are now Rush and Cass Streets, on North Water Street. Burns's was near the foot of Wolcott Street, on the bank of the river. The east end of the Chicago and Galena Freight Dépôt covers the spot.

The place where the fight commenced was between the Widow Clarke's and the lake. The trees are still standing which stood there at that day.

"Lee's Place" was about a fourth of a mile above where Halstead Street crosses the South Branch.

Captain Wells was killed near the foot of Twelfth Street, on the Lake Shore path.

The "Oak Woods" were, in 1862, "Camp Douglas," just beyond the southern limits of the city, on the Lake Shore. "Chicago University" and the grave of the late Stephen A. Douglas, who owned the property, occupy a portion of the tract.

The place of the parley was about at the intersection of the Archer Road and Clarke Street.

[2] See page 56.   [3] See page 197.

[4] James Rhea was a native of New Jersey, and was lieutenant and adjutant of "Rhea's levies" in 1791. He was ensign and second lieutenant of infantry in 1799, and was promoted to first lieutenant in 1800. He was commissioned a captain in July, 1807, and resigned at Fort Wayne at the close of 1812.—Gardner's *Dictionary of the Army*, page 377.

tary of the White River, within the limits of the present Scott County, in Southern Indiana, on the 3d of September.[a] They first killed two bee-hunters of the settlement;[1] and between sunset and dark they murdered one man, five women, and sixteen children.[2] Only two men and five children escaped.[3] These made their way, under the cover of the night, to the house of a settler six miles distant. One hundred and fifty mounted riflemen, under Major John M'Coy, gave chase to the murderers the next day.[b] They followed them twenty miles, but they escaped during the night. The militia of Scott, Jefferson, Clarke, and Knox Counties were soon assembled, and were joined[c] by about three hundred and fifty volunteers from Kentucky, under Colonel Geiger, for the purpose of destroying the towns of the Delawares, on the White River, who were suspected of being the murderers. Evidence of the innocence and even friendliness of those Indians was not wanting, and they were spared. From that time until the close of the war, the settlers in that region lived in a continual state of fear and excitement.[4]

[a] 1812.
[b] September 4.
[c] September 7.

For several days the Indians, in large numbers, had been seen hovering in the woods around Fort Wayne, and on the night of the 5th of September they commenced a series of attacks by firing upon the sentinels, without effect. Up to that time, the Miamis in the neighborhood, who had resolved to join the British, had made great professions of friendship, hoping, no doubt, to gain possession of the fort by a surprise. This hypocrisy availed them nothing, so they cast off all disguise and opened hostilities. On the morning of the 6th they were invisible, and some of the soldiers ventured out of the fort. They had not proceeded seventy yards when bullets from a concealed foe killed two of their number. Their companions hastened back, carrying the bodies of their comrades with them.

On the night of the 6th the whole body of Indians, supposed to have been six hundred strong, attacked the fort. They attempted to scale the palisades, but so vigilant and skillful were the garrison that the savages were not permitted to do the least damage. Perceiving such assaults to be useless, they resolved to employ strategy in the morning. Two logs were formed into the shape of cannon, and placed in battery before the fort. A half-breed, with a flag, approached and informed the commandant that the British, then on their march, had sent them two battery cannon, and that if a surrender was not immediately made, the fort would be battered down. He also threatened a general massacre of the garrison within three days, as a re-enforcement of seven hundred Indian warriors were expected the next day. The troops were not frightened by the "Quaker guns." They were aware that friends were on the way to relieve them,[5] and resolved to hold out while their provisions lasted. For nearly three days after the menace there was quiet. Then the savages renewed the at-

---

[1] Jeremiah Payne and Frederick Kaupfman.
[2] These were Henry Collings and his wife; the wife of Jeremiah Payne and eight of her children; Mrs. Richard Collings and seven of her children; Mrs. John Morris and her only child, and Mrs. Morris, the mother of her husband.
[3] Mrs. Jane Biggs and her three children, and the aged William Collings and Captain John Morris, with two of the children (John and Lydia) of Mrs. Collings who was murdered. They all escaped to the house of Zebulon Collings.—Dillon's *History of Indiana*, page 492.
[4] Mr. Zebulon Collings, to whose house the fugitives from The Pigeon Roost escaped, has left on record the following vivid account of the sense of peril felt by the settlers during those dark days between the summer of 1812 and 1815: "The manner in which I used to work was as follows: on all occasions I carried my rifle, tomahawk, and butcher-knife, with a loaded pistol in my belt. When I went to plow, I laid my gun on the plowed ground, and stuck up a stick by it for a mark, so that I could get it quick in case it was wanted. I had two good dogs. I took one into the house, leaving the other out. The one outside was expected to give the alarm, which would cause the one inside to bark, by which I would be awakened, having my arms always loaded. I kept my horses in a stable close to the house, having a port-hole so that I could shoot to the stable-door. During two years I never went from home with a certainty of returning, not knowing the minute I might receive a ball from an unknown hand; but, in the midst of all these dangers, that God who never sleeps nor slumbers has kept me."—Dillon's *History of Indiana*, page 493.
[5] General Harrison, then at Piqua in command of Kentucky troops, sent Major William Oliver, a gallant officer, with four Shawnoese, to Fort Wayne to assure the garrrison of speedy re-enforcement. They pushed through the wilderness for about sixty miles. Oliver was in Indian costume. When they approached the fort they came upon the out-guards of the savages. With great skill they evaded them, made their way through the lines of the besiegers, and, with fleet foot, gained the fort. Oliver and his companions remained there until the close of the siege.—*Early History of the Maumee Valley*, by H. L. Hosmer, page 32.

tack,[a] and kept up a fire at intervals for twelve hours. On the following day they raised a tremendous war-whoop, to frighten the garrison, and again commenced an assault, with as little success as on previous occasions. The patient little garrison remained unharmed; and on the 12th, the besiegers fled precipitately, having heard of the approach of a large re-enforcement for the fort. That evening the deliverers arrived, and Fort Wayne was saved.[1]

[a] September 9, 1812.

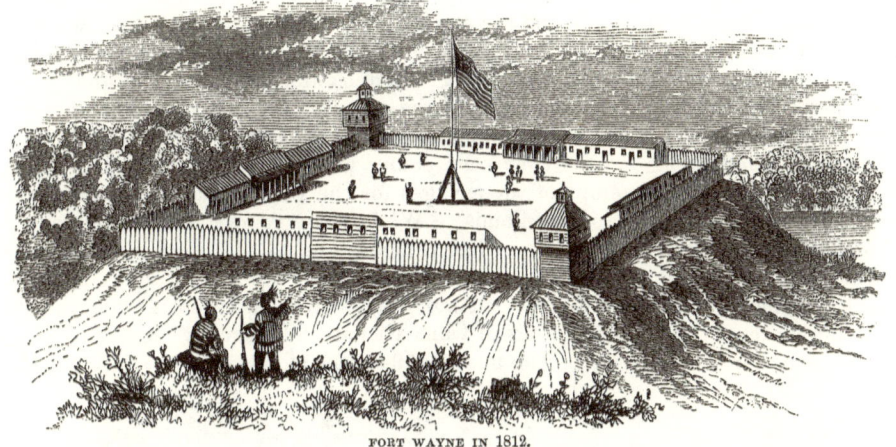

FORT WAYNE IN 1812.

Before they left, the Indians destroyed every thing outside the fort—live-stock, crops, and dwellings. Among the latter was the house of Captain Wells, who was killed at Chicago. It was on his reservation of rich bottom lands on the north side of the St. Mary's River, opposite the present city of Fort Wayne, and not more than half a mile distant from it. When I visited the spot in the autumn of 1860, in company with the venerable Mr. Hedges, already mentioned,[2] and the Hon. I. D. G. Nelson, more than twenty apple-trees of an orchard planted by Captain Wells—the oldest in Northern Indiana, having been set out in 1804 or 1805—were yet standing, shorn of beauty, huge, gnarled, and fantastical, but fruit-bearing still. They were on the land of Mr. Edward Smith, on the east side of the road from Fort Wayne to White Pigeon. In Mr. Smith's garden, which was within the inclosure of the orchard, only a few yards westward of a group of larger trees, was the grave of the Little Turtle. Its place is marked in our little sketch of that group

THE LITTLE TURTLE'S GRAVE.

of five apple-trees by the figures in the foreground. There the Little Turtle was buried in the middle of July, 1812, and his nephew, Co-is-see, pronounced a funeral oration at his grave. His residence was then at Eel River, about fifteen miles northwest of Fort Wayne. He had come to the fort to be treated by the garrison surgeon for the gout, and died there.[3] Mr. Hedges was at his funeral.

---

[1] Thomson's *Sketches of the War*, page 56; M'Afee, page 127.   [2] See page 44.
[3] Mr. Drake, in his *Book of the Indians*, quotes the following notice of the Little Turtle's death from one of the public prints of the day: "Fort Wayne, 21 July, 1812.—On the 14th instant the celebrated Miami chief, the Little Turtle, died at this place, at the age of sixty-five years. Perhaps there is not left on this continent one of his color so distinguished in council and in war. His disorder was the gout. He died in a camp, because he chose to be in the open air. He met

By the side of his remains reposed those of his sister, the wife of Captain Wells. Their graves were unhonored, but I was informed that the kinsfolk of the noted man were about to erect a neat monument to mark the place of their sepulture.

Fort Wayne, delineated on page 315, was built, as we have seen (page 56), in the autumn of 1794. It was not on the site of the old French stockade, known as Fort Miami;[1] nor on that of the one which was occupied by an English garrison, consisting of a captain's command, at the time of Pontiac's conspiracy in 1763. At that time the old Fort Miami was a ruin, and the stockade to which reference is here made was in perfect order. It was about half a mile from the present bridge across the Maumee, on the east bank of the St. Joseph. The commander was a surgeon, and his profession was the cause of his own death and the capture of the garrison by the Indians at that time. He was asked by an Indian girl to go out of the fort to see a sick savage at the Miami village near by, where a young woman of the tribe, chosen for the purpose, to show the contempt of the savages for the English, murdered him. The garrison became prisoners to the Miamis.[2] When, three years later, George Croghan visited the spot, the fort was "somewhat ruinous." He found forty or fifty Indian cabins at the village across the Maumee (that "stood on both sides of the St. Joseph"), besides "nine or ten French houses." Among the latter was that of Drouet de Richardville, a French trader, and father of Chief Richardville, already mentioned as the successor of the Little Turtle.[3] The fort of 1794–1812 stood on the bank of the Mau-

BRIDGE AT THE HEAD OF THE MAUMEE, AT FORT WAYNE.

mee (see map on page 266), at the junction of the present Main and Clay Streets, Fort Wayne. The Wabash and Erie Canal passes through a portion of it. It was a

---

his death with great firmness. The Agent for Indian Affairs had him buried with the honors of war, and other marks of distinction suited to his character." A writer, quoted by Mr. Drake, says that he saw the Little Turtle, soon after St. Clair's defeat, at Montreal, and described him as about six feet in height, sour and morose, and apparently crafty and subtle. He wore Indian moccasins, a blue petticoat that came half way down his thighs, and a European waistcoat and surtout. On his head was a cap that hung half way down his back, bespangled with about two hundred silver brooches. In each ear were two rings, the upper parts of each bearing three silver medals about the size of a dollar, and the lower parts quarters of a dollar. They fell more than twelve inches from his ears. One from each ear fell over his breast, the others over his back. He also had three large nose jewels of silver, cunningly painted. Little Turtle was of mixed blood—half Mohican and half Miami. Colonel Johnston, who knew him well, called him "the gentleman of his race."

[1] The French governor of Louisiana mentioned this stockade in a letter in 1751. It was situated near the St. Mary's, probably in the vicinity of the canal aqueduct. The dim outlines of this fort were traced by Wayne in 1794, and by Colonel Johnston in 1800.—Lecture by J. L. Williams before the congregation of the First Presbyterian Church of Fort Wayne, March 7th, 1860.

[2] Oral statement of Colonel John Johnston, of Dayton, Ohio, to the writer, who knew the murderess, she being a resident of the Miami village when he went to Fort Wayne in the year 1800. Colonel Johnston gave me the names of the United States commanders of the fort in regular succession, as follows: Colonels J. F. Hamtramck, and Thomas Hunt; Majors John Whistler, Thomas Pasteur, and Zebulon M. Pike; Captains Nathan Heald, James Rhea, and Hugh Moore; and Colonel Joseph H. Vose. The fort was abandoned in 1818. Captain Vose was a citizen of Manchester, and had been commissioned a captain in the Twenty-first Infantry in April, 1812. Colonel Johnston, in a letter written in 1859, said that Captain Vose was the only army officer within his knowledge, in 1812, who publicly professed Christianity. He was in the constant habit of assembling his men on the Sabbath and reading the Scriptures to them, and conversing with them on religious subjects.—Williams's Lecture, p. 12. Captain Vose was promoted to major during the War of 1812. In 1842 he received the commission of colonel. He died at the New Orleans barracks, just below the city, on the 15th of July, 1845.

[3] Dillon's *History of Indiana*, p. 403.

well-built stockade, with two block-houses and comfortable barracks, and of sufficient strength to defy the Indians, but not the British with cannon. A large and substantial bridge now spans the Maumee from near the site of Fort Wayne to the plains on which the Miami village stood. The sketch on page 316 was taken from near the line of the eastern side of the fort. At the centre of the picture is seen the point of confluence of the St. Mary's and the St. Joseph's rivers, which form the Maumee.

While these demonstrations against Fort Wayne were in progress, similar efforts were made against Fort Harrison, on the Wabash. At sunset on the day of the Pigeon Roost massacre,[a] two young haymakers near Fort Harrison were killed and scalped by a party of Indians. The crack of the murderers' muskets was heard at the fort, and excited the vigilance of Captain Zachary Taylor, the commander of the garrison, who was just recovering from an attack of bilious fever. On the following morning the bodies of the young men were taken to the fort and buried. Late that evening[b] old Joseph Lenar came to the fort with a flag, followed by about forty Indians, one fourth of them women. The men were chiefs of the several tribes—Winnebagoes, Kickapoos, Pottawatomies, Shawnoese, and some Miamis—who still adhered to the fortunes of the Prophet. They came from his town near Tippecanoe, on the Wabash, where he was still busy in stirring up the Indians against the white people. One of Lenar's party, a Shawnoese who could speak English, told Taylor that their leader would speak to him in the morning about food for his company. Friendly Miamis had warned Taylor of the hostile disposition of all the neighboring tribes, and he was perfectly on his guard.

[a] September 3, 1812.

[b] September 4.

The garrison consisted of only about fifty men, of whom, on account of the prevailing fevers, not much more than a dozen were free from the care of Dr. Clark, the surgeon. Only six privates and two non-commissioned officers could mount guard at a time. Yet now, in the presence of impending danger, some of the convalescents went freely upon duty. The arms of the garrison were examined with great care that evening; and, when every thing necessary for watchfulness and security had been arranged, the commander, weak and exhausted, lay down and fell asleep. His slumbers were short. Toward midnight he was aroused by the firing of his sentinels. Springing from his couch, he hastened to the parade and ordered every man to his post. It was soon ascertained that the lower block-house (on the left of the picture of the fort on page 315), had been set on fire by the savages. It was the most important point in the fort excepting the magazine, for there were the contractor's stores—the supplies for the garrison. The guns, at this time, had "begun to fire pretty smartly" on both sides, and the attack and defense were fairly begun at a little past eleven, with great vigor.

The chief efforts of the commander were directed to the extinguishment of the fire. General confusion reigned, and efforts for the safety of the fort were, for a while, put forth feebly. The entire garrison were either sick or faint with fatigue, and for a time the utter destruction of the whole fortification seemed inevitable. The block-house was consumed, and the fort was thus opened to the savage foe. This exposure and their horrid yells dismayed the little garrison, and for a moment they regarded all as lost, and gave up in despair. Two of the stoutest and most trusted of the soldiers leaped the palisades, and attempted to escape, leaving their companions to their fate. Nothing saved the fort and garrison but the presence of mind, courage, prudence, and energy of the commander. The fire was about to communicate to the barracks, when he shouted, "Pull off the roofs nearest the block-house, pour on water, and all will be well!" His voice gave new courage to his troops. Water was brought in buckets, and several of the men, led by Dr. Clark, climbed to the roof, cut off the boards, and by great exertions, in the face of bullets and arrows, they subdued the flames, and saved the menaced buildings. Only eighteen or twenty feet of the fort was opened by the fire, and up to this time only one man had been killed

318   PICTORIAL FIELD-BOOK

The Indians driven from Fort Harrison.   Relief sent to the Garrison.   Character and Services of Captain Taylor.

and two wounded. Before daylight the breach was covered by a breastwork as high as a man's head, in spite of the incessant firing of the foe, and only one man was killed (none wounded) in the fort. At six o'clock in the morning, when the garrison returned the fire more briskly, after a conflict of almost eight hours, the savages retired beyond the reach of the guns of the fort, and then proceeded to destroy or drive off the live-stock—horses, hogs, and cattle—found in the neighborhood. Fortunately for the garrison, the standing corn around the fort was left unharmed. Their food having been destroyed with the block-house that contained it, and their cattle being driven away, they were compelled to subsist for several days on that delicious and nourishing green corn.

One of the men who leaped the pickets and fled from the fort returned toward morning badly wounded. He approached the gate, and begged, "for God's sake," to be let in. Captain Taylor was near, but, not recognizing the voice, and believing it to be a trick of the Indians to get the gate open, he ordered the soldiers near to shoot the man. Fortunately for him, he had run to the other bastion with the same supplication, where his voice was recognized, and he was told to lie quietly behind some empty barrels at the foot of the pickets until morning. He did so, and was saved. His companion had been literally cut in pieces by the savages within a few yards of the fort. The entire loss of the garrison was only three men killed and three wounded, and all but two of the latter met with disaster because of disobedience of orders.[1]

useful, and modest of public officers.[2]

On the 5th[a] Captain Taylor effectually repaired the breach in the fort made by the fire by placing in the opening strong pickets made of the logs of the guard-house; and he furnished a messenger with dispatches for Vincennes, asking for relief. This was a difficult task, for the Indians hovered about the fort for several days. At length the messenger made his way through their circumvallating line, during a dark night, and soon afterward General Hopkins, with Kentucky Volunteers, marched up the valley on an expedition against the Indians on the head waters of the Wabash, and gave ample relief to the sick, weary, and worn soldiers at Fort Harrison.

[a] September, 1812.

The soldierly qualities displayed by Captain Taylor in the defense of his post against such fearful odds won for him promotion to a major by brevet, and from that time until his death, nearly forty years afterward, which occurred while he was President of the United States, he was one of the most reliable,

---

[1] Captain Taylor's Dispatch to Governor Harrison, dated "Fort Harrison, September 10, 1812."
[2] Zachary Taylor was born in Orange County, Virginia, on the 24th of September, 1784. His father removed with his family to Kentucky the following year, and settled near the site of the present city of Louisville, then known as The Falls of the Ohio. Zachary entered the army when about twenty-five years of age as first lieutenant of infantry. Two years afterward (May, 1810) he was promoted to captain, and at about the same time he was married to Margaret Smith, a young lady of good family in Maryland. When war was declared he was in command of Fort Harrison, and for his

OF THE WAR OF 1812.

| Attack on Fort Madison. | Repulse of the Savages. | Biography of Zachary Taylor. |

Simultaneous with the attack on Fort Harrison, an attempt was made by a party of the British allies to capture a small military post a short distance from the site of the present city of St. Louis, on the bank of the Mississippi River. The place was called Bellevue, and the stockade Fort Madison. The post was very ineligibly situated, and totally unfitted for defense. The savages appeared before it on the afternoon of the 5th of September.[a] They were fierce Winnebagoes, two hundred strong. The garrison, under Lieutenants Hamilton and Vasques, consisted of a small party of the First Regiment of United States Light Infantry. The approach of the foe was heralded by the shooting and scalping of one of the garrison within thirty yards of the fort. For three days the Indians kept up the assault, with frequent attempts to fire the block-houses and barracks. Buildings outside were burnt, and all the live-stock were slaughtered. The gallant little garrison defended the imperiled fort, with great spirit and perseverance, until ten o'clock on the night of the 8th, when the enemy withdrew. With the exception of the man murdered at the commencement of the attack, not one of the garrison was seriously injured. One of the men was slightly wounded in the nose.

[a] 1812.

services there in defending it, in September, 1812, he was breveted a major. He was an active and useful officer in the West during the remainder of the war. When the army was reduced at the close of the contest, he was deprived of his commission of major, and recommissioned a captain, in consequence of which he resigned. He was soon afterward called back to the service by President Madison, and commissioned a major in the Third Infantry, and placed in command of a post at Green Bay. In 1819 he was promoted to lieutenant colonel, and in that position he remained until 1832, when President Jackson commissioned him a colonel. He served with distinction in the "Black Hawk War" that year, and remained in command of Fort Crawford, at Prairie du Chien, until 1836, when he was sent to Florida to operate against the Seminole Indians. His services there were of great importance, and at the close of 1837 he was breveted brigadier general. He remained in charge of all the troops in Florida until 1840, when he was appointed to the command of the southwestern division of the army. Fort Gibson was made his head-quarters in 1841, and the same year he purchased an estate near Baton Rouge, Louisiana, and placed his family there. When, in 1845, war with Mexi-

GENERAL TAYLOR'S RESIDENCE AT BATON ROUGE.

co was imminent, he was ordered to take post in Texas with an army of observation, as it was called. It soon became an army of invasion. In the war that ensued he gained, in quick succession, several brilliant battles; and when the conflict was ended, and he returned home, he was greeted with the wildest enthusiasm. Congress honored him with the commission, by brevet, of major general, its thanks, and also with a ponderous gold medal, "in the name of the republic, as a tribute due to his gallant conduct, valor, and generosity to the vanquished." The "Whig" party nominated him for the presidency of the grateful republic, and he was elected to that high office in November, 1848. He entered upon the exalted duties of his office on the 4th of March, 1849, and died at the presidential mansion, in Washington City, on the 9th of July, 1850, at the age of sixty-five years.

The portrait of General Taylor, given on page 318, is from a daguerreotype taken after his return from Mexico. The picture of his residence is a fac-simile of a pencil-sketch made by the venerated hero himself for the author, in November, 1848. In his letter covering the drawing, he says, "The sketch, you will perceive, is rude, but the best I can offer to you at this time. Indeed, the building is rude in itself, and scarcely worthy of being sketched. I hope, however, that this may be suited to your purposes." It was the residence of Colonel Dixon, the English commander at Baton Rouge, when the fort there was taken by the Spaniards, under Don Bernardo de Galvez, in 1779, and that commander then made it his residence. It was demolished in 1859.

CHAPTER XVI.

> 'They rise, by stream and yellow shore,
>   By mountain, moor, and fen ;
> By weedy rock and torrent hoar,
>   And lonesome forest glen !
> From many a moody, moss-grown mound,
>   Start forth a war-worn band,
> As when, of old, they caught the sound
> Of hostile arms, and closed around,
>   To guard their native land."
>
>   J. M'LELLAN, JR.

WE have observed that troops, in ample numbers, were sent to the relief of Forts Harrison and Wayne. Whence came they? What spirit animated them when pushing eagerly into the wilderness among hostile Indians, after the disasters in the Northwest — the utter failure of Hull's campaign, which had created such great expectations on the part of both government and people? Let us consult contemporary records and traditions for an answer.

Those sad disasters on the Northwestern frontier, aroused, as we have before observed, the most intense feelings of indignation and mortified pride throughout the whole country, and especially in the region west of the Alleghany Mountains and beyond the Ohio River, which was thereby exposed to Indian raids and British invasion. When intelligence of those disasters spread over that region, a burning desire to wipe out the disgrace was universal; and there was a general uprising of sentiment and action for the recovery of all that had been lost, the extermination of the brutal savages, and the expulsion of their British allies from the soil of the Republic.[1]

Even before the formal declaration of war Kentucky had made military preparations for the event. Her quota of the one hundred thousand detached militia which the President was authorized to summon to the field was almost ready when the fiat went forth. Early in May, Governor Scott,[2] in obedience to instructions from the War Department, had organized ten regiments (the quota of his state), and filled

---

[1] "The War," a weekly paper, published in the City of New York, by Samuel Woodworth, the poet, gives the following glimpses of the spirit of the people at that time in its issue of September 19, 1812: "The citizens of Albany, immediately on hearing of the surrender of General Hull, commenced a subscription for raising a regiment of volunteers. Very liberal subscriptions were made for the comfort and convenience of those who might offer their services. A regiment of volunteers is also raising in the City of Baltimore, and $15,000 have already been subscribed for the purpose of furnishing the men with every thing necessary for their comfort. Fifteen hundred men are immediately to march from Virginia, to rendezvous at Point Pleasant, on the Ohio. The *ladies* of Richmond volunteered their services to make tents, knapsacks, etc., for the soldiers, and in five days all things were ready. When the news of the fall of Detroit reached Lexington, in Kentucky, instead of deploring the loss, the citizens immediately set about repairing it. An immense number of volunteers immediately came forward, among whom were several members of Congress, and shouldered their muskets in their country's cause. The greatest enthusiasm prevails throughout the whole Western country; almost every man has volunteered his services, and, if we may judge from appearances, it will not be long before our Western brethren will wipe away the stain upon the American arms by the ignominious surrender of Detroit and the American army under General Hull.

"The citizens of New York are forming patriotic associations for the purpose of raising funds to assist the families of volunteers and drafts detached for the defense of the borders, who may be in want during their absence on duty. Large supplies of vegetables, coffee, tea, chocolate, sugar, etc., have also been sent to the troops stationed in and about the harbor. This conduct is worthy of imitation."

[2] Charles Scott was a native of Cumberland County, Virginia. He was a corporal in a militia company under Braddock in the campaign of 1755, and was a distinguished officer in the Revolution. See Lossing's *Field-Book of the Revolution*. For a brief biographical sketch of him and his signature, see the same, Note 3, ii., 147.

them without difficulty with volunteers, making an effective force of five thousand five hundred men.

Governor Meigs, of Ohio, was equally active and vigilant. He promptly responded to the call for troops to accompany Hull to Detroit, as we have seen; and when he was informed of the danger that menaced Hull's command, he immediately ordered out the remaining portion of the quota of detached militia, twelve hundred in number, to rendezvous at Urbana, on the border of the wilderness, under Brigadier General Tupper. And when the fall of Detroit was known, he sent expresses in every direction to the militia generals of the frontier, with orders to adopt energetic measures for defense within their respective commands, and to advise the inhabitants on the borders of the wilderness to associate and erect block-houses for the defense and accommodation of families. He also sent arms and ammunition to different parts from the public stores at Urbana.[1]

Governor Harrison, of Indiana, with his usual vigilance, promptness, and forecast, had already caused block-houses and stockades to be erected in various parts of his territory as defenses against the hostile Indians, and the militia were placed in a state of preparation for immediate action when called upon. He had been authorized by the national government to take command of all the troops of the territories of Indiana and Illinois in prosecuting the war against the Indians commenced in the autumn of 1811, and to call on the Governor of Kentucky for any portion of the contingent of that state which was not in service. Under that authority he went to Kentucky, by invitation of Governor Scott, to confer respecting the troops of that state. Kentucky was forever freed from apprehensions of Indian incursions, and her sons, who had suffered, were eager to assist their neighbors over the Ohio in their efforts to drive the murderous hordes back into the wilderness.

Harrison repaired to Frankfort, where the military were paraded and he was honored with a public reception. He remained there several days, and met many of the most eminent military men and civilians in the state. He comprehended in all its length and breadth the difficulties and dangers to which Hull was exposed, and expressed his opinions freely at a dinner-party in Lexington, whereat Henry Clay was one of the guests. That gentleman and others urged him to present his views to the government.[2] He did so in a letter, dated the 10th of August, in which he suggested a system of military operations in the Northwest. He expressed his fears of the result of the fall of Mackinack, by which the Indian tribes might be let loose upon Detroit, and "meet, and perhaps overpower, the convoys and re-enforcements" which had been, or might be, sent to Hull. After speaking of those re-enforcements, he said: "I rely greatly upon the valor of these troops; but it is possible that the event may be adverse to us, and if it is, *Detroit must fall*, and with it every hope of re-establishing our affairs in that quarter until the next year."

Before this letter reached the War Department, Detroit had fallen, and Chicago too, and the worst fears of the people of the West were realized. But these disasters, instead of depressing them, gave them increased elasticity and strength. The whole total of society bordering upon the Ohio River heaved, like a storm-smitten ocean in its wrath, with patriotic emotions. The murders by the Indians which soon followed, and the alliance of the British with such fierce barbarians, excited a vehement cry for retributive justice. Christian civilization, national pride, and an enlightened patriotism, all pleaded for vindication, and nobly was that plea responded to. When a call for troops was made, men of every class and condition of life—farmers, merchants, lawyers, physicians, and young men innumerable—flocked to the recruiting stations and offered their services. Tenfold more men than were needed might have

---

[1] Reply of Governor Meigs to the memorial of the citizens of Chillicothe, Ohio, on the subject of protecting the frontier.—Niles's *Weekly Register*, September 26, 1812.
[2] *Memoirs of the Public Services of William Henry Harrison*, by James Hall, p. 160.

been mustered in Kentucky alone. Nor was Ohio, in proportion to its population, behind its elder sister state in practical enthusiasm. Governor Meigs was indefatigable in his efforts; and the people every where responded to the call of local officers, as well as of the chief magistrate, with the greatest alacrity, to form an ample army for both protection and conquest. It was resolved to recover all that had been lost within the territory of the United States, and to take Malden, the focus of the British-Indian power in the Northwest.

At this moment the venerable Isaac Shelby, one of the heroes of King's Mountain, appears upon the stirring scene as the successor of General Scott in the executive chair of the State of Kentucky. With his usual sagacity, he surveyed the field of operations determined upon, and strongly recommended the government to appoint a Board of War for the region west of the Alleghanies, to prevent the delays caused by the operations of what is termed, in our day, "red-tape policy"—in other words, the absolute control, by a central power hundreds of miles away, of minor movements which the exigency of the hour might demand as of vast importance. "If such a board," he said, "was now organized, and I had the control of the present armament, I would pledge myself the Indians would have cause to lament this campaign, and their temerity in joining the British and deserting the friendship of the United States." Governor Shelby's advice was not utterly disregarded; but no practical results followed. The War Department promised to "think about it," and no conclusion seems ever to have been reached.

Governor Harrison was very popular, and it was the general desire of the volunteers and militia of the West, who had been gathering at different points since the declaration of war was made, that he who had shown such soldierly qualities in the little campaign that ended at Tippecanoe the previous year, should now be their leader against the British and Indians. Governor Scott, Harrison's warm personal friend, was anxious to place him in chief command of all the Kentucky troops, but he could not do so legally, for the Governor of Indiana was not a citizen of that state. But Scott was not a man to allow technicalities to interfere with great concerns in time of danger; so he invited several prominent men, among whom were Shelby (the governor elect), Henry Clay (the Speaker of the National House of Representatives), and Thomas Todd, Judge of the United States District Court, to meet him and consult upon the subject. They unanimously requested the governor to make the appointment; and accordingly he issued a commission[a] to Harrison, by which he was invested with the title of "Major General of the Militia of Kentucky" by brevet. By a commission dated three days earlier, President Madison appointed him a brigadier general in the Army of the United States.

[a] August 25, 1812.

On the 27th of August Harrison was at Cincinnati, and in a letter of that date to Governor Meigs, after mentioning his appointment, he said: "It remains for your excellency to determine what assistance I shall derive from your state. The Kentucky troops which are placed at my disposal are two regiments of infantry and one of riflemen, now at this place; three regiments of infantry, one of dragoons, and one of mounted riflemen, in full march to join me, and making in the aggregate upward of four thousand men. The three regiments which are now here will march immediately for Urbana; and should the report of the capture of General Hull's army prove untrue, I shall join them either at that place or before they reach it, and proceed to Detroit without waiting for the regiments in my rear."[1]

In addition to the Kentucky troops here referred to, others were dispatched for the protection of the Territories of Illinois and Indiana.[2] Some of those destined for the

---

[1] Autograph letter, August 27, 1812.

[2] "The regiment commanded by Colonel Barbour," says M'Afee, "when ordered into service at the call of Governor Harrison, was directed to rendezvous at the Red Barracks, with a view of marching to the aid of Governor Edwards, at Ruskin's, in the Illinois Territory. The regiments of Colonels Wilcox and Miller were ordered to rendezvous at Louis-

Gathering of Troops.   Departure for the Wilderness.   Harrison commissioned a Brigadier General.

latter region having been called, by the exigencies of current events, to Ohio, Harrison thought it desirable to raise an additional force for Indiana. In compliance with his request, Governor Shelby issued a proclamation early in September for the raising of a large corps of mounted volunteers, to repair immediately to Vincennes; and all of the Kentucky troops destined for that post were placed under the command of the venerable soldier of the Revolution, Brigadier General Samuel Hopkins. That proclamation brought hundreds of Kentuckians, from all parts of the state, to the standard of the Union. Every body seemed willing to march for the defense of the frontiers; and the question was not, Who will go? but, Who shall stay?[1] Before the 1st of October, Kentucky had more than seven thousand of her sons in the field. At about the same time, in obedience to an order from the Secretary of War, two thousand troops under General Robert Crooks, from Western Pennsylvania, and fifteen hundred under General Joel Leftwich,[2] from Western Virginia, proceeded to join the Army of the Northwest.

Before leaving Frankfort, General Harrison had issued an address to the people of Kentucky, accompanied by another from General Scott, calling for five hundred mounted volunteers. The Honorable Richard M. Johnson, who had distinguished himself in Congress, also issued an address for the same purpose; and they had the desired effect. The latter gentleman, and John Logan, and William S. Hunter, Esqs., were appointed aids to the general; and when he departed for Cincinnati, Johnson was left to lead on such mounted troops as might be raised by the 1st of September.

On the 28th of August Harrison issued a general order from his head-quarters at Cincinnati, directing all the troops under his command to continue their march toward Dayton on the following morning, and prescribing in detail the discipline and tactics to be observed.[3] The troops marched early; and on the morning of the 31st, when they had passed Lebanon a short distance, forty miles from Cincinnati, Harrison overtook them, and was received with the most hearty cheers of welcome from the whole line. They reached Dayton on Tuesday, the 1st of September, and while on his march toward Piqua the following day the commanding general was overtaken by an express bearing to him the commission of brigadier general from the President, with instructions to take command of all the forces in the Territories of Indiana and Illinois, and to co-operate with General Hull, and with Governor Howard of the Missouri Territory.

Harrison was embarrassed by the instructions which accompanied the appointment, and he refrained from accepting it until he should have definite information from the War Department as to his relations to General Winchester, of the Regulars, to whom

---

ville and on the Ohio below, for the purpose of marching to Vincennes to protect the Indiana Territory. Colonels Barbee and Jennings were at first ordered to the same place; but, in consequence of the perilous situation of the Northwestern Army, they were now directed, by express, to rendezvous at Georgetown on the 1st of September, and pursue the other regiments, by the way of Newport and Cincinnati, for the Northwestern frontiers. The regiment of Colonel Poague was called to rendezvous at Newport, on its way to the Northwestern Army; and a regiment of dragoons, under Colonel Simrall, was likewise directed to proceed for the same destination."—*History of the Late War in the Western Country*, page 109.   [1] M'Afee, page 111.   [2] Died April 20, 1846.

[3] On the same day General Harrison, who had heard of the fall of Detroit and Chicago, and knew the danger to which Fort Wayne would be exposed, wrote as follows to the Secretary of War: "I shall march to-morrow morning with the troops I have here, taking the route of Dayton and Piqua. The relief of Fort Wayne will be my first object, and my after operations will be guided by circumstances until I receive your instructions. Considering my command as merely provisional, I shall cheerfully conform to any other arrangements which the government may think proper to make. The troops which I have with me, and those which are coming from Kentucky, are perhaps the best materials for forming an army that the world has produced. But no equal number of men was ever collected who knew so little of military discipline, nor have I any assistants that can give me the least aid, if there was even time for it, but Captain Adams, of the 4th Regiment, who was left here sick, and whom I have appointed deputy adjutant general until the pleasure of the President can be known. No arms for cavalry have yet arrived at Newport, and I shall be forced to put muskets in the hands of all the dragoons. I have written to the quarter-master at Pittsburg to request him to forward all supplies of arms, equipments, and quarter-master's stores as soon as possible. I have also requested him to send down a few pieces of artillery without waiting your order, and wait your instruction as to a farther number. There is but one piece of artillery, one iron four-pounder, any where that I can hear of in the country. If it is intended to retake the posts that we have lost, and reduce Malden this season, the artillery must be sent on as soon as possible." He also complained of a want of facility for getting money on drafts. Such were the inadequate preparations made by the government for the promotion of the war in the Northwest, when it was first commenced.

had been assigned the chief command of the Army of the Northwest. The original object in the formation of that army having been co-operation with Hull in the capture of Malden, and the reduction and occupation of Canada West, the whole aspect of affairs had been changed by the loss of Hull and his army. Harrison suggested to the Department the importance of having one military head in the Northwest; and, with the justification of pressing necessity, he laid aside his usual modesty, and preferred his own claim to that distinction, on the ground of his superior knowledge of the country and the savages with whom they had to contend, and the universally expressed desire of the troops that he should be their chief leader. Having made this response to the government by the express who brought his commission and instructions, Harrison pressed forward in the path of duty to Piqua, on the bank of the Great Miami, with the intention of there resigning his command into the hands of General Winchester. He had two thousand troops with him, and two thousand were on their way to join him.

Piqua was reached on the 3d of September, and there Harrison was informed of the critical situation of Fort Wayne, and of the rumored marching from Malden, on the 18th of August, of a large force of British and Indians under Major Muir, with the intention of joining the savages in the siege of that place. Winchester, to whom Harrison had written, had not arrived. There would be great danger in delay, and Harrison resolved not to wait for his superior, but, retaining command, send detachments immediately forward to the relief of the menaced garrison. For this purpose he detached Lieutenant Colonel John Allen's regiment of Regulars, with two companies from Lewis's and one from Scott's regiments, with instructions to make forced marches until their object should be accomplished.[1] At the same time he dispatched a messenger, as we have seen, to assure the garrison of Fort Wayne of approaching relief.[2] Already seven hundred mounted men, under Colonel Adams, had advanced to Shaw's Crossing of the St. Mary's River, not far from Fort Wayne. The troop was composed of citizens of Ohio of all ages and conditions, who, in hearing of the disasters northward, and the perils of Fort Wayne, had hastened to the field. "Such, indeed, was the ardor of the citizens," says a contemporary, "that every road leading to the frontiers was invaded with unsolicited volunteers."[3] The exasperation in the West against the British and Indians was intense.

Harrison had observed some restlessness among the troops under the restraints of discipline. On the morning of the 5th[a] he addressed them briefly, read the Articles of War, endeavored to impress their minds with the importance of discipline and obedience, told them that the danger to which Fort Wayne was then exposed demanded an immediate forced march for its relief, and requested those who could not endure the life of a true soldier to leave the ranks. Only one man did so, when his companions, thinking him too feeble to walk, carried him on a rail to the banks of the Great Miami, and gave him a "plunge bath," not, perhaps, in strict accordance with the fashion prescribed by Priessnitz. The effect was salutary, and murmurings ceased. Such discipline, exercised by the soldiers themselves, was a hopeful sign for the commander.

[a] September, 1812.

Colonel John Johnston, the Indian agent, was residing at Piqua.[4] At the request of Harrison, he sent some Shawnoese to old Fort Defiance, at the mouth of the Au Glaize River, to ascertain whether any British troops had gone up the Maumee Valley. Logan, a powerful half-breed, was sent to Fort Wayne for information. Both parties were successful, and returned with important messages. No British troops had passed up the Maumee, and Fort Wayne was closely besieged by the savages.

---

[1] M'Afee, page 121.   [2] See note 5, page 314.   [3] M'Afee, page 121.
[4] For the purpose of neutralizing, if possible, the effects of British influence over the tribes of Ohio, a council had been held at Piqua on the 15th of August. Governor Meigs, Thomas Worthington, and Jeremiah Morrow were the commissioners on the part of the United States. Every thing promised success; but while the council was in progress news of the fall of Detroit and Chicago reached Piqua, and frustrated the plans of the white people.

The Army in the Wilderness.   Preparations for Battle.   Fort Wayne relieved.   Destruction of Indian Towns.

Harrison was compelled to wait at the Piqua until the morning of the 6th[a] for flints. At dawn of that day his forces were under motion, and before eight o'clock they had fairly plunged into the great wilderness beyond the borders of civilization. In order to march rapidly and easily, the troops had left most of their clothing and baggage at Piqua; and on the afternoon of the 8th, they overtook Allen's regiment at St. Mary, sometimes called "Girty's Town,"[1] or the First Crossing of the St. Mary River. There they were joined by Major R. M. Johnson, with a corps of mounted volunteers. The army in the wilderness numbered two thousand two hundred men. Indian spies were seen hovering around the camp that night, who, it was afterward said, reported that "Kentuck was crossing as numerous as the trees."   [a] Sept., 1812.

The morning of the 9th was dark and lowering, but the troops were in good spirits, and reached Shane's, or the Second Crossing of the St. Mary, before sunset, where they found Colonel Adams, with his mounted Ohio Volunteers. Being now in the vicinity of Fort Wayne, the army marched in battle order on the following day, expecting an attack. They moved slowly and cautiously. Scouts were out continually, and Logan and another Shawnoe acted as guides. On the night of the 11th they fortified their camp in expectation of an attack, and many alarms occurred during the darkness, caused by the discovery of Indian spies who were lurking around the verge of the pickets.

The march was resumed at a very early hour on the morning of the 12th in battle order. An encounter was expected at a swamp five miles from Fort Wayne. But no foe was visible there. The savages had all fled, as we have before observed,[2] and Fort Wayne, on that warm, bright September day, was the scene of great rejoicing. The liberating army encamped around the fort that night, excepting a party of horsemen, who made an unsuccessful pursuit of the savages; and on the following morning, reconnoitring parties were sent out in every direction, but did not discover the dusky foe.

Harrison now called a council of officers, to whom he submitted a plan of operations, which was adopted. He had determined to strike the neighboring Indians with terror by a display of power. He accordingly divided his army, and sent out detachments to destroy whatever of Indian possessions might be found. One detachment, under Colonel Simrall (who arrived in camp with three hundred and twenty dragoons on the 17th), laid waste the Little Turtle's town, on the Eel Run,[b] excepting the buildings erected by the United States for the now deceased chief, on account of his friendship since the treaty of Greenville in 1794.[3] Another detachment, under Colonel Samuel Wells, was sent to the Elk Hart River, a tributary of the St. Joseph, of Michigan (sometimes called the St. Joseph of the Lake), sixty miles distant, to destroy the town of the Pottawatomie chief O-nox-see, or Five Medals,[4] which was accomplished;[c] and Colonel Payne, with another detachment, to the forks of the Wabash, and laid in ashes[d] a Miami village there, and several others lower down.[5] Around all of these villages were corn-fields and gardens, but no living thing was seen. The Indians had deserted

[b] Sept. 19.
[c] September 16.
[d] September 15.

---

[1] Now the village of St. Mary, in Mercer County, Ohio, on the site of Fort St. Mary, erected by Wayne, and commanded by Captain John Whistler before he built Fort Dearborn at Chicago. The notorious Simon Girty occupied a cabin at that place for some time.   [2] See page 315.
[3] While the Little Turtle lived most of the Miamis remained faithful to the Americans, but soon after his death, in the summer of 1812, the great body of them joined the hostile savages.
[4] This village, like all the others, was deserted. Before the door of the chief, upon a pole, hung a red flag, with a broom tied above it; and at the tent of an old warrior a white flag was flying from a pole. The body of the old warrior was in a sitting posture, the face toward the east, and a bucket containing trinkets by its side. In one of the huts was found a Cincinnati newspaper containing an account of General Harrison's army. The troops found a large quantity of dried corn, beans, and potatoes, which furnished them and their horses with food.
[5] In one of these was found the tomb of a chief, built of logs and daubed with clay. His body was laid on a blanket, with his gun and his pipe by his side, a small tin pan on his breast containing a wooden spoon, and a number of ear-rings and brooches.

them. The severest blow that a savage can receive, especially at that season of the year, is to deprive him of food and shelter. So, when the torch was applied to the cabins, the knife destroyed the corn and the vegetables.

General James Winchester arrived at Fort Wayne on the 18th of September, and on the following day General Harrison formally resigned all command into his hands. The change produced almost a mutiny among the soldiers. They were greatly attached to Harrison. Winchester was a wealthy citizen of Tennessee, and had not for many years had any military experience. He had been a subordinate officer in the army of the Revolution, but for thirty years had lived in ease and opulence in Tennessee. His deportment was too aristocratic to please the great mass of the troops, and this, added to their expectations of more severe discipline from an officer of the Regulars, caused a large number of them to positively refuse at first to serve under the new commander. It required all the address of Harrison (popular as he was, and as ready as were his followers to comply with all his wishes), together with the persuasions of the other officers, to reconcile them to the change. It was effected, but only when they were allowed to indulge the hope that their beloved general might be reinstated in command.[1]

[a] September, 1812.

Harrison left Fort Wayne on the evening of the 19th,[a] and returned to St. Mary, where he intended to collect the mounted men from Kentucky, and prepare for an expedition against Detroit. "From Fort Wayne," he wrote, "there is a path, which has been sometimes used by the Indians, leading up the St. Joseph's, and from thence, by the head waters of the River Rezin [Raisin], to Detroit. By this route it appears to me very practicable to effect a *coup-de-main* upon that place, and if I can collect a few hundred more mounted men, I shall attempt it."[2] To the accomplishment of this design he prepared to lend all his energies. Already there was a respectable force of mounted men at St. Mary, and others were on the march to that place.

[b] September.

Harrison went to Piqua to perfect his arrangements. There, on the 24th,[b] he received a dispatch from the Secretary of War in reference to his letter concerning the acceptance of a brigadier's commission, which opened thus:

"The President is pleased to assign to you the command of the Northwestern Army, which, in addition to the regular troops and rangers in that quarter, will consist of the volunteers and militia of Kentucky, Ohio, and three thousand from Virginia and Pennsylvania, making your whole force ten thousand men." It then went on to instruct him to first provide for the defense of the frontiers, and then to retake Detroit with a view to the conquest of Canada. He was assured that every exertion would be made to send him a train of artillery from Pittsburg, in charge of Captain Gratiot, of the Engineers, who would report to him as soon as some of the pieces could be got ready. He was also informed that Major Ball, of the 2d Regiment of Dragoons, would join him; and that such staff officers as he might legally appoint would be approved by the President. "Colonel Buford, deputy commissioner at Lexington," he said, "is furnished with funds, and is subject to your orders." More ample powers than had ever been given to any officer of the American army since Washington was invested with the authority of a military dictator were intrusted to him in the following closing sentence in the dispatch: "You will command such means as may be

---

[1] At St. Mary's, Harrison wrote to Governor Shelby as follows: "My situation here is very embarrassing, so much so that I have determined within the two hours past to propose to General Winchester to recognize me as commander-in-chief, or to relinquish all command whatever, unless it is of the mounted forces which I have prepared, and with which I shall strike a stroke somewhere. You will hear from another quarter the very serious difficulty which was to be encountered before the men of Scott's, Allen's, and Lewis's regiments could be reconciled to the command of General Winchester. I fear that the other three regiments will prove still more refractory."—Autograph Letter, September 22d, 1812.

[2] Autograph Letter to General Shelby, dated "St. Mary, 22d September, 1812." I have before me an autograph note from General Harrison to Governor Meigs, of similar purport, dated at St. Mary, the 20th of September. "But it must be kept profoundly secret," he wrote.

practicable. *Exercise your own discretion, and act in all cases according to your own judgment.*" With such ample powers invested in a commander-in-chief, Shelby's "Board of War" would have been quite useless. Harrison had reason to be proud of the honor conferred, and the "special trust and confidence" reposed in him; while his soldiers, rejoicing in the fact, appeared ready and eager to follow whithersoever he might lead.

General Winchester, with about two thousand men, left Fort Wayne on the morning of the 22d of September (each soldier carrying six days' provisions) for the Maumee Rapids. He moved cautiously down the left bank of that river, to avoid a surprise, in three divisions, his baggage in the centre, and a volunteer company of spies, under Captain Ballard, supported by Garrard's dragoons, moving about two miles in advance. Winchester intended to halt at Fort Defiance, at the confluence of the Maumee and Au Glaize Rivers, fifty miles from Fort Wayne, and there await re-enforcements from Harrison at St. Mary. They encountered Indians on the way. Some of the spies were killed; among them Ensign Leggett, of the Seventeenth United States Infantry, who, with four others of a Woodford (Kentucky) company, had been permitted to push forward to reconnoitre the vicinity of Fort Defiance. They were all killed and scalped. When their fate was made known in the camp, Captain Ballard[1] was ordered out with his spies and forty of Garrard's dragoons to bury the bodies. This sad office they undertook on the morning of the 27th, and when within two miles of the place of the massacre they discovered an Indian ambuscade. A conflict ensued. Garrard's troops charged upon the savages, when they fled in dismay, closely pursued for some distance, and found refuge in the swamps, where cavalry could not penetrate.

These Indians were the advance of a heavy force—heavy by comparison only—under Major Muir, consisting of two hundred British regulars, one thousand savages, under Colonel Elliott, and four pieces of cannon. They were making their way up the Maumee on its southern side to attack Fort Wayne. Their artillery and baggage had been brought to Defiance in boats from Malden, and with them they were marching by land to Fort Wayne. Fortunately for the little army under Winchester, a shrewd subaltern of Scott's regiment (Sergeant M'Coy) had been captured and taken before Muir, who was then twelve miles above Fort Defiance. He was questioned closely, and in his answer he magnified Winchester's army fourfold. He also told Muir that another army equally large was coming down the Au Glaize to join Winchester. The exaggerated facts given to the British commander by his own credulous and excited scouts made him believe the stories of M'Coy; and when he heard of the defeat of his advance by Ballard and Garrard, he ordered a retreat to Fort Defiance, where he re-embarked his artillery and baggage.

Relying upon his boats for facility in retreating, in the event of a defeat, Muir resolved to give battle about four miles above Fort Defiance, at the ford of a creek on the north side of the Maumee, where Wayne crossed in 1794; but when, on the morning of the 28th, he attempted to form his line of battle there, he found, to his great mortification and alarm, that about three fourths of his Indian allies had deserted him. They had heard of M'Coy's stories, and, associating them with Muir's retrograde movement, and the re-embarkation of his artillery and baggage, they became greatly alarmed, and abandoned the expedition. Thus weakened, Muir conceived himself to be in great danger. He hastened back to Defiance, and fled twenty miles

---

[1] Captain Bland Ballard was a distinguished citizen of Kentucky. He was born in Fredericksburg, Virginia, October 16, 1761, and at this time was just past fifty years of age. He had been in Kentucky since 1779. He was with General Clark when he invaded the Ohio country in 1781, where he was severely wounded. In all that service, as a spy and otherwise, Ballard was exceedingly active. He was with Wayne in his campaigns. He joined Allen's regiment in 1812, and, as we have seen in the text, was wounded at the Raisin and taken prisoner. He frequently represented Shelby County in the Kentucky Legislature. Ballard County, Kentucky, was so called in his honor, and Blandville, the county seat, bears the Christian name of Captain Ballard. He was living, at the age of eighty-seven years, in 1847. For a fuller account of him, see Collins's *Historical Sketches of Kentucky*, page 171.

Winchester arrives at Fort Defiance.   Re-enforcements gathering.   Their March toward Fort Defiance.

down the Maumee before he halted, leaving some faithful mounted Indians behind to watch the movements of the Americans.

Winchester, in the mean time, was moving cautiously forward. He could receive no certain intelligence concerning the force and position of the enemy. Two scouts (Hickman and Riddle) had gone completely around the invaders on the 26th without seeing them,[1] and others were equally unsuccessful on the 27th and 28th.[a] When the army approached the creek where Muir expected to make a stand, Winchester was informed of its advantageous position for the enemy, and crossed to the southeast side of the Maumee to avoid him. There they discovered the trail of the invader, with his artillery. Ignorant of the alarm of Muir, they encamped on a rise of ground and fortified their position. Then a council of war was held. Some officers were in favor of sending a detachment in pursuit of the retreating foe, but the general and a majority determined otherwise. Their provisions were almost exhausted, and the unknown force of the enemy caused prudence to ask for strength in re-enforcements.[2] Several mounted parties were sent out to reconnoitre, and expresses were detached to General Harrison at St. Mary, asking for relief by sending men and food. It was soon ascertained that the enemy had left Fort Defiance, and on the 30th Winchester moved down the river to a high bank of the Maumee, within a mile of the fort, and again formed a fortified camp. On the 1st of October Colonel Lewis made a reconnoissance in force, and ascertained that the enemy was entirely gone.[3]

[a] September, 1812.

While Winchester was making his way toward Fort Defiance, the troops that were gathering in the rear of the army had mostly arrived at St. Mary. These consisted of three regiments from Kentucky, commanded respectively by Colonels Joshua Barbee, Robert Poague, and William Jennings (the latter riflemen), and three companies of mounted riflemen, from the same state, under Captains Roper, Bacon, and Clark. Also a corps of mounted men from Ohio, under Colonel Findlay, who, as we have seen, had been active with General Hull. These had been raised pursuant to a call of Governor Meigs and General Harrison, at the beginning of September, and rendezvoused as early as the 15th at Dayton. They were intended to operate against some of the hostile Indian towns.

On the 21st of September, Harrison ordered Colonel Jennings to proceed with his regiment down the Au Glaize to establish an intermediate post between St. Mary and Fort Defiance, and to escort provisions to the latter place for the use of Winchester on his route to the Rapids of the Maumee. When Jennings had marched between thirty and forty miles, he found the Indians hovering round his camp at night, and his scouts brought intelligence that they were in considerable force toward Fort Defiance; so he halted and constructed a stockade on the bank of the Ottawa River, a tributary of the Au Glaize, not far from the present Kalida (the Greek for *beautiful*), the capital of Putnam County, Ohio. It was named Fort Jennings, in honor of the commander of the detachment. At the same time Colonel Findlay was ordered to attack some Ottawa towns[4] farther eastward, on Blanchard's Fork, below Fort Findlay, in the same county.[5]

[b] September.

Winchester was informed of the march of Jennings with provisions, and on the 29th,[b] his army being half famished, he sent Captain Garrard

---

[1] They crossed the Maumee to the south side, and took as direct a route as they could to the Au Glaize. They crossed that stream, and descended it along its eastern shore to its mouth at Defiance. Two miles below the confluence of the streams they crossed the Maumee, and returned up the north side to the army.

[2] At about this time Peter Navarre (whom we shall meet hereafter), who had piloted the British as far as the Rapids, deserted them, and pushed on to meet Winchester and inform him of the approach of the enemy.—Hosmer's *Early History of the Maumee Valley*, page 34.

[3] M'Afee, pages 102–138, inclusive; Thomson's *Sketches of the Late War*, ch. iv.; Perkins's *History, etc., of the Late War*; Brackenridge's *History of the Late War*, pages 55–58, inclusive.

[4] The emphasis in the word Ottawa being in the middle syllable, these were called 'Tawa towns. The Lower 'Tawa town was on Blanchard's Fork, on the site of the present village of Ottawa, two miles below the Upper 'Tawa town.

[5] See page 257.

Harrison's Autumn Campaign arranged.   Patriotism of the Women of Kentucky.   Troops ready for an Advance.

with dragoons to assist in escorting to his camp a brigade of pack-horses with supplies. Garrard was successful, and returned, after a tour of thirty-six hours, in a drenching rain. Winchester was still in his fortified camp near Fort Defiance, and Garrard was received at that beautiful spot in the wilderness with the lively satisfaction of the famished when fed.

During the few days of suspense concerning the extent of his command General Harrison formed projects for the immediate future, which inexorable circumstances compelled him to abandon, to some extent. He had now, as commander-in-chief, arranged with care the plan for an autumn campaign, which contemplated the seizure and occupation of the strategic position at the foot of the Maumee Rapids, and possibly the capture of Detroit and Malden. His base of military operations, having the Rapids as the first object to be possessed, was a line drawn along the margin of the swampy region from St. Mary to Upper Sandusky, the former to be the principal deposit for provisions, and the latter for artillery and military stores. He intended to march his army in three divisions: the right column to be composed of the Virginia and Pennsylvania troops, to rendezvous at Wooster, the capital of the present Wayne County, Ohio, and proceed from thence, by Upper Sandusky, to the Rapids. The centre column, to consist of twelve hundred Ohio militia, to march from Urbana, where they were then collected, to Fort M'Arthur, and follow Hull's road to the Rapids. The left column, to be composed of the regulars under Colonel Wells and four regiments of Kentucky volunteers, to proceed down the Au Glaize to the Maumee from St. Mary, and from their confluence pass on toward the Rapids. He designed to send the mounted horsemen, by way of the St. Joseph of the Lake, to make the *coup-de-main* on Detroit, already alluded to; but this project was abandoned, for, should they take that post without the support of infantry, they might be compelled to abandon it, and would thereby expose the inhabitants to the fury of the Indians, who must be exasperated by the movement. Harrison therefore determined to employ them in making destructive forays upon Indian towns, and sweep the savages from the line of march from the Rapids to Detroit, when the troops should all be ready to move.

Harrison now made urgent appeals for supplies of every kind. He sent an express to Pittsburg to hurry forward the cannon and ordnance stores to Wooster; and, as the troops were nearly destitute of winter clothing, he and Governor Shelby appealed to the inhabitants of Kentucky for voluntary contributions. It was generously responded to. A thousand needles were speedily put in motion in fair hands; and many a poor soldier, as he stood sentry on the banks of the Maumee or the Raisin a few weeks later, had reason to feel grateful to the patriotic women of Kentucky.

On the 1st of October there were nearly three thousand troops at St. Mary. Harrison resolved to employ the portion of the left wing, under Winchester, at Defiance, as a corps of observation, and to make that place an important deposit for provisions, preparatory to the advance of that corps upon the Rapids. This movement was to commence as soon as the artillery should arrive at Upper Sandusky, and the other supplies had accumulated along the base of operation. A corps of observation was also to be placed at Lower Sandusky, which, with Defiance, would form the extremities of a second base when the Rapids should be occupied. These arrangements for operations were exceedingly judicious for an economical use of supplies, and a perfect defense of the frontier while the troops were concentrating at the Rapids.

The mounted men, consisting of the companies of Roper, Clark, and Bacon, and the volunteers under Major Richard M. Johnson, were formed into a regiment. They elected Johnson their colonel; and these, with the Ohio mounted men under Findlay, formed a small brigade, which Harrison placed in charge of General Edward W. Tupper, of Gallia County, Ohio, a gentleman about fifty years of age, who had, by his own exertions, raised about a thousand men for the service. This brigade was destined for the expedition against Detroit, by way of the St. Joseph, which the general hoped to set in motion soon. A few hours after it was organized, an express from Winchester reached Harrison with the intelligence of his encounter with the invading force under Muir. At almost the same moment, an express arrived from Governor Meigs, with a letter to him from General Kelso, who was in command of some Pennsylvania troops on the shore of Lake Erie, informing him that, as late as the 16th of September, some British regulars, Canadian militia, and two thousand Indians, had left Malden with two pieces of artillery for Fort Wayne.

These dispatches created a great stir in camp. Three days' cooked provisions, with ammunition and other military stores, were immediately issued to the troops, and a command for a forced march was given. Three hours afterward General Harrison was in the saddle, and his whole corps were following him toward the wilderness in a drenching rain, and the road filled with deep mud. They reached the camp of Colonel Jennings at twilight, and officers and men, from the general down, slept in the cold, damp air, without tents, and nothing between them and the water-pools on the surface of the flat ground but brush from the beech-trees. There Harrison was met by another express from Winchester, notifying him of the flight of the enemy down the Maumee. The rapid march was stayed. Barbee's regiment was ordered back to St. Mary, and Poague's was directed to cut a road to Fort Defiance from Camp Jennings. The mounted men, more than a thousand in number, pressed forward in five lines, making an imposing appearance in the stately forest, where the leaves were just assuming the gorgeous autumnal hues. The troops were disappointed and depressed because of the flight of the enemy; and the commanding general was vexed when he discovered that Winchester's alarm was quite unnecessary. He reached that officer's camp at sunset. His soldiers bivouacked three miles in the rear. Early the next morning they marched down to the confluence of the Maumee and Au Glaize, and encamped there around the ruined intrenchments of old Fort Defiance.

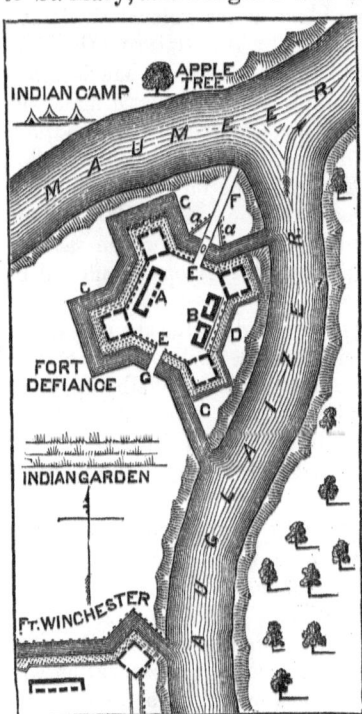

FORT DEFIANCE.[1]

Harrison found the troops under Winchester in a deplorable condition, and one regiment in a state of open mutiny. He ordered the "alarm" instead of the "réveille" to be beaten on the following morning. This brought all the troops to arms. They were drawn up in a hollow square, when, to the surprise and delight of the soldiers, Harrison, their beloved general, appeared among them. It was with difficulty that they restrained their voices, for shouts of welcome were ready to burst from their lips. He addressed them as a kind father would talk to his children. He shamed the malcontents by saying that while he lamented the fact of their mutiny, and was mor-

---

[1] This fort was constructed of earth and logs, with a ditch extending around it, except on the Au Glaize side. At each angle was a block-house, connected by a line of pickets at their nearest angles. Outside the fort there was a *glacis*, or sloping wall of earth, eight feet thick, and outside of this the ditch, fifteen feet wide and eight feet deep. The *glacis* next to the ditch was supported by a log wall, and by *fascines*, or fagots, on the side next to the Au Glaize. Pickets, eleven feet long and one foot apart projected from the wall diagonally over the ditch, forming a *fraise* of formidable appearance. The diagram, showing the relative position of the fort to the two rivers at their confluence, and to a new fort afterward built by Winchester, may be explained as follows: A, officers' quarters; B, store-houses; C C C C, the ditch; E E, gateways; F, a dry ditch, eight feet deep, used for the safe procurement of water from the river, with pickets (*a a*) guarding it; G, draw-bridge.

tified on their account, it was of no consequence to the government, as he had now more troops than he needed, and was in expectation daily of receiving large re-enforcements from Pennsylvania and Virginia. As they had come to the woods expecting to find all the comforts and luxuries of home, they must be disappointed, and he gave them liberty to return. But he could not refrain from alluding to the mortification which he anticipated they would experience from the reception they would meet from the old and the young, who had greeted them on their march to the scene of war as their gallant neighbors. Then he appealed to their pride as soldiers and their patriotism as citizens. He told them that his government had made him commander-in-chief of the army in which they were serving, and assured them that ample supplies of provisions and other stores were on the way. When he had concluded, and the veteran Scott addressed them, saying, "You, my boys, will prove your attachment for the service of your country and your general by giving him three cheers," the wilderness instantly rang with shouts of applause, and before the sun went down perfect harmony and good feeling prevailed in the camp.

General Harrison selected a site for a new fort on the bank of the Au Glaize, about eighty yards above Old Fort Defiance, and ordered the immediate assignment of fatigue parties to construct it. General Winchester at the same time moved his camp from the Maumee to the Au Glaize, about half a mile above the site of the new fort. This movement was made on the 4th of October. That evening Harrison, accompanied by Colonel Johnson and his original battalion (composed of Johnson's, Ward's, and Ellison's companies), turned their faces toward St. Mary, where, three days afterward, their term of enlistment having expired, they were discharged. Poague's regiment was directed to return to the old Ottawa towns, twelve miles from St. Mary, after the road to Defiance should be completed, and erect a stockade there. They did so, and Poague named it Fort Amanda, in honor of a loved one in Kentucky. General Winchester was left in command of the left wing of the army, with instructions to facilitate the transportation of supplies to Fort Defiance, and to occupy a position at the Maumee Rapids as speedily as possible. When he left Winchester, Harrison expected to have all necessary supplies for advancing against Detroit within a fortnight.

Before leaving Fort Defiance Harrison ordered General Tupper to lead the mounted men, then over nine hundred in number, down the Maumee to the Rapids, and beyond if desirable, to disperse any detachments of the enemy, civilized or savage, that might be found, and to return to St. Mary by the "'Tawa" or Ottawa towns on Blanchard's Fork of the Au Glaize. But this order was not executed on account of several disturbing causes, namely, extensive damage to powder and scarcity of food, which made it difficult to provide adequate supplies for an expedition that might occupy a week or ten days; the sudden appearance of hostile Indians, who menaced Winchester's camp; dissatisfaction of some of the Kentucky troops with Tupper and his command; misunderstanding between Winchester and Tupper, and the unfriendly conduct of the former toward the latter; the weakening of Tupper's forces by the withdrawal of Kentucky troops and Simrall's dragoons; and finally the dismissal of Tupper from the command of the expedition by Winchester, who gave it to Colonel Allen, of the regulars, and which caused the Ohio troops to cross the Au Glaize, and positively refuse to march under any other than their own chosen leader.[1] The chief difficulty seems to have arisen from conflict between regular officers and volunteers; and thus terminated the expedition, said Tupper, "at one time capable of tearing the British flag from the walls of Detroit."[2]

---

[1] M'Afee, pages 148, 149; Tupper's Letter to General Harrison from Urbana, October 12, 1812; Brackenridge, page 59; Perkins, page 97.

[2] Letter to General Harrison from Urbana, dated October 12th, 1812. M'Afee, who gives a more detailed account of this affair than any other writer, says, "Some of the Kentuckians were not inclined to march under Tupper unless

Instead of returning to St. Mary, Tupper took the most direct route to Urbana by way of Hull's road, from near the present town of Kenton, where he immediately prepared for another and independent expedition to the Rapids. Winchester preferred charges against him for alleged misconduct at Defiance, and Harrison ordered his arrest, but the accused being far on his way toward the Rapids, as we shall observe presently, when the order was given, the prosecution was stayed. At Tupper's request a court of inquiry afterward investigated the matter, and he was honorably acquitted.

While on his way from Defiance to St. Mary, General Harrison was informed, by express from Fort Wayne, that the Indians were again menacing that post. At St. Mary he found Colonel Allen Trimble at the head of five hundred mounted men of Ohio, who came to join Tupper in the expedition against Detroit. These were immediately dispatched to the relief of Fort Wayne, with instructions to proceed to the St. Joseph of the Lake, about sixty miles distant, and destroy the town of the hostile Pottawatomie chief White Pigeon. The troops were disappointed, and at Fort Wayne about one half of Trimble's command refused to go farther. The gallant colonel pushed on with the remainder, destroyed two Pottawatomie villages, and would have killed or captured the inhabitants had not a treacherous guide given them timely warning of danger.

At St. Mary Harrison found some penitent Miami chiefs who had joined the enemy. They had come at the summons of messengers, and were prepared to deny their guiltiness, or to palliate it, as circumstances might dictate. They found Harrison well informed concerning their bad conduct, and they cast themselves upon the mercy of the government. As proof of their sincerity, they sent five chiefs to Piqua as hostages until the decision of the President should be made known. Thither General Harrison repaired, where he found some of Tupper's troops. He passed over to Urbana, and then southeastward to Franklinton, on the west bank of the Scioto, opposite the present city of Columbus, the capital of Ohio, whose site was then covered by the primeval forest. There, in the heart of Ohio, and at a convenient point for the concentration of troops and supplies from a distance, Harrison established his head-quarters, and occupied much of the remainder of the autumn and early winter in laborious preparations for an advance on Detroit and Canada—collecting troops and creating dépôts for supplies, building stockades and block-houses, cutting roads, and dispersing or overawing the hostile Indians, who might be excessively mischievous on the flank and rear. Poague speedily completed Fort Amanda on the Au Glaize, Colonel Barbee erected another at St. Mary, which was called Fort Barbee, and before the 1st of November the new stockade at Defiance, built chiefly of logs, was completed and named Fort Winchester.

I visited the ruins of Fort Defiance on a warm sunny day late in September, 1860. I came up the Maumee Valley by railway from Toledo on the previous evening, and arrived at Defiance Station at midnight. The village of Defiance,[1] lying mostly on the Maumee, upon the beautiful plain at the confluence of that river and Au Glaize, was shrouded in a chilling fog. Warned of the danger of the night air in that valley

---

accompanied by some field officer from Winchester's command. Colonel Allen therefore tendered his services to accompany General Tupper in any capacity he might choose to receive him. The offer was accepted. But General Winchester, having misunderstood the nature of the arrangement between them, issued an order directing Colonel Allen to take the command and march toward the Rapids. This caused a serious misunderstanding between the two generals. Colonel Allen, however, having informed General Winchester correctly on the subject, the order was immediately rescinded. The greater part of the men having by this time refused to proceed directly to the Rapids, General Tupper marched them over the Au Glaize, and proceeded to the Ottawa towns, where he professed to expect re-enforcements from Ohio." This account agrees substantially with that of Tupper in his letter to Harrison, in which he says, " It is a duty I owe to Colonel Allen to say that I have not the smallest reason to believe he was privy to the orders of General Winchester."

[1] Defiance is the county seat of Defiance County, about fifty miles northeastward from Fort Wayne. It was laid out in 1822, and from its eligible situation and fertility of the country around—the rich Black Swamp region—seems destined to become a place of much importance.

at that season of the year, I felt as if fever and ague were inhaled at every inspiration while walking a long distance to a hotel. There all was darkness. A slumbering attendant was finally aroused, and I was directed by the feeble light of a small candle to a most cheerless bedroom at one o'clock in the morning. After an early breakfast I went out to find the historical localities of the place, and was fortunate enough to be introduced to Mr. E. H. Leland and Doctor John Paul, who kindly accompanied me to them. We first visited the interesting remains of Fort Wayne on the point of land where the two ruins meet. We found the form of the *glacis* and ditch very distinctly marked, the remains of the former rising six or eight feet above the bottom of the latter. The shape of the fort was perfectly delineated by those mounds and the ditch. Some large honey-locust-trees were growing among the ruins. These have appeared since the fort was abandoned in 1795. One of them, with a triple stem, standing in the southeastern angle of the fort, measured fifteen feet in circumference. These ruins are likely to be preserved. The banks were covered with a fine sward, and they were within an inclosure containing about two acres of land, which the heirs of the late Curtis Holgate presented to the town.

We visited the site of Fort Winchester, a little above Defiance, on the bank of the Au Glaize, and found the remains of many of the pickets protruding from the ground. Across a ravine, just above the fort, was the garrison burying-ground. We returned to the village, crossed the long bridge which spans the Maumee, and from the heights of Fail's Grove, on the eastern side of the river, obtained a comprehensive view of the two streams at their confluence, the site of the fort, and the village of Defiance. The sketch there made is here given. The meeting of the waters is seen toward the left, those of the Maumee flowing in from the right to meet those of the Au Glaize, over which, in the distance, a bridge is seen. The group of trees (the honey-locusts spoken of) seen near the centre of the picture mark the site of Fort Defiance. In the foreground is seen a garden extending from the highway at the foot of the heights of Fail's Grove to the bank of the Maumee, with waving broom corn then ripe and ready for the knife.

SITE OF FORT DEFIANCE.

On our return to the village we visited on the way, near the margin of the Maumee, an aged and gigantic apple-tree, coeval, no doubt, with the one near Fort Wayne.[1] We found it carefully guarded, as a sort of "lion" of the place, by a high board fence, the ground around it, within the inclosure, thickly covered with burr-bearing weeds. It was upon the Southworth estate, and access to it might be had only through a small house near. That tree was a living monument of the French occupation of the spot, as a trading station, long before any other Europeans had penetrated that remote wilderness. It measured about fifteen feet in circumference eighteen inches from the ground. The figure standing by it affords a fair criterion for judging of

[1] See page 334.

APPLE-TREE AT DEFIANCE.

its size, by comparison with the body of a stout man. We returned to Defiance in time for dinner, and left with the early train for Fort Wayne.[1]

Let us resume the narrative of events in the Northwest in the autumn of 1812.

We left General Harrison at Franklinton, General Tupper at Urbana, and General Winchester at Fort Defiance, all engaged in preparations to move forward to the Rapids of the Maumee, and thence to Detroit. While the movement of the troops in Western Ohio and Eastern Indiana, just related, were in progress, stirring events of a like nature occurred in the region nearer the Mississippi River.

We have already noticed the departure of troops from Kentucky for Vincennes, and the messengers sent to that post by Captain Taylor, asking immediate aid for Fort Harrison on the Wabash.[2] This call was immediately responded to. Colonel William Russell, of the Seventh United States Regiment of Infantry, just arrived at Vincennes, departed at once for Fort Harrison with about twelve hundred men, consisting of three companies of Rangers, two regiments of Indiana militia, under Colonels Jordan and Evans, and Colonel Wilcox's regiment of Kentucky Volunteers. Lieutenant Richardson, of the regulars, was directed to follow with eleven men as an escort for provisions. By a forced march Russell and his party reached Fort Harrison on the 16th, much to the joy of Captain Taylor, without encountering the foe. Not so the provision escort. That was attacked by the savages on the 15th, who killed more than one half of the detachment and captured all of the provisions. Another provision train that followed immediately afterward was more fortunate. The savages were not seen. The great body of the Indians seemed to have fled from the vicinity, and Russell and his troops, except Wilcox's regiment, returned to Vincennes.

At about this time the Indians of Illinois and Northern Indiana, persuaded, like the rest of the savages under the influence of Tecumtha, after the fall of Mackinaw, Detroit, and Chicago, that the time was at hand when the white people might be driven beyond the Ohio River, every where showed signs of hostilities. These were so menacing that Ninian Edwards, the Governor of the Illinois Territory, called on the executive of Kentucky for aid. That aid was on its way in the person of Colonel Barbour and his command, when it was diverted to Vincennes, on account of the dangers impending over Fort Harrison. Edwards had sent out spies, and was persuaded that no time was to be lost in making preparations for offensive and defensive operations against the savages. He combined the scattered militia of his Territory, and caused several companies of Rangers to be encamped on the Mississippi, above St. Louis, and on the Illinois River. These served to keep the Indians in check for a time. Meanwhile Governor Shelby had made the stirring appeal[a] to the Kentuckians already alluded to.[3] He told them of the "extensive combination of the savages, aided by the British from Canada," who were momentarily expected on the frontier settlements of Illinois and Indiana. Twenty-one persons, he said, had already been murdered not more than twenty miles north of the Ohio! "It is hoped," he remarked, "that it will rouse the spirit and indignation of the freemen of Kentucky, and induce a sufficient number of them to give their services to their country for a short period." He asked them to rendezvous at Louisville on the 18th of the month, with thirty days' provisions. "Kentuckians," he said, "ever pre-eminent for their patriotism, bravery, and good conduct, will, I am persuaded, on this occasion, give to the world a new evidence of their love of coun-

[a] September 8, 1812.

---

[1] See page 43. [2] See page 197. [3] See page 323.

Wealth and Patriotism of Kentucky illustrated.   Hopkins's Expedition against Illinois Indians.   Insubordination.

try, and a determination, at every hazard, to rescue their fellow-men from the murders and devastations of a cruel and barbarous enemy."[1]

This address, as we have seen, was responded to with wonderful alacrity. Hundreds more than were needed were at Louisville on the appointed day, and were turned back with feelings of the keenest disappointment. One old veteran, who had suffered from savage cruelty, and had fought the dusky foe in the early days of Kentucky settlement, although greatly chagrined when he found his company rejected, said, "Well, well, Kentucky has often glutted the market with hemp, flour, and tobacco, and now she has done so with volunteers." This was a truthful exposition, in few words, of the wealth and patriotism of Kentucky.

General Samuel Hopkins, under whom the Kentucky Volunteers were placed, made his head-quarters at Vincennes. The troops continued to arrive and were mustered into the service from the 21st of September until the 2d of October, when Hopkins, then convalescing after a severe attack of fever, found himself at the head of almost four thousand men, about two thousand of them expert riflemen, on horseback. His little army was speedily organized,[2] and on the 10th of September he started with the mounted riflemen for the Indian country by the way of Fort Harrison. The chief design of the expedition was to march an annihilating force upon the principal Kickapoo and Peoria Indian villages on the waters of the Illinois River, the former supposed to be about eighty miles distant, and the latter one hundred and twenty miles.

Hopkins and his two thousand horsemen crossed the Wabash on the afternoon of the 14th,[a] and made their first encampment that night three miles from Fort Harrison. Before them lay magnificent level prairies, covered with tall grass, both dry and green. The guides passed a satisfactory examination as to their knowledge of the route, and the plans of the general were unanimously approved by a council of officers. On resuming the second day's march, every thing promised well excepting the lack of discipline and evident restlessness under restraint manifested by the troops. Indeed, so far as military discipline was concerned, they constituted little more than a vast mob, and it was soon found that every man was disposed to be a law unto himself. Every hour of the march revealed to the commanding general evidences of the fact that his army was as combustible as the dry grass around them. The symptoms of discontent, seen even at Vincennes, now assumed the positive forms of complaint and murmuring. The guides were suspected of ignorance or disloyalty; and food and forage, it was alleged, were becoming alarmingly scarce. Finally, while halting on the fourth day's march, a major, whose name is withheld, rode up to the commanding general, and in an insolent manner peremptorily ordered him to march the troops back to Fort Harrison. Not long afterward a violent wind arose that blew directly toward them, and very soon it was discovered that the prairie was on fire at the windward. They saved themselves by burning the grass around their camp. It was believed that this was the work of the Indians, and it gave the finishing blow to the expedition. The troops would not march farther. Hopkins called a council of officers,[b] when it was decided by them to return, as their men were utterly unmanageable. The mortified commander then called for five hundred volunteers to follow him to the Illinois. Not one responded to his summons. His authority had vanished. They even refused to sub-

[a] October, 1812.

[b] October 20.

---

[1] Address of Governor Shelby, issued at Frankfort September 8, 1812.
[2] Four regiments were at first formed, to be commanded respectively by Colonels Samuel Caldwell, John Thomas, James Allen, and Young Ewing. These constituted two brigades, the first to be commanded by General James Ray, an early adventurer in Kentucky and experienced Indian fighter,[*] and the other by General Jonathan Ramsey. After this arrangement was made, another, under Colonel Samuel South, was organized. George Walker was appointed judge advocate of the little army, Pierce Butler adjutant general, Majors William Trigg and William A. Lee aids to General Hopkins, William Blair and Joseph Weisiger volunteer aids, and John C. Breckinridge the general's secretary.

[*] For an account of the early adventures of General Ray, see Collins's *Kentucky, its History, Antiquities, and Biography*, page 458.

mit to his leadership on their return, and he *followed* his army back to Fort Harrison, where they arrived on the 25th.[1] Thus ended an apparently formidable and promising expedition. Yet it was not unfruitful of good. It alarmed the Indians, gave them a sense of the real power of the white people, and made them more cautious and circumspect. That imposing force had marched eighty or ninety miles in the Indian country without show of opposition any where.

While Hopkins's expedition was in motion, another, under Colonel Russell, composed of two small companies of United States Rangers, marched from Vincennes[a] to unite with a small body of mounted militia under Governor Edwards (who assumed the chief command), for the purpose of penetrating the region toward which General Hopkins was marching, and to co-operate with him. Their combined force numbered nearly four hundred men, rank and file. They penetrated deeply into the Indian country, but, hearing nothing of Hopkins, and being too few to attempt much, they contented themselves with some minor exploits. They fell suddenly and furiously upon the principal Kickapoo town, twenty miles above Peoria, at the head of Peoria Lake, and drove the Indian inhabitants into a swamp, through which for three miles they were vigorously pursued, the invaders finding themselves frequently waist-deep in mud and water. The fugitives fled in dismay across the Illinois River. Many of the pursuers passed over, and brought back canoes with dead Indians in them. Twenty lifeless warriors lay prone in the path of the returning victors. Doubtless many more perished in the morass and the stream. The town, with a large quantity of corn and other property, was destroyed. The spoils brought away were eighty horses, and the dried scalps of several white persons who had been murdered by the savages.[2] The expedition returned, after an absence of thirteen days, with no other serious casualty than four men wounded, not one of them mortally.

[a] October 11, 1812.

General Hopkins discharged the mutinous mounted men, and organized another expedition against the Indians. This force, twelve hundred and fifty strong, was composed chiefly of foot soldiers, and the object of the expedition was the destruction of the Prophet's town, and other Indian villages on the Upper Wabash. His troops consisted of three regiments of Kentucky militia, commanded respectively by Colonels Barbour, Miller, and Wilcox; a small company of regulars, under Captain Zachary Taylor; a company of Rangers, commanded by Captain Beckers; and a company of scouts or spies, led by Captain Washburne. The greater portion of them rendezvoused at Vincennes, and moved up the Wabash Valley to Fort Harrison, where they arrived on the 5th of November. Six days afterward they marched from the fort up the road made by Harrison a year before, and, at the same time, seven boats, filled with provisions, forage, and military stores, well guarded by Lieutenant Colonel Barbour with a battalion of his regiment, moved up the river. The Indians were supposed to be on the alert, and the march was cautiously pursued. The streams were full of water, and the passage of swamps and low lands was extremely difficult and fatiguing. They did not cross the Wabash as Harrison did, but, for sufficient reasons, marched up the east side of that stream.

So difficult was the march that the expedition did not reach the Prophet's town until the 19th, when Hopkins dispatched Adjutant General Butler, with three hundred men, to surprise a Winnebago village of about forty houses on the present Wild Cat Creek, a mile from the Wabash, and about four miles below the Prophet's town. The village was deserted. Flames soon laid it in ashes. The Prophet's town, about equal in size, and a large Kickapoo village just below it, containing about one hund-

---

[1] Hopkins's Report to Governor Shelby, dated Fort Harrison, October 26, 1812; Dillon's History of Indiana, page 497; M'Afee, page 158.
[2] Colonel William Russell's Letter to General Gibson, the acting governor of Indiana, dated "Camp Russell, October 31, 1812."

| The Indians attack a Burial Party. | Sufferings of the Kentucky Soldiers. | Close of Hopkins's military Career. |

red and sixty huts, with all their winter provision of corn and beans, were utterly destroyed.

It was not until the 21st that any Indians were discovered. On that day they fired upon a small party of soldiers, and killed one man. On the following morning sixty horsemen, under Colonels Miller and Wilcox, went out to bury the dead, when they were suddenly attacked by Indians in ambush, and lost eighteen men, killed, wounded, and missing, in the skirmish that ensued.[1] The rendezvous of the savages, in a strong position on the Wild Cat, was soon discovered, and preparations were made for dislodging them, when they decamped and disappeared. The season was far advanced, the cold was increasing, and ice was beginning to form in the river. These circumstances, and the fact that many of the troops, especially the Kentuckians, were "shoeless and shirtless"—clad in the remnants of their summer clothes, caused an order to be issued on the 25th for a return to Fort Harrison and Vincennes.[2] "We all suffered very much," said Pierre La Plante, of Vincennes, who was one of the troops, "but I pitied the poor Kentuckians. They were almost naked and barefoot—only their linen hunting-shirts—the ground covered with snow, and the Wabash freezing up."[3]

With this more successful expedition ended General Hopkins's military career. In general orders, issued at Vincennes on the 18th of December following, he said: "The commander-in-chief now closes his command, and, in all probability, his military services forever." Most of the volunteers were now discharged, and Illinois and Indiana experienced a season of comparative repose.

---

[1] This detachment was composed of Captain Beckers's company of Rangers, a small number of mounted militia, and several army officers.
[2] General Hopkins's Letter to Governor Shelby, November 27, 1812.
[3] Dillon's *History of Indiana*, Note, page 502.

Y

CHAPTER XVII.

"How dread was the conflict, how bloody the fray,
Told the banks of the Raisin at the dawn of the day;
While the gush from the wounds of the dying and dead
Had thaw'd for the warrior a snow-sheeted bed.

"But where is the pride that a soldier can feel,
To temper with mercy the wrath of the steel,
While Proctor, victorious, denies to the brave
Who had fallen in battle, the gift of a grave?"

ALL through the months of October, November, and December,[a] General Harrison labored incessantly and intensely in making preparations for a winter campaign in the Northwest. The nation was feverish and impatient. Ignorance of military necessities allowed unjust and injurious censures and criticisms to be made—unjust to the officers and soldiers in the field, and injurious to the cause. The desire of the people to recover all that Hull had lost would brook no restraint, nor listen to any excuse for delay. A winter campaign was demanded, and Harrison was not a man to shrink from any required duty. He knew that much was expected of him; and day and night his head and hands were at work, with only the intermissions required by the necessity for taking food, indulging in sleep, and the observance of the Sabbath. Taking all things into consideration, his task was Herculean, and to some men would have been appalling. He was compelled to create an army out of good but exceedingly crude materials. He was compelled to reconcile many differences and difficulties in order to insure the harmony arising from perfect discipline. He was compelled to concentrate forces and supplies at some eligible point, like the Rapids of the Maumee, while perplexed with the greatest impediments. His operations were necessarily threefold in character — preparative, offensive, and defensive, in a wilderness filled with hostile savages controlled and supported by British regulars. A frontier, hundreds of miles in extent, must be protected at all hazards from the hatchet and the knife. The season was becoming more and more inclement. From the fortieth degree of latitude northward (the direction of his projected march) was a region of dark forests and black swamps. The autumnal rains had commenced, filling every stream, and making every morass brimful of water. Through these, roads and causeways for wagons and pack-horses must be cut and constructed, over which supplies of every kind, with men and artillery, must be conveyed. Block-houses were to be built, magazines of provisions established, and a vigilant watch kept upon the savages who might prowl upon flanks and rear. All this had to be done with undisciplined troops prone to self-reliance and independence, with great uncertainty whether volunteers would swell his army for invasion to the promised dimensions of ten thousand men.

Yet, in view of all these labors and difficulties, Harrison was cheerful and hopeful. "I am fully sensible of the responsibility invested in me," he wrote to the Secretary of War on the 13th of October. "I accepted it with full confidence of being able to effect the wishes of the President, or to show unequivocally their impracticability. If the fall should be very dry, I will take Detroit before the winter sets in; but if we should have much rain, it will be necessary to wait at the Rapids until the Mi-

[a] 1812.

ami of the Lake [Maumee, or Miami of the Lakes] is sufficiently frozen over to bear the army and its baggage."

Nine days later Harrison wrote, "I am not able to fix any period for the advance of the troops to Detroit. It is pretty evident that it can not be done upon proper principles until the frost shall become so severe as to enable us to use the rivers and the margin of the lake for transportation of the baggage and artillery upon the ice. To get them forward through a swampy wilderness of near two hundred miles, in wagons or on pack-horses, which are to carry their own provisions, is absolutely impossible." He then referred to a suggestion of a Congressman that the possession of Detroit by the enemy would probably be the most effectual bar to the attainment of peace, then hoped for, and observed, " If this were really the case, I would undertake to recover it with a detachment of the army at any time. A few hundred pack-horses, with a drove of beeves (without artillery or heavy baggage), would subsist the fifteen hundred or two thousand men which I would select for the purpose until the residue of the army could arrive. But, having in view offensive operations *from* Detroit, an advance of this sort would be premature, and ultimately disadvantageous. No species of supplies are calculated on being found in the Michigan Territory. The farms upon the Raisin, which might have afforded a quantity of forage, are nearly all broken up and destroyed. This article, then, as well as the provisions for the men, is to be taken from this state—a circumstance which must at once put to rest every idea for a land conveyance at this season, since it would require at least two wagons with forage for each one that is loaded with provisions and other articles. My present plan is," he continued, " to occupy Upper Sandusky, and accumulate at that place as much provision and forage as possible, to be taken from thence upon sleds to the River Raisin. At Defiance, Fort Jennings, and St. Mary, boats and sleds are preparing to take advantage of a rise of water or a fall of snow."

At this time, the troops moving on the line of operations which passed from Franklinton (head-quarters) and Delaware, by Upper to Lower Sandusky, composed of the brigades from Virginia and Pennsylvania, and one of Ohio, under General Simon Perkins,[1] were designated in general orders, and known as the right wing of the army;

---

[1] Simon Perkins was born at Norwich, Connecticut, on the 17th of September, 1771. His father was a captain in the army of the Revolution, and died in camp. He emigrated to Oswego, New-York, in 1795, where he spent three years in extensive land operations. A portion of the "Western Reserve," in Ohio, having been sold by the State of Connecticut, the new proprietors invited Mr. Perkins to explore the domain, and report a plan for the sale and settlement of the lands. He went to Ohio for that purpose in the spring of 1798. He spent the summer there in the performance of the duties of his agency, and returned to Connecticut in the autumn. This excursion and these duties were repeated by him for several successive summers. He finally married in 1804, and settled on the "Reserve" at Warren. So extensive were the land agencies intrusted to him, that in 1815 the state land-tax paid by him into the public treasury was one seventh of the entire revenue of the state. Mr. Perkins was the first post-master on the "Reserve," and to him the post-master general intrusted the arrangement of post-offices in that region. For twenty-eight years he received and merited the confidence of the department and the people. At the request of the government, in 1807 he established expresses through the Indian country to Detroit. His efforts led to the treaty of Brownsville in the autumn of 1808, when the Indians ceded lands for a road from the "Reserve" to the Maumee, or Miami of the Lakes. In May of that year he was commissioned a brigadier general of militia, in the division commanded by Major General Wadsworth. On hearing of the disaster to Hull's army at Detroit, he issued orders to his colonels to prepare their regiments for active duty. In him was assigned the duty of protecting a large portion of the Northwestern frontier. "To the care of Brigadier General Simon Perkins I commit you," said Wadsworth on parting with the troops of the *Reserve*, "who will be your commander and your friend. In his integrity, skill, and courage, we all have the utmost confidence." He was exceedingly active. His scouts were out, far and near, continually. His public accounts were kept with the greatest clearness and accuracy for more than forty years. "No two officers in the public service at that time," testifies the Honorable Elisha Whittlesey, "were more energetic or economical than Generals Harrison and Perkins." When, in 1813, General Harrison was sufficiently re-enforced to dispense with Perkins's command, he left the service [February 28, 1813], bearing the highest encomiums of the commander-in-chief of the Army of the Northwest. President Madison, at the suggestion of Harrison and others, sent him the commission of colonel in the regular army, but duty to his family and the demands of a greatly increasing business caused him to decline it.

General Perkins was intrusted with the arrangement and execution, at the head of a commission, of the extensive canal system of Ohio. From 1826 until 1838 he was an active member of the "Board of Canal Fund Commissioners." They were under no bonds and received no pecuniary reward. In the course of about seven years they issued and sold state bonds for the public improvements to the amount of four and a half millions of dollars. Among the remarkable men who settled the "Western Reserve," General Simon Perkins ever held one of the most conspicuous places, and his influence in social and moral life is felt in that region to this day. He died at Warren, Ohio, on the 19th of November, 1844. His widow long survived him. She died at the same place in April, 1862. To their son, Joseph Perkins, Esq., of Cleveland, I am indebted for the materials for this brief sketch, and the likeness of the patriot on the next page.

Tupper's brigade, that was to move on Hull's road, by Fort M'Arthur, was called the centre; and the Kentuckians under Winchester were styled the left wing. The Virginia and Pennsylvania troops were employed in escorting the artillery and military stores toward Upper Sandusky; the Ohio troops conveyed provisions from Manary's Block-house, near the head of the Great Miami, twenty miles north of Urbana, to Forts M'Arthur and Findlay, on Hull's road; while the Kentuckians were traversing the swamps of the St. Mary and the Au Glaize, and descending those rivers in small craft, to carry provisions to Fort Winchester (Defiance) on the left wing.[1]

Northwestern Ohio, particularly the settlements on the *Western Reserve*,[2] had been alive with excitement and patriotic zeal during all the autumn, and General Wadsworth, commander of the 4th Division of the Ohio Militia (the boundaries of which comprised the counties of Jefferson and Turnbull, thus embracing at least one third of the state) was continually, vigilantly, and efficiently employed in the promotion of measures for the defense of the frontier from the Maumee to Erie, and for the recovery of Michigan. In politics General Wadsworth was a Democrat of the Jefferson school. He had watched with interest and indignation the course of Great Britain for many years, and when the Congress of the nation declared war against her, he rejoiced in the act as a righteous and necessary one. He had been an active soldier of the Revolution,[3] and now, when his country needed his

---

[1] M'Afee, pages 103, 104.

[2] The charter of Connecticut, granted in 1662, covered the country from Rhode Island, or, as expressed, "Narragansett River," on the east, to the Pacific on the west. When New York, New Jersey, and Pennsylvania claimed dominion above the line of the southern boundary of the province, difficulties appeared. These were disposed of. In 1786 the State of Connecticut ceded to the United States all the lands within the charter limits westward of Pennsylvania, excepting a tract one hundred and twenty miles in length westward, adjoining that state. The cession was accepted. This was called the *Connecticut* or *Western Reserve*; and many settlers went there from the State of Connecticut. A part of the Reserve, containing half a million of acres, was granted by the state to the inhabitants of New London, Fairfield, and Norwalk, whose property had been burnt by the British during the Revolution. This was known as *The Fire Lands*. The remainder of the *Reserve* was sold in 1795, and the proceeds of the sale were devoted to the formation of the present school fund of Connecticut.

[3] Elijah Wadsworth was born in Hartford, Connecticut, on the 4th of November, 1747, and became a resident of Litchfield before the Revolution. After the battle of Bunker's Hill he volunteered to go to Boston, but his purpose was frustrated, when he engaged heartily in raising Colonel Elisha Sheldon's troop of light-horsemen. He was commissioned a lieutenant of the company of which Benjamin Tallmadge was captain. He served with zeal during the entire war. He commanded the guard in whose custody Major André was placed immediately after his arrest.

Wadsworth was a man of great energy. He went early to Ohio, and was part owner of the "Western Reserve." He made his residence at Canfield, Ohio, in 1802, and was always a leading man in that section of the new state, and was

services, he cheerfully offered them. Although he was sixty-five years of age, he entered upon active military duties with energy with the late venerable Elisha Whittlesey, of Canfield,[1] and the late Honorable Benjamin Tappen, of Steubenville, Ohio, as his aid-de-camp. The former accompanied him to Cleveland from Canfield,[2] and the latter soon joined him there.

General Wadsworth was at his house in Canfield when intelligence of the surrender of Hull reached him.[3] The alarming rumors that prevailed concerning the imminence of an invasion called for immediate and energetic action. Wadsworth at once issued orders to the several brigadier generals of his division to muster the militia for the protection of the frontier from the immediate incursions of the British and their savage allies. Already citizens of the region adjacent to Canfield had formed a corps of dragoons, under Captain James Dowd. This company was ordered into the service; and so promptly did it respond to the call, that by noon the following day (Sunday, August 23d, 1812), it was on its march toward Cleveland as an honorary escort

---

very efficient in the organization of the crude material of pioneer life into well-balanced society, the establishment of schools, etc. His aid was essential in the establishment of the state government, and when the militia was enrolled he was chosen major general of the 4th Division. In that office he was found when war broke out in 1812. His services in the war are recorded in the text. On his tomb-stone at Canfield are the following words: "Major General Elijah Wadsworth moved into Canfield in October A.D. 1802, and died December 30, 1817, aged 70 years, 1 month, and 17 days."

[1] Elisha Whittlesey was born in Litchfield County, Connecticut, on the 19th of October, 1783. His father, a practical farmer, was a member of the Connecticut Legislature seventeen consecutive sessions, and was a member of the State Convention that ratified the Constitution of the United States. The subject of this brief memoir was a pupil of Rev. Thomas Robbins, of Danbury, Connecticut, who died only a few years ago, and also of the eminent Moses Stuart, of Andover. He studied law, and was admitted to practice at Fairfield in the winter of 1805. He commenced practice at New Milford, but in June, 1806, he emigrated to Ohio, and settled at Canfield, Turnbull County, which place was his home when in private life. In the autumn of that year he was admitted to practice in the Supreme Court of Ohio, and at the first session of the Court of Common Pleas thereafter he was appointed prosecuting attorney, which office he held sixteen years. When the war broke out he was appointed aid to General Wadsworth. On the retirement of General Wadsworth from the service, Mr. Whittlesey was appointed brigade major in General Simon Perkins's corps, and was with that officer during the remainder of his campaign in Northern Ohio in 1812-'13. He was sent by General Harrison from the Rapids of the Maumee, after the defeat of General Winchester at the Raisin, to ask the Legislature of Ohio to pass a law providing for the payment of such Ohio troops as should remain in service after their time of enlistment should expire. He was successful.

Mr. Whittlesey resumed his profession after the war. He served as a member of the Ohio Legislature from 1820 to 1822 inclusive, when he was elected to Congress, in which he served fourteen consecutive years. During all that time he was a member of the Committee on Claims, full one half of that time its chairman, and was never absent, excepting on public business, but for *one day*, for which, in the settlement of his accounts, he deducted the sum of eight dollars—a day's salary! President Harrison appointed him auditor of the treasury of the Post-office Department in March, 1841. He resigned it in 1843. President Taylor appointed him comptroller of the treasury in June, 1849. He offered his resignation to President Pierce, but that gentleman, knowing the value of an honest man in that responsible station, would not accept it. In March, 1857, he tendered his resignation to President Buchanan. He accepted it in May, saying, "The Lord knows I do not wish you to resign at all." On the 10th of April, 1861, President Lincoln called him from his home to occupy the same responsible position. He cheerfully responded to the call of his country, although seventy-eight years of age, and faithfully discharged the duties of his office until a few days before his death, which occurred on Wednesday, the 7th day of January, 1863, when in the eightieth year of his age.

[2] Canfield, the capital of Mahoning County, Ohio, was then the residence of General Wadsworth, and also of Mr. Whittlesey.

[3] It came in the form of a letter written by Alfred Kelley, and signed by twelve other citizens of Cleveland. B. Fitch, of Ellsworth, was the bearer of it.

for the commanding general. They marched by the way of Hudson,[1] twenty-five miles from Cleveland, and breakfasted there, at Oviatt's, on the morning of the 24th.[a] Soon after resuming their march they met some of Hull's paroled army, who had been landed from British boats at Cleveland. Their stories increased the panic caused by startling rumors, and many of the inhabitants along the lake were fleeing from their homes eastward or toward the Ohio, to avoid the apprehended oncoming evils. Wadsworth tried to allay the excitement, but it was rolling over the frontier in an almost resistless flood. When the cavalcade entered Cleveland that afternoon at four o'clock, it created great joy among the few inhabitants there. Two or three hours later Colonel Cass arrived at Cleveland from Detroit on his way to Washington City, and at the request of General Wadsworth he was accompanied to the seat of government by ex-governor Samuel Huntington, then at Cleveland,[2] as bearer of an important letter to the Secretary of War. In that letter Wadsworth informed the secretary that he had called out about three thousand of the militia of his division, to rendezvous at Cleveland, but was compelled to acknowledge them destitute of arms, ammunition, and proper equipments for a campaign, as well as the difficulty of feeding them. Properly estimating the value of the great Northwest to the Union, and the importance of these troops for its protection, as well as in the efforts to be made for the recovery of Michigan, "so dishonorably given up to the enemy," he urged the government to extend its immediate and unceasing aid in supplying the wants of this little army then hastening to the field. "The fate of the Western country," he said, "is suspended on the decision the government shall make to this application."[3]

[a] August, 1812.

General Wadsworth did not wait for a reply. Necessity demanded instant action. He took the responsibility of appointing commissioners of supplies, and giving receipts to those who furnished them in the name of the government.[4] The people, with equal faith in the wisdom of the general and the justice of the government, responded without hesitation to the call for provisions and forage. Nor was that faith disappointed. By a letter dated the 5th of September, Wadsworth's course was sanctioned by the War Department, and he was invested with full power to take measures for supplying his troops and giving efficiency to their service.

Intelligence came to Wadsworth almost hourly of the distress of the inhabitants on the Raisin, and along the lake shore eastward as far as the Huron River, who, in violation of the agreements of the capitulations at Detroit, were being plundered by the Indians even of their boots and shoes. Their homes were broken up by the marauders, and many of the inhabitants were fleeing for their lives. The benevolent Wadsworth was exceedingly anxious to send them relief, and it was with real joy that he welcomed the arrival at Cleveland, on the 26th of August, of General Simon Perkins with a large body of troops. He resolved to send him forward to the Huron immediately with a thousand men, to erect block-houses and protect the inhabitants.

---

[1] The capital of the present Summit County, Ohio. It was the first settlement made in the county. In the division of the Western Reserve among the purchasers from Connecticut, this section fell to the lot of David Hudson, who commenced a settlement in the year 1800. Mr. Hudson died in March, 1836, aged seventy-five years.

[2] Huntington was governor of Ohio from 1808 to 1810. In the latter part of his life he resided at Painesville, in Lake County, where he died in 1817. He lived in Cleveland for a while before making his residence at Painesville. As an illustration of the wonderful growth of American cities, and the rapid settlement and clearing of the country westward of the Alleghany Mountains, I mention the fact that Governor Huntington, when approaching Cleveland from the east one night, and only two miles from it, was attacked by a pack of wolves. He beat them off with his umbrella, and made his escape to the town through the fleetness of his horse. That was only about fifty years ago. Cleveland now [1867] contains more than 50,000 inhabitants.

[3] MS. Letter of General Wadsworth to the Secretary of War, dated Cleveland, August 25, 1812.

[4] The commissioners appointed were Aaron Norton, Eleazer Hicock, and Ebenezer Murray. The people sold to them, on the terms offered, as cheaply as if paid in gold and silver. They gave a certificate in writing stating the article furnished, its quantity and value, with a promise to pay for it when the government should remit funds for the purpose. Property abandoned by frightened inhabitants was taken, appraised, and inventoried. A fatigue party would harvest a field of grain, while an officer kept an exact account of the whole matter, and the owners were afterward remunerated. In the final settlement hardly a single case of dissatisfaction occurred.—Statement of Hon. Elisha Whittlesey to the author.

Re-enforcements for Winchester. March to Detroit suspended. Attempted Lodgment at the Maumee Rapids.

General Reazin Beall[1] was also directed to go westward on a similar errand; and preparations for their departure were nearly completed, when Wadsworth received dispatches from the Secretary of War saying that the President intended to adopt the most vigorous measures "to repair the disasters at Detroit," and to prosecute with increased ardor the important objects of the campaign. Wadsworth was directed to forward fifteen hundred men to the frontier as quickly as possible, with directions to "report to General Winchester, or officer commanding" there, at the same time promising an adequate supply of arms and ammunition. Arrangements for the movement were speedily made, and Perkins and Beall, who had been employed by Governor Meigs in opening a road from Mansfield, in the interior of Ohio (now capital of Richland County), to Lower Sandusky, were ordered toward the latter place. Some clashing of authority between Wadsworth and Meigs, and some complaints concerning affairs in the region bordering on Lake Erie, caused Harrison, who (as we have seen) was made commander-in-chief of the Northwestern Army, to make a personal examination of matters there toward the close of October. He found General Wadsworth near the mouth of the Huron River, at the head of eight hundred men. Beall, with about five hundred, was at Mansfield. The two corps were consolidated and placed under General Perkins, with orders to proceed to Lower Sandusky, and open a road thence to the Rapids of the Maumee; a severe task, for it was necessary to causeway it about fifteen miles. This was accomplished. Harrison returned to his head-quarters at Franklinton early in November, and on the 15th of that month was compelled to inform the War Department that he doubted the propriety of attempting to penetrate Canada, or to proceed farther than the Rapids during the winter, owing to the insurmountable difficulties in the way of transporting forage and supplies. "I know it will be mortifying to Kentucky," Harrison wrote to Governor Shelby, "for this army to return without doing any thing; but it is better to do that than to attempt impossibilities. I wish to God the public mind were informed of our difficulties, and gradually prepared for this course. In my opinion, we should in this quarter disband all but those sufficient for a strong frontier guard, convoys, etc., and prepare for the next season."

General Tupper had made another unsuccessful attempt to establish a permanent lodgment at the Maumee Rapids, and this failure doubtless gave nerve to Harrison's convictions. We left Tupper at Urbana, after his difficulties with Winchester at Defiance. He pushed forward along Hull's road to Fort M'Arthur, and there he speedily prepared an expedition to the Rapids, consisting of six hundred and fifty mounted men who volunteered for the service. He had sent Captain Hinkson, at the head of a company of spies, to reconnoitre at the Rapids, who returned with a British captain, named Clarke, as his prisoner. The result of the reconnoissance was information that there were three or four hundred Indians, and about seventy-five British regulars at the Rapids, who were there for the purpose of carrying off a quantity of corn at that post. Tupper immediately notified General Winchester of his intended expedition, and, on the 10th,[a] moved forward with his command along Hull's road toward the Rapids, taking with him a light six-pounder, and five days' provisions in the knapsacks of the men.   [a] November, 1812.

The roads were wretched, and Tupper was compelled to leave his little cannon at a block-house on the way. From Portage River, twenty miles from the Rapids, he sent forward a reconnoitring party, following slowly with his whole command. Within a few miles of the Rapids he met his spies returning with information that the enemy were still there. Halting until twilight, he marched forward to a ford

---

[1] Reazin Beall, of Pennsylvania, was an ensign in the United States Infantry in 1792, and was in the third sub-legion the same year. He was adjutant and quartermaster the following year. He served under Wayne for a while, and resigned at the beginning of 1794. From the 8th of September till the 3d of November, 1812, he was a brigadier general of Ohio volunteers. He represented Ohio in Congress from 1813 till 1815. He died on the 20th of February, 1842.—Gardner's *Dictionary of the Army*, page 59.

about two miles above the Rapids. Thence spies were again sent forward, and returned, saying, "They are closely encamped, and are singing and dancing." Tupper resolved to attack them at dawn, and orders were given to cross the river immediately. The sky was clear, and the weather intensely cold. The men were much fatigued, yet the excitement gave them strength. Tupper dashed into the icy flood at the head of his men, and crossed with the first section in safety; but the water, waist-deep at times, and flowing in a swift current, confused and swept from their feet many of the next division. They were exposed to great perils, but none were lost. After ineffectual attempts to accomplish the undertaking, those who had crossed were recalled, and the whole body retired to the woods and encamped.

Early the next morning Tupper sent to Winchester for re-enforcements and food; and some spies went down the river, showed themselves opposite the enemy's camp, and tried to entice them across. They failed, when Tupper moved down with his whole body, and displayed the heads of his columns in the open space between the river and the woods. This frightened the enemy. "The squaws," said a contemporary writer,[1] "ran to the woods; the British ran to their boats, and escaped. The Indians, more brave than their allies, paraded, and fired across the river, but without effect." They used muskets and a four-pound cannon. Tupper then fell back, hoping the savages in a body would venture across the Maumee, but they did not. Some mounted Indians were seen to go up the stream, and at the same time some of Tupper's men, contrary to orders, entered a field to pull corn, while others pursued a drove of hogs in the same direction. The latter were suddenly assailed by a party of mounted savages who had crossed unperceived, and four of Tupper's men were killed. The Indians, excited by the shedding of blood, fell upon the left flank of the white army, but were repulsed. Almost at the same moment, a large body of the savages, under the notable chief Split-Log, who rode a fine white horse, crossed the river above the advance of Tupper's column. They were driven back by Bentley's battalion with some loss, and the Ohio troops were not again annoyed by them. Late in the evening Tupper and his men turned their faces toward Fort M'Arthur, for their provisions were almost exhausted, and their nearest point of sure supply was forty miles distant.

Winchester, in the mean time, having received Tupper's first message, had sent a detachment, under Colonel Lewis, of four hundred and fifty men, to co-operate with the Ohio troops. Tupper's appeal for men and food, which reached him later, was forwarded to Lewis as soon as it was received by Winchester, and the former pushed forward by a forced march to the relief of the imperiled ones. Finding Tupper's camp deserted, apparently with haste, and in it two dead men scalped, Lewis supposed he had been defeated. Under this impression, he retreated to Winchester's camp. Thus ended this bold attempt to take position at the Rapids. The intentions of the projector failed, but the expedition had the effect to frighten the British and Indians away before they had gathered up the corn; and averted, for the time, a contemplated blow by the savages upon the alarmed French settlements on the Raisin, at the instigation of their British allies.[2]

---

[1] M'Afee, page 170. See also Brackenridge, page 61.

[2] Just before the approach of Tupper the following note (of course, written by one of the British allies) from the Indians was sent to the inhabitants on the Raisin:

"*The Hurons and other tribes of Indians, assembled at the Miami Rapids, to the inhabitants of the River Raisin.*

"FRIENDS,—Listen: you have always told us that you would give us any assistance in your power. We therefore, as the enemy is approaching us, within twenty-five miles, call upon you all to rise up and come here immediately, bringing your arms along with you. Should you fail at this time, we will not consider you in future as friends, and the consequences may be very unpleasant. We are well convinced that you have no writing forbidding you to assist us.

"We are your friends at present.
"Round + Head,
his mark.
"Walk-in- + the-Water,"
his mark.

Services of Captain Logan.   His Death.   Wa-pagh-ko-netta and its notable Indians.

At about this time the American service in the Northwest lost a valuable friend. It was the settled policy of the government not to employ the Indians in war, but there were occasions when exceptions to the rule became a necessity. It was so in Ohio. There was an active, intelligent, and influential chief, a nephew of Tecumtha (son of his sister), who, when a boy, having been captured by General John Logan, of Kentucky, received that gentleman's name, and bore it through life. His wife had also been a captive to a Kentuckian (Colonel Hardin), and both felt a warm attachment to the white people. Major Hardin (then in the Army of the Northwest, and son of Colonel Hardin) and Logan were true friends, and highly esteemed each other. Logan had much influence with his tribe, and when the war broke out he asked for employment in the American service. It was granted, because he might have been made an enemy. He accompanied Hull to Detroit, and was exceedingly active as a scout. We have also seen that Harrison employed him on a mission to Fort Wayne.

Soon after the return of Tupper from the Rapids, Logan and his followers were sent toward that post to reconnoitre. They met a strong opposing party, and, to save themselves, scattered in every direction. Captain Logan, with two friends (Captains John and Bright Horn), made his way to Winchester's camp, where he related their adventures. His fidelity was ungenerously suspected, and he was believed to be a spy. His pride and every sentiment of manhood were deeply wounded by the suspicion, and he resolved to vindicate his character by actions rather than by words. He started[a] with his two friends for the Rapids, with the determination to bring in a prisoner or a scalp. They had not gone far when they were made prisoners themselves by a son of Colonel Elliott and some Indians, among whom was Win-ne-meg, or Win-ne-mac—the Pottawatomie chief who bore Hull's dispatch from Fort Wayne to Chicago.[1] He was now an ally of the British. He knew Logan well, and rejoiced in being the captor of an old enemy. The latter resolved to make a desperate effort for liberty. His companions were made to understand significant signs, and at a concerted signal they attacked their captors. Logan shot Win-ne-meg dead. Elliott and a young Ottawa chief were also slain. Logan was badly wounded, so was Bright Horn; but they leaped upon the backs of horses of the enemy and escaped to Winchester's camp. Captain John followed the next morning with the scalp of the Ottawa. Logan's honor and fidelity were fully vindicated, but at the cost of his life—his wound was mortal. After he had suffered great agony for two days, his spirit returned to the Great Master of Life. Proctor had offered, it is said, one hundred and fifty dollars for his scalp. It was never taken from his head. His body was carried in mournful procession, by Major Hardin and others, to Wa-pagh-ko-netta,[2] where his family resided, and was buried

[a] November 22, 1812.

---

[1] See page 305.

[2] This is a small village in Allen County, Ohio, on the Au Glaize River, about ten miles from St. Mary. After the Shawnoese were driven from Piqua by General Clark in 1780, they established a village here, and named it Wa-pagh-ko-netta, in honor of a chief of that name. Colonel John Johnston informed me that he knew the chief well. He said he had a club-foot, and thinks the name had some relation to that deformity. Colonel Johnston resided at Wa-pagh-ko-netta for some time. The Society of Friends, or Quakers, had a mission there for a number of years. It was the home of Blue Jacket, spoken of in our account of the invasion of the country by Wayne, in 1794. Buckongahelos also resided there; also the celebrated Black Hoof, who was a native of Florida, whose birthplace was on the Suwanee. He remembered the removal of that tribe from their southern home to the forests of Pennsylvania and Ohio. He was at the defeat of Braddock in 1755. In all the wars with the white people in his region, from that time until the treaty of Greenville in 1795, he was a popular leader, and could always command as many men for the war-path as he desired. He was a party to the treaty at Greenville, and was ever faithful to his pledges there made. Tecumtha could not seduce him, and he was the faithful friend of the Americans in the war with Great Britain which we are now considering. A few weeks after the burial of Logan [January, 1813], he visited General Tupper's camp at Fort M'Arthur. While sitting by the fire with the general, a scoundrel militia-man, Colonel Johnston informed me, fired a pistol ball at him through the logs of the block-house, which entered his cheek, passed through his mouth, cut off his palate, and lodged in his neck. He would never have the ball removed, but would call the children to feel of it, and then would tell them of his wrongs. Colonel Johnston gave him a healing plaster for his wound in the form of a bank-note of the denomination of one hundred dollars. Colonel Johnston says he was one of the most perfectly formed men he ever saw. He was naturally cheerful and good-natured. He lived with his wife faithfully for forty years. His stature was small, and his eyesight remained perfect during his whole life.

there with mingled savage rites and military honors. The scalp of the slain Ottawa, raised upon a pole, was carried in the funeral procession and then taken to the council-house. Logan's death was mourned as a public calamity, for he was one of the most intelligent, active, and trustworthy of Harrison's scouts.

At this time the Miamis, nearly all of whom had become wedded to the interests of the British, were assembled, with some Delawares from White River, in towns on the Mississiniwa, a tributary of the Wabash, fifteen or twenty miles from its confluence with the latter stream, near the boundary-line between the present Wabash and Grant Counties, Indiana. They were evidently there for hostile purposes, and General Harrison resolved to destroy or disperse them. He detached for the purpose Lieutenant Colonel John B. Campbell, of the Nineteenth Regiment of United States Infantry,[1] composed mainly of Colonel Simrall's regiment of Kentucky dragoons; a squadron of United States volunteer dragoons, commanded by Major James V. Ball; and a corps of infantry, consisting of Captain Elliott's company of the Nineteenth United States Regiment, Butler's Pittsburg Blues, and Alexander's Pennsylvania Riflemen. A small company of spies and guides were attached to the expedition.

Campbell left Franklinton, the head-quarters of the Army of the Northwest, on the 25th of November, with his troops, instructed by Harrison to march for the Mississiniwa by way of Springfield, Xenia, Dayton, Eaton, and Greenville, so as to avoid the Delaware towns. He was also instructed to save, if he could do so without risk to the expedition, Chiefs Richardville (then second chief of the Miamis), Silver Heels, and the White Lion, all of which, with Pecan, the principal chief of the Miamis, and Charley, the leader of the Eel River tribe, were known to be friendly to the white people. The son and brother of Little Turtle were also to be saved, if possible; also old Godfroy and his wife, who were true friends of the Americans.

It was the middle of December before the expedition left Dayton, on account of delay in procuring horses. Their destination was eighty miles distant. Each soldier was required to carry twelve days' rations, and a bushel of corn for forage. The ground was hard frozen and covered with snow, and the weather was intensely cold, yet they marched forty miles the first two days. On the third they made a forced march, and during that day and night they advanced another forty miles, when they reached the Mississiniwa, and fell upon a town inhabited by a number of Miamis and Delawares. Eight warriors were slain, and eight others, with thirty-two women and children, were made prisoners. The town was laid in ashes with the exception of two houses, which were left for the shelter of the captives. Cattle and other stock were slaughtered.

Campbell left the prisoners in charge of a sufficient guard, and pushed on down the river three miles to Silver Heels's village with Simrall's and Ball's dragoons. It was deserted; so also were two other towns near. These were destroyed, with many cattle. They captured several horses, and with these and a very small quantity of corn they returned to the scene of their first victory, and encamped for the night on the shore of the Mississiniwa. The camp was about two hundred yards square, and fortified with a small redoubt at each angle. The infantry and riflemen were posted in front, on the bank of the river, Captain Elliott's company on the right, Butler's in the centre, and Alexander's on the left. Major Ball's squadron occupied the right

---

Black Hoof was often asked to sing the songs of the worship of his people, but nothing could induce him to do so. He would not even repeat the words to the white man. His was like the refusal of the Hebrew captive to sing the songs of Zion on the banks of the rivers of Babylon. Black Hoof was the principal chief of the Shawnoese for many years before his death, which occurred at Wa-pagh-ko-netta about the year 1830, at the age, it was believed, of one hundred and ten years.

[1] John B. Campbell was a native of Virginia, and nephew of Colonel Campbell, who was distinguished at the battle of King's Mountain in 1780. He was commissioned lieutenant colonel of the Nineteenth Regiment of Infantry in March, 1812. For his good conduct in the expedition mentioned above he was breveted a colonel. In April, 1814, he was commissioned a colonel in the Eleventh Infantry, and was distinguished and severely wounded in the battle of Chippewa on the 5th of July following. He died of his wounds on the 28th of August, 1814.

and one half of the rear line, and Colonel Simrall's regiment the left and other half of the rear line. Between Ball's right and Simrall's left there was a considerable opening. Major Ball was the officer of the day.

At midnight the sentinels reported the presence of Indians, and a fire was seen down the river. The greatest vigilance was exercised, and the *réveille* was beaten at four o'clock in the morning. Adjutant Payne immediately summoned the field officers to a council at the fire of the commander to consult upon the propriety of going on twelve miles farther down the river, to attack one of the principal towns there. While the officers were in council, half an hour before dawn,[a] the camp was startled by terrific yells, followed immediately by a furious attack of a large body of savages who had crept stealthily along the margin of the river. Every officer flew to his post, and in a few moments the lines were formed, and the Indians were confronted with a heavy fire. The attack was made upon the angle of the camp, formed by the left of Captain Hopkins's troops and the right of Captain Garrard's dragoons of Simrall's regiment. Captain Pierce, who commanded at the redoubt there, was shot and tomahawked, and his guard retreated to the lines. The conflict soon became general along the right flank and part of the rear. The Pittsburg Blues promptly re-enforced the point assailed, and gallantly kept the savages at bay. For an hour the battle raged furiously. It was finally terminated, between dawn and sunrise, by a well-directed fire from Butler's Pittsburg corps, and desperate charges of cavalry under Captains Trotter, Markle,[1] and Johnson, when the Indians fled in dismay, leaving fifteen of their warriors dead on the field. Campbell had lost eight killed and forty-two wounded. Several of the latter afterward died of their wounds.[2] Campbell had one hundred and seven horses killed. What the whole loss of the Indians was could not be ascertained, but it is supposed that they carried away as many mortally wounded as they left dead on the field. Little Thunder, a nephew of Little Turtle, was in the engagement, and performed great service in inspiring his people with confidence by stirring words and gallant deeds. Although Silver Heels, a friend of the Americans (and who was with their army on the Niagara frontier the following year), was not present, nearly all of the prisoners were of his band. He did every thing in his power to persuade his young warriors to remain neutral, but in vain.

Rumors reached Campbell immediately after the battle that Tecumtha, with five or six hundred warriors, was on the Mississiniwa, only eighteen miles below. Without calling a council, the commander immediately ordered a retreat for Greenville. He sent a messenger (Captain Hite) thither for re-enforcements and supplies, for he expected to be attacked on the way. Fortunately the savages did not pursue. It was a dreadful journey, especially for the sick and wounded, in that keen winter air. They moved slowly, for seventeen men had to be conveyed on litters. Every night the camp was fortified by a breastwork. At length, wearied and with little food, they met provisions with an escort of ninety men under Major Adams. The relief was timely and most grateful. All moved forward together, and on the 25th, with three hundred men so frostbitten as to be unfit for duty, the expedition arrived at Greenville. More than one half the corps that a month before had gone gayly to the wilderness were now lost to the service for a while. They had accomplished their errand, but at a great cost.[3] The commander-in-chief of the army of the Northwest,

[a] December 18, 1812.

---

[1] Joseph Markle, afterward a distinguished citizen of Pennsylvania. He died in 1867.

[2] Lieutenant Colonel Campbell's official report to General Harrison, dated at Greenville, December 25th, 1812; M'Afee, page 178; Dillon's *History of Indiana*, page 510; Thompson's *Sketches of the War*, page 62. Lieutenant Colonel Campbell sent a brief dispatch to Harrison on the morning after the battle, misdated December 12th instead of December 18th, and addressed from "Two miles above Silver Heels."

[3] "I have on this occasion," wrote Campbell to Harrison, "to lament the loss of several brave men and many wounded. Among the former are Captain Pierce, of the Ohio Volunteers, and Lieutenant Waltz, of Markle's troops. Pierce was from Zanesville; Lieutenant Waltz was of the Pennsylvania corps. He was first shot through the arm, and then through the head. Captain Trotter was wounded in the head." Lieutenant Colonel Campbell highly commended these

in a general order, congratulated Lieutenant Colonel Campbell on his success, and commended him for his obedience to orders, his gallantry, and his magnanimity.[1]

These expeditions against the savages produced salutary effects, and smoothed the way for the final recovery of Michigan. They separated the friends and enemies of the Americans effectually. The line between them was distinctly drawn. There were no middle-men left. The Delawares on the White River, and others who desired to be friendly, and who had been invited to settle on the Au Glaize in Ohio, now accepted the invitation.[2] The other tribes, who had cast their lot with the British, were made to feel the miseries of war, and to repent of their folly. So severe had been the chastisement, and so alarmed were the tribes farther north, who received the fugitives from the desolated villages on the Wabash and the Illinois at the close of 1812, that Tecumtha's dream of a confederacy of Indians that should drive the white man across the Ohio was rapidly fading as he awoke to the reality of an unsuspected power before him, and the folly of putting his trust in princes—in other words, relying upon the promises of the representatives of the sovereignty of England to aid him in his patriotic schemes. Before the war was fairly commenced, the spirits of the Indians, so buoyant because of the recent misfortunes of the Americans in the Northwest, were broken, and doubt and dismay filled the minds of all excepting those who were under the immediate command and influence of the great Shawnoese leader.

As winter came on the sufferings and difficulties of Harrison's invading army were terrible, especially that of the left wing under Winchester, which was the most advanced, and the most remote from supplies. Early in November typhus fever was slaying three or four of his small command daily, and three hundred were upon the sick-list at one time. So discouraging became the prospect at the beginning of December of reaching even the Rapids, that, having proceeded about six miles below the Au Glaize, Winchester, partly from necessity and partly to deceive the enemy, ordered huts to be built for the winter shelter of the troops. Clothing was scanty, and at times the whole corps would be without flour for several days. These privations were owing chiefly to the difficulty of transportation. The roads were wretched beyond the conception of those who have not been in that region at the same season of the year. It was swamp, swamp, swamp, with only here and there a strip of terra firma in plight almost as wretched. The pack-horses sank to their knees, and wagon-wheels to their hubs in the mud. Wasting weariness fell upon man and beast in the struggle, and the destruction of horses was prodigious. "The fine teams which arrived on the 10th at Sandusky with the artillery," wrote Harrison to the Secretary of War on the 12th of December, "are entirely worn down; and two trips from M'Arthur's block-house, our nearest deposit to the Rapids, will completely destroy a brigade of pack-horses." It was sometimes found impossible to get even empty wagons through the mire, and they were abandoned, the teamsters being glad to get out with their horses alive; and sometimes the quarter-master, taking advantage of suddenly frozen mud, would send off a quantity of provisions, which

---

officers, also Lieutenant Colonel Simrall, Major M'Donnell, Captains Hite and Smith, and Captains Markle, M'Clelland, Garrard, and Hopkins. Lieutenants Hedges, Basye, and Hickman were among the wounded.

[1] "It is with the sincerest pleasure," said General Harrison, in a general order, "that the general has heard that the most punctual obedience was paid to his orders in not only saving all the women and children, but in sparing all the warriors who ceased to resist, and that, even when vigorously attacked by the enemy, the claims of mercy prevailed over every sense of their own danger, and this heroic band respected the lives of their prisoners. Let an account of murdered innocence be opened in the records of Heaven against our enemies alone. The American soldier will follow the example of his government, and the sword of the one will not be raised against the fallen and the helpless, nor the gold of the other be paid for the scalps of a massacred enemy."

[2] The Delawares had emigrated from Pennsylvania about fifty years before, where they had had an acquaintance with the white people for as long a period under the most favorable circumstances. They had experienced the justice and kindness of William Penn and his immediate successors. They were settled on the Au Glaize, about half way between Piqua and Wa-pagh-ko-netta. Some of them went farther east, and settled on the banks of the Scioto, within the limits of the present Delaware country, whose name is derived from these Indians. Buckongahelos, already mentioned, and an eminent chief named Kill-buck, were of this tribe.

would be swamped and lost by a sudden thaw. Water transportation was quite as difficult. Sometimes the streams would be too low for loaded boats to navigate; then they would be found crooked, narrow, and obstructed by logs; and again sudden cold would produce so much ice that it would be almost impossible to move forward. Then sleds would be resorted to until a thaw would drive the precious freight to floating vessels again. Such is a glimpse of the difficulties encountered in that wilderness of Northern Ohio; but it affords a faint idea of the hardships of the little invading army trying to make its way toward Detroit. All this was endured by the patriotic soldiers without scarcely a murmur.

In view of all these difficulties, the enormous expense of transportation, and the advantages which dishonest contractors were continually taking, Harrison suggested to the War Department, at about the middle of December, that if there existed no urgent political necessity for the recovering of Michigan and the invasion of Canada during the winter, the amount of increased expenditure of transportation at that season of the year might be better applied to the construction of a small fleet that should command the waters of Lake Erie—a suggestion made by Hull, but little heeded, early in the year.[1] The response came from the pen of a new head of the War Department. Dr. Eustis[2] had resigned, and James Monroe, the only man in the cabinet who had experienced actual military service, had succeeded him. With a more perfect knowledge of military affairs, he better comprehended the character of the campaign; and, having perfect confidence in the commander-in-chief of the Northwestern Army, he reiterated the instructions of his predecessor to Harrison, directing him to conduct the campaign according to his own judgment, promising, at the same time, that the government would take immediate measures for securing the command of Lake Erie. Only on two points were positive instructions given: First, in the event of penetrating Canada, not to promise the inhabitants any thing but the protection of life, liberty, and property; and, secondly, not to make any temporary acquisitions, but to proceed so surely that any position which he might obtain would be absolutely permanent.

Early in December a detachment of General Perkins's brigade reached Lower Sandusky (now Fremont, Ohio), and repaired an old stockade there which had protected an Indian store. The remainder of the brigade arrived soon afterward. On the 10th a battalion of Pennsylvania troops made their appearance there, with twenty-one pieces of artillery, which had been escorted from Pittsburg by Lieutenant Hukill. Very soon afterward a regiment of the same troops and part of a Virginia brigade arrived, speedily followed by General Harrison, who made his head-quarters there on the 20th. He remained but a little while. There he received the second dispatch [December 25th] from Lieutenant Colonel Campbell, giving a more detailed account of his expedition to the Mississiniwa. Harrison at once repaired to Chillicothe to consult with Governor Meigs on the propriety of fitting out another expedition in the same direction, to complete the work begun by destroying the lower Mississiniwa towns. The project was abandoned.

The whole effective force in the Northwest did not exceed six thousand three hundred infantry,[3] and a small artillery and cavalry force; yet Harrison determined

---

[1] See page 251.

[2] William Eustis was born in Cambridge, Massachusetts, on the 10th of June, 1753. He was graduated at Harvard College at the age of nineteen, and chose the practice of medicine for his profession. He entered the Continental Army of the Revolution as a regimental surgeon, and served in that capacity during the war. He was at the Robinson House, opposite West Point, while Arnold occupied it as his head-quarters. He commenced the practice of his profession at Boston at the close of the war. He was an ardent politician, and was a representative of Massachusetts in the National Congress, of the Republican party, from 1801 till 1805. President Madison appointed him Secretary of War in 1809, and he retained the office until the autumn of 1812, when he resigned. He was appointed minister to Holland in 1814. After his return he was chosen to a seat in Congress again, which he held for nearly two terms from 1820. In 1823 he was chosen governor of Massachusetts. He was then seventy years of age. He died in 1825, while holding that office, in the seventy-second year of his age.

[3] Harrison's Letter to the Secretary of War, January 4, 1813.

to press forward to the Rapids, and beyond if possible. From Lower Sandusky he dispatched Ensign Charles S. Todd, then division judge advocate of the Kentucky troops, to communicate instructions to Winchester. He was accompanied by two white men and three Wyandottes. He bore oral instructions from General Harrison to General Winchester, directing the latter to advance toward the Rapids when he should have accumulated twenty days' provisions, and there commence building huts, to deceive the enemy into the belief that he intended to winter there; at the same time to prepare sleds for an advance toward Malden, but to conceal from his troops their intended use. He was also to inform Winchester that the different lines of the army would be concentrated at the Rapids, and all would proceed from thence toward Malden, if the ice on the Detroit River should be found strong enough to bear them. Young Todd performed this dangerous and delicate duty with such success that he received the highest commendations of his general.

Meanwhile Leslie Combs, another Kentuckian, a brave and spirited young man of scarcely nineteen years, who had joined Winchester's army as a volunteer on its march from Fort Wayne to Defiance, had been sent by Winchester to Harrison on an errand fraught with equal peril. He bore a dispatch to Harrison communicating the fact that the left wing had moved toward the Rapids on the 30th of December. Combs traversed the pathless wilderness on foot, accompanied by a single guide (A. Ruddle), through snow and water, for at least one hundred miles, enduring privations which almost destroyed him. He, too, performed his mission so gallantly and satisfactorily that his general thanked him. These two messengers, who passed each other in the mazes of the great Black Swamp fifty years ago—young, ambitious, patriotic, and daring—performed other excellent service during the war, as we shall have occasion to observe. Combs and Todd are still [1867] living; both residents of Kentucky, enjoying a green old age, and wearing the honors of their country's gratitude. I had the pleasure of meeting them both during 1861, and listening to interesting narrations of their experiences in that war. Portraits and biographical sketches of these heroes may be found in future pages of this work.[1]

While on his march toward the Rapids, Winchester received a letter from Harrison recommending him to abandon the movement, because, if, as Lieutenant Colonel Campbell, in his second dispatch,[a] had been informed, Tecumtha was on the Wabash with five or six hundred followers, he might advance rapidly and capture or destroy all the provisions in Winchester's rear. It was this second dispatch of Campbell, as we have seen, that sent Harrison in such haste back to Chillicothe, to consult with Governor Meigs.

[a] December 25.

Winchester did not heed the cautious suggestions of his superior, but pressed on toward the Rapids. General Payne, with six hundred and seventy men, was sent forward to clear the way. Payne went down the Maumee several miles below old Fort Miami, but saw no signs of an enemy. The remainder of the army arrived at the Rapids on the 10th of January, 1813, and established a fortified camp on a pleasant eminence of an oval form, covered with trees and having a prairie in the rear. This was a little above Wayne's battle-ground in 1794, opposite the camp-ground of Hull at the close of June, 1812, and known as Presque Isle Hill.[2] On the day of their arrival, an Indian camp, lately deserted, was discovered. Captain Williams, with a small detachment, gave chase to the fugitives, whom he overtook and routed.

---

[1] Combs's sufferings were very severe. He carried a heavy musket and accoutrements, a blanket, and four days' provisions. The snow commenced falling on the morning after his departure, and continued without intermission for two days and nights. On the third day of their march Combs and his companion found the snow over two feet deep in the dense forest. Ruddle had been a captive among the Indians in this region and knew the way, and the method of encountering such hardships as they were now called upon to confront. The storm detained them, their provisions became scarce, and for several nights they could find no place to lie down, and sat up and slept. Hunger came to both on the sixth day of their journey, and illness to young Combs. Nothing but his ever unfliching resolution kept him up. On the ninth evening they reached Fort M'Arthur, and were well cared for by General Tupper. Combs lay prostrated with sickness for several days. [2] See page 257, and map of the Maumee in this vicinity, page 55.

The enlistments of the Kentucky troops would expire in February, and Harrison had requested Winchester to endeavor to raise a new regiment among them to serve six months longer. Inaction and suffering had greatly demoralized them. There was so much insubordination among them that Winchester had little confidence in their strength. Harrison, on the contrary, believed that active service would quicken them into good soldiers, and did not hesitate to include them in those on whom he would most rely in his expedition against Malden. Events justified that faith and confidence.

Winchester was now satisfied that the pleadings of humanity would speedily summon him to the Raisin. First came rumors that the enemy, exasperated by their want of success in their recent movements, were preparing at Malden an expedition to move upon Frenchtown, on the Raisin, for the purpose of intercepting the expedition from Ohio on its way to Detroit. These rumors were speedily followed by messengers from Frenchtown,[a] made almost breathless by alarm and rapid traveling, bringing intelligence that the Indians whom Williams had scattered had passed them on their way to Malden, uttering threats of a sweeping destruction of the inhabitants and their habitations on the Raisin. Others soon followed,[b] deeply agitated by alarm, and, like the first, earnestly pleaded for the shield of military power to avert the impending blow. The troops, moved by the most generous impulses, were anxious to march instantly to the defense of the alarmed people. Harrison, the commander-in-chief, was at Upper Sandusky,[1] sixty-five miles distant, and could not be consulted. Winchester called a council of officers. The majority advised an immediate march toward the Raisin, between thirty-five and forty miles distant by the route to be traveled. This decision was approved by Winchester's judgment and humane impulses, and on the morning of the 17th he detailed Colonel Lewis and five hundred and fifty men in that direction. A few hours afterward Colonel Allen was sent with one hundred and ten men. Lewis's instructions were "to attack the enemy, beat them, and take possession of Frenchtown and hold it." These overtook Lewis and his party at Presque Isle, a point on Maumee Bay a little below, opposite the present city of Toledo, about twenty miles from the Rapids. There Lewis was told that there were four hundred British Indians at the Raisin, and that Colonel Elliott was expected with a detachment from Malden to attack Winchester's camp at the Rapids. This information was sent by express to General Winchester, whose courier was on the point of starting with a message to General Harrison, informing him of the movement toward the Raisin, and suggesting the probable necessity of a co-operating force from the right wing.

Colonel Lewis remained all night at Presque Isle. The weather was intensely cold, and strong ice covered Maumee Bay and the shore of Lake Erie. On that glittering bridge the Americans moved early and rapidly on the morning of the 18th, and were within six miles of their destination before they were discovered by the scouts of the enemy. On the shore of the lake, in snow several inches in depth, the little army calmly breakfasted, and then marched steadily forward through timber lands to an open savanna in three lines, so arranged as to fall into battle order in a moment. The right, composed of the companies of M'Cracken, Bledsoe, and Matson,

[a] January 13, 1813.

[b] January 14th and 16th.

---

[1] Upper Sandusky, the present capital of Wyandot County, Ohio, is not the place above alluded to. The "Upper Sandusky" made famous during the Indian wars, and as the rendezvous of Americans in the war of 1812, was at Crane Town (so called from an eminent chief named Tarhe or Crane), four miles northeast from the court-house in the present village of Upper Sandusky. After the death of Tarhe in 1818, the Indians transferred their council-house to the site of the modern Upper Sandusky, gave it its present name, and called the old place Crane Town.

Old Upper Sandusky was a place of much note in the early history of the country. It was a favorite residence of the Wyandot Indians, and near it Colonel Crawford had a battle with them and was defeated in June, 1782. Crawford was murdered by fire and other slow tortures which the savages inflicted on leading prisoners. A full account of events in this vicinity may be found in Howe's *Historical Collections of Ohio.*

General Harrison built Fort Ferree, a stockade about fifty rods northeast of the court-house in the present Upper Sandusky.

was commanded by Colonel Allen; the left, led by Major Green, was composed of the companies of Hamilton, Williams, and Kelley; and the centre, under Major Madison, contained the corps of Captains Hightown, Collier, and Sebrees. The advanced guard was composed of the companies of Captains Hickman, Glaives, and James, and were under the command of Captain Ballard, acting as major. The chief of the little army was Colonel Lewis.

Frenchtown,[1] at the time in question, was a flourishing settlement containing thirty-three families, twenty-two of whom resided on the north side of the Raisin. Gardens and orchards were attached to their houses, and these were inclosed with heavy pickets, called "puncheons," made of sapling logs split in two, driven in the ground, and sometimes sharpened at top. The houses were built of logs of good size, and furnished with most of the conveniences of domestic life. Two days after the surrender of Detroit, as we have seen, this place was taken possession of by Colonel Elliott, who came from Malden for the purpose with authority from General Brock. The weapons and horses of the inhabitants were left on parole, and protection to life and property was promised. The protection was not given, and for a long time the inhabitants were plundered not only by the Indians, but by Canadians, French, and British,[2] and were kept in a state of almost continual alarm by their threats. In the autumn two companies of the Essex (Canadian) militia, two hundred in number, under Major Reynolds, and about four hundred Indians, led by Round-head and Walk-in-the-water,[3] were stationed there, and these composed the force that confronted Colonel Lewis when he approached Frenchtown on the 18th of January, 1813, and formed a line of battle on the south side of the Raisin, within a quarter of a mile of the village. Lewis's force numbered less than seven hundred men, armed only with muskets and other light weapons. The enemy had a howitzer[4] in position, directed by bombardier Kitson, of the Royal Artillery.

When within three miles of Frenchtown Colonel Lewis was informed that the enemy was on the alert and ready to receive him; and as the Americans approached the village on the south side, the howitzer of the foe was opened upon the advancing column, but without effect. Lewis's line of battle was instantly formed, and the whole detachment moved steadily forward to the river, which was hard frozen, and in many places very slippery. They crossed it in the face of blazing muskets, and then the long roll was beaten, and a general charge was executed. The Americans rushed gallantly up the bank, leaped the garden pickets, dislodged the enemy, and drove him back toward the forests. Majors Graves and Madison attempted to capture the howitzer, but failed. Meanwhile the allies were retreating in a line inclining eastward, when they were attacked on their left by Colonel Allen, who pursued them more than half a mile to the woods. There they made a stand with their howitzer and small-arms, covered by a chain of inclosed lots and groups of houses, and having in their rear a thick, brushy wood, full of fallen timber. While in this position Majors Graves and Madison moved upon the enemy's right, while Allen was sorely pressing his left. The enemy fell back into the wood, closely pursued, and the conflict became extremely hot on the right wing of the Americans, where both whites and Indians were concentrated. The contest lasted from three o'clock until dark, the enemy all the while slowly retreating over a space of not less than two miles, gallantly contesting every foot of the ground. The detachments returned to the village in the evening, and encamped for the night on the ground which the ene-

---

[1] The Raisin, on which Frenchtown was situated, was called Sturgeon River by the Indians, because of the abundance of that fish in its waters. It flowed through a fertile and attractive region, and late in the last century a number of French families settled upon its banks, and engaged in farming, and trading with the Indians. Because of the abundance of grapes on the borders of the stream they called it *Riviere aux Raisins*, and on account of the nationality of the settlers the village was called Frenchtown. It is now Monroe, Michigan.

[2] Statement to the author by the Hon. Laurent Durocher, of Monroe (Frenchtown), who was an actor in the scenes there during the war of 1812. [3] See note 3, page 279.

[4] A *howitz* or *howitzer* is a kind of mortar or short gun, mounted on a carriage, and used for throwing bomb-shells.

my had occupied. American officers occupied the same buildings in which the British officers had lived. The troops had behaved nobly. There had not been a single case of delinquency. "This amply supported," as was said, "the double character of Americans and Kentuckians," and fully vindicated the faith and judgment of General Harrison. Twelve of the Americans were killed and fifty-five wounded. Among the latter was Captain B. W. Ballard,[1] who gallantly led the van in the fight; also Captains Paschal, Hickman,[2] and Richard Matson.[3] The loss of the enemy must have been much greater, for they left fifteen dead in the open field, while the most sanguinary portion of the conflict occurred in the wood. That night the Indians gathered their dead and wounded, and, on their retreat toward Malden, killed some of the inhabitants and pillaged their houses.

As soon as his little army was safely encamped in the village gardens, behind the strong "puncheon" pickets, and his wounded men comfortably housed, on the night of the battle,[a] Colonel Lewis sent a messenger to General Winchester with a brief report of the action and his situation.[4] He arrived at Winchester's camp before dawn, and an express was immediately dispatched to General Harrison with the tidings. [a January 18, 1813.]

Lewis called a council of officers in the morning, when it was resolved to hold the place and wait for re-enforcements from the Rapids. They were not long waiting. From the moment when intelligence of the affair at Frenchtown was known in Winchester's camp, the troops were in a perfect ferment. All were eager to press northward, not doubting that the victory at the Raisin was the harbinger of continued success until Detroit and Malden should be in the possession of the Americans. It was also apparent that Lewis's detachment was in a critical situation; for Malden, the principal rendezvous of the British and Indians in the Northwest, was only eighteen miles from Frenchtown, and that every possible method would be instantly put forth to recover what had been lost, and bar farther progress toward Detroit. Accordingly, on the evening of the 19th,[b] General Winchester, accompanied by Colonel Samuel Wells, of Tippecanoe fame, marched from the Maumee toward Frenchtown with less than three hundred men, it being unsafe to withdraw more from the camp at the Rapids. He arrived at Frenchtown at three o'clock in the afternoon of the next day, crossed the river, and encamped the troops in an open field on the right of Lewis's forces,[5] excepting a small detachment under Captain Morris, left behind as a rear-guard with the baggage. Leaving Colonel Wells in command of the re-enforcements, after suggesting the propriety of a fortified camp, Winchester, with his staff, recrossed the Raisin, and established his head-quarters at the house of Colonel Francis Navarre, on the south side of the river, and more than half a mile from the American lines.[6] [b January.]

---

[1] Captain Bland W. Ballard was a son of Captain Ballard, of Winchester's army. He was acting major at the time when he was wounded.

[2] Hickman led a party of spies under Wayne from December, 1794, until June, 1795.

[3] Matson was afterward with Colonel R. M. Johnson in the battle of the Thames.

[4] Colonel Lewis's full report to General Winchester was written two days afterward, dated "Camp at Frenchtown, January 20, 1813, on the River Raisin." The facts in our narrative of the battle were drawn chiefly from this report.

[5] It is asserted that Colonel Lewis recommended the encamping of the re-enforcements within the picketed gardens, there being plenty of room on his left. Wells being of the regular army, precedence gave him the *right* of Lewis, and military rule would not allow him to take position on his left. This observance of etiquette proved to be exceedingly mischievous.

[6] The view of Colonel Navarre's house, the head-quarters of Winchester, given on page 354, represents it as it appeared in 1813, with a "puncheon" fence in front. General Winchester occupied the room on the left of the entrance-door. The room was a long one, fronting east (we are looking at the house in a southeast direction), and had a large fireplace. In this room the Indians who came to trade with Navarre rested and slept. The trees seen on the west side of the house are still there—venerable pear-trees (originally brought from Normandy), which were planted there by the early settlers. Those which remain still bear fruit. In 1830 the old Navarre House was altered by the son of the owner in 1813. He made additions to it, and raised the roof so as to make it two stories in height. Like the original, the structure of 1830 was a log edifice. When I visited the spot in the autumn of 1860, it had undergone another change. The log-house of 1830 had been clap-boarded, and it was then the residence of the rector of the Episcopal church in Monroe. It stood back a little from Front Street, within the square bordered by Front, Murray, Humphrey, and Wads-

WINCHESTER'S HEAD-QUARTERS.

According to the testimony of an officer of the expedition, very little vigilance was exercised by General Winchester. Spies were not sent out to reconnoitre, nor any measures adopted for strengthening the camp. A large quantity of fixed ammunition, sent to Winchester's quarters from the Rapids, was not distributed, although the re-enforcements had only ten rounds of cartridges each; and the urgent recommendation of Colonel Wells that the quarters of the commander-in-chief and the principal officers should be with the troops was unheeded.[1]

On the morning of the 21st Winchester requested Peter Navarre and his four brothers to go on a scout toward the mouth of the Detroit River. Peter was still living when I visited the Maumee Valley in the autumn of 1860, and accompanied me from Toledo to the Rapids. He was a young man at the time in question, full of courage and physical strength. He and his brothers complied with Winchester's request with alacrity. They saw a man, far distant, coming toward them on the ice. He proved to be Joseph Bordeau, whose daughter Peter afterward married. He had escaped from Malden, and was bringing the news that the British would be at the Raisin, with a large body of Indians, that night. Peter hastened back to Winchester with this intelligence. Jacques La Salle, a resident of Frenchtown, in the interest of the British, was present, and asserted, in the most positive language, that it must be a mistake. Winchester's fears were allayed. Peter was dismissed with a laugh, and no precautions to insure safety were taken by the general.[2] Another scout confirmed this intelligence during the afternoon. The general was still incredulous. Late in the evening news came to Lewis's camp that a very large force of British and Indians, with several pieces of heavy artillery, were at Stony Creek, only a few miles distant, and would be at Frenchtown before morning. The picket-guard was immediately doubled, and word was sent to the commanding general. He did not believe a word of it; but Colonel Wells, who did believe the first rumor brought by Bordeau, had meanwhile hastened to the Rapids with Captain Lanham for re-enforcements, leaving his detachment in charge of Major M'Clanahan.

When the late evening rumors had been communicated to Winchester, the field officers remained up, expecting every moment to receive a summons to attend a council at head-quarters. They were disappointed. The general disbelieved the alarming rumors; and before midnight a deep repose rested upon the camp, as if some trusted power had guaranteed perfect security. The sentinels, as we have observed, were well posted, but, owing to the severity of the weather, no pickets were sent out upon the roads leading to the town. All but the chief officers in Lewis's camp and some better-informed inhabitants seemed perfectly free from apprehension. At head-quarters the night was passed by the general and his staff in sweet slumber; but just as the *réveille* was beaten, between four and five o'clock in the morning, and the drummer-boy was playing the *Three Camps*, the sharp crack of the sentinels'

---

worth Streets. I am indebted to the kind courtesy of Mrs. Sarah A. Noble, of Monroe (Frenchtown), Michigan, for the foregoing facts, and for the above sketch of Winchester's quarters as it appeared in 1813.

[1] Major Elijah M'Clanahan to General Harrison, dated "Camp on Carrying River, January 26, 1813." Carrying River was eighteen miles from Winchester's camp, on the Maumee, on the way toward the Raisin.
[2] Oral statement of Peter Navarre to the author.

Attack on Frenchtown by Proctor and his Fellow-savages.   A terrible Struggle.   A Panic and Massacre.

muskets firing an alarm was heard by still dull ears. These were followed immediately by a shower of bombshells and canister-shot hurled from several pieces of ordnance, accompanied by a furious charge of almost invisible British regulars, and the terrible yells of painted savages. The sounds and missiles fell upon the startled camp with appalling suddenness, giving fearful significance to the warnings, and a terrible fulfillment of the predictions uttered the previous evening. Night had not yet yielded its gloomy sceptre to Day. The character and number of assailants were unknown. All was mystery, terrible and profound; and the Americans had nothing else to do but to oppose force to force, as gallantly as possible, until the revelations of daylight should point to strategy, skill, or prowess for safety and victory.

The exposed re-enforcements in the open field were driven in toward Lewis's picketed camp, after bravely maintaining a severe conflict for some time. At this moment General Winchester arrived, and endeavored to rally the retreating troops behind a "puncheon" fence and second bank of the Raisin, so that they might incline to the right, and find shelter behind Lewis's camp. His efforts were vain. The British and their savage allies were pressing too heavily upon the fugitives; and when at length a large body of Indians gained their right flank, they were thrown into the greatest confusion, and fled pell-mell across the river, carrying with them a detachment of one hundred men which Lewis had sent out for their support. Seeing this, Lewis and Allen joined Winchester in his attempt to rally the troops behind the houses and fences on the south side of the Raisin, leaving the camp in the gardens in charge of Majors Graves and Madison. But all efforts to stop the flight of the soldiers were vain. The Indians, more fleet than they, had gained their flank, and swarmed in the woods on the line of their retreat, while those who made their way along a narrow lane leading from the village to the road from the Rapids were shot down and scalped by the savages skulking behind the trees and fences. Others, who rushed into the woods hoping to find shelter there from the fury of the terrible storm, were met at every turn by the bloody butchers, and scarcely one escaped. Within the space of a hundred yards, near Plum or Mill Creek, nearly one hundred Kentuckians fell under the hatchets of hired savages, who snatched the "scalp-locks" from their heads, and afterward bore them in triumph to Fort Malden to receive the market price for that precious article of commerce.[1] Death and mutilation met the fugitives on every side, whether in flight or in submission, and all about that little village the snow was crimsoned with human blood. On that dreadful morning it was on the part of the allies of the British a war of extermination.[2]

---

[1] "Never, dear mother, if I should live a thousand years, can I forget the frightful sight of this morning, when handsomely-painted Indians came into the fort, some of them carrying half a dozen scalps of my countrymen fastened upon sticks, and yet covered with blood, and were congratulated by Colonel Proctor for their *bravery!* I heard a British officer, who, I was told, was Lieutenant Colonel St. George, tell another officer, who, I believe, was Colonel Vincent, that Proctor was a disgrace to the British army—that such encouragements to devils was a blot upon the British character."—Letter of A. G. Tustin, of Bardstown, Kentucky, to his mother, dated Fort Malden, January 23, 1813.

[2] No rule of civilized warfare was observed. Blood and scalps were the chief objects for which the Indians fought. They seemed disposed not to take any prisoners. A party of fifteen or twenty, under Lieutenant Garrett, after retreating about a mile, were compelled to surrender, when all but the young commander were killed and scalped. Another party, of forty men, were more than one half murdered under similar circumstances. Colonel Allen, who had been wounded in the thigh in the attempt to rally the troops, after abandoning all hope, and escaping about two miles in the direction of the Maumee, was compelled, by sheer exhaustion, to sit down upon a log. He was observed by an Indian chief, who, perceiving his rank, promised him his protection if he would surrender without resistance. He did so. At the same moment two other savages approached with murderous intent, when, with a single blow of his sword, Allen laid one of them dead upon the ground. His companion instantly shot the colonel dead. "He had the honor," says M'Afee, "of shooting one of the first and greatest citizens of Kentucky."

John Allen was born in Rockbridge County, Virginia, on the 30th of December, 1772. His father emigrated with him to Kentucky in 1780, and settled about a mile and a half below the present town of Danville, in Boyle County. In 1784 the family removed to another part, five miles from Bardstown, and in a school in that then rude village young Allen received his education. He studied law in Staunton, Virginia, for four years, and commenced its practice in Shelbyville, Kentucky, in 1795. He was following his profession successfully there when the war broke out in 1812, when he raised a regiment of riflemen for service under Harrison. He was killed, as we have seen, at the massacre on the River Raisin, on the 22d of January, 1813, at the age of forty-one years. Allen County, Kentucky, was so named in his honor.

Winchester made Prisoner.   Proctor repulsed.   Winchester forced to surrender his Army.   Major Madison.

General Winchester and Colonel Lewis were made prisoners by Round-head,[1] at a bridge about three fourths of a mile from the village, stripped of their clothes except shirt, pantaloons, and boots, and in this plight were taken to the quarters of the British commander, who proved to be Colonel Proctor, the unworthy successor of the worthy Brock in the command at Detroit and Amherstburg. He was in Fort Malden, at the latter place, when intelligence of Lewis's occupation of Frenchtown reached him, and he made immediate preparations to drive the Americans back. The British and Indians expelled from Frenchtown on the 18th had fallen back with their howitzer to Brownstown, where Proctor joined them, on the evening of the 20th, with a detachment of the 41st Regiment, one hundred and forty in number, under Lieutenant Colonel St. George; the Royal Newfoundland Regiment, under Colonel Vincent; and a part of the 10th Veteran Battalion and some seamen. These, with Reynolds's militia and a party of the Royal Artillery, with three three-pounders and the howitzer already mentioned, made a white force about five hundred strong. The Indians, under Round-head and Walk-in-the-Water, numbered about six hundred. With these Proctor advanced from Brownstown on the morning of the 21st, and halted at Swan Creek, twelve miles on the way. There he remained until dusk, when the march was resumed. So great was the lack of vigilance on the part of the Americans that Proctor's troops and guns were made ready for assault before their presence was positively known. Then followed the attack just recorded.

While the right wing of Lewis's army and Winchester's re-enforcements were suffering destruction, the left and centre, under Majors Graves and Madison, were nobly defending themselves in the garden picketed camp. They maintained their position manfully against the powerful assault of the enemy. The British had planted their howitzer within two hundred yards of the camp (and eastward of it), behind a small house about forty rods from the river, upon the road to Detroit. It was a formidable assailant, but it was soon silenced by the Kentucky sharp-shooters behind the pickets, who first killed the horse and driver of the sleigh that conveyed ammunition, and then picked off thirteen of the sixteen men in charge of the gun. It was soon drawn back so far that its shot had no effect on the "puncheon;" and at ten o'clock, perceiving all efforts of his white troops to dislodge the Americans to be fruitless, Proctor withdrew his forces to the woods, with the intention of either abandoning the contest, or awaiting the return of his savage allies, who were having their feast of blood beyond the Raisin. When the assailants withdrew, the Americans quietly breakfasted.

While the troops were eating, a white flag was seen approaching from the British line. Major Madison, believing it to be a token of truce while the British might bury their dead, went out to meet it. It was borne by Major Overton, one of General Winchester's staff, who was accompanied by Colonel Proctor. He brought an order from General Winchester directing the unconditional surrender of all the troops as prisoners of war. This was the first intelligence received by the gallant left wing that their chief was a captive. Proctor had dishonorably taken advantage of his situation to extort that order from him. He assured Winchester that as soon as the Indians, fresh from the massacre from which he had escaped, should join his camp, the remainder of the Americans would be easily captured, concealing from him the fact that they had already driven the British back to the woods. He represented to the general that, in such an event, "nothing would save the Americans from an indiscriminate massacre by the Indians." Totally ignorant of the condition of the remnant of his little army, and horrified by the butchery of which he had just been a witness, Winchester yielded, and sent Major Overton with the orders just mentioned.

Madison, surprised and mortified, refused to obey the order except on conditions.

[1] See page 291. It was with great difficulty that Proctor persuaded Round-head to release his prisoner, or to give up the military suit he had stripped from him.

"It has been customary for the Indians," he observed, "to massacre the wounded and prisoners after a surrender; I shall therefore not agree to any capitulation which General Winchester may direct, unless the safety and protection of all the prisoners shall be stipulated." The haughty Proctor stamped his foot, and said, with a supercilious air, "Sir, do *you* mean to dictate to *me!*" "I mean to dictate for myself," Madison replied, with firmness. "We prefer selling our lives as dearly as possible rather than be massacred in cold blood." Proctor, who was scorned by Brock for his jealousy and innate meanness, and is remembered with dislike by the Canadians, who knew him as innately cruel and cowardly,[1] quailed before the honest, manly bravery of Madison, and solemnly agreed that all private property should be respected; that sleds should be sent the next morning to remove the sick and wounded to Amherstburg; that the disabled should be protected by a proper guard; and that the sidearms of the officers should be returned when the captives should reach Malden. Proctor refused to commit these conditions to writing, but pledged his honor as a soldier and a gentleman that they should be observed. Madison was ignorant of Proctor's poverty in all that constituted a soldier and man of honor, and trusted to his promises. On the conditions named, he and his officers agreed to surrender themselves and their men prisoners of war.

Before the surrender was fairly completed the Indians began to plunder, when Major Madison ordered his men to resist them, even with ball and bayonet. The cowardly savages quailed before the courage of the white captives, and none of the prisoners were again molested by them while on their way to Malden. Quite different was the fate of the poor wounded men who were left behind. Having secured his object, Proctor violated his word of honor, and left them exposed to savage cruelty. Rumors came that Harrison was approaching, and the British commander, more intent on securing personal safety than the fulfillment of solemn promises, left for Malden with most of his savage allies, within an hour after the surrender, leaving as a "guard" only Major Reynolds and two or three interpreters. Proctor did not even name a guard, nor spoke of conveyances for the wounded after leaving Frenchtown; and when both Winchester and Madison reminded him of his promises and the peril of the wounded, he refused to hear them. It is evident that from the first that inhuman officer intended to abandon the wounded prisoners to their fate. Among them was Captain Hart, brother-in-law of Henry Clay, and inspector general of the Army of the Northwest. He was anxious to accompany the prisoners to Malden, but Captain Elliott, son of the notorious Colonel Elliott, who had known Hart intimately in Kentucky, assured him of perfect safety at Frenchtown, and promised to send his own conveyance for him the next morning. Elliott assured all the wounded that they need not apprehend danger, and that sleds from Malden would come for them in the morning.

The wounded were taken into the houses of the kind-hearted villagers, and cared for by Drs. Todd and Bowers, of the Kentucky Volunteers, who were left behind for the purpose. In every mind there was an indefinable dread when Proctor and his motley crew departed; and when it was known that he had promised his savage allies a "frolic" at Stony Creek, only about six miles from the Raisin, not only the wounded soldiers, but the villagers, and Major Reynolds himself, felt a thrill of horror, for there could be no doubt that the drunken Indians, after their debauch, would return to Frenchtown to glut their appetites for blood and plunder. Even those who remained went from house to house, after Proctor's departure, in search of plunder.

The night following the battle was a fearful one at Frenchtown. Day dawned with hope, but the sun at his rising[a] found the inhabitants [a] January 23, 1812.

---

[1] Tecumtha, as we shall observe hereafter, regarded Proctor as a coward, and by threats compelled him to make a stand on the Thames; and the venerable Robert Reynolds, of Amherstburg, and other survivors of the British army in Canada with whom I have conversed, spoke of him with contempt as a boasting coward.

and prisoners in despair. Instead of the promised sleds from Malden, about two hundred half-drunken savages, with their faces painted red and black in token of their fiendish purposes, came into the village. The chiefs held a brief council, and determined to kill and scalp all the wounded who were unable to travel, in revenge for the many comrades they had lost in the fight. This decision was announced by horrid yells, and the savages went out upon their bloody errand. They first plundered the village; then they broke into the houses where the wounded lay, stripped them of every thing, and then tomahawked and scalped them. The houses of Jean B. Jereaume and Gabriel Godfrey, that stood near the present dwelling of Matthew Gibson, sheltered a large number of prisoners. In the cellar of Jereaume's house was stored a large quantity of whisky. This the savages took in sufficient quantities to madden them, when they set both dwellings on fire. A number of the wounded, unable to move, were consumed. Others, attempting to escape by the doors and windows, were tomahawked and scalped. Others, outside, were scalped and cast into the flames, and the remainder, who could walk, were marched off toward Malden. When any of them sank from exhaustion, they were killed and scalped.

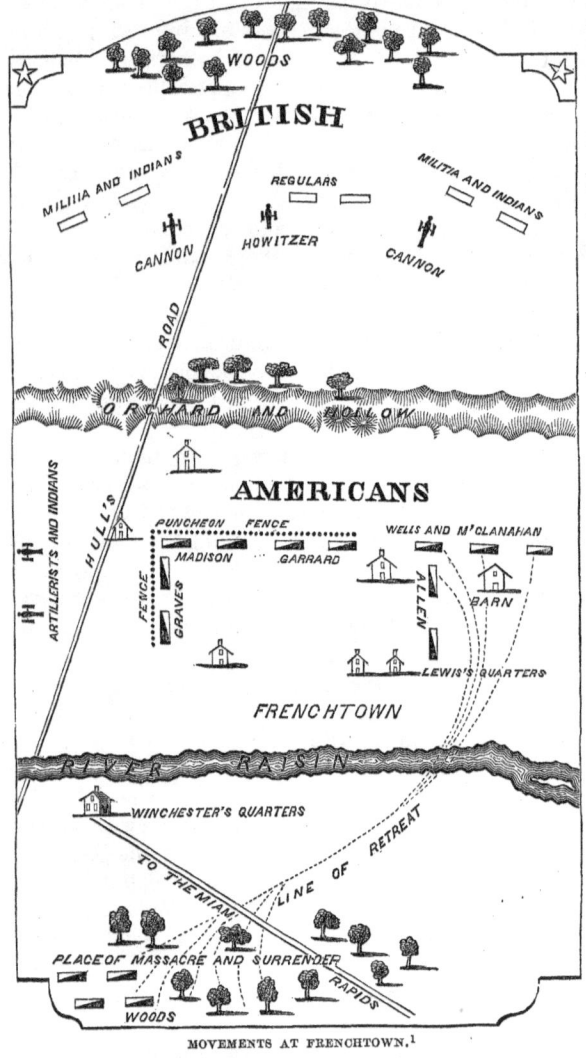

MOVEMENTS AT FRENCHTOWN.[1]

Doctor Todd, who had been tied and carried to Stony Creek, informed Elliott of what was going on at the Raisin, and begged him to send conveyances for the wounded, especially for Captain Hart; but that young officer coolly replied, "Charity begins at home; my own wounded must be carried to Malden first." He well knew that an hour more would be too late for rescue.[2]

Major Graves was never heard of after the Maumee. Captain Hickman was murdered in Jereaume's house. Captain Hart was removed from that house by Doctor

---

[1] This is from a sketch sent to Colonel William H. Winder by Lieutenant Colonel Boerstler, in a letter dated "Buffalo, 17th February, 1813. I send you," he says, "a hasty sketch of the situation of the troops at Frenchtown." He obtained it from some subordinate officer among the prisoners from the Raisin, who were paroled, and passed through Buffalo. He says, "The prisoners have passed through to the number of four hundred and sixty-two. The general and field officers are not yet sent across."—*Autograph Letter*.

[2] Elliott had been in Lexington, where he was very ill of fever for a long time in the family of Colonel Thomas Hart, the father of Captain Hart. During that illness he had received many attentions from the young man whom he now basely deserted in his hour of greatest need.

Todd, before the massacre was commenced, to the dwelling of Jacques Navarre, about a mile up the river (now the Wadsworth brick house), under the charge of a friendly Pottawatomie chief. Hart offered him one hundred dollars to convey him in safety to Malden. The chief attempted it. Hart was placed on a horse, and when passing through the village, near the house of François La Salle[1] (who was suspected of complicity with the British), a Wyandot savage came out, and claimed the captain as his prisoner. A dispute arose, and they finally settled it by agreeing to kill the prisoner, and dividing his money and clothes between them. So says the most reliable recorded history.[2] Local tradition declares that the Pottawatomie attempted to defend Captain Hart when the Wyandot shot and scalped him. There are many versions of the tragedy. He was buried near the place of his murder, but the exact spot is not known.

RESIDENCE OF LA SALLE.

Proctor arrived with his prisoners at Amherstburg on the morning of the 23d of January, and on the 26th proceeded to Sandwich and Detroit.[3] Some of them were sent to Detroit, and others were forwarded to Fort George, on the Niagara, by way of the Thames. These suffered much from the severity of the weather and bad treatment of their guards. At Fort George they were mostly paroled, on condition that they should not "bear arms against his majesty or his *allies* during the war, or until exchanged." "Who are his majesty's allies?" inquired Major Madison. The officer addressed, doubtless ashamed to own the disgrace in words, said, "His majesty's allies are known." General Winchester, Colonel Lewis,[4] and Major Madison,[5] were sent to Quebec, and at Beauport, near that city, they were confined until the spring of 1814, when a general exchange of prisoners took place.

---

[1] I am indebted to Mrs. Sarah A. Noble for this sketch of La Salle's house, as it appeared at the time. It stood in front of the ford, was built of logs, and between it and the river was a "puncheon" fence. The "Laselle Farm" was known some time as the "Humphrey Farm." It is now [1867] the property of the Honorable D. A. Noble.

[2] Nathaniel G. T. Hart was a son of Colonel Thomas Hart, who emigrated to Kentucky from Maryland, and settled in Lexington. Captain Hart was born at Hagerstown, in Maryland. One of his sisters married Henry Clay, another married James Brown, long the United States minister at the French Court. Hart was making a fortune in mercantile pursuits when the war of 1812 broke out, when (at the age of about twenty-seven years) he was in command of the *Lexington Light Infantry*, a company which was organized by General James Wilkinson, who was its first captain, in 1787. Under its fourth captain (Beatty) it was with Wayne in the campaign of 1794. Hart was its seventh captain, and was at the head of it in the expedition to the Raisin. When I visited Lexington in April, 1861, I called on the then commander of the company, Captain Samuel D. M'Cullough, who showed me the crimson silk sash of Captain Hart in his possession, which was torn and had blood-stains upon it. Cassius M. Clay, now [1867] American minister to the Court of St. Petersburg, commanded this company in the United States army in Mexico. In the battle of Buena Vista its flag was the regimental color of the Kentucky cavalry. On the 18th of January, 1861, a flag was presented to this company (now called the "Lexington Old Infantry") at the Odd Fellows Hall in Lexington, by General Leslie Combs, in behalf of the donor, David A. Sayre. On that occasion the United States band from the barracks at Newport, Kentucky, performed the musical part of the ceremonies. The *Star-spangled Banner* was sung, and the roll of all the captains, from 1789 to 1861, was called. The only survivors of the company when Hart was captain, who were present, were, Thomas Smith, of Louisville; Lawrence Daly, of Fayette County; and Judge Levi L. Todd, of Indianapolis. The latter, who was Hart's successor as captain, gave the opening address.

[3] A few days after the massacre at the Raisin Proctor ordered all the inhabitants there to leave their houses and move to Detroit. It was mid-winter and severely cold. The snow was very deep, and they suffered dreadfully. Some conveyances were sent down from Detroit for them. For a while Frenchtown was a desolation, and the remains of the massacred were unburied.

[4] William Lewis was in Gaither's battalion at St. Clare's defeat in 1791. He was then captain, and was appointed to the same position in the 3d Regiment of Infantry the following year. He resigned in 1797. In August, 1812, he was commissioned Lieutenant Colonel of Kentucky Volunteers, and, as we have seen, behaved gallantly at Frenchtown. He was a native of Virginia. His death occurred near Little Rock, Arkansas, on the 17th of January, 1825.

[5] George Madison was a native of Virginia, where he was born in 1763. He was a soldier in the Revolution, although he was only a lad of twelve years when it broke out. He was with General Clarke in the Northwest, and was at the head of a company in St. Clair's defeat in 1791, where he was wounded. He was also wounded in an attack by the In-

War-cry of the Kentuckians.   Honor conferred on Proctor.   Shamefulness of the Act.   "Guardians of Civilization."

The loss of the Americans in the affair at the Raisin was nine hundred and thirty-four. Of these, one hundred and ninety-seven were killed and missing; the remainder were made prisoners. Of the whole army of about a thousand men, only thirty-three escaped. The loss of the British, according to Proctor's report, was twenty-four killed, and one hundred and fifty-eight wounded. The loss of their Indian allies is not known. The event was a terrible blow to Kentucky. It caused mourning in almost every family. The first shock of grief was succeeded by intense exasperation, and the war-cry of Kentucky soldiers after that was, *Remember the River Raisin!*

[a] January 26, 1812. At Sandwich Proctor wrote his dispatch[a] to Sir George Prevost, the commander-in-chief in Canada, giving an account of his expedition to Frenchtown, and highly commending the conduct of his savage allies.[1] His private representations were such that the evidently deceived Assembly of Lower Canada passed a vote of thanks to him and his men, and the equally duped Sir George promoted him to the rank of brigadier general " until the pleasure of the Prince Regent should be known."[2] That "pleasure" was to confirm the appointment, and thereby the British government indorsed his conduct.

I visited Frenchtown (now Monroe), in Michigan, early in October, 1860. I went down from Detroit by railway early in the morning, after a night of tempest—mingled lightning, wind, and rain. The air was cool and pure, and the firmament was overhung with beautiful cloud-pictures. I bore a letter of introduction to the Honorable D. S. Bacon, a resident of the place for almost forty years, who kindly spent the day with me in visiting persons and places of interest on that memorable spot.

Crossing the bridge to the north side of the stream, we passed down Water Street toward the site of La Salle's, the camp of Colonel Lewis, and other places connected with the battle and massacre already described. We met the venerable Judge Du-

---

dians in the camp of Major John Adair the following year. For more than twenty years he was auditor of public accounts in Kentucky. When Kentucky was asked for troops in 1812 he took the field. He was kept a prisoner at Quebec for some time. In 1816 he was nominated for the office of governor of Kentucky. He was so beloved and popular that his opponent withdrew in the heat of the canvass, declaring that nobody could resist that popularity. He was elected, but died on the 14th of October the same year.

[1] "The zeal and courage of the Indian Department," he said, "were never more conspicuous than on this occasion, and the Indian warriors fought with their usual bravery."

[2] It seems hardly possible that the Canadian Assembly or Sir George Prevost could have known the facts of the horrors of Frenchtown, and Proctor's inhuman abandonment of the prisoners, or they would have punished rather than rewarded the commander on that occasion. Sir George, in his general order announcing the promotion of Proctor, actually said, "On this occasion the gallantry of Colonel Proctor was most nobly displayed in his *humane and unwearied exertions, which succeeded in rescuing the vanquished from the revenge of the Indian warriors!*" British writers, unable to offer the shadow of an excuse for Proctor's conduct, either avoid all mention of the massacre, or endeavor to shield him from the scourge of just criticism by affecting to disbelieve the fact that he agreed to give protection to the wounded, or accepted the surrender on any conditions whatever. "Indeed," says James, with an air of triumph in discussion, "General Winchester was not in a condition to dictate terms," because he was "stripped to his shirt and trowsers, and suffering exceedingly from the cold."—*Account of the Military Occurrences of the Late War*, etc., i., 188. But the testimony of eye and ear witnesses to the fact are too abundant for any honest-minded man to doubt. Before all his men, in the presence of Colonel Proctor, not twenty rods from the house of François Lasalle, Major Madison declared the conditions that had been agreed upon. The late Judge Durocher, who was present, informed me that he heard these conditions announced, and that Proctor assented to them by his silence. This is in confirmation of Winchester's statement in his report, written at Malden on the 23d of January, the day after the surrender.

It gives the writer no pleasure to record the cruelties of savages and the unchristian conduct of British commanders who employed them. He would prefer to bury the knowledge of these things in oblivion, and let the animosities which they engender die with the generation of men who were actors in the scenes; but when a Pharisee, affecting to be the "guardian of civilization," preaches censorious homilies to an equal in virtue and dignity, it is sometimes a wholesome service to prick the bubble of his pride with the bodkin of just exposure. When the British government, in its pride or blindness, lectures that of the United States on lust for power, barbarity in warfare, and kindred subjects, as it did during the late civil war in the United States, an occasional lifting of the veil from the records of the censor's own shortcomings may be productive of a wholesome humility and a practical desire for reform. Posterity will point the finger of scorn toward the conduct of the government of that empire, and the journalists and publicists in its interest, during the trials of the government and loyal people of the United States in their late struggles against foul conspiracy and frightful rebellion, as unworthy of an enlightened and Christian nation. That conduct—the manifestation of the intense selfishness of the aristocracy of rank and wealth which have ever ruled England—will always appear darkly in the history of nations as a crime against humanity, and a libel upon the character of the overwhelming majority of the English people. The employment of bloody savages to butcher their relatives in America; the demoniac treatment of captive Sepoys in India; the encouragement of frightful atrocities in China, and the open sympathy with conspirators against a beneficent government for the avowed purpose of establishing a despotism whose corner-stone should be HUMAN SLAVERY, should forever close the lips of the English government when it attempts to lecture others on humanity, or claims to be, *par excellence*, the "guardian of civilization."

rocher, already mentioned in the narrative as one of the actors in the scenes there—a short, dark-complexioned man of French descent—who pointed out the spot, in an open lot between Water Street and the river, not far from where we were standing, a little westward of La Salle's house, where Captain Hart was murdered by the Indians. Promising me another and longer interview at his office, we left Judge Durocher, and passed on to the site of La Salle's dwelling, then the property of Hon. D. S. Noble, delineated on page 359, a part of which yet remains, with a pear-tree planted there during the last century. Not far below this we came to the railway and the common road leading from the Raisin to Detroit. On the corner of the latter, not far from the site of the houses of Godfrey and Jereaume, where the wounded were burned and massacred, was a large brick house, the residence of Matthew Gibson. Very near it, in an orchard, might be seen the remains of the cellars of those buildings. From that point, around which the battle was fought, and near which the

MONROE, FROM THE BATTLE-GROUND.

Americans were driven across the Raisin just before the massacre on the south side of the stream, I made the above sketch (looking westward) of the river, the railway bridge, and the distant town. Gibson's house is seen in the foreground, on the right; the railway bridge, on four piers in the water, with the town beyond it, is seen in the centre; and by the distant trees, seen immediately beyond the point on the left, is indicated the spot near which Winchester was captured. Returning to the village, I called upon Judge Durocher, who, in the course of a pleasant interview of an hour, gave me many items of information concerning the events we have been considering. He spoke of Winchester as a "fussy man," quite heavy in person, and illy fitted for the peculiar service in which he was engaged. He also assured me that after the defeat of the Americans at Frenchtown, Proctor endeavored to persuade the Indians to destroy the French settlements there, because he believed the inhabitants to be favorable to the United States. It was even proposed to the Indians in council, and another cold-blooded massacre, not by the permission, but at the instigation of Proctor, was only prevented by the firmness of the friendship which the Pottawatomies bore to the inhabitants on the Raisin. Judge Durocher was seventy-four years of age when I visited him. A little less than a year afterward he was borne to the grave.[1]

---

[1] Laurent Durocher was the son of a French Canadian, and was born at St. Genevieve Mission, in Missouri, in 1786. His father died when he was young, and his uncle sent him to a college in Montreal to be educated. At the close of his

Our next visit was to the head-quarters of Winchester, delineated on page 354, which was occupied by the rector of the Protestant Episcopal church in Monroe. It was too unlike the original to claim the service of the pencil, and we proceeded to the house of James Knaggs, one of the oldest inhabitants of that region, and a remarkable character, who, as an Indian fighter and volunteer soldier, performed good service during the war of 1812. He had just returned from some toil at a distance, and, octogenarian as he was, he seemed vigorous in mind and body. He was a stout-built man, about eighty years of age. His birth-place was at Roche de Bout, on the Maumee, a little above the present village of Waterville. His father was an Englishman, and his mother a Mohawk Valley Dutch woman.[1] From early life he was familiar with the Indians and the woods. He had been a witness of the treachery and cruelty of the savages, and his family had suffered severely at their hands. When speaking of the Indians and his personal contests with them, his vengeful feelings could hardly be repressed, and he talked with almost savage delight of the manner in which he had disposed of some of them.[2]

Soon after Wayne's campaign Knaggs settled at Frenchtown, and became a farmer. In 1811 he established a regular ferry at the Huron River, on the road to Detroit, with only Indians as companions and neighbors. These, excited against all Americans by British emissaries, were very troublesome, and Knaggs had frequent conflicts with them in some form. When Hull was on his way toward Detroit, Knaggs joined the army as a private in Captain Lee's company of dragoons—"River Raisin men the best troops in the world," as Harrison said[3]—and became very expert and efficient in the spy, scout, or ranger service. He was engaged in the various conflicts near the Detroit River, already described, and in 1813 was in the battle of the Thames, under Colonel Richard M. Johnson. While with Hull at Sandwich, attached to Colonel M'Arthur's regiment, he performed important scout service. On one occasion, accompanied by four men, he penetrated the country as far as the site of the present village of Chatham, on the Thames, and there captured a Colonel M'Gregor, a burly British officer, and a Jew named Jacobs, and carried them to Hull's camp. He tied M'Gregor to a horse, and thus took him to the head-quarters of his chief. After the surrender M'Gregor offered five hundred dollars for the capture of Knaggs, dead or alive. The Indians were constantly on the watch for him, and he had many

---

studies, in 1805, he settled at Frenchtown. At the beginning of the war of 1812, he, with other young Frenchmen of that region, joined the army of General Hull for a year. They were at the Raisin when Hull surrendered, and gave themselves up to Captain Elliott. During the remainder of the war he was charged by the American commander with several important trusts. When, in 1818, Monroe County was organized, Durocher was chosen its clerk. He held that office for about twenty years. He was for six years a member of the Territorial Council of Michigan, and in 1835 was a member of the Convention that framed the state Constitution. He was a member of the state Legislature, a justice of the peace, judge of probate, and circuit judge, and at the time of his death, on the 21st of September, 1861, was clerk of the city of Monroe. The funeral services at the time of his burial were held in St. Anne's Catholic church of Monroe, where Father Joos officiated.

Laurent Durocher

[1] Knaggs's mother lived at or near Frenchtown at the time of the battle there, and was one of those whom Proctor ordered to Detroit. She was then eighty years of age. Thinly clad (having been robbed by the Indians), she proceeded in an open *traineau*, and reached Detroit in safety. When asked how it happened that she did not perish, she replied, "My spunk kept me warm."

[2] On one occasion, as he informed me, while he kept the ferry on the Huron, he flogged a troublesome Indian very severely. That night a brother of the savage came to Knaggs's cabin at a late hour to avenge the insult. Hearing a summons, but not knowing the visitor, Knaggs went out, when the gleam of a knife-blade in the starlight warned him of danger. He ran to a spot where he had a large club, pursued by a savage, who, in striking at him with his knife, cut off the skirt of the only garment that Knaggs had on. The latter seized the club, turned upon his assailant, felled him to the ground, and beat him until every bone in his body was broken. Although nearly fifty years had elapsed since the occurrence, Mr. Knaggs became much excited while relating it.

[3] I am indebted to Mr. Lyon, of Detroit, for the following copy of the first muster-roll of the "Raisin men," under Cornet Isaac Lee:

Cornet, Isaac Lee. *Sergeant*, James Bentley. *Corporal*, John Ruland. *Privates*, James Knaggs, Louis Drouillard, Orrin Rhodes, Michael M'Dermot, Scott Rolle, Samuel Dibble, Robert Glass, Cyrus Hunter, James Rolle, Silas Lewis, Samuel Youngs, John Murphy, Thomas Noble, Francis Moffatt, Daniel Hull, John Reddull, John Creamer.

From October, 1813, to April, 1814, Captain Lee commanded a large company of dragoons. His lieutenants were George Johnson and John Ruland. The late Judge Laurent Durocher was cornet. Johnson was a very brave officer, and in the battle of Maguaga he actually commanded Smyth's dragoons.

narrow escapes. This made him feel bitterly toward them.

At the battle of the Thames, Knaggs identified the body of Tecumtha; it is said, he having been long acquainted with the great Shawnoe. He was absent in Ohio on his parole when the battle of the Raisin occurred. He was the youngest of five brothers, all of whom were active in military service. His four brothers served as spies with Captain Wells, who was killed at Chicago. One of them was captured in the war of 1812, and carried a prisoner to Halifax. They were all men of strong convictions, and each, until the day of his death, hated both the British and their Indian allies, for they had all suffered at their hands.

Mr. Knaggs seemed in fine health and spirits when I visited him; but, a little more than three months afterward, he died suddenly. His death occurred on the 23d of December, 1860.[1]

I returned to Detroit by the evening train, filled with reflections concerning the events of the day, and those which made the Raisin terribly conspicuous in the annals of the war. I remembered that some of the newspapers of the day censured Harrison for not promptly supporting Winchester; and that in the political campaign of 1840, when Harrison was elected President of the United States, his enemies cited his alleged shortcomings on this occasion as evidence that his military genius and services, on which his fame mostly rested, were myths. But contemporary history, and the well-settled convictions of his surviving companions in arms whom I met in the Northwest, as well as the gallant engineer, Colonel Wood, who afterward fell at Fort Erie,[2] fully acquit General Harrison of all blame or lack of soldierly qualities on that occasion. It was not until the night of the 16th that he was informed by a messenger that General Winchester had arrived at the Rapids, and meditated a forward movement. The latter intimation alarmed Harrison, and he made every exertion to push troops forward from Upper Sandusky, where he was then quartered, sixty miles from the Rapids by way of the Portage River, and seventy-six miles by Lower Sandusky. He immediately ordered his artillery to advance by way of the Portage, with an escort of three hundred men, under Major Orr, with provisions; and he pressed forward himself, as speedily as possible, by the way of Lower Sandusky, where one regiment and a battalion were stationed, under the command of General Perkins. This battalion was ordered to march immediately, under Major Cotgrove, and Harrison determined to follow it the next morning. He was just rising from his

---

[1] I am indebted to Mr. William H. Bowlsby, a photographer in Monroe, for the likeness of Mr. Knaggs. It was taken from life by that gentleman. The signature was written in my note-book by Mr. Knaggs when I visited him.

[2] Lieutenant Colonel Wood, then Harrison's chief engineer, with the rank of captain, afterward said, "What human means within the control of General Harrison could prevent the anticipated disaster, and save that corps which was already looked upon as lost, as doomed to inevitable destruction? Certainly none, because neither orders to halt nor troops to succor him [Winchester] could be received in time, or at least that was the expectation. He was already in motion, and General Harrison still at Upper Sandusky, seventy miles in his rear. The weather was inclement, the snow was deep, and a large portion of the Black Swamp was yet open. What would a Turenne or a Eugène have done, under such a pressure of embarrassing circumstances, more than Harrison did?"

bed when a messenger came with the tidings of the advance of Lewis upon Frenchtown. Perkins was immediately ordered to press forward to the Rapids the remaining troops under his command. After hastily breakfasting, he and Perkins proceeded in a sleigh. They were met on the way by an express with intelligence of Lewis's victory at the Raisin. This nerved Harrison to greater exertions. He pushed forward alone and on horseback, through the swamps filled with snow, in daylight and in darkness, and, after almost superhuman efforts, he reached the Rapids early on the morning of the 20th. Winchester had departed for the Raisin the previous evening, and Harrison could do nothing better than wait for his oncoming troops, under Perkins and Cotgrove, and the artillery by the Portage. What remained at the Rapids of Winchester's army, under Colonel Payne, were sent forward toward the Raisin, and Captain Hart, the inspector general, was sent to inform Winchester of the supporting movements in his rear.

Alas! the roads were so almost impassable that the troops moved very slowly. After the utmost exertions they were too late. News came to Harrison, at ten o'clock on the morning of the 22d, of the attack of the British and Indians on the Americans at Frenchtown. The fraction of Perkins's brigade which had arrived at the Rapids was sent forward, and Harrison himself hastened toward the Raisin. He met the affrighted fugitives, who told doleful stories of the scenes of the morning, and assured the commander that the British and Indians were in pursuit of the broken army of Winchester toward the Rapids. This intelligence spurred on the re-enforcements. Other fugitives were soon met, who declared that the defeat of Winchester was total and irretrievable, and that no aid in Harrison's power could win back the victory of the enemy. A council of officers was held at Harrison's head-quarters in the saddle, when it was decided that a farther advance would be useless and imprudent. A few active men were sent forward to assist the fugitives in escaping, while the main body returned to the Rapids. There another council was held, which resulted in an order for the troops, numbering not more than nine hundred men, to fall back to the Portage (about eighteen miles), establish there a fortified camp, wait for the arrival of the artillery and accompanying troops, and then to push forward to the Rapids again.

The latter movement was delayed on account of heavy rains. On the 30th of January Colonel Leftwitch arrived with his brigade, a regiment of Pennsylvania troops, and a greater part of the artillery, and on the 1st of February General Harrison moved toward the Rapids with seventeen hundred men. He took post on the right bank of the river, upon high and commanding ground, at the foot of the Rapids, and there established a fortified camp, to which was afterward given, in honor of the governor of Ohio, the name of Fort Meigs. All the troops that could be spared from other posts were ordered there, with the design of pressing on toward Malden before the middle of February; but circumstances caused delay, and the Army of the Northwest tarried for some time on the bank of the Maumee before opening the campaign of 1813 in that region.

CHAPTER XVIII.

"Oh! now the time has come, my boys, to cross the Yankee line,
We remember they were rebels once, and conquered John Burgoyne;
We'll subdue those mighty Democrats, and pull their dwellings down,
And we'll have the States inhabited with subjects to the crown."
                                    SONG—THE NOBLE LADS OF CANADA.

IN preceding chapters the military events in the Northwest, where the war was first commenced in earnest, have been considered in a group, as forming a distinct episode in the history. By such grouping, in proper order, the reader may obtain a comprehensive view of the entire campaign of 1812 in that region, which ended with the establishment of General Harrison's head-quarters on the banks of the Maumee early in February, 1813.

We will now consider the next series of events, in the order of time, in the campaign of 1812, which occurred on the Northern frontier, from Lake Erie to the River St. Lawrence. The movements in the Northwest already recorded claim precedence, in point of time, over those on the Northern frontier of only seven days, Hull having initiated the former by the invasion of Canada on the 12th of July, and a squadron of British vessels having opened the latter by an attack on Sackett's Harbor on the 19th of the same month. The parties in these movements, between the scenes of which lay an almost unbroken wilderness of wood and water of several hundred miles, were absolutely independent of each other in immediate impulse and action.

When war was declared the United States possessed small means on the northern frontier for offensive or defensive operations. The first warlike measure was the construction, at Oswego, on Lake Ontario, of the brig *Oneida*, by Christian Berg and Henry Eckford, under the direction of Lieutenant Melancthon Woolsey, of the United States Navy. She was commenced in 1808, and was launched early in 1809. She was intended chiefly for employment in the enforcement of the revenue laws on the frontier, under the early embargo acts. For a similar purpose, a company of infantry and some artillery were posted at Sackett's Harbor, at the eastern end of Lake Ontario,[1] in 1808; and in March, 1809, militia detachments were stationed on the southern shores of the St. Lawrence, opposite Kingston, to prevent smuggling. This duty gave rise to many stirring scenes on the frontier in the violation and vindication of the revenue laws, which were generally evaded or openly defied until the spring of 1812, when a more stringent embargo act was passed.[a]   [a] April 4, 1812.

The Legislature of the State of New York, as vigilant as the national government, took measures early for enforcing the laws on the Canada frontier of that commonwealth. In February, 1808, the governor ordered five hundred stand of arms to be deposited at Champion, in the present county of Jefferson; and the following year an arsenal was built at Watertown,[2] on the Black River, twelve miles

---

[1] The Indians gave this an almost unpronounceable and interminable name, which signified "Fort at the mouth of Great River." It received its name from Augustus Sackett, the first settler. It was constituted an election district in 1805, and in 1814 it was incorporated a village. During the war of 1812 it was the chief military post on the Northern frontier. Millions of dollars have been expended there for fortifications and war vessels, yet prosperity as a village seems not to have been its lot. It contains less than one thousand inhabitants.

[2] The engraving of the Arsenal Building on the following page is from a sketch made by the writer in 1855. It was erected at a cost of about two thousand dollars. It is still [1867] standing, on the south side of Arsenal (formerly Columbia) Street, between Benedict and Madison Streets. It was maintained by the state as an arsenal until 1850, when it was sold.

War Materials at Watertown.   The Militia there in Command of General Brown.   The detached Militia of the State.

ARSENAL BUILDING, WATERTOWN.

eastward of Sackett's Harbor, under the direction of Hart Massey,[1] where arms, fixed ammunition, accoutrements, and other war supplies were speedily gathered for use on the Northern frontier. In May, 1812, a regiment of militia, under Colonel Christopher P. Bellinger, was stationed at Sackett's Harbor, a part of which was kept on duty at Cape Vincent. Jacob Brown, an enterprising farmer from Pennsylvania, who had settled on the borders of the Black River about four miles from Watertown, and had been appointed a brigadier general of militia in 1811, was then in command of the first detachment of New York's quota of the one hundred thousand militia which the President was authorized to call out by act of Congress.[a] When war was declared he was charged with the defense of the frontier from Oswego to Lake St. Francis, a distance of two hundred miles.[2]

[a] April 10, 1812.

---

[1] Mr. Massey was one of the earlier settlers of Watertown. The first religious meeting there was held in his house. He was collector of the port of Sackett's Harbor at the time in question, and held that office all through what was called "Embargo times" and the War. He died at Watertown in March, 1853, at the age of eighty-two years.

[2] By a General Order issued from the War Department on the 21st of April, 1812, the detached militia of the State of New York were arranged in two divisions and eight brigades. STEPHEN VAN RENSSELAER, of Albany, was appointed major general, and assigned to the command of the First Division; and BENJAMIN MOOERS, of Plattsburg, was appointed to the same office, and placed in command of the Second Division.

The eight brigadiers commissioned for the service were assigned to the several brigades as follows: 1st brigade, GERARD STEDDIFORD, of the city of New York; 2d, REUBEN HOPKINS, of Goshen, Orange County; 3d, MICAJAH PETTIS, of Queensbury, Washington County; 4th, RICHARD DODGE, of Johnstown, Montgomery County; 5th, JACOB BROWN, of Brownsville, Jefferson County; 6th, DANIEL MILLER, of Homer, Cortland County; 7th, WILLIAM WADSWORTH, of Geneseo, Ontario County; 8th, GEORGE M'CLURE, of Bath, Steuben County.

This force was farther subdivided into twenty regiments, and to the command of each a lieutenant colonel was assigned, as follows:

First Brigade: 1st regiment, *Beekman M. Van Buren*, of the city of New York; 2d, *Jonas Mapes*, of the city of New York; 3d, *John Ditmas*, of Jamaica, Queens County.

Second Brigade: 4th regiment, *Abraham J. Hardenbergh*, of Shawangunk, Ulster County; 5th, *Martin Heermance*, of Rhinebeck, Duchess County; 6th, *Abraham Van Wyck*, of Fishkill, Duchess County.

Third Brigade: 7th regiment, *James Green*, of Argyle, Washington County; 8th, *Thomas Miller*, of Plattsburg, Clinton County; 9th, *Peter I. Vosburgh*, of Kinderhook, Columbia County.

Fourth Brigade: 10th regiment, *John Prior*, of Greenfield, Saratoga County, and 11th, *Calvin Rich*, of Sharon, Schoharie County, to be attached to the regiments from General Veeder's division; 12th, *John T. Van Dalfsen*, of Coeyman's, Albany County, and 13th, *Putnam Farrington*, of Delhi, Delaware County, to be attached to the regiments from General Todd's division.

Fifth Brigade: 14th regiment, *William Stone*, of Whitestown, Oneida County; 15th, *Thomas B. Benedict*, of De Kalb, St. Lawrence County.

Sixth Brigade: 16th regiment, *Farrand Stranahan*, of Cooperstown, Otsego County; 17th, *Thomas Mead*, of Norwich, Chenango County.

Seventh Brigade: 18th regiment, *Hugh W. Dobbin*, of Junius, Seneca County; 19th, *Henry Bloom*, of Geneva, Cayuga County; 20th, *Peter Allen*, of Bloomfield, Ontario County.

To the Eighth Brigade was assigned the regiment of light infantry under Colonel Jeremiah Johnson, of Brooklyn, Kings County, and the regiment of riflemen under Colonel Francis M'Clure, of the city of New York.

General Van Rensselaer assigned to the several brigades the following staff officers:

Brigades.	Brigade Majors and Inspectors.	Brigade Quartermasters.	Brigades.	Brigade Majors and Inspectors.	Brigade Quartermasters.
1	Theophilus Pierce.	Charles Graham.	5	Robert Shoemaker.	Henry Seymour.
2	John Dill.	Robert Heart.	6	Thomas Greenley.	Nathaniel R. Packard.
3	Michael S. Van der Cock.	Dean Edson.	7	Julius Keyes.	Henry Wells.
4	Moses S. Cantine.	Leon'd H. Gansevoort.	8	Joseph Lad.	Jeremiah Anderson.

I have compiled the above statement from General Van Rensselaer's first General Order, issued from his head-quarters at Albany on the 18th of June, 1812.* The following paragraph from his second General Order, issued on the 13th of July, indicates the special field of operations to which General Van Rensselaer was assigned: "Major General Stephen Van Rensselaer having been requested to repair to the command of the militia heretofore ordered into the service, and to be hereafter ordered into the service of the United States for the defense of the Northern and Western frontiers of this state *between St. Regis and Pennsylvania*, enters upon his command this day." In the same Order General Van Rensselaer declared that all the militia comprehended in the brigades organized by his General Order of the 18th of June, "together with the corps commanded by Lieutenant Colonels Swift, Flemming, and Bellinger, were subject to his division orders."

---

* General Van Rensselaer's MS. Order Book from June 18th to October 1st, 1812.

| Seizure of British Vessels on Lake Ontario. | Retaliation expected. | Northern Militia called out. |

In May, 1812, the schooner *Lord Nelson*, owned by parties at Niagara, Upper Canada, and laden with flour and merchandise, sailed from that port for Kingston. She was found in American waters, captured by the *Oneida*, under Lieutenant Commanding Woolsey, and condemned as a lawful prize for a violation of the Embargo Act. About a month later,[a] another British schooner, the *Ontario*, was captured at St. Vincent, but was soon afterward discharged; and at about the same time, still another British schooner, named *Niagara*, was seized, and sold because of a violation of the revenue laws. These events, as was expected, soon led to retaliation. When news of the declaration of war reached Ogdensburg, on the St. Lawrence, eight American schooners—trading vessels—lay in its harbor. They endeavored to escape[b] to Lake Ontario, bearing away affrighted families and their effects. An active Canadian partisan named Jones, living not far from the present village of Maitland, had raised a company of volunteers to capture them. He gave chase in boats, overtook the fugitive unarmed flotilla at the foot of the Thousand Islands,[1] a little above Brockville, captured two of the schooners (*Sophia* and *Island Packet*), and emptied and burned them. The remainder retreated to Ogdensburg.[2]

[a] June 14, 1812.

[b] June 29.

It was believed that this movement was only the beginning of more active and extensive ones, offensive and defensive, on the part of the British—that several of the Thousand Islands were about to be fortified, and that expeditions of armed men in boats were to be sent over to devastate the country along the northern frontier. General Brown and Commander Woolsey, vested with full authority, took active measures to repel invasion and protect the lake coast and river shores. In a letter to the former, Daniel D. Tompkins, Governor of New York, informed him of the declaration of war, and directed him to call out re-enforcements for Bellinger from the militia of Jefferson, Lewis, and St. Lawrence Counties, and to arm and equip them, if necessary, from the arsenals at Watertown, and at Russel, farther north on the Grosse River. Colonel Benedict, of St. Lawrence, was ordered to guard the frontier from Ogdensburg to St. Regis. Measures were also taken to concentrate a considerable force at Ogdensburg and Cape Vincent, for the twofold purpose of guarding the frontier and keeping Kingston in a state of alarm, that being the chief naval station where the British built vessels for service on Lake Ontario.

Jh. B. Benedict

On the 11th of July the inhabitants on the frontier were alarmed by a rumor that Commander Woolsey and his *Oneida* had been captured by the enemy, and that a squadron of British vessels were on their way from Kingston to recapture the *Lord Nelson* and destroy Sackett's Harbor. General Brown immediately repaired to the Harbor. The rumor was a false one, but a part of it was the precursor of truth in a similar form. Eighteen days afterward Commander Woolsey saw from his mast-head, at early dawn, a squadron of five British vessels of war off Stony Island, beating toward the Harbor with the wind dead ahead. These proved to be the *Royal George*, 24; *Prince Regent*, 22; *Earl of Moira*, 20; *Simcoe*, 12; and *Seneca*, 4, under the command of Commodore Earle, a Canadian. On the way up they captured a boat returning from Cape Vincent; and by the crew (who were released), they sent word to Bellinger, the commandant at Sackett's Harbor, that all they wanted was the

---

[1] This group of islands, lying in the St. Lawrence River, just below the foot of Lake Ontario, fill that river for twenty-seven miles along its course, and number more than fifteen hundred. A few of them are large and cultivated, but the most of them are mere rocky islets, covered generally with stunted hemlocks and cedar-trees, which extend to the water's edge. Some of them contain an area of only a few square yards, while others present many superficial square miles. Canoes and small boats may pass in safety among all of them, and there is a deep channel for steamboats and other large vessels, which never varies in depth or position, the bottom being rocky. The St. Lawrence here varies from two to nine miles in width. The boundary-line between the United States and Canada passes among them. It was determined in 1818. The largest of the islands are *Grand* and *Howe*, belonging to Canada, and *Carleton, Grindstone*, and *Wells's*, belonging to the United States. They have been the theatre of many historic scenes and legendary tales during two centuries and a half.

[2] *History of St. Lawrence and Franklin Counties*, by Franklin Hough, M.D., pages 620, 621.

Oneida and the *Lord Nelson*, at the same time warning the inhabitants that if the squadron should be fired upon, the town should be burned.

Perceiving the peril to which the *Oneida* was exposed, Woolsey weighed anchor and attempted to gain the lake. He failed, returned, and moored his vessel just outside of Navy Point, on which the ship-house now [1867] stands, in such position that her broadside of nine guns might be brought to bear on the enemy. The remainder of her guns were taken out, to be placed in battery on land. An iron thirty-two-pounder, designed for the *Oneida*, but found to be too heavy, had already been placed on a battery of three nine-pounders upon the bluff at the foot of the main street of the village, on which the dwelling of the commander of the naval station there now stands. That heavy gun had been lying near the shore, partly imbedded in the mud, for some time, and from that circumstance had acquired the name of *The Old Sow*. These cannon, with two brass nine-pounders in charge of an artillery company under the command of Captain Elisha Camp, and two sixes fished out of the lake from the wreck of an English ship near Duck Island, composed the heavy metal with which to combat the approaching British squadron. The soldiers for the same purpose comprised only a part of Bellinger's regiment, Camp's Sackett's Harbor Artillery, which promptly volunteered for thirty days' service, the crew of the *Oneida*, and three hundred militia. At the first appearance of the enemy alarm-guns were fired, and couriers were sent into the country in all directions to arouse the militia. At sunset nearly three thousand had arrived or were near, but they were too late. Victory had been lost and won early in the day.

Woolsey, the best engineer officer present, left his brig in charge of his lieutenant, and took the general command on shore. He placed the 32-pounder in charge of Captain William Vaughan, a sailing-master of eminence then living at Sackett's Harbor,[1] and directed Captain Camp to manage the others in battery. Meanwhile the enemy were slowly drawing near; and by the time Woolsey was prepared to receive them, the British flag-ship *Royal George*, closely followed by the *Prince Regent*, were close enough for action. Vaughan opened it at eight o'clock by a shot from the big gun, which was harmless, and drew from the people on the *Royal George* a response of derisive laughter, which could be plainly heard on the shore. This was followed by some shots from those two vessels in the advance at the distance of a mile, which were quickly answered by Vaughan. The firing was kept up for about two hours, the squadron standing off and on, out of range of the smaller guns.

WILLIAM VAUGHAN.

---

[1] From the widow of Captain Vaughan, yet [1867] living at Sackett's Harbor, I received the following brief sketch of his life: He was born in the middle of August, 1776, at Wilkes-Barré, in the Valley of Wyoming, Pennsylvania. He was two years old when the massacre took place there, and his mother fled with him over the mountains. At the age of eighteen years he visited Canada. The posts of Oswego, Fort Carleton, and Presentation, or Oswegatchie, were then held by the British, and he was compelled to have a passport to go from post to post on the soil of the United States. He returned to Canada in 1797, after these posts were given up, and engaged in lake navigation. He was a pilot on Lake Ontario for many years, and when the war broke out he was appointed a sailing-master. He served with great activity during the war. We shall meet him occasionally in the course of our narrative. After the war he returned to the occupation of mariner, and was master, at different times, of six steamboats on Lake Ontario. About the year 1850 his spine received an injury by his falling on the ice while rescuing a man and two women from destruction among floating ice agitated by high winds. He never recovered. He died at Sackett's Harbor on the 10th of December, 1857, aged eighty-one years.

The most of the enemy's shot fell against the rocks below the battery. One of these (a thirty-two-pound ball) came over the bluff, struck the earth not far from Sackett's mansion (then occupied by Vaughan's family), and plowed a deep furrow into the door-yard.[1] It was immediately caught up by Sergeant Spier, who ran with it to Captain Vaughan, exclaiming, "I've been playing ball with the red-coats, and have caught 'em out. See if the British can catch back again." At that moment the *Royal George* was wearing to give a broadside, when Vaughan's gun sent back the captive ball with such force and precision[2] that it struck her stern, raked her completely, sent splinters as high as her mizzen top-sail yard, killed fourteen men, and wounded eighteen![3] The flag-ship had already received a shot that went through her sides, and another between wind and water. The *Prince Regent* had lost her fore-topgallant-mast, and the *Earl of Moira* had been hulled. The laughter of the enemy had been changed into wailing. Disaster suggested the exercise of discretion, and a signal of retreat was speedily given after the returned ball had made its destructive passage through the ship. The squadron put about and sailed out of the harbor, while the band on shore played Yankee Doodle, and the troops and the citizens greeted their departure with loud cheers. Nothing, animate or inanimate, on shore had been injured in the least by the cannonading of two hours' duration.[4] It was a serene Sabbath morning, and the village at evening was as quiet as if nothing remarkable had happened.

The command of the waters of Lake Ontario was now an object of great importance to both parties. To obtain this advantage required the speediest preparation of armed vessels. The British had several afloat already; the Americans had but one. The only hope of the latter of securing the supremacy of the lake rested upon their ability to convert merchant vessels afloat into warriors. These were schooners varying in size from thirty to one hundred tons burden, and susceptible of being changed into active gun-boats. Eight of them, as we have observed, were at Ogdensburg when war was declared. Two had been destroyed, and six now remained. To capture and destroy them was an important object to the British; to save and arm them was a more important object to the Americans. To accomplish the former result, the British sent the *Earl of Moira*, 14, and *Duke of Gloucester*, 10, down the St. Lawrence to Prescott, opposite Ogdensburg, to watch or seize the imprisoned vessels. To accomplish the latter, the Americans sent a small force in the same direction, consisting of the schooner *Julia* (built by the late venerable Matthew M'Nair, of Oswego, and named in honor of his daughter), armed with a long thirty-two and two long sixes, bearing about sixty volunteers, under the command of Lieutenant H. W. Wells, from the *Oneida*, with Captains Vaughan and Dixon; also a rifle corps under Noadiah Hubbard, in a Durham boat. These sailed from Sackett's Harbor on the evening of the 30th of July, unmindful of the superior force of the enemy. "Our means are humble," General Brown wrote to Governor Tompkins on that day,[a] "but, with the blessing of Heaven, this republican gun- [a July 30, 1812.]

---

[1] One of Captain Vaughan's gunners was Julius Torrey, a negro, who was a great favorite, and known in camp as Black Julius. He served at his post with the greatest courage and activity. As the enemy was beyond the reach of small-arms, most of the troops were inactive spectators of the scene.—Hough's *History of Jefferson County*, page 464.

[2] Although the gun was well managed, the range of the shot had been a little wild because of their size. The gun was a thirty-two-pounder, but the largest balls to be found at Sackett's Harbor were twenty-fours. These were made to fit by wrapping them in pieces of carpet. The British thirty-two was just the shot needed for precision. The smaller shot used on that occasion were brought from the Taberg Works, near Rome, only a week before.

[3] On my way to Sackett's Harbor in the summer of 1860, I saw at Big Sandy Creek an old seaman named Jehaziel Howard, who was at Sackett's Harbor at this time, and from him I learned some of the facts above stated. His statement concerning the number of killed and wounded by that last shot from the thirty-two-pounder was made on the authority of James Dutton, who deserted to the British a few days before the battle. Dutton told the British commander that the Americans were very weak, and had no cannon. Their experience in the action made them suspect him of being a spy. They threatened to have him tried as such. Taking counsel of his fears, he deserted from the British and returned to the American camp. He was on the *Royal George* at the time of the action.

[4] *The War*, i., 82; Cooper's *Naval History of the United States*, ii., 326, 327; Hough's *History of Jefferson County*, 462–464; oral statements to the author by Captain (now Colonel) Camp, the late Amasa Trowbridge, M.D., and Jehaziel Howard.

A Fight on the St. Lawrence.   Riflemen at Sackett's Harbor.   Chauncey chief Commander on Lake Ontario.

boat may give a good account of the *Duke* and the *Earl;* and a successful termination of this enterprise will give us an equal chance for the command of the lake."

The *Julia* and her Durham consort went to the St. Lawrence that night. Although it was very dark, they arrived in safety at Cape Vincent. At early dawn, under a deeply-clouded sky, they pressed forward among the Thousand Islands, the wind blowing down the river, and, at three o'clock in the afternoon,[a] met the two British vessels off Morristown, eleven miles above Ogdensburg. They anchored at once, and opened fire upon each other. The action lasted more than three hours, during which the cannonading was almost incessant, and yet the *Julia* was only slightly injured by a single shot, and not one of the Americans was killed or wounded. The *Earl of Moira* was hulled several times, and both of the British vessels withdrew toward the Canada shore. Night came with intense darkness, but frequent flashes of lightning in the southern horizon revealed surrounding objects for a moment. With the aid of the Durham and her own yawl, the *Julia* made her way to Ogdensburg before morning,[b] when Lieutenant Wells left her in charge of Captain Vaughan, and returned to Sackett's Harbor. The armistice that soon followed[1] enabled the *Julia*, with the six schooners in her wake, to make her way to the lake.[c] Meanwhile the guns of the *Earl* and *Duke* were landed at Elizabethtown (now Brockville), and placed in battery there.[2]

[a] July 31, 1812.
[b] August 1.
[c] September 5.

Early in August Captain Benjamin Forsyth arrived at Sackett's Harbor with a well-drilled company of riflemen. These were the first regular troops seen on that frontier, and were welcomed with much satisfaction. General Brown urged Forsyth to open a recruiting station at once, hoping to enlist two full companies of the sharpshooters. At the same time, the national government was putting forth vigorous efforts for acquiring the supremacy of the lakes. The appointment of a proper commander-in-chief of the navy to be created on them, who might properly superintend its formation, was the first and most important measure. Fortunately for the service, Captain Isaac Chauncey was chosen for this responsible and arduous duty. He was then at the head of the navy yard at Brooklyn, New York. He was one of the best practical seamen of his time, possessed a thorough knowledge of ships in whole and in detail, and was in the constant exercise of energy and industry of the highest order. On the 31st of August he was commissioned for that special service, and on the following day, Paul Hamilton, the then Secretary of the Navy, sent him a cipher alphabet and numerals, by which he might make secret communications to the Department.[3]

CIPHER ALPHABET AND NUMERALS.

[1] See note 2, page 293.
[2] Letter of General Brown to Governor Tompkins, August 4, 1812. Hough's *History of Jefferson County*, page 465, 466. Hough's *History of St. Lawrence and Franklin Counties*, page 622. Written Statement to the Author by the late Amasa Trowbridge, M.D.
[3] "After your arrival upon the lakes," wrote Mr. Hamilton, "you may experience some difficulty and risk in sending your dispatches to me; and you may find it necessary to employ a cipher in your communications, especially such of them as might do the service an injury by falling into the hands of the enemy. Under such circumstances, you will communicate to me in cipher by the following alphabet whenever you may judge it expedient." Here follows the cipher alphabet and numerals, of which a fac-simile is above given. The original is in the possession of the New York Historical Society. It was presented by the Rev. Mr. Chauncey, a son of the commodore, on the 5th of February, 1861.

American and British Squadrons on Lake Ontario.   Elliott sent to Lake Erie.   Chauncey's first Cruise.

Chauncey entered upon his new duties immediately after the receipt of his orders. In the first week in September he sent forward forty ship-carpenters, with Henry Eckford at their head. Others soon followed; and Commander Woolsey was directed to purchase some merchant vessels for the service. On the 18th of the same month, one hundred officers and seamen, with guns and other munitions of war, left New York for Sackett's Harbor, and Chauncey arrived there himself on the 6th of October. The schooners *Genesee Packet, Experiment, Collector, Lord Nelson, Charles and Ann,* and *Diana,* were purchased, and manned and named respectively in the same order, *Conquest, Growler, Pert, Scourge, Governor Tompkins,* and *Hamilton.* Their armament consisted principally of long guns mounted on circles, with a few lighter ones that could be of very little service. Add to these the *Oneida* and *Julia* already in the service, and the entire flotilla, exclusive of the *Madison,* 24 (whose keel was laid before Chauncey's arrival[1]), mounted only forty guns, and was manned by four hundred and thirty men, the marines included. The *Oneida* carried sixteen guns, therefore there was an average of only five guns each among the remainder of the squadron. The British, at the same time, had made for service, on Lake Ontario, the ships *Royal George,* 22, and *Earl of Moira,* 14; and schooners *Prince Regent,* 16, *Duke of Gloucester,* 14, *Simcoe,* 12, and *Seneca,* 4. These, in weight of metal, were double the power of the American, while there was a corresponding disparity in the number of men.[2]

Lake Erie, over which also Chauncey was appointed commander, was separated from Ontario by the impassable cataract of Niagara, and vessels for use on the waters of the former had to be constructed on its shores, or at Detroit, where the unfinished brig *Adams,* captured at the surrender of Hull, had been built. For the purpose of creating a fleet there, Chauncey sent Lieutenant Jesse D. Elliott with orders for purchasing vessels similar to those given to Commander Woolsey. We shall consider some of Elliott's earlier operations presently.

Chauncey first appeared on Lake Ontario as the commander of a squadron on the 8th of November, a cold, raw, blustery day, with his broad pennant fluttering over the *Oneida,* his flag-ship, accompanied by six small vessels,[3] and bound on an expedition to intercept the entire British squadron on their return from Fort George, on the Niagara River, whither they had gone from Kingston with troops and munitions of war. Chauncey took his station near the False Ducks, some small islands nearly due west from Sackett's Harbor, on the track to Kingston, and in the afternoon of the 9th[a] fell in with the *Royal George,* Commodore Earl's flag-ship, making her way for the latter place. Chauncey chased her into the Bay of Quinté, and lost sight of her in the darkness of the night that soon followed. On the morning of the 10th[b] he captured and burnt a small schooner, and soon afterward espied the *Royal George* headed for Kingston. He gave chase with most of his squadron,[4] followed her into Kingston Harbor, and there engaged both her and five land batteries[5] for almost an hour. These were more formidable than Chauncey supposed; and a brisk wind having arisen, and the night coming on, he withdrew and anchored. The breeze had become almost a gale the next morning,[c] so Chauncey weighed anchor and stood out lakeward. The *Tompkins, Hamilton,* and *Julia* chased the *Simcoe* over a reef of rocks, and so

[a] November, 1812.

[b] November.

[c] November 11.

---

[1] The *Madison* was launched on the 26th of November, only forty-five days after her keel was laid. Henry Eckford was her constructor.

[2] Cooper's *Naval History of the United States,* ii., 328.

[3] The *Oneida* was commanded by Lieutenant Woolsey; the *Conquest* by Lieutenant Elliott; the *Hamilton* by Lieutenant M'Pherson; the *Governor Tompkins* by Lieutenant Brown; the *Pert* by Mr. Arundel; the *Julia* by Mr. Trant; and the *Growler* by Mr. Mix. The last three named were sailing-masters.

[4] In this chase Captain Elliott, in the *Conquest,* gallantly led, followed by the *Julia, Pert,* and *Growler.* The *Oneida* brought up the rear. She allowed the smaller vessels to make the attack. When, at half past three, she opened her carronades on the *Royal George,* that vessel was quick to cut her cables, and run up to the town.

[5] There was a battery on both India and Navy Points. Three others guarded the town; and some movable cannon were brought to bear on the American vessels.

riddled her that she sank before reaching Kingston. Soon afterward the *Hamilton* captured a large schooner from Niagara. The prize was sent past Kingston under convoy of the *Growler*, hoping to bring out the *Royal George*, but that vessel had been so much damaged in the action that she was compelled to haul on shore to keep from sinking. She had received several shots between wind and water, some of her guns were disabled, and a number of her crew had been killed.

The gale continued on the 12th, and during the following night a heavy snow-storm set in. Chauncey was undismayed by the fury of the elements. He had set his heart on obtaining the supremacy of the lake at all hazards, and he continued his cruise. Informed that the *Earl of Moira* was off the Real Ducks, he attempted to capture her. She was on the alert. A schooner that she was convoying was seized, but the warrior escaped. During the day Chauncey saw the *Royal George*, and two schooners that he supposed to be the *Prince Regent* and *Duke of Gloucester*, but they did not seem disposed to meet him.

In this short cruise Commodore Chauncey captured three merchant vessels, destroyed one armed schooner, and disabled the British flag-ship, and took several prisoners,[1] with a loss on his part of only one man killed and four wounded.[2] The loss of the British is not found on record.

Leaving the *Governor Tompkins*, *Conquest*, *Hamilton*, and *Growler* to blockade Kingston harbor until the ice should do so effectually, Chauncey sailed on the 19th, in the *Oneida*, for the head of the lake, accompanied by the remainder of the squadron. "I am in great hopes," he wrote to Governor Tompkins, "that I shall fall in with the *Prince Regent*, or some of the royal family which are cruising about York. Had we been one month sooner, we could have taken every town on this lake in three weeks; but the season is now so tempestuous that I am apprehensive we can not do much more this winter." His anticipations were realized. He was driven back by a gale in which the *Growler* was dismasted, and the ice formed so fast that all the vessels were in danger. He retired to Sackett's Harbor, and early in December the lake navigation was closed by the frost.[3]

While Chauncey was commencing vigorous measures for the construction of a navy at the east end of Lake Ontario, the land forces there and on the St. Lawrence were not idle, although no very important service was performed there during the remainder of 1812. The vigilant Captain Forsyth made a bold dash into Canada late in September. Having been informed that a large quantity of ammunition and other munitions of war were in a British store-house at Gananoqui, on the shores of the Lake of the Thousand Islands, in Canada,[4] and not heavily guarded, Forsyth asked and obtained permission of General Brown to make an attempt to capture them. He organized an expedition of one hundred and four men, consisting of seventy riflemen and thirty-four militia, the latter officered by Captain Samuel M'Nitt, Lieutenant Brown, and Ensigns Hawkins and Johnson. They set out from Sackett's Harbor on the 18th of September, and on the night of the 20th they left Cape Vincent in boats, threading their way in the dark among the upper group of the Thousand Islands. They landed a short distance from the village of Gananoqui, only ninety-five strong, without opposition; but as they approached the town they were confronted by a party of sixty British regulars and fifty Canadian militia drawn up in battle order, who poured heavy volleys upon them. Forsyth dashed forward with his men with-

---

[1] Among the prisoners was Captain Brock, brother of Major General Brock, who had been killed recently at Queenstown. He had some of his brother's baggage with him.

[2] Mr. Arundel, the commander of the *Pert*, was badly injured by the bursting of one of her guns, and a midshipman and three seamen were slightly wounded. Mr. Arundel refused to leave the deck, and was afterward knocked overboard by accident and drowned.

[3] Chauncey's Letter to Governor Tompkins, November 15, 1812; Cooper's *Naval History*, ii., 333 to 337 inclusive.

[4] Gananoqui is pleasantly situated at the mouth of the Gananoqui River, where it enters the upper portion of the St. Lawrence, known as the Lake of the Thousand Islands. It is in the town of Leeds, in Canada West, nearly opposite the town of Clayton (old French Creek), New York.

out firing a shot until within a hundred yards of the enemy, when the latter fled pell-mell to the town, closely pursued by the invaders. There the fugitives rallied and renewed the engagement, when they were again compelled to flee, leaving ten of their number dead on the field, several wounded, and eight regulars and four militia-men as prisoners. Forsyth lost only one man killed and one slightly wounded. For his own safety, he broke up the bridge over which he had pursued the enemy, and then returned to his boats, bearing away, as the spoils of victory, the eight regulars, sixty stand of arms, two barrels of fixed ammunition comprising three thousand ball-cartridges, one barrel of gunpowder, one of flints, forty-one muskets, and some other public property. In the store-house were found one hundred and fifty barrels of provisions, but, having no means of carrying them away, Captain Forsyth applied the torch, and store-house and provisions were consumed.[1] The public property secured on this occasion was given to the soldiers of the expedition as a reward for their valor.

While Forsyth was away on his expedition, Brigadier General Richard Dodge arrived at Watertown[a] with a detachment of Mohawk Valley militia. He outranked General Brown, and on his arrival he ordered that officer to proceed to Ogdensburg, at the mouth of the Oswegatchie River, to garrison old Fort Presentation, or Oswegatchie, at that place.[2] General Brown was chagrined by this unlooked-for order, but, like a true soldier, he immediately obeyed it. A part of Captain Forsyth's company went with him; and three weeks later, at the request of the governor, General Dodge sent to Brown[b] the remainder of the riflemen, and the artillery companies of Captains Brown, King, and Foot, in all one hundred and sixty men, with two brass 9-pound cannon, one 4, and an ample supply of muskets and munitions of war.

[a] September 21, 1812.

[b] October 12.

APPEARANCE OF FORT OSWEGATCHIE IN 1812.

General Brown arrived at Ogdensburg on the 1st of October. Already the militia had been employed in some hostile movements. At about the middle of September information reached Ogdensburg that some British bateaux, laden with stores, were ascending the St. Lawrence. It was resolved to capture them. A gun-boat, with a brass six-pounder and eighteen men, under Adjutant Daniel W. Church, accompanied by a party under Captain Griffin, in a Durham boat, went down the river in the night, and encountered the enemy near Toussaint Island. The Durham boat was lost in the affray, and the gun-boat was in great peril at one time. It was saved, however. The expedition was a failure. Five of Church's men were wounded, and one was killed. The British lost several in killed and wounded. They were led by Adjutant Fitzgibbon.[3]

On the day after General Brown's arrival at Ogdensburg,[c] about forty British bateaux, escorted by a gun-boat, were seen approaching Prescott from below, and as they neared the town a battery at that place opened upon Og-

[c] October 2.

---

[1] Letter of General Brown to Governor Tompkins, September 23, 1812; Letter from Utica, September 29, 1812, published in *The War*, page 71. The same letter appears in Niles's *Weekly Register*, October 10, 1812.
[2] A particular account of this fort will be given hereafter.
[3] Hough's *History of St. Lawrence and Franklin Counties*, page 624.

densburg to cover the flotilla.¹ The heavy guns at the latter place consisted of a brass six-pounder under the charge of Adjutant Church, and an iron twelve-pounder managed by Joseph York, sheriff of the county, and a volunteer citizen. These replied to the British battery for a while. On the following day the firing from Prescott was renewed, but was not answered; and on Sunday morning, the 4th,[a] two gun-boats and twenty-five bateaux, filled with about seven hundred and fifty armed men, under Colonels Lethbridge and Breckinridge, went up the river almost a mile, and then turned their prows toward Ogdensburg, with the evident intention of attacking it. Forsyth's riflemen were encamped at the time near the old fort on the west side of the Oswegatchie, and General Brown, with regulars and militia, were stationed in the town.² The whole American force amounted to about twelve hundred effective men. These were immediately drawn up in battle order to receive the invaders. When the latter had approached to within a quarter of a mile of the town, nearly in mid-channel, the Americans opened such a severe fire from their two cannon that the enemy retreated in confusion and precipitation, with the loss of three men killed and four wounded.³ About thirty rounds were fired from each of the two cannon, and the action lasted two hours.⁴ Not one of the Americans was injured in the action, but some damage was done to the town by the cannon-shot of the British. "This enterprise," says Christie, a British author, "undertaken without the sanction of the commander of the forces, was censured by him, and the public opinion condemned it as rash and premature."⁵

[a] October, 1812.

Eighteen days after the repulse of the British at Ogdensburg, Major Guilford Dudley Young, and a small detachment of militia, who were chiefly from Troy, New York, performed a gallant exploit at St. Regis, an Indian village lying upon the boundary-line between the United States and Canada. The dusky inhabitants of that settlement were placed in a very embarrassing position when war was declared. Their village lay within the boundaries of both governments, and up to that time the administration of their internal affairs, managed by twelve chiefs, had been nominally independent of both. The annuities and presents from both governments were equally divided among them, and in all matters of business and profits every thing was in common. That this relation should not be disturbed, commissioners, appointed by the two governments, agreed that the Indians should remain neutral, and that the troops of both parties should avoid intrusion of their reservation. But they became objects of suspicion and dread. The settlers in that region had been horrified with tales of Indian massacres remotely and recently, and these people could not pass the boundaries of their domain without being regarded as possible enemies. So vigilant was this general fear that the Indians were compelled, when they went abroad, to carry a pass from some well-known white inhabitant, among the most prominent of whom, appointed by the chiefs, was Captain Polley, late of Massena Springs.⁶

---

¹ William E. Guest, Esq., whom I met at Ogdensburg in the summer of 1860, in some of his published "Recollections" of that place, speaking of the affair, says, "The villagers came out in large numbers, and stood in Washington Street, near the residence of Mr. Parish. Among them were a number of ladies, who felt safe, as no balls had as yet come into the village. While all were intently watching, with great excitement, the movements of the contending parties, a 12-pound shot, with its clear, singing, humming sound, passed over our heads, in the line of State Street, as near as we could judge, and fell in the rear of the village. A sudden change came over the scene. It became an intimate matter to all, and the ladies beat a rapid retreat." When I was in Ogdensburg in 1855, and made a sketch of the old Courthouse, printed in a note in Chapter XXVII. of this work, I was informed that that ball passed through the building, and a hole made by it was pointed out to me.

² The subordinate commanders on this occasion were Colonel Benedict, Major Dimock, Adjutant Hoskin, and Captains Forsyth, Griffin, Hubbard, Benedict, and M'Nitt. — *Ogdensburg Palladium*, October 6, quoted in *The War*, i., 78.

³ One account says that one of their gun-boats was disabled, and another that "two of their boats were so knocked to pieces as to render it necessary to abandon them."

⁴ Hough's *History of St. Lawrence and Franklin Counties*, page 625. Letter from Plattsburg, dated October 9, in Niles's *Weekly Register*, iii., 126. Christie's *Military Operations in Canada*, page 81.

⁵ Christie's *Military Operations in Canada*, page 81.

⁶ These passes stated that the bearer was a quiet, peaceable person. It was their custom to hold these passes up on approaching a white person that they might not be alarmed. On the other hand,

These restrictions curtailed their hunting and fishing, and they were reduced to such great extremities that they were compelled to apply to Governor Tompkins for relief.[1] The governor listened to their request, and during the war they received about five hundred rations daily from the United States government stores at French Mills,[2] now Fort Covington, on the Salmon River.

The neutrality agreement was violated by Sir George Prevost, the British commander-in-chief in Canada, who placed Captain M'Donell and a party of armed Canadian voyageurs in the village of St. Regis "for the security of that post," to "guard against any predatory incursions of the enemy, to inspire confidence in the Indians," and to give "support and countenance" to "Monsieur de Montigny, captain and resident agent at the village."[3] The real object appears to have been the seduction of the Indians from their neutrality by persuading them to join the British standard. In this they were successful, as the presence of more than eighty St. Regis warriors in the British army at different places on the frontiers subsequently fully proves.[4]

Major Young was stationed at French Mills when M'Donell took post at St. Regis, and he wished to attempt the capture of the whole party at about the 1st of October. William L. Gray, an Indian interpreter, was then running a mill on the site of the present village of Hogansburg, two miles above St. Regis, and consented to be Young's guide. He took him and his command along an unfrequented way, that brought them out suddenly upon the eastern banks of the St. Regis, opposite the village. The stream was too deep to ford, and, having no boats, Major Young was compelled to abandon the project at that time. The British intruders were alarmed; but as day after day wore away without farther molestation, M'Donell settled down into a feeling of absolute security. From that state he was soon aroused. Young left French Mills, with about two hundred men, on the night of the 21st of October, at eleven o'clock, crossed the St. Regis, at Gray's Mills, at half past three in the morning,[a] in a boat and canoe and a hastily-constructed raft, and before dawn arrived within half a mile of St. Regis, where they concealed themselves, while taking some rest and refreshment, behind a gentle hill westward of the village. Having carefully reconnoitred the position, the little party moved in three columns toward the British part of the village, at the northern extremity of which, not far from the ancient and famous church, stood the houses of Montigny and M'Donell, in which the officers and many of the men of the British detachment were stationed. Captain Lyon, editor of the Troy *Budget*, moved with his company along the road upon the bank of the St. Regis, so as to gain the rear of Montigny's house and a small blockhouse, while Captain Tilden and his company made a detour westward, partly in rear of M'Donell's, for the purpose of reaching the St. Lawrence and securing the boats of the enemy. Major Young, with the companies of Captains Higbie and M'Neil, moved through the village in front. Thus the enemy was surrounded. Lyon was first discovered by the British sentinel and attacked. Young was then within one hundred and fifty yards of Montigny's house. At that instant an ensign of the enemy, attempting to pass in front after being ordered to stand, was shot dead; and a few minutes afterward complete success crowned the enterprise of the gallant major. Forty prisoners (exclusive of the commander and the Catholic priest), with their arms and accoutrements, thirty-eight muskets, two bateaux, a flag, and a quantity of bag-

[a] October 22, 1812.

---

the Indians required persons traveling across their domain to exhibit passes. As few of these Indians could read, a device (see preceding page) was adopted to obviate the difficulties which that deficiency might give rise to. If a person was going through to French Mills, a simple bow was drawn on the paper; if he was intending to visit St. Regis village, an arrow was added to the bow.

[1] The letter written to Tompkins for that purpose was signed by the mark and name of Lewis Cook, one of the chiefs of the St. Regis Indians, and a colonel in the service of the United States.
[2] Hough's *History of St. Lawrence and Franklin Counties*, page 156.
[3] Letter of Adjutant Baynes to Captain M'Donell.
[4] Le Clerc, who succeeded Montigny as agent, raised a company of warriors there, and crossed over to Cornwall. These participated in several engagements during the war.—Hough's *St. Lawrence and Franklin Counties*, page 156.

gage, including eight hundred blankets found at the Indian agent's house, were the fruits of the victory. The British had seven men killed, including a lieutenant, ensign, and sergeant, while the Americans were all unhurt. The late distinguished civilian, William L. Marcy,[1] who was a lieutenant in Lyon's company, and assailed the block-house, was the captor of the flag that waved over it. He bore it in triumph back to French Mills, where Young and his party arrived the same day, at eleven o'clock, with the prisoners and spoils — the latter in the captured bateaux, by way of Salmon River.[2] The prisoners were sent to Bloomfield's head-quarters at Plattsburg. Early in January Major  Young and his detachment returned to Troy, and with his own hand presented that British flag — the first trophy of the kind that had ever been taken on land—to the people of the State of New York in the capital at Albany.[3]

Soon after the affair at St. Regis the British retaliated by an expedition to French Mills, which captured the company of Captain Tilden stationed there. Le Clerc also captured Mr. Gray, the interpreter, and sent him to Quebec, where he died in the hospital.

During a brief sojourn at the Massena Springs, on the Racquette River, in the summer of 1855, I visited St. Regis, or *Ak-wis-sas-ne*, the place "where the partridge drums," as the Indians called it.[4] I rode out to Hogansburg, ten miles eastward of

---

[1] The public career of Mr. Marcy is too well known to require more than a passing notice here. He was then twenty-six years of age, and had studied law, and was practicing it in Troy. He served with credit in the New York State militia during a greater part of the war. In 1821 he was appointed adjutant general of the state. In 1829 he was made a justice of the Supreme Court of the state. In 1831 he was elected to a seat in the United States Senate, and in 1833, governor of the State of New York, which office he held, by re-election, six years. In 1845 President Polk called him to his cabinet as Secretary of War, and in 1853 he became one of President Pierce's constitutional advisers as Secretary of State. On the 4th of March, 1857, he retired to private life, and just four months afterward he died suddenly at Ballston, New York, while reading in his bed, at the age of seventy years.

[2] Major Young's dispatch to General Bloomfield, October 24, 1812; Thomson's *Historical Sketches*, etc.; Hough's *History of St. Lawrence and Franklin Counties*; statement of Rev. Eleazer Williams to the author.

[3] That ceremony took place on the 5th of January, 1813, at one o'clock in the afternoon. Major Young, with a detachment of his Troy volunteers, entered Albany. The soldiers bore two fine living eagles in the centre of the detachment, and the trophy-colors in the rear, while a band played *Yankee Doodle*. They passed through Market Street (near Broadway), and up State Street, to the Capitol, where they were greeted by an immense crowd who thronged the building. The governor was too ill to be present, and Colonels Lamb and Lusk acted as his representatives. Major Young, after an appropriate speech, delivered the trophy to those gentlemen, and received from Colonel Lusk a complimentary response.

Guilford Dudley Young was born at Lebanon, Connecticut, in June, 1776, and in 1798 married Miss Betsey Huntington, of Norwich. In 1805 he settled in Troy, New York, where he engaged in mercantile pursuits. He raised a corps of volunteers in the summer of 1812, and joined the service on the St. Lawrence frontier under Colonel Benedict. Because of his exploit at St. Regis he was promoted to major in the 29th Regular Infantry in February, 1813, and was raised to the rank of lieutenant colonel two months afterward. He was disbanded in 1815, and soon afterward joined Miranda's Mexican expedition. He left New York for that purpose in July, 1816. In August, the following year, he was in Fort Sombrero, with two hundred and sixty-nine men, when it was encircled by three thousand five hundred Royalists. While standing exposed on the ramparts on the 18th of August, 1818, a cannon-shot from the enemy took off his head.

[4] During the colonial period, when the northern frontiers of New England were harassed by savages, three children, were carried off by them from Groton, Massachusetts. They consisted of two boys and a girl named Tarbell. The girl escaped and returned home, but the boys were taken to Canada and adopted into the families of their captors—some Caughnawaga Indians, near Montreal. In the course of time they married daughters of chiefs. Their intercourse with the savages was not very pleasant, and the village priest advised them to seek new homes. They, with their wives and wives' parents (four families) departed in a bark canoe, went up the St. Lawrence, and landed upon the beautiful point on which St. Regis stands. There they resolved to remain. They called the place, on account of the abundance of partridges, as above noticed. In 1760, when they had made themselves comfortable houses, with cultivated fields around them, they were joined by Father Anthony Gordon, a Jesuit priest, and a colony from Caughnawaga. Gordon named the place St. Regis. Gordon erected a church of logs and covered it with bark. This was burned two years afterward, when a small wooden church was erected in its place, and the first bell ever heard in St. Regis was hung in its tower. The common belief has been that this was the bell carried off from Deerfield by the Indians, after the destruction of that village by fire in 1704; and with that belief Mrs. Sigourney wrote her beautiful poem entitled THE BELL OF ST. REGIS, in which occurs these stirring lines:

"Then down from the burning church they tore
The bell of tuneful sound;
And on with their captive train they bore
That wonderful thing toward their native shore,
The rude Canadian bound.

Massena, with some friends, over a newly cleared but pleasant country, with the great Wilderness of Northern New York lying on our right, and far in the southeast the blue summits of the Green Mountains bounding the horizon. We dined at Hogansburg in company with the late Rev. Eleazer Williams, the reputed "Lost Prince" of the house of Bourbon, who was then pastor of a little congregation of Episcopalians, whose  place of worship had just been erected in a pleasant pine grove on the borders of that village of two hundred inhabitants. Mr. Williams was connected with the Indians in that region during the War of 1812. He was with Major Young in his first attempt to surprise the British at St. Regis, and was afterward in military service at Plattsburg, in a company of volunteer Rangers. He gave me some useful information concerning the events of the war in that region, and showed me a portrait of himself, painted in water-colors in 1814, in which he appears in military costume, and his features and complexion not exhibiting the least indication of Indian blood. Mr. Williams's biography, written by the Rev. Mr. Hanson, and published under the title of *The Lost Prince*, is a remarkable book. It contains a most strange story.[1]

From Hogansburg we rode up to St. Regis, a poor-looking village situated upon a gently elevated plain at the head of Lake St. Francis, just below the foot of the Long Saut Rapid, on a point between the mouths of the St. Regis and Racquette Rivers. It is surrounded by broad commons, used as a public pasture, with small gardens near the houses. In front of the village, in the St. Lawrence, lie some beautiful and fertile islands, upon which is raised the grain for the subsistence of the villagers; and on the opposite shore of the great river is the Canadian village of Cornwall. We first visited the remains of the cellar of Montigny's house, where Captain M'Donell and some of the British soldiers were captured by Young, at the mouth of the St.

<pre>
          *   *   *   *   *   *   *   *   *   *
               It spake no more till St. Regis's tower
                 In northern skies appeared;
               And their legends extol that pow-wow's power,
               Which lulled that knell like a poppy-flower,
               As conscience now slumbereth a little hour
                 In the cell of a heart that's seared."
</pre>

The bell carried from Deerfield was taken to Caughnawaga, and hung in the church of St. Louis there, where it still remains.

[1] A dark mystery has ever brooded over the fate of the eldest son of Louis the Sixteenth, King of France, who was ten years of age at the time of his father's murder by the Jacobins. The Revolutionists, after the downfall of Robespierre and his fellows, declared that he died in prison, while the Royalists believed that he was sent to America. Curious facts and circumstances pointed to the Rev. Mr. Williams, a reputed half-breed Indian of the Caughnawaga tribe, as the surviving prince, who for almost sixty years had been hidden from the world in that disguise. The claim that he was the Dauphin—the "Lost Prince"—was set up for him, and the fact that he was not possessed of Indian blood was fairly established by physiological proofs. Scars produced by scrofula and inoculation for the small-pox, described as marking the person of the Dauphin, marked the person of Mr. Williams with remarkable exactness. The book in question brings all of these proofs of identity to view. But the world was incredulous. The word of the Prince de Joinville, an interested son of Louis Philippe, was put in the balance against that of a poor missionary of the Episcopal church in America, and the latter was outweighed. Mr. Williams died in 1859, in that obscurity in which his life had been passed. The question that so excited the American public a few years ago—"Have we a Bourbon among us?"—has not been asked for a long time. The remains of the reputed "Lost Prince" rest in peace near the banks of the St. Regis.

Regis. We then called at the house of the parish priest (Father Francis Marcoux), but had not the pleasure of seeing him, he having gone over to Cornwall, his servant said, to attend a horse-race. The gray old church, built of massive stone, its walls five feet thick, its roof covered with shingles and its belfry with glittering tin-plate, stood near. Its portal was invitingly open, and we entered. We found it quite plain in general construction, but the altar and its vicinity were highly ornamented and gilded. Upon the walls hung some rude pictures. Across the end over the entrance was a gallery for the use of strangers. The Indian worshipers usually kneel or sit on the floor during the service. The full liturgy of the Roman Catholic Church was used there, and the preaching was in the Mohawk language.[1] The present church edifice was erected in 1792. The dilapidated spire had lately been taken down, and the belfry was covered with a cupola surmounted by a glittering cross. Near the vestry-room, within the inclosure, was a frame-work on which hung three bells; the two upper ones made of the first one ever heard in St. Regis, mentioned in note 4, page 376.[2] The lower and larger one was cast in Troy in 1852, and had not yet been placed in the tower.

OLD CHURCH IN ST. REGIS.

While sketching the old church[3] I was surrounded by the Indian children, all curious to know what I was about; while an old Indian woman stood in the door of a miserable log house near by, looking so intently with mute wonder, apparently, that I think she did not move during the half hour I was engaged with the pencil. The children kept up a continual conversation, intermingled with laughter, all of which came to the ear in sweet, low, musical cadences, like the murmuring of brooks. This is in the British portion of the town.

Just after leaving the church we met the venerable Captain Le Clerc, already mentioned, who had lived in St. Regis fifty-seven years. He accompanied us to the house of François Dupuy, one of the two merchants then in St. Regis. Dupuy's store and

---

[1] A full and interesting account of St. Regis may be found in Hough's *History of St. Lawrence and Franklin Counties.*
[2] This bell became cracked more than thirty years ago, and it was recast in two small ones. The Indians, suspicious that some of the (to them) sacred metal might be abstracted at the bell-founder's, sent a deputation to watch the process, and see that every particle of the old bell went into the crucible.
[3] In this view is seen the old church on the right, a specimen of many of the houses in the village on the left, and in the extreme distance, near the centre, the dwelling of the parish priest. A tall flag-staff stands near the inclosure. The bells mentioned in the text are just behind the two Lombardy poplars on the right.

dwelling were on the forty-fifth parallel of north latitude, which is the dividing-line here between the United States and Canada. That line passed through his house; and while an attendant was preparing some lemonade for us within the dominions of Queen Victoria, we were sitting in the United States, but *in the same room*, waiting to be served. On the margin of the street opposite Dupuy's stood one of the cast-iron obelisks, three feet and a half in height, which are placed at certain intervals along that frontier line as boundary monuments. Upon its four sides were cast appropriate inscriptions, in raised letters.[1]

BOUNDARY MONUMENT.

We left St. Regis toward the evening of a delightful day, and reached Massena just as the guests of the hotel were assembling at the supper-table. At twilight I walked leisurely down to the springs on the margin of the swift-flowing Racquette, and under the pavilion that covers the principal fountain of health I met a venerable man, who informed me that he was one of the first settlers in that region. He was in the War of 1812 as a soldier, and fought in some of the battles on the Niagara frontier. He was badly wounded at Black Rock by the explosion of a bombshell that came from a battery on the Canada side. "I was knocked down," he said, "had my breast-bone stove in, and three ribs broken." He was at Fort Erie at the time of the sanguinary sortie, but was unable to walk on account of his wounds. That veteran was Captain John Polley, already mentioned. He was then seventy-two years of age. He had seen all the country around him bloom out of the wilderness, and had outlived most of the companions of his youth.

Let us resume the historical narrative:

While active operations were in progress at the eastern end of Lake Ontario and along the St. Lawrence River, important events were transpiring toward the western end of the lake and on the Niagara frontier. That frontier, extending along the Niagara River from Lake Erie to Lake Ontario, a distance of thirty-five miles, was the theatre of many stirring scenes during the war we are considering. The Niagara River is the grand outlet of the waters of the upper lakes into Ontario, and divides a portion of the State of New York from that of Canada. Half way between the two lakes that immense body of water pours over a limestone precipice in two mighty cataracts, unequaled in sublimity by any others on the surface of the globe.

At the time we are considering that frontier was sparsely settled. Buffalo[2] was a little scattered village of about one hundred houses and stores, and a military post of sufficient consequence to invite the torch of British incendiaries at the close of 1813, when all but two dwellings were laid in ashes. It was only about sixty years ago that the tiny seed was planted of that now immense mart of inland commerce, containing one hundred thousand inhabitants. Where now are long lines of wharves, with forests of masts and stately warehouses, was seen a sinuous creek, navigable for small vessels only, winding its way through marshy ground into the lake, its low banks fringed with trees and tangled shrubbery. In 1814 it was a desolation, and the harbor presented the appearance delineated in the engraving on the following page.

A little south of Buffalo, stretching along Buffalo Creek, were the villages of the Seneca Indians, on a reservation of one hundred and sixty thousand acres of land, and then inhabited by about seven hundred souls. Two miles below Buffalo was Black Rock, a hamlet at the foot of Lake Erie and of powerful rapids, where there

---

[1] On the west face, "BOUNDARY, AUGUST 9, 1842." On the east, "TREATY OF WASHINGTON." On the north, "LIEUTENANT COLONEL I. B. B. ESTCOURT, H. B. M. COMMISSIONER." On the south, "ALBERT SMITH, U. S. COMMISSIONER."
[2] Buffalo was laid out by the Holland Land Company in 1801, and was called New Amsterdam.

THE PORT OF BUFFALO IN 1813.

was a ferry; and almost opposite was Fort Erie, a British post of considerable strength. Nine miles below, at the Falls of Elliott's Creek, was the village of Williamsville; and at the head of the rapids, above Niagara Falls, were the remains of

REMAINS AT FORT SCHLOSSER.

old Fort Schlosser, about a mile below Schlosser Landing, near which is yet standing an immense chimney that belonged to the English "mess-house," or dining-hall of the garrison that were stationed there several years before the Revolution.[1] Opposite Schlosser, at the mouth of the Chippewa Creek, was the small village of Chippewa, inhabited by Canadians and Indians. At the Falls, on the American side, was the hamlet of Manchester; and seven miles below, at the foot of the Lower Rapids, was Lewiston, a little village, with a convenient landing at the base of a bluff. Opposite Lewiston was Queenston, overlooked from the south by lofty heights, sometimes called The Mountain. It was the landing-place for goods brought over Lake Ontario for the inhabitants above. At the mouth of

---

[1] The English built a stockade here in the year 1760, and named it Fort Schlosser, in honor of the meritorious officer who was in command there at the time. It was about a mile from the Niagara River. The frame of the mess-house was prepared at Fort Niagara, at the mouth of the river, while the French were in possession there. It was intended for a Catholic church at that place. The English took it to the site of the new fort, and put it up there. It disappeared in the course of time, leaving nothing but the huge chimney. Around it a small building was erected, in which Judge Porter resided for several years after his removal to the Niagara frontier. The building was consumed when the British devastated that shore in 1813. Slight traces of old French works on the bank of the river, and of Fort Schlosser, more in the interior, may now be seen. I am indebted to the late Colonel P. A. Porter, of Niagara Falls village (who was killed in battle during the late Civil War), for the above sketch of the great chimney and the little building attached to it.

Schlosser Landing was made famous at the close of 1837 by the destruction there of the American steamer *Caroline* by a party of British from Canada. At that time a portion of both Canadian provinces were in insurrection against the British government. Navy Island, on the Niagara River, just above Schlosser, was made a rendezvous for the insurgents of that neighborhood and their American sympathizers, and the steamboat *Caroline* was brought down from Buffalo to be used as a ferry-boat between the island and Schlosser Landing. On the night of the 29th of December, 1837, she was moored at Porter's store-house, Schlosser's Landing, having crossed the ferry several times during the day.

Niagara River, on the American side, was (and still is) Fort Niagara, a strong post, erected by the combined skill and labor of the French and English engineers and troops at different times.¹ Just above the fort was the little village of Youngstown; and opposite this, on the Canada shore, was Fort George. Between the fort and the lake was the village of Newark, now Niagara. Along both banks of the river, its whole length, a farming population was scattered. Such was the Niagara frontier at the opening of the war of 1812. The reader will have occasion frequently to refer to the map of it on the following page.

Major General Stephen Van Rensselaer, appointed by Governor Tompkins the commander-in-chief of the detached militia of the state, with Solomon Van Rensselaer, the adjutant general of New York, as his aid and military adviser,² and John Lovett, of Troy, as his secretary, arrived at Fort Niagara on the 13th of August,³ and assumed command of the forces on that frontier. On the following day he made his head-quarters at Lewiston, seven miles farther up the river. General Amos Hall, commander of the militia of Western New York, was then at the little hamlet of Manchester, at Niagara Falls, with a few troops; and detachments of the same kind were scattered along the whole line of the river, a distance of thirty-five miles. But the whole force in the field, to guard that frontier from a threatened invasion of the enemy, did not amount to more than a thousand men.⁴ These were scantily clothed, indifferently fed, and were clamorous for pay. There was not a single piece of heavy ordnance along the entire frontier, nor artillerists to man the light field-pieces in their possession. Of ammunition there were not ten rounds for each man. They had no tents. The medical department was in a most destitute condition, and insubordination was the rule and not the exception.⁵

General Dearborn had been instructed[a] to make such demonstrations on the frontier as should prevent re-enforcements being sent to Malden by Hull at Detroit. This duty was wholly neglected, and, as late as the 8th of August, the commanding general wrote to the Secretary of War, saying, "Till now I did not consider the Niagara frontier as coming within the limits of my command." This extraordinary assertion was made in the face of no less than five dispatches from the War Department, in which such allusions were made to that frontier as to expressly, or by implication, give him to understand that the entire line of the Niagara River and the lakes were under his jurisdiction.⁶ And on the very next

[a] June 26, 1812.

The tavern there being crowded, several persons went on the boat to lodge for the night. At midnight a body of armed men from the Canada shore came in a boat, rushed on board, exclaiming "Cut them down! give no quarter!" and chased the unarmed occupants astern. Some were severely injured, one man was shot dead on the wharf, and twelve more were never heard of afterward. The boat was towed out into the river, set on fire, and left to the current above the cataract. It sunk near Iris Island, and on the following morning charred remains of the vessel were seen below the Falls. It was supposed that more than one of the missing men perished in the flames or the turbulent waters. At one time the diplomatic correspondence between the two governments concerning this outrage threatened a war.

¹ A particular account of the fort will be given hereafter.
² General Stephen Van Rensselaer was not a military man. He was possessed of great wealth, extensive social influence, and was a leading Federalist. His appointment was a stroke of policy to secure friends to the war among that party. It was only on condition that Solomon Van Rensselaer, who had been in military service, should accompany him, that he consented to take the post. It was well understood that Colonel Van Rensselaer would be the general, in a practical military point of view.
³ On reaching Utica, on his way westward, General Van Rensselaer was called to Sackett's Harbor by rumors of hostile movements in that quarter. From there he went on a tour of inspection along the frontier to Ogdensburg, to learn the condition of troops, and the means for offensive or defensive operations along the St. Lawrence frontier.
⁴ See note 2, page 366.
⁵ *Narrative of the Affair at Queenstown in the War of 1812*, by Solomon Van Rensselaer, page 10.
⁶ On the 26th of June the Secretary of War wrote to General Dearborn, then at Albany: "Your preparations, it is presumed, will be made to move in a direction for *Niagara*, Kingston, and Montreal." On July 15th he wrote: "On your arrival at Albany your attention will be directed to the security of *the northern frontier by the lakes*." On the 20th he wrote more explicitly, saying: "You will make such arrangements with Governor Tompkins as will place the militia *detached by him for the Niagara and other posts on the lake under your control*." July 29th he wrote: "Should it be advisable to make any other disposition of these restless people [the warriors of the Seneca Indians], you will give orders to Mr. Granger and the *commanding officer at Niagara*." On the 1st of August the same functionary wrote: "You will make a diversion in favor of him [General Hull] at *Niagara* and *Kingston* as soon as may be practicable." Yet, with these

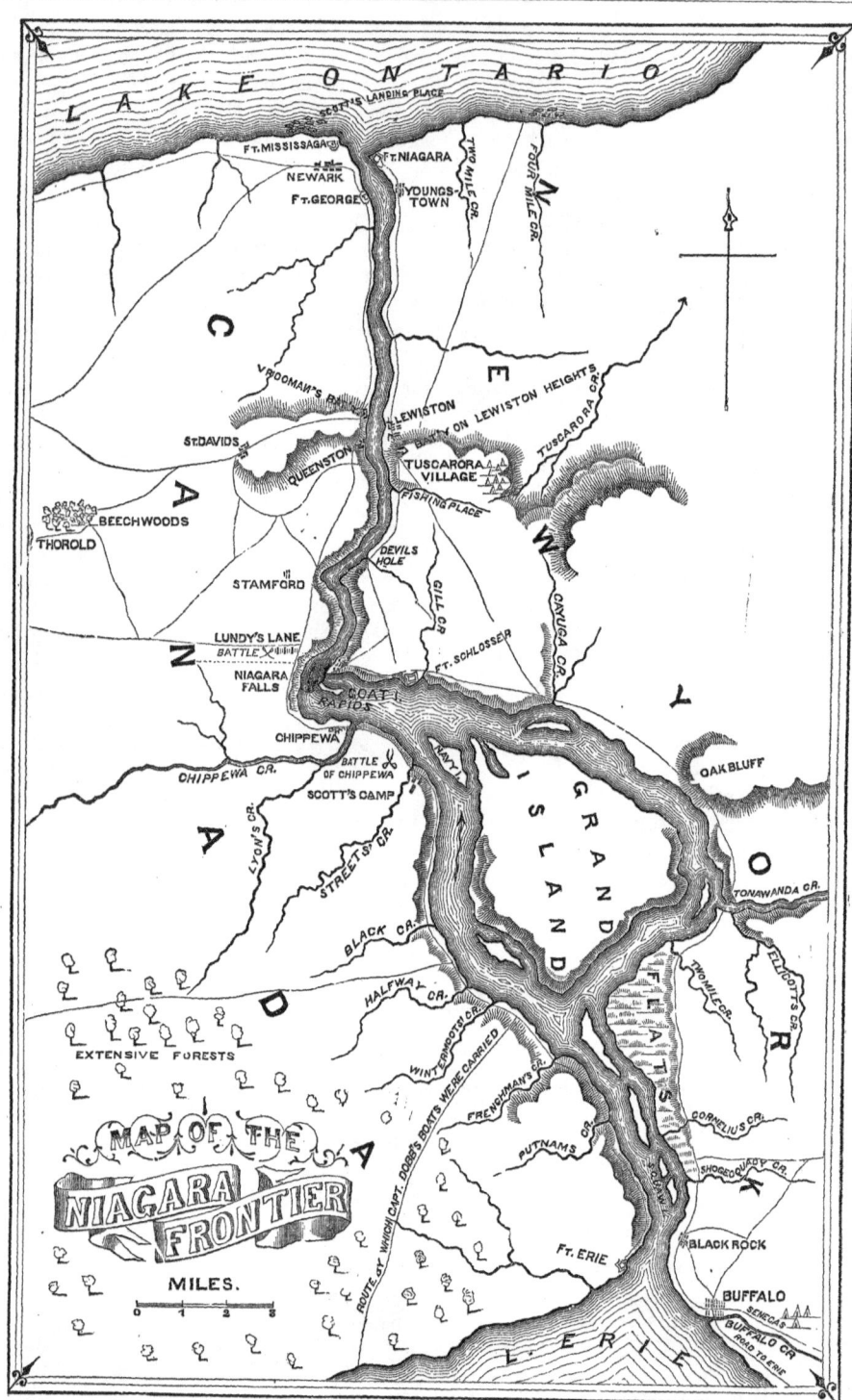

letters in his possession, General Dearborn, on the 8th of August, declared that until then he did "not consider the Niagara frontier as coming within the limits of his command!"

Effect of the Armistice. Solomon Van Rensselaer's Diplomacy. Service expected of the Army on the Niagara Frontier.

day[a] he signed an armistice agreeing to a cessation of hostilities along that entire dividing line between the two countries. That armistice still farther delayed preparations for offensive or defensive operations on the part of the Americans, and, on the 1st of September, the entire effective force under General Van Rensselaer on the Niagara frontier was only six hundred and ninety-one men, instead of five thousand, as he had been promised![1] Notwithstanding Dearborn had been ordered peremptorily to put an end to the armistice, he continued it until the 29th of August,[2] for the purpose, as he alleged,[3] of forwarding stores to Sackett's Harbor —a matter of small moment compared with the accruing disadvantages. Within the period of the armistice, Brock was enabled, after the capture of Hull and the Territory of Michigan, to return leisurely with his troops and prisoners to the Niagara frontier. When the armistice was ended, and Van Rensselaer was so weak in men and munitions of war, the British confronted him, on the opposite side of a narrow river, with a well-appointed and disciplined, though small army, commanded by skillful and experienced officers, while every important point from Lake Ontario to Lake Erie, along the British side of the Niagara, was carefully guarded or had been materially strengthened.

[a] August 9, 1812.

Some of the most disastrous effects of the armistice were parried by a successful effort at diplomacy on the part of Colonel Solomon Van Rensselaer, the commanding general's aid, who was sent to Fort George to confer with the British general, Sheaffe, on the details of the operations of that agreement. Van Rensselaer insisted upon the unrestricted navigation of Lake Ontario for both parties, and this point was unexpectedly yielded,[4] restrictions upon the movements of troops, stores, etc., being confined to the country above Fort Erie. This was of vital importance to the Americans; for the much-needed supplies for the army, ordnance, and other munitions of war collected at Oswego could only be taken to the Niagara by water, the roads were in such a wretched condition. By this arrangement, the vessels at Ogdensburg, already mentioned, were released,[5] to be converted into warriors; and Colonel Fenwick, at Oswego, moved forward over the lake to Niagara with a large quantity of supplies.

General Van Rensselaer[6] was charged with the duty of not only defending the frontier from invasion, but of an actual invasion of Canada himself. This was a part of the original plan of the campaign. While Hull invaded the province from Detroit, it was to be penetrated on the Niagara and St. Lawrence frontiers. But Van Rensselaer found himself in a most critical situation, and doubtful whether he could even protect the soil of his own state from the foot of the invader. The arrival of

---

[1] Van Rensselaer's *Narrative*, etc., p. 10.

[2] On the 29th of August General Dearborn issued an order in which he declared the armistice at an end, and yet the express bearing the order to the Niagara frontier did not reach General Van Rensselaer until the 12th of September.— MS. Letter of Colonel Solomon Van Rensselaer to his Wife, dated Lewiston, September 12, 1812.

[3] Dearborn to the Secretary of War, August 27, 1812.

[4] This was on the 21st of August. Four days afterward General Brock arrived with Hull and the regulars of his army as prisoners.

[5] As soon as Van Rensselaer obtained the concession, an express was sent to Oswego, Sackett's Harbor, and Ogdensburg, ordering those vessels up.

[6] Stephen Van Rensselaer was the fifth in lineal descent from Killian Van Rensselaer, the earliest and best known of the American *Patroons*. He was born at the manor-house in Albany, New York, on the first of November, 1764. Being the eldest son, he inherited the immense estate of his father, and was the last of the *Patroons*. He was educated first at Princeton College and then at Harvard University. He was graduated at the latter institution in 1782. He became an active politician, and was a warm supporter of Washington and the national Constitution. In 1795 he was elected lieutenant governor of his native state, and held the office six consecutive years. He was a rising man in the political scale, when the overthrow of the Federal party in 1800 impeded his advancement. Although a Federalist and opposed to the war in 1812, when his country was committed to the measure he patriotically laid aside all party feelings and gave it his hearty support. He was not a military man, and his appointment to the major generalship of the detached militia was a stroke of policy rather than the deliberate choice of a good military leader. He did not long remain in the service. He was in Congress during several consecutive sessions, and by his casting vote in the delegation of New York he gave the presidency to John Quincy Adams in 1824. Then his political life closed. He was foremost in good works. The "Rensselaer School" at Troy, New York, attests his liberality, and his activity in religious societies was marked and useful. For many years he was President of the Board of Canal Commissioners. That was his position at the time of his death, which occurred on the 26th of January, 1840, in the seventy-fifth year of his age.

Colonel Fenwick, on the 4th of September, with ordnance and stores gave some relief, but the evidence of preparations for invasion on the part of the British became daily more and more positive and alarming.

At the middle of September Van Rensselaer informed both Governor Tompkins and General Dearborn of the gloomy prospects before him, and pleaded for re-enforcements, saying, "A retrograde movement of this army upon the back of that disaster which has befallen the one at Detroit would stamp a stigma upon the national character which time would never wipe away. I shall therefore try to hold out against superior force and every disadvantage until I shall be re-enforced."[1] But as late as the 26th of September General Dearborn could give him no sure promises of timely re-enforcements, while in the same letter that officer expressed a hope that Van Rensselaer would not only be able to meet the enemy, but to carry the war into Canada. "At all events," he said, "we must calculate on possessing Upper Canada before winter sets in."[2]

Soon after this regular troops and militia began to arrive on the Niagara frontier. The former assembled at Buffalo and its vicinity, the latter at Lewiston; and when, in the first week of October,[a] General Van Rensselaer invited Major General Hall, of the militia of Western New York, Brigadier General Smythe, of the regular army and then inspector general, and the commandants of the United States regiments to meet him in council, he proposed a speedy invasion of Canada. "I propose," he said, "that we immediately concentrate the regular force in the neighborhood of Niagara and the militia here [Lewiston], make the best possible dispositions, and at the same time the regulars shall pass from Four-mile Creek to a point in the rear of the works of Fort George and take it by storm; I will pass the river here, and carry the heights of Queenstown. Should we succeed, we shall effect a great discomfiture of the enemy by breaking their line of communication, driving their shipping from the mouth of this [Niagara] river, leaving them no rallying-point in this part of the country, appalling the minds of the Canadians, and opening a wide and safe communication for our supplies. We shall save our land, wipe away part of the score of our past disgrace, get excellent barracks and winter quarters, and at least be prepared for an early campaign another year."[3] This proposed council was not held, owing to the failure of General Smyth to comply with the request of General Van Rensselaer,[4] and the latter was left wholly to the resources of himself and his military family in forming his plans. They were deliberately matured, and preparations for invading Canada went vigorously on. To-

[a] October 5, 1812.

---

[1] Letter to Governor Tompkins, September 17, 1812.   [2] Dearborn to Van Rensselaer, September 26, 1812.
[3] Letter of General Van Rensselaer to General Dearborn, Lewiston, October 8, 1812.
[4] This will be noticed in the next chapter.

Lieutenant Elliott on Lake Erie.   Preparations for capturing British Vessels.   Co-operation of the Military.

ward the middle of October the American forces on the frontier were considered sufficient to warrant the undertaking.

While these preparations were in progress, a daring and successful exploit was performed near Buffalo, that won great applause for the actors and infused new spirit into the troops. We have already observed that Lieutenant Jesse D. Elliott, of the United States Navy, was sent by Commodore Chauncey to superintend the erection of a fleet on Lake Erie. By a letter from the commander, dated the 7th of September, he was instructed to report himself to General Van Rensselaer, on the Niagara frontier, consult with him as to "the best position to build, repair, and fit for service" such vessels as might be required to retain the command of Lake Erie, and, after selecting such place, to "purchase any number of merchant vessels or boats that might be converted into vessels of war or gun-boats," with the advice of General Van Rensselaer, and to commence their equipment immediately. He was also instructed to take measures for the construction of two vessels of three hundred tons each, six boats of considerable size, and quarters for three hundred men. These, and a variety of other relevant duties, were committed to the charge of Lieutenant Elliott by Chauncey, who said, "Knowing your zeal for the service and your discretion as an officer, I feel every confidence in your industry and exertions to accomplish the object of your mission in the shortest time possible."[1] Elliott was then twenty-seven years of age.

Black Rock, two miles below Buffalo, was selected as the place for Lake Erie's first dock-yard in fitting out a navy. While busily engaged there, early in October, in the duties of his office, Elliott was informed that two British armed vessels had come down the lake, and anchored under the guns of Fort Erie. These were the brigs *Adams*, Lieutenant Rolette commander, and *Caledonia*, commanded by Mr. Irvine, the former a prize captured when Hull surrendered, and its name was changed to *Detroit*, the latter a vessel owned and employed by the Northwestern Fur Company on the Upper Lakes.[2] They were both well armed and manned,[3] and it was understood that the *Caledonia* bore a valuable cargo of skins from the forest. They appeared in front of Fort Erie on the morning of the 8th of October, and the zealous Elliott, emulous of distinction, immediately conceived a plan for their capture. Timely aid offered. On that very day a detachment of seamen for service under him arrived from New York. They were unarmed, and Elliott turned to the military authorities for assistance. Lieutenant Colonel Winfield Scott was at Black Rock. He entered warmly into Elliott's plans, and readily obtained the consent of General Smyth, his commanding officer, to lend his aid. Captain Towson, of the Engineers' Corps (2d Regiment of Artillery), was detailed, with fifty men, for the service, and the cordial acquiescence of General Smyth was evinced by a note, marked "confidential," to Colonel Winder, of the 14th Regiment, then encamped near Buffalo, in which he said, "Be pleased to turn out the hardy sailors in your regiment, and let them appear, under the care of a non-commissioned officer, in front of my quarters, precisely at three o'clock this evening. Send also all the pistols, swords, and sabres you can borrow at the risk of the lenders, and such public swords as you have."[4]

Towson joined Elliott with arms and ammunition for the seamen, and both were accompanied by citizens. The combined force, rank and file, was one hundred and twenty-four men.[5] All the preparations for the enterprise were completed by four

---

[1] Letter of Chauncey to Elliott, "Navy Yard, New York, September 7, 1812."   [2] See page 270.
[3] The *Detroit* mounted six 6-pounders and mustered fifty-six men, besides thirty American prisoners. The *Caledonia* mounted two small guns and mustered twelve men, besides ten American prisoners.
[4] Manuscript Letter of General Smyth to Colonel Winder, October 8, 1812. It is proper here to remark that, through the kind offices of Mrs. Aurelia Winder Townsend, of Oyster Bay, Long Island, daughter of General Winder, the papers of that gallant officer were placed in my possession. Free use has been made of them in the course of this work.
[5] Lieutenant Elliott, in his official report to the Secretary of the Navy, October 9, 1812, says there were one hundred in the expedition—fifty in each boat. The list furnished by him, and here given in full, makes the number one hundred and twenty-four, as follows:
Commanders, Jesse D. Elliott, Isaac Chauncey.
Sailing-masters, George Watts, Alexander Sisson.

o'clock in the afternoon. Two large boats had been fitted up at Shogeoquady[1] Creek, just below Black Rock, and then were taken to the mouth of Buffalo Creek in the evening. The expedition embarked at midnight, and at one o'clock in the morning[a] it left the creek silently, while scores of people on shore, who knew that an important movement was on foot, waited with anxiety in the gloom. At three o'clock the sharp crack of a pistol, followed by the flash and roll of a volley of musketry, a dead silence, and the moving of two dark objects down the river, proclaimed that the enterprise had been successful. A shout of joy rang out upon the night air from the shore between Buffalo and Black Rock, and lanterns and torches in abundance flashed light across the stream to illuminate the way of the victors.[2] The surprise and success were complete. The vessels were captured and the men in them made prisoners. "In less than ten minutes," wrote Elliott, "I had the prisoners all seized, the topsails sheeted home, and the vessels under weigh."[3] The *Detroit* was taken by the boat conducted by Elliott in person, assisted by Lieutenant Roach,[4] of the Engineers, and the *Caledonia* by the other boat conducted by Sailing-master Watts,[5] assisted by the military under Captain Towson. The first was taken with scarcely any opposition, the second after very brief resistance. The wind was light—too light to allow the vessels thereby to stem the current and reach the open lake; so they ran down the stream in the darkness, but not without annoyance. The turmoil of the capture, the shouts of the citizens at Black Rock and Buffalo, and the display of lights along the American shore, called every British officer and soldier to his post. The guns of Fort Erie, of two or three batteries, and of fly-

[a] October 9, 1812.

Captain of Engineers and Marines, N. Towson.
Lieutenant of Engineers and Marines, Isaac Roach.
Master's Mates, William Peckham, J. E. M'Donald, John S. Cummings, Edward Wilcox.
Ensign, William Presman.
Boatswain's Mates, Lawrence Hanson, John Rack, James Morrell.
Quarter Gunners, Benjamin Tallman, John Bird, Hawk, Noland, Vincent, Osborn, M'Cobbin, John Wheeler.
Seamen, Edward Police, James Williams, Robert Craig, John M'Intire, Elisha Atwood, William Edward, Michael S. Brooks, William Roe, Henry Anderson, Christopher Bailey, John Exon, John Lewis, William Barker, Peter Davis, Peter Deist, Lemuel Smith, Abraham Patch, Benjamin Myrick, Robert Peterson, Benjamin Fleming, Gardiner Gaskill, Anthony De Kruse, William Dickson, Thomas Hill, John Reynolds, Abraham Fish, Jerome Sardie, John Tockum, William Anderson, John Jockings, Thomas Bradley, Hatten Armstrong.
Soldiers, Jacob Webber, Jesse Green, Henry Thomas, George Gladden, James Murray, Samuel Baldwin, John Hendrick, Peter Evans, William Fortune, Daniel Martin, John M'Guard, Samuel Fortune, John Garling, Zachariah Wise, John Kearns, Thomas Wallager, Thomas Houragua, Peter Peroe, Edward Mahoney, Daniel Holland, Mathias Wineman, Moses Goodwin, Lishurway Lewis, William Fisher, John Fritch, James Roy, James M'Gee, James M'Crossan, William Weimer, Thomas Leister, Joseph Davis, Benjamin Thomas, James M'Donald, Thomas Ruark, J. Wicklin, W. Richards, James Tomlin, James Boyd, James Neal, John Gidleman, William Knight, M. Parish, James M'Coy, Daniel Fraser, John House, Jacob Stewart, William Kemp, Hugh Robb, Anson Crosswell, Charles Lewis, John Shields, Charles Le Forge, John Joseph, Henry Berthold, James Lee, Isaac Murrows, George Eaton, Thomas C. Leader, William Cowenhoven, John J. Lord, Charles Le Fraud, Elisha Cook, John Tolenson, John G. Stewart, William Fryer, Cyrenus Chapin, Alexander M'Comb, Thomas Davis, Peter Orenstock, William C. Johnson.
 I am indebted to Colonel Gleason F. Lewis, of Cleveland, for the above "Roll of Honor," and I take pleasure in here acknowledging my indebtedness to that gentleman for many kind services in aid of my labors. His attention to the business of procuring pensions and bounties for the soldiers of the War of 1812 and their families for many years, gives him, probably, a more thorough knowledge of that subject, as relates to the Army of the Northwest, than any other man in the country.

[1] This is an Indian word, and is variously spelled Shogeoquady, Shojeoquady, Seajaquady, and Skajoekuda.
[2] *Reminiscences of Buffalo*, by Henry Lovejoy.   [3] Letter to the Secretary of the Navy, October 9, 1812.
[4] Isaac Roach was born in the District of Southwark, Philadelphia, on the 24th of February, 1786. After the attack on the *Chesapeake* in 1807 [see page 157], Roach, then twenty-one years of age, organized an artillery company in Philadelphia. In 1812 he obtained the appointment of second lieutenant in the Second Regiment U. S. Artillery, and joined that regiment under Lieutenant Colonel Scott in July. He volunteered to accompany the expedition against the British brigs, and led fifty of his associates in the attack. He was then adjutant of the regiment; and so anxious were the men to accompany him, that when he passed along the line to select them, his ears were saluted with the exclamations, "Can't I go, sir?"—"Take me, Adjutant"—"Don't forget M'Gee"—"I'm a Philadelphia boy," etc. Roach was wounded in the battle at Queenstown soon afterward, and he returned home. He soon afterward joined the staff of General Izard. He was made a prisoner at the Beaver Dams the next year. He had many adventures in attempts to escape, and was finally successful. He was about to take the field under General Scott as assistant adjutant general, when peace came. He commanded successively Forts M'Henry, Columbus, and Mifflin, until 1823, when he was commissioned major by brevet. He retired from the army in 1824. In 1838 he was elected Mayor of Philadelphia, and was appointed Treasurer of the Mint soon afterward. He died December 29, 1848.
[5] Watts was killed on the 28th of November following, while assisting Lieutenant Holdup and others in spiking some cannon at the little village of Waterloo, on the Canada side of the Niagara, a short distance below Fort Erie. The ball that killed Watts passed through Holdup's hand. The former died in the arms of the latter.

ing artillery, all guided by the lights that gleamed over the waters, were brought to bear upon the vessels.[1] The *Detroit* was compelled to anchor within reach of the enemy's guns, while the *Caledonia* ran ashore, and was beached under the protection of the guns of an American battery between Buffalo and Black Rock.[2] The guns of the *Detroit* were all removed to her larboard side, and a mutual cannonading was kept up for some time.[3] Efforts were made by tow-line and warps to haul her to the American shore. These failed; and, regarding the destruction of the *Detroit* as certain in her exposed position, Elliott cut her cable and set her adrift. At that moment he discovered that his pilot had left. For ten minutes she went blindly down the swift current, and then brought up on the west side of Squaw Island, near the American shore, but still exposed to the guns of the enemy.[4] The prisoners, forty-six in number, were immediately landed below Squaw Island, but the current was so strong that the boats could not return to the vessel. She was soon boarded by a party of the British Forty-ninth Regiment, then stationed at Fort Erie, but they were driven off by some citizen soldiers of Buffalo, who, with a six-pound field-piece, crossed over to Squaw Island in a scow and boldly attacked them.[5] She was then placed in charge of Lieutenant Colonel Scott, at Black Rock, who gallantly defended her. Each party resolved that the other should not possess her, and the cannons of both were brought to bear upon the doomed vessel during the remainder of the day. At a little after sunset Sir Isaac Brock arrived, and made preparations to renew the attempt to recover the *Detroit*, with the aid of the crew of the *Lady Prevost*; but before these were perfected a party of the Fifth United States Infantry set her on fire and she was consumed.[6] The *Caledonia* was saved, and afterward performed good service in Perry's fleet on Lake Erie.

In this really brilliant affair the Americans lost only two killed and five wounded. The loss of the British is not known.[7] The *Caledonia* was a rich prize, her cargo

---

[1] The movements on the Canadian shore were under the direction of the gallant Major Ormsby, the British commandant there. The first shot from the flying artillery crossed the river and instantly killed the brave Major William Howe Cuyler, of Ontario, General Hall's aid-de-camp, who had taken a deep interest in the expedition. He had been in the saddle all night, and had just left a warehouse where rigging was procured for warping in the *Detroit*, and was guiding the vessels with a lantern in his hand, when the fatal ball struck him and he fell dead. His body was carried by Captain Benjamin Bidwell and others to the house of Nathaniel Sill. The death of the gallant and accomplished Cuyler was widely mourned. Obituary notices appeared in the newspapers; and "*The War*," printed in New York, published a poem "*To the Memory of Major Cuyler*," in six stanzas, in which the following lines occur:

"In Freedom's virtuous cause alert he rose,
In Freedom's virtuous cause undaunted bled;
He died for Freedom 'midst a host of foes,
And found on Erie's beach an honored bed."

[2] She was grounded a little above what is now the foot of Albany Street. The injured on board the *Caledonia* were brought on shore in a boat. It could not quite reach the land on account of shoal water, when Doctor Josiah Trowbridge, yet [1867] a resident of Buffalo, waded in and bore some of them to dry land on his back. They were taken to the house of Orange Dean, at the old ferry (now foot of Fort Street, opposite the angle in Niagara Street), and well cared for. While Doctor Trowbridge was taking a musket-ball from the neck of a wounded man, a twenty-four-pound shot entered the house, struck a chimney just over their heads, and covered them with bricks, mortar, and splinters. Another shot of the same weight demolished a trunk on the deck of the *Caledonia*, scattered its contents, consisting of ladies' wearing apparel, among the rigging, passed on, and was buried in the banks of the river. Two small boys (Cyrus K. St. John and Henry Lovejoy), who came down from Buffalo to see the fight, exhumed the shot and carried it home as a trophy of their valor.—*Narrative of Henry Lovejoy*.

[3] Elliott, who was on board the *Detroit*, hailed the British commander, and threatened to place his prisoners on the decks if he did not cease firing. The enemy disregarded the menace. "One single moment's reflection," said Elliott in his official dispatch, "determined me not to commit an act that would subject me to the imputation of barbarity."

[4] Her position was nearly opposite Pratt's Iron Works.

[5] These were principally members of an independent volunteer company of Buffalo, of which the late Ebenezer Walden was commander. They first brought their six-pounder to bear upon the enemy at the point where the Black Rock Ice-house stood in 1860, Doctor Trowbridge acting as gunner. When the regular gunner came they crossed over to Squaw Island.—Statement of Doctor Trowbridge to the Author.

[6] Through the intrepidity of Sailing-master Watts, some of her guns were taken out of her during the cannonade, and saved to do excellent duty in a land-battery between Black Rock and Buffalo.

[7] Elliott's official Letter to the Secretary of the Navy, October 9, 1812; Cooper's *Naval History*, ii., 331; Letter of General Sir Isaac Brock to Sir George Prevost, October 11, 1812, quoted in Tupper's *Life of Brock*, page 313.

being valued at two hundred thousand dollars. The gallantry of all—Americans and British—on this occasion was highly commendable. Elliott[1] made special mention of several of his companions,[2] and Congress,[a] by a vote, awarded to that officer their thanks, and a sword, with suitable emblems and devices.[3] The exploit sent a thrill of joy throughout the United States, because it promised speedy success in efforts to obtain the mastery of Lake Erie, while it produced a corresponding depression on the other side, for a similar reason. "The event is particularly unfortunate," wrote General Brock, "and may reduce us to incalculable distress. The enemy is making every exertion to gain a naval superiority on both lakes, which, if they accomplish it, I do not see how we can possibly retain the country."[4]

[a] Jan. 26, 1813.

JESSE D. ELLIOTT.

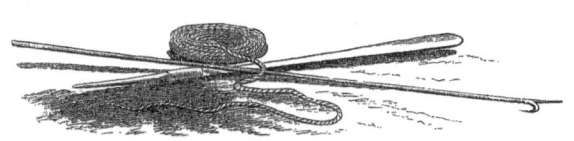

[1] Jesse Duncan Elliott was born in Maryland in 1785. He entered the naval service of the United States as midshipman in April, 1806, and in 1810 was promoted to lieutenant. After his gallant exploit near Buffalo he joined Chauncey at Sackett's Harbor. In July, 1813, he was promoted to master commandant over thirty lieutenants, and appointed to the command of the brig *Niagara*, 20, built on Lake Erie. He was second in command in Perry's engagement on the 10th of September, 1813, and for his conduct on that occasion Congress voted him a gold medal. After that battle he returned to Lake Ontario, and was there actively employed until November the same year, when he was assigned the command of the sloop-of-war *Ontario*, then just completed at Baltimore. This vessel was one of Decatur's squadron that performed good service in the Mediterranean Sea in 1815. Elliott was promoted to the rank of captain in 1818, and subsequently had command of squadrons on several stations, as well as of the navy yards at Boston and Philadelphia. On account of alleged misconduct in the Mediterranean, he was tried by a court-martial in 1840. The result was a sentence of four years' suspension from the service. In 1843 the President remitted the remainder of his suspension. He died on the 18th of December, 1845. Commodore Elliott became involved in a controversy concerning his conduct in the Battle of Lake Erie, which ceased only with his death. That controversy, and the excitement growing out of his placing an image of President Jackson on the *Constitution* frigate as a figure-head, will be noticed hereafter.

[2] He specially commended for their gallant services Captain Towson and Lieutenant Roach, of the Second Regiment of Artillery; Ensign Prestman, of the Infantry; Captain Chapin, and Messrs. John Macomb, John Town, Thomas Dain, Peter Overstocks, and James Sloan, residents of Buffalo. He also particularly noticed Sailing-master Watts, who commanded the boat that boarded the *Caledonia*.

[3] Journal of Congress, January 26, 1813.

[4] Letter of General Brock to Sir George Prevost, October 11, 1812.

CHAPTER XIX.

> "September the thirteenth, at midnight so dark,
> Our troops on the River Niagara embark'd;
> The standard of Britain resolved to pull down,
> And drive the proud foes from the heights of Queenstown."
>
> OLD SONG—THE HEROES OF QUEENSTOWN.

OR several weeks General Van Rensselaer had felt the pressure of public impatience, manifested by letters and the press. It had been engendered by the extreme tardiness displayed in the collection of troops on the frontier for the invasion of Canada, about which much had been said and written menacingly, boastfully, and deprecatory. That impatience had begun to be seriously manifested by his troops early in October.[1] Homesickness, domestic claims, idleness in the camp, and bodily sufferings and growing inclemency of the season, combined to affect the temper of the men most injuriously. Their calls to be led to battle became daily more and more urgent and imperious, until the volcanic fires of mutiny completely undermined the camp, and threatened a total overthrow of the general's authority. He perceived the necessity of striking the enemy at once at some point, or allow his army to dissolve, and all the toils and expenses of the campaign to be lost. He formed his plans, and, as we have observed, endeavored to counsel with the field officers under his command, but failed. General Alexander Smyth, his second in command, had lately arrived. He was a proud Virginian, an officer of the regular army (inspector general), and an aspirant for the chief command on the frontier. Unlike the true soldier and patriot, he could not bend to the necessity of obedience to a militia general, especially one of Northern birth and a leading Federalist, who, for the time, was made his superior in rank and position. His temper was exhibited in his letter to Van Rensselaer[a] announcing his arrival on the frontier.[2] It was supercilious, dictatorial,

[a] September 29, 1812.

---

[1] General Van Rensselaer was placed in a most delicate situation. It was well known that, politically, both he and his aid, Colonel Solomon Van Rensselaer, had been opposed to the war, and the unavoidable delays were construed by some into intentional immobility in order to frustrate the designs of the government. These suspicions were unjust and ungenerous in the extreme, for no purer patriot and conscientious and truthful man than Stephen Van Rensselaer ever lived. "A flood of circumstances," wrote Lovett, Van Rensselaer's secretary, "such as a great desire for forage, for provisions, for every thing to make man comfortable; the most inclement storm which I ever experienced at this season of the year; indeed, innumerable circumstances had convinced the general, as early as the beginning of the month, that a blow must be struck, or the army would break up in confusion, with intolerable imputations on his own character."—Manuscript Letter to Abraham Van Vechten, Buffalo, October, 21, 1812.

[2] The following is a copy of General Smyth's letter:

"I have been ordered by Major General Dearborn to Niagara, to take command of a brigade of United States troops, and directed, on my arrival in the vicinity of your quarters, to report myself to you, which I now do. I intended to have reported myself personally, but the conclusions I have drawn as to the interests of the service have determined me to stop at this place for the present. From the description I have had of the river below the Falls, the view of the shore below Fort Erie, and the information received as to the preparations of the enemy, I am of opinion that our crossing should be effected between Fort Erie and Chippewa. It has, therefore, seemed to me proper to encamp the United States troops near Buffalo, there to prepare for offensive operations. Your instructions or better information may decide you to give me different orders, which I will await."

This letter was offensive, first, because the subordinate officer not only failed to report himself in person, as he was bound in duty to do, but assumed perfect independence by choosing his own theatre of action; and, secondly, because the writer, an entire stranger to the country, just arrived, went out of his way to intrude his opinions upon his commanding general as to military operations, when he knew that that general had been there for weeks, and was neces-

and impertinent, and gave ample assurance that he would not cordially co-operate with the chief in command. So undutiful was his conduct that many were of opinion that coercive measures should be used to bring him to a sense of duty.[1] When politely requested by Van Rensselaer to name a day for a council of officers, he neglected to do so. Day after day passed, and Smyth made no definite reply, when the commanding general resolved to act upon his own responsibility, and "gratify his own inclinations and that of his army" by commencing offensive operations at once. On the 10th of October he prepared to attack the British at Queenston, opposite Lewiston, before dawn the next morning.[2]

QUEENSTON IN 1812.

Van Rensselaer considered his forces ample to assure him of success. They numbered more than six thousand. Sixteen hundred and fifty regulars, under General Smyth, were between Black Rock and Buffalo, commanded by Colonels Winder, Parker, and Milton, and Lieutenant Colonel Scott. In the vicinity were three hundred and eighty-six militia, under Lieutenant Colonels Swift and Hopkins. At Lewiston, where Van Rensselaer had his head-quarters, Brigadier General Wadsworth com-

---

sarily familiar with every rood of the ground and every disposition of the enemy. Van Rensselaer, true gentleman as he was, quietly rebuked the impertinence by informing General Smyth that for many years he had had "a general knowledge of the banks of the Niagara River and of the adjacent country on the Canada shore," and that he had now "attentively explored the American side with the view of military operations." "However willing I may be," he said, "as a citizen soldier, to surrender my opinion to a professional one, I commonly make such surrender to an opinion deliberately formed upon a view of the whole ground. . . . . All my past measures have been calculated for one point, and I now only wait for a competent force. As the season of the year and every consideration urges me to act with promptness, I can not hastily listen to a change of position, mainly connected with a new system of measures and the very great inconvenience of the troops."—*Van Rensselaer to Smyth*, 30th September, 1812.

Speaking of the conduct of General Smyth on this occasion, a contemporary officer says, "It is presumed this temper produced a spirit of insubordination destructive to the harmony and concert which is essential to cordial co-operation, and that the public service was sacrificed to personal sensibility."—*Wilkinson's Memoir*, i., 566. "Was I to hazard an opinion," says Wilkinson in another place, "it should be that his designs were patriotic, but that his ardor obscured his judgment, and that he was more indiscreet than culpable."—*Memoirs*, i., 581.

[1] *A Narrative of the Affair at Queenstown in the War of* 1812, by Solomon Van Rensselaer, page 19.

[2] Queenston (originally Queen's Town) was at this time a thriving little village, and one of the principal dépôts for merchandise and grain in that region. Its prosperity was paralyzed by the Welland Canal, which cut off most of its trade. The view here given is from a sketch made in 1812, from the north part of the village, looking southward up the Niagara River. On the right are seen the Heights of Queenston, and on the left the heights of Lewiston. The river is here about six hundred feet in width. The village was upon a plain of uneven surface at the foot of the Heights. This plain at Queenston is seventy feet above the river, and slopes gradually to the lake, where the bank is only a few feet above the water. The Heights rise two hundred and thirty feet above the river.

manded a corps of militia almost seventeen hundred strong, and near him was the camp of Brigadier General Miller, with almost six hundred men. Five hundred and fifty regulars under Lieutenant Colonel Fenwick, and eight hundred of the same class of troops under Major Mullany, were in garrison at Fort Niagara. There were, in the aggregate, three thousand six hundred and fifty regulars, and two thousand six hundred and fifty militia.

The British force on the western bank of the Niagara River, regular militia and Indians, numbered about fifteen hundred. Their Indian allies, under John Brant, were about two hundred and fifty strong. Small garrisons held Fort Erie, at the foot of Lake Erie, and two or three batteries, on rising ground, opposite Black Rock. The erection of Fort Erie had then just been commenced, but for want of funds had been left unfinished. Major Armand commanded there. A small detachment of the 41st Regiment, under Captain Bullock, and the flank companies of the 2d Regiment of the Lincoln Militia, under Captains Hamilton and Roe, was at Chippewa, where there was a dilapidated old block-house called Fort Welland. The flank companies of the 49th Regiment, under Captains Dennis and Williams, and a considerable body of militia, were at Queenston, and, with the exception of detached parties of militia along the whole line of the river to watch the movements of the Americans, the remainder were at Fort George, the head-quarters of Major General Brock, under General Sheaffe. At every mile between Fort George and Queenston, batteries were thrown up. On Queenston Heights, south of the village, and half way up the mountain, was a redan battery, mounting some 18-pounders and two howitzers; and on Vrooman's Point,[1] about a mile below, was another battery, on which was mounted a twenty-four-pound carronade *en barbette*. This gun commanded both Lewiston and Queenston Landing.

VIEW FROM THE SITE OF VROOMAN'S BATTERY.

Van Rensselaer had made himself thoroughly acquainted with the condition of the enemy. His officers, while on official visits to the various posts, had been vigilant and observing,[2] and he was so well satisfied that a favorable time for an invasion of

---

[1] The picture represents a view of the Niagara River and shores from Vrooman's Point. In the foreground are the remains of the battery. On the right is seen Queenston and the Heights, with Brock's monument; on the left, Lewiston and its heights; and in the centre, Niagara River and the Lewiston Suspension Bridge. We are looking southward, up the Niagara River.

[2] Colonel Solomon Van Rensselaer, who visited the British head-quarters on business several times, says that on the last occasion he saw two beautiful brass howitzers, of small size, calculated to be carried on pack-horses, the wheels about the size of a wheel-barrow. He remarked to Colonel M'Donell and other British officers who accompanied him, "These, at all events, are old acquaintances of mine. I feel partial to them, and must try to take them back." He recognized them as formerly belonging to Wayne's army when he was in service under him. They were among the

Canada had arrived that he made arrangements on the 10th of October to assail Queenston at three o'clock the next morning.[1] During that evening thirteen large boats, capable of bearing three hundred and forty full-armed and equipped men, were brought down on wagons from Gill's Creek, two miles above the Falls, and placed in the river at Lewiston Landing, under cover of intense darkness. The flying artillery under Lieutenant Colonel Fenwick, and a detachment of regulars under his command, were ordered up from Fort Niagara, and General Smyth was directed to send down detachments from his brigade at Buffalo to support the movement. Colonel Solomon Van Rensselaer was appointed to the command of the invading force,[2] an arrangement which seems to have given umbrage to some of the officers of the regular army on the frontier.

The river at Lewiston, at the foot of the lower rapids, is always a sheet of violent eddies, the middle current running about four miles an hour. To prevent confusion and disaster, experienced boatmen were procured, and the command of the flotilla was intrusted to Lieutenant Sims, who was considered "the man of the greatest skill for the service."[3] Before midnight every thing was in readiness. Clouds had been gathering in immense masses all the evening, and at one in the morning a furious northeast storm of wind and rain was sweeping over the country. But the zeal of the troops was not cooled by the drenching rain. At the appointed hour they were all at the place of debarkation, with Van Rensselaer at their head. Lieutenant Sims entered the foremost boat, and soon disappeared in the gloom. The others could not follow, for he had taken nearly all the oars with him! They waited for him to discover and correct his mistake, but in vain. He went far above the intended crossing-place, moored his boat to the shore, and fled as fast as the legs of a traitor or coward could carry him. The soldiers endured the fierce blasts and the falling flood until almost daylight, when they were marched to their respective cantonments, and the enterprise was for a moment abandoned. The storm continued unabated twenty-eight hours, and during that time all the soldiers remained in their deluged camps.

The general-in-chief again determined to seek the council of his brother officers, hoping the patience of his troops would brook farther delay. He was mistaken. The miscarriage and the desertion of Sims increased their ardor, and Van Rensselaer found himself compelled to renew the attempt at invasion immediately. He was willing, for valuable re-enforcements were near. Lieutenant Colonel Chrystie had arrived at Four-mile Creek late in the evening of the 10th, with three hundred and fifty newly-enlisted regulars, a part of the Thirteenth Regiment of Infantry, commanded respectively by Captains Wool, Ogilvie, Malcolm, Lawrence, and Armstrong, with thirty boats and military stores. Chrystie had hastened to head-quarters, and offered the services of himself and men in the execution of the enterprise in hand, but he was too late. Every arrangement was completed. Colonel Van Rensselaer was

---

British trophies of victory taken at Detroit, and were brought down to be sent to England. Nicholas Gray, who was inspector general of New York the following year, with the rank of colonel, and who was then acting engineer, made a valuable reconnoissance of the whole frontier. His manuscript report to General Van Rensselaer is before me. His outline map, accompanying the report, I found useful in constructing the *Map of the Niagara Frontier* on page 382.

[1] Van Rensselaer was deceived by an erroneous report of a spy whom he had sent across the river on the morning of the 10th to gain information. He returned with the false report that General Brock, with all his disposable force, had moved off in the direction of Detroit.

[2] General Van Rensselaer's Letter to the Secretary of War, October 14, 1812.

[3] On that evening Colonel Van Rensselaer wrote to his wife: "I go to storm an important post of the enemy. Young Lush and Gansevoort attend me. I must succeed, or you, my dear Harriet, will never see me again. If so, let me entreat you to meet my fall with fortitude; and be assured, my dear, lovely, but unfortunate wife, that my last prayer will be for you and my dear children."—MS. Letter, Lewiston, October 10, 1812. This letter is before me. It is much blotted by the tears of the soldier's wife, as I was informed by her daughter.

moving with his men to the landing-place, where only boats enough for the transportation of the troops appointed for the perilous service had been provided.

When the storm abated immediate preparations were made for the second attempt at invasion. Brock was watching the Americans with the eye of a vigilant and skillful commander. The river that divided the belligerents was narrow, and every open movement by each party might be observed by the other. Preparations were therefore made with great caution. Brock was deceived. The strong force at Fort Niagara, and the detention of Chrystie's troops at Four-mile Creek, made him suspect that an attack, if made soon, would be upon Fort George.

Three o'clock in the morning of the 13th was the appointed hour for the expedition to embark from the old Ferry-house at Lewiston Landing for the base of Queenston Heights. The command was again intrusted to Colonel Solomon Van Rensselaer. Lieutenant Colonel Chrystie was exceedingly anxious to have the honor of chief in the enterprise, and pleaded his rank and experience, as compared with that of the aid-de-camp of the general-in-chief, in favor of his claim. But Van Rensselaer would not change his general arrangements. It was agreed, however, that Colonel Van Rensselaer should lead a column of three hundred militia, and Lieutenant Colonel Chrystie should lead another composed of the same number of regulars, so that each might share in the hazards and glory of the expedition. Chrystie refused to waive his rank in favor of Van Rensselaer, but consented to receive orders from him. This technical distinction between waiving of rank and yielding obedience may be clear to military minds, but it is quite imperceptible to the common sense of a civilian.

At an early hour in the evening of the 12th,[a] Chrystie marched with three hundred men from Fort Niagara by an interior road, and reached Lewiston before midnight. Lieutenant Colonels Stranahan, Mead, and Bloom, with three regiments, marched at about the same time from Niagara Falls,[1] and also reached Lewiston in good season. Meanwhile Lieutenant Colonel Scott had arrived at Schlosser, two miles above the Falls, at the head of his regiment, where he was informed that an expedition against the enemy of some kind was in motion at Lewiston.[2] Young,

[a] October, 1812.

---

[1] To avoid attracting the attention of the British, these regiments left the Falls at different hours; Stranahan's started at seven in the evening, Mead's at eight, and Bloom's at nine.

[2] This fact was communicated to Scott by Colonel James Collier, now (1867) a citizen of Steubenville, Ohio. "He was adjutant of the same regiment (Colonel Henry Bloom's) wherein I was paymaster," wrote Arad Joy, Esq., of Ovid, New York, to the author in March, 1852. In a letter to me, written on the 20th of February, 1860, Colonel Collier says: "The regiment to which I was attached was stationed at the Falls. I had been down to head-quarters at Lewiston, seven miles below, on the 12th of October, and the orders for the marching of the troops at the Falls for that place were confided to me. About sunset I rode up to the head of the Rapids, a mile above our camp, and was surprised to see a detachment of troops pitching their tents. The officer in command, whom I did not then know, but who, I thought, was the finest specimen of a man I ever saw, was standing alongside of his horse near by. His rank I knew from his dress. I rode up to him and inquired if he was encamping for the night. 'Yes,' he replied. 'Then, sir,' I said, 'I think you can not know what is to be going on in the morning.' 'No, sir,' he said, 'I have not heard from head-quarters for several days. Is there any thing in the wind, sir?' I remarked that we were to cross the river the next morning and attack the enemy on the Heights of Queenston; that I had the orders for the marching of the troops to that post, but that, of course, they did not include his command. 'I am Colonel Scott,' he said; 'will you allow me to look at your orders?' They were handed to him, and the moment he had read them he was in the saddle, his tents were struck, and his command under marching orders. The next I saw of the gallant soldier was on the Heights of Queenston in a perfect blaze of fire, and then, as now, head and shoulders taller than any man in the country."

Many years afterward, when Scott, as a major general, was bearing more years and many honors, Colonel Collier met him in Washington City, and the first words Scott addressed to him were, "I was indebted to you for my first fight. I have always felt under great obligations to you. If it had not been for you, colonel, what would have been my position? Seven miles from the battle-field, sir, and the first battle of a campaign! Why, sir, I should never have got over it during my life!" "It is pleasant now," wrote Colonel Collier, "in the sunset of my days, to recall this little incident, connected as it is with the greatest captain of the age in which he lives." A few months after receiving this letter, I had the pleasure of spending a day or two with Colonel Collier at Cleveland, on the occasion of the inauguration of the statue of Commodore Perry. He is a hale, erect gentleman, of what is called "the old school" in manners, and most delightful entertainer of company in conversation.

ardent, and eager for adventure and glory, he immediately mounted his horse, and dashed toward head-quarters as speedily as the horrid condition of the road would allow. He presented himself to the commanding general, and earnestly solicited the privilege of taking a part in the invasion with his command. "The arrangements for the expedition are all completed, sir," said General Van Rensselaer. "Colonel Van Rensselaer is in chief command. Lieutenant Colonels Chrystie and Fenwick have waived their rank for the occasion, and you may join the expedition as a volunteer, if you will do the same." Van Rensselaer wisely determined not to have a divided command. Scott was unwilling to yield his rank; but he pressed his suit so warmly that it was agreed that he should bring on his regiment, take position on the heights of Lewiston with his cannon, and co-operate in the attack as circumstances might warrant. Scott hastened back to Schlosser, put his regiment in motion, and by a forced march through the deep mud reached Lewiston at four o'clock in the morning.[a] Again he importuned for permission to participate directly in the enterprise, but in vain. His rank would be equal, on the field, to that of Colonel Van Rensselaer, who had originated and planned the whole affair,[1] and who the commanding general resolved should have the honor of winning the laurels to be obtained by leadership.

[a] October 13, 1812.

The night of the 12th was intensely dark, yet every thing was in readiness for the invasion at a little after three o'clock in the morning.[b] Mr. Cook, a citizen of Lewiston, had assumed the direction of the boats, and provided men to man them; Mr. Lovett, Van Rensselaer's secretary, had been placed in charge of an eighteen-pound gun in battery on Lewiston Heights, with instructions to cover the landing of the Americans on the Canada shore; and the six hundred men, under Van Rensselaer and Chrystie, were standing in a cold storm of wind and rain at the place of embarkation. It had been arranged for them to cross over and storm and take possession of Queenston Heights, when the remainder of the troops were to follow in a body and drive the British from the town. But there were only thirteen boats, and these were not sufficient to carry more than about one half of the troops intended for the capture of the Heights.[2] The regulars having reached the boats first, the companies of Wool, Malcolm, and Armstrong were immediately embarked, with forty picked men from Captain Leonard's company of artillery at Fort Niagara, under Lieutenants Gansevoort and Rathbone, and about sixty militia. When all were ready, Van Rensselaer gave the word to advance, and leaped into the boat containing the artillerists. Major Morrison was ordered to follow with the remainder of the troops on the return of the boats.

[b] October 13.

The struggle with the eddies was brief. Within ten minutes after leaving Lewiston Landing the boats struck the Canada shore "at the identical spot aimed at," just above a huge rock now seen lying in the edge of the water under the Lewiston suspension bridge. There the militia were landed; the regulars debarked a little below the rock.[3] Three of the thirteen boats had lost their way; the remaining ten now returned to the American shore.

The enemy were on the alert. The movements of the Americans had been discov-

---

[1] See note 2, page 381.

[2] This inadequate number of boats seems to have been owing to remissness in Quarter-master-general Porter's department. The quarter-master, then stationed at the Falls, had written to Van Rensselaer, "I can furnish you boats at two or three days' notice to carry over 1200 or 1400 men." A sufficient number for six or seven hundred were ordered, and the matter was left in charge of Judge Barton, the quarter-master's agent. He had forwarded only thirteen at the appointed hour. General Van Rensselaer has been censured for not having boats enough. It was no fault of his.

[3] The view of the landing-place seen on the next page I sketched from a point a few yards below the Canadian end of the Lewiston Suspension Bridge. The rock mentioned in the text is a prominent object in the picture. It is at the foot of the rapids, where the river sweeps in a curve around Queenston Heights, a portion of which occupies a large part of the sketch. Above is seen the suspension bridge, with its steadying-chains attached to the shore; and on the side of the opposite bank, looking up the river, the position of the railway, that lies upon a narrow shelf cut in the almost perpendicular shore of the river, is marked by a train of cars. The toll-house seen at the end of the bridge, on the right, shows the direction of the road from the bridge to the village of Queenston, not an eighth of a mile distant.

ered by the sentinels, and Captain Dennis, of the Forty-ninth Regiment of British Regulars, stationed at Queenston, with sixty grenadiers of that corps, Captain Hatt's company of York volunteer militia,[1] a small body of Indians, and a three-pound field-piece, took position on the sloping shore, a little north of the site of the suspension bridge, to resist the debarkation. Their presence was first made known by a broad flash, then a volley of musketry that mortally wounded Lieutenant Rathbone, by the side of Colonel Van Rensselaer, before landing, and random shots from the field-piece along the line of the ferry at the moment when the boats touched the shore. These were answered by Lovett's battery on Lewiston Heights, when the enemy turned and fled up the hill toward Queenston, pursued by the regulars of the Thirteenth, under Captain Wool, the senior officer present, in the absence of Lieutenant Colonel Chrystie, who was in one of the missing boats.[2] On the margin of

LANDING-PLACE OF THE AMERICANS AT QUEENSTON.

the plateau on which Queenston stands Wool ceased pursuit, drew his men up in battle order, and was about to send to Colonel Van Rensselaer for directions, when that officer's aid, Judge Advocate Lush, came hurrying up with orders to prepare to storm the Heights. "We are ready," promptly responded the gallant Wool. Lush hastened back to the chief commander on the shore, and in a few minutes returned with orders for Wool to advance. He was moving rapidly over the plateau toward the foot of the Heights, when the order for storming was countermanded, and the troops were brought to a halt near the present entrance to the village from the bridge. Captain Dennis, meanwhile, had been strengthened by the arrival on the Heights of the Light Infantry under Captain Williams, and a company of the York militia under Captain Chisholm; and just as Wool's command had taken their resting position in battle order, Dennis and his full force, already mentioned, fell heavily on the right flank of the Americans. At the same time, Williams and Chisholm opened a severe fire in their front from the brow of the Heights. Without waiting for farther orders, Wool wheeled his column to the right and confronted the force of the enemy on the plain, where with deadly aim his men poured a very severe fire into their ranks. Van Rensselaer and the militia had taken a position on the left of the Thirteenth in the mean time. The engagement was severe but short, and the enemy were compelled to fall back to Queenston. Both parties suffered much—the Americans most severely. Of the ten officers of the Thirteenth who were present, two were killed and five were seriously wounded. The former were Lieutenant Valleau[3] and Ensign Morris;[4] the latter were Captains Wool, Malcolm, and Armstrong, and Ensign

---

[1] Captain Samuel Hatt was one of the most esteemed and richest men in the province. He entered the service under the impulses of the purest patriotism only, and took this subordinate station.

[2] The three missing boats were commanded respectively by Lieutenant Colonel Chrystie, Captain Lawrence, and an unknown subaltern. Chrystie's boat was driven by the currents and eddies upon the New York shore, and he ordered Lawrence's back, while the third fell into the hands of the enemy, it having struck the shore at the mouth of the creek, just north of Queenston.

[3] John Valleau was commissioned first lieutenant of the Thirteenth Regiment on the 24th of March, 1812.

[4] Robert Morris, appointed ensign in the Thirteenth Regiment March 12, 1812.

Lent.[1] The militia suffered very little; but Colonel Van Rensselaer was so badly wounded in several places that he was compelled to relinquish the command. A bullet passed through both of Wool's thighs, and both Malcolm[2] and Armstrong[3] were wounded in the left thigh. A considerable number of the Americans were made prisoners.

While Wool and his command were engaged with the enemy on the plain, those upon the Heights kept up a desultory fire upon the Americans, which the latter could not well respond to. Perceiving this, Van Rensselaer ordered the whole detachment to fall back to the beach below the hill, in a place of more security. They did so, but were not absolutely sheltered from the fire of the enemy above. One man was killed and several were wounded by their shots.

It was now broad daylight, and the storm had ceased. While the detachment was forming for farther action on the margin of the river, a fourth company of the 13th, under Captain Ogilvie, crossed and joined them. No time was to be lost. The Heights must be stormed and taken, or the expedition would be a failure. Lieutenant Colonel Chrystie had not been heard from. Van Rensselaer was disabled. All the other officers were young men. Not a single commission was more than six months old, and Captain Wool, the senior of them all in rank, was only twenty-three years of age—too young, Van Rensselaer thought, to be intrusted with an undertaking so important. He had never been under fire before that morning, and was already badly wounded. True, in the fight just ended, his metal had given out the ring of that of a true soldier. The alternative was great risk and a chance for honor, or total abandonment of the enterprise and the pointings of the finger of scorn. The choice was soon made. Wool had asked for orders; had been told that the capture of the Heights was the great object of the expedition; and, notwithstanding his severe flesh wounds and the inexperience of himself and his men, he had expressed his eagerness to make the attempt. Van Rensselaer ordered him to that duty, and at the same time he directed his aid-de-camp Lush to follow the little column and shoot every man who should falter, for symptoms of weak courage had already appeared.

Elated with the order, young Wool almost forgot his bleeding wounds. He was light and lithe in person, full of ambition and enthusiasm, and beloved by his companions in arms.[4] All followed him cheerfully. Ordering Captain Ogilvie, with his

---

[1] James W. Lent, Jr., appointed ensign in the Thirteenth Regiment May 1, 1812. In March, 1813, he was promoted to first lieutenant of artillery. He was retained in 1815, and became active in the quarter-master's department in 1816. Left the service in 1817.

[2] Richard M. Malcolm was commissioned captain in the Thirteenth Regiment of Infantry on the 8th of April, 1812. In March, 1813, he was promoted to major, and in June, 1814, to lieutenant colonel of the same regiment. He was disbanded in June, 1815.—Gardner's *Dictionary of the Army*, page 307.

[3] Henry B. Armstrong, yet [1867] living, is a son of General John Armstrong, the Secretary of War in 1814. He was commissioned a captain in the Thirteenth Regiment in April, 1812; promoted to major the following year; in June, 1813, distinguished himself at Stony Creek; became lieutenant colonel of the First Rifle Regiment in September, 1813, and was disbanded in June, 1815. Although nearly eighty years of age when the Great Rebellion broke out in 1861, he went to Washington City and tendered to the government the services of himself and two sons. He then resided on an ample estate in Red Hook, Duchess County, New York.

[4] John Ellis Wool, now (1867) a major general in the army of the United States, is a son of a soldier of the Revolution who was with General Wayne at the taking of Stony Point in the summer of 1779. He was born in Newburg, Orange County, New York, in 1788. His father died when he was only four years of age, when he was taken into the family of his grandfather, James Wool, five of whose sons bore arms in the old war for independence. During his residence with his grandfather in Rensselaer County, young Wool attended a common country school. At the age of twelve years, with a slender education, he entered the service of a merchant in Troy, New York, as clerk. At eighteen he engaged in the business of selling books and stationery in the same town, and continued in that avocation until fire swept away all his worldly goods. He then commenced the study of law with John Russell, in Troy, in a small building recently standing on Second Street, nearly opposite General Wool's present residence. War with Great Britain was soon afterward looked upon as inevitable, and young Wool, feeling the old fire of his father stirring within him, left his books to seek usefulness and honor in the field. Upon the recommendation of De Witt Clinton he obtained a commission as captain in the 13th United States Regiment in the spring of 1812. It is dated March 14, 1812. War was declared in little more than ninety days afterward, and in September his regiment, under Lieutenant Colonel Chrystie, was ordered to the

RUSSELL'S LAW OFFICE.

Scaling Queenston Heights. General Brock at Fort George. His Expectation of an Invasion.

fresh troops to take the right of the column, he sprang forward and commenced the perilous ascent, guided by Lieutenants Gansevoort and Randolph, who were well acquainted with the way. The picked artillerists led the column; and in many places the precipice was so steep that the troops were compelled to pull themselves up by means of bushes. They were concealed from the enemy by the shelter of the rocks and shrubbery; and near the top of the acclivity they struck a fisherman's path, which the enemy supposed to be impassable, and had neglected to guard it.

While Wool and his little band were scaling the Heights, the British were making movements under great uncertainty. The vigilant Sir Isaac Brock at Fort George, about seven miles distant, had heard the cannonading before dawn. He aroused his aid-de-camp, Major Glegg, and called for Alfred, his favorite horse, presented to him by Sir James Craig. He had been in expectation of an invasion at some point for several days, and only the night before he had given each of his staff special instructions.[1]

Niagara frontier. His gallant bearing there is recorded in the text. Because of his bravery at Queenston he was promoted to major in the 29th Regiment of Infantry in April, 1813. For his gallant conduct at Plattsburg, in September, 1814, he was promoted to lieutenant colonel in December following. He was retained in the army in 1815, and on the 29th of September, 1816, was appointed inspector general of division, and in 1821 inspector general of the army of the United States, with the rank of colonel. In 1826 he was made a brigadier general by brevet "for ten years' faithful service." His reports to the government on matters pertaining to the service were always models of their kind, and always elicited encomiums. His discipline was always perfect and most efficient, and his sleepless vigilance has made him on all occasions one of the most trusted officers in the service.

In 1832, General Wool was sent to Europe to collect information connected with military science. He received great attention, especially in France, where, on one occasion, he formed one of the suite of Louis Philippe at a grand review of 70,000 men. In November of the same year he accompanied the King of Belgium at a review of 100,000 troops, and visited the fortifications of Antwerp. In 1835, when hostilities with France were anticipated, General Wool made a thorough inspection of all the sea-coast defenses, and submitted an admirable report to government. In 1836 he was ordered to the service of removing the Cherokee Indians to Arkansas. In that mission he displayed some of the highest traits of a soldier and statesman. In 1838, while the Canadian provinces were disturbed by insurrection, Wool was sent to the wilds of Maine to look after the defenses of the border. In the Mexican war his services as a tactician, disciplinarian, and as an administrative and executive officer in the field were of incalculable benefit to the country. These are all recorded by the pen of the grateful historian. For his gallant conduct in that war he was breveted a major general, and on his return home he was every where met with the most enthusiastic greetings. As tokens of approbation, three swords were presented to him, one by the citizens of Troy, another by the State of New York, and a third by the United States.

Toward the close of 1853, when filibustering expeditions were fitted out on the Western coast, the command of the *Department of the Pacific* was intrusted to General Wool. It was a post of great labor and trust, involving as it did international questions of a delicate nature, and peculiar relations with Indian tribes. His activity, vigilance, and untiring energy in that field were wonderful. In the spring of 1855 he made a tour of inspection and reconnoissance through the distant Territories of Oregon and Washington. On the breaking out of hostilities in that region in the fall of 1855, Wool repaired to the scene of trouble, and was efficient in ending them. He remained in California until near the close of President Pierce's administration, when he was relieved, and placed in command of the *Department of the East*, comprising the whole country eastward of the Mississippi River. He was every where received with the greatest enthusiasm, and especially at Troy, his place of residence. He was there engaged in the quiet routine of his office when the rising tide of the great rebellion, that broke out at the close of 1860, commanded his attention. With his wonted energy, he warned and entreated the national government to prepare for a great emergency; and when, in April, 1861, Fort Sumter was attacked, and the national capital was menaced by the rebels, General Wool conceived and executed such efficient measures at New York, that it is not too much to say that he was one of the chief instruments in the salvation of the republic from the hand of the destroyer. In July he entered upon active service at Fortress Monroe as commander of that post, where he stood in the delicate and most important position of sentinel at the portal opening between the loyal and disloyal territories of the republic. He remained there almost a year, when he was commissioned a full major general in the army of the United States, and transferred to the command at Baltimore and vicinity. In 1863 he retired to private life.

[1] Beacons had been placed at convenient distances between Kingston and Fort George to give notice in the event of an invasion, but in the confusion they were not lighted. The late Honorable William Hamilton Merritt, M.P., then a

But so confident was he that the attack would be made from Fort Niagara, that he considered the demonstration above as only a feint to conceal that movement; yet, as a vigilant soldier, he instantly resolved to obtain personal knowledge of the situation of affairs. Mounting Alfred, he pushed toward Queenston at full speed, followed by his aids, Major Glegg and Colonel M'Donell. The journey of seven miles was made in little more than half an hour. Arriving at Queenston, Sir Isaac and his companions rode up the Heights at full gallop, exposed to a severe enfilading fire of artillery from the American shore. On reaching the redan battery, half way up the Heights,[1] they dismounted, took a general view of affairs, and pronounced them favorable. Suddenly the crack of musketry in their rear startled them. Wool and his followers had successfully scaled the Heights, and were close upon them. Brock and his aids had not time to remount. Leading their horses at full gallop, they fled down the slope to the village, followed by the twelve men who manned the battery. A few minutes afterward the Stars and Stripes—the symbol of the Union—the insignia of the Republic—were waving over the captured redan, and greeting the rays of the early morning sun, then struggling in fitful gleams through the breaking clouds. This was the third time within three months that the standard of the United States had been victoriously displayed on the soil of Canada.[2] Wool's triumph for the moment was complete.

Brock immediately dispatched a courier to General Sheaffe at Fort George with orders to push forward re-enforcements, and, at the same time, open fire upon Fort Niagara. He then took command of Captain Williams's detachment of one hundred men, and hastened up the slope toward the battery, behind which Captain Wool had placed his little band, with their faces toward Queenston, to await an attack. Dennis soon joined Brock with his detachment, when a movement was made to turn the American flank. The vigilant Wool perceived it, and immediately sent out fifty men to keep the flanking party in check, and to take possession of the "Mountain," or crown of the Heights, where the monument now stands. But they were too few for the purpose, and even when re-enforced they were too weak to stem the steady advance of the veteran enemy. The whole detachment fell back with some confusion. The enemy, inspirited by this movement, pressed forward, and pushed the Americans to the verge of the precipice, which overlooks the deep chasm of the swift-flowing river more than two hundred feet below. Wool's little band was in a most perilous position. Death by ball, bayonet, or flood seemed inevitable, and Captain Ogilvie raised a white handkerchief on the point of a bayonet in token of surrender. The incensed Wool sprang forward, snatched away that token of submission, addressed a few spirited words to his officers and soldiers, begging them to fight on so long as the ammunition should last, and then resort to the bayonet. Waving his sword, he led his inspirited comrades to a renewal of the conflict with so much impetuosity that the enemy broke and fled down the Heights in dismay, and took shelter in and behind a large stone building near the edge of the river. Sir Isaac was amazed and mortified; and to his favorite grenadiers he shouted, "This is the first time I have seen the Forty-ninth turn their backs!" His voice and the stinging rebuke of his words checked them. At the same time Lieutenant Colonel M'Donell brought up two flank companies of York Volunteers, under Captains Cameron and Howard, which had just arrived from Brown's Point, three miles below. The fugitives had rallied, and Sir Isaac turned to lead them up the Heights. His tall figure was a conspicuous object for the American sharp-shooters. First a bullet struck his wrist, wounding it slightly. A moment afterward, as he shouted "Push on the York Volunteers," another bullet entered his breast, passed out through his side, and left a

---

major at the head of a corps of cavalry, called the Niagara Dragoons, immediately dispatched a courier to Brock. He reached Fort George early, but found Brock about ready to take the saddle.

[1] A *redan* is a rampart in the following form, \/, having its angle toward the enemy, and open in the rear.
[2] At Sandwich by Hull (see page 262); at Gananoqui by Forsyth (see page 373); and at Queenston by Wool.

death-wound. He fell from his horse at the foot of the slope, and lived long enough to request those around him to conceal his death from the troops, and to send some token of his remembrance to his sister in England. But his death could not be concealed more than a few minutes. When it became known, the bitter words "Revenge the general!" burst from the lips of the Forty-ninth. M'Donell assumed the command, and, at the head of them and the York Militia, one hundred and ninety strong, he charged up the hill to dispute with Wool the mastery of the Heights. The struggle was desperate, and the Americans, doubtful of the issue, spiked the cannon in the redan. Both parties were led gallantly and fought bravely. But when M'Donell fell mortally wounded,[1] and Dennis and Williams were both severely injured, and were compelled to leave the field, the British fell back in some confusion to Vrooman's Point, a mile below, leaving the young American commander and his little band of two hundred and forty men masters of Queenston Heights, after three distinct and bloody battles, fought within the space of about five hours. Taking all things into consideration—the passage of the river, the nature of the ground, the rawness of the troops (for most of the regulars were raw recruits), the absence of cannon, and the youth and wounds of the American commander, the events of that morning were, "indeed, a display of intrepidity," as Wilkinson afterward wrote, "rarely exhibited, in which the conduct and the execution were equally conspicuous. . . . Under *all* the circumstances, and on the *scale* of the operations, the impartial soldier and competent judge will name this brilliant affair a *chef-d'œuvre* of the war."[2]

It was now about ten o'clock in the morning. Although bleeding and in much pain, Wool would not leave the field, but kept vigorously at work in preparations to defend the position he had gained. He drew his troops up in line on the Heights fronting the village, ordered Gansevoort and Randolph to drill out the spiked cannon in the redan, and bring it to bear upon the enemy near Vrooman's, and sent out scouts to watch the movements of the foe.

Meanwhile re-enforcements and supplies were slowly crossing the river. In the passage they were greatly annoyed by the fire from the one-gun battery on Vrooman's Point. The first that arrived on the Heights was a detachment of the Sixth Regiment under Captain M'Chesney; another, of the Thirteenth, under Captain Lawrence; and a party of New York state riflemen, under Lieutenant Smith. These were immediately detached as flanking parties. They were soon followed by others, and before noon Major General Van Rensselaer, Brigadier General Wadsworth, Lieutenant Colonels Scott, Fenwick, Stranahan, and Major Mullany, were on the Heights, while a few militia were slowly

---

[1] Lieutenant M'Donell was a brilliant and promising young man. He was the attorney general of Upper Canada, and was only twenty-five years of age. He was wounded in five places, one bullet passing through his body, yet he survived twenty hours in great agony. During that time he constantly lamented the fall of his commander.—Tupper's *Life*, etc., *of Brock*, page 322.

[2] *Wilkinson's Memoirs*, i., 577. The officers who participated with Captain Wool, and received from him, in his report to Colonel Van Rensselaer, special commendation, were Captain Peter Ogilvie, and Lieutenants Kearney, Hugunin, Carr, and Sammons, of the Thirteenth, Lieutenants Gansevoort and Randolph, of the light artillery, and Major Lush, of the militia. Captain Ogilvie resigned in June, 1813. Lieutenant Stephen Watts Kearney, who was a native of New Jersey, was retained in the service in 1815, having risen to the rank of captain. He was made a major by brevet in 1823, and full major in 1829. In the spring of 1833 he was promoted to lieutenant colonel of dragoons, and to colonel of the same in 1836. In 1846 he was promoted to brigadier general, went into the war with Mexico, and made conquest of the province of New Mexico. For his gallant conduct there and in California he was made major general by brevet. In March, 1847, he was appointed Governor of California. He died in October, 1848. His brother, Philip Kearney, who lost an arm in the battles before the city of Mexico, was a brigadier general in the army raised to put down the Great Rebellion in 1861, and was killed in battle near Fairfax Court-house, in Virginia, September 1, 1862. Lieutenant Daniel Hugunin was a representative in Congress for New York from 1825 to 1827. He died in Wisconsin in 1850. Lieutenant Gansevoort, who had been in the artillery service since 1806, was distinguished a little more than a month later at Fort Niagara. He became captain of artillery in May, 1813, and left the service in March, 1814. Lieutenant Thomas Beverly Randolph was aid-de-camp to General Carrington and captain of infantry in the spring of 1813. He resigned in 1815. He was lieutenant colonel of Hamtramck's regiment of Virginia volunteers in Mexico in 1847. Lieutenant Stephen Lush (acting major at Queenston) was aid to General Izard, and dangerously wounded before Chippewa in October, 1814.

passing over the river. Van Rensselaer took immediate steps for fortifying the position, under the direction of Lieutenant Totten, of the Engineers, and dispatched an aid-de-camp to hasten the passage of the militia.

Lieutenant Colonel Scott, as we have observed, arrived at Lewiston with his command at four o'clock that morning. He placed his heavy guns in battery on the shore under the immediate command of Captains Towson and Barker. Having received permission from Van Rensselaer to cross over as a volunteer and take command of the troops on the Heights, he reached the Canada shore, with his adjutant Roach, just after Wadsworth, with a small detachment of volunteers, had crossed without orders. He unexpectedly found that officer upon the mountain, and immediately proposed to limit his own command to the regulars; but the generous and patriotic Wadsworth promptly waived his rank, and said, "You, sir, know professionally what ought to be done. I am here for the honor of my country and that of the New York militia." Scott at once assumed the general command, at the head of three hundred and fifty regulars and two hundred and fifty volunteers, the latter under General Wadsworth and Lieutenant Colonel Stranahan. Assisted by the skillful Lieutenant Totten, Scott placed them in the strongest possible position to receive the enemy and to cover the ferry, expecting to be re-enforced at once by the militia from the opposite shore. He was doomed to most profound mortification and disappointment.

While Scott was absent for a short time, superintending the unspiking of the cannon in the redan, a troop of Indians suddenly appeared on the left, led by Captain Norton, a half-breed, but under the general command of Chief John Brant, a young, lithe, and graceful son of the great Mohawk warrior and British ally of that name in the Revolution. Brant made his first appearance in the field on this occasion. He was dressed, painted, and plumed in Indian style from head to foot. His lieutenant and most valued companion was a dark, powerfully-built chief known as Captain Jacobs. Another was Norton, the half-breed just mentioned. They and their followers were the allies of the British, and came mostly from the settlements of the Six Nations, on the Grand River, in Canada.[1]

It was between one and two o'clock in the afternoon when this cloud of dusky warriors swept along the brow of the mountain in portentous fury, with gleaming tomahawks and other savage weapons, and fell upon the American pickets, driving them in upon the main line of the militia in great confusion. The fearful war-whoop struck terror to many a white man's heart, and the militia were about to fly ignobly, when Scott appeared, his tall form—head and shoulders above all others—attracting every eye, and his trumpet-voice commanding the attention of every ear. He instantly brought order out of confusion. He suddenly changed the front of his line; and his troops, catching inspiration from his voice and acts, raised a shout and fell with such fury upon the Indians that they fled in dismay to the woods after a sharp, short engagement. But they were soon rallied by the dauntless Brant,[2] and contin-

---

[1] The British found considerable difficulty in inducing these Indians to join them. The authorities of the United States used every effort in their power to keep the Indians from the contest on both sides, knowing their cruel mode of warfare. Cornplanter, the venerable Seneca chief, did all in his power to keep his race neutral. At the request of the United States government, he induced their influential chiefs, named respectively Blue Eyes, Johnson, Silver Heels, and Jacob Snow, to visit the Indians on the Grand River, talk with them about remaining neutral, and bring back an answer. In a manuscript letter before me from Robert Hoops to Major Van Campan, is an interesting account of a meeting at Cornplanter's to hear their report. Mr. Hoops, Francis King, and John Watson were the white representatives present. Blue Eyes made the report. He said the Indians told him that they did not want to go to war, but remarked, "It is the President of the United States makes war upon us. We know not your disputes. The British talk much against the Americans, and the Americans talk much against the British. We know not which is right. The British say the Americans want to take our lands. We do not want to fight, nor do we intend to disturb you; but if you come to take our land, we are determined to defend ourselves." The three commissioners cautioned the Senecas not to use strong drinks, to keep quietly at home, and refrain from engaging in the war. Had the British been equally mindful of the claims of civilization, the historian would have many less atrocities to record.

[2] John Brant, whose Indian name was *Ahyouwaighs*, was a son of Joseph Brant, or *Thayendanegea*, and was born at the Mohawk village, on the Grand River, in Canada, on the 27th of September, 1794, and was only eighteen years of

ued to annoy the Americans until Scott, at the head of a considerable portion of his army, made a general assault upon them, and drove them from the Heights. At the same time, General Sheaffe was seen cautiously approaching with re-enforcements from Fort George, his troops making the road near Vrooman's all aglow with scarlet. Lieutenant Colonel Chrystie had just arrived upon the battle-field for the first time. He had crossed and recrossed the river, but did not appear upon the Heights until in the afternoon,[1] when he took command of the Thirteenth Regiment, and ordered Captain Wool, who had endured toil and suffering for more than twelve hours, to the American shore to have his wounds dressed.

At Vrooman's, General Sheaffe, who had succeeded Brock in command, joined the fragments of the different corps who had been driven from the Heights when Brock was killed, with heavy re-enforcements.

John Brant

age when he appeared as leader on the battle-field at Queenston. He received a good English education at Ancaster and Niagara, and was a diligent student of English authors. He loved nature, and studied its phenomena with discrimination. He was manly and amiable, and at the time in question was in every respect an accomplished gentleman. On the death of his father in 1807, he became the *Tekarihogea*, or principal chief of the Six Nations, although he was the fourth and youngest son. As such he took the field in 1812 in the British interest, and was engaged in most of the military events on the Niagara frontier during the war. At the close of the contest he and his young sister Elizabeth took up their residence at the home of their father, at the head of Lake Ontario, where they lived in the English style, and dispensed hospitalities with a liberal hand. The reader will find a full account of this residence and of the family at the time in question in Stone's *Life of Joseph Brant.* Young Brant went to England in 1821 on business for the Six Nations, and there took occasion to defend the character of his father from aspersions in Campbell's *Gertrude of Wyoming.* He was successful in his proof, but the poet had not the generosity or manliness to strike the calumnies from his poem, and there they remain to this day. On his return Brant went to work zealously for the moral improvement of his people, in which he was successful. In 1827 Governor Dalhousie appointed him to the rank of captain in the British army and Superintendent of the Six Nations. He was elected a member of the Provincial Parliament in 1832 for the county of Haldimand, which comprehended a good portion of the territory originally granted to the Mohawks. Technical disability gave the seat to another, after he had filled it for a while. But during that very summer the competitors were both laid in the grave by that terrible scourge, *Asiatic cholera.* He died at the Mohawk village where he was born, at the age of forty-eight years, and was buried in the same vault with his father, in the burying-ground of the Mohawk Church, a short distance from Brantford, in Canada, over which has been erected a substantial mausoleum,

BRANT'S MONUMENT.

represented in the engraving. This monument will be noticed more particularly presently.

[1] The conduct of Lieutenant Colonel Chrystie on this occasion was not wholly reconcilable with our ideas of a true soldier. In a manuscript letter before me, written by Colonel Solomon Van Rensselaer to General Wilkinson in January, 1816, he accuses Chrystie with cowardice, and says Captain Lawrence, whose boat Chrystie ordered back at the crossing (see note 2, page 395), openly charged him with it. Van Rensselaer gives it as his opinion that much of the bad conduct of the militia in refusing to cross the river in the afternoon was owing to the example of this officer. On the other hand, General Van Rensselaer makes honorable mention of him in his report written the next day, and he

He moved cautiously. Near Vrooman's he left two pieces of artillery to command the town, filed to the right, and crossed the country to the little village of St. David's, three miles westward of Queenston, and by that circuitous route, after marching and countermarching as if reconnoitring the American lines, he gained the rear of that portion of the Heights on which they were posted, and formed in Elijah Phelps's fields on the Chippewa road.[1] There he was joined by the 41st Grenadiers and some militia and Indians from Chippewa, when the whole British army confronting that of the Americans was more than one thousand strong, exclusive of their dusky allies.[2] The Americans, according to the most careful estimate, did not exceed six hundred in number.

When Sheaffe appeared, General Van Rensselaer was on the Heights. He immediately crossed the river to push forward re-enforcements. He failed. The militia, who had been so brave in speech and clamorous to be led against the enemy, refused to cross. The smell of gunpowder, even from afar, seems to have paralyzed their honor and their courage. Van Rensselaer rode up and down among them, alternately threatening and imploring. Lieutenant Colonel Bloom, who had been wounded in action and had returned, and Judge Peck, who happened to be at Lewiston, did the same, but without effect. Van Rensselaer appealed to their patriotism, their honor, and their humanity, but in vain. They pleaded their exemption as militia, under the Constitution and laws, from being taken out of their own state! and under that miserable shield they hoped to find shelter from the storm of indignation which their cowardice was sure to evoke. Like poltroons as they were, they stood on the shore at Lewiston while their brave companions in arms on Queenston Heights were menaced with inevitable destruction or captivity. All that Van Rensselaer could do was to send over some munitions of war, with a letter to General Wadsworth, ordering him to retreat if in his judgment the salvation of the troops depended upon such movement, and promising him a supply of boats for the purpose. But this promise he could not fulfill. The boatmen on the shore were as cowardly as the militia on the plain above. Many of them had fled panic-stricken, and the boats were dispersed.

Wadsworth communicated Van Rensselaer's letter to the field officers. They perceived no chance for re-enforcements, no means for a retreat, and no hope of succor from any human source except their own valor and vigorous arms. They resolved to meet the oncoming overwhelming force like brave soldiers. Scott sprang upon a log, his tall form towering conspicuous above all,[3] and addressed the little army in a few stirring words as the British came thundering on. "The enemy's balls," he said, begin to thin our ranks. His numbers are overwhelming. In a moment the shock must come, and there is no retreat. We are in the beginning of a national war. Hull's surrender is to be redeemed. Let us, then, die arms in hand. The country demands the sacrifice. The example will not be lost. The blood of the slain will make heroes of the living. Those who follow will avenge our fall and their country's wrongs. Who dare to stand?" "All! all!" was the generous response; and in that spirit they received the first heavy blow of the enemy on their right wing.[4]

---

was promoted to the office of inspector general. He did not live long enough to test his mettle fairly. He died at Fort George, in Canada, on the 22d of July, 1813.   [1] MS. Journal of Captain William Hamilton Merritt.

[2] Sheaffe's re-enforcements, with whom he marched from Fort George, consisted of almost four hundred of the 41st Regiment, under Captain Derenzy, and about three hundred militia. The latter consisted of the flank companies of the 1st Regiment of Lincoln Militia, under Captains J. Crooks and M'Ewen; the flank companies of the 4th Regiment of Lincoln Militia, under Captains Nellis and W. Crooks; Captains Hall's, Durand's, and Applegarth's companies of the 5th Regiment of Lincoln Militia; Major Merritt's Yeomanry Corps, and a body of Swayzee's Militia Artillery under Captains Powell and Cameron. Those from Chippewa were commanded by Colonel Clark, and consisted of Captain Bullock's company of Grenadiers of the 41st Regiment; the flank companies of the 2d Lincoln Regiment, under Captains Hamilton and Rowe, and the Volunteer Sedentary Militia. Brant and Jacobs commanded the Indians. Two three-pounders, under the charge of Lieutenant Crowther, of the 41st Regiment, accompanied the troops.

[3] General Scott was six feet five inches in height. He was then slender, graceful, and commanding in form; for several years before his death he was ponderous, yet exceedingly dignified in his appearance.

[4] Scott was in full-dress uniform, and, being taller than his companions, was a conspicuous and important mark for

Battle on Queenston Heights.   Perils of the Americans.   Heroes and Cowards made Prisoners of War.

Sheaffe opened the battle at about four o'clock by directing Lieutenant M'Intyre, with the Light Company of the 41st on the left of his column, supported by a body of militia, Indians, and negroes under Captain Runchey, to fall upon the American right. They fired a single volley with considerable execution, and then charged with a tremendous tumult, the white men shouting and the Indians ringing out the fearful war-whoop and hideous yells. The Americans were overpowered by the onslaught and gave way, for their whole available force did not much exceed three hundred men. Perceiving this, Sheaffe ordered his entire line to charge, while the two field-pieces were brought to bear upon the American ranks. The effect was powerful. The Americans yielded and fled in utter confusion toward the river, down the slope by the redan, and along the road leading from Queenston to the Falls. The latter were cut off by the Indians, and forced through the woods toward the precipices along the bank of the river. Others, who had reached the water's edge, were also cut off from farther retreat by a lack of boats. Meanwhile the American commander had sent several messengers with flags, bearing offers to capitulate. The Indians shot them all, and continued a murderous onslaught upon the terrified fugitives. Some of them were killed in the woods, some were driven over the precipices and perished on the rocks or in the rushing river below, while others escaped by letting themselves down from bush to bush, and swimming the flood. At length Lieutenant Colonel Scott, in the midst of the greatest peril, reached the British commanding general, and offered to surrender the whole force.[1] The Indians were called from their bloody work, terms of capitulation were soon agreed to, and all the Americans on the British side became prisoners of war. These, to the utter astonishment of their own commanders, amounted to about nine hundred, when not more than six hundred, regulars and militia, were known to have been on the Canada shore at any time during the day, and not more than half that number were engaged in the fight on the Heights. The mystery was soon explained. Several hundred militia had crossed over during the morning. Two hundred of them, under Major Mullany, who crossed early in the day, were forced by the current of the river under the range of Vrooman's battery, and were captured. Two hundred and ninety-three, who were in the battle, were surrendered; and the remainder, having seen the wounded crossing the river, the painted Indians, and the "green tigers," as they called the 49th, whose coats were faced with green, skulked below the banks, and had no more to do with the battle than spectators in a balloon might have claimed. But they were a part of the invading army, were found on British soil, and were properly prisoners of war. The British soldiers, after the battle, plucked them from their hiding-places, and made them a part of the triumphal procession with which General Sheaffe returned to Fort George.[2]

---

the enemy. He was urged to change his dress. "No," he said, smiling, "I will die in my robes." As in the case of Washington on the field of Monongahela, the Indians took special aim at Scott, but could not hit him.

[1] Scott fixed a white cravat on the point of his sword as a flag of truce, and, accompanied by Captains Totten (from whose neck the "flag was taken") and Gibson, made his way along the river shore, under shelter of the precipice, to a gentle slope, up which they hastened to the road leading from the village to the Heights, exposed to the random fire of the Indians. Just as they reached the road they were met by two Indians, who sprang upon them like tigers. They would not listen to Scott's declaration that he was under the protection of a flag and was going to surrender. They attempted to wrench his sword from him, when Totten and Gibson drew theirs. The Indians, who were armed with rifles, instantly fired, but without effect, and were about to use their knives and tomahawks, when a British sergeant, accompanied by a guard, seeing the encounter, rushed forward, crying Honor! honor! took the Americans under his protection, and conducted them to the presence of General Sheaffe. — *Life and Services of General Winfield Scott*, by Edward Mansfield, page 44.

[2] The authorities consulted in compiling the foregoing account of events on the Niagara frontier, in this and the preceding chapter, are as follows: Official Reports of Generals Van Rensselaer and Sheaffe, Lieutenant Colonel Chrystie and Captain Wool; oral and written statements of Captain (now Major General) Wool to the Author; MS. Order and

The entire loss of the Americans during that eventful day, according to the most careful estimates, was ninety killed, about one hundred wounded, and between eight and nine hundred made prisoners, causing an entire loss, in rank and file, of about eleven hundred men. The British loss in killed, wounded, and prisoners (the latter taken in the morning), was about one hundred and thirty. The number of Indians engaged and their loss is not positively known.[1] Captain Norton was wounded, but not severely. All parties engaged in the fight on that day behaved with exemplary courage, and deserved, as they received, the encomiums of their respective generals, and the thanks of their respective governments.[2]

Brigadier General Wadsworth was in command when the army was surrendered. He delivered his sword to General Sheaffe in person. The ceremony of formal surrender occurred at near sunset, when the prisoners, officers, and men were marched to the village of Newark (now Niagara), at the mouth of the Niagara River. There the officers were quartered in a small tavern, and placed under guard. While waiting for an escort to conduct them to the head-quarters of General Sheaffe, a little girl entered the parlor and said that somebody in the hall wanted to see the "tall officer." Scott, who was unarmed, immediately went out, when he was confronted by the two Indians who had made such a violent assault upon him while bearing a flag of truce. Young Brant immediately stepped up to Scott and inquired how many balls had passed through his clothing, as they had both fired at him incessantly, and had been astonished continually at not seeing him fall. Jacobs, at the same time, seized Scott rudely, and attempted to whirl him around, exclaiming, "Me shoot so often, me sure

---

Letter Books of General Stephen Van Rensselaer; MS. correspondence of Colonel Solomon Van Rensselaer; Oral Narratives of Soldiers in the Battle at Queenston, living in Canada in 1860; Perkins's *History of the Late War*; Brackenridge's *History of the Late War*; Thornton's *Historical Sketches of the Late War*; Colonel Solomon Van Rensselaer's *Narrative of the Affair at Queenston*; Ingersoll's *Historical Sketch of the Second War, etc.*; Niles's *Weekly Register*; the *War*; Stone's *Life of Brant*; *Sketches of the War*, by an anonymous writer; Armstrong's *Notices of the War* of 1812; Mansfield's *Life and Services of General Winfield Scott*; Baylis's *Battle of Queenston*; Files of the *New York Herald*, or semi-weekly *Evening Post*; James's *Military Occurrences of the Late War*; Auchinleck's *History of the War of* 1812; Tupper's *Life and Correspondence of Sir Isaac Brock*; Christie's *Military Operations in Canada*; Jarvis's *Narrative*; Manuscript Journal of Major Merritt; Symonds's Battle of *Queenston Heights*.

[1] British writers widely disagree in their estimates concerning the Indian force on that occasion. It is known that there were some with Dennis in the morning, that others accompanied Sheaffe from Fort George in the afternoon, and that he was joined on the Heights by others from Chippewa. I think the Six Nations were represented on that day by about two hundred and fifty warriors.

[2] General Sheaffe named almost every commissioned officer engaged in the battle as entitled to high praise. He specially commended Captain Holcroft, of the Royal Artillery, for his skillful and judicious use of the ordnance in his charge; also Lieutenant Crowther for similar service. He gave credit to Captain Glegg, Brock's aid-de-camp, for great assistance; also to Lieutenant Fowler, assistant deputy quarter-master general, Lieutenant Kerr, of the Glengary Fencibles, Lieutenant Colonels Butler and Clarke, and Captains Hall, Durand, Rowe, Applegarth, James Crooks, Cooper, Robert Hamilton, M'Ewen, and Duncan Cameron. Lieutenants Richardson and Thomas Butler, and Major Merritt, of the Niagara Dragoons, were all highly spoken of. He added to the list of honor the names of Volunteers Shaw, Thomson, and Jarvis. The latter (G. S. Jarvis) wrote an interesting account of the battle. He was attached to the light company of the Forty-ninth Regiment. Upon Major General Brock, his slain aid-de-camp (Colonel M'Donell), and Captains Dennis and Williams, he bestowed special and deserved encomium for their gallantry.

In contrast with this dispatch of General Sheaffe to Sir George Prevost, written at Fort George on the evening of the day of battle, is that of General Van Rensselaer to General Dearborn, written at Lewiston on the following day. He gives a general statement of important events connected with the battle, but when he comes to distribute the honors among those who are entitled to receive them, he omits the name of every officer who was engaged in storming and carrying the Heights of Queenston, the chief object of the expedition. The name of Captain Wool, the hero of the day until the tide of victory was turned against the Americans, is not even mentioned. Byron defined military glory as "being shot through the body, and having one's name spelled wrong in the gazettes." Worse fate than that would have been that of Wool and the storming-party had History confined her investigations to Van Rensselaer's report. He expressed his great obligations to General Wadsworth, Colonel Van Rensselaer, Lieutenant Colonels Scott, Chrystie, and Fenwick, and Captain Gibson, all of whom were gallant men, and performed their duties nobly in the after part of the day, but not one of them had a share in the capture of the Heights, the defeat of Major General Brock, and the winnings of victory. Van Rensselaer was wounded and taken to Lewiston before daylight. Fenwick was wounded while crossing the river and taken prisoner. Chrystie was not on the battle-field until the morning victories were all won under Wool. How General Van Rensselaer could have made such a report is a mystery. It is due to his candor and sense of justice to say that he was doubtless misled by the reports of interested parties, for as soon as he perceived the injustice that was done to brave officers, he did all in his power to remedy the evil. In his report to Colonel Van Rensselaer, on the 23d of October, Captain Wool made special mention of the officers who acted with him on that day, and these General Van Rensselaer took occasion to name in a special manner in a letter to Brigadier General Smyth announcing his resignation, written at Buffalo on the 24th. In a letter to Captain Wool in December following, General Van Rensselaer said, "I was not sufficiently informed to do justice to your bravery and good conduct in the attack of the enemy on the Heights of Queenston." He then expressed the hope that the government would notice his merits on that occasion.

to have hit somewhere!" The indignant officer thrust the savage from him, exclaiming, "Hands off, you villain! You fired like a squaw!" Both assailants immediately loosened their knives and tomahawks from their girdles, and were about to spring upon Scott, while Jacobs exclaimed, "We kill you now!" when the assailed rushed to the end of the hall, where the swords of the captured officers stood, seized the first one, drew the blade from its steel scabbard as quick as lightning, and was about to bring the heavy weapon with deadly force upon the Indians, when a British officer entered, seized Jacobs by the arms, and shouted for the guard.[1] Jacobs turned fiercely upon the officer, exclaiming, "I kill you," when Scott, with the heavy sabre raised, called out, "If you strike I'll kill you both." For a moment the eyes of the group gleamed with fury upon their antagonist, and a scene was presented equal to any thing in the songs of the Troubadours or the sagas of the Norsemen. The gust of passion was momentary, and then the Indians put up their weapons and slowly retired, muttering imprecations on all white men and all the laws of war.[2] "Beyond doubt," says his biographer,[3] "it was no part of the young chief's design to inflict injury upon the captive American commander. His whole character forbids the idea, for he was as generous and benevolent in his feelings as he was brave." It is believed that their visit to Scott was one of curiosity only, for, having tried so repeatedly to hit him with their bullets, they were anxious to know how nearly they had accomplished their object. But it can not be denied that the exasperation of the Indians against Scott, because of their losses on the Heights, was very great—so great that while he remained at Niagara he could not move from his lodgings in safety, even to visit the head-quarters of General Sheaffe,[4] without a guard.

When General Sheaffe marched in triumph from Queenston to Newark, he took with him the body of the slain General Brock, which had been concealed in a house near where he fell. The march had a twofold aspect. It was a triumphal and a funeral procession. At Newark the body was placed in the government house,

NEW MAGAZINE AT FORT GEORGE.

and there it lay in state three days, when it was buried[a] in a new cavalier bastion in Fort George, whose erection he had superintended with great interest. By the side of Brock's remains were laid those of his provincial aid-de-camp, Lieutenant Colonel M'Donell.[5] The funeral ceremonies

[a] October 16, 1812.

---

[1] This was Colonel Coffin, who had been sent by General Sheaffe, with a guard, to invite the American officers to his table at his quarters. [2] Stone's *Life of Brant*, ii., 514; Mansfield's *Life of Scott*, page 46.
[3] William L. Stone. At the close of his *Life of Joseph Brant*, Stone gives an interesting sketch of the life of John Brant.
[4] Roger H. Sheaffe was a native of Boston, Massachusetts, and was a lad living there with his widowed mother at the opening of the Revolution. Earl Percy's head-quarters were at their house while the British occupied the town, and his lordship became much attached to the boy; so much so that, with the consent of his mother, he took him away with him at the evacuation to provide for him. He gave him a military education, placed him in the army, and procured commissions and promotions for him as fast as possible. His promotion to major general was acquired on account of meritorious service. He was stationed in Canada at the breaking out of the war. He at once stated frankly his reluctance to serve against his native country, and solicited a transfer to some other field of duty. His request was not granted. For his gallant conduct, and winning victory on the Heights of Queenston, he was created a baronet, and ever afterward was known as Sir Roger Sheaffe. General Sheaffe was born on the 17th of July, 1763, and entered the British army on the 1st of May, 1778.
[5] The cavalier bastion where Brock and his aid were buried is near what is known as the new magazine, in Fort

were arranged by his other aid, Captain Glegg;[1] and when they were over, the Americans at Fort Niagara and at Lewiston fired minute-guns, as a mark of respect due to a brave enemy, by command of Major General Van Rensselaer. An armistice for a few days had been agreed upon by Van Rensselaer and Sheaffe, which gave the

George. That magazine is represented in the engraving on the preceding page. Behind it are seen the earthen ramparts of the fort as they appeared when I visited it in 1860. The place of the bastion is indicated by the hollow and opening in the fence on the right of the picture.

[1] The following was the order of the procession: 1. Fort-major Campbell. 2. Sixty men of the Forty-first Regiment, commanded by a subaltern. 3. Sixty of the militia, commanded by a captain. 4. Two six-pounders firing minute-guns. 5. Remaining corps and detachments of the garrison, with about two hundred Indians, in reverse order, forming a street through which the procession passed, extending from the government house to the garrison. 6. Band of the Forty-first Regiment. 7. Drums, covered with black cloth and muffled. 8. Late general's horse, fully caparisoned, led by four grooms. 9. Servants of the general. 10. The general's body-servant. 11. Surgeon Muirhead, Doctor Moore, Doctor Kerr, and Staff-surgeon Thorn. 11. Rev. Mr. Addison. Then followed the body of Lieutenant Colonel M'Donell, with the following gentlemen as pall-bearers: Captain A. Cameron, Lieutenant Robinson (late chief justice of Canada), J. Edwards, Lieutenant Jarvis, Lieutenant Ridout, and Captain Crooks. The chief mourner was the brother of the deceased.

The body of General Brock followed, with the following pall-bearers: Mr. James Coffin, Captains Vigoreaux, Derenzy, Dennis, Holcroft, and Williams, Major Merritt, Lieutenant Colonels Clarke and Butler, and Colonel Claus, supported by Brigade Major Evans and Captain Glegg. The chief mourners were Major General Sheaffe, Ensign Coffin, Lieutenant Colonel Myers, and Lieutenant Fowler. These were followed by the civil staff, friends of the deceased, and the inhabitants.

General Brock had become greatly endeared to the Canadians. Gentlemanly deportment, kind and conciliating manners, and unrestrained benevolence were his prominent characteristics. He died unmarried, precisely a week after he had completed his forty-third year. His dignity of person has already been described. I have been unable, after diligent efforts, to obtain his portrait or his autograph. His contemporaries gave many tokens of respect to his memory after his death. "Canadian farmers," says Howison, in his *Sketches of Canada*, "are not overburdened with sensibility, yet I have seen several of them shed tears when a eulogium was pronounced upon the immortal and generous-minded deliverer of their country." The Prince Regent, in an official bulletin, spoke of his death as having been "sufficient to have clouded a victory of much greater importance." The muse was invoked in expressions of sympathy and sorrow. Among poetical effusions which the occasion elicited was the following, written by Miss Ann Bruyeres, "an extraordinary child of thirteen years old," the daughter of the general's warm friend, Lieutenant Colonel Bruyeres, of the Royal Engineers:

"As Fame alighted on the mountain's crest,
She loudly blew her trumpet's mighty blast;
Ere she repeated Victory's notes, she cast
A look around and stopped. Of power bereft,
Her bosom heaved, her breath she drew with pain,
Her favorite Brock lay slaughtered on the plain!
Glory threw on his grave a laurel wreath,
And Fame proclaims, 'A hero sleeps beneath.'"

Brock's biographer observes, in alluding to Fame being twice mentioned in the above lines, that it was singular that "the mournful intelligence of Sir Isaac Brock's death was brought from Quebec to Guernsey [his native country] by the ship *Fame*, belonging to that island, on the 24th of November, two days before it was known in London."—Tupper's *Life of Brock*, page 330.

By direction of a resolution of the House of Commons on the 20th of July, 1813, a military monument by Westmacott was erected to his memory in St. Paul's Cathedral, London, at a cost of nearly eight thousand dollars. It is in the western ambulatory of the south transept, and contains an effigy of the hero's body reclining in the arms of a British soldier, while an Indian pays the last tribute of respect. The monument bears the following inscription: "Erected, at the public expense, to the memory of MAJOR GENERAL SIR ISAAC BROCK, who gloriously fell on the 13th of October, MDCCCXII., in resisting an attack on Queenston, in Upper Canada." In addition to this, twelve thousand acres of land in Upper Canada were bestowed on the four surviving brothers of General Brock, and each were allowed a pension of one thousand dollars a year for life, by a vote of the British Parliament.

IN MEMORY OF GENERAL BROCK.

BROCK'S MONUMENT.

The Canadians could never seem to honor him enough. In 1816 they struck a small medal to his memory; and soon afterward steps were taken in the province to erect a suitable monument on Queenston Heights, not far from the spot where he fell. They raised a lofty Tuscan column, 135 feet in height from the base to the summit. The diameter of the base of the column was seventeen and a half feet. On the summit was a pedestal for a statue. Within was a spiral staircase around a central shaft. In the base was a tomb, in which the coffins containing the remains of Brock and M'Donell were deposited on the 13th of October, 1824. Their remains were conveyed from Fort George to their last resting-place in a hearse drawn by four black horses, followed by an immense military and civic procession, while artillery fired a salute of minute-guns. This monument stood, the pride of the Canadians, until the middle of April, 1840, when a miscreant named Lett, a fugitive from Canada, who had become implicated in the disturbances there in 1837 and 1838, attempted to destroy it with gunpowder. He succeeded in so injuring it that it became necessary to pull it down. A meeting was held on the Heights in July following, at which the late Sir Allan M'Nab made a stirring speech, when it was resolved to erect a new monument. It was estimated that eight thousand persons were present, and a salute was fired by the Royal Artillery. That meeting and the new monument will be considered in the next chapter.

Lovett on Lewiston Heights. Transfer of Colonel Van Rensselaer from Queenston to Albany. His Reception.

two commanders an opportunity for the exchange of those humane courtesies which should never be lost sight of amid the tumults of war.[1]

Let us turn back and consider for a moment what occurred on the American side in connection with the battle of Queenston. At Lewiston, Lovett,[2] as we have seen, was placed in charge of an eighteen-pounder in battery on the Heights,[3] where he performed good service in covering the party that crossed before daylight. It being dark, he stooped close to the gun to observe its aim, when it was discharged, and the concussion so injured his ears that he was much deaf ever afterward. Soon after this Colonel Van Rensselaer was brought over from the Canada shore with five bleeding wounds. He had been sick with fever, and had left his bed to attend to preparations for the invasion. The disease and his wounds so prostrated him that for several days his life was in extreme peril.[4] It was not until five days after the battle that he could be moved from Lewiston. Then a cot was rigged with cross-bars and side-poles, on which he was carried, on the 18th,[a] to Schlosser by a detachment of Major Moseby's militia riflemen. On the following day he was taken by the same party by land and water to Buffalo.[5] There he remained until the 9th of November,

* October, 1812.

and was then conveyed to his home at Mount Hope, near Albany, accompanied, as he had been since his removal from Lewiston, by Mr. Lovett. They were met in the suburbs of Albany by a cavalcade of citizens, and Van Rensselaer was received with the honors of a victor.[6]

---

[1] The correspondence between the generals may be found in Van Rensselaer's *Narrative*, already alluded to.

[2] John Lovett was a resident of Albany when the war broke out, and was a leading man in the profession of the law there. General Van Rensselaer, his early friend, invited him to become his aid and military secretary. "I am not a soldier," said Lovett. "It is not your *sword*, but your *pen* that I want," replied Van Rensselaer. Mr. Lovett was elected to a seat in Congress in 1813, when he renewed his acquaintance with Governor Meigs, and through his influence purchased a tract of land on the Maumee, and commenced a settlement which he named Perrysburg, in honor of the gallant hero of Lake Erie. There he resided, but he was early cut off by the prevailing fever of the country. He died at Fort Meigs in August, 1818, at the early age of fifty-two years. For a more extended sketch of Mr. Lovett's life, see *Reminiscences of Troy*, by John Woodworth.

[3] This battery was called Fort Gray, in honor of Nicholas Gray, acting engineer, under whose supervision it was arranged.

[4] Arad Joy, Esq., who was paymaster of Colonel Henry Bloom's regiment, and acting quartermaster on the day of the battle, wrote to me on the 15th of March, 1852, giving me an account of his experience on the Lewiston side of the river. He had charge of the wagons that conveyed the wounded to the hospital on the ridge road, two miles from the village. Of Van Rensselaer he says: "The loss of blood caused him to be chilly. He sat upon a board across the top of the wagon-box, without a groan; and as we met the soldiers going to the river to cross, he would call out at the top of his voice, 'Go on, my brave fellows, the day is our own.' It cheered up and encouraged them. He was taken to good quarters in a private house. The head surgeon, with his instruments, was along. We carried him into the house and seated him on a chair. His boots were filled with blood, which was gushing from his thigh, and plainly to be seen through his pantaloons. The boots, at Van Rensselaer's request, were cut from his feet."

[5] At Buffalo, on the 24th, Van Rensselaer used a pen for the first time since receiving his wounds, and wrote to his wife. That letter is before me. It is filled with expressions of gratitude toward General Van Rensselaer, and concludes by saying: "I congratulate you on the birth of our little boy. That this should have taken place on the same night I made the attack on the British is singular. He must be a soldier."

[6] Solomon Van Rensselaer was born in Greenbush, opposite Albany, in the old house known as the Garret mansion,

Events at the Mouth of the Niagara River.   Account of Fort Niagara.   Disposal of the American Prisoners.

While the stirring events at Queenston were in progress in the morning, there was a lively time at Forts George and Niagara.[1] So soon as Brock heard the state of affairs at Queenston, he sent down word to Brigade Major Evans, who had been left in charge of Fort George, to open a cannonade upon Fort Niagara. He did so, and received a sharp reply from the south block-house of the American fortress, which was in charge of Captain M'Keon. That officer turned his guns upon the village of Newark also when charged with hot shot, and several buildings were set on fire. The cannonade continued some time, when Evans, aided by Colonel Claus and Captain Vigoreux, of the Royal Engineers, opened a severe bombardment upon Fort Niagara. Already the bursting of a twelve-pounder had deprived the Americans of their best weapon. This fact, and the exposed condition of the fort under the attack of shells, caused Captain Leonard, the commandant of the garrison, to abandon it. The troops had not proceeded far when they observed British boats, filled with armed men, leaving the Canada shore for Fort Niagara, evidently with the intention of securing a lodgment there. M'Keon immediately returned with his little force, remained there unmolested over night, and was joined by the remainder of the garrison the next morning.

The American militia officers and privates captured at Queenston were paroled and sent across the river, but those of the regular army were detained as prisoners of war for exchange.[2] These were sent to Quebec, and from there, in a *cartel*,[3] to Boston, except twenty-three, who were claimed as British subjects, and were sent to England to be tried for treason.[4] The energetic action of Lieutenant Colonel Scott then and

---

in 1774. His father was a brave officer of the Revolution (Henry Killian Van Rensselaer), who was severely wounded in the thigh in a battle near Fort Ann in 1777. He was then a colonel. The bullet, which was not extracted until after his death, forty years later, is still in the possession of the family. It was flattened by striking the thigh bone. His son Solomon inherited his military disposition, and at the age of eighteen years entered the army under Wayne as a cornet of cavalry in the same battalion with the late President Harrison. He was promoted to the command of a troop [July 1, 1798] before he was twenty. He was shot through the lungs in the battle at the Rapids of the Miami or Maumee in August, 1794. In 1798, when war with France seemed inevitable, Washington sent for Van Rensselaer, inquired about the state of his wounds, and soon afterward [January, 1800] he was appointed a major of cavalry. When the army was disbanded he went into civil pursuits, but was called to the responsible post of Adjutant General of New York in January, 1801. He held that office when the war broke out, and at the solicitation of his uncle, General Van Rensselaer, he took a position on his staff. His services at Queenston have been recorded in the text. That event closed his military life, except as major general of the militia in 1819. Monroe appointed him post-master at Albany, and he held that position until removed by Van Buren. He was a delegate to the Whig Convention that nominated his friend Harrison for the presidency in 1839. Harrison reinstated him in the post-office at Albany, from which he was removed by John Tyler. He died at his residence at Cherry Hill, about a mile south of State Street, Albany, on the 24th of April, 1852, in the seventy-eighth year of his age. Cherry Hill is a most beautiful spot, westward of the rural extension of Pearl Street. It overlooks the Hudson, and commands a fine view of the country eastward of the river. I remember a visit to that mansion several years ago (then occupied by his daughters) with much pleasure. His residence during the war of 1812 was called Mount Hope, and is a little south of Cherry Hill.

[1] Fort Niagara was commenced as early as 1679, when La Salle, a French explorer, inclosed a small spot there with palisades. In 1687, De Nonville, a French commander, constructed a quadrangular fort there with four bastions. The Senecas attacked, a fatal disease followed, and the fort was abandoned. In 1725, the French, who still occupied the spot, built quite a strong fortification there. It was taken from them by Sir William Johnson, with a force of British and Indians, in 1759. It then covered about eight acres, having been enlarged and strengthened from time to time until it had become a regular fort of great resisting power. It never again passed into the hands of the French. During the Revolution it was the rendezvous of the Tories and Indians, who desolated Central New York, and sent predatory parties into Pennsylvania. "It was the head-quarters," says Deveaux, "of all that was barbarous, unrelenting, and cruel. There were congregated the leaders and chiefs of those bands of murderers and miscreants who carried death and desolation into the remote American settlements. There civilized Europe reveled with savage Americans, and ladies of education and refinement mingled in the society of those whose only distinction was to wield the bloody tomahawk and the scalping-knife. There the squaws of the forests were raised to eminence, and the most unholy unions between them and officers of highest rank smiled upon and countenanced. There, in the strong-hold, like a nest of vultures, securely for some years they sallied forth and preyed upon the distant settlements of the Mohawk and Susquehanna valleys. It was the dépôt of their plunder. There they planned their forays, and there they returned to feast until the time of action came again."—*Deveaux's Falls of Niagara*. Fort Niagara remained in possession of the British until 1796. It was then commanded by Colonel Smith, who led the British in the fight at Concord in 1775. It has been well observed that "Colonel Smith may with propriety be said to have participated in both the opening and closing acts of the American revolution."

[2] The following is a list of the regular officers who were surrendered: Colonel Scott, Lieutenant Colonels Christie and Fenwick (the former slightly, the latter badly wounded), Major Mullany, Captains Gibson, M'Chesney, and Ogilvie, Lieutenants Randolph, Kearney, Sammons, Hugunin, Fink, Carr, Turner, Totten, Bailey, Phelps, Clarke (wounded), and M'Carty, and Ensign Reeve.

[3] A cartel ship is a vessel commissioned in time of war to carry prisoners for exchange, or messages from one belligerent to another.

[4] At the beginning of the war the American prisoners were cruelly treated. Much testimony on the subject was collected by a committee of Congress, appointed for the purpose, in the summer of 1813. It was in evidence that when

afterward saved them from death. When the prisoners were about to sail from Quebec, a party of British officers came on board the *cartel*, mustered the captives, and commenced separating from the rest those who, by their accent, were found to be Irishmen. These they intended to send to England for trial as traitors in a frigate lying near, in accordance with the doctrine that a British subject can not expatriate himself.[1] Scott, who was below, hearing a tumult on deck, went up. He was soon informed of the cause, and at once entered a vehement protest against the proceedings. He commanded his soldiers to be absolutely silent, that their accent might not betray them. He was repeatedly ordered to go below, and as repeatedly refused. The soldiers obeyed him. Twenty-three had already been detected as Irishmen, but not another one became a victim. The twenty-three were taken on board the frigate in irons. Scott boldly assured them that if the British government dared to injure a hair of their heads, his own government would fully avenge the outrage. He at the same time as boldly defied the menacing officers, and comforted the manacled prisoners in every possible way. Scott was exchanged in January, 1813, and at once sent a full report of this affair to the Secretary of War. He hastened to Washington in person, and pressed the subject upon the attention of Congress. A bill was introduced to vest " the President of the United States with powers of retaliation."[2] It originated in the Senate, and would have passed both houses but for the conceded fact that such powers were already fully contained in the general constitutional powers of the President to conduct the war. Fortunately for the credit of common humanity, the President never had occasion to exercise that power to the extent of life-taking, for the British government wisely and prudently abstained from carrying out in practice, in the case of American prisoners, its cherished doctrine of perpetual allegiance.[3]

---

prisoners arrived at Plymouth they were sent to Mill prison for one day and night, and all the food allowed them " for the twenty-four hours were three small salt herrings, or about the same weight of salted codfish, or half a pound of beef, one and a half pounds of black bread, a little salt, etc." On the second day they were paroled, and sent twenty-four miles from Plymouth, at the expense of the prisoners, where they were allowed scarcely sufficient to drive starvation away. It was testified that the prisoners were kept in a half-starved state, it being " the policy of the British government," according to the memorial of "James Orne, Joseph B. Cook, Thomas Humphries, and others," as they solemnly believed, " to select the sickly to be first sent in cartels, and keep the hale and hardy seamen until they become sickly, thus rendering the whole of these gallant sons of Neptune who escape death, when they return to their homes, at least for some time, perfectly useless to themselves, and quite so to their country, from their debilitated state."

American prisoners were actually hired out in the British service, as appears by the following advertisement in a Jamaica paper:

"Port Royal, 25th Nov., 1812.

"Masters of vessels about to proceed to England with convoy are informed that they may be supplied with a limited number of American seamen (prisoners of war) to assist in navigating their vessels, on the usual terms, by applying to

"GEORGE MAUDE, *Agent*."

[1] See page 85.

[2] Only two months after the passage of the act, Scott himself, as commander in the capture of Fort George, selected from his prisoners twenty-three, to be confined in the interior of the country, to abide the fate of those sent to England from Quebec.

[3] The British government had a precedent not only in a notable case in its own history, but in the action of a neighboring nation. In the reign of Queen Elizabeth, Doctor Storey, a native of England, quitted his country and became a subject of Spain. He was received at the English Court as embassador from his adopted country. He was indicted in England for treason, when he pleaded his Spanish citizenship. It availed him nothing. His plea was overruled, and he was condemned and executed. Colonel Townley, an Englishman born, became naturalized in France, but on being seized while bearing arms against England, was executed for treason. The French decree of Trianon declared that no Frenchman could be naturalized abroad without the consent of the emperor, and that such that may be naturalized abroad without his consent could not bear arms against France. The American judiciary had also furnished a precedent. Isaac Williams, an American, received a lieutenant's commission from the French government in 1792, and served in the French navy. In 1799 he was tried before Chief Justice Ellsworth for having accepted a privateer's commission from the French Republic to commit acts of hostility against Great Britain, contrary to the laws of the United States and of the late treaty with Great Britain. The judge decided that the prisoner was a citizen of the United States, and that the emigration of a citizen implies no consent of the government that he should expatriate himself.—See Perkins's *History of the Political and Military Events of the Late War*, page 288. A farther notice of this subject, and the views of the government of the United States, expressed by Secretary Monroe, will be found in another portion of this work.—See Index.

The final result of Scott's humane and courageous conduct in this matter was very gratifying to himself. Almost three years after the event at Quebec he was greeted by loud huzzas as he was passing a wharf on the East River side of New York City. It came from a group of Irishmen who had just landed from an emigrant ship. They were twenty-one of the twenty-three prisoners for whom he had cared so tenderly. They had just returned after a long confinement in English prisons. They recognized their benefactor, and, says Scott's biographer, " nearly crushed him by their warm-hearted embraces."—Mansfield's *Life of Scott*.

Resignation of General Van Rensselaer.   Smyth his Successor.   Smyth's pompous Proclamations.

General Van Rensselaer was disgusted with the jealousies of some of the regular officers and the conduct of the militia. He was also convinced that the profession of arms was not the sphere in which he would be most useful. On the 24th of October he resigned the command of the troops on the Niagara frontier to General Smyth, and soon afterward obtained from Governor Tompkins permission to leave the service.[1] Smyth's pride was gratified, and it was soon displayed in a series of pompous proclamations, which created both merriment and disgust. He promised so largely and performed so little that he became the target for ridicule and satire by all parties. In his first proclamation, issued on the 10th of November, he displayed a lack of common courtesy and good taste by offensive reflections upon Generals Hull and Van Rensselaer.[2] "One army," he said, "has been disgracefully surrendered and lost. Another has been sacrificed by a precipitate attempt to pass it over at the strongest point of the enemy's lines with most incompetent means. The cause of these miscarriages is apparent. The commanders were popular men, destitute alike of theory and experience in the art of war." "In a few days," he continued, "the troops under my command will plant the American standard in Canada. They are men accustomed to obedience, silence, and steadiness. They will conquer or they will die. Will you stand with your arms folded and look on this interesting struggle? . . . . . . Must I turn from you, and ask men of the Six Nations to support the government of the United States? Shall I imitate the officers of the British king, and suffer our ungathered laurels to be tarnished by ruthless deeds?[3] Shame, where is thy blush? No. Where I command, the vanquished and the peaceful man, the child, the maid, and the matron, shall be secure from wrong. The present is the hour for renown. Have you not a wish for fame? Would you not choose in future times to be named as one of those who, imitating the heroes whom Montgomery led, have, in spite of the seasons, visited the tomb of the chief, and conquered the country where he lies?"

[1] General Van Rensselaer reached Albany on Saturday morning, the 31st of October, when he was honored by a public reception. On the 30th the Common Council of Albany appointed three of their members, namely, Teunis Van Vechten, Isaac Hansen, and Peter Boyd, a committee for the purpose. These on the same day issued a little handbill, calling upon the people to meet at the public square the next morning at eight o'clock. The committee also recommended that such "as are accommodated with horses or carriages to repair to the house of Widow Douw, on the Albany and Schenectady turnpike, for the purpose of escorting Major General Van Rensselaer to his mansion-house; and the residue of the citizens are requested to proceed to the hay-scales, and there join the escort." The reception was imposing, and highly gratifying to the general. Two days afterward he received a letter from the debtors in the Albany jail, who had experienced his bounty, congratulating him on his return.

[2] "I take the liberty," wrote a correspondent of General Van Rensselaer from Geneseo, "to inclose you a copy of a handbill from General Smyth, which was circulated yesterday and the day before about Batavia. As far as I have been able to observe, *men of all parties* unite in reprobating the attack he makes upon other commanders. I suspect, indeed, that the attack is the main, *real object of the handbill*." Autograph Letter of Samuel M. Hopkins, November 14, 1812.

[3] Soon after the commencement of hostilities it was rumored at Buffalo that the British had taken possession of Grand Island, in the Niagara River, which belonged to the Senecas, one of the Six Nations. Red Jacket, the chief of the Senecas, called the nation to a council, and thereat a desire was expressed to go and drive the invaders off. At a subsequent council, where there was a large attendance of the nation, a formal declaration of war against the Canadas was made in these words:

"We, the chiefs and councilors of the Six Nations of Indians, residing in the State of New York, do hereby proclaim to all the war-chiefs and warriors of the Six Nations that war is declared on our part against the provinces of Upper and Lower Canada. Therefore we hereby command and advise all the war-chiefs and warriors of the Six Nations to call forth immediately the warriors under them, and put them in motion to protect their rights and liberties, which our brethren, the Americans, are now defending."*

This is believed to have been the first Indian declaration of war ever committed to writing. Although the services of the Indians were offered to General Smyth, he declined them, because the government of the United States, acting in the interest of common humanity, had resolved not to employ the savages in the war unless compelled to.

* Alluding to this council, Mr. Lovett, General Van Rensselaer's military secretary, then in attendance at Buffalo on Colonel Solomon Van Rensselaer, said: "The spirit of insubordination seems to have worked its way among the sons of Belial, our red brethren. Without the leave or knowledge of Mr. Granger [the Indian Superintendent], they have had a great council back in the bush. To purge away this horrid sin of disobedience, Mr. G., the good Moses of these shabby Israelites, ordered them to tread back their steps unsanctified by his behests, and to cast to the wind the wampum, and the belts, and all the records of their abominable council, and to repair, one and all, before the high-priest of the temple at Buffalo, to have their souls scrubbed from all political sins. The day before yesterday hither they came—sachems, chiefs, and warriors—old and young, squaws and pappooses—with all of intermediate grades. Such a thorough shaking of the beggar-bag of poor motley human nature I never before saw. With great humility all confessed their sins, received absolution, and washed their souls in whisky. All got drunk, wallowed all night in the mud, and the next day went home to their wigwams pure and humble, chanting the praises of Moses."—Autograph Letter to General Van Rensselaer, November 6, 1812.

Smyth and his Proclamations ridiculed.

In another proclamation he said: "Companions in arms! the time is at hand when you will cross the stream of Niagara to conquer Canada, and to secure the peace of the American frontier. You will enter a country that is to be one of the United States. . . . . Whatever is booty by the usages of war shall be yours." He offered two hundred dollars apiece for horses for artillery that might be captured. He then boasted of the superiority of the American soldiers and weapons, and unnecessarily offended the Federalists, many of whom were in the ranks, by saying to the volunteers, "Disloyal and traitorous men have endeavored to dissuade you from doing your duty." In his address to "The Army of the Centre," as he called the little force under his command, he said: "Soldiers of every corps! it is in your power to retrieve the honor of your country, and to cover yourselves with glory. Every man who performs a gallant action shall have his name made known to the nation. Rewards and honors await the brave, infamy and contempt are reserved for cowards. Companions in arms! you come to vanquish a valiant foe. I know the choice you will make. Come on, my heroes! and when you attack the enemy's batteries, let your rallying-word be, 'The cannon lost at Detroit, or death!'"[1]

When these proclamations in quick succession appeared, the general's friends smiled, the enemy laughed, and the Opposition press teemed with squibs and epigrams. He was called "Alexander the Great," "Napoleon the Second," etc. A wag in the *New York Evening Post* wrote of "General Smyth's Bulletin No. 2:"

> "Just so! (and every wiser head
> The likeness can discover)
> We put a *chestnut* in the fire,
> And pull the embers over;
> A while it waxes hot and hotter,
> And eke begins to hop,
> And after much confounded pother,
> Explodes a mighty *Pop!!!*"

General Smyth's invasion of Canada will be noticed presently.

---

[1] General Smyth's magniloquence was equaled only by Ross Bird's, a captain of the Third United States Infantry, who, in great indignation because of some offense, offered to resign his commission. His letter closed with the following words: "In leaving the service I am not abandoning the cause of Republicanism, but yet hope to brandish the glittering steel in the field, and carve my way to a name which shall prove my country's neglect; and when this mortal shall be closeted in the dust, and the soul shall wing its flight to the regions above, in passing by the pale-faced moon I shall hang my hat on brilliant Mars, and make a report to each superlative star, and, arriving at the portals of heaven's high chancery, shall demand of the attending angel to be ushered into the presence of Washington!

"Ross Bird, Captain.

"Washington, September 13, 1813.
"*To Lieutenant Colonel C. C. Russell.*"

Captain Bird had been in the army as early as 1791, and had lately been promoted to major of infantry in the new army.

CHAPTER XX.

"Alas for them! their day is o'er,
Their fires are out from shore to shore;
No more for them the wild deer bounds—
The plow is on their hunting-grounds."
CHARLES SPRAGUE.

AT the middle of August, 1860, I visited the theatre of events described in the preceding chapter. I went down to Niagara Falls from Buffalo in a railway train on the afternoon of the 16th. A violent thunder-storm greeted our arrival at five o'clock. As business, not pleasure, was my errand to that great gathering-place of the fashionable and of tourists in summer, I rode to the northern part of the village, and took lodgings at the quiet "Niagara House," where I found room in abundance in chamber and at table. On the following morning, accompanied by the late Colonel P. A. Porter, then a resident of Niagara Falls village, I crossed the suspension bridge, rode up the western bank of the river to Street's Creek, opposite Navy Island, and visited the battle-ground of Chippewa with Colonel Cummings, a surviving aid of the British general Riall, who commanded in that engagement. Of that visit and its results I shall write hereafter.

I returned to the *Niagara House* in time for dinner, and at four o'clock started in an old, dusty light wagon, with a jaded horse, for Lewiston, seven miles down the river. It was at an hour when every body was on the road, and every horse and vehicle were employed. I was left without choice, and felt thankful that I was not compelled to go afoot. The driver was a rather rough-cast boy of sixteen years, with a freckled face, a turned-up nose, a mischievous gray eye, sandy hair, and rather intelligent, but uneducated. The horse seemed tipsy as well as tired, for he was constantly leaving the right lines of the highway. His coat was an uncertain brick color, and rough; the harness had dotted him with black bare spots; his tail and mane were thin and frizzled; one of his ears drooped, and his gait, at best, was decidedly "gawky." I was anxious to reach Lewiston in time to cross the suspension bridge to Queenston, and visit places of interest there before sunset, and at the start the boy commenced lashing the beast unmercifully. I remonstrated. "Hain't ye in a hurry?" he asked. "Yes, but you shall not torture the poor horse in that way," I replied. Such mercy surprised him. "Why, darn it," he said, impatiently, "I'm so used to whippin' I can't help it. I never knowed a man afore who cared a whip-snap for a hired hoss. He is lazy, mister—lazy," and he gave the poor animal another severe stroke. So inveterate was the boy's cruel habit that he would not relinquish it until I took the whip from him, and threatened to leave him by the road side. Even then he would rise occasionally and kick the horse; harmlessly, however, for his toes were ambitiously getting ahead of his shoes.

We jogged on at a fair rate of speed, and met numerous "turn-outs" superior to our own, of which we were not specially proud. Among them was a jaunty little wagon and a span of black ponies, driven at full speed by the owner, the wife of a New York city editor. Her establishment was the "observed of all observers," but we were not jealous; indeed, all thoughts of the road and its frequenters soon faded when, at five o'clock, we reached the brow of Lewiston Heights and beheld the magnificent panorama before us. At the turn of the road, where it descends the Heights, I alighted, and from the site of Fort Gray,[1] now marked by slight mounds, I obtained a view of land and water both grand and beautiful. On the left was seen Queenston Heights, on which stands the new monument erected to the memory of General Brock. At their base lay the village of Queenston. Farther westward a glimpse of St. David's was obtained; and northwestward, as far as the eye could reach, the level country was dotted with woods and well-cultivated farms. At our feet lay the village of Lewiston; and stretching away to the northeast was the vast plain, much of it covered with the primeval forest. In the centre was the glittering line of the blue Niagara River. Near its mouth the eye could discern the spires of Niagara (old Newark), on the Canada side, and the village of Youngstown, with the mass of old Fort Niagara beyond, on the American side. The whole horizon northward was bounded by the dark line of Lake Ontario, over which was brooding a thunder-storm, flashing fire and bellowing angrily as it moved sullenly eastward.

Leaving this grand observatory with reluctance, we made our way down the sinuous road to Lewiston, every where meeting, in the descent, geological evidences that this bank was the shore of an ancient lake when the Falls of Niagara were doubtless at this place, and that the plain on which the village stands was its bed. The ridge is composed of sand and gravel, and the usual *débris* thrown up by a large body of water in character essentially different from the surrounding surface. The summit of the Heights is here thirty-four feet above the level of Lake Erie.[2]

We passed through Lewiston[3] (a village of about one thousand souls, very pleasantly situated) without halting, and crossed the Niagara River to Queenston, over the suspension bridge, a magnificent structure, with a roadway eight hundred and fifty feet in length, twenty feet in width, and sixty feet above the water.[4] We were at Wadsworth's Tavern, in Queenston, and had engaged lodgings for the night before six o'clock; and we immediately rode from there up the Heights to Brock's Monument, near the summit. A short distance above the residence of David Thorburn, Esq. (then the superintendent of the Six Nations of Indians in Canada), at the turn of the road from the highway to the Falls, well up the acclivity, we passed a burying-ground which marks the site of the redan battery.[5] Soon after passing this, we came to the eastern entrance to the monument grounds (about forty acres in extent), and the lodge of the keeper, George Playter, a loyal old man, whose kind courtesies I remember with pleasure. The gate is of wrought iron, highly ornamented, with cut-stone piers surmounted with the arms of the hero. The lodge is also of cut stone. From the entrance an easy carriage-way winds up the hill to an avenue one hundred feet wide, which terminates at the monument in a circle one hundred and eighty feet in diameter.

---

[1] See note 3, page 407.

[2] Lake Ontario is 334 feet lower than Lake Erie. The current of the Niagara River that connects them is not very rapid above Schlosser and below Lewiston, and the river makes nearly the whole of that descent in the space of nine miles. It falls perpendicularly at the great cataracts, 154 feet on the Canada side of Goat Island, and 163 feet on the American side. It is supposed that the river originally flowed over the face of the precipice at Lewiston. By the gradual wearing away of the rocks in the lapse of ages, the Falls have receded seven miles, becoming continually lower. "The precipice over which the present Falls flow is composed of solid limestone, with shale above and below. The wearing away of the shale above has formed the Rapids, and the disintegration of that below has left the limestone in overhanging masses until they break off with their own weight."—French's *Gazetteer of the State of New York*.

[3] Lewiston was so named in honor of Morgan Lewis, who was an officer in the Revolution, and governor of the State of New York in 1804.

[4] This bridge was destroyed by a gale of wind at the close of 1863. Fortunately no life was lost. The *Lockport Journal* relates the following incident in connection with its destruction: "During the day upon which the Lewiston bridge was carried off by the wind, a boy, whose parents reside in Canada, but is at work in Lewiston, went over to Canada on a short visit to his parents. Just before the bridge went down, the boy proposed starting for his place of business in Lewiston. His father accompanied him. As they reached the bridge it was swaying to and fro over the boiling waters far beneath. The boy hesitated a moment, but, as this motion of the bridge was not unusual, he stepped upon it, his father still with him, and proceeded to cross. They both went to about the middle, when the rapid and unusual motion of the bridge greatly increased their fear. The father turned about, and the boy went on, both running at their fastest speed for the opposite shore. They had just time to reach the shore on each side before the structure was borne away."

[5] See page 398.

The monument is built of the limestone of the Heights, quarried near the spot. It is placed upon a slightly-raised platform within a dwarf-walled inclosure, seventy-five feet square, with a *fosse* around the interior. At each angle of this inclosure is placed massive military trophies, wrought out of the same stone as that of the monument, and about twenty feet in height. The monument is built upon a foundation of wrought stone forty feet square and ten feet thick, resting upon the solid rock of the mountain. Upon this stands, in a grooved plinth, a basement, thirty-eight feet square and twenty-seven feet in height, under which, in heavy stone sarcophagi, are the remains of General Brock and Lieutenant Colonel M'Donell. On the exterior angles of this basement are placed well-carved lions rampant, seven feet in height, supporting shields with the armorial bearings of the hero. On the north side of this basement is an inscription in bold letters,[1] and upon brass plates in the interior of the column are epitaphic inscriptions.[2]

Upon the basement is the pedestal of the column, little more than sixteen feet square, and just thirty-eight feet in height. Upon a panel on each of three sides of this pedestal is an emblem in low relief, and on the north side, facing Queenston, is a representation of a battle scene in high relief, in which Brock is represented at the head of his troops, wounded.

The column is of the Roman composite order, ninety-five feet in height. The shaft is fluted, and is ten feet in diameter at its base, with an enriched plinth, on which are carved the heads of lions and wreaths in bold relief. The flutes terminate in palms. The capital of

BROCK'S MONUMENT ON QUEENSTON HEIGHTS.

---

[1] The following is a copy of the inscription:

"UPPER CANADA has dedicated this monument to the memory of the late MAJOR GENERAL SIR ISAAC BROCK, K.B., Provincial Lieutenant Governor and Commander of the Forces in this Province, whose remains are deposited in the vault beneath. Opposing the invading enemy, he fell in action near these Heights on the 13th of October, 1812, in the forty-third year of his age. Revered and lamented by the people whom he governed, and deplored by the sovereign to whose service his life had been devoted."

[2] On one plate is the following:

"In a vault underneath are deposited the mortal remains of MAJOR GENERAL SIR ISAAC BROCK, K.B., who fell in action near these Heights on 13th October, 1812, and was entombed on the 16th of October at the bastion of Fort George, Niagara, removed from thence, and reinterred under a monument to the eastward of this site, on the 13th October, 1824; and, in consequence of that monument having received irreparable injury by a lawless act on the 17th of April, 1840, it was found requisite to take down the former structure and erect this monument; the foundation-stone being laid, and the remains again reinterred with due solemnity, on 13th October, 1853."

The other plate has the following inscription:

"In a vault beneath are deposited the mortal remains of Lieutenant Colonel JOHN M'DONELL, P.A.D.C., and Aid-de-camp to the lamented MAJOR GENERAL SIR ISAAC BROCK, K.B., who fell mortally wounded in the battle of Queenston, on the 13th October, 1812, and died on the following day. His remains were removed and reinterred with due solemnity, on 13th October, 1853."

the column is sixteen feet square, and twelve feet six inches in height. On each face is sculptured a figure of Victory, ten feet six inches in height, with extended arms grasping military shields as volutes. The acanthus and palm leaves are enwreathed in antique style. From the ground to the gallery at the top of the column is a spiral staircase of cut stone, comprising two hundred and thirty-five steps, lighted by loopholes in the flutings of the column. On the abacus is a cippus upon which stands a statue of BROCK, in military costume, seventeen feet in height, the left hand resting on a sword, and the right arm extended with a baton.[1] This monumental column is exceeded in height by only one of a similar character in the world. That is the one erected by Sir Christopher Wren, in London, to commemorate the great fire that desolated that city in 1666. It is only twelve feet higher than Brock's.[2]

It was sunset when I completed the sketch of the monument, in which is included a distant view of Lewiston Heights, seen on the right, and the village of Lewiston and the plain beyond, seen on the left. Heavy clouds rolling up from the west, and rumbling thunder in the distance, gave warning of an approaching storm. This fact and the lateness of the hour prevented my ascending the shaft to obtain the magnificent panoramic view from its summit, from which, it is said, small villages may be seen southward, the battle-ground of Lundy's Lane or Niagara, the white spray from the cataract, and the turmoil of the great whirlpool, in addition to the vast stretch of land and water seen at other parts of the compass.

We made our way down the Heights to the village just in time to avoid the storm which fell simultaneously with the darkness. It was severe, but short. The stars were visible soon after it passed by, and I found my way to the house of Mr. Joseph Winn, on the road to the suspension bridge. He was an old resident of Queenston, and familiar with every locality there connected with the battle, although he was not in the engagement. He kindly offered to be my guide in the morning. The night was a tempestuous one, but the sky was cloudless at dawn. At an early hour I visited the landing-place of the Americans near the suspension bridge, and made the sketch printed on page 395. I then followed the high bank of the river some distance, and made my way to the stone building in which the British took refuge after being repulsed by Wool;[3] but the sketch I then made was lost a few days afterward.

---

[1] This monument was designed by W. Thomas, Esq., of Toronto, and was erected under his superintendence. The contractor was Mr. J. Worthington.

[2] We have observed that a former monument to the memory of Brock was shattered by powder in 1840. The act produced the greatest indignation throughout Canada. A meeting was held on Queenston Heights in June following, composed of about eight thousand people. One of the most active men on that occasion was the late Sir Allan M'Nab. There was a military parade and salutes with artillery. In Toronto the day was observed as a solemn holiday. All the public offices were closed, and business was generally suspended. Delegations and crowds of citizens flocked to Queenston from Kingston, Toronto, Cobourg, and Hamilton. The lieutenant governor, Sir George Arthur, and his staff, were there. Sir George presided. He addressed the meeting. Chief Justice Robinson, Sir Allan M'Nab, and several others, also made speeches. A number of Brock's surviving soldiers were also present. Resolutions were passed ; and when the public proceedings were ended, six hundred persons sat down to a dinner under a pavilion erected on the spot where the hero fell, at which Chief Justice Robinson presided. The result of the affair was the formation of a building committee for the erection of a new monument, of which Sir Allan M'Nab was chairman.* The money for the purpose was raised by the voluntary subscriptions of the militia and Indian warriors of the province. A grant from the Provincial Parliament enabled the committee to lay out the grounds, and erect the gate and keeper's lodge. The foundation-stone was laid on the 13th of October, 1853, and on the same day the remains of Brock and M'Donell were reinterred with imposing ceremonies. The day was very fine. There were pall-bearers and chief mourners.† When the remains were deposited in their last resting-place, the corner-stone was laid by Lieutenant Colonel M'Donell, brother of one of the dead heroes. The late Honorable William Hamilton Merritt, M.P., delivered an address, in which he spoke highly of the character and services of the Indians in the War of 1812. Mr. Thorburn, Indian agent, responded in their behalf, and read an address from the chiefs present, which breathed sentiments of loyalty and affection for the English queen. As a mark of respect, an American steam-boat at Lewiston lowered its flag to half mast.

[3] See page 398.

---

* The following named gentlemen constituted that committee : Sir Allan M'Nab, M.P. ; Chief Justice Sir John Brush Robinson ; Honorable Mr. Justice M'Lean ; Honorable Walter H. Dickson, M.L.C. ; Honorable William Hamilton Merritt, M.P. ; Honorable Thomas Clark Street, M.P. ; Colonel James Kerby ; Colonel John M'Dougal ; David Thorburn, Esq. ; Lieutenant Garrett ; Colonel Robert Hamilton ; and Captain H. Munro.

† The pall-bearers were Colonels E. W. Thompson, W. Thompson, Duggan, Stanton, Kerby, Crooks, Zimmerman, Caron, Thorne, Servos, Clark, Wakefield, and Miller. Among the chief mourners were Colonel Donald M'Donell, the deputy adjutant general for Canada East, Colonel Taché, Lieutenant Colonel Irvine, the survivors of 1812, and the chiefs of the Six Nations.

From the river I went up the Heights to the site of the *redan*, and then to the point where the Americans were crowded to the verge of the precipice. This was accomplished before breakfast.

When I came out of the dining-room at Wadsworth's, I found the venerable Major Adam Brown in the little parlor. He was a native of Queenston. At the time of the battle he was a lieutenant in the 1st Battalion of the Lincoln Militia under Colonel Claus, then at Fort George, and was not in the engagement. He was in command of a hundred men at the battle of Niagara (Lundy's Lane), and was in active service during a greater part of the war. While I was writing some memoranda of his conversation in my note-book, he spoke to a person behind me whom I had not noticed, and asked, "Were you the chief who was with the Indians at the dedication of the monument?" "I was, sir," replied a pleasant voice. I turned and observed a fine-looking, dark-complexioned, well-dressed man, whose features and expression revealed traces of the Indian race. We both arose at the same moment. I introduced myself and inquired his name. He informed me that he was George Henry Martin Johnson, a descendant, in the fourth generation, of Sir William Johnson, of the Mohawk Valley, and now *Tekarihogea*, or commander-in-chief of the Six Nations of Indians in Canada, his father having been the official successor of John Brant. To me this meeting was interesting and fortunate. I intended to visit the settlements of the Six Nations, on the Grand River, during this tour, but was doubtful concerning the best route, and the most important place for obtaining desired information. All was now plain, and, before we parted, arrangements were made for Mr. Johnson to meet me at Brantford a few days later.

On the day of my arrival at Queenston, a committee, appointed for the purpose, had decided upon the exact spot where Brock fell. I visited it in company with Major Brown. A space sixty feet square, within which was to be placed a memorial-stone, had been staked out, and in the centre, the very spot, as the committee supposed, where the hero fell, was marked.[1] As early as 1821, John Howison, in his *Sketches of Upper Canada*, had said, "General Brock was killed close to the road that leads through Queenston village, and an aged thorn-bush now marks the place where he fell when the fatal ball entered his vitals." The spot marked by the committee is about twenty rods west of the "road that leads through Queenston," and a little eastward of the "aged thorn-bush," which had become a tree twenty feet in height, with two large stems, when I saw it. Near the site a workman was fashioning the blocks of freestone of which the monument was to be composed, and from him I obtained a sketch of it. After making

MONUMENT WHERE BROCK FELL.

---

[1] I was told that some old residents of the village declared that the place where Brock fell was westward of the thorn-tree, and at least twenty paces from the spot selected. James Cooper, a blacksmith, who was within six feet of Brock when he fell, said it was west of the thorn-tree; and Henry Stone, who lived in the stone house near the field, declared that he saw the blood of Brock on rocks west of the tree.

a drawing of the spot, showing the old thorn-tree on the right, and the stately monument on the Heights in the distance, I introduced, in proper place and proportions, the sketch of the memorial-stone to mark the place which Howison said " may be called classic ground." It is a small affair, being only about four feet in height. The ground around it was to be inclosed in an iron railing. The Prince of Wales (Albert Edward) was at that time[a] making a tour in Canada, receiving tokens of loyalty every where. He visited Queenston very soon after I was there, and laid the corner-stone of the little monument with imposing ceremonies.[1]

[a] August, 1860.

I left Queenston for Niagara at about nine o'clock, after riding to the point in the northern part of the village where the " old fort," or barracks, were situated, near the residence of Mr. E. Clements, of the Customs. We immediately passed a creek and deep ravine, and soon came to the first brick house below Queenston, on the left of the road, the residence of the venerable Solomon Vrooman, pleasantly situated, and surrounded by evidences of the highest and most thrifty cultivation. He was the owner of the point on which the battery bearing his name was situated,[2] and participated in the battle by assisting in manning the nine-pounder that was mounted there. I called to see him, and spent half an hour with him most agreeably. He was a slender man, seventy-six years of age. His native place was in the Mohawk Valley, but he had lived in Canada since the days of his young manhood. He went with me to the spot where the battery was, and pointed out the very prominent mounds that yet remain, near a barn, from which I made the sketch printed on page 391. He told me that one hundred and sixty shot were thrown from that battery during the day, wholly for the purpose of obstructing the passage of the river by the Americans.[3] Its range of the old ferry and the new crossing-place at the present suspension bridge was point-blank and effectual. On one occasion during the afternoon, some Americans, trying to escape from Queenston by swimming the river, were brought by the current within rifle-shot distance of the battery, when one of the men in his company raised his piece to fire. Vrooman knocked up the piece, exclaiming indignantly, " Shame on you! none but a coward would fire upon men thus struggling for their lives!"

Solomon Vrooman

The road from Vrooman's to Niagara was one of the most delightful that I had ever traveled. Most of the way it skirted the high bank of the winding river, which was covered with stately trees, through which continual glimpses of the American shore could be obtained. Landward were seen broad fields, from which bountiful harvests were pouring into barns, or green waving Indian corn, or numerous orchards, whose trees were so heavily laden with fruit that they drooped like weeping willows. As we approached Niagara we passed through first an aromatic pine grove, and then a narrow forest of oaks, beeches, maples, and evergreens, and emerged upon an open plain, the property of the government, with the mounds of abandoned Fort George,

---

[1] The Prince of Wales arrived at Queenston on the 17th of September, and on the following day he laid the corner-stone of the little monument. Near the spot was erected a triumphal arch, on which, in large letters, were the words "VICTORIA—WELCOME." The veterans of 1812, who were present, formed a guard of honor for the young prince. In the background were the St. Catharine's Riflemen with a brass band. A silver trowel was presented to the prince with which to perform the ceremony. Upon it was engraved the following inscription: "Presented to His Royal Highness ALBERT EDWARD, Prince of Wales, by the Brock Monument Committee, on Queenston Heights, 18th September, 1860." On one side of the monument was placed the following inscription: "This stone was placed by his Royal Highness ALBERT EDWARD, Prince of Wales, on the 18th of September, 1860." On the other side, "Near this spot Sir Isaac Brock, K.B., Provisional Lieutenant Governor of Upper Canada, fell on the 13th of October, 1812, while advancing to repel the invasion of the enemy."   [2] See Map on page 382.

[3] The battery was crescent-shaped. Engineer Gray, in his manuscript report now before me, thus describes it: "It is built *en barbette* (that is, without embrasures), and has a high breastwork to the river. On the north, a frame house, intended for a barn; on the west is a gun, mounted *en barbette* (on the top of the breastwork), and flanked by the skeleton of a house. Within five rods of this runs the highway to Fort George."

on the bank of the river, breaking the monotony of the level far to the right. There were no fences to obstruct the view or the travel on the plain. Cattle were feeding on the short grass, and here and there a footman or a horseman might be seen. We turned out of the beaten road to the right, and drove across the plain to one of the angles of the fort. There I left horse and driver, clambered up the steep grassy sides of the embankment, and commenced a hasty exploration of the interior of the fort. The breastworks in all directions were quite perfect, and the entire form of the fort could be traced without difficulty. There were two or three houses within the works, and the parade and other portions were devoted to the cultivation of garden vegetables.

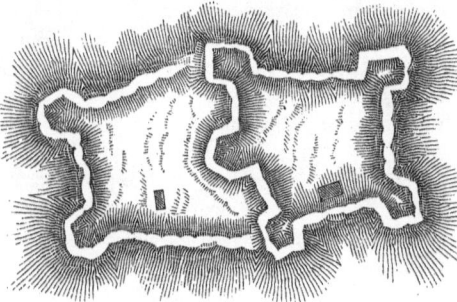

PRESENT OUTLINES OF FORT GEORGE.

In the most southerly part of the fort, about three hundred yards from the river, is an old powder magazine, built by the French within a stockade. It was occupied as a dwelling by the family of an English soldier named Lee when I was there in 1860. The higher building seen in the picture is the old magazine. It was covered with slate, and its walls, four and a half feet thick, were supported by three buttresses on each side.

FRENCH MAGAZINE AT FORT GEORGE.

The buildings on the left are more modern. The interior of the magazine is arched, and the doors were originally covered with plates of copper fastened by copper nails.

Mrs. Lee was an intelligent woman, very communicative, and free in the dispensation of the hospitalities of her humble abode. We were refreshed with cakes, harvest-apples, and cold spring-water. She filled a small basket with copper coins and other relics, and as I parted with her she wished me good luck in my journeyings. I clambered over an irregular and steep bank northward of the old magazine, visited the site of the "cavalier battery" where Brock and M'Donell were buried, and sketched the "new magazine," erected by the British in 1812, delineated on page 405. It is of brick. Near it was a small house occupied by an Irish family, and the magazine was used as a pig-sty.

From Fort George we rode to Niagara, half a mile below, halted long enough to obtain refreshments for ourselves and the horse, and then rode out over the garrison reservation, northeastward of the town, to Fort Mississaga,[1] a strong earth-work with a castle, which was constructed by the British during the war of 1812. Cattle were grazing upon the plain; the waters of Lake Ontario, ruffled by a breeze, were sparkling in the distance, and the whole scene was one of quiet and repose. Such, indeed, is

---

[1] *Mississaga* or *Massasauga* is the Indian name of a small black or dark brown rattlesnake, twelve or fourteen inches in length, which usually inhabits tamarack and cranberry swamps in Northwestern Ohio and Canada West. This is the name of an Indian tribe; also of a large stream in Canada West that empties into Lake Huron. In the little view of Fort Mississaga given on the next page, Fort Niagara is seen on the right in the distance, and Lake Ontario on the west.

the impression on the mind in Canada, as compared with "the States." The turmoil and bustle that marks an American population in large or small numbers, was but slightly manifested there. I found apparent stagnation in Queenston; and Niagara, though a fine

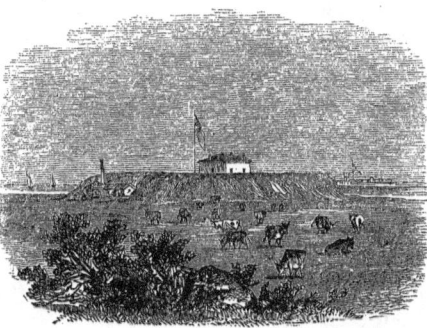
DISTANT VIEW OF FORT MISSISSAGA.

and pleasant town in appearance, with a population of about twenty-five hundred, seemed to be reposing in almost perfect rest. It was formerly called Newark, and the present city occupies the site of the little village which the Americans destroyed in 1813. It was one of the oldest towns in the province, having been settled by Colonel Simcoe when he was the lieutenant governor.[a] It was a place of considerable trade before the opening of the Welland Canal, about thirty years ago, and is now, as then, the capital of the Niagara District.

[a] 1791.

We found the gate of Fort Mississaga wide open, and walked in without leave.

INTERIOR VIEW—FORT MISSISSAGA IN 1860.

Not a human face was visible. I went up to and around the ramparts, and, taking a position over the entrance-gate, from which I could see most of the interior and Fort Niagara beyond, I sketched the scene. In this view are seen the barracks and the castle, with Fort Niagara across the river in the extreme distance. The castle is built of brick. The walls are eight feet in thickness, and covered with stucco. While engaged with the sketch I was startled by a voice near me. It was that of the whole garrison, comprised in the person of Patrick Burns, who told me to make as many sketches as I pleased, for the fort was uninhabited except by his own family.

At an early hour we started on our return to Niagara Falls. I attempted to drive, but soon became discouraged by the eccentric movements of the horse, when the boy told me for the first time that he was "as blind as a bat." But I have no reason to complain of the animal, for he carried us back in safety, and in time for dinner and for departure by the evening train for the West. Having placed my luggage in charge of a proper person at the suspension bridge station, I crossed that marvelous hanging viaduct on foot, along the carriage-road under the railway gallery, with my satchel in hand. As I left the bridge to ascend to the station on the Canada shore I was hailed by a custom-house officer, of whose business I had not the least suspicion until informed by him. Believing my assurance that the satchel contained nothing contraband, he allowed me to pass, after I had expressed a wish, good-naturedly, that the United States might soon be annexed to Canada, so that revenue officers might be allowed to engage in some other employment.

On entering the cars on the Canada side I met Chief Johnson. We traveled together as far as St. Catharine, eleven miles, where I intended to spend a day or two, and agreed upon the time when we should meet at Brantford. The impressions made by the time spent at St. Catharine, the persons I met at that famous gathering of invalids around a mineral spring, a visit to the battle-ground of the Beaver Dams, the journey to Hamilton, and a ride to Stony Creek, a place made famous in the annals of the war we are now considering by a conflict and the capture of two American generals, are always summoned by memory with great pleasure. Of these I shall hereafter write.

On Tuesday evening, the 20th of August, I arrived at Hamilton, at the head of Lake Ontario, by the Great Western Railway, and spent the night at the "Royal Hotel." Early on the following morning I rode out to Stony Creek, seven miles, and returned in time to take the cars at meridian for Paris in company with a young Quadroon chief of the Six Nations, named M'Murray, whose mother, wife of the Reverend Dr. M'Murray, of Niagara, was a half-breed Indian woman, and sister to the first wife of H. R. Schoolcraft, Esq. He was one of the finest formed and most attractive young men, in person and feature, I have ever met.

The road from Hamilton to Paris, nearly thirty miles, passes through a very picturesque country. For five miles it skirts the northern high bank of the great marsh that extends from Burlington Bay to Dundas, and follows, a greater portion of the way, a line parallel with Dundas Street, or the Governor's Road. At Paris,[1] a large town, situated partly on a high rolling plain, and partly in a deep valley, on Smith's Creek and the Grand River, I left the Great Western Railway, and took passage for Brantford, seven miles southward, on the Buffalo and Huron Road, which here intersects it. The country was hilly most of the way, but at Brantford it spreads out into a beautiful plain, or high gravelly ridge, overhanging an extensive and well-cultivated region. The town derives its name from the great Mohawk[2] chief, the Indians having a ford across the Grand River here, which they called "Brant's Ford," it being near his residence.[3] The situation of the town, on the north or right bank of the Grand River, is a healthful one. That river is navigable to within less than three miles of the village. The deficiency in that distance is supplied by a canal. The population is about four thousand.

Early on the morning after my arrival at Brantford I was met by Chief Johnson, who had come up to the village the previous evening for the purpose. We left at six o'clock for the Onondaga Station, about nine miles below, from which we walked to Mr. Johnson's house, half way between the villages of Onondaga and Tuscarora, the former inhabited by white people, and the latter wholly by the Indians. Onondaga is on the north side of the river, and Tuscarora on the south. We passed several pure-blooded Indians on the way, some of them, who remain pagans, wearing portions of the ancient savage costume; but most of them, men and women, were dressed in the style of the white people around them.

---

[1] Paris was so named on account of the gypsum, or "plaster of Paris," which abounds there.

[2] The word Mohawk, in that language, signifies "flint and steel."

[3] Those of the Six Nations who joined the British during the Revolution were promised by the governors of Canada, Carleton and Haldimand, that they should be well provided for at the close of the war. But in the treaty of peace in 1783, no provision was made for the Indians. At that time the Mohawks, with Brant at their head, were temporarily residing on the American side of the Niagara River, near its mouth. The Senecas offered them a home in the Genesee Valley, but Brant and his followers had resolved not to live in the United States. He went to Quebec to claim from Governor Haldimand the fulfillment of his promise. He had fixed his eye upon a large tract of land on the Bay of Quinté. But the Senecas did not wish them to go so far away, and they chose a large tract on the Grand River. This matter being settled, Brant went to England at the close of 1775, and during the remainder of his life he devoted much of his time to the moral improvement of his people.

The grant of land on the Ouise, or Grand River, which Brant, in the behalf of the Indians, procured in 1784, comprised an area of twelve hundred square miles, or, as Brant expressed it when asked how much would satisfy them, "six miles each side of the river from its mouth to its source." The whole country thus granted was fertile and beautiful. Of all that splendid domain, running up into the country from Lake Erie toward Lake Huron to the Falls of Elora, the Indians now retain only comparatively small tracts in the vicinity of Brantford. In 1830 the Indians made a surrender to the government of the town plot of Brantford, when it was surveyed and sold to actual settlers. It soon grew into a large and thriving village.

On our way we also passed the old mission-house, constructed of logs in 1827, for the residence of the Reverend Robert Lugger, the predecessor of the present missionary among the Indians there. It is near the left bank of the Grand River; and from the road where the sketch was made is a fine view of the beautiful valley through which that stream winds its way toward Lake Erie.

MISSION-HOUSE ON THE GRAND RIVER.

A walk of a mile and a half brought us to "Chiefswood," the residence of Mr. Johnson, situated on a gentle eminence, with beautiful grounds sloping to the banks of the Grand River, and surrounded by his farm of two hundred acres of excellent land. It is a modest, square mansion, two stories in height, built of brick, and stuccoed. There I was cordially welcomed by Mrs. Johnson, a handsome and well-educated woman, daughter of a clergyman of the Church of England, and the mother of three fine-looking, healthy children. While awaiting preparations for breakfast, Mr. Johnson proceeded to his business office, leaving me to amuse myself with the curiosities which adorned the little parlor. On a table were several rare Indian relics, and the daguerreotypes of some Indian chiefs. Among the latter was one of Mr. Johnson himself, in the military costume of commander-in-chief of the Six Nations, as seen in the engraving. In precisely this garb he appeared, in compliment to my curiosity, when he came to invite me to breakfast. The coat and breeches were white cloth, and the scarf and sash were rich specimens of Indian work, composed of cloth, ribbons, beads, and porcupine quills.

In one hand he holds a handsome curled-maple handled, silver-mounted pipe-tomahawk,[2] and in the other a most formidable weapon, composed of the shank of a deer, with the bare shin-bone for a handle, dried in the angular position seen in the small engraving on the following page, and holding a thick glittering blade, which may be used either in giving deadly

ORNAMENTAL TOMAHAWK.

---

[1] It will be observed, in the signature of Mr. Johnson, that a character in the form of a **Z** precedes the word "chief." This indicates an arm bent at the elbow, and signifies that the head chief is the right arm of the nation.

[2] These ornamental tomahawks are not for practical use. The handle, fourteen inches in length, contains a tube that answers the purpose of the stem of a pipe, and the head of the tomahawk is arranged as a pipe-bowl. In this specimen the blade and handle are connected by a silver chain. The blade is brass except the steel edge.

blows or as a scalping-knife. These, with a silver *calumet*, or pipe of peace, compose a part of the regalia of the civil and military heads of the Six Nations. These arti-

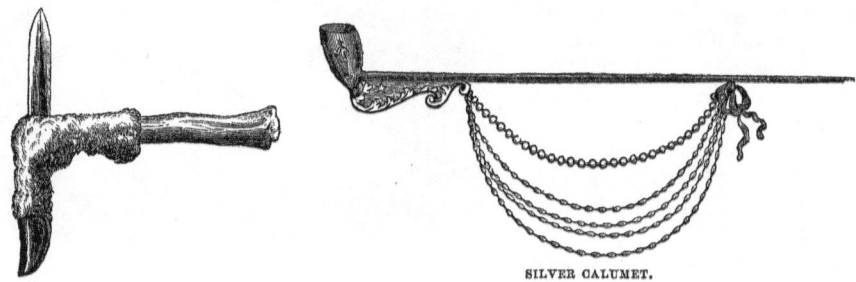

SILVER CALUMET.

DEER-SHANK WEAPON.

cles had been long in possession of the nation.[1] On the table was also a daguerreotype of Oshawahnah, the lieutenant of Tecumtha at the battle of the Thames, and who in 1861 was yet living on Walpole Island, in Lake St. Clair, off the coast of Michigan. Mr. Johnson kindly presented to me the likeness of himself and of that venerable chief. That of the latter, with some facts concerning him, will be given hereafter.

By the side of the fireplace hung an undressed deerskin sheath which attracted my attention. I drew from it an ancient scalping-knife, half consumed by rust, as seen in the little picture. Its history, as related to me by Mr. Johnson, is curious. When he was  about to break ground for the foundation of his house, two or three years previous to my

ANCIENT SCALPING-KNIFE.

[a] August, 1860. visit,[a] the venerable Whitecoat, a centenarian chief then living at Tuscarora Village, came to him, and, pointing to the huge stump of a tree that had been felled within the prescribed lines of the building, said, "Dig there, and you will find a scalping-knife that I buried seventy years ago. You know," he continued, "that before the laws of the white man governed us, it was the duty of the nearest of kin of a wounded man to avenge his death by shedding the blood of the murderer in like manner, and that the weapon so employed was never afterward used, but buried. I thus took vengeance for my brother's blood, and at the foot of that tree I buried the fatal knife. Dig, and you'll find it." Johnson did so, and found nothing but the rusty blade, to which he has affixed a wooden handle, made like the original. Whitecoat was among the warriors who were in the battle at Queenston. More than twenty of his companions on that occasion were living in the Grand River settlements in 1860. The whole number of the Six Nations, with the Chippewas, in those settlements was about three thousand. Of these about five hundred were pagans. The latter are chiefly Cayugas, who are usually of purer blood than the others, and consequently retain more of the Indian feeling and dislike of the Christians—the personification of hated civilization.

---

[1] I saw and sketched these objects at the store of Mr. Allan Cleghorn, in Brantford, whose great interest in the welfare of the Indians in that vicinity caused him to be elected to a chieftaincy among them, according to the old Indian custom—a compliment equivalent to the presentation of the "freedom of a city" to meritorious men.

The silver *calumet*, or pipe of peace, used at councils and in making treaties, above delineated, was quite old. On the broad, ornamented silver plate under the bowl and part of the stem was the following inscription: "To the Mohawk Indians, from the Nine Patentees of the Tract near Schoharie, granted in 1769." On one side of the bowl was the figure of a white man, and on the other that of an Indian. These were connected with the representation of the sun on the front of the bowl by a union chain. Suspended from the stem in a festoon was, first, a silver chain, and then strings of wampum. The stem was eighteen inches in length.

The sword seen in the picture was presented to Mr. Johnson in 1849 by T. D. Beverly, Esq., of Three Rivers, Canada, because of the chief's speech to the Six Nations (when assembled on the queen's birthday), in deprecation of the action of the Canadian Parliament in paying Mr. M'Kenzie and "other rebels" for their losses during the civil war in 1837 and 1838. It was an elegant sword.

Mr. Johnson was born near Brantford on the 7th of October, 1818. He was a lineal descendant of Sir William Johnson, through Sir John Johnson, whose son Jacob was his grandfather. His military commission as chief of the Six Nations gave him the rank and pay of colonel. His influence was powerful, and he had the esteem of his people and of the white inhabitants.

Immediately after breakfast I bade adieu to Mrs. Johnson and her interesting little family, and left "Chiefswood" for Brantford, accompanied by the kind-hearted leader in his own conveyance. We went by the way of Onondaga and Mohawk or "The Institute," where Brant first settled. Near the former village Mr. Johnson has a farm, on the verge of which, and close by the town, is a free Episcopal church, built of brick, and devoted to the use of the poor white people of that section. For that noble purpose Mr. Johnson gave the ground and a considerable sum of money. In the village, which is pleasantly situated on a plain, is a small Methodist chapel and some neat cottages. Only here and there an Indian family were seen, and these were found in a state of excitement and grief because of the death of a fine lad, a grandson of Brant, who had been killed by being thrown from a horse that morning.

We reached the old Mohawk church (the first of the kind erected in the province) toward noon, found the door open, and entered. Some carpenters were at work repairing the exterior, but in no way changing its form from what it was originally. It is of wood, and was erected in the year 1783. It is a very plain, unpretending structure within and without.

MOHAWK CHURCH.

The only ornament, except the upholstery of the pulpit and the upper part of the frames inclosing the Ten Commandments, is a representation of the royal arms of England, handsomely carved and gilt, attached to the wall over the entrance-door, inside. Back of the pulpit are two black tablets with the Commandments inscribed upon them. On the right of it is another tablet, on which is written the Lord's Prayer, and on the left another, with the Apostles' Creed, all in the Mohawk language.[1] In front of the little chancel is a neat font. The seats have high backs. The one seen in

INTERIOR OF MOHAWK CHURCH.

the corner, at the right of the pulpit, was pointed out to me as that which Brant and

---

[1] The following is a copy of the Lord's Prayer, as written upon the tablet in the old Mohawk church:
"Shoegwaniha Karouhyakouh teghsiderouh, Wagwaghseanadokeaghdiste; Sayanertsherah aodaweghti; Tsineaghsereh egh neayaweane ne oughweatsyake tsioni nityouht ne Karouhyakouh. Takyouh ne Keah weghniserate ne niyadeweghniserake oegwanadarok: Neoni toedagwarighwyastea ne tsiniyoegwatswatouh, tsiniyouht ne oekyouhha tsitsyakhirighwiyoesteanis ne waonkhiyatswatea. Neoni toghsa tagwaghsharinet tewadadeanakeraghtoeke: Nok toe-

his family occupied when he resided there. The area of the interior is only about thirty by forty feet, and is lighted by four arched windows on each side. The timber for the church was floated down the Grand River, sawed and dressed by hand, and carried to the spot by the Indians. The communion service, still used in the church, was presented to the Mohawks by Queen Anne. It has been generally supposed that the bell was also a gift of the royal lady; but, on examination, I found the following "card" of the manufacturer cast upon it: "John Warner, Fleet Street, London, 1786." It was doubtless brought from England at about that time by Brant.

Near the south side of the church is the tomb of Brant and his son and official successors. His original family vault was built of wood. It fell into decay, and in 1850 the inhabitants of the vicinity erected a new and substantial tomb, composed of light brown sandstone. The public ceremonies on the occasion were conducted chiefly by the Freemasons (Brant being a member of that order), assisted by a large gathering of the people from the surrounding country and from the States, especially from the Mohawk Valley, full five thousand in number. Upon a massive slab which composes the top of the tomb are appropriate inscriptions commemorative of both father and son.[1] A picture of the tomb may be seen on page 401. In front of the church, near the entrance-gate to the grounds, is the grave of the maternal grandfather of Chief Johnson, who was in the train of young Brant at the battle of Queenston. A stone slab, with an appropriate inscription, covers his grave.[2]

After sketching the exterior and interior of the ancient church and Brant's tomb, and visiting the much-altered house, a few rods distant, where the great chieftain lived, we went to the "Mohawk Institute," the central point of missionary effort among the Six Nations, commenced and continued by "The Society for the Propagation of the Gospel in Foreign Parts."[3] Their first missionary to the Mohawks was sent in the year 1702, and from that time to this they have followed the waning tribe and its confederates in the old league with motherly solicitude. This company have maintained a missionary among the Six Nations in Canada ever since their migration thither. They have contributed largely to the repairs of the old Mohawk church, erected a new one in Tuscarora Village, and now maintain at the "Institute" about sixty Indian scholars. These were under the charge of the Reverend Abraham Nelles, the missionary of the station, and his excellent wife, who had been in that useful field of labor since 1829. His family had had ecclesiastical connection with the Six

---

dagwayadakoh tsinoewo niyodaaheah: Ikea iese saweauk ne kayanertsherah, neoni ne kashatsteaghsera, neoni ne œweseaghtshera, tsiniyeaheawe neoni tsiniyeaheawe. *Amen.*"

[1] The following are copies of the inscriptions:

"This tomb is erected to the memory of THAYENDANEGEA, or Captain JOSEPH BRANT, Principal Chief and Warrior of the Six Nations Indians, by his Fellow-Subjects, admirers of his fidelity and attachment to the British Crown. Born on the banks of the Ohio River, 1742; died at Wellington Square,* U. C., 1807.

"It also contains the Remains of his Son AHYOUWAIGHS, or Captain JOHN BRANT, who succeeded his Father as *Tekarihogea*, and distinguished himself in the war of 1812-15. Born at the Mohawk Village, U. C., 1794; died at the same place, 1833. Erected 1850."

The tomb is surrounded by a heavy wooden fence.

[2] The following is a copy of the inscription:

"In memory of GEORGE MARTIN, Mohawk Chief. Born at Kanajohara, U. S., Dec. 23, 1767; died at Grand River, C. W., Feb. 18, 1853, aged 86 years."

Chief Johnson has in his possession a silver medal, presented to his grandfather more than seventy years ago by George the Third. On one side is a profile of the king. On the other is a landscape. In the foreground is a lion in repose, and a wolf approaching him with awe. In the distance is a representation of the Mohawk church on Grand River and the mission-house near.

[3] This society was incorporated by Parliament in 1701. It is the successor or continuation of an earlier one, in 1561, under the title of *The Company for the Propagation of the Gospel in New England and Parts Adjacent in America*. It was composed partly of members of the Church of England and partly of Protestant Dissenters.

---

* Wellington Square is a pleasant little village in Nelson Township, situated on Lake Ontario, eight miles from Hamilton, and now (1867) contains between four and five hundred inhabitants. There, north of the beach which divides Lake Ontario from Burlington Bay, Brant made his abode, in a handsome two-storied mansion, beautifully situated, long before the present village had existence. There he lived, in the English style, until his death. His widow (third wife), Catharine, was forty-eight years of age at the time of his death. She preferred the customs of her people, and soon after her husband's departure she left Lake Ontario and returned to Mohawk, on the Grand River. Her son and daughter remained at the "Brant house" on Lake Ontario, and lived in elegant style for several years.

Nations for a century and a half. His faithfulness as a teacher of temporal and spiritual things merits and receives the highest commendations. He resided at the old mission-house, near Tuscarora, delineated on page 241, until 1837, when he took up his abode at Mohawk.

Unfortunately, our visit was at vacation time, and we were deprived of the coveted pleasure of seeing a group of threescore Indian children under instruction. We spent two hours very agreeably with the kind missionary and his family at the "Institute" and the parsonage at the glebe. These have each two hundred acres of fertile land, at the head of the Grand River, attached to them, and are separated by the canal, which carries the navigation of the river up to Brantford. We crossed the canal in a canoe, and at the parsonage, an old-fashioned dwelling near the old "Institute" building, with beautiful grounds around it, we saw many curious things connected with the mission. Among them was one half of the massive silver communion plate presented by Queen Anne to the Mohawks in 1712. The other half, a duplicate of this, was lent to a church on the Bay of Quinté. Upon each was engraved the royal arms of England and "A. R."—Anne Regina—with the following inscription in double lines around them: "THE GIFT OF HER MAJESTY ANNE, BY THE GRACE OF GOD, OF GREAT BRITAIN, FRANCE, AND IRELAND, AND OF HER PLANTATIONS IN NORTH AMERICA, QUEEN, TO HER INDIAN CHAPEL OF THE MOHAWKS." In addition to the three pieces given in the picture was a plate, nine inches in diameter, for receiving collections. Mr. Nelles also showed us a well-preserved folio Bible, which was printed in London in 1701, and was sent to the Mohawks with the communion plate. On the cover are the following words in gilt letters: "FOR HER MAJESTY'S CHURCH OF THE MOHAWKS, 1712."

COMMUNION PLATE.

We dined with the excellent missionaries, and then rode to Brantford, a mile and a half distant, where, after a brief tarry, I bade adieu to Mr. Johnson and the Six Nations, when I had only an hour in which to travel seven miles to Paris to take the evening train for Hamilton or Toronto. I had procured a fleet and powerful horse, and in a light wagon, with a small boy as driver, I traveled the excellent stone road, or "pike," between the two places on that hot afternoon with the speed of the trotting-course, yet with apparent ease to the splendid animal. I had four minutes to spare at Paris.

That beautiful day, spent with the Six Nations and their military chief and spiritual guide, will ever remain a precious treasure in the store-house of memory. I could think of little else while on my journey that evening from Paris to Toronto. Of my visit to that former capital of Upper Canada, known as York in the War of 1812, I shall hereafter write.[1]

Let us return from our digression from the strict path of history to the Niagara frontier, which we so recently left, and consider the record of events there during the remainder of 1812, after the battle at Queenston.

The British had erected some batteries on the high banks, a little back of the Niagara River, just below Fort Erie, at a point where an invasion by the Americans

---

[1] The Indian name was *Darondo* or *Taronto*, signifying "Trees on the Water." This was in allusion to the long, low, sandy point (now an island), within which was the Bay of Toronto. On that point were, and still are, many trees. The distance is so great that from the shore at the city they seem to be *on the water*. When Colonel Simcoe became lieutenant governor of the Upper Province he endeavored to Anglicize the settlers by making them familiar with English names and things. With this object in view he gave English names to all places, and the Indian name of *Taronto* was changed to *York*, in honor of the Duke of York. It was known for many years as Little York.

might be reasonably expected. From these batteries they opened a severe fire on the morning of the 17th of November upon Black Rock opposite, then a place of quite as much importance as Buffalo in some respects. There were the head-quarters of the little army under General Smyth, and there was the fine residence of General Peter B. Porter, who was then in command there of a body of New York militia, and made

GENERAL PORTER'S RESIDENCE, BLACK ROCK.[1]

that dwelling his head-quarters. There were some slight fortifications near Black Rock, but the heaviest cannon upon the breastwork was a six-pounder. All day long, at intervals, the British kept up the fire, at one time hurling a 25-pound shot against the upper loft of Porter's residence, and soon afterward dropping another ball, of the same weight, through the roof, while he was there at dinner. At length a bomb-shell was sent into the east barrack with destructive power. It exploded the magazine, fired the buildings, and destroyed a portion of the valuable furs captured on board the *Caledonia* a few days before.[a] This exploit being one of the chief objects of the cannonade and bombardment, both ceased at sunset.

[a] October 9, 1812.

Very little noise was heard along that frontier for a month afterward except the sonorous cadences of General Smyth's proclamations. At length British cannon opened their thunders. Breastworks had been raised in front of Newark, opposite Fort Niagara, at intervals all the way up to Fort George, and behind them mortars and a long train of battery cannon had been placed. At six o'clock on the morning of the 21st of November these commenced a fierce bombardment of Fort Niagara, and at the same time a cannonade was opened from Fort George and its vicinity. From dawn until the evening twilight there was a continual roar from five detached batteries on the Canada shore, two of them mounting twenty-four-pounders. From these batteries two thousand red-hot shot were poured upon the American works, while the mortars, from five and a half to ten and a half inches calibre, were showering bomb-shells all day long. The latter were almost harmless, but the former set fire to several buildings within the fort, which, by the greatest exertions, were saved. The garrison, meanwhile, performed their duty nobly. They were quite sufficient in number, but lacked artillery and ammunition. The gallant Lieutenant Colonel George M'Feely[2] was the commander, and Major Armistead, of the United States Engineer Corps, performed the most important services at the guns and in extinguishing the flames. Captain M'Keon commanded a 12-pounder in the southeast block-house; Captain Jacks, of the 7th Regiment of Militia Artillery, was in charge of the north block-house, where he was greatly exposed to a raking fire of the enemy; and Lieutenant Rees, of the 3d United States Artillery, managed an eighteen-pounder in the southeast battery, which told heavily upon a British battery with a twenty-four-pounder *en barbette*. He was soon badly wounded in the shoulder by the falling of a part of the parapet. On the west battery an eighteen and a four pounder were directed by Lieu-

---

[1] This is from a sketch made by the writer in the summer of 1860, from a pier in the Niagara River. The house is upon the high shore of the river. It was then owned by Mr. Lewis F. Allen.

[2] M'Feely was commissioned a major in March, 1812, and in July was promoted to lieutenant colonel. He became colonel of infantry in April, 1814, and was disbanded in June, 1815.

tenant Wendal, and on the mess-house,[1] Doctor Hooper, of the New York Militia, had charge of a six-pounder. South of Fort Niagara, and a dependency of it, was the "Salt Battery," so called, mounting an eighteen and a four pounder. It was directly in range of Fort George, and annoyed the garrison there exceedingly. It was commanded by Lieutenants Gansevoort and Harris, of the 1st Artillery. From these several batteries on the American side many a destructive missile went on terrible errands during the day. Newark was on fire several times before night, and the buildings in Fort George were also fired, and one of its batteries was silenced.[2] During the day an American twelve-pounder burst and killed two men. Two others were killed by the enemy's fire, and a lieutenant and four men were wounded. These were the casualties of the day on the American side. What injury was done to the British is not known. A shot from the Salt Battery sunk a sloop lying at the wharf on the Canada side. Night ended the artillery duel, and it was not renewed in the morning.

We have observed that General Smyth expressed his opinion to General Van Rensselaer, on his arrival on the frontier, that the proper place to cross the Niagara River for the invasion of Canada was somewhere between Fort Erie and Chippewa.[3] A few days after the bombardment of Fort Niagara, Smyth attempted to act upon that opinion. His proclamation had stirred the people of Western New York, and large numbers had flocked to his standard; for his flaming sentences warmed their zeal, and they believed that all his glowing hopes would be realized and his flattering promises would be fulfilled. On the 27th of November, when Smyth called the troops to a general rendezvous at Black Rock, they numbered about four thousand five hundred. They were composed of his own regulars, and the Baltimore Volunteers under Colonel Winder, the Pennsylvania Volunteers under General Tannehill, and the New York Volunteers under General Peter B. Porter. With these he felt competent to invade Canada successfully.

As early as the 25th, General Smyth issued orders for "the whole army to be ready to march at a moment's warning." "The tents," he said, "will be left standing. Officers will carry their knapsacks. The baggage will follow in convenient time." After giving directions for the embarkation of the troops in the boats provided by Colonel Winder, to whom that important service was intrusted, he gave the following directions for forming the troops in battle order on the Canada shore: "Beginning on the right, as follows: Captain Gibson's Artillery; the Sixth and Thirteenth Infantry; Captain Towson's Artillery; the Fourteenth and Twenty-third Infantry as one regiment; Captain Barker's and Captain Branch's Artillery; the Twelfth and Twentieth Infantry; Captain Archer's Artillery; General Tannehill's Infantry; a company of Riflemen; the Infantry of Colonel Swift and Colonel M'Clure; a company of Riflemen; General Porter's Infantry; Captain Leonard's Artillery; a battalion of Riflemen on each flank, in a line perpendicular to that formed by the main army, extending to the front and rear."[4]

---

[1] The Indians were jealous of any attempts of the French to build any thing like a fort among them. The French succeeded by stratagem. They obtained permission to erect a great wigwam, or dwelling, and then induced the Indians to go on a long hunt. When they returned the walls were so advanced that they might defy the savages. They completed the building in a way that they might plant cannon on the top, and used it as a mess-house. Under it was a deep dungeon, and in that dungeon was a well. It is believed that political prisoners from France were confined in that dark prison. The water of the well was poisoned at one time, and a story was believed by superstitious soldiers that at midnight the headless body of a Frenchman might be seen sitting on the margin of the well, where he had been murdered.

[2] Thompson, in his *Historical Sketches of the Late War*, page 80, says, "Such was the spirited earnestness of both officers and men at this battery, that when, in the most tremendous of the bombardment, they had fired away all their cartridges, they cut up their flannel waistcoats and shirts, and the soldiers their trowsers, to supply their guns." He also speaks of the wife of an Irish artilleryman, named Doyle, who had been made a prisoner at Queenston, and to whom a parole had been refused, determined to resent the act by taking her husband's place as far as possible. On the occasion now under consideration she took her place at the mess-house, and supplied the six-pounder there with hot shot. Regardless of the shot and shell that fell around her, she never quitted her station until the last gun had been fired.

[3] See Smyth's letter to Van Rensselaer, note 2, page 389.

[4] Manuscript order, November 25, 1812: *Winder Papers*. In that order the directions for attack were given as follows:

| Arrangements for Crossing the Niagara River. | The British, forewarned, are forearmed. | Passage of the River. |

^a November, 1812.

Every thing was in readiness on the 27th^a for invasion, and arrangements were made for the expedition to embark at the navy yard below Black Rock at *réveille* on the morning of the 28th. Seventy public boats, capable of carrying forty men each; five large private boats, in which one hundred men each could be borne; and ten scows for artillery, with many small boats, were pressed into the service, so that three thousand troops, the whole number to be employed in the invasion, might cross at once. That evening Smyth issued his final order, directing Lieutenant Colonel Boerstler to cross over at three o'clock in the morning with the effective men of Colonel Winder's regiment, and destroy a bridge about five miles below Fort Erie, capture the guard stationed there, kill or take the artillery horses, and, with the captives, if any, return to the American shore. Captain King was directed to cross at the same time at the "Red House," higher up the river, to storm the British batteries. It was left to the discretion of Boerstler to march up the Canada shore to assist King, or to return immediately after performing his allotted work at the bridge. "It is not intended to keep possession," said the order. "Let the wounded be kept from the public eye to-morrow. You [Colonel Winder] will remain on this bank and give directions."[1]

General Smyth had so long and loudly proclaimed his designs against Canada, and had so fairly indicated his probable point of invasion, that the authorities on the other side were prepared to meet him at any place between Fort Erie and Chippewa. Major Ormsby, of the Forty-ninth, with a detachment of that and the Newfoundland regiment, was at the fort. The ferry opposite Black Rock was occupied by two companies of militia under Captain Bostwick. Two and a half miles from Fort Erie, at a house on the Chippewa road, was Lieutenant Lamont, with a detachment of the Forty-ninth, and Lieutenant King, of the Royal Engineers, with a three and six pounder, and some militia artillerymen. Near the same spot were two batteries, one mounting an eighteen and the other a twenty-four pound cannon, also under Lamont. A mile farther down was a post occupied by a detachment under Lieutenant Bartley; and on Frenchman's Creek, four and a half miles from Fort Erie, was a party of seventy under Lieutenant M'Intyre. Lieutenant Colonel Cecil Bisshopp was at Chippewa with *Cecil Bisshopp* a part of the Forty-first Regulars, some militia and militia artillery, and near him was Major Hatt with a small detachment of militia. The whole number of British troops, scattered along a line of twenty miles, did not, according to the most reliable estimates, exceed one thousand men.

^b November.

Before the appointed hour on the morning of the 28th,^b the boats were in readiness under the general superintendence of Lieutenant Angus, of the navy, at the head of a corps of marines and seamen, assisted by Lieutenant Dudley, Sailing-master Watts, of *Caledonia* fame,[2] and several other naval officers. *Saml Angus* It was a cold and dreary night.

^c November 29.

At three in the morning^c the advanced parties left the American shore for their respective destinations. One, under Lieutenant Colonel Boerstler, consisted of about two hundred men of Colonel Winder's regiment, in eleven boats; and the other, under Captain King, was composed of one hundred and fifty regular soldiers, and seventy sailors under Lieutenant Angus, in ten boats. King's party were discovered upon the water a quarter of a mile from the shore, and were

---

"1. The artillery will spend some of their first shot on the enemy's artillery, and then aim at the infantry, raking them where it is practicable. 2. The firing of musketry by wings or companies will begin at the distance of two hundred yards, aiming at the middle and firing deliberately. 3. At twenty yards' distance the soldiers will be ordered to trail arms, advance with shouts, fire at five paces' distance, and charge bayonets. 4. The soldiers will be *silent*, above all things, attentive at the word of command, load quick and well, and *aim low*."

[1] Manuscript order of General Smyth to Colonel Winder, November 27, 1812: *Winder Papers.*   [2] See page 386.

Incidents of the Attempt to invade Canada on the Upper Niagara.

so warmly assailed by volleys of musketry and shot from a field-piece at the Red House, that six of the ten boats were compelled to return. The other four resolutely landed in good order, in the face of the storm of bullets and grape-shot from flying artillery; and before King could form his troops on the shore, Angus and his seamen, with characteristic impetuosity, rushed into the hottest fire and suffered considerably. King formed his corps as quickly as possible, and the enemy were soon dispersed. He then proceeded to storm and take in quick succession two British batteries above the landing-place, while Angus and his seamen rushed upon the field-pieces at the Red House, captured and spiked them, and cast them, with their *caissons*,[1] into the river. In this assault Sailing-master Watts was mortally wounded while leading on the seamen.[2] Angus and his party returned to the landing-place, with Lieutenant King, of the Royal Artillery, wounded and a prisoner. Supposing the other six boats had landed (for it was too dark to see far along the shore), and that Captain King and his party had been taken prisoners, Angus crossed to the American shore in the four boats. This unfortunate mistake left King, with Captains Morgan and Sproull, Lieutenant Houston, and Samuel Swartwout, of New York, who had volunteered for the service with the little party of regulars, without any means of crossing. King waited a while for re-enforcements. None came, and he went to the landing-place for the purpose of crossing, with a number of the British artillerists whom he had made prisoners. To his dismay, he discovered the absence of all the boats. He pushed down the river in the dark for about two miles, when he found two large ones. Into these he placed all of his officers, the prisoners, and one half of his men. These had not reached the American shore when King and the remainder of his troops were taken prisoners by a superior force.

Boerstler and his party, in the mean time, had been placed in much peril. The firing upon King had aroused the enemy all along the Canada shore, and they were on the alert. Boerstler's boats became separated in the darkness. Seven of them landed above the bridge, to be destroyed, while four others, that approached the designated landing-place, were driven off by a party of the enemy. Boerstler landed boldly alone, under fire from a foe of unknown numbers, and drove them to the bridge at the point of the bayonet. Orders were then given for the destruction of that structure, but, owing to the confusion at the time of landing, the axes had been left in the boat. The bridge was only partially destroyed, and one great object of this advance party of the invading army was not accomplished. Boerstler was about to return to his boats and recross the river, because of the evident concentration of troops to that point in overwhelming numbers, when he was compelled to form his lines for immediate battle. Intelligence came from the commander of the boat-guard that they had captured two British soldiers, who informed them that the whole garrison at Fort Erie was approaching, and that the advance guard was not five minutes distant. This intelligence was correct. Darkness covered every thing, and Boerstler resorted to stratagem when he heard the tramp of the approaching foe. He gave commanding orders in a loud voice, addressing his subordinates as field officers. The British were deceived. They believed the Americans to be in much greater force than they really were. A collision immediately ensued in the gloom. Boerstler ordered the discharge of a single volley, and then a bayonet charge. The enemy broke and fled in confusion, and Boerstler crossed the river without annoyance.[3]

---

[1] A *caisson* is an ammunition chest or wagon in which powder and bomb-shells are carried. [2] See page 386.
[3] Colonel Winder's manuscript report to General Smyth, December 7, 1812. Winder had attempted to re-enforce the troops on the Canada shore, but failed. On the return of Angus and his party, he was ordered to cross the river with two hundred and fifty men. Within twenty minutes after the order was given, he and his troops were battling with the current and the floating ice. Winder's boat was the first and only one that touched the Canada shore, the current having carried the others below. The enemy, with strong force and a piece of artillery, disputed his landing. Resistance would be vain, and Winder ordered a retreat, after losing six men killed and twenty-two wounded. On his return he formed his regiment at once, to join in the embarkation at dawn.
In the report above cited Colonel Winder paid the following compliment to Captain Totten, of the Engineers, who,

It was sunrise when the troops began to embark, and so tardy were the movements that it was late in the afternoon when all were ready. General Smyth did not make his appearance during the day,[1] and all the movements were under the direction of his subordinates. A number of boats had been left to strand upon the shore, and became filled with water, snow, and ice; and as hour after hour passed by, dreariness and disappointment weighed heavily upon the spirits of the shivering troops. Meanwhile the enemy had collected in force on the opposite shore, and were watching every movement. At length, when all seemed ready, and impatience had yielded to hope, an order came from the commanding general "to disembark *and dine!*"[2] The wearied and worried troops were deeply exasperated by this order, and nothing but the most positive assurances that the undertaking would be immediately resumed kept them from open mutiny. The different regiments retired sullenly to their respective quarters, and General Porter, with his dispirited New York Volunteers, marched in disgust to Buffalo.

[a] November 28, 1812. Smyth now called a council of officers.[a] They could not agree. The best of them urged the necessity and expediency of crossing in force at once, before the enemy could make formidable preparations for their reception. The general decided otherwise, and doubt and despondency brooded over the camp that night. The ensuing Sabbath dawn brought no relief. Preparations for another embarkation were indeed in progress, while the enemy, too, was busy in opposing labor. It was evident to every spectator of judgment that the invasion must be attempted at another point of the river, when, toward evening, to the astonishment of all, the general issued an order, perfectly characteristic of the man, for the troops to be ready at the navy yard, at eight o'clock the next morning,[b] for embarkation.

[b] November 30. "The general will be on board," he pompously proclaimed. "Neither rain, snow, or frost will prevent the embarkation," he said. "The cavalry will scour the fields from Black Rock to the bridge, and suffer no idle spectators. While embarking, the music will play martial airs. *Yankee Doodle* will be the signal to get under way.... The landing will be effected in despite of cannon. The whole army has seen that cannon is to be little dreaded.... Hearts of War! to-morrow will be memorable in the annals of the United States."[3]

"To-morrow" came, but not the promised achievement. All the officers disapproved of the time and manner of the proposed embarkation, and expressed their opinions freely. At General Porter's quarters a change was agreed upon. Porter proposed deferring the embarkation until Tuesday morning, the 1st of December, an hour or two before daylight, and to make the landing-place a little below the upper end of Grand Island. Winder suggested the propriety of making a descent directly upon Chippewa, "the key of the country." This Smyth consented to attempt, intending, as he said, if successful, to march down through Queenston, and lay siege to Fort George.[4] Orders were accordingly given for a general rendezvous at the navy yard at three o'clock on Tuesday morning, and that the troops should be collected in the woods near by on Monday, where they should build fires and await the signal for gathering on the shore of the river. The hour arrived, but when day dawned only fifteen hundred were embarked. Tannehill's Pennsylvania Brigade were not present. Before their arrival rumors had reached the camp that they, too, like Van Rensselaer's militia at Lewiston, had raised a constitutional question about being led out of their state. Yet their scruples seem to have been overcome at this time, and they would

---

at the time of his death in 1864, was Chief Engineer of the Army of the United States: "It is with great pleasure I acknowledge the intelligence and skill which Captain Totten, of the Engineers, has yielded to the works which are raising. To him shall we be indebted for what I believe will be a respectable state of preparation in a short time."

[1] Thomson's *Historical Sketches, etc.*, page 85.
[2] General Smyth's dispatch to General Dearborn, December 4, 1812.
[3] Autograph order, Winder Papers, dated "Head-quarters, Camp near Buffalo, Nov. 29, 1812."
[4] Smyth's dispatch to General Dearborn, December 4, 1812.

Smyth's Council of Officers.   The Invasion of Canada abandoned.   Disappointment and Indignation of the Troops.

have invaded Canada cheerfully under other auspices. But distrust of their leader, created by the events of the last forty-eight hours, had demoralized nearly the whole army. They had made so much noise in the embarkation that the startled enemy had sounded his alarm bugle and discharged signal-guns from Fort Erie to Chippewa. Tannehill's Pennsylvanians had not appeared, and many other troops lingered upon the shore, loth to embark. In this dilemma Smyth hastily called a council of the regular officers, utterly excluding those of the volunteers from the conference, and the first intimation of the result of that council was an order from the commanding general, sent to General Porter, who was in a boat with the pilot, a fourth of a mile from shore, in the van of the impatient flotilla, directing the whole army to debark and repair to their quarters.[1] This was accompanied by a declaration that the invasion of Canada was abandoned at present, pleading, in bar of just censure, that his orders from his superiors were not to attempt it with less than three thousand men.[2] The regulars were ordered into winter quarters, and the volunteers were dismissed to their homes.

This order for debarkation, and the fact that just previously a British major, bearing a flag of truce, had crossed the river and held an interview with General Smyth, caused the most intense indignation, and the most fearful suspicions of his loyalty[3] in the army, especially among the volunteers, whose officers he had insulted by neglect. The troops, without order or restraint, discharged their muskets in all directions, and a scene of insubordination and utter confusion followed. At least a thousand of the volunteers had come from their homes in response to his invitation, and the promise that they should certainly be led into Canada by a victor. They had imposed implicit confidence in his ability and the sincerity of his great words, and in proportion to their faith and zeal were now their disappointment and resentment. Unwilling to have their errand to the frontier fruitless of all but disgrace, the volunteers earnestly requested permission to be led into Canada under General Porter, promising the commanding general the speedy capture of Fort Erie if he would furnish them with four pieces of artillery. But Smyth evaded their request, and the volunteers were sent home uttering imprecations against a man whom they considered a mere blusterer without courage, and a conceited deceiver without honor. They felt themselves betrayed, and the inhabitants in the vicinity sympathized with them. Their indignation was greatly increased by ill-timed and ungenerous charges made by Smyth, in his report to General Dearborn, against General Porter, in whom the volunteers had the greatest confidence.[4] His person was for some time in danger. He was compelled to double the guards around his tent, and to move it from place to place to avoid continual insults.[5] He was several times fired at when he ventured out of his marquee. Porter openly attributed the abandonment of the invasion of Canada to the cowardice of Smyth. A bitter quarrel ensued; and soon resulted in a challenge by the general-in-chief for his second in command to test the courage of both by a duel.[6] In direct violation of the Articles of War, these superior officers of

---

[1] Autograph statement of Colonel Winder.

[2] General Smyth's report to General Dearborn, December 4, 1812.

[3] It is proper to say, in justice to General Smyth, that there were no just grounds because of that event for any suspicions of his loyalty. Colonel Winder had been to the British camp with a flag two days before, to make some arrangement about an exchange of prisoners, and this visit of the British major was doubtless in response.

[4] General Porter was a partner in business with Mr. Barton, the army contractor for the Niagara frontier, and General Smyth alluded to him in his report as "the contractor's agent." He charged him with "exciting some clamor" against the measures of General Smyth, and said, "He finds the contract a losing one at this time, and would wish to see the army in Canada, that he might not be bound to supply it."

[5] His friend Colonel Parker, a Virginian, in an autograph letter before me, written to Colonel Winder on the second of December, said: "Major Campbell will inform you of the insult offered to the general last evening, and of the interruption to our repose last night. God grant us a speedy relief from such neighbors!"—*Winder Papers.*

[6] There appears to have been much quarreling among the officers on that frontier during the autumn of 1812. Only three months before, Porter and Colonel Solomon Van Rensselaer had such a bitter dispute that it resulted in a challenge from Porter, but they never reached the dueling-ground on Grand Island. General Stephen Van Rensselaer watched them closely after he heard of the challenge, and was prepared to arrest them both when they should attempt to go to the island.—Statement of Solomon Van Rensselaer, among the Van Rensselaer papers.

the *Army of the Centre*, with friends, and seconds,[1] and surgeons,[2] put off in boats from the shore near Black Rock, in the presence of their troops, at two o'clock in the afternoon of the 12th of December, to meet each other in mortal combat on Grand Island.[3] They exchanged shots at twelve paces' distance. Nobody was hurt. An expected tragedy proved to be a solemn comedy. The affair took the usual ridiculous course. The seconds reconciled the belligerents. General Porter acknowledged his conviction that General Smyth was "a man of courage," and General Smyth was convinced that General Porter was "above suspicion as a gentleman and an officer."[4]

Thus ended the melodrama of Smyth's invasion of Canada. The whole affair was disgraceful and humiliating. "What wretched work Smyth and Porter have made of it," wrote General Wadsworth to General Van Rensselaer from his home at Geneseo, at the close of the year. "I wish those who are disposed to find so much fault could know the state of the militia since the day you gave up the command. It has been 'confusion worse confounded.'"[5] The day that saw Smyth's failure was indeed "memorable in the annals of the United States," as well as in his own private history. Confidence in his military ability was destroyed, and three months afterward he was "disbanded," as the *Army Register* says; in other words, he was deposed without a trial, and excluded from the army.[6] Yet he had many warm friends who clung to him in his misfortunes, for he possessed many excellent social qualities. He was a faithful representative of the constituency of a district of Virginia in the national Congress from 1817 to 1825, and again from 1827 until his death, in April, 1830.

---

[1] Lieutenant Colonel Winder was Smyth's second, and Lieutenant Angus was Porter's.
[2] The surgeon on that occasion was Dr. Roberts, and the assistant surgeon was Dr. Parsons, afterward surgeon of Perry's flag-ship *Lawrence*, in the battle on Lake Erie, and now [1867] a resident of Providence, Rhode Island.
[3] This is a large island, containing 20,000 acres, dividing the Niagara River into two channels. (See map on page 382.) On this island the late Mordecai Manasseh Noah proposed to found a city of refuge for his co-religionists, the Jews, and memorialized the Legislature of the State of New York on the subject in 1820. The project failed because the chief rabbi in Europe disapproved of it. Noah erected a commemorative monument there, but it and his scheme have passed away.
[4] In a letter of Lieutenant Angus to Colonel Winder the next day, he said: "A meeting took place between General Smyth and General Porter yesterday afternoon on Grand Island, in pursuance of previous arrangements. They met at Dayton's tavern, and crossed the river with their friends and surgeons. Both gentlemen behaved with the utmost coolness and unconcern. A shot was exchanged in as intrepid and firm a manner as possible by each gentleman, but without effect. . . . . . The hand of reconciliation was then offered and received."—Autograph letter, *Winder Papers*. Another account says that the party returned to Dayton's, where they supped and spent a convivial evening together.
[5] Autograph letter to General Van Rensselaer, December 30, 1812.
[6] General Smyth petitioned the House of Representatives to reinstate him in the army. That body referred the petition to the Secretary of War—the general's executioner! Of course, its prayer was not answered. In that petition he asked for the privilege of "dying for his country." This phrase was a subject for much ridicule. At a public celebration of Washington's birthday in 1814 at Georgetown, in the District of Columbia, the following sentiment was offered at the table during the presentation of toasts: "General Smyth's petition to Congress to 'die for his country:' May it be ordered that the prayer of said petition be granted."
A wag wrote on a panel of one of the doors of the Hall of Representatives—

> "All hail, great chief! who quailed before
> A *Bisshopp* on Niagara's shore;
> But looks on *Death* with dauntless eye,
> And begs for leave to bleed and die.
>   Oh my!"

CHAPTER XXI.

"'By the trident of Neptune,' brave Hull cried, 'let's steer:
It points out the track of the bullying *Guerriere:*
Should we meet her, brave boys, "Seamen's rights!" be our cry:
We fight to defend them, to live free or die.'
The famed *Constitution* through the billows now flew,
While the spray to the tars was refreshing as dew,
To quicken the sense of the insult they felt,
In the boast of the *Guerriere's* not being the *Belt*."
SONG, "CONSTITUTION AND GUERRIERE."

"Ye brave Sons of Freedom, whose bosoms beat high
For your country with patriot pride and emotion,
Attend while I sing of a wonderful *Wasp*,
And the *Frolic* she gallantly took on the ocean."
OLD SONG.

IN preceding chapters we have considered the prominent events of the war on land, and perceive in the record very little whereof Americans should boast as military achievements. The war had been commenced without adequate preparations, and had been carried on by inexperienced and incompetent men in the Council and in the Field. Brilliant theories had been promulgated and splendid expectations had been indulged, while Philosophy and Experience spoke monitorily, but in vain. The visions of the theorists proved to be "dissolving views"—unsubstantial and deceptive—when tested by the standard of practical results. At the close of the campaign in 1812, the *Army of the Northwest*, first under Hull and then under Harrison, was occupying a defensive position among the snows of the wilderness on the banks of the Maumee; the *Army of the Centre*, first under Van Rensselaer and then under Smyth, had experienced a series of misfortunes and disappointments on the Niagara frontier, and was also resting on the defensive; while the *Army of the North*, under Bloomfield, whose head-quarters were at Plattsburg, had made less efforts to accomplish great things, and had less to regret and more to boast of than the others. Yet it, too, was standing on the defensive when the snows of December fell.

Different was the aspect of affairs on the water. The hitherto neglected navy had been aggressive and generally successful. We have already observed the operations of one branch of it, with feeble means, in the narrow waters of Lake Ontario, under Chauncey;[1] let us now take a view of its exploits on the broad ocean, where Thomson had declared in song,

"Britannia rules the waves."

The naval superiority of England was every where acknowledged; and the idea of the omnipotence of her power on the sea was so universal in the American mind, that serious expectations of success in a contest with her on that theatre were regarded as absurd. The American newspapers—then, as now, the chief vehicles of popular information—had always been filled with praises of England's naval puissance and examples of her prowess; while the British newspapers, reflecting the mind of the ruling classes of that empire, were filled with boastings of England's power, abuse of all other people, and supercilious sneers at the navies of every other nation on the

[1] See page 371.

face of the earth. That of the United States, her rapidly growing rival in national greatness and ever the object of her keenest jealousy, was made the special target for the indecorous jeers of her public writers and speakers. The *Constitution*, one of the finest vessels in the navy of the United States, and which was among the first to humble the arrogance of British cruisers, was spoken of as "a bundle of pine boards, sailing under a bit of striped bunting;" and it was asserted that "a few broadsides from England's wooden walls would drive the paltry striped bunting from the ocean."[1] It was with erroneous opinions like these that the commander of the *Alert* attacked the *Essex*,[a] and, as we shall observe presently, was undeceived by a conclusive argument. Yet, in spite of conscious inferiority of strength in men and metal, the distrust of the nation, and the defiant contempt of the foe, the little navy of the United States went boldly out upon the ocean to dispute with England's cruisers the supremacy of the sea.[2]

[a] August 13, 1812.

When war was declared, the public vessels of the United States, exclusive of one hundred and seventy gun-boats, numbered only *twenty*, with an aggregate armament of litle more than five hundred guns. These were scattered. Four of them had wintered at Newport, Rhode Island; four others in Hampton Roads, Virginia; two were away on foreign service; two were at Charleston, South Carolina; two were at New Orleans; one was on Lake Ontario; and five were laid up "in ordinary."[3] In view of this evident inefficiency of the American navy to protect its commerce, there was much alarm among the few merchants whose ships had gone abroad before the laying of the embargo, which saved many hundreds of detained vessels from exposure to capture or destruction, and thus furnished materials for the privateers that soon swarmed upon the ocean. These merchants sent a swift-sailing pilot-boat to the coasts of Northern Europe with the news of the declaration of war, and with directions for the American commercial marine in the harbors of Russia, Sweden, Denmark, and Prussia, to remain there until the war should cease. By this timely movement a greater part of the American shipping in those ports was saved from the perils of British privateering. A sketch of that important branch of the American naval service during the war will be presented in a group in another part of this work. It is

---

[1] This was alluded to in the following stanzas of a song of the time:

"Too long our tars have borne in peace
With British domineering;
But now they've sworn the trade should cease—
For vengeance they are steering.
First gallant Hull, he was the lad
Who sailed a tyrant-hunting,
And swaggering Dacres soon was glad
To strike to '*striped bunting*.'"

[2] "While, therefore," says an English writer, "a feeling toward Americans bordering on contempt had unhappily possessed the mind of the British naval officer, rendering him more than usually careless and opinionative, the American naval officer, having been taught to regard his new foe with a feeling of dread, sailed forth to meet him with the whole of his energies aroused."—*Naval Occurrences of the Late War*, etc., by William James.

[3] The following is a list of those vessels, their rated and actual armament, the names of the commanders of those afloat, and the designation of those in "ordinary," or laid up for repairs or other purposes:

Name.	Rated.	Mounting.	Employed.	Name.	Rated.	Mounting.	Employed.
Constitution	44	58	Capt. Hull.	John Adams	26		Capt. Ludlow.
United States	44	58	Capt. Decatur.	Wasp	16	18	Capt. Jones.
President	44	58	Com. Rodgers.	Hornet	16	18	Capt. Lawrence.
Chesapeake	36	44	Ordinary.	Siren	16		Lieut. Carroll.
New York	36	44	Ordinary.	Argus	16		Crane.
Constellation	36	44	Ordinary.	Oneida	16		Woolsey.
Congress	36	44	Capt. Smith.	Vixen	12		Gadsden.
Boston	32		Ordinary.	Nautilus	12		Sinclair.
Essex	32		Capt. Porter.	Enterprise	12		Blakely.
Adams	32		Ordinary.	Viper	12		Bainbridge.

There were four bomb-vessels in ordinary, named respectively *Vengeance*, *Spitfire*, *Ætna*, and *Vesuvius*. The gun-boats were all numbered, from "1" to "170," and during the War of 1812 were distributed as follows:
In New York, 54; New Orleans, 26; Norfolk, 14; Charleston, S. C., 2; Wilmington, N. C., 2; St. Mary's, 11; Washington, 10; Portland, 8; Boston, 2; Connecticut and Rhode Island, 4; Philadelphia, 20; Baltimore, 10. Of these only sixty-two were in commission. Eighty-six were in ordinary, and some were undergoing repairs. There had been an increase of five to the number, and some slight changes of position, when the war broke out.

proposed now to consider the events of the regular service only, excepting where necessity may compel an incidental allusion to the other.

At the time of the declaration of war, Commodore Rodgers, with his flag-ship *President*, 44; *Essex*, 32, Captain Porter; and *Hornet*, 18, Captain Lawrence, was in the port of New York. The *Essex* was overhauling her rigging; the others might be ready for service at an hour's notice. On the 21st of June Rodgers received the news of the declaration of war, and with it orders for sailing immediately. He had dropped down the bay that morning with the *President* and *Hornet*, and toward noon had been joined by a small squadron under Commodore Decatur, whose broad pennon floated from the *United States*, 44. Her companions were the *Congress*, 38, Captain Smith, and *Argus*, 16, Lieutenant Commandant St. Clair.

Rodgers had received information that a large fleet of Jamaica-men had sailed for England under a strong convoy, and he believed that they must then be sweeping along the American coast in the current of the Gulf Stream. When his sailing orders arrived he resolved to make a dash at that convoy, and within an hour after receiving his dispatch from the Navy Department he had weighed anchor. With the united squadron he passed Sandy Hook that afternoon. In the evening he spoke an American merchantman that had seen the Jamaica fleet, and had been boarded by the British frigate *Belvidera*, 36. Rodgers crowded sail and commenced pursuit. Thirty-six hours elapsed, and the enemy were yet invisible; but an English war-vessel was espied on the northeastern horizon, and a general chase of the whole squadron commenced in that direction. The wind was fresh, and the enemy was standing before it.[1] The fleet *President* outstripped her companions, and rapidly gained on the fugitive. At four o'clock she was within gun-shot of the enemy, off Nantucket Shoals, when the wind fell, and the heavier *President* — heavier, because she had just left port — began to fall behind.

To cripple the stranger was now Rodgers's only hope of success. With his own hand he pointed and discharged one of his forecastle chase-guns, *the first hostile shot of the war fired afloat*.[2] It went crashing through the stern-frame of the stranger and into the gun-room with destructive effect, driving her people from the after part of the vessel. This was immediately followed by a shot from the first division below, directed by Lieutenant Gamble, which struck and damaged one of the stranger's stern-chasers. Rodgers fired again, and was followed immediately by Gamble, whose gun bursted, and killed and wounded sixteen men. It blew up the forecastle of the *President*, and threw Rodgers several feet into the air. In his descent one of his legs was broken. This accident caused a pause in the firing, when a shot from a stern-chaser of the stranger came plunging along the *President's* deck, killing a midshipman and one or two men.

It was now twilight, and the British ship having her spars and rigging imperiled by the *President's* fire, that vessel having yawed[3] for the purpose, began to lighten by cutting away her anchors, staving and throwing overboard her boats, and starting two tons of water. She gained headway; and, as a last resort, the *President* fired three broadsides, but with little effect. Unwilling to lighten his own ship, as it would impair his ability for a cruise, Rodgers ordered the pursuit to be abandoned at midnight.[a] The British vessel, it was afterward ascertained, was the frigate *Belvidera*, 36, Captain Richard Byron, that had boarded the American merchantman just mentioned. Her commander displayed great skill in saving his vessel. She sailed for Halifax for repairs,[4] and gave the first information there

[a] June 23, 1812.

---

[1] The commander of the English vessel had not heard of the declaration of war, and when he saw the squadron he stood toward it. But when he saw them suddenly take in their studding-sails and haul up in chase of him, frequently wetting the sails to profit by the lightness of the wind, he suspected hostility.

[2] The first on land was in the amphibious fight at Sackett's Harbor a month later. See page 368.

[3] To *yaw* is to steer wild, or out of the line of the ship's course.

[4] The *Belvidera* was badly injured in her hull, spars, and rigging. The *President* received a number of shots in her sails and rigging, but was not materially injured.

of the actual existence of war, so positively communicated to her by the *President*. In this action the American frigate had twenty-two men killed and wounded, sixteen of whom were injured by the bursting of the gun. The *Belvidera* lost seven killed and wounded by shot, and several others by splinters. Captain Byron was wounded in the thigh by the latter.[1]

R Byron

Rodgers now continued the chase after the Jamaica-men. Cocoanut shells, orange skins, and other evidences of his being in their track, were seen upon the water off the Banks of Newfoundland on the first of July. On the ninth the commander of an English letter-of-marque captured by the *Hornet* reported that he had seen the fleet on the previous evening, when he counted eighty-five sail, convoyed by a two-deck ship, a frigate, a sloop-of-war, and a brig. This intelligence stimulated Rodgers to greater exertions, and he continued the chase, ineffectually on account of fogs, until the 13th, when he was within a day's sail of the chops of the Irish Channel. Then he relinquished pursuit, sailed southwardly, and passed within thirty miles of the Rock of Lisbon, in sight of Madeira, the Western Islands, and the Grand Banks of Newfoundland, without falling in with a single vessel of war, and entered Boston Harbor after a cruise of seventy days. He had captured seven English merchantmen, recaptured an American vessel from a British cruiser, and brought in about one hundred and twenty prisoners. Many of the seamen of the squadron were sick of the scurvy, and several had died.

The news carried into Halifax by the *Belvidera* created a profound sensation there. The commandant of that naval station, Rear Admiral Sawyer, took measures immediately to collect a squadron for the purpose of cruising in search of Rodgers's ships or any other American vessels. Within a week, the *African*, 64, Captain Bustard; the *Shannon*, 38, Captain Broke; the *Guerriere*, 38, Captain Dacres; the *Belvidera*, 36, Captain Byron; and the *Æolus*, 32, Captain Lord James Townsend, were united in one squadron, under the command of Captain Broke, the senior officer, who made the *Shannon* his flag-ship. This force appeared off New York early in July, and made several captures, among them the United States brig *Nautilus*, 14, of Tripolitan fame,[2] Lieutenant Commandant Crane. She had arrived at New York just after Rodgers left, and went out immediately for the purpose of cruising in the track of the English West Indiamen. On the very next day she fell in with the British squadron, and, after a short and vigorous chase, was compelled to strike her colors to the *Shannon*, and surrender one hundred and six men. The *Nautilus* was *the first vessel of war taken on either side* in that contest. A prize crew was placed in her, and she was made one of Broke's squadron.[3] She was afterward fitted with sixteen 24-pound carronades, and commissioned as a cruiser.

THE CONSTITUTION IN 1860.

The *Constitution*, 44,[4] Captain Isaac

---

[1] Rodgers's journal and British account of the engagement, in Niles's Weekly Register, iii., 26; American account in the *Boston Centinel*, by an officer of the squadron; Cooper's *Naval History*, ii., 150.   [2] See page 120.

[3] In naval nomenclature, a number of vessels under one commander, less than ten, are called a *squadron;* more than ten, a *fleet*.

[4] The *Constitution* was built at Hart's ship-yard, in Boston, where Constitution Wharf now is, at a cost of $302,718. She was made very strong. Her frame was of live-oak, and her planks were bent on without steam, as it was thought that process softened and weakened the wood. She was launched on the 21st of October, 1797 (see page 100), in the presence of a great gathering of people. She did not start upon a cruise until the following season, when she was commanded by Captain James Nicholson, who died in New York on Sunday, the 2d of September, 1804, in the sixty-ninth

Hull, returned from foreign service at about the time of the declaration of war, and went into Chesapeake Bay, where she shipped a new crew, and on the 12th of July sailed from Annapolis on a cruise to the northward.[1] She was out of sight of land on the 17th, sailing under easy canvas with a light breeze, when, at one o'clock in the afternoon, she descried four vessels northward, heading westward. At four o'clock she discovered a fifth sail in a similar direction, which had the appearance of a vessel of war. By this time the other four were so near that they were distinguished as three ships and a brig. They were in sight all the afternoon, evidently watching the *Constitution*. At half past six a breeze sprang up from the southward, which brought the latter to the windward of the last discovered vessel. She was a British frigate. Hull determined to bear down upon and speak to her; and, to be ready for any emergency, he beat to quarters, and prepared his ship for action. The wind was very light, and the two frigates slowly approached each other during the evening. At ten o'clock the *Constitution* shortened sail and displayed a private signal. The lights were kept aloft for an hour without receiving an answer. At a quarter past eleven they were lowered, and the *Constitution* made sail again under a light breeze that prevailed all night. Just before dawn the stranger tacked, wore entirely round, threw up a rocket, and fired two signal-guns.

In the gray of early morning three other vessels were discovered on the starboard quarter of the *Constitution*, and three more astern, and at five o'clock a fourth was seen in the latter direction. The American cruiser had fallen in with Broke's squadron, and the vessel with which she had been manœuvring all night was the *Guerriere*, 38, Captain Dacres. The squadron was just out of gun-shot distance from the *Constitution*, and the latter found herself in the perilous position of having two frigates on her lee quarter, and a ship of the line, two frigates, a brig, and a schooner astern. The brig was the captured *Nautilus*.

Now commenced one of the most remarkable naval retreats and pursuits ever recorded. The *Constitution* was not powerful enough to fight the overwhelming force closing around her, and Hull perceived that her safety depended upon celerity in flight. There was almost a dead calm. Her sails flapped lazily, and she floated almost independently of the helm on the slowly undulating bosom of the sea. In this

---

year of his age. She was so stanch a ship that the name of *Ironsides* was given her. She always was favored with excellent commanders and performed gallant service. Some years ago the Navy Department concluded to break her up and sell her timbers, as she was thought to be a decided "invalid." The order had gone forth, when the execution of it was arrested by the voice of public opinion, called forth by the magic wand of a poet—the pen of Dr. Oliver Wendell Holmes, who wrote and published the following stirring protest against making merchandise of her:

"Ay, tear her tattered ensign down!
 Long has it waved on high,
And many an eye has danced to see
 That banner in the sky.
Beneath it rung the battle-shout,
 And burst the cannon's roar;
The meteor of the ocean air
 Shall sweep the clouds no more.

Her deck, once red with heroes' blood—
 Where knelt the vanquished foe,
When winds were humming o'er the flood,
 And waves were white below—

No more shall feel the victor's tread,
 Or know the conquered knee;
The harpies of the shore shall pluck
 The eagle of the sea!

O! better that her shattered hulk
 Should sink beneath the wave;
Her thunders shook the mighty deep,
 And there should be her grave.

Nail to the mast her holy flag,
 Set every threadbare sail,
And give her to the God of Storms,
 The lightning and the gale!"

"*Old Ironsides*" was saved, repaired, and converted into a school-ship. Such is her vocation now [1867]. She was lying at Annapolis in that capacity when the Great Rebellion broke out in 1861. Our little sketch exhibits her under full sail, as she appeared there in the autumn of 1860. When the Naval Academy was temporarily removed from Annapolis to Newport, Rhode Island, on account of the Rebellion, the *Constitution* took her place at the latter station. Her latest commander in the war of 1812–'15, Rear Admiral Charles Stewart, yet [1867] survives, at the age of ninety-one years. He is sometimes called *Old Ironsides*. His achievements in the *Constitution* will be noticed hereafter.

[1] The following is a list of the officers of the *Constitution* at that time: *Captain*, Isaac Hull; *Lieutenants*, Charles Morris, Alexander S. Wadsworth, Beekman V. Hoffman, George C. Read, John T. Shubrick, Charles W. Morgan; *Sailing-master*, John C. Alwyn; *Lieutenants of Marines*, William S. Bush, John Contee; *Surgeon*, Amos E. Evans; *Surgeon's Mates*, John D. Armstrong, Donaldson Yeates; *Purser*, Thomas J. Chew; *Midshipmen*, Henry Gilliam, Thomas Beatty, William D. Salter, Lewis Germain, William L. Gordon, Ambrose L. Field, Frederick Baury, Joseph Cross, Alexander Belcher, William Taylor, Alexander Eskridge, James W. Delancy, James Greenleaf, Allen Griffin, John Taylor; *Boatswain*, Peter Adams; *Gunner*, Robert Anderson.

listlessness there was danger. Down went her boats with long lines attached, and the sweeps were bent in towing her with the energy of men struggling for life and liberty. Up from her gun-deck was brought a long eighteen-pounder, and placed on her spar-deck as a stern-chaser, while another, of the same weight of metal and for a similar purpose, was pointed off the forecastle. Out of the cabin windows, when saws and axes had made them broad enough, two twenty-four pounders were run, and all the light cannon that would draw was set. She was just beginning to get under headway, with a gentle northwest wind blowing, when exertion was stimulated by the booming of the bow-guns of the *Shannon*. For ten minutes she sent forth her shot, but without effect, for she was yet beyond range. Again the breeze died away. Soundings showed twenty fathoms of water. A kedge[1] might be used. All spare rope was spliced and attached to one which was carried out half a mile ahead and cast into the deep. Quickly and strongly the crew "clapped on and walked away with the ship, overrunning and tripping the kedge as she came up with the end of the line."[2] This was frequently repeated, and the frigate moved off in a manner most mysterious to her pursuers. At length they discovered the secret and adopted the method, when the *Constitution*, having a little breeze, fired a shot at the *Shannon*, the nearest ship astern. At nine o'clock that vessel, employing a large number of men in boats and with a kedge, was gaining rapidly on the flying frigate. A conflict, unequal and terrible, seemed impending and inevitable, yet on board the *Constitution* the best spirit prevailed. Nearer and nearer drew the *Shannon*, and almost as closely the *Guerriere* was now pursuing on the larboard quarter of the imperiled vessel. All hope was fading, when a light breeze from the south struck the *Constitution* and brought her to windward. With such consummate skill did Captain Hull take advantage of the wind and bear gallantly away, that the admiration of the enemy was excited in the highest degree. As she came by the wind she brought the *Guerriere* nearly on her lee beam, when that vessel opened a fire from a broadside. The shot fell short, the blessed breeze that had come like a Providence at the critical moment died away, and the boats were again got out to tow by both parties. So anxious was Broke to get the *Shannon* near enough for action, that nearly all the boats of the squadron were employed for the purpose,[3] while the men of the *Constitution* made up in spirit what they lacked in numbers. Thus the race continued hour after hour all that day and night, the pursuers and the pursued sometimes towing, sometimes kedging.

The dawn of the second day of the chase was glorious. The sun rose with unusual splendor. Not a cloud was seen in the firmament. The sea was smooth, and a gentle wind was abroad, sufficient to make the murmur of ripples under the bow of the vessels fall pleasantly on the ear. All of the ships were on the same tack, and three of the English frigates were within long gun-shot of the *Constitution* on her lee quarter. The five frigates were clouded with canvas from their truck to their decks. Eleven sail were in sight. The scene was a most beautiful and exciting one. No guns were fired, for the distance between the belligerents widened. Either better sailing qualities or superior seamanship gave advantage to the *Constitution*. With that pleasant breeze she gained on her antagonists, and at four o'clock in the afternoon she was four miles ahead of the *Belvidera*, the nearest English ship. At seven heavy clouds began to brood over the sea, with indications of a squall. The *Constitution* prepared for it. It burst with fury—wind, lightning, and rain—but left that

---

[1] Kedge, or kedger, is a small anchor with an iron stock, used for keeping a vessel steady or warping it along.
[2] Cooper, ii., 156.
[3] Coggeshall, in his *History of the American Privateers and Letters of Marque*, relates (page 12) that his friend, Captain Brown, who was a prisoner on board the *Shannon*, was amused to hear Captain Broke and his officers converse about the "Yankee frigate." At one period of the chase they were so confident of capturing her that a prize-crew were already appointed to conduct her in triumph to Halifax. To all their questions about her, as she was seen speeding before them, Captain Brown had but one answer, namely, "Gentlemen, you will never take that frigate."

good frigate unharmed. The pursuers and the pursued lost sight of each other for a while in the murky vapor. In less than an hour the squall had passed to leeward, and the *Constitution*, sheeted home, her main and top-gallant sails set, was flying away from the enemy at the rate of eleven knots. At twilight the pursuers were in sight, and at near midnight they fired two guns. Away went the *Constitution* before the wind, and at six in the morning the topsails of the British vessel were seen from the American, beginning to dip below the horizon. At a quarter past eight the Englishman relinquished the pursuit, and hauled off to the northward; and a few days afterward the British fleet separated for the purpose of cruising in different directions. Thus ended a chase of sixty-four hours, chiefly off the New England coast, remarkable alike for its length, closeness, and activity. It was a theme for much newspaper comment, and a poet of the day, singing of the exploits of the *Constitution*, referred to this as follows:

> " 'Neath Hull's command, with a tough band,
>   And naught beside to back her,
> Upon a day, as log-books say,
>   A fleet bore down to thwack her.
> A fleet, you know, is odds, or so,
>   Against a single ship, sirs;
> So 'cross the tide her legs she tried,
>   And gave the rogues the slip, sirs."

A few days after Rodgers left New York, Captain Porter sailed from that harbor in the *Essex*, 32, from the mast-head of which fluttered a flag bearing conspicuously the words, "FREE TRADE AND SAILORS' RIGHTS." He captured several English merchant vessels soon after leaving Sandy Hook, making trophy bonfires of most of them on the ocean, and their crews his prisoners. After cruising southward for some weeks in disguise, capturing a prize now and then, he turned northward again, and met with increased success. One night, by the dim light of a mist-veiled moon, he chased a fleet of English transports bearing a thousand soldiers toward Halifax or the St. Lawrence, convoyed by the frigate *Mercury*, 36, and a bomb vessel. They were sailing wide, and he captured one of the transports, with one hundred and fifty men, before dawn, without attracting the attention of the rest of the fleet, for no guns were fired.

A few days after this,[a] while sailing in the disguise of a merchantman, her gun-deck ports in, top-gallant masts housed, and sails trimmed in a slovenly manner, the *Essex* fell in with a sail to windward. The stranger came bearing down gallantly, when the *Essex* showed an American ensign, and kept away under short sail, as if trying to avoid a contest. This emboldened the English vessel. She followed the *Essex* for some time, and finally running down on her weather quarter, set her national colors, and, with three cheers from her people, opened fire. She was soon undeceived, and her temerity was severely punished. The ports of the *Essex* were knocked out in an instant, and the fire of the enemy was responded to with terrible effect. The assailant was so damaged and disconcerted that the conflict was made short. It was a complete surprise. A panic seized her people, and, in spite of the efforts of her officers, they fled below for safety.[1] Scarcely eight minutes had elapsed from the firing of the first gun, when the stranger, which proved to be the British ship *Alert*, Captain T. L. P. Laugharne, mounting twenty 18-pound carronades and six smaller guns, struck her colors and was reported to be in a sinking condition. When Lieutenant Finch, of the *Essex*, went on board to receive her flag, he found seven feet water in the hold. She was a stanch vessel, and had been built for the coal trade. She was purchased for the British navy in 1804, and the complement of her crew was one hundred and thirty men and boys. She was every way inferior to the *Essex*, whose armament was forty 32-pound carronades and six long twelves, and her complement of men was three hundred and twenty-five. The capture of the *Alert* possesses no special historical interest excepting from the fact that

[a] August 13, 1812.

---
[1] It is said that some of them, after their exchange, were executed for deserting their guns.

she was *the first British national vessel captured in the war.* The *Alert* had three men wounded, while the *Essex* sustained no injury whatever.

The *Essex* was now crowded with prisoners, and Porter became conscious of the fact that they had entered into a plot to rise and take the vessel from him. The leaks of the *Alert* being stopped, and all things put in fair seaworthy condition, Porter made an arrangement with Captain Laugharne[1] to convert her into a *cartel* ship. When this was accomplished, the prisoners were placed on board of her, and she was sent into St. John's, Newfoundland. On her return to the United States she was fitted up for the government service.

The *Essex* continued her cruise to the southward, and on the thirtieth of August, just at twilight, fell in with a British frigate in latitude 36° N. and longitude 62° W.[2] Porter prepared for action, and the two vessels stood for each other. Night fell, and Porter, anxious for combat, ran up a light. It was answered at the distance of about four miles. The *Essex* sought the stranger in that direction, but in vain, and when the day dawned she had disappeared. Five days afterward Porter fell in with "two ships of war to the southward and a brig to the northward—the brig in chase of an American merchant ship."[3] The *Essex* pursued, when the brig attempted to pass and join the other two vessels. The *Essex* headed her, turned her course northward, and continued the chase until abreast the merchantman, when, the wind being light, the brig escaped by the use of her sweeps.

When the *Essex* showed her colors to the merchantman, the two British vessels at the southward discovered them, fired signal-guns, and gave chase. At four o'clock in the afternoon they were in the wake of the *Essex* and rapidly gaining upon her, when Porter hoisted the American colors, and fired a gun to the windward, expecting to escape by some manœuvre in the approaching darkness. At sunset the larger of the two vessels was within five miles, and rapidly shortening the distance between her and the *Essex.* Porter determined to heave about after dark, and, if he could not pass his pursuer, give her a broadside and lay her or board. The crew were in fine spirits, and when this movement was proposed to them they gave three hearty cheers. Preparations for action were immediately made. The *Essex* hove round and bore away to the southwest, but the night being dark and squally, Porter saw no more of the enemy. Supposing himself cut off from New York and Boston by a British squadron, he made for the Delaware.[4]

Soon after Captain Porter reached the Delaware a circumstance occurred which created quite a sensation in the public mind for a few days. A week after the declaration of war a writer in a New York paper charged Captain Porter with cruelly treating an English seaman on board of the *Essex* who refused to fight against his countrymen, pleading, among other reasons, that if caught he would be hung as a deserter from the British navy. This story reached Sir James Lucas Yeo, commander of the frigate *Southampton,* then on the West India station. By a prisoner in his hands, who was sent home on parole, he forwarded a message to Porter which ap-

---

[1] Thomas Lamb Polden Laugharne entered the British navy in 1798, at the age of twelve years. He was a most faithful and active officer, and advanced steadily to the post of commander, which he attained in 1811. He was appointed to the command of the sloop *Alert* in February, 1812. His last appointment afloat was to the *Achates,* 18, in which he cruised in the Channel until November, 1815. In 1823 he became inspecting commander in the coast-guard, was advanced to post-captain, when he retired from the service on half-pay. He is yet [1867] living.

[2] The reader who may consult a modern map while studying this account should remember that at that time the longitude was calculated from the meridian of Greenwich, in England. In modern American maps it is calculated from Washington City, the national capital.

[3] Manuscript letter of Captain Porter to the Secretary of the Navy, dated "At sea, September 5, 1812."

[4] Porter's manuscript letter, September 5, 1812. That letter is before me. It contains a rough sketch of the nautical movement just described. "Considering this escape a very extraordinary one," he wrote, "I have the honor to inclose you a sketch of the position of the ships at three different periods, by which you will perceive at once the plan of effecting it." According to a letter from an officer of the *Shannon,* that frigate was the larger of the two vessels that chased the *Essex* on that occasion, and the other vessel, instead of being a "ship of war," as Porter supposed, was the *Planter,* a recaptured West Indiaman. In the light of this fact we perceive that Porter's escape was not very "extraordinary." The American merchantman mentioned in the text was the *Minerva,* from Cadiz. She was burnt by the English on the morning succeeding the chase.

peared in the following language on the 18th of September, 1812, in the *Democratic Press,* printed in Philadelphia: "A passenger of the brig *Lyon,* from Havana to New York, captured by the frigate *Southampton,* Sir James Yeo commander, is requested by Sir James Yeo to present his compliments to Captain Porter, commander of the American frigate *Essex*—would be glad to have a *tête-à-tête* any where between the Capes of Delaware and the Havana, where he would have the pleasure to break his own sword over his damned head, and put him down forward in irons."

To this indecorous challenge Captain Porter replied as follows on the same day: "Captain Porter, of the United States frigate *Essex,* presents his compliments to Sir James Yeo, commanding H. B. M.'s frigate *Southampton,* and accepts with pleasure his polite invitation. If agreeable to Sir James, Captain Porter would prefer meeting near the Delaware, where Captain P. pledges his honor to Sir James that no other American vessel shall interrupt their *tête-à-tête.* The Essex may be known by a flag bearing the motto FREE TRADE AND SAILORS' RIGHTS, and when that is struck to the *Southampton* Captain P. will deserve the treatment promised by Sir James.[1] Here the matter ended. The coveted *tête-à-tête* never occurred.

The *Constitution* did not long continue idle after her escape from Broke's squadron. She remained a short time in Boston to recuperate, and on the 2d of August sailed eastward in hope of falling in with some one of the English vessels of war supposed to be hovering along the coast from Nantucket to Halifax. Hull,[2] her commander, was specially anxious

---

[1] The original of Porter's acceptance is in the possession of Doctor Leonard D. Koecker, of Philadelphia, who kindly allowed me to make from it the *fac-simile* of the paragraph given in the text.

[2] Isaac Hull was born at Derby, Connecticut, in 1775. He first entered the merchant service, and in 1798 became a fourth lieutenant in the infant navy of the United States, under Commodore Nicholson. In 1800 he was promoted to first lieutenant under Commodore Talbot. In 1804 he commanded the brig *Argus,* and distinguished himself at the storming of Tripoli and the reduction of Derne. He was made captain in 1806, and was in command of the *Constitution* when the war broke out. Of his achievements in her the text furnishes a detailed account. Commodore Hull served in the American navy, afloat and ashore, with the rank of captain, thirty-seven years. He commanded in the Mediterranean and Pacific, and had charge of the navy yards at Boston and Washington. He was a member of the Naval Board for several years. Commodore Hull died at his residence in Philadelphia on the 9th of February, 1843. His remains rest in *Laurel Hill Cemetery,* and over them is a beautiful altar-tomb of Italian marble, made by John Struthers and Sons. It is a copy of the tomb of Scipio Barbato at Rome, chastely ornamented, and surmounted by an American eagle in

to fall in with that famous frigate before whom he had been compelled to fly when she was part of a squadron, and of whom it had been said,

> "Long the tyrant of our coast
>   Reigned the famous *Guerriere;*
> Our little navy she defied,
>   Public ship and privateer:
> On her sails, in letters red,
>   To our captains were displayed
> Words of warning, words of dread:
>   'All who meet me have a care!
> I am England's *Guerriere.*' "[1]

The commander of the *Guerriere* had boastfully enjoined the Americans to remember that she was not the *Little Belt*,[2] and this offensive form of menace increased Hull's desire to meet her and measure strength with her.

The *Constitution* ran not far from the shore down to the Bay of Fundy without meeting a single armed vessel. She then bore away southward off Cape Sable, and eastward to the region of Halifax, but with a like result. Hull now determined to cruise eastward of Nova Scotia to the Gulf of St. Lawrence, with the hope of interrupting vessels making their way to Halifax or Quebec. In this new field he made some winnings, but the promise of much harvest was too small to detain him. He turned his prow southward, and on the nineteenth, at two o'clock in the afternoon, in latitude 41° 40′, and longitude 55° 48′,[3] his heart was gladdened by the discovery of a sail from his mast-head, too remote, however, for her character to be determined.

The *Constitution* immediately gave chase to the stranger, and at half past three o'clock it was discovered that she was a frigate, and doubtless an enemy. Hull let his ship run free until within a league of the stranger to leeward, when he began to shorten sail and deliberately prepare for action. The stranger at once showed signs of willingness for a fight. Hull cleared his ship, beat to quarters, hoisted the American colors, and bore down gallantly on the enemy, with the intention of bringing her into close combat immediately.

---

full relief, in the attitude of defending the national flag, on which it stands. There is a cannon-ball under the flag, on which rests one of the eagle's talons. Upon the south side of the tomb is the name of ISAAC HULL. On the north side is the following inscription, written by his friend Horace Binney, Esq.: "FEBRUARY IX., MDCCCXLIII. In affectionate devotion to the private virtues of ISAAC HULL, his widow has erected this monument." The above likeness of Hull is from an engraving by Edwin, from a painting by Stewart.

[1] A feminine warrior—an Amazon. The *Guerriere* was originally a French ship, and was captured on the 19th of July, 1806, by the British ship *Blanche*, Captain Lavie. She was built at L'Orient upon a sudden emergency, and her timbers, not having been well seasoned, were in a somewhat decaying state at this time, it is said.

[2] See page 184.
[3] See note 2, page 440.

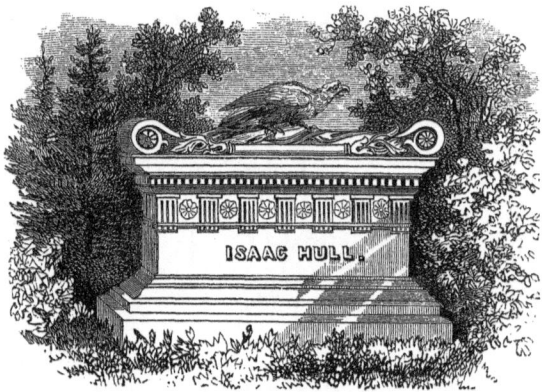

HULL'S MONUMENT.

> "'Clear ship for action!' sounds the boatswain's call;
> 'Clear ship for action!' his three mimics bawl.
> Swift round the decks see war's dread weapons hurled,
> And floating ruins strew the watery world.
> 'All hands to quarters!' fore and aft resounds,
> Thrills from the fife, and from the drum-head bounds;
> From crowded hatchways scores on scores arise,
> Spring up the shrouds, and vault into the skies.
> Firm at his quarters each bold gunner stands,
> The death-fraught lightning flashing from his hands."

Comprehending Hull's movement, the Englishman hoisted three national ensigns,[1] fired a broadside of grape-shot, filled away, and gave another broadside on the other tack, but without effect. The missiles all fell short. The stranger continued to manœuvre for about three quarters of an hour, endeavoring to get in a position to rake and prevent being raked, when, disappointed, she bore up and ran under topsails and jib, with the wind on the quarter. The *Constitution*, following closely, yawed occasionally to rake and avoid being raked, and firing only a few guns as they bore, as she did not wish to engage in a serious conflict until they were close to each other.

It was now about six in the evening. These indications on the part of the enemy to engage in a fair yard-arm and yard-arm fight caused the *Constitution* to press all sail to get alongside of the foe. At a little after six the bows of the American began to double the quarter of the Englishman. Hull had been walking the quarter-deck, keenly watching every movement. He was quite fat, and wore very tight breeches. As the shot of the *Guerriere* began to tell upon the *Constitution*, the gallant Lieutenant Morris, Hull's second in command, came to the captain and asked permission to open fire. "Not yet," quietly responded Hull. Nearer and nearer the vessels drew toward each other, and the request was repeated. "Not yet," said Hull again, very quietly. When the *Constitution* reached the point we have just mentioned, Hull, filled with sudden and intense excitement, bent himself twice to the deck, and then shouted, "Now, boys, pour it into them!" The command was instantly obeyed. The *Constitution* opened her forward guns, which were double shotted with round and grape, with terrible effect. When the smoke that followed the result of that order cleared away, it was discovered that the commander, in his energetic movements, had split his tight breeches from waistband to knee, but he did not stop to change them during the action.[2]

The concussion of Hull's broadside was tremendous. It cast those in the cockpit of the enemy from one side of the room to the other, and, before they could adjust themselves, the blood came streaming from above, and numbers, dreadfully mutilated, were handed down to the surgeons. The enemy at the same time was pouring heavy metal into the *Constitution*. They were only half pistol-shot from each other, and the destruction was terrible. Within fifteen minutes after the contest commenced the stranger's mizzen-mast was shot away, her main yard was in slings, and her hull, spars, sails, and rigging were torn in pieces. The English vessel brought up in the wind as her mizzen-mast gave way, when the *Constitution* passed slowly ahead, poured in a tremendous fire as her guns bore, luffed short round the bows of her antagonist to prevent being raked, and fell foul of her foe, her bowsprit running into the larboard quarter of the stranger. In this situation the cabin of the *Constitution* was set on fire by the explosion of the forward guns of her enemy, but the flames were soon extinguished.

Both parties now attempted to board. The roar of great guns was terrible, and

---

[1] This is alluded to in an old song called "Halifax Station," written and very extensively sung soon after the event commemorated occurred:

> "Then up to each mast-head he straight sent a flag,
> Which shows on the ocean a proud British brag;
> But Hull, being pleasant, he sent up but one,
> And told every seaman to stand true to his gun."

[2] Statement of Lieutenant B. V. Hoffman.

the fierce volleys of musketry on both sides, together with the heavy sea that was running, made that movement impossible. The English piped all hands from below, and mounted them on the forward deck for the purpose; and Lieutenant Morris, Alwyn, the master, and Lieutenant Bush, of the Marines, sprang upon the taffrail of the *Constitution* to lead their men to the same work. Morris was severely but not fatally shot through the body; Alwyn was wounded in the shoulder; and a bullet through his brain brought Bush dead to the deck. Just then the sails of the *Constitution* were filled, and as she shot ahead and clear of her antagonist, whose fore-mast had been severely wounded, that spar fell, carrying with it the main-mast, and leaving the hapless vessel a shivering, shorn, and helpless wreck, rolling like a log in the trough of the sea, entirely at the mercy of the billows.

> "Quick as lightning, and fatal as its dreaded power,
> Destruction and death on the *Guerriere* did shower,
> While the groans of the dying were heard on the blast.
> The word was, 'Take aim, boys, away with the mast!'
> The genius of Britain will long rue the day.
> The *Guerriere*'s a wreck in the trough of the sea;
> Her laurels are withered, her boasting is done;
> Submissive, to leeward she fires her last gun."—OLD SONG.

The *Constitution* hauled off a short distance, secured her own masts, rove new rigging, and at sunset wore round and took a favorable position for raking the wreck.

JAMES RICHARD DACRES.

A jack that had been kept flying on the stump of the enemy's mizzen-mast was now lowered, and the late Commodore George C. Read, then a third lieutenant, was sent on board of the prize. She was found to be the *Guerriere*, 38, Captain James Richards Dacres, one of the vessels which had so lately been engaged in the memorable chase of her present conqueror, and which Hull was anxious to meet. The lieutenant asked for the commander of the prize, when Captain Dacres appeared. "Commodore Hull's compliments," said Read, "and wishes to know if you have struck your flag?" Captain Dacres, looking up and down, coolly and dryly remarked, "Well, I don't know; our mizzen-mast is gone, our main-mast is gone, and, upon the whole, you may say we *have* struck our flag." Read then said, "Commodore Hull's compliments, and wishes to know whether you need the assistance of a surgeon or surgeon's mate?" Dacres replied, "Well, I should suppose you had on board your own ship business enough for all your medical officers." Read replied, "Oh no; we have only seven wounded, and they were dressed half an hour ago."[1]

---

[1] Statement of Captain William B. Orne, in the New York *Evening Post*. He commanded the American brig *Betsey*, and when returning from Naples in the summer of 1812, she was captured by the *Guerriere*. Captain Orne was a prisoner on board of her at the time of the action, and was treated by Captain Dacres with the greatest courtesy. When that commander's interview with Read was concluded, he turned to Orne and said, "How have our situations been changed! You are now free, and I am a prisoner."

James Richard Dacres was a son of Vice Admiral J. R. Dacres, who was in command of the British schooner *Carleton*, on Lake Champlain, in the fight with Arnold's flotilla in 1776. Young Dacres entered the royal navy in 1796, on board the *Sceptre*, 64, commanded by his father. His first service was against the French, in which he exhibited excellent qualities. He was promoted to the command of the sloop *Elk* in 1805, and the next year was transferred to the *Bacchante*, 24. He was appointed to the command of the *Guerriere* in March, 1811. She then carried 48 guns, and was called "a worn-out frigate." See O'Byrne's *Naval Biography*. He was wounded in the action with the *Constitution*. He was unanimously acquitted by the court-martial at Halifax that tried him for surrendering his ship. He commanded the

The *Constitution* kept near her prize all night. At two in the morning a strange sail was seen closing upon them, when she cleared for action, but an hour later the intruder stood off and disappeared. At dawn the officer in charge of the *Guerriere* hailed to say that she had four feet water in her hold and was in danger of sinking. Hull immediately sent all his boats to bring off the prisoners and their effects.[1] That duty was accomplished by noon, and at three o'clock the prize crew was recalled. The *Guerriere* was too much damaged to be saved; so she was set on fire, and fifteen minutes afterward she blew up, scattering widely upon the subsiding billows all that was left of the boastful cruiser that was "not the *Little Belt*."[2]

> "Isaac did so maul and rake her,
> That the decks of Captain Dacre
> Were in such a woful pickle
> As if Death, with scythe and sickle,
> With his sling or with his shaft,
> Had cut his harvest fore and aft.
> Thus, in thirty minutes, ended
> Mischiefs that could not be mended;
> Masts, and yards, and ship descended
> All to David Jones's locker—
> Such a ship, in such a pucker!"—OLD SONG.

The *Constitution* arrived at Boston on the 30th of August, and on that day Captain Hull wrote his official dispatch to the Secretary of War, dated "U. S. frigate *Constitution*, off Boston Light." He was the first to announce to his countrymen the intelligence of his own victory. That intelligence was received with the most lively demonstrations of joy in every part of the republic, and dispelled for a moment the gloom occasioned by the recent disasters at Detroit in the surrender of General Hull. When the *Constitution* appeared in Boston Harbor, she was surrounded by a flotilla of gayly-decorated small boats, and the hundreds of people who filled them made the air tremble with their loud huzzas. At the wharf where he landed he was received with a national salute by an artillery company, which was returned by the *Constitution*. An immense assemblage of citizens were there to greet him and escort him to quarters prepared for him in the city, and the whole town was filled with tumultuous joy. The streets through which the triumphal procession passed were decorated with flags and banners. From almost every window ladies waved their white handkerchiefs, and from the crowded side-pavements shout after shout of the citizens greeted the hero. Men of all ranks hastened to pay homage to the conqueror. A splendid public entertainment was given him and his officers by the inhabitants of Boston, and almost six hundred citizens, of both political parties, sat down to the banquet in token of their appreciation of the gallant commander's

---

Tiber from 1814 to 1818. He continued in service afloat. In 1838 he attained flag rank, answering to our commodore, and in 1845 was appointed commander-in-chief at the Cape of Good Hope, his flag-ship being the *President*, 50. Vice Admiral Dacres died in England, at an advanced age, on the 4th of December, 1853. The preceding likeness of Captain Dacres (Vice Admiral of the Red) is from a print published in London in October, 1831.

[1] "I feel it my duty to state that the conduct of Captain Hull and his officers to our men has been that of a brave enemy, the greatest care being taken to prevent our men losing the smallest trifle, and the greatest attention being paid to the wounded."—Captain Dacres's Report to Vice Admiral Sawyer, September 7, 1812.

[2] Three days before the action between the *Constitution* and *Guerriere*, the *John Adams*, Captain Fash, from Liverpool, was spoken by the English frigate. Upon Fash's register, which he deposited at the New York Custom-house, the following lines were found written:

"Captain Dacres, commander of his Britannic majesty's frigate *Guerriere*, of 44 guns, presents his compliments to Commodore Rodgers, of the United States frigate *President*, and will be very happy to meet him, or any other American frigate of equal force to the *President*, off Sandy Hook, for the purpose of having a few minutes' *tête-à-tête*."

To this fact a poet of the day, an American gentleman then living at St. Bartholomew's, thus alluded:

> "This Briton oft had made his boast
> He'd with his crew, a chosen host,
> Pour fell destruction round our coast,
>   And work a revolution;
> Urged by his pride, a challenge sent
> Bold Rodgers, in the *President*,
>   Wishing to meet
>   Him *tête-à-tête*,
> Or one his equal from our fleet—
> Such was the *Constitution*."

services.¹ The citizens of New York raised money for the purchase of swords to be presented to Captain Hull and his officers; and the Corporation offered the gallant victor the freedom of the city in a gold box,ᵃ with an appropriate inscription.² Hull was also requested by the same Corporation to sit for his portrait, to be hung in the picture-gallery of the City Hall.³ In Philadelphia the citizens, at a general meeting, resolved to present to Captain Hull "a piece of plate of the most elegant workmanship, with appropriate emblems, devices, and inscriptions," and that "a like piece of plate be presented to Lieutenant Morris, in the name of the citizens of Philadelphia." They also resolved to present tokens of their gratitude to the other officers of the *Constitution*. The Congress of the United States, by resolution, voted a gold medal to Captain Hull,⁴ and fifty thousand dollars to be dis-

ᵃ December 28, 1812.

¹ A stirring ode was sung at the table. It was written for the occasion by the late L. M. Sargent, Esq., then an eminent and highly esteemed citizen of Boston. The victory of Hull, so complete, and obtained over a foe so nearly equal in strength, gave promise of future successes on the ocean, and inspired the most doubting heart with hope. This hope was expressed in the following closing stanza of Mr. Sargent's ode:

"Hence be our floating bulwarks
    Those oaks our mountains yield;
'Tis mighty Heaven's plain decree—
    Then take the watery field!
To ocean's farthest barriers, then,
    Your whitening sails shall pour;
Safe they'll ride o'er the tide
    While Columbia's thunders roar;
While her cannon's fire is flashing fast,
    And her Yankee thunders roar."

² This is a merely complimentary act, by which a person, for gallant or useful services, is honored with the nominal right to all the privileges and immunities of a citizen by the government of a city. When Andrew Hamilton, of Philadelphia, nobly defended the liberty of the press, and procured the acquittal of John Peter Zenger, a New York printer, who was accused of libel by the governor in 1735, the Corporation of New York presented that able lawyer the freedom of the city in a gold box for his noble advocacy of popular rights. When Washington Irving returned to New York, after twenty years' absence in Europe, the freedom of the city was given to him as a compliment for his distinction as an American author when successful ones were rare.

The ceremony of presentation to Captain Hull took place in the Common Council Chamber of the City Hall. A committee, consisting of Aldermen Fish and Mesier, and General Morton, introduced Hull to the Common Council, when De Witt Clinton, the mayor, arose and addressed him. He then presented him with the diploma, elegantly executed in vellum,* and a richly-embossed gold box, with a representation of the battle between the *Constitution* and *Guerriere* painted in enamel. Hull responded in a few low and modest words, after which the mayor administered to him the freeman's oath.

³ In that gallery hang the portraits of the successive governors of the State of New York. On that account it is known as the Governors' Room.

⁴ On one side of this medal, represented of the exact size of the original in the above engraving, is seen the likeness of Captain Hull in profile, with the legend ISACUS HULL PERITOS ARTE SUPERAT JUL. MDCCCXII. ANG. CERTAMINE FORTES. This legend (and date) seems to refer to the skill of Hull in escaping from the British fleet the previous month, for it asserts that his stratagem overmatched the experienced English. On the reverse of the medal is seen a naval engagement, in which the *Guerriere* is represented as receiving the deadly shots that cut away her mizzen-mast. The legend is HORÆ MOMENTO VICTORIA, and the exergue INTER CONST. NAV. AMER ET GUER. NAV. ANGL.—the abbreviation of words indicating action "between the American ship *Constitution* and the English ship *Guerriere*."

* The form of words in which this instrument is expressed will be found in another part of this work, where an account is given of a similar honor conferred on General Jacob Brown.

tributed as prize-money among the officers and crew of the victor, whose example was "highly honorable to the American character and instructive to our rising navy."[1]

It is difficult to comprehend at this time the feeling which this victory of the Americans created on both sides of the Atlantic. The British, as we have observed, looked with contempt upon the American navy, while the Americans looked upon that of England with dread. The naval flag of England had seldom been lowered to an enemy during the lapse of a century, and the people had come to believe her "wooden walls" to be impregnable. Dacres himself, though less a boaster than most of his countrymen in command, had similar faith. He believed that an easy victory awaited him whenever he should be so fortunate as to meet *any* American vessel in conflict; and he constantly expressed a desire to show how quickly he would make the "striped bunting" trail in his presence. Very great, then, was the disappointment of the commander of the *Guerriere*, the service, and the British people, when Hull's victory was accomplished. The Americans, on the other hand, as we have observed, had little confidence in the power of their navy, and at that time they were cast down by the heavy blow to their hopes in the misfortunes of the Army of the Northwest at Detroit. This victory, therefore, so unexpected and so complete, was like the sudden bursting forth of the morning sun, without preceding twilight, after a night of tempest, and the joy of the whole people was unbounded. It was natural for them to indulge in many extravagances, yet these were only the mere demonstrative evidences of a new-born faith that had taken hold of the American mind. This victory was, therefore, of immense importance, inasmuch as it gave the Americans confidence, and dispelled the idea of the absolute omnipotence of the British navy. Its momentous bearing upon the future of the war was at once perceived by statesmen and publicists on both sides, and zealous discussions at once arose concerning the relative strength, and force, and armament of the two vessels, and the comparative merits of the two commanders as exhibited in their conduct before and during the action.

There was a tendency on the part of the Americans to overestimate the importance of the victory and the powers of their seamen, and there was an equal tendency of the organs of British opinion to underestimate it, and to detract from the merits of the conqueror by disparaging the strength and condition of the *Guerriere*. The very writers who had spoken of the *Constitution* as "a bundle of pine-boards" now called her one of the stanchest vessels afloat; and the *Guerriere*, which they had praised as a frigate worthy of the exhibition of British valor when she was captured from the French, and able to drive "the insolent striped bunting from the seas," was now spoken of as "an old worn-out frigate," with damaged masts, a reduced complement, and "in absolute need of thorough refit," for which "she was then on her way to Halifax." Yet the London *Times*, then, as now, the leading journal in England, and then, as now, the bitter enemy of the United States, and implacable foe of every supposed rival or competitor of England, was compelled, in deep mortification, to view the affair as a severe blow struck at Britain's boasted supremacy of the seas. "We have been accused of sentiments unworthy of Englishmen," it said, "because we described what we saw and felt on the occasion of the capture of the *Guerriere*. We witnessed the gloom which that event cast over high and honorable minds; we participated in the vexation and regret; and it is the first time we have ever heard that *the striking of the English flag on the high seas to any thing like an equal force* should be regarded by Englishmen with complacency and satisfaction. . . . . It is not merely that an English frigate has been taken, after, what we are free to confess, may be called a brave resistance, but that it has been taken by a *new enemy*, an enemy unaccustomed to *such triumphs, and likely to be rendered insolent and confident by them*. He must

---

[1] Resolutions of the House of Representatives, November 5, 1812.

be a weak politician who does not see how important the first triumph is in giving a tone and character to the war. *Never before in the history of the world did an English frigate strike to an American;* and though we can not say that Captain Dacres, under all circumstances, is punishable for this act, yet we do say that there are commanders in the English navy who would a thousand times rather have gone down with their colors flying than have set their brother-officers so fatal an example." William James, one of the most bitterly partisan and unscrupulous historians of the war, was constrained to say, "There is no question that our vanity received a wound in the loss of the *Guerriere*. But, poignant as were the national feelings, reflecting men hailed the 19th of August, 1812, as the commencement of an era of renovation to the navy of England."[1]

The advantage in the action, in guns, men, and stanchness, was undoubtedly on the side of the *Constitution*, yet not so much as to make the contest really an unequal one. The vessels rated respectively 44 and 38, while the *Constitution* actually carried in the action 56, and the *Guerriere* 49. The latter was pierced for 54 and carried 50 when she was captured from the French.[2] Her gun-deck metal was lighter than that of the *Constitution*, but the rest of her armament was the same. Notwithstanding this disparity, the weight of the respective broadsides, according to the most authentic account, could not have varied very materially.[3] The crew of the *Constitution* greatly outnumbered that of the *Guerriere*, being 468 against 253. That of the latter had a great advantage in experience and discipline; for they had been long in naval service, while the crew of the *Constitution* was newly shipped for this cruise, and mostly from the merchant service.

According to the official report of Captain Hull, the action lasted thirty minutes, while Dacres said its duration was two hours and twelve minutes. This discrepancy may be reconciled by the consideration that the British commander probably counted from the time when the *Guerriere* fired her first gun, which the *Constitution* did not respond to, and the American commander computed from the moment when he poured in his first broadside. The *Guerriere* was made a wreck—the *Constitution* was severely wounded in spars and rigging. The American loss was seven killed and seven wounded. The British loss was fifteen killed, forty-four wounded, and twenty-four (including two officers) missing. Dacres was severely wounded in the back.

At that time there were more captains in the navy than vessels for them to command; and Captain Hull, with noble generosity and rare contentment with the laurels already won, gave up the command of his frigate for the sole purpose of giving others a chance to distinguish themselves. Captain Bainbridge, one of the oldest officers in the service, and then in command of the *Constellation*, 38, which was fitting out for sea at Washington, was appointed Hull's successor. He was made a flag officer, and the *Essex*, 32, and *Hornet*, 28, was placed under his command. He hoisted his broad pennant on board the *Constitution*, and sailed from Boston on a cruise on the 15th of September. Captain Charles Stewart was assigned to the command of the *Constellation;* and not long afterward, Lieutenant Morris, Hull's second in command, who was severely wounded when gallantly attempting to lead a boarding-party to the decks of the *Guerriere*, was promoted to captain. Of Bainbridge's cruise I shall write presently. Let us now consider a most gallant exploit of the *Wasp*, an inferior member of the United States Navy.

The sloop-of-war *Wasp*, 18, was considered one of the finest and fastest sailers of her class. She was built immediately after the close of the war with Tripoli, and was thor-

---

[1] *Naval Occurrences*, page 116.
[2] Captain Lavie's Letter to Lord Keith, July 26, 1806. "*Le Guerriere*," he said, "is of the largest class of frigates, mounting fifty guns, with a complement of 317 men."
[3] By actual weighing of the balls of both ships by an officer of the *Constitution*, it was found that the American 24's were only three pounds heavier than the English 18's on that occasion, and that there was nearly the same difference in favor of the latter's 32's.—Cooper's *Naval History*, etc., ii., 173, Note *.

oroughly manned and equipped. She mounted sixteen 32-pound carronades and two long 12's, and also carried, usually, two small brass cannon in her tops. Her officers were always proud of her, as an admirable specimen of their country's naval architecture. At the kindling of the war she was on the European coast, the only government vessel, excepting the *Constitution*, then abroad; and at the time of the declaration of hostilities by the American Congress, she was on her way home as bearer of dispatches from the diplomatic representatives of the United States in Europe. Her commander was Captain Jacob Jones, a brave officer, in whose veins ran much pure, indomitable Welsh blood.[1]

On the thirteenth of October, 1812, the *Wasp* left the Delaware on a cruise, with a full complement of men, about one hundred and thirty-five in number. She ran off southeasterly to clear the coast and strike the tracks of vessels that might be steering north for the West Indies, and on the sixteenth encountered a heavy gale, which carried away her jib-boom, and with it two of her crew. The storm abated on the following day;[a] and toward midnight, when in latitude thirty-seven north, and longitude sixty-five west, his watch discovered several sail, two of them appearing to be large vessels. Ignorant of the true character of the strangers, Captain Jones thought it prudent to keep at a respectful distance until the morning light should give him better information. All night the *Wasp* kept a course parallel with that of the stranger vessels. At dawn she gave chase, and it was soon discovered that the strangers were a fleet of armed merchant vessels under the protection of the British sloop-of-war *Frolic*, mounting sixteen thirty-two-pound carronades, two long six-pounders, and two twelve-pound carronades on her forecastle. She was manned with a crew of one hundred and eight persons, under Captain Thomas Whinyates,[2] who had been her commander for more than five years. She was con-

[a] October 18, 1812.

---

[1] Jacob Jones was born in the year 1770, near the village of Smyrna, Kent County, Delaware. His father was a farmer, and the maiden name of his mother was likewise Jones. He received a good academic education, and at the age of eighteen years commenced the study of medicine and surgery. He began the practice of his profession at Dover, in his native state, but did not pursue it long. He found the field well occupied, and, being active and ambitious, resolved to abandon his profession for one more lucrative. He received the appointment of clerk of the Supreme Court for Kent County. Of this business he became wearied, and entered the service of his country as a midshipman in the year 1799. He made his first cruise under Commodore Barry, and was on board the frigate *United States* when she bore Ellsworth and Davie to France as envoys extraordinary of the United States to the government of that country. He was promoted to lieutenant in February, 1801. When the war with Tripoli broke out he sailed in the *Philadelphia* under Bainbridge, and after the disaster that befell that vessel he was twenty months a captive among the semi-barbarians of Northern Africa. He was commissioned master commandant in April, 1810, and was appointed to the command of the brig *Argus*, which was stationed for the protection of our commerce on our southern maritime frontier. In 1811 he was transferred to the command of the *Wasp*, and in the spring of 1812 was dispatched with communications from the United States government to its embassadors in France and England. While on that duty war between the United States and Great Britain was declared by the former. Soon after his return, he went on the cruise which resulted in his capture of the *Frolic*, and the recapture of his own and the prize vessel by a British frigate. In March, 1813, he was promoted to captain, and ever afterward bore the title of Commodore. After the peace he was employed alternately at home and abroad; and, finally, in his declining years, he retired to his farm in his native state, where he enjoyed a serene old age. He died at Philadelphia in July, 1850, at the age of eighty years. The likeness is copied from an engraving by Edwin, from a portrait painted by the late Rembrandt Peale.

[2] Thomas Whinyates entered the British navy in 1798, and obtained his first commission in September, 1799. He was promoted to the rank of commander in May, 1805, and, after having command of the bomb *Zebra* almost two years, he was promoted to the command of the *Frolic* in

voying six merchantmen from Honduras. Four of these vessels were large, and mounted from sixteen to eighteen guns each.[1]

It was Sunday morning. The sky was cloudless, the atmosphere balmy, and a stiff and increasing breeze from the northwest was giving white crests to the billows.

Jones soon perceived that the hostile sloop was disposed to fight, and was taking position so as to allow the merchantmen to escape by flight during the engagement. The top-gallant yards of the *Wasp* were immediately sent down, her top-sails were close-reefed, and she was otherwise brought under short fighting canvas. The *Frolic* also carried very little sail, and in this condition they commenced a severe engagement at half past ten o'clock in the morning. The *Wasp* ranged close up on the starboard side of the *Frolic*, after receiving a broadside from her at the distance of fifty or sixty yards, and then instantly delivered her own broadside, when the fire of the Englishman became so accelerated that the *Frolic* appeared to fire three guns to the *Wasp's* two. The breeze had increased, and the sea was rolling heavily.

Within five minutes after the action commenced the main-top-mast of the *Wasp* was shot away. It fell, with the main-top-sail yard, and lodged across the larboard and fore and fore-top-sail braces, rendering the head yards unmanageable during the remainder of the action. In the course of three minutes more her gaff and main-top-gallant-mast was shot away, and fell heavily to the deck; and at the end of twenty minutes from the opening of the engagement, every brace and most of the rigging was disabled. She was in a forlorn condition indeed, and had few promises of victory.

But, while the *Wasp* was receiving these serious damages in her rigging and tops, the *Frolic* was more seriously injured in her hull. The latter generally fired when on the crest of the wave, while the former fired from the trough of the sea, and sent her missiles through the hull of her antagonist with destructive force. The two vessels gradually approached each other until the bends of the *Wasp* rubbed against the *Frolic's* bows; and, in loading for the last broadside, the rammers of the *Wasp's* gunners were shoved against the sides of the *Frolic*.[2] Finally, the combatants ran foul of each other, the bowsprit of the *Frolic* passing in over the quarter-deck of the *Wasp*, and forcing her bows up into the wind. This enabled the latter to throw in a close raking broadside that produced dreadful havoc.

The crew of the *Wasp* was now in a state of the highest excitement, and could no longer be restrained. With wild shouts they leaped into the tangled rigging before Captain Jones could throw in another broadside, as he intended before boarding his enemy, and made their way to the decks of the *Frolic*, with Lieutenants Biddle and Rodgers, who, with Lieutenants Booth, Claxton,[3] and Rapp, had exhibited the most undaunted courage throughout the action.[4] But there was no one to oppose them. The last broadside had carried death and dismay into the *Frolic*, and almost cleared her decks of active men. The wounded, dying, and dead were strewn in every di-

---

March, 1807. He was commissioned a post-captain in August, 1813, and in 1846 was placed on the list of retired rear admirals.

[1] The *Frolic* had left the Bay of Honduras with about fourteen sail under convoy. When off Havana her commander first heard of the declaration of war. The British vessels experienced the same gale which the *Frolic* encountered, and they were separated. The *Frolic* sustained quite serious damage, having had her main yard broken in two places, and her main-top-mast badly sprung, besides other injuries. In this condition she entered upon the engagement. During the engagement the merchant vessels with the *Frolic* escaped. See James's *Naval Occurrences*.

[2] Captain Jones's Report to the Secretary of the Navy, November 24, 1812.

[3] "Lieutenant Claxton," says Captain Jones, in his report to the Secretary of the Navy, "who was confined by sickness, left his bed a little previous to the engagement, and, though too indisposed to be at his division, remained upon deck, and showed, by his composed manner of noticing its incidents, that we had lost by his illness the services of a brave officer."

[4] John (or, as he was familiarly called, Jack) Lang, a seaman of the *Wasp*, who had once been impressed into the British service, and was hot with the fire of retaliation, jumped on a gun with his cutlass, and was springing on board the *Frolic*, when Captain Jones, wishing to give the enemy another broadside, called him down. But his impetuosity overcame his sense of obedience, and in a moment he leaped upon the bowsprit of the *Frolic*. The crew were all alive with excitement. Seeing this, Lieutenant Biddle mounted the hammock-cloth to board. The crew caught the signal, and followed with the greatest enthusiasm. Lang was from New Brunswick, New Jersey.

rection. Several surviving officers were standing aft, the most of them bleeding, and not a common seaman or marine was at his station, except an old tar at the wheel, who had kept his post throughout the terrible encounter. All who were able had rushed below to escape the raking fire of the *Wasp*.

The English officers cast down their swords in submission, and Lieutenant Biddle, who led the boarding-party, springing into the main rigging, struck the colors of the *Frolic* with his own hand, not one of the enemy being able to do so. The prize passed into the possession of the conquerors after a contest of three quarters of an hour, when every one of her officers were wounded, and a greater part of her men were either killed or severely injured. Not twenty persons on board of her remained unhurt.[1] Her aggregate loss in killed and wounded was estimated at ninety men. The *Wasp* had only five killed and five wounded.

The *Frolic* was so injured that when the two vessels separated both her masts fell, and with tattered sails and broken rigging covered the dead on her decks. She had been hulled at almost every discharge from the *Wasp*, and was virtually a wreck before her colors were struck.

The heat of the battle was scarcely over when Captain Jones prepared to continue his cruise in his victorious little vessel. He had placed Lieutenant Biddle in command of the shattered *Frolic*, with orders to take her into Charleston, or some other Southern port, and was about to part company with his prize, when a strange vessel was seen bearing down upon them. Neither the *Wasp* nor her prize was in a condition to resist or flee. The rigging of the latter was so cut, and her top-sails so nearly in ribbons, that it would have been folly to attempt either.

The strange sail drew near, and heaving a shot over the *Frolic*, and ranging up near the *Wasp*, convinced them both that the most prudent course would be to submit at once. Within two hours after the gallant Jones had gained his victory he was compelled to surrender his own noble vessel and her prize. The captor was the British ship-of-war *Poictiers*, of seventy-four guns, commanded by Captain John Poo Beresford.[2] She proceeded to Bermuda with her prizes, where the American prisoners were exchanged, and departed for home. From New York Captain Jones sent his account of the occurrences to the Secretary of the Navy—a report that was received with the greatest satisfaction.[3]

The victory of the *Wasp* over the *Frolic*—the result of the first combat between the vessels of the two nations of a force nearly equal—occasioned much exultation in the United States. The press teemed with laudations of Captain Jones and his gallant companions, and a stirring song commemorative of the event was soon upon the lips of singers at public gatherings, in bar-rooms, workshops, and even by ragged urchins in the streets. The name of the author, if ever known, has been long forgotten, but the following lines are remembered by many a gray-haired survivor of the War:

> "The foe bravely fought, but his arms were all broken,
>   And he fled from his death-wound aghast and affrighted;
> But the *Wasp* darted forward her death-doing sting,
>   And full on his bosom, like lightning, alighted.
> She pierced through his entrails, she maddened his brain,
>   And he writhed and he groan'd as if torn with the colic;
> And long shall John Bull rue the terrible day
>   He met the American *Wasp* on a *Frolic*."

---

[1] Captain Whinyates's dispatch to Admiral Sir J. Borlase Warren, from the ship *Poictiers*, October 23, 1812. The loss of the *Frolic* must have been about one hundred.

[2] Report of Captain Jones to the Secretary of the Navy, November 24, 1812; Whinyates's dispatch to Admiral Warren, October 23, 1812.

[3] According to general usage, a court of inquiry was held on the conduct of Captain Jones in giving up the *Wasp* and her prize. The opinion of the court was, "That the conduct of the officers and crew of the *Wasp* was eminently distinguished for firmness and gallantry in making every preparation and exertion of which their situation would admit."

A WASP ON A FROLIC.

Charles, the Philadelphia caricaturist, materialized the idea, and sent forth a colored picture, called A WASP ON A FROLIC, OR A STING FOR JOHN BULL, that sold by hundreds during the excitement in the public mind.[1]

Captain Jones was everywhere received with demonstrations of gratitude and admiration on his return to the United States. In the cities through which he had occasion to pass, brilliant entertainments were given in his honor. The Legislature of Delaware, his native state, appointed a committee to wait on him with their thanks, and to express "the pride and pleasure" they felt in recognizing him as a native of their state, and at the same time voted him thanks, an elegant sword, and a piece of silver plate with appropriate engravings. The Common Council of New York, on motion of Alderman Lawrence, voted him a sword, and also the "freedom of the city." The Congress of the United States, on motion of James A. Bayard, of Delaware, appropriated twenty-five thousand dollars as a compensation to Captain Jones and his companions for their loss of prize-money occasioned by the recapture of the *Frolic*. They also ordered a gold medal to be presented to the cap-

GOLD MEDAL AWARDED BY CONGRESS TO CAPTAIN JONES.

tain, and a silver one to each of his officers. The captain also received a more substantial token of his country's approbation by being promoted by Congress to the command of the frigate *Macedonian*, which had lately been captured from the British and taken into the service.[2]

---

[1] Under the picture were the following lines :

"A *Wasp* took a *Frolic*, and met Johnny Bull,
Who always fights best when his belly is full.
The *Wasp* thought him hungry by his mouth open wide,
So, his belly to fill, put a sting in his side."

[2] The following are the names of the officers of the *Wasp* at the time of the action : Jacob Jones, *Commander*; George W. Rodgers, James Biddle, Benjamin Booth, Alexander Claxton, and Henry B. Rapp, *Lieutenants*; William Knight, *Sailing-master*; Thomas Harris, *Surgeon*; George S. Wise, *Purser*; John M'Cloud, *Boatswain*; George Jackson, *Gunner*; George Van Cleve, A. S. Ten Eyck, Richard Brashear, John Holcomb, William J. M'Cluney, C. J. Baker, and Charles Gaunt, *Midshipmen*; Walter W. New, *Surgeon's Mate*.

The engraving is a representation of the medal, full size. On one side is a bust of Captain Jones. Legend—JACOBUS JONES, VIRTUS IN ARDUA TENDIT. On the reverse are seen two ships closely engaged, the bowsprit of the *Wasp* between

Lieutenant Biddle honored and rewarded.

Lieutenant Biddle shared in the honors. The Legislature of Pennsylvania voted him thanks and a sword, and a number of leading men in Philadelphia presented him with a silver urn, bearing an appropriate inscription, and a representation of the action between the *Wasp* and the *Frolic*.[1] He was shortly afterward promoted to the rank of master commandant, and received command of the *Hornet* sloop-of-war. Poetry wreathed coronals for the brows of all the braves of that fight, and in the Portfolio for January, 1813, a rather doleful poem appeared in commemoration of the gallantry of Biddle, of which the following is a specimen:

THE BIDDLE URN.

"Nor shall thy merits, Biddle, pass untold.
When covered with the cannon's flaming breath,
Onward he pressed, unconquerably bold;
He feared dishonor, but he spurned at death."

the masts of the *Frolic*. Men on the bow of the *Wasp* in the act of boarding the *Frolic*. The main-top-mast of the *Wasp* shot away. Legend—VICTORIAM HOSTI MAJORI CELERRIME RAPUIT. Exergue—INTER WASP. NAV. AMERI. ET FROLIC NAV. ANG. DIE XVIII OCT. MDCCCXII.

[1] This urn and the silver medal presented to Lieutenant Biddle for his share in the capture of the *Frolic* are in possession of Lieutenant James S. Biddle, of Philadelphia. Also the gold medal afterward presented to the hero in acknowledgment of his services in capturing the *Penguin*. The following is the inscription on the urn:

"To Lieutenant James Biddle, United States Navy, from the early friends and companions of his youth, who, while their country rewards his public services, present this testimonial of their esteem for his private worth. Philadelphia, 1813."

CHAPTER XXII.

"The chiefs who our freedom sustained on the land,
    Fame's far-spreading voice has eternized in story;
By the roar of our cannon now called to the strand,
    She beholds on the ocean their rivals in glory.
        Her sons there she owns,
        And her clarion's bold tones
Tell of Hull and Decatur, of Bainbridge and Jones;
    For the tars of Columbia are lords of the wave,
And have sworn that old Ocean's their throne or their grave."

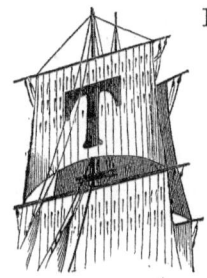

HE victory won by the *Wasp* was followed, precisely a week later,[a] by another more important. Commodore Rodgers sailed in the *President* from Boston on a second cruise, after refitting, accompanied by the *United States*, 44, Captain Decatur, and *Argus*, 16, Lieutenant Commanding Sinclair, leaving the *Hornet* in port. The *President* parted company with her companions on the 12th of October, and on the 17th fell in with and captured the British packet *Swallow*. The *United States* and *Argus*, meanwhile, had also parted company with each other, and the former had sailed to the southward and eastward, hoping to intercept British West Indiamen. Decatur was soon gratified by better fortune in the estimation of a soldier. At dawn on Sunday morning, the 25th,[b] when in latitude 29° and west longitude 29° 30′, not far from the island of Madeira, the watch at the main-top discovered a sail to windward. There was a stiff breeze and a heavy sea on at the time. It was soon discovered that the stranger was an English ship-of-war, under a heavy press of sail. Decatur resolved to overtake and engage her, and for that purpose he spread all his canvas. The *United States* was a good sailer, and she rapidly reduced the distance between herself and the fugitive she was pursuing. The enthusiasm of her officers and men was unbounded; and as the gallant ship drew nearer and nearer to the enemy, shouts went up from the decks of the *United States* loud enough to be heard by the British before the American vessel was near enough to bring her guns to bear.

At about nine in the morning Decatur had so nearly overtaken his prospective antagonist that he opened a broadside upon her. The balls fell short. The *United States* was soon much nearer, when she opened another broadside with effect. This was responded to in kind. Both vessels were now on the same tack, and continued the action with a heavy and steady cannonade with the long guns of both, the distance between them being so great that carronades and muskets were of no avail for some time. Almost every shot of the *United States* fell fearfully on the enemy, who finally perceived that safety from utter destruction might only be found in closer quarters. When the contest had lasted about half an hour, the stranger, with mutilated spars and riddled sails, bore up gallantly for close action. The *United States* readily accepted the challenge, and very soon afterward her shot, sent by the direction of splendid gunnery, cut the enemy's mizzen-mast so that it fell overboard. Not long afterward the main yard of the foe was seen hanging in two pieces, her main and fore top-masts were gone, her fore-mast was tottering, no colors were seen floating over her deck, and her main-mast and bowsprit were severely wounded, while the *United States* remained almost unhurt. The stranger's fire had become feeble,

a October 25, 1812.

b October.

Capture of the *Macedonian*.   Incidents of the Battle.   Comparison of the *United States* and *Macedonian*.

and Decatur filled his mizzen-top-sail, gathered fresh way, tacked, and came up under the lee of the English ship, to the utter discomfiture of her commander, who, when he saw the American frigate bear away, supposed she was severely injured and about to flee from him. With that impression her crew gave three cheers;[1] but when the *United States* tacked and brought up in a position for more effectual action than before, the British commander, perceiving farther resistance to be vain, struck her colors and surrendered. As the *United States* crossed the stem of the vanquished vessel, Decatur hailed and demanded her name. "His majesty's frigate *Macedonian*, 38, Captain John S. Carden," was the response. An officer was immediately sent on board. She had suffered terribly in every part during a combat of almost two hours. She had received no less than one hundred round shot in her hull alone, many of them between wind and water. She had nothing standing but her fore and main masts and fore yard. All her boats were rendered useless except one. Of her officers and crew, three hundred in number, thirty-six were killed and sixty-eight were wounded.[2] The loss of the *United States* was only five killed and six wounded.[3] The *Macedonian* was a very fine vessel of her class, only two years old, and, though rated at 36, she carried forty-nine guns—eighteen on her gun-deck and thirty-two pound carronades above. The *United States* mounted thirty long 24's on her main deck, and twenty-two 42-pound carronades and two long 24's on her quarter-deck and forecastle. She

---

[1] The cannonade by the *United States* was so incessant that her side toward the enemy seemed to be in a blaze. Carden supposed she was on fire, and this belief caused the exultation on his ship. A contemporary rhymer wrote as follows:

"For Carden thought he had us tight,
 Just so did Dacres too, sirs,
But brave Decatur put him right
 With Yankee doodle doo, sirs.
They thought they saw our ship in flame,
 Which made them all huzza, sirs,
But when the second broadside came,
 It made them hold their jaws, sirs."

See an allusion to this battle in Note 1, page 140, quoted from Cobbett's *Register*.

[2] Captain Carden thus stated his casualties: "*Killed*: 1 master's mate, the school-master, 23 petty officers and seamen, 2 boys, 1 sergeant, and 7 privates of marines—total, 36. *Wounded dangerously*: 7 petty officers and seamen. *Severely*: 1 lieutenant, 1 midshipman, 18 petty officers and seamen, 4 boys, and 5 private marines—total, dangerously and severely, 36. *Wounded slightly*: 1 lieutenant, 1 master's mate, 26 petty officers and seamen, and 4 private marines—total, 32. According to the muster-roll found on board of the *Macedonian*, she had seven impressed American seamen among her crew, two of whom were killed in the action. Another had been drowned at sea, while compelled to assist in boarding an American vessel. Their names were Christopher Dodge, Peter Johnson, John Alexander, C. Dolphin, Mayer Cook, William Thompson, John Wallis, and John Card. During the whole war, American seamen, similarly situated, were compelled to fight against their countrymen. When the fact became known that there were impressed Americans on the *Macedonian*, the exasperation of the people against Great Britain, because of her nefarious practice, was intensified.

[3] *Killed*: Boatswain's mate, 1 seaman, and 3 marines. *Wounded*: 1 lieutenant, 4 seamen, and 1 marine. The lieutenant (John M. Funk) and one seaman (John Archibald) died of their wounds.

The following is a list of the officers of the *United States*: *Commander*, Stephen Decatur. *Lieutenants*, William H. Allen, John Gallagher, John M. Funk, George C. Read, Walter Wooster, John B. Nicholson. *Sailing-master*, John D. Sloat. *Surgeon*, Samuel R. Trevitt. *Surgeon's Mate*, Samuel Vernon. *Purser*, John B. Timberlake. *Midshipmen*, John Stansbury, Joseph Cassin, Philip Voorhees, John P. Zantzinger, Richard Delphy, Dugan Taylor, Richard S. Heath, Edward F. Howell, Archibald Hamilton, John M'Can, H. Z. W. Harrington, William Jamieson, Lewis Hinchman, Benjamin S. Williams. *Gunner*, Thomas Barry. *Lieutenants of Marines*, William Anderson, James L. Edwards.

There was a boy only twelve years of age on board the *United States*, the son of a brave seaman, whose death had left the lad's mother in poverty. When the crew were clearing the ship for action, the boy stepped up to Decatur and said, "I wish my name may be put down on the roll, sir." "Why so, my lad?" asked the commander. "So that I may have a share of the prize-money," was the earnest reply. Pleased with the spirit of the boy, Decatur granted his request. The boy behaved gallantly throughout the contest. At the close of the action Decatur said to him, "Well, Bill, we have taken the ship, and your share of the prize-money may be about two hundred dollars;* what will you do with it?" "I will send half to my mother, and the other half shall send me to school." The commander was so pleased with the right spirit of the boy that he took him under his protection, procured a midshipman's berth for him, and superintended his education.—Putnam's *Life of Decatur*, page 193.

---

* Congress decreed that in the distribution of prize-money arising from capture by national vessels, one half should go to the United States, and the other half, divided into twenty equal parts, should be distributed in the following manner: to captains, 3 parts; to the sea lieutenants and sailing-masters, 2 parts; to the marine officers, surgeons, pursers, boatswains, gunners, carpenters, master's mates, and chaplains, 2 parts; to midshipmen, surgeon's mates, captain's clerks, school-master, boatswain's mates, gunner's mates, carpenter's mates, steward, sail-makers, master at arms, armorers, and coxswains, 3 parts; to gunner's yeomen, boatswain's yeomen, quarter-masters, quarter-gunners, coopers, sail-maker's mates, sergeants and corporals of marines, drummers and fifers, and extra petty officers, 3 parts; to seamen, ordinary seamen, marines, and boys, 7 parts.

was manned with a crew of four hundred and seventy-eight. In men and metal the *United States* was heavier than the *Macedonian*, "but," says Cooper, "the disproportion between the force of the two vessels was much less than that between the execution."[1]

Captain Carden fought his ship skillfully and bravely, and when he came on board the *United States*, and offered his sword to Captain Decatur, the latter generously remarked, "Sir, I can not receive the sword of a man who has so bravely defended his ship, but I will receive your hand." Suiting the action to the word, Decatur took the gallant Carden's hand, and led him to his cabin, where refreshments were set out and partaken of in a friendly spirit by the two commanders.[2]

When he took possession of his prize, Decatur found her not fatally injured, and he determined to abandon his cruise and take her into an American port. His own vessel was speedily repaired. The *Macedonian* was placed in the charge of Lieutenant Allen, who, with much ingenuity, so rigged her as to convert her into a barque, when captor and captive sailed for the United States. Decatur arrived off New London on the 4th of December,[3] and at about the same time his prize entered Newport Harbor.

> "Then quickly met our nation's eyes
> The noblest sight in nature—
> A first-rate *frigate* as a prize
> Brought home by brave DECATUR."—OLD SONG.

Both vessels made their way through Long Island Sound, the East River, and Hell Gate, at the close of the month, and on the 1st of January, 1813, the *Macedonian* anchored in the harbor of New York, where she was greeted with great joy as a "New-year's gift." "A more acceptable compliment could not have been presented to a joyous people," said one of the newspapers. "She comes with the compliments of the season from Old Neptune," said another. "Janus, the peace-loving, smiled," said a third, more classical. The excitement of a feast had then scarcely died away,

---

[1] *Naval History of the United States*, ii., 179. See the official dispatches of Decatur and Carden; Clark's *Naval History*; Waldo's *Life of Stephen Decatur*; *The War*; Niles's *Register*; Memoir of Decatur, in the *Analectic Magazine*, i., 502.

[2] All of the private property of the officers and men of the *Macedonian* was given up to them. Among other things claimed and received by Captain Carden was a band of music and several casks of wine, the whole valued at eight hundred dollars. Of this generous conduct Captain Carden spoke in the highest terms. Hull's generosity to Captain Dacres, as we have seen, elicited the praise of that officer. The American newspapers called attention to the fact that the British commander of the *Poictiers*, when he captured the *Wasp* and her prize from Jones, would not permit officers or men to retain any thing except the clothes on their backs. See *The War*, i., 115.

Decatur and Carden had met before. It was in the harbor of Norfolk, just before the beginning of the war, that they were introduced to each other. Before they parted Carden said to Decatur, "We now meet as friends; God grant we may never meet as enemies; but we are subject to the orders of our governments, and must obey them." "I heartily reciprocate the sentiment," replied Decatur. "But what, sir," said Carden, "would be the consequence to yourself and the force you command if we should meet as enemies?" "Why, sir," responded Decatur, in the same playful spirit, "if we meet with forces that might be fairly called equal, the conflict would be severe, but the flag of my country on the ship I command shall never leave the staff on which it waves as long as there is a hull to support it." They parted, and their next meeting was on the deck of the *United States*, under the circumstances recorded in the text.

John Surman Carden was born on the 15th of August, 1771, at Templemore, Ireland. His father, Major Carden, of the British army, perished in the war of the American Revolution. This, his eldest son, entered the British navy as captain's servant in 1788 in the ship *Edgar*. In 1790 he became midshipman in the *Perseverance* frigate. He was made lieutenant in 1794. He received the commission of commander in 1798. He was appointed to the command of the *Ville de Paris* in 1808, and in 1811 to that of the *Macedonian*. He was acquitted of all blame in the surrender of his ship to Decatur. Parliament was full of his praise, and the cities of Worcester and Gloucester, and the borough of Tewksbury, honored him with their "freedom." He was made a rear admiral in 1840, and died at Bonnycastle, Antrim, Ireland, in May, 1858, at the age of eighty-seven years.

[3] Decatur's official dispatch to the Secretary of the Navy was dated "At Sea, October 30, 1812. Lieutenant Hamilton, a son of the Secretary of the Navy, was sent with it to his father, at Washington, immediately after the arrival of the *United States* at New London. He bore the flag of the *Macedonian* to the seat of government, where he arrived on the evening of the 8th of December, at which time a ball was in progress which had been given in honor of the naval officers. The Secretary of the Navy (Paul Hamilton) and his wife and daughter were present. The first intimation of the arrival of their son and brother was his entrance into the hall of the brilliant assembly, bearing the trophy. Captains Hull and Stewart received it, and bore it to the accomplished wife of President Madison, who was present. The pleasure of the occasion was changed to patriotic joy, and at the supper one of the managers offered as a toast, "*Commodore Decatur, and the officers and crew of the frigate United States.*"

Decatur's arrival at New London was hailed with joyful demonstrations. The city authorities presented him the public thanks, and a ball was given in his honor.

for only three days before[a] a splendid banquet had been given, at Gibson's City Hotel, to Hull, Jones, and Decatur, by the Corporation and citizens of New York,[1] and the newspapers of the land speedily became the vehicles of the "effusions" of a score of poets, who caught inspiration from the shouts of triumph that filled the air. Woodworth, the printer-poet, and author of *The Old Oaken Bucket*, "threw together, on the spur of the moment," as he said, a dozen stirring stanzas, of which the following is the first:

[a] December 29, 1812.

> "The banner of Freedom high floated unfurl'd,
> While the silver-tipp'd surges in low homage curl'd,
> Flashing bright round the bow of Decatur's brave bark,
> In contest an *eagle*—in chasing, a *lark*."

And J. R. Calvert wrote a banquet-song, which became immensely popular, of which the following is the closing stanza:

> "Now charge all your glasses with pure sparkling wine,
> And toast our brave tars who so bravely defend us;
> While our naval commanders so nobly combine,
> We defy all the ills haughty foes e'er can send us!
> While our goblets do flow,
> The praises we owe
> To Valor and Skill we will gladly bestow.
> And may grateful the sons of Columbia be
> To DECATUR, whom Neptune crowns *Lord of the Sea!*"

Decatur's victory, following so closely upon others equally brilliant, produced the most profound sensations in the United States and in England. In the former they were impressions of encouragement and joy; in the latter, of disappointment and sorrow. The victor was highly applauded for his soldierly qualities and generosity by each service; and he was spoken of with the greatest enthusiasm by his countrymen. Public bodies, and the Legislatures of Massachusetts, New York, Maryland, Pennsylvania, and Virginia gave him thanks, and to these each of the two latter added a sword. The same kind of weapon was presented to him by the city of Philadelphia; and the city of New York voted[a] him the freedom of the city in addition to the honor of a banquet jointly with Hull and Jones, and requested his portrait for the picture gallery in the City Hall. The Corporation of New York also gave the gallant crew of the *United States* a banquet at the City Hotel.[2] The national Congress, by unanimous vote, thanked Decatur, and gave him

[a] December 17.

---

[1] This banquet was given on the day after the freedom of the city was presented to Captain Hull. He and Decatur were present, but Jones was absent. At five o'clock about five hundred gentlemen sat down at the tables. De Witt Clinton, the mayor, presided. The room "had the appearance of a marine palace," said an eye-witness. It was "colonnaded round with the masts of ships, entwined with laurels, and bearing the national flags of all the world. Every table had upon it a ship in miniature, with the American flag displayed. In front, where the President sat, with the officers of the navy and other guests, and which was raised about three feet, there appeared an area of about twenty feet by ten covered with green sward, and in the midst of it was a real lake of water, in which floated a miniature frigate. Back of all this hung a main-sail of a ship thirty-three by sixteen feet."—*The War*, i., 119. Decatur sat on the right of the President, and Hull on the left. When the third toast—"Our Navy"—was given with three cheers, the great main-sail was furled, and revealed an immense transparent painting, representing the three naval battles in which Hull, Jones, and Decatur were respectively engaged. Other surprises of a similar nature were vouchsafed to the guests, and the whole affair was one long to be remembered by the participants.

[2] This banquet was given on Thursday, the 7th of January, 1813, at two o'clock in the afternoon, under the direction of Aldermen Van Der Bilt, Buckmaster, and King. The room had the same decoration as at the time of the banquet given to Hull, Jones, and Decatur, a few days before. The sailors, numbering about four hundred, marched to the hotel in pairs, and were greeted by crowds of men and women in the streets, loud cheers from the multitude, and the waving of handkerchiefs from the windows. The band of the 11th Regiment, among whom was an old trumpeter who had served under Washington, received them with music at the door. At the table they were addressed by Alderman Van Der Bilt, who was responded to by the boatswain of the *United States*. In the evening they went to the theatre by invitation of the manager, which was communicated to them in person by Decatur. The whole pit was reserved for them. The orchestra opened with *Yankee Doodle*. The drop curtain, in the form of a transparency, had on it a representation of the fight between the *United States* and *Macedonian*. Children danced on the stage. They bore large letters of the alphabet in their hands, which, being joined in the course of the dance, produced in transparency the names of HULL, JONES, and DECATUR. Then Mr. M'Farland, as an Irish clown, came forward and sang a comic song of seven stanzas, written for this occasion, beginning,

> "No more of your blathering nonsense
> 'Bout Nelsons of old Johnny Bull;
> I'll sing you a song, by my conscience,
> 'Bout JONES, and DECATUR, and HULL.

a splendid gold medal, with appropriate devices and inscriptions.[1] From that time until now that commander's name is the synonym of honor and gallantry in the es-

GOLD MEDAL AWARDED TO DECATUR.

timation of his countrymen. His subsequent career added lustre to his renown as the conqueror of the *Macedonian.*

We have already observed that Hull generously retired from the command of the *Constitution* for the purpose of giving some brother-officer an opportunity for gallant achievements in her, and that Captain Bainbridge was his appointed successor. A small squadron, consisting of the *Constitution*, 44; *Essex*, 32; and *Hornet*, 18, were placed in his charge. When Bainbridge entered upon his duty in the new sphere of flag-officer, the *Constitution* and *Hornet* were lying in Boston Harbor, and the *Essex*, Captain Porter, was in the Delaware. Orders were sent to the latter to cruise in the track of the English West Indiamen, and at a specified time to rendezvous at certain ports, when, if he should not fall in with the flag-ship of the squadron, he would be at liberty to follow the dictates of his own judgment. Such contingency occurred, and the *Essex* sailed on a very long and most eventful cruise in the South Atlantic and Pacific Oceans. That cruise will form the subject of a portion of a future chapter.

Bainbridge[2] sailed from Boston with the *Constitution* and *Hornet* on the 26th of

---

> Dad Neptune has long, with vexation,
> Beheld with what insolent pride
> The turbulent, billow-washed nation
> Has aimed to control the salt tide.
>   CHORUS—Sing lather away, jonteel and aisy,
>   By my soul, at the game hob-or-nob,
>   In a very few minutes we'll plase ye,
>   Because we take work by the job."

[1] On one side of the medal is a profile of Decatur's bust, with the legend STEPHANUS DECATUR NAVARCHUS, PUGNIS PLURIBUS VICTOR. On the reverse is a representation of a naval engagement, one of the vessels representing the *Macedonian* much injured in spars and rigging. Over them is the legend OCCIDIT SIGNUM HOSTILE SIDERA SURGUNT. Exergue—INTER STA. UNI. NAV. AMERI. ET MACEDO. NAV. ANG. DIE XXV OCTOBRIS MDCCCXII.

[2] William Bainbridge was born at Princeton, New Jersey, on the 7th of May, 1774, and at the age of fifteen years went to sea as a common sailor. He was promoted to mate in the course of three years, and became a captain at the age of nineteen. When war with the French became probable, he entered the navy with the commission of a lieutenant but the position of a commander, his first cruise being in the *Retaliation*, which was captured. He was promoted to post-captain for good service in the year 1800, and took command of the frigate *Washington*. His career in the Mediterranean has been already mentioned in preceding chapters of this work. Between the war with Tripoli and that of 1812 Captain Bainbridge was employed alternately in the naval and merchant service. After the successful cruise of the *Constitution* in 1812, he took command of the navy yard at Charlestown, Massachusetts. After the war he went twice to the Mediterranean in command of squadrons to protect American commerce there. For three years he was president of the Board of Navy Commissioners, and he prepared the signals which were in use in our navy until lately. For several years Commodore Bainbridge suffered severely from bodily ill health, and finally died at his residence in Philadelphia, on the 27th of July, 1833, at the age of fifty-nine years. His funeral was celebrated on the 31st. The Cincinnati Society attended, with a large concourse of citizens, and his body was laid in the earth with military honors by the United States Marines and a fine brigade of infantry, under the command of the late Colonel J. G. Watmough. His remains rest

Bainbridge on the Coast of Brazil. The *Hornet* challenges a British Vessel. Cruise of the *Constitution* down the Coast.

October.[a] He touched at the appointed rendezvous,[1] and arrived off Bahia, or San Salvador, Brazil,[2] on the 13th of December. He immediately sent in Captain Lawrence, with the *Hornet*, to communicate with the American consul there, when that commander discovered in the port the English sloop-of-war *Bonne Citoyenne*, 18, Captain Greene, about to sail for England with a very large amount of specie. Lawrence invited Greene to go out upon the open sea with his vessel and fight, pledging himself that the *Constitution* should take no part in the combat, but the British commander prudently declined the invitation. The *Hornet* then took a position to blockade the English sloop, and the *Constitution* departed[b] for a cruise down the coast of Brazil, keeping the land aboard. Three days afterward, at about nine o'clock in the morning, when in latitude 13° 6′ south and longitude 38° west, or about thirty miles from shore, southeasterly of San Salvador, Bainbridge discovered two vessels in shore and to the windward. The larger one was seen to alter her course, with an evident desire for a meeting with the *Constitution*. The latter was willing to gratify her, and for that purpose tacked and stood toward the stranger. At meridian they both showed their colors and displayed signals, but

[a] 1812.

[b] December 26.

BAINBRIDGE'S MONUMENT.

beneath a plain white marble obelisk in Christ Church-yard in Philadelphia, and near it is a modest monument to mark the resting-place of his wife, Susan Heyleger. The following is the inscription on Bainbridge's monument: "WILLIAM BAINBRIDGE, United States Navy. Born in Princeton, New Jersey, 7th of May, 1774. Died in Philadelphia 28th of July, 1833. PATRIA VICTISQUE LAUDATUS." See the Medal, page 463.

Bainbridge was about six feet in height, and well built. His complexion was fair, his eyes black and very expressive, and his hair and whiskers very dark. He was considered a model as an officer and a man in the navy.

[1] The places specified were Port Praya, in the island of St. Jago, and Fernando de Noronha, an island in the Atlantic 125 miles from the extreme eastern cape of Brazil. It is now used as a place of banishment by the Brazilian government. The *Constitution* and *Hornet* appeared in the character of British vessels, and at both places letters were left, directed to Sir James L. Yeo, of the *Southampton*. They contained commonplace remarks, and also orders, in sympathetic ink, for Captain Porter, should they fall into his hands, he having been informed that letters at those places for him would be directed to Yeo. The stratagem succeeded. The whole transaction was in accordance with the privileges of war, and yet a writer in the London *Quarterly Review* charged Porter with being guilty of an improper act in opening a letter directed to another person!

[2] This is one of the most important places in South America, and until 1763 was the seat of the viceroyalty of Brazil, when it was transferred to Rio de Janeiro. It contains a population of 100,000, of whom one third are white, one third mulattoes, and the remainder negroes.

the latter were mutually unintelligible. The stranger was seen to be an English frigate. Bainbridge at once prepared for action, when the Englishman hauled down his colors, but left a jack flying. Both ships ran upon the same tack, about a mile apart, when, at almost two o'clock, the British frigate bore down upon the *Constitution* with the intention of raking her. The latter wore and avoided the calamity, and at two o'clock, both ships being on the same tack, the *Constitution* fired a single gun across the enemy's bow to draw out her ensign again. A general cannonade from both vessels immediately ensued, and a furious battle was commenced. When it had raged half an hour the wheel of the *Constitution* was shot away, and her antagonist, being the better sailer, had a great advantage for a time. But Bainbridge managed his crippled ship with such skill that she was the first in coming to the wind on the other tack, and speedily obtained a position for giving her opponent a terrible raking fire. The combatants now ran free with the wind on their quarter, the stranger being to the windward of the *Constitution*. At about three o'clock the stranger attempted to close by running down on the *Constitution's* quarter. Her jib-boom penetrated the latter's mizzen rigging, but suffered most severely without receiving the least advantage. She lost her jib-boom and the head of her bowsprit by shots from the *Constitution*, and in a few minutes the latter poured a heavy raking broadside into the stern of her antagonist. This was followed by another, when the fore-mast of the English frigate went by the board, crashing through the forecastle and main deck in its passage. At that moment the *Constitution* shot ahead, keeping away to avoid being raked, and finally, after manœuvring for the greater part of an hour, she forereached her antagonist, wore, passed her, and luffed up under her quarter. Then the two vessels lay broadside to broadside, engaged in deadly conflict, yard-arm to yard-arm. Very soon the enemy's mizzen-mast was shot away, leaving nothing standing but the main-mast, whose yard had been carried away near the slings. The stranger's fire now ceased, and the *Constitution* passed out of the combat of almost two hours' duration at a few minutes past four o'clock, with the impression on the mind of her commander that the colors of the English frigate had been struck. Being in a favorable weatherly position, Bainbridge occupied an hour in repairing damages and securing his masts, when he observed an ensign still fluttering on board of his antagonist. He immediately ordered the *Constitution* to wear round and renew the conflict. Perceiving this movement, the Englishman hauled down his colors, and at six o'clock in the evening First Lieutenant George Parker[1] was sent on board to inquire her name and to take possession of her as a prize.[2] She proved to be the *Java*, 38, Captain Henry Lambert, and one of the finest frigates in the British navy. She was bearing, as passenger to the East Indies, Lieutenant General Hyslop (just appointed governor general of Bombay), and his staff, Captain Marshall and Lieutenant Saunders, of the Royal Navy, and more than one hundred other officers and men destined for service in the East Indies.

The *Java* was a wreck. Her main-mast had gone overboard during the hour that Bainbridge was repairing. Her mizzen-mast was shot out of the ship close by the deck, and the fore-mast was carried away about twenty-five feet above it. The bowsprit was cut off near the cap, and she was found to be leaking badly on account of wounds in her hull by round shot. The *Constitution* was very much cut in her sails

---

[1] The officers of the *Constitution* in this action were—*Captain*, William Bainbridge. *Lieutenants*, George Parker, Beekman T. Hoffman, John T. Shubrick, Charles W. Morgan. *Sailing-masters*, John C. Alwin, John Nichols. *Chaplain*, John Carleton. *Lieutenants of Marines*, William H. Freeman, John Contee. *Surgeon*, Amos A. Evans. *Surgeon's Mates*, John D. Armstrong, Donaldson Yeates. *Purser*, Robert C. Ludlow. *Midshipmen*, Thomas Beatty, Lewis Germain, William L. Gordon, Ambrose L. Fields, Frederick Baury, Joseph Cross, Alexander Belcher, William Taylor, Alexander Eskridge, James W. Delancy, James Greenleaf, William D. M'Carty, Z. W. Nixon, John A. Wish, Dulaney Forest, George Leverett, Henry Ward, John C. Long, John Packet, Richard Winter. *Boatswain*, Peter Adams. *Gunner*, Ezekiel Darling. *Acting Midshipman*, John C. Cumings.

[2] On this very day, and at that very hour, Hull and Decatur were at the public banquet given them in the city of New York. See page 457.

and rigging. Many of her spars were injured, but not one was lost. She went into the action with her royal yards across, and came out of it with all three of them in their proper places. There are conflicting accounts concerning the loss of the *Java* in men. Her commander, Captain Lambert, was mortally wounded, and her other officers were cautious about the number of her men and her casualties. According to a muster-roll found on board of her, made out five days after she sailed, her officers and crew numbered four hundred and forty-six. These were exclusive of the more than one hundred passengers, many of whom assisted in the engagement, and of whom thirteen were killed. The British published account states the loss of men on the *Java* to have been twenty-two killed, and one hundred and one wounded, while Bainbridge reported her loss, as nearly as he could ascertain from the British officers at the time, at sixty killed, and one hundred and one wounded. This was, doubtless, below the real number. Indeed, Bainbridge inclosed to the Secretary of the Navy evidences of a much larger loss in wounded. It was a letter, written by one of the officers of the *Java* to a friend, and accidentally dropped on the deck of the *Constitution*, where it was found and handed to Bainbridge. The writer, who had no motive of public policy for concealing any thing from his friend, stated the loss to be sixty-five killed, and one hundred and seventy wounded.[1] The *Constitution* lost only nine killed and twenty-five wounded. Bainbridge was slightly hurt in the hip by a musket-ball; and the shot that carried away the wheel of the *Constitution* drove a small copper bolt into his thigh, which inflicted a dangerous wound, but did not cause him to leave the deck before midnight.

The *Java*, as has been observed, was a superior frigate of her class. She was rated at thirty-eight, but carried forty-nine. The *Constitution* carried at that time forty-five guns, and had one man less at each than the *Java*. On the whole, the preponderance of strength was with the latter. Bainbridge might have saved the hull of his prize by taking it into San Salvador, but, having proof that the Brazilian government was favorable to that of Great Britain, he would not trust the captured frigate there. He was too far from home to think of conducting her to an American port; so, after lying by the *Java* for two days, until the wounded and prisoners, with their baggage, could all be transferred to the *Constitution*, he ordered the battered frigate to be fired. She blew up on the 31st, when Bainbridge proceeded to San Salvador with his prisoners, and found the *Bonne Citoyenne* about to attempt passing the *Hornet* and putting to sea. His arrival frustrated the plan. Having landed and paroled his prisoners,[a] Bainbridge sailed for the United States on the 6th of January, 1813.[2]   [a] January 3, 1813.

The *Constitution* arrived at Boston on Monday, the 15th of February, and Bainbridge immediately dispatched Lieutenant Ludlow with a letter to the Secretary of the Navy. When Bainbridge landed he was greeted with the roar of artillery and the acclamations of thousands of citizens. A procession was formed, and he was escorted to the Exchange Coffee-house, the bands playing Yankee Doodle, and the throngs in

---

[1] Letter from H. D. Corneck to Lieutenant Peter V. Wood, in the Isle of France, dated on board the *Constitution*, January 1, 1813. After speaking of the death of a friend in the battle, he said, "Four other of his messmates shared the same fate, together with sixty men killed, and one hundred and seventy wounded."

[2] The following is a list of the British military and naval officers paroled: *Military*, one lieutenant general, one major, one captain. *Naval*, one post captain, one master and commander, five lieutenants, three lieutenants of marine, one surgeon, two assistant surgeons, one purser, fifteen midshipmen, one gunner, one boatswain, one ship carpenter, two captain's clerks—total, thirty-eight. Captain Lambert died on the day after the landing (January 4). Bainbridge treated all of his prisoners with the greatest tenderness and consideration. Silver plate to a large amount, presented to General Hyslop by the colony of Demarara, and which would have been lawful prize, was returned to that gentleman, who thanked Bainbridge for his kind courtesy, and presented him his sword (which Bainbridge would not receive when it was offered in token of surrender) in farther testimony of his gratitude. And yet, in the face of all this, James, the earliest, as he was the most mendacious of the British historians of the war, and one most quoted by British writers now, says (*Naval Occurrences, etc.*, page 188), "The manner in which the *Java's* men were treated by the American officers reflects upon the latter the highest disgrace." In a letter to a friend, written when homeward bound, Bainbridge exhibited his goodness of heart in thus speaking of the death of his antagonist: "Poor Lambert, whose death I ncerely regret, was a distinguished, gallant, and worthy man. He has left a widow and two helpless children! But untry makes provision for such sad events."

the streets, balconies, and windows cheering loudly, the ladies waving their handkerchiefs. The streets were strung with banners and streamers, and Commodores Rodgers and Hull, who walked with Bainbridge in the procession, received a share of the popular honors. The victory was announced at the theatre that night, and produced the wildest enthusiasm. The Legislature of Massachusetts being in session, they passed a resolution of thanks to Bainbridge and his officers and crew,[1] and on the 2d of March a splendid banquet was given at the Exchange Coffee-house to Bainbridge and the officers of the *Constitution*.[2]

The capture of the *Java*, the fourth brilliant naval victory in a brief space of time, caused great exultation throughout the United States, and the *Constitution* was popularly called from that time *Old Ironsides*. Orators and rhymers, the pulpit and the press, made the gallant exploits of Bainbridge the theme of many words in verse and prose.[3] The Common Council of New York presented to him the freedom of the city in a gold box,[4] and ordered his portrait painted for the picture-gallery in the City Hall.[5] The city of Albany did the same;[6] and the citizens of Philadelphia pre-

NEW YORK GOLD BOX.

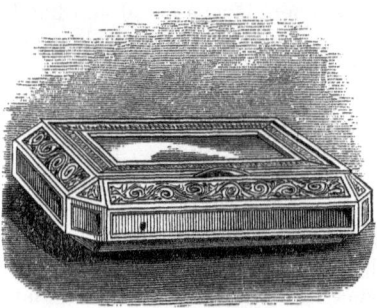

ALBANY GOLD BOX.

sented him with an elegant service of silver plate, the most costly piece of which was a massive urn, elegantly wrought.[7] The Congress of the United States voted their

---

[1] By the Senate on the 19th of February, and by the House of Representatives on the 20th.

[2] The procession was formed in Faneuil Hall by Major Tilden, and was escorted by the *Boston Light Infantry* and the *Winslow Blues*, under Colonel Sargent. The Honorable Christopher Gore presided at the table, assisted by Harrison Grey Otis, Israel Thorndike, Arnold Willis, Thomas L. Winthrop, Peter C. Brooks, and William Sullivan as vice-presidents. Intelligence had just come that the British Orders in Council had been repealed, and that peace might be soon expected. Elated by this news, the Honorable Timothy Dexter offered the following toast: "The British Orders in Council revoked, and our national honor gallantly retrieved. Now let us shut the temple of Janus till his double face goes out of fashion." An ode was sung at the banquet, written, on request of the committee of arrangements, by the late L. M. Sargent, Esq.

[3] One of the most popular songs of the day was composed in honor of the capture of the *Java*, and called "Bainbridge's Tid re I," in which, after every verse, the singer gives a sentence in prose, winding up with the chorus "Tid re I, Tid re I, Tid re id re I do." The following is a specimen of that kind of song, once so popular:

"Come, lads, draw near, and you shall hear,
    In truth as chaste as Dian, O!
How Bainbridge true, and his bold crew,
    Again have tamed the lion, O!
'Twas off Brazil he got the pill
    Which made him cry *peccavi*, O
But hours two, the *Java* new,
    Maintained the battle bravely, O!

"But our gallant tars, as soon as they were piped to quarters, gave three cheers, and boldly swore, by the blood of the heroes of Tripoli, that, sooner than strike, they'd go the bottom singing

Tid re I, Tid re I, Tid re id re I do."

[4] This box is three inches in diameter and one inch in depth. On the inside of the lid is the following inscription: "The Corporation of the City of New York to Commodore William Bainbridge, of the United States frigate *Constitution*, in testimony of the high sense they entertain of his gallantry and skill in the capture of his Britannic Majesty's ship JAVA on the 29th of December, 1812."

[5] The portrait was painted by John Wesley Jarvis. The engraving on page 459 is from a copy of that picture.

[6] The box presented by the city of Albany is of oblong form, and is faithfully delineated in the engraving. It is three inches and a half long and three fourths of an inch deep. On the inside of the lid is the following inscription: "A tribute of respect by the Common Council of the City of Albany to Commodore William Bainbridge for his gallant naval services in the late war with Great Britain." This box is in the possession of the gallant commander's daughter, Mrs. (Mary Bainbridge) Charles Joudon, of Philadelphia.

[7] This urn is eighteen inches in height. The lid is surmounted by an eagle about to soar. Below each massive

thanks to Bainbridge and his companions in arms, and also fifty thousand dollars in money, because of the necessary destruction of their prize. They also ordered a gold medal to be struck in honor of the commander,[1] and silver ones for each of his officers, in token of the national approbation of their conduct.

BAINBRIDGE MEDAL.

The conflict between the *Constitution* and *Java* was the closing naval engagement of the year, and, with the previous victories won by the Americans, made the deepest impressions upon the public mind in both hemispheres. The United States cruisers, public and private, had captured about three hundred prizes from the British during that first six months of war. The American war-party—indeed, the whole American people, excepting a few Submissionists, were made exultant by these events, and the gloom caused by the failure of the land forces was dispelled. The views of the Federalists, who had always favored a navy, were justified, and the opposition to it, on the part of the Democrats, ceased. The British people were astounded by these heavy and ominous blows dealt at their supremacy of the seas, and some of the leading newspapers scattered curses broadcast. One of them, a leading London paper, with that vulgarity which too often disgraced journalism on both sides of the Atlantic at that time, petulantly expressed its apprehensions that England might be stripped of her maritime superiority " by a piece of striped bunting flying at the mast-head of a few fir-built frigates, manned by a handful of bastards and outlaws !"

But this impotent rage soon subsided, and British writers and speakers, compelled to acknowledge the equality of the American people in all that constitutes the true

dle is a head of Neptune. On one side of the urn is the representation of the wrecked *Java* and the triumphant *Constitution*, and on the other the following inscription : "Presented by the citizens of Philadelphia to Commodore William Bainbridge, of the U. S. frigate *Constitution*, as a testimonial of the high sense they entertain of his skill and gallantry in the capture of the British frigate *Java*, of 49 guns and 500 men, and of their admiration of his generous and magnanimous conduct toward the vanquished foe. Loss in the action of 29th December, 1812—C., 9 killed, 25 wounded ; J., 60 killed, 101 wounded."

After the death of Bainbridge's widow, his plate was distributed among his surviving children. The urn and other silver pieces, and the New York gold box, belong to Mrs. Susan (Bain-

BAINBRIDGE URN.

bridge) Hayes, widow of Captain Thomas Hayes, of the United States Navy, a resident of Philadelphia. To her kind courtesy I am indebted for the privilege of making sketches of the urn and boxes. She also has in her possession the sword presented to Bainbridge by Hyslop (see Note 2, page 461). It is a straight dress sword, in a black leather scabbard. Also another sword, with basket guard and elegant gilt mountings. Also a Turkish cimeter.

[1] On one side of the medal is a bust of Bainbridge, and the legend " GULIELMUS BAINBRIDGE PATRIA VICTORISQUE LAUDATUS." Reverse, a ship, the stumps of her three masts standing, and her conqueror with only a few shot-holes in her sails. Legend—" PUGNANDO." Exergue —" INTER CONST. NAV. AMERI. ET JAV. NAV. ANGL. DIE XXIX. DECEM. MDCCCXII."

greatness of a nation, labored hard to show that in all cases the American vessels, in force of men and metal, were greatly superior to those of the British encountered. They even went so far as to assert that the American frigates were all "seventy-fours in disguise !" These assertions were iterated and reiterated long after the war had ceased, to the amusement of thoughtful men, who clearly perceived the truth when the smoke had cleared away. The most notable exhibition of this folly is seen in three volumes, one on the naval and two on the military occurrences of that war, written by William James. These, as we have observed, were among the earliest of the elaborate writings concerning that war, and have, ever since their appearance, been the most frequently quoted by those British and British-American writers and speakers who delight in abusing the government and people of the United States. The spirit manifested on every page bears evidence of the poverty of the author in all that constitutes a candid and veracious historian.[1]

Having now considered in groups the military and naval events of the war during the first year of the contest, excepting those in the extreme southern boundaries of the Republic, which will be noticed hereafter, let us glance at the civil affairs of the United States, having relation to the subject in question, before entering upon a description of the stirring campaign of 1813.

The second session of the Twelfth Congress commenced on the 2d day of November.[a] It was the eve of the popular election of Presidential electors.

[a] 1812.

President Madison had been nominated for the office for a second term by a Congressional caucus, as we have already observed,[2] as the Democratic candidate; and the Legislature of New York had nominated De Witt Clinton, a nephew of the late Vice-president, and of the same political faith, for the same office. The Federalists, conscious of their inability to elect a candidate of their own, coalesced with the Clintonian Democrats. This course was decided upon in a Convention of Federalist leaders from all the states north of the Potomac, held in secret session, in the city of New York, in September.[b] If the war must go on, they regarded Clinton as

[b] 1812.

the possessor of greater executive ability than Madison, and better able to conduct it vigorously; but their chief desire and hope was to bring about an early peace by the defeat of Madison, the repeal of the British Orders in Council[3] having opened a door for that consummation so devoutly wished for. Jared Ingersoll, of Pennsylvania, a moderate Federalist, was nominated by the Convention for Vice-president. George Clinton having died, Elbridge Gerry, as we have seen,[4] was nominated for Vice-president by the Madisonians.

When the elections occurred, nearly all the Federalists and a fraction of the Democratic party voted for the Clintonian electors. All of the New England States, excepting Vermont, chose such electors.[5] New York did the same, in consequence of the adroit management of Martin Van Buren, a politician thirty years of age, who then appeared prominently for the first time.[6] There was a similar result in New Jersey,

---

[1] William James was an English emigrant to the United States early in the present century. He was a veterinary surgeon (or "horse doctor," as they are called in this country) in Philadelphia, but was unsuccessful in his profession. He left that city for his native country, thoroughly disgusted with every thing American, because the people had not appreciated his talents. His chief employment after his return seems to have been abuse of the Americans, their public men, their government, and their writers. He wrote angry reviews of some American books on the naval and military history of the War of 1812, and these were published, in 1817 and 1818, in three volumes. The first was entitled "*A Full and Correct Account of the* NAVAL OCCURRENCES *of the Late War, etc.*," and the other two, "*A Full and Correct Account of the* MILITARY OCCURRENCES *of the Late War, etc.*" They are not histories, but violent tirades, and manifest, as the *Edinburg Review* remarked, "bitter and persevering antipathy" to the Americans. "Almost every original remark made by the author upon them," said the *Review*, "bears traces of the unworthy feeling we have just mentioned." In considering his performance in the light of two generations of thought and investigation, the truth of the motto on the title-page of his volume on the *Naval Occurrences*, quoted from Murphy's Tacitus, is very manifest. "Truth is always brought to light by time and reflection, while *the lie of the day* lives by bustle, noise, and precipitancy." James died in 1827.   [2] See page 225.   [3] See page 245.   [4] See page 226.

[5] In Massachusetts, so strongly Democratic, only a few months before, the "peace electors," as the Clintonians were called, obtained a majority of 24,000.

[6] Owing to the dissonance in the Democratic party in New York, caused by the dissensions between the Madisonians and Clintonians, the Federalists chose nineteen out of the twenty-three members of Congress. Those of New Hamp-

and for a time the re-election of Madison appeared doubtful. But before Congress had been in session six weeks it was definitely ascertained, from the official canvass, that Madison had one hundred and twenty-eight out of the two hundred and eighteen electors chosen, and that a large majority of the Congressmen elect were friends of the administration. This result was regarded, under the circumstances, as a very strong expression of the public in favor of the war; and the war-party in and out of Congress were greatly strengthened. They were also encouraged by the aspect of affairs abroad. Intelligence of apparent disasters to the English in Spain, the triumph of Bonaparte in the terrible battle of Borodino, and his victorious march upon Moscow, filled them with the hope that England, struggling with all Europe against her, must speedily be compelled to withdraw her soldiers and seamen from America, and give up the contest here, or else fall a prey to the conquering Corsican. But they were doomed to an early disappointment of their hopes by disasters that fell thick and fast upon the French army, exposed to Russian snows and Russian cohorts. It was evident, too, from the returns of the late elections, that the Opposition were growing stronger every day.

Among the earliest national measures proposed in Congress was a plan for increasing the army twenty thousand men, making the whole establishment fifty-six thousand. The President, in his fourth annual message,[a] after giving a general statement of the position of affairs in relation to the war, called the attention of the national Legislature to the necessity of measures for the vigorous prosecution of it. A bill was introduced into the House of Representatives to raise the pay of private soldiers from six to eight dollars a month, to guarantee recruits against arrest for debt, and to give them their option to enlist for five years or for the war. In the same bill was a clause allowing the enlistment of minors without the consent of their parents or masters. This elicited a very spirited debate, in which Josiah Quincy engaged with his usual vigor. He declared it to be an interference with the rights of parents and masters, and warned the House that if the bill passed with that "atrocious principle" contained in it, it would be met in New England by the state laws against kidnapping and man-stealing. He opposed it as bearing particularly hard upon the North, where the laborers are the yeomanry and the minors, while at the South the laborers were slaves, and exempted by law from military duty. The planter of the South, he said, can look around upon his fifty, his hundred, and his thousand human beings, and say, "These are my *property*"—property tilling the land, and enriching the owner in war as well as in peace; while the farmer of the North has "only one or two *ewe lambs*—his children, of which he can say, and say with pride, like the Roman matron, 'These are my ornaments.'" These, by the proposed law, might be taken from him, and his land must remain untilled.[1]

[a] November 4, 1812.

Williams, of South Carolina, the chairman of the Military Committee, retorted fiercely. In reply to Quincy's assertion that the bill contained an "atrocious principle," he charged the great Federal leader with uttering an "atrocious falsehood." His language was so offensively supercilious that it drew admonitions even from John Randolph. He argued well in favor of an increase of the army. "The British regular force in the Canadas," he said, "could not be estimated less than twelve thousand men. In addition to these were the Canadian militia, amounting to several thousands, and three thousand regulars at Halifax. To drive this force from the field, the St. Lawrence must be crossed with a well-appointed army of twenty thousand men, supported by an army of reserve of ten thousand. Peace is not to be expected

shire were all Federalists, and that party carried the Legislature of New Jersey and more than half of its Congressional delegation.

[1] A question upon similar premises arose in the Convention of 1787, when it was proposed to make three out of every five slaves count as persons in determining the representation of the states in Congress. It was observed that while the slaves were called *persons* for a political purpose, they were only *chattels* at other times, and could not be called into the military service of the country. This was a grievous wrong toward the non-slaveholding states.

but at the expense of a vigorous and successful war. Administrations have in vain sued for it, even at the expense of the sarcastic sneers of the British minister. The campaign of 1813 must open in a style and vigor calculated to inspire confidence in ourselves and awe in the enemy. Nothing must be left to chance; our movements must every where be in concert. At the same moment we move on Canada, a corps of ten thousand men must threaten Halifax from the province of Maine. The honor and character of the nation require that the British power on our borders should be annihilated the next campaign. Her American provinces once wrested from her, every attempt to recover them will be chimerical, except by negotiation. The road to peace thus lies through Canada." The bill passed the House of Representatives, but the objectionable clause received only four votes in the Senate.

The expensive volunteer system was taken up in Congress, and the law authorizing the employment of that species of soldiers was repealed. Another was substituted, which authorized the enlistment of twenty regiments of regulars to serve twelve months, to whom a bounty of sixteen dollars should be given. It also provided for the appointment of six major generals and six brigadier generals, and a corresponding increase of subordinate officers. Party spirit was aroused in the debate that ensued, and the discussion took a range so wide as to include the whole policy and conduct of the war. Mr. Quincy led off[a] with great bitterness and the keenest sarcasm. "He denounced the invasion of Canada," says Hildreth,[1] "as a cruel, wanton, senseless, and wicked attack, in which neither plunder nor glory was to be gained, upon an unoffending people, bound to us by ties of blood and good neighborhood; undertaken for the punishment, over their shoulders, of another people three thousand miles off, by young politicians fluttering and cackling on the floor of that house, half hatched, the shell still on their heads, and their pin-feathers not yet shed—politicians to whom reason, justice, pity, were nothing, revenge every thing; bad policy, too, since the display of such a grasping spirit only tended to alienate from us that large minority of the British people anxious to compel their ministers to respect our maritime rights. So thought the people of New England, and hence the difficulty of getting recruits. The toad-eaters of the palace—party men in pursuit of commissions, fat contracts, judgeships, and offices for themselves, their fathers, sons, brothers, uncles, and cousins—might assert otherwise, but the people had spoken in the late elections. There were in New England multitudes of judicious, patriotic, honest, sober men, who, if their judgments and their consciences went with the war, would rush to the standard of their country at the winding of a horn, but to whom the present call sounded rather as a jewsharp or a banjo. . . . . . If the government would confine itself to a war of defense, it should have his support; but for a war of conquest and annexation, whether in East Florida[2] or Canada, he would not contribute a single dollar. Nor was he to be frightened from this ground by the old state cry of British connection, raised anew by a pack of mangy, mongrel blood-hounds, for the most part of very recent importation, their necks still marked with the collar, and their backs sore with the stripes of European castigation, kept in pay by the administration to hunt down all who opposed the court."

[a] January 5, 1813.

This contemptuous speech drew a most vigorous reply from Mr. Clay, the Speaker of the House, who felt himself specially aimed at by the expression "unfledged politicians." He charged the Federalists, says Hildreth, "with always, throughout the whole controversy with Great Britain, thwarting the plans of their own government; clamoring alike against the embargo, against the non-intercourse, against the non-importation; when the government were at peace, crying out for war; and, now the government were at war, crying out for peace; falsely charging the President with

---

[1] *History of the United States*, second series, iii., 381.
[2] The revolutionary and military operations in that quarter will be noticed hereafter.

being under French influence;[1] heaping all kinds of abuse on Bonaparte; assailing Jefferson with impotent rage; spiriting up chimeras of Southern influence and Virginia dictation, as if the people did not choose their own presidents; going even so far as to plot the dissolution of the Union." Mr. Clay then presented a most pathetic picture of the wrongs inflicted upon, and miseries endured by, American seamen under the operations of the impressment system, to which Great Britain clung tenaciously. "As to the gentleman's sentimental protest against the invasion of Canada," he said in substance, " was Canada so innocent, after all? Was it not in Canada that the Indian tomahawks were whetted? Was it not from Malden and other Canadian magazines that the supplies had issued which had enabled the savage bands to butcher the garrison of Chicago? Was it not by a joint attack of Canadians and Indians that Michillimackinac had been reduced? What does a state of war present? The combined energies of one people arrayed against the combined energies of another, each aiming to inflict all the injury it can, whether by sea or land, upon the territories, property, and persons of the other, subject only to those mitigated usages practiced among civilized nations. The gentleman would not touch the British Continental possessions, nor, for the same reason, it was supposed, her West India islands. By the same rule, her innocent soldiers and sailors ought to be protected; and as, according to a well-known maxim, the king could do no wrong, there would seem to be nobody left whom, on the gentleman's principles, we could attack, unless it were Mr. Stephen,[2] the reputed author of the Orders in Council, or the Board of Admiralty, under whose authority our seamen were impressed." . . . . Mr. Clay's "plan was," he said, "to call out the ample resources of the country to the fullest extent, to strike wherever the enemy could be reached, by sea or land, and to negotiate a peace at Quebec or Halifax."

Measures were adopted for strengthening both the army and navy, and the more perfect organization of each. The President was authorized to cause the construction of four ships of seventy-four guns each, and six frigates and six sloops-of-war;[3] to issue treasury notes to the amount of five millions of dollars, and to create a new stock for a loan of sixteen millions of dollars.[4] A bill was also passed, chiefly through the untiring efforts of Langdon Cheves and John C. Calhoun, representatives from South Carolina, by which the bonds of merchants given for goods imported from Great Britain and Ireland after the declaration of war, and seized under the provisions of the Non-importation Act, were canceled. For six weeks after the news of war reached England exportations had been allowed to go on;[5] and the goods to which the law in question would apply were valued, at invoice prices, at more than

---

[1] Quincy had said, in the speech just quoted from, that the "administration, under French influence and dictation, had for twelve years ruled the country with authority little short of despotic;" and then referred to the continuous rule of "a narrow Virginia clique, to the exclusion from office and influence of all men of talents, even of their own party, not connected with that clique." [2] Author of *War in Disguise.* See page 140.

[3] According to a careful estimate made by the Secretary of the Navy, the force of *three* frigates would not be more than equal to one 74-gun ship. The expense of building and equipping a frigate of 44 guns, estimated from the actual cost of the *President*, was $220,910; the cost of a 74, $333,000. The annual expense of keeping a frigate of that size in service was estimated at $110,000, and that of a 74 at $210,110. The result from these calculations was, that while the expenses of a 74 were something less than those of two frigates of 44 guns each, her value in service was equal to three frigates.—See Perkins's *History of the Political and Military Events of the Late War*, page 150. This estimate determined Congress to build 74's.

[4] The following were the Treasury estimates of expenditures for the year 1813:

    For the civil list, and interest and reimbursement of a part of the principal of the public debt....$8,500,000
    For the army, not including the new levies..17,000,000
    For the navy, not including the proposed increase..4,925,000
        Total...$30,425,000

The total appropriations made for the service of the year amounted to $39,975,000. Such was the amount necessary to meet the entire expenses of the government of the United States fifty years ago, when it was waging a war with Great Britain. The expenditures of the government for a year (1863) during the late civil war was $865,234,000.

[5] This was under a false impression made by Mr. Russell, the American *Chargé d'Affaires*, that in consequence of the repeal of the Orders in Council the Non-Intercourse Act would be suspended. Immediately after the repeal (June 23d, 1812), all the American ships then in British ports commenced loading with British goods.

eighteen millions of dollars, and were worth double that amount in the American market. This act conciliated the mercantile interest.

Cheves, who was chairman of the Committee of Ways and Means, endeavored to procure a partial repeal of the Non-importation Act, but failed. The restrictive system was regarded with great favor as a powerful weapon in the hands of the Americans, and its friends adhered to it with the greatest tenacity, believing it to be a policy potent in hastening the ruin of England. The Federalists failed to support the measure because the repeal was not complete, and on account of the provision in it for the more strict enforcement of what was left.

We have already observed that a retaliatory law, first suggested by Colonel Scott on account of some prisoners taken at Queenston, and who had been sent to England as deserters because they were Irishmen, was passed.[1] It was so framed as not only to meet the special case of those persons, but such Indian outrages under British sanction as had been committed at the River Raisin.[2] Happily, there was no occasion for enforcing the law.

On the 13th of January, Mr. Calhoun, from the Committee on Foreign Relations, made an able report. It had been looked for with great interest. In that report the subject of *impressment* held a conspicuous place. The President, as we have observed, only a week after the declaration of war,[a] proposed an immediate armistice, on conditions at once just and honorable to both nations. It was rejected by the British in terms of peculiar reproach and insult. At about the same time the British Orders in Council were repealed conditionally, but the practice of impressment was defended as just and expedient, and would not be allowed to become a subject for negotiation by the British authorities. Thus matters stood when the Report on Foreign Relations was presented. After alluding to the above facts, the committee proceeded to say that "the impressment of our seamen, being deservedly considered a principal cause of the war, the war ought to be prosecuted until that cause be removed. To appeal to arms in defense of a right, and to lay them down without securing it, or a satisfactory evidence of a good disposition in the opposite party to secure it, would be considered in no other light than a relinquishment of it. . . . The manner in which the friendly advances and liberal propositions of the Executive have been received by the British government has, in a great measure, extinguished the hope of amicable accommodations. . . . War having been declared, and the case of impressment being necessarily included as one of the most important causes, it is evident it must be provided for in the pacification. The omission of it in a treaty of peace would not leave it on its former ground; it would, in effect, be an absolute relinquishment, an idea at which the feelings of every American must revolt. The seamen of the United States have a claim on their country for protection, and they must be protected. If a single ship is taken at sea, and the property of an American citizen wrested from him unjustly, it rouses the indignation of the country. How much more deeply, then, ought we to be excited when we behold so many of this gallant and highly meritorious class of our fellow-citizens snatched from their families and country, and carried into a cruel and afflicting bondage? It is an evil which ought not, which can not be longer tolerated. Without dwelling on the sufferings of the victims, or on that wide scene of distress which it spreads among their relatives through the country, the practice is, in itself, in the highest degree degrading to the United States as a nation. It is incompatible with their sovereignty; it is subversive of the main pillars of their independence. The forbearance of the United States under it has been mistaken for pusillanimity."

To effect a change in the British policy respecting impressments, the committee

[a] June 26, 1812.

---

[1] See page 408.
[2] The British authorities excused themselves on the plea that they could not restrain the Indians. This was no justification. The root of the iniquity was in the employment of the savages as allies.

Manifesto of the Prince Regent.   Charges against the Government of the United States.

recommended the passage of an act, which was appended to their report, similar to one proposed by Mr. Russell to Lord Castlereagh several months before, prohibiting, after the close of the present war, the employment, in public or private vessels, of any persons except American citizens, this prohibition to extend only to the subjects or citizens of such states as should make reciprocal regulations. An act to that effect, which passed the House on the 12th of February, was adopted by the Senate on the last day of the session,[a] against very warm opposition of some of the war-party, who considered it as a humiliating concession.   [a] March 3, 1813.

Only four days before the presentation of their report[b] by the Committee on Foreign Relations, the Prince Regent, acting sovereign of Great Britain, issued a manifesto[c] concerning the causes of the war, and the subjects of blockade and impressment. He declared that the war was not the consequence of any fault of Great Britain, but that it had been brought on by the partial conduct of the American government in overlooking the aggressions of the French, and in their negotiations with them. He alleged that a quarrel with Great Britain had been sought because she had adopted measures solely as retaliative as toward France; and that, as those measures had been abandoned by a repeal of the Orders in Council, the war was now continued on the question of impressment and search. On this point the Prince Regent took such a decisive position, that the door for negotiation which the recommendation of the Committee on Foreign Affairs proposed to open seemed irrevocably shut. "His royal highness," said the manifesto from his palace at Westminster, " can never admit that in the exercise of the undoubted and hitherto undisputed[1] right of searching neutral merchant vessels in time of war, and the impressment of British seamen when found therein, can be deemed any violation of a neutral flag, neither can he admit the taking of such seamen from on board such vessels can be considered by any neutral state as a hostile measure or a justifiable cause of war." After reaffirming the old English doctrine of the impossibility of self-expatriation of a British subject, the manifesto continued: "But if, to the practice of the United States to harbor British seamen, be added their assumed right to transfer the allegiance of British subjects, and thus to cancel the jurisdiction of their legitimate sovereign by acts of naturalization and certificates of citizenship, which they pretend to be as valid out of their own territory as within it,[2] it is obvious that to abandon this ancient right of Great Britain, and to admit these naval pretensions of the United States, would be to expose the very foundations of our maritime strength."   [b] January 13. [c] January 9.

The manifesto charged the United States government with systematic efforts to inflame their people against Great Britain, of ungenerous conduct toward Spain, Great Britain's ally, and of deserting the cause of neutrality. " This disposition of the government of the United States—this complete subserviency to the ruler of France—this hostile temper toward Great Britain," said the prince, " are evident in almost every page of the official correspondence of the American with the French government. Against this course of conduct, the real cause of the present war, the Prince Regent solemnly protests. While contending against France in defense not only of the liberties of Great Britain, but of the world, his Royal Highness was entitled to look for a far different result. From their common origin—from their common interest—from their professed principles of freedom and independence, the United States was the last power in which Great Britain could have expected to find a willing instrument and abettor of French tyranny."[3]

---

[1] For a refutation of this erroneous assertion, see Chapter VII.
[2] This right of citizenship, acquired by naturalization and the transfer of allegiance, has long ago been tacitly acknowledged by the British authorities. Indeed, the claim set up by the Prince Regent was practically abandoned during the War of 1812, for, excepting in the case of the Irishmen made prisoners with Colonel Scott, the British never claimed British-born prisoners as subjects. See page 408.
[3] In the manifesto the Prince Regent also solemnly declared that "the charge of exciting the Indians to offensive

This manifesto, adroitly framed for effect in the United States as well as at home, was approved by both houses of Parliament, and sustained in an address to the throne. It reached America at about the close of the twelfth Congress, and its avowals of the intended adherence of the British government to the practice of impressment stood before the people side by side with the declarations of the report of their Committee on Foreign Affairs, in which it was declared that it was against that practice the war was waging, and that it ought to be waged until the nefarious business was abandoned by the enemy.

While pondering these documents, the Americans were suddenly called by the march of events to contemplate other most important subjects in connection with the war. John Quincy Adams was then the American minister at the Russian court. His relations with the Emperor Alexander were intimate and cordial. When intelligence of the declaration of war reached St. Petersburg the Czar expressed his regret. On account of the French invasion of his territory he was on friendly terms with Great Britain, and his prime minister, Romanzoff, suggested to Mr. Adams[a] the expediency of tendering the mediation of Russia for the purpose of effecting a reconciliation. Mr. Adams favored it, but for a while the victorious march of Bonaparte toward Moscow, the heart of the Russian empire, delayed the measure. The final defeat of the invader secured present tranquillity to the Czar, and he sent instructions to M. Daschkoff, his representative at Washington, to offer to the United States his friendly services in bringing about a peace. This was formally done on the 8th of March, 1813, only four days after President Madison, in his second inaugural address, had laudably endeavored to excite anew the enthusiasm of the people in the vigorous prosecution of the war.

[a] September 20, 1812.

At about this time official intelligence had been received by the government of the result of Napoleon's invasion of Russia. He had indeed reached Moscow after fearful sufferings and losses, but when he rode into that ancient capital of the Muscovites at the head of his staff, on the 15th of September, it was as silent as the Petrified City of the Eastern tale. The inhabitants had withdrawn, and the great Kremlin in which he slept that night was as cheerless as a magnificent mausoleum. His slumbers were soon disturbed. The Russians had not *all* left. For hours a hundred unlighted torches had been held by the hands of Russian incendiaries. When the great bell of the metropolitan cathedral tolled out the hour of midnight, these were kindled by flint and steel, and instantly a hundred fires glared fearfully from every direction upon the couch of the great Corsican. The city was every where in flames, and the wearied French army were compelled to seek shelter in the desolate country around the blackened ruins of that splendid town.

On that fearful night the star of Napoleon's destiny had reached its meridian. Ever afterward it was seen slowly descending, in waning splendor, the paths of the western sky. He perceived in the destruction of Moscow the fearful perils of his situation, and sought to avert them. He proposed terms of peaceful adjustment, but the emperor flung them back with scorn. Retreat or destruction was the alternative. He chose the former; and late in October, with one hundred and twenty thousand men, he turned his face toward France. For a few days the sky was clear and the atmosphere was genial. Then came biting frosts and blinding snow-storms, while clouds of fiery Cossacks smote his legions on flank and rear with deadly blows. Suf-

---

measures against the United States is equally void of foundation." This denial was iterated and reiterated by British statesmen and publicists, and has been ever since. It is very natural for a civilized and Christian people to repel the charge of complicity with savage pagans in the practices of merciless and barbarous warfare. It is commendable, and evinces a proper sense of the heinousness of the offense against civilization; but the official declarations of even a prince, were he many times more virtuous than that libertine regent of England, can not set aside the indelible records of history or the verdict of mankind. There are too many positive statements concerning such complicity to doubt it. In addition to those given in the preceding pages of this work, many more may be found in Niles's *Weekly Register*, ii., 342.

fering and death held high carnival among the fugitives. Bonaparte saw that all was lost, and he hastened to France, bearing almost the first intelligence of the terrible disaster. He lost during the campaign one hundred and twenty-five thousand slain in battle, one hundred and thirty-two thousand by fatigue, hunger, disease, and cold, and one hundred and ninety-three thousand made prisoners; in all, *four hundred and fifty thousand men!* Notwithstanding this fearful loss of life, he had scarcely reached Paris when he issued an order for a general conscription, in number sufficient to take the places of the dead. At the same time Russia, Sweden, Denmark, Prussia, and Spain coalesced for the purpose of striking the crippled conqueror a crushing blow, and early in 1813 they sent large armies toward the Elbe to oppose him. His conscripts were already in the field, and with three hundred and fifty thousand men he invaded Germany, fought and won the great battle of Lutzen,[a] and, after other conflicts, seated himself in Dresden, agreeably to an armistice, and listened to offers of mediation on the part of Austria, with a view to closing the war.

[a] May 2, 1813.

The intelligence from Europe was disheartening to the war-party, for it was evident that the coalition of the great powers of Europe against the French would so relieve England that she might prosecute the war in America with great vigor. The President had been at all times anxious for peace on honorable terms. He perceived a chance for its accomplishment through Russian mediation, and he at once accepted the offer of M. Daschkoff. That acceptance was followed by the nomination of Albert Gallatin, the Secretary of the Treasury, and James A. Bayard, a representative of Delaware in the Senate of the United States, as commissioners or envoys extraordinary, to act jointly with Mr. Adams to negotiate a treaty of peace with Great Britain at St. Petersburg. At the same time, William H. Crawford, of Georgia, a Peace Democrat, was appointed to succeed the lately deceased Joel Barlow[1] as minister at the French court. Of the result of the efforts for peace through Russian mediation I shall hereafter write.

The reverses of Napoleon, as we have observed, discouraged the war-party, and gave corresponding joy to the Federalists, especially to the wing of that organization known as the Peace-party, whose head-quarters were at Boston. There they celebrated the Russian triumphs with public rejoicings.[2] In other places, too, these vic-

---

[1] Mr. Barlow, as we have seen, was an ardent Republican (see page 94). In October, 1812, the Duke de Bassano, at Napoleon's request, invited Barlow to meet the emperor at Wilna, in Poland, the nominal object of which was to complete a commercial treaty with the United States, for which the American minister had long importuned. It was believed by some that the real object was to make an arrangement by which French ships, manned by American sailors, might be brought into play against Great Britain. Whatever was the object remains a mystery. Barlow obeyed the royal summons immediately, and traveled day and night. The weather was very inclement. The country had been wasted by war, and he suffered many privations. In consequence of these and exposure to the weather, he was attacked with inflammation of the lungs, which caused his death in the cottage of a Jew at Zarnowice, near Cracow, on the 22d of December, 1812. Of course, the object of his mission was not accomplished. His last poem, dictated, it is said, from his death-bed, was a withering expression of resentment against Napoleon for the hopes which he had disappointed.

[2] Services were held in King's Chapel, on the 26th of March, 1813, in commemoration of the victories of the Russians over Napoleon, who aimed, it was said, "at the empire of the world." One hundred and fifty amateurs and professional gentlemen assisted in the performance of sacred music. Among other pieces sung was the following recitative, composed for the occasion: "For the hosts of Gallia went in with their chariots and with their horsemen into the North, and the Lord chased them with fierce warriors, winter blasts, and famine; but the children of Sclavia, safe and unhurt, through all the danger passed." The closing prayer was made by the Reverend Mr. Chauncey.

The services in the church were held in the forenoon. In the afternoon many hundreds of the citizens of Boston and the neighboring country sat down to a public dinner. M. Eustaphieve, the Russian consul for New England, was a guest. The room was appropriately decorated. Among the ornaments was a portrait of the Russian emperor, with the words, "*Alexander, the deliverer of Europe.*" Harrison Gray Otis made a speech on the occasion, in which he declared his conviction that the check given to Napoleon by Russia had rescued our country from its greatest danger—the influence of the French policy. Several songs were sung. One of them contained the following verse:

"Hail, Russia! may thy conq'ring bands
Sad Europe from her chains release;
Exalt the hopes of farthest lands,
And give us back an exiled PEACE!"

An ode was sung, to the air of "Ye Mariners of England," which concluded thus:

"Then fill to Alexander!
For him a garland twine,
While shaded by our oaks, we taste
The virtues of the vine.

tories were hailed with joy, and became the themes for song and oratory,[1] to the great disgust of the war-party and their newspaper organs, who censured the President for his haste in snatching at Russian mediation.

During the session of Congress which closed on the 3d of March, 1813, there had been some important changes in President Madison's Cabinet. Public clamor against him had caused Dr. Eustis to resign the War bureau, and the affairs of that department were conducted for several weeks by Mr. Monroe, the Secretary of State. John Armstrong, who had been appointed a brigadier general in the army of the United States, and succeeded General Bloomfield in command at New York, was appointed Secretary of War,[a] and Paul Hamilton was dismissed from the Navy Department to make way for William Jones,[b] who had been a ship-master in earlier life, was an active Philadelphia politician of the Democratic school, and at the time was Commissary of Purchases for the army. Madison's Cabinet, at the opening of the campaign of 1813, was composed as follows: James Monroe, Secretary of State; John Armstrong, Secretary of War; William Jones, Secretary of the Navy; Albert Gallatin, Secretary of the Treasury; and William Pinkney, Attorney General.

[a] January 13, 1813.
[b] January 12.

<blockquote>
And when those oaks adorn our hills,
Or bear our thunders far,
Let each soul
Fill his bowl
To vict'ry and the Czar—
And give a long and loud huzza
To vict'ry and the Czar."
</blockquote>

[1] On the 5th of June, 1813, the late G. W. P. Custis, the adopted son of Washington, addressed a large audience at Georgetown, in the District of Columbia, on the Russian victories. That address drew from the Russian minister at Washington a very complimentary letter, and a request for a copy to be transmitted to Russia. That letter, dated "June 21, 1813," was accompanied by a small medal containing a likeness of the Emperor Alexander. "Permit me to express to you my gratitude," said M. Daschkoff, "that of my family, and of all my countrymen who shall peruse your oration, for the zeal and interest you have displayed in our cause; and allow me to send you a small medal, with the likeness of Alexander the First, the only one which is now in my possession."—*MS. Letter.*

CHAPTER XXIII.

> " Oh, lonely is our old green fort,
> Where oft, in days of old,
> Our gallant soldiers bravely fought
> 'Gainst savage allies bold ;
> But with the change of years have passed
> That unrelenting foe,
> Since we fought here with Harrison,
> A long time ago."
>   SONG—OLD FORT MEIGS.

OTHING of importance in military movements occurred during the dead of winter, in 1813, excepting the terrible affair at Frenchtown, on the River Raisin, already described,[1] and some hostile demonstrations on the St. Lawrence frontier at Elizabethtown and Ogdensburg by the opposing parties. The campaign of that year opened almost simultaneously on the shores of Lake Ontario, in the Valley of the Maumee, and on the coasts of Virginia.

Let us first consider the military events in the Northwest, where we left General Harrison, with a portion of his gallant little army, encamped amid the snows in the dark forests that skirted the Rapids of the Maumee.[2]

The position chosen by Harrison for a strong advanced post, which would give him facilities for keeping open a communication with Ohio and Kentucky, allow him to afford protection to the inhabitants on the borders of Lake Erie, and to operate against Detroit and Malden, was one of the most eligible in the Northwest, and its possession gave the British much uneasiness. Harrison's plan was to form simply a fortified camp, and to prosecute the winter campaign with vigor. For this purpose he endeavored to concentrate troops there, and prepared to push on to the vicinity of Brownstown, for the purpose of operating directly against Malden while the Detroit River was bridged with ice. Considering the destruction of the enemy's vessels, frozen up in the vicinity of Malden, of great importance, he sent a small force, under Captain Langham,[3] to perform that service. On the 2d of March[a] they set off in sleighs, with six days' provisions, and well equipped with combustibles. The party was one hundred and seventy strong. The particular incendiaries were under the immediate command of M. Madis, a Frenchman of European military experience, then conductor of artillery. They were instructed to leave the sleighs at Middle Bass Island, and, with their feet muffled in moccasins, proceed noiselessly, under cover of night, to the work of destruction. Harrison advanced with a supporting detachment, but on his arrival at Maumee Bay,[b] not far below the present city of Toledo, he met Langham and his party returning. They had found the lake open, and of course the plan of the expedition was frustrated. The mildness of the winter had been remarkable; the roads were consequently almost impassable. There was no ice competent to bear troops and munitions of war.

[a] 1813.

[b] March 3.

Harrison now abandoned all hopes of moving forward until spring, and continued the work of fortifying his camp with great vigor, for the preservation of his stores,

---

[1] See Chapter XX.   [2] See page 364.
[3] Augustus L. Langham, of Ohio, was an ensign in a rifle corps in 1808. He resigned in 1809, and in March, 1812, was commissioned a captain in the Nineteenth Regiment of Infantry. He distinguished himself at Fort Meigs. In August following he was promoted to major, was retained in 1815, and resigned in October, 1816.

collected there in great quantity. His troops were then about eighteen hundred in number, and were employed on the works under the skillful direction of that competent officer, Captain Wood, the chief engineer of Harrison's army, Captain Gratiot,[1] then lying prostrate with illness that long continued. "The camp," said Captain Wood, was about twenty-five hundred yards in circumference, the whole of which, with the exception of several small intervals left for batteries and block-houses, was to be picketed with timber fifteen feet long, from ten to twelve inches in diameter, and set three feet in the ground. Such were the instructions of the engineer; and so soon as the lines of the camp were designated, large portions of the labor were assigned to each corps in the army, by which means a very laudable emulation was easily excited. To complete the picketing, to put up eight block-houses of double timbers, to elevate four large batteries, to build all the store-houses and magazines required to contain the supplies of the army, together with the ordinary fatigues of the camp, was an undertaking of no small magnitude. Besides, an immense deal of labor was likewise required in excavating ditches, making *abatis*, and clearing away the wood about the camp; and all this was to be done, too, at a time when the weather was inclement, and the ground so hard that it could scarcely be opened with the mattock and pickaxe. But in the use of the axe, mattock, and spade consisted the chief military knowledge of our army; and even that knowledge, however trifling it may be supposed by some, is of the utmost importance in many situations, and in ours was the salvation of the army. So we fell to work, heard nothing of the enemy, and endeavored to bury ourselves as soon as possible."[2]

But the work so vigorously commenced was abandoned soon afterward, when the general and the engineer left the camp—the former to visit his sick family at Cincinnati, and to urge forward troops and supplies for his army; the latter to superintend the erection of defensive works at Sandusky. The camp at the Rapids was left in charge of Colonel Leftwich, of the Virginia militia, who appears to have resolved to desert the post as soon as possible. Regardless of the danger to the stores, and comfort and safety of those he might leave behind, he not only allowed all work upon the fortifications to cease, but permitted the soldiers to burn the collected picketings for fuel, instead of getting it from the woods within pistol-shot of the camp. On his return from Sandusky on the 20th of February, Captain Wood, to his great mortification, perceived the utter neglect of Leftwich, and the destruction of the works on the lines commenced before he left. The consequence of this conduct of Leftwich, whom Wood called "an old phlegmatic Dutchman, who was not even fit for a pack-horse master, much less to be intrusted with such an important command," was great exposure of the garrison to the inclement weather, and the stores to imminent peril from the enemy. When, on the expiration of their term of enlistment, the Virginia troops under Leftwich, and others from Pennsylvania, left for home, only about five hundred men remained at the Rapids under Major Stoddard, with which to maintain possession of an unfinished line of circumvallation calculated to contain an army of two thousand men.

Harrison's greatest concern during the winter of 1813 was the possibility of not keeping soldiers enough in the field for the spring campaign, as the terms of the en-

---

[1] Charles Gratiot was a native of Missouri, and was appointed second lieutenant of Engineers in October, 1806, and captain in 1808. Harrison appointed him his chief engineer in 1812. He was promoted to major in 1815, lieutenant colonel in 1819, colonel and principal engineer in 1828, and on the same day (May 24) was breveted brigadier general. He left the service in December, 1838.

[2] The lines of the camp, inclosing about eight acres, were very irregular. They were upon a high bank, about one hundred feet above the river and three hundred yards from it. On the land side, commencing at the run, was a deep ravine that swept in a crescent form quite round to the rear.

listment of different corps would soon expire. To provide for such contingency, he called for volunteers from Kentucky and Ohio, and met with cordial responses.[1] He was preparing to collect about four thousand men at the Rapids for an early movement against Malden, when he received instructions from General Armstrong, the new Secretary of War, which deranged all his plans. By these he was directed to continue his demonstrations against Malden, but only as a diversion in favor of attempts to be made upon Canada farther down. He was enjoined not to make an actual attack upon the enemy until the consummation of measures for securing the command of Lake Erie, then just inaugurated, and to be completed at Presque Isle (now Erie, Pennsylvania) by the middle of the ensuing May. Much to his mortification and alarm, he was directed to dispense with militia as much as possible, and to fill up the 17th, 19th, and 24th Regiments of Regulars for service in the ensuing campaign. He was informed that two other regiments of regulars had been ordered to be raised, one in Kentucky and the other in Ohio. Should the old regiments not be filled in time, he was permitted to make up the deficiencies from the militia. With these he was to garrison the different posts, hold the position at the Rapids, and amuse the enemy by feints.

This interference with his plans annoyed Harrison exceedingly, and he ventured to remonstrate with the Secretary of War. He gave him his views[a] very freely, and with them some valuable and much-needed information concerning the country to be defended and the Indian tribes in alliance with the British. He explained the causes of apprehended danger in attempting to carry out the new programme, and assured the Secretary of War that the regular force to be relied on could not be raised in time for needed service, and that, even if it should, it would be too small for the required duty—so evidently inadequate that enlistments would be discouraged.[2] Armstrong, who seldom bore opposition patiently, did not like to be remonstrated with, but he prudently forbore farther interference in the conduct of the campaign in the Northwest at that time.[3]

[a] March 18, 1813.

General Harrison was yet at Cincinnati late in March, actively engaged in endeavors to forward troops and supplies to the Rapids. Informed that the lake was almost free of ice, that the Virginia and most of the Pennsylvania troops would leave at the ex-

---

[1] Harrison requested that a corps of fifteen hundred men might be raised in Kentucky immediately, and marched to his head-quarters without delay. The Legislature of Kentucky was then in session, and Harrison's request was submitted to them in a confidential message by Governor Shelby. A law was immediately passed offering additional pay of seven dollars a month to any fifteen hundred Kentuckians who would remain in the service till a corps could be sent to relieve them. This offer was accompanied by an appeal to their patriotism from the Legislature, which reached them on the 8th of February. They had suffered much, and were very anxious to return home, so they would only promise to remain an indefinite time, but said that if the general was ready to lead them against the enemy they would follow him without additional pay. Similar appeal to the Ohio and Pennsylvania troops met with similar success, but the Virginians would not remain. Meanwhile the Legislature of Kentucky passed an act for detailing three thousand men from the militia, of which fifteen hundred were to march for Harrison's camp, and Governor Meigs ordered two regiments to be organized for the same service.

[2] In a letter to Governor Shelby, at about this time, Harrison said: "Last night's mail brought me a letter from the Secretary of War in which I am restricted to the employment of the regular troops raised in this state to re-enforce the post at the Rapids. There are scattered through this state about one hundred and forty recruits to the 19th Regiment, and with these I am to supply the place of the brigades from Pennsylvania and Virginia, whose time of service will now be daily expiring. By a letter from Governor Meigs I am informed that the Secretary of War disapproved the call for militia which I had made on this state and Kentucky, and was on the point of countermanding the orders. I will just mention one fact, which will show the consequences of such a countermand. There are upon the Au Glaize and St. Mary's Rivers eight forts, which contain within their walls property to the amount of half a million of dollars from actual cost, and worth now to the United States four times that sum. The whole force which would have had charge of all these forts and property would have amounted to less than twenty invalid soldiers."—Autograph Letter, March 21, 1813.

[3] Armstrong attempted to arrange the military force of the country on the plan adopted by General Washington in the Revolution. On the 19th of March he promulgated a general order, dividing the whole United States into nine military districts, as follows: 1, Massachusetts, with Maine and New Hampshire; 2, Rhode Island and Connecticut; 3, New York below the Highlands and New Jersey; 4, Pennsylvania and Delaware; 5, Maryland and Virginia; 6, Georgia; 7, Louisiana. The rest of the States and Territories being divided between the 8th and 9th, the first embraced the seat of war at the west end of Lake Ontario, and the other the Niagara portion, Lake Ontario, and the St. Lawrence and Lake Champlain.

On the 12th of March commissions were issued for eight new brigadiers, namely, Cushing, Parker, Izard, and Pike, of the old army, and Winder, M'Arthur, Cass, Howard, and Swartwout. The latter succeeded Morgan Lewis as quarter-master with the rank of brigadier.

piration of their term on the 2d of April, and that the enemy were doubtless informed of the situation of affairs at the Rapids by a soldier who had been made a prisoner by them, he anticipated an early attack upon his camp there. It was, therefore, with the greatest anxiety that he awaited promised re-enforcements from Kentucky. The governor had ordered a draft of three thousand militia (fifteen hundred of them for Harrison's army) as early as the middle of February, to be organized into four regiments, under Colonels Boswell, Dudley, Cox, and Caldwell, forming a brigade to be commanded by Brigadier General Green Clay.[1] The regiments under the first two named officers rendezvoused at Newport, opposite to Cincinnati, at about the first of April. Those companies which had arrived there earlier had been sent forward to the Rapids on forced marches, by the way of Urbana and "Hull's Trace," and the commander-in-chief followed soon afterward, leaving the remainder of the Kentuckians designed for his command to be forwarded as quickly as possible. He arrived at camp on the 12th of April, and was gratified by finding more than two

VIEW OF CINCINNATI FROM NEWPORT IN 1812.[2]

---

[1] In a letter dated at "Frankfort, March 5, 1813," Governor Shelby invited Mr. Clay to accept the command of the brigade as brigadier general. Clay accepted the office, and in a letter, dated on the 16th of the same month, the governor sent him his commission. In the first letter, now before me, the governor said that, had it been designed to cross into Canada at once, he should have taken command of the Kentucky troops in person.

[2] This view of Cincinnati in 1812 is from an old print. It then contained about two thousand inhabitants.

hundred patriotic Pennsylvanians remaining, who had been persuaded to do so by their chaplain, Dr. Hersey.[1]

Under the direction of Captain Wood, the fortified camp, which had been named in honor of the governor of Ohio, had assumed many of the features of a regular fortification, and was dignified with the name of Fort Meigs. It was evident that its defense would be the chief event in the opening of the campaign. Harrison had been informed while on his way of the frequent appearance of Indian scouts in the neighborhood of the Rapids, and of little skirmishes with what he supposed to be the advance of a more powerful force. Alarmed by these demonstrations, he dispatched a messenger from Fort Amanda with a letter to Governor Shelby, urging him to send to the Maumee the whole of the three thousand militia drafted in Kentucky. This was in violation of his instructions from the War Department respecting the employment of militia, but the seeming peril demanding such violation, he did not hesitate for a moment. Expecting to find Fort Meigs invested by the British and Indians, he took with him from Fort Amanda all the troops that could be spared from the posts on the St. Mary and the Au Glaize, about three hundred in all, and descended by water from his point of departure with the intention of storming any British batteries which he might find employed against his camp. He was agreeably disappointed on his arrival by the discovery that the enemy was not near in great force. But that enemy, vigilant and determined, was preparing to strike at Fort Meigs a destructive blow.

When the ice began to move in the Detroit River and the lake, Proctor formed his plans for an early invasion of the Maumee Valley. Ever since his sanguinary operations at Frenchtown he had been using every art and appliance in his power to concentrate at Amherstburg a large Indian force for the purpose. He fired the zeal of Tecumtha and the Prophet by promises of future success in all their schemes for confederating the savage tribes, and by boasting of his ample power to place in the hands of his Indian allies Fort Meigs, its garrison, and immense stores. So stimulative were his promises that, at the beginning of April, Tecumtha was at Fort Malden with almost fifteen hundred Indians. Full six hundred of them were drawn from the country between

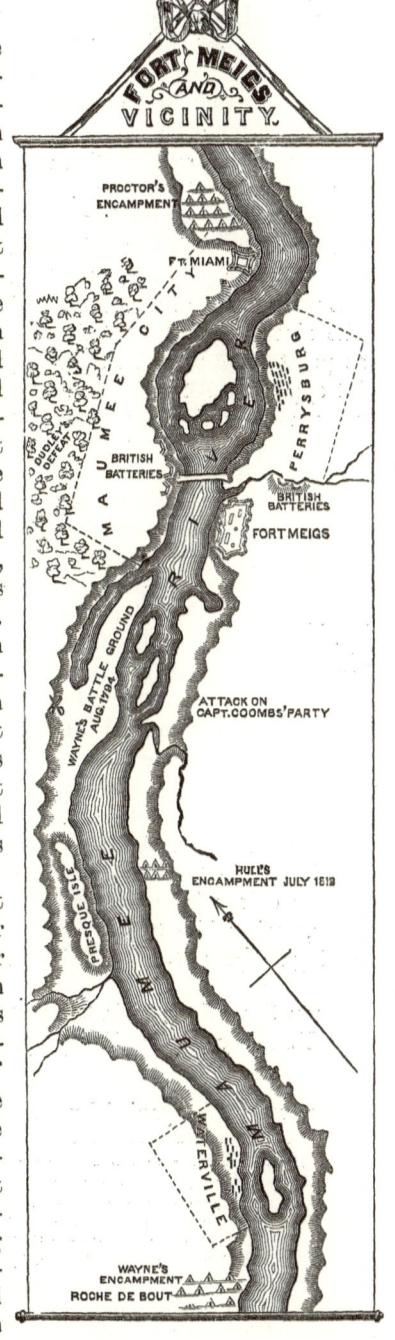

---

[1] These patriotic men informed the general that they were very anxious to go home to put in their spring seeds, but that they would never leave him until he thought that their services could be spared without danger to the cause. On the arrival of the three Kentucky companies he discharged the Pennsylvanians.

Lake Michigan and the Wabash, much to the satisfaction of Harrison when he discovered the fact, for it so relieved him of apprehensions of peril to his posts from that direction that he countermanded his requisition on Governor Shelby for *all* the drafted men from Kentucky.

Proctor was delighted with the response of the savages to his call, and visions of speedy victory, personal glory, and official promotion filled his mind. He became more boastful than ever, and more supercilious toward the Americans at Detroit. He ordered the Canadian militia to assemble at Sandwich on the 7th of April,[a] when he assured them that the campaign would be short, decisive, successful, and profitable. On the 23d[b] his army and that of his savage allies, more than two thousand in number,[1] were in readiness at Amherstburg; and on that day they embarked on a brig and several smaller vessels, accompanied by two gun-boats and some artillery. On the 26th they appeared at the mouth of the Maumee, about twelve miles below Fort Meigs; and on the 28th they landed on the left bank of the river, near old Fort Miami, and established their main camp there.[2] From that point Proctor and Tecumtha, who were well mounted, rode up the river to a point opposite Fort Meigs to reconnoitre. They were discovered at the fort, when a shot from one of the batteries sent them back in haste.[3] Captain Dixon, of the Royal Engineers, was immediately sent up with a fatigue party to construct batteries upon a commanding elevation nearly opposite the fort, in front of the present Maumee City, but incessant rains, and the wretched condition of the roads, so retarded the progress of the work that they were not ready for operations until the first day of May.

[a] 1813.
[b] April.

The approach of the enemy in force had been discovered by Captain Hamilton, of the Ohio troops, on the 28th, while reconnoitring down the river with a small force. Peter Navarre, one of Harrison's most trustworthy scouts, yet (1867) living in Ohio, first saw them. Hamilton sent him in haste to Fort Meigs with the intelligence, when Harrison instantly dispatched him with three letters, one for Upper Sandusky, one for Lower Sandusky, and one for Governor Meigs, at Urbana.[4] Although Fort Meigs was quite strong, several block-houses having been erected in connection with the lines of intrenchment and pickets, and a good supply of field-pieces had been mounted, Harrison was convinced, from the character and strength of the enemy, that his post was in imminent peril. He knew that General Green Clay was on his march with Kentuckians; and as soon as Navarre was furnished with his letters, he dispatched Captain William Oliver, the commissary to the fort, an intelligent, brave, and judicious officer (who had performed similar service for him), with an oral message to Clay, urging him to press forward by forced marches. Oliver bore to Clay the following simple note of introduction:[5]

"Head-quarters, Camp Meigs, 28th April, 1813.

"DEAR SIR,—I send Mr. Oliver to you, to give you an account of what is passing here. You may rely implicitly upon him. Yours,

"WILLIAM HENRY HARRISON."

Oliver was accompanied by a single white man and an Indian. He was escorted

---

[1] The combined force under Proctor consisted of 522 regulars, 461 militia, and about 1500 Indians; total, 2482. The Americans at Fort Meigs did not exceed 1100 effective men.

[2] See the map on the preceding page, which covers the entire historic ground at and around the Maumee Rapids from Roche de Bout—perpendicular rock—where the river has a considerable fall, and where Wayne was encamped in 1794 (see page 54), to Proctor's encampment near Fort Miami at the time we are considering. It shows the place of Hull's encampment in 1812 (see page 257), and Wayne's battle-ground in 1794 (see page 55), with the site of Fort Meigs, and of incidents connected with the siege about to be described in the text; also the present Maumee City on one side of the river, Perryville on the other, and the rail and wagon bridges across. Between Fort Meigs and Perryville is seen a stream. It courses through the ravine mentioned in Note 2, page 474.

[3] Statement of Reverend A. M. Lorraine, in the *Ladies' Repository*, March, 1845.

[4] Oral statement of Navarre to the author.

[5] The original is before me, and a *fac-simile* of it appears on the opposite page. It is one of the papers of General Clay kindly placed in my hands by his son, General Cassius M. Clay, our late minister at the Russian Court. It is written on a half sheet of foolscap paper, and is thoroughly soiled by contact with mud and water.

beyond the immediate danger that surrounded the camp by a company of dragoons under Captain Garrard. He found General Clay at Fort Winchester (Defiance) with twelve hundred Kentuckians, three companies of his command, as we have observed,[1] having been sent forward by Harrison at the close of March. Clay had left Cincin-

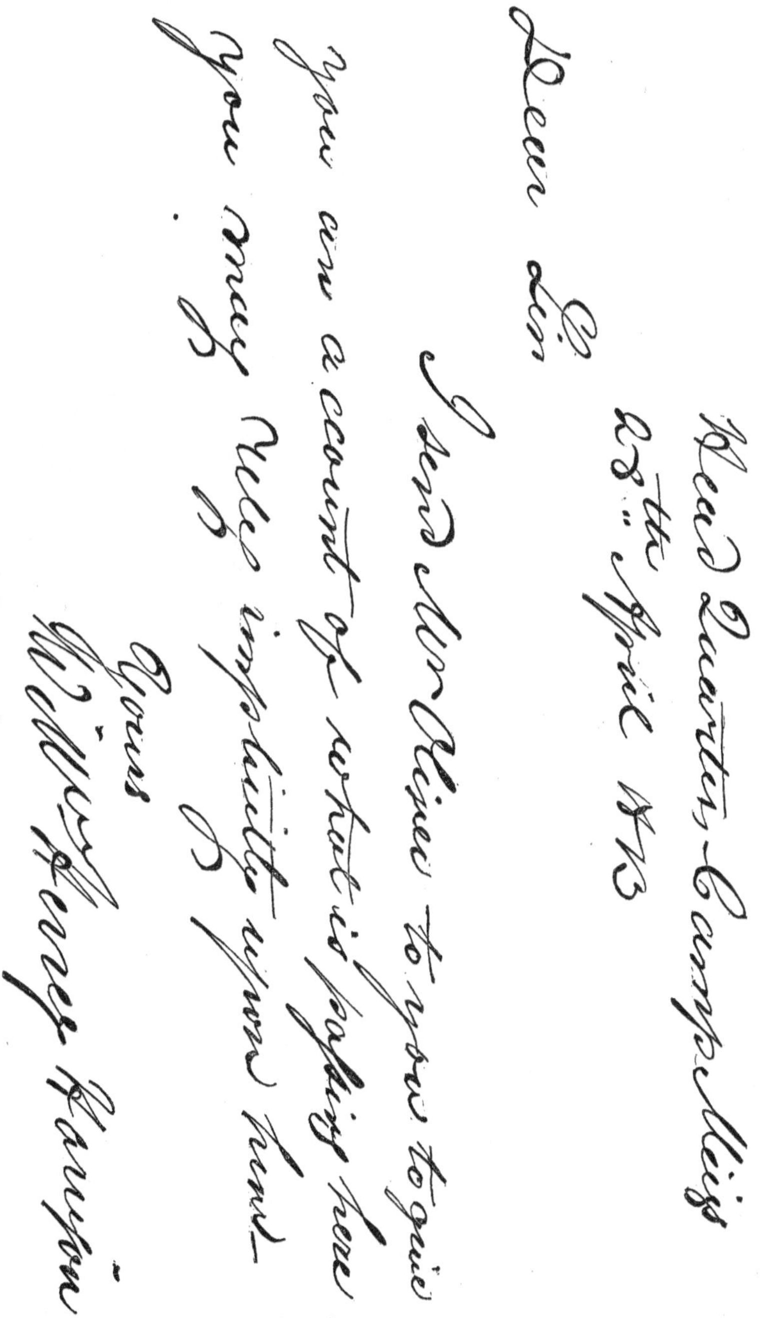

> Head Quarters Camp Meigs
> 23th April 1813
>
> Dear Sir
>
> I send Mr Oliver to you to give you an account of what is passing here you may rely implicitly upon him
>
> Yours
> Will Henry Harrison

FAC-SIMILE OF HARRISON'S LETTER.

---

[1] See page 476.

nati early in April, after issuing a stirring address[1] to his troops[a] in General Orders, and followed Winchester's route to the Maumee.[2] At Dayton he was overtaken by Leslie Combs, of Kentucky, a bold and ardent young man of nineteen years, whose services as scout and messenger in the late campaign, which ended so disastrously at the Raisin, were well known to General Clay. He at once commissioned Combs captain of a company of riflemen as spies or scouts, to be selected by him from Dudley's corps.

[a] April 7, 1813.

At St. Mary's block-house Clay divided his brigade. He sent Dudley to the Au Glaize, while he descended the St. Mary himself with Colonel Boswell's corps. Both divisions were to meet at Defiance. While on their way down the Au Glaize, intelligence reached Dudley of the perilous condition of Harrison at Fort Meigs. At a council of officers it was resolved to apprise the commander-in-chief of the near approach of succor. Who shall undertake the perilous mission? was the important question. It required some person acquainted with the country. Young Combs, eager for patriotic duty and distinction, volunteered to go. "When we reach Fort Defiance," he said, "if you will furnish me a good canoe, I will carry your dispatches to General Harrison, and return with his orders. I shall only require four or five volunteers from my own company, and one of my Indian guides to accompany me." A murmur of approbation ran through the company, and his offer was joyfully accepted by Dudley with words of compliment and gratitude.[3] They reached Defiance the following morning. It was the first of May. As soon as a canoe could be procured Combs embarked on his perilous mission, accompanied by two brothers named Walker, and two others named respectively Paxton and John-

Leslie Combs

---

[1] "Kentuckians," he said, "stand high in the estimation of our common country. Our brothers in arms who have gone before us to the scene of action have acquired a fame which should never be forgotten by you—a fame worthy your emulation. . . . . . Should we encounter the enemy, *remember the fate of your* BUTCHERED BROTHERS *at the River Raisin—that British treachery produced their slaughter!*"

[2] As it may be interesting to the reader to know what constituted the private outfit of an officer of the army at that time for service in the field, I subjoin the following "*list of articles for camp*" prepared for General Clay:

"Trunk, portmanteau and fixtures, flat-iron, coffee-mill, razor-strop, box, etc., inkstand and bundle of quills, ream of paper, three halters, shoe-brushes, blacking, saddle and bridle, tortoise-shell comb and case, box of mercurial ointment, silver spoon, mattress and pillow, three blankets, three sheets, two towels, linen for a cot, two volumes M'Kenzie's Travels, two maps, spy-glass, gold watch, brace of silver-mounted pistols, umbrella, sword, two pairs of spurs—one of silver. CLOTHES: Hat, one pair of shoes, one pair of boots, regimental coat, great-coat, bottle-green coat, scarlet waistcoat, blue cassimere and buff cassimere waistcoat, striped jean waistcoat, two pair cotton colored pantaloons, one pair bottle-green pantaloons, one pair queen-cord pantaloons, one pair buff short breeches, one pair red flannel drawers, one red flannel waistcoat, red flannel shirt, five white linen shirts, two check shirts, nine cravats, six chamois, two pair thread stockings, three pair of thread socks, hunting shirt, one pair of woolen gloves, one pair of leather gloves."

"A complete ration" at that time was estimated at fifteen cents, and was composed and charged as follows: meat, five cents; flour, six cents; whisky, three cents; salt, soap, candles, and vinegar, one fourth of a cent each.

[3] Captain Combs is yet (1867) living in his native state of Kentucky, vigorous in mind and body, and bearing the title of general by virtue of his commission as such in the militia of his state. He is descended, on his mother's side, from a Quaker family of Maryland. His father, a Virginian, was a "Revolutionary Officer and a Hunter of Kentucky." So says a simple inscription on his tomb-stone. Leslie was the youngest of twelve children. He joined the army in 1812, when just past eighteen years of age, and was at once distinguished for his energy and bravery. He was employed, as we have seen (page 350), on perilous duty, and never disappointed those who relied upon him. He was made a captain and wounded near Fort Meigs, and narrowly escaped death. He was paroled, and late in May, 1813, returned home. He commenced the study of law, and was not again in the field until 1836, when he raised a regiment for the southwestern frontier at the time of the revolution in Texas. He became very active in political life. His home was Lex-

son; also by young *Black Fish*, a Shawnoese warrior.[1] With the latter at the helm, the other four engaged with the rowing, and himself at the bow in charge of the rifles and ammunition of the party, Combs pushed off from Defiance, amid cheers and sad adieus (for few expected to see them again), determined to reach Fort Meigs before daylight the next morning. The voyage was full of danger. Rain was falling heavily, and the night was intensely black. They passed the Rapids in safety, but not until quite late in the morning, when heavy cannonading was heard in the direction of the fort. It was evident that the expected siege had commenced, and that the perils of the mission were increased manifold. For a moment Combs was perplexed. To return would be prudent, but would expose his courage to doubts; to remain until the next night, or proceed at once, seemed equally hazardous. A decision was soon made by the brave youth. "We must go on, boys," he said; "and if you expect the honor of taking coffee with General Harrison this morning, you must work hard for it." He went forward with many misgivings, for he knew the weakness of the garrison, and doubted its ability to hold out long. Great was his satisfaction, therefore, when, on sweeping around Turkey Point,[2] at the last bend in the river by which the fort was hidden from his view, he saw the stripes and stars waving over the beleaguered

UP THE MAUMEE VALLEY.

camp. Their joy was evinced by a suppressed shout. Suddenly a solitary Indian appeared in the edge of the woods, and a moment afterward a large body of them were observed in the gray shadows of the forest, running eagerly to a point below to cut off Combs and his party from the fort. The gallant captain attempted to dart by them on the swift current, when a volley of bullets from the savages severely wounded Johnson and Paxton—the former mortally. The fire was returned with effect, when the Shawnoese at the helm turned the prow toward the opposite shore.[3] There the voyagers abandoned the canoe, and, with their faces toward Defiance, sought safety in flight. After vainly attempting to take Johnson and Paxton with them, Combs and *Black Fish* left them to become captives, and at the end of two days and two nights the captain reached Defiance, whereat General Clay had just arrived. The Walkers were also there, having fled more swiftly, because unencumbered. Combs and his dusky companion had suffered terribly.[4] The former was unable to assume

ington, and he was a neighbor and warm personal friend of Henry Clay throughout the long public career of that great man. The friendship was mutual, and Clay always felt and acknowledged the power of General Combs. He was always a fluent, eloquent, and most effective speaker, and now, when he has passed the goal of "threescore and ten years," he never fails to charm any audience by his words of power, his apt illustrations, and genial humor.

[1] He was a grandson of *Black Fish*, a noted warrior who led the Indians in the attack on Boonsboro', in Kentucky, in 1778.

[2] In the above picture, a view of a portion of the Maumee Valley, as seen from the northwest angle of Fort Meigs, looking up the river, Turkey Point is seen near the centre, behind the head of Hollister's Island, that divides the river. A clump of trees, a little to the right of the three small trees in a row near the bank of the river, marks the place. The Maumee is seen flowing to the right, and to the left the plain, when I made the sketch in the autumn of 1860, was covered with Indian corn, some standing and some in the shocks. A canal for hydraulic purposes is seen in the foreground. It flows immediately below the ruins of Fort Meigs.

[3] It was first thought that the Indians were friendly Shawnoese. So thought *Black Fish*; but when he discovered his mistake, he exclaimed, "Pottawatomie, God damn!"

[4] Paxton was shot through the body, but recovered. During the political campaign of 1840, when General Harrison

the command of his company, but he went down the river with the re-enforcements, and took an active part in the conflict in the vicinity of Fort Meigs. There we shall meet him again presently.[1]

The British had completed two batteries nearly opposite to Fort Meigs on the

SITE OF THE BRITISH BATTERIES FROM FORT MEIGS.[2]

[a] April, 1813. morning of the 30th,[a] and had mounted their ordnance. One of them bore two twenty-four-pounders, and the other three howitzers—one eight inches, and the other two five and a half inches calibre. In this labor they had lost some men by well-directed round shot from the fort, but neither these missiles nor the drenching rain drove them away. Harrison had not been idle in the mean time. His force was much inferior to that of the enemy in numbers, but was animated by the best spirit. On the morning after the British made their appearance near, he addressed his soldiers eloquently in a General Order;[3] and when he discovered the foe busy in erecting batteries on the opposite shore that would command his works, he began the construction of a *traverse*, or wall of earth, on the most elevated ground through the middle of his camp, twelve feet in height, on a base of twenty feet, and three hundred yards in length. During its construction it was concealed by the tents. When these were suddenly removed to the rear of the traverse, the British engineer, to his great mortification, perceived that his labor had been almost in vain. Instead of an exposed camp, from which Proctor had boasted he would soon "smoke

---

was elected President of the United States, General Combs spoke to scores of vast assemblies in his favor. On one occasion he was in the neighborhood of Paxton's residence, who took a seat on the platform by the side of the speaker. Combs related the incident of the voyage down the Maumee and their joy at the sight of the old flag on that morning. "Here," said he, "is the man who was shot through the body. Stand up, Joe, and tell me how many bullets it would have taken to have killed you at that measure." "*More than a peck!*" exclaimed Paxton.

[1] I met General Combs at Sandusky City in the autumn of 1860, when he gave me an interesting account of his operations in the Maumee Valley at that time. Speaking of his return to Defiance, he said, "*Black Fish* made his way to his native village, while I pushed on toward Defiance. It rained incessantly. I was compelled to swim several swollen tributaries to the Maumee, and was dreadfully chafed by walking in wet clothes. My feet were lacerated by traveling in moccasins over burnt prairies, and my mouth and throat were excoriated by eating bitter hickory-buds, the only food that I tasted for forty-eight hours. For days afterward I could not eat any solid food. I was placed on a cot in a boat, and in that manner descended the river with my gallant Kentucky friends."

[2] The above little picture, sketched in the autumn of 1860 from the ruins of Croghan Battery (so named in honor of the gallant defender of Fort Stephenson), Fort Meigs, looking northwest, shows the scattered village of Maumee City in the distance, with the site of the British batteries in front of it. This is indicated in the picture by the distant bluff with two houses upon it, immediately beyond the two little figures at the end of the railway-bridge in the middleground. When I visited the spot in 1860, the ridge on which the cannon were planted, lower than the plain on which the village stands, was very prominent. Behind it was a deep hollow, in which the British artillerymen were securely posted. On the brow of the plain, just back of the British batteries, indicated by the second bluff with one house upon it, was afterward the place of encampment of Colonel Johnson. The railway-bridge, seen in the middle-ground of this picture, has a common passenger-bridge by the side of it. Between the extreme foreground and the railway embankment is the ravine mentioned in a description of Fort Meigs on page 474, and indicated in the map on page 488 by a stream of water.

[3] "Can the citizens of a free country," he said, "who have taken arms to defend its rights, think of submitting to an army composed of mercenary soldiers, reluctant Canadians, goaded to the field by the bayonet, and of wretched, naked savages? Can the breast of an American soldier, when he casts his eyes to the opposite shore, the scene of his country's triumphs over the same foe, be influenced by any other feelings than the hope of glory? Is not this army composed of the same materials with that which fought and conquered under the immortal Wayne? Yes, fellow-soldiers, your general sees your countenances beam with the same fire that he witnessed on that glorious occasion; and, although it would be the height of presumption to compare himself with that hero, he boasts of being that hero's pupil.* To your posts, then, fellow-citizens, and remember that the eyes of your country are upon you!"

* Wayne's battle-ground in 1794, and the theatre of his victory, were in sight of the soldiers thus addressed. Harrison was Wayne's aid-de-camp on that occasion, and, as we have observed on page 53, was one of his most useful officers.

OF THE WAR OF 1812.   483

British and Indians cross the River. | A Gun-boat. | Fort Meigs attacked. | Colonel Christy

out the Yankees"—in other words, speedily destroy it with shot and shell, he saw nothing but an immense shield of earth, behind which the Americans were invisible and thoroughly sheltered. Proctor accordingly modified his plans, and sent a considerable force of white men under Captain Muir, and Indians under Tecumtha, to the eastern side of the river, under cover of the gun-boats, with the evident intention of preparing for an attack on the fort in the rear. When night fell the British batteries were yet silent, and remained so; but a gun-boat, towed up the river near the fort under cover of the darkness, fired thirty shots without making any other impression than increasing the vigilance of the Americans, who reposed on their arms. Early in the morning the gun-boat went down the river barren of all honor.

Late in the morning on the 1st of May,[a] notwithstanding heavy rain-clouds were driving down the Maumee Valley, and drenching every thing with fitful discharges, the British opened a severe cannonade and bombardment upon Fort Meigs, and continued the assault, with slight intermissions, for about five days,[1] but without much injury to the fort and garrison. The fire was returned occasionally by eighteen-pounders. The supply of shot for these and the twelve-pounders was very small, there not being more than three hundred and sixty of each. They were used with judicious parsimony, for it was not known how long the siege might last. The British, on the contrary, appeared to have powder, balls, and shells in great abundance, and they poured a perfect storm of missiles—not less than five hundred—upon the

[a] 1813.

---

[1] A survivor of the War of 1812, and one of the most active and remarkable men of the day when the late civil war broke out, was Colonel William Christy. He was acting quarter-master at Fort Meigs, and had charge of all the stores and flags there at that time. He was only twenty-two years of age, yet he had, by his energy and patriotism, secured the love and confidence of General Harrison in a remarkable degree. When the first gun was fired upon Fort Meigs, Harrison called him to his side, and said, "Sir, go and nail a banner on every battery, where they shall wave so long as an enemy is in view." Christy obeyed, and there the flags remained during the entire siege.

Mr. Christy was born in Georgetown, Kentucky, on the 6th of December, 1791. At an early age he went with his father to reside near the Ohio, not far distant from Cincinnati. He was left an orphan at the age of fourteen years. He studied law, and entered upon the duties of that profession in 1811. When war was declared he joined the army under Harrison. That officer knew his father, and kindly gave the son of his old friend a place in his military family as aid-de-camp, and, as we have just observed, he was made acting quarter-master at Fort Meigs. He behaved gallantly there in the sortie in which Captain Silver was engaged, and in which his company suffered terribly. Christy was in subordinate command in that fight, and received the commendations of his general. He was promoted to lieutenant in the old First Regiment of United States Infantry. After the close of the Harrison campaign, which resulted in victory at the Thames, he was ordered to join his regiment, then at Sackett's Harbor. There General Brown appointed him adjutant, and he was in active service in Northern New York for some time. When the army was disbanded, Christy was retained, and was stationed for a while in New Orleans. He left the army in 1816, and commenced the career of a commission merchant in New Orleans. He married there, and soon amassed a fortune, which he lost, however, by the dishonesty of a partner. He resumed the practice of the law, and in 1826 published his "Digest" of the Decisions of the Supreme Court of the State of Louisiana. Again he amassed a large fortune. He espoused the cause of Texas, and soon afterward lost his property, but gained the praise of being "the first filibuster in the United States." His nature was impulsive, and during his residence of more than forty years in New Orleans he had several "affairs of honor," growing out of political quarrels chiefly. He was a ready and fluent speaker, and during the campaign when Harrison was candidate for the Presidency, Colonel Christy accompanied his chief in person throughout Ohio, and made more than one hundred speeches in his behalf. His kindness of heart and ungrudging hospitality ever gained him hosts of warm friends.

fort all of the first day, and until eleven o'clock at night.[1] One or two of the garrison were killed, and Major Stoddard, of the First Regiment, a soldier of the Revolution, who commanded the fort when Leftwitch retired, was so badly wounded by a fragment of a shell that he died ten days afterward.[2]

On the morning of the 2d the British opened a third battery of three twelve-pounders upon the fort from the opposite side of the river, which they had completed during the night, and all that day the cannonade was kept up briskly. Within the next twenty-four hours a fourth battery was opened.[3] That night a detachment of artillerists and engineers crossed the river, and mounted guns and mortars upon two mounds for batteries already constructed in the thickets by the party that crossed on the 30th, within two hundred and fifty yards of the rear angles of the fort. One of these, nearest the ravine already mentioned, was a mortar battery; the other, a few rods farther southward, was a three-gun battery. Expecting an operation of this kind, the Americans had constructed traverses in time to foil the enemy; and when, toward noon of the 3d, the three cannon and the howitzer opened suddenly upon the rear angles of the fort, their fire was almost harmless. A few shots from eighteen-pounders, directed by Gratiot, who was convalescing, soon silenced the gun-battery, and the pieces were hastily drawn off and placed in position near the ravine.

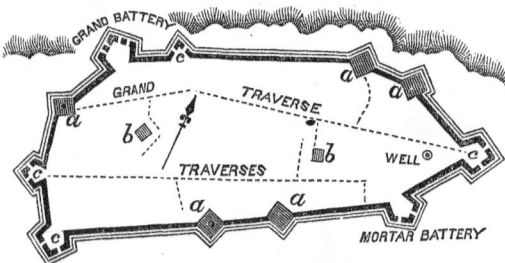

PLAN OF FORT MEIGS.[4]

Shot and shell were hurled upon the fort more thickly and steadily on the 3d than at any other time, but with very little effect. This seemed to discourage the besiegers, and on the 4th the fire was materially slackened. Then Proctor sent Major Chambers with a demand for the surrender of the post. "Tell General Proctor," responded Harrison, promptly, "that if he shall take the fort it will be under circumstances that will do him more honor than a thousand surrenders." Meanwhile the cannonading from the fort was feeble, because of the scarcity of ammunition. "With plenty of it," wrote Captain Wood, "we should have blown John Bull from the Miami." The guns were admirably managed, and did good execution at every discharge. The Americans were well supplied with food and water[5] for a long siege, and could well afford to spend time and weary the assailants by merely defensive warfare sufficient to keep the foe at bay. They exhibited their confidence and spirit by frequently mounting the ramparts, swinging their hats, and shouting defiance to their besiegers. Nevertheless, Harrison was anxious. Hull and Winchester had failed and suffered. The foe was strong, wily, and confident. So he looked hourly and anxiously up the Maumee for the hoped-for re-enforcements. Since Navarre and Oliver went out, he had heard nothing from

---

[1] As the enemy were throwing large numbers of cannon-balls into the fort from their batteries, Harrison offered a gill of whisky for every one delivered to the magazine-keeper, Thomas L. Hawkins. Over one thousand gills were thus earned by the soldiers.—Howe's *Historical Collections of Ohio*, page 532. An eyewitness (Reverend A. M. Lorraine) relates that one of the militia took his station on the embankment, watched every shot, and forewarned the garrison thus: "Shot," or "bomb," as the case might be; sometimes "Block-house No. 1," or "Look out, main battery," "Now for the meat-house," "Good-by, if you *will* pass." At last a shot hit him and killed him instantly.

[2] Amos Stoddard was a native of Massachusetts, and was commissioned a captain of artillery in 1798. He was retained in 1802. In 1804 and '05 he was governor of the Missouri Territory. He was promoted to major in 1807. He was deputy quarter-master in 1812, but left the staff in December of that year. He died of tetanus, or lockjaw, on the 11th of May, 1813. He was the author of "Sketches of Louisiana," published in 1810.

[3] These were named as follows, as indicated on the above map: *a*, Mortar; *b*, Queen's; *c*, Sailor's; and *d*, King's.

[4] This plan is from a sketch made by Joseph H. Larwell, on the 19th of July, 1813. All the dotted lines represent the *traverses*. *a a a a a* indicate the block-houses; *b b*, the magazines; *c c c c*, minor batteries. The grand and mortar batteries and the well are indicated by name.

[5] During the first three days of the siege the Americans were wholly dependent upon the rain for water. Those who were sent to fetch it were exposed to the fire of the enemy. On the fourth they had completed a well within the fort which gave them an ample supply.

abroad. His suspense was ended at near midnight on the 4th, when Captain Oliver, with Major David Trimble and fifteen men who had come down the river in a boat, made their way into the fort as bearers of the glad tidings that General Clay and eleven hundred Kentuckians were only eighteen miles distant, and would probably reach the post before morning.

Captain Oliver had found Clay at Fort Winchester on the 3d. The cannonading at Fort Meigs was distinctly heard there, and Clay pressed forward as speedily as possible with eighteen large flat scows, whose sides were furnished with shields against the bullets of Indians who might infest the shores of the river. It was late in the evening when the flotilla reached the head of the Rapids, eighteen miles from the scene of conflict. The moon had gone down, and the overcast sky made the night so intensely dark that the pilot refused to proceed before daylight. It was then that Trimble and his brave fifteen volunteered to accompany Captain Oliver to the fort, to cheer the hearts of Harrison and his men by the tidings of succor near. It did cheer them. Harrison immediately conceived a plan of operations for Clay, and dispatched Captain Hamilton and a subaltern in a canoe to meet the general, and say to him with delegated authority, "You must detach about eight hundred men from your brigade, and land them at a point I will show you, about a mile or a mile and a half above Camp Meigs. I will then conduct the detachment to the British batteries on the left bank of the river. The batteries must be taken, the cannon spiked, and carriages cut down, and the troops must then return to the boats and cross over to the fort. The balance of your men must land on the fort side of the river, opposite the first landing, and fight their way into the fort through the Indians. The route they must take will be pointed out by a subaltern officer now with me, who will land the canoe on the right bank of the river, to point out the landing for the boats."

This explicit order reveals much of Harrison's well-devised plan. He knew that the British force at the batteries was inconsiderable, for the main body were still near old Fort Miami, and the bulk of the Indians with Tecumtha were on the eastern side of the river. His object was to strike simultaneous and effectual blows on both banks of the stream. While Dudley was demolishing the British batteries on the left bank, and Clay was fighting the Indians on the right, he intended to make a general sally from the fort, destroy the batteries in the rear, and disperse or capture the whole British force on that side of the river.

It was almost sunrise when Clay left the head of the Rapids. He descended the river with his boats arranged in solid column, as in a line of march, each officer having position according to rank. Dudley, being the senior colonel, led the van. Hamilton met them, in this order, about five miles above the fort. Clay was in the thirteenth boat from the front. When Harrison's orders were delivered, he directed Dudley to take the twelve front boats and execute the commands of the chief concerning the British batteries, while he should press forward and perform the part assigned to himself.

Colonel Dudley executed his prescribed task most gallantly and successfully. The current was swift, and the shores were rough, but his detachment effected a landing in fair order. They ascended to the plain on which Maumee City stands unobserved by the enemy, and were there formed for marching in three parallel columns, the right led by Dudley, the left by Major Shelby, and the centre, as a reserve, by Acting Major Morrison. Captain Combs, with thirty riflemen, including seven friendly Indians, flanked in front full a hundred yards distant.[1] In this order they moved through the woods a mile and a half toward the British batteries, which were playing briskly upon Fort Meigs, when the columns were so disposed as to inclose the enemy in a

---

[1] At the request of General Clay, Captain Combs furnished him with minute information respecting the operations under Dudley, in a letter dated May 6, 1815. The writer has kindly furnished me with a copy of that letter, from which the main facts of this portion of the narrative have been drawn.

crescent, with every prospect of capturing the whole force. Dudley had failed to inform his subalterns of his exact plans, and that remissness was a fatal mistake. Shelby's column, by his order, penetrated to a point between the batteries and the British camp below, when the right column, led by Dudley in person, raised the horrid Indian yell, rushed forward, charged upon the enemy with wild vehemence, captured the heavy guns and spiked eleven of them without losing a man. The riflemen, meanwhile, had been attacked by the Indians, and, not aware of Dudley's designs, thought it their duty to fight instead of falling back upon the main body. This was the fatal mistake. The main object of the expedition was fully accomplished, although the batteries were not destroyed. The British flag was pulled down, and as it trailed to earth loud huzzas went up from the beleaguered fort.

Harrison had watched the moment with intense interest from his chief battery, and when he saw the British flag lowered, he signaled Dudley to fall back to his boats and cross the river, according to explicit orders. Yet the victors lingered, and sharp firing was heard in the woods in the rear of the captured batteries. Harrison was indignant because of the disobedience. Lieutenant Campbell volunteered to carry a peremptory order across to Dudley to retreat, but when he arrived the victory so gloriously won was changed into a sad defeat. Humanity had caused disobedience, and terrible was the penalty. At the moment when the batteries were taken, as we have just observed, Indians in ambush attacked Combs and his riflemen. With quick and generous impulse, Dudley ordered them to be re-enforced. A greater part of the right and centre columns instantly rushed into the woods in considerable disorder, accompanied by their colonel. Thirty days in camp had given them very little discipline. It was of little account at the outset, for, disorderly as they were, they soon put the Indians to flight, and relieved Combs and his little party. That work accomplished, discipline should have ruled. It did not. Impelled by the enthusiasm and confidence which is born of victory, and forgetful of all the maxims of prudence, they pursued the flying savages almost to the British camp. Shelby's column still held possession of the batteries when this pursuit commenced, but the British artillerists, largely re-enforced, and led by the gallant Captain Dixon, soon returned and recaptured them, taking some of the Kentuckians prisoners, and driving the others toward their boats.[1] Meanwhile the Indians had been re-enforced, and had turned fiercely upon Dudley. His men were in utter confusion, and all attempts at command were futile. Shelby had rallied the remnant of his column and marched to the aid of Dudley, but he only participated in the confusion and flight. The Kentuckians were scattered in every direction through the woods back of where Maumee City now stands, making but feeble resistance, and exposed to the deadly fire of the skulking savages. The flight became a rout, precipitate and disorderly, and a greater part of Dudley's command were killed or captured, after a contest of about three hours. Dudley, who was a heavy, fleshy man, was overtaken, tomahawked, and scalped, and his captive companions, including Captain Combs and his spies, were marched to old Fort Miami as prisoners of war. Of the eight hundred[2] who followed him from the boats, only one hundred and seventy escaped to Fort Meigs.[3]

---

[1] When Proctor was apprised of the approach of the detachment under Dudley, he supposed it to be the advance of the main American army, and he immediately recalled a large portion of his force on the eastern side of the river. About seven hundred Indians were among them, led by Tecumtha. They did not arrive in time to participate in the battle, but they allowed Proctor to send large re-enforcements from his camp.

[2] The exact number of officers and private soldiers were, of Dudley's regiment, 761; Boswell's, 60, and regulars, 45—total, 866.—Manuscript Reports among the Clay papers.

[3] General Harrison censured Colonel Dudley's men in General Orders on the 9th of May, signed by John O'Fallon, his acting assistant adjutant general. "It rarely occurs," he said, "that a general has to complain of the excessive ardor of his men, yet such appears always to be the case whenever the Kentucky militia are engaged. Indeed, it is the source of all their misfortunes." After speaking of the rash act in pursuing the enemy, he remarked, "Such temerity, although not so disgraceful, is scarcely less fatal than cowardice." In a letter to Governor Shelby on the 18th, General Harrison censured Colonel Dudley. "Had he retreated," he said, "after taking the batteries, or had he made a disposition to retreat in case of defeat, all would have been well. He could have crossed the river, and even if he had

While these tragic scenes were transpiring on the left bank of the river, others equally stirring were in progression in the vicinity of Fort Meigs. General Clay had attempted to land the six remaining boats under his command nearly opposite the place of Dudley's debarkation, but the swiftness of the current, swollen by the heavy rains, drove five of them ashore. The other, containing General Clay, with Captain Peter Dudley and fifty men, kept the stream, separated from the rest, and finally landed on the eastern bank of the river opposite to Hollister's Island. There they were assailed by musketry from a cloud of Indians on the left flank of the fort, and by round shot from the batteries opposite. Notwithstanding the great peril, Clay and his party returned the Indians' attack with spirit, and reached the fort without the loss of a man.

Colonel Boswell's command in the other boats, consisting of a part of the battalions of Kentucky militia under Major William Johnson, and two other companies of Kentucky levies, landed near Turkey Point. He was immediately ordered by Captain Hamilton, General Harrison's representative, to fight his way into the fort. The same Indians who assailed Clay disputed his passage. Boswell arranged his men in open order, marched boldly over the low plain,[1] engaged the savages on the slopes and brow of the high plateau most gallantly, and reached the fort without suffering very serious loss. There he was greeted by thanks and shouts of applause, and met by a sallying-party[2] coming out to join him in an immediate attack upon that portion of the enemy with whom he had just been engaged, pursuant to Harrison's original plan of assailing the foe on both sides of the river at the same time. There was but a moment's delay. Boswell on the right, Major Alexander and his volunteers on the left, and Major Johnson in the centre, was the order in which the party advanced against their dusky foe. They fell upon the savages furiously, drove them half a mile into the woods at the point of the bayonet, and utterly routed them. In their zeal the victors were pursuing with a recklessness that, if continued, would have resulted in disaster like that which overwhelmed Dudley. Fortunately, General Harrison, always on the alert, had taken a stand, with a spy-glass, on one of his batteries, from which he could survey the whole field of operations. He discovered a body of British and Indians gliding swiftly along the borders of the woods to cut off the retreat of the pursuers, when he dispatched a volunteer aid (John T. Johnson, Esq.) to recall his troops. It was a perilous undertaking. The gallant aid-de-camp had a horse shot under him, but he succeeded in communicating the general's orders in time to allow the imperiled detachment to return without much loss.

General Harrison now ordered a sortie from the fort against the enemy's works on the right, near the deep ravine. For this purpose three hundred and fifty men were

---

lost one or two hundred men, he would have brought over a re-enforcement of six hundred, which would have enabled me to take the whole British force on this side of the river." Harrison did not then know that Dudley had sacrificed the greater portion of his little army and his own life in the humane attempt to save Combs and his party from destruction. Combs afterward called General Harrison's attention to the injustice of his censure. It was too late; it had passed into history, and has been perpetuated by the pens of successive chroniclers.

William Dudley was a citizen of Fayette County, Kentucky, at that time, but was a native of Spottsylvania County, Virginia. He was a magistrate in Kentucky for many years, and was highly esteemed. He was overtaken, as we have observed in the text, by the Indians, and shot in the body and thigh. When last seen he was sitting on a stump in a swamp, defending himself against a swarm of savages. He was finally killed, and his body was dreadfully mutilated. I was informed by Abraham Miley, of Batavia, Ohio, who was in Fort Meigs at the time of the siege, that when the body of Dudley was found a large piece had been cut from the fleshy part of his thigh by the savages, which they doubtless ate.

[1] See picture on page 481, and note 2 on the same page.
[2] Composed of Pennsylvania and Virginia Volunteers (the former, except a small company, known as the *Pittsburg Blues*, and the latter the *Petersburg Volunteers*), a company of the Nineteenth United States Regiment under Captain Waring, and Captain Dudley's company, who had followed Clay into the fort. The *Pittsburg Blues* were commanded by Captain James Butler, son of the General Butler who fell at St. Clair's defeat in 1791. See pages 47 and 48. The Virginians were under Captain M'Crea.

detailed, and placed under the command of Colonel John Miller,[1] of the regular service. They consisted of the companies of United States troops under Captains Langham, Croghan, Bradford, Nearing,[2] Elliott,[3] and Gwynne,[4] and Lieutenant Campbell; Major Alexander's[5] volunteers, and a company of Kentucky militia under Captain Sebree.[6] Miller was accompanied by Major George Todd, of the Nineteenth Infantry, and led his command with the greatest bravery. They charged with the fiercest impetuosity upon the motley foe, eight hundred and fifty strong, drove them from their batteries at the point of the bayonet, spiked their guns, and scattered them in confusion in the woods beyond the ravine toward the site of the present village of Perrysburg. The enemy fought desperately, and Miller lost several of his brave men. At one moment the utter destruction of Sebree's company seemed inevitable. They were surrounded by four times their number of Indians, when Gwynne, of the Nineteenth, perceiving their peril, rushed to their rescue with a part of Elliott's company. They were saved. The object of the sortie was accomplished, and the victors returned to the fort with forty-three prisoners, followed by the enemy, who had rallied in considerable force.[7]

After these sorties on the 5th the siege of Fort Meigs was virtually abandoned by Proctor. The result of that day's fighting, combined with the ill success of all preceding efforts to reduce the fort, were so disheartening that his Indian allies deserted him, and the Canadian militia turned their faces homeward.[8] The splendid Territory of Michigan had been promised to the Prophet as a reward for his services in the capture of Fort Meigs, and Tecumtha was to have the person of General Harrison, whom he had hated intensely since the battle of Tippecanoe in 1811, as his peculiar trophy. These prom-

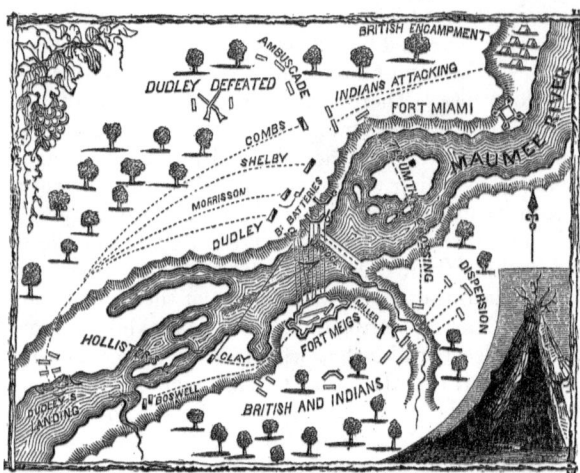

SIEGE OF FORT MEIGS.

---

[1] Colonel of the Nineteenth Regiment of Regulars. He was a native of Ohio, and was commissioned colonel on the 6th of July, 1812. He was transferred to the Seventeenth Infantry in May, 1814. In 1818 he left the army. He was governor of Missouri from 1828 to 1832, and a representative in Congress from 1837 to 1843. He died at Florisant, Missouri, on the 18th of March, 1846.

[2] Abel Nearing was from Connecticut. He survived the siege, but died on the 13th of September following from the effects of fever.

[3] Captain Elliott was a nephew of the notorious Colonel Elliott in the British service, and then with Proctor, and of Captain Jesse Elliott, of the United States Navy, on Lake Erie at that time.

[4] David Gwynne, as first lieutenant and regimental paymaster, had accompanied Colonel J. B. Campbell against the Mississinawa Towns (see page 346). He was made captain in March, 1813. In August he was made brigade major to General M'Arthur, and in 1814 was raised to major of riflemen. He left the army in 1816, and died near St. Louis in 1849.

[5] Major Alexander was a brave officer. He commanded a rifle company, Pennsylvania Volunteers, in Campbell's expedition against the Mississinawa towns in December, 1812.

[6] Uriel Sebree was a captain in Scott's Kentucky Volunteers in August, 1812, and was with Major Madison at Frenchtown, under Winchester. He was a gallant officer.

[7] The Americans lost in this sortie 28 killed and 25 wounded.—*MS. Report.*

[8] "I had not the option of retaining my position on the Miami. Half of the militia had left us. . . . Before the ordnance could be withdrawn from the batteries I was left with Tecumtha and less than twenty chiefs and warriors—a circumstance which strongly proves *that, under present circumstances at least, our Indian force is not a disposable one, or permanent, though occasionally a most powerful aid.*"—Proctor's Dispatch to Governor Prevost.

In his dispatch to Sir George Prevost from Sandwich on the 14th of May Proctor fairly acknowledged himself defeated, and, admitting that he had no data for judging how many the Americans had lost in killed, "conceived" the number to have been between a thousand and twelve hundred ; whereupon Sir George deceived the Canadians and falsified history by asserting, in a General Order, he had "great satisfaction in announcing to the troops the brilliant result of an action which took place on the banks of the Miami River," and "which terminated in the *complete defeat of the enemy*, and capture, dispersion, or destruction of thirteen hundred men !" By a comparison of the most reliable accounts

ises were all unfulfilled. The Indians left in disgust, and probably nothing but Tecumtha's commission and pay as brigadier in the British army secured his farther services in the cause.

Proctor's eyes saw his savage allies leaving him and his Canadian militia discontented, and his ears heard the startling intelligence that Fort George, on the Niagara frontier, was in the hands of the Americans, and that re-enforcements were coming from Ohio for the little army at Fort Meigs.[1] He saw nothing before him, if he remained, but the capture or dispersion of his troops, and he resolved to flee. With the design of concealing this fact that he might move off with safety, he again sent Captain Chambers to demand the surrender of the fort. Harrison regarded the absurd message as an intended insult, and requested that it should not be repeated. It was the last friendly communication between the belligerents.[2]

Proctor attempted to bear away from his batteries his unharmed cannon, but a few shots from Fort Meigs made him withdraw speedily. A parting response in kind from one of his gun-boats, in return, slew several, among them Lieutenant Robert Walker, of the Pittsburg Blues, whose grave may yet be identified within the remains of the fort by a plain, rough stone, with a simple inscription, that stands at its head.[3] This was the last life lost in the siege. In the same vessels that brought him to the Maumee, Proctor returned to Amherstburg with the remains of his little army, leaving behind him a record of infamy on the shores of that stream in the wilderness equal in blackness to that upon the banks of the Raisin.[4] Here, in few words, is the record, attested by Captain Wood, of the Engineers, and others.[5] On the surrender of Dudley's command the prisoners were marched down to Fort Miami with an escort, and there, under the eye of Proctor and his officers, the Indians, who had already plundered them and murdered many on the way,[6] were allowed to shoot, tomahawk, and scalp more than twenty of them. This butchery was stopped by Tecumtha, who proved himself to be more humane than his British ally and brother officer, Henry Proctor.[7]

REMAINS OF WALKER'S MONUMENT.

---

on both sides, the loss of the Americans during the siege may fairly, it seems, be put down at about 80 killed, 270 wounded, and 470 prisoners. The British loss was 15 killed, 47 wounded, and 44 made prisoners.

[1] We have observed (page 478) that Peter Navarre was sent from Fort Meigs with a letter to the Governor of Ohio. That energetic man immediately sent messengers in all directions for volunteers, and he was very soon on his way to the relief of the beleaguered garrison. His march was arrested by the flight of the besiegers.

[2] Harrison's dispatches to the Secretary of War, May 9, 1813; Proctor's dispatch to Sir George Prevost, May 14, 1813; M'Afee's *History of the Late War;* Perkins's and Thomson's *Sketches, etc.;* Captain Wood's Narrative, cited by M'Afee; Major Richardson's Narrative; Auchinleck's *History of the War of 1812;* General Clay's Letter to General Harrison, May 13, 1813; Captain Combs's Letter to General Clay, May 5, 1815; General Harrison to Governor Shelby, May 18, 1813; Armstrong's *Notices of the War of 1812;* Onderdonk's MS. *Life of Tecumseh;* Speech of Eleutheros Cook, Esq., of Sandusky City, at Fort Meigs, June 11, 1840; Narratives of Rev. A. M. Lorraine and Joseph R. Underwood, eyewitnesses, quoted by Howe; Hosmer's *Early History of the Maumee Valley;* oral statements to the Author by Peter Navarre.

[3] The little monument, which contained only the words, Lieutenant Walker, May 9, 1813, had been greatly mutilated, when I visited the spot in the autumn of 1860, by relic-seekers, those modern iconoclasts whose business, when thus pursued, is simply infamous. The remains of the stone, as delineated in the picture, were only about five inches above the ground. It is of limestone, and was wrought by a stone-cutter in the garrison not long after his burial. A few rods east of it is the grave of Lieutenant M'Culloch, who was killed during the summer by Indians while out hunting.

[4] See the close of Chapter XVII.

[5] In Howe's *Historical Collections of Ohio,* page 533, may be found a very interesting narrative of the horrid events at Fort Miami, by Joseph R. Underwood, who was present. It is more circumstantial than the letter of Captain Combs to General Clay, mentioned below.

[6] Major Richardson, of the British army, who wrote an account of events under Brock and Proctor in the West, says that the Indians who made the attack, in spite of the efforts of the guard, were some who had taken no part in the battle. "An old and excellent soldier," he says, "of the name of Russell, of the Forty-first, was shot through the heart while endeavoring to wrest a victim from the grasp of his assailant."

[7] Major Richardson, just quoted, says, in speaking of the massacre: "More than forty of these unhappy men had fallen beneath the steel of the infuriated party, when Tecumtha, apprised of what was doing, rode up at full speed, and, raising his tomahawk, threatened to destroy the first man who resisted his injunction to desist.

General Leslie Combs, then, as we have seen, a captain of spies, and one of the prisoners, in a letter to General Clay, already alluded to, gave a very particular account of the affair. A copy of that letter, furnished by General Combs in 1861, is before me. He says that the prisoners, on their march toward Fort Meigs, met a body of Indians, who, in the

I visited the theatre of events just described, on the 24th of September, 1860, and had the singular good fortune to be accompanied by L. H. Hosmer, Esq., of Toledo, author of *The Early History of the Maumee Valley*, and the venerable Peter Navarre (a Canadian Frenchman), General Harrison's trusty scout, already mentioned.[1] Navarre resided about twenty miles from Toledo, and had come into the city on business two or three days before. Mr. Hosmer, aware of my intended visit at that time, had kindly detained him until my arrival. Only two days before, I had enjoyed a long conversation at the "West House," in Sandusky City, with General Leslie Combs, who had just visited Fort Meigs for the first time since he was there as a soldier and prisoner in 1813. That visit had recalled the incidents of the campaign

PETER NAVARRE.

most vividly to his mind, and he related them to me with his usual enthusiasm and perspicuity. With the soldier's description in my memory, and the historian and scout at my side, I visited Fort Meigs and its historical surroundings under the most favorable circumstances.

The night of my arrival at Toledo had been a tempestuous one—wind, lightning, rain, and a sprinkle of hail. The following morning was clear and cool, with a blustering wind from the southwest. We left the city for our ride up the Maumee Valley at nine o'clock, in a light carriage and a strong team of horses. Mr. Hosmer volunteered to be coachman. Our road lay on the right side of the river; and when nearly seven miles from Toledo we came to the site of Proctor's encampment, on a level plateau a short distance from the Maumee, upon land owned, when we visited

---

presence and without the interference of General Proctor, Colonel Elliott, and other officers, as well as the British guard, commenced robbing the captives of clothes, money, watches, etc. Combs showed his wound as a plea for consideration, but without effect. He too was stripped. As they passed on, the prisoners saw ten or twelve dead men, naked and scalped, and near them two lines of Indians were formed from the entrance of a triangular ditch in front to the old gate of the fort, a distance of forty or fifty feet. Between these the prisoners were compelled to run the gauntlet, and in that race many were killed or maimed with pistols, war-clubs, scalping-knives, and tomahawks. The number of prisoners thus slaughtered, without Proctor's attempt at interference, was estimated at a number nearly, if not quite equal to those slain in battle.

When the surviving prisoners were all inside, the savages raised the war-whoop and commenced loading their guns. The massacre already accomplished, and this preparation for a renewal of it, were made known to Tecumtha, who hastened to the fort with all the rapidity of his horse's speed, and, more humane than his white ally, instantly interposed and saved the lives of the remainder. Elliott then rode in, waved his sword, and the savages retired.

Drake, in his *Life of Tecumtha*, says that the warrior authoritaively demanded, "Where is General Proctor?" Seeing him near, he sternly inquired of him why he had not put a stop to the massacre. "Your Indians can not be commanded," replied Proctor, who trembled with fear in the presence of the enraged chief. "Begone!" retorted Tecumtha, in perfect disdain. "You are unfit to command; go and put on petticoats!"

The half-naked prisoners were taken in a cold rain-storm that night, in open boats, to the mouth of Swan Creek, and thence to Malden. After a brief confinement there they were sent across the river, and at the mouth of the Huron were left to find their way to the nearest settlement in Ohio, fifty miles distant.

[1] Peter Navarre was a grandson of Robert Navarre, a French officer who came to America in 1745. He settled at Detroit, and there Peter was born about the year 1790, and, with his father and family, settled at the mouth of the Maumee in 1807. At that time Kan-tuck-ee-gun, the widow of Pontiac, was living there with her son, Otussa. She was very old, and was held in great reverence. Navarre was at the Prophet's Town, on the Wabash, with a French trader, when Harrison arrived there just before the battle of Tippecanoe, but escaped. He joined Hull's army at the Rapids, was with him at Detroit, and, after the surrender, returned to the Raisin and enlisted in Colonel Anderson's regiment. He was there when Brock was ordered to surrender (see page 291), but was afterward compelled to accompany the British as a guide up the Maumee, where, as we have seen, he deserted and fled to Winchester's camp. He was an eyewitness of the massacre at the River Raisin. After that, Navarre and his brothers were employed as scouts, and performed excellent service. He is a stout-built man, of dark complexion, and is now [1867] about eighty years of age. He speaks English imperfectly, as the Canadian French usually do. The above portrait is from a daguerreotype taken in Toledo when he was about seventy years of age, and kindly presented to me by Mr. Hosmer.

it, by Henry W. Horton. Across a small ravine, a few rods farther southward, were the remains of old Fort Miami, famous, as we have seen, in Wayne's time, as one of the outposts of the British, impudently erected in the Indian country within the acknowledged territory of the United States.[1] It was upon the land of Benjamin Starbird, whose dwelling was just beyond the southern side of the fort. It was a regular work, and covered about two acres of land. The embankments were from fifteen to twenty feet in height. They were covered with heavy sward, and fine honey-locust and hickory trees were growing upon them. These were in full leaf, and the grass was very green,

RUINS OF FORT MIAMI.

when we were there. From the northwest angle of the fort I made the accompanying sketch, which includes the general appearance of the mounds. On the right is seen a barn, which stands within the triangular outwork, at the sally-port mentioned by Captain Combs in his narrative, substantially given in Note 7, page 489, where he was compelled to run the gauntlet for his life; and on the left a glimpse of the Maumee. All about the old fort is now quiet. For more than fifty years peace has smiled upon the Maumee Valley; and Proctor and Tecumtha, Elliott and The Prophet, and the other savages of the war, white and red, are almost forgotten, except by those families who suffered from their cruelty.

From Fort Miami we rode up to Maumee City, opposite Fort Meigs, a pleasant little village of about two thousand inhabitants, situated at the head of river navigation, eight miles from Toledo. It is the capital of Lucas County, Ohio, and was laid out in 1817 by Major William Oliver and others, within a reservation of twelve miles square. The bank of the river, curving gracefully inward here, is almost one hundred feet in height. Nearly opposite lies the little village of Perrysburg, and between them is a fertile, cultivated island of two hundred acres, with smaller islands around it. Directly in front are seen the mounds of Fort Meigs and a forest back of them; and up the Maumee are the considerable islands known respectively as Hollister's and Buttonwood, or Peninsula. The latter view is delineated in the sketch on the next page, taken from the main road along the brow of the river bank in front of the village. In it is seen the magnificent elm-tree that stood near the old "Jefferson Tavern;" and in the middle, in the distance, over Hollister's Island, is seen Turkey Point, memorable in connection with the adventures of Combs and the landing of Boswell. That elm is famous. We have observed that, at the beginning of the siege, the water used by the garrison was taken from the river at great risk. From the thick foliage of this elm several bullets from rifles in the hands of Indians went on death-errands across the river to the water-carriers. These were returned by Kentucky riflemen, and tradition says that not less than six savages were brought to the ground out of that tree by those sharp-shooters.

From Maumee City we rode three miles up to Presque Isle Hill[2] (the scene of Wayne's operations), wandered over the battle-ground of The Fallen Timber,[3] and

---

[1] See page 54.   [2] See page 55.   [3] See Map on page 55.

sketched Turkey-Foot's Rock, given on page 55. We then returned to the bridges (common carriage and railway bridge), and crossed to Fort Meigs, the form of which we found distinctly marked by the mounds of earth. That of the Grand Traverse[1] was from four to six feet in height, and all were covered with green sward. The fort originally included about ten acres, but was somewhat reduced in size before the second siege, which we shall notice presently. The places of the blockhouses were visible, and the situation of the well, near the most easterly angle of the fort, was marked by a shallow pit, and a log in an upright position, seven or eight feet in height.[2]

UP THE MAUMEE, FROM MAUMEE CITY.

On leaving the fort we strolled along the ravine on its right and rear to the site of the British battery captured by Colonel Miller. There yet stood the primeval forest-trees—the very woods in which Tecumtha and his Indians were concealed. A little brook was flowing peacefully through the shallow glen, and the high wind that

WELL AT FORT MEIGS.

[1] See Plan of Fort Meigs on page 484.

[2] That log has a history. In 1840, General Harrison, then living at North Bend, on the Ohio, was nominated for President of the United States. It was said that the hero lived in a log cabin, was very hospitable, and was ever ready to give the traveler a draught of hard cider. Politicians, who are always anxious to find something to charm the popular mind, took the hint, and when the partisans of the general, during the political canvass that ensued, held large meetings, they erected a log cabin, and had a barrel of cider for the refreshment of all comers. In a short time there were log cabins in every city and village in the land. The partisans of the general made a capital "hit," and he was elected by an overwhelming majority. During that canvass a mass meeting of his partisans in Northern Ohio was appointed to be held at Fort Meigs, and, on the day previous to the time appointed for it, logs were taken there for the purpose of building a cabin. On that night some political opponents in the neighborhood spoiled the logs by sawing them in two. The cabin-building was abandoned. One of the logs was placed in an upright position in the nearly-filled old well, a large hole was bored in the end, a small pole was inserted, and upon it was raised a banner before the eyes of the assembled multitude,* having on it a rude picture of a man sawing a log, and the words "LOCO FOCO ZEAL." In those days the Democratic party were called *Loco Focos*, the origin of which name was as follows: A faction of the Democratic party met to organize in the city of New York, when some opponents suddenly turned off the gas. This trick had been played before, and they were prepared. In an instant loco foco matches were produced from their pockets, and the gas-lamps relighted. From that time they were called the Loco Foco Party, and it became the general name, in derision, of the whole Democratic party.

* This meeting was held on the 11th day of June. It was estimated that forty thousand persons were present. The orator of the day was Eleutheros Cooke, Esq., of Sandusky City. The Reverend Mr. Badeau, the clergyman who officiated, was the chaplain of Harrison's army, and in the fort at the siege.

made the great trees rock was scarcely felt in the quiet nook. There we three—historian, scout, and traveler—had a "picnic" on food brought from Toledo, and clear water from the brook, and at one o'clock we departed for the city, passing down the right bank of the Maumee. Just after leaving the fort we rode through Perrysburg, a pleasant village about the size of Maumee City, and the capital of Wood County, Ohio. It was laid out in 1816, and named in honor of the gallant victor on Lake Erie three years before.

When we arrived at the ferry station opposite Toledo, the boat had ceased running because of low water. The wind had been blowing stiffly toward the lake all day, and expelled so much water from the river that the boat grounded in attempting to cross, so we left our team to be sent for, were borne over in a skiff at the moderate price of three cents apiece, and were at the "Oliver House" in time for a late dinner, and a stroll about the really fine little city of Toledo[1] before sunset. At that hour I parted company with Mr. Navarre, with heartfelt thanks for his services, for he had been an authentic and intelligent guide to every place of interest at and around Fort Meigs. I spent a portion of the evening with General John E. Hunt (a brother-in-law of General Cass), who was born in Fort Wayne in 1798. His father was an officer under General Wayne at the capture of Stony Point, on the Hudson, in 1779, and composed one of the "forlorn hope" on that occasion. Although General Hunt was only a boy at the time, he was attached to General Hull's military family during the entire campaign which ended so disastrously at Detroit at midsummer.

At ten o'clock in the evening I bade good-by to kind Mr. Hosmer, and went up the Maumee Valley by railway to Defiance, where I landed at midnight, as already mentioned,[2] in a chilling fog.

---

[1] Toledo is on the left bank of the Maumee River, near its entrance into Maumee Bay, at the lake terminus of the Wabash and Erie Canal. It covers the site of Fort Industry, a stockade erected there about the year 1800, near what is now Summit Street. It stretches along the river for nearly a mile and a half, and the business was originally concentrated at two points, which were two distinct settlements, known respectively as Port Lawrence and Vistula. Toledo was incorporated as a city in 1836, and has now [1867] almost twenty thousand inhabitants. Little more than thirty years ago Ohio and Michigan disputed firmly for the possession of Toledo—a prize worth contending for, for it is a port of great importance. They armed, and an inter-state war seemed inevitable for a while. It was finally settled by Congress, and Toledo is within the boundaries of Ohio. For a full account of this "war," see Howe's *Historical Collections of Ohio*, and Major Stickney's narrative in Hosmer's *Early History of the Maumee Valley*. [2] See page 332.

CHAPTER XXIV.

"Sound, oh sound Columbia's shell!
  High the thundering pæan raise!
Let the echoing bugle's swell,
  Loudly answering, sound his praise!
'Tis Sandusky's warlike boy,
  Crowned with Victory's trophies, comes!
High arise, ye shouts of joy,
  Sound the loud triumphant sound,
    And beat the drums."   C. L. S. JONES.

S soon as General Harrison was certain that Proctor had abandoned the attempt to gain possession of the Maumee Valley and had returned to Malden, he placed the command of the troops at Fort Meigs in charge of the competent General Clay, and started for Lower Sandusky and the interior, to make provision for the defense of the Erie frontier against the exasperated foe. He left the fort under an escort of cavalry commanded by Major Ball, whose horses had been sheltered by the traverses during the siege. He arrived at Lower Sandusky on the 12th of May, where he met Governor Meigs with a large body of Ohio volunteers pressing forward to his relief. Believing that their services would not be needed immediately, he thanked them cordially for their promptness and zeal, and directed them to be disbanded. He then hastened toward Cleveland, and ordered the country along the shores of Lake Erie, from the Maumee to the Cuyahoga, to be thoroughly reconnoitred. Having thus provided for the immediate safety of the frontier settlements, he took up his quarters again at Franklinton, and inaugurated measures for meeting the future exigencies of the service in that region by the establishment of military posts not far from the lake, one of the most important of which was at Lower Sandusky. The general was delighted with the evidences of spirit, courage, and patriotism that appeared on every side. The Ohio settlements were alive with enthusiasm. The advance of Proctor had spread general alarm throughout the state, and hundreds, discerning the peril that menaced their homes, had hastened to the field at the call of the patriotic Governor Meigs. These revelations of strength and will assured Harrison that when he should call for aid, the sons of Ohio would immediately appear in power.

While these events were occurring in the extreme Northwest, the naval preparations were going on vigorously at Presque Isle (Erie), and another and efficient arm of the service had been created, or rather materially strengthened. Richard M. Johnson, a representative of Kentucky in Congress, who had been with Harrison the previous autumn, had proposed to the Secretary of War the raising of a regiment of mounted men in his state, to traverse the Indian country from Fort Wayne along the upper end of Lake Michigan, round by the Illinois River, and back to the Ohio near Louisville. The secretary approved the plan, and early in January[a] laid it before Harrison. The general perceived its utter impracticability in winter. Campbell's expedition to the Mississiniwa Towns[1] had taught him that. "Such an expedition in the summer and fall," he said, "would be highly advantageous, because the Indians are then at their towns, and their corn can be destroyed. An attack upon

[a] 1813.

---
[1] See page 347.

a particular town in the winter, when the inhabitants are at it, as we know they are at Mississiniwa, and which is so near as to enable the detachment to reach it without killing their horses, is not only practicable, but, if the snow is on the ground, is perhaps the most favorable. But the expedition is impracticable to the extent proposed."[1]

The projected incursion was abandoned, but Johnson was authorized[a] to raise a full regiment of mounted men in Kentucky, to serve under General Harrison. As soon as Congress adjourned, he hastened homeward and entered zealously upon the business of recruiting. He published his authority with a stirring address.[b] The regiment was soon raised; and toward the close of May, Johnson was at the head of several companies, on their way to the appointed general rendezvous at Newport, opposite Cincinnati, when a note from one of General Harrison's aids was handed to him. It had already been read to the commanders of the advanced companies, and produced the greatest dissatisfaction among the troops. After thanking all patriotic citizens who had taken up arms in defense of the country in general terms, the note assured them that as the enemy had "fled with precipitancy from Camp Meigs," there was no "present necessity for their longer continuance in the field." Disappointment, chagrin, anger, and depression took the place of patriotic zeal for a moment; but Johnson soon allayed these feelings. He did not choose to regard the note as an order for disbanding *his* troops, and he pressed forward to Newport. There he met General Harrison, when arrangements were made for the regiment to enter the United States service, to traverse a portion of the Indian country according to Johnson's original plan, and to rendezvous at Fort Winchester on the 18th of June. It was believed that the fleet on Lake Erie, designed to co-operate with the army, would be ready at that time for a movement against Malden and Detroit. The regiment arrived at Dayton on the 28th of May, and there the final organization was completed.[2] Under the brave Johnson that regiment performed important service.[3]

[a] February 26, 1813.

[b] March 22.

Proctor appears to have been disheartened, for the moment, by his failure before Fort Meigs, and on his return to Malden he disbanded the Canadian militia, and cantoned the Indians at different places in the neighborhood. Some of them were employed as scouts, others hunted, but the most of them lived upon rations furnished by the British commissariat. Meanwhile British emissaries, white and red, were busy among the tribes of the Northwest, stirring them up to make war on the Americans. A Scotchman and Indian trader, named Dickson, was one of the most efficient of these agents. He was sent, before Proctor moved for the invasion of the Maumee Valley,

[1] General Harrison's Letter to the War Department, January 4, 1813.

[2] Richard M. Johnson was appointed *Colonel*; James Johnson, *Lieutenant Colonel*; Duval Payne and David Thompson, *Majors*; R. B. M'Afee (the author of a *History of the War in the West*, already quoted frequently), Richard Matson, Jacob Elliston, Benjamin Warfield, John Payne, Elijah Craig, Jacob Stucker, James Davidson, S. R. Combs, W. M. Price, and James Coleman, *Captains*; Jeremiah Kertly, *Adjutant*; B. S. Chambers, *Quarter-master*; Samuel Theobalds, *Judge Advocate*; L. Dickinson, *Sergeant-major*; James Suggett, *Chaplain* and *Major of the Spies*; L. Sandford, *Quartermaster general*; Doctors Ewing, Coburn, and Richardson, *Surgeons*.

[3] Richard Mentor Johnson was born at Bryant's Station, five miles northeast of Lexington, Kentucky, on the 17th of October, 1781. At the age of fifteen years he acquired the rudiments of the Latin language, and then entered Transylvania University as a student. His mental and physical energies were remarkable. He chose the law for a profession, and he soon took a conspicuous place in that avocation. During the excitement in the Southwest at the beginning of the present century, when hostilities between the Spaniards at New Orleans and the settlers of the Mississippi Valley seemed imminent, young Johnson took an active part, and volunteered, with others, to make an armed descent on New Orleans. Before he was twenty-two years of age he was elected to a seat in the Kentucky Legislature, where he served two years. He was elected to Congress in 1807, and took his seat when he was just twenty-five years of age. He took a prominent position from the beginning. He held that seat by continued re-election until 1819. In the debates in Congress and movements in the field he was very active during the Second War for Independence. These will find proper notice in the text.

When, in 1819, Colonel Johnson retired from Congress, he was immediately elected to a seat in the Kentucky Legislature. He was chosen a representative of his state in the Senate of the United States, where he served his country faithfully

to visit all the tribes for that purpose on the Illinois and Mississippi Rivers, from Prairie du Chien to Green Bay, making desolated Chicago the grand rendezvous for his savage recruits. There he had collected more than one thousand of them early in June.[a] He marched them across Michigan to Detroit, and barely missed falling in with Colonel Johnson and his mounted men at White Pigeon's Town on the way.[1] His influence had been such that the Indians were incited to many acts of violence in the Territories of Illinois and Missouri. They were even so bold as to invest Fort Madison, and at one time it was apprehended that the powerful Osage nation would rise in open war against the Western frontier. But that calamity was arrested by prompt measures in Illinois and Missouri.

[a] 1813.

Tecumtha had not ceased, since their return to Malden, to urge Proctor to renew the attempt to take Fort Meigs. Proctor was reluctant; but, toward the close of June, he consented, and an expedition was organized for the purpose. At about that time, a Frenchman, taken prisoner on the field of Dudley's defeat, and kept at Malden ever since, escaped. As the enemy suspected, he fled to Fort Meigs, and informed General Clay of the preparations to attack him. Clay immediately communicated the fact to Harrison at Franklinton, and Governor Meigs at Chillicothe. It was rumored that the expected invading force was composed of nearly four thousand Indians and some regulars from the Niagara frontier. The vigilant Harrison was quickly in the saddle. He did not believe Fort Meigs to be the object of attack, but the weaker posts of Lower Sandusky, Cleveland, or Erie. He ordered the Twenty-fourth Regiment of United States Infantry, under Colonel Anderson, then at Upper Sandusky, to proceed immediately to Lower Sandusky. Major Croghan, with a part of the Seventeenth, was ordered to the same post, and also Colonel Ball with his squadron of cavalry.[2] Harrison followed, and on the evening of the 26th he over-

ten years. Then [1829] he again took a seat in the Lower House, and held that position until 1837, when, having been elected Vice-president of the United States, he took his place as President of the Senate. At the end of his official term he retired from public life, and passed the remainder of his days on his farm in Scott County, Kentucky, excepting a brief period, when he was again in the Legislature of that state. While engaged in that service at Frankfort, he was prostrated by paralysis, and expired on the 15th of November, 1850. In the cemetery near Frankfort, Kentucky, is a splendid monument erected to the memory of soldiers of the Commonwealth who had fallen in battle. Within its inclosure is a beautiful monument, made of slightly clouded Italian marble, to the memory of Colonel Johnson, bearing the following inscriptions: on one side of the pedestal, "RICHARD MENTOR JOHNSON, born at Bryant's Station, Kentucky, on the 17th day of October, 1781; died in Frankfort, Kentucky, on the 15th of

JOHNSON'S MONUMENT.

November, 1850." On the opposite side: "To the memory of Colonel Richard M. Johnson, a faithful public servant for nearly half a century, as a member of the Kentucky Legislature, and Representative and Senator in Congress; author of the Sunday Mail Report, and of the laws for abolishing imprisonment for debt in Kentucky and in the United States. Distinguished by his valor as colonel of a Kentucky regiment at the battle of the Thames. For four years Vice-president of the United States. Kentucky, his native state, to mark her sense of his eminent services in the cabinet and in the field, has erected this monument in the resting-place of her illustrious dead."

On the northeast side of the pedestal is a bust of Johnson in low relief; and on the southwest side an historical group, in the same style, in which he is represented as shooting Tecumtha at the battle of the Thames. Some remarks on that subject will be found in our account of that battle.

[1] Dickson's recruits are represented by eyewitnesses as being the most savage and cruel in their nature. The principal chief among them was Mai-pock, whose girdle was covered with human scalps as trophies of his prowess. "It is remarkable," says M'Afee, "that after the savages joined the British standard to combat for 'the Defenders of the Faith,' victory never again declared for the allies in the Northwest. For the cruelties they had already committed, and those which were threatened by this inhuman association, a just God frowned indignant on all their subsequent operations."—*History of the Late War*, page 298.

[2] General Harrison had just held an important council with the Shawnoese, Delaware, Wyandot, and Seneca Indians

Johnson's Reconnoissance to the Raisin.   At Fort Stephenson.   Departure for the Wilderness, and Recall.

took Colonel Anderson. Scouts had reported the appearance of numerous Indians on the Lower Maumee, and the general selected three hundred men to make a forced march to Fort Meigs. He arrived there himself on the 28th, and then ordered Colonel Johnson, who had come down from Fort Winchester with his seven hundred men after forty days of hard service in traversing the Wilderness, to make a reconnoissance toward the Raisin to procure intelligence. Obedience followed command. The movement was successful. Johnson ascertained that there was no immediate danger of an invasion from Malden in force. Satisfied of this, Harrison left Fort Meigs on the 1st of July, escorted by seventy mounted men under Captain M'Afee as far as Lower Sandusky. From there he went to Cleveland, escorted by Colonel Ball, to make farther defensive provisions. There he left Ball and his cavalry in charge, and returned to his head-quarters after ordering Colonel Johnson, with his mounted men, to take post at the Huron River. That efficient officer again promptly obeyed. He arrived at Lower Sandusky on the 4th of July. Flags were flying, and music filled the air. The garrison of Fort Stephenson,[1] under Major Croghan, were about to celebrate the day with appropriate ceremonies, and, at their request, Colonel Johnson delivered a patriotic oration. Toasts were given, and good cheer abounded. But duty called from pleasure, and the mounted men resumed their saddles to press onward to the Huron. An order from the War Department arrested them. Johnson was directed to turn back, and hasten to the defense of the Illinois and Missouri Territories, then, in the opinion of the authorities there, seriously menaced by Dickson and his savage followers. He was disappointed and mortified; but, after writing to Harrison expressing his strong desire to remain in the army destined for Detroit and Malden, he turned his horse's head again toward the Wilderness. The commander-in-chief urged the Department to comply with Johnson's wishes, assuring the Secretary that Dickson's savages were on the Detroit. The order was countermanded, and, when far on his way toward the Mississippi as an obedient soldier, Johnson was recalled. It was well for the country that he was left to serve under the direct command of General Harrison at that time.

Late in July the British had collected on the banks of the Detroit nearly all of the warriors of the Northwest, full twenty-five hundred in number. These, with Proctor's motley force already there, made an army of about five thousand men. Early in the month bands of Indians began to appear in the vicinity of Fort Meigs, killing and plundering whenever opportunity offered. Tecumtha, meanwhile, had become

---

at his head-quarters at Franklinton. Circumstances had made him suspect their fidelity to their promises of strict neutrality. It was a crisis when all should be made plain. He required them to take a decided stand for or against the Americans; to remove their families into the interior, or the warriors must accompany him in the ensuing campaign, and fight for the United States. The venerable *Ta-he*, who was the acknowledged representative of them all, assured the general of their unflinching friendship, and that the chiefs and warriors were anxious to take part in the campaign. He accepted their assurances as true, and told them he would let them know when he wanted them. "But," he said, "you must conform to our mode of warfare. You are not to kill defenseless prisoners, old men, women, or children. By your good conduct I shall be able to tell whether the British can restrain their Indians if they wish to do so." He then told them that he had heard of Proctor's promise to deliver him into the hands of Tecumtha. "Now," he said, jocularly, "if I can succeed in taking Proctor, you shall have him for your prisoner, provided you will treat him as a squaw, and only put petticoats upon him, for he must be a coward who would kill a defenseless prisoner."

[1] Fort Stephenson was erected in the summer of 1812. Lower Sandusky (now the village of Fremont) was a mere trading-post, the only buildings being a government store and a Roman Catholic mission-house in charge of two priests. Thomas Butler, who had been in Wayne's army, was charged with the duty of selecting the site and superintending the construction of a stockade at that place. He drew the lines of the fort around the store-house, about one hundred yards in one direction, and about fifty yards in the other. The men employed in the work were a company under Captain Norton, of Connecticut, who were ordered to Lower Sandusky by Governor Meigs for the purpose. Sergeant Erastus Bowe, of Tiffin, Ohio, one of the three known survivors of the detachment in 1860, was the first to break ground, saying, "Captain, I don't think there will be much fighting here, but I believe I will make a hole here." His remark was caused by the general belief that the British would never be able to penetrate so far. The pickets for the fort were cut near the present railway station, and in the course of twenty-five days they were all set. A block-house was constructed on the northeast corner, and another in the middle of the north side of the fort. Croghan strengthened the fort in the summer of 1813 by the erection of two more block-houses, one of which was built against the middle block-house on the north side, and the other on the southwest corner. He also constructed an embankment and ditch, and in the block-house on the northeast angle placed his six-pounder.—*Statement of Erastus Bowe in the "Sandusky Democrat," July* 27, 1860. The other two known survivors of the constructors of the fort at that time were Samuel Scribner, of Marion, and Ira Carpenter, of Delaware, Ohio.

very restive under the restraints of inaction, especially when he saw so large a body of his countrymen ready for the war-path, and he at last demanded that another attempt should be made to capture Fort Meigs. He submitted to Proctor an ingenious plan by which to take the garrison by stratagem and surprise. He proposed to land the Indians several miles below the fort, march through the woods, unobserved by the garrison, to the road leading from the Maumee to Lower Sandusky in the rear, and there engage in a sham-fight. This would give Clay an idea that some approaching re-enforcements had been attacked, and he would immediately sally out with the garrison to their aid. The Indians would form an ambuscade, rise, and attack the unsuspecting Americans in their rear, cut off their retreat, and, rushing to the fort, gain an entrance before the gates could be closed.[1] Proctor accepted the plan and arranged for the expedition, but the vigilance and firmness of General Clay defeated the well-devised scheme and saved the fort.

On the 20th of July Proctor and Tecumtha appeared with their combined forces, about five thousand strong, at the mouth of the Maumee.[2] General Clay immediately dispatched a messenger to Harrison, at Lower Sandusky, with the information. The commander-in-chief, doubtful what post the enemy intended to attack, sent the messenger (Captain M'Cune) back with an assurance for General Clay that he should have re-enforcements if needed, and a warning to beware of a surprise. He then removed his head-quarters to Seneca Town,[3] nine miles farther up the Sandusky River, from which point he might co-operate with Fort Meigs or Fort Stephenson, as circumstances should require. There, with one hundred and forty regulars, he commenced fortifying his camp, and was speedily joined by four hundred and fifty more United States troops under Lieutenant Colonel Paul,[4] of the infantry, and Ball, of the dragoons; also by M'Arthur and Cass, of Ohio, who had each been promoted to brigadier general. Colonel Theodore Deye Owings was also approaching with five hundred regulars from Fort Massac, on the Ohio River.

Tecumtha attempted to execute his strategic plan. On the afternoon of the 25th,[a] while the British were concealed in the ravine already described, just below Fort Meigs, the Indians took their prescribed station on the Sandusky road, and at sunset commenced their sham-fight. It was so spirited, and the yells of the savages were so powerful, that the garrison had no doubt that the commander-in-chief, with re-enforcements, had been attacked. They were exceedingly anxious to go out to their aid. Fortunately, General Clay was better informed. Captain M'Cune had just returned from a second errand to General Harrison, after many hair-breadth escapes in penetrating the lines of the Indians swarming in the woods. Although Clay could not account for the firing, yet he was so certain that no Americans were engaged in the contest, whatever it might be, that he remained firm, even when officers of high rank demanded permission to lead their men to the succor of their friends, and the troops were almost mutinous because of the restraint. Clay's firmness saved them from utter destruction. A heavy shower of rain, and a few cannon-

[a] July, 1813.

---

[1] Statement of Major Richardson, of the British army.
[2] Proctor commanded the white troops in person. Dixon, of the Royal Artillery, commanded the Mackinaw and other Northern tribes; Tecumtha those of the Wabash, Illinois, and St. Joseph; and Round-Head (see page 291) those of the Chippewas, Ottawas, and Pottawatomies of Michigan.—Harrison's Letter to the Secretary of War, Seneca Town, August 4, 1813.
[3] The Indians who occupied this region were called "the Senecas of Sandusky"—why does not appear, for they were composed of Cayugas chiefly, with a few Oneidas, Mohawks, Onondagas, Tuscaroras, and Wyandots. They numbered about four hundred souls at the close of the war, and were the remnant of the tribe of Logan, the chief immortalized by Mr. Jefferson. In 1817 and 1818 forty thousand acres of land lying on the east side of the Sandusky River were granted to them. In 1831 they ceded their lands to the United States, and went west of the Mississippi. Seneca County, of which Tiffin is the county seat, derived its name from these so-called Seneca Indians. The fortified camp of Harrison assumed the form of a regular work known as Fort Seneca, having a stockade and ditch, and occupied several acres of a plain on the bank of the Sandusky. Slight remains of the work were yet visible in 1860.
[4] George Paul was a major of Pennsylvania militia under General Harrison. He afterward resided in Ohio, and entered the service again early in the war. He was commissioned a lieutenant colonel in April, 1813, and colonel at the close of June following. He resigned in October, 1814.

shot hurled from the fort in the direction of the supposed fight, put an end to the firing, and that night was as quiet at Fort Meigs as in a time of peace. The strategy of Tecumtha had failed, to the great mortification of the enemy. Ignorant of the strength of the fort and garrison,[1] they did not attempt an assault. After lingering around their coveted prize about thirty hours, the besiegers withdrew[a] to Proctor's old encampment, near Fort Miami, and on the 28th the British embarked with their stores and sailed for Sandusky Bay, with the intention of attacking Fort Stephenson. A large number of their savage allies marched across the country for the purpose of co-operating with Proctor in the siege. Intelligence of this movement was promptly communicated to Harrison by General Clay.

[a] July 27, 1813.

Fort Stephenson was garrisoned by one hundred and sixty men, under the command, as we have observed, of a gallant young Kentuckian, Major George Croghan, of the Regular Army, then only twenty-one years of age. Their only ordnance was an iron six-pounder cannon, and their chief defenses were three block-houses, circumvallating pickets from fourteen to sixteen feet in height, and a ditch about eight feet in width and of equal depth.

Already an examination of Fort Stephenson by General Harrison had convinced him that it would be untenable against heavy artillery, and, in orders left with Major Croghan, he said, "Should the British troops approach you in force with cannon, and you can discover them in time to effect a retreat, you will do so immediately, destroying all the public stores. You must be aware that to attempt to retreat in the face of an Indian force would be vain. Against such an enemy your garrison would be safe, however great the number."

On the receipt of the intelligence from General Clay, General Harrison called around him in council[b] M'Arthur, Cass, Ball, Wood, Hukill, Paul, Holmes, and Graham, and it was unanimously agreed that Fort Stephenson was untenable, and that, as the approaching enemy had cannon, Major Croghan ought immediately to comply with the standing order of his general. Believing that the innate bravery of Croghan would make him hesitate, General Harrison immediately dispatched to him an order to abandon the fort.[2] The bearers started at midnight, and lost their way in the dark. They did not arrive at Fort Stephenson before eleven o'clock the next day, when the forest around was swarming with Indians.

[b] July 29.

Major Croghan consulted his officers concerning a retreat, when a majority agreed with him that such a step would be disastrous, and that the post might be maintained. A few moments after the conference, he placed in the hands of the messengers from General Harrison the following answer to his chief:[c] "SIR,—

[c] July 30, 1813.

---

[1] The garrison numbered, in rank and file, only about eighteen hundred men. There were a little over two thousand at the close of May, but full two hundred had died of camp fever.

[2] The order was sent by a white man (Conner) and two Indians, who found some difficulty in the performance of their mission. The following is a copy of the order: "SIR,—Immediately on receiving this letter you will abandon Fort Stephenson, set fire to it, and repair with your command this night to head-quarters. Cross the river and come up on the opposite side. If you should deem and find it impracticable to make good your march to this place, take the road to Huron, and pursue it with the utmost circumspection." The order was dated 29th July.

I have just received yours of yesterday, ten o'clock P.M., ordering me to destroy this place and make good my retreat, which was received too late to be carried into execution. We have determined to maintain this place, and, by heavens! we can."

This positive disobedience of orders was not intended as such. The gallant young Kentuckian gladly perceived sufficient latitude given him in the clause of the earlier order, in which the danger of a retreat in the face of an Indian force was mentioned, to justify him in remaining, especially as the later order did not reach him until such force was apparent. But the general could not permit disobedience to pass unnoticed, and he immediately ordered Colonel Wells to repair to Fort Stephenson and supersede Major Croghan.[1] The latter was ordered to head-quarters at Seneca Town. He cheerfully obeyed the summons, and made so satisfactory an explanation to General Harrison that he was directed to resume his command the next morning, with written instructions similar to the ones he had before received. Croghan was now more determined than ever to maintain the post.

General Harrison kept scouts out in all directions watching for the foe. On the evening of Saturday, the 31st of July, a reconnoitring party, lin-

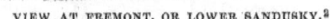

VIEW AT FREMONT, OR LOWER SANDUSKY.[2]

[1] Colonel Wells was escorted by Colonel Ball, with his corps of dragoons, and bore the following letter to Major Croghan: "SIR,—The general has just received your letter of this date informing him that you had thought proper to disobey the order issued from this office, and delivered to you this morning. It appears that the information which dictated the order was incorrect, and as you did not receive it in the night, as was expected, it might have been proper that you should have reported the circumstances and your situation before you proceeded to its execution. This might have been passed over, but I am directed to say to you that an officer who presumes to aver that he has made his resolution, and that he will act in direct opposition to the orders of his general, can no longer be intrusted with a separate command. Colonel Wells is sent to relieve you. You will deliver the command to him, and repair, with Colonel Ball's squadron, to this place. By command, etc., A. H. HOLMES, Assistant Adjutant General."

On the way, about half a mile southwest of the present village of Ballsville, Colonel Ball's detachment were attacked by about twenty Indians, and quite a severe skirmish ensued. Seventeen of the Indians were killed; and, until within a few years, an oak-tree stood on the site of the contest, bearing seventeen marks of a hatchet, to indicate the number of Indians slain.

[2] This view was taken from the verge of the hill, near where the howitzer, or mortar, of the British was planted after landing, so as to be brought to bear upon the fort. In the front is seen a magnificent elm-tree, of large growth at the time of the invasion. Tradition avers that an Indian, who climbed into its top to reconnoitre Fort Stephenson, was shot by one of the Kentucky riflemen in the garrison. In this view we are looking down the Sandusky River. In the little cove, seen nearly over the roof of the small building nearest the left of the picture, is the place where the British landed. The island opposite is seen more to the left. In the extreme distance are store-houses, at which point the British gun-boats were first discovered by the garrison. On the extreme right is the gas-house, and over it, on the east side of the river, is the elevated plain where Croghanville was laid out, and where the Indians were first seen.

gering upon the shores of Sandusky Bay, about twenty miles from Fort Stephenson, discovered the approach of Proctor by water. They hastened back, stopping at the fort on the way at about noon the next day.[a] Croghan was on the alert. Already many Indians had appeared upon the eminence on the eastern side of the Sandusky River (where Croghanville was laid out in 1817), and had scampered away after a few discharges of the six-pounder in the fort.

[a] August 1.

At four o'clock that afternoon the British gun-boats, with Proctor and his men, appeared at a turn in the river more than a mile distant. In the face of shots from the six-pounder they advanced, and, in a cove not quite a mile from the fort, the British landed, with a five-and-a-half-inch howitzer, opposite a small island in the stream. At the same time the Indians displayed themselves in the woods in all directions, to cut off a retreat of the garrison.

General Proctor entered immediately upon the business of his errand. His attacking force consisted of a portion of the Forty-first Regiment, four hundred strong, and several hundred Indians. Tecumtha, with almost two thousand more, was stationed upon the roads leading from Fort Meigs and Seneca Town, to intercept apprehended re-enforcements from those directions.

Having disposed of his forces so as to cut off Croghan's retreat, General Proctor sent Colonel Elliott, accompanied by Captain Chambers with a flag of truce, to demand the instant surrender of the fort. These officers were accompanied by Captain Dixon, of the Royal Engineers, who was in command of the Indian allies.

Major Croghan sent out Second Lieutenant Shipp,[1] as his representative, to meet the flag. After the usual salutations, Colonel Elliott said: "I am instructed to demand the instant surrender of the fort, to spare the effusion of blood, which we can not do should we be under the necessity of reducing it by our powerful force of regulars, Indians, and artillery."

"My commandant and the garrison," replied Shipp, "are determined to defend the post to the last extremity, and bury themselves in its ruins, rather than surrender it to any force whatever."

"Look at our immense body of Indians," interposed Dixon. "They can not be restrained from massacring the whole garrison, in the event of our undoubted success."

"Our success is certain," eagerly added Chambers.

"It is a great pity," said Dixon, in a beseeching tone, "that so fine a young man as you, and as your commander is represented to be, should fall into the hands of the savages. Sir, for God's sake, surrender, and prevent the dreadful massacre that will be caused by your resistance."

Shipp, who had lately dealt with the same foe at Fort Meigs, coolly replied: "When the fort shall be taken, there will be none to massacre. It will not be given up while a man is able to resist."

Shipp was just turning to go back to the fort, when an Indian sprung from a bushy ravine near and attempted to snatch his sword from him. The indignant American was about to dispatch the savage, when Dixon interfered. Croghan, who had stood upon the ramparts during the conference, observed the insult, and shouted, "Shipp, come in, and we will blow them all to hell!" The ensign hastened into the fort, the flag returned, and the British opened a fire immediately from their gun-boats, and from the five-and-a-half-inch howitzer which they had landed. For some reason, never

---

[1] Edmund Shipp, Jr., was a native of Kentucky, and was appointed ensign of the 17th regiment of infantry in May, 1812. He was promoted to second lieutenant in March, 1813, and distinguished himself in the defense of Fort Meigs the following year. After the affair at Fort Stephenson he became General M'Arthur's brigade major. In March, 1814, he was promoted to first lieutenant, and to captain in May, and at the close of the war was retained in the service. He died at Bellefontaine, Ohio, on the 22d of April, 1817. On the 13th of February, 1835, the Congress of the United States voted a sword, to be received by his nearest male relative, in testimony of their sense of his services at Fort Stephenson.—Gardner's *Dictionary of the Army.*

until recently explained, they commenced the attack in great haste, before proper arrangements were made.[1]

All night long, five six-pounders, which had been landed from the British gun-boats, and the howitzer upon the land, played upon the stockade without serious effect. They were answered occasionally by the solitary cannon in the fort, which was shifted from one block-house to another, so as to give the impression that the garrison had several heavy guns. But their supply of ammunition was small, and Major Croghan determined to use his powder and ball to better advantage than firing at random in the dark. He silenced the gun, and ordered Captain Hunter,[2] his second in command, to place it in the block-house at the middle of the north side of the fort, so as to rake the ditch in the direction of the northwest angle, the point where the foe would doubtless make the assault, it being the weakest part. This was accomplished before daylight, and the gun, loaded with a half charge of powder and a double charge of slugs and grapeshot, was completely masked.

During the night the British had dragged three six-pounders to a point of woods on ground higher than the fort, and about two hundred and fifty yards from it (near the spot where the court-house in Fremont now stands, westward of Croghan Street), and early in the morning they opened a brisk fire upon the stockade from these and the howitzer. Their cannonade produced but little effect, and for many hours the little garrison made no reply. Proctor became impatient. That long day in August was rapidly passing away, and he saw before him only a dreary night of futile effort in his present position. His Indians were becoming uneasy, and at length he resolved to storm the fort. At four o'clock in the afternoon he concentrated the fire of all his guns upon the weak northwest angle. His suspected purpose was now apparent. Toward that weak point Croghan directed his strengthening efforts. Bags of sand and sacks of flour were piled against the pickets there, and the force of the cannonade was materially broken.

At five o'clock, while the bellowing of distant thunder in the western horizon, where a dark storm-cloud was brooding, seemed like the echo of the great guns of the foe, the British, in two close columns, led by Brevet Lieutenant Colonel Short and Lieutenant Gordon, advanced to assail the works. At the same time a party of grenadiers, about two hundred strong, under Lieutenant Colonel Warburton, took a wide circuit through the woods to make a feigned attack upon the southern front of the fort, where Captain Hunter and his party were stationed. Private Brown, of the Petersburg Volunteers, with half a dozen of his corps and Pittsburgh Blues, happened to be in the fort at the time. Brown was skilled in gunnery, and to him and his companions was intrusted the management of the six-pounder in the fort.

As the British storming-party under Lieutenant Colonel Short advanced, their artillery played incessantly upon the northwestern angle of the fort, and, under cover of the dense smoke, they approached to within fifteen or twenty paces of the outworks before they were discovered by the garrison. Every man within the fort was at his post, and these were Kentucky " sharp-shooters !" They instantly poured upon the assailants such a shower of rifle-balls, sent with fatal precision, that the British line was thrown into momentary confusion. They quickly rallied. The axe-men

---

[1] The late Hon. Elisha Whittlesey, in his address at Fremont (Lower Sandusky), on the forty-fifth anniversary of the defense of Fort Stephenson, explained the cause. Aaron Norton, of Portage County, Ohio, told him that on that Sunday afternoon, in total ignorance of the proximity of the British and Indians, he was approaching the fort on the opposite side of the Sandusky, when he discovered quite a large body of Indians scattered along the bank of the river, half concealed by bushes. He wheeled his horse and fled in the direction of Seneca. The startled Indians fired several shots at him, but without effect. This occurrence was doubtless communicated to the British commander. He knew Harrison was near, and feared that he might sally forth from his fortified camp with re-enforcements from Cleveland or Mansfield, beat back Tecumtha, and fall upon him at Sandusky ; hence his haste in assailing the fort.

[2] James Hunter was a native of Kentucky, and was adjutant of the Kentucky mounted riflemen in the battle of Tippecanoe. He was wounded there. He was promoted to captain in the 17th regiment of infantry in March, 1812. He left the army in May, 1814. On the 13th of February, 1835, the Congress of the United States voted him a sword because of his distinguished services at Fort Stephenson.—Gardner's *Dictionary of the Army*.

| Storming of Fort Stephenson. | Slaughter of the Assailants. | The British and Indians repulsed. |

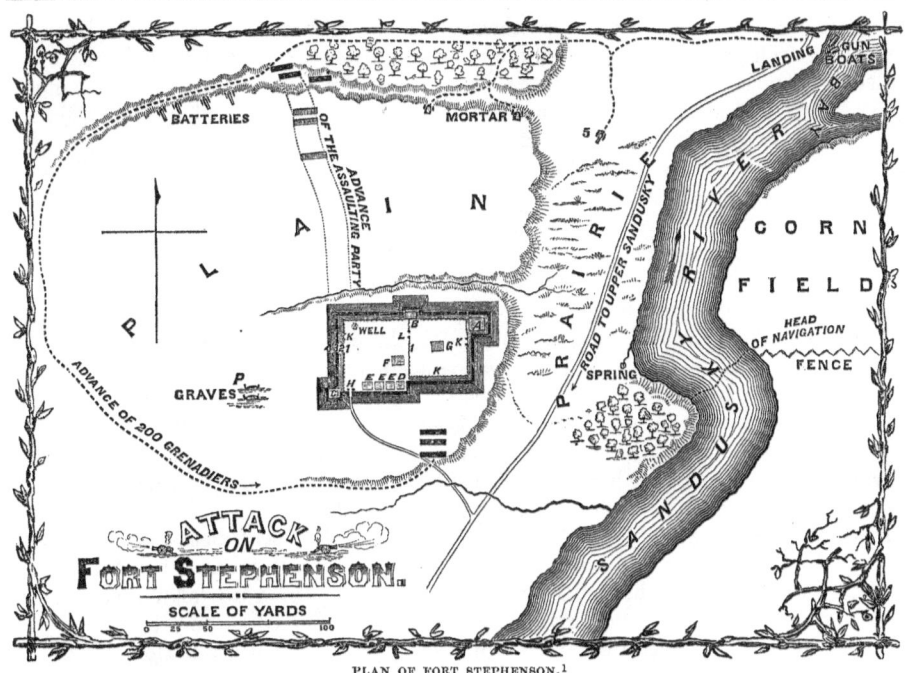

PLAN OF FORT STEPHENSON.[1]

bravely pushed forward over the glacis, and leaped into the ditch to assail the pickets. Lieutenant Colonel Short was at the head of the gallant party, and when a sufficient number of men were in the ditch behind him, he shouted, "Cut away the pickets, my brave boys, and show the damned Yankees no quarter!" Now was the moment for the voice of the unsuspected six-pounder to be heard. The masked port flew open instantly. The gun spoke with terrible effect. Slugs and grapeshot streamed along that ditch overflowing with human life, and spread terrible havoc there. Few escaped. A similar attempt was made by the second column of the storming-party, when another discharge from the six-pounder and a destructive volley of rifle-balls ended the contest. Brevet Lieutenant Colonel Short and Lieutenant Gordon, of the Forty-first Regiment, Laussaussiege, of the Indian department, and twenty-five privates, were left dead in the ditch,[2] and twenty-six of the wounded were made prisoners. Captain Dixon and Captain Muir, and Lieutenant M'Intyre, of the Forty-first Regiment, were slightly wounded and escaped. A precipitate and confused retreat immediately followed this repulse. Warburton and his grenadiers did not reach the south front of the fort until after the disaster. They were assailed with a destructive volley from Hunter's corps, and fled for shelter to the adjacent woods.

The whole loss of the garrison was one man killed and seven slightly wounded. The loss of the British in killed and wounded, according to the most careful estimates, was one hundred and twenty. The cowardly Indians, as usual when there was open

---

[1] EXPLANATION OF THE PLAN.—1, line of pickets; 2, embankment from the ditch to and against the pickets; 3, dry ditch; 4, outward embankment or glacis; A, block-house first attacked by cannon; B, bastion or block-house from which the ditch was raked by the six-pounder in the fort; C, guard block-house; D, hospital while attacked; E E E, military store-houses; F, commissary's store-house; G, magazine; H, fort gate; K K K, wicker gates; L, partition gate; 5, position of the five six-pounders of the British on the night of the 2d of August; P, the graves of Lieutenant Colonel Short and Lieutenant Gordon, who were killed in the ditch. The mortar or howitzer shifted position, as indicated on the plan. In the first assault there were only four six-pounders in battery, only one being left in the first position near the river. This Plan was first published, from the official drawing, in the *Port Folio* for March, 1815, and soon afterward in Thomson's carefully prepared *Historical Sketches of the Late War*. The graves of the two British officers are a few yards northeastward from the junction of High and Market Streets.

[2] It is said that Lieutenant Colonel Short, when he fell, twisted a white handkerchief on the end of his sword as a supplication for that mercy which his battle-cry a moment before denied to his foe.

fighting or great guns to face, kept themselves out of harm's way in a ravine near by, and the whole battle was fought by the small British force, who behaved most gallantly. During the night Proctor sent Indians to gather up the dead and wounded, and at three o'clock in the morning[a] the invaders sailed down the Sandusky, leaving behind them a vessel containing clothing and military stores. At about the same hour the gallant Major Croghan wrote a hurried note to General Harrison, informing him of his victory and the retreat of Proctor.

[a] August 3.

The assault lasted only about half an hour. The dark storm-cloud in the west passed northward, the setting sun beamed out with peculiar splendor, a gentle breeze from the southwest bore the smoke of battle far away over the forest toward Lake Erie, and in the lovely twilight of that memorable Sabbath evening the brave young Croghan addressed his gallant little band with eloquent words of praise and grateful thanksgiving. As the night and the silence deepened, and the groans of the wounded in the ditch fell upon his ears, his generous heart beat with sympathy. Buckets filled with water were let down by ropes from the outside of the pickets; and as the gates of the fort could not be opened with safety during the night, he made a communication with the ditch by means of a trench, through which the wounded were borne into the little fortress and their necessities supplied.[1]

Intelligence of this gallant defense caused the liveliest sentiments of admiration throughout the country, and congratulations were sent to Major Croghan from every quarter. His general, in his official report, spoke of him in words of highest praise.[2] The ladies of Chillicothe, Ohio, purchased and presented to him an elegant sword;[3] and the Congress of the United States voted him the thanks of the nation.[4] Twenty-two years later the Congress gave him a gold medal, in commemoration of his signal service on that day. Posterity will ever regard his name with honor.[5]

---

[1] Major Croghan's Report to General Harrison, August 5, 1813; General Harrison's Report to the Secretary of War, August 5, 1813; M'Afee's *History of the Late War*, pages 322 to 328; Auchinleck's *History of the War of 1812*, pages 184 to 187; James's *Military Occurrences, etc.*, pages 262 to 266; *Niles's Register*, August 14, 1813; The *Port Folio*, March, 1815; *The War*, volume ii., pages 39, 43, 47, 49, 51, 61; Address of Colonel Elisha Whittlesey at Fremont, August 2, 1858; Address of Homer Everett, Esq., at Fremont, February 24th and 25th, 1860; Perkins's *History of the Late War*, pages 223, 224; *Sketches of the War* (Rutland, 1815), pages 166 to 168; Atwater's *History of Ohio*, pages 226 to 229; Dawson's *Life of General Harrison*, pages 249 to 251; MS. of Dr. Brainerd, quoted by Homer Everett, Esq.

[2] "I am sorry," wrote General Harrison to the Secretary of War on the 4th of August, "that I can not transmit you Major Croghan's official report. He was to have sent it to me this morning, but I have just heard that he was so much exhausted by thirty-six hours of continued exertion as to be unable to make it. It will not be among the least of General Proctor's mortifications to find that he has been baffled by a youth who has just passed his twenty-first year. He is, however, a hero worthy of his gallant uncle, General George Rogers Clarke."

[3] This gift, at their request, was presented to him by Samuel Finley and Joseph Wheaton, with the following letter bearing the signatures of the donors:

"CHILLICOTHE, August 13, 1813.

"SIR,—In consequence of the gallant defense which, under Divine Providence, was effected by you and the troops under your command, of Fort Stephenson, at Lower Sandusky, on the evening of the 2d inst., the ladies of the town of Chillicothe, whose names are undersigned, impressed with a high sense of your merits as a soldier and a gentleman, and with great confidence in your patriotism and valor, present you with a sword. Mary Finley, Mary Sterret, Ann Creighton, Eliza Creighton, Eleanor Lamb, Nancy Waddle, Eliza Carlisle, Mary A. Southward, Susan D. Wheaton, of Washington City, Richamah Irwin, Judith Delano, Margaret M'Lanburg, Margaret Miller, Elizabeth Martin, Nancy M'Arthur, Jane M'Coy, Lavina Fulton, Catharine Fullerton, Rebecca M. Orr, Susan Wake, Ann M. Dunn, Margaret Keys, Charlotte James, Esther Doolittle, Eleanor Buchannan, Margaret M'Farland, Deborah Ferree, Jane M. Evans, Frances Brush, Mary Curtis, Mary P. Brown, Jane Heylin, Nancy Kerr, Catharine Hough, Eleanor Worthington, Martha Scott, Sally M'Lean."

To this letter Major Croghan replied at Lower Sandusky on the 25th of August:

"LADIES OF CHILLICOTHE,—I have received the sword which you have been pleased to present to me as a testimonial of your approbation of my conduct on the 2d instant. A mark of distinction so flattering and unexpected has excited feelings which I can not express. Yet, while I return you thanks for the unmerited gift you have thus bestowed, I feel well aware that my good fortune (which was bought by the activity of the brave soldiers under my command), has raised in you expectations from my future efforts which must, I fear, be sooner or later disappointed. Still, I pledge myself (even though fortune should not be again propitious) that my exertions shall be such as never to cause you in the least to regret the honors you have been pleased to confer on your 'youthful soldier.'"

[4] On the 8th of February, 1814, the Committee on Military Affairs reported a resolution, among others similar, to request *the President* to present an elegant sword to Colonel Croghan. This resolution was passed by at the time, and never called up again.

[5] George Croghan was a son of Major William Croghan, of the Revolutionary army. His father was a native of Ireland; his mother was a sister of General George Rogers Clarke, sometimes called the Father of the Northwest. He was born at Locust Grove, near the Falls of the Ohio (now Louisville), in Kentucky, on the 15th of November, 1791. He

| Medal presented to Croghan. | A Visit to Sandusky. | A Ride to Castalian Springs. |

GOLD MEDAL AWARDED TO GENERAL CROGHAN.[1]

It was a soft, hazy, half sunny day, late in September,[a] when I visited the site of Fort Stephenson and the places of events that made it famous. I had come up by railway during the early hours of the morning from pleasant Sandusky City, where I had spent two or three days with friends, vainly endeavoring to visit Put-in-Bay, where Perry's fleet rendezvoused before the battle which gave him victory and immortality. The excursion steam-boat to that and other places had been withdrawn for the season, and the wind was too high to make a voyage thither in a sail-boat safe or pleasant. I was less disappointed than I should otherwise have been, by the discovery that an artist (Miss C. L. Ransom), then in Sandusky City, had made careful drawings of the historical points about Put-in-Bay. I had the pleasure of meeting her, and availing myself of her courteous permission to copy such of her drawings as I desired. Of these more will be said when giving an account of the naval battle near there.

In company with Mr. Barney, with whom I was staying, I visited the famous Castalian Springs, at the village of Castalia, five or six miles south from Sandusky City. They flow up from subterranean fountains, almost as limpid as air, and in volume so great that along the outlet, which is called Cold Creek, in its course of three miles through a beautiful prairie of three thousand acres to Sandusky Bay, no less than

[a] September 24, 1860.

---

was graduated at William and Mary College, in Virginia, in the summer of 1810; entered its law school, and remained there until the fall of 1811, when he joined the army under Harrison at Vincennes. He was volunteer aid to Colonel Boyd at the battle of Tippecanoe. On account of his services in the Wabash expedition, he was appointed a captain of infantry in the spring of 1812, and in August he marched with the forces under General Winchester to the relief of General Hull in Canada. In March, 1813, he was promoted to major, and became aid-de-camp to General Harrison. In that capacity he distinguished himself in the defense of Fort Meigs, and the sortie on the 5th of May under the gallant Colonel Miller. For his gallantry at Fort Stephenson he was breveted a lieutenant colonel, and was appointed colonel of a rifle corps in February, 1814. At the close of the war he was retained in service, but married in 1817 and resigned. In 1824 he was appointed postmaster at New Orleans, and returned to the service in 1825 as inspector general, with the rank of colonel. In 1835 Congress awarded him a gold medal for his gallantry at Fort Stephenson. He died at New Orleans on the 8th of January, 1849.

[1] On Tuesday, the 27th of January, 1835, a joint resolution passed the House of Representatives, authorizing the President of the United States to "present a gold medal to General Croghan" (he was then inspector general of the army), and swords to several officers under his command. These were Captain James Hunter, and Lieutenants Benjamin Johnson and Cyrus A. Baylor, of the Seventeenth Regiment, Lieutenant John Meek, of the Seventh Regiment, and Ensigns Edward Shipp and Joseph Duncan. The latter was afterward Governor of Illinois.

Lieutenant Johnson was promoted to captain of a rifle corps in March, 1814, and left the service at the close of the war. Lieutenant Baylor also left the service at the close of the war. Lieutenant Meek resigned in May, 1814. He was appointed military store-keeper at Little Rock, Arkansas, in the summer of 1838, and was removed, on a change of administration, in 1841. Ensign Duncan was promoted to first lieutenant of infantry in July, 1814, and was disbanded in 1815. He was a representative in Congress from Illinois from 1827 to 1835, Governor of Illinois from 1834 to 1838, and died at Jacksonville on the 15th of January, 1844.

It is proper to observe that the representation of the fort and its surroundings, on this medal, presented to General Croghan, is incorrect. It was not a regular fort, but a picketed inclosure, with rudely-built block-houses. The Sandusky River is here a narrow stream, and not such an expanse of water as the place of the vessels represent. It may have been intended for Sandusky Bay.

fourteen sets of mill-stones were kept in motion by it. In a rough scow we hovered over the centre of the spring, and, peering down into its clear, mysterious depths, saw logs, and plants, and earth in grotto form, made iridescent by the light in the aqueous prism.[1] We intended to visit the somewhat marvelous cave in the range of limestone about two miles from the springs, but the day was too far spent when I had completed my sketch of the fountains to allow us to do so. We returned to the town by the way of Mr. Barney's fine vineyard, and arrived at sunset. I spent the evening with General Leslie Combs at the "West House," and in a public meeting.[2] The next day was the Sabbath, and on Monday morning I started by railway for Lower Sandusky with impressions which have crystallized into pleasant memories of a delightful little city on a slope overlooking one of the finest bays that indent the southern shores of Lake Erie.[3] On our way we stopped a few minutes at the little village of Clyde, where the railways from Cleveland and Toledo and from Cincinnati and Sandusky City cross each other. There a crowd had collected to see and hear the late Judge Douglas, then one of the candidates for the presidency of the United States, who was traveling for his political health, weary and wayworn. Eager eyes, vociferous shouts, loud huzzas, and the swaying of a little multitude, is the picture of a few minutes of time impressed upon the memory. An hour later I was in Fremont, as the old village of Lower Sandusky was named a few years ago in honor of the accomplished explorer in earlier years, and general in the army of the republic during a portion of the late Civil War.

LOWER CASTALIAN SPRING.

Very soon after my arrival I was favored with the company of Messrs. Sardis Birchard and Homer Everett (residents of the village, and familiar with its history) in a pilgrimage to places of interest in and around that shire-town of Sandusky County.[4]

---

[1] The Castalian Springs are great natural curiosities, and are much visited. There are two, known respectively as Upper and Lower. They are about one fourth of a mile apart, and are connected by a race. At the lower one, where Messrs. Cochrane and Weston had a flouring-mill, a dike had been raised (seen in the above sketch) to give more fall to the water. The two springs are of about equal dimensions. That of the lower one, which I visited, is about sixty feet in depth. The water is so limpid that a white object an inch in diameter may be plainly seen lying on the bottom. The temperature of the water is about 40° Fahrenheit, and holds in solution lime, soda, magnesia, and iron. It petrifies every thing with which it comes in contact. This process makes the mill-wheels indestructible. About a mile and a half from the springs is a limestone ridge covered with alluvium. From beneath this these springs appear to flow, and are doubtless the first appearance on the earth of a little subterranean river, like that of the Eutaw in South Carolina. [2] See page 490.

[3] Sandusky City is the capital of Erie County, Ohio. It was named Portland when it was first laid out in 1817, when there were only two log houses there, one on the site of the "Veranda Hotel," and the other about sixty rods east of it. The town stands upon an inexhaustible quarry of the finest limestone. It was a favorite resort of the Indians, and previous to the War of 1812 it was known as Ogontz's Place, Ogontz being the name of a Wyandot chief who resided there. A writer in the *American Pioneer*, i., 199, says the name of Sandusky is derived from that of a Polish trader who was with the French when they were establishing their line of trading-posts on the Maumee and Wabash Rivers. His name was Sanduski, and established himself near the present village of Fremont. His trading operations were confined to the river and bay there, and these became known to both Indians and Europeans as Sanduski's River and Sanduski's Bay. Sanduski quarreled with the Indians, fled to Virginia, and was there killed by some of those who followed him.

On the peninsula, across the bay opposite Sandusky, is a rough monument, erected there by the order and at the expense of the late Honorable Joshua R. Giddings, to perpetuate the memory of the spot where he and twenty-one others had a skirmish with the Indians on the 29th of September, 1812. He was a substitute for an older brother, and was only fourteen years of age. The regiment to which he belonged was commanded by Colonel Richard Hayes, and the little company, who had been ordered on duty on the peninsula after the defeat of General Hull, was led by Captain Colton. They had two skirmishes with the savages, in which, of the twenty-two soldiers, six were killed, and an equal number were wounded. Mr. Giddings was the youngest soldier of the regiment.

[4] This town stands at the head of the navigation of Sandusky River, eighteen or twenty miles from Sandusky Bay

The site of Fort Stephenson is in the bosom of the village of Fremont. It occupies about two thirds of the square bounded by Croghan, High, Market, and Arch

SITE OF FORT STEPHENSON.[1]

Streets. The dwelling of the late Honorable Jacques Hurlburd stands within the area of the old stockade, and a few yards south of the block-house in which was placed the cannon that swept the ditch. The northwest angle, where the British made their chief assault, is at the junction of High and Croghan Streets. Near the house of Dr. J. W. Wilson, on Croghan Street, was the head of the ravine and small stream of water (see Plan of Fort Stephenson on page 503) between the stockade and the British battery. It was to the shelter of that ravine that the affrighted Indians fled after the first discharge of rifle-balls from the garrison.

From the site of the fort we went to the brow of the hill overlooking the landing-place of the British. When I had finished my sketch (printed on page 500) we visited the *Good Bess*, the iron six-pound cannon that performed such fearful service in the defense of the fort.[2] I then rode, in company with Mr. Birchard, to old Cro-

---

by its course. Here, at the Lower Rapids of the Sandusky, the Indians were granted a reservation by the treaty of Greenville. The French had a trading-station here at an early day. Here was the residence of a band of Wyandot Indians, called the Neutral Nation. They had two villages. They were "cities of refuge" for all. Whoever sought safety in them found it. During the bloody wars between the Iroquois and the Europeans, this band of Indians were always peace-makers. Their two towns were walled, and remains of their works may yet be seen. Indian tribes at war recognized them as neutral. Those coming from the West might enter the Western City, and those from the East the Eastern City. The inhabitants of one city might inform those of the other that war-parties had been there, but who they were, or where from, must never be mentioned. At length the inhabitants of the two cities quarreled, and one destroyed or dispersed the other.—Stickney's *Lecture* at Toledo, 1845, quoted by Howe.

[1] This view is from the northern side of Croghan Street, opposite the residence of Dr. J. W. Wilson. The building seen in the centre is the late residence of Honorable Jacques Hurlburd. Croghan Street descends to the left, to the business part of the village, and High Street passes to the right. On the extreme left, on High Street, is seen a barn. This is just beyond the southwest angle of the fort, where Croghan placed a block-house. At the foot of the bank on Croghan Street is the site of the ditch swept by the six-pounder, and a little way eastward from the corner of High Street is the place where the body of Lieutenant Colonel Short was found. In 1850, when the street and side-walk were being regulated, the brass piece at the top of a sword-scabbard was found upon that spot, supposed to have belonged to Lieutenant Colonel Short. It is now in the possession of Sardis Birchard, Esq., of Fremont.

PART OF SHORT'S SWORD-SCABBARD.

The ground occupied by Fort Stephenson belongs to Chester Edgerton, Esq. The citizens have manifested a laudable desire to purchase the property, that it may be converted into a public square, and the site kept free from buildings.

[2] The garrison named the piece the *Good Bess*. It was taken to Pittsburg, where it remained until it was presented to the Corporation of Lower Sandusky (Fremont) in 1850. It was then nicely mounted as a field-piece, and is used on the anniversary of the battle for salutes, and sometimes by political parties. The breech is somewhat mutilated, it having been spiked by contending political parties at different times. It was carefully preserved in a small building on Croghan Street, between Forest Street and the site of the fort.

Works of Art. Journey to Toledo. General Harrison's Military Character assailed and vindicated.

ghanville, on the eastern side of the Sandusky, and afterward to the place of Ball's skirmish with the Indians, mentioned in Note 1, page 500. It was between the dwelling of Mr. Villetti (the residence of Mr. Birchard) and Mr. Platt Brush, on the road from Fremont to Tiffin and Columbus. The oak-tree, with the hatchet-marks, stood on the west side of the road, near Mr. Brush's house.

At Mr. Villetti's I enjoyed the pleasure of seeing some valuable paintings belonging to Mr. Birchard, among them the fine picture of *The Dog and Dead Duck*, a work of art of the Dusseldorf school that attracted much attention during the exhibition in the Crystal Palace in New York in 1854. Leaving his attractive gallery, we returned to the village, stopping on the way in the "Spiegel Wood," a lovely spot not far from the banks of the winding Sandusky, where he was erecting an elegant summer mansion.

The day was now far spent. Dark clouds were gathering in the western sky, and in that direction I was soon moving swiftly over the railway toward Toledo, thirty miles distant. I arrived at the "Oliver House," in that city, a few minutes before a heavy thunder-storm burst upon it and the surrounding country. On the following day I made the visit to Fort Meigs, up the Maumee Valley, already described on pages 490 to 493 inclusive.

After the repulse of the British at Fort Stephenson, very little of importance occurred in the Northwest until the battle on Lake Erie, at near the middle of September, when the aspect of affairs in that quarter was entirely changed. Harrison's regular force in the field did not exceed two thousand men, yet he considered them sufficient for all present purposes. The din of a second invasion of the state had again aroused the people, and hundreds of volunteers had flocked to the field only to be again disbanded. These volunteers were offended. They regarded the action of the general as an indication that he believed them to be, as soldiers, unworthy of his confidence; and their indignant officers, in published resolutions, attacked the military character of General Harrison, and declared that they would never again rally to his flag. His personal and political enemies joined in the hue and cry; and men sitting at home in ease, utterly ignorant of military affairs, assailed him with jeers as an imbecile or a coward, because he did not, with his handful of regulars and a mass of raw troops, push forward against Malden and Detroit, before the tardily-building navy was completed. Misrepresentation followed misrepresentation, for the purpose of poisoning the public mind. Fearing their effects, his general, field, and staff officers, fourteen in number,[1] held a meeting at head-quarters, Lower Seneca Town,[a] and in an address to the public, drawn up by General Cass, they expressed their entire confidence in the military abilities of their chief, and their belief that his course "was such as was dictated by military wisdom, and by a due regard to our circumstances and to the situation of the enemy."

[a] August 14, 1813.

Up to this time General Harrison's efforts had been mainly directed to defensive measures; now, the fleet at Erie being nearly ready, and Captain Perry, who was to command it, having received orders to co-operate with Harrison, the latter bent all his energies to the creation of a well-appointed army for another invasion of Canada. Let us leave General Harrison for a while at his head-quarters at "Camp Seneca," and consider the naval preparations to co-operate with him.

We have observed that General Hull's advice respecting the creation of a fleet on Lake Erie, before attempting an invasion of Canada, was unheeded,[2] and that the army of the Northwest was involved in disaster, and its commander was covered with a cloud of disgrace. The event taught the rulers wisdom, and they profited by

---

[1] General Cass; Colonels Wells, Owings, Paul, and Bartlett; Lieutenant Colonels Ball and Morrison; Majors Todd, Trigg, Smiley, Graham, Croghan, Hukill, and Wood. The gallant Croghan, in a special letter on the 27th, silenced the slanderers who were making political capital of Harrison's order for him to evacuate Fort Stephenson, and his disobedience. "The measures recently adopted by him," wrote Croghan, "so far from deserving censure, *are the clearest proofs of his keen penetration and able generalship*." [2] See page 251.

the lesson. They resolved to dispute the supremacy of the lakes with the British, and to Commodore Chauncey was intrusted the necessary preparations.

During the summer and autumn of 1812, Captain Oliver H. Perry, of Rhode Island, a zealous naval officer twenty-seven years of age, was in command of a flotilla of gun-boats on the Newport station. He was very anxious for service in a wider field of action—on the lakes or the broad ocean—where he might encounter the enemy and win distinction. In November[a] he offered his services for the lakes; and on the first of February following[b] he received a cordial letter from Chauncey, in which that gentleman said, "You are the very person that I want for a particular service, in which you may gain reputation for yourself and honor for your country." This service was the command of a naval force on Lake Erie. Perry was delighted; and his joy was complete when, on the 17th of the same month, he received orders from the Secretary of the Navy to report to Commodore Chauncey, at Sackett's Harbor, with all of the best men of his flotilla in Narraganset Bay. Before sunset that day he had dispatched Sailing-master Almy, with fifty men and officers, for the eastern shore of Lake Ontario. Two days afterward another company of fifty men were sent to the same destination, under Sailing-master Champlin; and on the 21st fifty more, under Sailing-master Taylor, left Providence and followed their companions. Twenty hours later Perry left his pleasant home in Newport, with his little brother Alexander, then only thirteen years of age, and was on his way in a sleigh. He stopped part of a day at Lebanon, in Connecticut, to visit his parents, and on the 28th he met Chauncey at Albany. They journeyed together northwardly through the Wilderness, and arrived at Sackett's Harbor on the evening of the 3d of March. There Perry remained a fortnight on account of an expected attack by the British. The menaces of danger ceased, and the young commander was ordered to proceed to Presqu' Isle (now Erie), and hasten the equipment of a little squadron then in process of construction there.[2] He arrived at Buffalo on the 24th,

[a] 1812.
[b] 1813.

PERRY'S RESIDENCE.[1]

[signature] Daniel Dobbins

[1] Perry's house, a well-preserved mansion, stood, when the writer sketched it in 1848, on the south side of Washington Square, Newport, a few doors from Thames Street. It was a spacious, square building, and was erected almost a century ago by Mr. Levi, a Jew. To that house Perry took his bride, a daughter of Dr. Mason, of Newport, and there she lived a widow almost forty years. She died in February, 1858.

[2] Erie was chosen for this purpose on the recommendation of Captain Daniel Dobbins, one of the most experienced navigators on Lake Erie. He suggested its advantages as a place for building gun-boats early in the autumn of 1812. The bay being completely land-locked, and its only entrance too shallow for large vessels to enter, but deep enough for the egress of gun-boats, he regarded it as the safest place on the lake for the construction of small vessels. He was appointed sailing-master in the navy at the middle of September, 1812,[*] and received instructions from the government to commence the construction of gun-boats at Erie. On the 12th of December he informed the Department that, under the lead of Ebenezer Crosby, a good ship-wright, and such house-carpenters as he could supply, he had two of the gun-boats—50 feet keel, 17 feet beam, and 5 feet hold—on the stocks, and would engage to have them all ready by the time the ice was out of the lake.

[*] On his return from Detroit he was sent by General David Mead with dispatches to Washington. There he was summoned to a Cabinet council, and was fully interrogated concerning the lakes. His opinions were received with deference; and such was the confidence of the Cabinet in his judgment that he was appointed sailing-master, and directed to construct gun-boats at Erie.

spent the next day in examining vessels on the stocks at the navy yard at Black Rock, then superintended by Lieutenant Pettigru, and made arrangements for having stores forwarded to him. He pressed onward by land, and at an inn on the way he was informed by the keeper, who had just returned from Canada, that the British were acquainted with the movements at Erie, and would doubtless soon attempt to penetrate the harbor, and destroy the naval materials collected there.

The harbor of Erie is a large bay, within the embrace of a low, sandy peninsula that juts five miles into the lake, and a bluff of main land on which the pleasant village of Erie, the capital of Erie County, Pennsylvania, stands. The peninsula has sometimes been an island when its neck has been cleft by storms, and the harbor has been entered from the west by small vessels. Within the memory of living men Presqu' Isle (the peninsula) has been a barren sand-bank; now it is covered by a growth of young timber. It is deeply indented toward its extremity by an estuary called Little Bay. The harbor is one of the finest on the lake when gained, but at the period in question, and until lately, its entrance was by a shallow channel, tortuous and difficult on account of sand-bars and shoals. Although Presqu' Isle was a place of historic interest in colonial times,[1] it was an insignificant village in 1812, and less than twenty years of age.[2] Many miles of wilderness, or a very sparsely-populated country, lay between it and the thick settlements; and the supplies of every

---

Captain Dobbins was an efficient man and faithful officer. He was duly appointed a sailing-master in the navy, and was highly esteemed by Commodore Perry. He was born in Mifflin County, Pennsylvania, on the 5th of July, 1776, and first visited Erie, with a party of surveyors, in 1796. It was then a wilderness. He was there with General Wayne at the time of his death. He settled there, and became a navigator on the lakes. He was at Mackinaw with his vessel, the *Salina*, when that place was captured by the British in 1812, and, with R. S. and William Reid, of Erie, he was paroled. At Detroit he was again made prisoner, and paroled unconditionally. He was very efficient in fitting out the squadron at Erie, and in the expedition, under Commodore Sinclair, that attempted to retake Mackinaw. After the war he was in command of the *Washington*, and in 1816 he conveyed troops in her to Green Bay. She was the first vessel, except a canoe, that ever entered that harbor. A group of islands in that vicinity were named Dobbins's Islands in honor of him. He was ordered to sea in 1826, when he resigned his commission in the navy, but remained in the government employment. In 1829 President Jackson appointed him commander of the revenue cutter *Rush*. He left active service in 1849, and died at the age of almost eighty-one, February 29, 1856. The likeness of Captain Dobbins, given on the preceding page, is from a portrait painted by Moses Billings, of Erie, when he was seventy-five years of age.

[1] Here was erected one of the chain of French forts in the wilderness which first excited the alarm and jealousy of the English colonies in America and the government at home. The remains of the ramparts and ditches, seen in the sketch on the opposite page, are very prominent upon a point overlooking the entrance to the harbor, which it commands, and a deep ravine, through which Mill Creek flows, within the eastern limits of the borough of Erie. The fort is supposed to have been erected early in 1749, that being the year when the French sent armed emissaries throughout the Ohio Valley to drive off the English traders. It was constructed under the direction of Jean Cœur (commonly written Joncaire in history), an influential Indian agent of the French governor general of Canada. This was intended by the French for an important entrepôt of supplies for the interior forts; but when Canada passed into the possession of the English, a hundred years ago, the fort was abandoned, and fell into decay. General Wayne established a small garrison there in 1794, and caused a block-house to be built on the bluff part of Mill Creek, at the lake shore of Garrison Hill. On his return as victor over the Indians in the Maumee Valley, he occupied a log house near the block-house. There he died of gout, and, at his own request, was buried at the foot of the flag-staff. His remains were removed to Radnor Church-yard, Pennsylvania, in 1809. The block-house fell into decay, and, in the winter of 1813–'14, another was built on its site; also one on the Point of the Peninsula of Presqu' Isle. The former remained until 1853, when some miscreant burnt it. It was the last relic of the War of 1812 in that vicinity. I am indebted to B. F. Sloan, Esq., editor of the *Erie Observer*, for the accompanying sketch of the block-house, made by Mr. Chevalier, of Erie. The view is from the edge of the water at the mouth of Mill Creek, just below the old mill. On the left is seen the open lake, and on the right of the block-house, where a small building is seen, was the place of the flag-staff and Wayne's grave.

WAYNE'S BLOCK-HOUSE AT ERIE.

[2] It was laid out in 1795, when reservations were made of certain lots for the use of the United States. The first white settler there was Colonel John Reid, from Rhode Island, who built a log cabin, enlarged it, and called it the *Presqu' Isle Hotel*, entertained travelers, soldiers, traders, speculators, and Indians, and laid the foundation of a large fortune. His son built the "Reid House," in Erie, one of the finest hotels in the country out of the large cities.

VIEW OF THE SITE OF THE FRENCH FORT AND ENTRANCE TO ERIE HARBOR.[1]

kind, but timber, for naval preparations, had to be brought from far-away places with great labor. Zeal and energy overcame all difficulties.

Perry arrived at Erie, as we have observed, on the 27th of March. He established his quarters at Duncan's "Erie Hotel," and entered upon the duties of his important errand by calling around him the employés of the government there. Much preliminary work had already been done under the direction of the energetic Sailing-master Dobbins and Noah Brown, a shipwright from New York. Forest-trees around Erie had been felled and hewn; the keels of two twenty-gun brigs and a clipper schooner had been laid at the mouth of Cascade Creek; two gun-boats were nearly planked up at the mouth of Lee's Run, between the present Peach and Sassafras Streets; and a third, afterward call-

MOUTH OF CASCADE CREEK.[2]

BLOCK-HOUSE.

[1] This view of the entrance to Erie Harbor was taken from the site of the old French *Fort de la Presqu' Isle*, mentioned in the note on the preceding page. The mounds indicating the remains of the fort are seen on the right, and near them, in the centre of the picture, is a small building used as a powder-house. On the bluff on the extreme right is seen a little structure, indicating the site of the block-house mentioned in the note on the preceding page, which is not far from the present light-house. On the left, in the extreme distance, is Presqu' Isle Point, and in the water, piers that have been constructed for the improvement of the entrance channel, and a light-house.

[2] This is a view of the site of the navy yard at the mouth of the Cascade Creek, and of a portion of the harbor of Erie, made by the author early in September, 1860. The creek and the gentle cascade, which gives its appropriate name, are seen in the foreground. Beyond it, and the small boats seen in its waters, is the beach where the *Lawrence*, *Niagara*, and *Ariel* were built. On the clay and gravel bluff at the extreme right, the fence marks the site of a block-house built to protect the ship-yard, whose stout flag-staff, with cross-pieces for steps, served as an observatory. From its top a full view of the lake over Presqu' Isle could be seen. The lower part of the block-house was heavy, rough logs; the upper, or battery part, was made of hewn timber.

In the distance, in the centre of the picture, is seen the landing at Erie, and on the left the pier and light-house at the entrance to the harbor. Just behind the bluff, in the distance, is the mouth of Lee's Run, where the *Porcupine* and *Tigress* were built. The cascade is about fifteen feet in perpendicular fall in its passage over a ledge of slate rock, and is about one mile from the public square in Erie.

ed *Scorpion*, was just commenced. To guard against surprise and the destruction of the vessels by the British, a volunteer company of sixty men, under Captain Foster, had been organized. Captain Dobbins had also formed a guard of the ship-carpenters and other mechanics engaged on the vessels.

On the arrival of Sailing-master Taylor, on the 3d of March, with officers and men, Perry hastened to Pittsburg to urge forward supplies of every kind for the completion and equipment of his little squadron. He had already ordered Dobbins to Buffalo for men and munitions; and on his return[a] he was gratified to find that faithful officer back and in possession of a twelve-pound cannon, four chests of small arms, and ammunition. The vessels, too, were in a satisfactory state of forwardness. They were soon off the stocks. Early in May the three smaller ones were launched, and on the 24th of the same month the two brigs were put afloat.[1]

[a] April 10, 1813.

At sunset of the day before the launching of the brigs,[b] Perry left Erie in an open four-oared boat, to join Chauncey in an attack upon Fort George, at the mouth of the Niagara River. The commodore had promised him the command of the marines in the enterprise. All night he buffeted the angry waves of Lake Erie, and arrived at Buffalo the next day. Perry was accompanied from Erie as far as Lewiston by his faithful coadjutor, Captain Dobbins. From that point the latter was sent back to Schlosser, to prepare boats for seamen who were to be sent up after the reduction of Fort George, and to the Black Rock navy yard, to hasten the equipment of some government vessels that were to join the growing squadron at Erie.

[b] May 23.

Fort George fell,[c] Fort Erie was evacuated and burnt, and the British abandoned the entire line of the Niagara River. This enabled Perry to take safely from that stream into Lake Erie and the sheltering arms of Presqu' Isle five vessels which Henry Eckford had prepared for warlike service, and which had been detained below Buffalo by the Canadian batteries. They were loaded with stores at the Black Rock navy yard; and on the morning of the 6th of June, oxen, seamen, and two hundred soldiers, under Captains Brevoort and Younge, who had been detailed to accompany Perry to Erie, with strong ropes over willing shoulders commenced warping or "tracking" them up the swift current. It was a task of incredible labor, and occupied full six days.

[c] May 27.

The little flotilla[2] sailed from Buffalo on the 13th. Perry was in the *Caledonia*, sick with symptoms of bilious remittent fever. Head winds prevailed. "We made twenty-five miles in twenty-four hours," wrote Doctor Usher Parsons, Perry's surgeon, in his diary.[3] It was not until the 19th that they entered the harbor of Erie, just in time to avoid the little cruising squadron of the enemy under the gallant Captain Finnis, of the Royal Navy, which had been on the look-out for them. Of this Perry had been informed, on his way, by men in a small boat that shot out from the southern shore of the lake, and he had prepared to fight. When the last vessel of the flotilla had crossed the bar at Erie, the squadron of the enemy hove in sight off Presqu' Isle Point.[4] Three or four days afterward the flotilla went up to the mouth of the Cascade Creek, where the two brigs and a gun-boat lay.

Perry's fleet was completed and finished on the 10th of July; but, alas! he had

---

[1] The timber for the vessels was found on the spot. Their frames were made of white and black oak and chestnut, the outside planking of oak, and the decks of pine. Many trees found their places as timber in the vessels on the very day when they were felled in the forest.

[2] It consisted of the prize brig *Caledonia* (see page 386); the schooner *Somers* (formerly *Catharine*), carrying one long 24; schooner *Amelia* (formerly *Tigress*), carrying one long 18; and schooner *Ohio*, carrying one long 24; the sloop *Contractor* (now called *Trippe*), carrying one long 18. The commanders of this flotilla from Buffalo to Erie were Perry, Almy, Holdup, Darling, and Dobbins.

[3] Doctor Usher Parsons, of Providence, Rhode Island, is the last surviving commissioned officer of Perry's fleet. I am greatly indebted to him for many valuable contributions to this portion of my work, both oral and written, especially for the use of his diary kept during the campaign of 1813. We shall meet him presently as the surgeon of the *Lawrence*, Perry's flag-ship, in the battle of the 10th of September.

[4] This cruising squadron consisted of the ship *Queen Charlotte*, mounting 17 guns; the fine schooner *Lady Prevost*, mounting 13 guns; the brig *Hunter*, a smaller vessel of 10 guns; the schooner *Little Belt*, of 3 guns; and the *Chippewa*, of 1 gun.

only men enough to officer and man one of the brigs, and he was compelled to lie idle in the harbor of Erie, an unwilling witness of the insolent menaces of the enemy on the open lake. The brig that was to bear his broad pennant was named (by order of the Secretary of the Navy, received on the 12th) *Lawrence*, in honor of the gallant captain of the *Chesapeake*, who had just given his life to his country.[a] The other brig was named *Niagara*, and the smaller vessels constructed at Erie were called respectively *Ariel* (the clipper schooner), *Porcupine*, and *Tigress*. But what availed these vessels without officers and crews? The two hundred soldiers lent as a guard for the flotilla on its voyage from Buffalo had been ordered back. Only Captain Brevoort, who was familiar with the navigation of the lake, remained, and he was assigned to the command of the marines of the *Niagara*. Perry was sick, and almost one fifth of his men were subjects for the hospital in the court-house, under Doctor Horsley, or the one near the site of Wayne's block-house, under Doctor Roberts. And yet the government, remiss itself in furnishing Perry with men, was calling loudly upon him to co-operate with Harrison. Twice within four days he received orders to that effect from the Secretary of the Treasury.[b] Harrison, too, was sending messages to him recounting the perils of the situation of his little army, and intelligence came that a new and powerful vessel, called *Detroit*, was nearly ready for service at Malden. This was coupled with the assurance that the veteran Captain Robert H. Barclay, who had served with Nelson at Trafalgar, had arrived with experienced officers and men, and was in chief command of the hostile squadron seen off Presqu' Isle. In the bitterness of a mortified spirit Perry wrote to Chauncey,[c] his chief, saying, "The enemy's fleet of six sail are now off the bar of this harbor. What a golden opportunity, if we had men! Their object is, no doubt, either to blockade or attack us, or to carry provisions and re-enforcements to Malden. Should it be to attack us, we are ready to meet them. I am constantly looking to the eastward; every mail and every traveler from that quarter is looked to as the harbinger of the glad tidings of our men being on the way. . . . . . Give me men, sir, and I will acquire both for *you* and myself honor and glory on this lake, or perish in the attempt. Conceive my feelings: an enemy within striking distance, my vessels ready, and not men enough to man them. Going out with those I now have is out of the question. You would not suffer it were you here. Think of my situation: the enemy in sight, the vessels under my command more than sufficient and ready to make sail, and yet obliged to bite my fingers with vexation for want of men."[1] Again, on the 23d of July, when Sailing-master Champlin had arrived with seventy men, Perry wrote to Chauncey: "For God's sake, and *yours*, and mine, send me men and officers, and I will have them all [the British squadron] in a day or two. Commodore Barclay keeps just out of the reach of our gun-boats. . . . . The vessels are all ready to meet the enemy the moment they are officered and manned. Our sails are bent, provisions on board, and, in fact, every thing is ready. Barclay has been bearding me for several days; I long to be at him." Then, with the most generous patriotism, he added, "However anxious I am to reap the reward of the labor and anxiety I have had on this station, I shall rejoice, whoever commands, to see this force on the lake, and surely I had rather be commanded by my friend than by any other. Come, then, and the business is decided in a few hours."

Perry's importunities were almost in vain. Few and mostly inferior men came to him from Lake Ontario, and, so far as the government was concerned, he was left to call them from the forest or the deep. When he gave Harrison the true reason for failing to co-operate with him, the Secretary of the Navy reproved him for exposing

[a] June, 1813.

[b] July 15-19.

[c] July 19.

---

[1] Two days afterward [July 21] the enemy were becalmed off the harbor, when Perry went out with three gun-boats from Cascade Creek to attack him. Only a few shots were exchanged, at the distance of a mile. One of Perry's shots struck the mizzen-mast of the *Queen Charlotte*. A breeze sprung up, and the enemy's squadron bore away to the open lake.

his weakness; and when he complained to Chauncey of the inferiority of the men sent to him—"a motley set, blacks, soldiers, and boys"—he received from the irritated commodore a letter so filled with caustic but half-concealed irony, that he felt constrained to ask for a removal from the station, because, as he alleged, he "could not serve longer under an officer who had been so totally regardless of his feelings."[1] A manly, generous letter from Chauncey soon afterward restored the kindliness of feeling between them.

In the mean time the post of Erie had been seriously menaced. General Porter, at Black Rock, sent word that the enemy were concentrating at Long Point, on the Canada shore of the lake, opposite Erie. At about the same time a hostile movement was made toward Fort Meigs, and the British fleet mysteriously disappeared. No doubt was entertained of a design to attempt the capture of Erie, with the vessels and stores, by a combined land and naval force. A panic was the consequence. The families of many citizens fled with their valuables to the interior. Already a block-

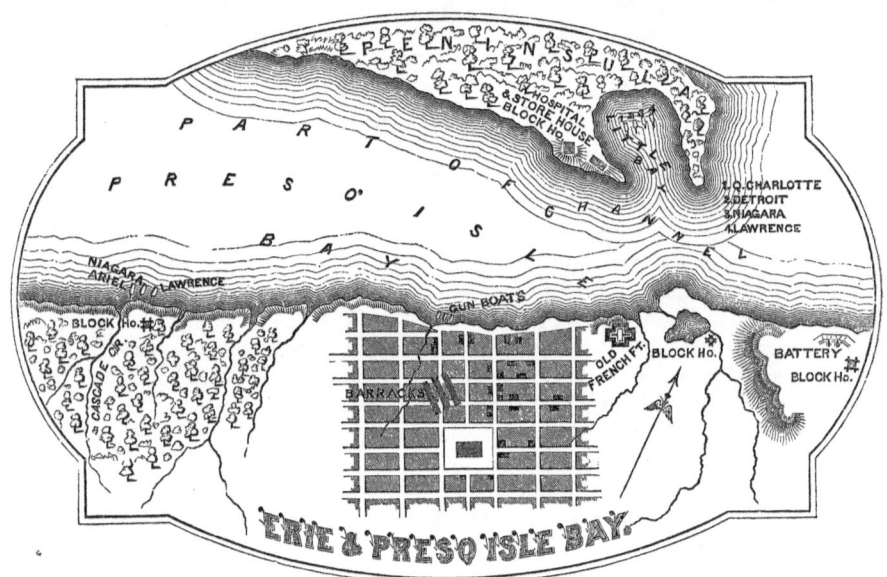

house had been erected on the bluff east of Cascade Creek to protect the ship-yard,[2] and a redoubt mounting three long twelve-pounders had been planted on the heights (now called Garrison Hill), near the present light-house, and named Fort Wayne. Barracks had been erected in the village,[3] and a regiment of Pennsylvania militia were encamped near Fort Wayne. The vessels were as well manned as possible, and boats rowed guard at the entrance to the harbor. But these means of defense were not considered sufficient, and Perry called on Major General David Mead, of Meadville, to re-enforce the troops with his militia. This was done,[4] and in the course of a few days upward of fifteen hundred soldiers were concentrated at a rendezvous near. But an invasion from the lake was not attempted, owing, as was afterward ascertained, to the difficulty of collecting a sufficient number of troops in time at Long Point.

At the close of July Perry had about three hundred effective officers and men at

---

[1] Letter to the Secretary of the Navy, dated on board the *Lawrence*, at Erie, August 10, 1813.
[2] See note 2, page 511.
[3] These occupied a portion of the space now bounded by Third and Fifth and State and Sassafras Streets. These objects and localities, and others, are indicated on the above map, in the construction of which I acknowledge aid kindly afforded me by Giles Sanford, Esq., of Erie. The public square is indicated by the white space on the village plan, and the court-house by the shaded square within it.
[4] Doctor Parsons wrote in his diary, under date of August 1, 1813, "General Mead, of Meadville, arrived two or three days ago, and, with his suite, came on board the *Lawrence* under a salute of thirty-two guns."

Passage of Vessels over Erie Bar.   First Cruise of Perry's Fleet.   Re-enforcements under Captain Elliott.

Erie, with which to man two 20-gun brigs and eight smaller vessels. The enemy disappeared and the lake was calm. He was so restive under the bearding of Barclay and the chafing from superiors, that he resolved with these to go out upon the lake and try the fortune of war. On Sunday, the first of August, he moved his flotilla down to the entrance of the harbor, intending to cross early the next morning. The lake was lower than usual, and the squadron would not float over the bar. Even the smaller vessels had to be lightened for the purpose, and at one time it was considered doubtful whether the *Lawrence* and *Niagara* could be taken out of the harbor at all. The flag-ship was tried first. Her cannon, not "loaded and shotted," as the historians have said (for they had been discharged in saluting General Mead), were taken out and placed on timbers on the beach, while the *Niagara* and smaller vessels lay with their broadsides toward the lake for her protection, in the event of the reappearance of Barclay.[1]

By means of "camels"[2] the *Lawrence* was floated over on the morning of the 4th, and by two o'clock that day her armament was all on board of her, mounted and prepared for action. The *Niagara* was taken over in the same way with very little trouble, and the smaller vessels reached the deep water outside[a] without much difficulty. The labor of this movement had been exciting and exhausting, and the young commander scarcely slept or partook of food during the four days. The enemy was expected every moment. Should he appear while the flotilla was on the bar, all might be lost. Fortunately, Commodore Barclay's social weakness—the inordinate love of public festivities—prolonged his absence, and his squadron did not heave in sight until the 5th, just as the *Niagara* was safely moving into deep water.[3] The *Ariel*, Lieutenant Packet, and *Scorpion*, Sailing-master Champlin, were sent out boldly to engage and detain the squadron. Barclay was surprised at this movement, and perceiving that his golden opportunity was lost, he bore away toward Long Point. The whole of Perry's flotilla was in perfect preparation before night. That evening it weighed anchor,[b] and stood toward Long Point on its first cruise. Perceiving no farther use for the militia, who were anxious to get into their harvest-fields, General Mead discharged them, and the armed citizens of Erie resumed their accustomed avocations.

[a] August 5, 1813.

[b] August 5.

Perry cruised between Erie and the Canada shore for two or three days, vainly searching for the enemy, who had gone to Malden to await the completion of the *Detroit*, a ship that would make the British force superior to that of the Americans. But the latter now received accessions of strength. On the 9th the squadron was joined at Erie by Captain Jesse D. Elliott,[4] who brought with him about one hundred officers and superior men. With these he manned the *Niagara* and assumed command of her. Thus re-enforced, Perry resolved to sail up the lake and report himself ready to co-operate with Harrison.

The squadron left Erie on the 12th[c] in double column, one line in regular battle order,[5] and rendezvoused in an excellent harbor called Put-in-Bay,[d]

[c] August.

[d] August 15.

---

[1] Manuscript corrections of the text of M'Kenzie's *Life of Perry*, by Captain Daniel Dobbins, who assisted in the movement. I am indebted for the use of these notes to his son, Captain W. W. Dobbins, of Erie, Pennsylvania.

[2] A "camel" is a machine invented by the Dutch for carrying vessels over shallow places, as bars at the entrance of harbors. It is a huge box or kind of scow, so arranged that water may be let in or pumped out at pleasure. One of them is placed on each side of a vessel, the water let in, and the camels so sunken that, by means of ropes under the keel and windlasses, the vessel may be placed so that beams may bear it, resting on the camels. The water in the camels is then pumped out, they float, and the vessel, raised by them, is carried over the shallow place.

[3] Captain Dobbins, in his MS. notes on M'Kenzie's *Life of Commodore Perry*, says that the citizens of Port Dover, a small village on Ryason's Creek, a little below Long Point, in Canada, offered Commodore Barclay and his officers a public dinner. The invitation was accepted. While that dinner was being attended Perry was getting his vessels over the bar, and thereby acquired power to successfully dispute the supremacy of Lake Erie with the British. At the dinner Captain Barclay remarked, in response to a complimentary toast, "I expect to find the Yankee brigs hard and fast on the bar at Erie when I return, in which predicament it will be but a small job to destroy them." Had Barclay been more mindful of duty, his expectations might have been realized. Captain Dobbins makes this statement on the authority of an old lake acquaintance, Mr. Ryason, who was at the dinner.   [4] See page 388.

[5] Perry's aggregate force of officers and men was less than four hundred. His squadron was composed as follows:

formed by a group of islands known as the North, Middle, and South Bass, Put-in-Bay, Sugar, Gibraltar, and Strontian,[1] and numerous small islets, some of them containing not more than half an acre. These lie off Port Clinton, the capital of Ottawa County, Ohio. Nothing was seen of the enemy; and on the following day, toward evening, the squadron weighed anchor and sailed for Sandusky Bay, when a strange sail was discovered off Cunningham (now Kelly) Island by Champlin, of the *Scorpion*, who had been sent out as a sort of scout. He signaled and gave chase, followed for a short time by the whole squadron. It was a British schooner reconnoitring. She eluded her pursuers by darting among the islands that form Put-in-Bay, under cover of the night. A heavy storm of wind and rain came with the darkness. The *Scorpion* partly grounded, the schooner ran ashore in the gale, and the squadron lay at anchor all night.[2] On the following morning the point of the peninsula off Sandusky Bay was reached, when Perry fired signal-guns, according to agreement, to apprise Harrison at his quarters at Camp Seneca of his presence. That evening Colonel E. P. Gaines, with a few officers and a guard of Indians, appeared on board the *Lawrence*, and informed Perry that Harrison, with eight thousand men—militia, regulars, and Indians—was only twenty-seven miles distant. Boats were immediately dispatched to bring the general and his suite on board. He arrived late in the evening of the 19th, during a heavy rain, accompanied by his aids, M'Arthur and Cass, and other officers composing his staff, and a large number of soldiers and Indians, twenty-six of the latter being chiefs of the neighboring tribes, whose friendship it was thought important to maintain. The plan of the campaign was then arranged by the two commanders. The 20th,[a] a bright and beautiful day, was spent in reconnoitring Put-in-Bay, with the view of concentrating the army there for transportation to Malden, and on the 21st the general returned to his camp.

[a] August, 1813.

Usher Parsons

As Harrison was not quite ready for the forward movement, Perry sailed[b] on a reconnoitring expedition toward Malden, first ordering the ever-trusty Captain Dobbins to hasten with the *Ohio* to Erie on the important errand of procuring additional stores. He found the enemy within the mouth of the Detroit River. The new vessel had not yet joined the squadron, and he resolved to strike a bold blow. Unfavorable winds made the measure very perilous; and before the elements were propitious he was prostrated by an attack of bilious remittent fever, then very prevalent in the squadron. His surgeon and chaplain, and his young brother Alexander, who had accompanied him from Rhode Island, were also severely ill, and the assistant surgeon, Doctor Parsons, was too weak from a similar attack to walk.[3] The enterprise was abandoned for the time, and

[b] August 23.

Lawrence, commanded by Commodore Perry; *Niagara*, Captain Elliott; *Caledonia*, Purser M'Grath; *Ariel*, Lieutenant Packet; *Somers*, Sailing-master Almy; *Tigress*, Master's-mate M'Donald; *Scorpion*, Sailing-master Champlin; *Porcupine*, Midshipman Senat; *Ohio*, Sailing-master Dobbins; *Trippe*, Lieutenant Smith.

[1] So named because of the quantity of that mineral found there.
[2] Parsons's Diary. MS. statement of Captain Champlin, communicated to the Author.
[3] "Though so ill as to be incapable of walking," says M'Kenzie, "with a humane self-devotion most honorable to him, he continued to attend at the bedside of the sick, to which he was carried, and to prescribe for them, not only on

Put-in-Bay. — A Reconnoissance by Perry. — The Circumspection of the British commander.

on the 27th,[a] at eight o'clock in the evening, the squadron again anchored in Put-in-Bay. There, on the 31st, Perry received from Harrison a re-en-

[a] August, 1813.

PUT-IN-BAY.

forcement of thirty-six men, to act as marines and supply the places of some of the sick.

At the end of a week's confinement Perry gave orders for another cruise, and on the first of September the squadron weighed anchor and sailed again for Malden, where he challenged Barclay, who did not then choose to respond, but, under shore batteries, lay securely and unmoved. On the following morning Perry sailed for Sandusky Bay, to communicate with General Harrison, and then, with his whole squadron, returned to anchorage in Put-in-Bay.[1]

board of the *Lawrence*, but of the smaller vessels, being lifted for the purpose in his cot, and the sick brought on deck for his prescriptions."—*Life of Perry*, i., 203.

Usher Parsons was born at Alfred, Maine, on the 18th of August, 1788. He chose the medical profession as a life-pursuit, and studied with Dr. John Warren, of Cambridge, Massachusetts. On the promulgation of the declaration of war he entered the navy as surgeon's mate. He volunteered to accompany Perry to Lake Erie with the crew of the John Adams. In the battle on Lake Erie, described in the next chapter, he was on the flag-ship *Lawrence* as acting surgeon, his superior being too ill to attend to his duties. Indeed, the duties of both Dr. Barton and Dr. Horseley devolved on Dr. Parsons when the battle was over. Speaking of him in a letter to the Secretary of the Navy, Perry said: "I can only say that in the event of my having another command, I should consider myself particularly fortunate in having him with me as a surgeon." In 1814 he served on the upper lakes under Commodore Sinclair. At the request of Perry, Parsons became the surgeon of the new frigate *Java*, 44, commanded by the hero of Lake Erie. After ten years' service in the navy he retired, settled as a physician and surgeon in Providence, Rhode Island, was professor in Brown University and other colleges, president of the Rhode Island Medical Society, and first vice-president of the National Medical Society. In 1822 he married a daughter of Rev. Dr. Holmes, of Cambridge, the author of the *Annals of America*. She died three years afterward, bearing one son, Dr. Charles W. Parsons, now [1867] president of the Rhode Island Medical Society. Dr. Parsons is the author of several medical works and historical discourses, and a well-written *Life of Sir William Pepperell, Bart*. Dr. Parsons is still [1867] in the enjoyment of perfect physical and mental health, at the age of seventy-nine years.

[1] Put-in-Bay Harbor is on the north side of Put-in-Bay Island, one of the largest of the group of about twenty in that neighborhood. The view of the harbor from Put-in-Bay Island, given above, is from a drawing made on the spot, in September, 1859, by Captain Van Cleve, a veteran Lake Ontario steam-boat commander, who kindly presented it to me. Directly in front is seen Gibraltar Island, and the place of "Perry's Look-out," delineated in the little picture at the beginning of the next chapter, is indicated by the flag. The smoke in the distance points out the place of the battle, ten miles in a northwardly direction from Put-in-Bay. The Bass Islands are seen on the right, and Rattlesnake Island on the left. The beaches of all are chiefly of white pebbles. The view is from Put-in-Bay Island, near the landing.

CHAPTER XXV.

"September the tenth, full well I ween,
   In eighteen hundred and thirteen,
The weather mild, the sky serene,
   Commanded by bold Perry,
Our saucy fleet at anchor lay
In safety, moor'd at Put-in-Bay;
'Twixt sunrise and the break of day,
   The British fleet
      · We chanced to meet;
Our admiral thought he would them greet
   With a welcome on Lake Erie."—OLD SONG.

"SAIL ho!" were the stirring words that rang out loud and clear from the mast-head of the *Lawrence* on the warm and pleasant morning of the 10th of September, 1813. That herald's proclamation was not unexpected to Perry. Five days before he had received direct and positive information from Malden that Proctor's army were so short of provisions that Barclay was preparing to go out upon the lake, at all hazards, to open a communication with Long Point, the chief deposit of supplies for the enemy on the banks of the Detroit River. Perry had made preparations accordingly; and, day after day, from the rocky heights of Gibraltar Island, now known as

PERRY'S LOOK-OUT, GIBRALTAR ISLAND, PUT-IN-BAY.[2]

"Perry's Look-out," he had pointed his glass anxiously in the direction of Malden.[1] On the evening of the 9th he called around him the officers of his squadron, and gave instructions to each in writing, for he was determined to attack the enemy at his anchorage the next day if he did not come out. His plan was to bring on a close action at once, so as not to lose the advantage of his short carronades. To each vessel its antagonist on the British side was assigned, the size and character of them having been communi-

---

[1] Perry also kept two of the smaller vessels as look-outs in the vicinity of the *Sisters* Islands.
[2] This little picture is from a painting made on the spot by Miss C. L. Ransom, who kindly permitted me to copy it (see page 505). "Perry's Look-out" is on the left, and is composed of limestone piled about fifty feet above the water. In front is a natural arch. On the summit is a representation of a monument proposed to be erected there, of which the corner-stone was laid several years ago with imposing ceremonies. On the left are seen the graves of some sailors who died of cholera. In the middle is seen Rattlesnake Island. On the right, in the extreme distance, is North Bass Island, and between the two is the passage toward Detroit. The Middle Bass is also seen on the right. This is a faithful copy of Miss Ransom's picture, with the exception of time. It has been made a moonlight scene, for effect, instead of a daylight one.

Near the site of the proposed monument, Jay Cooke, an eminent banker, has a fine dwelling, and on the foundations

cated to him by Captain Brevoort,[1] whose family lived in Detroit. The *Lawrence* was assigned to the *Detroit;* the *Niagara* to the *Queen Charlotte,* and so on; and to each officer he said, in substance, Engage your antagonist in close action, keeping on the line at half-cable length from the vessel of our squadron ahead of you.

It was about ten o'clock when the conference ended. The moon was at its full, and it was a splendid autumn night. Just before they parted, Perry brought out a large square battle-flag, which, at his request, Mr. Hambleton,[2] the purser, had caused to be privately prepared at Erie. It was blue, and bore, in large letters, made of white muslin, the alleged dying words of the gallant commander of the *Chesapeake,* "DON'T GIVE UP THE SHIP!" "When this flag shall be hoisted to the main-royal mast-head," said the commodore, "it shall be your signal for going into action." As the officers were leaving, he said, "Gentlemen, remember your instructions. Nelson has expressed my idea in the words, 'If you lay your enemy close alongside, you can not be out of your place.' Good-night."

PERRY'S BATTLE-FLAG.[3]

The cry of "Sail ho!" was soon followed by signals to the fleet of "Enemy in sight;" "Get underweigh;" and the voices of the boatswains sounding through the squadron and echoing from the shores the command, "All hands up anchor, ahoy!" At sunrise the British vessels were all seen upon the northwestern horizon—

"Six barques trained for battle, the red flag displaying,
By Barclay commanded, their wings wide outspread,
Forsake their strong-hold, on broad Erie essaying
To meet with that foe they so lately did dread."—OLD BALLAD.

A light wind was blowing from the southwest. Clouds came upon it from over the Ohio wilderness, and in passing dropped a light shower of rain. Soon the sky became serene, and before ten o'clock, when, by the aid of the gentle breeze in beat-

---

prepared for that monument he caused to be erected, in 1866, a small one, composed of yellowish limestone. It is about ten feet in height, and surmounted by a bronze vase for flowers. On its sides are naval devices of the same metal.

[1] Henry Brevoort, of New York, was commissioned Second Lieutenant in Third Infantry in 1801. He commanded transports on Lake Erie, and in May, 1811, was promoted to captain. He distinguished himself in the battle of Magua-ga (see page 279), and also as commander of marines in the *Niagara* in the battle of Lake Erie. He received a silver medal for his gallantry there. He was promoted to major in 1814, and was disbanded in 1815. In 1822 he was made United States Indian Agent at Green Bay.—Gardner's *Dictionary of the Army.*

[2] Samuel Hambleton was a native of Talbot County, Maryland, where he was born in 1777. He was first a merchant, then a clerk in the Navy Department, and in 1806 was appointed purser in the navy. After the battle of Lake Erie, the officers and crews of the American squadron appointed him prize agent, and more than $200,000 passed through his hands. He left the lake in 1814, and performed good service afloat and ashore for many years. He died at his residence in Maryland, near St. Michael's, called "Perry's Cabin," January 17, 1851.

[3] This is a picture of the flag as seen in the Trophy Room of the Sanitary Fair in the City of New York in the month of April, 1864. It is between eight and nine feet square. The form of the letters is preserved in the engraving. They are about a foot in length, and might be seen at a considerable distance.

The following lines, in allusion to this flag, are from a fine poem on *The Hero of Lake Erie,* by Henry T. Tuckerman, Esq.:

"Behold the chieftain's glad, prophetic smile,
As a new banner he unrolls the while;
Hear the gay shout of his elated crew
When the dear watchword hovers to their view,
And Lawrence, silent in the arms of death,
Bequeaths defiance with his latest breath!"

ing and strong arms with oars, the squadron had passed out from the labyrinth of islands into the open lake, within five or six miles of the enemy, not a cloud was hanging in the firmament, nor a fleck of mist was upon the waters. It was a splendid September day.

Perry was yet weak from illness when the cry of "Sail ho!" was repeated to him by Lieutenant Dulaney Forrest. That announcement gave him strength, and the excitement of the hour was a tonic of rare virtue. The wind was variable, and he tried in vain to gain the weather-gage of the enemy by beating around to the windward of some of the islands. He was too impatient to fight to long brook the waste of precious time in securing an advantage so small with a wind so light. "Run to the leeward of the islands," he said to Taylor, his sailing-master.[1] "Then you will have to engage the enemy to leeward," said that officer, in a slightly remonstrant manner. "I don't care," quickly responded Perry; "to windward or to leeward, they shall fight to-day." The signal to wear ship followed immediately, when the wind shifted suddenly to the southeast, and enabled the squadron to clear the islands, and to keep the weather-gage. Perceiving this, Barclay hove to, in close order, and awaited Perry's attack. His vessels, newly painted and with colors flying, made an imposing appearance. They were six in number,[2] and bore sixty-three carriage-guns, one on a pivot, two swivels, and four howitzers. Perry's squadron numbered nine vessels, and bore fifty-four carriage-guns and two swivels.[3] Barclay had *thirty-five* long guns to Perry's *fifteen*, and possessed greatly the advantage in action at a distance. In close action, the weight of metal was with the Americans, and for that reason Perry had resolved to close upon the enemy at once. The British commander had one hundred and fifty men from the royal navy, eighty Canadian sailors, two hundred and forty soldiers, mostly regulars, and some Indians. His whole force, officers and men, was a little more than five hundred. The American commander had upon his muster-roll four hundred and ninety names. Of these the bearers of one hundred and sixteen were sick, and most of them too weak to go upon deck. About one fourth of Perry's crew were from Rhode Island; one fourth were regular seamen, American and foreign; about one fourth were raw volunteers, chiefly from Kentucky; and about another fourth were negroes.

At a little past ten o'clock Perry's line was formed according to the plan arranged the previous evening, the *Niagara* in the van. The *Lawrence* was cleared for action, and the battle-flag, bearing the words "DON'T GIVE UP THE SHIP," in letters large enough, as we have observed, to be seen by the whole squadron, was brought out and displayed. The commodore then addressed his officers and crew a few stirring words, and concluded by saying, "My brave lads! this flag contains the last words of Captain Lawrence. Shall I hoist it?" "Ay, ay, sir!" they all shouted, as with one voice, and in a moment it was run up to the main-royal mast-head of the flag-ship, amid cheer after cheer, not only from the *Lawrence*, but the whole squadron. It was the signal for battle.

---

[1] William Vigeron Taylor was of French descent. He was a captain in the merchant service, and entered that of the navy under Perry as sailing-master. Perry esteemed him highly, and made him sailing-master of his flag-ship on Lake Erie. He rendered efficient service in the fitting out of the squadron. In the battle on the 10th of September he received a wound in the thigh, but kept the deck until the close. On the return of the *Lawrence* to Erie, Mr. Taylor was sent with dispatches to Chauncey. In 1814 he was commissioned a lieutenant in the navy. He was promoted to commander in 1831, and to post captain in 1841. He commanded the sloops *Warren* and *Erie* in the Gulf of Mexico. After his promotion to post captain he was placed in command of the ship-of-the-line *Ohio*, and took her around Cape Horn to the Pacific. He was then sixty-eight years of age. On the 11th of February, 1851, he died of apoplexy, in the seventy-eighth year of his age.

It is proper here to mention that most of the biographical sketches of the officers of Perry's squadron contained in this chapter are compiled from a paper on the subject from the pen of Dr. Usher Parsons, published in the *New England Historical and Genealogical Register for January*, 1863.

[2] These were as follows: Ship *Detroit*, 19 guns, 1 in pivot, and 2 howitzers; ship *Queen Charlotte*, 17, and 1 howitzer; schooner *Lady Prevost*, 13, and 1 howitzer; brig *Hunter*, 10; sloop *Little Belt*, 3; and schooner *Chippewa*, 1, and 2 swivels.

[3] These were as follows: Brig *Lawrence*, 20 guns; brig *Niagara*, 20; brig *Caledonia*, 3; schooner *Ariel*, 4; schooner *Scorpion*, 2, and 2 swivels; sloop *Trippe*, 1; schooner *Tigress*, 1; and schooner *Porcupine*, 1. The *Ohio*, Captain Dobbins, had gone to Erie for supplies, and was not in the action.

OLIVER H. PERRY.[1]

As the dinner-hour would occur at the probable time of action, the thoughtful Perry ordered refreshments to be distributed. The decks were then wetted and sprinkled with sand so that feet should not slip when blood should begin to flow. Then every man was placed in proper position. As the squadron moved slowly and silently toward the enemy, with a gentle breeze, at the rate of less than three knots, the *Niagara*, Captain Elliott, leading the van, it was discovered that Barclay had made a disposition of his force that required a change in Perry's prescribed order of battle. It was instantly made, and the American squadron moved to the attack in the order best calculated to cope with the enemy. Barclay's vessels were near together. The flag-ship *Detroit*,

[1] Oliver Hazard Perry was born in South Kingston, Rhode Island, on the 23d of August, 1785. His father was then in the naval service of the United States. He entered the navy as midshipman at the age of fifteen years, on board the sloop-of-war *General Greene*, when war with France seemed inevitable. He first saw active service before Tripoli, in the squadron of Commodore Preble. He was commissioned a lieutenant in 1810, and placed in command of the schooner *Revenge*, attached to Commodore Rodgers's squadron in Long Island Sound. She was wrecked, but his conduct in saving public property was highly applauded. Early in 1812 he was placed in command of a flotilla of gun-boats in Newport Harbor. After his victorious battle on Lake Erie in 1813, he was promoted to post-captain, and at the close of the war he was placed in command of the *Java*, 44, a first-class frigate, and sailed with Decatur for the Mediterranean Sea.

VIEW OF PERRY'S BIRTH-PLACE.

On his return, while his vessel was lying in Newport Harbor, in mid-winter, a fearful storm arose. He heard of the wreck of a merchant vessel upon a reef six miles distant. He immediately manned his barge and said to his crew, "Come, my boys, we are going to the relief of shipwrecked seamen; pull away!" He rescued eleven almost exhausted seamen from death.

On account of piracies in the West Indies, the United States government determined to send a little squadron there for the protection of American commerce. Perry was assigned to the command of it, and in 1819 he sailed in the *John Adams*, accompanied by the *Nonsuch*. In August he was attacked by the yellow fever, and on his birthday (August 23d) he expired, at the age of thirty-four years. He was buried at Port Spain, Trinidad, with military honors. His death produced a most profound sensation throughout the United States, for it was regarded as a great public calamity. Tributes of national grief were displayed, and the Congress of the United States made a liberal provision for his family, and his mother, who was dependent on him for support. In 1826 his remains were conveyed from Trinidad to Newport in the sloop-of-war *Lexington*, and landed on the 27th of November. On Monday (December 4th) following he was interred with funeral honors due to his rank. His coffin rested in a sort of *catafalco*, the lower part being in the form of a boat. The canopy was decorated with stars and

CATAFALCO.

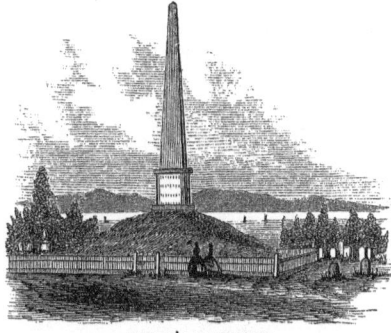

PERRY'S MONUMENT.

trimmed with black curtains, and at each corner were black plumes. The State of Rhode Island afterward caused to be erected a substantial granite monument to his memory. It stands upon a grassy mound on the west side of the Island Cemetery, and at the base rest the remains of the commodore and the deceased of his family. The monument bears the following inscriptions. *East side:* "OLIVER HAZARD PERRY. At the age of 27 years he achieved the victory of Lake

19, was in the van supported by the schooner *Chippewa*, with one long 18 on a pivot, and two swivels. Next was the brig *Hunter*, 10; then the *Queen Charlotte*, 17, commanded by Finnis. The latter was flanked by the schooner *Lady Prevost*, 13, and the *Little Belt*, 3. Perry, in the brig *Lawrence*, 20, moved forward, flanked on the left by the schooner *Scorpion*, under Champlin, bearing two long guns (32 and 12), and the schooner *Ariel*, Lieutenant Packet, which carried four short 12's. On the right of the *Lawrence* was the brig *Caledonia*, Captain Turner, with three long 24's. These were intended to encounter the *Chippewa*, *Detroit*, and *Hunter*. Captain Elliott, in the fine brig *Niagara*, 20, followed, with instructions to fight the *Queen Charlotte*; while Almy, in the *Somers*, with two long

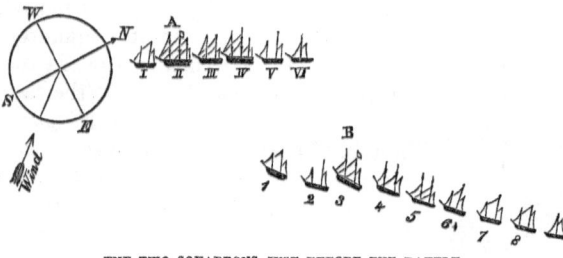

THE TWO SQUADRONS JUST BEFORE THE BATTLE.

32's and two swivels, Senat, in the *Porcupine*, with one long 32, Conklin, in the *Tigress*, with one long 24, and Holdup, in the *Trippe*, one long 32, were left in the rear to engage the *Lady Prevost* and *Little Belt*.[1]

The sun was within fifteen minutes of meridian when a bugle sounded on board the *Detroit* as a signal for action, and the bands of the British squadron struck up "Rule Britannia." A shout went up from that little squadron, and a 24-pound shot from the enemy's flag-ship was sent booming over the water toward the *Lawrence*, then a mile and a half distant. It was evident that Barclay appreciated the advantage of his long guns, and wished to fight at a distance, while Perry resolved to press to close quarters before opening his fire.

That first shot from the enemy fell short. Another, five minutes later, went crashing through the bulwarks of the *Lawrence*. It stirred the blood of her gallant men, but, at the command of Perry, she remained silent. "Steady, boys! steady!" he said, while his dark eye flashed with the excitement of the moment — an excitement which was half smothered by his judgment. Slowly the American line, with the light wind abeam, moved toward that of the enemy, the two forming an acute angle of about fifteen degrees.

"Sublime the pause, when down the gleaming tide
The virgin galleys to the conflict glide;
The very wind, as if in awe or grief,
Scarce makes a ripple or disturbs a leaf."—H. T. TUCKERMAN.

Signals were given for each vessel to engage its prescribed antagonist. At five minutes before twelve the *Lawrence* had reached only the third one in the enemy's line, and was almost as near the *Queen Charlotte* as the *Detroit*, with the *Caledonia* half-cable length behind, and the *Niagara* abaft the beam of the *Charlotte* and opposite the *Lady Prevost*.

The battle now began on the part of the Americans. The gallant young Champlin,

---

Erie, September 10, 1813." *North side:* "Born in South Kingston, R. I., August 23, 1785. Died at Port Spain, Trinidad, August 23, 1819, aged 34 years." *West side:* "His remains were conveyed to his native land in a ship-of-war, according to a resolution of Congress, and were here interred December 4, 1826." *South side:* "Erected by the State of Rhode Island."

In person Commodore Perry was tall and well-proportioned, of exquisite symmetry, and graceful in every movement. He was every inch a *man*. He possessed splendid talents; was prudent and brave in the highest degree. In private life he was gentle, and his conjugal love and faithfulness were perfect. His respect for his wife amounted to reverence, and he was ever ready to acknowledge her salutary influence. Doctor Parsons relates that his first remark on regaining the *Lawrence*, after the battle, was addressed to his friend Hambleton, the purser. He said, "The prayers of my wife have prevailed in saving me."

[1] The above diagram shows the position of the two squadrons when the American was approaching that of the British in battle order. A is the British squadron, and its vessels are designated by Roman numerals. I., *Chippewa*; II., *Detroit*; III., *Hunter*; IV., *Queen Charlotte*; V., *Lady Prevost*; VI., *Little Belt*. B is the American squadron, and the vessels are designated by Arabic numerals. 1, *Scorpion*; 2, *Ariel*; 3, *Lawrence*; 4, *Caledonia*; 5, *Niagara*; 6, *Somers*; 7, *Porcupine*; 8, *Tigress*; 9, *Trippe*. I have been furnished with these diagrams by Commodore Stephen Champlin, of the U. S. Navy, the commander of the *Scorpion* in the battle.

then less than twenty-four years of age, who still (1867) lives to enjoy a well-earned reputation,[1] had already fired the first (as he did the last) shot of the battle from the guns of the *Scorpion*.

> "But see that silver wreath of curling smoke—
> 'Tis Barclay's gun! The silence now is broke.
> Champlin, with rapid move and steady eye,
> Sends back in thunder-tones a bold reply."

This was followed by a cannonade from Packet,[2] of the *Ariel;* and then the *Lawrence*, which had begun to suffer considerably from the enemy's missiles, opened fire upon the *Detroit* with her long bow-gun, a twelve-pounder. The action soon became general. The smaller, slow-sailing vessels had fallen in the rear, and when the battle began the *Trippe* was more than two miles from the enemy.

The *Scorpion* and *Ariel*, both without bulwarks, fought bravely, and kept their places with the *Lawrence* throughout the entire action. They did not suffer much, for the enemy concentrated his destructive energies upon the *Lawrence* and neglected the others. From the *Detroit*, the *Hunter*, the *Queen Charlotte*, and even from the *Lady Prevost*, shots were hurled upon the American flag-ship, with the determination to destroy her and her gallant commander, and then to cut up the squadron in detail. No less than thirty-four heavy guns were brought to bear upon her. The *Caledonia*, with her long guns, was enabled to do good ex-

FIRST POSITION IN THE ACTION.[3]

---

[1] Stephen Champlin was born in South Kingston, Rhode Island, on the 17th of November, 1789. His father was a volunteer soldier in the Revolution. His mother was a sister of Commodore Perry's father, making the two commanders first cousins. He went to sea as a sailor at the age of sixteen years, and at the age of twenty-two, having passed through all grades, he was captain of a ship that sailed from Norwich, Connecticut. On the 22d of May, 1812, he was appointed sailing-master in the navy, and commanded a gun-boat, under Perry, at Newport. As we have seen, he was sent to Lake Erie. On his arrival here he was appointed to the command of the *Scorpion*, which he gallantly managed throughout the battle. Subsequently to the battle he was placed in command of the *Queen Charlotte* and *Detroit*, two prize-ships taken from the enemy. In the spring of 1814 he was placed in command of the *Tigress*, under Commander Sinclair, and, with Captain Turner, he blockaded the port of Mackinaw. His services on the Upper Lake will be noticed in the future text. Suffice it to say here that he was severely wounded in the thigh while in that service by canister-shot, and taken prisoner. That wound has been troublesome to him until this hour. In 1816 he was appointed to the command of the *Porcupine*, and conveyed a party of topographical engineers to the Upper Lakes, who were to consider the boundary-line between the United States and Great Britain. His wound prevented his doing much active service. He was ordered to the steam-ship *Fulton* at New York, and had left her but a short time when she blew up. In 1842 he was placed in command of the naval rendezvous at Buffalo, and was successful in shipping apprentices for the service. In 1845 he was ordered to the command of the *Michigan* at Erie, and continued there about four years and a half. A few years ago he was placed on the reserve list, with full pay, and remains so. He now bears the title of commodore. He resides at Buffalo, and, with the exception of the sufferings caused by his wound, he is in the enjoyment of fair health, at the age of seventy-eight years. He is a stout, thick-set man, of middle size. He is the last survivor of the nine commanders in Perry's squadron in the great battle in 1813.

[2] John H. Packet was a native of Virginia. He received his warrant as midshipman in 1809, and was commissioned a lieutenant a few days before this battle. He was with Bainbridge when the *Constitution* captured the *Java*. He served at Erie some years after the battle, and died there of fever.
The acting sailing-master of the *Ariel* in the battle, Thomas Brownell, was from Rhode Island, and went to Erie as master's-mate, where he was promoted. He was commissioned a lieutenant in 1843, when he was placed on the retired list. He now (1867) resides at Newport, Rhode Island. He was always an active and esteemed officer.

[3] This diagram shows the position of the vessels at the beginning of the action. The British vessels, A, are indicated by Roman numerals, and the American vessels, B, by Arabic. I., *Chippewa;* II., *Detroit;* III., *Hunter;* IV., *Queen*

ecution from the beginning, but the shot of the carronades from the *Niagara* fell short of her antagonist. Of her twenty guns, only a long 12 was serviceable for a while. Shifting another, Elliott brought two to bear with effect, and these were served so vigorously that nearly all of the shot of that calibre were exhausted. The smaller vessels meanwhile were too far astern to be of much service.

Perry soon perceived that he was yet too far distant to damage the enemy materially, so he ordered word to be sent from vessel to vessel by trumpet for all to make sail, bear down upon Barclay, and engage in close combat. The order was transmitted by Captain Elliott, who was the second in command, but he failed to obey it himself.[1] His vessel was a fast sailer, and his men were the best in the squadron, but he kept at a distance from the enemy, and continued firing his long guns. Perry meanwhile pressed on with the *Lawrence*, accompanied by the *Scorpion*, *Ariel*, and *Caledonia*, and at meridian exactly, when he supposed he was near enough for execution with his carronades, he opened the first division of his battery on the starboard side on the *Detroit*. His balls fell short, while his antagonist and her consorts poured upon the *Lawrence* a heavy storm of round shot from their long guns, still leaving the *Scorpion* and *Ariel* almost unnoticed. The *Caledonia* meanwhile engaged with the *Hunter*, but the *Niagara* kept a respectful distance from the *Queen Charlotte*, and gave that vessel an opportunity to go to the assistance of the *Detroit*. She passed the *Hunter*, and, placing herself astern of the *Detroit*, opened heavily upon the *Lawrence*, now, at a quarter past twelve, only musket-shot distance from her chief antagonist. For two hours the gallant Perry and his devoted ship bore the brunt of the battle with twice his force, aided only by the schooners on his weather-bow and some feeble shots from the distant *Caledonia* when she could spare them from her adversary the *Hunter*. During that tempest of war his vessel was terribly shattered. Her rigging was nearly all shot away; her sails were torn into shreds; her spars were battered into splinters; her guns were dismounted; and, like the *Guerriere* when disabled by the *Constitution*, she lay upon the waters almost a helpless wreck. The carnage on her deck had been terrible. Out of one hundred and three sound men that composed her officers and crew when she went into action, twenty-two were slain and sixty-one were wounded. Perry's little brother had been struck down by a splinter at his side, but soon recovered.[2] Yarnall,[3] his first lieutenant, had come to him bleeding, his nose swelled to an enormous size, it having been perforated by a splinter, and his whole appearance the impersonation of carnage and ill luck, and said, "All the officers in my division are cut down; can I have others?" They were sent; but Yarnall soon returned, again wounded and bleeding profusely, with the same sad story. "I have no more officers to furnish you," replied Perry; "you must endeavor to make out by yourself." The brave lieutenant did so. Thrice wounded, he kept the deck, and directed every shot from his battery in person. Forest, the second lieutenant, fell stunned at Perry's feet;[4] and the gallant Brooks,

---

Charlotte; V., *Lady Prevost*; VI., *Little Belt*. 1, *Scorpion*; 2, *Ariel*; 3, *Lawrence*; 4, *Caledonia*; 5, *Niagara*; 6, *Somers*; 7, *Porcupine*; 8, *Tigress*; 9, *Trippe*;

[1] Dr. Usher Parsons's *Discourse* on the Battle of Lake Erie, delivered before the Rhode Island Historical Society, February 16, 1852, page 10.

[2] Two musket-balls had already passed through his hat, and his clothes had been torn by splinters.

[3] John J. Yarnall was a native of Pennsylvania, and was commissioned a lieutenant in July, 1813, having been in the service as midshipman since 1809. Ten days after the battle on Lake Erie he was sent to Erie with the *Lawrence*, and soon afterward was ordered to the *John Adams*. He was appointed commander of the *Epervier* in 1815. She was lost at sea with all on board. The State of Virginia presented Lieutenant Yarnall with a sword soon after the battle of Lake Erie. It was exhibited at the head-quarters of the Old Soldiers at Cleveland, on the occasion of the dedication of the statue of Perry in that city in September, 1860. I copied the following inscription from the blade: "In testimony of the undaunted gallantry of Lieutenant John J. Yarnall, of the United States ship *Lawrence*, under Commodore Perry, in the capture of the whole English fleet on Lake Erie, September 10, 1813, the State of Virginia bestows this sword." It was brought from Wheeling to Cleveland by Mr. Fleming, of the former place.

[4] He was struck in the breast by a spent grape-shot. Perry raised him up, assured him that he was not hurt, as there

Death of Lieutenant Brooks. Terrible Scenes on board the *Lawrence*. Strange Conduct of Captain Elliott.

so remarkable for his personal beauty,[1] a son of an honored soldier of the old war for independence, and once governor of Massachusetts, was carried in a dying state to the cockpit, where balls were crashing through, his mind more exercised about his beloved commander and the fortunes of the day than himself. When the good surgeon, Parsons, who had hastened to the deck on hearing a shout of victory, returned to cheer the youth with the glorious tidings, the young hero's ears were closed—the doors of the earthly dwelling of his spirit were shut forever.[2]

While the *Lawrence* was being thus terribly smitten, officers and crew were anxiously wondering why the *Niagara*—the swift, stanch, well-manned *Niagara*—kept aloof, not only from her prescribed antagonist the *Queen Charlotte*, now battling the *Lawrence*, but the other assailants of the flag-ship. Her commander himself had passed the order for close conflict, yet he kept far away; and when afterward censured, he pleaded in justification of his course his perfect obedience to the original order to keep at "half-cable length behind the *Caledonia* on the line." It may be said that his orders to fight the *Queen Charlotte*, who had left *her* line and gone into the thickest of the fight with the *Lawrence* and her supporting schooners, were quite as imperative, and that it was his duty to follow. This he did not do until the guns of the *Lawrence* became silent, and no signals were displayed by, nor special orders came from Perry. These significant tokens of dissolution doubtless made Elliott believe that the commodore was slain, and himself had become the chief commander of the squadron. He then hailed the *Caledonia*, and ordered Lieutenant Turner[3] to

---

were no signs of a wound, and, thus encouraged, he soon recovered from the shock. The ball had lodged in his clothes. "I am not hurt, sir," he said to the commander, "but this is my shot," and coolly put it in his pocket.

[1] John Brooks was a native of Massachusetts. He studied medicine with his father. Having a military taste, he obtained the appointment of lieutenant of marines, and was stationed at Washington when the war broke out. He was sent to Lake Erie under Perry; and at Erie, while the squadron was a-building, he was engaged in recruiting for the service. There he raised a company of marines for the squadron. He was an excellent drill officer, and gave great promise of future distinction. So intense was his agony when he fell, his hip having been shattered by a cannon-ball, that he begged Perry to shoot him. He died in the course of an hour. "Mr. Brooks," says Doctor Parsons, "was probably surpassed by no officer in the navy for manly beauty, polished manners, and elegant personal appearance."

[2] The scenes on board the *Lawrence*, as described to me by Doctor Parsons, must have been extremely terrible. The vessel was shallow, and the ward-room, used as a cockpit, to which the wounded were taken, was mostly above water, and exposed to the shots of the enemy; while nothing but the deck-planks separated it from the terrible tumult above, caused by the groans and shrieks of the wounded and dying, the deep rumbling of the gun-carriages, the awful explosions of the cannon, the crash of round-shot as they splintered spars, stove the bulwarks, dismounted the heavy ordnance, and cut the rigging, while through the seams of the deck blood streamed into the surgeon's room in many a crimson rill. When the battle had raged half an hour, and the crew of the *Lawrence* were falling one by one, the commodore called from the small skylight for the doctor to send up one of his six assistants. In five minutes the call was repeated and obeyed, and again repeated and obeyed, until Parsons was left alone. "Can any of the wounded pull a rope?" inquired Perry. The question was answered by two or three crawling upon deck to lend a feeble hand in pulling at the last guns in position.

Midshipman Lamb had his arm badly shattered. While moving forward to lie down, after the doctor had dressed the wound, a round-shot came crashing through the side of the vessel, struck the young man in the side, dashed him across the room, and killed him instantly. Pohig, a Narraganset Indian, badly wounded, was released from his sufferings in the same way by another ball that passed through the cockpit. No less than six round-shot entered the surgeon's room during the action.

Some of the incidents witnessed by the doctor were not so painful. A cannon-ball passed through a closet containing all the brig's crockery, dashing a greater portion of it in pieces. It was an illustration—that ball from John Bull—of "a bull in a china-shop." The commodore's dog had secreted himself in that closet when the war of battle commenced, and when the destructive intruder came he set up a furious barking—"a protest," said the doctor, "against the right of such an invasion of his chosen retirement."

We have observed that Lieutenant Yarnall was wounded, yet kept the deck. He had his scalp badly torn, and "came below," said the doctor, "with the blood streaming over his face." Some lint was applied to the wound and confined by a handkerchief, and the lieutenant was then directed to come for better dressing after the battle, as he insisted upon returning to the deck. It was not long before he again made his appearance, having received a second wound. On the deck were stowed some hammocks stuffed with reed-tops, or "cat-tails," as they are popularly called. These filled the air like down, and had settled like snow upon the blood-wet head and face of Yarnall. When he made his appearance below, his visage was ludicrous beyond description; his head appeared like that of a huge owl. The wounded roared with laughter, and cried out, "The devil has come among us!"

[3] Daniel Turner was a native of New York. He was appointed a midshipman in 1808, and in 1813 was commissioned a lieutenant. He was efficient in getting the little lake squadron ready for service. In its first cruise across the lake, young Turner, less than twenty-one years of age, commanded the *Niagara*. On the arrival of Captain Elliott, he was ordered to the third ship, the *Caledonia*, and managed her gallantly during the action. He continued in the lake service the following year, and was made a prisoner and sent to Montreal. He was exchanged, and accompanied Perry in the *Java* to the Mediterranean. For his services in the battle of Lake Erie his native state presented him with an elegant sword. He was at one time commander of the naval station at Portsmouth; at another of the Pacific squadron, and always performed his duties with the greatest promptness. He was temperate, brave, generous, and genial. He was

leave the line and bear down upon the *Hunter* for close conflict, giving the *Niagara* a chance to pass for the relief of the *Lawrence*. The gallant Turner instantly obeyed, and the *Caledonia* fought her adversary nobly. The *Niagara* spread her canvas before a freshening breeze that had just sprung up, but, instead of going to the relief of the *Lawrence*, thus silently pleading for protection, she bore away toward the head

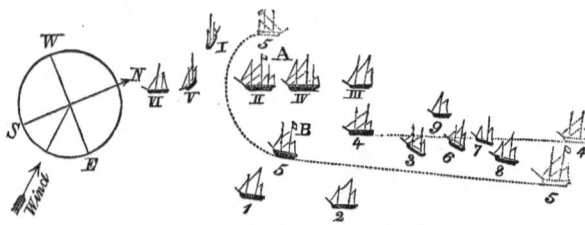

SECOND POSITION IN THE BATTLE.[1]

of the enemy's squadron, passing the American flag-ship to the windward, and leaving her exposed to the still galling fire of the enemy, because, as was alleged in extenuation of this apparent violation of the rules of naval warfare and the claims of humanity, both squadrons had caught the breeze and moved forward, and left the crippled vessel floating astern. Elliott seemed to notice her only by sending a boat to bring round shot from her to replenish his own scanty store.

As the *Niagara* bore down she was assailed by shots from the *Queen Charlotte*, *Lady Prevost*, and *Hunter*, and returned them with spirit. It was while she was abreast of the *Lawrence's* larboard beam, and nearly half a mile distant, that Perry performed the gallant feat of transferring his broad pennant from one vessel to the other. He had fought as long as possible. More than two hours had worn away in the conflict. His vessel lay helpless and silent upon the almost unruffled bosom of the lake, utterly incapable of farther defense. His last effective heavy gun had been fired by himself, assisted by his purser and chaplain. Only fourteen unhurt persons remained on his deck, and only nine of these were seamen. A less hopeful man would have pulled down his flag in despair; but Perry's spirit was too lofty to be touched by common misfortunes. From his mast-head floated the admonition, as if audibly spoken by the gallant Lawrence, DON'T GIVE UP THE SHIP. In the dash of the *Caledonia* and the approach of the long-lagging *Niagara* he felt the inspiration of hope; and when he saw the latter, like the priest or the Levite, about to "pass by on the other side," unmindful of his wounds, resolutions like swift intuitions filled his mind, and were as quickly acted upon. The *Niagara* was stanch, swift, and apparently unhurt, for she had kept far away from great danger. He determined to fly to her deck, spread all needful sail to catch the stiffening breeze, bear down swiftly upon the crippled enemy, break his line, and make a bold stroke for victory.

With the calmness of perfect assurance, Perry laid aside his blue nankeen sailor's jacket which he had worn all day, and put on the uniform of his rank, as if conscious that he should secure a victory, and have occasion to receive as guests the conquered commander and officers of the British squadron.[2] "Yarnall," he said, "I leave the *Lawrence* in your charge, with discretionary powers. You may hold out or surrender, as your judgment and the circumstances shall dictate." He had already ordered his boat to be lowered, his broad pennant, and the banner with its glorious words, to be taken down,[3] but leaving the Stars and Stripes floating defiantly over the battered

---

made master commander in 1825, and post-captain in 1835. He died on the 4th of February, 1850, leaving a widow and one daughter, who still survive him.

[1] This shows the relative position of the two squadrons at the time when the *Niagara* bore down upon the head of the British line, the change of her course after Perry took command of her, and the penetration of that line by her. One dotted line, from 4 to 4, shows the attack of the *Caledonia* on the *Hunter*, and the other, from 5 to 5, the course of the *Niagara* as described on this and the next page. The vessels of the British squadron, A, are designated by Roman numerals, thus: I., *Chippewa*; II., *Detroit*; III., *Hunter*; IV., *Queen Charlotte*; V., *Lady Prevost*; VI., *Little Belt*. Those of the American squadron, B, are designated by Arabic numerals, thus: 1, *Scorpion*; 2, *Ariel*; 3, *Lawrence*; 4, *Caledonia*; 5, *Niagara*; 6, *Somers*; 7, *Porcupine*; 8, *Tigress*; 9, *Trippe*.

[2] Letter of Rev. Francis Vinton, D.D., son-in-law of Commodore Perry, to the Author.

[3] This was rolled up and cast to him, after he had entered his barge, by Hosea Sargent, now [1867] living at Cambridge, Massachusetts.

hulk. With these, his little brother, and four stout seamen for the oars,¹ he started upon his perilous voyage, anxiously watched by Yarnall and his companions.

> "A soul like his no danger fears;
> His pendant from the mast he tears,
> And in his gallant bosom bears,
>   To grace the bold *Niagara*.
> See! he quits the *Lawrence's* side,
> And trusts him to the foaming tide,
> Where thundering navies round him ride,
>   And flash their red artillery."—OLD SONG.

He stood upright in his boat, the pennant and the banner half folded around him, a mark for the anxious eyes of his own men and for the guns of the enemy.² The latter discovered the movement. Barclay, who was badly wounded, and whose flagship was almost dismantled, well knew that if Perry, who had fought the *Lawrence* so gallantly, should tread the quarter-deck of the fresh *Niagara* as commander, his squadron would be in great danger of defeat. He therefore ordered great and little guns to be brought to bear upon the frail but richly-laden vessel—laden with a hero of purest mould. Cannon-balls, grape, canister, and musket-shot were hurled in showers toward the little boat during the fifteen minutes that it was making its way from the *Lawrence* to the *Niagara*.³ The oars were splintered, bullets traversed the boat, and the crew were covered with spray caused by the falling of heavy round and grape-shot in the water near. Perry stood erect, unmindful of danger. His men entreated him to be seated, for his life at that critical moment seemed too precious to be needlessly exposed to peril. It was not foolhardiness nor thoughtlessness, but the innately brave spirit of the man, that kept him on his feet. At length, when his oarsmen threatened to cease labor if he did not sit down, he consented to do so. A few minutes later they were all climbing to the deck of the *Niagara*, entirely unharmed, and greeted with the loud cheers of the Americans, who had watched the movement

---

¹ One of these was Thomas Penny, who died in the Naval Asylum, near Philadelphia, in 1863, at the age of eighty-one years.

² Perry's portrait belonging to the city of New York, and hanging in the Governor's Room, from which ours on page 521 was copied, is what artists call a kit-kat, or three-quarters length. It was painted by John Wesley Jarvis, and represents Perry standing, with the banner floating like a huge scarf from his shoulders.

³ Among the survivors of the Battle of Lake Erie whom I have met was John Chapman, a resident of Hudson, Ohio, a small, energetic man, who related his past experience in an attractive, dramatic style. He was in the British fleet as gunner, maintop-man, and boarder in the *Queen Charlotte*, and claimed the distinction of having fired the first shot at the *Lawrence* from a 24-pounder. He also said that he aimed a shot at Commodore Perry when making his perilous passage from the *Lawrence* to the *Niagara*. Mr. Chapman was a native of England. He came from there in the transport *Bostwick* early in 1812, and landed at Quebec. From that city he went up the St. Lawrence in May, and took post in Fort George, on the Niagara River. He afterward went up to assist in the erection of Fort Erie. He was present at the surrender of Hull, and participated in the battle of Queenston Heights. In the summer of 1813 he was placed on board the schooner *Lady Prevost*, at Long Point, and arrived at Malden about three weeks before the battle of Lake Erie. He was with Proctor at the attack on Fort Stephenson. He was one of the survivors in the fatal ditch (see page 503), and escaped to the woods under cover of the darkness. On the return of Proctor to Malden he went on board the *Queen Charlotte*, and was with her in the battle. He was sent to Ohio with other prisoners, and was one of those who were held as hostages for the safety of the Irishmen under Scott who were sent to England, as mentioned on page 408. He was released on the 20th of October, at Cleveland. He went immediately to Hudson, a few miles distant, where he resided until his death in 1865. I am indebted to the Rev. T. B. Fairchild, of Hudson, for the substance of the above brief sketch of the public career of Mr. Chapman, and to the soldier himself for his likeness, taken in the spring of 1862.

with breathless anxiety. Perry was met at the gangway by the astonished Elliott. There stood the hero of the fight, blackened with the smoke of battle, but unharmed in person and unflinching in his determination to win victory—he whom the commander of the *Niagara* thought to be dead. There were hurried questions and answers. "How goes the day?" asked Elliott. "Bad enough," responded Perry; "why are the gun-boats so far astern?" "I'll bring them up," said Elliott. "Do so," responded Perry. Such is the reported substance of the brief conversation of the two commanders,[1] at the close of which Elliott pushed off in a small boat to hurry up the lagging vessels. Having given his orders to each to use sails and oars with the greatest vigor, he went on board the *Somers*, and behaved gallantly until the close of the action.

At a glance Perry comprehended the condition and capabilities of the *Niagara*. There had been few casualties on board of her, and she was in perfect order for conflict. He immediately ran up his pennant, displayed the blue banner, hoisted the signal for close action, and received quick responses and cheers from the whole squadron; hove to, altered the course of the vessel, set the proper sails, and bore down upon the British line, which lay half a mile distant. Meanwhile the gallant Yarnall, after consulting Lieutenant Forrest and Sailing-master Taylor, had struck the flag of the *Lawrence*, for she was utterly helpless, and humanity required that firing upon her should cease. As the starry flag trailed to the deck a triumphant shout went up from the British. It was heard by the wounded on the *Lawrence*. When informed of the cause, their hearts grew almost still, and in the anguish of chagrin they refused to be attended by the surgeon, and cried out, "Sink the ship! sink the ship! Let us all sink together!"[2] Noble fellows! they were worthy of their commander. In less than thirty minutes after they had offered themselves a willing sacrifice for the honor of their country's flag, they were made joyful by hearing the step and voice of their beloved commander again upon the deck of the *Lawrence*.

Perry's movement against the British line was successful. He broke it; passed at half pistol-shot distance between the *Lady Prevost*[3] and *Chippewa* on his larboard, and the *Detroit*, *Queen Charlotte*, and *Hunter* on his starboard, and poured in tremendous broadsides right and left from double-shotted guns. Ranging ahead of the vessels on his starboard, he rounded to and raked the *Detroit* and *Queen Charlotte*, which had got foul of each other.[4] Close and deadly was his fire upon them with great guns and musketry. Meanwhile, the *Lawrence* having drifted out of her place in the line, her position against the *Detroit* was taken by the *Caledonia*, Captain Turner; the latter's place in line, as opposed to the *Hunter*, was occupied by the *Trippe*, commanded by Lieutenant Holdup.[5] These gallant young officers had exchanged signals

---

[1] Mr. Hambleton, the purser of the *Lawrence*, has left on record an account of this interview between Perry and Elliott. "As Perry reached the deck of the *Niagara*," he says, "he was met at the gangway by Captain Elliott, who inquired how the day was going. Captain Perry replied, Badly; that he had lost almost all of his men, and that his ship was a wreck, and asked what the gun-boats were doing so far astern. Captain Elliott offered to go and bring them up; and, Captain Perry consenting, he sprang into the boat and went off on that duty.—Hambleton's *Journal*, cited by M'Kenzie.

[2] Oration by George H. Calvert, at Newport, Rhode Island, on the 10th of September, 1853, on the occasion of the celebration of the fortieth anniversary of the Battle of Lake Erie.

[3] Lieutenant Buchan, the commander of the *Lady Prevost*, was shot through the face by a musket-ball from Perry's marines. Perry saw him standing alone, leaning on the companion-way, his face resting on his hand, and looking with fixed gaze toward the *Niagara*. His companions, unable to endure the terrible fire, had all fled below. Perry immediately silenced the marines on the quarter-deck. He afterward learned that the strange conduct of Buchan was owing to sudden derangement caused by his wound. Poor fellow! he was a brave officer, and had distinguished himself under Nelson.

[4] The position of the *Detroit* and *Queen Charlotte* at this time may be seen by reference to II. and IV. in the diagram on page 526. In the same diagram the course of the *Niagara* in breaking the British line may be seen along the dotted line from 5 to 5.

[5] Thomas Holdup was a native of South Carolina, and was an inmate and pupil of the Orphan Asylum in Charleston. He became a *protegé* of General Stevens, of that city, who obtained a midshipman's warrant for him in 1809. He was on board the *John Adams*, at Brooklyn, in 1812,

to board the *Detroit*, when they saw the *Niagara* with the commodore's pennant bearing down to break the British line. Turner followed her closely with the *Caledonia;* and the freshened breeze having brought up the *Somers*, Mr. Almy,[1] the *Tigress*, Lieutenant Concklin,[2] and the *Porcupine*, Acting Master Senat,[3] the whole American squadron except the *Lawrence* was, for the first time, engaged in the conflict. The fight was terrible for a few minutes, and the combatants were completely enveloped in smoke.

Eight minutes after Perry dashed through the British line the colors of the *Detroit* were struck, and her example was speedily followed by all the other vessels of Barclay's squadron, excepting the *Little Belt* and *Chippewa* (I. and IV. in the annexed diagram), which attempted to escape to leeward. Champlin with the *Scorpion*, and Holdup with the *Trippe*, made chase after the fugitives, and both were overtaken and brought back to grace the triumph of the victor, the *Little Belt* by the former, and the *Chippewa* by the latter. It was in this chase that Champlin fired the last gun in that memorable battle. "So near were they to making their escape," says Champlin in a letter to the author, "that it was 10 o'clock in the evening before I came to an anchor under the stern of the *Lawrence* with the *Little Belt* in tow."

POSITION OF THE SQUADRONS AT THE CLOSE OF THE BATTLE.[4]

It was three o'clock in the afternoon when the flag of the *Detroit* was lowered. The roar of cannon ceased; and as the blue vapor of battle was borne away by the breeze, it was discovered that the two squadrons were intermingled.[5] The victory was complete. The flag of the *Lawrence* had indeed been struck to the enemy, but she had not been taken possession of. She was yet free, and, with a feeble shout

---

and, with others, volunteered for the lake service. He performed gallant service near Buffalo toward the close of the year, and was commissioned a lieutenant. In April, 1813, he went to Erie with men, and assisted in fitting out the squadron there. He fought his vessel bravely in the action of the 10th of September, and he and Champlin pursued the two fugitives of the British squadron. He was in service on the upper lakes the following year, and there was invited to the *Java* by Perry. He had married, and declined the offer of a good post on that vessel. He subsequently commanded several different vessels, and was promoted to master commandant in 1825. He was commissioned post-captain in 1836. He died suddenly while in command of the Washington Navy Yard, in January, 1841. His widow, who was a Miss Sage, died soon afterward. By act of the Legislature of South Carolina he assumed the name of his benefactor, with a promise that he should inherit his fortune. From that time [1815] he is known as Thomas Holdup Stevens. He was possessed of a high order of literary ability, and was beloved by all. His son, Thomas Holdup Stevens, behaved gallantly in the naval action off Hilton Head in the late civil war.

[1] Thomas C. Almy was a native of Rhode Island, of Quaker parentage. He became a sailor in early life, and at the age of twenty-one years he was commander of a ship. He was in the flotilla at Newport, went to Lake

ALMY'S SWORD.

Erie, and was efficient, useful, and brave there. He died at Erie in December, 1813, only three months after the battle that has made his name immortal. His disease was pneumonia.

The annexed engraving is a picture of the hilt of the sword awarded to Almy, and which was given to his next of kin. On one side of the blade are the words "Thomas C. Almy, Sailing-master commanding, Lake Erie, 10th September, 1813." On the other side the words "Altius ibunt qui ad summa nituntur," with a little view of ships-of-war.

[2] Augustus H. M. Concklin was a native of Virginia. He was appointed midshipman in 1809, and lieutenant in 1813. He followed Elliott to Erie. On a dark night in 1814 his vessel was captured by a party in boats off Fort Erie. He left the service in 1820, while stationed at Portsmouth, New Hampshire.

[3] George Senat was a native of New Orleans, of French extraction. He commenced active life as a sailor, but of his career previous to his joining the squadron at Erie nothing appears on record. He served on the upper lakes in 1814. On his return to Erie he became involved in a quarrel with Sailing-master M'Donald. A duel ensued, and young Senat was killed. They fought at what is now the corner of Third and Sassafras Streets, Erie.

[4] In this, as in the preceding diagrams, furnished by Commodore Champlin, the British vessels are designated by Roman numerals, and the American vessels by Arabic numerals. This diagram shows the relative position of the vessels of the two squadrons at the close of the battle. The respective numbers indicate the same vessels as in the other diagrams. [5] See the above diagram and note of explanation.

L L

that floated not far over the waters, her exhausted crew flung out the flag of their country from her mast-head.[1]

This triumph was a remarkable one in American and British history. Never before had an American fleet or squadron encountered an enemy in regular line of battle, and never before, since England created a navy, and boasted that

"Britannia rules the wave,"

had a whole British fleet or squadron been captured. It was a proud moment for Perry and his companions.

"As lifts the smoke, what tongue can fitly tell
The transports which those manly bosoms swell,
When Britain's ensign down the reeling mast
Sinks to proclaim the desperate struggle past!
Electric cheers along the shattered fleet,
With rapturous hail, her youthful hero greet;
Meek in his triumph, as in danger calm,
With reverent hands he takes the victor's palm;
His wreath of conquest on Faith's altar lays,[2]
To his brave comrades yields the meed of praise."—H. T. Tuckerman.

When Perry's eye perceived at a glance that victory was secure, he wrote, in pencil, on the back of an old letter, resting it upon his navy cap, that remarkable dispatch to General Harrison whose first clause has been so often quoted—

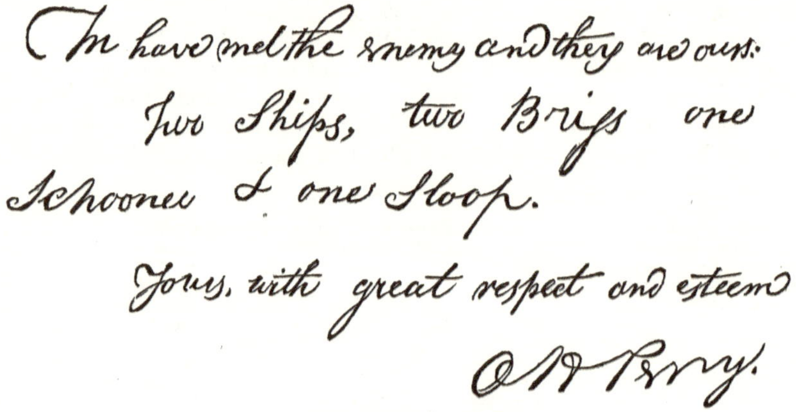

"We have met the enemy, and they are ours: two ships, two brigs, one schooner, and one sloop. Yours, with great respect and esteem, O. H. Perry."

We have met the enemy and they are ours:
Two Ships, two Brigs one
Schooner & one Sloop.
Yours, with great respect and esteem
O H Perry.

FAC-SIMILE OF PERRY'S DISPATCH.

A few minutes afterward, when, as Bancroft says, "a religious awe seemed to come over him at his wonderful preservation in the midst of great and long-continued danger,"[3] he wrote to the Secretary of the Navy as follows:

"U. S. Brig *Niagara*, off the Western Sister,[4] Head of Lake Erie, September 10, 1813, 4 P.M.

"Sir,—It has pleased the Almighty to give to the arms of the United States a signal victory over their enemies on this lake. The British squadron, consisting of two ships, two brigs, one schooner, and one sloop, have this moment surrendered to the force under my command after a sharp conflict.

"I have the honor to be, sir, very respectfully, your obedient servant,

"O. H. Perry.

"Honorable William Jones, Secretary of the Navy."

[1] "The shattered *Lawrence*," says Dr. Parsons, "lying to the windward, was once more able to hoist her flag, which was cheered by a few feeble voices on board, making a melancholy sound compared with the boisterous cheering that preceded the battle."—*Discourse*, page 13.

[2] See Perry's Dispatch to the Secretary of the Navy, printed above.

[3] *New York Ledger*.

[4] This is the most southwardly of three islands near the western end of Lake Erie, named respectively Eastern Sister, Middle Sister, and Western Sister, lying in a line from the southwest to the northeast. It was a little westward of the island named in the dispatch that the battle occurred.

These hurried but admirably-worded dispatches were sent by the same express to both Harrison and the Secretary of the Navy.[1] Then the ceremony of taking possession of the conquered vessels, and receiving the formal submission of the vanquished, was performed. Perry gave the signal to anchor, and started for his battered flag-ship, determined, on her deck, and in the presence of her surviving officers and crew, to receive the commanders of the captured squadron. "It was a time of conflicting emotions," says Dr. Parsons, "when he stepped upon deck. The battle was won and he was safe, but the deck was slippery with blood, and strewn with the bodies of twenty officers and men, seven of whom had sat at table with us at our last meal, and the ship resounded every where with the groans of the wounded. Those of us who were spared and able to walk met him at the gangway to welcome him on board, but the salutation was a silent one on both sides; not a word could find utterance."[2]

The next movement in the solemn drama was the reception of the British officers, one from each of the captured vessels. Perry stood on the after-part of the deck, and his sad visitors were compelled to pick their way to him among the slain. He received them with solemn dignity and unaffected kindness. As they presented their swords, with the hilts toward the victor, he spoke in a low but firm tone, without the betrayal of the least exultation, and requested them to retain their weapons. He inquired, with real concern, about Commodore Barclay and his fellow-sufferers from severe wounds; and he made every captive feel, at that sad and solemn moment, the thrill of pleasure excited by the conduct of a Christian gentleman in the moment of the adversity of the recipient of his kindness.

> "A chastened rapture, Perry, fills thy breast;
> Thy sacred tear embalms the heroes slain;
> The gem of pity shines in glory's crest
> More brilliant than the diamond wreath of fame."

When this sad ceremony was over, the conqueror, exhausted by the day's work upon which he had entered with fever-enfeebled body, lay down upon the deck in the midst of his dead companions, and, surrounded by prisoners, and with his hands folded over his breast, and his drawn sword held in one of them, he slept as sweetly as a wearied child.[3]

There was yet another sad service to be performed. The dead of the two squadrons were yet unburied. When twilight—the rich, glowing twilight at the end of a gorgeous September day—lay upon the bosom of the lake like a luminous, deepening mist, the bodies of all the slain, excepting those of the officers, wrapped in rude shrouds, and with a cannon-ball at the feet of each, were dropped, one by one, into the bosom of the clear lake, at the close of the beautiful and impressive burial service of the Anglican Church.

> "'Neath the dark waves of Erie now slumber the brave,
> In the bed of its waters forever they rest;
> The flag of their glory floats over their grave;
> The souls of the heroes in memory are blessed."—W. B. TAPPAN.

---

[1] The gallant Lieutenant Dulaney Forrest was Perry's chosen courier. He was a native of the District of Columbia, and had been in the service since 1809, when he was appointed midshipman. He was with Bainbridge when the *Constitution* captured the *Java*. He was acting lieutenant on board Perry's flag-ship, and was chief signal officer. His conduct was brave, and he was greatly beloved by his companions. He bore to Washington not only the dispatches of his commander, but the flags captured from the British. Forrest also took with him the blue banner with the words of Lawrence, mentioned on page 520. Forrest accompanied Perry to the Mediterranean in the *Java*. He was commissioned a lieutenant at that time. He died of fever in 1825.

Colonel Peter Force, of Washington City, has a piece of every flag captured in this battle, and of nearly every trophy-flag of the war. They were all taken to Washington, where, in course of time, through neglect, they fell into decay. The pieces in the possession of Mr. Force are carefully preserved in a scrap-book, with the place and date of their capture recorded, and make an interesting collection of bits of bunting.

The intelligence of the victory on Lake Erie was carried to Pennsylvania from Detroit by Samuel Doclue, Samuel Burnett, and Cyrus Bosworth. The first was a mail-carrier from Detroit to Cleveland; the second from Cleveland to Warren, Ohio, and the third from Warren to Pittsburg. They were all three living at the time of the inauguration of Perry's statue at Cleveland in September, 1860. Mr. Bosworth participated in that celebration.

[2] *Discourse*, page 14.   [3] Calvert's *Oration*, page 21.

| Burial of Officers on the Shore. | Sad Effects of the Battle. | "Ill luck" of the British. |

^a September 11, 1813. The moon soon spread her silver sheen over their common grave, and all but the suffering wounded slumbered until the dawn.^a

The two squadrons weighed anchor at nine o'clock and sailed into Put-in-Bay Harbor, and there, twenty-four hours afterward, on the margin of South Bass Island,

THE BURIAL-PLACE.

from which, on the right, may be seen the channel leading out toward Canada, and on the left the open way toward Detroit, where now willow, hickory, and maple-trees cast a pleasant shade in summer, three American and three British officers[1] were buried^b with the same solemn funeral rites, in the presence of their respective countrymen.[2]

^b September 12.

The light of the morning of the 11th revealed sad sights to the eyes of the belligerents. Vessels of both squadrons were dreadfully shattered, especially the two flag-ships. Sixty-eight persons had been killed and one hundred and ninety wounded during the three hours that the battle lasted. Of these, the Americans lost one hundred and twenty-three, twenty-seven of whom were killed; the British lost one hundred and thirty-five, forty-one of whom were killed.[3] Barclay, of the *Detroit* (the British commander), who had lost an arm at Trafalgar, was first wounded in the thigh, and then so severely injured in the shoulder as to deprive him of the use of the other arm. Finnis, of the *Queen Charlotte*, the second in command, was mortally wounded, and died that evening. Both were gallant men; and justice to all demands the acknowledgment that the Americans and British carried on that terrible conflict with the greatest courage, fortitude, and skill. It is also just to say that the British experienced what is called "ill luck" from the beginning. First, the wind suddenly turned in favor of the Americans at the commencement of the action, giving them the weather-gage; then the two principal British commanders were struck down early in the action; then the rudder of the *Lady Prevost* was disabled, which caused her to drift out of the line; the entanglement of the *Detroit* and *Queen Charlotte* gave the *Niagara*, under Perry, an opportunity to rake them severely; and, lastly, the men of the British squadron had not, with the exception of those from the Royal Navy, received the training with guns

---

[1] These were Lieutenant Brooks and Midshipmen Lunt and Clarke, of the American service, and Captain Finnis and Lieutenants Stokoe and Garland, of the British service. The view here given of the burial-place of these officers I copied, by permission, from one of the paintings of Miss C. L. Ransom, already mentioned.

[2] Samuel R. Brown, who arrived at Put-in-Bay Island on the evening of the 9th, and from the head of it was a witness of the battle at about ten miles distant, was present at the burial. "An opening on the margin of the bay," he says, "was selected for the interment of the bodies. The crews of both fleets attended. The weather was fine; the elements seemed to participate in the solemnities of the day, for every breeze was hushed, and not a wave ruffled the surface of the water. The procession of boats—the neat appearance of the officers and men—the music—the slow and regulated motion of the oars, striking in exact time with the notes of the solemn dirge—the mournful waving of the flags—the sound of the minute-guns from the different ships in the harbor—the wild and solitary aspect of the place—the stillness of nature—gave to the scene an air of melancholy grandeur better felt than described. All acknowledged its influence, all were sensibly affected."—*Views on Lake Erie*, printed in Albany in 1814.

[3] The American loss was distributed as follows: On the *Lawrence*, 83; *Niagara*, 27; *Caledonia*, 3; *Somers*, 2; *Ariel*, 4; *Trippe* and *Scorpion*, 2 each. Besides the officers mentioned in Note 1, above, the British lost in wounded Midshipman Foster, of the *Queen Charlotte*; Lieutenant Commanding Buchan and First Lieutenant Roulette, of the *Lady Prevost*; Lieutenant Commandant Brignall and Master's Mate Gateshill, of the *Hunter*; Master's Mate Campbell, commanding the *Chippewa*; and Purser Hoffmeister, of the *Detroit*.

Doctor Horseley, the surgeon of the squadron, being ill, the duties devolved wholly upon his young assistant, Doctor Usher Parsons, then only twenty-five years of age. During the action he removed six legs, which were nearly divided by cannon-balls. On the morning of the 11th he went on board the *Niagara* to attend to her wounded, and then those of the other vessels requiring surgical attention were sent to the *Lawrence*. The skill of Doctor Parsons is attested by the fact that of the whole ninety-six wounded only three died. He modestly attributed the result to fresh air, good spirits caused by the victory, and the "devoted attention of the commodore."

Importance of Perry's Victory.   *Its Effects.*   *How his Cannon were afterward used.*

that most of the Americans had just experienced, for they came out of port the morning of the battle.¹

Perry's victory proved to be one of the most important events of the war. At that moment two armies, one on the north and the other on the south of the warring squadrons, were waiting for the result most anxiously. Should the victory remain with the British, Proctor and Tecumtha were ready at Malden, with their motley army five thousand strong, to rush forward and lay waste the entire frontier. Should the victory rest with the Americans, Harrison, with his army in the vicinity of Sandusky Bay, was prepared to press forward by land or water for the seizure of Malden and Detroit, the recovery of Michigan, and the invasion of Canada. All along the borders of the lake within sound of the cannon in the battle (and they were heard from Cleveland to Malden²), women with terrified children, and decrepit old men, sat listening with the deepest anxiety; for they knew not but with the setting sun they would be compelled to flee to the interior, to escape the fangs of the red blood-hounds who were ready to be let loose upon helpless innocency by the approved servants of a government that boasted of its civilization and Christianity. Happily for America—happily for the fair fame of Great Britain—happily for the cause of humanity—the victory was left with the Americans, and the savage allies of the British were not allowed to repeat the tragedies in which they had already been permitted to engage. Joy spread over the northwestern frontier as the glad tidings went from lip to lip. That whole region was instantly relieved of the most gloomy forebodings of coming evil. That victory led to the destruction of the Indian confederacy, and wiped out the stigma of the surrender at Detroit thirteen months before. It opened the way for Harrison's army to repossess the territory then surrendered, and to penetrate Canada. It was speedily followed by the overthrow of British power in the Canadian peninsula and the country bordering on the upper lakes, and the absolute security forever of the whole northwestern frontier from British invasion and Indian depredations. From that moment no one doubted the ability of the Americans to maintain the mastery of our great inland seas, and the faith of the people in this ability was well expressed by a poet of the time, who concluded an epic with the following lines:

> "And though Britons may brag of their ruling the ocean,
> And that sort of thing—by the Lord I've a notion—
> I'll bet all I'm worth—who takes it?—who takes?—
> Though they're lords of the *sea*, we'll be lords of the *lakes*."³

The effect of this victory upon the whole country was electric and amazingly in-

---

¹ The great guns used by Perry, and those captured by him from the British, remained in the United States Naval Depôt at Erie until the autumn of 1825, when they were transferred to the Naval Station at Brooklyn. They were about to be removed through the agency of Dows, Cary, and Meech, who had prepared a line of boats for the just completed Erie Canal. The happy thought occurred to some one that these cannon might be used for telegraphic purposes in connection with the celebration of the first opening of the canal. They were accordingly placed at intervals of about ten miles along the whole line of the canal. When the first fleet of boats left Buffalo on that occasion, the fact was announced to the citizens of New York in one hour and twenty minutes by the serial discharges of these cannon. This announcement, literally conveyed in "thunder-tones" from the lake to the sea-board, was responded to in like manner and in the same space of time.—Statement of Orlando Allen to the Buffalo Historical Society, April, 1863.

The authorities consulted in the preparation of the foregoing account of the Battle of Lake Erie are the official dispatches of Perry and Barclay; Niles's Register; The War; Port Folio; Analectic Magazine; Political Register; M'Kenzie's Life of Perry; Life of Elliott, by a citizen of New York; Cooper's Naval History; Discourses by Parsons, Burgess, and Calvert; oral and written statements communicated to the author by the survivors; Brown's *Views on Lake Erie*, and Log-book of the *Lawrence*, kept by Sailing-master Taylor.

² I was informed by Captain Levi Johnson, whom I met at Cleveland in the autumn of 1860, that he and others were engaged in the last work upon the new court-house, which stood in front of the present First Presbyterian Church, on the day of the battle. They thought they heard thunder, but, seeing no clouds, concluded that the two squadrons had met. He and several others went down to the lake bank, near the present residence of Mr. Whittaker, on Water Street. Nearly all the villagers assembled there, numbering about thirty. They waited until the firing ceased. Although the distance in a straight line was full seventy miles, they could easily distinguish the sounds of the heavier and lighter guns. The last five reports were from the heavy guns. Knowing that the Americans had the heaviest ordnance, they concluded that victory remained with them, and with that conviction they gave three cheers for Perry. Miss Reynolds, sister of the venerable Robert Reynolds, of the British army, whom I also visited in the autumn of 1860, told me that she listened to the firing during the whole battle. The distance was less than forty miles.

A letter dated at Erie, September 24, 1813, says that a gentleman from the New York state line heard at his house the cannonading on the lake *one hundred and sixty miles distant!* It was heard at Erie, and at first was supposed to be distant thunder.

³ *Analectic Magazine*, iii., 84.

spiriting. There had been a prevailing apprehension that the failures of 1812 were to be repeated in 1813. This victory dissipated those forebodings, and kindled hope and joy all over the land.

"O'er the mountains the sun of our fame was declining,
    And on Thetis' billowy breast
The cold orb had reposed, all his splendor resigning,
    Bedimmed by the mists of the West.
The prospect that rose to the patriot's sight
    Was cheerless, and hopeless, and dreary;
But a bolt burst the cloud, and illumined the night
    That enveloped the waters of Erie."—OLD SONG.

It is difficult at this time to imagine the exultation then felt and exhibited every where. Illuminations,[1] bonfires, salvos of artillery, public dinners, orations, and songs were the visible indications of the popular satisfaction in almost every city, village, and hamlet within the bounds of the republic. The newspapers teemed with eulogies of the victor and his companions, and the pulpit and rostrum were resonant with words of thanksgiving and praise. The lyre[2] and the pencil[3] made many con-

---

[1] The City Hall and other buildings in New York were splendidly illuminated on the evening of Saturday, October 23, 1813. There was a band of music in the gallery of the portico, and transparencies were exhibited showing naval battles; also the words of Lawrence, "DON'T GIVE UP THE SHIP," and those of Perry's dispatch, "WE HAVE MET THE ENEMY, AND THEY ARE OURS." The last-named transparency was exhibited at the theatre, with a picture of the fight between the *Hornet* and *Peacock*.

[2] Many songs were written and sung in commemoration of Perry's victory. One of the most popular of these was *American Perry*, which commences thus:

"Bold Barclay one day to Proctor did say,
    I'm tired of Jamaica and Cherry;
So let us go down to that new floating town,
    And get some American Perry.*
        Oh, cheap American Perry!
        Most pleasant American Perry!
We need only all bear down, knock, and call,
    And we'll have the American Perry."

[3] Among the caricatures of the day was one by Charles, of Philadelphia, representing John Bull, in the person of the king, seated, with his hand pressed upon his stomach, indicating pain, which the fresh juice of the pear, called perry,

will produce. *Queen Charlotte*, the king's wife (a fair likeness of whom is given), enters with a bottle labeled PERRY, out of which the cork has flown, and in the foam is seen the names of the vessels composing the American squadron. She says, "Johnny, won't you have some more Perry?" John Bull replies, while writhing in pain produced by perry, "Oh! Perry!!! Curse that Perry! One disaster after another—I have not half recovered of the bloody nose I got at the Boxing-match." This last expression refers to the capture of the *Boxer* by the American schooner *Enterprise*. This caricature is entitled "*Queen Charlotte and Johnny Bull got their dose of Perry.*" This will be better per-

* See the next note on this page.

tributions to the popular demonstrations of joy, and public bodies testified their gratitude by appropriate acts. The Legislature of Pennsylvania voted thanks and a gold medal to Perry; also thanks and a silver medal to every man engaged in the battle.[1]

THE PERRY MEDAL.

The corporate authorities of New York ordered the illumination of the City Hall in honor of the victory;[2] and the National Congress voted thanks and a gold medal to both Perry and Elliott, to be adorned with appropriate devices,[3] and silver ones, with

THE ELLIOTT MEDAL.

the same emblems, to the nearest male relatives of Brooks, Lamb, Clarke, and Claxton, who were slain. Three months' extra pay was also voted for each of the commissioned officers of the navy and army who served in the battle, and a sword to

---

ceived by remembering that one of the principal vessels of the British squadron was named the *Queen Charlotte*, in honor of the royal consort. In a ballad of the day occurs the following lines:

"On Erie's wave, while Barclay brave,
 With *Charlotte* making merry,
He chanced to take the belly-ache,
 We drenched him so with *Perry*."

[1] *The War*, page 127.   [2] See note 1, page 534.
[3] On one side of Perry's medal is a bust of the commodore, surrounded by the following words: "OLIVERUS H. PERRY. PRINCEPS STAGNO ERIENSE. CLASSAM TOTAM CONTUDIT." On the reverse a squadron of vessels closely engaged, and the legend "VIAM INVENIT VIRTUS AUT FACIT." Exergue: "INTER CLASS. AMERI. ET BRIT. DIE X. SEP. MDCCCXIII."
On one side of Elliott's medal is a bust of the commander, and the words "JESSE D. ELLIOTT. NIL ACTUM REPUTANS SI QUID. SUPRESSET AGENDUM." On the reverse a squadron engaged, and the legend "VIAM INVENIT VIRTUS AUT FACIT." The exergue the same as on Perry's.

each of the midshipmen and sailing-masters "who so nobly distinguished themselves on that memorable occasion."¹ In after years, when the dead body of Perry was buried in the soil of his native state, her Legislature caused a monument to be erected to his memory,² for she claimed, with much justice, a large share of the glory of the battle of Lake Erie for her sons.³

The effect of this victory was deeply impressive on the British mind, and the newspapers in the provinces and the mother country indulged in lamentations over the want of vigor in the prosecution of the war manifested by the ministry. "We have been conquered on Lake Erie," said a Halifax paper,[a] "and so we shall be on every other lake, if we take as little care to protect them. Their success is less owing to their prowess than to our neglect." A London paper consoled the people by saying,[b] "It may, however, serve to diminish our vexation at the occurrence to learn that the flotilla in question was not any branch of the British Navy. . . . . It was not the Royal Navy, but a local force—a kind of mercantile military." Others, conscious of the inability of the British force in Canada to cope with the Americans, urged the necessity of extending the alliance with the Indians. "We dare assert," said a writer in one of the leading British Reviews,⁴ "and recent events have gone far in establishing the truth of the proposition, that the Canadas can not be effectually and durably defended without the friendship of the Indians, and command of the lakes and the River St. Lawrence." He urged his countrymen to consider the interests of the Indians as their own; "for men," he said, "whose very name is so very formidable to an American, and whose friendship has recently been shown to be of such great importance to *us*, we can not do too much."

[a] October, 1813.
[b] November.

The name of Perry is cherished with increasing reverence by successive generations; and the vast population that now swarm along the southern borders of Lake Erie regard the battle that has made its name immortal in history as a classical possession of rare value. Only a few weeks after the victory, Washington Irving, in a chaste biographical sketch of Commodore Perry,⁵ said: "The last roar of cannon that died along her shores was the expiring note of British domination. Those vast internal seas will perhaps never again be the separating space between contending nations, but will be embosomed within a mighty empire;⁶ and this victory, which decided their fate, will stand unrivaled and alone, deriving lustre and perpetuity from its singleness. In future times, when the shores of Erie shall hum with busy population; when towns and cities shall brighten where now extend the dark and tangled forests; when ports shall spread their arms, and lofty barks shall ride where now the canoe is fastened to the stake; when the present age shall have grown into venerable antiquity, and the mists of fable begin to gather round its history, then will the inhabitants look back to this battle we record as one of the romantic achievements of the days of yore. It will stand first on the page of their local legends and in the marvelous tales of the borders."

This prophecy of the beloved Irving has been fulfilled. The archipelago that embraces Put-in-Bay has become a classic region. At Erie, and Cleveland, and Sandusky, and Toledo, where the Indian then "fastened his canoe to a stake," "ports

---

¹ We have observed in Note 2, page 519, that Mr. Hambleton, purser of the *Lawrence*, was chosen prize agent. A board of officers from Lake Ontario, assisted by Henry Eckford, naval constructor, prized the captured squadron at $225,000. Commodore Chauncey, the commander-in-chief on the lakes, received one twentieth of the whole sum, or $12,750. Perry and Elliott each drew $7140. The Congress voted Perry $5000 in addition. Each commander of a gun-boat, sailing-master, lieutenant, and captain of marines, received $2295; each midshipman, $811; each petty officer, $447; and each marine and sailor, $209.—Miss Laura G. Sanford's *History of Erie*, page 273.   ² See page 521.

³ Perry took with him from Rhode Island, as we have seen (page 509), a large number of men and officers. It was by them chiefly that the vessels built at Erie were constructed. The commodore and three of his commanders—Champlin, Almy, and Turner, and five other officers—Taylor, Brownell, Breese, Dunham, and Alexander Perry, were from Rhode Island. In the fight forty-seven of the fifty-five guns of the squadron were commanded by Rhode Islanders.

⁴ *New Quarterly Review and British Colonial Register*, No. 4; S. M. Richardson, Cornhill, London.

⁵ *Analectic Magazine*, December, 1813.

⁶ He had just heard of Harrison's victorious invasion of Canada, and it was believed at that time that the upper province would assuredly become a portion of the United States.

spread their arms;" and every year the anniversary of the battle is somewhere celebrated with appropriate ceremonies. Already the corner-stone of a monumental shaft in commemoration of the battle has been laid upon Perry's Look-out on Gibraltar Island;[1] and in the beautiful city of Cleveland—an insignificant hamlet on the bleak lake shore in 1813, now [1867] a mart of commerce with about fifty thousand inhabitants—a noble statue of Perry, wrought of the purest Parian marble by a resident artist, has been erected by the city authorities.[2]

I was present, as an invited guest, at the inauguration of that statue of Perry on the 10th of September, 1860. Never will the impressive spectacles of that day, and the influence of the associations connected with them, be effaced from memory. The journey thither, the mementoes of history seen on the way, and the meeting of scores of veterans of the War of 1812 at the great gathering, made a deep impression on the mind. I left my home on the Hudson, with my family, on the morning of the 6th,[a] with the intention of stopping at Erie (where a portion of Perry's squadron was built) on my way to Cleveland. It was a day like one in midsummer—sultry and showery; yet in the railway carriage, whose steeds never grow weary, and wherein shelter from sun and rain are ever afforded, we traversed during the day, with very little fatigue or inconvenience, more than the entire length of the State of New York, through the Hudson and Mohawk valleys and the great levels westward, to Buffalo, a distance of three hundred and seventy miles. There I left my family in charge of the veteran Captain Champlin, one of the heroes of the fight, to accompany him by water to Cleveland; and early the next morning[b] I pushed on by railway to Erie, where I had the good fortune to meet Captain W. W. Dobbins, son of the gallant officer of that name already mentioned. He kindly accompanied me to the places of interest about Erie— the site of Fort Presqu' Isle[3]—of Wayne's block-house—of Fort Wayne, on Garrison Hill, by the light-house[4]—of the navy yard at the mouth of Cascade Creek,[5] and the old tavern where Perry made his head-quarters before and after the battle. When, at the close of the day, we returned to the village, heavy black clouds were brooding over the lake in the direction of the great conflict, and the deep bellowing of the distant thunder gave a vivid idea of the tumult of the battle heard from that very spot almost half a century before. I had completed my sketches and observations, and I spent the evening pleasantly and profitably with Captain Dobbins and his venerable mother, to whom I am indebted for kind courtesies and valuable information.[6] At almost two o'clock in the morning[c] I left Erie in the railway cars for Cleveland, just after a heavy thunder-shower had passed over that region, making the night intensely dark, and drenching the country.

[a September, 1860.]
[b September 7.]
[c September 8.]

We arrived at Cleveland at six o'clock in the morning. Heavy mists were scurrying over the lake upon the wings of fitful gusts, and dashes of rain came down frequently like sudden shower-baths. For almost three hours I waited at the wharf where the passengers on the boat from Buffalo were to land. She was *The Western Metropolis*—a magnificent vessel—one of the finest ever built on the lakes. All night

---

[1] See picture on page 518. On the 4th of July, 1852, the national anniversary was celebrated on Put-in-Bay Island by five companies of Ohio volunteer militia. Their encampment was the first ever seen there since Harrison left it with his troops in the autumn of 1813. At that time it was agreed to take measures for erecting a monument in commemoration of the victory, and *The Battle of Lake Erie Monument Association was formed*. A Constitution was adopted, and General Lewis Cass, of Detroit, was appointed provisional president of the association. J. G. Camp, E. Cooke, E. Bill, A. P. Edwards, and J. A. Harris, were appointed a provisional executive committee.

[2] The project of erecting a statue of Perry at Cleveland originated with the Hon. Harvey Rice, of that city, who, as member of the Common Council, brought the subject before that body in June, 1857, in a series of resolutions. A committee was appointed to take the matter in hand, composed of Harvey Rice, O. M. Oviatt, J. M. Coffinberry, J. Kirkpatrick, and C. D. Williams. They contracted with T. Jones and Sons, of Cleveland, to erect a monument surmounted by a statue of Perry, for the sum of eight thousand dollars. The designs of monument and statue were made by William Walcutt, the sculptor, of Cleveland, and the figures were executed by him.

[3] See page 511. [4] See note 1, page 510. [5] See page 511.

[6] Mrs. Dobbins is of English and Irish extraction, and was married to Mr. Dobbins at Cannonsburg, Pennsylvania, early in the year 1800, by whom she had ten children.

long she had battled with the storm, yet she was so stanch that her passengers had slept securely and soundly. A fine state-room had been assigned to Captain Champlin. Among the survivors of the war who accompanied him was Captain Asel Wilkinson, of Colden, Erie County, New York, who was the pilot of the *Ariel*—a tall, slender man, seventy-two years of age. He stood at the helm of his vessel all through the battle of the 10th of September. His cartridge-box was shot from his side by a cannon-ball, and the thunder of the great guns brought the blood from his ears and nose, and permanently impaired his hearing. I received many reminiscences of the fight from his lips during a brief hour that I spent with him. His vigor of mind and body gave promise of years of future usefulness, but his days were nearly numbered. On the 4th of July, 1861, he was in Buffalo with his wife to participate in the celebration of the day. When they were passing the corner of Pearl and Mohawk Streets he suddenly fell to the pavement and expired.

Asel Wilkinson

In the midst of a furious thunder-storm we rode to the residence of a gentleman on Euclid Street, to the hospitalities of which we had been invited, and there we found a pleasant home during our brief sojourn in Cleveland. It was the last day of the week. On Monday the appointed ceremonies were to be performed, and visitors were pouring into the "Forest City" by thousands from every direction. That evening the hotels and large numbers of private houses were filled with guests. Mr. Bancroft (the historian), who was one of the chosen orators for the occasion, had arrived; also a large delegation from Rhode Island, including Governor Sprague, Mr. Bartlett, the Secretary of State, Dr. Parsons, Bishop Clarke, and Captain Thomas Brownell, who was the acting sailing-master of the *Ariel* in the battle. Members of the Perry family and scores of the survivors of the war were also there, and the bright and beautiful Sabbath found Cleveland full of strangers.

It was indeed a bright and beautiful Sabbath. The storm-clouds were gone, and the first cool breath of autumn came from the lake and gave warning of the approaching season of hoar-frost. At an early hour Euclid Street — magnificent Euclid Street — was full of animation. Crowds were making their way to "Camp Perry," on the county fair-grounds, the head-quarters of the military, who were under the command of Brigadier General J. W. Fitch. In the spacious marquee of that officer we met, just before the hour for morning religious services (in which Bishop Clarke led), most of the Rhode Island delegation, Governor Dennison, of Ohio, and his staff, and Benjamin Fleming, of Erie, a lively little man, then seventy-eight years of age, who was a maintopman in the *Niagara* during the battle. He was yet living in 1863, and was one of three survivors of the battle who are

BENJAMIN FLEMING.

residents of Erie.[1] Fleming was a native of Delaware.[2] He was dressed in full sail-

---

[1] The other two were John Murray, a marine from Pennsylvania, aged about seventy-three, and Jesse Wall, a colored man, aged about seventy-four years, who was a fifer on board the *Niagara*.

[2] Benjamin Fleming was born in Lewiston, Delaware, on the 20th of July, 1782. He entered the naval service on

or's costume, and on his right breast, in the form of a shield, on which was inscribed his name and the occasion, was the silver medal presented by the State of Pennsylvania.[1]

There we also met Dr. Nathan Eastman, of Medina, Ohio, who, as volunteer surgeon, assisted in dressing the wounds of those injured in the battle who were taken to the marine hospital at Erie. He was afterward appointed assistant surgeon, and spent the dreary winter of 1813–14 in that capacity on board the prize-ships *Detroit* and *Queen Charlotte*,

PERRY'S LANTERN.

for some soldiers were on those vessels and upon Put-in-Bay Island. There was also Hosea Sargent, of Cambridge, Massachusetts, a survivor of the *Lawrence*, who handed Perry his flag as he was leaving his vessel for the *Niagara*. A mute relic of the battle was also on the ground. It was Perry's signal lantern, and belonged to Lieutenant Selden, of the "Wayne Guards" of Erie, who were present. It was made of tin, with windows of scraped horn, and had a venerable appearance.

Monday dawned gloomily. The sky was lowering with heavy clouds, the temperature was chilling, and as the time approached for the commencement of the public ceremonies there were indications of early rain. But these hindered nothing. At an early hour I went to the City Hall, the head-quarters of the "soldiers of 1812," and assisted in the interesting task of making a register of the names and ages of those who were present, about three hundred in number.[2] The air was full of martial music, the streets and buildings were gay with banners, and as the appointed time for uncovering the statue drew near, the public square of ten acres, in the centre of which it stood, began to fill with people. I had made my way with difficulty through the crowd from the old soldiers' head-quarters to the stage erected for the conductors of the pageant and invited guests. Mr. Bancroft soon arrived, alone, but was followed almost immediately by the mayor of the city, the committee of arrangements, Dr. Parsons (the associate orator), the Perry family, and other invited guests. Very soon the immense military and civic procession came filing into the square in gay and sombre costumes, accompanied by a miniature brig *Lawrence*, on wheels, drawn by four horses. The inclosure was filled with the living sea, and broad Ontario and Superior Streets were crowded with people as far as the eye could reach. "All Cleveland is out!" exclaimed a gentleman at my elbow. "All creation, you had better say," responded another. It was estimated that fifty thousand strangers were present.

The ceremonies before the statue were opened by prayer from the lips of the Reverend Dr. Perry, of Natchez, Mississippi. Then Mr. Walcutt, the sculptor, unveiled the statue. There it stood, upon a green mound, surrounded by an iron railing, imposing, beautiful, and remarkable because of its extreme whiteness.[3] Tens of thousands of voices sent up loud cheers as that chaste work of art was clearly revealed, for, just as the covering was removed, rays of sunlight, that had struggled through

---

[1] board the frigate *Essex* in 1811, and at New York volunteered for the lake service. He was with Elliott at the capture of the *Caledonia* and *Adams*. See list of names in Note 5, page 385. He had lived in Erie ever since the war. Two of his sons were in a Pennsylvania regiment during the late Civil War, and both were wounded in the battles before Richmond. See page 535.

[2] Among these were Benjamin Le Reaux, aged seventy-seven years. He was from La Salle City, Illinois. He was a small, lively, sparkling-faced man, and was dressed in the same military suit of gray in which, as orderly sergeant, he fought under General Scott in the battle of Niagara, or Lundy's Lane. He was in Jesup's command. A history of that gray uniform will be given hereafter. Mr. Le Reaux's father was a Frenchman, and served as captain under Lafayette.

[3] The monument and statue, represented on the following page, present to the eye one of the most chaste memorials of greatness to be found in the country. Indeed, it is believed that nothing equals it. The pedestal is of Rhode Island granite, twelve feet in height, on one side of which is sculptured, in low relief, the scene of Perry's passage from the *Lawrence* to the *Niagara*. On one side of it is a small statue of a *Sailor-boy*, bareheaded, and on the other one of a *Midshipman*, with his cap on, in the attitude of listening. The statue is of Parian marble, and remarkable for its purity. It is eight feet in height, but at the altitude of the top of the pedestal or monument it appears life-size. The entire height of the monument, including the base, is twenty-five feet.

PERRY'S STATUE.

the clouds, fell full upon it. Mr. Walcutt made a brief address, which was responded to by Mayor Senter. Then followed Mr. Bancroft's oration,[1] and an historical discourse by Dr. Parsons.[2] Oliver Hazard Perry, the only surviving son of the commodore, addressed the people briefly, when the masonic ceremonies of dedication were performed. The proceedings closed with a song, written by E. G. Knowlton, of Cleveland, and sung by Ossian E. Dodge.

I had been invited to dine with the veterans of 1812, and when the ceremonies before the statue were ended, I hastened from the crowded city to the old soldiers' banquet-hall in the railway buildings on the margin of the lake. The scene was a most interesting and remarkable one. Almost three hundred survivors of the war, who had been participants in its military events, were seated at the table, with their commander for the day (General J. M. Hughes), and Deacon Benjamin Rouse, the president of the Old Soldiers' Association, at their head. There were very few among them of feeble step. Upon every head not disfigured by a wig lay the snows that never melt. It was a dinner-party, I venture to say, that has no parallel in history. The ages of the guests (excepting a few younger men, like myself, who were permitted by courtesy to be present) ranged from *fifty-seven* to *ninety* years.[3] The average was about *seventy* years; and the aggregate age of the company was about twenty thousand years!

When I left the banquet-hall a spectacle of rare beauty met the eye. The high banks of the lake in front of the city were covered with men, women, and children, thousands in number, who had come out to be witnesses of a promised sham-fight on the lake, in nearly exact imitation of the real one forty-seven years before. I climbed the steep bank, up a long flight of stairs at the foot of Warren Street, to a good position for observation, and found myself by the side of Mr. Fleming, the jolly little maintop-man of the *Niagara*, with his sailor's dress and silver medal. The clouds had dispersed, and the afternoon was almost as bright and serene as when the old battle was waged. One by one the vessels representing the belligerent squadrons of Perry and Barclay went out from the mouth of the Cuyahoga, not "with a light breeze" alone, but by the more certain power of steam-tugs. Captain Champlin commanded the mock-American squadron, and Mr. Chapman[4] that of the mock-British.

---

[1] Immediately after the conclusion of Mr. Bancroft's address, he was presented with a cane, made of the timber of the *Lawrence*, by the "Wayne Guards," of Erie. The head is of gold, and the ferule a spike from the *Lawrence*.

[2] During the delivery of Dr. Parsons's discourse, an intelligent old man, named Quinn, from Pittsburg, Pennsylvania, came upon the stand, and reported himself as the man who made the cordage used in rigging the vessels of Perry's squadron. He had with him, in a box, the identical tools that were used in that service.

[3] The oldest man among them was a colored soldier named Abraham Chase. He was ninety. Two of them (S. F. Whitney and Richard M'Cready) were only fifty-seven. They were boys in the service.   [4] See page 527.

A singular coincidence occurred. As in the real battle, so in this, there was a light breeze at first, which freshened before the close. It was an exciting scene, and little Fleming fairly danced with exhilaration as he observed the flashes—the booming of great guns—the fleet enveloped in smoke—Champlin, like Perry, leaving the *Lawrence* and going to the *Niagara*, and the latter sweeping down, breaking the Chapman-Barclay's line and winning victory. With this extraordinary pageant closed the public ceremonies of the day.[1]

On the following day, accompanied by the Rev. T. B. Fairchild, of Hudson, Ohio, I visited several persons and places in Cleveland connected with its history. Among the former were Judge Barr, to whose kind courtesy, through the medium of letters, I was under many obligations, and the widow of Dr. David Long, a daughter of John Wadsworth, one of the earliest settlers in that region. She was a resident of Cleveland at the time of the battle.[2] When I visited her[a] she and Levi Johnson and his wife were the only survivors of the inhabitants of that place in 1813. At the time of Hull's surrender there was great alarm at Cleveland, and Mrs. Long was the only woman who remained. Her husband would not desert the sick there, and she would not desert her husband. At that time they had no military protection, but in the spring of 1813 Major Jesup was stationed there with two companies of Ohio militia. These were joined in May by Captain Stanton Sholes, now [1867] a resident of Columbus, Ohio,[3] with a company of United States Artillery from Pennsylvania. He was cordially welcomed by Governor Meigs, and made his quarters at Major Carter's tavern. He immediately set about felling the timber on the site of the present city of Cleveland, with which to build a small stockade fort. This was erected near the present light-house, about fifty yards from the lake.

[a] September, 1860.

[1] At the close of the public proceedings the members of the Masonic Order who were present dined together at the Weddell House. H. L. Hosmer, Deputy Grand Master of Ohio, presided. The banqueters were enlivened by toasts and speeches, and the festivities closed with a song written for the occasion by William Ross Wallace, and sung by Ossian E. Dodge—a song of three stanzas, of which the following stirring one is the conclusion:

"Roll, roll, ye waves! eternal roll!
For ye are holy from his might:
Oh, Banner, that his valor wreathed,
Forever keep thy victor-light!
And if upon this sacred lake
Should ever come invading powers,
Like him may we exulting cry,
WE'VE MET THE FOE, AND THEY ARE OURS!"

[2] Dr. Long's dwelling was on the site of the present light-house at Cleveland. It still exists, but at some distance from the place where it was built. It now stands on the north side of Frankfort Street, between Bank and Water Streets. It is a small building, one story, about 20 by 26 feet square.

[3] Mr. Sholes is a native of Connecticut, born before the breaking out of the Revolutionary War, and is now [1867] about ninety-six years of age. His father was a British soldier at the capture of Quebec from the French, and served four years in our old war for independence. In early life Captain Sholes engaged in the business of a sailor, and visited many parts of the world. He quit the ocean in 1803, and settled in the State of New York. After a few years he took up his abode on the banks of the Ohio River, about twenty miles below Pittsburg. In May, 1812, he received from President Madison a captain's commission in the second division United States Artillery, with orders to recruit a company of one hundred men for five years. This he accomplished, and in May, 1813, arrived with them at Cleveland, as we have observed. He served faithfully in the Northwest, during the hostilities in that region, under Harrison. I am indebted to Captain Sholes for much valuable information concerning operations there. He is an honored hero of two wars, for before the close of the Revolution he ran away from home, and entered the service of his country as a boy-soldier.

He also erected a comfortable hospital. During that summer he was on active duty there, but two days before the battle on the lake he received orders from General Harrison to break up his encampment, and, with his company and all the government boats at Cleveland, move on to the mouth of the Maumee, preparatory to a speedy invasion of Canada.

[a] 1860.

I left Cleveland on the morning of the 12th of September[a] for Southern Ohio, and the residence and tomb of General Harrison. Of the incidents of that journey I shall hereafter write. Let us occupy a few moments in considering the farther movements of the lake squadron so lately in battle. We left them in Put-in-Bay on the morning of the 12th,[b] after the sad task of burying the slain officers had been performed.

[b] September, 1813.

In the course of the day after the battle Perry visited the wounded Barclay on board the battered *Detroit*. They met there for the first time face to face, and it was the beginning of a lasting personal friendship. His kindness to Barclay and his men on this occasion elicited the praises of that officer in his official dispatch. Every thing that friend could do for friend was performed by the victor toward the captive.[1]

Perry now prepared for the transportation of Harrison's army to Canada. For that purpose he placed all the wounded Americans on board the *Lawrence*, and the wounded *British* on board the *Detroit* and *Queen Charlotte*,[2] and arranged the *Niagara* and the lighter vessels of both squadrons as transports. He made the *Niagara* his flag-ship; and on board of her, on the 13th, while a furious gale from the southwest was sweeping over the lake, he wrote a detailed account of the battle for the Secretary of the Navy.[3] The shattered British vessels were made to suffer by that storm. It drove heavy swells into the harbor, which so shook the *Detroit* that her masts fell upon her decks with a terrible crash, wrecking every thing near them. The main and mizzen masts of the *Queen Charlotte* also fell; and there lay the three vessels helpless hulks. They were converted into hospital ships. The crippled *Lawrence*, devoted to the same uses, sailed sluggishly for Erie on the 21st,[c] and was soon followed by the *Detroit* and *Queen Charlotte*.[4] She arrived

[c] September.

Captain Sholes is the subject of an extraordinary physiological change. For fifty years he was bald and wore a wig. Then he was afflicted with severe headache, for the relief of which cloths dipped in warm water and wrung out were applied. The pain ceased and a new growth of hair commenced. In the summer of 1864, as I was informed by his pastor, Rev. Mr. Byers, his head was thickly covered with glossy, snowy-white hair, so long that it was combed back from the forehead and tied with a ribbon at his neck. His face, also, which was formerly much wrinkled, had become smooth, "with much of the restored fairness of youth."

[1] While Perry was on the *Detroit*, two savages, who had been concealed in the hold of the vessel, were brought to him. They were Indian chiefs, and had been taken on board clothed in sailors' suits, and, with others, were placed in the tops as sharp-shooters. The noise of great guns and the dangers of the fight unnerved them, and they had fled to the hold in terror. When brought before Perry they expected torture or scalping. Their astonishment was great when he spoke kindly to them, directed them to be fed, and sent them on shore with assurances of protection from the Indians friendly to the Americans.

[2] The prisoners conveyed to Erie were sent to Pittsburg, in the interior, for greater security. The wounded were well cared for.

[3] In this dispatch Perry spoke in terms of praise of all his officers who were conspicuous in the battle. Captain Elliott received a bountiful share, contrary to the judgment and wishes of many of Perry's officers. They expressed their opinions freely in disparagement of Elliott. A quarrel between the two commanders and their friends ensued. The controversy was revived in after years by Mr. Cooper, the historian of the United States Navy, and old animosities were awakened to unwonted vigor. They have now slept for many years, and I do not choose to disturb them by any remarks here. The public verdict has determined the relative position of the two commanders in the history of the country. So let it be.

[4] The *Lawrence*, *Detroit*, and *Queen Charlotte* were afterward sunk in Little Bay (see map on page 514), on the northerly side of the harbor of Erie. The *Niagara* was kept at *Erie* as a receiving ship for a long time. She was finally abandoned, and also sunk in Little Bay. Here her bottom, partly covered by sand, may still be seen. In 1837 the *Detroit* and *Queen Charlotte* were purchased of the government, and raised by Captain George Miles, of Erie. They were converted into merchant ships, but in the course of five or six years they became useless. The *Detroit* lay at Buffalo some time, when she was purchased by the hotel-keepers at Niagara Falls, with which to make a spectacle for the visitors there in the summer. They placed a live bear and other animals on board of her, and sent her adrift above the Falls, in the presence of a great crowd of people, who expected to see her plunge over the great cataract. But she lodged in the rapids above, and there went to pieces. Such was the end of Commander Barclay's flag-ship *Detroit*. Pieces of the *Lawrence* have been sought for as Relics by the curious, and many canes and

at Erie on the 23d, and was greeted by a salute of seventeen guns on shore. A month later,[a] when Canada had been successfully invaded by Harrison, and Perry, as his volunteer aid, had shared in the honors of victory, the *Ariel* sailed into Erie with these commanders, who were accompanied by Commodore Barclay, then admitted to his parole, and Colonel E. P. Gaines. These officers took lodgings at Duncan's, Perry's old head-quarters, yet standing (glorious because of its associations, though in ruins), on the corner of Third and French Streets.[1] They were received with the booming of cannon, the shouts of the people, and the kindly greeting of every loyal heart. The town

[a] October 22, 1813.

PERRY'S QUARTERS.

was illuminated in the evening, and the streets were enlivened by a torch-light procession, bearing transparencies, made at the suggestion and under the direction of the accomplished Lieutenant Thomas Holdup.[2] On one of these were the words "Commodore Perry, 10th of September, 1813;" on another, "General Harrison, 5th of October, 1813;" on another, "Free Trade and Sailors' Rights;" and on a fourth, "Erie." The *Niagara* arrived the same afternoon, and other vessels soon followed.[3]

THOMAS HOLDUP STEVENS.

The succeeding winter was passed in much anxiety by the inhabitants of Erie on account of an expected attack by the British and Indians, who, it was reported, were preparing to cross the lake on the ice from the Canada shore. False alarms were frequent, and midnight packings of valuables preparatory to an exodus were quite common. The summer brought guaranties of repose, and during the last half of the year 1814 only a company of volunteers were stationed there, most of them at the block-house at Cascade Creek.[4]

---

other articles have been made of the wood. Captain Champlin and Dr. Parsons, survivors of the battle, both have chairs made from the oak wood of the flag-ship. Our little engraving on the opposite page shows the form of Champlin's chair. I saw the stern-post of the *Lawrence* in possession of Captain W. W. Dobbins, at Erie.

[1] This is known as the "Erie Hotel." The above picture shows its appearance when I sketched it, in September, 1860. The most distant window of the second story, seen in the gable of the main building, and boarded up, was pointed out to me as the one that lighted the room occupied by Perry.

[2] See Note 5, page 528. [3] Doctor Parsons's Diary. Miss Laura G. Sanford's *History of Erie*.

[4] Three men were executed at Erie for desertion in the autumn of 1814. One of them was a young man of some standing, named Bird, who had fought gallantly on the *Niagara* in the battle on Lake Erie. His offense could not be overlooked, and he was shot. It was thought by some that his pardon, under the circumstances, might not have been detrimental to the public good. A doleful ballad, called *The mournful Tragedy of James Bird*, was written, and became very popular throughout the country, drawing tears from unrefined and sensitive listeners. Older readers will doubtless remember with what pathos the singers would chant the following, which was the last of the eleven verses of the ballad:

"See, he kneels upon his coffin! sure his death can do no good.
 Spare him! Hark! Oh God! they've shot him; his bosom streams with blood.
 Farewell, Bird! farewell forever! Friends and home he'll see no more!
 But his mangled corpse lies buried on Lake Erie's distant shore."

www.ingramcontent.com/pod-product-compliance
Lightning Source LLC
Chambersburg PA
CBHW021812300426
44114CB00009BA/139